Organization Development

Joan V. Gallos, Editor

Foreword by Edgar H. Schein

Organization Development

A Jossey-Bass Reader

JOSSEY-BASS
A Wiley Imprint
www.josseybass.com

Published by Jossey-Bass
A Wiley Imprint
989 Market Street, San Francisco, CA 94103-1741   www.josseybass.com

Jossey-Bass books and products are available through most bookstores. To contact Jossey-Bass directly call our Customer Care Department within the U.S. at 800-956-7739, outside the U.S. at 317-572-3986, or fax 317-572-4002.

Jossey-Bass also publishes its books in a variety of electronic formats. Some content that appears in print may not be available in electronic books.

Credits are on page 1055

Library of Congress Cataloging-in-Publication Data

Organization development: a Jossey-Bass reader / Joan V. Gallos, editor; foreword by Edgar H. Schein.
    p. cm.—(The Jossey-Bass business & management series)
  Includes bibliographical references and index.
  ISBN-13: 978-0-7879-8426-7 (pbk.)
  ISBN-10: 0-7879-8426-4 (pbk.)
  1. Organizational change. I. Gallos, Joan V. II. Series.
  HD58.8.O72825 2006
  658.4'06—dc22
          2006010541

Printed in the United States of America
FIRST EDITION
PB Printing   10 9 8 7 6 5 4 3 2

The Jossey-Bass

Business & Management Series

To Lee—Amor tussisque non celantur

—⟶⟶⟶— Contents

Small Group

Large Group

Intergroup

Organization

Editor's Interlude

Consulting Process

Consulting Phases and Tasks

Contracting

Facilitation

Integrating Systems

Utilizing Diversity

Creating Learning Organizations

Creating Humane Organizations

Fostering Growth and Development

Editor's Interlude

CHANGES IN THE FIELD

Practitioner Perspective

Scholarly Perspective

On-line instructor's guide available at
http://bcs.wiley.com/he-bcs/Books?
action=index&bcsId=3160&itemId=
0787984264

—— Foreword: Observations on the State of Organization Development

SOME HISTORICAL NOTES

Organization development as a practice evolved in the 1950s out of the work of the National Training Labs (NTL) on group dynamics and leadership. At the same time, a number of social psychology departments and business schools were discovering that traditional industrial psychology no longer met the varied needs of organizations. The concepts and tools available in the early days of the field were mostly diagnostic and individual oriented, and therefore did not fully respond to the problems that many organizations were facing. Of particular importance to OD's beginning was the discovery in the T-groups (T for training) of the power of "experiential" learning in groups and in the organizational arena. This combining of new forms of intervention and new concepts of group dynamics and leadership in effect created the field of OD.

OD had come a long way by the mid-1960s. This led Dick Beckhard, Warren Bennis, and me to start to design the Addison-Wesley series on organization development. We knew that we wanted a book series rather than a single book on OD because the field was, even at that time, too diverse to lend itself to a single volume. Some practitioners saw the future in terms of new ways of looking at interpersonal dynamics. Some saw it as a new set of values for how organizations should be managed. Some focused on group and intergroup problems. Still others tried to conceptualize how a total change program for an organization would look. Many different approaches were proposed on how best to deal with organizational issues and the management of change. No one model dominated the scene, and various "experimental interventions" within organizations were the order of the day.

The most radical of these experiments was to introduce the T-group into organizational units, even work groups, to leverage the impact of here-and-now experiential learning and feedback for individual and organizational growth. But as we now know, such experiments also revealed the limitations of face-to-face feedback across hierarchical lines. Telling the boss exactly what you think of him or her has not really worked out, though the current efforts to employ 360-degree feedback is clearly a contemporary version of those original experiments.

My own involvement in the field centered on efforts to understand the deeper dynamics of personal and organizational change. I had encountered deep change processes in my earlier studies on "brainwashing" of prisoners of war and civilians captured by the Chinese communists in the early 1950s—what I came to call coercive persuasion (Schein, Schneier, & Barker, 1961). When I took on my first job in the Sloan School in 1956, I observed similar coercive persuasion processes in the indoctrination of new hires by large corporations. But exposure to experiential learning through work with NTL led me to the conclusion that coercive persuasion works only when the target person is a captive. If people can walk away from unpleasant learning situations, they will do so. Learning, therefore, has to be based on a collaboration between consultant (coach) and client (learner), the understanding of which led me to define and describe "process consultation" as the group and organizational equivalent of Rogerian therapy for the individual (Schein, 1969, 1999). In that regard, I have always considered process consultation as an essential philosophy underlying organization development, not just a tool to be taken off the shelf when needed.

Probably the biggest impact on the evolution of OD as a field—I know this is true in my case—was the result of the actual experience that individuals had as consultants to managers in real organizations. Though research was always an important dimension of OD practice, there is no doubt in my mind that the *essential* learning about change and how to manage it came from our own experiential learning. For example, in my historical analysis of the rise and fall of the Digital Equipment Corporation, where I was a consultant for thirty years, I pointed out how Ken Olsen, the founder and my primary client, influenced my insights on how to conduct organizational surveys (Schein, 2003). He wanted me to do an engineering department survey, and when I asked him when he wanted to see the results, he said, "I don't want to see the results. If problems are uncovered, I want them fixed." His surprising response led me to the concept of *upward* cascading of survey results—that is, having each group analyze and categorize its own data before anything was shared with the next higher level. This approach empowered groups to fix their own problems and to feed upward only the things that higher levels of management alone could handle.

Working with clients also made highly visible the impact of deep cultural assumptions on how organizations design themselves, determine their strategy, and develop the basic processes that they use to get the work done. It became increasingly clear to me that culture is not just about the soft stuff of communication, rewards, and morale. It is deeply connected to the fundamental issues of organizational goals and means. The deep explanation of why Digital Equipment Corporation was successful—and why, in the end, it failed as a business—is all about the cultural DNA in that organization that made innovation an imperative and more central than concerns about business efficiency. Similarly, in my work with Ciba-Geigy in the late 1970s, I could see clearly how the company's acquisition strategy was far more dominated by self-image and cultural identity than by any pure economic or market criteria (Schein, 2004).

SOME CURRENT OBSERVATIONS

What has happened to the field of organization development in the last forty years? The answer is evident in this volume. OD has evolved, yet it has maintained a conceptual core and its diversity. If one scans the table of contents, it is evident that the core has a number of elements: a concern with process, a focus on change, and an implicit as well as explicit concern for organizational effectiveness. At the same time, there is a healthy diversity of views on what processes to focus on, how to manage change, and which values should inform the concept of "organizational health."

There is as yet no consensus on what the basic goals of organization development should be. Some practitioners would argue that OD's role is to "reform" organizations: to introduce humanistic values and ensure that organizations become "better" places to work for their employees. Others would argue that OD should help client systems be more effective at whatever it is the clients are trying to do within their cultural contexts. Client values should not be challenged unless they cross some broad ethical boundary. Still others would argue that the two positions converge, in that only organizations that operate by certain humanistic values can be effective in the long run anyway.

And finally, some would argue, as I would, that organizations are complex systems and that "health" therefore has to be defined in systemic terms: does the organization have a clear identity, the requisite variety, the capacity to learn, and sufficient internal alignment among its subsystems to function. Obviously, if the system has evil goals, OD practitioners would not work with it, but systems operate in all kinds of cultural contexts and have many different kinds of value sets. In this view of the field, the role of OD is more to help the system work its internal processes of alignment and integration than to challenge or to try to change those values.

The question has been raised about whether OD is a viable and growing concern or if the field has lost its momentum. To answer that question, one must first recognize how many elements of OD have evolved into organizational routines that are nowadays taken for granted: better communications, team building, management of intergroup competition, and change management, to name just a few. At the same time, as this volume suggests, the field is continuing to grow in defining concepts and tools to tackle the even tougher problems of change and organizational dynamics in an increasingly global and diverse world. Two current issues for the field to address strike me as paramount:

1. The difficulty of creating a viable organization (system) that is geographically dispersed and consists of subsystems that are genuinely different national and occupational cultures. The positive aspects of diversity are highly touted, but the problems of alignment and integration of diverse cultural elements remain a major challenge.

2. The ongoing difficulty of getting upward informational flow in hierarchies, as illustrated by all the recent disasters in NASA and in the slow response to the New Orleans flooding from Hurricane Katrina. Even the best of managers find themselves isolated and therefore ignorant of what is really going on below them. I see little evidence that OD practice has found a cure for that fundamental organizational pathology.

Organization development will continue to flourish as a field, however, because its practitioners are unique in their concern with human processes. OD practitioners have learned as a core part of their training that process is as important as content—and sometimes more important—and often is a strong reflection of content. Process at the individual, group, or intergroup levels is what OD practitioners understand and can improve. Communications, meetings designs, feedback, physical arrangements and the design of workspaces, and the work itself are all processes of which OD has strong knowledge. As long as OD continues to explore and enhance these human processes, it will fulfill an essential role in the broad scheme of human affairs. Readers of this book will find a broad array of intellectual resources and tools to further their understanding of and involvement in this growing field of OD.

May 2006   EDGAR H. SCHEIN
                                                            Sloan Fellows Professor of
                                                            Management Emeritus,
                                                            Massachusetts Institute of
                                                            Technology Sloan School
                                                            of Management
                                                            Cambridge, Massachusetts

⸺⁓⸺ Introduction

This is a book about the power and possibilities of organization development (OD) and planned change. It celebrates OD's proud legacy of embracing the social and behavioral sciences in service to individual and organizational growth. It acknowledges OD's contributions to theory and practice: understanding how organizations work and developing methods for their improvement. It charts the evolution and impact of a field that set out more than half a century ago to release human potential at work and foster the role of learning and renewal in organizations. The death of OD has been vastly exaggerated, and the chapters in this volume suggest a vital role for OD in today's competitive, bottom-line-focused world of constant change. OD is poised for a renaissance. This project was developed to support that.

The book is intended as a resource for both newcomers and experienced practitioners. Those new to the field can read it cover to cover and explore OD's foundation, scope, purpose, methods, and possibilities. Experienced practitioners will find chapters that capture best thinking on a range of topics—resources for fine-tuning skills, learning about intervention options, envisioning OD's future, or reflecting on the larger issues in growth and change. The field of organization development has a powerful and influential heritage, a solid core, evolving applications and approaches, and important contributions to make.

This book is intentionally inclusive in content; it seeks to stretch the field's traditional boundaries. It applauds an approach to planned change that has expanded in scope and possibility along with the changing nature of organizations, the environment, and theoretical advances in the organizational and social sciences. OD is at its best when it enacts its own values for learning, growth, and change. The chapters in this volume promote an understanding of OD as a diverse set of approaches to organizational health and effectiveness in an increasingly competitive and complex world. Taken together, they remind readers that organization development is more than tools and techniques. OD's core values—participation, openness to learning, equity and fairness, valid information, informed choice, shared commitment—can foster processes that engage people in useful and significant ways to address a wide range of operational, technical, and strategic concerns. OD artfully weds process with content in a search for lasting solutions to tough challenges.

—⁓—

Organization development began as a field of promise and possibility. Long before others, OD's founders understood the inefficiencies, pain, and downsides of organizational life, and they set out to do something about them. They brought open minds, entrepreneurial spirits, and irrepressible optimism to the challenge, convinced that new ways of organizing and managing were possible. They were carriers of America's historic faith in progress and initiative. They believed in democracy, openness, and the worth of every individual. Above all, they believed in learning and experimentation. They knew they did not have all the answers—or even all the questions. But they were confident that both were waiting to be found. Their faith and hard work spawned a revolutionary intellectual movement—a paradigm shift—and changed forever how the world understood people, work, and organizations. Their efforts gave rise to the organizational and applied behavioral sciences, and OD developed a powerful array of ideas and practices for understanding and improving organizations, many of which are discussed in this volume.

But much has changed since OD's humble beginnings in the human relations movement of the 1950s. Technology, globalization, competitive pressures, industry shifts, worldwide markets, increasing workplace diversity, and a host of social and economic forces have altered the world of work, the ways we organize for collective action, and the meaning of organizational complexity. To its credit, OD has evolved since its early days in response. This volume charts those shifts. For OD to stay relevant and influential, however, this growth and development must continue. Equally important, OD needs to keep faith in its own significance, wisdom, and resilience—and a sharp eye on the ways that OD's original charter can guide or limit its contributions.

The scholarly and professional literatures ring with practitioners and academics arguing about which projects, concerns, and methods of change can claim the OD label, or squabbling over semantical distinctions between developing organizations and changing them. Some insist on a singular allegiance to the field's human development roots and draw a tight boundary around the parameters of the field. They resist the ways that OD's task, intervention options, and points of system entry have expanded commensurate with the increasing complexity of the world and our understanding of it—and that OD's methodologies and values are relevant and needed for working with the gamut of organizational issues: efficiency, continuous improvement, accountability, technology, strategic planning, and politics as well as individual and interpersonal concerns. At the other extreme, some define the field so loosely as to include almost anything and everything connected to human problem solving and change at work. Practitioners trained in a variety of disciplines in and outside the management arena—from psychology to engineering—add to the confusion by bringing their own spin to planned change, often with little knowledge of OD's core purpose and values or interest in building on and advancing its practices. Internal and external critics label OD as foundering, lost, stuck at the organizational margins, failing to honor and practice its values. Some suggest a mercy killing. Others trade eulogies in memory of its passing. This book sounds a more optimistic note.

OD has clearly been shaped by its parentage. Its roots in traditions that emphasize people and potential are a source of OD's strength, as well as its limitations. The power of OD's legacy and contributions is in the field's enduring respect for the human side of enterprise and its role in productivity and innovation. Supporting, developing, and fully utilizing human creativity, initiative, and expertise are keys to any organization's success. A vibrant OD field needs to live its core values while adapting its methods and approaches to address the major strategic issues and operational challenges that organizations face. OD's heritage is empowering when it is viewed as a rich source of possibilities. But OD risks marginality or irrelevance if that heritage is defined in terms of traditional tools and techniques, an ideology that has to be zealously defended, or the pursuit of openness and humanism as ends in themselves.

OD has been criticized on the one hand for being too narrow, and on the other for not knowing what it really is or where it is going. There is some merit in both indictments, but a fuller view recognizes OD as a field whose basic aspirations and scope of work are increasingly complex and intrinsically paradoxical. Its mystery, majesty, and challenges are in its openness to a collaborative search for the best forms and approaches to organizing that meet a client system's unique circumstances. The field initially evolved more than half a century ago because organizational change was difficult, frustrating, and prone to failure. Things are no simpler today.

The increasing diversity of people, environments, goals, knowledge, and organizational practices and processes reinforces OD's core assumption that there is no one-size-fits-all definition or path to organizational health and effectiveness. Human contribution, creativity, and commitment are essential. But so are the organizational efficiencies and smart strategic choices that ensure organizational survival in an increasingly competitive work world. As OD's founders reminded us more than fifty years ago, individuals and organizations share a common goal, and when both meet their needs, both benefit. OD knows something important about the route to that shared destination. And OD practitioners rise best to the challenge when they expand their horizons and welcome new insights and possibilities, regardless of source, that help all do their work better.

OD, for example, has an increasingly important role to play in a world where individuals have morphed into human capital, where "lean and mean" too often replaces an emphasis on quality of work life, where an unrelenting focus on bottom-line profits trumps loyalty and learning, and where ethical decision making across sectors seems akin to standing on shifting sands. No other field is better prepared or set to address these kinds of challenges or to understand their long-term impact on organizational innovation, productivity, and survival. To do that well, OD needs to keep its values straight, its resolve strong, and its eye on the prize: improved organizational health and effectiveness.

ORGANIZATION OF THE BOOK

This book was developed with that prize in mind. In deciding what to include, I have kept one question in mind: What are the tools and insights that will help consultants, change agents, and leaders improve organizational health and effectiveness? All the classic OD ideas, tools, and approaches that meet that test are represented and updated in this volume. But readers will also find boundary-stretching materials rarely included in traditional OD works, new pieces that expand understandings in key areas, and suggestions for strengthening OD's future impact and relevance. There is little sense in producing a new book that tells the same old story.

This volume is divided into eight parts. Each section is introduced by an Editor's Interlude that frames the issues to be examined, describes the rationale for material included, and introduces each of the chapters. The book flows from past to future: context (how come), process (how), content (what), purpose (why), and possibilities (what else). More specifically, Part One, "The OD Field: Setting the Context, Understanding the Legacy," explores the field's historical roots, evolution over time, and distinctive theory and practice focus. The state of OD today and tomorrow is clearly linked to where and how it all began. Part Two, "The OD Core: Understanding and Managing Planned Change," examines consistencies in OD's change model over time, the concept of planned change, intervention theory, a range of action technologies, and two change models that fall outside conventional boundaries but add rich wisdom to the field. The chapters in Part Three, "The OD Process: Diagnosis, Intervention, and Levels of Engagement," examine OD activities on multiple levels (individual, small group, large group, intergroup, and organization) and offer opportunities for OD practitioners to explore their own interpretive frameworks.

External consultants have played a central role from the field's inception, and Part Four, "OD Consulting: Leading Change from the Outside," addresses a range of issues related to consulting effectiveness: values, process, tasks, contracting, facilitation, and coaching. At the same time, there are also key leadership roles for insiders: top leadership, internal consultants, motivated organizational citizens. Part Five, "OD Leadership: Fostering Change from the Inside," explores skills and understandings relevant to launching and nourishing organization development from different positions within the organization.

The chapters in Part Six, "OD Focus: Organizational Intervention Targets," offer change agents a map of the more significant areas where OD can apply its methods for meaningfully involving people in critical choices: strategy, organizational design, the structure of work, workspace ecology, and culture, as well as workforce, team, and leadership development. OD professionals who understand where, why, and how to intervene in a broad array of circumstances are more likely to have the tools that fit the needs of different client systems.

The final two parts of the book suggest an expanded future for OD. A powerful vision is the antidote for a splintered field that has lost its way. Part Seven, "OD Purpose and Possibilities: Seeing the Forest for the Trees," reminds readers that OD's core purpose is to improve organizational health and effectiveness. The chapters here suggest a range of possibilities for what that might look like: a passionate community of leaders, deep collaboration across boundaries, a well-integrated system, well-leveraged diversity, compassionate organizations, organizations that learn *and* teach. OD's possibilities are constrained only by the limits of its creativity. Finally, Part Eight, "OD and the Future: Embracing Change and New Directions," identifies four areas of major change in the external environment and the nature of work where OD's traditions and methods can be brought to bear—technology, globalization, the growing knowledge economy, and the environment—and offers perspectives on the field's future from those engaged in theory and practice.

ACKNOWLEDGMENTS

There are multiple people to thank, and it is hard to know where to begin. Many have contributed in different ways to this project. Let me start by thanking Ed Schein. His Foreword to this volume is a rich and personal perspective on OD: a special gift from someone who helped shape the field. But for me, Ed deserves appreciation for more than that. He has influenced my thinking about change, learning, and organizations in significant ways. Thank you again, dear Professor Schein, from a former student of more years ago than either of us needs to admit.

Exploring OD's history for this project provided opportunities to reflect on my own. And I know my life and work would be different had I not met Chris Argyris at orientation on the first day of graduate school. He introduced me to a field I never knew existed, and his casual suggestion—"Why don't you take my course?"—set a new career in motion. Chris's work is well represented in this volume for reasons I don't have to explain. But it gave me great pleasure to reflect again on the full extent of his impact, reconnect with him over this volume, and hear about his perceptions of a field he helped launch and grow.

Terry Deal deserves special thanks for his inimitable magic and charm and his regular "How the hell are you?" phone greetings. Terry also provided valuable feedback on my chapter in this volume. And deep appreciation goes to respected colleagues Phil Mirvis, Bill Torbert,

Michael Sales, and Bob Marshak, who found time in their busy lives to write original chapters for this volume—with short turnaround time—when I realized that their particular perspectives needed to be represented here.

The size of the volume should be some indication of all the work required to get it to press. Kathe Sweeney, senior editor in the business and management division at Jossey-Bass, launched the project with her vision and sustained it with her usual support, trust, and good cheer. Jessie Mandle, my touchpoint at Jossey-Bass, handled preproduction details with professionalism and warmth. And the Jossey-Bass production team members were first class, as always. I appreciated their attention to detail—and their efforts to get my all-time favorite colors into the cover design. Production editor Susan Geraghty deserves special mention and thanks.

On the local front, there are many people to thank. Homer Erekson, dean of the Henry W. Bloch School of Business and Public Administration at the University of Missouri-Kansas City, is a good colleague, supportive dean, and friend. My faculty colleagues in the Bloch School's Department of Public Affairs—Robyne Turner, David Renz, Bob Herman, Arif Ahmed, Nick Peroff, Greg Arling, and Abby York—are impressive in their efforts to promote organization and community development. They graciously tolerated the ways in which this project consumed my time and focus. And a special thank you to Henry Bloch for welcoming me at a critical time in my own career development to the school that he so generously supports. The energizing and entrepreneurial spirit of the Bloch School keeps me hopping—and I love it.

My graduate assistants, Alice Peed and Ben Nemenoff, deserve thanks. Alice got plenty of exercise carrying books back and forth from the library, followed by exciting opportunities to rest up in front of the copying machine. Thanks, Alice. Ben's many contributions were invaluable. His attention to detail, technology skills, and strong work ethic helped with references, endnotes, and getting all the right pages, versions, chapters, folders, and files in order. We're all in good shape if Ben is any example of the leaders of tomorrow. Sheri Gilbert tackled the complex job of securing permissions and worked with impressive speed and professionalism. Thank you, Sheri.

Every woman needs girlfriends, and I have some great ones. Three deserve particular note here. Sandy Renz is my rock and all-around buddy. I am blessed by her warmth and caring. Marge Smelstor provides unending support on multiple fronts—and is the source of the fabulous wisewoman sculpture with whom I now share an office. Beth Smith, leader extraordinaire in the Kansas City nonprofit community, is a source of wisdom and affection—and enthusiastically reads everything I write.

My family is the greatest, and the three boys on the home front deserve thanks beyond what can be written here. My sons, Brad and Chris Bolman, are talented young men who enrich my life. In addition, Brad lent his technology and file-organizing skills to the project—and his music, juggling, and magic tricks sustained the editor. Chris Bolman, chilled-out entertainer, poet, and soon-to-be investment banker, contributed to the teaching materials that accompany this volume. And Lee Bolman, my husband, best friend, and closest colleague, has earned all the credit and appreciation offered here. He is cheerfully available 24/7 to his high-maintenance spouse. During this project, he read drafts, replaced hard drives, chauffeured crippled Dalmatians to swim class, cooked fabulous meals, and more. Thank you, dear. As the years go by, I appreciate and love you more.

May 2006   JOAN V. GALLOS
                                          Kansas City, Missouri

—〰— About the Editor

Joan V. Gallos is Professor of Leadership in the Henry W. Bloch School of Business and Public Administration at the University of Missouri-Kansas City, where she has also served as Professor and Dean of Education, Coordinator of University Accreditation, Special Assistant to the Chancellor for Strategic Planning, and Director of the Higher Education Graduate Programs. Gallos holds a bachelor's degree *cum laude* in English from Princeton University, and master's and doctoral degrees from the Harvard Graduate School of Education. She has served as a Salzburg Seminar Fellow; as President of the Organizational Behavior Teaching Society; as editor of the *Journal of Management Education*; on numerous editorial boards, including as a founding member of *Academy of Management Learning and Education*; on regional and national advisory boards including the Organizational Behavior Teaching Society, The Forum for Early Childhood Organization and Leadership Development, the Missouri Council on Economic Education, the Kauffman and Danforth Foundations' Missouri Superintendents Leadership Forum, and the Mayor's Kansas City Collaborative for Academic Excellence; on the national steering committee for the *New Models of Management Education* project (a joint effort of the Graduate Management Admissions Council and the AACSB (the International Association for Management Education); on the W. K. Kellogg Foundation College Age Youth Leadership Review Team; on the University of Missouri President's Advisory Council on Academic Leadership; and on civic, foundation, and non-profit boards in greater Kansas City. Dr. Gallos has taught at the Radcliffe Seminars, the Harvard Graduate School of Education, the University of Massachusetts-Boston, and Babson College, as well as in executive programs at Harvard's Kennedy School of Government, the Harvard Graduate School of Education, the University of Missouri, Babson College, and the University of British Columbia. She has published on professional effectiveness, gender, and leadership education; is coauthor of the book *Teaching Diversity: Listening to the Soul, Speaking from the Heart* (Jossey-Bass, 1997); received the Fritz Roethlisberger Memorial Award for the best article on management education in 1990; and was finalist for the same prize in 1994. In 1993, Gallos accepted the Radcliffe College *Excellence in Teaching* award. In 2002–2003, she served as Founding Director of the Truman Center for the Healing Arts, based in Kansas City's public hospital, which received the 2004 *Kansas City Business Committee for the Arts Partnership Award* as the best partnership between a large organization and the arts.

PART ONE

The OD Field

Setting the Context, Understanding the Legacy

The state of OD today is clearly linked to where and how the field began. OD's roots are anchored in the larger human relations movement of the 1950s. They were nourished by ideas in good currency in subsequent decades that promoted self-expression, individual agency, the release of human potential, and expectations for human growth in the workplace—the same forces that supported parallel growth in the budding fields of social and developmental psychology. Specific developments in a number of key areas fueled OD's meteoric rise: the T-group movement and other forms of laboratory education in the United States, sociotechnical systems thinking from the British Tavistock Institute, development of survey research methods, and expanding interests within and outside the academy in issues of individual and group effectiveness. Academics and early practitioners in the field such as Kurt Lewin, Chris Argyris, Abraham Maslow, Douglas MacGregor, Edgar Schein, and Rensis Likert promoted the value of learning from experience, modeled the importance of linking theory and practice, and gave OD its distinctive dual focus on understanding how organizations can and should operate by working to improve them. At its inception, OD was revolutionary in developing and applying its theories of people and change to organizational life and functioning. Understanding the field of organization development today requires knowing something about this history.

The first two chapters in Part One, excerpts from Richard Beckhard's classic *Organization Development: Strategies and Models* and from W. Warner Burke's influential *Organizational Development: A Normative View,* present the historical roots and purposes of OD in the words of two individuals who have significantly shaped the field. It seems right to begin with Beckhard's classic definition. Legend has it that he and his colleague Robert Tannenbaum gave the field its name in the 1950s while sitting around a kitchen table. Their reasoning went something like this: if *individual development* is the term for human growth and change in response to challenge and opportunities, then the growth and development of organizations and large social systems logically should be called *organization*—not *organizational*— *development.* These two historic articles are followed by an astute analysis of the current state of the field by Philip H. Mirvis, written for this volume. Mirvis updates his classic two-part history of evolutionary and revolutionary shifts in OD. He examines how current theories, processes, applications, and possibilities in the field—the new, new OD—are explained by understanding shifts in OD's knowledge base, its development as a social and intellectual movement, the influences of its clients and practices, and ongoing changes in the larger sociopolitical and industrial context of work.

Part One closes with an exploration and update on the interplay between theory and practice in the OD field. The early days of OD were marked by a dynamic and ready exchange of knowledge between the scholarly and practitioner communities. That is not as true today, but such reciprocity is the key to keeping OD fresh and relevant. John R. Austin and Jean M. Bartunek explore academic and practitioner approaches to organizational knowledge. They distinguish between scholarly efforts to theorize about the organizational goals and dynamics of change and the grounded understandings of intervention and implementation that come from change agents laboring in the organizational trenches. The authors outline key research and theoretical contributions in each area, situate OD in the larger field of change management, argue for better linking of academic and practice-based learning about organizational change, and suggest strategies for forging such links.

CHAPTER ONE

What Is Organization Development?

Richard Beckhard

O rganization development is an effort (1) *planned,* (2) *organization-wide,* and (3) *managed* from the *top,* to (4) increase *organization effectiveness* and *health* through (5) *planned interventions* in the organization's "processes," using *behavioral-science* knowledge.

1. It is a *planned change* effort.

An OD program involves a systematic diagnosis of the organization, the development of a strategic plan for improvement, and the mobilization of resources to carry out the effort.

2. It involves the total "*system.*"

An organization-development effort is related to a total organization change such as a change in the culture or the reward systems or the total managerial strategy. There may be tactical efforts which work with subparts of the organization but the "system" to be changed is a total, relatively autonomous organization. This is not necessarily a total corporation, or an entire government, but refers to a system which is relatively free to determine its own plans and future within very *general* constraints from the environment.

3. *It is managed from the top.*

In an organization-development effort, the top management of the system has a personal investment in the program and its outcomes. They actively participate in the *management* of the effort. This does not mean they must participate in the same *activities* as others, but it does mean that they must have both knowledge and *commitment* to the goals of the program and must actively support the methods used to achieve the goals.

4. It is designed to *increase organization effectiveness* and *health.*

To understand the goals of organization development, it is necessary to have some picture of what an "ideal" effective, healthy organization would look like. What would be its characteristics? Numbers of writers and practitioners in the field have proposed definitions which, although they differ in detail, indicate a strong consensus of what a healthy operating organization is. Let me start with my own definition. An effective organization is one in which:

a. The total organization, the significant subparts, and individuals manage their work against *goals* and *plans* for achievement of these goals.

b. Form follows function (the problem, or task, or project determines how the human resources are organized).

c. Decisions are made by and near the sources of information regardless of where these sources are located on the organization chart.

d. The reward system is such that managers and supervisors are rewarded (and punished) comparably for:

short-term profit or production performance,

growth and development of their subordinates,

creating a viable working group.

e. Communication laterally and vertically is *relatively* undistorted. People are generally open and confronting. They share all the relevant facts including feelings.

f. There is a minimum amount of inappropriate win/lose activities between individuals and groups. Constant effort exists at all levels to treat conflict and conflict-situations as *problems* subject to problem-solving methods.

g. There is high "conflict" (clash of ideas) about tasks and projects, and relatively little energy spent in clashing over *interpersonal* difficulties because they have been generally worked through.

h. The organization and its parts see themselves as interacting with each other *and* with a *larger* environment. The organization is an "open system."

i. There is a shared value and management strategy to support it, of trying to help each person (or unit) in the organization maintain his (or its) integrity and uniqueness in an interdependent environment.

j. The organization and its members operate in an "action-research" way. General practice is to build in *feedback mechanisms* so that individuals and groups can learn from their own experience.

Another definition is found in John Gardner's set of rules for an effective organization. He describes an effective organization as one which is *self-renewing* and then lists the rules:

> The *first rule* is that the organization must have an effective program for the recruitment and development of talent.
>
> The *second rule* for the organization capable of continuous renewal is that it must be a hospitable environment for the individual.
>
> The *third rule* is that the organization must have built-in provisions for self-criticism.
>
> The *fourth rule* is that there must be fluidity in the internal structure.
>
> The *fifth rule* is that the organization must have some means of combating the process by which men become prisoners of their procedures (Gardner, 1965).

Edgar Schein defines organization effectiveness in relation to what he calls "the adaptive coping cycle," that is, an organization that can effectively adapt and cope with the changes in its environment. Specifically, he says:

The sequence of activities or processes which begins with some change in the internal or external environment and ends with a more adaptive, dynamic equilibrium for dealing with the change, is the organization's "adaptive coping cycle." If we identify the various stages or processes of this cycle, we shall also be able to identify the points where organizations typically may fail to cope adequately and where, therefore, consultants and researchers have been able in a variety of ways to help increase organization effectiveness (Schein, 1965).

The organization conditions necessary for effective coping, according to Schein, are:

- The ability to take in and communicate information reliably and validly.
- Internal flexibility and creativity to make the changes which are demanded by the information obtained (including structural flexibility).
- Integration and commitment to the goals of the organization from which comes the willingness to change.
- An internal climate of support and freedom from threat, since being threatened undermines good communication, reduces flexibility, and stimulates self-protection rather than concern for the total system.

Miles and others (1966) define the healthy organization in three broad areas—those concerned with task accomplishment, those concerned with internal integration, and those involving mutual adaptation of the organization and its environment. The following dimensional conditions are listed for each area:

In the task-accomplishment area, a healthy organization would be one with (1) reasonably clear, accepted, achievable and appropriate goals; (2) relatively understood communications flow; (3) optimal power equalization.

In the area of internal integration, a healthy organization would be one with (4) resource utilization and individuals' *good fit* between personal disposition and role demands; (5) a reasonable degree of cohesiveness and "organization identity," clear and attractive enough so that persons feel actively connected to it; (6) high morale. In order to have growth and active changefulness, a healthy organization would be one with innovativeness, autonomy, adaptation, and problem-solving adequacy.

Lou Morse (1968), in his thesis on organization development, wrote:

> The commonality of goals are cooperative group relations, consensus, integration, and commitment to the goals of the organization (task accomplishment), creativity, authentic behavior, freedom from threat, full utilization of a person's capabilities, and organizational flexibility.

5. Organization development achieves its goals through *planned interventions* using behavioral-science knowledge.

A strategy is developed of intervening or moving into the existing organization and helping it, in effect, "stop the music," examine its present ways of work, norms, and values, and look at alternative ways of working, or relating, or rewarding. The interventions used draw on the knowledge and technology of the behavioral sciences about such processes as individual motivation, power, communications, perception, cultural norms, problem-solving, goal-setting, interpersonal relationships, intergroup relationships, and conflict management.

SOME OPERATIONAL GOALS IN AN ORGANIZATION-DEVELOPMENT EFFORT

To move toward the kind of organization conditions described in the above definitions, OD efforts usually have some of the following operational goals:

1. To develop a self-renewing, *viable* system that can organize in a variety of ways depending on tasks. This means systematic efforts to change and loosen up the way the organization operates, so that it organizes differently depending on the nature of the task. There is movement toward a concept of "form follows function," rather than that *tasks* must *fit* into existing structures.

2. To optimize the effectiveness of both the stable (the basic organization chart) and the temporary systems (the many projects, committees, etc., through which much of the organization's work is accomplished) by built-in, *continuous improvement mechanisms*. This means the introduction of procedures for analyzing work tasks and

resource distribution, and for building in continuous "feedback" regarding the way a system or subsystem is operating.

3. To move toward *high collaboration* and *low competition* between interdependent units. One of the major obstacles to effective organizations is the amount of dysfunctional energy spent in inappropriate competition—energy that is not, therefore, available for the accomplishment of tasks. If all of the energy that is used by, let's say, manufacturing people disliking or wanting to "get those sales people," or vice versa, were available to improve organization output, productivity would increase tremendously.

4. To create conditions where conflict is brought out and managed. One of the fundamental problems in unhealthy (or less than healthy) organizations is the amount of energy that is dysfunctionally used trying to work around, or avoid, or cover up, conflicts which are inevitable in a complex organization. The goal is to move the organization towards seeing conflict as an inevitable condition and as problems that need to be *worked* before adequate decisions can be made.

5. To reach the point where decisions are made on the basis of information source rather than organizational role. This means the need to move toward a *norm* of the *authority of knowledge* as well as the authority of role. It does not only mean that decisions should be moved down in the organization; it means that the organization manager should determine which is the best source of information (or combination of sources of information) to work a particular problem, and it is there that the decision-making should be located.

SOME CHARACTERISTICS OF ORGANIZATION-DEVELOPMENT EFFORTS

Most successful organization-development efforts have the following characteristics:

1. There is a *planned* program involving the whole system.

2. The *top* of the organization is *aware of* and *committed to* the program and to the management of it. (This does not necessarily mean that they participate exactly the same way as other levels of the organization do, but that they *accept the responsibility* for the management.)

3. It is related to the *organization's mission*. (The organization development effort is not a program to improve effectiveness in the abstract. Rather it is an effort to improve effectiveness aimed specifically

at creating organization conditions that will improve the organization's ability to achieve its mission goals.)

4. It is a *long-term* effort.

In my own experience, usually at least two or three years are required for any large organization change to take effect and be maintained. This is one of the major problems in organization-development efforts, because most reward systems are based on rewarding the achievement of short-term "profit" objectives. Most organization leaders are impatient with improvement efforts which take extended time. Yet, if real change is to occur and be maintained, there must be a commitment to an extended time, and a willingness to *reward* for the *process* of movement toward goals, as well as toward the specific achievement of short-term goals.

5. Activities are *action-oriented*.

(The types of interventions and activities in which organization members participate are aimed at changing something *after* the activity.)

In this respect, OD activities are different from many other training efforts where the activity itself, such as a training course or a management workshop, is designed to produce increased knowledge, skill, or understanding, which the individual is then supposed to transfer to the operating situation. In OD efforts, the group builds in connections and follow-up activities that are aimed toward *action programs*.

6. It focuses on *changing attitudes and/or behavior*. (Although processes, procedures, ways of work, etc., do undergo change in organization-development programs, the major target of change is the attitude, behavior, and performance of people in the organization.)

7. It usually relies on some form of *experienced-based learning* activities.

The reason for this is that, if a goal is to change attitudes and/or behavior, a particular type of learning situation is required for such change to occur. One does not learn to play golf or drive a car by getting increased knowledge about how to play golf or drive a car. Nor can one change one's managerial style or strategy through receiving input of new knowledge alone. It is necessary to examine present behavior, experiment with alternatives, and begin to practice modified ways, if change is to occur.

8. OD efforts work *primarily with groups*.

An underlying assumption is that groups and teams are the basic units of organization to be changed or modified as one moves toward organization health and effectiveness. Individual learning and personal change do occur in OD programs but as a fallout—these are not the *primary* goals or intentions.

KINDS OF ORGANIZATION CONDITIONS THAT CALL FOR OD EFFORTS

An essential condition of any effective change program is that somebody in a *strategic position* really *feels the need* for change. In other words somebody or something is "hurting." To be sure, some change efforts that introduce new technologies do not fit this generalization. As a general rule, if a change in people and the way they work together is contemplated, there must be a *felt need* at some strategic part of the organization. Let me list a few of the kinds of conditions or felt needs that have supplied the impetus for organization-development programs.

1. The need to change a *managerial strategy.*

It is a fact that many managers of small and large enterprises are today re-examining the basic strategies by which the organization is operating. They are attempting to modify their total managerial strategy including the communications patterns, location of decision-making, the reward system, etc.

2. The need to make the organization *climate more consistent* with both individual needs and the changing needs of the environment.

If a top manager, or strategically placed staff person, or enough people in the middle of the hierarchy, really feel this need, the organization is in a "ready state" for some planned-change effort to meet it.

3. The need to *change "cultural" norms.*

More and more managers are learning that they are really managing a "culture" with its own values, ground rules, norms, and power structure. If there is a felt need that the culture needs to be changed, in order to be more consistent with competitive demands or the environment, this is another condition where an organization development program is appropriate. For example, a large and successful food company, owned by two families, had operated very successfully for fifty years. All positions above the upper middle of the structure were restricted to members of the family; all stock was owned by the family; and all policy decisions were made by a family board. Some of the more progressive members of the family became concerned about the state of the enterprise in these changing times. They strongly felt the need for changing from a family-owned, family-controlled organization to a family-controlled, professionally-managed organization. The problem to be dealt with, then, was a *total change* in the *culture* of the organization, designed to arrive at different norms, different ground rules, and so forth.

This required a major, long-term change-effort with a variety of strategies and interventions, in order for people to accept the new set of conditions. This was particularly true for those who had grown up within the other set of conditions.

4. The need to change *structure* and *roles*.

An awareness by key management that "we're just not properly organized," that the work of (let's say) the research department and the work of the development department should be separated or should be integrated; that the management-services function and the personnel function should report to the same vice-president; or that the field managers should take over some of the activities of the headquarters staff, etc. The *felt* need here and the problems anticipated in effecting a major structural or role change may lead to an organizational-development effort.

5. The need to improve *intergroup collaboration*.

As I mentioned earlier, one of the major expenditures of dysfunctional energy in organizations is the large amount of inappropriate competition between groups. When this becomes noticeable and top managers are "hurting," they are ready to initiate efforts to develop a program for increasing intergroup collaboration.

6. The need to *open* up the *communications system*.

When managers become aware of significant gaps in communication up or down, or of a lack of adequate information for making decisions, they may *feel* the need for action to improve the situation. Numbers of studies show that this is a central problem in much of organization life. Blake and Mouton (1968) in their Grid OD book report studies of several hundred executives in which the number one barrier to corporate excellence is communications problems, in terms not only of the communication structure, but also of the *quality* of the communication.

7. The need for *better planning*.

One of the major corollaries of the increasing complexity of business and the changing demands of the environment is that the planning function, which used to be highly centralized in the president's or national director's office, now must be done by a number of people throughout the organization. Most people who are in roles requiring this skill have little formal training in it. Therefore, their planning practices are frequently crude, unsophisticated, and not too effective. An awareness of this condition by management may well lead to an organization-wide effort to improve planning and goal-setting.

8. The need for coping with *problems of merger.*

In today's world, it is more and more common for companies to merge, for divisions of organizations to merge, for church organizations to merge, for subgroups doing similar tasks to merge. In every merger situation, there is the surviving partner and the merged partner. The human problems concerned with such a process are tremendous and may be very destructive to organization health. Awareness of this, and/or a feeling of hurting as the result of a recent merger, may well cause a management to induce a planned program for coping with the problem.

9. Need for *change in motivation* of the *work force.*

This could be an "umbrella" statement, but here it specifically refers to situations which are becoming more and more frequent where there is a need for changing the "psychological ownership" condition within the work force. For example, in some large companies there are planned efforts under way to change the way work is organized and the way jobs are defined. Herzberg, Mausner, and Snyderman's (1959) work on "job enlargement" and "job enrichment" and the application of this in many organizations is evidence of the need. The Scanlon plans, a shared-reward system, are examples of specific, company-wide efforts to change the motivations of a work force (Lesieur, 1958).

10. Need for *adaptation* to a *new environment.*

If a company moves into a new type of product due to a merger or an acquisition, it may have to develop an entirely different marketing strategy. If a company which has been production-oriented becomes highly research-oriented, the entire organization has to adapt to new role relationships and new power relationships. In one advertising agency the historic pattern was that the account executives were the key people with whom the clients did all their business. Recently, due to the advent of television and other media, the clients want to talk directly to the television specialist, or the media specialist, and have less need to talk with the account executive. The environment of the agency, in relation to its clients, is dramatically different. This has produced some real trauma in the agency as influence patterns have changed. It has been necessary to develop an organization-wide effort to examine the changed environment, assess its consequences, and determine ways of coping with the new conditions.

CHAPTER TWO

Where Did OD Come From?

W. Warner Burke

E ven though OD may be characterized as evolutionary with respect to the field's beginnings, we must start somewhere. There was not a "big bang" or "blessed event." Thus, considering three forerunners or precursors will help us to understand the beginnings, that is, where OD came from. These three precursors are sensitivity training, sociotechnical systems, and survey feedback.

SENSITIVITY TRAINING

From a historical perspective, it would be interesting to know how many events, interventions, and innovations that occurred around 1946 had lasting impact through the subsequent decades. Apparently once World War II was over, people were somehow freer to pursue a variety of creative endeavors. Both sensitivity training, later "housed" at the National Training Laboratories (NTL), and a similar yet different version of human relations training, independently founded at the Tavistock Institute in London, began about that time.

On the U.S. side, sensitivity training, or the T-group, as it was to be labeled later (*T* meaning *training*), derived from events that took place in the summer of 1946 in New Britain, Connecticut. Kurt Lewin, at the time on the faculty of the Massachusetts Institute of Technology (MIT) and director of the Research Center for Group Dynamics, was asked by the director of the Connecticut State Inter-Racial Commission to conduct a training workshop that would help to improve community leadership in general and interracial relationships in particular. Lewin brought together a group of colleagues and students to serve as trainers (Leland Bradford, Ronald Lippitt, and Kenneth Benne) and researchers (Morton Deutsch, Murray Horwitz, Arnold Meier, and Melvin Seeman) for the workshop. The training consisted of lectures, role playing, and general group discussion. In the evenings, most researchers and trainers met to evaluate the training to that point by discussing participant behavior as they had observed it during the day. A few of the participants who were far enough from their homes to stay in the dormitory rooms at the college in New Britain asked if they could observe the evening staff discussions. The trainers and researchers were reluctant, but Lewin saw no reason to keep them away and thought that, as participants, they might learn even more.

The results were influential and far-reaching, to say the least. In the course of the staff's discussion of the behavior of one participant, who happened to be present and observing, the participant intervened and said that she disagreed with their interpretations of her behavior. She then described the event from her point of view. Lewin immediately recognized that this intrusion provided a richness to the data collection and analysis that was otherwise unavailable. The next evening many more participants stayed to observe the staff discussions. Participant observations alone didn't last, of course, and three-way discussions occurred among the researchers, trainers, and participants. Gradually, the staff and participants discovered that the feedback the participants were receiving about their daytime behavior was teaching them as much or more than the daytime activities. The participants were becoming more sensitive to their own behavior in terms of how they were being perceived by others and the impact their behavior was having on others. This serendipitous and innovative mode of learning, which had its beginning that summer in Connecticut, has become what Carl Rogers labeled "perhaps the most significant social invention of the century" (1968, p. 265).

Sensitivity training, T-groups, and laboratory training are all labels for the same process, consisting of small group discussions in which the primary, almost exclusive, source of information for learning is the behavior of the group members themselves. Participants receive feedback from one another regarding their behavior in the group, and this feedback becomes the learning source for personal insight and development. Participants also have an opportunity to learn more about group behavior and intergroup relationships.

T-groups are educational vehicles for change, in this case individual change. During the late 1950s, when this form of education began to be applied in industrial settings for organizational change, the T-group became one of the earliest so-called interventions of organization development.

As the T-group method of learning and change began to proliferate in the 1950s, it naturally gravitated to organizational life. Sensitivity training began to be used as an intervention for organizational change; in this application the training was conducted inside a single organization, and members of the small T-groups were either organizational "cousins"—from the same overall organization but not within the same vertical chain of the organization's hierarchy—or members of the same organizational team, so-called family groups. As French and Bell (1978) reported, one of the first events to improve organizational effectiveness by sensitivity training took place with managers at some of the major refineries of Exxon (then known as Esso) in Louisiana and southeast Texas. Herbert Shepard of the corporate employee relations department and Harry Kolb of the refineries division used interviews followed by three-day training laboratories for all managers in an attempt to move management in a more participative direction. Outside trainers were used, many of them the major names of the National Training Laboratories at the time, such as Lee Bradford and Robert R. Blake. Paul Buchanan conducted similar activities when he was with the Naval Ordnance Test Station at China Lake, California. He later joined Shepard at Esso.

At about that time, Douglas McGregor of the Sloan School of Management at MIT was conducting similar training sessions at Union Carbide. These events at Esso and Union Carbide represented the early forms of organization development, which usually took the form of what we now call team building (Burck, 1965; McGregor, 1967).

Also during that period, the late 1950s, McGregor and Richard Beckhard were consulting with General Mills. They were fostering what now would be called a sociotechnical systems change. They helped to change some of the work structures at the various plants so that more teamwork and increased decision making took place on the shop floor; more bottom-up management began to occur. They didn't want to call what they were doing "bottom-up," nor were they satisfied with "organizational development." This label also became, apparently independently, the name for the work Shepard, Kolb, Blake, and others were doing at the Humble Refineries of Esso.

Even though McGregor and Beckhard were initiating organizational change that involved a sociotechnical perspective, they called what they were doing organization development rather than sociotechnical systems. Across the Atlantic at the Tavistock Institute, the sociotechnical label stuck.

SOCIOTECHNICAL SYSTEMS

In the United Kingdom at about the same time that sensitivity began in the United States, Eric Trist and Ken Bamforth of the Tavistock Institute were consulting with a coal mining company. Prior to their consultative intervention, coal was mined by teams of six workers. Each team selected its own members and performed all of the work necessary, from extraction of the coal to loading to getting it above ground. Teams were paid on the basis of group effort and unit productivity, not individual effort. Teams tended to be quite cohesive.

Problems arose when new equipment and a change in technology were introduced. With this introduction a consequent change in the way work was conducted occurred. Rather than group work, individualized labor became the norm. Work therefore became both more individualized and specialized; that is, jobs were more fractionated. Gradually, productivity decreased and absenteeism increased.

Trist and Bamforth suggested a new approach that combined the essential social elements of the previous mode of work—team as opposed to individualized effort—yet retained the new technology. As a consequence of the company's management implementing what Trist and Bamforth suggested, productivity rose to previous levels, if not higher, and absenteeism significantly decreased. The specifics of this early work, including the documented measurements and outcomes, are reported in Trist (1960) and Trist and Bamforth (1951).

Shortly thereafter, A. K. Rice, another Tavistock consultant and researcher, conducted similar experiments and changes in two textile mills in Ahmedabad, India. The results of his interventions, which involved combining important social factors while, again, maintaining a group effort with the technological changes, were much the same: increased productivity and reduced damage and costs (Rice, 1958).

The approach pioneered by Trist, Bamforth, Rice, and their colleagues at Tavistock is based on the premise that an organization is simultaneously a social and a technical system. All organizations have a technology, whether it is producing something tangible or rendering a service, and this technology is a subsystem of the total organization. All organizations also are composed of people who interact to perform a task or series of tasks, and this human dimension constitutes the social subsystem. The emphasis of OD is typically on the social subsystem, but both subsystems and their interaction must be considered in any effort toward organizational change.

SURVEY FEEDBACK

Organization development has been influenced by industrial or organizational psychology. This influence is perhaps manifested most in the third precursor to OD, survey feedback. Industrial or organizational psychologists rely rather extensively on questionnaires for data collection and for diagnosis and assessment. Leadership questionnaires, for example, typically have been associated with the group of psychologists at Ohio State University in the 1950s. Questionnaires for organizational diagnosis, however, are more likely to be associated with the psychologists of the 1950s and 1960s at the Institute for Social Research at the University of Michigan. Rensis Likert, the first director of the institute, started by founding the Survey Research Center in 1946. Kurt Lewin had founded the Research Center for Group Dynamics at MIT. With his untimely death in 1947, the Center was moved to the University of Michigan later that year. These two centers initially constituted Likert's institute. The two primary thrusts of these centers, questionnaire surveys for organizational diagnosis and group dynamics, combined to give birth to the survey feedback method. As early as 1947 questionnaires were being used systematically to assess employee morale and attitudes in organizations.

One of the first of these studies, initiated and guided by Likert and conducted by Floyd Mann, was done with the Detroit Edison Company. From working on the problem of how best to use the survey data for organization improvement, the method now known as survey feedback evolved. Mann was key to the development of this method. He noted that when a manager was given the survey results, any resulting improvement depended on what the manager did with the information. If the manager discussed the survey results with his or her subordinates, however, and failed to plan certain changes for improvement jointly with them, nothing happened—except, perhaps, an increase in employee frustration with the ambiguity of having answered a questionnaire and never hearing anything further.

Briefly, the survey feedback method involves two steps. The first is the survey, collecting data by questionnaire to determine employees' perceptions of a variety of factors, most focusing on the management of the organization. The second step is the feedback, reporting the results of the survey systematically in summary form to all people who answered the questionnaire. Systematically, in this case, means that feedback occurs in phases, starting with the top team of the organization and flowing downward according to the formal hierarchy and within functional units or teams. Mann (1957) referred to this flow as the "interlocking chain of conferences." The chief executive officer, the division general manager, or the bureau chief, depending on the organization or subunit surveyed, and his or her immediate group of subordinates receive and discuss feedback from the survey first. Next, the subordinates and their respective groups of immediate subordinates do the same, and so forth downward until all members of the organization who had been surveyed hear a summary of the survey and then participate in a discussion of the meaning of the data and the implications. Each functional unit of the organization receives general feedback concerning the overall organization and specific feedback regarding its particular group. Following a discussion of the meaning of the survey results for their particular groups, boss and subordinates then jointly plan action steps for improvement. Usually, a consultant meets with each of the groups to help with data analysis, group discussion, and plans for improvement.

This is a rather orderly and systematic way of understanding an organization from the standpoint of employee perceptions and processing this understanding back into the organization so that change can occur, with the help of an outside resource person. Not only was it a direct precursor to and root of organization development, but it is an integral part of many current OD efforts.

Current OD efforts using survey feedback methodology do not, however, always follow a top-down, cascading process. The survey may begin in the middle of the managerial hierarchy and flow in either or both directions, or may begin at the bottom and work upward, as

Edgar Schein (1969) has suggested. For more information about and guidelines for conducting survey feedback activities, see David Nadler's book in the Addison-Wesley OD series (Nadler, 1977).

Finally, it should be noted that there are other forerunners or precursors to OD. A case in point is the activity prior to World War II at the Hawthorne Works of Western Electric. There the work of Mayo (1933), Roethlisberger and Dickson (1939), and Homans (1950) established that psychological and sociological factors make significant differences in worker performance.

The work at Hawthorne and its consequent popularity and impact occurred some two decades prior to the three precursors I chose to discuss in some depth. Thus, sensitivity training, sociotechnical systems, and survey feedback had a much greater and more direct influence on the beginnings of OD.

THEORETICAL ROOTS

Organization development has other roots in the area of concepts, models, and theories. Some people in or related to the burgeoning field of OD in the 1960s not only were doing but were thinking and writing as well. Some took an individual viewpoint, others a group perspective, and still others more of a macro view with the total organization as the frame of reference.

What follows is a synopsis of some of the thinking of a fairly select group of people who have helped to provide most of the theoretical and conceptual underpinnings of organization development. Ten theorists or conceptualizers were selected to represent the theory that is associated with organization development, because no single theory or conceptual model is representative or by itself encompasses the conceptual field or the practice of OD. What we have now is a group of minitheories that have influenced the thinking and consultative practice of OD practitioners. I refer to them as minitheories because each helps to explain only a portion of organizational behavior and effectiveness.

The ten theories or theory categories were selected because they best represent the theory we do have within the field of OD. Some prominent names in the field of OD were not included because their contributions have been more descriptive than theoretical, such as Blake and Mouton's (1978) Managerial Grid, a model of managerial styles; more practice-oriented, such as Beckhard (1969); Schein (1969); and Walton (1969); or more broadly explanatory and provocative, such as Bennis

(1966, 1967, 1969, 1970). The selection is a matter of judgment and certainly could be debated. Moreover, some of these theorists would not consider themselves to be OD practitioners. In fact, I have heard Frederick Herzberg state that he did not associate himself with the field. B. F. Skinner may never have heard of organization development. In other words, these theorists did not elect themselves into OD. I have chosen them because I believe that their thinking has had a large impact on the practices of OD.

The ten theories are presented in three major categories:

- The individual approach to change (Maslow and Herzberg, expectancy theorists Vroom and Lawler, job satisfaction theorists Hackman and Oldham, and Skinner)
- T-group approach to change (Lewin, Argyris, and Bion)
- The total system approach to change (Likert, Lawrence and Lorsch, and Levinson)

INDIVIDUAL PERSPECTIVE

Psychologists have taken two major approaches to the understanding of human motivation: need theory and expectancy theory. One of the early proponents of need theory was Murray; later representatives were Maslow and Herzberg. Expectancy theory, a more recent approach to understanding human motivation, is usually associated with Lawler and Vroom. Applications of need theory in organizations have centered around job design, career development, and certain aspects of human relations training, whereas expectancy theory has been applied with respect to both needs and rewards systems.

Need Theory—Maslow and Herzberg

According to Maslow (1954), human motivation can be explained in terms of needs that people experience in varying degrees all the time. An unsatisfied need creates a state of tension, which releases energy in the human system and, at the same time, provides direction. This purposeful energy guides the individual toward some goal that will respond to the unsatisfied need. The process whereby an unsatisfied need provides energy and direction toward some goal is Maslow's definition of motivation. Thus, only unsatisfied needs provide the sources of motivation; a satisfied need creates no tension and therefore no motivation.

Maslow contended that we progress through this five-level need system in a hierarchical fashion and that we do so one level at a time. The hierarchy represents a continuum from basic or psychological needs to safety and security needs to belongingness needs to ego-status needs to a need for self-actualization.

It is on this last point, a single continuum, that Herzberg parts company with Maslow. Herzberg (1966; Herzberg, Mausner, & Snyderman, 1959) maintains that there are two continua, one concerning dissatisfaction and the other concerning satisfaction. It may be that the two theorists are even more fundamentally different in that Herzberg's approach has more to do with job satisfaction than with human motivation. The implications and applications of the two are much more similar than they are divergent, however.

Specifically, Herzberg argues that only the goal objects associated with Maslow's ego-status and self-actualization needs provide motivation or satisfaction on the job. Meeting the lower-order needs simply reduces dissatisfaction; it does not provide satisfaction. Herzberg calls the goal objects associated with these lower-level needs (belonging, safety, and basic) hygiene or maintenance factors. Providing fringe benefits, for example, prevents dissatisfaction and thus is hygienic, but this provision does not ensure job satisfaction. Only motivator factors, such as recognition, opportunity for achievement, and autonomy on the job ensure satisfaction.

Herzberg's two categories, motivator factors and maintenance or hygiene factors, do not overlap. They represent qualitatively different aspects of human motivation.

It is important to note one other point of Herzberg's. He states that not only does the dimension of job dissatisfaction differ psychologically from job satisfaction, but it is also associated with an escalation phenomenon, or what some have called the principle of rising expectations: the more people receive, the more they want. This principle applies only to job dissatisfaction. Herzberg uses the example of a person who receives a salary increase of $1000 one year and then receives only a $500 increase the following year. Psychologically, the second increase is a cut in pay. Herzberg maintains that this escalation principle is a fact of life, and that we must live with it. Management must continue to provide, upgrade, and increase maintenance factors—good working conditions, adequate salaries, and competitive fringe benefits—but should not operate under the false assumption that these factors will lead to greater job satisfaction.

Job enrichment, a significant intervention within OD and a critical element of quality-of-work-life projects, is a direct application of Herzberg's theory and at least an indirect one of Maslow's.

Expectancy Theory—Lawler and Vroom

Expectancy theory (Lawler, 1973; Vroom, 1964) has yet to have the impact on organization development that need theory has had, but it is gaining in acceptance and popularity. This approach to understanding human motivation focuses more on outward behavior than on internal needs. The theory is based on three assumptions:

1. People believe that their behavior is associated with certain outcomes. Theorists call this belief the *performance-outcome expectancy.* People may expect that if they accomplish certain tasks, they will receive certain rewards.

2. Outcomes or rewards have different values (*valence*) for different people. Some people, for example, are more attracted to money as a reward than others are.

3. People associate their behavior with certain probabilities of success, called the *effort-performance expectancy.* People on an assembly line, for example, may have high expectancies that, if they try, they can produce 100 units per hour, but their expectancies may be very low that they can produce 150 units, regardless of how hard they may try.

Thus, people will be highly motivated when they believe (1) that their behavior will lead to certain rewards, (2) that these rewards are worthwhile and valuable, and (3) that they are able to perform at a level that will result in the attainment of the rewards.

Research has shown that high-performing employees believe that their behavior, or performance, leads to rewards that they desire. Thus, there is evidence for the validity of the theory. Moreover, the theory and the research outcomes associated with it have implications for how reward systems and work might be designed and structured.

Job Satisfaction—Hackman and Oldham

Hackman and Oldham's (1980) *work design model* is grounded in both need theory and expectancy theory. Their model is more restrictive in that it focuses on the relationship between job or work design and worker satisfaction. Although their model frequently leads to what is called job enrichment, as does the application of Herzberg's motivator-hygiene theory, the Hackman and Oldham model has broader implications. Briefly, Hackman and Oldham (1975) contend that there are three primary psychological states that significantly affect worker satisfaction:

1. Experienced meaningfulness of the work itself

2. Experienced responsibility for the work and its outcomes

3. Knowledge of results, or performance feedback

The more that work is designed to enhance these states, the more satisfying the work will be.

Positive Reinforcement—Skinner

The best way to understand the full importance of the applications of B. F. Skinner's (1953, 1971) thinking and his research results is to read his novel, *Walden Two* (1948). The book is about a utopian community designed and maintained according to Skinnerian principles of operant behavior and schedules of reinforcement. A similar application was made in an industrial situation in the Emery Air Freight case. By applying Skinnerian principles, which are based on numerous research findings, Emery quickly realized an annual savings of $650,000. (The Emery case is discussed more fully later in this section.)

Skinner is neither an OD practitioner nor a management consultant, but his theory and research are indeed applicable to management practices and to organizational change. For Skinner, control is key. If one can control the environment, one can then control behavior. In Skinner's approach, the more the environment is controlled the better, but the necessary element of control is the reward, both positive and negative. This necessity is based on a fundamental of behavior that Skinner derived from his many years of research, a concept so basic that it may be a law of behavior, that people (and animals) do what they are rewarded for doing. Let us consider the principles that under-lie this fundamental of behavior.

The first phase of learned behavior is called *shaping,* the process of successive approximations to reinforcement. When children are learning to walk, they are reinforced by their parents' encouraging comments or physical stroking, but this reinforcement typically follows only the behaviors that lead to effective walking. *Programmed learning,* invented by Skinner, is based on this principle. To maintain the behavior, a sched-ule of reinforcement is applied and, generally, the more variable the schedule is, the longer the behavior will last.

Skinner therefore advocates positive reinforcement for shaping and controlling behavior. Often, however, when we consider controlling behavior, we think of punishment ("If you don't do this, you're gonna get it!"). According to Skinner, punishment is no good. His stance is not based entirely on his values or whims, however. Research clearly shows that, although punishment may temporarily stop a certain behavior, negative reinforcement must be administered continuously for this certain process to be maintained. The principle is the opposite of that for positively reinforced behavior. There are two very practical concerns here. First, having to reinforce a certain behavior continu-ously is not very efficient. Second, although the punished behavior may be curtailed, it is unlikely that the subject will learn what to do; all that is learned is what *not* to do.

Thus, the way to control behavior according to Skinnerian theory and research is to reinforce the desirable behavior positively and, after the shaping process, to reinforce the behavior only occasionally. An attempt should be made to ignore undesirable behavior and not to punish (unless, perhaps, society must be protected) but, rather, to spend time positively shaping the desired behavior. The implica-tions of Skinner's work for organizations is that a premium is placed on such activities as establishing incentive systems, reducing or elim-inating many of the control systems that contain inherent threats and punishments, providing feedback to all levels of employees regarding their performance, and developing programmed-learning techniques for training employees.

The application of Skinner's work to OD did not occur systemati-cally until the 1970s. Thus, his influence is not as pervasive as is Maslow's, for example. Skinner's behavior-motivation techniques as applied to people also raise significant questions regarding ethics and values: Who exercises the control, and is the recipient aware? Thus, it is not a question of whether Skinner's methodology works, but rather how and under what circumstances it is used.

GROUP PERSPECTIVE
The Group as the Focus of Change—Lewin

The theorist among theorists, at least within the scope of the behavioral sciences, is Kurt Lewin. His thinking has had a more pervasive impact on organization development, both directly and indirectly, than any other person's. It was Lewin who laid the groundwork for much of what we know about social change, particularly in a group and by some extrapolation in an organization. Lewin's interest and, easily determined by implication, his values have also influenced OD. As a Jew who escaped Hitler's Germany in the 1930s, it was not coincidental that Lewin was intensely interested in the study of autocratic versus democratic behavior and matters of influence and change (Marrow, 1969). Thus, his own and his students' research findings regarding the consequences of such variables as participative leadership and decision making have had considerable impact on the typical objectives of most if not all OD efforts.

According to Lewin (1948, 1951), behavior is a function of a person's personality, discussed primarily in terms of motivation or needs, and the situation or environment in which the person is acting. The environment is represented as a field of forces that affect the person. Thus, a person's behavior at any given moment can be predicted if we know that person's needs and if we can determine the *intensity* and *valence* (whether the force is positive or negative for the person) of the forces impinging on the person from the environment. Although Lewin borrowed the term *force* from physics, he defined the construct psychologically. Thus, one's perception of the environment is key, not necessarily reality. An example of a force, therefore, could be the perceived power of another person. Whether or not I will accomplish a task you want me to do is a function of the degree to which such accomplishment will respond to a need I have and how I perceive your capacity to influence me—whether you are a force in my environment (field).

Lewin made a distinction between *imposed* or induced forces, those acting on a person from the outside, and *own* forces, those directly reflecting the person's needs. The implications of this distinction are clear. Participation in determining a goal is more likely to create its own forces toward accomplishing it than is a situation in which goal determination is imposed by others. When a goal is imposed on a person, his or her motives may match accomplishment of the goal, but the chances are considerably more variable or random than if the goal is determined by the person in the first place. Typically, then, for imposed or induced goals to be accomplished by a person, the one who induced them must exert continuous influence or else the person's other motives, not associated with goal accomplishment, will likely determine his or her behavior. This aspect of Lewin's theory helps to explain the generally positive consequences of participative management and consensual decision making.

Another distinction Lewin made regarding various forces in a person's environment is the one between *driving* and *restraining* forces. Borrowing yet another concept from physics, quasi-stationary equilibria, he noted that the perceived status quo in life is just that—a *perception*. In reality, albeit psychological reality, a given situation is a result of a dynamic process and is not static. The process flows from one moment to the next, with ups and downs, and over time gives the impression of a static situation, but there actually are some forces pushing in one direction and other, counterbalancing forces that restrain movement. The level of productivity in an organization may appear static, but sometimes it is being pushed higher—by the force of supervisory pressure, for example—and sometimes it is being restrained or even decreased by a counterforce, such as a norm of the work group. There are many different counterbalancing forces in any given situation, and what is called a force-field analysis is used to identify the two sets of forces.

Change from the status quo is therefore a two-step process. First, a force-field analysis is conducted, and then the intensity of a force or set of forces is either increased or decreased. Change can be fostered by adding to or increasing the intensity of the forces Lewin labeled *driving forces*—that is, forces that push in the desired direction for change. Or change can be fostered by diminishing the opposing or restraining forces. Lewin's theory predicts that the better of these two choices is to reduce the intensity of the restraining forces. By adding forces or increasing the intensity on the driving side, a simultaneous increase would occur on the restraining side, and the overall tension for the system—whether it is a person, a group, or an organization—would intensify. The better choice, then, is to reduce the restraining forces.

This facet of Lewin's field theory helps us to determine not only the nature of change but how to accomplish it more effectively. Lewinian theory argues that it is more efficacious to direct change at the group level than at the individual level.

If one attempts to change an attitude or the behavior of an individual without attempting to change the same behavior or attitude in the group to which the individual belongs, then the individual will be a deviate and either will come under pressure from the group to get back into line or will be rejected entirely. Thus, the major leverage point for change is at the group level—for example, by modifying a group norm or standard. According to Lewin (1958):

> As long as group standards are unchanged, the individual will resist change more strongly the farther he is to depart from group standards. If the group standard itself is changed, the resistance which is due to the relation between individual and group standard is eliminated. (p. 210)

Adherence to Lewinian theory from the standpoint of application involves viewing the organization as a social system, with many and varied subsystems, primarily groups. We look at the behavior of people in the organization in terms of (1) whether their needs jibe with the organization's directions, usually determined by their degree of commitment; (2) the norms to which people conform and the degree of that conformity; (3) how power is exercised (induced versus own forces); and (4) the decision-making process (involvement leading to commitment).

Changing Values Through the Group—Argyris

It is not possible to place the work of Chris Argyris in one category, one theory, or one conceptual framework. He has developed a number of minitheories whose relationship and possible overlap are not always apparent. He has always focused largely on interpersonal and group behavior, however, and he has emphasized behavioral change within a group context, along the same value lines as McGregor's (1960) Theory Y. The work described in *Management and Organizational Development: The Path from XA to YB* (Argyris, 1971) best illustrates this emphasis. Since Argyris has made many theoretical contributions, we shall briefly cover his work chronologically.

Argyris's early work (1962) may be characterized as emphasizing the relationship of individual personality and organizational dynamics. His objective was to look for ways in which this relationship could be "satisficed," with the person and the organization both compromising so that each could profit from each other. *Satisficed* is a word formed by combining *satisfied* and *suffice* and it means that there is an improvement but that it is less than optimal for each party. Although the relationship may never be optimal for both parties, it could still be better for both. For this relationship between the individual and the organization to be achieved, the organization must adjust its value system toward helping its members to be more psychologically healthy, less dependent on and controlled by the organization. The individuals must become more open with their feelings, more willing to trust one another, and more internally committed to the organization's goals.

In his thinking, research, and writing during the late 1960s and early 1970s, Argyris became more clearly associated with organization development. His thrust of this period was in (1) theorizing about competent consultation, and especially about the nature of an effective intervention, and (2) operationalizing organizational change in behavioral terms by McGregor's Theory Y. Regarding the first aspect, Argyris (1970) contends that, for any intervention into an organization-social system to be effective, it must generate valid information, lead to free, informed choice on the part of the client, and provide internal commitment by the client to the choices taken. More on this aspect of Argyris's work is provided in Chapter 5. For the second aspect, Argyris connects behaviors (he calls them Pattern A) with McGregor's Theory X and Theory Y (Pattern B). Argyris specifies the behavioral manifestations of someone who holds either of the sets of assumptions about human beings in organizations that were postulated earlier by McGregor (1960). Pattern A behaviors are characterized as predominantly intellectual rather than emotional, conforming rather than experimenting, individually oriented rather than group oriented, involving closer rather than open communications, and generally mistrusting rather than trusting. This pattern is the opposite of interpersonally competent behavior. Thus, Pattern B is an extension of Argyris's earlier facets of interpersonal competence.

More recently, Argyris has turned his attention to the gaps in people's behavior between what they say (he calls it espoused theory) and what they do (theory in action). People may say that they believe that McGregor's Theory Y assumptions about human beings are valid, for example, but they may act according to Pattern A. Argyris goes on to argue that as people become more aware of these gaps between their stated beliefs and their behavior, they will be more motivated to reduce the differences, to be more consistent. In one project Argyris tape-recorded managerial staff meetings, analyzed the recorded behaviors, and then showed the managers where their actions were not consistent with their words (Argyris, 1973). More recently, in collaboration with Don Schön, Argyris studied and elaborated the learning process involved in obtaining greater self-awareness and organizational awareness about human effectiveness (Argyris & Schön, 1978). Argyris and Schön argue that most organizations accomplish no more than "single-loop learning," that problems are solved or fixed and a single loop of learning is accomplished. For significant organizational improvement and for ensuring long-term survival and renewal, however, change must occur in more fundamental ways. Although problems must be solved in a single loop, new ways of learning how to solve problems must be learned as well. Another loop is thus added to the learning cycle, what Argyris and Schön refer to as "double-loop learning." Single-loop learning is like adjusting a thermostat to a standard that has already been established, whereas double-loop learning means confronting the current standard and creating a new one. This process of learning is analogous to if not the same as the way OD is sometimes defined as a planned process of change in the organization's culture—how we do things and how we relate to one another.

The Group Unconscious—Bion

Most people believe that everyone has an unconscious. Freud has clearly had an effect. Wilfred Bion believes, as others do, that there is also a group unconscious—a collective unconscious that is more than the sum of the individual unconsciouses—and he gives compelling but complex arguments (Bion, 1961; Rioch, 1970).

Bion believes that every group is actually composed of two groups, the work group and the basic-assumption group; that is, every group behaves as if it were two groups, one concerned with group accomplishment and rational actions, the other concerned with activity that stems from the unconscious and is irrational. Bion does not mean simply that a group is both rational and irrational. He goes far beyond this commonly accepted dichotomy.

The *work group* is the aspect of group functioning that is concerned with accomplishing what the group is composed to do, the task at hand.

The work group is aware of its purpose, or at the outset knows that its initial task is to establish clarity of purpose. The work group is sure about, or quickly becomes sure about, roles and responsibilities in the group. The work group is also clearly conscious of the passage of time and the procedures and processes needed to accomplish the task.

How many times have you been a member or leader of a group that fit such a description? I suspect that it has not been very often, if ever. Bion states that groups do not behave in this clearly rational and sensible way because there is always another group operating simultaneously—the *basic-assumption* group.

Bion theorizes that all groups function according to basic assumptions, that groups operate as if certain things are inevitable. Perhaps an analogy will help to explain. In the early days of automobiles, many people made the basic assumption that no motorized vehicle could go faster than a horse, and these people acted accordingly. In fact, some of them eventually lost money because they bet heavily on that assumption. The point is that they acted as if their belief were true and inevitable.

According to Bion, basic-assumption groups may take, at least predominantly, one of three forms: the dependency group, the fight-flight group, and the pairing group. The *dependency group* assumes that the reason the group exists is to be protected and to be assured of providence by its leader. The group members act immaturely, childishly, and as if they know little or nothing as compared with the leader. The leader is all powerful and wise. In the dependency group, the leader is typically idolized. We mortals are neither omnipotent nor omniscient, however, and the group members soon realize that they must seek a "new messiah." The cycle then repeats itself with a new leader.

The *fight-flight* group assumes that it must preserve itself, that its survival is at stake, so group members act accordingly. Taking action is the key to survival, as in the proverbial army command: "Do something even if it's wrong!" It is the *group* that must be preserved, so individuals may be sacrificed through fight or abandonment (flight). The leader's role in this basic-assumption group is clear: to lead the group into battle or retreat. The best leader is one who acts in a paranoid manner, assuming, "They're out to get us, gang!" Eventually and inevitably the leader will not meet all the group's demands, at which point the group panics and searches for a new leader.

In the *pairing* group the assumption is that the group's purpose is to give birth to a new messiah. The leader in this case is purely incidental, and the group must quickly get on with the business of bringing forth the new savior. Two members therefore pair off to procreate. The two may be both male, both female, or male and female, but the basic assumption is that when two people pair, the pairing is sexual in nature, even though it takes the innocent form of establishing a subcommittee. Although new life and hope may be provided, the new messiah, as the Christian Messiah, will soon be done away with. All the basic-assumption groups behave as if the leader must be replaced or, to use Bion's more dramatic and graphic terminology, as if the leader must be crucified.

Although the work group and the basic-assumption group are functioning simultaneously, their degree of activity varies. At times the work group is predominant and at other times the basic-assumption group holds sway.

Bion was never an OD practitioner; he was a psychotherapist. His theory, however, is applicable to interventions with teams, consultations with leaders, and diagnoses of possible processes of collusion. For a direct application and extension of the latter group or organizational dynamic, see Harvey's "Abilene Paradox" (1974), an extension of Bion's theory that explains collusive behavior on the part of members of a group.

For the OD practitioner serving as a consultant to an organizational team, Bion's theory is particularly useful for diagnosing internal problems, especially those concerning team members' relationships with the leader. For example, when subordinates defer to the boss for most if not all decisions, a basic-assumption mode of dependency may be occurring, with the work group mode being submerged. Calling this process to the attention of the group may break the basic-assumption mode and help to facilitate the group's task accomplishment. An OD practitioner might intervene with a comment like, "We seem to be looking to (the boss) for practically all of our problem solutions," and follow up with a question such as, "Don't we have experience among us that we could tap into more?" Helping a work group to stay focused on its task is a way of preventing flight and another example of how to apply Bion's theory.

TOTAL SYSTEM PERSPECTIVE
Participative Management, The One Best Way— Likert

Likert is best known for two concepts: the *linking pin* notion of management and the four-system model of organizations. He is also known for his unequivocal advocacy of participative management as the approach to be taken by managers, regardless of organizational type. Likert's method for organization development is survey feedback. We shall consider each of these concepts briefly.

Likert's (1961) idea of the linking pin originated from his desire to design organizations in a more decentralized form without eliminating the hierarchical structure. He also wanted to incorporate more opportunity for group activity, especially group decision making, in the managerial process. Thus, each manager is simultaneously a member of two groups, one in which he or she manages and is the leader and one in which he or she is a subordinate and follows the leadership of a boss. By being a member of both these hierarchical groups, the person becomes a key link within the vertical chain of command. This linkage manifests itself primarily in activities involving communication and resolution of conflict. The manager-subordinate, therefore, is the primary conduit for information and facilitates the resolution of conflict, by virtue of the linking position, when there are differences between the two vertically connected organizational groups. An organization chart is drawn so that groups overlap vertically rather than in the more traditional way, as separate boxes connected only by lines.

Likert (1967) has described four major models or systems of organization design: the *autocratic,* the *benevolent autocratic,* the *consultative,* and the *participative.* He uses seven organizational functions to describe the four models differentially: *leadership, motivation, communication, interaction and influence, decision making, goal setting,* and *control.* His "Profile of Organizational Characteristics," a diagnostic questionnaire, is organized according to these seven functions and four models. Organization members' answers to the questionnaire provide a perceptual profile of the organization. The profile is derived from the respondents' views of how the seven functions are managed and depicts which of the four systems seems to be predominant, at least in the eyes of the respondents.

Likert not only argues that there is one best way to manage, he also espouses one best way to conduct an organization development effort. His method is survey feedback, the survey instrument being his Profile of Organizational Characteristics and the feedback being organized and analyzed according to the four-system model of organizational management. In an organization development effort, then, Likert's approach is highly data-based, but the diagnosis is largely limited to the functions he deems important. Once the survey data are collected, they are given back in profile form to organizational family units—to a boss and his or her team. This group then considers the data in light of their particular situation and organizational mandate, then decides on a plan for changes they want to make, and finally takes the necessary action for implementing the plan. Approximately a year later, the organization should take another survey to check progress and to plan and implement further changes.

Although organizational change agents may be uncomfortable with Likert's one best way and may prefer an approach that is more contingent and perhaps more flexible, they can be very sure of the direction and the objectives of the change effort.

It All Depends—Lawrence and Lorsch

For an organization to operate efficiently and effectively, one person cannot do everything, and every organizational member cannot do the same thing. In any organization, therefore, there is a division of labor. Lawrence and Lorsch (1967, 1969) call this differentiation. In an organization with many divisions, some people must provide coordination, so that what the organization does is organized in some fashion. Lawrence and Lorsch label this process integration. Their approach is sometimes referred to as a theory of differentiation-integration. A more appropriate label, however, and the one they prefer, is *contingency theory.* They believe that how an organization should be structured and how it should be managed depend on several factors, primarily the organization's environment, or its marketplace. The central elements of the Lawrence and Lorsch contingency theory are differentiation, integration, the organization–environment interface, and the implicit contract between the employees and management.

Differentiation means dividing up tasks so that everything that needs to be done is accomplished. To determine the degree of differentiation in an organization, Lawrence and Lorsch consider four variables:

1. *Goal certainty.* Are goals clear and easily measured or ambiguous and largely qualitative?

2. *Structure.* Is the structure formal, with precise policy and procedures, or loose and flexible, with policy largely a function of current demand?

3. *Interaction.* Is there considerable interpersonal and intergroup communication and cooperation or very little?

4. *Timespan of feedback.* Do people in the organization see the
results of their work quickly or does it take a long time?

The more that units within an organization differ from one
another along these four dimensions, the more differentially structured the organization is. Some units may be very sure of their goals
while others are not so sure, and some units may follow strict and precise work procedures while other units are still trying to formulate
working procedures. It should be clear, therefore, that highly differentiated organizations are more difficult to coordinate. In a pyramidal organization, the coordination and the resolution of conflict are
handled by the next higher level of management. When organizations
are simultaneously highly differentiated and decentralized with respect
to management, Lawrence and Lorsch argue that integrator roles are
needed, that certain people must be given specific assignments for
coordinating and integrating diverse functions. These people may or
may not be in key decision-making positions, but they ensure that
decisions are made by someone or by the appropriate group.

Should an organization be structured in centralized (pyramidal)
or decentralized fashion? We already know the answer: It depends. But
on *what* does it depend? Lawrence and Lorsch state that it depends
primarily on the organization's environment, on whether the environment is complex and rapidly changing, as in the electronics industry, or relatively simple (one or two major markets) and stable (raw
materials forthcoming and predictable and market likely to remain
essentially the same in the foreseeable future). The more complex the
environment, the more decentralized and flexible management should
be. Lawrence and Lorsch's reasoning is that, the more rapidly changing the environment, the more necessary it is that the organization
have people monitoring these changes, and the more they should be
in a position to make decisions on the spot. When the organization's
environment is not particularly complex and when conditions are relatively stable, management should be more centralized, since this way
of structuring is more efficient.

Lawrence and Lorsch consider matters of conflict resolution
because conflicts arise quickly and naturally in a highly differentiated
organization and the management of these conflicts is critical for efficient and effective organizational functioning. Moreover, if the organization is highly differentiated and decentralized, conflict is even
more likely.

Finally, how well an organization operates is also a function of the nature of the interface between management and employees. Lawrence and Lorsch recognize the importance of individual motivation and effective supervision. They tend to view motivation in terms of expectancy, believing that employees' motivation (and morale) is based on the degree to which their expectations about how they should be treated are actually met by management in the work environment.

In summary, Lawrence and Lorsch are known as contingency theorists. They advocate no single form of organizational structure or single style of management. The structure and the style depend on the business of the organization and its environment—how variable or how stable it is.

Lawrence and Lorsch have been among the most influential theorists for OD practitioners. There is something appealing about the idea of considering contingencies before acting.

The Organization as a Family—Levinson

Harry Levinson believes that an organization can be psychoanalyzed and that an organization operates like a family, with the chief executive officer as the father. According to Levinson, all organizations "recapitulate the basic family structure in a culture." Thus, the type of organization Levinson understands best, of course, is the family-owned business, and his theory about organizations and how they operate and change has its roots in Freudian psychology (Levinson, 1972a, 1972b).

Levinson does not look at organizations exclusively through psychoanalytical glasses, however. He is well aware that structure, the type of business, and the outside environment affect the internal behavioral dynamics of organizations. More important for Levinson's diagnosis of an organization, however, is the nature of the organization's personality (we might call it culture). He believes that an organization has a personality, just as an individual does, and that the health of an organization, like that of a person, can be determined in terms of how effectively the various parts of the personality are integrated. He refers to this process as *maintaining equilibrium*. Levinson also believes that implicit psychological contracts exist between management and employees, based on earlier experiences from family life. If the employees behave themselves (are good boys and girls), the parents (management) will reward them appropriately. Thus, the psychological contract is characterized by dependency. Note that this aspect of Levinson's theory is similar to Argyris's theory.

Continuing the psychoanalytic paradigm, Levinson theorizes that the chief executive officer represents the ego ideal for the organizational family and that this ideal, for better or for worse, motivates the kinds of people who are attracted to the organization in the first place, the interaction patterns among people in the organization, especially in matters of authority, and the kinds of people who are promoted. If a chief executive officer stays in office for a long time, the personality of the organization slowly crystallizes over the years; those who aspire to the ego ideal stay in the organization, and those who do not, leave. Accordingly, Levinson believes that history is a critical factor in diagnosing an organization.

Levinson is a clinical psychologist who became more interested in organizational health than in individual psychodynamics as a result of his work at the Menninger Clinic. He has applied the principles of individual clinical therapy to his consulting practice with organizations. His approach as a consultant is (1) to immerse himself as deeply as possible in the psychodynamics of the organization; (2) to take a thorough history of the organization, just as a clinician would in the initial session with a patient; (3) to work predominantly with top management, since they tend to shape the personality of the organization and are therefore in the best position to change it; and (4) to pay particular attention to the stress factors in the organization and to how organizational members cope. In regard to this last point, Levinson is considered the "great worrier" among OD theorists. He worries about executive stress (Levinson, 1975) and about the incidence in an organization of such variables as psychosomatic illnesses, absenteeism, and business pressures, such as the all-out emphasis many organizations place on meeting the "bottom line." Levinson is very interested in what people do with their energy, in whether human energy in the organization is directed toward goal accomplishment or toward coping with stress.

In summary, as a consultant, Levinson uses the clinical case method in diagnosis, intervenes primarily at the top of an organization, and bases his theory on psychoanalysis. In his own words:

> You've got to take into account all the factors in an organization, just as you gather all the main facts of a person's life in taking a case history. But you need a comprehensive theory like psychoanalysis to make sense of all the facts, to make it hang together in a useful way. (1972a, p. 126)

SUMMARY

At the risk of oversimplification, I have summarized ten theorists' views by categorizing them according to their perspectives and emphases and according to potential applications of their theoretical approaches. A summary of these factors is given in Table 2.1. Keep in mind that there is no single, all-encompassing theory for organization development. What we have are several minitheories that help us understand certain aspects of organizational behavior and OD. Taken together and comparatively, they become more useful to the practitioner who must cope with an ever-changing, complex, total organization.

Perspective	Theorist	Emphasis	Application
Individual	Maslow and Herzberg	Individual needs	Career development, job enrichment
	Vroom and Lawler	Individual expectancies and values	Reward system design, performance appraisal
	Hackman and Oldham	Job satisfaction	Job and work design, job enrichment
	Skinner	Individual performance	Incentive systems, reward system design
Group	Lewin	Norms and values	Changing conformity patterns
	Argyris	Interpersonal competence and values	Training and education
	Bion	Group unconscious, psychoanalytic basis	Group behavior diagnosis
System	Likert	Management style and approach	Change to participative management
	Lawrence and Lorsch	Organizational structure	Change contingent on organizational environment
	Levinson	Organization as a family, psychoanalytic basis	Diagnosis of organization according to familial patterns

Table 2.1. Summary of Primary OD Theorists According to Their Perspectives, Emphases, and Applications.

CHAPTER THREE

Revolutions in OD

The New and the New, New Things

Philip H. Mirvis

———∿∿∿———

*O*D is dead. Long live OD! This is the current-day construction of the state of organization development. Leading scholar-practitioners (for example, Bradford & Burke, 2004; Worley & Feyerherm, 2003) ask, "Is OD in crisis?" The typical answer is *yes, but* . . . new ideas, problems, and people in the field hold promise for turning things around. How fascinating that this same position (sometimes expressed by the same folks!) was in currency when I began studying OD as a graduate student in the 1970s, researching it as a scholar in the 1980s, and practicing it as a consultant in the 1990s. Frankly, I have said the same thing myself.

The advance of OD knowledge has slowed as the field became the intellectual captive of the mainstream organizational behavior and theory disciplines. I concluded this in part one of my two-part history of OD (Mirvis, 1988). But even as practice was offering solid, proven methods to address organizational challenges that centered on competitiveness, restructuring, mergers and acquisitions, quality improvement, team building, and personal growth, practitioners were distancing themselves from OD and its values. Indeed, by the 1990s, former ODers were calling themselves experts in strategy implementation or human resources and joking publicly during their consultations about OD's pre-occupation with soft things—the "birds and bunnies"—in contrast to real-time problems and their hard-hitting tools of change management.

One contributor to a 1998 OD practitioners' conference, for example, noted that over one hundred thousand websites proffered advice and assistance on change management, including the "Big Five" and all the major management, strategy, information technology, and human resource consulting firms (Davis, 1998). The title of his talk, drawn from an advertisement about updating a tired auto brand, said it plainly: "Change Management: Not Your Father's OD." That trend continues: a 2006 Google search for change management generated 383,000,000 sites.

In part two of my essay (Mirvis, 1990), however, I took a contrary tack. I contended that new knowledge continued to enliven and move the field forward and that there were more innovative change efforts under way than imagined. Leading practitioners were stretching OD beyond its conceptual boundaries. The artist's creative drive and spiritualist's search for meaning were intermixing with and extending the applied science of OD.

To illustrate, I made a seemingly heretical point that laboratory training, once the wellspring of OD but later peripheral to it, was a vital source of innovation. The basic T-group, developed after World War II and popularized in the 1960s, had become passé. But by the 1990s, working people were going to workshops to meditate, manage stress, and tap the creative potential of their right lobes; experience risk in raft trips or reverie on mountain treks; and explore new ways to manage their time, space, and lives.

An alert observer could argue that these programs aim at personal development and better represent the continued flowering of the human potential movement than they do OD's blossoming. In rejoinder, I point to the "power lab" and its successor, the "power and systems lab," both developed by Barry Oshry (1999), as revolutionary advances in laboratory education aimed at core processes of organizing. I also cite Bill Torbert's "The Theater of Inquiry" (1989), which draws from the performing arts, and M. Scott Peck's community-building workshops (1993) based on psychospiritual principles, which both seek to stimulate new forms of organizing. The widespread appeal of organizational theater (Nissley, Taylor, & Houden, 2004) and soul work in business (Mirvis, 1997), accompanied by a wave of fresh theorizing on the aesthetic and spiritual dimensions of OD, are indicative of how laboratory education continues as a primary source of R&D for the field.

Another notion that runs contrary to beliefs about OD's death centers on action research, the field's prime methodology. I have argued that although action research has become "old hat," it has new potential in participatory research (Brown & Tandon, 1983) and action science (Argyris, Putnam, & Smith, 1985). The former gives change experts and clients equal sway in defining the problems in human systems. The latter offers frameworks to unpack assumptions and test shared commitments to action. I have pointed as well to the promise of then nascent ideas about appreciative inquiry (Cooperrider & Srivastva, 1987), scenario planning (Schwartz, 1991), and future search conferences (Weisbord, 1992) that were just making their way into practice.

It is clear today that these then revolutionary ideas turned OD's traditional building blocks of problem diagnosis, solution brainstorming, and action planning into a Rubik's cube: a look into future opportunities serves to unearth current problems; an emphasis on what's working well in a human system helps ameliorate what's wrong. Furthermore, my earlier commentaries gave only modest attention to what would turn into booming interest in organization learning (Senge, 1990)—a topic that generates 145 billion Internet hits today.

A crabbed academic might contend that organization learning (OL, as it has been mainstreamed via an acronym) is more an amalgam of familiar ideas than a revolutionary new paradigm (Mirvis, 1996). This understates the market appeal of the idea that organizations can learn and the power of the movement to generate innovative "fifth discipline" change tools and methodologies (Senge, Roberts, Ross, Smith, & Kleiner, 1994). Peter Senge and colleagues have since developed a new type of action-research methodology that involves the "presencing" of desired futures and prototyping of new actions (Senge, Scharmer, Jaworski, & Flowers, 2004). With edited volumes (for example, Reason & Bradbury, 2001) and a new journal on the subject, who would deem action research "old hat" today?

Although new kinds of laboratory education and action inquiry are not standard fare in most change management efforts today, this chapter argues that the field lives on vitally through new theories and practices. Consider, for example, the case of Ben and Jerry, two visionaries out of the business mainstream who sponsored OD in their company in the late 1980s and into the 1990s, and who pride themselves on being "weird."

BACK TO THE FUTURE: OD AT BEN & JERRY'S

The story of these two ice cream entrepreneurs has an antiestablishment New Age quality. The "boys," childhood friends, dropped out of college in the late 1960s, worked at odd jobs, and in 1978 together opened a small ice cream shop in Burlington, Vermont, with scant know-how and capital. Neither Ben nor Jerry had any intention of becoming "businessmen." Both were committed to making the best ice cream and having fun while doing so.

More than this, the founders believed that business draws from the community and is obliged to give something back. In the early days, this meant free ice cream to loyal customers and worthy charities. As the company grew to sales of over $50 million, Ben & Jerry's (B&J) embraced what it calls a "social mission" that ranged from making regular donations to social change groups to introducing "Peace Pops" (ice cream bars) whose profits go to the peace movement.

Ben and Jerry had tried to introduce this "funky" and socially responsible orientation inside the company. In the late 1980s, it became evident to the founders, managers, and employees that the company's external image of "funk, fun, and love" was inconsistent with the atmosphere inside. The company was always short on ice cream and long on hours, pressure, and problems. I was commissioned to begin organization development and bring people and the company together (Mirvis, 1991).

Diagnosis

Three months of interviews with key managers and staff in B&J showed them committed to the company and comfortable in an environment where they could "be themselves." At the same time, however, organizational structures and systems were not keeping pace with growth, people lacked clear roles and did not agree about corporate priorities, and the human organization had not jelled behind any encompassing company mission.

The intent of the OD effort was to help the board of directors take ownership of the company's mission and cede operating responsibilities to management. In turn, it was to empower managers to run the company in a unified and responsible fashion. There were pragmatic issues to address: managers did not see themselves as a team, nor had they worked together to formulate goals and responsibilities. There were also matters of principle: many managers had no prior experience leading a company dedicated to social responsibility. And several did not fully buy into socially oriented company policies, including active association with the peace movement. Overall, people were chafing at the founders' mandate to have "fun" at work while achieving record production at superior quality standards.

An Out-of-Doors Retreat

The managers went to an off-site retreat where all were blindfolded, roped together in their three work-related clusters, and charged with locating three inner tubes symbolically lashed together about seventy-five yards away. Members of each cluster shouted instructions or demanded them, took stabs at leading, and then pulled back in frustration, while other groups stumbled along vainly searching for the "goal." One group finally located the tubes, cheered for its own success, and chided the others. This exercise provided a window into current company dynamics and led to an examination of teamwork, competition, and cooperation throughout the rest of the retreat.

The managers climbed ropes, worked on problem-solving initiatives, and trekked in the out-of-doors, all in service of finding new ways to work together. One evening they talked about their personal values through the medium of "mind maps." The managers all recorded on a silhouette the persons and events that had most shaped their character, how they wanted to be thought of in the company and by peers, and what mark they wanted to leave behind. Several spoke of scarring experiences in Vietnam; poignant efforts to cope with family trials; the impact that mothers, fathers, and now spouses and children had on them. Many cried. There were hugs and cheers.

The next evening, the clusters had the opportunity to put on skits about their part in the organization. The manufacturing cluster drew from a popular game and had peers guess the company's priorities from conflicting clues. The marketing and sales group selected a member to wear a beard like one of the founders and joined him in songs and dance about the trials of competing with less socially responsible companies and the seeming folly of having fun at work.

The search for the inner tubes was repeated at the end of the retreat. The groups quickly joined forces to analyze the problem, work out a plan, figure out roles and responsibilities, and establish procedures to stay in touch with one another. They reached the goal in one-third the time. The retreat concluded with each attendee's selecting of a "totem" to represent his or her experiences and developing a personal action plan for the months ahead.

Follow-Up

The retreat was the beginning of months of team building with the newly created management group. Each working cluster was charged with developing a mission statement and goals for its area. The groups met together several times to mark progress and coordinate directions. At one session, managers drew pictures illustrating the degree of alignment between functions and the overall vision of the company. In one, the founders were depicted as the sun, functions as orbiting planets, and the market as a streaking comet, adding brilliance to the solar system but threatening to pull the planets out of orbit. The result was a series of cluster goal statements, an action agenda for the next year, and closer interpersonal and work relationships.

Did these interventions make a difference? Managers rated themselves as more of a team, and functions reported that they were more aligned. But the founders were worried that the "funk and fun" was lost in all of this "business." Moreover, the managers became something of a threat to the founders, who were having trouble letting go.

Subsequently, the founders, through the board of directors, configured the cluster goals into a broader statement of the company's economic, product, and social mission. The management team and founders met to examine their differences. Prior to the meeting, the founders had said publicly that management "wasn't weird enough" and expressed worry that the company's social mission was being sacrificed to growth. The managers took this to heart. Each came wearing a mask of either Ben or Jerry and buttons saying "We Are Weird." They then worked with the founders on issues of trust and empowerment, fleshed out how the two bodies would work together, and made a point that the company would remain committed to high-quality production, good works, *and* fun.

Following the session, several action committees were formed to bring neglected aspects of the mission statement to life. A safety committee helped the company achieve record performance in that regard. A joy committee was formed to ensure that spirit was kept alive, and a budget committee met to formulate B&J's first one-year plan. Several months later, the company's mission statement was unveiled at an all-employee meeting. Ben introduced the social mission to the tune of "What's Wrong with Love?" Jerry described product aspirations, including the introduction of low-fat ice cream. The general manager detailed the company's economic mission to the sounds of "Money, Money." The day was completed when Mr. Clean arrived to celebrate the new "cleanliness campaign."

OLD-FASHIONED AND NEWFANGLED OD

The work at B&J illustrates both the evolutionary and revolutionary character of OD.

Building on the Old

The B&J story shows how OD theory and practice have advanced incrementally over the years. The simple notion of getting people together, away from day-to-day organization life, and helping them open up about their life stories dates back to workshops at the National Training Laboratories (NTL) in the 1960s. Interventions aimed at team building came into OD in the 1970s. Beckhard (1972), for example, urged practitioners to attend to goals, responsibilities and roles, and work processes in addition to interpersonal dimensions and group development. Team building at B&J incorporated these structural and task-related considerations.

At the start of the OD work, company management did not see itself as a team, nor was it functioning as one. This made starting change at the top and building a management team logical and consistent with OD's traditional top-down change model (Shephard, 1975). Diagnosis also revealed that B&J was suffering from typical problems faced by fast-start, high-growth enterprises (Greiner, 1972). Management systems were "underorganized." Thus interventions were sequenced to enable management to come together as a team, work through conflicts with the founders, and redesign their structure and work systems—all standard OD protocol (Blake & Mouton, 1976).

The 1980s and 1990s brought concepts like vision and alignment into OD vocabulary and practice. These were readily incorporated into the change efforts at B&J. Accordingly, Ben, Jerry, and the board set to work devising an integrative three-part mission statement, and the managers drew pictures to illustrate their alignment with the company's mission.

Introducing the New

OD efforts at B&J also illustrate revolutionary ideas and new practices. For instance, the goals of the change program were not simply to improve relationships and organizational effectiveness—traditional OD aims. They were also to develop a sense of unity in the company culture and gain commitment to a complex business mission. To these ends, the inner tube exercises and theatrical skits emphasized the role of metaphor in creating change, an idea imported from the "new games" movement in experiential education (for example, Bacon, 1983) and new theories on the link between corporate culture and symbolic communication (for example, Hatch, 1993). How better to embody a unifying culture than for product-minded Ben to talk of love, fun-loving Jerry to speak about products, and managers to put the founders' images on their faces in a symbolic gesture of unity and weirdness when defining their roles and responsibilities?

B&J managers would have to grapple with the ambiguity and paradox of a three-part mission that gave equal emphasis to quality products, economic performance, and social responsibility. New theorizing on the generative power of paradox (Quinn & Kimberly, 1984) shaped the design and content of discussions on such issues as balancing business efficiency with social change in cause-related product marketing and shifting the message from antiwar to pro-peace in the branding of the ice cream pop. Subsequent redesign of the organization to balance pressures for production and the formation of a joy committee to realize Jerry's philosophy reflected Forisha-Kovach's notion of flexible organizing (1984), whereby a firm re-creates itself to manage the paradoxes of change.

Philosopher of science Gunther Stent (1972) contends that many scientific discoveries are ahead of their time. They are ignored or marginalized until they congeal into a new paradigm and, in the case of a field like OD, its practitioners and clients are ready for them. What were some of the other new ideas that informed the change effort at B&J?

At its inception, OD was oriented primarily toward personal growth and interpersonal relations (Tannenbaum & Davis, 1969). Its emphasis on human development drew from the humanistic theories of Maslow (1954). Its interpersonal emphasis was informed by understanding social orientations (Schutz, 1958), styles of interaction (Bales, 1951), and emotional congruence (Luft, 1963). The field took broader directions, however, as theorizing focused on people's reference groups and identities (Smith, 1977), intergroup dynamics (Alderfer, 1977), and the distribution of power in organizations (Pfeffer, 1981). Accordingly, new forms of intervention were developed to help people surface and speak to their identities, confront structural and ideological differences, and redress power imbalances. At B&J, the evocative mind maps, metaphorical exercises on intergroup conflict, and heated and heartfelt talk about trust and empowerment exemplified this broader OD thrust.

On the organizational side, OD was originally applied to the human problems in social systems. This deepened as theorizing delved into the sociocultural roots of organizing (Schein, 1985) and identified characteristics of strong company cultures (Deal & Kennedy, 1982). By reaching deeply into organizational beliefs, values, and purpose, the interventions at B&J aimed at organizational transformation (Levy, 1986; Bartunek & Louis, 1988) by bringing the company's complex mission to life. B&J was at the leading edge of a revolutionary movement that aimed at transforming not only the company but also the role of business in society. At the same time, B&J still resonated with the humanistic and democratic foundations of traditional OD. Thus, as one manager put it, the work mixed old-fashioned values with new fangled ideas (Lager, 1994). This mixing of old and new can be traced to both the evolutionary and the revolutionary development of OD.

EVOLUTION VERSUS REVOLUTION IN OD

Distinctions between evolutionary and revolutionary models have been drawn by theorists from many disciplines. Table 3.1 compares evolutionary and revolutionary characteristics of development. Evolutionary models are premised on continuity: they assume that processes of variation, selection, and retention are ongoing, slow, and gradual. The sequence is linear and orderly; development unfolds in incremental stages.

What is the result of evolutionary versus revolutionary development? Evolution is renewal as developed from a system's existing base. This means that OD has evolved by building on past knowledge and practices, incorporating and socializing new members in core traditions, and adapting gradually by "fine-tuning" its roster of interventions and applying itself to new problems and situations. By comparison, revolution involves death and birth. Revolutions in OD saw old ideas discarded and new ones embraced, a new community of practice often at odds with old mores, and new forms of intervention birthed for new circumstances.

Evolution	Revolution
The Process	
Continuous	Discontinuous
Linear, orderly	Nonlinear, chaotic
Sequenced, incremental	Reciprocal, simultaneous
The Results	
Renewal, fine-tuning	Death, rebirth
Quantitative change	Qualitative change
New content	New context
Path to known state	Odyssey to unknown state

Table 3.1.   Evolutionary Versus Revolutionary Models of Development.

To extend this line of thinking, evolution creates quantitative change, whereas revolution leads to qualitative change. This is addressed conceptually by Golembiewski, Billingsley, and Yaeger's distinction between *alpha, beta,* and *gamma* types of change (1976). Alpha represents increases or decreases in the quantity of a system variable or its measurement. Gamma refers to a fundamental change in the relationship of variables in a system.

Evolution yields new content, whereas revolution involves a change in context. This distinction is neatly drawn by Davis (1987), who contends that content changes occur within the confines of what is known about today and the future, whereas context changes involve the creation of the future. Hernes (1976) makes a similar distinction between transitions and transformations in a social system. My translation is that transitions follow a path to a known state; transformation is an odyssey to an unknown world.

The notion that revolutionary changes are more profound and have more significant consequences is well established in scientific discourse. In a review of this subject, Smith (1982a), drawing from biology, distinguishes between morphostatic and morphogenetic change. The former involves natural mutations or changes in the appearance of an organism or ecosystem. The latter are changes in the essence or core of the phenomena in question. Core changes in OD's paradigms marked its revolutionary periods.

NEW THEORY: FROM CHANGE TO TRANSFORMATION

Kurt Lewin's fundamental contributions (1935, 1936) to the understanding of change begin with his dynamic theory of personality and principles of topological psychology. His placement of the individual within a social field stressed the role of psychological, as opposed to physical and physiological, influences on behavior and provided a framework for mapping the "dynamic tension" between forces that might facilitate or hinder change. Lewin's stages of change in a social field—unfreezing, movement, refreezing—provided an integrative frame for conceptualizing the processes behind how people and social systems change (1948).

A key concept for Lewin was reflected in his proposition that motivation for change must be generated before change can occur. Ed Schein, who was trained by Alex Bavelas (one of Lewin's students), found this crucial in his studies of attitude change among prisoners of the Chinese communists during the Korean War. Contemporary change theories seemed trivial and superficial to Schein (1995) when applied to the profound changes that the prisoners had undergone. Lewin's basic model, however, offered him the theoretical foundation for a solid theory of change.

Schein (1964) in turn identified a roster of mechanisms of change. Meanwhile, a fuller explication of the dynamics of change in social systems appeared in volumes by Lippitt, Watson, and Westley (1958) and by Bennis, Benne, and Chin (1961). The period from 1960 to 1970 saw, in effect, the revolutionary birthing of OD. Scholars fleshed out methods and strategies for intervening in organizations, defined the roles of the client and the change agent, and defined OD as an effort to increase organizational health and effectiveness through planned changes and the use of behavioral science knowledge (Beckhard, 1969). The first OD textbooks, the Addison-Wesley series of professional OD books, countless seminars and workshops, and myriad company projects affirmed Lewin's oft-quoted point that there is nothing as practical as a good theory.

Organizational Transformation

But then came new theorizing, originally from family systems studies, on differences between first- and second-order change (Watzlawick, Weakland, & Fisch, 1974). In the former, the workings of a system may be altered, but the supersystem and paradigm that define it are unchanged. In the latter, the supersystem and paradigm are altered. In OD, this is the difference between organizational transition and transformation (Ackerman, 1986).

This distinction had a dramatic impact on conceptions of change in OD. Bartunek and Moch (1987) expanded the framework to differentiate among adaptations within a system, changes to the system overall, and changes in the surrounding supersystem that reverberate throughout, or first-, second- and third-order change. Kilmann and Covin (1988) referenced the impact of organization transformation (OT) on OD core beliefs and values, as well as on extant managerial paradigms. In a review of dozens of OT cases and interviews with key participants, Blumenthal and Haspeslagh (1994) provided a more colloquial distinction between OD and OT: in the latter, interventions are "bigger, deeper, and wider."

Model I and II

Another aspect of this new change perspective comes from Gregory Bateson. Bateson, working with a team of sea mammal specialists, observed that dolphins have a second-layer scanning system that monitors how they translate signals into actions, as well as checks for defects in their information processing, signal interpretation, and programming to guide pursuit. In *Steps to an Ecology of the Mind* (1972), he located a second-order self-correction capability in the human mind and contended it enables us to learn how to learn.

Chris Argyris (1974) looked deeply into this model of learning for personal change and found a gap between people's "espoused theory" (what they say are the beliefs and values behind their actions) and their "theory in use" (the beliefs and values implied by what they do). This gap, he asserted, results from people's defining situations to control their environment, maximize winning, minimize negative feelings, and make their actions seem rational and level headed. When actions don't yield desired results, people engage in what Argyris and Schön (1974) call single-loop learning: they devise new actions without exploring underlying motivations and assumptions. In double-loop learning, by comparison, attention turns to the collection of valid information, surfacing of conflicting views, and exercise of free choice and commitment by all involved.

Argyris and Schön (1978) later identified the organizational analogs of these defensive routines. Learning is muddled further in organizations because problems threaten to bring to light gamesmanship behind decisions. The implication in change situations is that new ideas and actions are not fully explored from the get-go, and the unexpected consequences yield denial, blame, and further action based on the same old assumptions and beliefs. Argyris and Schön (1978) call this Model I learning, or first-order change. In their alternative, Model II, groups combine inquiry and advocacy to publicly test assumptions, definitions of the situation, and so forth. These activities open up a second loop of inquiry whereby a system scans itself and learns how it learns. This, according to Argyris and Schön, exemplifies second-order change.

This revolutionary conception of human learning and change has been carried forward under the general label of reflective practice (Schön, 1983). The double-loop framework has been translated into such learning tools as a "left-hand column" exercise that helps individuals monitor themselves during interactions and a "ladder of inference" to check their cause-and-effect understandings of the situation at hand. People are urged to self-monitor whether they are engaged in "inquiry" or "advocacy." Torbert, expanding on domains of self-reflection, counsels that the inquirer attend to purposes, thinking, behavior, and the outside world (Fisher, Rooke, & Torbert, 2000).

All these methods and the double-loop logic behind them are today part of almost every OD tool kit. They have reached the mass market and become integral elements in work focused on enhancing personal mastery and examining mental models through Senge's framework for organization learning. But how are they reflected in organization transformation work?

High-Stage Organizing

Bill Torbert (1987) was one of the first to develop theory that expressed double-loop learning and reflective practice in the form of organizational structures and processes. The first step toward "high-stage" organizing for Torbert involves the development of an "openly chosen structure." Here the identity of the organization moves from tasks to what Torbert terms the "*deep structure*" or the underlying contract through a continuous process of testing, renegotiating, and renewing surface structures. This refers to an organization whose culture supports an open examination of beliefs and values and encourages the search for new modes of organizing.

The next level for Torbert is called the *foundational community*. Here people freely choose a more egalitarian and inclusive mode of organizing and adopt a high-minded purpose for their enterprise. Ben & Jerry's aimed to be such a community. The highest stage of organizing is a culture guided by liberating disciplines. Here self-study and continual adaptation define the mode of operation in the organization. Kiefer and Senge (1984) characterize this as a "metanoic" organization exemplifying a fundamental shift of mind. Vaill (1984) describes an organization as imbued with "process wisdom."

How does an organization reach this high stage of organizing? Vaill (1982) identified the characteristics of high-performance work teams as building blocks, and Lawler (1986) devised principles for high-involvement management. OD as a field responded with a focus on deep cultural change. Nelson and Burns (1984), for example, identified a range of cultural interventions to move an organization through stages of reactivity and responsiveness toward proactivity and sustained high performance. Senge stressed the importance of team learning and systems thinking. Still, this kind of deep change was by no means depicted as a natural or organic evolution for organizations. On the contrary, moving to high-stage organizing requires transformation of a company's guiding beliefs and purposes.

What makes OT different from OD in large-scale change? In many frameworks, a transformational leader is essential (Tichy & Devanna, 1986). This is charismatic leadership as anticipated by Berlew (1974) in his formulation of organizational excitement. Effective leadership has always been integral to the OD change paradigm. OT, however, challenged leaders with purposing their organization (Vaill, 1982) and stewarding its guiding beliefs (Davis, 1984). According to Peters and Austin (1985), leaders had to show a passion for excellence. Meanwhile, Kiefer and Stroh (1984) stressed the importance of leading through a motivating vision and meaningful sense of purpose. Senge lessens the burden on the single leader by stressing shared vision.

These themes became part of every guidebook on leading organizational transformation (for example, Nadler, Shaw, & Walton, 1995; Kotter, 1996). Standard texts were rebranded to include both OD and OT in their titles (French, Bell, & Zawaki, 1994). But operationalizing these theories on transformation—with their emphasis on self-and-system inquiry, collective learning, purposeful leadership, and deep culture change—would hinge on new change processes and the involvement of new actors. Here, too, OD moved forward in the 1980s and 1990s in revolutionary new directions.

NEW PROCESSES: FROM PROBLEMS TO POSSIBILITIES

Lewin's action research (1948) was the source of OD's change model. Its phases of diagnosis, problem analysis, intervention, evaluation, and feedback flow from the work of Lewin and his students, as does OD's emphasis on participatory processes. There were, however, many contributors to the development of the revolutionary idea that social science methods could be applied to practical problems. In *How We Think,* Dewey (1933) identified five phases of reflective thinking— encounter a problem, intellectualize, hypothesize, reason, and test hypotheses in action—that are reflected in action research. Rogers (1969) stressed the importance of experiential versus cognitive learning and emphasized how adults approach learning as problem solving. All these ideas fit neatly into the notion that action research was to be used in OD as a step-by-step problem-solving process (Frohman, Sashkin, & Kavanaugh, 1976).

Rethinking Problem Solving

In the 1970s, leading scholars began to question the mechanistic application of OD to problem solving. Argyris's first writings on "action science" (1970) critiqued the behavioral assumptions behind traditional scientific research and generalized the principles of action research to intervention theory. He called for valid information, free choice, and psychological commitment when individuals intervene to change behavior. Susman and Evered (1978), in turn, saw action research as extended from the tradition of hermeneutics (with its emphasis on open-ended interpretation rather than close-ended theory) and based in existentialism (with its emphasis on freedom of choice rather than causal determinism). These views raised questions about how problems are defined in OD and who has voice in their solution.

At the same time, fundamental questions were being raised about the epistemology of positivistic social science and the framing of problems and solutions by its methods. One notable critic was Don Michael (1973), whose *Learning to Plan and Planning to Learn* was a treatise on system learning disabilities. He noted that long-range requirements to acknowledge and live with uncertainty, accept role ambiguity and conflict, and expect and embrace errors run counter to short-term organizational preferences for predictability, order, and control.

My own work with Michael concentrated on what makes it so difficult for a system to learn from its mistakes (Michael & Mirvis, 1977). In a chapter in *Failures in Organization Development and Change,* we cited the gap between the simplified, linear, cause-and-effect "maps" that underlay models of planned change and the complex, interconnected "terrain" that people actually encounter in action. We also acknowledged the difficulty organizations have in gathering and making sense of the information needed to figure out what went wrong. Here the culprits range from denial and discounting to blaming and flank protection—behaviors that emanate from mental models and social system beliefs that all actions based on knowledge and undertaken with skill are supposed to turn out right. To intervene in this cycle, we advised decision makers to expect errors and undertake action as experiments, not so much to be right as to learn and continuously improve.

Other new ideas on the framing of social problems and how to address them developed on many fronts. In the case of remodeling problem-solving processes, new understandings of the link between cause-and-effect and problems-to-solutions were devised in fields as diverse as gestalt psychology, with its focus on paradox; communication theory, with its depictions of the "double-bind"; and quantum physics, with its interests in time-space interaction (for example, Capra, 1976).

Problems as Paradoxes

The fields of organizational behavior and organizational theory embraced paradox in the 1980s. The notion of paradox offered new ways to depict group dynamics, OD, and the dynamics of change (Quinn & Kimberly, 1984; Smith & Berg, 1987). It also made its way into the professional vocabulary. Tom Peters, coauthor of the best-selling business book *In Search of Excellence,* offered paradoxical messages to managers: change from tough-mindedness to tenderness and from concern with hard data and balance sheets to soft stuff like values, vision, and integrity. Long-term success, according to Peters, means appreciating that soft is hard. Indeed, Peters and Waterman (1982) framed the principles behind excellence as a series of organizational design and culture paradoxes that winning companies had successfully resolved. Naisbitt (1982), in a broader vein, saw a "megatrend" in movement away from "either-or" toward a "both-and" mind-set.

Practice-oriented thinkers, in turn, developed the implications. Such exercises as the nominal group technique had been popular tools to identify the importance of problems and rank solutions quickly. To promote paradoxical thinking, Mason and Mitroff (1981) proposed a dialectical method that has two groups work from different assumptions, analyze a situation, and compare their conclusions. Mitroff (1983) also introduced the idea that organizational stakeholders often have different and incompatible values, outlooks, and interests that cannot be satisfied through linear problem solving. Instead, it would be necessary to reframe the conflict situation at a higher level of abstraction—moving, say, from an individual to a systemic level—to identify and then address common concerns.

A wide range of interventions to promote paradoxical thinking and problem solving came into OD during this era. Janusian thinking, named after the two-faced Greek god who could look forward and back, was recommended by Quinn (1988) as a means to confront competing values in organization design. An organization would oscillate over time between, say, centralization and decentralization, thereby balancing the paradox of control and autonomy through time pacing. Evans and Doz (1992) illustrated how simultaneous attention to strategic "dualities" could be facilitated by having different national groups, with their distinct worldviews, unpack cultural assumptions behind strategic options.

On the behavioral side, research from gestalt theory showed how "damned if you do, damned if you don't" dilemmas prevent people from breaking out of problem paradigms. Resistance to change was redefined in paradoxical form as "skilled incompetence." Argyris (1982) used the transcription of interactions to help people see that concealing their true intentions sent mixed messages throughout an organization. Paradoxical interventions of staying with and going deeper into resistance, rather than trying to overcome it, were adapted to group development and used as a means for a group to inquire into its "stuckness" and thence move in bold new directions (Smith & Berg, 1987).

Time-Space

Another kind of paradoxical thinking applies to views of time-space. In order to understand stars, biologist Francisco J. Varela (1976) reasoned, we need to think about data from telescopes in terms of "it" (the star) and "the processes of becoming it" (what we actually see).

Thus Davis (1987) recommended this "future perfect" outlook to simultaneously envision a corporation's future—the "it"—and the processes of becoming it. This informed a whole roster of new OD interventions aimed at reframing time-space.

Change planners, as one example, proposed *what-if* theorizing and crisis simulations to enable operators to anticipate accidents and rehearse responses (Churchman, 1971). Scenario planning, first used widely at Royal Dutch Shell, is a method for anticipating the future by investigating the nature and impact of uncertain and important driving forces. The goal is to craft a number of diverging stories about possible futures based on different sets of assumptions. In OD, scenario planning–type activities enable organizations to "re-perceive" their situations and play out the implications of different action strategies (de Geus, 1991). Schwartz (1991) contends that scenarios are akin to organizational stories in that they have a plot, winners, and losers. They enable organization members to, in effect, "rehearse the future."

Search conferences are another way to examine people's multiple realities and different perspectives on the future (Weisbord, 1992). In the 1970s, pioneers Ron Lippitt and Eva Schindler-Rainman assembled as many as three hundred people at a time to scan the environment, assess their social system (past, present, and future), then move into action planning and dealing with constraints (Schindler-Rainman & Lippitt, 1980). Another set of pioneers, Emery and Trist (1973), introduced open-system thinking and the importance of differentiating between "my facts," "your facts," and a search for "our facts."

Emery and Purser (1996) explicated key OD considerations in the design of search conferences. On the analytic side, they likened a future search to a puzzle as people confront a "messy" situation where nothing readily seems to fit together. On the process side, they noted that competing group dynamics of fight-or-flight and dependency (Bion, 1961) need careful attention lest they divert people from task completion. They recommended an indirect approach, as in the game of Go, whereby groups continually re-form around new ideas and interpretations, ultimately yielding a broader view of the system and its possible futures.

A close look reveals that the foregoing methods and strategies represent new variants of action research. Philosopher of science Jurgen Habermas (1971) makes the point that science can be applied to test theories, solve problems, and guide discovery. Certainly, early OD turned action research toward problem solving. The revolution, however, turned it toward deep inquiry into what is behind problems and applied it toward systemic ills. It is not accidental that synergistic thinking of this sort can lead to startling discoveries, reconciling paradoxes, and even setting an organization on a new course. The act of creation, writes Arthur Koestler (1964), comes from bisociation: putting together competing stimuli, forces, urges, and forms in a new arrangement. He documents this experience among artists, scientists, and musicians. The resulting "aha's" are indicative of generative learning—learning, according to Senge (1990), that enhances our capacity to create.

NEW ROLES: FROM CLIENTS TO COCREATORS

Action research has a commitment to democratic change. Lewin, born in Prussia and educated in Berlin, experienced anti-Semitism firsthand, and it would inform his life's work. In 1933, he left Nazi Germany for the United States to seek academic and personal freedom (Marrow, 1969). During World War II, Lewin collaborated with Margaret Mead in the now famous studies to reduce civilian consumption of rationed foods. There they discovered that telling a group of housewives about how to change their cooking habits and selling them on the need were less effective than giving them information and having them discuss the situation to reach a group conclusion. Reflecting on the study, Pasmore (2001) writes that the results confirmed Lewin's already strong beliefs in democracy and in action research as a tool for advancing science while dealing with societal needs.

Lewin's contribution to workplace change began shortly after the war. A team of his students worked with Alfred Marrow's Harwood manufacturing company to enhance productivity by using action research. The studies demonstrated the power of participative management. Workers were encouraged to experiment with different methods, discuss them among themselves, and choose those that they agreed were most effective. The workers increased their own quotas. In confirmation of this finding, Lewin and his students conducted experimental studies with boys' clubs that demonstrated the superiority of democratic versus autocratic and laissez-faire styles of leadership.

In the context of OD, these studies confirmed that a participatory change process was far superior to an expert-centered approach. Benne (1964) argued that the democratic ethos stressed the opportunity for people collaboratively to define the problems they encounter in living and working together.

Who's Involved in Change and How?

By the 1970s, questions were raised about OD's democratic ethos. Standard OD practices and texts framed action research as "consultation" involving a "contract" between change agent and organizational client. Soul-stirring books, such as Freire's *Pedagogy of the Oppressed* (1972), questioned the tendencies of change agents to align themselves with society's elites and implement change from the top down. Papers on the partisan diagnosis of social problems (Guskin & Chesler, 1973), the role of researcher as advocate for vested interests (Laue & Cormick, 1978), and the ethics of OD interventions (Walton & Warwick, 1973) began to appear. In some quarters, a more radical and inclusive participatory model was urged. Problem definition would explicitly focus on the ideologies and values underlying social systems. Data gathering would involve all people implicated in or concerned with the situation at hand. And interventions would address the political economy of the interests involved in a change effort (Brown & Tandon, 1983). This model would, in essence, truly democratize the change process.

European Experiments in Work Democracy

Eric Trist in the United Kingdom, Fred Emery in Australia, Einar Thorsrud in Norway, and other European scholar-practitioners first demonstrated how a democratically oriented form of change could be practiced in organizations. The sociotechnical design of work systems, a radical notion challenging the principles of scientific management, was derived from the famous Welsh coal mine studies in the 1950s and village-level experiments in work redesign in India in the 1960s. Sociotechnical system work design—methods to optimize the relationship between social and technical factors in the workplace—became a prominent intervention in organizations (Trist, 1981). From the 1970s onward, it was implemented through cooperative labor-management bodies and works councils throughout Europe.

Emery and Trist (1973) extended this democratic frame to apply to what they termed social ecology, which aimed to optimize the relationship between a firm and other interests in society. Trist's subsequent involvement in communities in North America further demonstrated the efficacy of bringing diverse people together to take responsibility for their community's future. This pioneer saw collaborations between social actors and social scientists as increasing social capacities to choose and attain a more desirable future (Trist, 1979).

The revolutionary idea of involving workers in changes in their work environment and involving citizens in community change has become normative throughout Europe. The sociodemocratic design of work arrangements is codified in EU policy; taught routinely in professional and trade schools; and continues to advance through countless academic, governmental, and industry-based action-research institutes and consortia (Toulmin & Gustavsen, 1996; Greenwood & Levin, 1998). In the United States, it has taken different directions in the practice of OD.

Getting the "Whole System in a Room"

Early on, OD practitioners would involve a diagonal slice of an organization in fact finding to get a more informed picture of system dynamics. Later, they would create temporary systems of representative people implicated in a change effort—create a collateral or parallel structure—to involve them in action planning and implementation. By the late 1970s and 1980s, the European work experiments began to influence practice in the United States. The National Commission on Productivity and Quality of Work Life was created to disseminate knowledge about new organizational practices and fund demonstration projects promoting labor-management cooperation (Seashore, Lawler, Mirvis, & Cammann, 1983). Pioneering projects in Bolivar (Tennessee) and Jamestown (New York) promoted improvement in work design through employee involvement. They also fostered systemwide changes such that remedial educational activities, day care, and other social services were integrated with community-wide economic development.

The revolutionary commitment to democratic participation in the OD change process came together in Weisbord's call to "get a whole system in the room" (1987). It heralded the start of large group interventions to expand both the scale and scope of OD (Bunker & Alban, 1997, 2005, and in Chapter 14 in this volume). Large-scale OD applications yield multiple and often competing understandings of problems, as well as many and varied ideas on how and when to address them. Bringing the whole system into the room creates a microcosm to identify system dynamics in real time, and a practice field on which to experiment with new ways of working together. Nowadays, large groups are formed to develop scenarios, conduct future searches, explore issues through Owen's "open space" format (1997), and produce what Dannemiller and Jacobs (1992) call real time strategic change.

Noel Tichy is a well-known academic change agent who applied these ideas in global corporations. General Electric's transformation through the 1980s and 1990s incorporated the methods under the rubric of action learning. At one time, GE had hundreds of "workout" programs aimed at streamlining work flow and cost reductions. The many methods for accelerating change through "fast cycle" change processes are detailed in Tichy's "Handbook for Revolutionaries," which is appended to the GE transformation story (Tichy & Sherman, 1993). In other companies, Tichy has facilitated multiple, simultaneous "value creation" workshops to grow business units, develop leadership talent, and lead efforts in corporate community service (Tichy & Cohen, 1997; Tichy & Cardwell, 2002).

On the OD practice side, new high-tech tools, ranging from electronic databases to intranet chat rooms to digital handheld devices, aid collective fact finding and analysis. And high-touch tools, ranging from graphic facilitation to theatrics, aim to humanize the OD process and give it life. These new designs and tools serve to transform people from participants in a change process to cocreators of their future.

NEW APPLICATIONS: FROM SELF TO SYSTEM

It is necessary to go back to the 1940s and 1950s to understand the societal conditions that preceded OD's birth. On the socioeconomic front, America's recovery from the Depression and victory in World War II joined Americans together in common cause. Whereas the industrial revolution pitted workers against management, ethnic group against ethnic group, and class against class, these later historic struggles bonded Americans. The image of America as a melting pot held hope for the assimilation of ethnic groups. Economic recovery provided secure jobs and prospects for upward mobility, including home ownership and weekend leisure. Although strikes still erupted in the auto, railroad, and coal industries, a postwar labor-management compact was devised for both sides to share in America's economic boom.

It was during this era that leading thinkers recognized the limits of Taylor's principles of scientific management (1911) and sought to promote better human relations in industry. Studies by Mayo and Roethlisberger at the Hawthorne Works showed that productivity would increase when factory lights were turned up but also when they were dimmed. The attention and care shown the workers, not the lighting, led to increased production (Roethlisberger & Dickson, 1939).

These studies heralded a new conception of motivation and management at work: rational-economic models were broadened to recognize social factors (Schein, 1965). Managers were urged to get to know their employees and respond to their emotional makeups. Human relations tracts, such as Carnegie's *How to Win Friends and Influence People* (1936), became guidebooks for handling people. By the 1950s, U.S. companies were sponsoring bowling teams, picnics, and social clubs as signs of their good association with people.

Problems arose when Carnegie's precepts were put into practice, however. Carnegie instructed readers to use tact, praise, or even a little hypocrisy. Whyte (1956) blew the whistle on this kind of duplicity in *The Organization Man,* where he opined that managers were being stripped of their individuality by social engineers and socialized to conform to a stifling organizational persona. Next came new models of human behavior at work, exemplified by McGregor's Theory X and Y managerial assumptions (1960). Meanwhile, others began to decry the problems wrought by big bureaucracy. Argyris (1957) found that the demands of the formal organization inhibit the self-actualization of healthy workers. Bennis (1966) concluded that the "bureaucratic solution" caused organizations to lose flexibility and adaptability to change. Pointing to a range of new ideas making their way into scholarship and society, Bennis and Slater (1968) began to wonder, "Is democracy inevitable?"

Laboratory Education: The T-Group

T-group training gave birth to OD. Interpersonal skill training has always been an integral part of management and organizational improvement, but most of the training was didactic instruction or on-the-job coaching. Moreover, it rested on the assumption that there was a discrete set of skills that people could learn and apply to become more effective. T-groups turned this assumption on its head: rules were not given; they emerged through human interaction. Strangers would come together with no set agenda, designated leader, roles, norms, or established modes of operation. Their "work" was to learn about social systems and themselves by creating their own rules and roles.

T-group training was itself an accidental discovery. Benne (1964) traces its genesis to a 1946 workshop among teachers and social workers aimed at promoting interracial understanding. Trainers guided group discussions of participants' back home experiences with race and led them through role plays to rehearse more effective ways of dealing with interracial attitudes and situations. Researchers in attendance observed the training and met nightly to compare notes on participant behaviors and group dynamics. One evening, a few participants asked to join the researchers. More came on subsequent evenings. By the end of the training, it was clear that this give-and-take was an intervention in its own right and a potent means of creating behavioral change.

The next year, these trainers and researchers, plus several others, designed a workshop in which an explicit part of the program involved "action-research" analysis of individual and group behavior followed by feedback to the participants. From 1948 to 1955, the basic skills training group, retitled the T-group, took center stage in laboratory training. From 1956 through 1965, the T-group methodology was refined and introduced as a new form of organizational training. NTL hosted off-site sessions with executives, managers, teachers, and administrators, and conducted several in-company labs for industrial organizations and government agencies. Soon T-groups would become part of full-blown development efforts in organizations.

T-groups also gave OD its initial emphasis on self-development. Early trainers believed deeply in personal growth. They argued that sensitivity training strengthened one's ego and self-image. Bennis (1964) stated the principles or "meta goals" behind this. T-groups expanded people's consciousness about aspects of themselves and others that had been taken for granted, and allowed them to recognize "choices" they made about behavior. T-groups enabled trainees to receive feedback on current behaviors and experiment with new ones. The training took place in the "cultural island" of a laboratory setting, free of the confining nature of the formal organization.

During this same era, scholars at Britain's Tavistock Institute developed leaderless, small-group workshops to promote social awareness and train leaders (Rice, 1969). They drew from psychoanalytic theory to conceptualize leadership roles and stages of group development to the point that Tavi-labs gained currency as an alternative method of laboratory education. West Coast "groupies" experimented with "encounter groups," and other innovators developed their own particular brands of sensitivity training.

Still, T-group training had its limitations. Chief among them was the challenge of transferring laboratory learning to organizational life. Bennis (1969) argued that the values and lessons learned in the lab did not prepare people to cope with power dynamics in organizations.

This disaffection with the old and drive to promote something new led a small band of trainers to explore alternative ways of sensitizing people to the realities of power and systems.

Power and Systems

This small band of innovators was actually espousing a radical redirection of the field. Assuming that laboratory training offered fertile soil for learning and enrichment, was there a way to keep the benefits yet refocus the experiences on power and system dynamics? That question was posed by a group of NTL associates to Barry Oshry as he reviewed the state of laboratory education in the 1970s. There was urgency in the question. Personal growth labs were irrelevant to blacks and women, it was reported. Interpersonal growth counted little when power was concentrated in the hands of a few white men, and systemic norms perpetuated oppression of people of color, women, and the "have-nots." Oshry took this to heart. He designed a "power lab" to expose power dynamics and provide an experimental forum to act out the drama of inequality in a simulated society.

As participants arrived at the first power lab, they were separated into two groups, the haves ("elites") and have-nots ("outs"), based on societal criteria of education, accomplishments, race, and gender. The have-nots were told to turn over their belongings to the "society": their clothes, toilet instruments, money, car keys, and shoes were given over to the elites. Each group then received a private briefing: the elites were ushered into lush quarters and informed that they were to retain as many resources as possible while ensuring that order was maintained, the outs were taken to a cramped section of the facility where they clanned together and devised schemes for recovering their belongings.

Thus began the first power lab. Over the course of the training, the elites devised the name, values, and norms of the society. They met with out-group members to discuss their demands and negotiate agreements whereby shoes, toilet articles, changes of clothes, and such would be exchanged for work—cooking meals, cleaning the facility, ensuring that the system worked. In a short time, however, the outs went on strike and adopted guerrilla tactics to press their demands. One day, the car of a staff member of the facility was disabled. Oshry met with the outs to inform them that the staffer was not part of the exercise. The outs would hear none of this. Eventually the car was fixed, but only after the outs secured keys to a car of their own. At another point, an elite was "kidnapped"; she was a well-known feminist and outspoken critique of top-down oppression in real life. In the lab, however, she had urged her fellow elites to stay firm and not give in to tyranny.

Oshry observed that the elites were splitting into camps: "autocrats" tried to maintain their power and hold on to resources; "democrats" favored sharing power, pooling resources, and working collaboratively with the outs. Among the outs, there were "good soldiers" who were patient and responsive to the elites, whereas "radicals" wanted to seize power and destroy the system. The largest block of outs were "invisible."

This early work gave birth to the power and systems lab, now peopled by participants in three hierarchical groups: the Tops, Middles, and Bottoms (Oshry, 1977). The Middles get more resources than the bottoms but fewer than the Tops. Their job is to "integrate" the society, while the Tops exercise leadership and the Bottoms work. In a short time, such labs came to be the education experience of choice among ODers interested in power and system dynamics.

OD on Power and Systems

The power lab showed how systemic norms perpetuate hierarchy. This led to fresh thinking about human and organization development. Early OD assumed that once people let down barriers, they could know, trust, and work with one another in an authentic and mutually productive fashion. The power lab demonstrated that people were prisoners of their group identities (Smith, 1982b): system positions defined people and constrained their action in organizations. More broadly, scholars began to focus on identity groups and how age, ethnicity, social background, and other demographic factors, as well as organizational position and status, served to define people, outlooks, and interests.

Accordingly, OD turned its attention to the problems of women and minorities and the promotion of multiculturalism. Bunker and Seashore (1977) conducted company workshops and consciousness-raising interventions aimed at redefining male-female relationships. Kanter (1977) enriched the field with a structural analysis of the roles of women and men in companies; her workshop built on the "Tale of O" became a popular intervention. In industry, black manager groups formed, many facilitated by ODers. Nowadays, diversity workshops are commonplace and include programs aimed at members of specific groups, as well as at valuing diversity throughout an organization (Cox, 1993; Thomas & Ely, 1996).

To this point, ODers had lumped resistance to change into two categories: personal and organizational. In his writings, Oshry (1999) showed how intimately the two were related. The Tops in power labs controlled information, centralized decisions, and bore organizational burdens. Bottoms gave up responsibility, felt oppressed, and channeled energy into self-protection. Middles lived in conflict, torn between the competing demands of Tops and Bottoms. (See the Sales chapter in this volume for an expanded exploration of these dynamics.)

Is there hope of reconciling these competing interests? Oshry's *Seeing Systems* (1995) compared passive, political, and robust system processes. The key to robustness rests in people's assuming responsibility for the overall system *and* their own function and roles. The power and systems lab continues to develop: new forms involve interactions with customers, the merging of simulated companies, and the creation of democratic enterprises. Interestingly, lessons from the labs parallel those from the field: the need to address paradox in systems; the importance of getting the whole system in the room; and the potential for people to become empowered, aligned, and making a difference.

NEW, NEW THEORY: COMPLEX ADAPTIVE SYSTEMS

Complexity science is a child of the late twentieth century, with roots in chaos theory, dynamical systems theory, fractal geometry, and other interdisciplinary logics. It is concerned with the study of emergent phenomena—behaviors and patterns—that occur at multiple levels of systems. Key to change theory is that phenomena emerge from nonlinear interactions in complex systems that veer between equilibrium and randomness (Holland, 1995; Kauffman, 1995). Living systems are most dynamic and change naturally at this "edge of chaos." Such systems are characterized as "complex adaptive systems" (CAS)—a term coined by theorists at the Sante Fe Institute.

Much of the scholarship on organizational effectiveness to this point had centered on adaptation: how organizations achieve fit with their changing environments. In complex systems characterized by "flux and flow," achieving organizational *fitness* is a better descriptor (Morgan, 1996). OD and all of organizational science are still fleshing out the meaning of this new line of theorizing for practice. One implication is that organization members have to inquire deeply into the nature of things and devise ways to continuously adjust to discontinuities. Michael and Mirvis (1977) likened the process to white-water rafting, an image taken up by Vaill (1996) in his depiction of management as a performing art.

Confirming New Directions

These new CAS concepts confirm the vitality of revolutionary developments in theory and practice already in motion in OD. Prigogine's work in chemistry (1984) highlights the importance of disequilibrium: it "dissipates" system structure so that the system can recreate itself in a new form. Shaw (1997) argues that change agents are well advised to empower lower-power and marginalized organizational interests to ensure that they do disturb the system. She gives what was once called "guerilla OD" a respectable platform as a legitimate source of transformation.

Another implication is that there is a need to confront paradox. In periods of high instability, complex systems hit a bifurcation point or fork in the road where change energies dissipate in ways that allow either an old attractor to reassert itself or a new one to shift the system into a new form. The paradoxical conclusions, that destruction is integral to creation and freedom essential to order, are the stuff of the new science popularized by Wheatley (1993). An influential volume by Brown and Eisenhardt (1998) provides a detailed roster of strategic "balancing acts" for systems at the edge of chaos. Key competencies are time pacing, improvisation, and what they term "co-adapting" among the many interests in the marketplace.

Two Chilean biologists, Humberto Maturana and Francisco J. Varela (1987), and astronomer Erich Jantsch (1980) identified the system property whereby small changes feed back on themselves and reverberate through the larger system. The dynamic, called *autopoieses* or self-organization, sets the path by which systems evolve. There are many applications of these ideas in the theory and practice of continuous, systemwide organization change (Stacey, 1996; Kelly & Allison, 1999).

For instance, organizations today rely on boundary-spanning roles and early warning systems to monitor and signal environmental turbulence. The sociotechnical system idea of creating localized "intelligent" systems in which analysis and control are exercised closest to the source of any "disturbance" is a foundation in semiautonomous work teams. At the enterprise level, electronic communication networks and communities of practice (Wenger, McDermott, & Snyder, 2000) help ensure that information flows across functional and hierarchical boundaries and that the right people can organize around it. These innovations provide the organizational architecture for knowledge work (Purser & Pasmore, 1992) and for facilitating inductive, deductive, and compressive patterns of knowledge creation in organizations (Nonaka, 1988).

As for understanding the paths that systems follow, a group originally gathered at MIT around Jay Forrester and the Meadows and refined several archetypal system dynamics that are featured in Senge's *The Fifth Discipline* (1990). Practicing participative and reflective openness (to see the system) and affecting control without controlling through localized action (to leverage small changes) are essential to adaptability in complex systems. Simulations are being developed to mimic system dynamics and help people engage in systems thinking on a collective scale (Senge et al., 1994). Ideas on enriching the options run from Hampden-Turner's maps of organizational dilemmas (1990) to Peters's parables about thriving on chaos (1987).

Some New, New Considerations

As CAS findings filter into and reinforce new directions in OD, they also suggest new, new considerations. Most accounts of organizational transformation emphasize how interventions need to be bigger, deeper, and wider. CAS advises us to think small—on the order of the movement of a butterfly's wing—and to value the importance of small wins. Pascale, Millemann, and Gioja (2000) took this perspective in analyzing transformational changes at Sears, Shell, and the U.S. Army. Abrahamson (2004) found that a series of small changes had large effects in the form of "recombinant" strategies whereby organizational capabilities are cloned, redeployed, or revived for change without pain.

Deborah Meyerson's account of tempered radicals (2001) shows mid-level executives effecting big change through coalitions of supporters and the leveraging of small wins. Keys to their success are personal passions that energize a system and a personal commitment to be their true selves. This study and others herald a fresh look at the power of the single individual in organizational transformation—a subject neglected in most discussions of OD.

Bob Quinn was one of the first scholars to address the importance of acknowledging and reconciling paradox in organizational transformation (Quinn & Cameron, 1988). In the next decade, however, he would inquire into the central role of the individual. In *Deep Change*, Quinn (1996) articulates his version of the hero's journey that begins with vulnerability and requires digging deep into self as the unacknowledged source of many organizational problems.

In a subsequent volume, Quinn (2000) articulated "advanced change theory" in which he claims that being transformational is a choice. His biographical studies of Jesus, Ghandi, and Martin Luther King Jr. highlight how each confronted personal flaws yet remained beacons of moral purpose. On this count, Gardner (1995) expounds on how leaders' life stories are an inspiration to followers when the leaders have overcome foibles and thereby reinforced their status as ordinary human beings. Advanced change theory requires that leaders disturb the system yet surrender control to the flow of events. This emphasizes self-leadership and makes personal transformation a sine qua non for organizational transformation. It echoes Ghandi's principle: be the change you seek to create.

Quinn's emphasis on personal transformation points to moral leadership as an attractor to pull a system in new, positive directions. This logic is consistent with findings that leaders at higher levels of moral and skill development are better equipped to effect organizational transformations (Torbert, 1991).

NEW, NEW PROCESS: OD AS ART

Leonard Shlain (1991) contends that the visionary artist is the first member of a culture to see the world in a new way. He shows how, almost simultaneously, a revolutionary physicist makes a discovery along the same lines. The general point is that visionary art anticipates the new before it is expressed in accepted theory or makes its way into professional fields of practice. There is a well-established literature on how the creative process of artists is comparable to the discovery of new paradigms in science. This raises questions about the arts as a creative medium for practitioners and OD practice.

One set of clues comes from Taylor and Hansen (2005), who differentiate presentational knowing from formal propositional knowledge and colloquial know-how. They contend that presentational forms of expression, such as drawing, music, and drama, tap into and represent people's tacit knowledge of themselves, others, and the world around them. Gagliardi (1996) goes further and suggests that more rational representations of reality depend on and grow out of aesthetic experiences and understanding.

It should be noted that there are theatrical references in theories of organization change, but most have metonymic flavor. Tichy and Devanna (1986) characterize transformation as a three-act drama involving awakening, visioning, and restructuring. Practice volumes speak about the dance of change (Senge et al., 1999), as well as refer to sculpting, gardening, music making, and jujitsu. In these instances, however, it is *as if* people were dancing, sculpting, making music, and so on: performing arts are a *metaphor* for collective or personal activity. In the case of large-scale organization change, by contrast, the drama is a *participatory experience,* and the whole system and its members are transformed by participation in these performances. It is in this sense that Victor Turner (1957), an anthropologist and scholar of Greek theater, sees cultural change as a universal drama in the form of upheaval, conflict, reordering, and finally reintegration.

Fresh possibilities for large-scale interventions come from the nascent field of organizational aesthetics (see, Strati, 1992; Gagliardi, 1996). The field encompasses aesthetic theories, analyses, and practical applications involving music, visual arts, literature, dance, and the like. The most popular for OD is drama (Mangham & Overington, 1987; Morgan, 1993). Today theater troupes in organizations raise awareness of familiar scripts and stimulate reflection and problem solving (Meisiek, 2002). Typically, however, the theater is performed by professionals. There are instances, however, when organization members are the show, and the performance aims to transform them and their organization.

The Theatre of Inquiry

The Theatre of Inquiry was launched to introduce the art of organizing guided by "living inquiry." People were invited to "taste-test" life choices by engaging in performances convened by Torbert: play the fool, act like a child, act your age, and so on (Torbert, 1989).

The Theater originated from Torbert's belief that the political-literary-philosophical frameworks people use to order their world were causing many of its problems: people basically lacked workable frameworks to organize the fundamentals of late twentieth-century life. The public performances of The Theater were Torbert's brand of laboratory education. Act one begins with a dance of collaborative inquiry, symbolizing birth, life, and death and offering opportunity for people to access deep feelings and the creative potential from reliving their life course.

As the performance continues, Torbert commences a dialogue between his different and competing personalities. At one early performance, these were intellectual and emotional, interpretive and judgmental, a New Age apostle and a southern good old boy. In later performances, the script would introduce Justin Thor, the Nordic embodiment of power; Teiresias, the blind Greek seer; Jederman, the Germanic conscience of everyman; and Jimminy Christmas, the imp.

Internal dialogues and playacting are important components in transformational change. The former allow people to reflect on how their frames of reference define their reality and guide everyday actions. By surfacing these personalities, actors can see how competing frames yield contradictory and paradoxical perceptions that either open or seal off new possibilities. Playacting provides a medium for acting out these personalities and experimenting with new ones.

In the last two acts of Torbert's The Theater of Inquiry, the audience practices physical, emotional, and intellectual exercises to develop inquiry skills and engage in open dialogue about themselves, their roles, and the implication of The Theater for Action. Torbert terms this self-study-in-action aimed at exploring the world, as well as one's own behavior, thinking, feeling, and attention (Torbert, 1978).

Torbert has taken the precepts of The Theater and applied them in a less theatric way to the redesign of an MBA program and several OD efforts with community groups and businesses. Today he has plenty of company. Tichy has change leaders write out a script, then act out and videotape an "old way/new way" production that differentiates between undesirable current practices and desired future ones. These videos, typically prepared by small groups in a matter of a few hours, are watched, rated, and reflected on by the large group in "night at the movies" exercises (Tichy & Cohen, 1997). Weisbord has participants enact and embellish future scenarios through dramatic skits (Weisbord & Janoff, 1995). And Oshry's power labs (1999) are an encompassing form of theater. Interestingly, Oshry has also become a playwright whose dramas, such as "Get Carter" and "What a Way to Make a Living," center on power and system dynamics.

Change as Theater

There are plenty of tracts advising managers on the use of performance artistry to get things done (Vaill, 1989; Watkins & Marsick, 1993; Zander & Zander, 2000). There are guidelines for improvising, a requisite skill for leading and mastering change (Hatch, 1997; Mirvis, 1998). And there are myriad examples of dance, drawing, mask making, circus performing, clowning, talisman making, theatrics, and so forth in personal development, team building, and whole-system change (for example, Nissley, 2002; Darso, 2004). How do theater and art broadly contribute to transformation?

That people are naturally acting is a key conclusion of Erving Goffman (1959), who conceived of social behavior as performances among actors who rehearse, go on stage, and enact their roles. Conceiving of change as theater gives these natural behaviors full expression. As a performing art, acting creates an alternative reality that frees the imagination, generates emotional energy, and opens new possibilities for self-expression. In turn, precisely because actors are playing and the experience is "make-believe," they can reflect from a distance and, in so doing, learn something about their art and themselves (Davies & Hancock, 1993).

In broader parallel, Carlson (1996) draws an interactive link between the aesthetic drama of theater and the social drama of life. To the extent that change is theater, a whole system can be put on stage to learn a new way of being and working together. Mirvis, Ayas, and Roth (2003) have staged transformation experiences for groups of 250 to 2,000 employees in a company. They and others draw parallels between the design of change processes and theater-like performances (see Czarniawska, 1997; Pine & Gilmore, 1999).

One question is to what extent change practitioners are *planning* a program versus *scripting* a story. Most change plans begin with a goal and lay out discrete activities that will lead to desired results—in effect a road map. The plan of a *search conference,* for instance, typically aims at defining a vision, a *workout* at cost cutting or streamlining, and a *ropes course and outdoor challenge exercise* at team building. These events are often nested in a larger plan of organization-wide change, with preparatory and follow-up activities, and they are supported by a myriad of tactical and logistical plans. All of this planning covers *what* is supposed to happen, *when,* and by *whom.* A script serves this function in performances. But a script goes deeper by elaborating and detailing *how* things should be done *for the sake of the drama.* This turns the practitioner's attention to *storytelling*—the essence of a script—and to the dramatization of activities that will bring the story to life.

In *To the Desert and Back* (Mirvis et al., 2003), the authors show how the construction of a warehouse of waste, filled with spoiled product, served as a wake-up call to the sixteen hundred staff members who were immersed in an unfamiliar and unexpected environment. The sight shocked them, the smells nauseated, and the sound effects superimposed another layer of showmanship: Mozart's *Requiem* was piped over loudspeakers. This act ended with an aptly staged scene: forklifts moved the pallets from the warehouse to a nearby pit, where the waste was buried. The metaphor was unmistakable.

Such experiences remind us of the life-giving power of art. Often that power concerns tragedy and the darker side of human nature. As Ed Schein (2001) puts it, art does and should disturb, provoke, inspire, and shock. In CAS logic, it can effect system disturbances. At the same time, art inspires and elevates. Hatch, Kostera, and Kozminski (2005) highlight these functions in their studies of chief executives whose artistic and spiritual "faces" variously disrupt a system and then attract it toward desired aims.

The notion that transformation follows nonlinear, reciprocally causal, and unpredictable directions is now well established. So is the idea that to understand and appreciate such patterns, we might turn to nontraditional forms of assessment, such as storytelling, video documentary, and performance art (Thompson, 1976; Mirvis, 1980; Strati, 1992). The methods and criteria of literary and theatric critics and of performing arts scholarship provide a rigorous yet subjective means for gauging the aesthetic dimensions of transformation. When assessing transformation as an art form that has engaged and changed a community of people, however, those methods and criteria seem less appropriate. Indeed, when looking at a painting, one could attend to such details as brush strokes, lighting, colors, and shapes, or focus on the arrangement of the canvas and its framing. In the end, though, what matters first and foremost is how the painting as a whole strikes the viewer. In commentary on the validity of art, Polanyi, Prosch, and Prosch (1977) observed that its truth is based in the experience it creates for those who see the artwork or, in the case of OD, those who participate in the experience.

NEW, NEW PROCESS: OD AS SPIRIT

However we characterize the growing interest in organizational spirituality and community, it is clear that vast numbers of people, from all walks of life, are searching for new relationships and attachments and for something more in their individual and collective lives. That this yearning is felt in the workplace is no surprise.

The paradox is that organizations today seem far less hospitable to community making. From the post–World War II period to the early 1980s, the American workplace, corporate and governmental, was a relatively secure setting in which to develop a career, make friends, give and receive social support, and participate in purposeful activities. Today workplaces are marked by multiple changes in ownership, large-scale layoffs, internal movement and individual job hopping, and temporary assignments or part-time work. They are ripe with fear, pressure, and impermanence. What are the prospects for community and spirit amid the spoils?

They seem to be growing. More than one hundred World Bank employees gather at one o'clock every Wednesday afternoon to discuss soul consciousness in their organization ("Companies Hit the Road Less Traveled," 1995). Countless companies have invited poet David Whyte (1994) to stir their staff with recitations on the preservation of soul in corporate America. Tom Chappel, health products company CEO and proponent of a prayerful business, is in demand on the lecture circuit. And the list goes on.

Many also point to a dramatic shift in the visibility in organizations of spirituality at the top, as well as in the ranks. Not long ago, the common leadership role model was the celebrity CEO. That star power is waning (Khurana, 2002) and replaced by growing appreciation for the humility of CEOs who, according to Jim Collins (2001), make the move from good to great. Current emphasis is on Greenleaf's notion of "servant leadership" or Covey's "principle-centered" approach—models that speak to a leader's inner sources of inspiration and outward embodiment of ideals. Not long ago, self-assessment involved self-scoring tests, measurements of personality type, and 360-degree feedback. Nowadays, development-minded leaders are returning to simpler and more timeless approaches: prayer, meditation, journaling, and spiritual retreats—methods traditionally classified under care for the soul.

On the academic side, I explored the notion of soul work in organizations (Mirvis, 1997) and noted the emergence of academic conferences and business books on the subject, including *Leading with Soul* (Bolman & Deal, 1995), *Spirit at Work* (Conger and Associates, 1994), and *Jesus, CEO* (Jones, 1995). The trend has continued, and spirituality in business has been a cover story in *Business Week* ("Religion in the Workplace," 1999) and *Fortune* ("God in Business," 2001). I have also been involved in the community-building movement and active in its reach over to business.

The Community-Building Experience

A group from fifty to seventy-five persons participates in a community-building workshop (CBW). The session begins with a reading of the "Rabbi's Gift," a story of a twelfth-century monastery restored after a wise rabbi advises that one of the monks is the messiah, though no one knows which one. This reading is followed by silent reflection and the group's unique wending through stages of pseudocommunity, chaos, and emptiness. The creation of community is emergent—not predictable, programmable, or reducible to a precise formula. Nor is it the inevitable result of the collective effort of people with good intentions. M. Scott Peck (1993), inventor of the CBW, asserts that the process cycles and deepens through frank and intimate communication.

Based on an amalgam of practices from Quakerism, twelve-step programs, human relations training, and psychotherapy, the workshop is premised on the notion that people come together when they inquire into their *differences,* discover what they have in *common,* and consciously embrace *unity.* There is, however, something new in the communication exercises in community building (CB) or "dialogue" groups. Drawing from humanistic psychology of the 1950s and 1960s, many human relations trainers stress the importance of dealing directly with "here and now" behavior and regard interpersonal feedback as key to the helping relationship (see Bradford, Gibb, & Benne, 1964). Indeed, to heighten self-awareness in sensitivity training, people are encouraged to mirror their reactions to others' behavior and offer interpretations. By comparison, participants in CBWs are urged to speak to the group as a whole, self-reflect, and be aware of their filtering and judgments—all in service to emptying themselves of what gets in the way of truly hearing another person. The idea, as expressed by William Isaacs (1999) with reference to dialogue groups, is that through one's "observing the observer" and "listening to one's listening," self-awareness of thoughts, feelings, and past and present experiences seeps gently into consciousness.

Offering Rogerian-type counseling in a group—to help people see themselves more clearly through questioning or clarifying—is discouraged. In CB lingo, this is "fixing"—a worthy aspiration but one that has to be "emptied" to experience self and others fully. It is worth noting that Peck, a medical doctor and psychotherapist, in no way equates community-building activities with group therapy. Nor does he see the process as a fertile medium for personal growth. The focus in CB is on collective development. Interpretive comments, if offered at all, are aimed at the group as a whole (see Bion, 1961).

Still, there are parallels between dynamics in therapy or encounter groups and CBWs. Community-building groups are apt to express dependency on leaders and manifest the myriad of unconscious conflicts that surface in other groups. But the intent is not to work through these by confronting them. Rather, the group serves as a container to hold up differences and conflicts for ongoing exploration. This keeps "hot" conversation "cooled," enables people to see the whole group mind, facilitates development of a group consciousness, and counteracts splitting, whereby people identify with a good part of the group and reject the bad.

This model reflects properties of what some call the quantum universe (Wilber, 1984; Talbot, 1986). The study of particle physics concludes that observation of a particle influences the quantum field around it: observing literally affects the observed (see Capra, 1976, 1982). David Bohm (1986), the physicist whose theories stimulated development of the dialogue process, generalized this to human behavior. By simultaneously self-scanning and inquiring with a group, people create a connective field between observer and the observed. Success at creating new collective dynamics lies in uncovering this tacit infrastructure.

Community Building and Transformation

Here is where CBW principles apply. At the start of a workshop, members establish aspirations to welcome and affirm diversity, deal with difficult issues, bridge differences with integrity, and relate with love and respect. At the same time, leaders are admonished that they cannot lead a group to community. They may empty themselves of feelings or commune with a coleader—and these behaviors may stimulate a group that has had enough of fight or flight to examine new behavior. Leaders and anyone present are always free to call a group into silence, slow discussion down, or offer thoughts for contemplation—all of which lend themselves to what Bohm (1989) describes as "superconductivity" in a group, where the elements of conversation, like electrons, move as a whole rather than as separate parts.

It is plausible to think of the heightened group consciousness in community-building workshops in the psychodynamic terms of bisociation—people reclaiming split-off ideas, feelings, and subgroups to reconstitute the group as a whole. But what of the spiritual connection with the unseen order of things? Testimonials abound about the creative breakthroughs that groups experience in Outward Bound programs, sports, the arts, meditation, therapy, and other mediums where the experience of wholeness translates into creative insight, action, or both. These are labeled "flow" experiences (Csikszentmihalyi, 1990) and attributed to the harmonious coevolution of mental and material forces (Bateson, 1979).

Several variants of the new science speak to this dynamic. There is complex order to be found in a chaotic system, and it can be unveiled by what scientists call a "strange attractor"—some means or method for surfacing the hidden relationships in nature. Wheatley (1993), among others, suggests that the human equivalent of this phenomenon is meaning. Theories of transpersonal psychology are on the same wavelength. But to Peck; Willis Harman, founder of the World Business Academy; and others, such notions of an implicit order come from the field of inquiry known as spiritual science: mind and matter coevolve and interpenetrate.

As novel and scientific sounding as these ideas might seem, they can be found in ancient Buddhist tracts, other tenets of Eastern thought, and many indigenous peoples' ways of understanding the world. They have also reached the West over the centuries in novels, poetry, and the arts; in the words of mystics; and in the deeds of heretics. It is customary to say that this kind of knowledge is inspired or revealed, rather than invented or discovered.

In an evocative essay, Diana Whitney (1995) describes spirit as energy, meaning, and epistemology. Her illustrations come from Native American traditions, Chinese medicine, the new science, and musings of organizational scientists. In many cultures, she notes, spirit is sacred. This moves us from the realms of philosophy and metaphor to matters of faith. It is clear enough that the world's great religions, as well as more personal or idiosyncratic ones, offer different ways of apprehending and expressing their revealed truths. Yet the comparative study of religions suggests that all have, at their core, a near-universal means of accessing spiritual knowledge. It is this that Harman (1988) calls their perennial wisdom.

In his deeper reflections, Bateson posits that social systems are gifted with wisdom. Some who go deep within themselves believe that humans have tacit knowledge of universal community and can cocreate a new order in line with it. This is the utopian aspiration for business outlined by Willis Harman and John Hormann in *Creative Work* (1990). They make the point that the central project of laborers and leaders in the Middle Ages was construction of great churches in honor of their god. The spiritual nature of their labor shifted as god moved from the center of the universe, and earthly science and material pursuits began to define who we are and why we work. Today they wonder if a new central project for civilization might emerge from our new consciousness and appreciation of what is at the center of our existence. Peck (1993) hopes so when he concludes *A World Waiting to Be Born* with the statement that utopia may be possible after all.

NEW, NEW PURPOSE: A BETTER WORLD

OD was birthed with utopian aspirations. Democracy and freedom were central to Lewin's work. Chin and Benne (1969) describe early OD as part of the normative reeducative tradition of change. Human relations training was applied to problems of race relations, repatriation of soldiers and POWs, and everyday estrangement and depersonalization in the world of work. The 1960s-type lab programs shared the assumption that personal and interpersonal factors inhibited human growth and relations. Argyris (1962) saw interpersonal incompetence as the key barrier to individual and group effectiveness. He and others argued that sensitivity training helped people learn to create more open and authentic relationships (Argyris, 1964).

But OD's focus had implications beyond personal and group development. Fromm (1955) postulated that man was moving from an ethic of having to an ethic of being. And Salk (1972) developed sigmoid curves to show how *being values* would have to transcend *ego values* to overcome the problems posed by population growth. These thinkers epitomized the view that changes in people's values and orientations were essential to the survival of society and the species, respectively. Bennis (1966) made the complementary case that changes in human values were essential to the survival of organizations.

OD's democratic humanism in the 1960s underwent a shift in the 1970s and 1980s. American notions of a melting pot changed, and the goal of a pluralistic society was embraced. The unequal distribution of power and resources became a focus of attention. In this context, OD focused on empowerment and technostructural forces in organizations. Ideas and practices developed in Europe were applied in the workplace. New theorizing about how beliefs and values undergird human behavior and social systems spanned many disciplines. Cognitive science came to the fore in social psychology, showing how people socially process information and construct meaning. Cultural anthropology enjoyed a renaissance. The logics of social constructivism (Gergen, 1982) helped explain the diversity of outlooks, values, and expectations of a pluralistic America.

In part one of my essay on the evolution of OD (Mirvis, 1988), I argued that even as OD turned its attention to valuing diversity and promoting egalitarianism, its main emphasis was on the practical problems faced by business organizations. The emergence of Japan as a formidable competitor, the rise of the shareholder's movement and its emphasis on short-term profitability, and finally the emergence of global capitalism with the fall of the Berlin Wall and the emergence of China, India, industrialized Mexico, Brazil, and other parts of Asia consumed much of OD's theorizing and practice. Interestingly, OD chose to deal with the fallout of job loss from downsizing, restructuring, and mergers; the increased stress on workers and working parents; and attendant feelings of distrust and exploitation. My study with Donald Kanter, *The Cynical Americans* (1989), documented the depth and breadth of disillusionment among American workers. It raised questions, as William Whyte had years before, as to what extent behavioral science engineering, including OD, was a culprit or at least a patsy in all of this.

To be fair, however, segments of the field carried OD's democratic values and urgings forward. Advances in social constructivism led to breakthrough methods for people to talk about, think through, and address the paradoxes of everyday existence and the problems of the world.

Positive Image, Positive Action

As interpreted by its practitioners, appreciative inquiry (AI) is about the search for the best in people, organizations, and the world around them. It is the art and practice of asking questions to strengthen a system's capacity to recognize and build on its untapped potential. When organizations connect to this positive change core, changes never thought possible are democratically mobilized.

The central ideas of AI—that a better life is possible by focusing on what you want more (not less) of and that change is easier when you amplify a group's positive qualities rather than try to fix the negative ones—are not new. Norman Vincent Peale's power of positive thinking (1952), Geoffrey Vickers' appreciative thinking in the art of judgment (1965), and timeless wisdom on turning problems into opportunities all speak to this. Cooperrider and Srivastva (1987) were revolutionary, however, in seeing the connection between positive image and positive action.

AI is part of a wave of fresh thinking about social problems and actions. The field of positive psychology, originating in medicine but extending to mental health, athletic performance, and community work, has gained adherents and now has a following in the discipline of positive organization scholarship (Seligman & Csikszentmihalyi, 2000; Cameron, Dutton, & Quinn, 2003). Such concepts as the psychology of abundance, studies of positive deviance, and interest in a "simpler way" (Wheatley & Kellner-Rogers, 1996) are part of professional parlance in many fields, including OD.

AI's roots connect to the logic of social construction and the notion that people's ability to construct new and better modes of organizing are based in human imagination and collective will. Language and words are the basic building blocks of this social reality. Hence much of the emphasis in AI concerns new ways of talking about the world (for example, Barrett, Thomas, & Hocevar, 1995; Kegan & Lahey, 2002). From this perspective, creating new and better ideas and images is a powerful way of changing organizations because we see what we believe. Many OD efforts involving AI follow a participatory process of discovery, dream, design, and destiny. Central in AI are the *principle of simultaneity,* whereby inquiry and change are tightly connected in the positive affirmation of what exists, and the *anticipatory principle* that puts idealized images of the future into the design of present actions.

Otto Scharmer, in concert with Peter Senge and colleagues, developed a complementary model termed the U that has people inquire into the source of human action (Senge et al., 2004). The emphasis is on inner knowing and on gaining new perspective on the world from it. Central is the notion that all of life is connected via fields of consciousness (McTaggart, 2002). These ideas draw from the font of revolutionary thinking about complex adaptive systems, quantum physics, tacit knowledge, and the spiritual sciences. Senge et al. (2004) have translated these ideas into a methodology for "presencing" the future: groups co-sense their inner life and the world around them, co-presence emerging forces, co-create new actions, and coevolve with transformations influenced by their own doings.

Cooperrider (1990) has advanced a "heliotropic hypothesis" that social systems evolve toward the most positive images they hold of themselves. These images are not necessarily conscious, nor are they often discussable. AI and the U model, however, provide methods to surface such images and promote inquiry into them. In CAS parlance, positive imaging can be the strange attractor to move a social system toward health. One also wonders if in presencing the future, people connect to the implicit order traditionally assigned to spirit.

Bringing the World Together

Even with these new, new methods, OD has continued to enact the importance of getting the whole system in the room. Recommendations advanced on how to improve information processing, elevate thinking, enrich inquiry, and forward learning point to the advantages of *holographic organization designs,* particularly in complex, rapidly changing situations where actions reverberate quickly. Such organizational designs—from work teams and cross-functional project groups to complex networks and communities of practice—seek to replicate wholeness. They embody the requisite variety needed to inform a system, as well as the diversity in perceptions and thoughts that yields positive friction in interactions and conversations. As a result, the holographic unit develops a more appropriately complicated picture of what is going on. This "whole" is then encoded into the culture of, say, a smaller business within a business, where accumulated learnings are concentrated and amplified.

On a related front, transorganizational development has mushroomed in the past two decades. Nowadays there are countless collaborative multistakeholder forums (Gray, 1989) where, for example, a company will work together with community groups and nongovernmental organizations (NGOs) to address everything from the impact of plants and facilities to community social service and socioeconomic development needs. Civil society groups and organizations increasingly collaborate across national boundaries on matters of mutual interest (Brown, 2001). Furthermore, there are multibusiness forums, often including NGOs, that address sustainability, ethical business practices, and problems as vast as HIV-AIDS and climate change.

These collaborative multiparty gatherings, forums, and networks are based on OD's knowledge of social systems and processes, facilitated with its social technologies, and often assisted by its practitioners. Carolyn Lukensmeyer (2005), as one example, convenes twenty-first-century town meetings whereby citizens in a community, in person or via teleconference, gain voice in public policy matters. She helped engage forty-five hundred New Yorkers in plans to rebuild lower Manhattan following the 9/11 devastation. Todd Jick worked with a diverse group of firefighters, widows and widowers, and executives representing people and businesses lost in the destruction to plan the memorial monument. Some time later, David Cooperrider worked alongside Kofi Annan of the United Nations and led leaders of businesses, countries, and global NGOs in setting an agenda for the Global Compact to address ten world-transforming development goals for the millennium. Cooperrider has also established a consortium of change agents, businesspeople, and civil society leaders under the title Business as an Agent of World Benefit. Its mandate is "Management Knowledge Leading Positive Change."

Globalization is OD's new stage, and the field's methods are being creatively used in consultations with global organizations, transnational forums and groups, or international networks of people. My own journey has taken to me to more than one hundred countries and to work on socioeconomic development with such global companies as Shell, Novo Nordisk, and Unilever (see Ayas & Mirvis, 2005). One intervention of interest is a "learning journey" in which hundreds of leaders in a company travel together to inform their strategies and intentions. (A chapter by Mirvis and Gunning on this intervention appears later in the volume.) The journeys, lasting up to a week, are multilayered, multisensory experiences that engage the head, heart, body, and spirit. They are tribal gatherings in that we typically wake at dawn, dress in local garb, exercise or meditate together, hike from place to place, eat communally, swap stories by the campfire, and sleep alongside one another in tents. In our daily experiences, we might meet monks or a martial arts master, talk with local children or village elders, or simply revel in the sounds and sights of nature. We spend considerable time in personal and collective reflections about who we are as a community, what we are seeing, and what this means for our work together. Throughout a journey, a team of researchers prepares a "learning history" that documents key insights for continued reflection.

In principle, knowledge about environmental and social conditions can be gleaned from text, talks, and conversations in any forum, whether at an office or on retreat. But the experience of being there physically and seeing firsthand adds texture and depth to knowledge and has greater consciousness-raising potential (Wuthnow, 1991). Consciousness raising requires internalization of the problem at hand and placing oneself psychologically into a situation (Prochaska, Norcross, & DiClemente, 1994). The learning journeys of Unilever apply action learning simultaneously to individual, work group, organization, and community development (Mirvis & Gunning, 2006). In the process, these journeys affect people's personal visions of their role as leaders, their operations and the spirit of their work group, and even the mission and purpose of Unilever's business in Asia.

In essence, such journeys aim to expand consciousness and in a fashion create a field in which businesspeople are connected to the world they meet along the way. Although such journeys are beyond the imagination and financial means of many organizations, they embody a spirit and intent that allows the whole system to "get into the room." The holographic form is also a mind-set: think globally, act locally.

SOURCING THE NEW IN OD

Revolution or evolution? OD has followed both paths since its inception. To compare the trajectories, consider how each explains the development of OD's knowledge base, the field's progression as a social and intellectual movement, and the influences of clients and practice (see Table 3.2).

OD Knowledge

Part one of my essay (Mirvis, 1988) made the case that OD's knowledge base was an amalgam of systems theory, action research, and client-centered consultation. It then progressed through what Kuhn (1970) calls "normal science" by drawing concepts from organizational behavior and theory, translating them into interventions, and testing their validity. All of this casts OD as a scientific endeavor whose knowledge base is *cumulative.*

Evolutionary Perspective on OD's History	Revolutionary Perspective on OD's History
OD's Knowledge	
Cumulative and universalistic	Contextual and particularistic
OD Movement	
Scientific and utilitarian	Humanistic and value based
OD Client Base	
Logical and pragmatic	Explorative and experimental
OD Practice and Practitioners	
Market-driven and professional	Visionary and disciple-like

Table 3.2.   Two Views of the History of Organizational Development.

Depicted in this way, OD, like traditional science, is premised on the assumption that there are *universal* laws about human and organizational behavior that can be manipulated experimentally and tested empirically. Knowledge obtained from one study can be generalized to the next and appropriate contingencies divined to guide OD practice. As a result, the once organic process of OD gave way to a more mechanical model of intervention in the 1970s and 1980s, which emphasized diagnostic protocols, instrumented assessments, and detailed planning before application of any treatment.

This evolutionary model fails to account for dramatic changes in OD's science base that challenged prevailing theories and the assumptions behind them (for example, Gibb, 2004; Reason & McArdle, 2006). Neither does it acknowledge how new thinking across disciplines pointed to new theories and understandings about heretofore "well understood" phenomena. Even as Stent (1972) argues that many scientific discoveries are ahead of their time, he adds that they are seldom unique. OD's knowledge has been shaped by family systems theory, quantum physics, breakthroughs in chemistry and biology, and developments in psychology and other social system sciences, as well as trends in the arts, spiritual matters, and social movements and innovations in society. Whenever the new emerges, many thinkers and doers are on a similar wavelength and moving in complementary directions.

Knowledge does not develop in a vacuum. Neither is it simply an accumulation of theory made into fact by empirical validation. Adherents to the sociorational school of thought contend that, on the contrary, knowledge develops as a function of its relevance and that new ideas take hold as a result of their intellectual and aesthetic appeal. Knowledge development is *contextual,* and knowledge is a social product shaped by the beliefs and values of its producers and consumers (Gergen, 1982).

OD has had its share of "fads" these part thirty years. Traditional science stands as defense against "quackery," and OD scientists have been rightly skeptical of new ideas based on unproven theories and unwarranted assumptions. Still, the field has been shaken by organizations and people undergoing changes that were neither anticipated nor accounted for by existing theories. Revolutions in knowledge arise during such times.

Kuhn (1970) argues that normal science persists until anomalies occur. Here the point is made that new social situations led to the generation of revolutionary new theories and new forms of intervention in OD. These theories and methods were born in a new context and came into (and went out of) fashion based on *particularistic* relevance and application, not their universality or generalizability.

OD Movement

In part one (Mirvis, 1988), I portrayed OD as an intellectual and social movement evolving through stages of utopian idealism and a crisis of direction over the merits of laboratory training to become an established scientific discipline. As a result, OD theories and methods gained scientific status, practice became *utilitarian,* and the intellectual movement behind OD evolved into quasi-stationary equilibrium.

This fits a rigid definition of science wherein the scientist is rational, and practice is defined by technique. The archetype is the *analytic scientist* (Mitroff & Kilmann, 1978) who gathers data and takes a detached, impersonal, and values-free perspective on phenomena. Practice, in turn, is driven primarily by science. OD in this depiction is a clearly defined field of study with rigid membership boundaries and agreed-on methods and procedures.

What this evolutionary model fails to account for is diversity within the discipline and periodic ferment over its content and methods. Wallace (1956) argues that societies go through periods of cultural distortion wherein basic assumptions about man and nature are questioned. Revolutionary movements among OD's academic proponents centered on challenges to the field's scientific canons in the 1970s and 1980s. During these epochs, applied scientists lost faith in the doctrine of logical positivism and questioned whose interests were served by science. They promulgated models and methods that were *humanistic* and *value-based.*

This type of scientist, concerned with personal and organizational development, fits the archetype of the *particular humanist* (Mitroff & Kilmann, 1978) who takes an involved, personal, and values-conscious perspective to the subject at hand. Practice is personalized; may draw from science, the arts, or the humanities; and is neither rigid nor exclusionary. Although many academic proponents of OD mimicked the thinking of established disciplines and methods of traditional science, others followed their own drummers and, in some cases, led a new parade.

OD Client Base

Part one (Mirvis, 1988) made the case that OD evolved with reference to a client base that sought a proven technical fix for problems. In its early phase, OD appealed to the most venturesome clients—early adopters, in the language of Everett Rogers (1962). His model of innovation adoption, however, shows that ideas need "scientific status" to reach later adopters and must be packaged and proven to reach the mass market. Thus OD theories became more specific and applications more mechanical in response to demand.

This thinking depicts OD consumers as *logical* and *practical*—responsive to the rigor of OD *theory,* constancy of *technique,* and reliability of *results.* The field came to be oriented less to ideas and ideals and more to the demands of the marketplace and what would sell. The inadequacy of this argument, however, is that it hinges on a simple and unidirectional model of product and industry life cycles.

A different look at the OD client base shows how the field has also been influenced by market shake-ups. New entrants on the demand side brought new needs and different criteria for evaluating the desirability of one or another OD intervention. Not all sought OD on the basis of its sound theory and proven track record. Isenberg (1984) found that many top executives make radical policy changes based on instincts and intuition. Some turned to new and untested forms of OD based on their feel for something new.

Developments within a client system may also make it more receptive to new forms of OD. Management succession and staff turnover change the makeup of a company and thus the preferences of its decision makers. Switching costs are low for OD clients who want to try something different. Furthermore, client sponsors undergo transformative personal experiences or find new meaning in their jobs and lives. Such consumers of OD are explorative and experimental. They seek the new based on their feelings, experience, or search for more meaning in their work.

Finally, client organizations in certain eras have been more receptive to radically new forms of management. Lindbloom (1959) differentiates between two modes of organizational planning and problem solving. In routine change situations, organizations undergo branch change: a new situation develops incrementally out of successive comparisons of present and future states. In nonroutine situations, by contrast, organizations undergo root change in which managers go back to the fundamentals and build a new situation from the ground up. This was certainly true in the last several decades and continues to be so in this era of globalization.

OD Practice and Practitioners

Finally, my evolutionary analysis (Mirvis, 1988) contended that practice and practitioners became less oriented to invention in the past two decades and more oriented toward standard application and niche selling. Early emphasis on discovery, experimentation, and theory building was supplanted by a reliance on tested, tried-and-true forms of intervention. The missionary zeal of early proponents, resting on faith in human potential, gave way to secular professionalism, sustained by scientific dogma.

This depicts practice as driven by the marketplace and along the way achieving modest professional stature. OD became an institution as an academic discipline and as a function within organizations. My projection at the time was that practice would add little new knowledge beyond what is known or easily knowable about people and organizations.

These conclusions, however, failed to acknowledge OD's permeability as an underbounded profession (Alderfer & Berg, 1977). This chapter offers a different picture of the potential of practice. In hindsight, it is apparent that practice-generated knowledge came from advances in laboratory education. New possibilities are emerging, too, from clients seeking to make root changes in their work cultures and practitioners who are part of the new, new movements in OD.

This, in essence, locates a source of the new in the minds and hearts of *visionaries* in the academy, in practice, and in client organizations, and in the passion and energy of committed *disciples*. These key innovators will buck market trends and search for, try out, and sponsor the new.

———

Argyris (1988) contends that to discover the new, scholars must visit universes that do not exist and entertain assumptions about human nature beyond the commonplace. In OD revolutions to date, this has meant forsaking positivistic formulations of science and exploring a world undefined by linear-causal logic (Tetenbaum, 1998). It has also meant seeing human nature as more than an amalgam of biological instincts and stimulus responses. Both of these changes were necessary for the discovery of new theory and its translation into new forms of intervention (Bushe, 1995; Gozdz, 1996). Both enabled applied scientists to join with client systems as co-creators of the new.

Inspiration will lead to the next new. Inventors of new theories and methods will apply passionate reason, as Vaill (1996) says, to new forms of OD in the lab and the field. They will join scientists from other disciplines, leading practitioners, and clients in a complementary search for the new. This will all be informed by prevailing social, political, and intellectual developments.

There is a risk that destructive forces in industry and the economy will counter these positive intentions. Terrorism, the clash of civilizations, and even the specter of ecological and social calamities loom. At the same time, there are opportunities in developing countries and post-communist Eastern Europe. I sense that these parts of the world will be responsive to new forms of OD and may host the most innovative and far reaching of future OD efforts. Furthermore, the many new global forums beckon OD know-how and promise to advance knowledge.

Whether the heliotropic properties of organizations can be actualized remains to be seen. It is clear, however, that OD will have to go back to the lab to find a means of applying itself fully to the industrial context ahead. New principles of change and a more developed definition of OD as an appreciative and generative science will have to emerge. The current revolution has to be consolidated and conditions created whereby revolutionary ideas of change can come forth again.

Intellectuals ranging from Koestler (1964) to Bateson (1972) have speculated that within the dichotomy between two worlds lies the creative spark of man and nature and the source of human potential. Hence much of the new thinking, research, and action in OD centers on the synthesis of competing forces and the resolution of paradoxes in service to creating the new.

The immediate implication for practice on a rational level is that clients and change agents will need to critically articulate their theories of change, apply them with flexibility and care, and learn from them through systematic study and reflection. At the same time, the field will need to encourage more intuition and creative expression in the formulation of theory and dig deeper to understand how the power of positive thinking and transformational techniques stimulate creativity in application.

My recommendation is for OD to draw deeply from Eastern and Western styles of thought and open itself further to pluralism— including more "weirdness." There are also exciting possibilities in the spread of OD to emerging markets and countries; its broader applications to peace making, social justice, and community building; and its deeper penetration into the mission of organizations (see Kahane, 2004; Ayas & Mirvis, 2004). All this may or may not prevent OD's often predicted death in the commercial marketplace. But it will ensure that the field continues to develop as both a theory-generating science and a practically purposeful discipline.

CHAPTER FOUR

Theories and Practices of Organizational Development

John R. Austin
Jean M. Bartunek

From its roots in action research in the 1940s and 1950s (Collier, 1945), and building on Lewin's insight that "there is nothing so practical as a good theory" (Lewin, 1951, p. 169), organizational development has explicitly emphasized both the practice and the scholarship of planned organizational change. Ideally, at least, research is closely linked with action in organizational development initiatives, and the solution of practical organizational problems can lead to new scholarly contributions (Pasmore & Friedlander, 1982; Rapoport, 1970).

Despite this more or less implicit expectation, there have been many disconnects between practitioners' and academics' approaches to contributing new knowledge. For example, action research as it was originally conceived became more and more practice and solution oriented and less focused on making a scholarly contribution (Bartunek, 1983). Some recent approaches to organizational development, such as many large-group interventions, have been implemented primarily by practitioners, with little academic investigation of their success. Some theories of change formulated by academics are not at all feasible to implement.

It is easy enough for academics to suggest that practitioners' work is not sufficiently novel and thought-out to contribute to scholarly understandings of change. However, it is also the case that many new methods of accomplishing planned organizational change have been developed by people who were focusing in particular on practice contributions (e.g., team building, sociotechnical systems, and large-group interventions, to name just a few). It is through practice that organizational improvement actually takes place. Another way to put this is that organizational development practitioners have a substantial knowledge base from which it is valuable for academics to draw, albeit one that is sometimes more tacit than explicit, just as practitioners may draw from academics' knowledge (e.g., Cook & Brown, 1999).

It is not only with respect to organizational development that there are separations between academic and practitioner approaches to organizational knowledge. Rynes, Bartunek, and Daft (2001), introducing a special research forum on academic-practitioner knowledge transfer in the *Academy of Management Journal,* referred to the "great divide" between academics and practitioners in organizational research. But they also argued that there are many reasons—academic, economic, and practical—why it is important that more explicit links be developed between academics and practitioners. For example, corporate universities are becoming more prominent, and training organizations such as the American Society for Training and Development are gaining substantially in membership. A recent Swedish law mandated that universities collaborate with their local communities in generating research (Brulin, 1998). Many work organizations are outsourcing some knowledge-generation activities to academics. Given organizational development's history, the development of understanding and appreciation of both academic and practitioner contributions is particularly crucial.

Several reviews of organizational development and change have been presented prior to this chapter (recent ones include Armenakis & Bedeian, 1999; Porras & Robertson, 1992; Weick & Quinn, 1999). These reviews have made important scholarly contributions to the understanding of such topics as variables involved in planned organizational change; the content, context, and processes of organizational change; and the degree to which such change is constant or sporadic. But prior reviews have not explicitly incorporated both practitioner and academic knowledge about organizational development. In contrast to these prior approaches, we focus on the kinds of emphases that characterize practitioner and academic knowledge regarding organizational development and do this using both academic and practitioner literatures. In so doing, we hope to break down some of the barriers that typically exist between organizational development practice and scholarship.

We divide the chapter into several sections. First we briefly compare contemporary and earlier organizational development emphases. Organizational development is an evolving field, and its emphases today are not the same as its initial emphases (Mirvis, 1990). The state of the field at the present time has implications for the types of knowledge needed by practitioners and academics.

Second, we use a distinction introduced by Bennis (1966) and modified by Porras and Robertson (1992) to distinguish different types of conceptual emphases between practice and academic scholarship on change. Third, on the basis of this distinction we situate organizational development within larger literatures on organizational change. Although in its early days organizational development was often seen to represent the majority of approaches to "planned change" in organizations, it is now recognized as one of many approaches to planned change. We situate it within various "motors" of change as these were described by Van de Ven and Poole (1995).

Fourth, we describe some contemporary organizational development interventions and the motors in practice that we see as important in them. Finally, we describe barriers to enhanced links between academics and practitioners and then suggest some strategies that may be used to reduce these barriers. This latter approach is in the spirit of the force field analysis approach developed originally by Lewin (1951) and used often by practitioners (Schmuck, Runkel, Saturen, Martell, & Derr, 1972).

We believe that the kinds of knowledge—or knowing, as Cook and Brown (1999) put it—of organizational development practice do not always link as well as they might with academic scholarship on change. But developing greater links is crucially important because at its core organizational development involves the promotion of change. In their interviews with a number of organizational development "thought leaders," Worley and Feyerherm (2001) found numerous recommendations for increased collaboration between organizational development practitioners and other change-related disciplines.

Our focus is on the theoretical and practical knowledge underlying today's organizational development practice. Worley and Varney (1998) remind us that the practice requires skill competencies as well as knowledge competencies. Skill competencies include managing the consulting practice, analysis, and diagnosis; designing and choosing appropriate interventions; developing client capability; and evaluating organizational change. In this chapter we examine the theories of change that inform the application of these skills. Detailed consideration of these skill competencies is beyond the scope of this chapter but can be found in other resources (Cummings & Worley, 2000; French & Bell, 1999).

ORGANIZATION DEVELOPMENT TODAY, NOT YESTERDAY

Early approaches to organizational development centered primarily on the implementation of humanistic ideals at work. The types of values emphasized included personal development, interpersonal competency, participation, commitment, satisfaction, and work democracy (French & Bell, 1999; Mirvis, 1988). The focus generally was within the workplace.

Over time, however, there has been a shift in emphases. In comparison to its early formulations, organizational development pays much more attention to the larger environment in which the business operates and aims at helping businesses accomplish their strategic objectives, in part through organizational alignment with the larger environment (e.g., Bunker & Alban, 1997; Church & Burke, 1995; Mirvis, 1988, 1990; Seo, Putnam, & Bartunek, 2001).

Early approaches placed considerable emphasis on individual and group development (e.g., Harrison, 1970), and although the term *whole organization* was used, the types of change fostered by organizational development often focused more on the group (e.g., team building) or on other organizational subunits. Given the organizational environment of the 1980s and beyond, individual development and group development have been less emphasized unless they are treated within the context of large systems change and the adjustment of an organization to its larger environment. Such adjustment often involves radical departure from the organization's prior strategic emphases (Nadler, Shaw, & Walton, 1995) and is sometimes referred to as *organizational transformation* (e.g., Nadler et al., 1995; Quinn & Cameron, 1988; Tichy & Devanna, 1986; Torbert, 1989) or *radical organizational culture change* (e.g., Cameron & Quinn, 1999).

Despite the shifts that have occurred in the understanding of organizational development's focus, there remains an emphasis on organizational development as humanistically oriented—as concerned about the people who make up an organization, not just the strategic goals of the organization. Thus, for example, Church, Waclawski, and Seigel (1999) defined organizational development as the process of promoting positive, humanistically oriented, large-system change. By humanistic they mean that the change is "about improving the conditions of people's lives in organizations" (p. 53). Beer and Nohria (2000) included organizational development within the category of capacity-building interventions in organizations, not as primarily economically oriented.

This shift in emphasis locates organizational development within the context of multiple types of organizational change efforts (Van de Ven & Poole, 1995). It cannot be discussed entirely separately from types of change that, at first glance, seem far removed from its emphases. However, there are still important distinctions between the practice knowledge and academic knowledge of organizational development and other types of planned change.

THE CONCEPTUAL KNOWLEDGE OF ORGANIZATIONAL DEVELOPMENT

Contemporary as well as past approaches to organizational development are based on more or less explicit assumptions about (1) the processes through which organizations change and (2) the types of intervention approaches that lead to change. These two phrases, which seem quite similar, actually represent two different conceptual approaches: one that is more likely to be addressed by academic writing on organizational development and one that is more likely to be addressed by practitioner writing. We use them to frame approaches to change that are presented primarily for academics and primarily for practitioners.

In 1966 Bennis distinguished between *theories of change* and *theories of changing*. Theories of change attempt to answer the question of how and why change occurs. Theories of changing attempt to answer the question of how to generate change and guide it to a successful conclusion. Porras and Robertson (1987, p. 4) expanded on Bennis's notion, relabeling the two different approaches as *change process theory* and *implementation theory*. (Although the categories are essentially the same, we will use Porras and Robertson's terms because they are much easier to distinguish.)

Porras and Robertson (1987, 1992) described change process theory as explaining the dynamics of the change process. This approach centers around the multiple types of variables involved in the accomplishment of planned change. In contrast, they described implementation theory as "theory that focuses on activities change agents must undertake in effecting organizational change" (p. 4). They included strategy, procedure, and technique theories as examples of implementation approaches.

Porras and Robertson's focus was primarily on organizational development interventions as explicitly defined. As noted earlier, however, the understanding of dynamics of change has been widened well beyond organizational development (e.g., Weick & Quinn, 1999; Van de Ven & Poole, 1995). Porras and Robertson also asserted that change process theory should inform implementation theory; that is, the findings of academic research should inform practice. There is awareness now that organizational development practice should also have an impact on academic knowledge (Rynes and others, 2001).

In this chapter we expand on the understandings of change process theory and implementation theory. We describe an array of change process theories using the model developed by Van de Ven and Poole (1995) for that purpose. We also describe several implementation models and suggest possible links between them and change process models.

We noted that academic writing tends to focus more on change process theory whereas practitioner writing focuses more on implementation theory. There has been relatively little interaction between the two types of theories; to some extent they occupy separate intellectual spaces and are held in more or less separate "communities of practice" (J. S. Brown & Duguid, 1991, 1999; Tenkasi, 2000). Change process theories tend to draw from empirical work grounded in academic fields such as psychology, sociology, economics, and anthropology. Implementation theories tend to draw from practitioner-oriented experiential work; they may emerge from the same academic disciplines as change process theories but do not make the connections explicit. It is hoped that this chapter suggests useful connections between the two.

Change Process Theories

Porras and Robertson (1992) concluded their review of organizational change and development research with a call for increased attention to theory in change research. Through attention to the variety of ways organizations might change, this call has been answered.

Researchers have approached the task of understanding organizational change from a dizzying array of perspectives. In their interdisciplinary review of about 200 articles on change, Van de Ven and Poole (1995) identified four ideal types of change theories. They labeled them as life cycle, evolution, dialectic, and teleology and located organizational development primarily within the teleological framework. These four types are distinguished by their underlying generative mechanisms, or *motors*. Van de Ven and Poole suggested that most change theories can be understood within one motor or in a combination of motors.

We found evidence of extensive theory development pertinent to organizational development based on each change motor. In the following sections we summarize recent change research categorized by the primary underlying motor of change. With Van de Ven and Poole (1995) we recognize that most change theories capture elements from different motors, although one motor is typically primary.

THE TELEOLOGICAL MOTOR. The teleological motor describes organizational change as the result of purposeful social construction by organization members. The motor of development is a cycle of goal formation, implementation, evaluation, and modification. Organizational change is goal driven; impetus for change emerges when actors perceive that their current actions are not enabling them to attain their goals, and the focus is on processes that enable purposeful activity toward the goals. The teleological motor can be found in most contemporary theories of organizational change. For example, recent extensions of evolutionary theories and institutional theories—evolutionary innovation and institutional agency—have adopted a teleological motor. Change leadership theories rely on the teleological motor as well. In the following we summarize some teleological change theories that have emerged or reemerged during the prior decade.

Strategic Change. Rajagopalan and Spreitzer (1996) observed that strategic change deals primarily with teleological change. Underlying most strategic change theories is the understanding that planned change triggered by goal-oriented managers can trigger change in both an organization and its environment. Following this teleological logic, several researchers have sought to understand the role of leadership in generating organizational change (Nutt & Backoff, 1997). Bass's transformational leadership framework (Bass, 1985; Bass & Avolio, 1994) posits that organizational change emerges as the result of leaders' attempts to develop their followers and transform follower goals to match more closely those of the organization. Other researchers view organizational change as the end result of cognitive development of organizational leaders (Hooijberg, Hunt, & Dodge, 1997; Torbert, 1991).

Cognitive Framing Theories. Several studies emphasize the importance of cognitive change by managers in creating organizational change. Reconceptualization of the context then leads to further cognitive change in a continuing iterative process (Barr, Stimpert, & Huff, 1992; Bartunek, Krim, Necochea, & Humphries, 1999; Weick, 1995). Gioia and Chittipeddi (1991) found that managerial efforts to communicate a planned change built cognitive consensus, which further enabled the change.

Change Momentum. Studies of change momentum within organizations have relied on the evolutionary motor to explain selection of organizational routines, which in turn create inertial forces (Amburgey, Kelly, & Barnett, 1993; Kelly & Amburgey, 1991). Jansen (2000) proposed a new conceptualization of momentum that focuses on teleological processes of change. She distinguished between inertia, the tendency of a body at rest to stay at rest or a body in motion to stay in motion, and momentum, the force or energy associated with a moving body. Evolutionary change theories deal primarily with inertia. However, momentum is a teleological theory. The force that keeps a change moving is goal driven and purposeful. Jansen found that change-based momentum, defined as the perception of the overall energy associated with pursuing some end state, fluctuated in a systematic way throughout a change process.

Theories of Innovation. Several researchers consider how individual attempts at innovation combine with environmental characteristics to generate organizational change (C. M. Ford, 1996; Glynn, 1996). Glynn proposed a theoretical framework for how individual intelligence combines with organizational intelligence to generate creative ideas. These ideas are then implemented provided that certain enabling conditions (adequate resources and support, incentives and inducements) are present. This process presents a model of organizational change that is driven by individual cognitions and collective sense-making processes within the organization. Oldham and Cummings (1996) and Drazin and Schoonhoven (1996) reported evidence of multilevel influences on organizational innovation driven by individual creative action. Amabile, Conti, Coon, Lazenby, and Herron (1996) built from an individual level of creativity to identify group- and organization-level constraints on individual creativity and subsequent organization-level innovation.

Taken together, research on innovation and creativity reveals a complex mix of predictors of organizational change. At the center of these predictors is the teleological assumption of goal-driven, purposeful action. As Orlikowski and Hofman (1997) noted, the specific decisions and immediate strategies may be unplanned improvisations, but they are guided by a goal-driven theme. Recent theorizing on organizational innovation highlights the interaction between purposeful action, sense making, organizational settings, and environmental jolts to trigger organizational change (Drazin, Glynn, & Kazanjian, 1999).

Organizational development in recent years reflects many of these approaches. As noted earlier, there is much greater emphasis now on accomplishing strategic ends (Bartunek et al., 1999; Jelinek & Litterer, 1988) and on the role of leadership in these processes (Nadler & Tushman, 1989). There has also been some attention paid to cognitive framing of different participants in a merger process (Marks & Mirvis, 2001). As part of the understanding of change processes, questions have been raised about resistance to change (for example, Dent & Goldberg, 1999).

THE LIFE CYCLE MOTOR. The life cycle motor envisions change as a progression through a predetermined sequence of stages. The ordering of the stages does not change, but the speed of progress and the triggers that lead to advancement through the process vary. Van de Ven and Poole (1995) noted that the "trajectory to the final end state is preconfigured and requires a specific historical sequence of events" (p. 515).

Whereas life cycle models of organizational change proliferated in the 1970s and 1980s (Quinn & Cameron, 1983), we found little continued theoretical development of this motor since 1995. One exception is in the area of entrepreneurship, where theorists continue to use a life cycle motor to understand the development and failure of new ventures (Hanks, Watson, Jansen, & Chandler, 1994), including self-organized transitions (Lichtenstein, 2000a, 2000b). Variations of the life cycle model, especially in conjunction with the teleological motor, are apparent in recent research on punctuated equilibrium. It emerges as a motor in several contemporary organizational development approaches discussed in the next section, such as transforming leadership (Torbert, 1989) and advanced change theory (Quinn, Spreitzer, & Brown, 2000).

Punctuated Equilibrium. The evolution-revolution framework of organizational change (Greiner, 1972) has formed the foundation of many recent organizational change theories (Mezias & Glynn, 1993) that have been used to describe dynamics in organizations. Greiner described the typical life cycle of an organization as consisting of extended evolutionary periods of incremental change interspersed with short revolutionary periods. This framework provides the basis for recent theories of strategic redirection (Doz & Prahalad, 1987), transformation (Laughlin, 1991), punctuated equilibrium (Tushman & Romanelli, 1985), and change archetypes (Greenwood & Hinings, 1993). During reorientations large and important parts of the organization—strategy, structure, control systems, and sometimes basic beliefs and values—change almost simultaneously in a way that leads to very different organizational emphases.

Whereas Tushman and Romanelli (1985) suggested the effectiveness of punctuated equilibrium approaches to change, others suggested some cautions in the use of this approach. Previously established competencies may be threatened by transformations (Amburgey et al., 1993). In addition, Sastry (1997) found that reorientation processes increased the risk of organizational failure unless evaluation processes were suspended for a trial period after the reorientation. However, certain change processes may enable successful reorientations. Mezias and Glynn (1993), for example, suggested that previously established routines may guide reorientations in such a way that competencies are not destroyed.

Questions have also been raised about how frequent true reorientations of the type suggested by Tushman and Romanelli are. Cooper, Hinings, Greenwood, and Brown (1996) recently suggested that instead of true reorientations, the types of change that typically occur involve one layer of orientation placed on top of another layer that represents the prior orientation. Reger, Gustafson, DeMarie, and Mullane (1994) also suggested that changes may often include this type of middle ground.

As noted earlier, punctuated equilibrium theories (Gersick, 1991; Tushman & Romanelli, 1985) emphasize the life cycle motor (the normal interspersing of evolutionary and revolutionary periods) but combine it with the teleological motor. Organizational actors, especially leaders, purposefully respond to environmental conditions that require a particular type of change in order to achieve effectiveness.

THE DIALECTIC MOTOR. The dialectic motor describes organizational change as the result of conflict between opposing entities. New ideas and values must directly confront the status quo. This motor builds from the Hegelian process of a thesis and antithesis coming into direct conflict. There are then several paths that may be taken, including separating the thesis and antithesis, attempting to create a synthesis of them, and attempting to embrace the differing perspectives (e.g., Baxter & Montgomery, 1996; Seo et al., 2001). Some argue that achieving a synthesis that appears to close off change may be less productive than developing organizational capacity to embrace conflicting approaches (cf. Bartunek, Walsh, & Lacey, 2000).

The dialectic motor often drives cognitive and political change theories and plays a prominent role in schematic change theories and communicative change models. It also forms the basis for a number of organizational development approaches outlined in the next section.

Schematic Change. Schematic models of change build from an understanding of individual cognitive processing to understand how changes occur in shared schemas. Schemas are cognitive frameworks that provide meaning and structure to incoming information (Mitchell & Beach, 1990). Organizational change is categorized by the level of change in the shared schemas. First order change occurs within a shared schema and second order change involves change in the shared schema (Watzlawick, Weakland, & Fisch, 1974).

Change in schemas typically occurs through a dialectic process triggered by the misalignment of a schema in use with the context (e.g., Labianca, Gray, & Brass, 2000). If a situation does not fit within an expected schematic framework, the person shifts to an active processing mode (Louis & Sutton, 1991). In this mode, the individual uses environmental cues to generate a new schema or modify an existing one. The direct comparison of the schema (thesis) to the context (antithesis) creates the change.

This schematic dialectic is applied to organizational change through change in shared schemas. Bartunek (1984) proposed that organizational schema change required a direct conflict between the current schema and the new schema. Such conflict between schemata underlies large-scale organizational changes including major industry change (Bacharach, Bamberger, & Sonnenstuhl, 1996), organizational breakup (Dyck & Starke, 1999), organizational identity change (Dutton & Dukerich, 1991; Reger et al., 1994), and organizational responses to new economic systems (Kostera & Wicha, 1996).

Communicative Change Theories. Drawing from notions of social construction (Berger & Luckmann, 1966) and structuration (Giddens, 1984), several theorists have begun to consider change as an element of social interaction. Change is recognized and generated through conversation and other forms of communication (Ford, 1999a; Ford & Ford, 1995). Organizations consist of a plurality of perspectives that are revealed through conversation (Hazen, 1994) that form the context for all organizational action. When different perspectives meet through conversation, either a synthesized perspective is generated or one perspective is spread. New and old perspectives coexist within the organization at the same time as the newer synthesized understanding diffuses through multiple conversations (Gilmore, Shea, & Useem, 1997). Whether the end result is synthesis or diffusion is partially determined by the significance of the perspectives and interaction to the identities of the participants (Gergen & Thatchenkery, 1996). Significant organizational change typically requires new organizational language that results from the conversational dialectic (Barrett, Thomas, & Hocevar, 1995) and that realigns discordant narratives and images (Faber, 1998).

THE EVOLUTIONARY MOTOR. The evolutionary motor focuses on change in a given population over time. It involves a continuous cycle of variation, selection, and retention. Evolutionary theories of organizational change focus on environmental conditions that create inertial pressures for organizational change. Change theories built around this motor begin with the assumption that one must understand the environmental setting of an organization in order to understand the dynamics of change. Organizations evolve based on their ability to respond and adapt to these powerful external forces. In the early 1990s the evolutionary motor was most evident in population ecology models. However, it is also the driving force of change in recent research on the rate of organizational change and in theories of institutional change.

Internal Change Routines. Research on organizational routines applies variation, selection, and retention to intraorganizational processes by considering how individual actions are selected and retained within the population of organization members.

Nelson and Winter (1982; see also Feldman, 2000) proposed that organizations develop routines, or patterns of action, that drive future action. Routines become more developed and complex as they are used. Routines that involve changing current routines are called modification routines. Like other organizational routines, modification routines can be relatively stable over time, leading the organization to approach organizational change in a consistent manner. Well-developed routines of organizational change enable an organization to adjust to different demands for change by modifying the content of the change but using a consistent process to manage the change (Levitt & March, 1988).

Experience with a certain type of change enables an organization to refine its routines for implementing that type of change. As a result, the organization develops expertise with that type of change and may be more likely to initiate similar changes in the future. For example, in their study of the Finnish newspaper industry, Amburgey et al. (1993) found that experience with a certain type of organizational change increased the likelihood that a newspaper would initiate a similar type of change again. They argued that this process occurs because the organization develops competence with the change type. Thus, costs of change are lowered and the organization is likely to see the change as a solution to an increasing number of problems.

Hannan and Freeman (1984) used the notion of organizational routines to explain how organizations attempt to increase the reliability of their actions and enable organizations to create conditions of stability in relatively unstable environments. They posited that these routines institutionalize certain organizational actions and create organizational inertia, which hinders the organization's ability to change. Kelly and Amburgey (1991) extended this model by showing that the same routinization processes that create inertia can also create momentum. Routines that institutionalize a certain rate of change create conditions that encourage change consistent with those routines. While disruptions in routines brought about by organizational change can destroy competencies (Levitt & March, 1988), that same organizational change can create competencies that make future organizational change more effective (Amburgey & Miner, 1992).

S. L. Brown and Eisenhardt (1997) found that organizations establish an internal pacing mechanism to operate in a constantly changing environment. For example, managers plan to release new versions of their products every nine months or set goals targeting a certain amount of income that needs to come from new products each year. While organizations continue to respond to environmental changes, they may devote a larger percentage of their resources to developing internal capabilities to change regardless of industry pressures.

Institutional Change. Institutional theory is often associated with stability rather than with change. Organizations grow more similar over time because the institutional environment provides resources to organizations that conform to institutional norms that create barriers to innovations (North, 1990; Zucker, 1987). However, as Greenwood and Hinings (1996) noted, theories of stability are also theories of change.

Institutional theory proposes that organizational actions are determined by the ideas, values, and beliefs contained in the institutional environment (Meyer & Rowan, 1977). Strong institutional environments influence organizational change by legitimating certain changes and organizational forms (DiMaggio & Powell, 1991). In order for an organizational change to be successful, it needs to be justified within the institutional system of values (D'Aunno, Sutton, & Price, 1991). In addition, broader institutional forces sometimes trigger organizational change (Greenwood & Hinings, 1993) or provide comparisons that in turn prompt such change (Fligstein, 1991; Greve, 1998).

Institutional change theories rely on the evolutionary motor to understand the dynamics of change. Isomorphic pressures on organizations act as a selection and retention process for validating organizational changes. However, institutional theorists emphasize that organizational actors play a part in creating the institutional forces that restrain them (DiMaggio & Powell, 1991; Elsbach & Sutton, 1992; Oliver, 1991; Suchman, 1995). Thus, institutional models of change have begun to build teleological motors into theories of institutional change by considering the strategic actions of institutional actors (Bloodgood & Morrow, 2000; Johnson, Smith, & Codling, 2000). For example, Creed, Scully, and Austin (forthcoming) illustrated how organizational activists selectively use available institutional logics to legitimate controversial changes in workplace benefits policies.

SUMMARY OF CHANGE PROCESS RESEARCH. Change process theory continues to develop and evolve. During the past decade new approaches to understanding change processes have emerged from each change motor identified by Van de Ven and Poole. Contemporary theorizing frequently draws from multiple motors with comparatively great attention to the teleological motor. Attempts to understand such multilevel issues as institutional agency, innovation, and temporal pacing of organizational change require that researchers build links between theories of individual change and theories of organizational change. Interactions between research on individual resistance to change, organizational-level political pressures, and institutional constraints can lead to further clarification of change process at each level. Thus, multilevel theorizing can expand our understanding of change processes and may lead to the identification of additional change motors.

Samples of Contemporary Interventions in Organizational Development

Several approaches to intervention characterize contemporary organizational development. It is neither possible nor desirable to give a complete list here. In this section, however, we identify some organizational development interventions that have been prominent since the early 1990s. We start at this date in order to capture trends present since Porras and Robertson's (1992) review of the field. (Some of these, however, were developed in advance of 1990.) All the approaches we summarized have been used in a number of countries around the globe.

Our review includes articles published in both academic and practitioner journals. It is not meant to be exhaustive, but illustrative of the theories that have drawn the most attention in the 1990s. These approaches include appreciative inquiry, learning organizations, and large-scale interventions. We also discuss employee empowerment. There is no one universally accepted method of accomplishing empowerment, but it is a more or less explicit goal of much organizational development work as well as an expected means through which organizational development efforts achieve their broader ends.

APPRECIATIVE INQUIRY. Cooperrider and Srivastva (1987) introduced appreciative inquiry as a complement to other types of action research. Since then appreciative inquiry has emerged as a widely used organizational development intervention. Since 1995, articles about appreciative inquiry have dominated practitioner journals such as the *OD Practitioner* and *Organization Development Journal* (e.g., Sorenson, Yaeger, & Nicoll, 2000). Appreciative inquiry builds from several important assumptions. First, social systems are socially constructed; people create their own realities through dialogue and enactment. Second, every social system has some positive working elements, and people draw energy for change by focusing on positive aspects of the system. Third, by focusing on building consensus around these positive elements and avoiding discussion of the negative aspects of the system, a group will create momentum and energy toward increasing the positives there.

Recent writings on appreciative inquiry highlight the social constructionist focus on dialogue as a way to enact a reality. Most articles and books on appreciative inquiry use case studies and frameworks for appreciative discussions to help practitioners lead appreciative inquiry interventions (Barrett, 1995; Bushe & Coetzer, 1995; Cooperrider, 1997; Rainey, 1996; Srivastva & Cooperrider, 1999). Driving these case studies is the observation that by focusing on the positive elements about "what is," participants create a desire to transform the system. In a recent critique of appreciative inquiry, Golembiewski (1998) argued for a more balanced examination of the benefits of this type of intervention and increased attention to how appreciative inquiry might connect with other approaches and theories of change.

Appreciative inquiry is playing an increasingly important global role. It has been successful as an approach to global consultation efforts (for example, Barrett, 1995; Barrett & Peterson, 2000), in part because it emphasizes appreciation of different approaches. Mantel and Ludema (2000), for example, described how appreciative inquiry creates new language that supports multiple positive ways of accomplishing things. This is particularly important in a global setting in which people are operating out of very different perspectives on the world (Tenkasi, 2000).

LARGE-GROUP INTERVENTIONS. As noted at the beginning of this chapter, the primary conceptual basis for organizational development has been action research. As it was originally designed, action research customarily begins by searching out problems to be addressed. However, Bunker and Alban (1997) recounted that by the 1970s some concern had been raised about this approach; Ronald Lippitt believed that starting with problems caused organization members to lose energy and to feel drained and tired. (Similarly, appreciative inquiry starts with positive, rather than negative, features of an organization.)

Lippitt saw problem solving as past oriented. He believed that focusing on the future, rather than the past, would be more motivating. Thus, he began to engage organization members in thinking about their preferred futures (Lippitt, 1980). Attention to a future organization member's desire is a first major emphasis of many large-group interventions. A second emphasis is on gathering "the whole system," or, if the whole system is not possible, representatives of a large cross section of the system (at least 10% of it), to contribute to future planning. One reason for the prominence of large-group interventions is recent emphasis on organizational transformation. Many (though not all) large-group interventions are designed to help accomplish transformation, based on the expectation that in order to transform a system, sufficient numbers of organization members with power to affect transformational processes must participate in change efforts. Filipczak (1995) noted that the typical aims of large-group interventions include such foci as changing business strategies, developing a mission or vision about where the company is headed in the next century, fostering a more participative environment, and initiating such activities as self-directed work teams or reengineering the organization.

A wide variety of large-group interventions have been developed in recent years (e.g., Bunker & Alban, 1997; Holman & Devane, 1999; Weber & Manning, 1998). A list of many of these, along with very brief summary descriptions of each, is presented in Table 4.1. To give a more concrete sense of the different types of large-group interventions, we briefly introduce two of the interventions currently in practice: the search conference and workout.

Search Conferences.   Search conferences represent one of the oldest forms of large-group interventions. They were originally developed in England by Emery and Trist (1973) in the 1960s, and have been further developed by Emery and Purser (1996). They have been used in a number of different countries (for example, Babüroglu, Topkaya, & Ates, 1996; Emery, 1996).

Search conferences basically take place in two- to three-day offsite meetings in which 20 to 40 organizational members participate. Participants are chosen based on their knowledge of the system, their diversity of perspectives, and their potential for active participation.

Intervention	Summary Description
Future Search	A 3-day conference aimed at helping representatives of whole systems envision a preferred future and plan strategies and action plans for accomplishing it.
Real-time strategic change	Conference aimed at enabling up to 3,000 organizational members consult on major issues facing their organization.
Open Space Technology	A loosely structured meeting that enables groups of organization members ranging in size from a small group to 1,000 individuals develop their own agendas in relationship to prespecified organizational concerns.
Search Conferences	Participative events that enable a diverse group of organization members to identify their desired future and develop strategic plans to implement to accomplish this future.
Participative design workshops	Workshops based on the search conference model in which groups of employees participate democratically in designing, managing, and controlling their own work.
Simu-real	Workshops in which organizational members work on real problems in simulated settings that enable them to learn how their organization approaches tasks and to determine what they would like to change.
Workout	Meetings in which groups of employees brainstorm ways to solve an organizational problem. Managers typically must accept or reject solutions in a public forum at the conclusion of the meeting.
Conference model	A series of conferences through which organization members study the correspondence between their own work and their desired future and develop new designs for work.
ICA strategic planning process*	A method designed to maximize the participation of community members in change processes that affect them by means of focused conversation, workshops, and event planning.

Table 4.1. Summary Listing of Large-Group Interventions.

Note: Descriptions of the interventions are taken from Bunker and Alban (1996) and Weber and Manning (1998).

*ICA stands for The Institute of Cultural Affairs.

Search conferences involve several phases, each of which includes multiple components. First the participants pool their perceptions of significant changes in their environment that affect their organization.

Next they focus attention on the past, present, and future of their organization, ending with the generation of a shared vision based on participants' ideals for a more desirable future. The intent is to develop long-term strategies that enhance the system's capacity to respond to changing environmental demands. In the final phase they work next steps, action plans, and strategies for dealing with the environment.

The conference structure is explicitly democratic, and participants are fully responsible for the control and coordination of their own work. All data collected are public. The expectation is that as diverse participants begin to see mutually shared trends in their environment, they will recognize a common set of challenges facing the organization and its members and will also recognize that these common challenges will require cooperation.

Workout. Workout is a process developed at General Electric that was aimed at helping employees address and solve problems without having to go through several hierarchical levels. It has been successful enough at GE that its use has been expanded to many other organizations.

Workout sessions involve several steps (Bunker & Alban, 1996). First, a manager introduces the problem on which a group with expertise pertinent to the problem will work. Then the manager leaves, and the employees work together for approximately two days on the problem. The manager returns, and the employees report proposals regarding how to solve the problems. On the spot, the manager must accept the proposals, decline them, or ask for more information. If the manager requests more information, the process that will follow in order to reach a decision must be specified.

No blaming or complaining is allowed. Employees who do not like something are responsible for developing a recommended action plan and then volunteering to implement it.

LEARNING ORGANIZATIONS. The idea that organizations and their members learn has been present for decades. However, most scholarly attention to learning focused on learning as an adaptive change in behavioral response to a stimulus, particularly the learning of routines (for example, Levitt & March, 1988). Learning was not necessarily viewed as desirable for the organization.

In the 1970s, however, Argyris and Schön (1978) introduced learning in a positive way, as a means of improving organizations. Argyris and Schön and others (for example, Feldman, 2000) argued that learning must include both behavioral and cognitive elements and involve the capacity to challenge routines, not simply enact them. This formulation was the basis for the learning organization, which in recent years has been one of the most popular business concepts. Communities of researchers and practitioners who study and practice learning organizations have emerged and grown rapidly (Easterby-Smith, 1997; Tsang, 1997).

More than any other written work, Peter Senge's (1990) best-selling book *The Fifth Discipline,* and the workbooks that have followed, *The Fifth Discipline Fieldbook* (Senge, Kleiner, Roberts, Ross, & Smith, 1994) and *The Dance of Change* (Senge et al., 1999), have been responsible for bringing the learning organization into the mainstream of business thinking (Seo et al., 2001). For Senge (1990), a learning organization is "an organization that is continually expanding its capacity to create its future" and for which "adaptive learning must be joined by generative learning, learning that enhances our capacity to create" (p. 14). Senge described five different "disciplines" as the cornerstone of learning organizations: (a) *systems thinking,* learning to understand better the interdependencies and integrated patterns of our world; (b) *personal mastery,* developing commitment to lifelong learning and continually challenging and clarifying personal visions; (c) *mental models,* developing reflection and inquiry skills to be aware, surface, and test the deeply rooted assumptions and generalizations that we hold about the world; (d) *building shared vision,* developing shared images of the future that we seek to create and the principles and guiding practices by which to get there; and (e) *team learning,* group interaction that maximizes the insights of individuals through dialogue and skillful discussion and through recognizing interaction patterns in teams that undermine learning. The workbooks describe ways to accomplish these disciplines and challenges to sustain the momentum of learning. For example, Senge et al. (1994) described "left-hand column" and "ladder of inference" methods to help increase the ability to recognize one's mental models. They described dialogue as a way in which group members can think together to foster team learning, and they described ways in which people might draw forth their own personal visions as a way of developing personal mastery.

The learning organization envisioned and promoted by Senge and his colleagues is only one of the many versions of learning organizations currently available, although most other authors owe at least some of their approach to Senge's work (for example, Garvin, 1993; Lipshitz, Popper, & Oz, 1996; Nevis, DiBella, & Gould, 1995; Watkins & Marsick, 1994). For example, Nevis et al. (1995) defined a learning organization as one that is effective at acquiring, sharing, and utilizing knowledge. Garvin (1993) viewed systematic problem solving and ongoing experimentation as the core of a learning organization.

We mentioned several intervention tools aimed at facilitating the development of learning organizations. An additional tool, learning histories, is particularly important. *Learning histories* are extended descriptions of major organizational changes that are designed to help organizations reflect on and learn from their previous experiences (Bradbury & Clair, 1999; Kleiner & Roth, 1997, 2000; Roth & Kleiner, 2000). They include an extensive narrative of processes that occur during a large-scale change event in an organization. The narrative is composed of the people who took part in or were affected by the change. They also include an analysis and commentary by "learning historians," a small group of analysts that includes trained outsiders along with insider members of the organization. The analysts identify themes in the narrative, pose questions about its assumptions, and raise "undiscussable" issues surfaced by it. Thus, learning histories are ways for organization members to reflect on events that happened and learn about underlying processes in their organizations from this reflection.

EMPOWERMENT. Although there has not been agreement on standard intervention processes to develop employee empowerment, there is little doubt that achieving empowerment is a major emphasis of much organizational development and similar consulting. It has been emphasized since Peter Block's (1987) influential book *The Empowered Manager.*

There is considerable variation in how empowerment is understood. For example, Ehin (1995) described empowerment as a frame of reference that incorporates deep, powerful, and intimate values about others, such as trust, caring, love, dignity, and the need for growth. In the context of work teams, Mohrman, Cohen, and Mohrman (1995) described empowerment as the capability of making a difference in the attainment of individual, team, and organization goals, and they suggested that it includes adequate resources and knowledge of the organization's direction. Thomas and Velthouse (1990), followed by Spreitzer (1996), focused on empowerment in terms of cognitive variables (task assessments) that determine motivation in individual workers.

Just as there are multiple definitions of empowerment, there are multiple mechanisms in organizations that may be used to help foster it. These may include structural factors (Spreitzer, 1996) and attempts to redesign particular jobs so that they include more of the individual task components that make up empowerment (Thomas & Velthouse, 1990). Most frequently, the means by which empowerment is discussed as being fostered in organizations is through participation in organizational decision making (for example, Hardy & Leiba-O'Sullivan, 1998) and enhancement of the organizational mechanisms (for example, knowledge, resources, or teams) that help employees participate in decision making (Bowen & Lawler, 1992).

The types of interventions we have described—appreciative inquiry, the various large-group interventions, and learning organizations—all include empowerment of employees as central components. In all of these interventions, it is groups of employees as well as managers who contribute to both organizational assessment (e.g., through appreciative inquiry and through various learning exercises, including the construction of learning histories) and organizational change (e.g., through planning solutions such as in workout sessions, and in reflecting future planning for the organization). Empowerment is both a means by which these interventions take place and an expected outcome of them.

Implementation Theories

Implementation theories address how actions generate change and what actions can be taken to initiate and guide change. Porras and Robertson distinguished types of implementation based on whether they focused on intervention strategy, procedure, or technique. Similar to the approach taken by Van de Ven and Poole (1995), we focus on four "motors" of change—four primary implementation approaches that are expected to accomplish the desired change. These motors come primarily from literature written for practitioners rather than literature written for academics. They are participation, self-reflection, action research, and narrative. Participation and action research have been cornerstones of organizational development practice for decades (French & Bell, 1999). However, what they mean in practice has evolved. Self-reflection and narrative, while implicit in some earlier organizational development work, have become much more prominent recently. It is not surprising that these methods play prominent roles in the organizational development interventions described earlier.

PARTICIPATION. Participation in organizational change efforts and, in particular, participation in decision making, formed the earliest emphases of organizational development (French & Bell, 1999). Such participation is still viewed as important, but the ways in which such participation is understood and takes place have expanded, and there is greater awareness that employees do not always wish to participate in change efforts (Neumann, 1989).

Earlier rationales for participation often centered on the expectation that employees were more likely to accept decisions in which they had participated. Now, however, the rationale for participation is somewhat different, as expectations of the role of employees in participation expand. In particular, there is now much more explicit emphasis on employees participating in *inquiry* about their organizations and contributing necessary *knowledge* that will foster the organization's planning and problem solving. This is illustrated in the roles of employees in the various large-scale interventions, as various participants are expected to reflect on and contribute knowledge about the organization's past as well as its future (e.g., in search conferences). It is also illustrated in the expectation that employees contribute to learning processes in their organizations, for example, through the various exercises designed to foster their own capacity and in their contribution to learning histories. Creative new means of participation such as GE's workout sessions give employees much more responsibility for solving problems and acknowledge much more employee knowledge than was often the case in the past.

SELF-REFLECTION. The growing interest in large-scale transformation in organizations has been accompanied by a similar interest in leadership of organizational transformation and thus in the development of leaders who can blend experience and reflection in order to create lasting organizational change. Torbert (1999) and Quinn et al. (2000) suggested that a primary means by which leaders accomplish this is through self-reflection and self-inquiry.

Torbert (1999) suggested that leaders need to develop the ability to reflect while acting so that they can respond to changing conditions and develop new understandings in the moment. Individual transformation involves an awareness that transcends one's own interests, preferences, and theories, enabling more holistic understanding of patterns of action and thought. Transformational leaders determine the appropriate method of transformation by cultivating a strong understanding of the context, including tradition, vision, and organization and individual capabilities. The exercise of transforming leadership affects the organization's capacity for transformation. In a longitudinal study of CEOs, Rooke and Torbert (1998) found that five CEOs that scored as transforming leaders based on Torbert's developmental scale supported 15 progressive organizational transformations, whereas five CEOs that did not score as transforming leaders supported no organizational transformations.

Advanced change theory (Quinn et al., 2000) proposed that by modeling a process of personal transformation, change agents enable deeper organizational change. This process demands that change agents be empowered to take responsibility for their own understanding (Spreitzer & Quinn, 1996) and develop a high level of cognitive complexity (Denison, Hooijberg, & Quinn, 1995). This generally requires a change in values, beliefs, or behaviors, which is generated by an examination of internal contradictions. The leader creates opportunities for reflection and value change through intervention and inquiry. The leader is constantly shifting perspectives and opening up values and assumptions for questioning. The more skilled organization leaders are at generating deep personal cognitive change, the more likely it is that the leaders will support or create deep organizational change.

ACTION RESEARCH. Action research consists of a set of theories of changing that work to solve real problems while also contributing to theory. While the original models of action research emphasized the solution of problems, models of action research developed in later years include a wider array of emphases. In particular, many contemporary action research models propose that change can be triggered through a process of direct comparison between action and theory.

Participatory Action Research. Participatory action research was developed largely by Whyte (1991) and his colleagues. It refers to a process of systematic inquiry in which those experiencing a problem in their community or workplace participate with researchers in deciding the focus of knowledge generation, in collecting and analyzing data, and in taking action to manage, improve, or solve their problem.

Action Science. Dialectic change theories envision change as the outcome of conflict between a thesis and antithesis. Action science focuses on how to bring the thesis and antithesis into conflict. Argyris and Schön's (1974) Model II learning and Argyris, Putnam, and Smith's (1985) action science model provide a common base for dialectic action science methods. Change is triggered by calling attention to discrepancies between action and espoused values. Highlighting differences between "*theories in use*" and "*espoused theories*" generates the impetus for change. Argyris focused on processes that enable double-loop learning and awareness of underlying values guiding action. Individuals work to expose the mental models driving their action and to identify the values and actions through which they influence their context.

Several other writers have expanded this approach to change by highlighting the importance of understanding how action is embedded in a broader system of values and meaning. For example, Nielsen (1996) called for "tradition-sensitive" change dialectic strategies in which the change agent directly links the change with biases in the shared tradition system.

Action Learning. Action learning, like action science, has a goal of changing behavior by comparing behaviors and theories. In an action science intervention, the individual compares theories in use with espoused theories. In an action learning intervention, the dialectic is between theoretical knowledge and personal experience. Revans (1980) outlined a process in which action learning groups work to understand social theories and ideas by applying them to a real situation. Participants use the theory to understand the logical implications of their experience and use the experience to internalize, refine, and make sense of the theory. Because of its group emphasis, action learning focuses on interpersonal interactions and their effects on project outcomes (Raelin, 1997).

Cooperative Inquiry. Cooperative inquiry was developed primarily by Reason and his colleagues (for example, Reason, 1999). Cooperative inquiry is an inquiry strategy in which those involved in the research are both co-researchers and co-subjects. It includes several steps. First, a group of people chooses an issue to explore and develops one or more means by which they will explore it. Then they carry out the agreed-upon action and report on its outcomes. Through this action and reflection they become more fully immersed in their experience and are led to ask new questions. Finally, they reconsider their original questions in light of their experience.

Action Inquiry. Action inquiry (or developmental action inquiry) has been developed primarily by Torbert and his collaborators (for example, Torbert, 1999). Briefly, it is concerned with developing researchers' capacities in real time to increase their attention by turning to its origin, to create communities of inquiry, and to act in an objectively timely manner. This is a manner by which they become increasingly able to get multiple types of feedback from their actions that can increase their ability to act and to achieve personal congruity.

NARRATIVE-RHETORICAL INTERVENTION. Narrative interventions highlight the role that rhetoric and writing can play in generating organizational change. This approach to change finds its theoretical roots in sense making (Weick, 1995) and interpretive approaches to organizations (Boje, 1991). Organizational actors partially create their reality through the retrospective stories that they tell about their experience and through future-oriented stories that they create as a pathway for action. Convergence of narratives by organization members drives collective sense making (Boyce, 1995).

Organizational change can be generated through sharing of stories and building consensus around new images of the future (for example, Ford, 1999b) in which the stories shift. The stories thus offer a goal toward which organization actors can work, and the role of the change agent is to assist organization members in reconceiving their understandings (Frost & Egri, 1994) by creating new stories. Ford and Ford (1995) identified four types of conversations that drive change: initiative, understanding, performance, and closure. Initiative conversations start a change process; understanding conversations generate awareness; performance conversations prompt action; and closure conversations acknowledge an ending.

Several current organizational development practices rely on a narrative theory of changing. Appreciative inquiry draws on narrative organizational development theories by challenging organization members to generate local theories of action. Barry (1997) identifies strategies from narrative therapy that can enable organizational change. These include influence mapping, problem externalization, identifying unique outcomes, and story audiencing. Using the case of a high-technology research organization, O'Connor (2000) illustrated how stories told during a strategic change link the change with the past to highlight anticipated future problems and accentuate how the past and present differ.

THE CONNECTION BETWEEN IMPLEMENTATION THEORIES AND CHANGE PROCESS THEORIES

It is possible to construct a rough map of the links between particular implementation motors, interventions, and change processes, especially as implementation motors would likely occur in the interventions described earlier. Such a rough map is depicted in Table 4.2. It indicates that implementation strategies have been developed primarily for the teleological motor, as this is expressed in its multiple forms. However, at least one organizational development intervention potentially applies to each of the other change process motors.

THE DIVIDE BETWEEN IMPLEMENTATION THEORIES AND CHANGE PROCESS THEORIES

The fact that some organizational development interventions are applicable to the different change process theories means that they represent *potential* means for fostering these different types of change. It does not mean that authors who describe the different types of change motors reference organizational development work or that the implementation models reference the change process theories. In most cases there is no explicit connection between them. To the contrary, we believe that there is a fairly strong divide between those who focus on change process models and those who focus on particular interventions and their underlying implementation models.

To test whether this appeared to be true, we took a closer look at where change process theories were being published and where implementation models and descriptions of interventions were published during the 1990s. We examined 209 articles published since 1990 whose central ideas involved change process theory and implementation theory. We only included articles that had obvious implications for change process or implementation theories.

Implementation Models

	Participation	Reflection	Action Research	Narrative
	Often used in appreciative inquiry, large-group interventions, learning organizations, empowerment	Often used in appreciative inquiry, large-group interventions, learning organizations	Often used in learning organizations, empowerment	Often used in appreciative inquiry, large-group intervention, learning organizations
Change Process Motors				
Teleological (e.g., strategy, cognitive framing, change momentum, continuous change)	X	X	X	
Life cycle (e.g., punctuated equilibrium/transformation)		X	X	
Dialectic (e.g., schema change, communication change)			X	X
Evolutionary (e.g., internal change routines, institutional change)			X	

Table 4.2. Possible Relationships Between Change Process Models and Implementation Models as Expressed in Contemporary Intervention Approaches.

Possible ways of implementing each change process model by means of one or more of the implementation approaches are indicated by X.

Table 4.3 provides a summary of our findings. It shows that for the most part there is a segregation between journals publishing theories of change processes and journals publishing implementation theories. Only a few journals consistently published both types of change research work. Those that appeared often in our investigation include *Organization Science, Journal of Management Studies,* and the *Strategic Management Journal* (although with a larger sample some others also fit into this category).

We sorted the journals into three groupings and sought to understand whether there were any fundamental difference among the groupings. The first, and perhaps most obvious, difference is that journals that published implementation theory articles had a larger percentage of authors with nonacademic affiliations (Table 4.3, column 3). While a majority of the implementation theory articles were written by authors with academic affiliations, virtually all of the change process theory articles were written by authors with academic affiliations. Second, a comparison of citations within the articles shows that while implementation theory articles referenced change process theory articles, authors of change process theory articles rarely cited

Journal	Number of Articles	Percentage of Implementation Theory	Percentage of Authors with Academic Affiliation
Academy of Management Journal	8	0	100
Administrative Science Quarterly	10	0	100
Academy of Management Review	16	13	93
Organization Studies	13	23	82
Strategic Management Journal	16	44	100
Organization Science	12	50	100
Journal of Management Studies	6	50	100
Journal of Organizational Change Management	18	72	89
Organization Development Journal	21	81	56
Journal of Applied Behavioral Science	14	86	57
OD Practitioner	34	88	29
Leadership and Organization Development	18	94	77
Other journal articles	15	47	
Books and book chapters	13	46	
Total	**209**	**50**	**82**

Table 4.3.   Change and Organizational Development Theory in the 1990s.

implementation theory articles. The findings suggest a low level of interaction between these two approaches to change theorizing. In particular, academic scholars are paying comparatively little attention to practices through which change is facilitated. The overlap of the two knowledge networks is created by the journals that publish both types of work and by a few individual researchers who publish in both theoretical areas. In general, there is relatively little information passing from one knowledge network to the other. Several knowledge transfer barriers limit the knowledge flows between these two networks. Attempts to create more integration between change process and implementation models need to find ways around these barriers.

Barrier 1: Different Knowledge Validation Methods

We found a wide array of knowledge validation strategies in the change process theory and implementation theory literatures. These are the methods used to convey the significance and legitimacy of authors' theories and conclusions. They include appeals to previous research, clear and logical research designs, appeals to the authors' expertise, and use of detailed cases. An author's choice of knowledge validation strategy is determined by the targeted audience of the article and the author's own understanding of what determines knowledge validity.

Examination of the articles reveals strong norms of homogeneity within journals and within articles. Authors tend to cite other articles that employ similar knowledge validation methods, and journals tend to favor a certain knowledge validation method. This homogeneity enables clear progression of research because it makes it easy for the reader to understand how the current article builds from previous similar work. However, it can also hinder knowledge transfer between knowledge networks. References to previous work are typically limited to work in journals that employ similar strategies for legitimating knowledge.

Method variety within a journal provides one potential pathway around this knowledge transfer barrier. For example, a few journals, such as *Organization Science,* publish research using a wide range of methods. However, this diversity at the level of the journal is not mirrored at the article level. Authors still tend to reference other research using similar methodologies.

Epistemological understanding about knowledge may act as a larger barrier to knowledge transfer than methodological homogeneity. Many change process articles use a hypothesis-testing format to identify generalizable knowledge about organizational change. Writers of these articles attempt to persuade the reader of the legitimacy of their theory and conclusions by highlighting links with previous research findings and carefully describing the methodology and analysis of the study.

Implementation articles, on the other hand, often do not attempt to generalize their findings. These authors provide detailed descriptions of the context of the study that readers can use to link the article and theory to their own situation. The contextual approach of implementation fits an expertise-based epistemology. That is, expertise is developed through experience in similar situations; practitioners can gain expertise by reading detailed cases and attempting to connect those cases with their personal experience. The detailed descriptions in case-based articles enable readers to determine whether and how the theory is applicable to their situations and how it contributes to their expertise.

Epistemological differences between change process and implementation articles are similar to Geertz's (1983) distinction between "*experience-near*" and "*experience-far*" concepts. People use experience-near concepts to explain what they experience and to describe the experience to others. The goal is to communicate a sense of the immediate context. Specialists use experience-far concepts to map their observations and categorize them as part of a larger abstract body of knowledge. Academics often dismiss experience-near approaches as not rigorous enough; practitioners often dismiss experience-far approaches as not applicable to many contexts.

Barrier 2: Different Goals and Audiences

The journals included in our review have differing goals and audiences. The grouping of journals according to their tendency to publish change process or implementation theory articles is consistent with the journal audience. Thus, journals geared toward managers or organizational development practitioners offer more guidance on how to affect change. For example, the mission of the *OD Practitioner* is to present information about state-of-the-art approaches to organizational development diagnosis and intervention. The articles in the *OD*

Practitioner include well-developed implementation theories that are supported by case studies, appeals to practice, and connections with previous articles and books regarding similar issues.

As one example, the *OD Practitioner* sponsored a recent special issue on appreciative inquiry, which is becoming a widely adopted organizational development intervention technique (Sorenson et al., 2000). Yet we found comparatively little acknowledgment of appreciative inquiry in more academically oriented research and writings on organizational change and development. The academic silence and practitioner enthusiasm about appreciative inquiry illustrates the significance of the practitioner/academic theoretical divide. As Golembiewski (1998) noted, appreciative inquiry challenges several assumptions of previous research on resistance to change (Head, 2000). Academic theorizing about change would benefit from more attention to the questions raised by appreciative inquiry practitioners. But as long as theoretical discussions of appreciative inquiry remain limited to practitioner-oriented journals, the theoretical implications risk being ignored by those developing and testing change process theories.

The journals with a mix of change process and implementation theories may provide some insight into the barriers between academic-practitioner knowledge transfer. We suggest some characteristics of these journals that may offer guidance on this issue. The *Strategic Management Journal* included several change-related articles that have a strong teleological element (Barr et al., 1992; Fombrun & Ginsberg, 1990; Gioia & Chittipeddi, 1991; Greve, 1998; Simons, 1994). As would be expected in a strategy journal, the primary focus is on managerial action. Discussions of research results lead naturally into implications for practicing managers or change agents. Although the research designs in *Strategic Management Journal* are similar to those reported in *Academy of Management Journal* and *Administrative Science Quarterly,* the teleological, planned-change focus is similar to that of the practitioner journals such as the *OD Practitioner* and the *Harvard Business Review.* This mix may provide a template for communicating practitioner experience to academic researchers. *Organization Science* also publishes both change process and implementation articles. Several *Organization Science* articles provide implementation theories grounded in change process research (for example, Bate, Khan, & Pye, 2000; Denison et al., 1995; Kimberly & Bouchikhi, 1995; Kuwada, 1998). The result is an emergent understanding of the process underlying change and how it can be influenced. These journals have an academic audience but may provide a channel for practitioner-developed theory because of their close affiliation with managerial concerns and their willingness to publish innovative process-driven work.

Barrier 3: Different Theoretical Antecedents

Some change process theories have recently paid more attention to implementation. This convergence is occurring as change process theorists build teleological motors into their existing models, since the teleological motor offers a natural common ground for integrating change process and implementation models. However, the similarity of converging approaches can be overlooked if the writers are unaware of each other's work. This is particularly the case when there are differing theoretical antecedents behind the change process theories.

One illustration of this barrier is found in recent work on institutional agency and dialectic action research. Foster (2000) showed how both streams of research have addressed the issue of how actors can initiate and guide change in existing institutional structures. Institutional theorists have used this line of inquiry to expand understanding of institutional change theories (Barley & Tolbert, 1997), whereas action research theorists have focused on improving change agent effectiveness in changing broad tradition systems (Nielsen, 1996).

Despite the similarity of interest, neither stream of research is drawing on the insights of the other stream. Institutional theorists struggle to identify skills and strategies that enable change to the institutional structure (Fligstein, 1997). Building from individual cognitive theories, action research writers have identified successful strategies for institutional change (Argyris et al., 1985). Recent action research work has explicitly tied actor strategies with changes in the tradition system (Austin, 1997; Nielsen, 1996), which is similar to the institutional structure. This recent focus of action research on tradition systems considers how change agents are constrained by pressure to connect their change strategy with widely held social values. Building from sociological theories of organizational fields, institutional researchers have outlined a process of isomorphism and legitimation that offers insight into what strategies will fit within a given field (DiMaggio & Powell, 1991; Greenwood & Hinings, 1996).

Further indication of the importance of theoretical commonalities for information transfer is shown through linkages between communicative change theories and narrative organizational development theories. Articles in these two areas of inquiry have more cross-referencing than any other set of change process theories and implementation theories. These fields draw from the same theoretical roots: social constructionism and social cognition. Recent articles (Ford, 1999b; O'Connor, 2000) acknowledge and build on previous work in both fields. Their common roots may enable easy transfer of research by providing a common language and understanding of acceptable method of inquiry. Schematic change theory and action research theories also have substantial overlap. However, cross-referencing is more pronounced in schematic change theory than in action research. Both change theories, communicative and schematic, use the dialectic motor. The close linkages with change process models suggest that the dialectic motor, like the teleological motor, may provide a fruitful framework for future integration of change process theories and implementation theories.

STRATEGIES FOR OVERCOMING BARRIERS TO KNOWLEDGE TRANSFER

A sense-making approach to knowledge transfer (Weick, 1979, 1995) assumes that individuals actively select information from their environment and make determinations about its relevance and meaning. Individuals compare the new information with their current cognitions and attempt to integrate it into their personal schemas or reject it as irrelevant. The barriers to knowledge transfer identified earlier cause individuals to reject the new information as irrelevant. Individuals do not see how the information fits within their schemas because the information does not fit their perception of valid knowledge validation methods or because it builds from an unknown theoretical tradition. For the information to be accepted and used, it must be linked in some way with the receiving individual's conception of relevant knowledge.

The notion of idea translation (Czarniawska & Joerges, 1996) provides some insights on how the sense-making process between change process theories and implementation theories is being limited. Czarniawska and Joerges proposed that ideas do not simply move unchanged from one local setting to another, but are transformed when moved into a new setting. They further proposed that ideas are ambiguous. They are given meaning through their connection with other logics, through action taken on them, and through the ways in which they are translated for new settings. Translation includes interpretation and materialization. Interpretation occurs when the idea is connected with other already-understood words and values. Understanding of the idea depends on what words and values the idea is connected with in this stage. The same idea will be interpreted differently by different individuals. The communicator can guide this stage in translation by offering suggested words and values to use to understand the new idea. It becomes embedded in a complex of ideas motivating the action, and this leads to further transformation of the idea as feedback may lead to its modification or rejection. The communicator has less control over this part of the process.

Change and organizational development theorists translate ideas through interpretation when they connect their work with widely known words, stories, and values. As an example, a change process theory may be translated into an implementation theory when the writer presents the planned, purposeful action of managers engaged in the change process. An implementation theory may inform a change process theory when the writer describes how a particular approach, such as action research, affected the outcome of the change process (e.g., a particular transformation attempt). Change process and implementation theorists translate ideas through materialization when they report on results of theoretically motivated change attempts. Through their description of the action, the theory is "made real" and is subsequently transformed.

There are some excellent templates for how translation between change process theory and implementation theory would look in practice. We describe some of them below.

Same-Author Translation

Writers may translate their own research for a new audience. Because the translation process changes the content of the idea, it may include subtle shifts. Eisenhardt and Brown's work on change pacing is one illustration of this type of translation. S. L. Brown and Eisenhardt developed a theory of change (1997) published in an academic journal. In subsequent publications, a *Harvard Business Review* article (Eisenhardt & Brown, 1998a) and a book (Eisenhardt & Brown, 1998b), they translated their change theory for a managerial audience. In the process of translation, their theory was transformed into an implementation theory. In their 1997 article S. L. Brown and Eisenhardt focused attention on the organization level of analysis to learn how organizations continuously change. They used a multiple-case inductive research method to develop a theory of continuous organizational change that identifies the significance of limited structure and extensive communication, experimental "probes" to attempt to understand the future, and transition processes that link the present with the future. These organizational practices combine to enable change through flexible sense-making processes. In their later journal article and book, Eisenhardt and Brown shifted their focus to managerial action. They built from their theory of change and recommended specific strategies for managing change in markets that are continually shifting. These recommendations include strategies for establishing performance metrics, generating transitions, and understanding and establishing rhythms. Taken together, the strategies provide an implementation theory based on organizational temporal rhythms and heedful engagement with the constantly shifting market. The authors illustrated their points with stories demonstrating how managers at well-known technology companies have enabled their companies to prosper in chaotic environments.

This translation process subtly changed the idea of time pacing. The focus moved from the organization level to the strategic, managerial level. The shift to managerial action provides a more explicit teleological focus to the theory. The translation also involves a different writing style that relies less on reporting the methodology and more on story telling. This changes the goal behind the writing from generalizability to contextualizing. The methodology in the 1997 article indicates limitations of the theory, whereas the stories in subsequent articles invite readers to find the commonality between the story and their own contexts. One aspect that made this translation easier to accomplish was that the academic methodology employed was iterative case analysis. Stories were already present in the initial data collection process, so the raw data for the translation were ready to be used.

Multiple-Author Translation

Multiple-author translation is more common than is same-author translation. This process is used regularly in the *Academy of Management Executive,* where, for example, there is a section devoted to research translations. In multiple-author translation, a researcher builds from other researchers' work and translates it for a new audience. An illustration of this approach is Jansen's (2000) research on change momentum. Jansen developed and tested a momentum change theory based on the concepts of energy flows and movement momentum. She observed that most academic theories of change that referred to momentum were actually confusing momentum with inertia. Several implementation theorists have identified the importance of generating energy in order to move a change forward (Jick, 1995; Katzenbach, 1996; Kotter, 1995; Senge et al., 1999). Jansen translated the momentum idea into a change process theory and showed how it complements other evolutionary and teleological change theories. By referring to the implementation theory articles, Jansen invited other researchers to draw from them.

Multiple-author translation is less direct than same-author translation. It remains unclear how influential the initial idea is to the translation process. The translator claims credit for the idea because it is new to the targeted audience, and uses appeals to previous writings on the idea to legitimate it. Appeals to practitioner articles show that the idea has managerial relevance, and appeals to academic research show that the idea has empirical validity. Translation is enabled if both appeals are included within the same article. Linking the practitioner with the academic research implies a link and thus a translation process between the two.

Common Language Translation

Another method of idea translation is to present implementation and change process theories side by side within the same article and show their commonalities (and, sometimes, differences). This is a common strategy for review articles, especially articles dealing with organizational learning and learning organizations (for example, Easterby-Smith, 1997; Miller, 1996; Tsang, 1997). The advantage of this strategy is that it explicitly calls attention to a stream of research of which the reader may be unaware and legitimates it by showing its links with research that has already been validated by the audience. This strategy invites the audience to continue the translation process by including the newly translated research in their own work.

The common strategy for language translation is the most direct strategy. It requires the author explicitly to link the ideas and explain that link using a rhetorical style suited to the audience. Whereas the single-author translation strategy requires the author to have a working understanding of how to communicate a single idea to multiple audiences, the common-language translation strategy requires the author to have an understanding of how to communicate diverse ideas to a single audience. This chapter is an example of common language translation.

Translating Implementation Theory to Change Process Theory

There are not as many examples of the explicit translation of practice work (implementation) to inform change process models as there are of translations from change process models to implementation models. However, some methods are being developed that may begin to address this gap.

The major method is one in which an individual member of an organization who is working to change it also studies the change or works in combination with an external researcher to study the change and to communicate about it to a scholarly audience. The first way this might happen involves insiders conducting their own action research projects (Coghlan, 2001; Coghlan & Brannick, 2001). When insiders then write about these projects for an external audience, they are translating their work for people who are likely to understand them from a slightly different perspective. A second way is through organizational members writing together with external researchers to describe and analyze a change process for a scholarly audience (Bartunek, Foster-Fishman, & Keys, 1996; Bartunek et al., 1999). This type of approach is referred to as *insider-outsider team research* (Bartunek & Louis, 1996). It is a kind of multiple-author approach, but one in which practitioners and academics are working jointly, rather than sequentially and independently, to make the work accessible to multiple audiences.

CONCLUSION

Research in organizational change and development has been increasing. Calls for more attention to theorizing about change processes have certainly been heeded. In addition, the variety of intervention types and underlying implementation models is considerably greater today than it was only a decade ago.

But to a large extent theorizing and practice, change process models and implementation models, have been developing separately.

There are significant gaps between the two theoretical knowledge networks, even as there are potential overlaps in the work in which they are engaged. Whether or not the two groups are aware of it, the limited information flow between practitioners working from and further developing implementation theories and academics refining change process models limits the development of both types of theorizing. The barriers to knowledge transfer that we have identified— different knowledge validation standards, goals and audience, and theoretical antecedents—lead us to believe that successful connections between change process models and implementation models require a translation process. On some occasions such translation processes have been demonstrated, and those demonstrations provide a model for what might be done.

It is customary in chapters of this type to comment on the state of theorizing in a given field. There are some areas that could clearly use further conceptual development in terms of both change process and implementation models. These include downsizing, mergers and acquisitions, and nonlinear changes in mature organizations. On the whole, however, as the review here has made evident, there are abundant examples of change process theories, many of which address phenomena that are pertinent to the practice of organizational development. There are also a growing number of implementation models. As shown in Table 4.2, there are multiple potential overlaps between the two types of approaches. Thus, the current state of theorizing seems to us to be one that has the potential for the development of much more explicit links and connections between change process and implementation theories in ways that would benefit both. Such potential has not been realized as yet. However, the translation efforts we have described suggest that the means exists to begin to accomplish this after more concerted efforts are made, and that this accomplishment will be of considerable value to both the theory and the practice of organizational development.

Because of its dual interest in theory development and practical application, organizational development can play an important role in the translation of research to practice and in developing research questions informed by practice. For this to happen, academics and practitioners alike would benefit from increased attention to translation rather than expecting the audience to do the translation on its own. To take this theorizing to the next level, it would be useful for scholars and practitioners to ask questions like the following: What can appreciative inquiry practice teach us about strategic change? or How is action research similar to institutional agency? How can an understanding of life cycles affect the use of narrative strategies in organization change? If organizational development practitioners and organizational scholars can learn to ask—and answer—these questions, they will make a contemporary contribution to theory and practice that is consistent with organizational development's original ideals.

PART TWO

The OD Core

Understanding and Managing Planned Change

The theories, practices, and beliefs of OD have influenced organizational improvement efforts for more than half a century. As the chapters in Part One illustrate, the field has evolved in scope and methods in response to client needs, social changes, learning from experience, advances in theory, and increasing complexities in the world of work.

At the same time, organization development has retained a core philosophy and logic that are reflected in consistencies over time in OD's change model. Central continuities in that model include the following:

1. *Change is intentional.* It begins with understanding an organization or a subsystem, which leads to identification of desired outcomes and the development of a grounded intervention strategy.

2. *Change is positive and purposive.* It is intended to improve organizational health and functioning and to enhance a system's overall adaptive capacities.

3. *Change is data-driven.* It reflects the particular circumstances, needs, and goals of the client organization—and it is the job of change agents to investigate, understand, and pay heed to all that in their work.

4. *Change is values-centered.* OD is underpinned by a deep concern for the people who make up an organization and by a belief that organizational effectiveness, innovation, and survival require respect for and attention to the human side of enterprise. At the same time, however, OD is not dogmatic. It seeks to understand a client system's organizational culture and context and to work with the organization to see how its values, beliefs, and norms tacitly inform its goals, strategies, and decisions.

5. *Change is action oriented.* It is rooted in the art and science of planned intervention—a change agent enters a social system to initiate specific activities that enhance learning and effectiveness. Successful interventions affect behavior, frames of reference, strategic directions, and the choices that people make. The intervention process is iterative: cycles of active experimentation, practice, and choice alternate with active reflection, testing, and integration.

6. *Change is based in experience, grounded in theory, and focused on learning.* OD is an action science that uses the best social and behavioral science thinking to resolve practical problems and develop a system's capacity for learning and renewal. In the process, the field tests its own theories of organizing and change and generates new ones: knowledge informs action, and action informs knowledge.

The first chapter in Part Two, "Kurt Lewin and the Planned Approach to Change: A Reappraisal," by Bernard Burnes, explores the many contributions of Kurt Lewin, the undisputed father of social psychology and action research. Lewin's approach to planned change and, in particular, his 3-Step Model—unfreezing, moving, refreezing—have dominated theory and practice for half a century, attracting both strong supporters and critics along the way. An appreciation of Lewin's thinking and fundamental impact on the field is vital.

Next is an excerpt from a classic by Chris Argyris, *Intervention Theory and Method: A Behavioral Science View.* Argyris is unique in the depth and wealth of his contributions to intervention theory. More than thirty years after the publication of this book, his thinking and writing on the topic remain the standard. Argyris has advanced thinking about OD as a values-based method of planned change. Successful interventions are grounded in four interrelated core values: valid information (directly observable and testable data), free and informed choice, internal commitment, and constant monitoring to ensure consistency between intention and action. In this chapter, titled "Effective Intervention Activity," Argyris explores the organizational realities that change agents face and proposes a workable model for successful interventions.

The next two chapters in Part Two explore different action technologies at the core of organization development work, and a third presents an influential contemporary complement. Linda Dickens and Karen Watkins, in "Action Research: Rethinking Lewin," examine the definition, development, and goals of action research, as well as a range of historical and current applications of the process. OD's change strategies are underpinned by theories and methods of action research: organizations are best understood and improved through an iterative series of intervention experiments and data gathering. Joseph A. Raelin's "Action Learning and Action Science: Are They Different?" introduces readers to the current generation of action technologies. Raelin compares action learning and action science, offering OD practitioners ways to use each method and assess their differential impact. "Toward a Theory of Positive Organizational Change," by David L. Cooperrider and Leslie E. Sekerka, explores the concept of appreciative inquiry as an OD intervention and change strategy. As the title of the chapter indicates, appreciative inquiry focuses on the positive capacities and strengths of a social system as the starting point for fostering its growth and development. The method is a counterpoint to OD's historic emphasis on problem solving: appreciative inquiry emphasizes what's right rather than what's wrong. The chapter is also a good example of OD's expanding methods and approaches.

Part Two closes with two important models of planned change that fall outside conventional boundaries for the field, the first by John P. Kotter in "Leading Change: Why Transformation Efforts Fail" and the second by David A. Nadler in "The Congruence Model of Change." Both are rich in wisdom and contribute in important ways to planning and managing effective change. A lively and vibrant field seeks and welcomes good ideas and practices, even from outside the family. OD is at its best when it is open to learning.

CHAPTER FIVE

Kurt Lewin and the Planned Approach to Change

A Reappraisal

Bernard Burnes

> *Freud the clinician and Lewin the experimentalist—these are the two men whose names will stand out before all others in the history of our psychological era.*

The above quotation is taken from Edward C. Tolman's memorial address for Kurt Lewin delivered at the 1947 Convention of the American Psychological Association (quoted in Marrow, 1969, p. ix). To many people today it will seem strange that Lewin should have been given equal status with Freud. Some fifty years after his death, Lewin is now mainly remembered as the originator of the three-step model of change (Cummings & Huse, 1989; Schein, 1988), and this tends often to be dismissed as outdated (Burnes, 2000; Dawson, 1994; Dent & Goldberg, 1999; Hatch, 1997; Kanter et al., 1992; Marshak, 1993). Yet, as this article will argue, his contribution to our understanding of individual and group behavior and the role these play in organizations and society was enormous and is still relevant. In today's turbulent and changing world, one might expect Lewin's pioneering work on change to be seized upon with gratitude, especially given the high failure rate of many change programs (Huczynski & Buchanan, 2001; Kearney, 1989; Kotter, 1996; Stickland, 1998; Waclawski, 2002; Wastell et al., 1994; Watcher, 1993; Whyte & Watcher, 1992; Zairi et al., 1994). Unfortunately, his commitment to extending democratic values in society and his work on field theory, group dynamics and action research, which, together with his three-step model, formed an interlinked, elaborate, and robust approach to planned change, have received less and less attention (Ash, 1992; Bargal et al., 1992; Cooke, 1999). Indeed, from the 1980s, even Lewin's work on change was increasingly criticized as relevant only to small-scale changes in stable conditions, and for ignoring issues such as organizational politics and conflict. In its place, writers sought to promote a view of change as being constant, and as a political process within organizations (Dawson, 1994; Pettigrew et al., 1992; Wilson, 1992).

The purpose of this article is to reappraise Lewin and his work. The article begins by describing Lewin's background, especially the origins of his commitment to resolving social conflict. It then moves on to examine the main elements of his planned approach to change. This is followed by a description of developments in the field of organizational change since Lewin's death, and an evaluation of the criticisms leveled against his work. The article concludes by arguing that rather than being outdated, Lewin's planned approach is still very relevant to the needs of the modern world.

LEWIN'S BACKGROUND

Few social scientists have received the level of praise and admiration that has been heaped upon Kurt Lewin (Ash, 1992; Bargal et al., 1992; Dent & Goldberg, 1999; Dickens & Watkins, 1999; Tobach, 1994). As Edgar Schein (1988, p. 239) enthusiastically commented:

> There is little question that the intellectual father of contemporary theories of applied behavioral science, action research and planned change is Kurt Lewin. His seminal work on leadership style and the experiments on planned change which took place in World War II in an effort to change consumer behavior launched a whole generation of research in group dynamics and the implementation of change programs.

For most of his life, Lewin's main preoccupation was the resolution of social conflict and, in particular, the problems of minority or disadvantaged groups. Underpinning this preoccupation was a strong belief that only the permeation of democratic values into all facets of society could prevent the worst extremes of social conflict. As his wife wrote in the preface to a volume of his collected work published after his death:

> Kurt Lewin was so constantly and predominantly preoccupied with the task of advancing the conceptual representation of the social-psychological world, and at the same time he was so filled with the urgent desire to use his theoretical insight for the building of a better world, that it is difficult to decide which of these two sources of motivation flowed with greater energy or vigour. (Lewin, 1948b)

To a large extent, his interests and beliefs stemmed from his background as a German Jew. Lewin was born in 1890 and, for a Jew growing up in Germany, at this time, officially approved anti-Semitism was a fact of life. Few Jews could expect to achieve a responsible post in the civil service or universities. Despite this, Lewin was awarded a doctorate at the University of Berlin in 1916 and went on to teach there. Though he was never awarded tenured status, Lewin achieved a growing international reputation in the 1920s as a leader in his field (Lewin, 1992). However, with the rise of the Nazi Party, Lewin recognized that the position of Jews in Germany was increasingly threatened. The election of Hitler as Chancellor in 1933 was the final straw for him; he resigned from the university and moved to America (Marrow, 1969).

In America, Lewin found a job first as a "refugee scholar" at Cornell University and then, from 1935 to 1945, at the University of Iowa. Here he was to embark on an ambitious program of research which covered topics such as child-parent relations, conflict in marriage, styles of leadership, worker motivation and performance, conflict in industry, group problem-solving, communication and attitude change, racism, anti-Semitism, anti-racism, discrimination and prejudice, integration-segregation, peace, war, and poverty (Bargal et al., 1992; Cartwright, 1952; Lewin, 1948a). As Cooke (1999) notes, given the prevalence of racism and anti-Semitism in America at the time, much of this work, especially his increasingly public advocacy in support of disadvantaged groups, put Lewin on the political left.

During the years of the Second World War, Lewin did much work for the American war effort. This included studies of the morale of frontline troops and psychological warfare, and his famous study aimed at persuading American housewives to buy cheaper cuts of meat (Lewin, 1943a; Marrow, 1969). He was also much in demand as a speaker on minority and intergroup relations (Smith, 2001). These activities chimed with one of his central preoccupations, which was how Germany's authoritarian and racist culture could be replaced with one imbued with democratic values. He saw democracy, and the spread of democratic values throughout society, as the central bastion against authoritarianism and despotism. That he viewed the establishment of democracy as a major task, and avoided simplistic and structural recipes, can be gleaned from the following extracts from his article on "the special case of Germany" (Lewin, 1943b):

> ...Nazi culture ... is deeply rooted, particularly in the youth on whom the future depends. It is a culture which is centred around power as the supreme value and which denounces justice and equality .... (p. 43)

> To be stable, a cultural change has to penetrate all aspects of a nation's life. The change must, in short, be a change in the "cultural atmosphere," not merely a change of a single item. (p. 46)

> Change in culture requires the change of leadership forms in every walk of life. At the start, particularly important is leadership in those social areas which are fundamental from the point of view of power. (p. 55)

With the end of the War, Lewin established the Research Center for group dynamics at the Massachusetts Institute of Technology. The aim of the Center was to investigate all aspects of group behavior, especially how it could be changed. At the same time, he was also chief architect of the Commission on Community Interrelations (CCI). Founded and funded by the American Jewish Congress, its aim was the eradication of discrimination against all minority groups. As Lewin wrote at the time, "We Jews will have to fight for ourselves and we will do so strongly and with good conscience. We also know that the fight of the Jews is part of the fight of all minorities for democratic equality of rights and opportunities . . ." (quoted in Marrow, 1969, p. 175). In pursuing this objective, Lewin believed that his work on group dynamics and action research would provide the key tools for the CCI.

Lewin was also influential in establishing the Tavistock Institute in the UK and its journal, *Human Relations* (Jaques, 1998; Marrow, 1969). In addition, in 1946, the Connecticut State Inter-Racial

Commission asked Lewin to help train leaders and conduct research on the most effective means of combating racial and religious prejudice in communities. This led to the development of sensitivity training and the creation, in 1947, of the now famous National Training Laboratories. However, his huge workload took its toll on his health, and on February 11, 1947, he died of a heart attack (Lewin, 1992).

LEWIN'S WORK

Lewin was a humanitarian who believed that only by resolving social conflict, whether it be religious, racial, marital, or industrial, could the human condition be improved. Lewin believed that the key to resolving social conflict was to facilitate learning and so enable individuals to understand and restructure their perceptions of the world around them. In this he was much influenced by the Gestalt psychologists he had worked with in Berlin (Smith, 2001). A unifying theme of much of his work is the view that ". . . the group to which an individual belongs is the ground for his perceptions, his feelings and his actions" (Allport, 1948, p. vii). Though field theory, group dynamics, action research and the three-step model of change are often treated as separate themes of his work, Lewin saw them as a unified whole with each element supporting and reinforcing the others and all of them necessary to understand and bring about planned change, whether it be at the level of the individual, group, organization, or even society (Bargal & Bar, 1992; Kippenberger, 1998a, 1998b; Smith, 2001). As Allport (1948, p. ix) states: "All of his concepts, whatever root-metaphor they employ, comprise a single well integrated system." This can be seen from examining these four aspects of his work in turn.

Field Theory

This is an approach to understanding group behavior by trying to map out the totality and complexity of the field in which the behavior takes place (Back, 1992). Lewin maintained that to understand any situation it was necessary that "[o]ne should view the present situation— the status quo—as being maintained by certain conditions or forces" (Lewin, 1943a, p. 172). Lewin (1947b) postulated that group behavior is an intricate set of symbolic interactions and forces that not only affect group structures, but also modify individual behavior. Therefore, individual behavior is a function of the group environment or "field," as he termed it. Consequently, any changes in behavior stem from changes, be they small or large, in the forces within the field (Lewin, 1947a). Lewin defined a field as "a totality of coexisting facts which are conceived of as mutually interdependent . . ." (Lewin, 1946, p. 240). Lewin believed that a field was in a continuous state of adaptation and that "[c]hange and constancy are relative concepts; group life is never without change, merely differences in the amount and type of change exist" (Lewin, 1947a, p. 199). This is why Lewin used the term "quasi-stationary equilibrium" to indicate that whilst there might be a rhythm and pattern to the behavior and processes of a group, these tended to fluctuate constantly owing to changes in the forces or circumstances that impinge on the group.

Lewin's view was that if one could identify, plot, and establish the potency of these forces, then it would be possible not only to understand why individuals, groups, and organizations act as they do, but also what forces would need to be diminished or strengthened in order to bring about change. In the main, Lewin saw behavioral change as a slow process; however, he did recognize that under certain circumstances, such as a personal, organizational, or societal crisis, the various forces in the field can shift quickly and radically. In such situations, established routines and behaviors break down and the status quo is no longer viable; new patterns of activity can rapidly emerge and a new equilibrium (or quasistationary equilibrium) is formed (Kippenberger, 1998a; Lewin, 1947a).

Despite its obvious value as a vehicle for understanding and changing group behavior, with Lewin's death, the general interest in field theory waned (Back, 1992; Gold, 1992; Hendry, 1996). However, in recent years, with the work of Argyris (1990) and Hirschhorn (1988) on understanding and overcoming resistance to change, Lewin's work on field theory has once again begun to attract interest. According to Hendry (1996), even critics of Lewin's work have drawn on field theory to develop their own models of change (see Pettigrew et al., 1989, 1992). Indeed, parallels have even been drawn between Lewin's work and the work of complexity theorists (Kippenberger, 1998a). Back (1992), for example, argued that the formulation and behavior of complex systems as described by chaos and catastrophe theorists bear striking similarities to Lewin's conceptualization of field theory. Nevertheless, field theory is now probably the least understood element of Lewin's work, yet, because of its potential to map the forces impinging on an individual, group, or organization, it underpinned the other elements of his work.

Group Dynamics

> ... the word "dynamics" ... comes from a Greek word meaning force ... "group dynamics" refers to the forces operating in groups ... it is a study of these forces: what gives rise to them, what conditions modify them, what consequences they have, etc. (Cartwright, 1951, p. 382)

Lewin was the first psychologist to write about "group dynamics" and the importance of the group in shaping the behavior of its members (Allport, 1948; Bargal et al., 1992). Indeed, Lewin's (1939, p. 165) definition of a "group" is still generally accepted: "... it is not the similarity or dissimilarity of individuals that constitutes a group, but interdependence of fate." As Kippenberger (1998a) notes, Lewin was addressing two questions: What is it about the nature and characteristics of a particular group which causes it to respond (behave) as it does to the forces which impinge on it, and how can these forces be changed in order to elicit a more desirable form of behavior? It was to address these questions that Lewin began to develop the concept of group dynamics.

Group dynamics stresses that group behavior, rather than that of individuals, should be the main focus of change (Bernstein, 1968; Dent & Goldberg, 1999). Lewin (1947b) maintained that it is fruitless to concentrate on changing the behavior of individuals because the individual in isolation is constrained by group pressures to conform. Consequently, the focus of change must be at the group level and should concentrate on factors such as group norms, roles, interactions, and socialization processes to create "disequilibrium" and change (Schein, 1988).

Lewin's pioneering work on group dynamics not only laid the foundations for our understanding of groups (Cooke, 1999; Dent & Goldberg, 1999; French & Bell, 1984; Marrow, 1969; Schein, 1988) but has also been linked to complexity theories by researchers examining self-organizing theory and nonlinear systems (Tschacher & Brunner, 1995). However, understanding the internal dynamics of a group is not sufficient by itself to bring about change. Lewin also recognized the need to provide a process whereby the members could be engaged in and committed to changing their behavior. This led Lewin to develop action research and the three-step model of change.

Action Research

This term was coined by Lewin (1946) in an article entitled "Action Research and Minority Problems." Lewin stated in the article:

In the last year and a half I have had occasion to have contact with a great variety of organizations, institutions, and individuals who came for help in the field of group relations. (Lewin, 1946, p. 201)

However, though these people exhibited:

... a great amount of good-will, of readiness to face the problem squarely and really do something about it ... These eager people feel themselves to be in a fog. They feel in a fog on three counts: 1. What is the present situation? 2. What are the dangers? 3. And most importantly of all, what shall we do? (Lewin, 1946, p. 201)

Lewin conceived of action research as a two-pronged process which would allow groups to address these three questions. First, it emphasizes that change requires action, and is directed at achieving this. Second, it recognizes that successful action is based on analyzing the situation correctly, identifying all the possible alternative solutions, and choosing the one most appropriate to the situation at hand (Bennett, 1983). To be successful, though, there has also to be a "felt-need." Felt-need is an individual's inner realization that change is necessary. If felt-need is low in the group or organization, introducing change becomes problematic. The theoretical foundations of action research lie in Gestalt psychology, which stresses that change can only successfully be achieved by helping individuals to reflect on and gain new insights into the totality of their situation. Lewin (1946, p. 206) stated that action research ". . . proceeds in a spiral of steps each of which is composed of a circle of planning, action, and fact-finding about the results of the action." It is an iterative process whereby research leads to action and action leads to evaluation and further research. As Schein (1996, p. 64) comments, it was Lewin's view that ". . . one cannot understand an organization without trying to change it. . . ." Indeed, Lewin's view was very much that the understanding and learning which this process produces for the individuals and groups concerned, which then feeds into changed behavior, is more important than any resulting change as such (Lewin, 1946).

To this end, action research draws on Lewin's work on field theory to identify the forces that focus on the group to which the individual belongs. It also draws on group dynamics to understand why group members behave in the way they do when subjected to these forces. Lewin stressed that the routines and patterns of behavior in a group are more than just the outcome of opposing forces in a forcefield. They have a value in themselves and have a positive role to play in enforcing group norms (Lewin, 1947a). Action research stresses that for change to be effective, it must take place at the group level, and must be a participative and collaborative process which involves all of those concerned (Allport, 1948; Bargal et al., 1992; French & Bell, 1984; Lewin, 1947b).

Lewin's first action research project was to investigate and reduce violence between Catholic and Jewish teenage gangs. This was quickly followed by a project to integrate black and white sales staff in New York department stores (Marrow, 1969). However, action research was also adopted by the Tavistock Institute in Britain, and used to improve managerial competence and efficiency in the newly nationalized coal industry. Since then it has acquired strong adherents throughout the world (Dickens & Watkins, 1999; Eden & Huxham, 1996; Elden & Chisholm, 1993). However, Lewin (1947a, p. 228) was concerned that:

> A change towards a higher level of group performance is frequently short lived; after a "shot in the arm," group life soon returns to the previous level. This indicates that it does not suffice to define the objective of a planned change in group performance as the reaching of a different level. Permanency at the new level, or permanency for a desired period, should be included in the objective.

It was for this reason that he developed his three-step model of change.

Three-Step Model

This is often cited as Lewin's key contribution to organizational change. However, it needs to be recognized that when he developed his three-step model Lewin was not thinking only of organizational issues. Nor did he intend it to be seen separately from the other three elements that comprise his planned approach to change (i.e., field theory, group dynamics, and action research). Rather Lewin saw the four concepts as forming an integrated approach to analyzing, understanding, and bringing about change at the group, organizational, and societal levels.

A successful change project, Lewin (1947a) argued, involved three steps:

• *Step 1: Unfreezing.* Lewin believed that the stability of human behavior was based on a quasi-stationary equilibrium supported by a complex field of driving and restraining forces. He argued that the equilibrium needs to be destabilized (unfrozen) before old behavior can be discarded (unlearnt) and new behavior successfully adopted. Given the type of issues that Lewin was addressing, as one would expect, he did not believe that change would be easy or that the same approach could be applied in all situations:

> The "unfreezing" of the present level may involve quite different problems in different cases. Allport . . . has described the "catharsis" which seems necessary before prejudice can be removed. To break open the shell of complacency and self-righteousness it is sometimes necessary to bring about an emotional stir up. (Lewin, 1947a, p. 229)

Enlarging on Lewin's ideas, Schein (1996, p. 27) comments that the key to unfreezing ". . . was to recognise that change, whether at the individual or group level, was a profound psychological dynamic process." Schein (1996) identifies three processes necessary to achieve unfreezing: disconfirmation of the validity of the status quo, the induction of guilt or survival anxiety, and creating psychological safety. He argued that ". . . unless sufficient psychological safety is created, the disconfirming information will be denied or in other ways defended against, no survival anxiety will be felt and consequently, no change will take place" (Schein, 1996, p. 61). In other words, those concerned have to feel safe from loss and humiliation before they can accept the new information and reject old behaviors.

• *Step 2: Moving.* As Schein (1996, p. 62) notes, unfreezing is not an end in itself; it ". . . creates motivation to learn but does not necessarily control or predict the direction." This echoes Lewin's view that any attempt to predict or identify a specific outcome from planned change is very difficult because of the complexity of the forces concerned. Instead, one should seek to take into account all the forces at work and identify and evaluate, on a trial and error basis, all the available options (Lewin, 1947a). This is, of course, the learning approach promoted by action research. It is this iterative approach of research, action, and more research which enables groups and individuals to move from a less acceptable to a more acceptable set of behaviors. However, as noted above, Lewin (1947a) recognized that without reinforcement, change could be short-lived.

• *Step 3: Refreezing.* This is the final step in the three-step model. Refreezing seeks to stabilize the group at a new quasi-stationary equilibrium in order to ensure that the new behaviors are relatively safe from regression. The main point about refreezing is that new behavior must be, to some degree, congruent with the rest of the behavior, personality, and environment of the learner or it will simply lead to a new round of disconfirmation (Schein, 1996). This is why Lewin saw successful change as a group activity, because unless group norms and routines are also transformed, changes to individual behavior will not be sustained. In organizational terms, refreezing often requires changes to organizational culture, norms, policies, and practices (Cummings & Huse, 1989).

Like other aspects of Lewin's work, his three-step model of change has become unfashionable in the last two decades (Dawson, 1994; Hatch, 1997; Kanter et al., 1992). Nevertheless, such is its continuing influence that, as Hendry (1996, p. 624) commented:

> Scratch any account of creating and managing change and the idea that change is a three-stage process that necessarily begins with a process of unfreezing will not be far below the surface.

LEWIN AND CHANGE: A SUMMARY

Lewin was primarily interested in resolving social conflict through behavioral change, whether this be within organizations or in the wider society. He identified two requirements for success:

1. To analyze and understand how social groupings were formed, motivated, and maintained. To do this, he developed both field theory and group dynamics.
2. To change the behavior of social groups. The primary methods he developed for achieving this were action research and the three-step model of change.

Underpinning Lewin's work was a strong moral and ethical belief in the importance of democratic institutions and democratic values in society. Lewin believed that only by strengthening democratic participation in all aspects of life and being able to resolve social conflicts could the scourge of despotism, authoritarianism and racism be effectively countered. Since his death, Lewin's wider social agenda has been mainly pursued under the umbrella of action research (Dickens & Watkins, 1999). This is also the area where Lewin's planned approach has been most closely followed. For example, Bargal and Bar (1992) described how, over a number of years, they used Lewin's approach to address the conflict between Arab-Palestinian and Jewish youths in Israel through the development of intergroup workshops. The workshops were developed around six principles based on Lewin's work:

> (a) a recursive process of data collection to determine goals, action to implement goals and assessment of the action; (b) feedback of research results to trainers; (c) cooperation between researchers and practitioners; (d) research based on the laws of the group's social life, on three stages of change—"unfreezing," "moving," and "refreezing"— and on the principles of group decision making; (e) consideration of the values, goals and power structures of change agents and clients; and (f) use of research to create knowledge and/or solve problems. (Bargal & Bar, 1992, p. 146)

In terms of organizational change, Lewin and his associates had a long and fruitful relationship with the Harwood Manufacturing Corporation, where his approach to change was developed, applied, and refined (Marrow, 1969). Coch and French (1948, p. 512) observed that at Harwood, "[f]rom the point of view of factory management, there were two purposes to the research: (1) Why do people resist change so strongly? and (2) What can be done to overcome this resistance?" Therefore, in both his wider social agenda and his narrower organizational agenda, Lewin sought to address similar issues and apply similar concepts. Since his death, it is the organizational side of his work which has been given greater prominence by his followers and successors, mainly through the creation of the organization development (OD) movement (Cummings & Worley, 1997; French & Bell, 1995).

OD has become the standard-bearer for Kurt Lewin's pioneering work on behavioral science in general, and approach to planned change in particular (Cummings & Worley, 1997). Up to the 1970s, OD tended to focus on group issues in organizations, and sought to promote Lewin's humanistic and democratic approach to change in the values it espoused (Conner, 1977; Gellermann et al., 1990; Warwick & Thompson, 1980). However, as French and Bell (1995) noted, since the late 1970s, in order to keep pace with the perceived needs of organizations, there has been a major broadening of scope within the OD field. It has moved away from its focus on groups and toward more organization-wide issues, such as socio-technical systems, organizational culture, organizational learning, and radical transformational change. Nevertheless, despite OD's attempts to modernize itself, in the last twenty years Lewin's legacy has met with increasing competition.

NEWER PERSPECTIVES ON CHANGE

By the early 1980s, with the oil shocks of the 1970s, the rise of corporate Japan, and severe economic downturn in the West, it was clear that many organizations needed to transform themselves rapidly and often brutally if they were to survive (Burnes, 2000). Given its group-based, consensual, and relatively slow nature, Lewin's planned approach began to attract criticism as to its appropriateness and efficacy, especially from the culture-excellence school, the postmodernists, and the processualists.

The culture-excellence approach to organizations, as promoted by Peters and Waterman (1982) and Kanter (1989), has had an unprecedented impact on the management of organizations by equating organizational success with the possession of a strong, appropriate organizational culture (Collins, 1998; Watson, 1997; Wilson, 1992). Peters and Waterman (1982) argued that Western organizations were losing their competitive edge because they were too bureaucratic, inflexible, and slow to change. Instead of the traditional top-down, command-and-control style of management, which tended to segment organizations into small rule-driven units, proponents of culture-excellence stressed the integrated nature of organizations, both internally and within their environments (Kanter, 1983; Watson, 1997). To survive, it was argued, organizations needed to reconfigure themselves to build internal and external synergies, and managers needed to encourage a spirit of innovation, experimentation, and entrepreneurship through the creation of strong, appropriate organizational cultures (Collins, 1998; Kanter, 1983; Peters & Waterman, 1982; Wilson, 1992).

For proponents of culture-excellence, the world is essentially an ambiguous place where detailed plans are not possible and flexibility is essential. Instead of close supervision and strict rules, organizational objectives need to be promoted by loose controls, based on shared values and culture, and pursued through empowered employees using their own initiative (Watson, 1997). They argue that change cannot be driven from the top but must emerge in an organic, bottom-up fashion from the day-to-day actions of all in the organization (Collins, 1998; Hatch, 1997). Proponents of culture-excellence reject as antithetical the planned approach to change, sometimes quite scathingly, as the following quotation from Kanter et al. (1992, p. 10) shows:

> Lewin's model was a simple one, with organizational change involving three stages; unfreezing, changing and refreezing . . . . This quaintly linear and static conception—the organization as an ice cube—is so wildly inappropriate that it is difficult to see why it has not only survived but prospered. . . . Suffice it to say here, first, that organizations are never frozen, much less refrozen, but are fluid entities with many "personalities." Second, to the extent that there are stages, they overlap and interpenetrate one another in important ways.

At the same time that the culture-excellence school was criticizing planned change, others, notably Pfeffer (1981, 1992), were claiming that the objectives, and outcomes, of change programs were more likely to be determined by power struggles than by any process of consensus-building or rational decision making. For the postmodernists, power is also a central feature of organizational change, but it arises from the socially constructed nature of organizational life:

> In a socially constructed world, responsibility for environmental conditions lies with those who do the constructing. . . . This suggests at least two competing scenarios for organization change. First, organization change can be a vehicle of domination for those who conspire to enact the world for others. . . . An alternative use of social constructionism is to create a democracy of enactment in which the process is made open and available to all . . . such that we create opportunities for freedom and innovation rather than simply for further domination. (Hatch, 1997, pp. 367–368)

The other important perspective on organizational change which emerged in the 1980s was the processual approach, which derives from the work of Andrew Pettigrew (1973, 1979, 1985, 1990a, 1990b, 1997). Processualists reject prescriptive, recipe-driven approaches to change and are suspicious of single causes or simple explanations of events. Instead, when studying change, they focus on the interrelatedness of individuals, groups, organizations, and society (Dawson, 1994; Pettigrew & Whipp, 1993; Wilson, 1992). In particular, they claim that the process of change is a complex and untidy cocktail of rational decision processes, individual perceptions, political struggles, and coalition-building (Huczynski & Buchanan, 2001). Pettigrew (1990a, 1990b) maintains that the planned approach is too prescriptive and does not pay enough attention to the need to analyze and conceptualize organizational change. He argues that change needs to be studied across different levels of analysis and different time periods, and that it cuts across functions, spans hierarchical divisions, and has no neat starting or finishing point; instead it is a "complex analytical, political, and cultural process of challenging and changing the core beliefs, structure and strategy of the firm" (Pettigrew, 1987, p. 650).

Looking at planned change versus a processual approach, Dawson (1994, pp. 3–4) comments that

> [a]lthough this [Lewin's] theory has proved useful in understanding planned change under relatively stable conditions, with the continuing and dynamic nature of change in today's business world, it no longer makes sense to implement a planned process for "freezing" changed behaviors. . . . The processual framework . . . adopts the view that change is a complex and dynamic process which should not be solidified or treated as a series of linear events . . . central to the development of a processual approach is the need to incorporate an analysis of the politics of managing change.

Also taking a processualist perspective, Buchanan and Storey's (1997, p. 127) main criticism of those who advocate planned change is

> . . . their attempt to impose an order and a linear sequence to processes that are in reality messy and untidy, and which unfold in an iterative fashion with much backtracking and omission.

Though there are distinct differences between these newer approaches to change, not least the prescriptive focus of the culture-excellence approach versus the analytical orientation of the processualists, there are also some striking similarities which they claim strongly challenge the validity of the planned approach to change. The newer approaches tend to take a holistic/contextual view of organizations and their environments; they challenge the notion of change as an ordered, rational, and linear process; and there is an emphasis on change as a continuous process which is heavily influenced by culture, power, and politics (Buchanan & Storey, 1997; Burnes, 2000; Dawson, 1994; Kanter et al., 1992; Pettigrew, 1997). Accompanying and offering support to these new approaches to change were new perspectives on the nature of change in organizations. Up to the late 1970s, the incremental model of change dominated. Advocates of this view see change as being a process whereby individual parts of an organization deal incrementally and separately with one problem and one goal at a time. By managers responding to pressures in their local internal and external environments in this way, over time, their organizations become transformed (Cyert & March, 1963; Hedberg et al., 1976; Lindblom, 1959; Quinn, 1980, 1982).

In the 1980s, two new perspectives on change emerged: the punctuated equilibrium model and the continuous transformation model. The former approach to change

> ... depicts organizations as evolving through relatively long periods of stability (equilibrium periods) in their basic patterns of activity that are punctuated by relatively short bursts of fundamental change (revolutionary periods). Revolutionary periods substantively disrupt established activity patterns and install the basis for new equilibrium periods. (Romanelli & Tushman, 1994, p. 1141)

The inspiration for this model arises from two sources: first, from the challenge to Darwin's gradualist model of evolution in the natural sciences (Gould, 1989); second, from research showing that whilst organizations do appear to fit the incrementalist model of change for a period of time, there does come a point when they go through a period of rapid and fundamental change (Gersick, 1991).

Proponents of the continuous transformation model reject both the incrementalist and punctuated equilibrium models. They argue that, in order to survive, organizations must develop the ability to change themselves continuously in a fundamental manner. This is particularly the case in fast-moving sectors such as retail (Greenwald, 1996). Brown and Eisenhardt (1997, p. 29) draw on the work of complexity theorists to support their claim for continuous change:

> Like organizations, complex systems have large numbers of independent yet interacting actors. Rather than ever reaching a stable

equilibrium, the most adaptive of these complex systems (e.g., intertidal zones) keep changing continuously by remaining at the poetically termed "edge of chaos" that exists between order and disorder. By staying in this intermediate zone, these systems never quite settle into a stable equilibrium but never quite fall apart. Rather, these systems, which stay constantly poised between order and disorder, exhibit the most prolific, complex and continuous change . . . .

Complexity theories are increasingly being used by organization theorists and practitioners as a way of understanding and changing organizations (Bechtold, 1997; Black, 2000; Boje, 2000; Choi et al., 2001; Gilchrist, 2000; Lewis, 1994; Macbeth, 2002; Shelton & Darling, 2001; Stacey et al., 2002; Tetenbaum, 1998). Complexity theories come from the natural sciences, where they have shown that disequilibrium is a necessary condition for the growth of dynamic systems (Prigogine & Stengers, 1984). Under this view, organizations, like complex systems in nature, are seen as dynamic nonlinear systems. The outcome of their actions is unpredictable but, like turbulence in gases and liquids, it is governed by a set of simple order-generating rules (Brown & Eisenhardt, 1997; Lewis, 1994; Lorenz, 1993; Mintzberg et al., 1998; Stacey et al., 2002; Tetenbaum, 1998; Wheatley, 1992). For organizations, as for natural systems, the key to survival is to develop rules which are capable of keeping an organization operating "on the edge of chaos" (Stacey et al., 2002). If organizations are too stable, nothing changes and the system dies; if too chaotic, the system will be overwhelmed by change. In both situations, radical change is necessary in order to create a new set of order-generating rules which allow the organization to prosper and survive (MacIntosh & MacLean, 2001).

As can be seen, the newer approaches to change and the newer perspectives on the nature of change have much in common. One of the problems with all three perspectives on change—incrementalism, punctuated equilibrium, and continuous change—is that all three are present in organizational life and none appears dominant. Indeed, Burnes (2000) even questions whether these are separate and competing theories, or merely different ways of looking at the same phenomenon: change. He points out that sectoral, temporal, and organizational life cycle differences can account for whether organizations experience incremental, punctuated equilibrium, or continuous change (Kimberley & Miles, 1980). He also draws on the natural sciences, in the form of population ecology, to argue that in any given population of organizations one would expect to see all three types of change (Hannan & Freeman, 1988). Therefore, rather like the Jungian concept of the light and dark, these various perspectives on change may be shadow images of each other, none of which by themselves are capable of portraying the whole (Matthews, 2002).

LEWIN'S WORK: CRITICISMS AND RESPONSES

From the 1980s onwards, as newer perspectives on organizational life and change have emerged, Lewin's planned approach has faced increasing levels of criticisms. This section summarizes the main criticisms and responds to them.

Criticism 1

Many have argued that Lewin's planned approach is too simplistic and mechanistic for a world where organizational change is a continuous and open-ended process (Dawson, 1994; Garvin, 1993; Kanter et al., 1992; Nonaka, 1988; Pettigrew, 1990a, 1990b; Pettigrew et al., 1989; Stacey, 1993; Wilson, 1992).

Response 1. These criticisms appear to stem from a misreading of how Lewin perceived stability and change. He stated:

> One should view the present situation—the status quo—as being maintained by certain conditions or forces. A culture—for instance, the food habits of a certain group at a given time—is not a static affair but a live process like a river which moves but still keeps to a recognizable form . . . . Food habits do not occur in empty space. They are part and parcel of the daily rhythm of being awake and asleep; of being alone and in a group; of earning a living and playing; of being a member of a town, a family, a social class, a religious group . . . in a district with good groceries and restaurants or in an area of poor and irregular food supply. Somehow all these factors affect food habits at any given time. They determine the food habits of a group every day anew just as the amount of water supply and the nature of the river bed determine the flow of the river, its constancy or change. (Lewin, 1943a, pp. 172–173)

Far from viewing social or organizational groups as fixed and stable, or viewing change as linear and unidimensional, it is clear that he understood the limits of stability at least as well as his critics. He argued that social settings are in a state of constant change but that, just like a river, the rate varies depending on the environment. He viewed change not as a predictable and planned move from one stable state to another, but as a complex and iterative learning process where the journey was more important than the destination, where stability was at best quasistationary and always fluid, and where, given the complex forces involved, outcomes cannot be predicted but emerge on a trial and error basis (Kippenberger, 1998a; Lewin, 1947a). Therefore, rather than being prescriptive, Lewin recognized the unpredictable (nonlinear) nature of change and, as Hendry (1996) notes, he adopted the same "contextualist" and learning approach favored by many of his critics. Indeed, as outlined earlier, some argue that Lewin's conception of stability and change is very similar to that of many complexity theorists (Back, 1992; Elrod & Tippett, 2002; Kippenberger, 1998a; MacIntosh & MacLean, 2001; Tschacher & Brunner, 1995).

We should also note that when Lewin wrote of "refreezing," he referred to preventing individuals and groups from regressing to their old behaviors. In this respect, Lewin's view seems to be similar to that of his critics. For example, the last stage in Kanter et al.'s (1992, p. 384) model of change is to "reinforce and institutionalize the change." More telling, though, is that when Elrod and Tippett (2002) compared a wide range of change models, they found that most approaches to organizational change were strikingly similar to Lewin's three-step model. When they extended their research to other forms of human and organizational change, they also found that "models of the change process, as perceived by diverse and seemingly unrelated disciplines [such as bereavement theory, personal transition theory, creative processes, cultural revolutions and scientific revolutions] . . . follow Lewin's . . . three-phase model of change . . ." (Elrod & Tippett, 2002, p. 273).

Criticism 2

Lewin's work is only relevant to incremental and isolated change projects and is not able to incorporate radical, transformational change (Dawson, 1994; Dunphy & Stace, 1992, 1993; Harris, 1985; Miller & Friesen, 1984; Pettigrew, 1990a, 1990b).

Response 2. This criticism appears to relate to the speed rather than the magnitude of change because, as Quinn (1980, 1982) pointed out, over time, incremental change can lead to radical transformations. It is also necessary to recognize that Lewin was concerned with behavioral change at the individual, group, organizational and societal levels (Dickens & Watkins, 1999), whereas rapid transformational change is seen as only being applicable to situations requiring major structural change (Allaire & Firsirotu, 1984; Beer & Nohria, 2000; Burnes, 2000; Cummings & Worley, 1997). Even in such situations, as Kanter et al. (1992) maintain, these "bold strokes" often need to be followed by a whole series of incremental changes (a "long march") in order to align an organization's culture and behaviors with the new structure. Lewin did recognize that radical behavioral or cultural change could take place rapidly in times of crisis (Kippenberger, 1998a; Lewin, 1947a). Such crises may require directive change; again, this may be successful in terms of structural change but research by Lewin and others has shown that it rarely works in cases where behavioral change is required (Lewin, 1947b; Kanter et al., 1992; Schein, 1996; Stace & Dunphy, 2001).

Criticism 3

Lewin stands accused of ignoring the role of power and politics in organizations and the conflictual nature of much of organizational life (Dawson, 1994; Hatch, 1997; Pettigrew, 1980; Pfeffer, 1992; Wilson, 1992).

Response 3. Given the issues that Lewin was addressing, this seems a strange criticism. Anyone seriously addressing racism and religious intolerance, as Lewin was, could not ignore these issues. As Bargal et al. (1992, p. 8) note, Lewin's approach to change required ". . . the taking into account differences in value systems and power structures of all the parties involved. . . ." This is clear from the following quotation (Lewin, 1946, p. 203):

> An attempt to improve intergroup relations has to face a wide variety of tasks. It deals with problems of attitude and stereotypes in regard to other groups and one's own group, with problems of development of attitudes and conduct during childhood and adolescence, with problems of housing, and the change of the legal structure of the

community; it deals with problems of status and caste, with problems of economic discrimination, with political leadership, and with leadership in many aspects of community life. It deals with the small social body of the family, a club or a friendship group, with the larger social body of a school or school system, with neighborhoods and with social bodies of the size of a community, of the state and with international problems.

We are beginning to see that it is hopeless to attack any one of these aspects of intergroup relations without considering the others.

One also needs to be aware that French and Raven's Power/Interaction Model (French & Raven, 1959; Raven, 1965), on which much of the literature on power and politics is based, owes much to Lewin's work (Raven, 1993). French was a longtime collaborator with Lewin and Raven studied at the Research Center for group dynamics in the 1950s. Both have acknowledged the importance and influence of his work on their perspective on power (House, 1993; Raven, 1993, 1999).

Criticism 4

Lewin is seen as advocating a top-down, management-driven approach to change and ignoring situations requiring bottom-up change (Dawson, 1994; Kanter et al., 1992; Wilson, 1992).

Response 4. Lewin was approached for help by a wide range of groups and organizations:

> They included representatives of communities, school systems, single schools, minority organizations of a variety of backgrounds and objectives; they included labor and management representatives, departments of the national and state governments, and so on. (Lewin, 1946, p. 201)

He clearly recognized that the pressure for change comes from many quarters, not just managers and leaders, and sought to provide an approach which could accommodate this. However, regardless of who identified the need to change, Lewin argued that effective change could not take place unless there was a "felt-need" by all those concerned; he did not see one group or individual as driving or dominating the change process but saw everyone as playing a full and equal part

(Lewin, 1947b). He believed that only by gaining the commitment of all those concerned, through their full involvement in the change process, would change be successful (Bargal et al., 1992; Dickens & Watkins, 1999; French & Bell, 1984). Consequently, rather than arguing that Lewin saw behavioral change as a top-down process, it would be more accurate to say that Lewin recognized that it could be initiated from the top, bottom, or middle but that it could not be successful without the active, willing, and equal participation of all.

CONCLUSION

Lewin undoubtedly had an enormous impact on the field of change. In reappraising Lewin's planned approach to change, this article seeks to address three issues: the nature of his contribution; the validity of the criticisms leveled against him; and the relevance of his work for contemporary social and organizational change.

Looking at Lewin's contribution to change theory and practice, there are three key points to note. The first is that Lewin's work stemmed from his concern to find an effective approach to resolving social conflict through changing group behavior (whether these conflicts are at the group, organizational, or societal level). The second point is to recognize that Lewin promoted an ethical and humanist approach to change that saw learning and involvement as being the key processes for achieving behavioral change. This was for two reasons: (1) he saw this approach as helping to develop and strengthen democratic values in society as a whole and thus acting as a buffer against the racism and totalitarianism which so dominated events in his lifetime; (2) based on his background in Gestalt psychology and his own research, he saw this approach as being the most effective in bringing about sustained behavioral change. The last point concerns the nature of Lewin's work. Lewin's planned approach to change is based on four mutually reinforcing concepts, namely field theory, group dynamics, action research, and the three-step model, which are used in combination to bring about effective change. His critics, though, tend to treat these as separate and independent elements of Lewin's work and, in the main, concentrate on his three-step model of change. When seen in isolation, the three-step model can be portrayed as simplistic. When seen alongside the other elements of Lewin's planned approach, it becomes a much more robust approach to change.

We can now examine the criticisms made of Lewin's planned approach to change. The main criticisms leveled at Lewin are that: (1) his view of stability and change in organizations was at best no longer applicable and at worst "wildly inappropriate" (Kanter et al., 1992, p. 10); (2) his approach to change is only suitable for isolated and incremental change situations; (3) he ignored power and politics; and (4) he adopted a top-down, management-driven approach to change. These criticisms were addressed above, but to recap:

1. There is substantial evidence that Lewin (1947a, p. 199) recognized that "[c]hange and constancy are relative concepts; group life is never without change, merely differences in the amount and type of change exist." There is also a substantial body of evidence in the social, and even physical sciences, to support Lewin's three-step perspective on change (Elrod and Tippett, 2002; Hendry, 1996).

2. As Dickens and Watkins (1999, p. 127) observed: Lewin's approach is ". . . intended to foster change on the group, organizational and even societal levels." In the main, he saw change as a slow process of working with and through groups to achieve behavioral and cultural change. However, writers as diverse as Quinn (1980, 1982) and Kanter et al. (1992) have recognized that an incremental approach can achieve organizational transformation. Lewin also recognized that, under certain crisis conditions, organizational transformations can be achieved rapidly (Kippenberger, 1998a; Lewin, 1947a). Nevertheless, in the main, even amongst Lewin's critics, the general view is that only structural and technical change can be achieved relatively speedily (Dawson, 1994; Kanter et al., 1992; Pettigrew et al., 1989, 1992; Wilson, 1992).

3. Given Lewin's concern with issues such as racial and religious conflict, the accusation that he ignored the role of power and politics is difficult to sustain. One of the main strengths of field theory and group dynamics is that they identify the forces within and between groups and show how individuals behave in response to these. In addition, the iterative, investigative, and learning approaches which lie at the heart of action research and the three-step model are also designed to reveal and address such issues (Bargal and Bar, 1992).

4. The issues Lewin sought to tackle were many and varied
(Cartwright, 1952; Lewin, 1948a). Lewin's sympathies were
clearly with the underdog, the disadvantaged, and the discrimi-
nated against (Cooke, 1999; Marrow, 1969). His assistance was
sought by a wide range of parties including national and local
government, religious and racial groups, and employers and
unions; his response emphasized learning and participation by
all concerned (Lewin, 1946). In the face of this, the charge that
he saw change as only being top-down or management-driven is
difficult to sustain.

Lewin's critics have sought to show that his planned approach to
change was simplistic and outmoded. By rejecting these criticisms,
and by revealing the nature of his approach, this article has also shown
the continuing relevance of Lewin's work, whether in organizations
or society at large. The need to resolve social conflict has certainly not
diminished since Lewin's day. Nor can one say that Lewin's approach
seems dated, based as it is on building understanding, generating
learning, gaining new insights, and identifying and testing (and retest-
ing) solutions (Bargal & Bar, 1992; Darwin et al., 2002). Certainly,
there seems little evidence that one can achieve peace, reconciliation,
cooperation, or trust by force (Olsen, 2002). Likewise, in organizations,
issues of group effectiveness, behavior, and change have not diminished in the half century since Lewin's death, though they may often
now be labeled differently. However, as in Lewin's day, there are no
quick or easy ways of achieving such changes, and Lewin's approach
is clearly still valuable and influential in these areas (Cummings &
Worley, 1997). This can be seen from the enormous emphasis that
continues to be placed on the importance of group behavior, involvement, and empowerment (Argyris, 1992; Handy, 1994; Hannagan, 2002;
Huczynski & Buchanan, 2001; Kanter, 1989; Mullins, 2002; Peters,
1982; Schein, 1988; Senge, 1990; Wilson, 1992). Indeed, the advent of
the complexity perspective appears to be leading to a renewed interest in Lewin's work (Back, 1992; Kippenberger, 1998a; MacIntosh &
MacLean, 2001; Tschacher & Brunner, 1995).

   In conclusion, therefore, though Lewin's contribution to organizational change has come under increasing criticism since the 1980s,
much of this appears to be unfounded and/or based on a narrow
interpretation of his work. In contrast, the last decade has also seen a

renewed interest in understanding and applying his approach to change (Bargal & Bar, 1992; Elrod & Tippett, 2002; Hendry, 1996; Kippenberger, 1998a; MacIntosh & MacLean, 2001; Wooten & White, 1999). In many respects, this should not come as a surprise given the tributes and acknowledgments paid to him by major figures such as Chris Argyris (Argyris et al., 1985) and Edgar Schein (1988). Above all, though, it is a recognition of the rigor of Lewin's work, based as it was on a virtuous circle of theory, experimentation, and practice, and which is best expressed by his famous dictum that ". . . there is nothing so practical as a good theory" (Lewin, 1943–1944, p. 169).

CHAPTER SIX

Effective Intervention Activity

Chris Argyris

───∿∿∿───

The world in which interventionists are asked to participate presents them with a difficult challenge. It tends to inhibit the very factors that have been identified as facilitating the creation of valid information. If it is to be of help, the client system needs to generate such information. Moreover, the diagnostic methods the system utilizes may accentuate the problem. The interventionist may therefore be faced with a client system that may perceive his view of competent problem solving and effective systems as not only different from, but antagonistic to, their views. How may he behave effectively under such conditions?

The first step in developing a model of effective and ineffective interventionist strategy is to define more precisely the probable discrepancies in values and strategies between the client system and the interventionist. Once this is made more explicit, we can ask the question: how can the interventionist behave competently under these conditions?

CONDITIONS FACED BY AN INTERVENTIONIST

Relationship Between Interventionist and Client

The most fundamental condition between the interventionist and client that we may identify may be stated as follows: There is a tendency toward an underlying discrepancy in the behavior and values of the interventionist and the client, and in the criteria which each uses to judge effectiveness. The potency of these discrepancies and challenges (Exhibit 6.1) will tend to be low in the routine, programmed activities between the interventionist and client system and high in the innovative, nonroutine activities—the activities that are most relevant for change. Let us explore these generalizations in more detail.

1. *Discrepancy between the interventionist's and client's views on causes of problems and designs of effective systems*
The interventionist holds views that tend to be different from the client's about effective relationships. For example, the interventionist tends to emphasize the importance of owning-up to, being open, and experimenting with ideas and feelings within a milieu whose norms include individuality, concern, and trust. The thrust of many client systems, in the name of effectiveness, is to inhibit these variables and emphasize defensive, relatively closed, nonexperimenting activities as well as norms that include conformity, mistrust, and antagonism.

The second discrepancy lies in the fact that the members of the client system tend to be unaware of the extent to which they are responsible for these conditions of ineffectiveness. Their tendency is to blame the system. Moreover, although many clients may berate these conditions, they also tend to view them as inevitable and natural, a view not shared by the interventionist.

Discrepant World

Discrepancy between own and client's views on causes of problems and designs of effective systems.
Discrepancy between own and client's views on effective implementation of change.
Discrepancy between own ideals and behavior.

Exhibit 6.1. Conditions Faced by an Interventionist.

The third discrepancy is derivable from the first two. The interventionist and the client system tend to hold discrepant views about the nature of strong leadership and effective organizations. They tend to value different human qualities as resources to build upon and make the foundations for change. For example, established management usually defines directive, controlling, task-oriented, rationally focused leadership as organization. The interventionist believes that such characteristics are most effective under certain conditions and that under a different set of conditions, effective leaders and organizations are able to create conditions for genuine participation and psychological success, where the expression of relevant feelings are legitimate.

These three discrepancies generate three major challenges for interventionists. How can they help to unfreeze the clients from their concepts of individual and group strengths? How can they help to unfreeze the client's view that defensive, time-consuming, relatively ineffective groups are natural? How can they help the clients see that they may be blind about the basic causes of their problems and at the same time, help develop the conditions where they can see and develop their potential for change?

2. Discrepancy between the interventionist's and client's views regarding effective implementation of change

Given the discrepancies in views regarding the nature of effective systems, leadership, and interpersonal relationships, we see there also exists a basic difference in views regarding the effective implementation of change. Client systems tend to evaluate the effectiveness of a change program in terms of the rationality of the new design, the smoothness with which it is master minded and sold to the members at all levels, and the degree to which there seems to be minimal overt resistance. The reader may recall the model of quasi-stationary equilibrium and change. In terms of that model, accepted change strategy tends to be one of management strengthening the pushing forces to overcome the restraining forces. This view is to be expected from people whose basic assumptions about the effective way to organize human effort are those we have discussed.

The interventionist view of effective change is fundamentally different. He believes that it is more effective to help everyone diagnose and reduce the restraining forces before energy and resources are placed into marshalling the pushing forces. The interventionist, therefore, believes that basic changes in human behavior should not be ordered from, or by, those above. The interventionist may place the client horse in front of water (it is the interventionist's job to create all sorts of water holes), but he or she cannot make the client drink. The door to effective change is locked from the inside. Ordering change, even if the order is a correct one and the interventionist is able to show a tested solution for the client to follow, tends to place the client in a situation of psychological failure. This is the case because it is the interventionist who is defining the goals and the paths to the goals, is setting the level of aspiration, and is activating the needs within the clients. Under these conditions, even if the program for change is a good one, the clients cannot have their positive interpersonal and administrative skills confirmed and expanded. They will not feel essential because it is the interventionist's skill and wisdom that are responsible for the success; nor will they be able to develop a sense of trust in themselves, their group, and their problem-solving activities. As we have noted previously, the interventionist strives, wherever possible, not only to help the system solve the particular problems at a particular time, but also to help the system learn how to develop its own solutions to these kinds of problems so that they can prevent their recurrence or, if they do recur, be able to solve them without consulting help.

This does not imply that an interventionist never makes interventions that may create conditions of psychological failure for the client. Conditions of psychological failure are not very potent when they are related to the routine, noninnovative activities between the client and the interventionist. Also, conditions for psychological failure tend not to have negative impact if the goals, paths, and level of aspiration being defined represent activities that are professional. The competence is naturally expected to be held by the interventionist and not the clients. People can enter conditions of psychological failure without feeling the failure very much *if* the activities they are performing are not rightly their responsibility.

Finally, if the client system contains many people who are relatively incompetent in interpersonal relationships or people who are experiencing crisis, the interventionist may frequently have to focus more on helping the system to survive than on developing its problem-solving competence. The important requirement is for the interventionist to be aware of the functionality of coercing change and to be able to specify the conditions under which it is relevant. Further on, we will specify the conditions under which manipulation may be necessary.

We must emphasize now that clients will probably tend to develop ambivalent feelings about being pushed and manipulated. On the one hand, such behavior may be consistent with their concept of effective leadership for change. On the other hand, they may also resent being placed in a dependent, submissive position. Another dimension of the ambivalence may be expressed as follows. Although the clients may not like being manipulated in certain directions by the interventionist, they may prefer this dependent relationship to the more threatening ones (1) of being held responsible for the change and (2) of learning that changes can be made effective with minimal direct application of unilateral power. If the interventionist can show that the latter possibility is a viable one, the clients may develop feelings of incompetence and, perhaps, guilt related to their previous behavior and preferred leadership styles.

3. *Discrepancy between the interventionist's ideals and behavior*
The third major discrepancy that interventionists may experience while in the client system is the discrepancy between their level of aspiration and their actual performance. The greater the discrepancy between the interventionist and the client system in terms of change strategy, value, and behavior, the greater the feelings of inadequacy the interventionist may experience. This, in turn, may lead to a higher probability that the interventionist will become less effective (especially under stress).

This generalization, if left without any qualifications, could be misleading. There are other conditions that influence the potential impact of this discrepancy upon the effectiveness of the interventionist. For example, the same degree of discrepancy with the more routine aspects of change may have significantly different consequences from a similar degree of discrepancy with the less routine aspects of change. An interventionist may feel little threat if he has discrepant views on the physical location of a meeting or on the construction of a letter of invitation to a conference. If, however, there are equally discrepant views between himself and the client on the proper way to diagnose the problem, confront conflict, and deal with differences, then the interventionist is faced with challenges of a significantly higher magnitude.

Also, the relative position of the interventionist's ideal aspiration, as compared with what he knows is the presently attainable ideal level of competence by himself and others, can modify the impact upon his effectiveness. Few things can be as debilitating to an interventionist as aspiring to levels much beyond his (or others') competence. For example, if an interventionist expects all of his interventions to be effective, he may be placing a difficult and unnecessary burden on himself. It may be more realistic to aspire to a much lower percentage of the interventions (during a given session) being effective. The more realistic level of aspiration will permit the interventionist not to become frightened by a failure; the higher aspiration may act to coerce him to return the clients to his intervention until they understand him so that he can succeed. Even if his intervention was valid, such activity would only serve to alienate the clients who had been told (by the interventionist) that they would be allowed to help to learn at their own pace.

Another factor in effectiveness is the degree to which interventionists accept the discrepancy between their actual and their ideal behavior. The more accepting they are of the discrepancy, the lower the probability is that they will become ineffective because of the discrepancy. The degree of acceptance of one's skill as an interventionist is influenced, we hypothesize, largely by the interventionist's previous history of successes and failures, plus the degree to which she conceives of herself as a person who is constantly learning.

Another highly interdependent variable is the degree of difficulty of the problem faced by the client system. If the problem is one at the frontier of professional knowledge, then the interventionist's reaction will probably be different from what it would be if the problem, or the solutions, were well-known. Presumably, the more the problem is at the frontier of professional knowledge, the greater the probability that interventionists can be accepting of the discrepancy between their competence and the requirements of the problem. It should be psychologically easier for interventionists to be patient with, or to terminate, a relationship when it can be shown that they are dealing with a highly difficult problem or a highly defensive client system.

MARGINALITY

As a major consequence of the discrepancies described, the interventionist tends to be a member of two overlapping, but discrepant, worlds (Exhibit 6.2). One world is that of the client; the other is that of the professional interventionist. The determiners of appropriate behavior in the client world tend to be different from those in the world in which the interventionist operates and toward which he wants to move the clients. If the interventionist behaves according to his own views, the clients' reactions may range from bewilderment to hostility, depending on how deviant the interventionist's behavior is considered to be. On the other hand, the more the interventionist behaves in accordance with the behavioral determiners of the client's present world, the less the client will experience a need to change. The clients may say to themselves, "The interventionist is behaving exactly as we do." If the interventionist attempts to behave according to the determiners of both worlds, he will experience himself, and be experienced by the client, as being conflicted, ambivalent, inconsistent, and unsure. The client and the interventionist will find it difficult to have the latter straddle both worlds.

Moreover, the greater the discrepancy between the present world of the clients and the new one, the greater the probability that the interventionist will experience himself as being consistently in new, ambiguous situations. For an excellent analysis of new situations, see Barker, Wright, and Gonick (1946).

For example, the writer has attempted to help two different organizations whose systems were examples of the extreme ends of correct manipulation (in one case) and overt hostility and destructive competition (in the other case). The strength of these factors was so great that the discrepancy between his views and the client system's views was also very great. Under these conditions, it was difficult to find situations within the client systems which could be used as an example of the impact of moderate manipulation or hostility. It was also difficult to find clients for or situations in which support could be developed for a new approach. Moreover, the clients seemed to be united against the interventionist every time he attempted to suggest a new strategy for coping with a particular problem.

Discrepant World

Own and client's views on causes of problems
Own and client's views on effective change
Own ideals and own behavior

Marginality

Membership in two overlapping but different worlds

Perpetual client mistrust

Minimal feedback about effectiveness

Exhibit 6.2.   Conditions Faced by an Interventionist.

The greater its ambiguity, the less parsimonious and effective will his behavior be and the less it will follow the most expeditious path to the goal. Errors and false steps will be made at the very time the interventionist strives to be cautious. This, in turn, may give the clients the impression that the interventionist is inept, lacks confidence in himself, and may even be unable to control his own behavior.

The interventionist may react ambivalently. He may withdraw from the situation lest he show his limitations, but, at the same time, may seek to advance even deeper into client territory with the hope that everything will work out. If he decides to enter the client's world and be like them, the clients may correctly wonder why they should hire someone whose way of reacting to stress is similar to theirs. If the interventionist reacts by retreating to his own world, he will tend to behave in a way that bewilders the clients. He will be seen as defending odd values and making queer points.

PERPETUAL CLIENT MISTRUST

On the other side of the argument, the clients, to the extent they take the interventionist seriously, will tend to place themselves in situations that are overlapping but incongruent with their established ways of behaving. The clients also become marginal people. They experience ambiguity; their behavior will tend to be less effective; they may make errors and take false steps precisely when they are trying to be careful. They will tend to feel inept and lack confidence in themselves and in each other.

Under these conditions, there is a high probability that the clients will tend to defend themselves by selecting those behaviors and values that maintain their present level of self-acceptance. There are three different types of psychological selectivity that clients may use to defend themselves: selective memory, selective exposure, and selective interpretation. For a review of the literature, see Rosenberg (1967). Briefly, this means that the clients may tend to forget controversial information suggested by the interventionist and recall in its place the information from their past substitutes for the controversial information. It means that the clients will expose themselves to learning the information that maintains their present degree of self-acceptance and their client systems, and that the clients will tend to interpret relatively threatening information in line with their values and their system's norms and not necessarily as the interventionist wishes that they react.

At the same time, the clients may become more questioning of the interventionist and may confront her. Since what they remember and interpret is more congruent with their values, it becomes even more difficult for them to understand and trust the interventionist. The interventionist becomes the symbol for the clients' feeling that they are in an unstructured and ambiguous situation, a condition in which psychological selectivity is particularly free to operate (Rosenberg, 1967).

It is understandable that clients may feel a need to place the interventionist under a continuing trial of mistrust and trust. Every major idea and every important bit of behavior will be questioned. The clients will tend to mistrust her in the sense that they will not be willing to entrust themselves to her.

The constant stress that might result could lead the interventionist to develop her own personal, perpetual trial. What am I doing here? Should I be an interventionist? Am I really competent? Self-inflicted trial and mistrust could lead to a decrease in one's own confidence, a greater degree of anxiety, and a higher probability of failure.

MINIMAL FEEDBACK ABOUT EFFECTIVENESS

Interventionists tend to fear being kept in the dark by their clients, especially in regard to their ineffectiveness or effectiveness. In the case of the former, if they are not told, they never know why their relationship is not going well, and they can do little to correct the relationship. Moreover, the belief by the interventionist that the clients are not leveling may strike the interventionist at a time of deep anxiety. He may wonder if he is behaving in a way that prevents clients from being open. If so, is he blind to this? Could he be manifesting some of the same behavior of which the clients are unaware? Could the clients be sending him cues which he is not receiving?

The probability that the interventionist will be kept in the dark by the clients about his negative impact is very high. As we have already pointed out, the clients tend to hold values which prevent them from speaking openly if that would mean entering the area of emotional and interpersonal issues. Moreover, if there is a tendency to give feedback, the feedback will tend to be highly evaluative and probably defensive of the clients' views. Thus, the interventionist lives in legitimate fear that people will not be open with him when they dislike what he is doing or when they are angry or hostile toward him.

Nor may the client be influenced by the interventionist's plea to him early in the relationship that he be open about negative feelings. For the client to do so would mean that he had developed the very competence that the interventionist is expecting to help him develop. Of course, most clients respond positively to this plea, partially because they honestly believe they are open, partially because they may believe it is easy to be open to an outsider, and partially because it is difficult to be against a value that is so close to the core of unconflicted people or, as this state is known colloquially, motherhood.

To summarize, interventionists may find themselves in a client system in which they experience (1) a discrepancy between their and the clients' views on causes of problems and designs of effective systems, (2) a discrepancy between their and the clients' views regarding effective implementation of change, and (3) a discrepancy between their own ideals and behavior. These discrepancies may create a relationship with the client in which the *initial* state is characterized by (1) the interventionist and the client being in marginal roles and under perpetual client trial and mistrust and (2) the interventionist receiving minimal information about his impact. Moreover, the interventionist and the clients tend to have different concepts of helping. The interventionist believes that he or she may:

HELP THE CLIENT	WHEN THE CLIENT PREFERS
1. to diagnose and reduce the restraining forces	1. to diagnose and increase the pushing, pressuring forces
2. to develop internal commitment to change	2. to develop external commitment to change
3. to use observed categories	3. to use inferred categories
4. to describe rather than evaluate	4. to evaluate rather than describe
5. to manipulate the environment	5. to manipulate people
6. to create conditions of psychological success	6. to create conditions of psychological failure
7. to share influence in groups	7. prescribed influence by the leader
8. to increase the members' feelings of essentiality to the client system and to self, thereby generating loyalty	8. to increase members' loyalty to the client system

9. to emphasize the effectiveness of group processes and the achievement of the objective(s)

9. to emphasize the achievement of the objective(s)

10. to generate problem-solving intergroup relationships

10. to generate competitive win–lose intergroup relationships

Effective Intervention Strategy

We may conclude from the preceding analysis that being an interventionist is an occupation built upon discrepancies resulting in challenging dilemmas. For example, how may an interventionist behave effectively with the client if the latter views the former's concept of effectiveness as being incorrect? Clients are faced with a similar dilemma. How can they keep the interventionist in dialogue if the latter does not prefer the client's mode of conversing?

One possibility that the interventionist may consider is to turn the dilemma into virtue and to use the dilemmas as leverage for the initial interactions between himself and the clients. For example, the interventionist will need to discover, as early as possible in the relationship, where the client system tends to fall on each of the ten dimensions described. How much agreement is there in preferences regarding effective individual, group, and intergroup activities? Do these agreements and disagreements relate to specific issues? If so, how potent are these issues?

As the answers to these questions begin to form, interventionists may begin to assess (1) the degree to which there exist discrepancies between themselves and the clients, (2) the probable causes of these discrepancies, (3) the resultant marginality that they will experience, and (4) the marginality the clients may experience if they seriously consider changing.

OPEN AND CLOSED CLIENT SYSTEMS

All the preceding information becomes an input for the interventionist to assess the probability that the client system is open to learning. This assessment is especially critical. The more closed a client system is, the lower is the probability that an interventionist can help the client system.

If the description of dysfunction in organization is recalled, it is not too difficult to see how client systems may become more closed than open. The lower levels may adapt to their system by fighting, by withdrawal, by apathy, by indifference, by goldbricking, by distorting information sent upwards, and by developing internal defensive establishments. Destructive intergroup rivalries, win–lose competitive relationships, and crises become dominant in the living system. At the upper levels, closedness and emphasis on stability, conformity, and mistrust may overcome openness, risk taking, individuality, and trust.

Such a system may easily become more concerned about surviving than about being effective. Defensive, survival-oriented activities (1) increase the probability that other systems will behave defensively toward them, (2) increase further survival-oriented activity *within* the system, and (3) decrease the probability that the system will be able to learn from the environment. Under these conditions, the system may become increasingly closed within, as well as with its relationships with other systems. The system will be less able to learn and will be less able either to be influenced by, or to influence, others. The more closed the system becomes, the more its learning and adaptive reactions will be defined by reference to the internal makeup of the system. But since the internal system is full of defensive activities, the behavior that it produces tends to be neither functional nor easily alterable.

An open system is one whose strategy for adaptation is less on building defensive forts and more on reaching out, learning, and becoming competent in controlling the external and internal environment so that its objectives are achieved and its members continue to learn. An open system not only is open to being influenced, but also its members strive to accept every responsibility that helps them increase their confidence in themselves and their group, and increase their capacity to solve problems effectively.

OPEN AND CLOSED SYSTEMS ARE NOT DICHOTOMOUS

It is important to emphasize that systems are rarely either completely open or completely closed. The degree of openness and closedness may be a function of:

1. The situation in which the system is placed. If the situation is confirmably threatening, then closedness may be a functional

response. For example, in one case it was suggested that internal organizational environments are created that make it necessary for a system to remain closed and survival oriented (while still producing its particular product). This type of closedness will be called *external* in that its cause lies primarily in the larger system in which the system in question is embedded.

In an analysis of a top operating group, it was suggested that all but two of the members had similar interpersonal styles. This led to a system milieu in which the individuals withdrew from conflict, hesitated to face reality, and so on (Argyris, 1965). Once the members became aware of the internal interpersonal environment, all but one agreed to change, but they found it difficult to do so. The problem was that their group's "life-style" was deeply rooted in individual defense mechanisms that were not amenable to competence-oriented change methods. This style of closedness may be identified as *internal* because its roots reside within the system.

2. The duration of the threat. A threat can produce momentary closedness if it is of short duration, or it can produce long-lasting closedness if it lasts for a long period of time.

3. The parts of the system affected by the threat. The degree of closedness tends to vary when the source of threat is related to peripheral, inner, or central aspects of the system. Peripheral aspects are those that have a low potency for the system, while inner aspects tend to have a high potency. We assume that one must pass through the peripheral in order to arrive at the inner aspects.

The central aspects can be peripheral or inner. The key differentiating property is that change in a central part will tend to create changes in the surrounding parts, be they inner or peripheral.

4. Whether or not the source of the threat is from within or without. The problem is dealing with the threat that the system's faces are very different when the threat emanates from within from those faces when the threat comes from the external environment.

5. The degree of control the system is able to manifest over the threat. The less control there is over the threat, the greater is the probability that the system will become closed. Closedness will also increase as the potency of the parts involved increases and as the duration of the threat increases.

Open and closed systems are therefore oversimplifications. What is more likely is that systems are more or less closed or open. The more the system seeks to create competent problem-solving activities, the more open it may be said to be. The more the system resists these processes, the more closed it may be said to be. The point to be emphasized is the hypothesis stating that the more open the system can be, the more it can learn from the interventionist; the more closed it is, the more it may need interventions that at the outset may be more mechanistic.

INTERVENTIONS TO TEST FOR THE DEGREE OF OPENNESS TO LEARNING

There are four types of interventions that can be used to assess the degree of learning readiness of the client system. All of them are derivable from the conditions necessary to generate valid information. The first type is to confront the client system with a dilemma of its own making. For example, they may report that they wish to reward individual initiative, yet they may have promoted several who are seen as individuals who do not cause disturbance. The assessment begins by watching how the clients react to the formulation of the dilemma. Do they experience it as a dilemma? Do they tend to deny its importance? Do they tend to react in ways that imply that the interventionist should not raise such issues openly? The more these questions are answered in the affirmative, the more closed is the system to learning.

Another test to assess openness to learning is noting how the clients prefer to tackle their problems. Do they prefer to have the interventionist do all the diagnosing, develop all the recommendations, and suggest action strategies? If so, the clients may be less interested in learning and more interested in being commanded or directed. The more intervention directs the change, the less internal responsibility the client may feel toward the changes, and the freer the clients will feel to direct their subordinates in the changes (if the interventionist directs us, we can direct them).

The degree to which the clients are able to deal openly with here-and-now observed categories, especially with regards to difficult issues and emotions, is a third test that the interventionist may use to assess the probable degree of openness to learning of the client system.

The degree to which the clients evaluate each other and create double binds for one another is a fourth criterion to test for the learning capacity of the system. The higher the tendency to evaluate and double bind each other, the greater the competitiveness among the members. The greater these forces, the higher the probability that the clients will focus more on win–lose relationships than on learning and problem solving.

UNILATERAL OR COLLABORATIVE DIAGNOSIS

There are two basic strategies that an interventionist may utilize to make the diagnostic test just described, indeed to make all types of diagnoses. These two strategies, for discussion purposes, may be described as existing at opposite ends of a continuum of subject involvement. One end is mechanistic, and the other organic.

A mechanistic diagnosis follows the model of mechanistic research. In the psychological literature, it is called the "attributive processes." The fundamental assumptions underlying the attributive processes are that the individual who is being the diagnostician (1) observes the behavior of those she is trying to understand, (2) makes certain decisions concerning ability and knowledge, (3) makes certain observations regarding the distinctiveness of the behavior, its consistency over time and over different modalities, and (4) develops from this her diagnosis (attributes intentions to the individual) which she then checks with other observers (Kelley, 1967; Jones & Gerard, 1967). In short, the model is of a sophisticated detective, who by the use of scientific methodology and confirmation of other sophisticated observers, infers what the client is doing and why.

The difficulties with such a diagnosis are similar to the difficulties already identified with mechanistic research. They tend to create a relationship of dependence upon the interventionist in which she may be held responsible for the validity of the diagnosis as well as the action consequences that may flow from it. Even when the interventionist is completely correct in her diagnosis and action recommendations, the result tends to be to place the clients in situations of psychological failure rather than psychological success because it is the interventionist who defines the goals, the path to the goals, and the level of aspiration for the clients. Sometimes mechanistic diagnosis may be necessary (as will be discussed later), but the more frequent mechanistic diagnoses are, the less the clients will develop their own competence in diagnosing their problems.

The alternative is a more organic diagnosis in which (1) the diagnostician and the clients join in the process of generation of data and observation of behavior, (2) the inferences from the observed categories are made by the clients with the aid of the interventionist, and (3) the checks of consistency over time and over modality are arrived at by a mutual and overt consensus.

Factors Facilitating Effective Interventionist Activity

Using the discrepancies between client and interventionist as a leverage for change is difficult to accomplish effectively in a relatively closed system. Collaborative diagnosis is even more difficult. Confrontation of threatening issues may seem almost impossible. If the attempt is made to accomplish these goals by designing and utilizing conditions that approximate psychological success, observed categories, minimally evaluative feedback, minimally contradictory information, shared influence, and feelings of essentiality, it may seem to be asking the interventionist to be superhuman. In some sense, this superhuman aspiration is implied. The aspiration is kept at a level of reality because no one expects the interventionist's behavior to be effective all the time or always to be congruent with the skills described.

A word of caution is in order at this point. The requirements already described, and those yet to be described, are ideals and can only be approximated. They represent overall aspirations rather than particular aspiration levels.

Medical doctors, for example, have definite and high professional standards. Few doctors ever achieve them; indeed, so few do that when one does he may be immortalized in the literature. However, the standards still remain as guideposts for assessing professional effectiveness. They may also serve as guideposts for keeping the clients' and interventionists' level of aspiration realistic about what and how much help can be given and received. If one truly understands the complexity, the difficulties involved, and the skills required to help others (and to be helped), it becomes easier to define a more modest and realistic level of aspiration. This, in turn, tends to reduce the anxiety of the interventionist, which may help him to be more effective.

The history of medicine again illuminates an important issue. When it was proposed that medical education be expanded to ten years of education, there was outcry and resistance by some but agreement and support from many. Medicine had become too helpful to be left to second-rate practitioners.

The same standards should be applied to behavioral science interventionists. Ten years of education may not be unrealistic. As in the case of medicine, our society had best get on with the task of designing the equivalent of medical schools for behavioral science interventionists before it discovers that the only professional help it can get to cure organizational and city dry rot comes from well-meaning, deeply motivated, but hopelessly outgunned (by the bureaucrats), interventionists.

Given this learning, let us turn to a discussion of five qualities that may be of help to an interventionist while under stress (Exhibit 6.3).

First, in a world with high potential for discrepancies in values and behavior, it is important for interventionists to have developed, and to have confidence in, their own philosophy of intervention. Second, interventionists need the capacity to perceive reality accurately, especially under stress. Third, they should be able to understand and encourage the client to express angry and hostile feelings openly. Fourth, interventionists should be able to learn from, and to trust, their own experience. Finally, they should be able to use the discrepancies, the mistrust, and the stress as vehicles for developing learning experiences for the clients.

It is important to note that the basis for all these qualities lies in the interventionist's awareness of self and probable impact on others and in acceptance of self. It is difficult to see how these five qualifications can be developed if the interventionist does not have a relatively high degree of self-awareness and self-acceptance.

Conditions Faced by an Interventionist

Discrepant World
Marginality
Perpetual Client Mistrust
Minimal Feedback About Effectiveness

Qualities Needed by an Interventionist

Confidence in own intervention philosophy
Accurate perception of stressful reality
Acceptance of the client's attacks and mistrust
Trust in own experience of reality
Investing stressful environments with growth experiences

Exhibit 6.3.   Five Qualifications That May Help an Interventionist.

CONFIDENCE IN OWN INTERVENTION PHILOSOPHY

There are two ways in which confidence in an intervention philosophy may be generated. The first is to have as complete and internally consistent a cognitive map as possible of the intervention theory. The second is to be as aware as possible of the motives being fulfilled when acting as an interventionist.

A cognitive map is relevant because it helps the interventionist assess the kind of terrain over which he must pass if he is to help the client with his substantive problems. A map also helps the interventionist see the way the different parts of the client's problem may be interrelated into a whole. For example, the model of the impact of the organization on the individual suggests that absenteeism, turnover, trade unionization, and withdrawal are all caused by the discrepancy between the individuals' needs and the organization's demands; that is, the informal employee culture results from the discrepancy as well as from the impact of directive leadership and managerial controls. The map of top management relations suggests that, with technically competent executives, the major causes of ineffective decision making and management by crisis (through fear and by detail), and the destructive intergroup rivalries are related to the norms of, and interpersonal relationships within, the executive system which, in turn, are related to the values executives hold about effective relationships.

The map also may help the interventionist in dealing with the process of change. For example, one of the major problems faced by the interventionist is, how can he remain authentic in a world that presses for nonauthenticity? How is he to behave when some managers strive to coerce him to manipulate others, to overlook certain defensive behavior, to agree with the key power people rather than confront them, and to accept a violation of his ethics because it is identified as temporary and good for the program?

Is an interventionist ready to parry a request by a superior for information about his subordinate, for example, by pointing out that if he gave information to the superior about his subordinate, how could the superior be certain the interventionist would not give information to the superior's superior? Has the interventionist thought through carefully the advantages and disadvantages of beginning a major change program at the top, or at the middle, of an organization?

Does the interventionist have a map of the kinds of interventions that he believes are most effective in helping others? For example, from this view, descriptive, directly verifiable, minimally evaluative, and minimally attributive interventions are defined as effective. Is the interventionist capable of behaving according to these self-imposed requirements even under stress?

Having a well-thought-out, articulated, and internalized (but always open to change) intervention strategy also leads to the interventionist being consistent and genuine as well as flexible. Consistency in intervention behavior means that the interventions are not related to different objectives, do not mirror different values, and do not manifest mutually contradictory behavior. The more the consistency, the easier it is for a client to come to understand the interventionist's philosophy or style of intervening. The easier it is to learn this style, the quicker the client may come to decide if he can use it as a vehicle for his personal growth and for resolution of the system's problems. Once having learned the interventionist's style and having come to experience it as dependable, the client will develop less fear that the personal growth will be contaminated with his or the interventionist's resolved problems.

Another important resultant of having a well-thought-through philosophy of intervention is an increase in the variety of effective behavior available to the interventionist. The interventionist who knows his basic position clearly, who has explored its outer limits carefully, and who is aware of its gaps and inconsistencies will probably tend to feel freer to generate and attempt a wide variety of behavior than the interventionist who is not thoroughly familiar with the consequences of his strategy.

Moreover, an intimate contact with the breadth and depth of his intervention strategy may also tend to lead to the capacity to know ahead of time when the interventionist is going to reach the limits of, or violate, his own style, to predict the conditions under which he will become defensive, and to be able to identify quickly the moments when he has unknowingly violated his values or when he has become defensive. To put this another way, two minimum conditions for being an effective interventionist are (1) to be aware of, and have control over, one's behavior, (2) to be able to predict when one will be in difficulty without realizing it. This may be an explanation for the increasing amount of literature that shows psychotherapists and T-group leaders of significantly different styles can be of help to individuals and groups. They present ideas clearly, easily, consistently, genuinely, and with minimal internal conflictedness.

#2. Like M.B.O.

The second dimension that may influence an interventionist's confidence in his strategy is related to his reasons for being interested in the processes of intervention. What needs are the predominant source of the interventionist's constructive intent? Are the needs those that cluster around being protective, being included, being loved, and controlling others? Or are the motivational sources for intervening related to helping others enlarge their self-awareness, their competence, and especially their capabilities to resolve important problems? The former cluster may indicate that the interventionist is in this profession partially to work through or find fulfillment of his own needs which may inhibit others' growth. The latter cluster may indicate that the interventionist's foundations for trying to be of help are competence centered.

It has already been suggested that adults may be viewed as representing self-systems that are relatively open (learning) and relatively closed (nonlearning, repetitive, and compulsive). The more closed the system, the less it will learn from the environment and the less it will be able to help others become open. The interventionist must strive constantly to enlarge his awareness of the proportion of his openness to his closedness, as well as the possible causes of each. This implies that the basic motivations for a person to become an interventionist should be significantly loaded with needs that help one's self and others to be open, to learn, and to increase one's own and others' awareness and competence.

The importance of being aware and accepting of one's motives for being an interventionist may be illustrated by several examples. One interventionist was in the midst of emphasizing the negative aspects of power to the clients when he was confronted about his own power needs. "Don't you go for power?" asked one executive. "That's not a fair question of a professor," added another laughingly. The interventionist became quite red; his face tightened. After a little stammering, he gave an honest and open view of his power needs. However, as far as the clients were concerned, as one put it, "Did you see him turn color? We hit him where it hurts most." There are several cases are presented of interventionists who, in an attempt to cope with the issue of power, became as manipulative and nongenuine as were the clients. Eventually they were confronted by the clients about their apparent comfort in being manipulators. They began their reply with the phrase, "Because we are concerned with you as clients . . . ". However, this was immediately challenged by the clients. How could they be manipulators and be concerned for people? As we shall see, their replies were unsatisfactory, and this contributed to their ineffectiveness.

Because of its prevalence, it may be important to pause for a moment and comment on the frequently heard motive for being an interventionist, namely, "I like people and I want to help them." This stance is usually one of apparent selfless devotion to others. Ironically, such a stance probably tends to reward the person who suppresses his needs and enhance his valuation of himself in helping others. As has been pointed out, man's growth is intimately tied to the growth of others. He cannot understand himself without understanding others, and he cannot understand others without understanding himself. Man tends to be incomplete, gaining his awareness and wholeness in relationship to others. Such a view questions the advisability—indeed the possibility—that individuals can or should be selfless. The stance of selflessness, if explored carefully, usually covers several unexamined needs operating within the individual while he is intervening. The selfish aspects of the individual's motives are simply hidden.

Moreover, the dichotomizing of selfishness and selflessness seems neither realistic nor useful. Selfish motives are always operating. The key, for an interventionist, is to be aware of his motives and to develop himself so that while he is fulfilling his needs, he can help others increase their awareness and acceptance of themselves and become more competent. This requires focusing upon the needs that make one more of an open, rather than closed, system and more competent and congruent.

ACCURATE PERCEPTION OF STRESSFUL REALITY

The interventionist needs to be able to perceive accurately, while under stress, his own internal world and the world around him. In terms of the former, it is important for him to be aware of, and in control over, those defense mechanisms which, if activated, could make him an inaccurate and an ineffective interactor. In addition, it is important for the interventionist to be able to describe reality helpfully while under stress. As has been pointed out, the most helpful descriptions of reality are those given in terms of observed categories with minimal evaluation so that they can be directly verifiable by the participants. However, to generate information that is directly verifiable by nonprofessionals, as well as professionals, requires that it remain as close to the "here-and-now" observable data as possible.

It should be emphasized that the meaning of here-and-now interventionists, as used in this book, is significantly different from the meaning of "here and now" in many psychotherapeutic activities. Some psychotherapists tend to use the here and now to help the client discover the unconscious structure active in the present but created in the past. Others use here-and-now data to help the client see that he uses the relationship to involve the therapist as a more or less unconscious object. Finally, others use the here-and-now data to generate enough evidence to make an interpretation to the patient, such as that he may be projecting, or he may be identifying with such-and-such a person, etc. (For illustrations, see Ezriel, 1952.) In all these examples, the here-and-now data are used to help the professional generate interpretations that go much beyond the directly verifiable observed category.

To the extent that the interventionist is capable of coping effectively with stress, he will be able to use the stress to help the client learn how he can cope more effectively with it. Equally important is that the interventionist may help the client learn more about him (interventionist). For example, the interventionist may help the client realize that one important way he has of validating the views being propounded by the interventionist is to watch him deal with stress. If the interventionist deals with stress by regressing to more primitive behavior, the client can justifiably wonder about the worthwhileness of the new values that the interventionist is suggesting to him. Many clients strive to develop a new set of values and new ways of behaving because the old ones do not tend to be effective under stress; indeed, they create stress. If the client comes to believe that the interventionist's values are not effective under stress or that he regresses to his client's values under stress, it would not make much sense to him to strive to learn the new values and new behavior.

Several years ago the writer was a faculty member in a course designed to educate new interventionists (all of whom had a doctorate degree and some experience in consulting). For four weeks the course seemed to go well. The interventionists were learning a great deal by participating as faculty in such activities as T-groups, community simulations, and general theory sessions. One day they were told that a client system had accepted the idea that all of the interns could come to the firm for several days of diagnosis. The clients realized that they were inviting interventionists with little experience. They were willing to take the risks.

The more the interventionist interns planned for the first confrontation session with the clients, the more anxious and tense they became. Soon they were, as a group, asking questions about the clients that questioned their integrity. Do these clients sell to people of color? Are they too money oriented? Are the clients going to manipulate the interns to become part of their sales campaign?

The anxiety reached the point where many of the group members answered the questions in the negative even though they had not yet met the clients. Then they confronted the faculty as to whether or not they should be asked to consult with clients whose values were significantly different from theirs!

The faculty responded by raising two sets of questions. First, how do interventionists reach the point where they judge a client negatively even before he arrives? Are not these views of the client fantasies? If they are, upon what do they base these fantasies? Since most interventionists said they had never consulted for such an organization, could the fantasies be projections of their own mistrust of themselves as competent interventionists?

The second set of questions was related to the issue: do the interventionists not have a special responsibility to consider working with clients whose values are different from their own? Are these not the clients who especially need their help?

When the clients arrived, they were willing and able to answer all the questions put to them. Yes, they wanted to make money. No, they did not want to do it illegally. Yes, they did sell to people of color. Moreover, the clients never raised any objections to several of the interventionists who sported beards when meeting with their customers (even though they admitted that a bearded observer could have upset a customer so much that it might have meant a loss of a sale).

In another case, a three-man consulting team spent about six months diagnosing the interpersonal relationships of a top management team. They kept detailed notes of their group and individual meetings with each other and the clients. At the end of their diagnosis, they recommended unanimously that the president should be discharged. (The recommendation was accepted by the board of directors.) A year later, the case was given to the writer to read as an example of a successful consulting relationship. After an analysis of the detailed documentation, the writer concluded (and the consulting team accepted as legitimate) that the consultants were unanimous in firing the president because he threatened them continually as individuals and as a team. Since there was a norm (within all the teams) to suppress their interpersonal problems in order to work with the clients, the issue was never explored.

ACCEPTANCE OF THE CLIENT'S ATTACKS AND MISTRUST

An interventionist who is capable of learning (and helping others to learn) from the client's stress is able to value the stresses produced by the client. She therefore encourages the client to express his misgivings, frustrations, hostilities, and mistrust, including those related to the interventionist. To the extent that the interventionist is accepting of herself, is relatively unconflicted, is able to perceive reality correctly, and is intellectually certain of her philosophy of intervention, she will tend to perceive the client's attack for what it is: the client's attempt to reduce his own anxiety and tension. The attack also has the potential of keeping the client in dialogue with the interventionist because the former expresses hostility; he offers to the latter and himself an opportunity to explore and discuss his feelings. A response to the effect that "I am sorry that I am upsetting you, and I can certainly understand how upsetting my position can be if it is valid," may lead the client to explore openly several feelings that are rarely analyzed openly, namely, hostility toward others and feelings of failure. An open attack, therefore, has the value of keeping the client and interventionist in dialogue; it is a sign that the interventionist is being taken seriously. It also provides further opportunity for self-examination and growth. *yay!. Fun! :~5*

TRUST IN OWN EXPERIENCE OF REALITY

An interventionist who has evidence from within herself and from the clients that under stress (1) she can perceive reality accurately, (2) she minimally contaminates the environment with her distortions, (3) she minimally regresses under stress, and (4) she respects client attacks and uses them as a basis for growth will tend to find it easier to trust her experience of the world and her repertoire of behavior available to her to deal with problems, especially when there is little here-and-now data to back up these feelings of trust. Given a relatively high degree of self-trust, the interventionist can focus on the task of helping the client begin to trust her and trust himself.

Self-trust also makes it possible for the interventionist to stand alone without him; then she will feel loneliness in addition to the feeling of standing alone. How? By standing alone, the interventionist is able to own up, to be open about, and to experiment with her views even though the clients may thoroughly disagree with her. If the disagreement continues for a long time, it is not unusual for the interventionist to feel some degree of loneliness; after all, everyone is disagreeing with her. Clients may say, in effect, "Why don't you give in? We are all in agreement that you are wrong!" If the interventionist views these comments as a rejection of her, then she will feel loneliness in addition to the feeling of standing alone. However, if she sees these comments as the client's way of defending herself, as his way of remaining in dialogue with the interventionist, then she will not tend to feel loneliness. This does not mean that the interventionist may never become angry. Indeed, there are moments when she does have to protect herself from a client who is so threatened that he not only wants to fight the interventionist, but may want to aggress against her. Anger is a valid defense against a real enemy.

INVESTING STRESSFUL ENVIRONMENTS WITH GROWTH EXPERIENCE

The interventionist attempts to utilize every dilemma, discrepancy, and conflict as an opportunity for everyone to learn. Thus, he may withdraw from the usual leadership pattern of controlling and manipulating people, but this does not mean he becomes uninvolved. One of the major tasks of the interventionist is to manipulate the environment (*not* the people) so that growth and learning can occur if the clients wish to enter the environment. The interventionist strives to create conditions of psychological success. Experiencing psychological success should help the clients increase their sense of self-confidence and trust in others. These conditions are the major foundations for effective groups and for effective problem-solving activity.

In striving to generate meaningful learning experiences from the environment, the interventionist runs several risks. One, he can develop client dependency. If the client sees that the interventionist is ahead of him, he may tend to become more dependent upon him. The learning that may then be achieved would be mostly the responsibility of the interventionist and would be difficult for the client to internalize as his own. This, in turn, can make the interventionist feel impatient with the client's progress. "What is wrong with the client?

He has learned it; why does he not behave differently?" The interventionist can become especially anxious if he believes that dependence upon him is wrong. He may feel a sense of failure and adapt by becoming more blind to the moments when he is influencing the client to become more dependent upon him.

Second, the interventionist may develop correct insights long before anyone else sees them. Clients who are anxious about their relationship with the interventionist may use what seem to them to be wild leaps of influence as valid reasons to infer that the interventionist is trying to pressure or embarrass them.

To summarize, the preceding discussion represents a model of interventionist effectiveness. The more an interventionist is able (1) to have confidence in his philosophy of intervening, (2) to regress minimally under stress, (3) to understand and use client attacks constructively, (4) to trust his own experience of reality and his repertoire of skills, and (5) to invest ambiguity with valid meanings, the greater is the probability that he will help to reduce the resisting forces in the relationship and help the clients and himself increase the pushing forces toward change. These conditions, in turn, increase the probability that the interventionist will experience himself, and be seen by others, as an effective interventionist.

The increased success will tend to feed back to, and alter, the inputs. It will tend (1) to reduce the discrepancy between his ideals and his actual behavior, (2) to decrease his need for, and dependence upon, formal power, and (3) to increase his feelings of validity about his intervention and change philosophy. The success will also tend to reduce his concern about (1) the marginality of being an interventionist, (2) the perpetual trial and mistrust, and (3) ignorance about his impact upon the clients. As the former three and latter three factors occur, the interventionist's competence in the use of the appropriate copying mechanisms may increase. A circular process is in action which should lead to increased interventionist effectiveness (Exhibit 6.4).

An interventionist who is able to accept his own and his clients' behavior even under conditions of stress will tend to find it easier to create relationships with the client that can produce effectiveness in intervention behavior. These behaviors include owning up to, being open toward, and experimenting with ideas and feelings. The interventionist strives to communicate and to help others communicate ideas and feelings by using observed categories and by minimizing attributions, evaluations, and contradictory comments.

Conditions Faced by an Interventionist

Discrepant world
Marginality
Perpetual Client Mistrust
Minimal Feedback about Effectiveness

Qualities Needed by an Interventionist

Confidence in own intervention philosophy
Accurate perception of stressful reality
Acceptance of the client's attacks and mistrust
Trust in own experience of reality
Investing stressful environments with growth experiences

Behavior of an Interventionist to Produce Effectiveness

Owning up to, being open toward, and experimenting with ideas and feelings.
Helping others to own up, be open, and experiment with ideas and feelings.
Contributing to the norms of individuality, concern, and trust.
Communicating in observed, directly verifiable categories, with minimal attribution, evaluation, and internal contradiction.

Exhibit 6.4.   Circular Process to Increase Interventionist Effectiveness.

CHAPTER SEVEN

Action Research
Rethinking Lewin

Linda Dickens
Karen Watkins

After fifty years of development, action research remains an umbrella term for a shower of activities intended to foster change on the group, organizational, and even societal levels. While most action research practitioners would agree that they are attending to institutional or personal constraints, they vary in their emphasis on different elements of the action research process to address those constraints. Participatory action researchers focus on participation and empowerment. Teacher action researchers rely on data to transform individual behavior. Organizational action researchers focus on research and data driven decision-making. There is, in fact, no definitive approach to action research, which is part of its strength but also part of its problem. Action research has not evolved into a unified theory, but has resulted, instead, in disparate definitions and characterizations (Peters & Robinson, 1984).

This article explores both historical and contemporary definitions, development, and goals of action research while acknowledging the differences among various action research approaches. Case examples are offered to depict the process in action. Finally, we consider the case of the manufacturing manager and propose possible approaches to intervention based on the action research framework.

DEVELOPMENT AND DEFINITIONS OF ACTION RESEARCH

Kurt Lewin developed the action research model in the mid-1940s to respond to problems he perceived in social action (Kemmis & McTaggart, 1988). Conducting research in a time of great social challenges brought about by World War II, Lewin worked toward achieving democratic inquiry within the social sciences. He believed that social problems should serve as the impetus for public inquiry within democratic communities. The war, writes Kemmis (1988), "galvanized views about democratic decision-making processes and participation in those processes by those affected by the decisions" (p. 5). As Lewin conceived it, action research necessitates group decision and commitment to improvement.

Noting the chasm between social action and social theory (Peters & Robinson, 1984) and the lack of collaboration between practitioners and researchers, Lewin called for social scientists to bridge the gap and combine theory building with research on practical problems (Cunningham, 1993). Without collaboration, practitioners engaged in uninformed action; researchers developed theory without application; and neither group produced consistently successful results. By using the methodology of action research, practitioners could research their own actions with the intent of making them more effective while at the same time working within and toward theories of social action. The marriage between theory and action could produce informed, improved behavior and encourage social change (Oja & Smulyan, 1989). Action researchers, then, generate context-bound, values-based knowledge and solutions from their public inquiries into system problems.

Lewin conceived of action research as a cycling back and forth between ever deepening surveillance of the problem situation (within the persons, the organization; the system) and a series of research-informed action experiments. His original formulation of action research "consisted in analysis, fact-finding, conceptualization, planning execution, more fact-finding or evaluation; and then a repetition of this whole circle of activities; indeed a spiral of such circles" (Sanford, 1970, p. 4; Lewin, 1946). Although Lewin first formulated the definition, he left scant work to describe and expand his early definitions. Argyris, Putnam, and Smith (1987) note that Lewin "never wrote a systematic statement of his views on action research" (p. 8). In fact he wrote only twenty-two pages that addressed the topic (Peters & Robinson, 1984). Perhaps because Lewin was unable to fully conceive his theory of action research before his death in 1947, he left the field open for other similarly-minded researchers to elaborate on, and at times reinterpret, his definition. Several subsequent definitions of action research illustrate how others have changed the definition to emphasize different aspects of the process.

According to Cunningham (1993), action research "is a term for describing a spectrum of activities that focus on research, planning, theorizing, learning and development. It describes a continuous process of research and learning in the researcher's long-term relationship with a problem" (p. 4). In his view, the action research approach is broken down into a series of units that are interrelated. Cunningham's definition suggests that the methodology encompasses a wide breadth of activities rather than one specific format. Although he reports that the process includes learning and development, he does not state explicitly whether or how action research leads to action or change and neglects mention of action research as a group process.

Sanford (Sanford, in Reason & Rowan, 1981) describes action research as a process of analysis, fact-finding, conceptualization, planning, execution, and then more fact-finding or evaluation, all followed by a repetition of the same pattern. While Sanford's definition conveys Lewin's iterative process of action research, it ignores the issue of changing the environment under study. The term "execution" has an element of action to it, yet does not adequately address the transformative change that Lewin intended. It implies, instead, an act or performance, with the action brought on the subject, rather than the subject as an active member of the process. The definition fails to mention the importance of the participants in the action research process and how they act as members of the change environment.

Argyris places action science clearly in the Lewinian action research tradition and emphasizes the features from Lewin's approach that are most consistent with action science in his definition of action research:

> Action research takes its cues—its questions, puzzles, and problems—from the perceptions of practitioners within particular, local practice contexts. It builds descriptions and theories within the practice context itself, and tests them through *intervention experiments*—that is,

through experiments that bear the double burden of testing hypotheses and effecting some (putatively) desirable change in the situation. (Argyris & Schön, 1991, p. 86)

In this definition, the interventions are an experimental manipulation, and problem-solving is the goal. Contribution to knowledge is in the area of research on intervention. Participants learn a mode of public, democratic reflection (the action science technology) and participate in solving self-diagnosed problems.

Elden and Chisholm (1993) identify emerging varieties of action research and label action research as originally conceived by Lewin as the classical model of action research. Heller (1976) argues that those who would differentiate their work from the classical, Lewin-influenced model may in fact misunderstand Lewin. For example, Lewin focused on classical experiments over social action, but at the same time sought to understand, through this research, the deeper causes that threatened democracy, itself a social action thrust. Elden and Chisholm (1993) believe that action research is focused at increasing systems' adaptive capacity, ability to innovate, and competence in self-design. Quoting Brown, they note that action research from the Northern school tends to be focused on reform, particularly organizational reform, while action research from the Southern school is more focused on social change, and that these differing purposes have everything to do with differences in approach. Heller (1976) notes that the distinguishing feature among these methodologies may be the choice of intervention approach. The model here best fits the classical model and the emphasis on organizational development or an organizational reform agenda.

Social scientists can apply these various definitions and the action research methods to multiple situations and within practically limitless settings. Cohen and Manion (1980) explain that they can be used to spur action; address personal functioning, human relations and morale; focus on job analysis; guide organizational change, plan and make policy; create innovation; solve problems; or develop theoretical knowledge. We note that—when implemented with close adherence to Lewin's principles of democratic participation and social action, and cycling between analyzing a situation and reconceptualizing or reframing that situation or problem—action research has significant potential to create space for organizational learning.

Response to the Traditional Scientific Paradigm

Gestaltist in origin (Foster, 1972), Lewin's arguments for action research stemmed from the limitations of studying social problems in a controlled, laboratory environment. He proposed that principles of traditional science be used to address social problems (Aguinis, 1993). Rather than study a single variable within a complex system, Lewin preferred to consider the entire system in its natural environment (the gestalt). He argued that scientists could research social phenomena "not by transforming them into quantifiable units of physical actions and reactions, but by studying the intersubjectively valid sets of meanings, norms, and values that are the immediate determinants of behavior" (Peters & Robinson, 1984, p. 115). Lewin brought together all the elements of science that had been separated rigidly in order to study social phenomena that could not be understood by using any one of those dispersed elements (Sanford, in Reason & Rowen, 1981).

Lewin believed that experimentation was an important part of any change effort. Action research was built on the traditional scientific paradigm of experimental manipulation and observation of effects (Clark, 1976). A change is made, and the results are studied in order to inform future change efforts. Similar to traditional science, action research yields a set of general laws expressed in "if/so" propositions (Peters & Robinson, 1984). Yet, beyond that, the methodologies diverge.

Whereas the traditional scientific paradigm reduces human phenomena to variables that can be used to predict future behavior, the alternative paradigm, of which action research is a part, describes what happens holistically in naturally-occurring settings (Perry & Zuber-Skerritt, 1994). Unlike traditional science, action research does not attempt to set tight limits and controls on the experimental situation. The action researcher approaches the subject, whether people or institution, in its natural state (Trist, 1976).

Both action research and traditional science share the goal of creating knowledge. The action research participants begin with little knowledge in a specific situation and work collaboratively to observe, understand, and ultimately change the situation, while also reflecting on their own actions. The situation and environmental conditions lead the direction of the research. Traditional science, on the other hand, begins with substantial knowledge about hypothetical relationships, seeking to "discover new facts, verify old facts, and to analyze their sequences, causal explanations, and the natural laws governing the data gathered" (Cunningham, 1993). It is exact in its measurement of cause and effect.

Another difference between traditional and action research lies in their approaches to action. While the former collects or establishes information for the purpose of learning and usually ends with the point of discovery, the latter intends to use any information to guide new behavior. Traditional science does not attempt to offer solutions to problems (Cohen & Manion, 1980). Chein, Cook, and Harding (1948) contend that action researchers differ from scientists in that they must not only make discoveries, but must also ensure that those discoveries are properly applied. Action researchers attempt to make scientific discoveries while also solving practical problems. Aguinas (1993) notes that, nevertheless, the separation between action research and science is greater than ever.

Participants in action research programs expect to be treated not as objects or even subjects, but as co-researchers engaged in "empowering participation" and in "co-generative dialogue" between "insiders and outsiders" (Elden & Levin, 1991). In action research, truth is in the process of inquiry itself. Was it reflexive and dialectical? Was it ethical, democratic, and collaborative? Did participants learn new research skills, attain greater self-understanding, or achieve greater self-determination? Did it solve significant practice problems or did it contribute to our knowledge about what will not solve these problems? Were problems solved in a manner that enhanced the overall learning capacity of the individuals or the system?

These are the types of questions that guide action research. They are unlike those that guide most research. On the other hand, they speak to the essence of management and organizational learning.

Critiques of Action Research

Action research has been criticized as either producing research with little action or action with little research (Foster, 1972); weak when merely a form of problem-solving and strong when also emancipatory (Peters & Robinson, 1984; Kemmis, in Kemmis & McTaggart, 1988); lacking the rigor of true scientific research (Cohen & Manion, 1980); and lacking in internal and external control (Merriam & Simpson, 1984), hence of limited use in contributing to the body of knowledge. Marris and Rein (in Cohen & Manion, 1980) argue that the principles of action and research are so different as to be mutually exclusive, so that to link them together is to create a fundamental internal conflict.

Many action research studies appear to abort at the stage of diagnosis of a problem or at the implementation of a single solution or strategy, irrespective of whether it resolves the problem. Individuals seeking to solve problems in complex, real-time settings find that the problems change under their feet, often before the more in-depth iterative search for solutions suggested by action research has achieved meaningful results.

These critiques hinge on whether or not action research must contribute to knowledge in the same manner as other forms of social science research and whether or not action research must end in a resolution of a problem in order to be valid (Watkins & Brooks, in Brooks & Watkins, 1994). There is little doubt from the works reviewed in this article, as well as from the case studies of action research projects, that these critiques are more academic than practical concerns of most action researchers.

Essential Goals of Action Research

The expectation to both make and apply discoveries reflects the two essential aims of action research: to improve and to involve. The goal of improvement is directed toward three areas: practice, the understanding of the practice by its practitioners, and the improvement of the situation in which the practice takes place (Carr & Kemmis, 1986; Brown et al., 1982). Indeed, action research is more effective when participants engage in self-reflection while they are critically reflecting on the objective problem (Brown et al., 1982). Researchers can meet the goal of improvement by taking strategic action and then examining these actions against their original hypotheses. The validity of the theory is judged by a simple criterion: whether it leads to improvement and change within the context. It must both solve a practical problem and generate knowledge.

The goal of involvement is no less important than improvement. The Lewinian approach states that participants in the environment or project are best suited to collaborate and develop hypotheses since they are grounded in the context. They know the subtle characteristics that might influence the implementation of any plan. Additionally, involvement encourages members' psychological ownership of facts; it allows for economical data collection; and teaches methods which can be used later for further development (Lippitt, 1979). In addition to owning the problem, the action researchers may acquire the skills necessary for continuous learning and problem-solving so that what is learned in the action research process is actually implemented.

Involvement speaks to the need for collaboration that Lewin considered vital to research. It is one critical element that distinguishes action research from other forms of social research (Peters & Robinson, 1984). The collaboration, according to Peters and Robinson, "must take place within a mutually acceptable ethical framework governing the collection, use and release of data" (p. 118).

The interdependence of improvement and involvement addresses Lewin's concern about the schism between theorists and practitioners. Action research can produce strong links among knowledge about learning, personal knowledge, and the commitment to further strategic action (Brown et al., 1982).

THE PROCESS OF ACTION RESEARCH

As noted, action research consists of a team of practitioners, and possibly theorists, who cycle through a spiral of steps including planning, action, and evaluating the result of action, continually monitoring the activity of each step in order to adjust as needed (Kemmis & McTaggart, 1988). The cyclical nature of action research recognizes the need for action plans to be flexible and responsive to the environment. Kemmis and McTaggart note that "Lewin's deliberate overlapping of action and reflection was designed to allow changes in plans for action as people learned from their own experience" (p. 8).

The action research team begins the cycle by identifying a problem in their particular context. Often, the outside facilitator is needed to unfreeze the group dynamics so that participants can proceed to make changes. After identifying the problem within its community, the action research team works within that context to collect pertinent data. Data sources might include interviewing other people in the environment, completing measurements, conducting surveys, or gathering any other information that the researchers consider informative. By collecting data around a problem and then feeding it back to the organization, researchers identify the need for change, and the direction that that change might take (Watkins, 1991). Following the guideline of involvement, all team members participate in the data collection phase.

After collecting the data, action research team members analyze it and then generate possible solutions to the identified problem. In addition, the team must make meaning of the data and introduce that meaning to the organization. The feedback to the community may act as an intervention itself, or the action researchers may implement more structured actions that create changes within the system. The interventions can be considered experimental, as the action research team members next test the effects of the changes they have implemented by collecting more data, evaluating the results, and reformulating thoughts or redefining the problem in the system.

The action researchers continue moving through this cycle until they have exhausted the problem that they identified initially. Possibly, completing one cycle adequately addresses the problem; more likely, however, the team might go through several iterations of problem identification and solving before the problem is both correctly identified and fully addressed. Figure 7.1 presents Lewin's model of action research—phases that he originally depicted as a spiral.

Models of Action Research

Action researchers can draw on many models to guide their research. Cunningham (1993) notes:

> The difficulty with any definition of action research is that the term can be used to summarize many activities which have the "veneer" of research and action. Two researchers attempting to solve the same problem could inevitably reach different conclusions and still meet the criteria of action research within some paradigm or another. (p. 25)

Different researchers using the action research method may disagree in their approach, while agreeing on fundamental philosophies or goals. The participants in any action research undertaking ultimately choose—either consciously or unconsciously—the particular route that directs the research.

Most action researchers agree that action research consists of cycles of planning, acting, reflecting or evaluating, and then taking further action. Because various forms of action research exist, practitioners may choose one or several methodologies to inform their action. Consequently, it may be difficult to identify a "pure" action researcher, that is, someone who follows only one particular methodology.

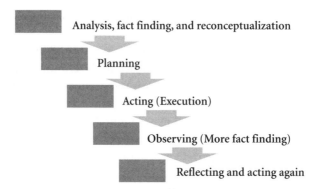

Figure 7.1.   Lewin's Action Research Model.

In addition to choosing from different methodologies, action researchers may differ in what they choose to emphasize in the action research cycle. Some emphasize experimentation, others show more concern with feedback, planning, or learning and theory building (Cunningham, 1993). Further, researchers may vary the duration of each cycle (Brown et al., 1982) depending on their particular purposes.

The professional expert model of action research (Whyte, 1991b) is based on the premise that a professional researcher contracts with an organization to "study a situation and a set of problems, to determine what the facts are, and to recommend a course of action" (p. 9). The professional expert leads the research effort in this situation, with relatively little direction or involvement provided by organizational members. Although this model can provide answers to problematic organizational questions, it does less to stimulate learning on the part of organizational actors. Members may not gain full comprehension or ownership of their problems and underlying values and, thus, may remain unable to address them adequately without continued outside consultation or intervention.

McTaggart (1991) differentiates between action research and participatory action research, which he suggests is more emancipatory than much of the action research undertaken. Participatory action research presupposes a commitment that all participants actually do research for themselves. Likewise, Kemmis (1988) stipulates that participants in the environment under investigation should be involved in every stage of the action research cycle; participatory action research theorists, on the other hand, suggest that some social scientists who undertake action research projects define "involvement" so broadly that participants actually engage minimally in the project. Participatory action research, then, serves as an extension of Lewin's original formulation, which focuses more on involvement than participation. Action research is truly participatory when members of the particular context design and conduct the research and reflect on its nature (McTaggart, 1991). The participants engage in research that changes first themselves and then their environment.

In summary, the literature offers a variety of applications of action research. While this allows practitioners to choose an approach that meets specific needs, it also makes difficult a common understanding. The existence of several explicit models of action research interferes with the development of a consistent and unified theory of action research. Few authors agree on a definition of action research; they may include certain elements of Lewin's theory while deemphasizing, or altogether ignoring, others. Most theorists agree on the collaborative nature of action research, yet fail to critically examine how individuals collaborate or, indeed, engage in action research. Some may acknowledge the ability of action research to improve social action, yet neglect the internal values and theories that define improvement and guide that action. The literature provides limited information on internal action research team processes, focusing instead on the intervention and its consequences. Cases are written from an expert point of view, while the perceptions of team members usually are neglected. Finally, the literature fails to clarify the interdependence of action and research. In the section which follows, we illustrate the classical model of research through a case study of two contrasting action research teams in a high technology company.

LEWIN'S MODEL IN ACTION, PART I: THE CASE OF TWO ACTION RESEARCH PROJECTS

Southwest Technologies (ST), a multinational, high technology company, began an action research project in conjunction with the University of the Southwest (the University) in order to study quality issues within two divisions, Stripe and Star. The more specific purpose of the venture was to establish corporate action research teams to identify and address social systems-related barriers to the implementation of the divisions' total quality management programs and to help facilitate the move toward self-directed work teams (Dickens, 1998). The "action" task would enable ST to move toward a more democratic work culture; the "research" task would contribute knowledge to the field of quality management in the workforce.

Stripe and Star were situated in separate buildings on the same corporate campus in the Southwest. Faculty from the local university approached the site manager to propose the formation of action research teams. Table 7.1 depicts the actions taken by each team over the course of one year as they relate to the action research process described above.

While using Lewin's spiral as a basic framework, Table 7.1 provides much greater detail about what action research actually demands from participants. It conveys the iterative nature of action research, emphasizing that it requires both parallel and serial stages of activity (Davis & Valfer, in Clark, 1976). The table also illustrates that teams may need to re-cycle through steps that received inadequate attention or that were not resolved. Areas in which each team appeared to struggle, continuing to attempt action around a problematic step without achieving resolution, become apparent in this chronology.

Even this level of detail, however, fails to capture the tensions, revisions and experimentation inherent in the process. Action research is not a methodology that can be implemented in discrete, orderly steps, as much of the theoretical literature suggests. Rather, it can go forward, backward, and all directions at once. Both teams became paralyzed or helpless. In this instance, the Stripe team got bogged down trying to identify a project that met with management approval, and we see the cycling again and again through planning and reflection with little or no action. On the other hand, the Star team moves methodically through goal setting to action but is then arrested in the middle of the process when they present their preliminary findings to management. At this point, both management and the team decide that the team does not have authority to address the problems identified. What becomes clear in these chronicles is that each step reveals new information and new demands that have the potential to affect the outcome of the action research process.

Stripe Action Research Team	**Star People Effectiveness Team**
Planning • forming the team • learning action research • selecting an area for research • agreeing on action	*Planning* • outlining goals • forming the team • studying empowerment • adopting action research • exploring the purpose of the team • seeking authority • facing conflict • agreeing on action
Acting	*Acting* • collecting the data
Reflecting • discussing team processes • confronting issues of membership and leadership • discussing team objectives • discussing team processes • organizing the data • reporting to managers • analyzing the data	*Reflecting* • reflecting on team and data collection processes • organizing and analyzing the data • coping with change • reconsidering our authority • organizing our feedback • reconsidering our authority and purpose • preparing for the QST presentation • presenting data to upper managers for reflection
Acting • creating individual projects	*Planning*
Reflecting • discussing team objectives • discussing team processes • discussing team purpose and objectives	
Planning • seeking authority • sharing our experiences • agreeing on action	
Acting • collecting the data	
Reflecting • organizing and analyzing the data • presenting the data to upper managers for reflection	

Table 7.1.   The Action Research Project at Southwest Technologies.

LEWIN'S MODEL IN ACTION, PART II: THE CASE OF THE MANUFACTURING MANAGER

The cases provide an opportunity to illustrate how action research might be used to intervene on a problematic organizational situation. Here, we see an interaction during a meeting between team members and management that leaves the participants dissatisfied with one another and with the outcome of the meeting.

The case of the manufacturing manager suggests several weaknesses and constraints within the team's functioning, as observed from the lens of action research. If action research intends to produce social change and practical solutions in a democratic forum, then we must ask how we can democratize this group. We look at ways to involve participants and improve the situation in a way that balances research and action.

How then would action researchers respond to the case? One possibility is to explore the issue of sanction—the necessary endorsements and permissions to act which are essential to action research. Does the team indeed have organizational sanction to proceed? If it once did, does it still? What is the nature of the sanction that the team has—what can it do, for how long, to whom? One paradox evident in this case is that a team may have the stated authority to act and still not feel an internal capacity to act. That is, they may experience a mandate without also experiencing empowerment to fulfill that mandate.

Another key observation is the role of management in sanctioning the project. As Goodman and Clark (in Clark, 1976) contend, "It is very difficult both to collect good data and to employ the data usefully without the broad support of the client system" (pp. 174–175). Foster (in Clark, 1976), Clark (1976), Greenwood, Whyte, and Harkavy (1993) and Seashore and Bowers (1963) all report that continued sanction is imperative to the enactment of the action research process. While the teams intended to be self-sufficient, they could not proceed without management approval. This case demonstrates again the critique that many action research teams yield research with little action.

We are intrigued by the juxtaposition of sanction and sanctuary—perhaps there is a way that a team that has not been sanctioned to take action also lacks sanctuary or safety. Certainly the thoughts of the team leader suggest this when he thinks, "You keep cutting us off at the knees." An action researcher might explore learned helplessness and empowerment issues with the team members and the manager within the context of sanction.

We have said that the two goals of action research are to involve and to improve. Team members must consider their own involvement, as well as the degree of collaboration with their manager. How can they involve the manager in a dialogue to identify a mutually acceptable improvement objective and then continue to involve him or her in subsequent iterations of the action research process? If involvement leads to psychological ownership, then what does the manager need in order to take ownership of the organization's project? Who is part of the system that must be involved? If this stakeholder has not been a part of the process, who else may also need to be involved in order for the team to have the necessary endorsements to proceed?

Based on the thought, "Whew, he finally came to our meeting. He's been invited to every session," group members might identify the manager's lack of involvement as a serious constraint. The response to this identified problem, then, is to create ways for the manager to be involved. In this case, simply inviting him to meetings has not been sufficient. Team members have the opportunity to reflect on their own efforts at involvement to date and must own up to the fact that they have been ineffective partners in the project. Group reflection might lead participants to acknowledge that they have failed at involvement and to generate new options. They must not only look at ways to involve the manager, but also at ways to involve themselves in involving the manager. Team members could request a commitment from the manager to attend specific meetings; they could, themselves, commit to briefing the manager thoroughly—through electronic mail, memos, phone calls, or short meetings—on a regular basis. They could solicit from the manager his own ideas about the best way to involve him.

Action research requires that a group have a specific goal. Cunningham (1993) notes that a problem that is too general cannot be tested. It is possible in this case that "identifying ways that each of us can help eliminate non-value-added work in our area" is too general a goal on which to act. The case does not delineate action steps surrounding non-value-added work (NVAW). At this point in the team's existence, team members are compelled to reconsider their goal. This meeting gives them the opportunity to co-create with the manager a goal that meets his needs as well as theirs and to collaborate on actions they might pursue. When the manager tells the group that the goal of eliminating non-value-added work is not a good idea, he may show little respect for the thought and research that the team members have dedicated to their task; but it also illustrates that the manager does not "own" the goal of eliminating NVAW. Most importantly, the team has the opportunity to question whether or not the goal of eliminating NVAW will indeed make a significant improvement in the organization.

The team's plan to develop individual projects intimates that they might not be able or willing to work with each other. When team members decided to develop individual projects, they may have colluded to inhibit teamwork and collaboration. Kemmis and McTaggart (1988) argue that "action research is not individualistic. To lapse into individualism is to destroy the critical dynamic of the group" (p. 15). Smith and Berg (1988) state that "in order to be a group, a collection of individuals must integrate the large array of individual differences that the members represent" (p. 90). Yet in this case, we see more indications of individualism than teamwork, more distrust than trust.

Action research intends to foster learning about one's self and one's environment. In this case, however, we actually see no evidence of learning. As the case is written, it appears that the team has done little besides decide to act on NVAW in the previous six months. Have team members, in fact, learned anything in the six months that they have been together? If they have, they could use this meeting as an opportunity to share their new knowledge with their manager. If they have not, then they need to acknowledge this and make a decision to disband or to reframe their approach.

In conclusion, this case offers many possibilities for action research interventions. Most notably, team members and the manager can increase their efforts at involvement and secure organizational sanction for their activities. The members might be more specific in their goal definition and ensure that everyone "owns" the goal. After the team members begin doing these things to improve their group, they can return their attention to improving their organizational environment— selecting a problem, collecting data, studying the data, experimenting, providing feedback, implementing changes, and continuing this cycle until they have accomplished their project. The case well illustrates the interdependence of group or involvement strategies with the improvement aims of action research.

CONCLUSION

Lewin's approach to action research, the classical model, conceived of a process whereby we would attain deeper and deeper understanding of a phenomenon through cycles of fact-finding or research and of taking action to implement what was learned in the research. Taking action is itself an experimental treatment on an organization or a community and can be studied to see whether or not the system or problem is transformed. Each of the variants discussed in this special issue has its roots in this Lewinian model. Participatory research has embraced the social change theme that underlies much of Lewin's work. Action learning focuses on transformation through individual and collective reframing of the problem—what Lewin called *reconceptualization*. Action science looks deeply into individual actions for their reflection of the underlying social perspective—whether more authoritarian or democratic in Lewin's terms—and through fact finding (Argyris's directly observable data) works to make explicit these tacit social perspectives and thereby to transform them (reconceptualization). Developmental action inquiry focuses on the readiness or developmental level of the individual or system to take action, to make a change. Collaborative inquiry emphasizes the power of asking questions and of collaboration. While these approaches no longer emphasize the hypothesis testing in the positivist tradition found in Lewin's work, there is nevertheless a thread that connects back to Lewin. Somehow we think he would have applauded the evolution and reinterpretation of his ideas evident in these pages.

CHAPTER EIGHT

Action Learning and Action Science

Are They Different?

Joseph A. Raelin

A number of epistemological technologies have evolved in the past fifty years bearing the term *action* as part of their reference label. Although not always credited, Kurt Lewin is this author's nomination as the founder of these so-called action technologies, in that they seem to have their genesis in his reference to action research as a means of conducting systematic inquiry into group phenomena.

The common basis for most of these technologies is that knowledge is to be produced in service of action. As opposed to "positivist" models that were designed to develop theories purposely separated from practice in order to predict truth, action research applied theory directly in the field, with scholars and practitioners collaborating. This approach acknowledged rather than rejected the role of personal feelings within the research context. Both theorists and practitioners would open themselves to inquiry as they sought to "unfreeze" the assumptions underlying their actions.

Evolving from action research are two of the most popular action technologies or strategies in use today, action learning and action science. Action learning, most practiced in Europe and first associated with the work of Reg Revans, is based on the straightforward pedagogical notion that people learn most effectively when working on real-time problems occurring in their own work setting. Action science, most practiced in the United States and associated with the work of Chris Argyris, is an intervention method based on the idea that people can improve their interpersonal and organizational effectiveness by exploring the hidden beliefs that drive their actions.

The purpose of this chapter is to distinguish these two technologies in a way that will assist those organization development practitioners who may serve as facilitators in both. Readers who are unfamiliar with either technology may consult the following descriptions of actional learning and action science. After reviewing their foundational similarities, we will consider the principal differences between the two methods and address some of the advantages and risks associated with each. Readers who serve as facilitators might wish to reflect on their intervention styles to determine if they have leanings toward one technology over the other. If they are capable of using both, they are invited to consider whether they should be using them sequentially or simultaneously.

WHAT IS ACTION LEARNING?

Action learning describes a developmental approach, used in a group setting but affecting the individual and organizational levels of experience, that seeks to apply and generate theory from real (not simulated) work situations. In Reg Revans's original conceptualization, learning results from the independent contributions of programmed instruction (designated P) and spontaneous questioning (designated Q); P constitutes information and skill derived from material already formulated, digested, and presented, typically through coursework, and Q is knowledge and skill gained by apposite questioning, investigation, and experimentation.

For Revans, Q was the component that produces most behavioral change since it results from interpretations of experience and knowledge accessible to the learner. These interpretations are bolstered by feedback from mutual learners who participate in a debriefing of the learner's workplace experiences. Hence, actions taken are subject to inquiry about their effectiveness, including a review of how one's theories were applied to practice. Participants learn as they work by taking time to reflect with peers who offer insights into their workplace problems.

In a typical action learning program, a series of presentations constituting programmed instruction might be given on a designated theory or theoretical topic. In conjunction with these presentations, students might be asked to apply their prior and new knowledge to a real project that is sanctioned by organizational sponsors and that has potential value, not only to the participant but also to the organizational unit to which the project is attached. Throughout the program, students continue to work on the projects with assistance from other participants as well as from qualified facilitators or advisers who help them make sense of their project experiences in light of relevant theory.

This feedback feature principally occurs in learning teams or "sets" typically composed of five to seven participants. During the learning team sessions, the students discuss not only the practical dilemmas arising from actions in their work settings, but also the application or misapplication of concepts and theories to these actions. Further, the group develops a social culture in its own right, which presents participants with lessons regarding group dynamics. Team members also provide encouragement to one another.

Not all organizational problems are solved or are even meant to be solved in action learning. Rather, the experience is designed to confront learners with the constraints of organizational realities, leading oftentimes to the discovery of alternative and creative means to accomplish their objectives.

WHAT IS ACTION SCIENCE?

Action science is an intervention approach, also aimed at the individual, team, and organizational levels of experience, for helping learners increase their effectiveness in social situations through heightened awareness of the assumptions behind their actions and interactions. Individuals' mental models—the images, assumptions, and stories of themselves and of others—are often untested and unexamined and, consequently, often erroneous. Action science brings these mental models into consciousness in such a way that new, more serviceable models can be formed. Action science thus calls for the deliberate questioning of existing perspectives and interpretations, a process referred to as *double-loop* learning. When a mismatch occurs between our values and our actions, most of us attempt to narrow the gap by trial-and-error learning. We also prefer to maintain a sense of control over the situation, over ourselves, and over others. In double-loop learning, we subject even our governing values to critical reflection, creating free and informed choice, valid information, and high internal commitment to any new behavior attempted.

Action scientists refer to the set of understandings with which we group the world as an "action model." In many organizational situations involving interpersonal interaction, especially those involving threat or embarrassment, we may automatically invoke a so-called Model I program. This program allows us to save face, avoid upset, and maintain control. Since this kind of reaction often produces self-reinforcing patterns that seal off self-discovery, action science facilitators work with participants to engage in Model II responses. These responses allow for the exploration of interpersonal differences and mutual responsibility.

Donald Schön prefers the term *reflection-in-action* to characterize the rethinking process in which someone attempts to discover how what he or she did contributed to an unexpected or expected outcome. In order to engage in reflection-in-action, participants might start by describing a situation and then, upon reflection, provide a frame that characterizes not only their intentions but also explains the inferences they draw from others' responses. Then, they might inquire as to how others in the group see it. Group members might reflect on these frames, offer feedback, and subsequently begin to surface and test their own underlying assumptions and respective reasoning processes.

The aim is to narrow inconsistencies between one's espoused theories and one's theories-in-use. Espoused theories are those characterizing what we say we will do. Theories-in-use describe how we "actually" behave. The goal of action science is to uncover our theories-in-use and, in particular, to distinguish between those that inhibit and those which promote learning.

———

The material that follows reviews these and other issues, drawing on transcriptions from actual facilitator interventions (either mine or those published by others) to illustrate the concepts in use. My hope is that by being more aware of the distinctions in action technologies, OD facilitators will be better able to illustrate the respective methods for participants and forecast their likely effects.

ARE THEY DIFFERENT?

Experienced facilitators tend to acknowledge a fair amount of similarity between action learning and action science. In both action technologies, the "work" within the group tends to focus on one individual at a time, yet the ultimate aim is improvement of interpersonal and organizational behavioral processes. Both emphasize the use of knowledge in service of action. Both are designed to be participatory and even collaborative. Each employs an experimental (as opposed to preset) methodology, predominantly conducted in a group setting. Each encourages the presence of a skilled facilitator who helps the group make use of actual situations, as opposed to simulated experiences.

There is also considerable focus on reeducation and reflection. This means that the participants, normally adult practitioners, seek to improve themselves, especially in regard to their human interactions and practices. They accomplish this primarily through critical self-reflection, which by raising consciousness tends to permit more control over one's actions.

Behind these similarities, which are also to some extent generic to action research, lie some significant differences, especially at the level of implementation. Hence, for someone who assumes a facilitation role, it becomes critical to know where, for example, action learning ends and action science begins.

We can begin to distinguish between the two technologies by applying a set of criteria formulated to analyze action research-type interventions. These criteria, in combination with real-world examples chosen to illustrate important qualitative differences in interaction style and process, will clarify the fundamental differences between the two.

Purpose

Although action learning and action science each seeks to benefit individuals by helping them become more effective in achieving useful action, especially in their organizations, action science goes deeper than action learning. It explicitly asks learners to examine the reasoning processes they use, based on the belief that a person can improve action only when his or her mental models become more explicit. As people in groups behave more consistently with their espoused beliefs and make their inferences known, the level of public discourse naturally improves. Action learning, on the other hand, does not require this level of depth. Although one's assumptions about action are typically examined, action learning is more concerned with behavioral change through public reflection on real work practices.

Consider an example. The vice president of a chain of retail outlets (lumber and hardware products) is concerned about low levels of commitment from the chain's part-time check-out clerks. He has undertaken a project aimed at determining why their motivation is lower than their full-time counterparts.

In an action learning set, the facilitator might start by having this executive, call him Joe, describe the project and anticipated intervention in clinical detail. In a fairly well-developed set, members may join in by probing the details and the assumptions underlying his plans and actions.

Let's say that Joe determines that the best way to obtain data from the part-time clerks would be through a series of focus groups made up of three or four clerks from each work shift. Someone in the group might challenge this methodology, pointing out that focus groups can be intimidating to part-timers and thus yield unreliable information. In this participant's view, Joe might be better off interviewing selected clerks individually or better yet, have someone else, with less status in the company, interview them.

Joe would then reflect on his intervention approach and decide whether to change his plans. Other questions from the facilitator might attempt to ascertain why Joe has chosen this project over others. Is it one that the company's president has a particular interest in, or is it a genuine concern of Joe's?

In some action learning sets, questions and responses of this nature might ensue for the entire duration of the meeting. Notice that the focus tends to be on one member alone, at least until time is allocated to another member or to the set as a whole. A lot of probing goes on, but it tends to focus on the member's plans and actions that typically take place or are about to take place in a separate work setting. When the focus shifts to the set itself, attention centers on how to make the group more effective as a learning vehicle for its membership. This might require learning how to apply active listening and offer feedback more effectively, how to check on one's assumptions about others, how to apply classroom theories in practice, and so on.

Now, contrast this with the dynamics that might occur in an action science group. Rather than spending a majority of time on Joe's plans and offering suggestions regarding useful interventions, the facilitator and group members will focus more directly on Joe and his organization. For example, the facilitator might start by asking Joe why this problem has been standing around looking for a solution. Joe might answer by saying it hasn't been a high priority and that management has assumed that the clerks' low motivation couldn't be helped. The facilitator might then ask Joe if he feels the same way as "management." Joe might answer that he has always been concerned but didn't feel that the president considered it a priority.

At this point, the facilitator might ask whether Joe, as a rule, disavows those issues with which he believes the president won't agree. Joe might explain that he carefully monitors what he says, as do others in management. No one, including himself, wants to be seen as contradictory.

In action science terms, Joe has not only offered an observation but also provided an initial inference regarding his perception of the behavior of others.

Although it might be possible to stop here, most action science facilitators would inquire whether Joe would like to pursue the issue further. Assuming he would, the facilitation could proceed using a number of different methods. For example, the facilitator might draw out Joe's inferences by asking what he assumes drives the president's behavior. The facilitator and group might also inquire what makes Joe and his colleagues so reluctant to bring up so-called contradictory issues with the president.

Another technique might be to have Joe write out a case in which he recounts a conversation with the president about a controversial issue. In the margin or on one side of the page adjoining the narrative, Joe would write down what he and the president were thinking when they responded in particular ways. A conceptual map might be drawn wherein Joe displays his action strategies using both Model I and Model II learning approaches. Joe might be invited to role-play a conversation with the president wherein he practices a Model II action strategy. Finally, an "on-line" conversation might be constructed whereby members of the group agree to role-play key figures in the scenario in order to demonstrate Joe's cognitive and behavioral responses. Whatever method is chosen, the ultimate purpose is to surface defensive or inhibiting behaviors blocking operating effectiveness.

Although both technologies seek to benefit the organization, action learning's impact is often more direct and short-term, as this example shows. Projects are undertaken that can have an immediate and projected residual impact on the sponsoring unit. Real problems also constitute the most appropriate data for analysis in action science. But it is only after a reasonable number of organizational members begin to operate under Model II assumptions that a sought-after cultural shift is likely to occur.

Finally, the example points out differences regarding the anticipated depth of change. Although both focus on interpersonal relationships (in this case, between Joe and his co-workers, particularly his boss), an action science intervention also intensifies the focus on Joe's intrapersonal cognitive awareness, namely, his perceptions about how he functions in given situations. Joe is also given the opportunity to examine the inferences behind his decisions to act or refrain from acting. Action learning does not require this level of cognitive awareness. The focus is more instrumental, that is, more concerned with perceptions about changing work behavior and work relationships.

Epistemology

Each of the two action technologies approaches the acquisition of knowledge in a distinct way. Action learning is concerned with making new ideas or recently acquired theories tacit by placing them into natural experience. It operates at a practical or rational level of discourse, seeking to make meaning from experience. It thus seeks to help participants enhance their sensitivity to the ways others perceive or react to them as well as how they, in turn, respond to others. With new information in hand, they *can* learn to change their communication patterns to become more effective in the workplace.

Action science, on the other hand, is concerned with making explicit or bringing into awareness individuals' theories-in-use. It operates at an emancipatory or reflective level of discourse, seeking to explore the very premises underlying the perceptions we formulate of our world. Hence, whereas action learning seeks to contextualize learning, action science decontextualizes practice so that participants can become more critical of their behavior and explore the premises of their beliefs.

Consider a case involving a participant in both an action learning and an action science group.

Dan is an upper level executive in a multinational firm headquartered in San Francisco. Although he is on a "fast track" to senior management, one flaw might derail his career: his tendency to "blow up" when others don't see things his way or when he perceives them as unsupportive. He presents an example of this to the group. Michelle, his boss, was planning to make a number of organizational changes that would affect his department. During the meeting in question, Dan accused Michelle of acting unfairly and irresponsibly. Michelle responded angrily and warned Dan not to talk to her in that way. The meeting escalated to a point of such emotional fury that it had to be terminated.

An action learning facilitator would encourage Dan to expound in detail about this scenario, testing out his assumptions about his and Michelle's behavior. With the support of the set, Dan might examine what he said that triggered such a strong emotional response by Michelle. Set members might exemplify how he broke the canons of healthy two-way communication by, for example, using accusations rather than descriptive statements. At this point, the focus would be on clarifying what happened through apposite questioning as a means of tracing the causes of the emotional outburst.

Once Dan understands what happened, the facilitator and set might consider ways to overcome this unfortunate sequence of events. Moreover, Dan might learn to improve the quality of his interactions with others who, like Michelle, might occasionally trigger an uncontrolled emotional response. The set would continue to propose ideas and use questioning to elicit recommendations from Dan himself.

Finally, a set adviser might ask Dan to role play a subsequent conversation with Michelle (or some other colleague). The person playing Michelle would be thoroughly prompted regarding her behavioral style. Dan would try to incorporate any suggestions from the set and would receive ongoing feedback about his revised communication style.

Action science intervention tends to require more direct facilitator intervention. For example, Chris Argyris, in working through an actual case from which this example was drawn (from his book *Reasoning, Learning and Action*), asked Dan to illustrate what made Michelle angry. He explained that he consciously or subconsciously challenged her and told her that she did not back him up. He went on to say that he had never criticized her that way before because they had developed a norm in their relationship of not criticizing one another. "She knows that I am very sensitive and I know that she is also very sensitive when it comes to feelings about her supportive role with subordinates."

At this point, Dan has acknowledged an espoused theory, namely, that he should not have been criticizing Michelle. However, he is unaware of his theory-in-use, which is, in effect, that when attacked, he responds in kind. Argyris used the following intervention:

> I can understand how you could resent her accusations as the conversation escalated. On the one hand, she was telling you not to attack her. On the other hand, she was, in your view, attacking and putting you down. So the first thing that hit me was that each of you is doing to the other what neither of you wants the other to do to you. Does it make sense to you that you are behaving in the same way?

As this case demonstrates (and this is a minor portion of the complete case, which goes on for twenty-nine pages), the facilitator in action science attempts to help the learner elicit the deepest defensive reactions that he or she brings either into the group or into workplace interactions. In this case, Dan is led to understand the preconceived inferences he draws from others' behavior and how his responses can lead to an escalation of error.

As in action learning, the facilitator also helps Dan design more constructive communication, but does so by probing his theory-in-use. He or she would help Dan recognize his deep defenses and learn to diagnose and implement his own actions with more insight. Finally, a session might be devoted to methods of uncovering the assumptions underlying behavior in Michelle's group. This could lead to an analysis of the defensive routines that reinforce ineffective exchanges (e.g., no one criticizes anyone else around here).

At the point of intervention, facilitators need to acknowledge whether they plan to engage in a practical or an emancipatory level of discourse. The practical level solicits inquiry regarding how others see someone who has been or is currently engaged in action. By using emancipatory discourse, action science takes the intervention into another, perhaps sequential, level. It becomes permissible to challenge not only the actor's theories-in-use but the questioner's perceptions and inferences to the point of challenging the entire system's assumptive frame of reference.

For many participants and even for the system under scrutiny, action science intervention can be threatening, as it has the potential to cause an entire reframing of the practice world. Even participants in responsible positions may not have sufficient authority or independence of action to challenge their cultures at the level of exposure sanctioned by action science.

Ideology

Although both approaches are committed to the expansion of participants' self-awareness, they use processes arising from different ideological foci. Action learning insists that learning emanate from the set participants themselves as they wrestle with live but puzzling natural phenomena. It refutes the view that knowledge can be reduced to a single all-inclusive perspective. Rather, it not only accepts but encourages contributions from different and contradictory points of view. The basis for inquiry can be expert advice or folk wisdom arising from a community of practice. However, the ultimate aim is to help members discover solutions to their own problems.

An example of this form of inquiry comes from Judy O'Neil, an action learning practitioner, who reported how, in a set she was observing, a set member (rather than the facilitator) suggested a strategy known as "stop and reflect." During stop and reflect periods, participants stop and take time to gather their thoughts—often in writing—and then publicly let others in the set know what they're thinking. In this particular set, the member introduced this technique when two other members simply could not agree on an intervention strategy. One of the members recalled what happened:

> Stop and reflect . . . [was] sort of mind shattering. We were going through a number of discussions where we were really at odds, that we just couldn't see each others' points of view. We finally did stop, and we wrote each thing down . . . And when we wrote it down, [the two points of view] were almost identical. By taking that little bit of time to actually understand the other person's viewpoint, we took a giant leap to where we were going.

Action science, in contrast, is committed to a particular kind of self-awareness, in particular, Model II double-loop learning. Accordingly, participants take personal responsibility to ensure that valid information is presented such that they and others in the group can make free and informed choices. Working toward win-win rather than win-lose solutions, participants operate under the criterion of justice to ensure a fair and mutual examination of personal data including feelings, assumptions, and inferences.

The different ideological foci expose participants to contrasting experiences. Action learning keeps the focus on project work under the assumption that the skills applied will generalize to other situations. Participants look to improve their effectiveness in their current work settings. Action science participants may be asked to create here-and-now, on-line scenarios to help them work through blockages arising from contrasts between their reasoning and their actions.

It is typically more comfortable to begin a team intervention using action learning, since its ideology does not prescribe a particular line of inquiry. As long as queries from set members focus on a target member's assumptions and actions and are considerate and empathic as opposed to self-interested and opinionated, they are generally endorsed. At the same time, it is sometimes advisable to move from an action learning to an action science intervention. Consider an example.

In one group I facilitated, a member talked about her struggle to create a unified team culture in a staff group drawn from two different organizations that had recently merged. She recounted one constraint after another, and for each, the group responded with myriad suggestions for overcoming the problem. Some issues involved interpersonal matters between particular staff members, others were structural concerns related to the roles these team members were to assume in the newly constituted team.

The forty-five-minute exchange was lively and frank. Other than offering a paraphrase to help her clarify her response to a vice president's request about formulating a mission statement, I saw little need to intervene. She finished her time slot by saying how much she appreciated everyone's suggestions and that she "might even use some of them." This was followed by an awkward silence. Another team member interrupted the silence by offering to "go next." At this point I asked if everyone was ready to move on. All nodded in agreement.

Nevertheless, I decided to make an intervention of the type that is more associated with action science ideology. As the next member began, I interrupted and said:

> Excuse me, Paul. I'm sorry for interrupting, but I detect that there may be unfinished business left over from Jennifer's work. Would you or anyone else mind if I shared my concerns? [No one voiced a concern, so I went on.] I would like to propose a different kind of dialogue from the kind we've typically had. It will require us to look a little deeper into our defenses and how we choose to handle them when faced with an event characterized by deep emotion.

I went on to describe my inferences regarding the group's feelings: we all "felt" for Jennifer in her role in the new team, but we may also have felt our efforts to provide suggestions were somewhat rebuffed. I illustrated my inference by referring to her comment about "possibly" using some of them. I then asked what reactions members, including Jennifer, had to my comments.

When people began to concur that they were somewhat perturbed by her apparent callousness, I asked if the group wanted to dig deeper into our interaction patterns as a group. It was at this point that the group chose to make a transition from an instrumental action learning orientation to an ideology that values introspection of intrapersonal reasoning processes and resulting interpersonal patterns.

The implication of this case suggests that OD practitioners, when serving as facilitators, may need to clarify ahead of time whether they will be pursuing action learning or action science change. Participants need to know in advance whether anticipated changes will arise from frequent questioning of their action interventions, common in action learning, or from in-depth exploration of their reasoning processes, more typical of action science. Likewise, organizational sponsors need to know whether they'll get a completed project of significance in addition to prospectively more effective interventionists or an organizational culture in which there is far more consistency (even under stressful conditions) between what people say they will do and what in fact they do.

Methodology

The methods employed in action learning and action science are compatible in the sense that both use groups as the primary vehicle of participation and both focus on real problems. Further, although group development can be a secondary goal of the experience, both tend to focus on one individual at a time. Both also attend to real problems occurring in the participants' work settings, though less so in action science. What differentiates the two is what is being processed at any given moment as well as the content of the discussion.

Action learning focuses more on problems arising from the handling or mishandling of "there-and-then" on-the-job project interventions. For example, PepsiCo's "Building the Business" leadership program for senior executives sandwiches a three-month "growth project" between preparatory five-day and culminating three-day workshops. In the first workshop, participants hear from CEO Roger Enrico regarding his model of leadership and receive feedback on their leadership styles. At this time, they also develop action plans and visualize obstacles they'll need to overcome in implementing their projects. The projects are substantial: combating private label competitors, for example, or working out joint ventures.

In the follow-up workshop, participants review their progress, including successes and shortcomings. Throughout the dialogue, they evaluate the contribution of Enrico's model of leadership as well as the application of their own theories of action to their project. This program demonstrates that although action learning is concerned with current problems, the issues tend to be strategic rather than here-and-now concerns arising from ongoing interactions among members of the set. Interpersonal issues may well surface, but their elicitation is designed more to increase the communication effectiveness among set members than to probe individual members' mental models. When the action learning set is functioning effectively, feedback to individuals is open, direct, and unburdened by hidden agendas.

Although concerned with workplace problems, an action science process is just as likely to focus on here-and-now interactions occurring among members of the group. Where workplace problems are chosen, the group process is designed to not only improve the work activity but also to serve as a means to help participants initiate Model II action models. Facilitators are also inclined to create on-line experiments to help participants focus on their mental models. For example, they might elicit the attributions and evaluations the participants are making about themselves, about others in the group, or about the situation being depicted. The idea is to slow participants down so they can focus on the inferential steps taken in leaping from data to conclusions.

One familiar method is known as "lefthand column." A page is split into two columns. Participants use the right-hand column to depict an actual or contemplated conversation with a co-worker. On the left-hand side, they write what they thought or felt but did not say. For example, on the right side, a participant (call her Darlene) might respond to a co-worker's unexpected absence from an important meeting by writing:

> That's all right that you couldn't make it in yesterday. I know you had a bad cough and, as it turns out, I was able to finish the proposal on my own anyway.

On the left side, Darlene writes:

> I was furious at you! How could you let me down like that. Without your cost analysis, the proposal didn't have a prayer. Big deal that you had a cough. I can't tell you how many times I've come in with far worse.

After presenting her left-hand column to the group, Darlene might be invited to respond to a number of queries leading to some extensive reflection. For example, what prevented her from saying all or some of her feelings? What inferential leaps was she making from the data to which she had access? If she had more data, would she be drawing the same conclusions? Were her espoused beliefs consistent with her own actions? What action strategies could she have engaged in to produce more effective consequences?

Management

Both approaches require the presence of a skilled facilitator, but the skills used are different and in some instances might even be contradictory. In classic action learning, the facilitator's role is clearly more passive than in action science. Revans conceived of the role as that of a "mirror" to merely reflect conditions in the set in such a way that members could learn by themselves and from each other. Others have suggested that the role of facilitator be elevated to that of a critical contributor of the overlooked P (programmed instruction) or of theory. P's role is to inform spontaneous inquiry and offer alternative frames of problems.

Moreover, creative problem-solving devices, such as synectics, which introduces metaphor or analogy in an informal interchange, can be introduced to stimulate group and individual problem exploration. Many standard group process techniques are also available to advance the development of learning teams, resulting in improved efficiency and effectiveness.

The amount of direct intervention taken by action learning facilitators will vary depending on each facilitator's comfort level. The early proponents called for infinite patience in order to permit skills in insight and inquiry to develop. Naturally, some early modeling of active listening might be required. Facilitators, however, were not to forget that the ultimate aim was to make the learner the center of the experience.

One way to talk about facilitator differences is by referring to the level of inference used to diagnose and intervene in the respective technologies. Facilitators and group members need to make inferences, since decisions often have to be reached without all the information being known or expressed. In action learning, facilitators tend to be content working at a low level of inference. For example, if a group member named Jane talks about avoiding a co-worker because "he is discourteous," the facilitator might ask Jane to describe what this co-worker does that leads to the inference of discourteousness.

In this instance, an explanation is required since the team may need to (1) determine how closely Jane works with this individual, (2) identify what he does that implies discourteousness, and (3) assuming that the behavior is indeed discourteous, suggest how she can learn to either work around the coworker or confront him to change the behavior. The inference in this case is considered to be low level, since a relatively small amount of information is needed to clarify the behavior in question.

Higher level inferences tend to concern such issues as trust, power, and defensiveness.

Action science facilitators, when given permission by members, will often probe into members' defensive behavior. For instance, a salesperson named Jay complained that his two colleagues broke a trust built on a "one for all" mentality that they had long agreed on. When encouraged to explain what they did, he alleged that they were planning to "ace him out of a commission" on a joint endeavor. However, he admitted that he had no real evidence of this presumed plot.

By engaging in an on-line simulation with some fellow team members who volunteered to play the part of his colleagues. Jay was able to work through his own fears of losing control in this three-way arrangement. He was able to analyze his fear of a loss of trust as his own defensive behavior arising from feelings of vulnerability whenever he had to work closely with others.

Although action science facilitators would subscribe to the action learning precept that the group eventually assume management of the experience, action science skills require considerable practice and development. It is difficult to learn how to surface inconsistencies between a participant's governing values and action strategies. Besides modeling, the facilitator needs to spend time actually teaching and demonstrating Model II learning skills. In working through individual and interpersonal problems, learners may have to reveal their defenses, placing themselves in a personally vulnerable position.

Facilitators thus need to be not only adequately trained but also active in helping the group member or members surface and deal with their feelings. Eventually, as the group gains confidence in using action science skills, learners can serve as cofacilitators and even begin to challenge the facilitator's action strategies. At this point, the facilitator and the membership can transform themselves into a collaborative learning community.

Risk

No group experience is without some threat to individual members, but action science potentially subjects participants to more personal threat than normally occurs in action learning sets. Action science intervention is inevitably psychological since it often explores innermost feelings and emotional reactions, some of which are protected by sophisticated personal defenses. As these defense mechanisms break down, members may feel vulnerable and exposed. Of course, they work through problems in the presence of a sensitive and well-trained facilitator and caring group members. Moreover, the action science session is not therapeutic, in that it aims at changes in work-based and interpersonal behavior rather than personality adjustment.

Action science participants often talk about the difficulty of leaving their group and having to face "the real world," both between sessions and after the training is over. They long for an organizational culture that appreciates their hard work and endorses double-loop learning as an organizational standard. It is unfortunately rare to find corporate management that collectively commits not only to acquiring and storing new knowledge but also to interpreting it in a way that reveals organizational patterns, processes, and defensive routines. Only in organizations with such management can the risk of action science be considered worthwhile in light of the potential learning afforded the organization.

Although it took five years of personal and interpersonal trial and development, the directorship of Monitor Co., a 350-person consulting firm, seems to have produced a predominant Model II learning pattern, according to their consultant, Chris Argyris. Their meeting transcripts, for example, illustrate significant reductions in the number of untested or undiscussable inferences and attributions that the directors make of each other. There is more encouragement of double-loop learning and inquiry, not only at the director level, but among staff consultants and even, in some cases, with clients.

Action learning subjects its participants to a different level of risk, which can again be characterized as instrumental. Normally, set members are working on a project in conjunction with learning team meetings. Although they are well-advised throughout the process, they may end up working on a project that they cannot bring to a successful conclusion. In some instances, a project may fail due to circumstances beyond a member's control. In other instances, a participant may attempt a change that goes beyond the organization's coping capacity.

In either case, failure may imply incompetence, leading to possible career derailment. The personal risk described here can be overcome by organizational support that conceives of failure or suboptimal performance as an opportunity for organizational learning. Lack of management support, however, can seriously expose the participant.

In one project, a commercial sales representative for a utility undertook a project to expand the company's economic development activity. Unfortunately, in the middle of the project, his supervisor was transferred. The new supervisor had little interest in the project and withdrew financial support. The project was scrapped, leaving the participant both resentful about the company's commitment to change and anxious about his future career progression.

Assessment

As action research technologies, both action learning and action science subscribe to an assessment that values participant learning as an ultimate goal. Both also have a secondary objective of changing the participants' organizational systems through more effective action by these same participants. Hence, both need to be evaluated against a meta-competency of learning to learn, such that the lessons of the training experience carry over to new and unique situations. As both technologies profess a learner-centered humanist philosophy, they also need to be evaluated against a standard of free consent.

A critical difference concerns the level of learning expected in each approach. Action learning primarily focuses on what Gregory Bateson terms *second-order learning*. In first-order learning, we move from using preexisting habitual responses (zero-order learning) to learning about them. In second-order, we learn about contexts sufficiently to challenge the standard meanings underlying our responses. Accordingly, action learning helps participants learn to challenge the assumptions and meanings they use in planning and undertaking their project interventions. As they perfect their reflective skills, they tend to develop confidence in transferring their learning outside the group context.

At Cable & Wireless PLC, a global telecommunications giant, a top leadership workshop features five-month projects undertaken by cross-business and cross-cultural teams. One project endeavored to improve customer value by coordinating account management activities around the world. Comparable projects have been undertaken at Grace Cocoa, which has been using a form of action learning called *action reflection learning* since 1993. The company's vice president of human resources credits action learning with helping managers become more proficient working across cultural boundaries, a key objective in a company that operates on five continents.

Although some action learning facilitators risk moving their sets into third-order learning, it is undoubtedly an important province of action science. Third-order learning brings the very premises of tacit theories in use into question. It is learning about the "context of contexts" so that participants can hold a virtual reflective conversation with their situations. In this way, action science reconceives our practice world to reveal the tacit processes that underlie our reasoning.

Action science intervention is more difficult to assess in that its effects can be measured only over the long run. Systemic change is likely to occur when a critical mass of organizational members begin to act in accordance with a Model II learning strategy. Action learning can bear nearly immediate results, at least in terms of finished and, in some instances, successful projects that can impact the organization's bottom line.

The participants' learning orientation is designed to be contagious. For example, a participant in one of our school's executive development programs designed as his action learning project a program to arrest the spread of an oral disease as part of his company's dental health program in less developed countries. His commitment to involve multiple stakeholders was so effective as to constitute an eventual framework for launching other strategic initiatives.

Throughout the planning process, however, little attention was paid to the possible negative consequences of using the company's charity as a public relations ploy. Such a probe might well have ensued, however, under action science effectiveness criteria, which would have sanctioned not only an examination of the project's underlying assumptions but also the very governing values of its genesis and operation.

CONCLUSION

To those practitioners interested in humanistically derived cognitive and behavioral change in organizations, there may not appear to be significant distinctions among the burgeoning action technologies in use today.

Nevertheless, at the point of implementation, these approaches may vary considerably in the impact they have on participants as well as on the organization or unit sponsoring the change. Hence, facilitators need to understand the philosophical assumptions underlying each approach. A number of significant distinctions between two of the more popular strategies have been drawn in this article and are summarized in Table 8.1.

Criteria	Action Learning	Action Science
Philosophical Basis	Humanism and action research	Humanism and action research
Purpose	Behavioral change through reflection on real practices	Behavioral change through articulation of reasoning processes and improved public disclosure
Time Frame of Change	Short and mid-term	Long-term
Depth of Change	Interpersonal and instrumental	Interpersonal and intrapersonal
Epistemology	Placing theories into tacit experience	Making explicit tacit theories-in-use
Nature of Discourse	Rational, making meaning from experience	Emancipatory, exploring the premises of beliefs
Ideology	Arising from intrinsic natural learning processes within the group	Subscribing to particularistic double-loop learning concerned with elicitation of mental models
Methodology	Processing of there-and-then problems occurring within one's own work setting	Processing of here-and-now reasoning or on-line interactions
Facilitator Role	Passive, functioning as mirror to expedite group processing	Active, demonstrating and orchestrating on-line Model II learning skills
Level of Inference	Low	High
Personal Risk	Political, peer dissatisfaction or career derailment resulting from poor project performance	Psychological, exposure of personal defenses and vulnerabilities
Organizational Risk	Moderate, needs top management and supervisory management support	Heavy, requires all management levels to expose their assumptions
Assessment	Project effectiveness, systemic change	Managerial effectiveness, systemic change
Learning Level	Second-order, challenging assumptions underlying practice interventions	Third-order, challenging premises underlying theories-in-use and underlying management's governing values

Table 8.1. Action Technology Criteria and Distinctions Between Action Learning and Action Science.

OD facilitators need to understand these distinctions so that they can forecast and illustrate respective methods and likely effects. Those who may be experienced in both approaches also need to know whether and how to shift gears in the midst of an intervention as they lead a group into transition, say from action learning to action science. As OD intervention strategies become more specialized, practitioners must become more skilled in their own theory and practice.

CHAPTER NINE

Toward a Theory of Positive Organizational Change

David L. Cooperrider
Leslie E. Sekerka

With increased focus on positive organizational scholarship, new ways of understanding the processes and dynamics of positive outcomes in organizations are rapidly emerging. The practice of organizational development and change is on the forefront of this shift in direction, moving from traditional change methods to approaches that feature appreciative inquiry. In the past, organizational interventions typically focused on error detection, gap analysis, and fixing problems. Today there are more applications that examine what contributes to the best of organizational life—as a starting point for change.

In this chapter, we discuss how appreciative inquiry, an organizational development and change process, contributes to positive organizational scholarship. We begin with a review of the technique's history and relate it to traditional practices. We then outline a theory that explains the understructure of appreciative inquiry, offering propositions to suggest how this process fosters positive organizational change. Drawing from work in the field, we use examples from religious, military, and corporate settings to create a model that describes our observations (Cooperrider, 2001).

THE FIELD OF ORGANIZATIONAL DEVELOPMENT AND CHANGE

Organizational development is an applied field, often focusing on organizational change. It took root in the 1960s and has grown continuously (Bennis, 1963; Chin & Benne, 2000). For the most part, the interventions in organizational development are problem-focused or deficit-based. They start with the question, " What is wrong?" It is assumed that a problem must be identified and then the appropriate intervention can be applied to "fix" the issue. In short, it is not exaggeration to say that most change efforts emerge from deficit-based inquiry.

Tracing the contours of this approach, scholars like Gergen (1997) and Weick (1984) have articulated some of the unintended consequences of deficit-based conversation, including how we limit ourselves by the way we frame and commonly make sense of the world. "It seems useful," writes Weick, "to consider the possibility that social problems seldom get solved, because people define these problems in ways that overwhelm their ability to do anything about them" (p. 40). Deficiency focus, root cause analysis, remedial action planning, machine metaphors, and intervention are all means designed to fix broken systems.

Management scholars also write about how to change organizations. Kotter, a leading expert in this area, writes about the essence of deficit-based change theory (1998). He advises executives to communicate negative information broadly and to even manufacture crisis: "when the urgency rate is not pumped up enough, the transformation process cannot succeed and the long-term future of the organization is put in jeopardy" (p. 5). Since deficit-based inquiry is so widely accepted, few people think to question this advice. While researchers have demonstrated the potential for increased organizational understanding when members focus on opportunity rather than threat (Jackson & Dutton, 1988), nevertheless, deficit inquiry continues to guide many in their quest for change. There is, however, an alternative way to think about change.

Appreciative Inquiry

Appreciative inquiry is a process of search and discovery designed to value, prize, and honor. It assumes that organizations are networks of relatedness and that these networks are "alive." The objective of appreciate inquiry is to touch the "positive core" of organizational life.

This core is accessed by asking positive questions. Humans have a tendency to evolve in the direction of questions that are asked most often. Appreciative inquiry operates from the premise that asking positive questions draws out the human spirit in organizations. In a self-organizing way, the organization begins to construct a more desirable future. This is a key objective of the technique. It is accomplished by bringing forth the positive change core of the organization, making it explicit and allowing it to be owned by all. It tends to follow a four-step process.

STEP 1: DISCOVERY. The assumption is that human systems are drawn in the direction of their deepest and most frequent explorations. The discovery phase, designed around an interview process, is a systematic inquiry into the positive capacity of the organization. Interestingly, the interviews are not conducted by outside consultants looking to define problems, but by members of the organization. This often occurs with a majority of the membership and stakeholders participating. In other words, there is a systemwide analysis of the positive core by its members. The argument is that as people throughout the organization become increasingly aware of the positive core, appreciation escalates, hope grows, and community expands.

STEP 2: DREAM. Appreciation becomes a form of power that attracts people into a transformational state. As they come together, they are asked to share their findings. As they describe the actual, the potentials—or possibilities—invariably emerge in the dialogue. Positive feedback loops begin to occur, and a dream begins to form. It is usually stated in terms of three elements: a vision of a better world, a powerful purpose, and a compelling statement of strategic intent. As Quinn describes it, "people are beginning to envision a productive community—deeply connected people who tightly hold a passionate purpose" (2000).

STEP 3: DESIGN. Once the dream is in place, attentions are directed toward how we would ideally redesign the organization to fully realize the dream. In normal change processes people tend to greatly resist any redesign. When they share a vivid dream of the potential of their organization, they are far more likely to cooperate in designing a system that might make that dream a reality. In fact, Cooperrider and his colleagues assert that in their experience, every time an organization has been able to articulate a dream, it has been immediately driven to create a design for that dream.

STEP 4: DESTINY. In the initial work on appreciative inquiry, the fourth step was called "delivery," and it emphasized typical notions of planning and implementation. Over the years, experienced practitioners in the technique realized that the process is really about the transformation of existing paradigms. As their cognitive and conversational scripts change, people discover that how they interpret the world makes a difference. They see that they actually do create the world in which they live! So instead of emphasizing planning and implementation, appreciative inquiry practitioners now emphasize giving the process away. Give it to everyone, and then *step back*. This sounds like a recipe for chaos. It is instead a recipe for self-organization and the emergence of the transformational process.

> Appreciative inquiry accelerates the nonlinear interaction of organization breakthroughs, putting them together with historic, positive traditions and strengths to create a "convergence zone" facilitating the collective re-patterning of human systems. At some point, apparently minor positive discoveries connect in accelerating manner and quantum change, a jump from one state to the next that cannot be achieved through incremental change alone, becomes possible. What is needed, as the "Destiny Phase" of AI (appreciative inquiry) suggests, are the network-like structures that liberate not only the daily search into qualities and elements of an organization's positive core but the establishment of a convergence zone for people to empower one another— to connect, cooperate, and co-create. Changes never thought possible are suddenly and democratically mobilized when people constructively appropriate the power of the positive core and . . . let go of accounts of the negative. (Cooperrider & Whitney, 1999, p. 18)

Appreciative inquiry is credited with having a revolutionary impact on organizational development (Quinn, 2000, p. 220). Ironically, the technique was never meant to revolutionize anything in the area of intervention practice. Instead, Cooperrider and his colleagues were searching for ways to enlarge the generative potential of grounded theory. It was first used in one of the world's leading hospitals, where the idea was to build a theory of the emergence of the egalitarian organization. That is, logic that seeks to create and maintain organizational arrangements that heighten ideal situations for all members in a given organization (Srivastva & Cooperrider, 1998).

The enactment of the study itself, however, created one change after another. Those engaged in the process began to realize what now seems obvious: inquiry itself can be an intervention. Inquiry *is* agenda setting, language shaping, affect creating, and knowledge generating. Inquiry is embedded in everything we do as managers, leaders, and agents of change. Because of the omnipresence of inquiry, we are often unaware of its presence. Nevertheless, we live in the worlds our inquiries create. These experiences suggested that the best intervention might be to simply be an inquirer, seeking to understand organizational life and to create a spirit of inquiry that invites others to collaboratively do the same. Inquiry itself *intervenes.*

Moments of Change

Appreciative inquiry has helped foster positive change in a range of unlikely situations. With observations from the field, we create a theory to describe the process of how relating emerges in a way that seems to help participants generate energy, life, and creativity. We believe there is a human desire to gain a deeper understanding of one another's strengths. Our experience demonstrated that when individuals explore the best of humanity, it draws them to seek further inquiry. To set the stage for presenting the underlying theory, let us consider the process in action.

Early in the 1990s on his first visit to Jerusalem, His Holiness the Dalai Lama proposed that if the leadership of the world's religions could get to know one another, the world would be a better place. To forward this goal, a series of planning meetings were convened where religious leaders with representatives from Buddhist, Christian, Hindu, Jewish, Muslim, and other spiritual traditions came together. The hope was to create a home for conversation between the world's religious leaders—a secure, private, small, and relatively unstructured forum where leaders could talk with one another, know one another in mutually respectful ways, and reflect on challenging world issues without binding any institution to another. Appreciative inquiry was selected as the method used to conduct the meetings and was later credited with creating many favorable outcomes (Cooperrider, 2000).

Following the above described "4-D cycle" (that is, discovery, dream, design, and destiny), the first session began with dyads randomly formed across religious lines. Picture a Greek Orthodox priest in an appreciative interview with a Muslim imam, or a sage from Hindu background with a rabbi. Within an hour, participants were working together to explore each other's experiences in shared dialogue. To foster the conversation, participants were asked:

> One could say a key task in life is to discover and define our life purpose, and then accomplish it to the best of our ability. Can you share a story of a moment or a period of time where clarity about life purpose emerged for you—for example, a time where you heard your calling, where there was an important awakening or teaching, where you felt the touch of the sacred, or where you received some guiding vision? Now, beyond this story, what do you sense you are supposed to do before your life, this life, is over? (Unpublished interview protocol, Cooperrider, 2000)

After the interviews, participants introduced their partners to the larger group using conversational discoveries about their strengths, personal meanings, and visions of a better world. During this process, the interpersonal chemistry in this interaction was spontaneous; the positive emotions of excitement were palpable. Despite the short-term nature of the meeting, its impact proved to be far-reaching. The vision generated by this group was for a global United Nations–like organization to sustain an enduring dialogue between people of all faiths. The hope was to end religious violence in the world and to bring the strengths of wisdom traditions to bear on our common global agendas for change. In their logic for such an entity, they quoted theologian Hans Kung, who said, "There will be no peace among nations until there is peace among religions, and there will be no peace among religions until there is dialogue" (1996). The appreciative conversations fostered by this inquiry led to the creation of a UN-like body among the world's religions, a global organization called the United Religions Initiative. A charter to instill this organization was signed at Carnegie Music Hall in June 2000, and to date there are over 100 centers located worldwide.

Beyond the small conversational setting, appreciative inquiry can also be deployed in a summit forum using a whole-scale methodology. Here, a systems approach is undertaken, bringing all of the organizational stakeholders together to conduct the inquiry. Groups of 100 to 2,000 people have gathered to advance appreciative inquiry initiatives in medical centers, universities, communities, educational systems, and companies in a variety of industries (Whitney & Cooperrider, 2000). For example, the U.S. Navy recently held several summits where the chief naval officer and hundreds of seamen, admirals, and individuals from all levels and functions of the system were engaged.

Full participation inspires the breakdown of communication barriers and becomes a process that engenders the full voice of the organization from every level. At Roadway Express, for example, dockworkers, senior executives, customers, truck drivers, teamsters, and other representatives of the system met in a series of summits across the country. Results from their Akron, Ohio, terminal produced an abundance of transformational innovations including immediate cost-saving ideas and new visions for their shared future. The stories of cooperation, trust, and breakthrough thinking shared at their summits became "news" that reverberated across their 25,000 employee system. This ignited a program called "leadership as storytelling," creating a learning culture that now calls for the spread of innovation and good news narratives on a sustained basis, throughout the company.

The process of inquiring appreciatively seeks to build union between people as they talk about past and present capacities. The focus is on achievements, assets, potentials, innovations, strengths, elevated thoughts, opportunities, benchmarks, high-point moments, lived values, traditions, strategic competencies, memorable stories, and expressions of wisdom. In sharing these appreciative reflections, members are led to insights into the corporate spirit and visions of valued and possible futures. Taking the positives into a gestalt, appreciative inquiry operates from the system's core, with the assumption that everyone has untapped inspiring accounts of the positive.

When the energy of people's collective relationship is linked to their positive core, it is possible to connect this awareness to any change agenda, and positive change is then suddenly and more democratically mobilized. What's more, these changes are often beyond what was thought possible. Conspicuously absent from this process are the vocabularies of deficit-based change (for example, gap analysis, root causes of failure, unfreezing, defensive routines, variances, diagnosis, resistance, and flaming platforms). Yet there is change! We ask: How can the power of nondeficit positive change in organizations be explained? How is valued change experienced and realized? To address these questions, we propose that a new theoretical framework is required.

A THEORY OF POSITIVE
ORGANIZATIONAL CHANGE

Our process begins with an assumption that organizations are centers of human relatedness. The model of positive organizational change involves three stages, moving from elevation of inquiry, to fusion of strengths, to activation of energy. Each stage is triggered by increases of inquiry into the appreciable world and the expansion of relatedness to others (see Figure 9.1). Organizations move through these stages in vivid form and in a wide range of diverse settings.

As in theories of group development, general stages in the process of positive change are discernable. There are movements toward inclusion and intimacy, as well as changes in affect, language, and awareness. New patterns of communicating and relating emerge, which appear to eclipse and dissipate prior means. As participants let go of the problem focus, there is room for positive conversation. This is especially notable when people collaboratively create a new vision, name their idea, and map out how it can come to fruition. Individual, group, and organizational strengths become stronger through heightened narrative and a buildup of group receptiveness through ritualizations.

As a result, both the organizational real and ideal become a part of lived experience. As individuals work together to look deeper into what they value most, an expansion of relatedness occurs. Our contention is that this experience generates positive emotions, which helps broaden and build resources needed to motivate, create, overcome adversity, and transform. Here Fredrickson's "broaden-and-build" theory (1998) is used as a framework, taking it from the individual to organizational level of analysis and highlighting new dimensions of elevation and extension. A choiceful act of inquiring appreciatively is elevated by positive emotion, coupled with the use and development of positive language and the creation of valued images of the future. Taken together, these components set the process of positive organizational change into motion. As depicted by the horizontal axis in our model, this process simultaneously works to extend positive relating between organizational members.

Organizations reflect our deepest assumptions about humanity. As such, our view is that they are living centers, alive with the capacity to create connections. Given this postulation, organizational development is a process where living human systems extend, differentiate,

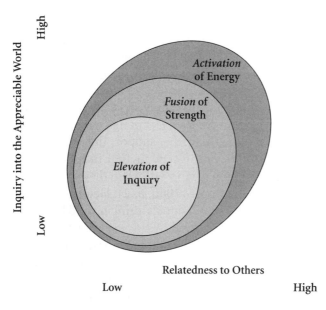

Figure 9.1.   A Model of Positive Organizational Change.

and create mutually enriching relationships, creating alignments of strength from the local level, expanding to the whole. The more extended these intimacies grow, through sharing and amplifications of strengths, virtues, resources, and creative capacities, the more developed the organizing becomes. As Wright suggests with his research on non-zero-sum approaches, the benefits are revealed as individuals move to accept the whole as a part of oneself (2001). We contend that as members engage in this process, they become aware of larger webs of relatedness.

Elevating Inquiry

When individuals reflect on a time when they were valued or appreciated, they experience a variety of positive emotions. Prior research links positive affect with broader thinking (Isen, Daubman, & Nowicki, 1987) and associates positive emotions with improved psychological health (Fredrickson, 2000, 2001). For instance, coping strategies related to the occurrence and maintenance of positive emotions (such as, positive reappraisal or infusing ordinary events with positive meaning) serve to help buffer against stress (Folkman & Moskowitz, 2000). These types of strategies help individuals handle crises with effective coping, sustain closer relationships, and hold a richer appreciation for life—all of which predict increased psychological well-being (Fredrickson, Mancuso, Branigan, & Tugade, 2000; Tugade & Fredrickson, 2004).

Given these findings, inquiry into the appreciable world is a vehicle for creating and developing positive change, not just within the present moment, but also over time. To further support this idea, Haidt's research on experiences of elevation reports that individuals are "surprised, stunned, and emotionally moved" when they see or experience unexpected acts of goodness (2000, p. 2). He suggests that witnessing good deeds influences individuals' thinking and behavior. The admiration and affection triggered by this experience seem to make affiliative behavior more likely, beyond the momentary experience. This helps to explain what occurs when members reflect on the goodness of organizational life—that a similar relational and prosocial orientation is produced by appreciation. If elevation is associated with future positive action, it holds great potential to favorably impact organizational communities. Interestingly, this emotion also appears to increase the likelihood that a witness to good deeds will be moved to enact good deeds (Haidt, 2000). Our prediction is that organizational elevation is petitioned by appreciative inquiry and contributes to an upward positive emotional spiral for the organization, as similarly described for individuals (Fredrickson, 2000).

We propose that inquiry into the positive, naturally occurring or deliberate, is a source of positive change as it elevates and extends the best of what is present in the organizational system. The foundation of positive change rests on elevation of inquiry into our strengths. Our theory suggests that inquiry and change are a simultaneous event, for the seeds of change are implicit in our questions. Our proposition is that human systems move in the direction of the questions they create, ask, and address in collaboration. More specifically:

> Human systems grow in the direction of what they persistently ask questions about. This propensity is strongest and most sustainable when the means and ends of inquiry are positively correlated. The single most prolific thing a group or organization can do, if its aims are to liberate the human spirit and consciously construct a better future, is to make the positive core the common and explicit property of all.

THE STAGES OF POSITIVE ORGANIZATIONAL CHANGE

Elevation of Inquiry

Both the vertical axis and first stage of the model are inquiry into the positive. As individuals come together, there is ever-widening capacity commensurate with how the world is viewed. As described earlier, when viewing both self and other in an appreciative light, relationships are generated based upon shared discovery. This leads individuals to work together to seek out the best in the entire system. As with experiences of elevation (Haidt, 2000), life-generating potentials emerge as organizational members share awareness of commonalities, beauty, and virtue found outside the self. In organizational research, leading thinkers such as Cameron (2002) and Khandwalla (1998) have proposed dimensions that depict organizational greatness. For our purposes, what is most relevant is that conceptions of elevated states are locally emergent through elevated inquiry, where the good, better, or possible are explored in and through an expanding web of relatedness. In practice, this elevated form of inquiry, in a socially constructive sense, replaces absolutist claims or the final word. It is an ongoing collaborative quest to understand and construct options for better living (Gergen, 1997). When exchanging stories of change, hope, courage, compassion, strengths, and creativity, organizational members are observed to experience mutual appreciation and surprise, as well as an eclipse of self-focusedness. As a result, an unexpected bonding between individuals often emerges.

Relatedness to Others

The horizontal axis of our model is "relatedness to others." The most powerful starting point for positive change involves a significant extension of organizational connectivity whereby the accessible strengths, opportunities, and potentials for development are multiplied from the local to the whole. This extension involves the creation of a field of relations across familiar contexts. Like a series of interconnected and expanding webs, it moves from the micro-system (face-to-face interpersonal) to the mesosystem (a cluster of microsystems involving two or more organizations) to the macrosystem (societies, cultures, and global connections). In ideal form, these relations, from the local to the whole, move in the direction of non-zero-sum dynamics (Wright, 2001).

Within the three-part series of these stages, there is an initial burst of elevation and extension in the first stage. Beginning with appreciative inquiry at a micro level, a positive dialogue of understanding evolves. As with the initial meeting with the interreligious group, when the process commences with positive-based questions, narratives of hope and strength lend to the depiction of human strengths and virtues. Participants in the inquiry begin to name and honor one another's uniqueness and specialties, which generates a process of language development and continued sharing. As a reservoir of stories and knowledge of specialties increases, our theory suggests that individuals experience specific positive emotions such as: admiration and appreciation; interest, curiosity, and surprise; and humility. In group dynamic terms, the inquiry magnifies the specialties of each (an in-depth valuing of diversities and multiplicities) and establishes a climate of safety and rich inclusion and respect.

Fusion of Strengths

With the initial phase of questioning, inquiry into the appreciable world and relatedness to others are elevated and extended. Organizational members seem to share a newfound mutual access to a world of strengths. However, our theory of nondeficit positive change must answer challenging questions such as, "What about our problems? If we ignore what is wrong in our organization, it merely postpones addressing the issue." Others may ask, "If dissatisfaction is not aroused and the tension not high enough, if we do not perform a diagnosis, how can we expect significant and lasting change to occur?" Our answer to these questions is to pose one of our own: Could it be that positive human experiences are not only indicators of well-being, but also generative sources of change?

Current research theorizes that positive emotions have the capability to alter the harmful impacts from negative emotions because they "broaden people's momentary thought–action repertoires *in a manner that is incompatible with the continuance of negative emotion*" (Fredrickson, 2000, emphasis added). Just like turning on a light in a room is incompatible with the darkness, the undoing capacity of emotions like contentment (incompatible with anger) and awe or surprise (incompatible with boredom) have broad transformational potential because a person's response cannot easily be simultaneously broad and narrow. It may be that building empathy between people and groups works to reduce prejudice, aggression, and violence because it taps into the broadening effects of appreciation and care, helping to create social bonds. Likewise, invoking amusement and laughter may work to de-escalate anger and interpersonal conflict as well as to combat stress and illness, tapping into the broadening effects of joy, which helps to build coping resources (Cousins, 1998). Could it be that finding ways to cultivate positive emotions will more quickly forge paths toward positive change and serve prominently as active ingredients in an upward spiral toward organizational well-being?

With this précis in mind, we are now positioned to better understand the movement of positive change from the first stage, the elevation of inquiry, to the second stage, a fusion of strengths. Returning once again to our scenario of the interreligious gathering, remember that their goal was to create a home for united conversation among all religions. In a span of four years, thousands of people shared a vision and worked together to create the United Religions. Working on all continents and across different cultures and faiths, those of differing spiritual traditions experienced unprecedented levels of cooperation in an inclusive, nonhierarchical, and decentralized organizational form. The participants characterized their experience through the distinct emotions of interest, awe, and curiosity and new relationships based upon a growing respect, openness, presence, and deep listening. Diverse stories of strength, achievement, and innovation were shared among conversations rich with language of life and creativity. Perhaps most salient was an honoring and proliferation of diversities, uniqueness, and specialties.

The relational energy obtained from the diversity of strengths in this group was enormous. Our theory proposes that participants' inquiry into the appreciable world leads to an elevation of inquiry, which contributes to an expansion of relatedness to others, that creates a fusion of strengths. Inquiry was pressed forward among the religious leaders by the experience of positive emotions, which helps individuals to draw on their combined strengths. As a result, the positive energy is much greater than what was available before participants began the process. In appreciative inquiry, movement within the technique (i.e., from discovery to dream) involves cultivating narrative-rich environments, reenactment of stories of human cosmogony, analysis of interdependent causes of success, relating to history as a positive possibility, metaphoric mapping or symbolizing of the system's positive core, and the enactment of visions of a valued future that people want to create. The aim is a fusion of strengths that connect organizational members to their shared positive core.

Exciting research opportunities exist as scholars work to understand the emergent capacities in groups and organizations, investiga-
tions that go beyond the individual level of analysis. For example,
it appears that there is an almost natural development moving
from appreciative awareness to an expanded cooperative awareness,
which emerges as a shared realization of collective empowerment.
Likewise, a new set of distinct emotions evolve with different action
tendencies, beyond what was experienced in the initial stage. Here,
emotional resources are viewed in a cooperative sense, where individuals become sources of contagious emotion, sharing and amplifying mutually felt inspiration, hope, and joy (Hatfield, Cacioppo, &
Rapson, 1994). These specific emotions appear to help move the
process forward, and are particularly predominant in the second stage.
Hope, for example, relates to the action tendency to join with others
and to create anew (Ludema, Wilmot, & Srivastva, 1997). Inspiration
is associated with the building of commitment and sense of purpose
(Kast, 1994). Joy connects with creativity, liberation, gratitude, and an
increasing propensity to serve (Fredrickson, 2000).

Activation of Energy

While many go through life accepting the status quo, arrangements or
presets as givens, and social structures as norms, elevation of inquiry
and a fusion of strengths persuades us otherwise. In this stage there is a
liberation of energy, once the relational construction of our world is
jointly owned. Through mutually experienced appreciation and story
sharing, there is an emergence of innovation, challenge, change, and
breakthrough. An intensification of the relational resources of imagination and mutual support is observable, and people begin to view
their world not as static constraint, but as mobilized energy.

As members experience the activation of group energy, they leave
their perceptions of constraint behind. For example, when representation from the entire organizational system of Roadway Express came
together to map their positive core, a process of creativity and innovation jettisoned forward. Ideas and bold discoveries emerged, in real
time with major immediate ramifications, such as their garage team
coming up with a million dollar annual cost-saving idea as a result of
their summit experience! In his analysis of creativity, Grudin (1990)
likens this activation beyond the status quo to abandonment and transcendence. He writes, "it is like leaving the world of effort and
abandoning oneself to an irresistible flow, like a canoeist drawn into

the main channel of a rapids, or a bodysurfer who catches a fine wave just below the crest" (p. 10).

To foster this surge of creative strength, we propose there is an experience that occurs between the appreciative reflection and the imagined future. It is here, in this synergistic moment of empowering continuity and novelty, that boldness emerges alongside of abandonment, and any sense of resistance evaporates. The result is a combination of courage and surrender, key elements in the study of creators (May, 1975). As scenarios in the fusion stage were marked by shifts in inspiration, hope, and joy, a shift is again fueled by the elicitation of specific positive emotions. In this phase, the process moves participants toward readiness for the task of creating.

Our contention is that these experiences contribute to courage, an acting from the heart and feeling of boldness which tells us to push forward when circumstances might otherwise frighten (Cavanagh & Moberg, 1999; Srivastva & Cooperrider, 1998). In addition, there is an abundance of excitement and enthusiasm, an energized force of interest, determination, and the desire to put one's passion into motion. During the activation of energy, there is a sense of affection and attraction that moves people to give beyond themselves, immerse themselves into the process, and join into caring relation with the world and others (Schneider & May, 1995).

Finally, there is a radical organizational restructuring from the entire process. From the elevation of inquiry, to the fusion of strengths, toward the activation of energy, not once during the positive change process have groups envisioned or called for increased command and control hierarchy. What always happens, without exception, is movement toward greater equalitarian relationships and self-organizing structures. These organizational forms are much like those described by Hock, in his work on bridging chaos and order (1999). One feature of this chaordic form of organizing, like in nature, is that it connects infinite diversity in a liberating environment with pattern and coherence at the level of the whole. Our theory suggests that as people touch each other at their positive core, searching for the best in each other and life's offerings, the energy leads to self-organizing units. When ignited through elevated inquiry, unions emerge (Hubbard, 1998). Even in the U.S. Navy, one of the most structured command-and-control bureaucracies, participants created a weblike metastructure of self-organizing groups to carry out the hundreds of projects envisioned in their appreciative inquiry summits.

So, what does the positive organizational change look like as it emerges in this stage? At the United Religion's global summit, one participant used the analogy of Indra's net, which is a mythological story about the cosmic web of interrelatedness extending infinitely in all directions of the universe. Every intersection of the intertwining web is set with a glistening jewel, in which all parts of the whole are reflected. Imagine an organization where the reflections that compose each entity are an endless amplification of the positive, mirroring one another, sparkling and reverberating every strength.

FROM THE LOCAL TO THE WHOLE

A truly elegant organizational form is one where relationships from the local to the whole allow for shared links to the essence of our appreciable world. It is one where there is an ongoing and open exchange of our unique and shared strengths between members. We propose that a focus on our best and on the positive features of our organizations, in relation to many change agendas, is all too frequently underestimated. As a result of limiting ourselves, there is a tide of growing cynicism about our capacity for creating sustainable change in our institutions. While the description offered of positive change may seem an exaggeration, or perhaps a romantic view of the possibilities, there is a mounting wave of research from both the laboratory and the field, inviting us to focus on these possibilities as avenues for further consideration and study.

Positive organizational scholarship has given us an opportunity for the creation of new knowledge, as researchers move to examine the best of organizational life. Our theory portrays positive organizational change as a progression through three movements. From the elevation of inquiry, to a fusion of strengths, to the activation of energy— change can extend in ways that have the capacity to create valued new futures. At the same time, the process plays a role in broadening and building our capacities and circumventing old patterns with the potential to create reserves for the future. Positive emotions are ignited, expanded, and edified in organizations where appreciative inquiry elevates further discovery and extends relatedness to others. This technique can illuminate an infinite array of strengths and capacities that are embedded in interrelationships, where the process of shared valuing and discovery leads to the creation of countless new connections in multiple directions. In summary, appreciative inquiry is a process that instills positive organizational change stemming from the local and expanding outward to the whole.

CHAPTER TEN

Leading Change
Why Transformation Efforts Fail

John P. Kotter

Over the past decade, I have watched more than 100 companies try to remake themselves into significantly better competitors. They have included large organizations (Ford) and small ones (Landmark Communications), companies based in the United States (General Motors) and elsewhere (British Airways), corporations that were on their knees (Eastern Airlines), and companies that were earning good money (Bristol-Myers Squibb). These efforts have gone under many banners: total quality management, reengineering, right sizing, restructuring, cultural change, and turnaround. But, in almost every case, the basic goal has been the same: to make fundamental changes in how business is conducted in order to help cope with a new, more challenging market environment.

A few of these corporate change efforts have been very successful. A few have been utter failures. Most fall somewhere in between, with a distinct tilt toward the lower end of the scale. The lessons that can be drawn are interesting and will probably be relevant to even more organizations in the increasingly competitive business environment of the coming decade.

The most general lesson to be learned from the more successful cases is that the change process goes through a series of phases that, in total, usually require a considerable length of time. Skipping steps creates only the illusion of speed and never produces a satisfying result. A second very general lesson is that critical mistakes in any of the phases can have a devastating impact, slowing momentum and negating hard-won gains. Perhaps because we have relatively little experience in renewing organizations, even very capable people often make at least one big error.

ERROR #1: NOT ESTABLISHING A GREAT ENOUGH SENSE OF URGENCY

Most successful change efforts begin when some individuals or some groups start to look hard at a company's competitive situation, market position, technological trends, and financial performance. They focus on the potential revenue drop when an important patent expires, the five-year trend in declining margins in a core business, or an emerging market that everyone seems to be ignoring. They then find ways to communicate this information broadly and dramatically, especially with respect to crises, potential crises, or great opportunities that are very timely. This first step is essential because just getting a transformation program started requires the aggressive cooperation of many individuals. Without motivation, people won't help and the effort goes nowhere.

Compared with other steps in the change process, phase one can sound easy. It is not. Well over 50 percent of the companies I have watched fail in this first phase. What are the reasons for that failure? Sometimes executives underestimate how hard it can be to drive people out of their comfort zones. Sometimes they grossly overestimate how successful they have already been in increasing urgency. Sometimes they lack patience: "Enough with the preliminaries; let's get on with it." In many cases, executives become paralyzed by the downside possibilities. They worry that employees with seniority will become defensive, that morale will drop, that events will spin out of control, that short-term business results will be jeopardized, that the stock will sink, and that they will be blamed for creating a crisis.

A paralyzed senior management often comes from having too many managers and not enough leaders. Management's mandate is to minimize risk and to keep the current system operating. Change, by definition, requires creating a new system, which in turn always demands leadership. Phase one in a renewal process typically goes nowhere until enough real leaders are promoted or hired into senior-level jobs.

Transformations often begin, and begin well, when an organization has a new head who is a good leader and who sees the need for a major change. If the renewal target is the entire company, the CEO is key. If change is needed in a division, the division general manager is key. When these individuals are not new leaders, great leaders, or change champions, phase one can be a huge challenge.

Bad business results are both a blessing and a curse in the first phase. On the positive side, losing money does catch people's attention. But it also gives less maneuvering room. With good business results, the opposite is true: convincing people of the need for change is much harder, but you have more resources to help make changes.

But whether the starting point is good performance or bad, in the more successful cases I have witnessed, an individual or a group always facilitates a frank discussion of potentially unpleasant facts: about new competition, shrinking margins, decreasing market share, flat earnings, a lack of revenue growth, or other relevant indices of a declining competitive position. Because there seems to be an almost universal human tendency to shoot the bearer of bad news, especially if the head of the organization is not a change champion, executives in these companies often rely on outsiders to bring unwanted information. Wall Street analysts, customers, and consultants can all be helpful in this regard. The purpose of all this activity, in the words of one former CEO of a large European company, is "to make the status quo seem more dangerous than launching into the unknown."

In a few of the most successful cases, a group has manufactured a crisis. One CEO deliberately engineered the largest accounting loss in the company's history, creating huge pressures from Wall Street in the process. One division president commissioned first-ever customer-satisfaction surveys, knowing full well that the results would be terrible. He then made these findings public. On the surface, such moves can look unduly risky. But there is also risk in playing it too safe: when the urgency rate is not pumped up enough, the transformation process cannot succeed and the long-term future of the organization is put in jeopardy.

When is the urgency rate high enough? From what I have seen, the answer is when about 75 percent of a company's management is honestly convinced that business-as-usual is totally unacceptable. Anything less can produce very serious problems later on in the process.

ERROR #2: NOT CREATING A POWERFUL ENOUGH GUIDING COALITION

Major renewal programs often start with just one or two people. In cases of successful transformation efforts, the leadership coalition grows and grows over time. But whenever some minimum mass is not achieved early in the effort, nothing much worthwhile happens.

It is often said that major change is impossible unless the head of the organization is an active supporter. What I am talking about goes far beyond that. In successful transformations, the chairman or president or division general manager, plus another five or fifteen or fifty people, come together and develop a shared commitment to excellent performance through renewal. In my experience, this group never includes all of the company's most senior executives because some people just won't buy in, at least not at first. But in the most successful cases, the coalition is always pretty powerful—in terms of titles, information and expertise, reputations and relationships.

In both small and large organizations, a successful guiding team may consist of only three to five people during the first year of a renewal effort. But in big companies, the coalition needs to grow to the twenty to fifty range before much progress can be made in phase three and beyond. Senior managers always form the core of the group. But sometimes you find board members, a representative from a key customer, or even a powerful union leader.

Because the guiding coalition includes members who are not part of senior management, it tends to operate outside of the normal hierarchy by definition. This can be awkward, but it is clearly necessary. If the existing hierarchy were working well, there would be no need for a major transformation. But since the current system is not working, reform generally demands activity outside of formal boundaries, expectations, and protocol.

A high sense of urgency within the managerial ranks helps enormously in putting a guiding coalition together. But more is usually required. Someone needs to get these people together, help them develop a shared assessment of their company's problems and opportunities, and create a minimum level of trust and communication. Off-site retreats, for two or three days, are one popular vehicle for accomplishing this task. I have seen many groups of five to thirty-five executives attend a series of these retreats over a period of months.

1 Establishing a Sense of Urgency
· Examining market and competitive realities
· Identifying and discussing crises, potential crises, or major opportunities

2 Forming a Powerful Guiding Coalition
· Assembling a group with enough power to lead the change effort
· Encouraging the group to work together as a team

3 Creating a Vision
· Creating a vision to help direct the change effort
· Developing strategies for achieving that vision

4 Communicating the Vision
· Using every vehicle possible to communicate the new vision and strategies
· Teaching new behaviors by the example of the guiding coalition

5 Empowering Others to Act on the Vision
· Getting rid of obstacles to change
· Changing systems or structures that seriously undermine the vision
· Encouraging risk taking and nontraditional ideas, activities, and actions

6 Planning for and Creating Short-Term Wins
· Planning for visible performance improvements
· Creating those improvements
· Recognizing and rewarding employees involved in the improvements

7 Consolidating Improvements and Producing Still More Change
· Using increased credibility to change systems, structures, and policies that don't fit the vision
· Hiring, promoting, and developing employees who can implement the vision
· Reinvigorating the process with new projects, themes, and change agents

8 Institutionalizing New Approaches
· Articulating the connections between the new behaviors and corporate success
· Developing the means to ensure leadership development and succession

Exhibit 10.1   Eight Steps to Transforming Your Organization.

Companies that fail in phase two usually underestimate the difficulties of producing change and thus the importance of a powerful guiding coalition. Sometimes they have no history of teamwork at the top and therefore undervalue the importance of this type of coalition. Sometimes they expect the team to be led by a staff executive from human resources, quality, or strategic planning instead of a key line manager. No matter how capable or dedicated the staff head, groups without strong line leadership never achieve the power that is required.

Efforts that don't have a powerful enough guiding coalition can make apparent progress for a while. But, sooner or later, the opposition gathers itself together and stops the change.

ERROR #3: LACKING A VISION

In every successful transformation effort that I have seen, the guiding coalition develops a picture of the future that is relatively easy to communicate and appeals to customers, stockholders, and employees. A vision always goes beyond the numbers that are typically found in five-year plans. A vision says something that helps clarify the direction in which an organization needs to move. Sometimes the first draft comes mostly from a single individual. It is usually a bit blurry, at least initially. But after the coalition works at it for three or five or even twelve months, something much better emerges through their tough analytical thinking and a little dreaming. Eventually, a strategy for achieving that vision is also developed.

In one midsize European company, the first pass at a vision contained two-thirds of the basic ideas that were in the final product. The concept of global reach was in the initial version from the beginning. So was the idea of becoming preeminent in certain businesses. But one central idea in the final version—getting out of low value-added activities—came only after a series of discussions over a period of several months.

Without a sensible vision, a transformation effort can easily dissolve into a list of confusing and incompatible projects that can take the organization in the wrong direction or nowhere at all. Without a sound vision, the reengineering project in the accounting department, the new 360-degree performance appraisal from the human resources department, the plant's quality program, the cultural change project in the sales force will not add up in a meaningful way.

In failed transformations, you often find plenty of plans and directives and programs, but no vision. In one case, a company gave out four-inch-thick note-books describing its change effort. In mind-numbing detail, the books spelled out procedures, goals, methods, and deadlines. But nowhere was there a clear and compelling statement of where all this was leading. Not surprisingly, most of the employees with whom I talked were either confused or alienated. The big, thick books did not rally them together or inspire change. In fact, they probably had just the opposite effect.

In a few of the less successful cases that I have seen, management had a sense of direction, but it was too complicated or blurry to be useful. Recently, I asked an executive in a midsize company to describe his vision and received in return a barely comprehensible thirty-minute lecture. Buried in his answer were the basic elements of a sound vision. But they were buried—deeply.

A useful rule of thumb: if you can't communicate the vision to someone in five minutes or less and get a reaction that signifies both understanding and interest, you are not yet done with this phase of the transformation process.

ERROR #4: UNDERCOMMUNICATING THE VISION BY A FACTOR OF TEN

I've seen three patterns with respect to communication, all very common. In the first, a group actually does develop a pretty good transformation vision and then proceeds to communicate it by holding a single meeting or sending out a single communication. Having used about .0001 percent of the yearly intracompany communication, the group is startled that few people seem to understand the new approach. In the second pattern, the head of the organization spends a considerable amount of time making speeches to employee groups, but most people still don't get it (not surprising, since vision captures only .0005 percent of the total yearly communication). In the third pattern, much more effort goes into newsletters and speeches, but some very visible senior executives still behave in ways that are antithetical to the vision. The net result is that cynicism among the troops goes up, while belief in the communication goes down.

Transformation is impossible unless hundreds or thousands of people are willing to help, often to the point of making short-term sacrifices. Employees will not make sacrifices, even if they are unhappy with the status quo, unless they believe that useful change is possible. Without credible communication, and a lot of it, the hearts and minds of the troops are never captured.

This fourth phase is particularly challenging if the short-term sacrifices include job losses. Gaining understanding and support is tough when downsizing is a part of the vision. For this reason, successful visions usually include new growth possibilities and the commitment to treat fairly anyone who is laid off.

Executives who communicate well incorporate messages into their hour-by-hour activities. In a routine discussion about a business problem, they talk about how proposed solutions fit (or don't fit) into the bigger picture. In a regular performance appraisal, they talk about how the employee's behavior helps or undermines the vision. In a review of a division's quarterly performance, they talk not only about the numbers but also about how the division's executives are contributing to the transformation. In a routine Q&A with employees at a company facility, they tie their answers back to renewal goals.

In more successful transformation efforts, executives use all existing communication channels to broadcast the vision. They turn boring and unread company newsletters into lively articles about the vision. They take ritualistic and tedious quarterly management meetings and turn them into exciting discussions of the transformation. They throw out much of the company's generic management education and replace it with courses that focus on business problems and the new vision. The guiding principle is simple: use every possible channel, especially those that are being wasted on nonessential information.

Perhaps even more important, most of the executives I have known in successful cases of major change learn to "walk the talk." They consciously attempt to become a living symbol of the new corporate culture. This is often not easy. A sixty-year-old plant manager who has spent precious little time over forty years thinking about customers will not suddenly behave in a customer-oriented way. But I have witnessed just such a person change, and change a great deal. In that case, a high level of urgency helped. The fact that the man was a part of the guiding coalition and the vision-creation team also helped. So did all the communication, which kept reminding him of the desired behavior, and all the feedback from his peers and subordinates, which helped him see when he was not engaging in that behavior.

Communication comes in both words and deeds, and the latter are often the most powerful form. Nothing undermines change more than behavior by important individuals that is inconsistent with their words.

ERROR #5: NOT REMOVING OBSTACLES TO THE NEW VISION

Successful transformations begin to involve large numbers of people as the process progresses. Employees are emboldened to try new approaches, to develop new ideas, and to provide leadership. The only constraint is that the actions fit within the broad parameters of the overall vision. The more people involved, the better the outcome.

To some degree, a guiding coalition empowers others to take action simply by successfully communicating the new direction. But communication is never sufficient by itself. Renewal also requires the removal of obstacles. Too often, an employee understands the new vision and wants to help make it happen. But an elephant appears to be blocking the path. In some cases, the elephant is in the person's head, and the challenge is to convince the individual that no external obstacle exists. But in most cases, the blockers are very real.

Sometimes the obstacle is the organizational structure: narrow job categories can seriously undermine efforts to increase productivity or make it very difficult even to think about customers. Sometimes compensation or performance-appraisal systems make people choose between the new vision and their own self-interest. Perhaps worst of all are bosses who refuse to change and who make demands that are inconsistent with the overall effort.

One company began its transformation process with much publicity and actually made good progress through the fourth phase. Then the change effort ground to a halt because the officer in charge of the company's largest division was allowed to undermine most of the new initiatives. He paid lip service to the process but did not change his behavior or encourage his managers to change. He did not reward the unconventional ideas called for in the vision. He allowed human resource systems to remain intact even when they were clearly inconsistent with the new ideals. I think the officer's motives were complex. To some degree, he did not believe the company needed major change. To some degree, he felt personally threatened by all the change. To some degree, he was afraid that he could not produce both change and the expected operating profit. But despite the fact that they backed the renewal effort, the other officers did virtually nothing to stop the one blocker. Again, the reasons were complex. The company had no history of confronting problems like this. Some people were afraid of the officer. The CEO was concerned that he might lose a talented executive. The net result was disastrous. Lower level managers concluded that senior management had lied to them about their commitment to renewal, cynicism grew, and the whole effort collapsed.

In the first half of a transformation, no organization has the momentum, power, or time to get rid of all obstacles. But the big ones must be confronted and removed. If the blocker is a person, it is important that he or she be treated fairly and in a way that is consistent with the new vision. But action is essential, both to empower others and to maintain the credibility of the change effort as a whole.

ERROR #6: NOT SYSTEMATICALLY PLANNING FOR AND CREATING SHORT-TERM WINS

Real transformation takes time, and a renewal effort risks losing momentum if there are no short-term goals to meet and celebrate. Most people won't go on the long march unless they see compelling evidence within twelve to twenty-four months that the journey is producing expected results. Without short-term wins, too many people give up or actively join the ranks of those people who have been resisting change.

One to two years into a successful transformation effort, you find quality beginning to go up on certain indices or the decline in net income stopping. You find some successful new product introductions or an upward shift in market share. You find an impressive productivity improvement or a statistically higher customer-satisfaction rating. But whatever the case, the win is unambiguous. The result is not just a judgment call that can be discounted by those opposing change.

Creating short-term wins is different from hoping for short-term wins. The latter is passive, the former active. In a successful transformation, managers actively look for ways to obtain clear performance improvements, establish goals in the yearly planning system, achieve the objectives, and reward the people involved with recognition, promotions, and even money. For example, the guiding coalition at a U.S. manufacturing company produced a highly visible and successful new product introduction about twenty months after the start of its renewal effort. The new product was selected about six months into the effort because it met multiple criteria: it could be designed and launched in a relatively short period; it could be handled by a small team of people who were devoted to the new vision; it had upside potential; and the new product-development team could operate outside the established departmental structure without practical problems. Little was left to chance, and the win boosted the credibility of the renewal process.

Managers often complain about being forced to produce short-term wins, but I've found that pressure can be a useful element in a change effort. When it becomes clear to people that major change will take a long time, urgency levels can drop. Commitments to produce short-term wins help keep the urgency level up and force detailed analytical thinking that can clarify or revise visions.

ERROR #7: DECLARING VICTORY TOO SOON

After a few years of hard work, managers may be tempted to declare victory with the first clear performance improvement. While celebrating a win is fine, declaring the war won can be catastrophic. Until changes sink deeply into a company's culture, a process that can take five to ten years, new approaches are fragile and subject to regression.

In the recent past, I have watched a dozen change efforts operate under the reengineering theme. In all but two cases, victory was declared and the expensive consultants were paid and thanked when the first major project was completed after two to three years. Within two more years, the useful changes that had been introduced slowly disappeared. In two of the ten cases, it's hard to find any trace of the reengineering work today.

Over the past twenty years, I've seen the same sort of thing happen to huge quality projects, organizational development efforts, and more. Typically, the problems start early in the process: the urgency level is not intense enough, the guiding coalition is not powerful enough, and the vision is not clear enough. But it is the premature victory celebration that kills momentum. And then the powerful forces associated with tradition take over.

Ironically, it is often a combination of change initiators and change resistors that creates the premature victory celebration. In their enthusiasm over a clear sign of progress, the initiators go overboard. They are then joined by resistors, who are quick to spot any opportunity to stop change. After the celebration is over, the resistors point to the victory as a sign that the war has been won and the troops should be sent home. Weary troops allow themselves to be convinced that they won. Once home, the foot soldiers are reluctant to climb back on the ships. Soon thereafter, change comes to a halt, and tradition creeps back in.

Instead of declaring victory, leaders of successful efforts use the credibility afforded by short-term wins to tackle even bigger problems. They go after systems and structures that are not consistent with the transformation vision and have not been confronted before. They pay great attention to who is promoted, who is hired, and how people are developed. They include new reengineering projects that are even bigger in scope than the initial ones. They understand that renewal efforts take not months but years. In fact, in one of the most successful transformations that I have ever seen, we quantified the amount of change that occurred each year over a seven-year period. On a scale of one (low) to ten (high), year one received a two, year two a four, year three a three, year four a seven, year five an eight, year six a four, and year seven a two. The peak came in year five, fully 36 months after the first set of visible wins.

ERROR #8: NOT ANCHORING CHANGES IN THE CORPORATION'S CULTURE

In the final analysis, change sticks when it becomes "the way we do things around here," when it seeps into the bloodstream of the corporate body. Until new behaviors are rooted in social norms and shared values, they are subject to degradation as soon as the pressure for change is removed.

Two factors are particularly important in institutionalizing change in corporate culture. The first is a conscious attempt to show people how the new approaches, behaviors, and attitudes have helped improve performance. When people are left on their own to make the connections, they sometimes create very inaccurate links. For example, because results improved while charismatic Harry was boss, the troops link his mostly idiosyncratic style with those results instead of seeing how their own improved customer service and productivity were instrumental. Helping people see the right connections requires communication. Indeed, one company was relentless, and it paid off enormously. Time was spent at every major management meeting to discuss why performance was increasing. The company newspaper ran article after article showing how changes had boosted earnings.

The second factor is taking sufficient time to make sure that the next generation of top management really does personify the new approach. If the requirements for promotion don't change, renewal rarely lasts. One bad succession decision at the top of an organization can undermine a decade of hard work. Poor succession decisions are possible when boards of directors are not an integral part of the renewal effort. In at least three instances I have seen, the champion for change was the retiring executive, and although his successor was not a resistor, he was not a change champion. Because the boards did not understand the transformations in any detail, they could not see that their choices were not good fits. The retiring executive in one case tried unsuccessfully to talk his board into a less seasoned candidate who better personified the transformation. In the other two cases, the CEOs did not resist the boards' choices, because they felt the transformation could not be undone by their successors. They were wrong. Within two years, signs of renewal began to disappear at both companies.

There are still more mistakes that people make, but these eight are the big ones. I realize that in a short article everything is made to sound a bit too simplistic. In reality, even successful change efforts are messy and full of surprises. But just as a relatively simple vision is needed to guide people through a major change, so a vision of the change process can reduce the error rate. And fewer errors can spell the difference between success and failure.

CHAPTER ELEVEN

The Congruence Model of Change

David A. Nadler

---~∾~---

Given how crucial organizational models are to each manager's ability to analyze and act upon a situation involving fundamental change, my colleagues and I have devoted much of our work to refining a model that is profoundly useful. This model guides managers to an understanding of the concept of *organizational fit*. It helps them answer the basic question, How do we understand and predict the patterns of organizational behavior and performance? Because if managers can't do that, they don't stand a chance of understanding and managing change throughout the enterprise.

SOME BASIC ORGANIZATIONAL COMPONENTS

The model provides a simple, straightforward way to understand not only how an organization looks as a system but also how it works—or doesn't. Let's begin by examining the elements that constitute the basic components of every organization. These are among the components we have to analyze to diagnose organizational fit.

Input

At any particular time, each organization operates with the following set of givens. Taken together, these three givens, or factors, constitute the *input* component of the organizational system.

THE ENVIRONMENT. This includes all of the forces, conditions, and players operating outside the boundaries of the organization. They can be customers, labor unions, competitors, suppliers, technological developments, regulatory restrictions, communities—the list goes on. The environment exerts powerful demands that the organization must successfully respond to or die. It exerts constraints on the organization, and it provides opportunities to capitalize on organizational competencies. An important note: this model applies equally to organizations and to discrete units within larger organizations; in the latter case, the parent organization becomes a huge factor in a unit's external environment.

In terms of organizational change remember this: virtually all large-scale change originates in the external environment. It does not bubble up from within the organization through some mysterious process of spontaneous generation. Something is happening "out there" that is causing so much anxiety that change is unavoidable. A case in point: back in the early 1970s, when I was on the staff of the Institute for Social Research at the University of Michigan, some of my colleagues and I got federal research money to investigate the relationship between quality and worker involvement. One day we headed out to One American Road in Dearborn, the worldwide headquarters of Ford Motor Company, to offer Ford executives the chance to participate in our groundbreaking project, at no cost to them. They listened incredulously to our research subject and then asked, "Why would we want to do that?"

About ten years later, Ford got interested. Why? Because the explosion in Japanese auto sales was sending shockwaves through Detroit, forcing U.S. carmakers to take a close look at Japanese management techniques—including quality and worker involvement. Faced with a threat of historic proportions, Ford launched a massive and fairly successful quality initiative of its own, captured in the ubiquitous advertising slogan, "At Ford, Quality is Job One." But quality didn't climb to the top of Ford's chart by itself; it took a lot of help from Toyota and Nissan and Honda. And that's the way major change almost always starts—from the outside.

RESOURCES. These are the organizational assets that have potential value in light of the demands, opportunities, and constraints of the environment. Resources can be tangible assets such as capital, plant, facilities, and numbers of people, or they can be intangible ones like customer relations or the creativity of key employees. And of course there's money. Keep in mind that current assets don't necessarily hold their value. AT&T, for example, viewed The Network—its nationwide system of in-ground copper wire—as one of its most valuable assets. As fiber optics made copper wire obsolete, however, AT&T found itself forced in 1990 to write off billions of dollars for that very same network.

HISTORY. This comprises the past events, activities, and crises that continue to influence the way the organization works today. Like people, organizations are massively influenced by their experience, perhaps more than they realize. In the late 1980s, I was trying to help Xerox managers figure out why it was having so little success with joint ventures and alliances. As it turned out, history was a major factor. Xerox, founded as the Haloid Corporation, had initially spent nearly fifteen years developing the process it was to call xerography. When it designed its revolutionary new copier in the late 1950s and sought a larger partner to assist with production, sales, and distribution, it contacted such major corporations as IBM, GE, and RCA—all to no avail. (Tom Watson, the legendary head of IBM, later described his refusal to buy into xerography as the biggest mistake of his career.) In the end Xerox introduced the copier on its own—and the result was one of the most successful product launches in recent history. As a result, however, there is a strong sentiment running through the organization's subconscious that states, "Real men don't do joint ventures." Just think, managers will tell you, of the billions that would have been lost if Xerox had found a partner. The historical lesson was clear and resonates to this day: winning means going it alone.

As I said at the outset, these three factors—the environment, resources, and history—represent the givens in an organization's situation. In a sense they are the hand each new leader is dealt as he or she tries to decide which cards to play in the process known as strategy.

Strategy

More specifically, *strategy* represents the set of decisions made by the enterprise about how to configure its resources vis-à-vis the demands, opportunities, and constraints of the environment within the context of history. Those decisions involve:

- *Markets.* Who are our customers, and which of their needs are we going to meet?
- *Offerings.* What is the set of products or services we will create to meet those needs?
- *Competitive basis.* What features will persuade customers to come to us rather than our competitors? Low cost? High quality? Cutting-edge technology? Exceptional customer service?
- *Performance objectives.* By what measures will we determine how successful the other elements of the strategy have been?

Keep in mind that I'm referring here to *business strategy,* not *corporate strategy.* As I'll explain in more detail later, there's a distinct difference. Corporate strategy, as opposed to what I've just described, makes fundamental decisions about what businesses the enterprise wants to be in and typically focuses on portfolio decisions. I'm also talking here about enacted—not espoused—strategy. Written strategies often have little or nothing to do with what's really happening. Henry Mintzberg says strategy is best seen not by standing at the front of a ship and looking at where you're going, but by standing at the stern and seeing where you've been (Mintzberg, 1994). There's a lot of truth to that.

Output

The ultimate purpose of the enterprise is to produce *output*—the pattern of activities, behavior, and performance of the system at the following levels:

- *The total system.* There are any number of ways to look at the output of the total system—goods and services produced, revenues, profits, employment created, impact on communities, and so on.
- *Units within the system.* The performance and behavior of the various divisions, departments, and teams that make up the organization.
- *Individuals.* The behavior, activities, and performance of the people within the organization.

Although this might seem basic, it's also extremely useful. Whenever I'm invited into a new situation and asked to offer a diagnosis, my first step is to try to understand the environment, resources, history, and strategy. Then I look at performance—the output side of the system—and measure it against the performance objectives embodied in the strategy. The existence of a gap between objectives and output—and the size of the gap—provides my first glimpse of the dimensions of that particular organization's problems.

THE OPERATING ORGANIZATION

At the heart of the congruence model is the *operating organization.* The operating organization is the transformation mechanism that takes the strategy, in the context of history, resources, and environment, and converts it into a pattern of performance. In this model, just as the all-encompassing organizational system has its basic components, the operating organization has its major components: its work, its people, the formal organizational arrangements, and the informal organizational arrangements. Analyzing these components will also be part of our diagnosis of organizational congruence. Let's examine each in turn.

Work

Work is the defining activity of any enterprise—the basic and inherent tasks to be performed by the organization and its parts. Visit a company you haven't been to in five years, and the offices—even entire buildings—may well be different. You may be unfamiliar with the new equipment people are using. For that matter, you might not recognize many of the people. But the work the people are doing, in terms of creating a category of goods or providing certain types of service, will be essentially the same.

For example, Dow Jones and Company, which for decades has been publishing the *Wall Street Journal,* now offers all kinds of online services, but the core work is still the same—collecting, processing, and distributing news and information of interest to the business community.

When trying to understand the characteristics of work in any organization, there are three elements to look at:

- *Skills and knowledge demands.* What do people need to know in order to do this work?
- *Rewards.* What are the psychic rewards people derive from their work? These can differ immensely from one industry to another. Producing pine boards, for example, offers significantly different rewards from designing business software which is different again from managing investment portfolios.
- *Uncertainty.* What is the degree of uncertainty associated with the work? What are the key sources of stress and uncertainty that have to be managed?
- *Impact of strategy.* What are the constraints or demands placed upon the work within the context of strategy? For example, Wal-Mart and Nordstrom are both general retailers, but strategic decisions about the basis on which each competes result in two very different operations. Wal-Mart competes on the basis of low cost and has developed purchasing, warehousing, distribution, and sales processes all designed to lower expenses and keep prices low. Nordstrom offers its affluent customers a unique shopping experience and selects its merchandise, designs its stores, and trains its salesforce accordingly.

People

In order to diagnose any organizational system you have to analyze four characteristics of the people who work there:

- What knowledge and skills do the people bring to their work?
- What are the needs and preferences of the people in the organization in terms of the benefits they expect to flow from their work?
- What are the perceptions and expectations they develop over time?
- What are the demographics? What does the workforce look like in terms of age, gender, and ethnicity as these factors relate to the work?

The Formal Organization

If all of us were genetically programmed to get up each morning, stream from our homes in lemminglike fashion to our places of work and voluntarily—perhaps even cheerfully—perform our assigned tasks, the model could stop with work and people. Clearly, however, that's not the way the world works, and to compensate for it organizations of every kind have developed formal organizational arrangements: structures, systems, and processes that embody the patterns each organization develops for grouping people and the work they do and then coordinating their activity in ways designed to achieve the strategic objectives.

The Informal Organization

So far the operating organization on the congruence model includes the work, the people, and the formal organizational arrangements. But there's a final element that's crucial to understanding how organizations actually operate. If you put three people together for more than fifteen minutes, it becomes obvious that another powerful force is at work. Here's what I mean.

Consider the city of New York. It has an extensive and intricate system of streets that perform several functions. One, of course, is to facilitate the flow of traffic (I'm speaking theoretically). Another is to store vehicles; this is commonly referred to as parking. But people in New York, despite their many lovable traits, are not known to be particularly tidy. So there's an additional work requirement: cleaning the streets. So how does the city juggle the competing demands of storage and cleaning? Alternate side of the street parking and cleaning, reinforced by street signs everywhere—"No parking this side of the street every Tuesday, Thursday, and Saturday, 8:30 to 11:30 A.M."—and a fleet of city tow trucks. In terms of our model the city has developed a formal organizational arrangement to accommodate the competing demands of two work requirements.

But that formal arrangement means that every morning, armies of New Yorkers have to move their cars to make way for the street sweepers and garbage trucks. So where do they go? To the other side of the street of course, where they double-park. But double-parking is illegal in New York City. Do these people get tickets? No. The slips of paper you see on the windshields of these double-parked cars just carry the phone numbers where the owners can be reached in a hurry by the owners of the cars they're blocking.

Where is this arrangement written down? Nowhere. But somehow eight million New Yorkers all know about it and make it work surprisingly well. What has emerged over time is an *informal organizational arrangement* that balances the demands of the work and the needs of the people.

The informal organization, then, includes the emerging arrangements and interaction patterns that overlap the formal structures and processes. More specifically it encompasses

- The *organizational culture*—the values, beliefs, and behavioral norms
- The informal rules and work practices
- The patterns of communications and influence
- The actual behavior of leaders, rather than their prescribed roles.

THE CONCEPT OF FIT

There's one more vital issue to discuss before leaving this central portion of the model.

Russell Ackoff, a noted systems theorist, has described it this way. Suppose for a moment that you could build your own dream car. You might take the styling of a Jaguar, the power plant of a Porsche, the suspension of a BMW, and the interior of a Rolls-Royce. Put them together and what have you got? Nothing. Why? Because they weren't designed to go together. They don't fit. You can see the concept brought to life nearly every time an all-star team of professional athletes takes the field. Inevitably, these temporary amalgams of world-class talents produce teams that are woefully less than the sum of their parts.

This concept of *fit* is crucial to understanding the organizational model I've been describing. In systems the interaction of the components is more important than the components themselves. In terms of the organization, its overall effectiveness relies on the internal congruence, or fit, of its basic components. The tighter the fit, the greater the effectiveness.

As an example, think about Sun Microsystems, one of the most successful companies in Silicon Valley. Founded in 1982, it was by 1996 experiencing an extraordinarily high degree of internal fit. CEO Scott McNealy redesigned the company in the early 1990s to create a structure he describes as "loosely coupled, tightly aligned" independent business units. Some are so independent, in fact, that some of their customers are Sun's competitors. That kind of formal structure in turn encourages independence, entrepreneurial innovation, and a heavy dose of competitiveness—all in keeping with the company's strategy.

At the same time, McNealy's own highly informal—sometimes to the point of quirky—personality has spawned a consciously anti-corporate operating environment. There are no assigned parking spaces or executive dining rooms, no luxurious corporate offices. Not surprisingly, that environment attracts the creative engineers and scientists Sun needs to produce the kinds of breakthroughs—such as the Java system for creating Internet materials that can be read by any computer—that have fueled the company's success.

For now, at least, each component of Sun's organization is aligned and in reasonable congruence. The structure and the work support the strategy, and the work provides the challenges and the operating environment provides the atmosphere to attract the highly skilled creative professionals the company's strategy requires. Somewhat remarkably, Sun maintained that degree of fit as it grew from a tiny start-up run by four twenty-seven-year-olds to a $7-billion-a-year corporation with 14,500 employees. Typically, exponential growth creates huge problems because it almost always throws some organizational component out of alignment. For instance, the demands of the work and the size of the workforce frequently result in controlling bureaucracies, which then destroy the entrepreneurial spirit that made the company successful in the first place. Somehow, so far, Sun has escaped that dilemma.

PRINCIPLES IMPLIED BY THE MODEL

This, then, is the essence of the congruence model: the greater the congruence among the internal components (see Table 11.1), the more effective organizations will be in transforming their strategies into performance. Conversely, the poorer the fit, the wider the gap between strategy and performance. For managers about to embark on change, identifying the points at which the organizational fit is breaking down is the vital first step in figuring out what has to change.

The full congruence model, with the various components discussed so far, implies three general principles that can boost the odds of success. Or if ignored, they can doom the effort to failure.

1. Make sure the new strategy fits the realities of the organization's resources and environment. In the mid-1990s, Apple Computer's

Fit	Issues
Individual-organization	To what extent individual needs are met by the organizational arrangements. To what extent individuals hold clear or distorted perceptions of organizational structures; the convergence of individual and organizational goals.
Individual-task	To what extent the needs of individuals are met by the tasks; to what extent individuals have skills and abilities to meet task demands.
Individual–informal organization	To what extent individual needs are met by the informal organization. To what extent the informal organization makes use of individual resources, consistent with informal goals.
Task-organization	To what extent organizational arrangements are adequate to meet the demands of the task; to what extent organizational arrangements tend to motivate behavior consistent with task demands.
Task–informal organization	To what extent the informal organization structure facilitates task performance; to what extent it hinders or promotes meeting the demands of the task.
Organization–informal organization	To what extent the goals, rewards, and structures of the informal organization are consistent with those of the formal organization.

Table 11.1.   Meaning of Fit for Each Component.

successive regimes stumbled from one disaster to another as they misjudged the external environment and underestimated their need to find a powerful partner to help stave off the growing dominance of Microsoft and the Windows operating system. At the same time, cost-cutting measures depleted and demoralized the ranks of first-class engineers who could provide Apple with the needed product innovations.

2. Make sure the strategy fits the formal structures, systems, and processes. Without that fit the most brilliant strategy is doomed from the start. When I first started working with Xerox, managers excitedly told me about their far-flung subsidiaries where lots of creative people were inventing new systems. The executive in charge explained that the major issue at that time was integration—how to get this array of innovative office systems to talk to each other. The company's solution was to set up each of the development groups as a separate independent operating unit. Well, if your strategic goal is integration, but your formal structure eliminates nearly all coordination and interaction among the units, you're almost certainly going to fail—and this attempt did.

3. Make sure there's fit among all the internal components of the organization—the strategy, the work, the formal and informal organizational arrangements, and the people. As I'll illustrate throughout this book, a lack of fit between any of the organizational components—between people and their work requirements, between formal structures and the informal operating environment, and so on—can produce huge problems. Whatever you do, don't assume that by changing one or two components of the model you will cause the others to fall neatly into place.

PART THREE

The OD Process

Diagnosis, Intervention, and Levels of Engagement

O rganization development efforts are always locally grounded. They begin with understanding the unique nature and circumstances of a particular client system. The quality of that diagnosis is essential to developing effective strategies for working with the reality of that social system. Diagnosis at its simplest is a two-part process. It involves gathering information and using appropriate theory and experience to interpret the meaning and implications of the data. OD's effectiveness and impact over time derive from its emphasis on teaching a client organization how to generate and use valid information to foster learning and growth. In the process, OD practitioners need to be mindful of the ways that diagnostic activities themselves both shape and limit intervention possibilities and the overall course of change.

Effective data gathering is more than constructing good questions—although it takes considerable skill to develop lines of inquiry that evoke openness, strong description, and deep reflection. Data gathering is an intervention in itself. Questions are never neutral. They focus attention on specific issues and areas while ignoring others. They plant seeds for learning, personal commitment, and change. Lines of inquiry always reflect the unique way that the asker sees the world—the formal and informal theories and beliefs about change, human nature, and organizational effectiveness that the change agent brings to the work. Questions also influence how respondents frame and make sense out of their world. We know from research and experience that people's beliefs and actions change in response to the questions they are asked and the interpretative frames that are used to make sense of their answers. Chris Argyris, for example, reminds us in Part Two how easily individuals and organizations can feel defensive or evaluated by the attempts of others to study and learn about them.

If good OD begins with good diagnosis, change agents need at least three key tools. First, they need solid theories and models about individuals, groups, and organizations that help them make sense of organizational complexity. Developing an organization requires a clear concept of what a "healthy" and "effective" organization looks like, how its members behave, and how all the parts fit together. Second, change agents need methods for surfacing and exploring their own interpretive frameworks and expanding their capacities for multiframe thinking. Organizations are complex and will only become more so. Multiple lenses enable change agents to bring a full range of perspectives and understandings to their work and increase the odds of addressing what is *really* going on in a client organization. Finally, change agents need a language to be able to talk about these theories, models, and methods. The abilities to help clients frame experience, explore the accuracy of that framing, and see alternative perspectives are central to good OD work. The chapters in Part Three support the development of these abilities. They provide insights for diagnosis and intervention activities on multiple levels: individual, small group, large group, intergroup, and organization. They also suggest ways to frame reality for client organizations and understand the benefits and limitations of different perspectives.

Chris Argyris, in "Teaching Smart People How to Learn," identifies individual behaviors that maximize success and learning for both the individual and the organization. The concepts and strategies offered are relevant for OD in two ways: they focus on individual dynamics of learning and defensiveness that must be understood and addressed for any successful intervention; they also support development of the self-awareness and openness to learning that inform effective change agent behavior.

Edgar Schein, in "Facilitative Process Interventions: Task Processes in Groups," lays out his concept of process consultation and provides a model for both diagnosing and intervening in small groups. As Schein reminds readers in the Foreword to this book, process consultation is more than a technique. Its focus on *how* work is done—not just on the content of the issue being addressed—is an important philosophical underpinning to the practice of OD.

Next, an excerpt from Barbara Bunker and Billie Alban's book, *Large Group Interventions,* identifies the unique dynamics in large groups and suggests strategies for effective intervention in them. Michael J. Sales follows with "Understanding the Power of Position: A Diagnostic Model," a chapter specifically written for this volume. Organizational position influences human behavior in tacit and often overlooked ways. The chapter explores these powerful role dynamics and their implications for diagnosis and for interventions addressing intergroup tensions in organizations. Part Three ends with "Reframing Complexity: A Four-Dimensional Approach to Organizational Diagnosis, Development, and Change," by Joan V. Gallos. My chapter proposes a multiframe model for diagnosing organizations and examines the important role of reframing in effective organization development and change.

CHAPTER TWELVE

Teaching Smart People
How to Learn

Chris Argyris

—◁◈▷—

Any company that aspires to succeed in the tougher business environment of the 1990s must first resolve a basic dilemma: success in the marketplace increasingly depends on learning, yet most people don't know how to learn. What's more, those members of the organization that many assume to be the best at learning are, in fact, not very good at it. I am talking about the well-educated, high-powered, high-commitment professionals who occupy key leadership positions in the modern corporation.

Most companies not only have tremendous difficulty addressing this learning dilemma; they aren't even aware that it exists. The reason: they misunderstand what learning is and how to bring it about. As a result, they tend to make two mistakes in their efforts to become a learning organization.

First, most people define learning too narrowly as mere "problem solving," so they focus on identifying and correcting errors in the external environment. Solving problems is important. But if learning is to persist, managers and employees must also look inward. They need to reflect critically on their own behavior, identify the ways they often inadvertently contribute to the organization's problems, and then change how they act. In particular, they must learn how the very way they go about defining and solving problems can be a source of problems in its own right.

I have coined the terms *single-loop* and *double-loop* learning to capture this crucial distinction. To give a simple analogy: a thermostat that automatically turns on the heat whenever the temperature in a room drops below 68 degrees is a good example of single-loop learning. A thermostat that could ask, "Why am I set at 68 degrees?" and then explore whether or not some other temperature might more economically achieve the goal of heating the room would be engaging in double-loop learning.

Highly skilled professionals are frequently very good at single-loop learning. After all, they have spent much of their lives acquiring academic credentials, mastering one or a number of intellectual disciplines, and applying those disciplines to solve real-world problems. But ironically, this very fact helps explain why professionals are often so bad at double-loop learning.

Put simply, because many professionals are almost always successful at what they do, they rarely experience failure. And because they have rarely failed, they have never learned how to learn from failure. So whenever their single-loop learning strategies go wrong, they become defensive, screen out criticism, and put the "blame" on anyone and everyone but themselves. In short, their ability to learn shuts down precisely at the moment they need it the most.

The propensity among professionals to behave defensively helps shed light on the second mistake that companies make about learning. The common assumption is that getting people to learn is largely a matter of motivation. When people have the right attitudes and commitment, learning automatically follows. So companies focus on creating new organizational structures—compensation programs, performance reviews, corporate cultures, and the like—that are designed to create motivated and committed employees.

But effective double-loop learning is not simply a function of how people feel. It is a reflection of how they think—that is, the cognitive rules or reasoning they use to design and implement their actions. Think of these rules as a kind of "master program" stored in the brain, governing all behavior. Defensive reasoning can block learning even when the individual commitment to it is high, just as a computer program with hidden bugs can produce results exactly the opposite of what its designers had planned.

Companies can learn how to resolve the learning dilemma. What it takes is to make the ways managers and employees reason about their behavior a focus of organizational learning and continuous improvement programs. Teaching people how to reason about their behavior in new and more effective ways breaks down the defenses that block learning.

All of the examples that follow involve a particular kind of professional: fast-track consultants at major management consulting companies. But the implications of my argument go far beyond this specific occupational group. The fact is, more and more jobs—no matter what the title—are taking on the contours of "knowledge work." People at all levels of the organization must combine the mastery of some highly specialized technical expertise with the ability to work effectively in teams, form productive relationships with clients and customers, and critically reflect on and then change their own organizational practices. And the nuts and bolts of management—whether of high-powered consultants or service representatives, senior managers or factory technicians—increasingly consists of guiding and integrating the autonomous but interconnected work of highly skilled people.

HOW PROFESSIONALS AVOID LEARNING

For fifteen years, I have been conducting in-depth studies of management consultants. I decided to study consultants for a few simple reasons. First, they are the epitome of the highly educated professionals who play an increasingly central role in all organizations. Almost all of the consultants I've studied have MBAs from the top three or four U.S. business schools. They are also highly committed to their work. For instance, at one company, more than 90 percent of the consultants responded in a survey that they were "highly satisfied" with their jobs and with the company.

I also assumed that such professional consultants would be good at learning. After all, the essence of their job is to teach others how to do things differently. I found, however, that these consultants embodied the learning dilemma. While they were the most enthusiastic about continuous improvement in their own organizations, they were also often the biggest obstacle to its complete success.

As long as efforts at learning and change focused on external organizational factors—job redesign, compensation programs, performance reviews, and leadership training—the professionals were enthusiastic participants. Indeed, creating new systems and structures was precisely the kind of challenge that well-educated, highly motivated professionals thrived on.

And yet the moment the quest for continuous improvement turned to the professionals' *own* performance, something went wrong. It wasn't a matter of bad attitude. The professionals' commitment to excellence was genuine, and the vision of the company was clear. Nevertheless, continuous improvement did not persist. And the longer the continuous improvement efforts continued, the greater the likelihood that they would produce ever-diminishing returns.

What happened? The professionals began to feel embarrassed. They were threatened by the prospect of critically examining their own role in the organization. Indeed, because they were so well paid (and generally believed that their employers were supportive and fair), the idea that their performance might not be at its best made them feel guilty.

Far from being a catalyst for real change, such feelings caused most to react defensively. They projected the blame for any problems away from themselves and onto what they said were unclear goals, insensitive and unfair leaders, and stupid clients.

Consider this example. At a premier management consulting company, the manager of a case team called a meeting to examine the team's performance on a recent consulting project. The client was largely satisfied and had given the team relatively high marks, but the manager believed the team had not created the value added that it was capable of and that the consulting company had promised. In the spirit of continuous improvement, he felt that the team could do better. Indeed, so did some of the team members.

The manager knew how difficult it was for people to reflect critically on their own work performance, especially in the presence of their manager, so he took a number of steps to make possible a frank and open discussion. He invited to the meeting an outside consultant whom team members knew and trusted—"just to keep me honest," he said. He also agreed to have the entire meeting tape-recorded. That way, any subsequent confusions or disagreements about what went on at the meeting could be checked against the transcript. Finally, the manager opened the meeting by emphasizing that no subject was off limits—including his own behavior.

"I realize that you may believe you cannot confront me," the manager said. "But I encourage you to challenge me. You have a responsibility to tell me where you think the leadership made mistakes, just as I have the responsibility to identify any I believe you made. And all of us must acknowledge our own mistakes. If we do not have an open dialogue, we will not learn."

The professionals took the manager up on the first half of his invitation but quietly ignored the second. When asked to pinpoint the key problems in the experience with the client, they looked entirely outside themselves. The clients were uncooperative and arrogant. "They didn't think we could help them." The team's own managers were unavailable and poorly prepared. "At times, our managers were not up to speed before they walked into the client meetings." In effect, the professionals asserted that they were helpless to act differently—not because of any limitations of their own but because of the limitations of others.

The manager listened carefully to the team members and tried to respond to their criticisms. He talked about the mistakes that he had made during the consulting process. For example, one professional objected to the way the manager had run the project meetings. "I see that the way I asked questions closed down discussions," responded the manager. "I didn't mean to do that, but I can see how you might have believed that I had already made up my mind." Another team member complained that the manager had caved in to pressure from his superior to produce the project report far too quickly, considering the team's heavy work load. "I think that it was my responsibility to have said no," admitted the manager. "It was clear that we all had an immense amount of work."

Finally, after some three hours of discussion about his own behavior, the manager began to ask the team members if there were any errors *they* might have made. "After all," he said, "this client was not different from many others. How can we be more effective in the future?"

The professionals repeated that it was really the clients' and their own managers' fault. As one put it, "They have to be open to change and want to learn." The more the manager tried to get the team to examine its own responsibility for the outcome, the more the professionals bypassed his concerns. The best one team member could suggest was for the case team to "promise less"—implying that there was really no way for the group to improve its performance.

The case team members were reacting defensively to protect themselves, even though their manager was not acting in ways that an outsider would consider threatening. Even if there were some truth to their charges—the clients may well have been arrogant and closed, their own managers distant—the way they presented these claims was guaranteed to stop learning. With few exceptions, the professionals made attributions about the behavior of the clients and the managers but never publicly tested their claims. For instance, they said that the clients weren't motivated to learn but never really presented any evidence supporting that assertion. When their lack of concrete evidence was pointed out to them, they simply repeated their criticisms more vehemently.

If the professionals had felt so strongly about these issues, why had they never mentioned them during the project? According to the professionals, even this was the fault of others. "We didn't want to alienate the client," argued one. "We didn't want to be seen as whining," said another.

The professionals were using their criticisms of others to protect themselves from the potential embarrassment of having to admit that perhaps they too had contributed to the team's less-than-perfect performance. What's more, the fact that they kept repeating their defensive actions in the face of the manager's efforts to turn the group's attention to its own role shows that this defensiveness had become a reflexive routine. From the professionals' perspective, they weren't resisting; they were focusing on the "real" causes. Indeed, they were to be respected, if not congratulated, for working as well as they did under such difficult conditions.

The end result was an unproductive parallel conversation. Both the manager and the professionals were candid; they expressed their views forcefully. But they talked past each other, never finding a common language to describe what had happened with the client. The professionals kept insisting that the fault lay with others. The manager kept trying, unsuccessfully, to get the professionals to see how they contributed to the state of affairs they were criticizing. The dialogue of this parallel conversation looks like this:

PROFESSIONALS: The clients have to be open. They must want to change.

MANAGER: It's our task to help them see that change is in their interest.

PROFESSIONALS: But the clients didn't agree with our analyses.

MANAGER: If they didn't think our ideas were right, how might we have convinced them?

PROFESSIONALS: Maybe we need to have more meetings with the client.

MANAGER: If we aren't adequately prepared and if the clients don't think we're credible, how will more meetings help?

PROFESSIONALS: There should be better communication between case team members and management.

MANAGER: I agree. But professionals should take the initiative to educate the manager about the problems they are experiencing.

PROFESSIONALS: Our leaders are unavailable and distant.

MANAGER: How do you expect us to know that if you don't tell us?

Conversations such as this one dramatically illustrate the learning dilemma. The problem with the professionals' claims is not that they are wrong but that they aren't useful. By constantly turning the focus away from their own behavior to that of others, the professionals bring learning to a grinding halt. The manager understands the trap but does not know how to get out of it. To learn how to do that requires going deeper into the dynamics of defensive reasoning—and into the special causes that make professionals so prone to it.

DEFENSIVE REASONING AND THE DOOM LOOP

What explains the professionals' defensiveness? Not their attitudes about change or commitment to continuous improvement; they really wanted to work more effectively. Rather, the key factor is the way they reasoned about their behavior and that of others.

It is impossible to reason anew in every situation. If we had to think through all the possible responses every time someone asked, "How are you?" the world would pass us by. Therefore, everyone develops a theory of action—a set of rules that individuals use to design and implement their own behavior as well as to understand the behavior of others. Usually, these theories of action become so taken for granted that people don't even realize they are using them.

One of the paradoxes of human behavior, however, is that the master program people actually use is rarely the one they think they use. Ask people in an interview or questionnaire to articulate the rules they use to govern their actions, and they will give you what I call their "espoused" theory of action. But observe these same people's behavior, and you will quickly see that this espoused theory has very little to do with how they actually behave. For example, the professionals on the case team said they believed in continuous improvement, and yet they consistently acted in ways that made improvement impossible.

When you observe people's behavior and try to come up with rules that would make sense of it, you discover a very different theory of action—what I call the individual's "theory-in-use." Put simply, people consistently act inconsistently, unaware of the contradiction between their espoused theory and their theory-in-use, between the way they think they are acting and the way they really act.

What's more, most theories-in-use rest on the same set of governing values. There seems to be a universal human tendency to design one's actions consistently according to four basic values:

1. To remain in unilateral control

2. To maximize "winning" and minimize "losing"

3. To suppress negative feelings

4. To be as "rational" as possible—by which people mean defining clear objectives and evaluating their behavior in terms of whether or not they have achieved them

The purpose of all these values is to avoid embarrassment or threat, feeling vulnerable or incompetent. In this respect, the master program that most people use is profoundly defensive. Defensive reasoning encourages individuals to keep private the premises, inferences, and conclusions that shape their behavior and to avoid testing them in a truly independent, objective fashion.

Because the attributions that go into defensive reasoning are never really tested, it is a closed loop, remarkably impervious to conflicting points of view. The inevitable response to the observation that somebody is reasoning defensively is yet more defensive reasoning. With the case team, for example, whenever anyone pointed out the professionals' defensive behavior to them, their initial reaction was to look for the cause in somebody else—clients who were so sensitive that they would have been alienated if the consultants had criticized them or a manager so weak that he couldn't have taken it had the consultants raised their concerns with him. In other words, the case team members once again denied their own responsibility by externalizing the problem and putting it on someone else.

In such situations, the simple act of encouraging more open inquiry is often attacked by others as "intimidating." Those who do the attacking deal with their feelings about possibly being wrong by blaming the more open individual for arousing these feelings and upsetting them.

Needless to say, such a master program inevitably short-circuits learning. And for a number of reasons unique to their psychology, well-educated professionals are especially susceptible to this.

Nearly all the consultants I have studied have stellar academic records. Ironically, their very success at education helps explain the problems they have with learning. Before they enter the world of work, their lives are primarily full of successes, so they have rarely experienced the embarrassment and sense of threat that comes with failure. As a result, their defensive reasoning has rarely been activated. People who rarely experience failure, however, end up not knowing how to deal with it effectively. And this serves to reinforce the normal human tendency to reason defensively.

In a survey of several hundred young consultants at the organizations I have been studying, these professionals describe themselves as driven internally by an unrealistically high ideal of performance: "Pressure on the job is self-imposed." "I must not only do a good job; I must also be the best." "People around here are very bright and hardworking; they are highly motivated to do an outstanding job." "Most of us want not only to succeed but also to do so at maximum speed."

These consultants are always comparing themselves with the best around them and constantly trying to better their own performance. And yet they do not appreciate being required to compete openly with each other. They feel it is somehow inhumane. They prefer to be the individual contributor—what might be termed a "productive loner."

Behind this high aspiration for success is an equally high fear of failure and a propensity to feel shame and guilt when they do fail to meet their high standards. "You must avoid mistakes," said one. "I hate making them. Many of us fear failure, whether we admit it or not."

To the extent that these consultants have experienced success in their lives, they have not had to be concerned about failure and the attendant feelings of shame and guilt. But to exactly the same extent, they also have never developed the tolerance for feelings of failure or the skills to deal with these feelings. This in turn has led them not only to fear failure but also to fear the fear of failure itself. For they know that they will not cope with it superlatively—their usual level of aspiration.

The consultants use two intriguing metaphors to describe this phenomenon. They talk about the "doom loop" and "doom zoom." Often, consultants will perform well on the case team, but because they don't do the jobs perfectly or receive accolades from their managers, they go into a doom loop of despair. And they don't ease into the doom loop, they zoom into it.

As a result, many professionals have extremely "brittle" personalities. When suddenly faced with a situation they cannot immediately handle, they tend to fall apart. They cover up their distress in front of the client. They talk about it constantly with their fellow case team members. Interestingly, these conversations commonly take the form of bad-mouthing clients.

Such brittleness leads to an inappropriately high sense of despondency or even despair when people don't achieve the high levels of performance they aspire to. Such despondency is rarely psychologically devastating, but when combined with defensive reasoning, it can result in a formidable predisposition against learning.

There is no better example of how this brittleness can disrupt an organization than performance evaluations. Because it represents the one moment when a professional must measure his or her own behavior against some formal standard, a performance evaluation is almost tailor-made to push a professional into the doom loop. Indeed, a poor evaluation can reverberate far beyond the particular individual involved to spark defensive reasoning throughout an entire organization.

At one consulting company, management established a new performance-evaluation process that was designed to make evaluations both more objective and more useful to those being evaluated. The consultants participated in the design of the new system and in general were enthusiastic because it corresponded to their espoused values of objectivity and fairness. A brief two years into the new process, however, it had become the object of dissatisfaction. The catalyst for this about-face was the first unsatisfactory rating.

Senior managers had identified six consultants whose performance they considered below standard. In keeping with the new evaluation process, they did all they could to communicate their concerns to the six and to help them improve. Managers met with each individual separately for as long and as often as the professional requested to explain the reasons behind the rating and to discuss what needed to be done to improve—but to no avail. Performance continued at the same low level and, eventually, the six were let go.

When word of the dismissal spread through the company, people responded with confusion and anxiety. After about a dozen consultants angrily complained to management, the CEO held two lengthy meetings where employees could air their concerns.

At the meetings, the professionals made a variety of claims. Some said the performance-evaluation process was unfair because judgments were subjective and biased and the criteria for minimum performance unclear. Others suspected that the real cause for the dismissals was economic and that the performance-evaluation procedure was just a fig leaf to hide the fact that the company was in trouble. Still others argued that the evaluation process was antilearning. If the company were truly a learning organization, as it claimed, then people performing below the minimum standard should be taught how to reach it. As one professional put it: "We were told that the company did not have an up-or-out policy. Up-or-out is inconsistent with learning. You misled us."

The CEO tried to explain the logic behind management's decision by grounding it in the facts of the case and by asking the professionals for any evidence that might contradict these facts.

Is there subjectivity and bias in the evaluation process? Yes, responded the CEO, but "we strive hard to reduce them. We are constantly trying to improve the process. If you have any ideas, please tell us. If you know of someone treated unfairly, please bring it up. If any of you feel that you have been treated unfairly, let's discuss it now or, if you wish, privately."

Is the level of minimum competence too vague? "We are working to define minimum competence more clearly," he answered. "In the case of the six, however, their performance was so poor that it wasn't difficult to reach a decision." Most of the six had received timely feedback about their problems. And in the two cases where people had not, the reason was that they had never taken the responsibility to seek out evaluations—and, indeed, had actively avoided them. "If you have any data to the contrary," the CEO added, "let's talk about it."

Were the six asked to leave for economic reasons? No, said the CEO. "We have more work than we can do, and letting professionals go is extremely costly for us. Do any of you have any information to the contrary?"

As to the company being antilearning, in fact, the entire evaluation process was designed to encourage learning. When a professional is performing below the minimum level, the CEO explained, "we jointly design remedial experiences with the individual. Then we look for signs of improvement. In these cases, either the professionals were reluctant to take on such assignments or they repeatedly failed when they did. Again, if you have information or evidence to the contrary, I'd like to hear about it."

The CEO concluded: "It's regrettable, but sometimes we make mistakes and hire the wrong people. If individuals don't produce and repeatedly prove themselves unable to improve, we don't know what else to do except dismiss them. It's just not fair to keep poorly performing individuals in the company. They earn an unfair share of the financial rewards."

Instead of responding with data of their own, the professionals simply repeated their accusations but in ways that consistently contradicted their claims. They said that a genuinely fair evaluation process would contain clear and documentable data about performance—but they were unable to provide firsthand examples of the unfairness that they implied colored the evaluation of the six dismissed employees. They argued that people shouldn't be judged by inferences unconnected to their actual performance—but they judged management in precisely this way. They insisted that management define clear, objective, and unambiguous performance standards—but they argued that any humane system would take into account that the performance of a professional cannot be precisely measured. Finally, they presented themselves as champions of learning—but they never proposed any criteria for assessing whether an individual might be unable to learn.

In short, the professionals seemed to hold management to a different level of performance than they held themselves. In their conversation at the meetings, they used many of the features of ineffective evaluation that they condemned—the absence of concrete data, for example, and the dependence on a circular logic of "heads we win, tails you lose." It is as if they were saying, "Here are the features of a fair performance-evaluation system. You should abide by them. But we don't have to when we are evaluating you."

Indeed, if we were to explain the professionals' behavior by articulating rules that would have to be in their heads in order for them to act the way they did, the rules would look something like this:

1. When criticizing the company, state your criticism in ways that you believe are valid—but also in ways that prevent others from deciding for themselves whether your claim to validity is correct.

2. When asked to illustrate your criticisms, don't include any data that others could use to decide for themselves whether the illustrations are valid.

3. State your conclusions in ways that disguise their logical implications. If others point out those implications to you, deny them.

Of course, when such rules were described to the professionals, they found them abhorrent. It was inconceivable that these rules might explain their actions. And yet in defending themselves against this observation, they almost always inadvertently confirmed the rules.

LEARNING HOW TO REASON PRODUCTIVELY

If defensive reasoning is as widespread as I believe, then focusing on an individual's attitudes or commitment is never enough to produce real change. And as the previous example illustrates, neither is creating new organizational structures or systems. The problem is that even when people are genuinely committed to improving their performance and management has changed its structures in order to encourage the "right" kind of behavior, people still remain locked in defensive reasoning. Either they remain unaware of this fact, or if they do become aware of it, they blame others.

There is, however, reason to believe that organizations can break out of this vicious circle. Despite the strength of defensive reasoning, people genuinely strive to produce what they intend. They value acting competently. Their self-esteem is intimately tied up with behaving consistently and performing effectively. Companies can use these universal human tendencies to teach people how to reason in a new way—in effect, to change the master programs in their heads and thus reshape their behavior.

People can be taught how to recognize the reasoning they use when they design and implement their actions. They can begin to identify the inconsistencies between their espoused and actual theories of action. They can face up to the fact that they unconsciously design and implement actions that they do not intend. Finally, people can learn how to identify what individuals and groups do to create organizational defenses and how these defenses contribute to an organization's problems.

Once companies embark on this learning process, they will discover that the kind of reasoning necessary to reduce and overcome organizational defenses is the same kind of "tough reasoning" that underlies the effective use of ideas in strategy, finance, marketing, manufacturing, and other management disciplines. Any sophisticated strategic analysis, for example, depends on collecting valid data, analyzing it carefully, and constantly testing the inferences drawn from the data. The toughest tests are reserved for the conclusions. Good strategists make sure that their conclusions can withstand all kinds of critical questioning.

So too with productive reasoning about human behavior. The standard of analysis is just as high. Human resource programs no longer need to be based on "soft" reasoning but should be as analytical and as data-driven as any other management discipline.

Of course, that is not the kind of reasoning the consultants used when they encountered problems that were embarrassing or threatening. The data they collected was hardly objective. The inferences they made rarely became explicit. The conclusions they reached were largely self-serving, impossible for others to test, and as a result, "self-sealing," impervious to change.

How can an organization begin to turn this situation around, to teach its members how to reason productively? The first step is for managers at the top to examine critically and change their own theories-in-use. Until senior managers become aware of how they reason defensively and the counterproductive consequences that result, there will be little real progress. Any change activity is likely to be just a fad.

Change has to start at the top because otherwise defensive senior managers are likely to disown any transformation in reasoning patterns coming from below. If professionals or middle managers begin to change the way they reason and act, such changes are likely to appear strange—if not actually dangerous—to those at the top. The result is an unstable situation where senior managers still believe that it is a sign of caring and sensitivity to bypass and cover up difficult issues, while their subordinates see the very same actions as defensive.

The key to any educational experience designed to teach senior managers how to reason productively is to connect the program to real business problems. The best demonstration of the usefulness of productive reasoning is for busy managers to see how it can make a direct difference in their own performance and in that of the organization. This will not happen overnight. Managers need plenty of opportunity to practice the new skills. But once they grasp the powerful impact that productive reasoning can have on actual performance, they will have a strong incentive to reason productively not just in a training session but in all their work relationships.

One simple approach I have used to get this process started is to have participants produce a kind of rudimentary case study. The subject is a real business problem that the manager either wants to deal with or has tried unsuccessfully to address in the past. Writing the actual case usually takes less than an hour. But then the case becomes the focal point of an extended analysis.

For example, a CEO at a large organizational-development consulting company was preoccupied with the problems caused by the intense competition among the various business functions represented by his four direct reports. Not only was he tired of having the problems dumped in his lap, but he was also worried about the impact the interfunctional conflicts were having on the organization's flexibility. He had even calculated that the money being spent to iron out disagreements amounted to hundreds of thousands of dollars every year. And the more fights there were, the more defensive people became, which only increased the costs to the organization.

In a paragraph or so, the CEO described a meeting he intended to have with his direct reports to address the problem. Next, he divided the paper in half, and on the right-hand side of the page, he wrote a scenario for the meeting—much like the script for a movie or play—describing what he would say and how his subordinates would likely respond. On the left-hand side of the page, he wrote down any thoughts and feelings that he would be likely to have during the meeting but that he wouldn't express for fear they would derail the discussion.

But instead of holding the meeting, the CEO analyzed this scenario *with* his direct reports. The case became the catalyst for a discussion in which the CEO learned several things about the way he acted with his management team.

He discovered that his four direct reports often perceived his conversations as counterproductive. In the guise of being "diplomatic," he would pretend that a consensus about the problem existed, when in fact none existed. The unintended result: instead of feeling reassured, his subordinates felt wary and tried to figure out "what is he *really* getting at."

The CEO also realized that the way he dealt with the competitiveness among department heads was completely contradictory. On the one hand, he kept urging them to "think of the organization as a whole." On the other, he kept calling for actions—department budget cuts, for example—that placed them directly in competition with each other.

Finally, the CEO discovered that many of the tacit evaluations and attributions he had listed turned out to be wrong. Since he had never expressed these assumptions, he had never found out just how wrong they were. What's more, he learned that much of what he thought he was hiding came through to his subordinates anyway—but with the added message that the boss was covering up.

The CEO's colleagues also learned about their own ineffective behavior. They learned by examining their own behavior as they tried to help the CEO analyze his case. They also learned by writing and analyzing cases of their own. They began to see that they too tended to bypass and cover up the real issues and that the CEO was often aware of it but did not say so. They too made inaccurate attributions and evaluations that they did not express. Moreover, the belief that they had to hide important ideas and feelings from the CEO and from each other in order not to upset anyone turned out to be mistaken. In the context of the case discussions, the entire senior management team was quite willing to discuss what had always been undiscussable.

In effect, the case study exercise legitimizes talking about issues that people have never been able to address before. Such a discussion can be emotional—even painful. But for managers with the courage to persist, the payoff is great: management teams and entire organizations work more openly and more effectively and have greater options for behaving flexibly and adapting to particular situations.

When senior managers are trained in new reasoning skills, they can have a big impact on the performance of the entire organization—even when other employees are still reasoning defensively. The CEO who led the meetings on the performance-evaluation procedure was able to defuse dissatisfaction because he didn't respond to professionals' criticisms in kind but instead gave a clear presentation of relevant data. Indeed, most participants took the CEO's behavior to be a sign that the company really acted on the values of participation and employee involvement that it espoused.

Of course, the ideal is for all the members of an organization to learn how to reason productively. This has happened at the company where the case team meeting took place. Consultants and their managers are now able to confront some of the most difficult issues of the consultant-client relationship. To get a sense of the difference productive reasoning can make, imagine how the original conversation between the manager and case team might have gone had everyone engaged in effective reasoning. (The following dialogue is based on actual sessions I have attended with other case teams at the same company since the training has been completed.)

First, the consultants would have demonstrated their commitment to continuous improvement by being willing to examine their own role in the difficulties that arose during the consulting project. No doubt they would have identified their managers and the clients as part of the problem, but they would have gone on to admit that they had contributed to it as well. More important, they would have agreed with the manager that as they explored the various roles of clients, managers, and professionals, they would make sure to test any evaluations or attributions they might make against the data. Each individual would have encouraged the others to question his or her reasoning. Indeed, they would have insisted on it. And in turn, everyone would have understood that act of questioning not as a sign of mistrust or an invasion of privacy but as a valuable opportunity for learning.

The conversation about the manager's unwillingness to say no might look something like this:

PROFESSIONAL #1: One of the biggest problems I had with the way you managed this case was that you seemed to be unable to say no when either the client or your superior made unfair demands. [Gives an example.]

PROFESSIONAL #2: I have another example to add. [Describes a second example.] But I'd also like to say that we never really told you how we felt about this. Behind your back we were bad-mouthing you—you know, "he's being such a wimp"—but we never came right out and said it.

MANAGER: It certainly would have been helpful if you had said something. Was there anything I said or did that gave you the idea that you had better not raise this with me?

PROFESSIONAL #3: Not really. I think we didn't want to sound like we were whining.

MANAGER: Well, I certainly don't think you sound like you're whining. But two thoughts come to mind. If I understand you correctly, you *were* complaining, but the complaining about me and my inability to say no was covered up. Second, if we had discussed this, I might have gotten the data I needed to be able to say no.

Notice that when the second professional describes how the consultants had covered up their complaints, the manager doesn't criticize her. Rather, he rewards her for being open by responding in kind. He focuses on the ways that he too may have contributed to the cover-up. Reflecting undefensively about his own role in the problem then makes it possible for the professionals to talk about their fears of appearing to be whining. The manager then agrees with the professionals that they shouldn't become complainers. At the same time, he points out the counterproductive consequences of covering up their complaints.

Another unresolved issue in the case team meeting concerned the supposed arrogance of the clients. A more productive conversation about that problem might go like this:

MANAGER: You said that the clients were arrogant and uncooperative. What did they say and do?

PROFESSIONAL #1: One asked me if I had ever met a payroll. Another asked how long I've been out of school.

PROFESSIONAL #2: One even asked me how old I was!

PROFESSIONAL #3: That's nothing. The worst is when they say that all we do is interview people, write a report based on what they tell us, and then collect our fees.

MANAGER: The fact that we tend to be so young is a real problem for many of our clients. They get very defensive about it. But I'd like to explore whether there is a way for them to freely express their views without our getting defensive.

What troubled me about your original responses was that you assumed you were right in calling the clients stupid. One thing I've noticed about consultants—in this company and others—is that we tend to defend ourselves by bad-mouthing the client.

PROFESSIONAL #1: Right. After all, if they are genuinely stupid, then it's obviously not our fault that they aren't getting it!

PROFESSIONAL #2: Of course, that stance is antilearning and overprotective. By assuming that they can't learn, we absolve ourselves from having to.

PROFESSIONAL #3: And the more we all go along with the bad-mouthing, the more we reinforce each other's defensiveness.

MANAGER: So what's the alternative? How can we encourage our clients to express their defensiveness and at the same time constructively build on it?

PROFESSIONAL #1: We all know that the real issue isn't our age; it's whether or not we are able to add value to the client's organization. They should judge us by what we produce. And if we aren't adding value, they should get rid of us—no matter how young or old we happen to be.

MANAGER: Perhaps that is exactly what we should tell them.

In both these examples, the consultants and their manager are doing real work. They are learning about their own group dynamics and addressing some generic problems in client-consultant relationships. The insights they gain will allow them to act more effectively in the future—both as individuals and as a team. They are not just solving problems but developing a far deeper and more textured understanding of their role as members of the organization. They are laying the groundwork for continuous improvement that is truly continuous. They are learning how to learn.

CHAPTER THIRTEEN

Facilitative Process Interventions

Task Processes in Groups

Edgar H. Schein

T his chapter will develop the concept of *facilitative process intervention*. In its broadest sense, "process" refers to how things are done rather than what is done. If I am crossing the street, that is *what* I am doing; the process is *how* I am crossing—am I walking, running, dodging cars, or asking someone to help me across because I feel dizzy? If I am talking to another person, that is *what* I am doing, but I may be looking at her, looking at the ground, jumbling or raising my voice, gesturing or standing very still, all of which is *how* I am doing the talking. But because process is everywhere and involves everything we do, how do we become aware of "it" and the consequences of different kinds of processes that we may be using unconsciously? How does a consultant/helper know what to focus on when trying to intervene to improve a situation and to stimulate learning in the client?

Imagine that you have been invited to a staff meeting to see if you can be helpful in making that group more effective. You may have been labeled the "facilitator" but what does that mean in terms of where you should focus your interventions, all the time being mindful of the fact that sitting quietly and observing is also an intervention with consequences? If you are the manager who has called the meeting, imagine yourself trying to make the meeting as effective as possible. What should you be paying attention to and what kinds of interventions should you be considering beyond the traditional focus on the agenda and the content of what members say? Figure 13.1 presents a set of general categories of observable events that the consultant could consider as possible foci of attention.

The cells in Figure 13.1 overlap and, in reality, the distinctions are not as clear-cut as the descriptions imply, but we need simplifying models if we are to make any sense at all of the complex data that typically confront us in human situations. All groups, and I am including a two-person relationship in this definition, always have three fundamental issues to deal with: (1) How to manage their boundaries, defining who is in and who is out and how to maintain their identity; (2) How to survive in their external environment by fulfilling their function or primary task; and (3) How to build and maintain themselves as functioning entities by managing their internal interpersonal relationships. These three basic issues are represented across the top of the figure.

If the group or relationship has existed for any length of time, one can observe each of the above issues, how the group functions at the

	Group boundary management	Group task accomplishment	Interpersonal and group management
Content	(1) Who is in and who is out	(2) Agenda	(3) Member feeling toward each other
Process	(4) Processes of boundary management	(5) Problem solving and decision making	(6) Interpersonal processes
Structure	(7) Recurring processes for maintaining boundaries	(8) Recurring task processes, organization structure	(9) Formal rules in relation to authority and intimacy

Figure 13.1. Possible Areas of Observation and Intervention.

three levels: (1) The *content* of what it works on; (2) What kinds of *processes* it uses to conduct its affairs; and (3) What *structures* are in place in the sense of stable, recurring ways of operating. These three foci of observation are represented along the side of the table. The consultant then must decide which process issues to focus on and when to shift to content or structure. We will begin with the *task* focus, the middle column, and a *content* focus inasmuch as that is most likely the reason why the consultant was called in initially.

TASK CONTENT—AGENDA MANAGEMENT (CELL 2)

The most obvious thing to focus on in any meeting or conversation is why the group is there in the first place. What is its primary task or function? What are the goals of the meeting? Why does the group exist at all? Every group or organization has an ultimate function, a reason for existence, a mission, and its goals and tasks derive from that ultimate function. However, a group may not be aware of its ultimate mission or members may not agree on its goals. In fact, one of the main functions of the consultant may be to help the group to understand its task and function.

The most observable aspect of task content is the actual subject matter that the group talks about or works on, what would typically be labeled its formal agenda. If the group has a secretary and keeps minutes, the content of the discussion is what will appear in the minutes. The consultant can keep close tabs on the task content to make sure that it stays "on track." I often find myself at the beginning of a meeting asking "What are we trying to do?" or "What is our goal for today?" or "What do we want to have accomplished by noon today?" (or whenever the group is scheduled to disband). Sometimes the consultant even creates the agenda if she has interviewed the participants and been asked to summarize what is collectively on their mind, or if she has been called in to make an educational intervention, to present some concepts, or conduct a focused exercise.

TASK PROCESS—GETTING THE WORK DONE EFFECTIVELY (CELL 5)

The arena in which I find myself working most of the time is the cell at the center of Figure 13.1—task process. Task process is often mismanaged by clients, and such mismanagement is often the reason why a group feels unproductive. People may not listen to one another or may misunderstand one another; people may interrupt one another, arguments and conflicts may develop, the group may not be able to make a decision, too much time may be spent on what might be regarded as trivial issues, disruptive side conversations may develop, and other behavior may be displayed that gets in the way of effective task work.

If one observes a variety of groups one may also become aware that different groups working on the very same task may approach it very differently. In one group the chair calls on people to give their input; another group's chair invites anyone to speak who cares to. In one group there is angry confrontation and arguing; in another group there is polite, formal questioning. In one group decisions are made by consensus, in another they are made by voting, and in a third they are made by the manager after listening to the discussion for a while.

Task processes are elusive. It is easy to experience and to observe them but hard to define and clearly segregate them from the content that is being worked on. Group members learn that they can partially control the content outcomes by controlling the process, as senators do when they filibuster or as debaters do when they destroy an opponent's argument or composure by ridicule, changing the subject, or in other ways diverting the process from what has been said. One of the toughest tasks for the consultant/helper is not to get seduced by the content, not to get so caught up in the actual problem the group is working on as to cease to pay attention to *how* it is working.

For a group to move forward on its primary task a certain number of process functions must be fulfilled. These functions are often associated with the leadership of the group or are considered to be the duties of the chair, but in well-functioning groups different members will fulfill them at different times, and the main role of the consultant will often be to *identify and fulfill the missing functions*. A simplifying model of the main task functions to be considered is presented in Exhibit 13.1.

In order for the group to make progress on a task, there must be some *initiating*. Someone must state the goal or problem, make proposals as to how to work on it, and set some time limits or targets. Often this function falls to the leader or to whoever called the group together in the first place, but as a group grows and gains confidence, initiating functions will increasingly come from a broader range of members.

Task Functions

Initiating
Information seeking
Information giving
Opinion seeking
Opinion giving
Clarifying
Elaborating
Summarizing
Consensus testing

Exhibit 13.1.   Necessary Functions for Task Fulfillment.

In order to make progress, there must be some *opinion seeking and giving* and *information seeking and giving* on various issues related to the task. The kinds of information and opinions a group seeks in pursuing its tasks are often crucial for the quality of the solution. The consultant should help the group to assess for itself whether sufficient time was given to the information and opinion-seeking functions. It is also important to distinguish seeking from giving and information from opinion. Groups often have difficulty because too many members give opinions before sufficient information seeking and giving has occurred, leading them to fruitless debate instead of constructive dialogue. The consultant can help by asking what kinds of information might be needed to resolve the issue.

Clarifying and *elaborating* are critical functions in a group in order to test the adequacy of communication and in order to build on the ideas of others toward more creative and complex ideas. If such activities do not occur, the group is not really using its unique strength. One of the most common and powerful interventions that the consultant can make is to ask clarifying questions or test his own listening by elaborating some of the ideas of members.

Summarizing is an important function to ensure that ideas are not lost because of either the size of the group or the length of discussion time. Effective summarizing includes a review of which points the group has already covered and the different ideas that have been stated, so that as decision points are reached, the group is operating with full information. One common problem I have observed in committees, task forces, and executive teams is that they tend to work sequentially and process one idea at a time, never gaining any perspective on the totality of their discussion. What is missing is the summarizing function. It can be fulfilled by having a recorder note ideas on a blackboard as the group proceeds so there is a visible summary before them at all times. Or a group member or the consultant can, from time to time, simply review what she has heard and draw out tentative generalizations from it for the group to consider.

Finally, the group needs someone periodically to test whether it is nearing a decision or should continue to discuss. *Consensus testing* could involve simply asking the question "Are we ready to decide?" or could involve some summarizing: "It seems to me we have expressed these three alternatives and are leaning toward number two; am I right?" The success of this function in moving the group forward will depend largely on the sensitivity of the person in choosing the right time to test, although ill-timed tests are still useful in reminding the group that it has some more discussing to do.

Within this broad structure of task functions we can identify a second simplifying model that focuses specifically on the stages of problem solving. Most meetings have a purpose, a function, a specific problem they are trying to solve.

GROUP PROBLEM SOLVING AND DECISION MAKING

Problem solving as a process is much discussed and little understood. The simplifying model of this process proposed below resembles many such models in the literature of our field and is chosen because it is particularly amenable to observation and analysis. The steps or stages I will describe and analyze are applicable to any kind of problem-solving process, whether it occurs in an individual manager's head, in a two-person group, in a large committee, or in the total organization.

The model distinguishes two basic cycles of activity—one that occurs prior to any decision or action, and one that occurs after a decision to act has been taken. The first cycle consists of three stages: (1) problem formulation, (2) generating proposals for action, (3) forecasting consequences of proposed solutions or testing proposed solutions and evaluating them conceptually before committing to overt action.

This cycle ends when the group has made a formal decision on what to do. The second cycle then involves: (4) action planning, (5) action steps, and (6) evaluation of the outcomes of the action steps, often leading back to the first cycle with problem redefinition. The basic reason for breaking the total process into stages is that when problem solving goes awry, it is generally because a given stage is mismanaged or is missing altogether.

In each stage there are characteristic common traps. Awareness of these traps can help the consultant to focus on when and where to intervene. Whether we are focusing on a two-person group, such as a client and me trying to establish a relationship, or a task force meeting that I have been asked to attend as part of getting acquainted with the client organization, there is always a task explicitly or implicitly defined, there are always problems to be solved, decisions to be made, and time and effort to be managed. How, then, should a group tackle and solve problems?

CYCLE 1: DECIDING WHAT TO DO

1. *Problem Formulation.* The most difficult step by far in problem solving is defining the problem. The difficulty arises in part because of a confusion between *symptoms* and *the problem.* A manager typically starts a problem-solving process when someone brings some difficulty to her attention or she discovers something that is not as it should be. Sales have fallen off, a schedule for delivery has not been met, an angry customer is on the phone, the production line has broken down, a valued subordinate has threatened to resign, or there is a fire in the shop. In a general theory of learning and change, this can be thought of as *disconfirmation.* Something is observed that was not expected and is undesirable.

However, none of the things observed are really "the problem" to be worked on. Rather, they are the symptoms to be removed. Before the manager can begin to solve the problem she must identify the causes of the symptoms, and this is often difficult because it may require further diagnosis. This may reveal not one "root cause" but possibly multiple and systemically interlocked causes that may or may not be accessible or changeable. For example, Manager X has called together his key subordinates to sit down to discuss "the problem" of declining sales. If the manager is not sensitive to the issue raised previously, he may soon be in the midst of a debate over whether to raise the advertising budget or send ten more salespeople into the field. But has he defined his problem? Has he even identified what the various alternative circumstances might be that could cause a reduction in sales and how these might be interrelated?

Falling sales could have any number of causes—erroneous sales forecast, which would imply doing nothing out in the field but something in the marketing department, or a new competitor suddenly entering the market, or a drop in product quality, or the loss of two key salespeople to a competitor, or a change in consumer taste. Without some preliminary diagnosis—which, incidentally, may take time and effort—the manager will not know what he should really be working on. The consultant can often play a key role at this stage because she is less likely to react to the time pressure the manager is under, and therefore is more likely to notice premature shortcuts in reasoning and misdiagnoses. Her role is often to help the group to slow down, to engage in a period of dialogue rather than debate, to recognize that it may be acting hastily on an ill-defined problem, and to show that the initial time invested in identifying what is *really* the problem will later pay off in less wasted time and effort.

Problems involving interpersonal relations are especially difficult to diagnose. A manager says he has a "problem" in motivating a subordinate, or coordinating with another department, or influencing his boss, or integrating the efforts of several people, or overcoming "resistance to change." Often these "problems" are felt as frustrations and tensions, with a minimum of clear understanding on the part of the manager of what is actually frustrating him or making him tense. He knows something is not right, but he does not know what the problem really is and therefore what he should do about it.

The most facilitative intervention in such cases is to help the client to be as concrete as possible in identifying the sources of frustration by engaging in a period of *exploratory* inquiry. The consultant can ask: "When did you last experience 'this problem'? What was going on? Can you give some additional examples of when you experienced the problem?" Only after a set of examples has been generated should the consultant begin to move toward *diagnostic* inquiry and a joint exploration of what the possible causes were. By carefully going over the incidents in detail and trying to identify which event actually triggered the frustration, the consultant can often help the group to define the real problem. The essential step is to have enough concrete incidents to be able to generalize a sense of the problem from them, and then to seek the patterns that tie them together.

This process, as shown in Figure 13.2, is a necessary step in any problem formulation and is the one most often skipped, leading to premature closure on what may be an incorrect diagnosis of the problem.

In the falling sales example, the group should carefully reconstruct exactly when and where all the instances of falling sales have occurred, and then determine what those instances have in common and how the various factors identified may interact with each other. Using some form of systems diagramming can be very helpful, especially in forcing the problem solvers to consider the interaction of causal factors (Senge, 1990; Senge et al., 1994).

2. *Producing Proposals for Solution.* Once the problem has been adequately formulated, the group can move on to producing ideas or courses of action that might resolve the problem or improve the situation. At this stage the most likely pitfall is that proposals are evaluated one at a time and that the group lapses into debate instead of developing a dialogue format. If that happens, the group fails to look at a whole array of possible ideas for a solution and never gains a perspective on the problem.

The consultant can help here by pointing out the consequences of premature evaluations—there is insufficient opportunity for ideas to be judged in perspective because they cannot be compared to other ideas, and the premature evaluation tends to threaten a given idea and the person who proposed it. Members whose ideas have been rejected early may feel less inclined to offer ideas at a later stage. The group should be encouraged to start this stage with some version of brainstorming—producing a number of ideas and keeping them all in front of the group before any of them are evaluated as such. Brainstorming is built on the rule that no evaluation of ideas should be permitted during the idea-production phase to stimulate the creativity that is needed at this point, and ideas should be separated from their proposers so that they can be viewed objectively. I often find myself going to the flipchart in this situation and offering to write down the ideas, thereby also making it easier to say "are there other ideas that we should be getting up here . . . ?"

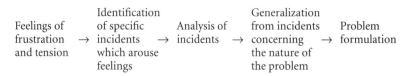

Figure 13.2.   Necessary Steps in Initially Formulating the Problem.

Once the group has a list of ideas, it can quickly weed out the obviously unworkable ones and explore the two or three ideas that look like they might work. The consultant should encourage systemic thinking at this point and invite the group to examine how the various ideas proposed interact and relate to each other. The consultant should also alert the group to the fact that just getting a number of ideas out does not in any way guarantee that the job of culling them and making a decision on which one to pursue will be easy or quick. In my experience when groups brainstorm they typically fail to allow enough time to evaluate the various ideas that they have produced.

3. *Forecasting Consequences and Testing Proposals.* Once a number of ideas for a solution have been proposed, it is necessary to forecast the consequences of adopting a particular solution and evaluate those consequences. This process is often difficult because *the criteria the group should be using to do its evaluating are either not clear or there is disagreement on which ones to use.* Such criteria might include (1) personal experience, (2) expert opinion, (3) surveying of existing data or information, and/or (4) planned tests or research. Personal experience and expert opinion are the easiest to fall back on but often the least valid. Surveys, focus groups, interviews, and other more formal research processes are likely to be more valid but also more time consuming and expensive. One of the consultant's key functions at this stage is to provide this range of alternatives and to enable the group to correctly match its validation method to the kind of idea it is trying to test.

For example, if the group is trying to decide between two products to develop, it should probably do some market research and test marketing; if the group is trying to decide whether to put surplus funds into capital expansion or investment programs, it should obtain advice from financial experts; or, if the group is trying to figure out how to overcome resistance to change to a new way of running the organization, it should run focus groups and involve future participants to get an idea of what their reactions will be. All too often a group uses just one validation method, no matter what ideas are being evaluated, and all too often that one method is based on someone's personal experience rather than any kind of formal inquiry.

At each stage of problem solving the discussion may reveal new features that lead to a reformulation of the problem. For example, in testing the idea that a new advertising campaign is needed, examining existing information may reveal that the old advertising campaign was perfectly sound. This discovery then raises the question of whether the initial formulation of the problem as "consumer sales resistance" was correct. The consultant should help the group to recognize that this kind of recycling—from initial formulation through idea production and idea testing to reformulation of the problem—is a very sound way to proceed even though it may take longer and initially appear to be inefficient. Reassurance from the consultant is usually necessary until a group becomes experienced in sensing its own problem-solving cycle because of the tendency to believe that constant reformulation of the problem is merely wasting time.

Cycle 1 ends with the group making a decision to move forward on an action item. That decision may be to gather more information, but it requires going outside the group meeting and doing something beyond considering alternatives. The next issue, then, is how the group actually makes decisions and how well the decision process is aligned with the kind of decision the group is making. A number of alternatives should be considered.

GROUP DECISION-MAKING METHODS

Decisions are involved at every stage of the problem-solving process but are only highly visible in the transition from cycle 1 to cycle 2, where the problem-solving unit commits itself to trying out a proposal for action or decides to gather more information before deciding on a particular proposal for solution. Prior to this step, the group has had to decide when and where to meet, how to organize itself, how to allocate time, by what procedures or rules to run its discussion (for example, with or without a formal chair, with or without Robert's Rules of Order), or how to tell when the problem has been sufficiently well formulated to move on to idea production. Often, group members do not recognize that they have made so many process decisions and that these have real consequences for the climate of the group and the quality of the problem solutions. The consultant must be prepared, therefore, to draw attention to the many available decision-making mechanisms by making an "educational intervention," which lays out the options discussed below. (The "Plop to Consensus" scheme was first developed by Robert Blake and others in NTL workshops in the early 1950s.)

In reviewing the different decision-making methods listed, it is important not to judge too quickly any one method as better than another. Each has its use at the appropriate time, and each method has certain consequences for future group operations. The important point is for the group to understand these consequences well enough to be able to choose a decision-making method that will be appropriate to the amount of time available, the past history of the group, the kind of task being worked on, and the kind of climate the group wants to establish.

1. *Decision by Lack of Response ("Plop").* The most common and perhaps least visible group decision-making method occurs when someone suggests an idea, and, before anyone else has said anything about it, someone else suggests another idea, until the group eventually finds one it will act on. All the ideas that have been bypassed have, in a real sense, been decided on by the group. But the decision has been simply a common decision not to support them, making the proposers feel that their suggestions have "plopped." The floors of most group meeting rooms are completely covered with plops. Notice that the tacit assumption underlying this method is that "silence means lack of agreement."

2. *Decision by Formal Authority.* Many groups set up a power structure or start with a power structure that makes it clear that the chair or someone in authority will make the decisions. The group can generate ideas and hold free discussion, but at any time the chair can say that, having heard the discussion, she has decided to do thus and so. This method is highly efficient. Whether it is effective depends a great deal on whether the chair is a sufficiently good listener to have culled the right information on which to base her decision.

Furthermore, if the group must move on to the next stage or implement the decision, the authority-rule method produces a minimum amount of group involvement. Hence it undermines the potential quality of the implementation of the decision. I have often sat in meetings where the chair has decided something after listening to the group for a few minutes, but the action ultimately taken proved to be somehow out of line with what the chair wanted. Upon later reconstruction it turned out that the group either misunderstood the decision or did not agree with it in the first place, and hence was neither able nor motivated to carry it out effectively.

3. *Decision by Self-Authorization or Minority.* One of the most common complaints of group members is that they feel "railroaded" in reference to some decision. Usually this feeling results from one, two, or three people employing tactics that produce action and therefore must be considered decisions, but which are taken without the consent of the majority. The tacit assumption in this case is that silence means consent.

One version of minority rule is "self-authorization." Self-authorization is where one member makes a proposal for what to do, no other proposals are offered, no one says anything negative, and so the group does what was proposed. The most popular version of this type of decision is what Jerry Harvey called the "Abilene Paradox" (1974), referring to his memory of when his family had an unpleasant drive to Abilene to have lunch only to discover later in the day that no one had wanted to go. One person had suggested it as a possibility, and everyone else had remained silent. The initiator and everyone else assumed that silence meant consent.

In my own experience this form of decision is most common and most dangerously inappropriate when used in choosing the *process* by which the group will work. Someone says "Let's run the meeting by Robert's Rules of Order" and, when no one challenges the suggestion even though they disagree, the group ends up using a method that no one wanted. Or, one person says, "Majority rules, right?" and when no one challenges the statement, the group finds itself making 8-to-7 decisions that get poorly implemented. When a self-authorized proposal is on the table it is often important for the consultant to say "Does the group agree with this? Is this what we want to do?"

A single person can railroad a decision, particularly if he is in some kind of convener role, by not giving opposition an opportunity to build up. The convener says, "I think the way to go at this is to each state our opinion on the topic to see where we all stand. Now my own opinion is . . . " Once he has given his own opinion, he turns to the person on his right and says, "What do you think, Joan?" When Joan has spoken, the convener points to the next person and the group is off and running, having in effect made a decision about how it is going to go about its work based on the convener's self-authorization. Another similar tactic is to say, "Well, we all seem to be agreed, so let's go ahead with John's idea," even though the careful observer may have detected that only John, the chair, and maybe one other person has spoken favorably about the idea. The others have remained silent. If the initiator is asked how he concluded there was agreement, chances are that he will say, "Silence means consent, doesn't it? Everyone had a chance to voice opposition." If one interviews the group members later, one sometimes discovers that an actual majority was against John's idea but each one hesitated to speak up because he thought that all the other silent ones were for it. They too were trapped by "silence means consent."

Perhaps the commonest form of minority rule is for two or more members to come to a quick and powerful agreement on a course of action, to challenge the group with a quick "Does anyone object?" and, if no one raises her voice in two seconds, to proceed with "Let's go ahead, then." Again the trap is the assumption that silence means consent both on the part of the initiators and on the part of the disagreers who are afraid to be in a minority of opposition. When the group operates this way, one often has a condition of "pluralistic ignorance"—where everyone makes an assumption about the opinions of members that turns out to be wrong, but no one checked. Or, at the extreme, we have "group think" (Janis, 1982), where a decision is made on the presumption of total agreement while a substantial minority (or even majority) may be in disagreement but has been silenced.

The consultant plays an important role with respect to these decision-making methods, primarily because they are rarely recognized and labeled as decision-making methods in the first place. Yet a great many group decisions, particularly pertaining to the important issue of group procedures, rules of order, and the like, are made in these rather rapid ways. For a group member to challenge such proceedings, to say, "We don't really agree," is often seen as blocking; hence there are strong pressures on group members to stay silent and let things take their course, even though they are not in agreement.

The consultant must first make the group aware of decisions it has made and the methods by which it has made them; then she must try to get the group members to assess whether they feel that these methods were appropriate to the situation. For example, the members may agree that the chairperson did railroad the decision, but they may also feel that this was appropriate because time was short and someone needed to make that decision quickly so the group could get on with more important things. On the other hand, the group might decide that a decision such as having each person in turn state his point of view introduces an element of formality and ritual into the group which undermines its ability to build creatively on ideas already advanced. The group might then wish to choose a different method of idea production. The important thing is to legitimize such process discussion and to have some observations available in case the group is finding it difficult to discern what the consultant is talking about.

4. *Decision by Majority Rule: Voting and/or Polling.* Next we come to more familiar decision-making procedures that are often taken for granted as applying to any group situation because they reflect our political system. One simple version is to poll everyone's opinion following some period of discussion, and, if a majority feels the same way, to assume that that is the decision. The other method is the more formal one of making a motion, getting a second or simply stating a clear alternative, and asking for votes in favor of it, votes against it, and abstentions.

On the surface this method seems completely sound, but surprisingly often decisions made by this method are not well implemented even by the group that made the decision. What is wrong? If one can get the group to discuss its process, or if one interviews members of the minority, it turns out that three psychological barriers to effective implementation exist: (1) the minority members often do not agree that the silent assumption of "majority rule" should apply, but they feel unable to challenge it; (2) the minority members often feel that there was an insufficient period of discussion for them to really get their point of view across; and, (3) the minority members often feel that the voting process has created two camps within the group, that these camps are now in a win-lose competition. Their camp lost the first round but it is just a matter of time until it can regroup, pick up some support, and win the next time a vote comes up.

In other words, voting creates coalitions, and the preoccupation of the losing coalition is not how to implement what the majority wants but how to win the next battle. If voting is to be used, the group must be sure that it has created a climate in which members feel they have had their day in court and where members feel obligated to go along with the majority decision. A key role for the consultant is to highlight for the group the pitfalls of each method and to get enough discussion of group climate to ensure that the group will choose an appropriate decision-making process.

5. *Decision by Consensus.* One of the most effective but also most time-consuming methods of group decision making is to seek consensus. Consensus, as I will define it, is not the same thing as unanimity.

Rather, it is a state of affairs where communications have been sufficiently open, and the group climate has been sufficiently supportive, to make all members of the group feel that they had a fair chance to influence the decision. Someone then tests for the "sense of the meeting," carefully avoiding formal procedures, such as voting. Polling can be effective in reaching consensus provided the group has accepted the principle that it will not go with a simple majority but will seek broader agreement.

If there is a clear alternative that most members subscribe to, and if those who oppose it feel they have had their chance to influence the decision, then a consensus exists. Operationally, it would be defined by the fact that those members who do not agree with the extended majority alternative nevertheless understand it clearly and are prepared to support it. It is a psychological state that must be tested for and might be described as follows: "I understand what most of you would like to do. I personally would not do that, but I feel that you understand what my alternative would be. I have had sufficient opportunity to sway you to my point of view but clearly have not been able to do so. Therefore, I will go along with what most of you wish to do and will do my best to implement it."

In order to achieve such a condition, time must be allowed for all group members to state their opposition and to state it fully enough to get the feeling that others really do understand them. This condition is essential if they are later to free themselves of preoccupation with the idea that they could have gotten their point of view across if others had only understood what they really had in mind. Only by careful listening to the opposition can such feelings be forestalled and effective group decisions reached.

The consultant can help the group to determine what kinds of decisions should be made by consensus, that is, which decisions are important enough to warrant the effort? One guideline he might suggest is that procedural decisions, those which pertain to *how* the group works, are the ones where it is most important that everyone be on board; hence these should probably be made by consensus. The group might decide to give complete authority to the chair, or it might decide to try for very informal discussion procedures, or it might wish to brainstorm some ideas. But whatever is decided, it should be completely clear to everyone and there should not be residual feelings of being misunderstood or desires to sabotage the group procedure.

6. *Decision by Unanimous Consent.* The logically perfect but least attainable kind of decision is where everyone truly agrees on the course of action to be taken. For certain key kinds of decisions it may be necessary to seek unanimity, but for most important ones consensus is enough, if it is real consensus. The consultant can help the group here by pointing out that the group may be setting too high a standard for itself in some cases. Unanimity is not always necessary and may be a highly inefficient way to make decisions. The important thing is to take some time to agree on which method to use for what kinds of tasks and in what kinds of situations.

A final thought—often the method of decision making is simply announced to the group by the convener or chair. If this is the case, the consultant must try to determine whether the group is comfortable with the method being used, and, if not, find an opportunity to raise with the chair the issue of whether she should permit some discussion by the group of how to handle the decision-making area. In my experience, conveners often tend to feel threatened by such discussion because they fear that they will lose control of the group, resulting in disorder and chaos. One way to reassure them is by pointing out that different ways of making decisions do not necessarily imply a disorderly communication process. If the consultant can provide some viable alternatives, he can often get the chair to experiment with different methods and draw her own conclusions.

CYCLE 2. ACTING, EVALUATING, AND REFORMULATING

All of cycle 1 involves steps that occur in discussion and that do not involve commitment to action unless the group chooses to gather additional data for idea evaluation. As the group reaches some consensus on a proposed solution and makes a decision to act, we go into cycle 2, the action cycle. Making the decision to act is not shown in the diagram but is represented by the act of crossing the boundary between cycle 1 and cycle 2. When a decision has been made on a given proposal or idea for solution, the problem-solving process is far from finished. The group must then still plan a detailed course of action, take action steps, and have some method to determine whether or not the action steps are solving the problem. This last step should be thought out in advance of taking action: "What information should we be looking at to determine whether or not our action steps are achieving the desired results?"

At any of these stages, it is again possible for the group to discover that it had not formulated the problem correctly and must revert back to cycle 1 for some new reformulation, as well as idea proposing and testing. Such recycling is entirely desirable and should not be considered a waste of time. It is far more costly to be working on the wrong problem and discover this only after expensive action steps have been taken, than it is to make a greater effort initially to define the problem correctly.

4. and 5. *Taking Action Steps.* The action planning stage can be treated as a new problem requiring its own problem formulation, idea production, and idea testing. If these substages are short-circuited or avoided, a good proposal may be carried out inadequately and the group will erroneously conclude that the proposal was deficient, instead of recognizing insufficient action planning as the culprit. Here again, the key role for the consultant may be to slow the group down and encourage them to plan carefully before leaping into action.

One of the major pitfalls of this stage is to make general plans without assigning clear responsibilities to specific members for specific actions. I have sat in many a group meeting where a decision was reached, the meeting was adjourned, and nothing happened because everyone thought that someone else would now do something. The clear allocation of responsibility for action not only ensures that action will be taken but provides a test of the decision in that the responsible implementer may raise questions about the decision that had not been considered before.

In some cases the whole second cycle is delegated to some other person or group. For example, the original problem-solving group decides "Let's beef up our advertising campaign." Once it has reached this decision, the group orders the advertising department to increase advertising on certain products. The group then relaxes and reverts to watching sales figures. Is this a sound approach? The answer in many cases is "No" because when different people perform cycle 2, they may neither understand clearly nor be particularly committed to the proposal or solution that the cycle 1 person or group has offered. They have not struggled with the problem definition or had a chance to see the reasons why other alternatives that may now occur to them have been rejected. They may also feel that the general proposal given to them is too unclear to permit implementation.

Equally problematic is the case where a management group delegates problem formulation (cycle 1) to a task force or a consulting organization and then waits for a diagnosis and proposal for action in writing. In nine cases out of ten, if the originating group has not involved itself in problem formulation and if the task force has not thought through action implementation (cycle 2), the management group will not like the proposal and will find an excuse to shelve it. Given these kinds of problems, it is desirable to ensure a high degree of overlap (or at least communication) between cycle 1 and cycle 2 members. The ideal situation would, of course, be that they are the same problem-solving unit. If that is not possible, the cycle 1 unit should provide for an interim phase that permits the cycle 2 unit to get completely on board before the two units sever their communication risk. One way to do this is to bring the implementer into the problem-solving process at the earliest possible stage, or, at least, to review completely with him all the steps the cycle 1 unit has gone through to arrive at a proposal for solution.

In such a review, the key process would be to permit the implementing unit to satisfy itself completely by asking as many questions as it would like concerning the reasons that certain other alternatives, which might strike it as better ones, were not selected. They should get satisfactory answers, or the cycle 1 group should go back and review the additional alternatives brought up by the implementing unit. The role of the consultant here is to help the group understand how difficult it is to communicate a complex action proposal to an implementer, and then to ensure this understanding early enough in the problem-solving process to institute protective measures against communication breakdown.

6. *Evaluating Outcomes.* To ensure adequate evaluation, the group should reach consensus on (1) the criteria for evaluation, (2) the timetable—when results should first be expected, and (3) who will be responsible for reporting back information to be evaluated. Once results are in, the group should be psychologically prepared to go back into cycle 1 with an effort to reformulate the problem, not merely to rush in with more solution alternatives. The group should always be prepared to reconsider what it sees as the problem, and the consultant should constantly raise the question "What problems are we working on?"

SUMMARY OF PROBLEM SOLVING AND DECISION MAKING

Problem solving can be thought of as consisting of two cycles, one of which involves primarily discussion and the other primarily action taking. The first cycle consists of the phases of problem identification and formulation, idea or proposal generation, and idea or proposal testing through attempting to forecast consequences. The most difficult stage is that of identifying and formulating the real problem, and often this stage requires additional data-gathering efforts before the problem can be clearly identified.

The second cycle involves action planning, action steps, and evaluation of outcomes. The action planning is itself a problem-solving process and should be treated as such. The major difficulty in the total cycle is making the transition from cycle 1 to cycle 2 if different parties are involved. Those who have to implement the decisions should be involved in the earliest possible stage.

The decision process itself can be handled by

1. lack of group response

2. authority rule

3. minority rule

4. majority rule

5. consensus and/or

6. unanimity.

It is important for a group to become aware of these different decision-making methods and to learn to choose an appropriate method for the kind of task or decision it is working on.

CHOOSING AN INTERVENTION FOCUS

Task issues such as the basic functions, the manner of cycling through the problem-solving process, and the methods of making decisions are so obviously relevant to effective group functioning that it is generally easy for the consultant to get the group to observe and manage them. But, one of the consultant's greatest dilemmas is choosing an intervention focus from among the many categories reviewed previously, that is, which behavior to bring to the group's attention.

The three key criteria for choosing from the array of possibilities are as follows:

1. The degree to which the consultant perceives the process issue to be related to the group's effectiveness

2. The degree to which the data about the process issue are sufficiently clear so that if attention is drawn to the issue, there is a reasonable probability that the group members will also have perceived what the consultant perceived

3. Whether or not the consultant can think of an intervention that will facilitate moving the process along instead of simply interrupting it

Obscure references to process issues that are not clearly visible will not enhance group learning, nor is it helpful to get a group preoccupied with how it is working when there is time pressure to make an important decision. The consultant must understand what the group views as its primary task and focus interventions on those task processes that relate clearly to that primary task.

WHAT ABOUT "TASK STRUCTURE?" (CELL 8)

If one observes a group for some period of time one will perceive that certain patterns recur, that some kinds of events happen regularly, and some kinds of events never happen. For example, one group always uses parliamentary procedure, whereas another refuses to vote on any issue even if they cannot resolve the issue by any other means. One group always has an agenda and follows it slavishly, whereas another waits until the meeting begins before generating a list of topics. Such regularities in the work of the group can best be thought of as the task structure of the group, relatively *stable, recurring* processes that help the group or organization accomplish its tasks.

In large organizations we think of the structure as being the formal hierarchy, the defined chain of command, the systems of information and control, and other stable, recurring processes that are taught to newcomers as "the way we work around here." But it is important to recognize that the concept of structure is only an extension of the concept of process in that it refers to those processes that are stable, recurring, and defined by members in the group as their "structure."

All groups require such regularities and stability to make their environment and working patterns predictable and, thereby, manageable. The assumptions that develop as the underlying premises of those patterns can then be thought of as part of the culture of the group. They become shared and taken for granted, and the structures that we can observe can be viewed as artifacts or manifestations of the culture of the group (Schein, 1992). The culture itself is not immediately visible because it is best thought of as the shared, taken for granted, underlying and unconscious assumptions that have evolved to deal with the various external and internal issues the group has had to face. But the culture will be reflected in the overt behavior and can be searched out through a joint process of inquiry between the outsider and members of the group. For most purposes it is sufficient to focus on the manifest artifacts, the visible behavior, always bearing in mind that they reflect important underlying assumptions that will eventually have to be taken into account. However, until the group itself is ready to look at its own culture, it is difficult for the consultant to focus on it.

The task structure that evolves in a group is composed of regularities that pertain specifically to the group's survival in its external environment. All groups face at least five basic survival problems. By being aware of them, the consultant can focus her observations and create a mental checklist of what to pay attention to.

1. *Mission/Primary Task.* What is the *fundamental mission* that justifies the group's existence—its *primary task?* The structural elements dealing with this issue are usually company charters, statements of philosophy or mission, formal agenda statements, and other efforts to document members' implicit understanding about the ultimate role of the group.

2. *Specific Goals and Strategies.* These are usually derived from the mission and are reflected in written goal statements, strategies, formal plans, publicly defined targets, and deadlines.

3. *Means to Use to Accomplish the Goals.* The structures for accomplishing goals are the defined formal organization, assigned task roles, and recurring procedures for solving problems and making decisions. The organization chart, lines of authority, job descriptions, and formally specified accountabilities all fall into this category.

4. *Measuring and Monitoring Systems.* Every group needs to know whether or not goals are being achieved. Formal information

and control systems are set up, and managerial planning, budgeting, and review processes are formalized.

5. *Systems for Fixing Problems and Getting Back on Course.* Measurement systems reveal when the group is off target or not accomplishing its goals. The group then needs processes for remedying situations, fixing problems, or getting itself back on course. Often solutions are invented ad hoc, but any group or organization has to be able to regularize remedial and corrective processes, and thus make them part of the structure of the group.

In a young group, the task structures will not be very stable, that is, the young group is not very "structured." As the group evolves, it keeps those processes that continue to work and comes to share the assumptions about itself that led to its success. The processes then become more visible and may be formally described in organization charts, manuals of procedure, rules of order, and other artifacts of the evolving culture. As these processes become more and more stable we talk of "bureaucracy" and "institutionalization."

Whether or not the consultant can intervene constructively in the task structure depends on the degree to which the group itself is conscious of that structure and needs to change it. In my experience the most powerful interventions in this area are the ones that enable the group to gain insight into its own unconscious assumptions. The visible external structures are easy to observe, but the underlying assumptions that created those structures are much harder to detect. Yet without insight into those assumptions, the group cannot learn how to function more effectively.

The final issue to be addressed, then, is whether the consultant can or should get involved in interventions aimed at structural issues. Observing the group and helping them to confront their own structures is certainly one kind of necessary intervention. More problematic is whether or not to get involved in structure and culture *change.* The main criterion continues to be that the consultant must be facilitative and helpful. If a group really wants me to get involved in working with their structure and culture I will do so, provided we clearly understand that changes in structure may entail change processes that will arouse high levels of anxiety and resistance because the evolved structures provide predictability, meaning, and security for the group members. Culture is embedded in structure, hence one cannot change structure without threatening accepted cultural assumptions.

CHAPTER FOURTEEN

Large Group Interventions and Dynamics

Barbara Bunker
Billie Alban

This chapter begins with a brief history to set the context for discussion of the unique dynamics in large group interventions. Large group interventions emerged at the confluence of three intellectual traditions: social psychology, psychoanalytic theory, and systems theory as applied to organizations.

Gestalt psychology, which emphasized the holistic configuration of psychological events as contrasted with atomistic theories, developed in Germany early in this century. It came to the United States in the late 1930s, as World War II was beginning, in the person of Kurt Lewin. Like many psychologists in his day, Lewin volunteered to assist the war effort on the home front. The following story describes an early experiment and how he became interested in the power of small groups to change people's behavior.

During the war, a severe meat shortage led to meat rationing. At the same time, certain parts of the cow such as the sweetbreads, liver, brains, and tongue went unused. The War Office wanted to promote full utilization of these. With Lewin's help, the War Office set up an experiment in which an audience of women heard a dietitian describe the nutritional value of these underused cuts of beef, give recipes, and demonstrate how to prepare them (Lewin, 1943). Then, half of the audience went home while the other half discussed what they had heard in small groups. At the end of the discussion, individuals were asked if they would make a public commitment to try the recipes. Those who were willing to do this made a verbal commitment in the presence of the group.

Six months later, when researchers checked with all the women who had heard the lecture, they found that the people who had participated in the discussion and had made the public commitment were much more likely to have bought and served these cuts than those who had only heard the lecture. Two questions emerged: "What goes on in groups that produces these changes in behavior?" and "How do we understand the power of groups over individuals?" To pursue these questions, the Laboratory for the Study of Group Dynamics was started at the Massachusetts Institute of Technology, with Lewin as its founder and head. For several decades thereafter, studies of groups and different aspects of group life were a major focus of research in social psychology. Much of what we take for granted in our understanding of group dynamics emerged from this line of research. Although Lewin died an untimely death in 1947, his students shared his interest in groups and in social problems. Ronald Lippitt, one of these, moved with Lewin when the Center for Group Dynamics was established at the University of Michigan. It later became the Institute for Social Research.

Lewin's interest in social change involved him and Lippitt with adult educator Leland Bradford and psychologist Kenneth Benne of Boston University in a project on race relations in 1946. They collaborated in planning and running a two-week training conference for community leaders on race relations in Connecticut (Marrow, 1969). During the conference, participants met in discussion groups that were observed by Lewin's students. The researchers met every evening to discuss their observations from that day and to develop theories about group process. The story goes that a few conference participants grew interested in these evening research discussions, appeared one evening, and asked to attend. Lewin agreed and the first discussion was so fascinating that more and more people began to attend, talking about and reflecting on their own experiences in the discussion groups.

This process of being part of a group and then reflecting on the process of that group gave birth to a new social innovation, what is commonly know as the *T-group* or sensitivity training group.

Building on this discovery, Bradford, Benne, and Lippitt founded the National Training Laboratories (now the NTL Institute), an organization dedicated to helping people learn about groups and about themselves as members and leaders of groups. During the 1950s and 1960s, the NTL summer campus in Bethel, Maine, was a hotbed of experimentation in experiential learning.

As it became clear during the 1960s that T-group training in organizations was not effective, the focus turned to problem solving and fixing the deficits in organizational functioning that could be identified. The method of choice was survey feedback, an action research method that collects data about how the people in an organization view the organization and the functioning of their unit and other units. It is used to identify sources of ineffectiveness so that attention can be paid to remedying the situation. Consultants collect and analyze data and feed these data back to units that then take action to deal with the issues.

Ron Lippitt, like other organizational consultants of his time, engaged in this process with organizations. As a researcher, however, he also studied the process. While listening to some tapes of problem-solving groups at work, he realized that their discussion caused him to lose energy and feel drained and tired. Since problem solving seemed to drain energy, perhaps he could find something that would engage people in a different way and thus generate energy. Ron Lippitt was a creative genius at designing processes. He began to think about how past-oriented problem solving is. It looks at what has happened and tries to fix it. What if you asked people to think about the future? What if you asked them what kind of future state they would like to have in their organization? Lippitt (1980, 1983) began to create activities that helped people to think their way into a "preferred future."

The 1970s were a time when the automobile industry was in decline in Michigan. Lippitt and his colleague, Eva Schindler-Rainman, got involved with a number of cities across the country, but especially in Michigan, in helping city leaders to bring together people from all parts of the community in order to think about and plan for the future of their city (Schindler-Rainman & Lippitt, 1980). Lippitt even created a system of voting with computer cards that allowed large groups of people to register their views. Then he immediately displayed the tally to the whole group. In some settings, Lippitt brought together as many as one thousand people, with remarkable results. Although many other consultants knew about the work that Lippitt and Schindler-Rainman were doing, they were not quick to adopt it. Only recently has the field looked back and acknowledged how visionary and ahead of its time this work was.

THE TAVISTOCK TRADITION

Parallel developments occurred in the United Kingdom, but from a different theoretical base than in the Lewinian tradition. The Tavistock Institute in London, England, was created to make social science knowledge applicable to individual, group, and system issues. Wilfred Bion, a psychiatrist and psychoanalyst associated with the Institute, found himself unable to treat his caseload of returning veterans from World War II because the numbers were too great. He decided to experiment with psychotherapy in groups rather than individually. His initial view was that he would treat each person in front of the others and that that might possibly have a positive effect on the observers. What he soon discovered was that a great deal more went on in groups than simply his interaction with the patient. The group itself had dynamics that could assist or sabotage the task; it even could attack and undermine him as the leader. Eventually, he wrote a book, *Experiences in Groups* (1961), in which he described three basic assumptions that can either facilitate or inhibit the primary task of the group: dependence, fight or flight, and pairing.

The Tavistock Institute began providing training in group processes using Bion's framework in 1957. These ideas were carried to the United States in the person of A. K. Rice, who began running conferences to train professionals in identifying and understanding group processes in work organizations.

Another central figure in the developments in Britain was Eric Trist, who, with Harold Bridger and Wilfred Bion, was one of the founders of the Tavistock Institute. Trist was a colleague of Bion in action research during the Second World War and an admirer of Lewin's work. Trist and his young colleague, Fred Emery, developed the idea of Socio-Technical Systems from studies they did in the British coal mines in the 1950s (Trist, Higgin, Murray, & Pollock, 1963). They developed a process for analyzing and achieving the best fit of social and technical systems in organizations that has been widely used in Europe, especially in Scandinavia, since the 1960s.

In the course of various consultations with industry, Trist and Emery were invited to help design a conference for the top leadership of Bristol/Siddeley, a recent merger of two aeronautical engineering companies. The organization's leader had in mind a leadership conference with invited speakers, but Emery and Trist had something different in mind. In their work at the Tavistock Institute, they had been studying the adjustment of industry to turbulent times, and they proposed a week-long exploration of the business environment, the aeronautics industry, and the desirable future role for Bristol/Siddeley; this was a clear departure from traditional organizational events. A compromise was achieved by preserving the days for the search process suggested by Trist and Emery and the late afternoons and evenings for speakers and discussion.

The week contained its points of stress and strain, but by the end, the group was talking like one company and had "redefined the business they were in" (Weisbord, 1992, p. 30). This was the first Search Conference (Trist & Emery, 1960). It was a dialogue among the participants that began with trying to understand the external world and then moved through explorations of the industry to their own company. The goal was a strategic action plan about the future.

SYSTEMS THEORY

The third stream in the development of large group interventions is the enormous impact that open systems theory has had on thought about organizations. Including the organization's environment as a key element in understanding organizational functioning was a paradigm shift. Understanding that changes in one part of the system affect the whole was another. Eric Trist credits Fred Emery with bringing the implications of Ludwig von Bertalanffy's thinking about biology (von Bertalanffy, 1950) into the Tavistock Institute. Emery was clearly one of the earliest to grasp the implications of systems theory and to use it in thinking about organizations as open systems. Later, colleagues Eric Miller and A. K. Rice (1967) published their book on organizations as open systems. In America, at the University of Michigan, social psychologists David Katz and Robert Kahn (1978) published the first edition of their now-classic open systems approach to organizations in 1966. But even though these ideas were in print, they were only gradually moved into the practice of organizational change.

One of the early published designs for working with the whole system in the room was Richard Beckhard's Confrontation Meeting, published later in the *Harvard Business Review* (Beckhard & Harris, 1967).

Beckhard invented the Confrontation Meeting out of a desire to shift the negative energy in a family business he was working with to a positive direction. This one-day intervention begins with heterogeneous groupings in which people consider what would need to change for life at work to be better. In other words, it begins with future possibilities. After the results are shared and organized, functional groups meet to develop four or five "promises," actions they can take in the direction of a better work environment. At the same time, they select a few priorities for management attention. At the end of the day, these actions and requests are shared and management responds. A two-hour follow-up meeting in about six weeks helps to sustain the changes and create others. This is the first design we know of that worked with all parts of the organization at the same time. It is not surprising that it emerged at the same time as Beckhard's work on complex systems change.

Training programs for consultants with open systems thinking at the core were started by the Gestalt Institute of Cleveland, Ohio, and the NTL Institute in the early 1970s. The A. K. Rice Institute also offered training in small, large, and intergroup dynamics from a systems perspective. Beckhard and Harris's book on complex systems change was published in 1977. Developments outside the field of organizational change also had an impact, for example, Jayaram's open systems planning model (1977) had wide effects on strategic planning and change in organizations. At a more experiential level, Barry Oshry (1996) developed a simulation in the mid 1970s called *The Power Lab,* which allowed participants to explore the dynamics of being at the bottom, middle, or top of any system. People who came to these three-day events lived in their assigned role and enacted and studied the system dynamics in a large group.

THE 1980S

The 1980s were a time when the field of organization development matured, or at least many of the senior practitioners in the field now had twenty years of experience. One of these senior practitioners, Marvin Weisbord, who was well known for his thoughtfulness about his own practice, used writing a book about the state of the field of organization development to reflect on his own extensive experiences working with organizations and to rethink the history of management practice in the United States. *Productive Workplaces* (1987) examined in a new light the contributions of Frederick Taylor, Douglas McGregor,

Eric Trist, Fred Emery, and Kurt Lewin to the way that organizations are run and changed. This reframing of management history was interlaced with Weisbord's own new practice theory.

One part of this new theory stressed the importance of "getting the whole system into the room" in order to create effective change. Drawing from all three traditions, Weisbord created the Future Search as a method to get the whole system to decide on its purposes. He believed that stakeholders outside the organization could contribute to rethinking what was needed in the fast-changing world of new customer requirements and new technology.

Weisbord's thinking struck a deep chord with many of us. It resonated with our own experience and frustrations. The notion of getting the whole system into the room was congruent with our experiences when we had worked to make change only to have it all come undone because of changes in other parts of the system. It felt like an idea whose time had come.

Other influences also affect the methods we describe but are difficult to fit into the three streams of influence. The work of W. Edwards Deming (1992), for example, and the total quality management movement have focused attention on what customers inside and outside the organization need and want. It has made it not only acceptable but critical to include stakeholders.

METHODS FOR GETTING THE WHOLE SYSTEM INTO THE ROOM

As we turn to the 1990s, it is now a great deal easier to talk about the ideas and assumptions that influenced these methods.

The two different forms of Search Conference originated in the Tavistock tradition with the Emery Search Conference. Weisbord and Janoff's Future Search was influenced heavily by the work of the Emerys and Eric Trist, but it has been modified by the Lewininan-NTL tradition.

Real Time Strategic Change and Large Scale Interactive Events, other methods for getting the whole system in the room (Dannemiller & Jacobs, 1992), come directly from the Lewinian-NTL tradition. The same is true for the ICA Strategic Planning Process and for Simu-Real. Work-Out also benefited from this tradition as well as being quite similar to Beckhard's Confrontation Meeting.

Four types of organizational redesign all came from Trist and Emery's original Socio-Technical Systems design, but each has been expanded to include large group events and participation by the whole system as well as by stakeholders. Participative Design is the next iteration of Fred Emery's commitment to democratic workplaces. According to recent statements by Emery (1995), it corrects some of the flaws in Socio-Technical Systems design and allows workers to truly control and be responsible for their own work.

Open Space Technology is difficult to categorize in terms of its theoretical roots. It was developed in the context of interest in organizational transformation. Harrison Owen (1992), who created it, has both NTL and analytic training. Rather than proceeding through a series of carefully orchestrated, structured experiences, participants in Open Space are challenged to find within themselves issues of deep importance and are invited to join others and discuss them. The agenda that the participants create makes possible the opening of whatever creative or emergent patterns there might be. Because no one knows in advance what they will be, the participants should be "prepared to be surprised." Theoretically, this seems close to the work of David Bohm (1990) and the work that is currently going on at MIT around the Dialogue Process, which emphasizes asking exploratory questions and examining assumptions and inferences (Senge, 1990). It is a nonlinear way of making progress under the assumption that deep structures can emerge if we allow them to. It is also the case, however, that psychoanalytic theory like Bion's may be very helpful in understanding the large group dynamics that occur, especially to the facilitator whose job it is to "hold the space"—that is, to maintain the integrity of the structure and process.

All of these methods of working in large groups are highly participatory. They fundamentally assume that people want to be engaged and to have a voice. But Open Space Technology assumes, to a greater degree than the other interventions, that people are capable of structuring their reality and of organizing themselves for the tasks at hand—and that being responsible for the events as well as the content will be energizing and lead to innovation.

With this background, now let us go on to look at the unique dynamics in large groups and how they impact interventions.

LARGE GROUP DYNAMICS

Are the psychological processes of large groups different from those in small groups? We find evidence of three issues that we believe it is critical to understand in order to work in large group settings.

THE DILEMMA OF VOICE

Large groups are, by definition, too large for people to have face-to-face interaction. In small groups of up to about a dozen people, each person has a reasonable chance to speak, be listened to, and be responded to. In small group dynamics, the expression "airtime" means the amount of time available for speaking. In an hour-long meeting of eight people, each person has about 7½ minutes for speaking. In such small groups, problems with speaking are not created by too little airtime. However, large groups have a structural airtime dilemma. Consider a group with fifty people who are in a meeting for thirty minutes. Each person can have just over half a minute. This means that she or he might be able to say a short sentence or two, but conversation and responding to others is not possible. Of course, that is not what happens. In large groups, typically, some people say quite a lot while others are silent.

This is the first major issue of large group dynamics. We are calling it *the dilemma of voice* (see also Main, 1975; Menzies, 1960). We use the word *dilemma* here as Glidewell (1970) uses it to describe a situation that cannot be changed or permanently resolved. Problems can be solved. Dilemmas, even in a good marriage, have to be lived with! In social settings, most people from individualistic countries like ours want to be recognized as individuals who have worth and a unique contribution to make. In a small group, we do this through our verbal contributions. We *individuate* ourselves by what we say in the group. People get to know us and what we can contribute. Through interaction, groups develop patterns of roles and members rely on each other.

In a large group, however, people always have the problem of feeling recognized, because it is difficult to get an opportunity to speak. This is a structural difficulty created by the time available and the number of people who want to use it. In addition, the sheer number of other people who are present is intimidating to some, especially those who prefer one-to-one interaction. Even those who do speak in large groups will not be able to know the reactions of others as easily as when fewer people are present.

For some, large groups are a challenge and they rise to it by trying to make themselves known. This can lead to a situation in which a few people do much of the speaking while others experience "the tyranny of the few." Resentments can grow because often the "big talkers" have taken on their role without having others offer it to them. Those who remain silent take on the role of quiet participant. It is easy for them to grow more and more passive and to feel more and more marginal to the group. Then, when they do have something to say, it is hard to break out of the passive role and speak.

One partial explanation for this phenomenon that comes from research on small groups is "diffusion of responsibility" (Latane & Darley, 1976). The idea is that as numbers increase, the personal sense of responsibility for the outcomes of the group decreases and this affects behavior. People in large groups are less likely to act when they see an occasion that calls for action. National attention focused on this phenomenon in the Kitty Genovese incident in New York City in 1964, when thirty-seven people stood by and did nothing while a woman was attacked and killed. The response by social psychologists was a flurry of research that focused on the processes that cause people to act even when they have something at risk (theories of altruism) and the processes that cause people not to act when others are in need (theories of deindividuation) (Zimbardo, 1970).

What do these large group events do to cope with this problem of individuation? Can people feel active and able to contribute in events with over five hundred participants? The genius of the methods in this book is that even in very large events, people spend much of their time in small groups doing specific tasks. In the search methods, the ICA Strategic Planning Process, all of the work design methods, and Real Time Strategic Change, the table group has structured interaction. Often, explicit directions call for everyone to have a minute or two to give his or her views before any discussion. The functional group roles of facilitator, recorder, reporter, and timekeeper are rotated for every new task so that everyone gets active and assumes responsibility. In the general sessions of the whole event, tables report out and ask questions so that each group has a voice. Dot voting, a process in which the participants each have a few sticky colored dots to place on wall charts for the items they believe are most important, also individuates people.

Simu-Real individuates people by placing them in their known work groups. Open Space accomplishes this by declaring people to be responsible for their own experience. It encourages them to be active and responsible about their own learning and goals, either by proposing what they want to do or by managing themselves so that they do not disengage. In other words, underlying the effectiveness of these large group events is the use of small group technology and processes that allow people to participate fully and feel engaged.

THE DILEMMA OF STRUCTURE IN LARGE GROUPS

If you have ever been in a crowd that was out of control or that was being harassed by onlookers or the police, you know some of the hidden fears that many people carry about large groups. They may fear that things will get out of control and that violence will occur. Experience with tense situations in groups varies. For some people, any perceived tension threatens violence. Others can be aware of tension before they become worried. When I (Barbara) lived in New York City in the 1960s, I occasionally went to events in a theater on the Lower East Side, a neighborhood that was known for sometimes becoming violent. I always went with experienced friends who could judge the level of tension, and they had us leave before anybody got hurt. I could not make those judgments by myself—any tension scared me.

Another fear in large groups is of potential chaos and total disorganization. How can so many people get organized and get something done? It could be bedlam! Thus, anxiety is always incipient in any large group situation. People and cultures differ in their response to these forces. Some people and some cultures tolerate more degrees of ambiguity than others.

Structure has the capacity to "bind" anxiety. It organizes experience and gives it coherence and meaning. Agendas, job descriptions, or organizational charts create a sense, at least symbolically, of order and purpose. The right amount of structure is reassuring and allows people to function in a healthy way. The dilemma is that we do not know how much anxiety exists and how much structure is needed. The paradox is that *too little structure* in a situation where more is needed will increase anxiety and is likely to produce acting out (jargon for behavior that alleviates anxiety rather than reaching objectives). In the same way, *too much structure* in situations that need less will also increase anxiety and lead to acting out.

So figuring out how much structure is needed is like walking a tightwire.

THE EGOCENTRIC DILEMMA

Employees' views of their organization are colored by their experience in their unit and the role that they carry. We each know only the most immediate part of the blind man's elephant. When the whole organization gathers in a large group, many people are unaware of the limitations of their organizational view. They believe that their view of things is accurate. The *egocentric dilemma* is the situation that obtains at the beginning of the large group event, when hundreds of people with differing pictures of organizational reality all act as if theirs is the only true reality.

In the same way that students who dislike the textbook in Barbara's organizational psychology course are stunned to discover that other students really like it and find it interesting, so, in organizations, the people on the shop floor are surprised by the views of the people in Marketing and vice versa. We look at the world through our own experience, egocentrically, often not appreciating the differences between us.

When the whole organization comes together in one place and begins to talk, people have the possibility of beginning to see things from other perspectives. The majority of methods assign people to heterogeneous max-mix groups for substantial amounts of time. Open Space and Work-Out cluster people around interests in specific issues. In these groups, people share views and begin to understand what it is like to be in different organizational roles. They also see the organization whole rather than partially.

THE CONTAGION OF AFFECT

The seminal contribution of Bion (1961) to our understanding of group life, the role of the unconscious affective dimensions that he calls *sentience,* helps us to understand how these affective forces can impede or further the primary task of the group.

What happens as groups get larger? One of the earliest works in social psychology, Le Bon's study (1896) of the crowd, also emphasizes how affect flows in larger groups. The simplest way to say it is that affect, like colds, can be caught. In other words, people begin to experience feelings because they feel them vicariously in others, not because they are all having the same experience. In large groups, this has serious implications. On the upside, Mardi Gras and other large crowd revelries are places where positive affect spreads. On the downside, Zimbardo (1970) demonstrated that people can join together in violent self-reinforcing cycles in groups.

The tone or affective center of large groups can be manipulated because affect is contagious. Politicians know this only too well. You can see it happening on national television when the political conventions are in session. It also happens in organizations, especially when not enough information is available for employees to make rational sense of what is happening. Secrecy and impending layoffs send waves of fear and rumors throughout organizations, often in the face of other information that is not trusted. The possibility of swirling affect is present in all large groups.

Affective contagion in a large group setting can be seen when people who have clearly had quite different experiences all profess the same emotion. In a debriefing of an outdoor "ropes" experience, we once watched forty people, who an hour before were clearly enjoying themselves and enthusiastically trying to get their entire group over a high wall, "catch" the negative affect of a very few members who were angry and upset about their own performance. In a few minutes, the entire group was describing the experience as "awful and a waste of time."

The potential for affective contagion in large groups has two implications. One concerns structure. Small groups interacting within the large group substantially reduce the probability of contagion. The second concerns professional facilitation. People who plan and manage large group events need to be trained and comfortable in dealing with a range of very strong feelings, as well as in understanding how affect can operate in these settings. This is a sophisticated competence that is developed over time with continued training.

CHAPTER FIFTEEN

Understanding the Power of Position

A Diagnostic Model

Michael J. Sales

K ees Boeke's lovely 1957 classic, *Cosmic View: The Universe in 40 Jumps,* reminds us of an obvious fact: we are all embedded in multiple social systems, from the microworld of the family to the macrocosm of the universe. Yet we rarely think of ourselves as system nodes. Those of us raised in cultures emphasizing individualism may have particular difficulty believing that our actions are significantly affected by our positions in social groupings or by the dynamics of such groups. We have been taught to see ourselves as autonomous agents who determine our own future. Challenging that idea insults something fundamental to our identity. Unfortunately, the belief that we are the full masters of our fates is an illusion.

This chapter builds on the ideas of a prominent systems theorist, Barry Oshry, with whom I have worked for over twenty years. It explores the power and influence of social systems. It examines why so much of human behavior in organizations is predictable, and what it takes for individuals and human systems to seize the full possibilities of the moment and act with independent thought. Life will never look the same again! The ideas developed in this chapter can serve as a model to diagnose behaviors and understand the deep structure of system forces in organizations. They also suggest strategies for implementing high-leverage interventions (Oshry, 1992, 1993, 1996, 1999, 2000, 2003).

Jean Jacques Rousseau said, "Man is born free, but everywhere he is in chains." The model of social analysis and social change presented here is in the tradition of that statement. Why is the suboptimal performance of human systems so commonplace? Why is the drudgery of system life accepted as a given? Why do so many human systems make the same mistakes over and over again?[1] What can be done about all this? This chapter addresses these questions and more.

The diagnostic concepts developed here fall into three categories:

1. A description of social systems on automatic pilot, where people operate reflexively without awareness of the interaction between deep system structure and everyday events.

2. A discussion of "robust" systems that are good at prospecting for opportunities and defending against threats. Robust systems present a vision of organizational and social possibilities.

3. Interventions that move social systems from their default, automatic, low-learning state to robustness, dynamism, and aesthetic beauty.

The sections that follow explore organizational issues as well as broader societal ones. They examine the power of position in social systems that can be used to maintain the status quo or create vibrant change. Every discipline has its own technical language (Foray, 2004), so I will be introducing a variety of terms; in keeping with the notion that good theory should be elegant and parsimonious, however, I strive to use scientific language that is familiar (Kaplan, 1964) and offer examples and illustrations throughout.

ON AUTOMATIC PILOT: SEEING SYSTEMS AS THEY USUALLY ARE

This tour of social systems begins with an analysis of organizations that strips organizational complexity down to essentials in order to show how core elements interact. The focus is on four key positions that people occupy in organizational systems, the challenges people face in those positions, the ways they typically meet the challenges, and the consequences. It also argues that the framework offered has applicability beyond workplace organizations: all social systems can basically be analyzed using these positional concepts.

A Four-Player Model

Organizational systems have four fundamental actors:

1. *Tops,* who have overall strategic responsibility for a system. They are the parents in a family, the principal of a school, the executives of an enterprise, the mayor of a town, and so on.

2. *Bottoms,* who do the specific work of the organization, producing its goods and services. In many organizations, they receive hourly or piecework pay and perform tasks defined in precise terms by others.

3. *Middles,* who stand between the Tops and the Bottoms and deliver information and resources developed in one part of the system to another. They are frequently referred to as managers or supervisors.

4. *Environmental Players,* who need the organization's goods and services to accomplish their own objectives. They are often called "customers" and can be internal or external to the organization. Internal customers rely on the productivity of other subsystems to do their own work. Any stakeholders who interface with the organization in ways that are important to both or either party (for example, vendors, regulators, community organizations, and educational institutions) are also environmental players.

Any organizational subsystem also will have its own Tops, Bottoms, Middles, and Environmental Players. An internal unit of an enterprise will have a Top who can be a Middle when the system is looked at through a wider-angle lens or a Bottom when the lens is pulled back further. For example, a police officer at an accident scene can be the Top when managing traffic flow and initiating emergency services on site, a Middle when calming down the drivers and passengers involved, and a Bottom when filling out multiple copies of the required accident report at headquarters.

Players in Each Position Face a Unique Set of Challenges

The generic conditions faced by organizational players in their various system positions constitute challenges that define the architecture of the space. Imagine rooms with the signs Top, Bottom, Middle, or Environmental Player on them. Anyone entering one of those rooms would be breathing the same air as others in it, looking at the same walls and windows, and so on. The activities in these rooms, however, differ greatly.

- *Tops live in an "overloaded" space.* They handle unpredictable, multiple sources of input. The more turbulence in the environment (for example, technological changes, globalization, disruptions in the labor force or resource availability, increased competition), the greater the overload.

- *Bottoms live in a "disregarded" space.* They see things that are wrong with the organization and how it relates to the larger environment. They feel powerless to do anything about it. Bottoms are frequently invisible to the Tops. Their input doesn't seem to count. The greater the turbulence of the system (that is, the more that Tops are overloaded), the greater the disregard for the Bottoms.

- *Middles live in a "crunched, torn, and 'disintegrated'" space.* Middles exist between Tops and Bottoms who want different or conflicting things from each other. Both Tops and Bottoms want Middles to handle their issues, frequently without regard for the impact on Middles or others. Middles spend much of their energy running back and forth between their Tops and Bottoms. As a result, they have little time for each other and are not an integrated group in the organization. In fact, they often do not see other Middles as part of the same "community." Middles are torn by their commitments, loyalties, and obligations to others. They are frequently seen by others as nice, but incompetent and ineffectual, or as defensive, bureaucratic, and expendable. Middles find themselves unable to act with independence of thought. Their behavior is too often reactive. The higher the level of turbulence (that is, the more that Tops and Bottoms are fighting), the greater the pressures and tearing.

- *Environmental Players live in a "neglected" space.* In a world where Tops are overloaded, Bottoms are disregarded, and Middles are torn, who has attention to focus outside the institution? The more turbulent the organization's situation, the more that the Environmental Players (for example, bankers, suppliers, regulators, local community members) find themselves "put on hold" (sometimes literally) while people inside the organization tend to something else.

People predominately occupy one position in organizations. However, as noted, the same person can be a Top, Bottom, Middle, or Environmental Player. And circumstances can shift positions over time. When the poorest of the poor lie awake at night feeling responsible for solving the problem of how to feed their family, they are Tops.[2] When Bill Clinton was forced to describe his sexual misadventures in excruciating detail to his nemesis, Kenneth Starr, he was a Bottom. When a dean is caught between the ever-conflicting demands of a downsized faculty and an administration facing state-mandated budget cuts, she's a Middle "living in a vise," no matter how impressive her title might sound (Gallos, 2002). Anytime you are put on hold by a customer service representative for more than a few minutes, you fully experience being an Environmental Player!

Occupants of Each Space Face Their Own Kind of Stress

Players in each organizational space work to survive in the context of their worlds. They are prone, however, to the defensive reactions of others.

- Tops are wary of any encounters and interactions that may increase their overload. They already have too much to do and too little time to do it. They limit their contact with others, even if they pay a price for doing so. Advice to be a "person of the people" and to lead by wandering around makes sense for Tops, but it is not an attractive strategy for those who already have too much to do. There are plenty of executives, for example, who don't leave their offices because they will predictably face "hallway hits" from a variety of parties who want something from them. As this chapter is being written, President Jacques Chirac of France—widely known as a lover of the spotlight—has become the invisible man in the face of France's fourteenth night of civil unrest. During what might be considered the worst crisis of his ten-year administration, Chirac has not appeared in public or addressed the media. One reason may be that he simply cannot take on anything more. The burden at the top is just too heavy (Sciolino, 2005).

• Bottoms are regularly excluded from decision making about their own lives. Consider, for example, the hundreds of thousands of manufacturing layoffs and offshoring steps announced in the last decade in the United States. Bottoms have every reason to be suspicious of the motives of Tops, Middles, and Environmental Players whose actions too often upend any sense of security for those at the bottom. Bottoms frequently bifurcate other people into "Us" and "Them"—those who are like us and whom we can trust, and those who are not like us and might do us harm.

• Middles are beset with demands from above and below, from peers in other parts of their organization, and from Environmental Players, such as customers. All want Middles to make the organization more responsive to their particular needs, regardless of the consequences for Middles and others of doing so. Middles frequently find it hard to get Tops or Bottoms to listen to them or to act differently toward each other. Every interaction becomes a demand that Middles take care of something they don't feel competent or influential enough to affect. Every request becomes another chance for a Middle to look bad.

• Chronically neglected customers and other Environmental Players resist giving organizations the help they might need to deal effectively with customer problems. Delays in delivery, payment of bills, responsiveness to complaints, and so on are met with varying degrees of annoyance and callousness, not empathy. This customer response is understandable, but it generates and sustains antagonistic feedback loops within the system that only accentuate customer dissatisfaction.

Again, these position-related dynamics exist in any complex hierarchical system. Because a significant body of research indicates that hierarchy is a permanent feature of virtually all human systems

(Conniff, 2005; Tannenbaum, 1974) and that all systems confront increasing levels of complexity (Emery & Trist, 1965), the framework offered here has universal applicability.

Predictable Conditions Are Met with Predictable, Reflexive Responses

The conditions of each system-space world are usually greeted by their own set of predictable reflexive responses. Oshry has observed human behavior over time and in a variety of laboratory-like conditions. Like other theorists, such as Argyris and Schön, he has concluded that most people, most of the time, react in an instinctive way under conditions of perceived stress. These automatic responses tend to worsen the conditions that people face (Argyris & Schön, 1977, 1978, 1996; Argyris, 1985). Recently, popular neuroscience has coined a term for these reflexive responses: the *amygdala hijack,* in reference to the amygdala, an almond-shaped structure in the brain. During the response, electrochemicals flood the thalamus and interfere with the ability to think clearly. The result is an emotional, fight-or-flight response. Once that kicks in, we're "in the soup!" (McGonagill, 2004).

OCCUPANTS OF TOP SPACES TYPICALLY RESPOND TO TOP OVERLOAD BY REFLEXIVELY "SUCKING RESPONSIBILITY UP TO THEMSELVES AND AWAY FROM OTHERS." Once they've done that, they are "burdened." George Bush's exclamation, "It's hard work! Being the president is a hard job!" in his first debate with John Kerry is a perfect example of a burdened Top talking. It is very difficult to bear a heavy load of responsibilities. Mr. Bush's lament is echoed by the findings of the Mayo Clinic's Executive Health program: executive stress driven by work overload is the number one health concern for senior organizational leaders ("Executive Stress," 2004).

A key feature of the Top automatic response is an assumption about responsibilities. The bigger the decision, the more likely it is that Tops will conclude that this is a problem that they must address alone or with a small number of other Tops. This only intensifies the loneliness and burden. And loneliness can have all sorts of ancillary consequences for physical and mental health, emotional accessibility in relationships, and executive effectiveness.

MOST BOTTOMS AUTOMATICALLY RESPOND TO THEIR CHRONIC STATE OF DISREGARD BY BLAMING OTHERS AND HOLDING "THEM" RESPONSIBLE.

They receive a lot of endorsement from other Bottoms and plenty of confirming evidence for their beliefs. Once Bottoms lock into blaming others, they experience their state as that of being oppressed: others are doing lousy things to them that they don't deserve and that therefore shouldn't be happening. Consider, for example, the unsuccessful job applicant who always blames his or her rejection on the stereotypical thinking and behavior of some other ethnic group: the Caucasians who blame affirmative action, or the people of color who lament the impact of racism on their job search difficulties. When these chronic perceptions are held in the face of contradicting data, they represent a case of Bottom oppression.

MIDDLES TYPICALLY RESPOND BY "SLIDING" AND LOSING INDEPENDENCE OF THOUGHT AND ACTION. Middles live in a world of disagreement with people above them and below them. They often stand between people inside and outside the organization. They are frequently stressed by the tensions between and among people in different sociopolitical-economic classes from their own. Middles respond to these conditions by making the conflicts of others their own. In doing so, they lose their objectivity. This inability to stay out of the middle increases the "tearing" nature of Middle life. Middles shuffle between parties in conflict or in pursuit of differing objectives. Unable to please everyone, they look weak and ineffectual to all. The Middle space has the greatest prospect for burnout of any in the system (Shorris, 1981).

The following is an example of "sliding into the middle." An employee in a sixty-person software company complains to her supervisor that a member of senior management is missing important technology developments that ought to be incorporated into the company's products. Her supervisor immediately defends the executive, describing how stressful his life is and how many technology conferences he goes to each month. Later in the day, the supervisor runs into the executive in question, who comments to the supervisor about the negative attitude of this same employee. The supervisor defends the employee, saying how hard she works and how much technical expertise she has. Neither the employee nor the executive respects the Middle's knowledge, and neither appreciates his effort to pacify the situation. Sliding into the middle of things doesn't necessarily solve problems. In fact, it often creates more.

NEGLECTED ENVIRONMENTAL PLAYERS REFLEXIVELY STAND BACK FROM THE DELIVERY SYSTEM AND HOLD "IT" RESPONSIBLE FOR WHATEVER

THEY ARE NOT GETTING THAT THEY FEEL THEY SHOULD. Customers want what they want when they want it and according to their specifications. They are dissatisfied with anything less. Because their stance rarely leads to changes in the delivery system, customers can frequently feel righteous and screwed. The relationship of most parents to their children's school district authorities is a good example of customers' standing back from a delivery system with which they could be intimately involved. Poorly informed parents, the vast majority of whom do not vote in school district elections, loudly lament (both to each other and the media) the poor functioning of teachers and local schools in general (Epstein, 2004).

Defensiveness Breeds Emotional Distance

To varying degrees, stress, blame, and low levels of learning are prominent features of most organizations. When Tops are overloaded, Bottoms disregarded, Middles crunched and torn, and Environmental Players neglected, everyone is vulnerable to feeling and being unseen and uncared for. Such feelings are then manifested behaviorally and attitudinally in a wide variety of ways. They also support the development of an intricate web of interpersonal feedback loops that Argyris and Schön (1996) call automatically defensive learning systems. Generally speaking, people with little feeling for others discount those others. The manifestations of these predictable stresses, however, vary by the nature of one's system space.

Bottoms tend to have a greater awareness of the commonality of their condition. They are also more amenable to unity of action than Tops, Middles, or Environmental Players. Bottoms, for example, establish unions and other collective efforts to protect workers' rights and improve work conditions. *The greater the sense of Bottom vulnerability, the more intense their "negative" solidarity can be* when they organize to struggle against a common foe. Radical Islamists, in their intense hatred of all things Western, are an example of a people who feel very Bottom to the point that they are willing to die in order to strike against perceived oppressors.

When Bottoms disagree, however, their relations can quickly turn ugly, as they are primed to see the world in right-wrong terms. Gang warfare is a good example of both the solidarity of Bottom groups and the hostility that they can show toward rivals. So are the commonplace office rumor mills, the personalized attacks among coworkers, and the occasional workforce violence (Kelleher, 1997) that can characterize life at the Bottom of an enterprise.

Tops tend to be separated from each other by specialization of function. Specialization is a way of managing overload and complexity by concentrating efforts in one area. However, hardening into a specialization can lead to disagreements over strategy. Tops are highly attuned to the needs of their own arena. They are rarely as sensitive to other domains. Organizational culture is significantly determined by which Tops "win" the battle for strategic direction. Teaching hospitals, for example, may tilt research activities in the direction of M.D. faculty led by clinical chiefs rather than toward their Ph.D. executives. In nonacademic health care research environments, the reverse could be true.

Because organizations are dominated by those who set the system's cultural tone, *Tops fight for relative status.* Tops make strategic alliances with other Tops, often to the disadvantage of other Tops and in elaborate games of intrigue. Some Tops are absorbed with the trappings of power: the biggest office, the largest salary, the best-looking trophy spouse, the most impressive title, and so on. These "alpha" behaviors often indicate who should get the most attention, respect, and money—and who should be most feared.

Middles are more emotionally distant from each other than the other sets of organizational actors. Middles spend their lives shuttling among Tops, Bottoms, and Environmental Players. Their roles are within the specialized silos that have been created for them and supported by the Tops. They are systemically dispersed and walled off from each other, with little available time or energy for independent thought or action.

When Middles do not experience themselves as part of any group, however, they develop what Oshry (1999) calls an "I" consciousness: what I know and care about is "me" and how I see the world; I don't see that others are like me because I'm not really integrated with them. There is irony in this, as Middles share so many problems and issues. This lack of integration also makes Middles vulnerable to seeming ineffectual because many things "fall between the cracks" and "get bumped up" to Tops.

This disconnectedness among Middles can be manifested in the context of very minor matters. A customer, for example, asks a Bottom at a Barnes and Noble store to accept a large number of quarters as payment for a book. The Bottom is not sure that quarters are an acceptable method of payment and asks a Middle running a particular operational function for help. The Middle responds by saying to the customer, "The accounting manager is away. You'll have to come back in two days to talk to her. I don't handle questions like this one." "I" consciousness often translates into "It's not my job."

When organizations merge and Tops celebrate the savings yielded by the purging of overlapping human resource pools, most of the time they are talking about eliminating Middles whose positions are perceived as deadwood. Chronically and systemically separated from each other and locked in "I" consciousness, Middles have no way to defend each other, nor a rationale for doing so. Anticipating all this can make them even more defensive in their relations with other organizational positions and with one another.

Finally, most systems have readily identifiable Environmental Players, such as customers and suppliers. These players may or may not join together, depending on the specifics of the situation. Nongovernmental organizations, for example, might work closely with official environmental authorities to force a corporation to address a pollution matter. But when they do work together, the likelihood for significant tension between the organization and its critics adds to stress, emotional distance, and distrust.

Dominance Dynamics Create Additional Challenges

Although anyone can experience the constraints, stresses, and conditions of these system spaces, the four positions (Tops, Middles, Bottoms, and Environmental Players) discussed thus far have been associated with particular roles. Oshry (1992, 1993, 1996), however, adds dominance itself as an additional analytical lens for understanding the impact of position in formal and informal systems. *Dominants* are those with access to resources. They make and enforce the rules; they establish cultural norms. Dominants behave like cultural Tops even if they don't have the title that makes their Top status official. They are distinguished from *Others*. Dominants influence a variety of cultural rules, such as how to dress; how to express oneself; and what constitutes good manners, appropriate beliefs, and commonly accepted values.

Dominant/Other issues and tensions are observable across arenas. Their impact, for example, can be seen in the intergroup dynamics of stable organizations (Deal & Kennedy, 1982). The question of who dominates and who doesn't is always at play during organizational mergers and acquisitions. The reality that many of the most menial, low-status jobs in America are held by non-English-speaking immigrants—many of whom are also not white—is another example of dominance dynamics in action.

Dominants and Others have complicated but relatively well-defined relationships:

- *Dominants experience Others as strange.* In the view of Dominants, Others are off, wrong, inappropriate, and scary. In the extreme, Others can seem downright sinful, disgusting, primitive, and polluting to Dominants.

- *Dominants typically act to preserve their culture* in the face of perceived or actual threats by Others. They stereotype, marginalize, ignore, suppress, trivialize, and exclude Others. They also educate Others in order to shape them to become more "normal." In the extreme, Dominants segregate, exile, enslave, and annihilate Others.

- *Others feel constrained, confused, oppressed, and angry in the context of a Dominant-controlled culture.* They frequently don't have any idea how to act.

- *Others manifest a variety of behavioral responses to their condition.* Some adopt the norms and values of the Dominants and assimilate. Some resist, rebel, and complain. Others respond by performing their duties with apathy.

Dominant/Other Dynamics Are Another Form of Reflex Responses

Like the reflex responses seen with Tops, Bottoms, Middles, and Environmental Players, the behaviors of Dominants and Others are largely unconscious and automatic to those who perform them. Those on the receiving end, however, are often very aware, especially if they don't like the behaviors. If asked, Dominants see themselves doing the "right" thing as mandated by tradition or norms ("We've always done it this way"). And they have absolute clarity about what it takes to maintain their system power (for example, "Immigrants threaten our way of life"). Others respond to constraints on their freedom imposed by Dominants with their own lack of consciousness, as if to say, "What else was I to do when they told me to [get rid of my Macintosh/cut my hair/go to that training program/stop bringing the *Gay Times* to lunch/wear a suit/learn English]?!"

Dominant/Other relations have a self-reinforcing quality. They are like a dance set into motion that neither partner has the ability or will to stop, which makes stereotypes hard to alter. The permanence of white racism and assumptions of racial superiority are strong examples of this dynamic (Feagin, 2001). Further, when organizational Tops are also cultural Dominants, and Bottoms are Others, the prospects for transformative change are severely limited. Both sets of actors lock into their own views even as the need for transformation and the tension between the parties grow.

THE VISION: ROBUST HUMAN SYSTEMS

The dynamics discussed thus far show that organizations and social systems—and the people in them—are on automatic pilot more than they realize. People play their positions as Tops, Bottoms, Middles, or Environmental Players unconsciously. Dominants and Others engage in predictable dances. No one sees choices or other options. These reflex responses increase stress and conflict throughout the system; simultaneously reduce satisfaction and learning; and drain the fortitude, resilience, and intelligence needed to face adversity or take advantage of opportunity. Human systems on automatic are brittle: they resist the honest emotionality and disputation that are fundamental to good decision making (Drucker, 1967).

This section of the chapter explores Oshry's alternative to automatic pilot, *robust systems*. Robust systems weather adversity and seize the moment when opportunity knocks. How a system functions when the people disagree is a good indicator of robustness. Rigid systems fear, defend against, and suppress differences. Robust systems welcome, value, and use differences well (Oshry, 1999, 2003).

Build Robustness by Understanding the Four Basic Elements of Systems

Using robust system thinking requires an understanding of four core concepts:

1. *Differentiation* refers to how and how much a system elaborates differences, tolerates internal richness, and interacts with a complex environment. A great university or a highly successful

corporation like General Electric is intricately differentiated. Each tolerates and interacts with a variety of people and produces a range of products and offerings. Similarly, a borderless, highly differentiated entity like Yahoo's network of message boards fits the bill.

2. *Homogenization* refers to commonality: shared understanding of a topic, norms, relevant knowledge, and so on. Architects, for example, are exposed to a common curriculum and are literate in the same range of basic shapes, materials, and tools. People around the world recognize the most popular Beatles songs. These are examples of homogenization.

3. *Integration* refers to the power of mission and direction on system members. Do people want the same goals and objectives? Do they support each other? Do they exhibit natural teamwork? Do they help others play their individual roles more expertly? Do they share information, identify group challenges, and so on? These are manifestations of integration.[3]

4. *Individuation* is a system's willingness to accommodate the distinctiveness of its members. Is an organization like a Norwegian shoreline, with coves, crags, and crannies, or is it a golf green, with every blade of grass the same height? Does a system encourage personal expression or conformity? Individuation is associated with personal freedom. World-class universities like Berkeley, Oxford, or Harvard have high levels of individuation. People there "do their own thing." Characters and eccentrics abound, adding color to the system like light through a stained-glass window.[4]

Balance the Elements to Create Robust Systems

Individuals and systems vary in their choices to emphasize either differentiation or homogenization, integration or individuation. These differences create tensions and mirror dynamics like those experienced by occupants of different system spaces discussed thus far: locked in reflex and unconscious of the limitations of their point of view. The results for organizations are predictable.

DIFFERENTIATION WITHOUT HOMOGENIZATION LEADS TO TERRITORIAL-ITY, SILOS, AND REDUNDANT RESOURCES. On the one hand, organizations that accentuate differentiation are likely to have finance departments, training programs, and hardware platforms for each distinctive division. Societies with thousands of subcultures are plagued by constant conflict. On the other hand, homogenization without differentiation is *boring* and imparts limited capacity for dealing with environmental variations. Think about a mom-and-pop bookstore in an environment that is dominated by Amazon, an oil company that has never heard of alternative energy, or a patriarchal religious regime with no interest in responding to women's rights. In each case, the system "knows" how to think and do as it currently does, but has no capacity for the new or different.

A robust system has a yeasty homeostasis between differentiation and homogeneity: there are enough shared values, norms, and knowledge for each system agent to act as a "holon" (Lipnack & Stamps, 1997), a pixel that contains the totality of a system. At the same time, there is also room for a variety of behavior and endeavor. A good example of differentiation and homogeneity in dynamic balance took place at 4:30 P.M. on September 11, 2001. The entire Congress of the United States stood on the steps of the Capitol in a city that had been attacked seven hours earlier, and spontaneously sang "God Bless America." At that dramatic moment of robustness for America, diverse voices blended and everyone and every region knew the same song.

INDEPENDENT PEOPLE COMMIT TO COMMON CAUSE WHEN INTEGRATION AND INDIVIDUATION ARE IN BALANCE. Integration without individuation suppresses entrepreneurial spirit and creativity. It is akin to generalized apathy. In the extreme, a Stalinistic state is a logical outcome: everyone is marching in formation but devoid of personality. In contrast, individuation without integration is chaos. People constantly bump into each other and act in an uncoordinated, self-focused fashion. The ability of the system as a whole to achieve its mission is impaired. The impact of the Pulitzer Prize–winning journalist Judith Miller's "running amok" at the *New York Times* is a prime example (Natta, Liptak, & Levy, 2005).

Robust systems encourage both common focus and individuality. The *Apollo* space missions, for example, captured in Tom Wolfe's *The Right Stuff* (1980) and in popular films, illustrate well how the astronauts related to their individual work, each other, and their common mission.

What It Looks Like When the Elements Work Together

There are good points of reference to inform our thinking on robust systems. The Boston Symphony Orchestra (BSO) is a highly *differentiated* system. It has many "product lines" and locations for its work, the two most prominent being Symphony Hall and Tanglewood. The BSO sponsors tours, has links to schools and civic organizations, engages in recording activities, publishes music, plays many types of music, and so on. But music is the BSO's *homogenization*. Everyone reads scores, is steeped in classical music, pays attention to the conductor, and so on. The conductor, musical score, and symphony traditions for quality and artistic expression *integrate* the organization. The BSO is one of the world's finest orchestras, and membership requires living up to established standards of excellence. At the same time, many of the musicians are individualists who could play almost anywhere—no one has to stay—but the diversity of opportunities, music, and activities makes the BSO an intriguing and exciting home for world-class musicians.

MOVING FROM REFLEXIVITY TO ROBUSTNESS

There are five principles for transforming reflexive rigidity to robustness:

1. Strive for true partnership.
2. Take leadership stands to guide behavior beyond the reflex of position.
3. Step into the fire of conflict.
4. Look for valuable enemies.
5. Don't stop thinking holistically about the system.

A Commitment to True Partnership Makes a Real Difference

Partnership is at the heart of robust systems (Oshry, 2000). It involves commitment to others, common mission, and a nuanced approach to differentiation, homogenization, integration, and individuation. Such military operations as those depicted in *Band of Brothers* and *Saving Private Ryan* and the early histories of the Beatles and the Rolling Stones are examples of what real partnership looks like.

Leadership Stands Create Systemic Partnership

Automaticity generates systemic vulnerability. Tops, Bottoms, Middles, and Environmental Players are set not to like by system dynamics each other or get along well. Their prospects for productive partnerships are limited. Taking a leadership stand from the vantage point of one's position, however, makes a difference. A stand is the opposite of a reflex: you have to think about it and come to it on your own. A stand is a statement about who you are. Specific strategies, behaviors, and commitment flow out of it. Systems have greater prospects for partnership when people throughout the organization lead by standing firm against the pull of unthinking reflex. There are stands for each of the positions.

TOPS CAN TAKE A STAND TO CREATE RESPONSIBILITY THROUGHOUT A SYSTEM. They can step back from the reflex response of sucking up work and responsibility and get everyone involved. This might mean sharing information so that others can see challenges and opportunities, developing more and different people to assume part of the Top's burden, or expanding people's involvement in important decision making. Sharing responsibility is not the same as avoiding it, but is also different from thinking no one else is willing to step up or knows how to do something. A closer look at a Top leadership stand illustrates the difference.

The Torah, the first five books of Moses, is "the word of God" for observant Jews. And Yom Kippur is the holiest day in the Jewish calendar. Picture the chief rabbi entrusting a six-year-old boy to hold the Torah during the Yom Kippur service at one of the country's largest synagogues. A thousand people are praying and watching the child with the Torah. Suddenly, a steel bar holding something behind the chair the boy is sitting in crashes to the ground. The boy holds on to the Torah with all his might. If the Torah is dropped, the synagogue must undergo thirty days of ritual cleansing. The young boy saves the day. Symbolically, Judaism itself is wrapped up in this moment: there is no Jewish boy without the Torah, and the Torah has no meaning without the Jewish boy holding it. That rabbi was a Top disseminating responsibility.

BOTTOMS CAN TAKE A LEADERSHIP STAND TO BE RESPONSIBLE FOR THEM-SELVES AND THE SYSTEM. This means stepping back from blaming others, especially higher-ups, and looking for opportunities to strengthen the organization, fix problems, and make a unique contribution by paying attention to something important that no one else does. A Bottom stand means moving from complaint to a project. Consider, for example, a young woman who joins the United Nations as a low-level administrator. She has no training as a diplomat or manager, but she develops positive relationships with mentors, learns about the system, and works on project after project. Over time, she becomes influential and a highly regarded senior director. The woman made the system's needs her own and ignored others who kept saying, "Why bother? You're never going to move up."

MIDDLES CAN TAKE A STAND TO MAINTAIN THEIR INDEPENDENCE OF THOUGHT AND ACTION. Oshry's work (2000) suggests a number of strategies:

> Be the Top when you can: act as if power resides in the Middle and does not just come from the Tops.
>
> Be the Bottom when you have to: say no to the Top when you know something is wrong or won't work.
>
> Coach those with problems: help others work better rather than being a repairman and making their conflicts yours.
>
> Develop facilitation skills: bring people in conflict together to work through the issues.
>
> Integrate with peers: find structured activities with others as the antidote to the dispersing nature of Middle space.

ENVIRONMENTAL PLAYERS CAN TAKE A STAND BY MAKING THE SYSTEM'S DELIVERY SYSTEMS WORK FOR THEM. They can step back from expecting the delivery system to take care of them and start seeing themselves as part the solution. Ordinary citizens getting involved in government to change a law, policy, or unresponsive agency demonstrates this kind of stand.

Step into the Fire: Real Conflict Is Good for You!

Conflict is inevitable in social systems as people pursue their own objectives, values, and needs for power. The workings of human systems situate people differently in relationship to each other: people will clash, alliances and loyalties will shift, and deals will be struck. Bottoms will be annoyed at Tops who try to create shared responsibility for systemic effectiveness: "I've got enough to do. Why should I worry about things that are your job?" Tops will resent Bottoms who want transparency and information: "Why are they trying to horn in on stuff they don't have the training to understand?" Middles will wonder what their job is: "If I'm not supposed to solve other people's problems, what *am* I supposed to do?" Others will be angry at Dominants for their blindness and wastefulness: "My kids are hungry, and you people are throwing away more than we could ever eat!" Dominants will be angered by Others: "You never have a right to steal from someone else, period!" Individualists will rebel against the judgment of the collective, integrationists at the eccentricities of a few. All of this is a given, so embrace conflict. Don't smooth over differences. Stand up for yourself in the fray, and expect others to do that for themselves.

Build Robustness by Valuing Enemies

It is easy for system antagonists to dehumanize each other as combatants in open warfare. However, system productivity requires them to work together. Total victory is attractive. Long-enduring stalemates are more commonplace and functional. People have much to learn from their system enemies. Think about Newt Gingrich working with Hillary Clinton on national health care issues, John McCain talking with the men who shot down his jet in Vietnam, or Bill Gates saving arch-rival Apple with a $150 million loan and Steve Jobs letting him do it! Yitzak Rabin once said, "You don't make peace with your friends." Rabin recognized the value of a good enemy. Robust systems come from individuals' identifying others who "scare" them in some way, reaching out to understand them, and looking for ways to work together.

Don't Stop Thinking About the System!

As this chapter illustrates, all human behavior sits on top of deep structure but still can influence its core. Clarity and choice are keys to social system transformation. A summary of the chapter's central ideas and a checklist for intervention are provided in Exhibits 15.1 and

15.2. Many forces came together over time to create the possibility for human flight, for example, and Charles Lindbergh's nonstop voyage to Paris marked a turning point in possibilities. Seeing systems clearly permits smart choices—choices that will liberate our full potential!

A four-player model can be applied to all systems:

1. Tops have overall responsibility for the system.
2. Bottom do the specific work.
3. Middles stand between Tops and Bottoms.
4. Environmental Players depend on the system to do what it does for them.

Each player operates in a unique "space" with specific conditions:

- Tops are overloaded.
- Bottoms are disregarded.
- Middles are crunched.
- Environmental Players are neglected.

The same person can be a Top, Bottom, Middle, or Environmental Player depending on the system or subsystem under study.

Players dealing with the unique conditions of their spaces act defensively toward others. Defensiveness increases emotional distance and diminishes compassion and empathy.

All system players respond reflexively from their role in ways that deepen their embeddedness in a particular space.

Human systems are also cultures with two key actors:

1. Dominants, who establish the rules and norms
2. Others, who are supposed to live by the Dominants' rules
3. Dominants and Others have complicated but limited relationships that influence the overall political tone of the culture.

Robust systems achieve a balance between four interconnected ecological elements:

- Differentiation and homogeneity
- Individuation and integration

There are five principles for transformation:

1. Forging and sustaining true partnership
2. Taking leadership stands
3. Embracing conflict for growth, truth, and trust
4. Identifying and working with "valuable enemies"
5. Pursuing "system sight" constantly

Exhibit 15.1.   Using the Power of Position to Diagnose Social Systems: A Summary.

❑ *Name the system under study.* Is it an entire organization or a subsystem? Is it an indecisive leadership team? A Bottom group on strike? What's your focus? What are the system's boundaries?

❑ *Identify the key actors in the system.* Who are the Tops, Bottoms, Middles, and customers and other key Environmental Players?

❑ *Pick a particular issue.* What specific dynamics need to be addressed (for example, burnout among the Tops, Middle communication processes, relations between Bottoms and Environmental Players)?

❑ *Map the larger context.* How do human system dynamics across spaces affect the space(s) of greatest interest to you?

❑ *Develop data-based "incident reports" on each part of the system under study.* Do the Tops, Bottoms, Middles, and Environmental Players appear to be dealing with predictable overload, disregard, crunch, and neglect? What strategies are they using to address these conditions?

❑ *Look for successes.* Are any of the players in the system *not* using reflexive, automatic strategies? If so, what are they doing that is different? How is that working out for them? For the system as a whole?

❑ *Use the cultural lens.* Who are the Dominants in this system? The Others? How are they different? What rules and norms do Dominants adhere to and Others disregard? What are the specific forms of their adaptation and relations? Are Dominants strident or mild, for example, in their critique of Others? Are the Others oriented to assimilation or rebellion?

❑ *Take a robustness pulse.* What is the balance between differentiation (the diversity in the system) and homogenization (the commonalities)? What are the dynamics between individuators (those who stand out as distinctive) and integrationists (those who support the overall purpose of the system)?

❑ *Develop an intervention strategy.* Where would you intervene and how? At the level of the automatic responses? In the development of system sight? By raising awareness of the need for balance between the core ingredients of robust systems?

❑ *Search for allies.* Who would be your allies? Why? What is the power of each facet of the system to create change? To block it? Do you have allies in every constituency that you need for success?

Exhibit 15.2.   A Checklist for Intervening in Social Systems.

Notes

1. In his review of the *Columbia* tragedy, former NASA trainer Peter Pruyn shows how the same learning failures that plagued the agency during the *Challenger* catastrophe persisted for years (and continue now) despite the "organizational renewal" that supposedly followed the *Challenger* explosion. This is an example of how entrenched antilearning is in organizations, and NASA leads federal agencies in low employee morale (Rosenbaum, 2005).

2. Russell Crowe's depiction of the prizefighter Jim Braddock in *Cinderella Man* is a vivid illustration of how people at the bottom of the social order can be a Top in the microsystem of the family.

3. Homogenization refers to knowledge, skills, and commonality in a frame of reference. It can even include speaking the same language. Integration is agreement on common purpose, woven together by a goal or agreed-on belief system.

4. Differentiation reflects how a system is structured to interact with its environment. The greater the differentiation, the more likely individuation flourishes. Different people are attracted to different functions. However, there are systems with high differentiation and low individuation, military organizations being prime examples.

CHAPTER SIXTEEN

Reframing Complexity

A Four-Dimensional Approach
to Organizational Diagnosis,
Development, and Change

Joan V. Gallos

I mproving organizations requires understanding them. Understanding anything as complex as modern organizations points to the importance of good theory. Although this may sound academic to those who labor in the organizational trenches, good theories are pragmatic and grounded. They explain and predict. They serve as frameworks for making sense of the world around us, organizing diverse forms and sources of information, and taking informed action. Theories come in all shapes and sizes. They may be personal—tacit mental schemas that individuals develop over time from their unique life experiences. They can be research-based—models that stem from formal exploration and study. Whatever the origin, theories guide human behavior and choice. The question is not whether to use theories, but rather which ones, how accurately they describe the richness of reality, and whether they enable us to view the trees without losing sight of the forest. Kurt Lewin, father of the applied social sciences, was right: there is nothing more practical than a good theory.

Good theories are at the core of effective organization development and change. Every effort to improve organizations is based on assumptions about how they work and what might make them better. Theory, therefore, facilitates the work of organization development (OD) professionals. It also presents them with two challenges: (1) sorting through the many models, frameworks, research studies, and findings that compete for attention; and (2) avoiding myopic or simplistic interpretations of complex organizational processes. This chapter addresses these challenges. It builds on the work of Bolman and Deal (2003) in proposing a multipronged approach to organizational diagnosis, development, and change.

More specifically, the chapter begins by developing Bolman and Deal's four frames as a diagnostic model that organizes the major schools of organizational thought and facilitates a comprehensive yet manageable approach to organizational complexity. It then examines the role of *reframing* in effective OD work, and explores ways to use the multiframe model to expand understandings of planned change, intervention strategy, and organization development. The purpose of this chapter is to enable OD professionals and others engaged in planned change to be more discriminating consumers of theory and advice, see new ways of working, and translate the myriad of prescriptions for organizational effectiveness into elegant diagnostic tools and intervention strategies.

SORTING COMPLEXITY: LEVERAGING THE PLURALISM IN ORGANIZATIONAL THEORY

Bolman and Deal (2003) view organizations as machines, families, jungles, and theater. The images result from the authors' work to synthesize and integrate the major traditions in organizational theory into four distinct areas: theories about organizational structure, human resource-related issues, political dynamics, and symbolic concerns. Each of the four areas—the authors call them *frames*—has its own delimited view of the organizational landscape, rooted in distinct academic disciplines. Each also has its own points of focus, underlying assumptions, action-logic, path to organizational effectiveness, and major advocates. Each captures an important slice of organizational reality, but alone is incomplete. Reliance on any one perspective can lead OD professionals to mistake a part of the field for the whole. Together, however, the four frames harness the pluralism in the organizational theory base, acknowledging its richness and complexity while organizing its major elements for easy access and application.

The *structural frame*, with its image of organization as machine, views organizations as rational systems. It reinforces the importance of designing structural forms that align with an organization's goals, tasks, technology, and environment (for example, Galbraith, 2001; Hammer & Champy, 1993; Lawrence & Lorsch, 1986; Perrow, 1986). Differentiation of work roles and tasks provides for clarity of purpose and contribution, but leads to the need for appropriate coordination and integration mechanisms.

The *human resource frame*, with its image of organization as family, captures the symbiotic relationship between individuals and organizations: individuals need opportunities to express their talents and skills; organizations need human energy and contribution to fuel their efforts. When the fit is right, both benefit. Productivity is high because people feel motivated to bring the best to their work. OD and the human resource frame both have roots in the work of such seminal theorists as Chris Argyris (1962), Abraham Maslow (1954), and Douglas McGregor (1960), who launched more than a half century of research and scholarship emphasizing the human side of enterprise and the importance of attending to the intra- and interpersonal dynamics in organizing.

The *political frame* sees an organization as a jungle, an arena of enduring differences, scarce resources, and the inevitability of power and conflict (for example, Cyert & March, 1963; Pfeffer, 1994; Smith, 1988). Diversity in values, beliefs, interests, behaviors, skills, and worldviews are enduring and unavoidable organizational realities. They are often toxic, but can also be a source of creativity and innovation when recognized and effectively managed.

Finally, the theater image of the *symbolic frame* captures organizational life as an ongoing drama: individuals coming together to create context, culture, and meaning as they play their assigned roles and bring artistry and self-expression into their work (for example, Weick, 1995; Cohen & March, 1974; Deal & Kennedy, 2000; Meyer & Rowan, 1983; Schein, 2004). Good theater fuels the moral imagination; it engages head and heart. Organizations that attend to the symbolic issues surrounding their own theater of work infuse everyday efforts with creativity, energy, and soul.

Table 16.1 outlines a four-frame approach to understanding organizations. It summarizes the underlying assumptions and images of organizations that underpin each perspective, as well as frame-specific disciplinary roots, emphases, implicit action-logics, and routes to organizational effectiveness.

Frame	Image of Organization	Disciplinary Roots	Frame Emphasis	Underlying Assumptions	Action-Logic	Path to Organizational Effectiveness
Structural	Machine	Sociology, industrial psychology, economics	Rationality, formal roles and relationships	1. Organizations exist to achieve established goals. 2. Specialization and division of labor increase efficiency and enhance performance. 3. Coordination and control ensure integration of individual and group efforts. 4. Organizations work best when rationality prevails. 5. Structure must align with organizational goals, tasks, technology, environment. 6. Problems result from structural deficiencies and are remedied by analysis and restructuring. (Adapted from Bolman & Deal, 2003, p. 45)	Rational analysis	Develop and implement a clear division of labor; create appropriate mechanisms to integrate individual, group, and unit efforts.
Human resource	Family	Psychology, social psychology	The fit between individual and the organization	1. Organizations exist to serve human needs. 2. People and organizations both need each other. 3. When the fit between individual and organization is poor, one or both suffer: each exploits or is exploited. 4. When the fit between individual and organization is good, both benefit. (Adapted from Bolman & Deal, 2003, p. 115)	Attending to people	Tailor the organization to meet individual needs, train the individual in relevant skills to meet organizational needs.

Table 16.1. A Four-Frame Approach to Understanding Organizations. (*continues*)

Frame	Image of Organization	Disciplinary Roots	Frame Emphasis	Underlying Assumptions	Action-Logic	Path to Organizational Effectiveness
Political	Jungle	Political science	Allocation of power and scarce resources	1. Organizations are coalitions of diverse individuals and interest groups. 2. Differences endure among coalition members: values, beliefs, information, interests, behaviors, worldviews. 3. All important organizational decisions involve scarce resources: who gets what. 4. Scarce resources and enduring differences make conflict inevitable and power a key asset. (Adapted from Bolman & Deal, 2003, p. 186)	Winning	Bargain, negotiate, build coalitions, set agendas, manage conflict.
Symbolic	Theater	Social and cultural anthropology	Meaning, purpose, and values	1. What is most important is not what happens but what it means to people. 2. Activity and meaning are loosely coupled: people interpret experiences differently. 3. People create symbols for conflict resolution, predictability, direction, hope. 4. Events and processes may be more important for what they express than what they produce. 5. Culture is the glue that holds organizations together through shared values and beliefs. (Adapted from Bolman & Deal, 2003, pp. 242–243)	Building faith and shared meaning	Create common vision; devise relevant rituals, ceremonies, and symbols; manage meaning; infuse passion, creativity, and soul.

Table 16.1.   A Four-Frame Approach to Understanding Organizations. *(continued)*

The power of these four frames for organizational diagnosis rests in the fact that organizations are messy and complex. They operate simultaneously on these four levels at all times, and can require special attention to address problems in one area while remaining strong and functioning in others. Organizations need a solid architecture—rules, roles, policies, formal practices, procedures, technologies, coordinating mechanisms, environmental linkages—that clearly channels resources and human talents into productive outcomes in support of key organizational goals. At the same time, organizations must deal with the complexity of human nature by facilitating workplace relationships that motivate and foster high levels of both satisfaction and productivity. Enduring differences of all kinds play a central role in organizational life. They lead to the ongoing need for managing conflict, disagreement, and differential levels of power and influence in order for the organization to accomplish a larger good. Finally, every organization must build and sustain a culture that aligns with organizational purposes and values, inspires and gives meaning to individual efforts, and provides the symbolic glue to coordinate the diverse contributions of many.

Staying ever mindful of these four parallel sets of dynamics cultivates solid diagnostic habits in a field like OD, where effectiveness requires a comprehensive, systemic perspective on an ambiguous, ever-shifting organizational landscape. But such mindfulness is not always easy. As human beings, we all rely on limited cognitive perspectives to make sense out of the world, readily fall back on habitual responses to problems and challenges, and remain blind to other options. Developmental limitations (Gallos, 1989, 2005) collude to sustain beliefs that our way of thinking and seeing the world is often "the only way"—when we only know how to use a hammer, the entire world begins to look like a nail. Such limitations keep us in our perceptual comfort zones and often away from the very experiences that challenge us to break frame and embrace "more complicated" socioemotional, intellectual, and ethical reasoning (Weick, 1979). In essence, good diagnosticians require multiple lenses to expand what they see and what it means. They are less apt to use them, however, without a framework that nudges them beyond their developmentally anchored propensities and into multiframe thinking.

To compound the issues, the ambiguity in organizational life leads to a host of possible explanations (and implicit solutions) for any problem. Take the simple case of two coworkers who engage regularly in verbal battles at work. Employing a human resource–based analysis of the situation, for example, might lead us to see a personality conflict between the two, clashing interpersonal styles, incompetence, immaturity, anger management issues, or some other intrapersonal problem for one or both of the employees. In this situation—as in all others—if we set out to find a people-blaming explanation, we will. And once we have determined that the problem requires people fixing, we will tackle it accordingly. We may invest in education and development: counseling, coaching, and training for one or both partners to help them behave appropriately at work, expand interpersonal capacities, build new skills and understandings, or negotiate differences more productively. Or we could fire one or both employees, then hire and train new ones. Both strategies are costly in their own way.

The verbal battles may, however, more accurately reflect overlapping job responsibilities: honest attempts to do their work keep the two employees repeatedly stepping on each other's toes. Although the expression of the problem is interpersonal, the cause is structural and relatively straightforward to address. Rewrite job descriptions, clarify role requirements, and eliminate the overlap, and the conflict should disappear—no need to change people or their skills. In their research across organizations, sectors, and nations, Bolman and Deal (2003) repeatedly found that the first and most common diagnosis of organizational inefficiency is interpersonal—blame people and explain everything that goes wrong as human error, folly, or treachery. Faulting individuals may be second nature to us all. But it blocks us from easily seeing structural weaknesses and other more subtle system dynamics. The tendency to look first for the people problem should raise a red flag for diagnosticians (such as OD professionals) whose values and traditions are strongly anchored in the human relations movement. Research on perception and human development confirms that what we expect to see is exactly what we will see.

Looking beyond people or structure offers additional possibilities. The verbal battles may be political, for example, rooted in the favoritism shown to one of the employees by a clueless boss who has unknowingly created a competitive work environment where the powerless grasp at any small share of the turf. The best intervention in that case is with the boss, who needs to learn to wield a supervisor's power with equity and justice. A focus on changing the coworkers or the structure bypasses the real source of the problem.

A fourth diagnostic alternative is to use a symbolic lens and explore the local meaning behind the actions. The coworkers' behaviors, for example, may be a reflection of a playful organizational culture where such verbal sparring is welcomed entertainment—a creative distraction from otherwise monotonous work, an expression of shared norms or ethnicity, or a sign of deep affection between the two. From a symbolic perspective, the verbal battles may warrant the organizational equivalent of a Tony Award for best performance in the theater of work. They are a sign of organizational health, not trouble.

A FOUR-DIMENSIONAL DIAGNOSTIC MODEL: ISSUES, CHOICE POINTS, AND AREAS OF FOCUS

As the foregoing examples illustrate, each of the four frames offers a diagnostic lens on a distinct set of organizational dynamics. Each also points to a frame-consistent course of action for intervention and change. If the problem is structural, tweak the structure. If the problem is with the people, teach, train, coach, counsel, or hire new ones. Issues of power and politics imply the need for strategies to empower, renegotiate, or share influence. Symbolic analyses focus on the meaning of organizational events to insiders and suggest ways to support the development of a healthy organizational culture. Although any of the frames may account for what's happening among those two coworkers, it is hard to know which one *really* does without first looking at them all. Any one frame may oversimplify a complex reality or send us blindly down the wrong path, squandering resources, time, and the change agent's credibility along the way.

A comprehensive diagnostic picture is better launched with four questions: What is going on structurally? What is happening from a human resource perspective? What's going on politically? What is happening on the symbolic front? Taken alone, each question encourages deep consideration of a slice of organizational life. Taken together, however, the four offer a systematic yet manageable way to approach and examine a full range of organizational possibilities. Table 16.2 outlines key issues and concepts from each frame. It provides a checklist of sorts, identifying a range of possible frame-specific issues to investigate, as well as potential areas of focus for data gathering and intervention.

Frame	Potential Issues and Areas to Investigate
Structural	Rules, regulations, goals, policies, roles, tasks, job designs, job descriptions, technology, environment, chain of command, vertical and horizontal coordinating mechanisms, assessment and reward systems, standard operating procedures, authority spans and structures, spans of control, specialization and division of labor, information systems, formal feedback loops, boundary scanning and management processes
Human resource	Needs, skills, relationships, norms, perceptions and attitudes, morale, motivation, training and development, interpersonal and group dynamics, supervision, teams, job satisfaction, participation and involvement, informal organization, support, respect for diversity, formal and informal leadership
Political	Key stakeholders, divergent interests, scarce resources, areas of uncertainty, individual and group agendas, sources and bases of power, power distributions, formal and informal resource allocation systems and processes, influence, conflict, competition, politicking, coalitions, formal and informal alliances and networks, interdependence, control of rewards and punishment, informal communication channels
Symbolic	Culture, rituals, ceremonies, stories, myths, symbols, metaphors, meaning, spirituality, values, vision, charisma, passions and commitments

Table 16.2.   Frame-Related Issues and Areas of Focus.

Finally, each frame can be understood as a unique set of central tensions that must be reconciled in making choices about structure, people, politics, and symbols. The tensions are universal and best thought of as endpoints on a series of continua with critical choice points in between that reflect trade-offs and balance between competing forces. For example, the design of an appropriate system of rules, roles, procedures, and structural relationships to facilitate organizational mission and purpose requires us to address four ongoing tensions:

1. *Differentiation and integration:* how to divide up the tasks and work to be done and then coordinate the diverse efforts of individuals and groups

2. *Centralization and decentralization:* how to allocate authority and decision making across the organization

3. *Tight boundaries and openness to the environment:* how much to buffer and filter the flow of people and information in and out of the organization

4. *Bureaucracy and entrepreneurism:* how to balance the requirement for consistency, predictability, and clarity with the need for autonomy, creativity, and flexibility

Working through these choices to achieve the right mix for any organization is hard and important work. But the aforementioned four tensions are only one piece of the larger work to be done. Again, each frame has its own central tensions. A look within the symbolic frame, for example, identifies different, yet equally significant, concerns:

1. *Innovation and respect for tradition:* how to foster newness and creativity while honoring the power and wisdom of the past

2. *Individuality and shared vision:* how to "get the whole herd moving roughly west" without sacrificing the originality and unique contributions of talented individuals

3. *Strong culture and permeable culture:* how to nurture shared values and norms while avoiding organizational repression and stagnation

4. *Prose and poetry:* how to balance an organization's needs for accuracy, objectivity, and accountability with its requirement for beauty, inspiration, and soul

Table 16.3 summarizes the central tensions for each of the four frames.

In working with these four sets of competing forces, it is important to remember that there is value for organizations on both ends of each continuum. The challenge for any organization is to find the balance between the two extremes that best fits its mission, purpose, values, and circumstances. All organizations need to divide up the work *and* integrate employee efforts. They foster the autonomy of individuals and units *and* the interdependence to accomplish common goals. They build on shared experience, skills, and values *and* utilize diversity to stay cutting-edge. They stay grounded in reality *and* embrace artistry and soul.

Frame	Central Tensions
Structural	Differentiation and integration Centralization and decentralization Tight boundaries and openness to the environment Bureaucracy and entrepreneurism
Human resource	Autonomy and interdependence Employee participation and authority decision making Self-regulation and external controls Meeting individual needs and meeting organizational needs
Political	Authority centered and partisan centered Similarity and diversity Empowerment and control Individual and collective
Symbolic	Innovation and respect for tradition Individuality and shared vision Strong culture and permeable culture Prose and poetry

Table 16.3.   Frame-Related Central Tensions.

The challenge for OD professionals then is to stay cognizant of the full range of universal dilemmas and tensions and open to working with each. We all have values or emotional preferences for one end of a continuum or the other. And as change agents, we may regularly push in only one direction. Those personal biases, however, do organizations a disservice.

OD work, for example, has historically favored such values as flexibility, autonomy, self-regulation, personal agency, and decentralization—positions that support individuality and entrepreneurial values and cast a negative shadow on the tight and bureaucratic. OD has historically preferred the poetry more than the prose. At the same time, we know that organizations require predictability, regularity, and consistency, and that people are empowered and more productive with clarity of purpose, means, and contribution. Rules, roles, policies, and standard operating procedures are a route to that needed clarity. Effective OD work is aided by an appreciation of all the options and choice points along the road to improved effectiveness. Attending simultaneously to the tensions in examining structure, people, politics, and symbols reminds change agents that there are multiple facets to organizing, each with its own contribution and promise. The four frames provide a map of the OD terrain that aids practitioners in knowing where they are, where they might go, and what they might gain or lose in choosing one direction or another. They also remind change agents that an important part of their job is reframing.

REFRAMING: USING AND TEACHING REFLECTION AND COGNITIVE ELASTICITY

Thus far, this chapter has looked at the four frames as a device for bringing all that we know about organizations to the work of making them more effective. Using them well, however, means engaging in a process of *reframing*—the practice of deliberately and systematically examining a complex situation from multiple perspectives. Reframing is a skill that requires both deep knowledge of alternative frames and practice in applying them so as to make frame flipping second nature.

Schön and Rein (1994) identify the important linkages among self-reflection, frames, and effective action. In the same way that a picture frame outlines and highlights a limited image from a larger visual landscape, our personal frames delineate and bound our experience. But we often don't realize this, for a number of reasons. People don't automatically think of themselves as choosing to take a personal and limited slant at the larger reality. They assume that what they see is what *is* and that any other perspective is distorted or wrong. The tacit nature of our preferred frames keeps us from seeing how they shape our perceptions and preferences. In addition, the nested nature of frames—frames can be individual, institutional, or cultural—compounds the problem. Individual frames are shaped by personal experiences with institutions, which have been influenced by a larger social and cultural milieu, and vice versa. These reciprocal influence loops reinforce and sustain each other. Schön and Rein (1994) believe that individuals can develop a "frame-critical rationality": personal capacities and strategies for understanding the content, impact, and limitations of their particular frame in action. This is a crucial first step on the road to reframing.

Reframing is a multistep process. Recognizing our preferred frame is important. But individuals also need to understand that expanding our frames of reference requires knowledge about alternative perspectives, appreciation for their potential contribution, opportunities to practice looking at the same situation through multiple lenses, and strategies for cross-frame diagnosis and reflection. The multiframe model developed in this chapter supports that by providing a comprehensive yet workable template for expanding choices, understanding alternatives, and managing social complexity. It also expands the contributions of change agents beyond traditional diagnosis and intervention.

In working with organizations to explore their structure, people, politics, and symbols, OD professionals are also assisting organizations in identifying their dominant institutional frame—the shared assumptions and logic that tacitly drive organizational actions and underpin reward systems and strategies. Although all organizations simultaneously function as machines, families, jungles, and theaters, few are skilled in regularly monitoring and managing the ongoing tensions and needs in all four areas. Recognizing this and understanding the content and contribution of each frame enable organizations to expand their institutional lenses, identify areas and issues historically ignored, and better balance attention across frames. Planned change now includes a useful metacurriculum on reframing and developing cognitive elasticity, with change agents modeling the process and benefits of cross-frame discourse (Kuhn, 1996). As a result, organizations enhance their capacities for multiframed analysis and action while building new levels of organizational awareness and learning. There are parallel gains for the individuals who lead and staff them, as well. Reframing demands a tolerance for ambiguity, an appreciation of the social construction of reality, and skills in relative thinking—all developmentally sophisticated capacities (Gallos, 1989). Teaching the art and craft of reframing actually encourages developmental growth. Change agents then play a significant role in both individual and organization development. William R. Torbert's chapter in Part Seven of this volume (Chapter Forty) illustrates well the concept of simultaneous individual and organization development.

OD AND THE FOUR FRAMES: MEANING AND METHOD

The four frames suggest strategies for diagnosing and improving an organization, as well as fostering the flexibility and multilevel learning necessary to ensure its long-term health. They also offer a way to reconceptualize OD and the field of planned change. Much has changed since OD's humble beginnings in the human relations movement of the 1950s. Technology, globalization, competitive pressures, economic models of human nature, and a host of social forces have altered the world of work, the ways we organize for collective action, and the meaning of organizational complexity. The organizational theory base has expanded to reflect increased understanding of these changes and their impact and to propel others by influencing managerial practice and metaconversations about effectiveness, organizing, and change. Although OD has evolved and grown since its early days in response to a host of environmental and theoretical shifts (Mirvis, 1988, 1990; see also Chapter Three), many still see the field as foundering, splintered, and unfocused (for example, Burke, 1997; Burke & Bradford, 2005; Greiner & Cummings, 2004; Wheatley, Griffin, Quade, & the National OD Network, 2003). Harvey (2005) even calls for its quiet death. This is no surprise.

The complexity of OD's task, points of system entry, and intervention options have expanded commensurate with the increasing complexity of the world and our ways of understanding it—and in ways that the field itself has neglected to embrace. Practitioners argue among themselves about where the boundaries of the field lie and which methods of planned change can claim the OD mantle and which cannot (or do not). Humanistic interventions of all kinds, for example, are inside OD's border, whereas reengineering and its industrial psychology–centered counterparts stand outside (Bradford & Burke, 2005; Burke, 1997). Multiple definitions of OD exist, some claiming strong allegiance to the movement's roots in human development, others embracing more technical interventions into strategy or structure (Cummings & Worley, 2005). At the same time, such OD methods as team building, feedback, data-based decision making, process consultation, and group problem solving are commonplace across organizational sectors and sizes, raising questions about the need for a field that promotes what has become obvious. Without a larger integrating framework for both diagnosis and intervention, OD risks becoming a series of incomplete or disconnected practices. The four frames provide an integrating structure for a struggling field. They situate OD practice within a larger conceptual map, helping practitioners more clearly see the organizational processes, dynamics, and issues to be explored and addressed, as well as those largely ignored or still uncharted.

In the language of this chapter, OD was conceived as a single-frame process to release human potential and facilitate ways to meet individual needs at work. But the impact of a single-frame process is limited in a multiframe world—and the organizational world is more multiframed than ever. Recognition of this requires an expanded and more generous definition of OD as a field that works with organizations as machines, families, jungles, and theater; appreciates the need for designing and managing multiframed change processes that address this reality; trains its practitioners on how and when to intervene in and on these different levels; and has at the ready a broad array of practices and processes to facilitate a multipronged approach to planned change and system health.

Solid values have always driven OD work, and the field must continue to support attention to the human side of enterprise, the fair and ethical treatment of people, and the creation of organizations that foster human initiative and dignity. A look at the front page of any newspaper reminds us how relevant and needed OD's values are today. A four-dimensional definition of the field, however, does not reject the humanistic values that have long underpinned OD work. On the contrary, it offers a more realistic and manageable way to create the organizational structures, workplace relationships, empowering systems, and healthy cultures that foster the release of human potential, productivity, and joy.

APPROACHING PLANNED CHANGE: THE PARADOX OF THE SPECIALIST AND THE GENERALIST

Richard Beckhard (1969) provides the seminal definition of organization development and identifies its five key components. OD is "(1) planned, (2) organization-wide and (3) managed from the top to (4) increase organization effectiveness and health through (5) planned interventions in the organization's 'processes,' using behavioral-science knowledge" (p. 9). The model presented in this chapter suggests a multiframed way to define this work and its outcomes. Table 16.4 provides a summary. It also raises an interesting conundrum for OD practitioners on how to optimize both their breadth and their specialization. There is value for effective change agents in both.

Frame	Focus of OD	Change Agent Role	Possible Intervention Options	Intended Meta-Outcome
Structural	Aligning structure to organizational mission and purpose	Analyst, organizational architect	Restructuring, infrastructure adjustments, vertical and lateral coordinating mechanisms, technology upgrades, environmental scanning, job design and redesign	Clarity, efficiency
Human resource	Facilitating the fit between individual and organizational needs	Facilitator, teacher, coach	Training and education, job and work redesign, hiring practices, job enrichment, workforce development, quality of work life programming, team building, process consultation, survey feedback, fostering participation, expanding of information networks, empowerment, diagnosis of the informal organization, norms, decision making, counseling, coaching	Satisfaction, motivation, productivity, empowerment

Table 16.4. Multiframed Organization Development. (*continues*)

Frame	Focus of OD	Change Agent Role	Possible Intervention Options	Intended Meta-Outcome
Political	Attuning the distribution of power, influence, and alliances to achieve organizational goals	Political strategist, community organizer, advocate	Charting power relationships, adjusting formal or informal networks, redistributing decision making, managing diversity, altering communication channels, clarifying or forging agendas, developing arenas to surface conflict, building or dismantling coalitions, rethinking formal and informal reward systems, advocacy and education	Competitive advantage, distributive justice
Symbolic	Creating a vision and culture that support organizational goals and individual creativity	Dramaturge, artist, poet	Vision and values work, culture analysis, framing opportunities, reframing challenge or conflict, creating rituals or ceremonies, using organizational histories and stories, training on how to give voice to the vision and develop charisma, rewarding heroes and heroines, fostering humor and play	Passion, spirit, creativity, soul

Table 16.4. Multiframed Organization Development. *(continued)*

Each of the four frames suggests an area for specialized attention and intervention. The advantages of specialization are that change agents can know more about a selected area, develop stronger skills in facilitating frame-related processes and diagnoses, and reflect their own values and talents. Designing formal vertical and lateral coordination networks, for example, is dramatically different from fostering a culture that respects humor and play. And given the realities of time, talent, and energy, it is basically easier to become a valued expert and resource on one set of dynamics than on them all.

Specialization involves real risks, however. OD practitioners may find themselves challenged in facing issues outside their area of expertise. Specialization can also tighten frame blinders so that change agents just don't see problems and options beyond their own perspective, the forest for the trees, or the benefit of reframing. They are particularly at risk if the environment shifts unexpectedly during a cycle of planned change, raising issues beyond their frame skill, focus, or comfort or suggesting alternative multiframe courses of action. Further, all OD practitioners need to remain generalists to some degree in their diagnostic work—at least long enough to understand what's *really* happening and to assess how well their talents and skills match current organizational needs. Competent OD professionals are specialists *and* generalists who need to embrace both sides of this core paradox.

This may seem like contradictory advice. Fletcher and Olwyler (1997) would disagree, however. Their work in understanding the role of paradox in optimal performance suggests the importance of simultaneously embracing two seemingly inconsistent paths without feeling the need to compromise on either. The most successful sprinters, for example, are simultaneously relaxed and tensed to meet the competition. Bill Gates is a genius in vision and in practicalities. Fletcher and Olwyler's work has been driven by recognition that highly successful people are universally contradictory but have learned to accept and use their contradictions for the creative resolution of what may seem to others to be irreconcilable conflicts. Just like musicians playing good counterpoint, these individuals have learned to play their competing melodies at the same time and celebrate the fact that each proudly holds its own. OD professionals are aided in their work when they successfully embrace the paradox of the specialist and the generalist and bring the benefits of both to their work.

IN CLOSING: A MULTIFRAME FUTURE FOR OD

This chapter begins with a promise to assist individuals committed to organizational improvement. It builds on the work of Bolman and Deal (2003) in laying out a four-frame model to harness the plurality in the organizational theory base to strengthen planned change efforts. It illustrates the possibilities and content of each frame; outlines key issues, inherent tensions, and areas of focus; proposes a four-dimensional approach to organizational diagnosis; highlights the power and benefits of reframing; and suggests frame-related strategies for intervention and change.

The chapter ends with advocacy for an expanded appreciation for OD as a field that embraces complexity and paradox, fosters both individual and organization development, and brings a full range of understandings about the interplay among organizational structure, people, politics, and symbols to its work. OD and its respect for the human side of organizing are needed more than ever. The field fulfills its mission and legacy best when its methods are underpinned by multiframed ways to understand and work with different layers of organizational reality; its change agents can assist organizations in identifying and expanding their current lenses; and its processes model the power of flexible thinking and the willingness to ask "What else might *really* be happening here?"

PART FOUR

OD Consulting
Leading Change from the Outside

E xternal consultants have played a central role in organization development from its inception. Many of the field's founders were university faculty who developed OD's theories and practices from their experiences with a variety of groups and organizations. Working as action researchers and interventionists, they helped client systems solve current problems in hopes of leaving the client better able to resolve future challenges. These individuals were valued as outsiders who brought new tools and perspectives about change and organizational processes. Their zeal helped spread the word of OD's success and led to invitations from other organizations. What began then as a fact of history soon became institutionalized in the field's definition of intervention and its methods of change. The model of the OD practitioner as a trained professional, external to the client organization or subsystem, has remained the norm. In some circles, the role of the OD consultant and the special nature of the collaborative relationship with a client system differentiate OD from other organizational improvement programs.

This history also translates into years of experience and theories about the OD consultant's role and about the strategies and values that inform a successful consultant-client relationship. Negotiating contracts, defining the client, differentiating roles and responsibilities, building trust and internal commitment, developing strategies for system diagnosis, testing theories and assumptions, serving the organization's (not the consultant's) needs, staying open to learning and responsive to feedback, establishing credibility, using oneself as a data point, and sustaining one's authenticity are a sample of the kinds of issues that the field has addressed over the years. Many of OD's consulting methods, innovations, and approaches have made their way into the mainstream and tacitly inform definitions of good consulting practice in other fields.

The articles in Part Four focus on good consulting in action. Taken together, they offer diverse strategies for leading organization development and change from the outside. Keith Merron, in "Masterful Consulting," presents a contemporary consulting model that enacts and extends many core principles of OD. Masterful consultants create a grounded, open, and collaborative relationship with their client organizations in service to organizational enhancement and learning. Peter Block demystifies the consulting process and outlines key consulting phases and tasks in an excerpt from his book *Flawless Consulting*. Marvin Weisbord, a thoughtful and well-respected senior consultant in the field, explains the importance and the nitty-gritty of contracting with a client system in his classic article, "The Organization Development Contract." The final two articles in Part Four— "The Facilitator and Other Facilitative Roles," by Roger Schwarz, and "The Right Coach," an excerpt from *The Art and Practice of Leadership Coaching,* by Howard Morgan, Phil Harkins, and Marshall Goldsmith—provide ways to understand and develop two essential capacities for OD consultants: facilitation and coaching skills.

CHAPTER SEVENTEEN

Masterful Consulting

Keith Merron

S am, an eager young consultant, was leading his first client engagement. Bright and aggressive, with a fresh MBA under his belt, he had been under the tutelage of one of the best partners in his consulting firm for three years. Now, having received a set of important distinctions and a proprietary consulting process, he was ready to strut his stuff. He did everything his partner taught him, and it seemed to work. He showed the clients all the important and relevant research that pointed to the flaws in the client organization. He used a team of bright consultants to gather and analyze data about the client, its competitors, and key trends in the industry. He showed the client the changes it needed to make to get ahead of the industry in its market space. At each step along the way, the client seemed eager, interested, engaged, and impressed with Sam's know-how.

At the final meeting, Sam's report was well received and a team of leaders in the client organization almost instantly accepted the recommendations he made. They assured Sam of their commitment to implementing these changes and even adopted his sensible timeline, which balanced a high degree of urgency with awareness that these things take time. At the end of this meeting, Sam was one happy consultant.

Months later, he could not have been more disappointed. For the first few weeks, the client began making plans to implement the recommendations. However, an unexpected dip in sales, coupled with some missed product development deadlines, caused the client to shelve some of Sam's recommendations. They assured him it was a temporary problem, and they would get back on track as soon as this temporary setback was addressed. They never did.

It was obvious to Sam that the process and the expertise he provided were right on target. The fault, clearly, lay in the client's lack of ability to deliver on its end and to stick with the plan. In debriefing with the partner about the failed effort, the partner pointed out some things Sam could have done differently, offering clever tricks of the trade that might have made a difference. The partner also pointed out that these things happen and that it was part of the learning process. "You are destined to do great things," the partner said. "Don't let it get you down."

The partner's sage counsel was welcome, and Sam was eager to tackle the next client opportunity with renewed vigor. Little did he know that it was almost inevitably doomed to fail. It would make money, but it wouldn't make a difference. Nor did the partner have any inkling of this. No one else in the firm did either. They were making plenty of money, in fact, with enough financial success that this and other failures were easily shrugged off. The failure pattern was left unexamined while the consulting firm got to continue the game.

Sam's story is repeated time after time in consulting engagements all over the world. Many consultants have seen outcomes like Sam's many times yet find themselves in the same scenario. Caught in the same pattern that most of the consulting world is following, they cannot see an alternative. As a result, many, if not most clients are either cynical about consultants or angry about how intractable the whole system is. Yet they too continue to participate in the pattern, hoping that the next time they hire a consultant, the outcome will be different. It rarely is.

SAVIOR AND PROBLEM SOLVER

To understand how to break out of this pattern, we need to go beneath the surface of the rules of typical consulting approaches and examine the goals and strategies that drive those rules. We will start with goals because the goals of consultants, as for any human being, form and inform the strategies they use.

Take a moment and ask yourself: What do you want as a consultant? Why do you consult in the first place? You could want many things. If you are like most consultants, however, your goals probably fall into one of three areas.

- To add value—fix a problem, plug a hole, introduce a new process or system
- To make a lot of money
- To make a profound difference—to shift the organization to a new level

The primary goals of many consultants employing the typical rules of consulting are to add value and to make a lot of money. The consultant typically offers help in the form of expert advice or an expert process. In a competitive bidding situation, often the consultant must also convince the client that this expertise cannot be found elsewhere and not only is it well worth it, but the client also is at risk of failing without it. In most cases, clients are inclined to believe this is so. In addition, the consultant will often leverage the talents of others to expedite the consulting process for the client.

These goals, to add value and to make money, get translated into strategies, which in turn directly affect the actions and outcomes of the client engagement. Let's begin with the primary strategy that drives most consultants' actions and behaviors.

The Savior Strategy

Every day, throughout the world, clients and consultants are participating in a silent and powerful contract, often unaware of its existence. It is the basis of what I call the *savior strategy*. To understand this strategy, we need to strip away the complexity of consulting and get down to its essential form.

At the core of any consulting activity is the desire by the client to get help and by the consultant to offer help. Help tends to take the following form:

- Client defines a problem.
- Client hires consultant to either solve the problem or tell the client how to solve it.
- Client pays for this service and sometimes implements the advice.

The desire to be helpful runs deep in the psychological makeup of most consultants. They have spent many years honing their craft, driven by this desire. More specifically, they have a belief in how organizations can be better run and a genuine desire to show clients the way.

Simultaneously, clients often have a deep desire to be helped. Rarely seeing consulting as an aid for growing or developing the organization, they often seek out consultants when something in the business is not working well or is "broken." Out of consultants' desire to help and clients' desire to have something "fixed" is born the savior strategy. To occur, the savior strategy requires two consenting parties—the helpers and the receivers of help. The helpers must be motivated to help and also believe they have a better way. The receivers of help must want to be saved, believe they are capable of changing, and believe that the helpers have a magic elixir obtainable only from the helpers.

Many consulting firms are brilliant at playing the savior game and preying on the fears of clients that, without the firm's help, the company is either doomed or in deep weeds. These consulting firms make impressive presentations, backed up by recent research, demonstrating the trends that are impinging on the company, followed by multiple examples of how clients have been helped enormously by the consulting firm's intervention. That these charts are often pseudoscientific is usually not evident, because the client so wants to believe that the consulting firm will save them. It is a lesson carried over from the snake oil salesman of the 1800s, who made a good living selling exotic elixirs to "cure all that ails you." When you want to be fixed or saved, you are easily prone to being convinced.

Preying on the client's need to be saved is a significant modus operandi for many consultants, particularly those that employ an "expert" model of consulting. What better way to hook the client into believing in the necessity of hiring the consultant than to cleverly participate in the game. To be fair, most consultants don't seek to "hook" the client at all (at least not consciously). They simply want to be of service and to add value in the best way they know how—by solving a problem. Nonetheless, both consultants and clients participate in the same implied contract. You, the client, need help. I have what you need. I'll sell it to you, and then you'll have it.

It sounds so wonderful. But the negative consequences of the implied contract can be severe. Once the consultant leaves, the client organization will not have more knowledge than it had before, because knowledge—the consultant's stock in trade—cannot be given away.

You can give people information; it's like giving them a bag of groceries. But knowledge transfers less easily. In the realm of human and organizational dynamics, knowledge must be learned and earned through exploration, deep shared thinking, and often struggle. Many consultants do indeed often have useful knowledge, but by the time it is transferred in the form of a presentation, report, or other form, it is rarely more than information. Since the knowledge behind that information is rarely transferred, it is never truly owned by the client organization. The bookshelves and credenzas of managers around the world are laden with well-crafted consultant presentations—collecting dust.

Yet in spite of this, clients are happy to pay for information and to expect positive results. This willingness to be "done to" and be "given to" is natural. Most organizations are overwhelmed, and they look for the quick fix. Most consultants are happy to oblige.

Secondary Strategies

The goal to add value and make a lot of money gets enacted and expressed through the primary savior strategy. This strategy, in turn, produces secondary strategies that support the desire to help and to make money. These strategies, in turn, determine the kinds of choices consultants make. The typical strategies of the consulting process fall into one of three categories: the consultant's relationship to his client; the consultant's relationship to knowledge; and the consultant's relationship with himself—his character, in other words.

In the arena of relationship to client, most consultants employ a strategy that gives them tacit power over the client, and they use that power to try to get the client to do what they believe is best for the client. In the arena of relationship to knowledge, most consultants claim and use specialized knowledge, processes, tools, and techniques as their primary added value. In the arena of relationship to self, most consultants seek to develop presentation and sales skills for gaining more business. Let's look at each more deeply and its consequences.

• *Create a "power over" relationship to the client.* Most consultants say they want a partnership with their clients. They talk about the importance of give and take and of working together to solve a problem. And indeed, in most cases that is what they desire. However, many consultants are unaware of the multiple ways their behavior implies a different relationship—one best described as having "power over" their clients.

Consultants who consciously or unconsciously employ a "power over" strategy do a number of things that are designed to maintain control over the client and the consulting process. For example, they chop up the business into parts in order to analyze it. On the face of it, this seems sound. However, the more consultants do the work, the more likely they will understand the business better than the client (at least those aspects relevant to the consulting engagement). Consultants then use this understanding as leverage to get clients to do what the consultants think is best for them. Additionally, many consultants control the consulting process as much as possible, convincing clients that these "tried and true" methods guarantee best results. Since consultants know these methods, and the clients do not, a "power over" dynamic is created or maintained. Finally, the very act of promising to deliver success feeds off the client's desire to be fixed or saved and puts them in a childlike position in relationship to the consulting "parent."

• *Claim and use specialized knowledge, processes, tools, and techniques as the primary added value.* Most often, the added value consultants provide in the form of knowledge, tools, and techniques is really worth something. So is the research they tailored to meet the unique needs of the client. Conducted by bright and eager consultants and led by savvy partners, consultants do provide useful analyses, sound techniques, and thoughtful recommendations, much of which has real value for the client. The only rub is the claim that it is specialized and unavailable elsewhere.

Consultants place a high value on being special, on having something the client cannot get anywhere else. Sometimes they claim that the knowledge may not be special, but the methods for implementing that knowledge are. However, rarely does a consultant have something a client can't get elsewhere. Many times I have seen consultants scramble to put together a presentation from a recent *Harvard Business Review* article, slap their logo on it, and claim to have specialized knowledge. Astonishingly, it works. They dazzle the client with presentations, delivered with panache. In truth, if this knowledge is this available, how special can it be? The real added value comes not from the information but from the ability to get clients to actually use this knowledge well. This ability is indeed a rare commodity among expert-based consultants.

• *Develop "self" skills for gaining more business.* Many consulting firms teach their new consultants the importance of presenting themselves well. Partners "dress for success" and encourage their more junior consultants to do the same. They place a high emphasis on conforming to the kind of social etiquettes that appeal to those in positions of power in their client organization. And they hone their influence and persuasion techniques. To many consulting firms, developing "self" is about outer image and presentation, not about the "inner self." Indeed, you might argue that the inner self has little to do with effective analysis. Masterful consultants take issue with this, however. One masterful consultant I know left her highly successful partnership in a firm, finally fed up with the overattention to image and inattention to issues of character and lack of true commitment to the client. In her words, "the hypocrisy of how the consulting firm ran counter to the very principles it taught clients and was too much for me to bear."

Each strategy can generate an endless number of actions. Many actions, however, fall into a typical set, represented in the last column in Table 17.1.

Many of the larger, more "successful" consulting firms use two additional and very questionable strategies as part of their financial wealth plan. They often use less experienced consultants and charge far more to the client to create high profits. And they offer high-margin "bolt-ons" ("how about some fries with your burger") as a critical added resource.

Although I think the typical approach in Table 17.1 is fair and close to reality, it is also a caricature. Few consultants truly operate exactly like this. Many do some of these things as well as some that are more masterful. Certainly, few consultants will ever admit that they are focusing primarily on making money. In subtle ways, however, they make choices that are not in the client's best interest. Sam was a great example. His mentor taught him that the client often can't see what it needs, and that he and other members of the consulting firm knew better than their clients. Had the client known better, it is reasoned, the client would not have needed to hire Sam's consulting firm in the first place. This frees up Sam to recommend things the consulting firm has to offer without hesitation or concerns.

Consultants everywhere are following the same process. In some cases, the consultant follows these strategies and actions and does indeed help solve the problem and leave the client satisfied. In some cases, it is a waste of effort: Remember those bookshelves of reports. collecting dust. Rarely, however, does advice giving or help in the forms most consultants provide make a difference. It rarely adds energy to the system. It does not challenge people to think differently, nor cultivate deeper understanding. It rarely penetrates the underlying patterns that form and shape the client and keep the client from achieving a higher level of performance.

What is the alternative? The consultant moves from being a savior and problem solver to being an empowering partner. This requires a fundamental shift in one's inner stance as a consultant.

Goals	Primary Strategy	Secondary Strategies	Actions
Make money Add value	Be a savior	Create a power-over relationship	Chop up the business into parts and analyze—use the analysis as the primary source of added value to the client
			Control the process to the extent possible
			Promise to deliver success and feed off the client's desire to be saved or fixed
		Claim and use specialized knowledge, processes, tools, and techniques as the primary added value	Offer value in the form of deep analysis and thoughtful recommendations
			Claim to have developed expertise unavailable to clients
			Dazzle the client with presentations and sound technique—delivery with panache
		Develop "self" skills for gaining more business	Attend to and develop one's image
			Hone one's influence and persuasion techniques

Table 17.1.   The Typical Game of Consulting.

EMPOWERING PARTNER

John left the debriefing session of the consulting engagement thinking he had done a decent job. He had helped the client accomplish the task, had met all his commitments, and felt satisfied his deliverable was better than most could have done. The debriefing went as expected, with nothing unusual. John shook hands with the client, leaving her with this message: "Sheryl, if you ever have any other work like this, please don't hesitate to call." Sheryl assured him she would. John was comforted by her response.

Months went by and there was no call. Through his connections John learned there were indeed two other similar projects that required his kind of expertise, yet he was never called. After eight months, he decided to take action. He called Sheryl to ask her why he was not considered. She gave him two reasons related to their internal decision making, both of which seemed compelling but did not persuade him. He asked her again if she was pleased with his work, and she indicated she was.

What John did not know, and would likely never find out from Sheryl, was that his work was adequate, but not great. He had done everything he could, but she felt no connection with him. Moreover, she felt that his work would not take them to the next level. He fulfilled the contract but did not impress. The problem wasn't his method or his reports. The problem was that he lacked the inner magic that inspired others to challenge their assumptions. He was good, but not masterful. Sadly, he yearned to be great, so not getting called back was painful. He didn't believe her answer to his question, yet had no way to probe deeper to learn what the real problem was. He felt rejected and confused.

Although much research exists on the practice of consulting, the profession is still far more art than science. John pays attention to the science and comes equipped with the latest techniques and models. But he lacks the artistry that is the essence of masterful consulting.

The Artistry of a Masterful Consultant

Like great painters, masterful consultants rely on more than simple technique. They know that each client situation is unique—a blank canvas. While there are principles to guide their actions, they must create anew the process and the relationship to produce the greatest effect. Where the painter works with paintbrush and palette, the masterful consultant works with "self."

All good consultants have an inventory of theories, models, tools, and techniques to draw on. Without them, most would be lost. Yet what differentiates master consultants from others has nothing to do with this inventory. It has all to do with the "feel" of the situation, with the ability to act effectively "in the moment"—to sense what is going on in a given situation and then take the action that meets that moment. To do this well requires consultants to divest themselves of the past and the future, of fears, anxieties, and desires, to be present, and then to take action without ego. Theory, models, instruments, and techniques can't teach this, because it arises from the consultant's inner stance—that invisible quality elusive to so many. The mastery of which I speak has to do with the ability to shift patterns in client organizations. That is the true magic of masterful consulting.

The Master Consultant's Goals and Strategies

Every organization is driven by a set of patterns. The way we hold meetings has a pattern. The way we communicate has a pattern. Our leadership style has a pattern. These patterns form, mold, and harden until they become the very culture of organizations. The goal of consulting mastery is simple: to have an impact on the fundamental patterns of the client organization in order to produce profound and deep change.

To accomplish this goal, masterful consultants adopt a primary strategy best characterized as an empowering partnership—one designed to shift the client organization to a new level of health and performance. An empowering partnership is one where both consultant and client are touched by each other. Together, they create an authentic, vulnerable relationship, where the client, the process, and the relationship itself are all explored, deepened, and enhanced. They see their work together as cocreative and filled with learning that is every bit as imaginative as it is well designed. Scottish philosopher David Hume said it well when he wrote: "The sweetest path of life leads through the avenues of learning, and whoever can open up the way for another, ought, so far, to be esteemed a benefactor to mankind." This avenue of learning traveled by an empowered relationship is the heart of the master consultant's primary strategy.

Following this primary strategy, masterful consultants use three secondary strategies, each fitting the three arenas of consulting: relationship with client, with knowledge, and with self.

1. *Master consultants develop a client-centered partnership.* They see clients as whole systems and encourage their clients to do the same. They are clear that clients have the capacity to grow. Therefore, they position themselves as guides or partners, not experts. Finally, they see their clients as responsible for the outcome while remaining a partner in the process.

2. *Master consultants share knowledge openly and freely.* They know that the key to effectiveness is in applying knowledge in real time. In addition, they know wherever possible to transfer knowledge and enhance the wisdom of their clients.

3. *Master consultants see the quality of their character as a catalyst for transformation and learning.* They recognize that the most important differentiator between good and great consultants is the quality of their character. As a result, they spend a great deal of time developing their inner self.

To better understand these three strategies, let's examine each one more thoroughly.

How Masterful Consultants Relate to Their Client Organizations

The empowering relationship masterful consultants form with their client organizations may be obvious to many, but it is also difficult to attain. Almost all consultants believe they form relationships with their client organizations with the intent to empower them. They say they create conditions in which the client owns the process or the outcome, and that their intent is to leave the client more capable than when the consulting process started. This mindset alone, however, is not what differentiates masterful consultants from others. It is the degree to which they behave congruently with it. While many consultants espouse the importance of the client owning the process and of creating a true partnership with the client, their behavior, too often, tells another story.

Let's look at one example. Craig is a competent consultant who believes strongly that his client needs to own the process and the outcome of the consultation, and he believes the members of the client organization need to implement his ideas themselves in order to grow. During a planning session to develop a two-year plan to execute a fairly radical Six-Sigma process throughout the company, Craig led the way. He offered a model for executing the ideas and walked the group of key executives and HR staff through each carefully designed step. They followed Craig's lead, feeling a need for his guidance in an area that seemed overwhelming and highly complex and made decisions consistent with Craig's framework. When members of the planning team offered ideas that Craig believed were unwise, he deftly and compassionately explained why and offered an alternative suggestion. The team felt persuaded by his viewpoint, never controlled. Based on initial positive feelings about Craig, all appeared to be going according to plan.

Had you looked at Craig's behavior more closely, however, you might have noticed signs of a less-than-ideal outcome. Throughout the meeting he made suggestions far more often than he asked questions or invited comments. When he did ask questions, it was almost always with an answer already in mind. Subtly, Craig steered the group toward the preexisting answer. Nor did he solicit feedback about how they were feeling about the process or decisions made. Additionally, numerous nonverbal signs were ignored, such as crossed arms and restive expressions suggesting that team members were disconnecting from the process. Regardless of these signs, Craig left feeling successful, having imparted his hard-earned wisdom to the members of the team. The CEO felt as if he got his money's worth. After all, wasn't he paying Craig for knowledge?

The missing ingredient here was that the team, while following Craig's lead, did not psychologically own the change process or the outcome, because they never had to think it through for themselves. As a result, they did a poorer job in the implementation phase than they did in the diagnosis. Midway through the process, the implementation stalled as other business concerns came to the fore. To this day, Craig blames the team members for their lack of commitment and ability to act with conviction, not himself for the subtle and mounting ways he precluded their own learning process.

In contrast to Craig's experience, masterful consultants keep their clients in the driver's seat, committed to their ownership of the outcome. It's a conscious process, one that calls for rigorous self-observation and attention to the potential to want to act in a heroic fashion and "fix" the client's problems. Masterful consultants seek feedback to minimize their own unconscious patterns that might result in taking power away from their client organizations. In other words, they walk their empowering talk. Unlike Craig, masterful consultants will more often ask questions than give answers. They act as facilitators, committed to having the planning team members think the process through for themselves. They might offer a model, but at the same time readily accept one of their client's if it achieves the outcomes of ownership and committed action necessary to implement change.

Masterful consultants know that the magic is not in the models, but rather in the intangibles: the learning process, the consultant's relationship to the client, and the consultant's character. Masterful consultants behave more congruently with their beliefs because they examine their own behavior deeply and fully. They are also deeply committed to the client having freedom of choice, ownership of the process, and valid information upon which to make decisions. They are far more consciously facilitative than someone like Craig. While Craig says he is committed to those same principles, his greater, unconscious commitment is to be "brilliant" in the eyes of the client—and to be "right."

Owning the outcome is one of three features of the client relationship that masterful consultants form. In addition, masterful consultants treat the whole system as the client, and wisely negotiate the dilemmas posed when the person paying them acts inconsistently with the needs of the whole system.

Underlying masterful consultants' success is their abiding commitment to a partnering relationship, one where power is shared equally between client and consultant during the change process. One thing that differentiates masterful consultants from others is the depth to which they hold true to this principle, not merely paying it lip service. In the act of defining a consultant-client relationship, for example, most masterful consultants have a very candid conversation with the client about mutual boundaries, expectations, and desires. While other consultants tend to wait to discuss their relationship until problems arise, masterful consultants deal with it up front. In the contracting phase of the consulting engagement, they will place as much if not more emphasis on defining the desired qualities of the interpersonal relationship as on the financial relationship. They discuss and agree upon who is in charge of which meetings, when and how to give feedback to each other, under what conditions either party can exit the relationship, expectations about honesty and vulnerability, and much more.

How Masterful Consultants Relate to Knowledge

Although I have argued strongly against the overemphasis on knowledge in the hierarchy of consulting abilities, I am not dismissing it altogether. Indeed, a threshold of knowledge is necessary to be even a half-decent consultant. The importance of knowledge was reinforced through the client interviews I conducted to understand their views of consulting mastery. When describing the most effective consultant they had ever worked with, many described how bright and knowledgeable the consultant was. Clients often spoke not only about the consultant's conceptual capability but also of his or her ability to see clearly through the fog of the client's difficulties. Similarly, the intellectual horsepower of each of the consultants I interviewed was quite evident. At the same time, none of them wore their intelligence on their sleeve. Quite the opposite; almost all were astoundingly humble.

Knowledge, then, is crucial to consulting mastery, as is the ability to think clearly. Without some threshold level of knowledge and a keen intellect, the consultant will not fulfill the client's tacit need to be given something (knowledge) the client believes it lacks.

In this day and age, both good and masterful consultants are more than adequately equipped with expert knowledge in their field and are able to communicate their knowledge effectively. In the knowledge arena, what distinguishes masterful consultants is the way they hold and use knowledge. They hold their knowledge with certainty and confidence, not arrogance. When they communicate, they often describe the complex set of unfolding dynamics in ways that create clarity out of confusion. Most important, masterful consultants are guided by a set of theories about change, which provide a map for how to navigate the complex and choppy waters of change. One master consultant I interviewed said it well:

> Too often consultants are walking around and they don't have a solid ground to stand on in terms of either a theory of change that they can use across multiple levels of system or a theory of phases of development. Without those two things, they are almost certainly going to end up basically leaning on tools and techniques.

In addition to offering concepts cleanly and simply, masterful consultants will pick and choose their spots when intervening in the client organization. Ever aware that the client must own the change and take action based on the knowledge offered, masterful consultants seek not to dazzle the client with knowledge. Instead, they guide and support the client toward the discoveries necessary for action. Even more important, they seek to create conditions in which these discoveries are so strongly experienced that the outcome is a profound commitment to change.

How Masterful Consultants Carry Themselves as People

The quality of character of masterful consultants is evident in how they talk, how they relate to others, and how they act. Behind these behaviors must be integrity, confidence, and humility. Behind this, deeper still, must be strong self-esteem, often born of years of self-reflection and intense inner work.

In my experience, masterful consultants strive to live by a set of principles. We all have principles that guide our actions, sometimes tacit and sometimes explicit. What distinguishes masterful consultants from others is their adherence to those principles, their commitment to examine themselves in relation to these principles, and their willingness and ability to self-correct. Ralph Waldo Emerson, the famous 19th-century transcendentalist philosopher, put it well: "Self-command is the main discipline."

Not surprisingly, the principles of self-command are not typically taught in most consulting training courses. Nor are they discussed in great detail in daily conversation among consultants. But they are held deeply by masterful consultants. Here are the principles they share (see Exhibit 17.1):

---

1 Always tell the truth, at the deepest levels.
2 Commit to learning—for self and for the client.
3 Bring my whole self in full partnership.
4 Play a big game.

Exhibit 17.1. The Masterful Consultant's Principles of Conduct.

- *Always tell the truth.* Be honest with oneself and with others at all times. Great consultants are typically courageous and value honesty before caution. At the same time, they find ways of speaking honestly in ways that others can hear. They do not bludgeon others with honesty. Instead, their honesty goes down easily because it is coupled with respect.

- *Commit to learning.* Take a stance in life. Great consultants are inquisitive. They spend far more time and energy exploring issues than they do offering answers. They respect and abide by the process of discovering, and they encourage answers to unfold rather than delivering them in machine-gun succession.

- *Bring my whole self.* Be vulnerable and be whole—mind, body, and spirit. Great consultants are acutely aware of their shadow self, and rather than deny or hide some areas of their self, they seek to bring them out. They see the process of consulting as a very human process and know that the more we know and respect our own self, the more we can understand, respect, and guide others.

- *Play a big game.* Work with others to make a larger difference. Great consultants don't get embroiled in either/or thinking. They focus on ways of working that expand possibilities to produce win-win outcomes and that open up vistas clients were not even aware of.

Simple as they may seem, these principles are profound in their implications. As I look back on the moments when I was less than successful, I can almost always trace them back to either avoiding or not embodying one of these principles. Masterful consultants know deep in their bones that failure in consulting is almost always attributable to violating one of those principles; therefore they strive to live by them impeccably—to be in command of self. Deviating from them creates an inner disturbance. Once they notice the deviation, they immediately correct course.

By saying that masterful consultants live by the principles I have described, I am not suggesting they are perfect. To the contrary, any principle or value is a beacon of light to strive for; not a rule to be gripped by. What differentiates masterful consultants from others is their commitment to the principles, their never-wavering intention to look themselves in the mirror, and their ability to self-correct without self-blame.

These qualities do not come easily. They are the result of years of self-exploration, self-examination, and the support of many others—therapists, counselors, coaches, mentors, friends, and family—all of whom challenge the consultant to live up to his or her full potential as a vehicle for positive change. It takes a strong sense of self—an unusually high level of self-esteem—to attain mastery, and it is driven by a continual commitment to self-awareness.

Underlying the four principles of conduct is a deeper awareness held by all masterful consultants. Masterful consultants do not see these principles as static. Nor do they see themselves as perfect. They see themselves on a journey toward realizing these principles, a destination that is never fully achieved. This is a journey toward being a more conscious and self-aware human being, not just a good consultant. It is a journey of self-discovery.

In short, these principles are a guide for how masterful consultants conduct themselves always. The principles determine the consultants' actions, decisions, and choices. It is their powerful inner guide, and in living by this guide, consultants become effective, trusted, and positively influential.

THE THREE STRATEGIES ARE AN INTEGRATED WHOLE

As a system, the goals and strategies of masterful consultants do not exist in isolation from one another. Trying to enact one strategy without the others is like a three-legged stool missing a leg. Inevitably, it will fall.

To illustrate, let's look at three examples. I know one consultant (let's call him Paul) who is quite brilliant and who has conceptualized a way of working with clients and helping them transform that is as well thought out as any I've ever seen. Paul also acts with the utmost of integrity. However, when he works with clients, they often feel that he is aloof, professorial, and sometimes self-absorbed. Paul has generated many new clients, but few stay with him over time. Fewer still call him back for more work. They rarely tell him the real reason for not continuing to work, masking it with excuses such as, "we aren't ready to go forward yet," or "we want to slow the process down for now." As a result, Paul has no clue why his client work comes up short. His relationship to knowledge is strong and his character impeccable. But his ability to connect to people in a heartfelt way just isn't there.

In contrast, I know another consultant (let's call her Sandy) who demonstrates enormous integrity in her dealings with others. Sandy has a wonderful way of engaging with clients, and they experience her as warm, caring, and appropriately empowering. Nonetheless, her Achilles' heel appears to be her ability to communicate her ideas clearly. While she is bright and holds a doctoral degree, she often speaks in a way that meanders or is verbose and tends to obfuscate her key points. As hard as Sandy tries, clients are often left confused. This is particularly problematic in that one reason an organization hires consultants is to help them better deal with their own uncertainty and confusion. Sandy's ability to relate effectively is clearly without question, and her integrity beyond reproach. But her relationship to knowledge is flawed. Consequently, she has difficulty obtaining work and, when working, sometimes has difficulty helping clients move in a clear, coordinated way.

Finally, I know a third consultant (Greg) who is clear thinking, holds knowledge in a way that supports clients and their learning, and establishes a strong partnership with them, yet his integrity is suspect. Frequently, Greg unconsciously acts in a self-serving manner. His need for work sometimes causes him to be too aggressive with clients, so that he comes across like a used car salesman. Greg sometimes "shapes the truth" to get what he wants. In other words, his character is compromised. As a result, clients often end up not trusting him, to the point of severing their work with him.

There are endless examples of consultants whose imbalance or inadequate capability in one of these fundamental arenas compromises their consulting effectiveness. In contrast, although all the masterful consultants I interviewed appear to have a particular strength, none of them is weak in any one of the arenas. They have worked hard to develop all three and recognize each of them as crucial to their consulting success.

THE LIFELONG JOURNEY TOWARD MASTERY

In the final analysis, mastery is not a destination, nor is it a thing one does. Instead it is a journey of a lifetime that knows no ending point (see Table 17.2). Although the ideas and examples in this chapter point the way, the best way to develop mastery is to develop one's inner stance. This, by its very nature, is through a lifelong journey of self-exploration, self-awareness, and self-discovery. Many spiritual traditions and psychoemotional practices offer guidance toward self-mastery, and there is no substitute for ongoing inner work. All of them operate from the basic premise that our inner stance guides our thoughts, and from our thoughts, all else follows.

Goals	Primary Strategy	Secondary Strategies	Actions
Make a difference	Empowering partnership	Develop a client-centered partnership	See the client as a whole system, and encourage the client to do the same
			Be clear that the client has the capacity to grow themselves, and position yourself as a guide and a partner, not an expert
			Keep the client responsible for the outcome, while you partner in the process.
		Share the knowledge openly and freely	Recognize that the key to effectiveness is how to apply knowledge in real time
			Seek to transfer knowledge and enhance the wisdom to the client
			Respect the client and build genuine trust
		See the quality of your inner stance as a catalyst for transformation and learning.	Recognize that the most important differentiator between good and great consultants is the quality of their inner stance
			Development your inner stance and act with integrity

Table 17.2. The Master Consultant's Model.

The thought manifests as the word;
The word manifests as the deed;
The deed develops into habit;
And the habit hardens into character;
So watch the thought and its ways with care;
And let it spring from love
Born out of concern for all beings.
As the shadow follows the body,
As we think, so we become.
                        —*From The Dhammapada*
                        (The Sayings of the Buddha)

All of the masterful consultants I know have been on the journey for a long time. They know that the source of their effectiveness and the deepening of their self-awareness are one and the same. They have each engaged in activities, practices, and disciplines designed to examine their thoughts, feelings, and beliefs and to find ways of being in the world that are more resourceful, capable, and ultimately satisfying.

CHAPTER EIGHTEEN

Flawless Consulting

Peter Block

C onsulting has a way of seeming vague and overly complicated. It doesn't have to be. It is possible to consult without error and to do so quite simply. The way to keep it simple is to focus on only two dimensions of consulting. Ask yourself two questions whenever you are with a client.

1. Am I being authentic with this person now?
2. Am I completing the business of the consulting phase I am in?

BEING AUTHENTIC

Authentic behavior with a client means you put into words what you are experiencing with the client as you work. *This is the most powerful thing you can do to have the leverage you are looking for and to build client commitment.*

There is a tendency for us to look for ways of being clever with a client. We agonize over ways of presenting our ideas, of phrasing the project so that it will appeal. Many times I have been with a client and found myself straining to figure out what will convince them that I am everything they are looking for. Projections of bottom line savings are made, solutions for sticky employee problems are suggested, confirmations that the client has been doing everything humanly possible are suggested with a nod and a smile.

It is a mistake to assume that clients make decisions to begin projects and use consultants based on purely rational reasons. More often than not, the client's primary question is: "Is this consultant someone I can trust? Is this someone I can trust not to hurt me, not to con me—someone who can both help solve the organizational or technical problems I have and, at the same time, be considerate of my position and person?" When I operate in too clever or manipulative a way, or lay it on too thick, clients pick this up. They are saying to themselves, "Wow! This guy is really laying it on thick. He is making me look like a fool if I say no." Line managers know when we are trying to maneuver them and, when it happens, they trust us a little less.

Lower trust leads to lower leverage and lower client commitment. Authentic behavior leads to higher trust, higher leverage, and higher client commitment. Authentic behavior also has the advantage of being incredibly simple. It is to literally put into words what you are experiencing.

Here are some examples.

Client says: Well, this audit shouldn't take you too long. Couple of days and you will be done. I wish I had some time to spend with you, but there are some really important things I must attend to. My secretary can give you some assistance. Also, don't take too much time from any of my people. They are under a lot of pressure.

Consultant experiences: Feeling unimportant, small. My work is being treated as a trivial matter. This is how I make my living, but to this character, I am an interruption.

Nonauthentic consultant response: This audit could have far-reaching implications. The home office is looking closely at these audits to assess our top divisions. They are also required by the company.

Authentic consultant response: You are treating this audit as though it is unimportant and small. Like a trivial matter. If it is an interruption, maybe we should reassess the timing. I would like you to treat it with more importance.

Client says: I want your opinion whether my people are making mistakes and what they should do to correct them. If you decide they are incompetent to operate this piece of equipment, I want you to report directly to me at once. With names and specifics.

Consultant experiences: Feeling like a judge, like I have to police the client's employees.

Nonauthentic consultant response: My report will describe how the equipment is being utilized and why there have been so many breakdowns. It will be up to you to take corrective actions.

Authentic consultant response: I feel I am being seen as a judge or police officer on this project. This is not the role I feel is most effective. I would like you to view me more as a mirror of what is happening now. You and your people can then evaluate what needs to be done and whether training is required. I am not a conscience.

—/w—

Client says: To really understand this problem, you have to go back thirty-five years when this operation was set up. It all started in November of 1946 on a Thursday afternoon. There were three people in this operation. At the time, their only function was to fill orders and answer the phone. George was the nephew of the sales manager and only had a high school education. Our customers were mostly on the East Coast and on and on and on and on.

Consultant experiences: Impatience, boredom. Spending too much time on history. Losing energy.

Nonauthentic consultant response: Silence. Encourage client to go on, assuming client will get to the point or that it is therapeutically essential for the client to go through all this detail.

Authentic consultant response: You are giving me a lot of detail. I am having trouble staying with your narrative. I am eager to get to the key current issues. What is the key problem now?

—/w—

Client says: If you will just complete your report of findings, my management group and I will meet later to decide what to do and evaluate the results.

Consultant experiences: Exclusion from the real action. Postponement of dealing with the problems.

Nonauthentic consultant response: There might be some information that I have not included in the report that would be relevant to your decision-making process. Or acquiescence.

Authentic consultant response: You are excluding me from the decision on what to do. I would like to be included in that meeting, even if including me means some inconvenience for you and your team.

—⁓—

In these examples, each initial client statement acts to keep the consultant distant in some way. Each is a subtle form of resistance to the consultant's help and serves to reduce its impact. The nonauthentic consultant responses deal indirectly and impersonally with the resistance. They make it easier for the client to stay distant and treat the consultant's concerns in a procedural way. The authentic responses focus on the relationship between the consultant and the client and force the client to give importance to the consultant's role and wants for the project. Simple direct statements by the consultant about the consultant-client interaction put more balance in the relationship; they work against either total client control or total consultant control. Imbalanced control in either direction acts to reduce internal commitment to the project and reduce the chance of successful implementation.

Authentic behavior by the consultant is an essential first part to operating flawlessly. Much of the rest of this book gives detailed and specific expression to what authentic behavior looks like in the context of doing consulting.

COMLETING THE REQUIREMENTS OF EACH PHASE

In addition to being authentic, flawless consulting demands a knowledge of the task requirements of each phase of the project. These requirements are the "business" of each phase and must be completed before moving on.

Here is a very brief description of the requirements of each phase.

Contracting

1. *Negotiating Wants.* Setting up a project requires the client and the consultant to exchange what they want from each other and

what they have to offer each other. Too often, consultants understate their wants and clients understate their offers.

2. *Coping with Mixed Motivation.* When clients ask for help, they always do so with some ambivalence. They want you to get involved and be helpful, but at the same time wish they had never met you. One hand beckons you, the other says stop. A requirement of contracting is to get this mixed motivation expressed early in the project so it won't haunt you later.

3. *Surfacing Concerns About Exposure and Loss of Control.* Most of the real concerns clients have about pursuing a consulting project with you are expressed quite indirectly. They ask about credentials, experience, results elsewhere, cost, timing, and more. Often what they are really concerned about is: (1) Are they going to be made to look or feel foolish or incompetent? and (2) Will they lose control of either themselves, their organization, or you the consultant? These concerns have to be addressed directly as part of the contracting phase.

4. *Triangular and Rectangular Contracting.* You have to know how many clients you have. Your client has a boss and you may have a boss. Your client's boss and your boss may have had a heavy hand in setting up this project. If so, they need to be part of the contract. At least, their roles need to be acknowledged between you and your client. If it is you, the client, and the client's boss, you have a triangular contract. Throw in your own boss and the triangle becomes a rectangle. Clarifying who is involved and getting them into the contract is a requirement of the contracting phase.

Discovery and Data Collection

1. *Layers of Analysis.* The initial problem statement in a consulting project is usually a symptom of other underlying problems. The task for the consultant is to articulate the different layers of the problem in a coherent and simple way.

2. *Political Climate.* Whether your client is a family or an organization, politics is affecting people's behavior and their ability to solve problems. Your task as consultant is to understand enough about the politics of the situation to see how it will affect your project and the implementation of your recommendations.

Too often we collude with the client in pretending that organizations are not political but solely rational.

3. *Resistance to Sharing Information.* The client always has some reluctance to give us the whole story or all the data we need to understand what's happening. This resistance, which often comes out indirectly with passive or questioning behavior during the data collection, has to be identified and expressed.

4. *Interview as a Joint Learning Event.* Once we begin to collect data, we have begun to change that organization. We are never simply neutral, objective observers. Beginning the process of our analysis portends the implementation process, and we need to see it that way. When sticky issues come up during the data collection phase, we need to pursue them and not worry about contaminating the data or biasing the study. Too often we see our role in the data collection phase as a passive one.

Feedback and the Decision to Act

1. *Funneling Data.* The purpose of data collection is to solve a problem, to get some action. It is not to do research for its own sake. This means the data needs to be reduced to a manageable number of items. Each of the final items selected for feedback to the client should be actionable—that is, they should be under the control of the client.

2. *Presenting Personal and Organizational Data.* As we collect data on equipment, or compensation, or information flow, we also pick up data on our client's management style. We learn about the politics of the situation, about people's attitudes about working in this place. One requirement of the feedback phase is to include this kind of information in our report. Personal and organizational data are not included to hurt anyone or to be gossipy, but as information on the context in which our recommendations might be implemented. It is also a unique kind of information that the client often cannot obtain from anyone else.

3. *Managing the Feedback Meeting.* The feedback meeting is the moment of truth. It is the moment of highest anxiety for both client and consultant—anxiety for the consultant because of

what is to be said, anxiety for the client because of what is to be heard. The consultant needs to keep control of this meeting so that the business of the meeting is covered. Presenting data to the client is only a part of the agenda: The main goal is to work on the decision about what to do. The more the feedback meeting can address what to do, the better the chance of implementation. The feedback meeting may be your last chance to influence the decision about implementation—so take advantage of the opportunity.

4. *Focusing on the Here and Now.* Another requirement of the feedback phase is identifying how the client is managing the feedback itself. Usually, the feedback process becomes victim to the same management problems that created the need for your services in the first place. If the organization is suffering from a lack of structure or direction, this will also affect how they handle your report. You need to be conscious of this and call it to your client's attention. If you are not meticulously aware of how your own project is being handled, you will simply become the latest casualty.

5. *Don't Take It Personally.* This is the toughest. The reaction of the client to your work is more a response to the process of dependency and receiving help than it is resistance to your own personal style. You do have your own peculiarities; so do I. If, however, you start agonizing about them, even to yourself, during the feedback process, you're in big trouble. The resistance you encounter during the process is resistance to the prospect of having to act on difficult organizational issues. Don't be seduced into taking it personally.

Engagement and Implementation

1. *Bet on Engagement Over Mandate and Persuasion.* Even though a decision has been made, the real work lies ahead. How we involve people will determine their commitment at each stage. The instinct is to focus too much on the decision and not value the importance of how people are brought together to make it work.

2. *Design More Participation Than Presentation.* Each meeting has to be an example of the new way of working and demonstrate that employee attitude will dictate success. This demands high

interaction and forms of proceeding. People will not invest in what they have been sold, even though it seems as though they just want you to be clear about what is expected from them.

3. *Encourage Difficult Public Exchanges.* Trust is built by dealing with the difficult issues early and publicly. Create room for doubt and cynicism right in the beginning. Reservations that are postponed will come back to haunt you. The way we handle the difficult conversations will determine the credibility of the project and their view of whether the consultant is an agent of the top or in service of all parties.

4. *Put Real Choice on the Table.* Bring people into the decision about change as early as possible. Commitment comes from having choice. Resist the temptation to package the whole solution early in the name of speed. Commitment may be more important than perfection. There are always several right answers to every question.

5. *Change the Conversation to Change the Culture.* Encourage dialogue that is void of blame, history, attention to who is not in the room, and that is too quick to action. Structure the conversation toward personal responsibility, questions of purpose and meaning, and what will be unique and new about this round of changes.

6. *Pay Attention to Place.* The structure of the way we come together has more impact on the attitude and commitment of our clients than we realize. The room itself, how we are seated, and the way we run the meeting carry strong messages about our intentions and who is important to success. Most of the places we meet reinforce high control, mandated strategies. When we have choice about the structure of the room, take advantage of it.

It's entirely possible to move through the phases and skip some of these task requirements. In contracting, for example, most of us are pretty good at assessing client wants. But if we fail to identify consultant wants or client offers as clearly as we assess client wants, we are in trouble. Wants skipped in the beginning are much harder to recover in later phases. An example is the consultant's desire to have the client manager support the project and tell his or her people about it. If this were not negotiated in the contracting phase, you would feel under-cut later when you went to collect data from people who don't really know why you were talking to them.

Another key task of contracting is to discuss the client's motivation to proceed with the project. Sometimes your desire to begin the project may lead you to minimize this discussion. You may never ask the client point blank whether they want to go ahead with the project and how much enthusiasm they have for it. If you find out later in the feedback meeting that the motivation is low, it may be too late to do anything about it.

Also, because of our desire to get a project going, most of us have a tendency to overlook and downplay the early resistance and skepticism we encounter. We delude ourselves into thinking that once clients get into the project, they will get hooked by it and learn to trust us. This can lead to our bending over more than we wish in the beginning, hoping that we will be able to stand up straight later on. This usually doesn't work. When we bend over in the beginning, we are seen by the client as someone who works in a bent-over position. When we avoid issues in the beginning, we are seen by the client as someone who avoids issues. It is difficult to change these images and expectations of us—particularly if the client wishes us to bend over and avoid.

By not confronting the tasks of each phase, we are left with accu-mulating unfinished business that comes back to haunt us. Unfinished business always comes out somewhere, and usually indirectly. The client who felt we were coercing in the beginning of the project, but never expressed it directly, is the client who endlessly questions our data in the feedback meeting. The endless questions are fueled by the early feeling of coercion, not by our faulty data. It will be much harder in the feedback meeting to rework those feelings of coercion than it would have been to discuss them in the contracting meeting when the project got started.

Finishing the business of each phase. Being authentic in stating what you are experiencing to the client. All you need to consult flawlessly.

But what about getting results and what about accountability?

RESULTS

By definition, being a consultant—and not a manager—means you have direct control and responsibility only for your own time and your own staff resources. The line manager is paid to take responsibility for what the line organization implements or doesn't implement. If the client manager takes your report and chooses to do nothing about it, that is the manager's right. In the final analysis, you are not responsible for the use of your expertise and recommendations. If consultants really believe that they should be responsible for implementing their recommendations, they should immediately get jobs as line managers and stop calling themselves consultants.

This desire to take responsibility for activities that rightly belong to our clients can become, in itself, a major obstacle to our consulting effectiveness. When we take over and act as if it is our organization (a wish we all have at times), the line manager is let off the hook. The organization may get the immediate problem solved, but will have learned little about how to do it for themselves. When something goes wrong with our system, as it must, we are either called back in again and again or the line organization will claim that our system was faulty to begin with. Both client overdependence and client disdain are bad for the consultant. It is essential to be clear on what you, the consultant, are responsible for and what the line manager is responsible for.

Accountability

Just because we are not responsible for what the client does with our efforts does not mean we don't care what happens in the end. In fact, it is deeply important to me what impact my consulting efforts have. I want my efforts to be used. Every time. If an engineer consultant is called in to fix a furnace in a plant, the engineer will make recommendations so the furnace will be fixed and operated to run perfectly forever. The problem is that the consultant doesn't control how that furnace is operated.

This is the deepest frustration of doing consulting. You know your recommendations are sound and should be followed, but you are not responsible for how the furnace is operated and need to accept that fact. All you can do is to work with clients in a way that increases the probabilities that they will follow the advice and make the effort to learn how to operate the furnace.

The key to increasing the chances of success is to keep focusing on how you work with clients. All we can really control is our own way of working, our own behavior, our own strategies of involving clients and reducing their reluctance to operate the furnace differently. This is what we should be held accountable for: How we work with clients. Not what clients do in managing or mismanaging their own operations.

The downside of our need to be useful is the desire to prove that our work led to good results. Needing to claim credit for the risks and efforts made by clients is a measure of our own inflation and the anxiety that underpins it. Our clients will know, even if they cannot name it easily, what contribution we made to their effort. Our need for concrete demonstration of our results is either to reassure our doubts or to serve our needs to market our services.

A big part of how I work with clients is based on whether my specific expertise is well-founded and whether my recommendations are sound. But both clients and I are assuming from the beginning that I know my stuff when it comes to technical skills. That leaves my consulting skills—how I contract, conduct discovery, collect data, feed it back, deal with resistance, engage in implementation—as the major factors contributing to my effectiveness. They are what affect consulting results.

If I—

know my area of expertise (a given),
behave authentically with the client,
tend to and complete the business of each consulting phase, and
act to build capacity for the client to solve the next problem on their own—

I can legitimately say I have consulted flawlessly. Even if no action results from my efforts. Even if the project aborts in the early, contracting phase. Even if my services are terminated the day I make my recommendations. Even if all these things happen, it is possible to call it a very competent job of consultation. If these things happen, it is not a happy consultation, for we all wish for the world to transform at our touch. But it is the best we can do.

This way of viewing consulting accountability restrains us from taking over for our clients and from uselessly pressuring them to do something they won't or can't do. I believe taking over client organizations, pressuring to be heeded, complaining about the way a manager manages—all reduce my effectiveness. Focusing on my own actions, expressing my awareness of what I am experiencing with the client and how we are working—all increase my effectiveness.

Our own actions, our own awareness—this is what we should be held accountable for. Fire me for not contracting well. For not confronting the client's low motivation until the feedback meeting. Fire me for packaging the recommendations so completely and perfectly that the client was afraid to touch them. But reward me for contracting solidly with three managers who terminated projects when a new vice president was announced. Reward me for not beginning a project when a plant manager said it was necessary, but all signs were to the contrary.

Completing the business of each phase. Behaving authentically with the client. That's what flawless consultation, consultation without failure, requires. In thirty years of consulting, all my failures (which I remember with distressing clarity) occurred either because I was so carried away by how I was going to solve the client's problem that I didn't pay attention to client motivation or because I wanted that client so badly that I didn't care what the contract looked like. In each case, I ignored some step in the consulting process, did not attend to the business of a particular phase, or chose not to deal authentically with my concerns about the client. Had I focused more on exactly how I was working with each client, these failures could have been avoided.

Failures can be avoided, but this doesn't mean a consultant can expect to see meaningful improvement as a result of every single project. Internal consultants often ask, "You mean if I behave authentically and take care of the business of each phase, I will win the support of a plant manager who up to now won't talk to me?" When they ask that question, they are expressing their skepticism. It is a rightful skepticism. No action by a consultant will guarantee results with a client. There are several reasons for this.

Each of us learns and uses information in different ways. It is often difficult for managers to accept help and be publicly open to suggestions. Privately they may be strongly affected by our work, and we may never know it. Pressuring clients to feel we have immediately helped them can be a tremendous obstacle to the learning we are trying to promote. If we can stay focused simply on the way we are working with clients, we will avoid compulsively pressuring the client, and the results will take care of themselves.

CHAPTER NINETEEN

The Organization Development Contract

Marvin Weisbord

I n OD consulting, the contract is central to success or failure. Most other kinds of contracts—employment, service, research, and so on—focus heavily on content, that is, the nature of the work to be performed, the schedule, and the money to change hands. Generally, these issues are negotiated through a proposal, which one party writes and the other accepts or rejects. The consulting contract most people are familiar with takes two forms: (1) You hire me to study the problem and to tell you what to do; (2) You hire me to solve the problem for you. I call these "expert" consulting contracts. In both cases the quality of the advice and/or the solution is the focus, and the consultant is a central figure.

But in OD consulting, the client is the central figure. He hires me to consult to him while he is working on his problem. I am helping him to achieve a better diagnosis of what has happened and what steps he must take to improve things. This is a form of collaboration which, if successful, also helps the client to achieve better working relationships with others, such as peers, bosses, and subordinates.

For that reason, in OD contracting, more so than with other kinds, the process by which content issues are pinned down is critical. Unless this negotiation is a model of the consultant's values and problem-solving behavior, the contract, when it's tested, probably won't stand up. More about testing will be discussed later in the chapter.

What do I mean by a contract? I mean an explicit exchange of expectations, part dialogue, part written document, that clarifies for consultant and client three critical areas:

1. What each expects to get from the relationship

2. How much time each will invest, when, and at what cost

3. The ground rules under which the parties will operate

WHAT EACH EXPECTS

Clients expect, and have a right to expect, change for the better in a situation that is making their lives hard. This situation, as my clients experience it, has three main components:

1. Organizational crises, that is, people leaving; excessive absenteeism; too high costs; too small a budget; unmanageable environmental demands; pressure from above; conflict between individuals or work groups

2. People problems, that is, one or more "significant people" who are especially problematic

3. Personal dilemmas, such as whether their job or career, is what they really want

The third component always grows in magnitude in direct proportion to the first two. Clients in a bind don't get much fun out of their work. They long for something simpler, better suited to their strengths, more consistent with their values. Above all, most clients long for outcomes. They want permanent "change" for the better, with no backsliding. I, on the other hand, see new outcomes as evidence that the client is learning a better way of coping. From my point of view the process—gathering information, becoming aware of deeper meanings, making choices—is my most important product. While the client identifies three kinds of difficult situations he wants to work on, I keep in mind three levels of improvement he might achieve:

1. Solution of the immediate crisis—changing structures, policies, procedures, relationships

2. Learning something about his own coping style—how he deals with crises, how he might do it better

3. Learning a process for coping better about whatever issue presents itself by continually becoming aware of and making choices

From my point of view, the existing problem is a vehicle for learning more about how to manage organizational life better. I have no preferences for the kinds of problems clients have. From my point of view, one issue will do as well as another.

However, clients rarely ask my direct help in cutting costs, reducing absenteeism, raising morale, or improving services. Instead, identifying me mainly with the "people" issue, they nearly always look for guidance in taking swift, painless, self-evident corrective actions toward those who contribute to their misery. I always ask prospective clients to name what outcomes they hope to achieve by working with me. Here are some typical replies:

- "Want others to understand our goals better"
- "Better communications, fewer misunderstandings"
- "_____ will shape up or ship out"
- "Better meetings—more excitement, more decisions made"

Notice that each of these statements is somewhat abstract, obviously "good," and very hard to measure. I never accept such generalities as adequate statements of a client's expectations. Instead, I push hard on outcomes. What would you see happening that would tell you communications are improving? How will you know when goals are clearer, or morale has gone up? What will people do? Will you be able to watch them do it? When I push at this level, I get more realistic statements:

- Pete will come to me with his gripes directly instead of going to Fred.
- Deadlines will be taken seriously and met more often.
- In meetings, decisions will be made, actions agreed upon, and names and dates put on them.

- I will understand how to set up the _____ unit, and will have agreement on whatever way I decide.
- We will have a new procedure for handling customer complaints.
- I will make a decision whether to keep or fire _____.

These statements are good short-run indicators of change. They are realistic expectations. Are changes like these worth the client's investment of time and money? Is there enough in it for her to go ahead? It's important that she be clear she is choosing to do whatever we do together because it's worth it to her (and not because it's this year's panacea, or somebody else tried it and liked it, or because she thinks her problems will go away). What does she want personally out of this? Easier life? What does that mean? And so on.

I expect some things too. Clients know that I work mainly for money and want to be paid on time. However, I try also to indicate some of my secondary motives for working with them.

For example, I crave variety. I like learning about and using my skills in various "content" areas—manufacturing and service industries, medicine, law enforcement, public education. I like to try new technologies, to break new theoretical ground, to write and publish my experiences. The chance to do something new increases my incentive with any client. So too does a client's ready acceptance of some of the responsibility for the crisis. If clients are well-motivated to work on their problems, so am I—and I tell them so. In doing this, I am trying to say that each of us has a right to some personal benefits from our relationship, apart from any benefits the organization may derive.

STRUCTURING THE RELATIONSHIP: TIME AND MONEY

OD, like much of life, is carried forward by a sequence of meetings between people. The central decision in any contract discussion is which people should sit in what room for how long and for what purpose. At some point it is essential to name those people, pick dates, and set a budget. The client has a right to know how much time I will invest in interviewing, or survey sampling, or the like, and how long our meetings will require. If I need time in between to organize data, I estimate how much. Often the initial contract is diagnostic, to be completed at a face-to-face meeting where the data will be examined, a common diagnosis arrived at, and next steps decided upon. Always, I work to clarify the costs of time and money, of each next step. Generally, this information will be written down.

In addition, there are some things I will and won't do, money aside. I know what these things are, and only mention them if the client does, on the premise that there's no point in solving a problem I don't have. For instance, I always turn down opportunities to work weekends. I'll work morning, noon, and night on any scheduled day if necessary. On weekends my contract is with my family. In addition, I have a strong value that when you work on your organization indicates how important you consider it. People get themselves into crises during the week. If they don't have time to get out of their crises during the week, they're never going to get out of them by working weekends. If a client doesn't agree, that makes me the wrong consultant for them. (Incidentally, I have never lost a client because of this policy.)

GROUND RULES

Ground rules speak to the process of our relationship. Sometimes I write them down, sometimes I don't. In any case, I try to get an understanding that includes these explicit agreements:

1. I supply methods, techniques, theory, and so on to help you understand and work better on your problems. You supply energy, commitment, and share responsibility for success. I do not study your problems and recommend expert solutions.

2. Part of my job is to raise sticky issues and push you on them. You have a right to say no to anything you don't want to deal with. If you feel free to say no, I'll feel free to push.

3. Tell me if I do something puzzling or irritating, and give me permission to tell you the same.

4. I have no special preferences for how you deal with others. Part of my job is to make you aware of what you do, and what possible consequences your actions have for me and for the people around you. My job is also to preserve and encourage your freedom of choice about what, if anything, you should do.

5. My client is the whole organization. That means I intend not to be seen as an advocate for anybody's pet ideas, especially ones

requiring your special expertise. However, I do advocate a certain process for problem solving, and recognize that some people oppose my process. I accept that risk.

8. Either of us can terminate on twenty-four hours' notice, regardless of contract length, so long as we have a face-to-face meeting first.

9. We evaluate all events together, face-to-face, and make explicit decisions about what to do next.

Contracting, like the seasons, is repetitive and continually renewable. If I have a long term contract (for example, four days a month for a year) I also have a separate contract for each meeting, which I present on a flipsheet and discuss at the outset. If I have a contract with a boss to help him build his team, I need to extend it to the team before we go to work. If I succeed with the team, and some members want to work with their teams, I need again to negotiate a new deal with the new people. Once, having worked with a team, I found the boss wanting to confront his boss. He wanted the whole team to do it with him, with me as consultant. I pointed out that that would require a temporary contract between him, his boss, and me. He set up a dinner meeting—the night before the confrontation—and his boss and I made a one-day contract which stood up very well the next morning.

In short, I'm never finished contracting. Each client meeting requires that I reexamine the contract. Does it cover everybody I'm working with? Is it clear what we're doing now? And why?

Moreover, contracting—while it deals ostensibly and mainly with content issues—has a process side crucial to its success. Consider, in some detail, where and how an OD contract is made.

OD contracts usually begin with a phone call or letter. Somebody has heard about what I did somewhere else. They wonder whether I can do it for (or with, or to) them. If I receive a letter, I respond with a phone call to the writer. If he calls first, I return his call at a time when I can spend ten minutes or more discussing what he wants and whether or not it makes sense to meet. This initial contact is crucial to any contract. Each of us is trying—over the phone—to decide whether he likes the other well enough to proceed. I try not to pre-judge the conversation. I want a face-to-face meeting if there's a chance of getting a solid contract. Here are some questions running through my mind:

1. How open is the caller with me? Me with him?

2. Is the caller window-shopping, maybe calling several consultants to find the "best deal" (whatever that means)? Does he really want me? Perhaps—as is often the case—he doesn't know what he wants. If that's so, I have a good chance to consult with him on the phone, helping him to clarify what he's after.

3. To which of his problems am I the solution? How does he name the issue?

4. What does he see as the solution? Is it a workshop? A meeting? A series of meetings? Magic?

5. Is his mind made up? Has he diagnosed his troubles and pre-scribed something already, which I'm to administer?

6. Does he have a budget? Is it adequate for his expectations? For mine? Is it likely to be worth my while to invest in a face-to-face meeting? I don't talk price on the phone, but I do test whether a budget exists or could be gotten together. If the answer is no, I decide not to pursue it further.

7. Assuming there is a budget, and a willingness on his part and mine to go forward, we need a meeting. Should anybody else be there? Who? Is the caller in a position to enter into a contract? If not, who is? His boss? Can he make the meeting? Is there another consultant I want to involve? If so, I ask whether I can bring an associate.

I end the phone call by clarifying that each of us intends to explore further whether there is a fit between the things my potential client needs help on and my skills and experience. I am investing up to a day at no fee. (If there are travel expenses involved, I test whether he will pay those.) At the end of that day, each of us will know whether to go further.

FIRST MEETING

I arrive, greet my prospective client, introduce myself and my associate to him and his associates. We have coffee and exchange pleasantries. Each of us is deciding, silently, privately, and maybe unconsciously, how much we like the other. We look for cues. We give cues. Early on, we get down to business—or appear to. The content issues might include:

1. Our backgrounds—potential clients need to know enough about me to feel I can help, before they'll put out major problems.

2. Problems in the client system—are they symptomatic of other things that are not being discussed? I always ask for examples in terms of observable behavior. "Communications" or "decision making" are not issues you can see, feel, or pin down. Who needs to talk to whom? Why? What do they do now? What do people do when they disagree? What patterns of behavior do the people present see in the organization?

3. What changes would the people I'm talking to like to see? What things would they observe happening that would tell them they are getting desired outcomes? This step in naming outcomes is important in reducing the level of fantasy around OD and what it can do.

4. What first event would be appropriate to moving the system in the desired direction? Nearly always, this event should be diagnostic. It should be an activity that will heighten the awareness of the people I'm meeting with about how the issues they raise are seen by others in the system—colleagues, subordinates, customers, students, peers, and so on. If the system is ready, the budget exists, and my reading of the willingness to proceed is good, I may propose a workshop activity, based on interviews. Sometimes I propose that the workshop start with interviews of each person as a first step in agenda-building (it's okay if no more than ten or twelve attend). Sometimes, it makes more sense to conduct it within the framework of a work group's regular weekly or monthly meetings. Sometimes, a survey questionnaire provides a database for a diagnostic meeting.

Whatever the event, we need a schedule, a place to meet, and a division of labor for organizing materials, sending out the agenda, and so on. These things can often be decided in the first meeting. Sometimes I agree to write a formal proposal and proceed from there. Always I try to close on the next step—what I will do, what the client will do, and by what date.

The above considerations focus mainly on content. However, there are several process issues surrounding this meeting which I'm continually working on too:

1. First among these is, "Do I like this person?" If there isn't a spark of fondness, or warmth, or empathy, then what am I feeling? Annoyance? Frustration? Wariness? Can I find something to like, respect, or admire about the other person? Usually, I can. Until I do, however, and until the other person finds it in me, I think our work on issues, possible next steps, logistics, and the like is largely fictional. It is a way of using the task at hand to help us get greater clarity about our relationship. Any time I'm uncertain about a relationship I believe my contract is in jeopardy, no matter what fine words are spoken or written on paper. Each time the relationship question gets a little more resolved, a little spark flies. I watch for it.

2. The client's depth of commitment is an issue for me. Does she really want to change things? Does she accept responsibility—at least a little bit—for the way things are? If she says, "I want you to change them," and I say, "Okay, but how open are you to changing?" Does she pull back, hem and haw? Or does she smile and admit the possibility? How open is she to understanding how what she does affects other people? My value about organizations improving themselves—that is, people learning to do things better with each other—is clear. I try to test how my client feels about that.

3. Part of client commitment is resources. Clients find money to do things they want to do. If money seems to be an insurmountable problem, I look to some other process issue—anxiety about failure, a boss who's negative about OD, fear of opening up "destructive issues," and so on. Helping the client get in touch with these possibilities, if I can, is valuable for both of us, whether I work with her again or not. How do it? By asking such questions as: What is the risk? What's the worst thing that could happen? How much exposure can you stand? I also ask what good things might happen, and whether the possible outcomes are worth the price.

In some ways OD is like playing the market. Every intervention is a calculated risk. There are no guarantees. The client will have problems no matter what he does. So will I. The question I continually confront is: Which problems would you rather have? The ones you have now? Or the ones you will have if you try to solve your current ones?

Once in a while, potential clients decide they would rather live with what they've got. I support this insight. It's better that both of us know it sooner rather than later.

More often this process leads to greater clarity and commitment on both our parts to make an intervention successful. My value set goes something like this: I want to find out what's real, what the environment will support, what's possible in this relationship, and then learn how to live with it. Of course I want to sell my services. I want to try new interventions. More than that, I want to be successful. I am learning to spot conditions under which I fail. An unclear contract ranks high on the list.

I resist entering untenable contracts, for I know deep down that they are like airplanes without fuel. No matter how beautiful they look, they won't fly. The fuel for an OD contract is (1) client commitment, (2) a good relationship between us, and (3) a clear structure for that relationship, symbolized by our ability to agree on what services I will perform, when, and at what costs in time and money.

STRUCTURING THE RELATIONSHIP

The third item above brings us to the specific first intervention. It has several criteria:

1. It is responsive to the client's perceived problem. She must see it as helping her gain greater clarity, insight, and control over whatever issues are bugging her. It is not based on my need to use any particular trick in my bag.

2. It names the people who will come together, when, for how long, and why. "Why" is generally for the client to answer, in her own words, but I help her shape the language if she has trouble. I make clear that the boss should tell people why they are there, as she sees it, and I will tell them what I see as my contract with them. It is never my job to tell people why they are there.

3. It involves some form of diagnosis. That means some systematic information is collected that will heighten the client's awareness and enlarge their freedom of choice. Sometimes this information fits some conceptual scheme, which I make explicit. Sometimes I help the client build a scheme from the information which will make sense to

her. Always, data collection, as I see it, must be done in such a way that the people who supply the information will recognize it as critical to their lives together when I collate it and hand it back. The more interpreting, or categorizing, I do in advance, the less likely this is to happen.

I ensure confidentiality and anonymity. Interpretation, I try to make clear, will result when people who supplied the information meet face-to-face to assign meaning to it. I try always to specify how much time people must give, what kinds of questions will be asked, and what will become of the answers. This structuring reduces anxiety and sets up reasonable expectations.

4. I establish that part of the contract is mutual feedback. I expect clients to confront me openly on my behavior when it doesn't make sense, to question anything I do, and to point out to me words or behavior that violate their sense of what's appropriate. In return, I expect to be open with them.

It is around this clause, I think, that all contracts are tested sooner or later. In a workshop the test may come in the form of protest that the activities are irrelevant to the agenda and a waste of time. In a one-to-one relationship the test may be something I did or said that really irritated the client. It takes some risk to let me know. In opening the issue, the client is checking to see whether I'm as good at handling deeds as I am at manipulating words.

I define testing the contract as an emotion-provoking exchange between the client and me in some risky situation. As a result our relationship will become more "real," more truly experimental, more like the action research model which I advocate as an appropriate way to live. I don't expect the burden for testing to rest entirely on the client. I test, too, whenever the time seems right, usually around something the client is doing which affects our relationship. Once, I noticed a client would continually express disappointment in others, and told him I was worried that one day—if not already—he was going to feel the same way about me. He owned up to the possibility, and assured me I would be the first to know, which, when the time came, I was. The confrontation deepened our relationship and strengthened the contract. It might have ended it, too.

I welcome ending a contract explicitly by having it tested and found wanting. Better a clean death than lingering agony. It is time to test (and maybe end) a contract when

- The client keeps putting things off
- Agreements are made and forgotten (by either side)
- The consultant appears to have a higher emotional stake in the outcomes than the client does
- The consultant asks for events, or activities, which intensify the feeling of crisis and pressure without much prospect for eventual relief
- The client looks to the consultant to do things which she, as manager of her own organization, should be doing—that is, arranging meetings, sending out agendas, carrying messages, and getting other people to do everything the client always wanted them to do but was afraid to ask
- The client is doing better and really doesn't need outside help

For me, a crisp, clean ending remains desirable, but sometimes elusive. In going over fourteen major contracts from the last four years, I found nine ended cleanly with no "unfinished business," three ended because the boss lacked commitment to continue, and two ended because organizational changes left a leadership vacuum and me uncertain who the client was.

In the case in which the boss lacked commitment, the intended follow-up meetings never took place, and I let things alone, feeling, I suppose, relatively little commitment myself. In the cases of organizational changes, it became plain that the interim leadership lacked either incentive or authority to keep up the contract, and I had other fish to fry.

It seems to me contracts have a natural life. Organizations eventually outgrow or tire of or cease needing a particular consultant, and vice versa. It's better for my client and me that we recognize explicitly when it's time to part.

CHAPTER TWENTY

The Facilitator and Other Facilitative Roles

Roger Schwarz

In this chapter, I begin by describing several facilitative roles—facilitator, facilitative consultant, facilitative coach, facilitative leader, and facilitative trainer—and explain how to choose an appropriate one. Then there is a description of the core values that guide these facilitative roles. For the rest of the chapter, I explain how to perform these roles in a way that is consistent with the core values.

CHOOSING A FACILITATIVE ROLE

Using facilitative skills enhances your leadership or consulting role and expertise. It is important to understand how the facilitative roles are similar and different and to select the appropriate one that accurately represents your relationship with the group. Table 20.1 shows five facilitative roles and how they are similar and different.

Facilitator	Facilitative Consultant	Facilitative Coach	Facilitative Trainer	Facilitative Leader
Third party	Third party	Third party or group member	Third party or group member	Group leader or member
Process expert	Process expert	Process expert	Process expert	Skilled in process
Content-neutral	Content expert	Involved in content	Content expert	Involved in content
Not substantive decision maker or mediator	May be involved in content decision making	May be involved in content decision making	Involved in content decision making in class	Involved in content decision making

Table 20.1.   Facilitative Roles.

The Facilitator Role

A facilitator is a substantively neutral third party, acceptable to all members of the group, who has no substantive decision-making authority. The facilitator's purpose is to help a group increase its effectiveness by diagnosing and intervening largely on group process and structure.

SUBSTANTIVELY NEUTRAL. By *substantively neutral,* I do not mean that you have no opinions on the issues that the group is discussing. That would be unrealistic and inhuman. Rather, I mean that you facilitate the discussion without sharing your opinions and so that group members cannot tell what you think about the group's issues; consequently, you do not influence the group's decisions. Group members are easily and justifiably annoyed by a facilitator who claims to be neutral and then acts in a way that is not.

To remain neutral requires listening to members' views, and remaining curious about how their reasoning differs from others (and from your private views) so that you can help the group engage in productive conversation. If you trade your curiosity for a belief that some members are right and others are wrong, or that the group as a whole is going in the wrong direction, you give up your ability to help group members explore their own views and differences and replace it with your desire to influence the content of discussion. If you find yourself invested in an issue or in having the group reach a particular outcome, or if you have expertise on the subject that makes it difficult for you to remain neutral, then consider serving in one of the other facilitative roles.

THIRD PARTY. A facilitator needs to be a third party because it is difficult to act neutrally in your own group. If you are a group member or leader, an individual would reasonably expect you to be involved in the content of discussion and to have a role in decision making.

The term *third party* is open to interpretation. Even if you are not a member of the immediate group that requests facilitation, members may not consider you a third party. This may happen, for example, if the group is seeking facilitation to address concerns with the division it is part of and you are an internal facilitator working in the larger division. To serve as a facilitator, the group requesting help needs to consider you a third party.

PROCESS EXPERT. A facilitator is content-neutral but also a process expert and advocate. As a process expert, you know what kinds of behavior, process, and underlying structure are more or less likely to contribute to high-quality problem solving and decision making, and you know which elements contribute to making an effective group. If you ask a group to use certain ground rules or if you identify certain ineffective behavior in the group, it is on the basis of this process expertise. Process expertise makes each of the four roles a facilitative role.

As a process expert, you advocate for processes, structures, and behaviors necessary for effective facilitation, such as appropriate membership, useful problem-solving methods, sufficient time, and ground rules. You inquire whether the group you are working with sees any problems with your design for the facilitation. For all of these decisions about the facilitation process, you are a partner with the group.

The Facilitative Consultant Role

Unlike the facilitator, a facilitative consultant is used for expertise in a particular area. The facilitative consultant is a third-party expert whose purpose is to help the client make informed decisions. The consultant does this by applying the area of expertise (marketing, management information systems, service quality, and so forth) to the client's particular situation, recommending a course of action, and in some cases implementing it for the client. Any substantive decision-making authority the consultant has results not from the role per se but from its being delegated by the client. A facilitative consultant uses facilitative skills while serving as an expert in a particular content area. Like the facilitator, the facilitative consultant may be external or internal to the organization. Internal human resource or organization development consultants often serve as facilitative consultants in an organization.

Facilitative skills are essential for expert consulting, which typically requires developing effective relationships, working with groups, and dealing with difficult conversations. The issues for which the expert consultant is called in are often ones about which members have strong and differing views. Consequently, the ability to help the group address the issues depends partly on the consultant's ability to effectively manage the process of exploring the issues. To paraphrase one of my clients, who is an expert consultant, "What do I do when I am talking to the client about what I found and what I recommend, and people start disagreeing with each other in front of me?" When this occurs, the facilitative consultant can help in the conversation while still being a participant in the content of the discussion. By integrating facilitative skills with expertise, the facilitative consultant increases the value provided to the clients.

The Facilitative Coach Role

In recent years, organizations have made coaches available for many of their executives and managers. A coach usually works one-on-one with people, helping them improve their effectiveness. Depending on her background, a coach may bring subject-area expertise in certain areas. At the heart of the facilitative coaching role is the ability to help people improve their effectiveness by helping them learn to rigorously reflect on their behavior and thinking.

When I coach clients—whether facilitative leaders, facilitators, or someone serving in another role—we explore difficult situations that they face, the outcomes they seek, and what it is about the situation that makes it difficult for them. Using the core values and principles described in this chapter, I help them think about how the way they are thinking and acting (or have thought and acted) contributes to the outcomes they seek as well as creating negative unintended consequences. Over time, clients develop the ability to do this kind of analysis themselves and produce the outcomes they seek with few unintended consequences.

A facilitative coach jointly designs the learning process with the client instead of assuming that she knows how the client can best learn. She also models mutual learning by exploring with the client how her coaching methods are helping or hindering the client's ability to learn. Facilitative coaches and clients explore the coaching relationship itself as a source of learning for both the client and the coach.

The Facilitative Trainer Role

Like the expert consultant, a trainer also has knowledge to share with participants; like the facilitative consultant, the trainer models the core values and ground rules and uses facilitative skills to enhance the participants' learning experience. When feasible, a facilitative trainer should work with the participants to design the training so that it meets their interests. During the training, the facilitative trainer regularly inquires whether the training is meeting the participants' needs and is flexible enough to modify the design if it isn't. The facilitative trainer also considers the training setting an opportunity for her own learning, not just for participant learning. This means she is open to changing her views and inviting participants to challenge her assumptions, just as the trainer herself challenges participants. The facilitative trainer also facilitates the interaction among participants to enhance learning.

In recent years, some trainers have changed their title to facilitator. To the degree that this signals a shift in trainers' recognizing the value of facilitative skills and integrating them into their work, it makes me hopeful. Yet calling a trainer a facilitator obscures the fact that the individual is expert in and has responsibility for teaching some particular topic. I use the term *facilitative trainer* to recognize both sets of responsibilities and skills.

The Facilitative Leader Role

The facilitative leader uses the core values and principles to help groups increase their effectiveness, which includes helping to create the conditions in which group members can also learn to use the core values and principles. The facilitative leader may be the formal leader of the group or just a group member. In either case, the facilitative leader role is the most difficult to fill because he needs to use his facilitative skills at the same time that he has strong views about the issue being discussed. For example, this requires that the facilitative leader openly state his views on a subject, explain the reasoning underlying those views, and then encourage others to identify any gaps or problems in his reasoning. Underlying the facilitative leader role is the premise that a group increases its effectiveness as members take on more responsibility for the group and increase their ability to learn from their experiences.

Choosing the Appropriate Role

The appropriate facilitative role is the one that accurately represents your relationship with the group; if you select an inappropriate role, you create problems for yourself and the group. One common problem occurs when an internal or external consultant or leader tries to serve as a facilitator, rather than as a facilitative consultant or facilitative leader.

Consider, for example, an internal HR manager who works with groups across the organization to develop and implement HR policy. The manager begins the group meeting by describing her role as a facilitator and asking for each group's thoughts about a particular policy. But the manager is an expert in the area of HR and has her own thoughts about what makes effective HR policy. When she realizes that the groups have ideas differing from those of HR, the "facilitator" begins asking leading questions in order to influence the group members' views without saying so explicitly, or she simply identifies some problems with others' proposals. Other group members begin to feel set up, believing that the HR person misled them about her role. At the same time, the manager is frustrated because she feels she cannot openly influence the group's ideas in the facilitator role. In this case, serving as a facilitative consultant or facilitative leader enables the manager to share subject-matter expertise, be involved in the decisions, and still use facilitative skills to improve the quality of the group's interaction.

A leader faces a similar problem in trying to serve as a neutral facilitator with his or her own group, or other groups in the organization. As a facilitator, the leader does not get a chance to openly share thoughts and feelings about the issue, to influence others and to be influenced, or to be involved in making decisions in which the leader has a legitimate role. Group members may need the leader's relevant information on the issue and find it hard to believe that the leader has no opinions. Acting as a facilitator, the leader may see a decline in the quality of the group's decisions, as well as his or her own commitment to group decisions. This can cause the leader to change group decisions that were made while he or she was serving as facilitator, which undermines both the leader's credibility and the role of a genuine facilitator. Serving in the facilitative leader role eliminates these problems.

In short, the facilitator role is appropriate for a situation in which you are not a member of the group, you have no stake in the issues, and no role in the group's decision making given your roles in the organization.

THE CORE VALUES OF THE SKILLED FACILITATOR APPROACH

Every third-party role is based on a set of assumptions about human behavior. Assumptions include values (things worth striving for) and beliefs (things considered to be true) that typically are accepted as valid without testing. Because assumptions clarify biases, identifying them is important.

Core Values

The skilled facilitator approach is based on four values: valid information, free and informed choice, internal commitment to those choices, and compassion (see Table 20.2).

Valid information means that you share information in a way that enables others to understand your reasoning and, ideally, to determine for themselves whether the information you have shared is accurate. This means sharing all information relevant to an issue, including your assumptions and your feelings about how the issue is being addressed. It means using specific examples so that other people can understand clearly what has been said and can determine independently whether the information is accurate. Valid information also means that others understand the information that you share with them. This means that you share not only your conclusions but also the reasoning by which you reach them. Having done so, you inquire whether others have information that is different from yours.

Core Value	Description
Valid information	• People share all relevant information. • People share information in such a way that others understand their reasoning. • People share information in such a way that others can independently validate it. • People constantly seek new information to determine whether past decisions should be changed on the basis of new, valid information.
Free and informed choice	• People define their own objectives and methods for achieving them. • Choices are not coerced or manipulated. • Choices are based on valid information.
Internal commitment	• People feel personally responsible for their choices; they own their decisions. • Commitment to action is intrinsic rather than based on reward or punishment.
Compassion	• People temporarily suspend judgment. • People are concerned for others and their own good. • People appreciate others' and their own suffering.

Table 20.2. Core Values.

Source: The first three core values come from the work of Chris Argyris and Donald Schön (Argyris, 1970; Argyris & Schön, 1974); I have added the fourth.

Free and informed choice means that you and others can define your own objectives and the methods for achieving them, and that these choices are based on valid information. When you make a free choice, you are not coerced or manipulated. Consequently, the facilitator does not change people's behavior. The facilitator provides information that enables people to decide whether to change their own behavior. If they decide to, the facilitator helps them learn how to change.

Internal commitment to the choice means that you feel personally responsible for the choices you make. You are committed to the decision because it is intrinsically compelling or satisfying, not because you will be rewarded or penalized for making that choice. If people are internally committed to a decision, there is little need for traditional over-the-shoulder monitoring to make sure they are really doing what they said they would do.

Compassion means adapting a stance toward others and ourselves in which we temporarily suspend judgment. It involves having a basic concern for the good of others that leads you to be concerned about their suffering. By *suffering* I mean simply the pain that people feel when their needs are not met. When you act with compassion, you infuse the other core values with your intent to understand, empathize with, and help others.

Compassion literally means "to suffer with" and is sometimes mistakenly thought of as having pity for others. Unfortunately, this pity-based compassion leads people to help others in a way they do not want to be helped, and to protect others in a way they do not want to be protected. The kind of compassion I am describing enables you to have empathy for others and for yourself in a way that holds you and others accountable for your actions, instead of unilaterally protecting yourself or others. This kind of compassion strengthens rather than diminishes the other core values.

The core values create a reinforcing cycle. People need valid information to make an informed choice. Compassion creates an environment in which people are willing to share valid information. When they make free and informed choices, they become internally committed to the choices. Compassion leads people to be concerned about others' free and informed choices, aside from their own. If people are internally committed to their decisions, they take responsibility for seeing that the decisions are implemented effectively. Internal commitment leads people to continue seeking new information to determine whether their decisions remain sound or should be revisited. Compassion leads people to avoid focusing on blame when things are implemented in a way that creates unintended consequences.

Guiding Facilitator and Group Behavior

Central to the Skilled Facilitator approach is the assumption that the same core values that increase your effectiveness as a facilitator increase the group's effectiveness. This means that when you act effectively, you are modeling effective behavior for group members. The notion that using the core values leads to effective process is not an untested assumption. It has been borne out by more than twenty-five years of research (Argyris, 1982, 1985, 1987, 1990; Argyris, Putnam, & Smith, 1985; Argyris & Schön, 1974). To examine how values serve as a guide for effective behavior, consider what happens when a group's actions are inconsistent with core values.

To take an example, group members often try to influence a decision by sharing information that supports their position and by withholding information that is inconsistent with it. They place a higher value on winning the discussion or protecting their own interests than on sharing valid information. Because valid information has been withheld, the group often makes poor decisions. The *Challenger* space shuttle disaster—caused by the failure of an O-ring, which some organizational members already believed might malfunction—is a vivid and tragic example of what can happen when valid information is withheld and choices are not as informed or free as they could be.

Group members are often asked to commit to achieving a goal without having any control over how they will accomplish the goal—or what it should be. They often become compliant, doing only what is minimally necessary to complete the task, expending extra effort only when they believe others are monitoring their work. Because of the lack of internal commitment, the group may fail to accomplish the goal.

The facilitator helps the group improve process by acting consistently with core values. In developmental facilitation, the group members develop the ability, over time, to identify when they have acted inconsistently with the core values and to correct their behavior—without a facilitator's help. In basic facilitation, the group uses a facilitator to help it act consistently with the core values, temporarily, while working with the facilitator.

You use the core values to guide your own behavior. You create valid information by sharing your observations and checking with the group about how members have acted consistently or inconsistently with core values and other principles of group effectiveness. By helping group members see the consequences of their behavior and by asking them whether they want to change, you enable the group to make free and informed choices. Consequently, members become committed to the choices they make during facilitation. By acting with compassion, you model your intent to understand, empathize, and help.

THE ROLE OF THE FACILITATOR

Having briefly described five facilitative roles, let us explore the facilitator role in detail. Essentially, the facilitator's role is to help the group improve its process in a manner consistent with the core values. The facilitator accomplishes this by helping the group establish ground rules for effective group process, identifying behavior that is inconsistent or consistent with the ground rules and core values, and helping members learn more effective behavior.

BASIC AND DEVELOPMENTAL FACILITATION

I divide facilitation into two types on the basis of the group's objectives (Table 20.3). In *basic facilitation,* the group seeks only to solve content problems, such as reducing the time for responding to customers or developing a strategy for marketing a new product. The group uses a facilitator to temporarily improve its process to solve the problem. Once the group solves its problem, the facilitation objective has been achieved. But the group has probably not improved its ability to reflect on and improve its process. Consequently, if other difficult problems arise, the group is likely to require a facilitator again.

In *developmental facilitation,* the group seeks to develop its process skills while solving problems. The group uses a facilitator to learn how to improve its process and applies newly developed skills to solving the problem. Once the group accomplishes its objectives, as in basic facilitation it has solved the problem. But the group will also have improved its ability to reflect on and manage the process. Consequently, if other difficult problems arise, the group remains less dependent on a facilitator than before. In practice, facilitation occurs on a continuum from purely basic to purely developmental, rather than as two discrete or pure types.

Characteristic	Basic Facilitation	Developmental Facilitation
Client objective	Solve a substantive problem	Solve a substantive problem while learning to improve the group's process
Facilitator role	Use facilitator's skills to temporarily improve group's process; take primary responsibility for managing the group's process	Help group develop its process skills; share responsibility for managing the group's process
Process outcome for client	Same dependence on facilitator for solving future problems	Reduced dependence on facilitator for solving future problems

Table 20.3.   Basic and Developmental Facilitation.

Choosing the Type of Facilitation

To help a group decide where on the basic-developmental facilitation continuum it needs help, it is useful to consider how your role differs with the approach. In basic facilitation, although the group can influence the process at any time, in general it expects you to guide the group, using what you consider effective group process. In developmental facilitation, members expect to monitor and guide the group's process and expect you to teach them how to accomplish this goal.

Basic and developmental facilitators intervene for different reasons. In general, as a basic facilitator you intervene when the group's process or other factors affecting the group interfere with its accomplishing a specific goal. Your intervention is designed to help the group accomplish the goal without necessarily learning how to improve process.

A developmental facilitator intervenes under the same conditions as a basic facilitator. But in addition, as a developmental facilitator you intervene when the group's process or other factors affecting the group hinder the group's long-term effectiveness, or when reflecting on the process will help members develop their process skills. Your intervention is designed to help the group learn how to diagnose and improve process. A fundamental difference between basic and developmental facilitation is doing something for a group in the former case and teaching a group how to do the same thing for itself in the latter case.

Throughout the chapter, I use the terms *basic facilitator* and *basic group* to refer to a facilitator and a group using basic facilitation. Similarly, I use *developmental facilitator* and *developmental group* to refer to a facilitator and a group using developmental facilitation.

Given that ineffective group process hinders a group's ability to solve substantive problems, basic facilitation is essentially limited. It helps a group solve one problem without exploring why it has trouble solving problems in general. In contrast, developmental facilitation identifies why the group, functioning as it does, has difficulty solving problems and helps the group learn how to address the fundamental causes. In doing so, developmental facilitation requires a group to reflect on its behavior and often change the basic values and beliefs that guide behavior in the group. In this sense, developmental facilitation is more systemic and produces deeper learning than basic facilitation.

When Is Developmental Facilitation Appropriate?

Still, developmental facilitation is not always the more appropriate choice for every group. The extent to which you use a basic or a developmental approach with a particular client depends on several factors. Obviously, the group's primary goal is a major one. A second important factor is time; a group unable to devote the time necessary for developmental facilitation should not pursue it. Even with adequate time available, if the group is a temporary one (such as a task force) then the investment required for developmental facilitation may not be worthwhile. A third factor is group stability. Even with a group initially learning to facilitate itself, if membership changes frequently or drastically the group may not be able to sustain the skills. A final factor is control over process. Unless the group has control over process, including how it makes decisions, developmental facilitation may be of limited use.

Even so, developmental facilitation is essential for some groups given their stated identity. For example, a truly self-directed work team must be self-facilitating; an organization that purports to be a learning organization has to have groups that can reflect on their actions in a manner consistent with developmental facilitation.

THE GROUP IS THE CLIENT

One significant implication of the core values and your objective to help groups improve their effectiveness is that your client needs to be the entire group rather than only the group leader. When you choose the group as your client, you are telling your clients that your responsibility is to help the group as a whole rather than only the leader (or a subset of the group). This simple choice has many implications. In practice, it means you offer valid information that enables the group to make a free and informed choice about whether to work with you, so that if they choose to do so they are likely to be internally committed to the process. It means that you do not automatically agree to the group leader's requests (say, to use a certain agenda or process) simply because they come from the group leader.

It can be scary to choose the group as your client. The leader has more authority and often more power than other group members. You may be afraid that if the group is your client you will alienate the leader and jeopardize future work with the group or the larger organization.

But if you meet the leader's needs at the expense of other group members, you lose your credibility with the group and your ability to facilitate. Viewed in this either-or way, you find yourself in a dilemma; either choice creates problems. The challenge is to recognize that the leader's role in the group is different and still treat the group as your client.

Facilitator's Responsibility for Group Outcomes

One challenging part of your facilitator role is deciding what responsibility you have for the group's outcomes. Some facilitators believe they are largely responsible; they reason that they are hired to help the group accomplish a task, such that if the group does not accomplish its objective then the facilitator considers himself at fault. Other facilitators believe that they have little responsibility for outcomes, reasoning that they are hired to help the group improve its process, so if the group does not accomplish its desired outcome, the facilitator is not at fault.

THE FACILITATOR'S CONTRIBUTION. Thinking about this systemically means thinking about your role and potential contribution rather than what you can be blamed for. As a facilitator, your contribution involves acting effectively so that you help the group accomplish its goals. To the extent that you act ineffectively, you contribute to the group's ineffective behavior and its consequences.

Consider, for example, a top management team that commits to making decisions by unanimous agreement but then votes six to four to install a new organization-wide intranet, although several members insist that the intranet will not meet divisional needs. Once installed and debugged, the computer intranet remains underused, largely because it cannot perform critical tasks needed by several divisions. As the facilitator, you are partly responsible for the effect of the group's poor decision if you have not shared with the group that several members' interests are not met in the decision, that the group is acting inconsistently with its own ground rule by voting, and that negative consequences can develop as a result of these behaviors.

A basic facilitator fulfills her responsibility to the group by designing an effective process for the group to accomplish its work, acting consistently with the core values, identifying for the group when members have acted inconsistently (or consistently) with principles of effective group behavior, and letting the group make free and informed choices on the basis of the facilitator's interventions. In addition, a developmental facilitator helps group members learn how to identify when they have acted inconsistently with principles of effective group behavior, how to explore the conditions that create the ineffective behavior, and how to change these conditions to generate more effective behavior.

Although you are not directly responsible for *what* the group decides, you are responsible for helping the group consider *how* its process leads to more or less effective decisions. Imagine that a group is trying to decide what data to use to predict the size of the market for a service. As facilitator, you do not offer an opinion about which are the best data to use. But you do help the group consider which criteria it uses to make the decision. If members disagree about the best data to use, you help them design a way to test their disagreement.

If the group makes a decision that creates a problem, you are responsible for helping the members analyze the process they used in making that decision. By determining where the group went wrong (perhaps there was an erroneous assumption), members can agree on what they will do differently next time.

PROCESS IS NECESSARY BUT NOT SUFFICIENT. If the content of a group's decisions improves as the process improves, it would seem to follow that all problems in a content decision flow from poor process—and therefore are partly the facilitator's responsibility. But they are not, for several reasons.

First, effective group process, and problem solving in particular, is based on assumptions that all relevant information is available and accurate and that the consequences of actions can be predicted accurately. Obviously, such assumptions are often incorrect. If the assumptions are violated, a group can make a content mistake even though the process is effective.

Second, effective group process is necessary but not sufficient for creating an effective group. An effective group also requires an effective structure and a supportive organizational context. An effective structure includes such elements as members who have appropriate knowledge and skills; well-designed, motivating jobs; and adequate time for members to complete the task. A supportive organizational context includes aspects of the larger organization that influence the group: a supportive culture, rewards consistent with the group's objectives, and various resources.

Finally, even if you facilitate effectively, the group may engage in ineffective process, because part of facilitating effectively is enabling the group to make free and informed choices, including choices about their own process. Sometimes you may feel you are abandoning a group by allowing it to make a free and informed choice that you are certain will have negative consequences. Or you may feel frustrated that a group does not seem to understand what you understand. For some facilitators, this is the hardest test of whether they enable the group to make a free and informed choice. Yet it may also be the most important test. If, by trying to help a group avoid poor process, you prevent the group from making its own choice, you act inconsistently with the core values being espoused. Ultimately, this reduces your credibility as facilitator. Also, it may suggest incorrectly to the client that the core values can be ignored if they are inconvenient or if the stakes are high.

Colluding with the Group

Collusion is a secret agreement or cooperation between parties that affects others. When you collude with a group, you are explicitly or implicitly asked (or you ask others) to act in a particular way but not to reveal that you are doing so, or why. Collusion is inconsistent with the facilitator's role, because it requires you to withhold valid information in a way that unilaterally places the interests of some group members above the interests of the group as a whole, which prevents the full group from making a free and informed choice. You can collude in several ways: with one or more members against one or more other members, with one or more members against a non–group member, and with a non–group member against one or more group members. Here are illustrative examples of the three forms of collusion:

- Jack, a group member, approaches you before a meeting. Jack says he wants to raise an issue in the meeting but does not want the group to know it is his issue. He is concerned that the issue will not get the attention it deserves if the group thinks he is raising it. Jack asks you to raise the issue "at an appropriate time" but to not tell the group where it originated. You agree.

- A task force is about to meet with Erika, the department head to whom it reports, to recommend changes in the department. (Erika is not a member of the task force.) It has been agreed that as the task force facilitator, you will facilitate the meeting. Before the meeting, the task force members realize they have made some assumptions about Erika that were not confirmed with her. The recommendations will work only if the assumptions are true. But they are reluctant to ask her about the assumptions, because a sensitive issue is involved. They ask you not to raise the assumptions in the meeting or to pursue them if Erika mentions them. You agree.

- Sven, a manager, tells you that a team that reports to him (and that he is not a member of) is spending too much time on an issue. Sven is especially concerned that the team is spending time discussing issues that are not in its charge. He asks you to attend fewer group meetings and, when facilitating, to steer the group away from those issues. You say, "OK, I'll see what I can do."

Colluding with group members is a solution that creates new problems and often makes the situation worse. In an attempt to help the group by colluding, you act inconsistently with the core values you espouse, reducing your effectiveness and credibility. Further, by shifting the responsibility for raising issues from a group member to you, you miss the opportunity to help group members develop their skills in dealing productively with difficult issues, and you reinforce ineffective group behavior. Over time, you may wonder why the group is overly dependent on you, without realizing how your own actions contributed to the very outcome you set out to avoid.

Even if you agree with this rational explanation, in any of these situations you may still feel a lot of emotion. You may feel angry if you attribute to a member that he intends to deceive others by asking you to act collusively. You may feel trapped if faced with choosing between meeting the request of a powerful member (who might pay your bill or salary) and acting inconsistently with your role and not helping the group. If members ask you to raise issues for them because they are worried about the consequences if they raise the issue themselves, you may feel sorry for them and want to protect them. In some of these situations, you may be naturally more compassionate than in others. The challenge is to respond out of compassion when it is not your immediate response—and to do so in a way that does not shift member responsibility onto you, because of how you are feeling about yourself or about others.

Dealing with Collusion

One way to avoid colluding with the group is to discuss, as part of the contracting process, what you as facilitator can and cannot do, explaining your reasoning. You can give examples of requests that you cannot fulfill because they would lead to collusion.

When you receive a request that requires you to collude with the group, you can explain how fulfilling the request obligates you to act inconsistently with the role of facilitator, which in turn reduces your ability to help the group in the long run. You can then ask the individual if he sees the situation differently. In this way, you can work with the person making the request to find a way for him to raise the issue directly with relevant individuals. You might begin by saying, "I think it's important that the group hear your concern, and I think it's appropriate for you to raise it with them because it's your concern. If I raise the issue in my role as facilitator, people might think I'm steering the conversation, which is inconsistent with my role. I can't raise the issue for you. But as soon as you raise it, I'll actively facilitate to help you and the other group members have as productive a conversation as possible. Do you see any of this differently? If not, do you want to talk about how you can have that conversation with the group?"

LEAVING THE ROLE OF FACILITATOR

I have emphasized how important it is to clarify your facilitator role and to act consistently with it. Yet sometimes it is appropriate to temporarily leave the facilitator role and serve in another role. This section considers the other roles, when it is beneficial to take them on, and what risks you face in doing so.

The Facilitator as Mediator

When is it appropriate to serve as a mediator? Before we discuss that question, let us explore the similarities and differences between the roles of facilitator and mediator.

COMPARING FACILITATION AND MEDIATION. People sometimes use the words *facilitation* and *mediation* interchangeably. According to Christopher Moore (1996, p. 15), "mediation is the intervention in a negotiation or a conflict of an acceptable third party who has limited or no authoritative decision-making power but who assists the involved parties in voluntarily reaching a mutually acceptable settlement of issues in dispute."

Although there are similarities between facilitation and mediation, there are also important differences. Both facilitation and mediation involve intervention by a neutral third party who is acceptable to the clients and who has no substantive decision-making authority. Both seek to help people reach a decision acceptable to all who are involved. The facilitator and the mediator share many of the same skills and techniques, but they apply them in varying situations and sometimes to accomplish different objectives. In general, mediation is more similar to basic facilitation than to developmental facilitation.

I see several distinctions between facilitation and mediation. First, they have differing objectives. Parties seeking a mediator have a conflict they have been unable to settle, so traditionally the objective of mediation has been to help the parties negotiate a settlement to a particular conflict. Note, however, that at least one approach to mediation (by Bush & Folger, 1994) also focuses on transforming relationships among participants and the participants themselves.

The objective of facilitation is to help a group improve its process for solving problems and making decisions so that the group can achieve goals and increase overall effectiveness. Although dealing with conflict can be a significant part of facilitation, it is not necessarily the primary focus. In addition, developmental facilitation seeks to help the group develop its own ability to improve the process for solving problems by teaching facilitative skills to the group.

Second, because a mediator helps parties resolve their conflict, the parties typically seek a mediator after they reach an impasse—that is, once they believe they can progress no further without third-party help. When a facilitator helps a group resolve conflict, she too is sometimes called in after the group has reached an impasse. But the facilitator often becomes involved earlier. For example, a group may seek basic facilitation because members understand that they do not have skills sufficient to manage the process of what is expected to be a difficult or complex discussion. A facilitator might also enter the process after the group has gone through a critical incident, such as a significant change in group membership or group mission.

Third, a facilitator works in the presence of the entire group, whereas a mediator may work with the parties together as well as separately. The potential problem with a facilitator playing the role of mediator is illustrated by the differences in the roots of the two words.

Mediate comes from a Latin word meaning "to come between"—in our context, to come between group members. *Facilitate* comes from a Latin word meaning "to make easy"—in our context, to make it easy for the group to be effective. One of the facilitator's goals is to help members improve their ability to work together effectively; serving as an intermediary usually limits achievement of this goal if members do not develop the skills for dealing directly with each other.

TEMPORARILY BECOMING A MEDIATOR. There are three common situations in which I am asked to move from facilitator to mediator by coming between members of the group: (1) in the beginning of a facilitation, when subgroups have concerns either about working with me as a facilitator or about working with the other subgroups; (2) during a facilitation, when a member or members want information raised in the group or some action taken without it being attributed to them; and (3) in a conflict, when the facilitation breaks down and one or more subgroups are unwilling to continue.

Acting as a mediator in these situations, I face a common risk of acting inconsistently with the core values, similar to collusion. Members share information with me outside of the group conversation and want me to use it to intervene in the full group. But because the members do not want the full group to know the source of the information (or even that it was shared with me), the members ask me to share the information for them or else act on their information without explaining that I am doing so (much like what is seen in the earlier examples of collusion). If I explicitly or implicitly agree not to share the information that was shared with me, and this becomes the basis of my intervention, then I cannot explain why I am intervening, and so I am withholding relevant information from the group. In addition, if the person who shared the information with me is not willing to identify herself in the full group, neither the group nor I can determine whether the information is valid.

The risk is actually a dilemma. If I act on the information given me without testing its validity or explaining my intervention, I act inconsistently with the core values I am espousing and may make an intervention that is ineffective. On the other hand, if I do not act on the information given me, the group and I miss an opportunity to get the group together initially or keep it from completely breaking down.

Returning to the three common situations I described earlier, in each one if certain interests are met then I can temporarily serve as a mediator without reducing the integrity of my facilitator role. In each situation, I seek first to serve as a facilitative coach, helping one or more members of the group raise concerns or questions about the other members in the full group (as I illustrated in the section on avoiding collusion). This role is still consistent with the facilitator role, as long as I am helping the group members raise their own issues. In any event, I do not agree to raise the issue for the members. Doing so could lead to a situation in which, after I raise the issue for the members, the members claim that they did not raise the issue with me. It also increases the group's dependence on me as the facilitator.

I may also meet with subgroups when I am beginning to work with a group, and one or more subgroups might have a concern about whether I am impartial and sensitive to their needs. Initially, I ask the subgroup what makes them reluctant to share this information in the full group, share my reasoning on the advantages of doing so, and ask what would need to happen for them to be willing to do so. If they are not yet willing to share these concerns in the full group, I consider it reasonable to meet separately with them to hear their concerns. If the concerns are relevant for the other subgroups, I help the subgroup figure out how to share these concerns in the full group, if they are willing.

I may temporarily act as mediator if conflict between subgroups threatens a complete breakdown in communication. I facilitated a union-management cooperative effort in which the seven union members of the union-management committee simultaneously closed their notebooks and walked out in the middle of a meeting. The discussion had become tense, and union members were frustrated by what they perceived to be management's efforts to undermine the process. As the facilitator, I saw two choices. I could stay in the room, let the union leave, and see the process unravel, along with the progress the committee had made. Or I could temporarily assume the role of mediator and talk with the union members, trying to find a way to help union and management members to work together again. I chose the latter course and spent the next six hours mediating in meetings and phone calls. The next morning, the union and management subgroups were back in the room, discussing why the process had broken down and exploring ways to prevent it from recurring.

When the facilitator meets with a subgroup, especially if the facilitator decides to mediate by conveying information between subgroups, the facilitator needs to state clearly that she or he is serving in the mediator role and the facilitator and subgroups need a clear agreement about what information, if any, the facilitator will share with the other subgroups. Without this agreement, a subgroup can easily feel that the facilitator has not acted neutrally, violated confidentiality, or colluded with another subgroup.

The facilitator acting as mediator entails advantages and disadvantages. Mediating can sometimes prevent a difficult conflict from escalating to the point where the group essentially breaks down and ceases to function. However, by agreeing to mediate, the facilitator may reduce the likelihood of the group developing the skills to resolve conflict. Also, working with a subgroup may lead group members to question the facilitator's neutrality. Therefore, before serving as mediator the facilitator should consider whether the advantages outweigh the disadvantages.

The Facilitator as Evaluator

As a facilitator, you face a role conflict whenever someone in the organization asks you to evaluate the performance of one or more members in the group. For example, a manager who is outside the facilitated group may be concerned about the performance of one of the members. She may ask you to evaluate the member to help her decide whether to take any corrective action. Alternatively, she may be considering promoting one of several members of the group and ask you to evaluate the members to help her make the promotion decision.

You face a potential role conflict in this situation because evaluating group members can jeopardize the members' trust in you. One reason members trust you is that the facilitator has no authority and adheres to the principle that the facilitator does not use information obtained within facilitation to influence decisions about group members that are made outside facilitation, except with the agreement of the group. Evaluating group members increases your power in the organization and therefore decreases the likelihood of members discussing openly information that they believe could prove harmful to them.

Still, it can be difficult to tell a manager that you cannot share information about subordinates, especially if you want to share positive information that can be used to help the subordinates' careers.

One way a manager can obtain this information from you, the facilitator, in a manner consistent with core values is to have the group member about whom the evaluation is being sought agree that you can share your observations with the manager. In this case, you would provide specific examples that you observe about the group member's behavior. You share these observations in the presence of the group member—ideally, in the presence of the entire facilitated group—and ask the evaluated group member (and other group members) whether they would make a different evaluation. Making your information available to all group members such that they can validate or disagree with it enables the members to make an informed choice about whether you have shared valid information with the manager. This can reduce member concerns about trust to the extent that they are based on concern about your sharing valid information. If you share all relevant information with the group, the information that you share during the evaluation session has already been discussed with group members as part of your facilitator role.

The Facilitator as Content Expert

Earlier in this chapter, I discussed when it is appropriate to serve as a facilitative consultant more than as a facilitator. Even if you decide to serve as a facilitator, the client may still ask you questions in an area in which you have expertise (marketing, performance management systems, finance, and so on).

The group is able to quickly obtain information when you serve as a content expert; doing so helps you feel good by showing the group you are knowledgeable about their work and that you can add value to their conversation. But offering this information also creates risks. One is that the group begins to see you as a *non*neutral third party, which reduces your credibility and ultimately your effectiveness. A second risk is that the group becomes dependent on you. Group members may grow sensitive to whether you approve of their decisions, which then affects the decisions they make.

The facilitator as content expert or information resource is an appropriate role if you and the group explicitly contract for it. In this situation, you can take several steps to reduce the risk that imparting expert information will negatively affect your facilitator role. First, acting as a content expert only when asked by the group, and only when the group reaches consensus to do so, reduces the prospect of meeting the needs of only some group members. Second, announcing to the group when you are temporarily leaving the role of facilitator and afterward that you are returning to the facilitator role reduces confusion about the role you are currently serving in. Finally, by avoiding serving as a content expert in the early stages of working with a group, you reduce the likelihood of the group coming to depend on you in this role.

People who facilitate groups in their own organizations are often asked by group members to play an expert role.

When the Content Is About Group Process: The Myth of Total Neutrality

It is a myth that you can always be neutral about the substance or content of a group's discussions while being partial about what constitutes effective group process. Recall that "substantively neutral" means a facilitator conveys no preference for any solution the group considers.

You are partial about what constitutes effective group process because that is your area of expertise. As a skilled facilitator, you know what kind of behavior is more or less likely to lead to effective problem solving and other important group outcomes—and you convey this knowledge through your actions as facilitator.

When I ask group members to follow certain ground rules (such as sharing all relevant information) or when I identify how members act inconsistently with the core values, I am also identifying my beliefs about what constitutes effective group process. When I use the core values to guide my own behavior, my behavior is a reflection of my theory of effective interpersonal process. In fact, embedded in each of my interventions is some prescription for effective behavior. In other words, because as facilitator I am always striving to model effective behavior, and because embedded in my behavior are beliefs about effective group process, I am constantly conveying my beliefs through my actions.

Consequently, the facilitator cannot be neutral about the content of a group's discussion when it involves how to manage group or interpersonal process effectively. In this case, your theory about what makes group process effective can be used to address the group's discussion of how to manage process effectively. As the group process becomes the subject of discussion, your comments about process focus on the group content. Consequently, you become involved in the content of the discussion. Because many management issues involve some aspect of interpersonal or group process, your theory of group effectiveness has implications for how groups handle many issues.

However, your role is not to impose upon the solution the principles that guide your intervention with the group.

CHAPTER TWENTY-ONE

The Right Coach

Howard Morgan
Phil Harkins
Marshall Goldsmith

Executive coaching is a precision tool for optimizing the abilities of leaders. Most often, coaching focuses on the leader's individual effectiveness. In other cases, the coaching aims more at the leader's effectiveness within a team environment or at his or her capacity to drive organizational change. Regardless of where coaching aims on the leadership spectrum, the executive coach works in close, trusted partnership with the leader. The coach applies experience, know-how, and insight to key areas, and judiciously pushes the client beyond his or her comfort zone to reach levels of performance greater than the client would have achieved alone—all within an accelerated time frame.

Despite this imperative, the coach selection process does not always receive the attention it deserves. In part, this results from lack of clarity about what coaching should accomplish and how it should accomplish it. This chapter describes what a coach does and what common attributes, skills, and orientations are common to successful coaches. It also looks at how to ensure fit between the coach and the organization's needs.

WHAT IS COACHING?

Coaching is not just for problems anymore. Ten years ago, coaching primarily concentrated on people with performance issues. A coach came on board because a leader's personal style had a negative impact on peers and reports, or because his or her skill set was inadequate—conditions that were leading to career derailment. Sometimes, the coach was simply a bulletproof way to communicate bad news about performance before dismissal. Coaching was often viewed pejoratively as something applied to failing leaders or as a last-ditch effort to salvage a career in which the organization had made a long-term investment it didn't want to throw away.

Today, that impression has turned 180 degrees. As the marketplace has become increasingly competitive and fast-moving, organizations now recognize they must work with speed and precision to enable key people to achieve critical business objectives. In response, coaching has embraced a whole new focus: how to take good people and make them the best they can be, positioning them to work more effectively and cohesively in their environments, and making the most of their capabilities. In other words, coaching is now most often applied to top performers whose leadership and growth potential are highly valued by the organization.

Performance issues will always arise in any development plan or in any dynamic that a leader must work through when trying to execute strategy or change. However, coaching is not intended to focus on those issues any more than absolutely necessary. The orientation is always forward, with a focus on efficiency, effectiveness, and impact. The personal and interpersonal challenges a coach encounters are no less complex than they were years ago, but the coach and coachee now work together, with a different kind of urgency and creative energy, to discover the best solutions to meet the organization's objectives.

Selecting the right coach is a challenge. Coaching is an approach, a viewpoint, and a technique as much as it is a profession. There are no defined backgrounds or sets of skills for coaches, just as there are no defined sets of problems or challenges. The coach is a highly specific resource of knowledge, expertise, intuition, and experience. He or she brings to the table the ability to deal with dynamic challenges. Although this dynamic character makes coaching difficult to codify, it also ensures that a good coach, with the right expertise, can work with a coachee to find a path to success. That path may differ from coach to coach, but the impact will still be positive.

What Coaching Isn't

To define what coaching is, let's examine what it isn't. Coaching often differs, for example, from consulting. Although a consultant and a coach both have a body of research or a theory from which to draw, the coach may very well not bring a model or framework into the engagement. As outsiders, neither coach nor consultant is likely to understand the client's business environment as well as the client does, but although the consultant provides ready-made answers, the coach's advice is extremely customized. Both consultant and coach rely on data gathering to interpret the organization's or individual's challenges. However, although the consultant uses that data to prepare a path for others to follow, the coach uses it to build the critical capabilities of key people so that they themselves can forge their own paths. Unlike the consultant, the coach works in partnership with the client to discover solutions together, finding them through careful listening, provocative questioning, enlightened guidance, and the right level of prompting at the right time. To a great degree, the coach's goal is to enable the client to find the right answers by him- or herself.

It is not surprising, therefore, that a successful relationship between coach and client depends on the highest levels of trust and openness. Nevertheless, boundaries do exist. Although coaching may sometimes feel like something halfway between the couch and the confessional, coaching is not therapy. The orientation is very different. Depending on personal background and skill, a coach may use some of the listening and analytical tools of therapy to build connection, trust, and openness. But although personal issues or deeper problems are likely to arise in the course of working together, the coach is not meant, and is usually not qualified, to provide more than supportive, confidential advice in those matters. Should serious personal issues emerge, a coach may be well positioned to provide a referral to a psychologist, counselor, or medical doctor. But, inasmuch as it is healthy to do so, a coach will maintain the focus of the engagement on moving the client forward, in line with business objectives. Although the client may control the pace and direction of a therapy session, the coach is being paid to facilitate the pace and direction of the coaching engagement— in the service of specific business-related goals.

Despite the coach's close working relationship with the client, the coach is not a substitute colleague or fellow executive. Many coaches have been successful in business in earlier incarnations, usually at the most senior levels. This provides a sense of comfort and familiarity in the client's world, allowing him or her to communicate in the same language. It also provides key insights into the complex and competing pressures of the client's work environment. This enables the coach to recognize a business opportunity or roadblock when it appears. However, the skills and interests that make the coach successful in coaching would probably not lead to success as a full-fledged member of the organization. If the coach were on board permanently, the orientation toward questioning, pushing the envelope, prompting alternative answers, and closely managing the personal dynamic might very well wear out the welcome. The coach's stay in the organization is meant to be short, usually less than two years, and longer only if intermittent challenges are pursued in a way that builds on the foundations that have already been established. A best practice coach, by design and ethic, is not in the business of creating a dependent relationship. Although this may be a sensible business model, akin to logging billable hours at a law firm, it violates one of the principle ethics of coaching: do everything in the service of the client, not in the service of oneself.

Skills and Attributes of Best Practice Coaches

Coaching takes place across a broad spectrum of areas, challenges, and situations. By its very nature, coaching is a flexible, adaptable, and fluid way of achieving measurable results. What are the skills and attributes that make for successful coaching? Chemistry, expertise, and experience are all very important—and we will define those in more detail shortly. But, the following sections help distinguish what it truly means to be a best practice coach.

TECHNICAL SKILLS. A best practice coach is able to

- Set the stage for the coaching engagement by establishing ground rules, reporting lines, confidentiality, and trust
- Assess the current situation fully and accurately
- Achieve alignment and agreement (with the coachee, client, and key stakeholders) around critical needs and achievable objectives
- Develop and execute an approach that will lead to a successful outcome

- Recognize emerging problems and opportunities in advance and adjust the plan accordingly
- Provide follow-up, to whatever degree necessary, to ensure sustainabilit

EXPERIENCE AND BACKGROUND. A best practice coach has

- A good working knowledge of the industry and the kind of organization for which the client is working
- A deep understanding of the coachee's level within the organization and the associated pressures, responsibilities, and relationships
- A keen knowledge of where his or her expertise starts and stops, and how that will match the client's needs
- The insight to judge whether the client is serious about working toward the kind of change, development, or direction the coach is able to drive
- The ability and resolve to assess personal fit and to go forward, or part ways accordingly
- The structure and discipline to manage the coaching relationship for the needs of the individual, whether the individual fully recognizes those needs or not
- The ability to distill a great deal of information while recognizing important patterns and uncovering key nuggets
- The ability to distinguish between matters of short-term urgency and long-term significance
- The ethics to maintain strict personal and business confidentiality

COACHING ATTRIBUTES. A best practice coach is able to:

- Put the coachee's needs ahead of his or her own ego
- Listen with nuance and sensitivity
- Establish the highest levels of trust, openness, and personal connection
- Ask probing questions that draw forth information the coachee could never have arrived at independently, despite superior knowledge and experience

- Understand the coachee's relationships with the insight of a participant-observer
- Make intuitive leaps that will lead the coachee to new levels of performance
- Judge actions or words to determine whether development is occurring at the appropriate rate and in the correct direction
- Match the coaching dynamic to the ever-shifting mood, attitude, and will of the coachee
- Back away from an area or direction that is not in the coachee's best interest to pursue or one that he or she is highly resistant to working on
- Change the coachee's behavior gradually, but steadily, even in the coach's absence
- Push the coachee to new levels without putting him or her in a position that would lead to compromise or embarrassment, or that would otherwise decrease the desire and willingness to change
- Create an independent capability in the coachee by building her strengths, instead of building reliance on the coach

Given this complex matrix of skills, attributes, and capabilities, it might seem that a best practice coach is born, not made. The hard truth, however, is that every coach learns through doing. The coach often begins his or her calling because of a passionate desire to take a leadership role in a particular area of expertise or interest. This passion carries the coach through a sometimes painful growth of skills and abilities in the service of his or her calling. A coach is always learning, growing, and developing key behaviors as they are required. Each of the best practice coaches we interviewed spoke of a two-way dynamic in coaching relationships, which is frequently described as teaching that flows in both directions, the coach providing insight to the client, while the client does the same for the coach.

A coach, like a leader, can be developed if she possesses the original passion. But this is a personal journey more than an educational attainment. Coaching accreditation programs probably can't teach the art of coaching any more than golf instruction can teach the art of golf. Skills can be learned and techniques replicated, but true understanding only comes from carefully honed practice in real-world situations.

We recognize that there are different levels of capabilities in the coaching profession, just as there are different categories of coaching. Higher levels can be attained over time, given limitations of experience, innovative capability, and personal growth.

Areas of Coaching Expertise

Another problem with the term coaching is that it describes the mode of the working relationship without differentiating the variety of aims and objectives.

In this chapter, we are generally talking about business or executive coaching. The distinction is most clear when compared to coaching that helps an individual achieve a personal aim such as happiness, work-life balance, wealth, or better relationships. There are several important exceptions to this distinction, and many coaches speak of the continuum between business and personal life encountered during any engagement; but, for the most part, executive or leadership coaching is meant to meet organizational needs.

Within that domain, we have made further differentiations. The following five categories seemed to provide adequate "boxes" for all of the coaches that were interviewed. A qualification is necessary, however. Some coaches were very firmly members of their particular box. Others recognized that although they belonged mainly in one category, there were aspects of their coaching that occasionally crossed over.

COACHING LEADERS/BEHAVIORAL COACHING. This is the largest and most inclusive category. Typically, the focus of such coaching is on a leader's behaviors, style, vision, or practice. The coach works with the coachee to understand and optimize his or her effectiveness in key relationships.

CAREER/LIFE COACHING. All coaching involves change, but coaching for transition focuses on change that is a part of distinct shifts in level or circumstance. Some coaches work on guiding a leader or leadership team through a major organizational shift such as occurs during a merger or acquisition. Others work at optimizing a leader's capabilities as required by a new level of responsibility. Still others define the career options for an individual who is seeking a new position, level of responsibility, environment, or role.

COACHING FOR LEADERSHIP DEVELOPMENT. Leadership development coaches work to instill a capability in the leader or leadership team to bring the organization to another level of effectiveness. In some cases, this means helping the leader become a coach himself or herself.

COACHING FOR ORGANIZATIONAL CHANGE. To some degree, coaching for organizational change is another catchall category, defined more by its variety than by any unifying approach. However, each of the coaches interviewed focused on the leader's ability to steer the organization through a period of change or to a distinctly different level of capability. Some coaches, for example, focused on developing the organization's capacity to innovate, others on the capacity of the leadership team to guide the organization through crisis and uncertainty. In any case, coaching for leadership behaviors, competitive strategy, team building, and change were common ideas acknowledged by each coach.

STRATEGY COACHING. Coaching for strategy, because it is more organizationally focused, can cover a broad range of challenges. Primarily, it is focused on coaching a leader or leadership team to understand its emerging competitive landscape, in order to dominate that future space, five to seven years down the road. Hardcore analysis, development and deployment of strategy, and implementation of organizational change are all aspects of strategy coaching. As a result, the coach must be able to guide the leader through the important stages of the journey. This means that coaching for personal effectiveness, leadership behaviors, team building, and organizational change can all be important to the engagement.

ENSURING FIT

Once the decision to hire a coach has been made, how does the client judge whether a particular coach will be a good fit for the coachee and the organization's needs? It is necessary to consider the appropriateness of the coach in terms of background, ability, organizational fit, and human chemistry. This will increase the likelihood of success.

Alignment of Values

Although alignment of values is rarely considered, a mismatch in values set leads to failure. The coach's values, demonstrated in his or her approach, methods, and personal philosophy, must be a good match for the organization. A hard-driving organization that values internal competition over team harmony, for instance, would not be well served by a coach who works to increase effectiveness by improving interpersonal relations. An organization oriented toward short-term profits might be out of line with a coach whose work is most effective at instilling long-range capabilities. Stark contrasts in these points of view will lead to conflict between coach and client, and result in a poor return on investment. It might even place the coachee in some degree of career jeopardy.

Wisdom, Insight, and Intuitive Leaps

Has the coach walked a mile in the coachee's shoes? The coach must be able to understand the challenges of the person being coached. Ideally, the coach has had direct, personal experience that relates to the coachee's current concerns and needs. Quite often, coaches who advise senior leaders have been senior leaders themselves, or have worked so closely with such people that familiarity is very high. It shouldn't be assumed, however, that because a coach works well with senior leaders, his or her ability transfers automatically to more junior levels. Pressures, responsibilities, challenges, and opportunities can be very different.

Experience provides the coach with credibility. The coach should know how to present him- or herself in a way that makes his or her messages heard and understood. It doesn't matter how wonderful the advice or counsel is. If the coach does not project credibility, the message will go unheeded.

Technical knowledge or expertise can also matter, but is not nearly as important as one might think. The coach, to a certain extent, can actually be well served by a lack of direct technical knowledge. This forces the coachee to articulate issues in greater detail, and opens the door for the fresh perspective of a newcomer. Regardless of the level of technical experience and understanding, the coach's questioning and insight must add value to the situation. If suggestions and questions are inappropriate or unhelpful, frustration will build.

But the expectations for the value that coaches provide should be even higher. Best practice coaches absorb information about the organization, the individual, the technical concerns, and the objectives—not just to steer the coachee appropriately, but also to bring him or her to entirely new levels of performance. The coach does so by making intuitive leaps.

He or she has an ability to see patterns and connect the dots in ways that the individual could never manage alone.

Evaluating the coach's experience, wisdom, and intuitive capabilities is no easy feat. One method of doing so is to ask concrete, behavior-based questions about past coaching engagements.

What Are the Coach's Other Dealings in the Industry?

Just as the network of senior leaders and board members is a tangled web, so the network of best practice coaches may extend beyond the client's organization to competitors. The client can be excused for asking the question, "Can the coach serve two masters?"

Confidentiality is not the issue. Coaches have strong personal ethics when it comes to confidentiality and would damage their reputations if they ever violated their obligations. Nevertheless, clients should consider how the coach's other dealings in the industry may affect the guidance being given. Can the coach be a committed partner in success? That's a judgment that can only be made based on the individuals involved.

On the other hand, many coaches that we surveyed frequently found themselves in exactly this scenario—and declared it to be a benefit rather than a detriment to their ability to provide service. A knowledge of the industry, the competitive landscape, the innovations taking place, and overall best practices are resources to the client in terms of crafting solutions unique to his or her circumstances. The essence of coaching is customized help. Whereas a consulting organization might provide the same plug-and-play advice, even to direct competitors, the coach is working in partnership with the client to discover unique solutions together.

Can the Coach Operate Effectively with More Than One Coachee in the Same Organization?

Quite often, the success of a coaching engagement with one leader will lead to the coach being retained by another leader in the same organization. The quality of results and impact can lead the coach to be passed around like an exciting new book that simply has to be read. In particular, if the coach has worked with a senior leader or CEO, it might be considered important for others to become schooled as well.

Each individual coach knows whether he or she can operate effectively with multiple leaders, or when tasked at different levels within the organization. Some coaches see that as a desired state because they are able to work most effectively at driving change, strategy, effectiveness, or team work when they become roving coaches. Some clients and coachees may view this with alarm when they consider possible breaches of trust and confidentiality. Certainly, trust and confidentiality are at issue, but problems can be avoided if the ground rules are clear and followed openly. In some organizations, the mandate for development is so insistent and clear that coaches will be working openly with superiors, colleagues, and reports to drive performance improvements. The organization needs to determine what is acceptable for its culture and direction.

Human Chemistry

Coaching is a partnership that thrives on trust, confidence, and forward progress. Coaches and coachees often develop a very strong relationship, even a strong friendship, during the course of working together. Best practice coaches are able to inspire that foundation from the very first stages of the engagement.

Nevertheless, a coachee will not obtain a great deal of benefit from someone he or she dislikes or, conversely, someone he or she likes a great deal but who is unwilling or unable to push him or her in the right direction. Personal likes and dislikes shouldn't be prime factors, but coaching will not be successful if the coachee is highly resistant to the coach. Where's the balance?

The client must make that decision by weighing all factors. For example, if the coachee is uncomfortable with assertive people but needs to develop more assertive behavior, a coach with a dominant and hard-driving personality may be the ticket. If a coachee is from the old school and does not respect the contributions of female reports, then a determined female coach may rearrange their worldview. There are times when likes and dislikes, personal preferences, and comfort levels and biases should be ignored.

Best practice coaches develop the human chemistry needed for success. By the end of any successful coaching relationship, the bond between coach and coachee will be present.

OD Leadership

Fostering Change from the Inside

External consultants have played a key role in the history of OD, but there are also key leadership roles for insiders: top leadership, internal consultants, motivated organizational citizens. The chapters in Part Five address general skills and understandings needed to launch or nourish development and change from different positions within an organization. The ideas address core issues in organization development, although none of the pieces were written as explicit contributions to the OD literature. To its benefit, OD informs its work with a variety of perspectives and insights. The field has a long history of welcoming relevant contributions from a range of disciplines and practices.

Part Five begins with an excerpt from Lee G. Bolman and Terrence E. Deal's classic book, *Reframing Organizations: Artistry, Choice, and Leadership.* The chapter explores change processes through four different lenses—structure, people, politics, and organizational symbols—and complements the Joan V. Gallos chapter, "Reframing Complexity: A Four-Dimensional Approach to Organizational Diagnosis, Development, and Change," in Part Three. Bolman and Deal provide an integrated framework for understanding different levels of issues that must be addressed for successful organizational change.

Although fewer organizations may have internal OD functions or internal consulting departments today than they did in OD's heyday, many still do. And, even without the title, internal consulting functions may be performed by human resource professionals or by individuals in training and development departments. Whatever they are called, internal consultants face a unique set of challenges and pressures. Alan Weiss takes a grounded look at those, as well as the strategies needed for effective service, in "What Constitutes an Effective Internal Consultant?"

OD from its inception has viewed the support of organizational leadership as essential to its success. Knowledge and commitment from those at the top demonstrate the seriousness of the change effort—and communicate the organization's willingness to support and reward its outcomes. Gene Boccialetti, in "Reversing the Lens: Dealing with Different Styles When You Are the Boss," offers suggestions for supporting and working effectively with diverse subordinates—an essential for fostering organization development and change. The chapter provides a different view of life at the top, enlarging the perspective offered by Michael J. Sales in "Understanding the Power of Position: A Diagnostic Model" in Part Three.

Initiation of change from the top is helpful, but it is not the only way. Individuals down through the organization may in fact understand the need for change better than those far above. Too often, however, they translate their subordinate role into a submissive stance toward those higher up in the organization. All organizations need leadership from individuals throughout their ranks, and benefit when those at the top and the bottom recognize and enact this. John Kotter, in "Relations with Superiors: The Challenge of 'Managing' a Boss," advocates for leading one's boss and explores skills and strategies for influencing upward.

The final chapter in Part Five is an excerpt from *The Leadership Challenge,* by James Kouzes and Barry Posner. It addresses an important issue across organizational positions: how to forge a sense of common vision and purpose. No organization development or change effort succeeds without it. Giving life, voice, and passion to a shared future sustains the hard work of change.

CHAPTER TWENTY-TWO

Reframing Change

Training, Realigning, Negotiating, Grieving, and Moving On

Lee G. Bolman
Terrence E. Deal

In 2002, the United States was almost the only nation not yet officially converted to the metric system. This seems strange, given that as far back as July 1958 the Federal Register contained provisions that "all calibrations in the U.S. customary system of weights and measurements carried out by the National Bureau of Standards will continue to be based on metric measurement and standards." It seems even more peculiar because in 1996 all federal agencies were ordered to adopt the metric system. For years, the United States has been urged to align its weights and measures with the rest of the world. Yet there has been little progress, even though America's adherence to a thousand-year-old English system (which the English have been slowly abandoning) has many costs. It handicaps international commerce, for example, and it led to measurement confusion in the design of the Hubble space telescope that cost taxpayers millions of dollars.

America's metric inertia illustrates a predictable dynamic of change that scuttles many bold new plans. Organizations spend millions of dollars on change strategies that either produce no change or make things worse. Mergers fail. Technology misses its potential. Strategies that are vital to success never make it into practice. This chapter opens by describing typical flaws in efforts to change organizations. It then moves from barriers to opportunities, developing a multiframe analysis of the change process to show how training, structural realignment, political bargaining, and symbolic rituals of letting go can achieve more positive outcomes. It goes on to describe an integrated model of the change process and concludes with a case study illustrating effective change.

A COMMON CHANGE SCENARIO

DDB Bank (a pseudonym) is one of the largest banks in Southeast Asia, with more than sixty branches and thirteen thousand employees, and a network of correspondent banks throughout the world. The bank has been uniformly profitable since its founding more than fifty years ago. Its loan portfolio is sound. Shareholders, capital markets, and government regulators universally give the bank high marks.

When he became general manager of DDB's main branch, Thomas Lo was one of a few managers dissatisfied with the bank's performance. In fourteen years with Citibank in various parts of the world, he had learned to think strategically and to feel at home in a dynamic, fast-moving organization. For years—generations, even—DDB's strategy had been very conservative. Its branches created a large deposit base. Particularly in rural areas, depositors stayed with DDB as long as they felt their money was safe and readily accessible. A low-cost deposit base enabled DDB to make loans at reasonable but profitable rates of interest—a key to the bank's solid profitability. It had stable, long-term relationships with both borrowers and depositors. In making decisions, managers could usually rely on explicit policies and procedures.

Staff and personnel policies also reflected DDB's reliance on stability and systems. Jobs and grades were defined in detail, with a clear career path from entry level position up to branch manager. Two main requirements governed upward movement: (1) complete the minimum time in grade, and (2) follow established rules and procedures to the letter. Meeting these criteria ensured a steady, predictable career.

The decision to hire Thomas Lo was controversial, and it split the management team. A faction led by Executive Vice President William Tun, head of all domestic branches, embraced the principle "If it's not broken, don't fix it." This group favored leaving well enough alone. An opposing group argued that the bank had to anticipate changes on the horizon. This contingent was led by Philip Neo, executive vice president in charge of corporate banking.

The more progressive group emphasized that the banking industry was becoming much more competitive as government regulation relaxed. This faction felt the traditional deposit base could no longer be taken for granted. To stay competitive, they maintained, DDB had to focus on superior customer service and innovative strategies to defend and extend its deposit base. Thomas Lo was recruited to make the main branch a role model for other DDB branches.

Lo hit the ground running. Within three months, a five-year plan was produced, and implementation got under way. Branch managers received targets for loans, deposits, and profitability. This last item got highest priority. Information systems were revamped so that targets could be monitored continuously. The main branch was reorganized. New positions for a marketing manager and a planning manager were added. Though Lo advertised these positions internally so as to appear to be in line with existing policies, his real intention was to hire outsiders and inject new blood into the main branch.

Lo also pressed for other changes. He argued for a new performance appraisal system to identify strong performers and move them rapidly upward. He wanted a more flexible salary scale: less emphasis on time in grade and more room for merit increases. He encouraged the human resource department to develop new career paths for moving people between branches and for making lateral transfers between branches and the head office. Most of the staff had degrees in accounting or economics, but Lo wanted a new breed of movers and shakers—even if their studies were unrelated to banking.

Six months later, Lo concluded that his innovations were having almost no effect on day-to-day activities. The problem was not open resistance but covert foot dragging. Some managers claimed they were working to implement the changes but offered many excuses for falling behind schedule. Others nodded their heads in public agreement but privately carried on doing things the old way. Lo began seriously considering leaving DDB to join a smaller, more dynamic investment banking firm.

Lo's story is all too familiar: hopeful beginnings, a turbulent middle, and a discouraging ending. Alert readers might note that Lo's story has parallels to other unsucessful change cases. Lo's subordinates may have felt that they were not resisting change but protecting the organization. Similarly, Thomas Lo had much in common with bosses in those failed situations: all bring fresh ideas to revitalize stodginess, and are frustrated with the difficulty of moving change through their organizations.

Lo's story illustrates an ironclad law: change rationally conceived usually fails. Like Lo, change agents misread or overlook unanticipated consequences of their actions. They march blindly down their chosen path despite warning signs that they are headed in the wrong direction. Over scores of change efforts, we continue to see managers whose strategies are limited because they are wedded to one or two frames. Some try to produce major change by redesigning formal structures, only to find people unable or unwilling to carry out new responsibilities. Others import new people or retrain old ones, only to find new blood and new ideas are rejected or assimilated, often disappearing without a trace.

Organizational change is a multiframe undertaking. It never works to retrain people without revising roles, or to revamp roles without retraining. Managers who anticipate that new roles require new skills and vice versa have much greater likelihood of success. Change also alters power relationships and undermines existing agreements and pacts. Even more profoundly, it intrudes on deeply rooted symbolic forms, traditional ways, and ritual behavior. Below the surface, the organization's social tapestry begins to unravel, threatening both time-honored traditions and prevailing cultural values and practices. In the remainder of the chapter, we look at the human resource, structural, political, and symbolic aspects of organizational change and integrate them with Kotter's model of the change process.

Each frame offers a distinctive view of major issues in change. The human resource frame focuses on needs and skills, the structural frame on alignment and clarity, the political frame on conflict and arenas, and the symbolic frame on loss of meaning and the importance of creating new symbols and ways. Each frame highlights a set of barriers and posits possibilities for making change stick.

CHANGE AND TRAINING

It sounds simplistic to point out that investment in change calls for collateral investment in training. Yet countless reform initiatives falter because managers neglect to spend time and money on developing necessary new knowledge and skills. In too many organizations, the human resource department is an afterthought no one really takes seriously.

In one large firm, for example, top management decided to purchase state-of-the-art technology. They were confident the investment would yield a 50 percent cut in cycle time from a customer order to delivery. Faster turnaround would yield a decisive competitive advantage. The strategy was crafted during hours of careful analysis. The new technology was launched with great fanfare. The CEO assured a delighted sales force it would now have a high-tech competitive edge. After the initial euphoria faded, though, the sales force realized its old methods were obsolete; years of experience were useless. Veterans suddenly felt like neophytes. When the CEO heard that the sales force was shaky about the new technology, he said, "Then find someone in human resources to throw something together. You know, what's-her-name, the new human resources vice president. That's why we hired her." A year later, the new technology had failed to deliver. The training never materialized. The company's investment ultimately yielded a costly, inefficient technology and a demoralized sales force. The window of opportunity was lost to the competition.

In contrast, a large hospital invested millions of dollars in a new integrated information system. The goal was to improve patient care by making updated information available to everyone involved in a treatment plan. Terminals linked patients' bedsides to nursing stations, attending physicians, pharmacy, and other services. To ensure that the new system would work, hospital administrators created a simulation lab. Individual representatives from all groups were brought into a room and seated at terminals. Hypothetical scenarios gave them a chance to practice and work out the kinks. Many, particularly physicians, needed to improve their computer skills. Coaches were there to help. Each group became its own self-help support system. Both skills and confidence improved in the training session. Relationships that formed across various functions were invaluable as the system was implemented.

From a human resource perspective, people have good reason to resist change. No one likes feeling anxious and incompetent. Changes in routine practice and procedure undermine existing knowledge and skills, and they undercut people's ability to perform with confidence and success. When asked to do something they don't understand, don't know how to do, or don't believe in, people feel puzzled, anxious, and insecure. Lacking skills and confidence to implement the new ways, they resist or even sabotage, awaiting the return of the good old days. Or, like Thomas Lo's subordinates, they may comply superficially while covertly dragging their feet. Even if they try to do what they are told, the results are predictably dismal. Sometimes, resistance is sensible; it produces better results than the new methods. Training, psychological support, and participation all increase the likelihood that people will understand and feel comfortable with the new methods.

Often overlooked in the training loop are those responsible for guiding the change. Kotter presents a vivid example of how training can prepare people to communicate the rationale for a new order of things. A company moving to a team-based structure developed by twenty top managers was concerned about how workers and trade unions would react. To make sure people would understand and accept the changes, the managers went through an intensive training regimen: "Our twenty 'communicators' practiced and practiced. They learned the responses, tried them out, and did more role plays until they felt comfortable with nearly anything that might come at them. Handling 200 issues well may sound like too much, but we did it. . . . I can't believe that what we did is not applicable nearly everywhere. I think too many people wing it" (Kotter & Cohen, 2002, p. 86).

CHANGE AND REALIGNMENT

Individual skills and confidence cannot guarantee success unless structure is also realigned to the new initiative. As an example, a school system created a policy requiring principals to assume a more active role in supervising classroom instruction. Principals were trained in how to observe and counsel teachers. Morale problems and complaints soon began to surface. No one had asked how changes in principals' duties might affect teachers. Nor had anyone thought to question existing agreements about authority. Was it legitimate, in teachers' eyes, for principals to spend time in classrooms observing them and suggesting ways to improve teaching? Most important, no one had asked who would handle administrative duties for which principals no longer had time. As a result, supplies were often delayed, parents felt neglected, and discipline deteriorated. By midyear, most principals were back to concentrating on their administrative duties and leaving teachers alone.

Structure confers clarity, predictability, and security. Formal roles prescribe duties and outline how work is to be performed. Policies and standard operating procedures synchronize diverse efforts into well-coordinated programs. Formal allocation of authority lets everyone know who is in charge, when, and over what. Change undermines existing arrangements, creating ambiguity, confusion, and distrust. People no longer know what is expected or what to expect from others. Everyone may think someone else is in charge when, in fact, no one is.

Consider another example. In the wake of changes in health care, a hospital was experiencing substantial employee turnover and absenteeism, a shortage of nurses, poor communication, and low staff morale. There were rumors of an impending effort to organize a union. A consultant's report identified several structural problems:

> One set related to top management. Members of the executive committee seemed to be confused about their roles and authority. Many believed all important decisions were made (prior to the meetings) by Rettew, the hospital administrator. Many shared the perception that major decisions were made behind closed doors, and that Rettew often made "side deals" with different individuals, promising them special favors or rewards in return for support at the committee meetings. People at this level felt manipulated, confused, and dissatisfied.
>
> Major problems also existed in the nursing service. The director of nursing seemed to be patterning her managerial style after that of Rettew.... Nursing supervisors and head nurses felt that they had no authority, while staff nurses complained about a lack of direction and openness by the nursing administration. The structure of the organization was unclear. Nurses were unaware of what their jobs were, whom they should report to, and how decisions were made. (McLennan, 1989, p. 231)

As the school and hospital examples both illustrate, when things start to shift people become unsure about their duties, how to relate to others, and who has authority to decide what. Clarity, predictability, and rationality give way to confusion, loss of control, and a sense that politics rather than policy rules. To minimize such difficulty, change efforts must anticipate structural issues and work to realign roles and relationships. In some situations, this can be done informally. In others, structural arrangements need to be renegotiated more formally.

CHANGE AND CONFLICT

Change invariably creates conflict. It spawns a hotly contested tug-of-war to determine winners and losers. Some individuals and groups support the change; others are dead set in opposition. Too often, conflicts submerge and smolder beneath the surface. Occasionally, they burst back into the open as outbreaks of unregulated warfare.

A case in point comes from a U.S. government initiative to improve America's rural schools. The Experimental Schools Project provided funds for comprehensive changes. It also carefully documented experiences of ten participating districts over a five-year period. The first year—the planning period—was free of conflict. But as plans became actions, hidden issues boiled to the surface. A Northwest school district illustrates a common pattern:

> In the high school, a teacher evaluator explained the evaluation process while emphasizing the elaborate precautions to insure the raters would be unable to connect specific evaluations with specific teachers. He also passed out copies of the check-list used to evaluate the [evaluation forms]. Because of the tension the subject aroused, he joked that teachers could use the list to "grade" their own [forms]. He got a few laughs; he got more laughs when he encouraged teachers to read the evaluation plan by suggesting, "If you have fifteen minutes to spare and are really bored, you should read this section." When another teacher pointed out that her anonymity could not be maintained because she was the only teacher in her subject, the whole room broke into laughter, followed by nervous and derisive questions and more laughter.
>
> When the superintendent got up to speak, shortly afterwards, he was furious. He cautioned teachers for making light of the teacher evaluators who, he said, were trying to protect the staff. Several times he repeated that because teachers did not support the [project] they did not care for students. "Your attitude," he concluded, "is damn the children and full speed ahead!" He then rushed out of the room.
>
> The superintendent's speech put the high school in turmoil. The woman who questioned the confidentiality of the procedure was in tears. Most teachers were incensed at the superintendent's outburst, and a couple said they came close to quitting. As word of the event spread through the system, it caused reverberations in other buildings as well. (Firestone, 1977, pp. 174–175)

After a heated exchange, conflict between the administration and teachers intensified. The school board got involved and reduced the superintendent's authority. Rumors he might be fired undermined his clout even more.

Such a scenario is predictable. As changes emerge, camps form: supporters, opponents, and fence-sitters. Conflict is avoided or smoothed over until eventually erupting in divisive battles. Coercive power may determine the winner. Often, the status quo prevails and change agents lose. From a political perspective, conflict is a natural part of life. It is managed through processes of negotiation and bargaining, where settlements and agreements can be hammered out. If ignored, disputes explode into street fights. Street fights have no rules. Anything goes. People get hurt, and scars last for years.

The alternative to street fights are arenas with rules, referees, and spectators. Arenas create opportunities to forge divisive issues into shared agreements. Through bargaining, compromises can be worked out between the status quo and innovative ideals. Welding new ideas onto existing practices is essential to successful change. One hospital administrator said, "The board and I had to learn how to wrestle in a public forum."

Mitroff describes a drug company facing competitive pressure to its branded, prescription drug from generic substitutes. Management was split into three factions: one group wanted to raise the price of the drug, another wanted to lower it, and still another wanted to keep it the same but cut costs (Mitroff, 1983). Each group collected information, constructed models, and developed reports showing that its solution was correct. The process degenerated into a frustrating spiral. Mitroff intervened to get each group to identify major stakeholders and articulate respective assumptions about them. All agreed the most critical stakeholders were physicians prescribing the drug. Each group had its own suppositions about how physicians would respond to a price change. But no one really knew. The three groups finally agreed to test their assumptions by implementing a price increase in selected markets.

The intervention worked through convening an arena with a more productive set of rules. Similarly, experimental school districts that created arenas for resolving conflict were more successful than others in bringing about comprehensive change. In the school district just cited, teachers reacted to administrative coercion with a power strategy of their own:

Community members initiated a group called Concerned Citizens for Education in response to a phone call from a teacher who noted that parents should be worried about what the [administrators] were doing to their children. The superintendent became increasingly occupied with responding to demands and concerns of the community group. Over time, the group joined in a coalition with teachers to defeat several of the superintendent's supporters on the school board and to elect members who were more supportive of their interests. The turnover in board membership reduced the administrator's power and authority, making it necessary to rely more and more on bargaining and negotiation strategies to promote the intended change. (Deal & Nutt, 1980, p. 20)

Changing always creates division and conflict among competing interest groups. Successful change requires an ability to frame issues, build coalitions, and establish arenas in which disagreements can be forged into workable pacts. One insightful executive remarked: "We need to confront, not duck, and face up to disagreements and differences of opinions and conflicting objectives. . . . All of us must make sure—day in and day out—that conflicts are aired and resolved before they lead to internecine war."

CHANGE AND LOSS

In the early 1980s, America's Cola wars—a battle between Coke and Pepsi—reached a fever pitch. The Pepsi Challenge—a head-to-head taste test—was making inroads in Coca-Cola's market share. In blind tests, even avowed Coke drinkers preferred Pepsi. In a Coke counterchallenge, held at its corporate headquarters in Atlanta, Pepsi again won by a slight margin. Later, Pepsi stunned the industry by signing Michael Jackson to a $5 million celebrity advertising campaign. Coca-Cola executives were getting nervous. They decided on a revolutionary strategy and struck back with one of the most important announcements in the company's ninety-nine-year history: Old Coke would be replaced with New Coke.

Shortly before 11:00 A.M. [on Tuesday, April 23, 1985], the doors of the Vivian Beaumont Theater at Lincoln Center opened to two hundred newspaper, magazine, and TV reporters. The stage was aglow with red. Three huge screens, each solid red and inscribed with the company logo, rose behind the podium and a table draped in red. The lights were low: the music began. "We are. We will always be. Coca-Cola. All-American history." As the patriotic song filled the theater, slides of Americana flashed on the center screen—families and kids, Eisenhower and JFK, the Grand Canyon and wheat fields, the Beatles and Bruce Springsteen, cowboys, athletes, and Statue of Liberty—and interspersed throughout, old commercials for Coke. Robert Goizueta [CEO of Coca-Cola] came to the podium. He first congratulated the reporters for their ingenuity in already having reported what he was about to say. And then he boasted, "The best has been made even better." Sidestepping the years of laboratory research that had gone into the program, Goizueta claimed that in the process of concocting Diet Coke, the company flavor chemists had "discovered" a new formula. And research had shown that consumers preferred this new one to old Coke. Management could then do one of two things: nothing, or buy the world a new Coke. Goizueta announced that the taste-test results made management's decisions "one of the easiest ever made." (Oliver, 1986, p. 132)

The rest is history. Coke drinkers rejected the new product. They felt betrayed, and many were outraged: "Duane Larson took down his collection of Coke bottles and outside of his restaurant hung a sign, 'They don't make Coke anymore' [. . . .] Dennis Overstreet of Beverly Hills hoarded 500 cases of old Coke and advertised them for $30 a case. He is almost sold out. . . . San Francisco *Examiner* columnist Bill Mandel called it 'Coke for wimps' [. . . .] Finally, Guy Mullins exclaimed, 'When they took old Coke off the market, they violated my freedom of choice—baseball, hamburgers, Coke—they're all the fabric of America'" (Morganthau, 1985, pp. 32–33).

Even bottlers and Coca-Cola employees were aghast: "By June the anger and resentment of the public was disrupting the personal lives of Coke employees, from the top executives to the company secretaries. Friends and acquaintances were quick to attack, and once proud employees now shrank from displaying to the world any association with the Coca-Cola company" (Oliver, 1986, pp. 166–167).

Coca-Cola rebounded quickly with Classic Coke. Indeed, the company's massive miscalculation led to one of the strangest, most serendipitous triumphs in marketing history. All the controversy, passion, and free publicity stirred up by the New Coke fiasco ultimately helped Coca-Cola regain its dominance in the soft drink industry. A brilliant stratagem, if anyone had planned it.

What led Coke's executives into such a quagmire? Several factors were at work. Pepsi was gaining market share. As the newly appointed

CEO of Coca-Cola, Goizueta was determined to modernize the company. A previous innovation, Diet Coke, had been a huge success. Most important, Coca-Cola's revered, long-time "Boss," Robert Woodruff, had just passed away. On his deathbed, he reportedly gave Goizueta his blessing for the new recipe.

In their zeal to compete with Pepsi, Coke's executives overlooked a central tenet of the symbolic frame. The meaning of an object or event can be far more powerful than the reality. Strangely, Coke's leadership had lost touch with their product's significance to consumers. To many people, old Coke was a piece of Americana. It was linked to cherished memories. Coke represented something far deeper than just a soft drink.

In introducing New Coke, company executives unintentionally announced the passing of an important American symbol. Symbols create meaning, and when a symbol is destroyed or vanishes people experience emotions akin to those at the passing of a spouse, child, old friend, or pet. When a relative or close friend dies, we feel a deep sense of loss. We unconsciously harbor similar feelings when a computer replaces old procedures, a logo changes after a merger, or an old leader is replaced by a new one. When these transitions take place in the workplace rather than in a family, feelings of loss are often denied or attributed to other causes.

Any significant change in an organization triggers two conflicting responses. The first is to keep things as they were, to replay the past. The second is to ignore the loss and rush busily into the future. Individuals or groups can get stuck in either form of denial or bog down vacillating between the two. Nurses in one hospital's intensive care unit were caught in a loss cycle for ten years following their move from an old facility. Four years after AT&T was forced to divest its local phone operations, an executive remarked: "Some mornings I feel like I can set the world on fire. Other mornings I can hardly get out of bed to face another day." Loss is an unavoidable by-product of change. As change accelerates, executives and employees get caught in endless cycles of unresolved grief.

In our personal lives, the pathway from loss to healing is culturally prescribed. Every culture outlines a sequence for transition rituals following significant loss: always a collective experience in which pain is expressed, felt, and juxtaposed against humor and hope. (Think of Irish actor Malachy McCourt who, as his mother lay dying, said to the distressed physician, "Don't worry, Doctor, we come from a long line of dead people.") In many societies, the sequence of ritual steps involves a wake, a funeral, a period of mourning, and some form of commemoration.

From a symbolic perspective, ritual is an essential companion to significant change. A military change-of-command ceremony is formally scripted. A wake is held for the outgoing commander, and the torch is passed publicly to the new commander in full ceremony. After a period of time, the old commander's face or name is displayed in a picture or plaque. Transition rituals initiate a sequence of steps that help people let go of the past, deal with a painful present, and move into a meaningful future. The form of these rites varies widely, but without them people are blocked from facing loss. They then vacillate between hanging on to the past and plunging into a meaningless future. Disruption of attachment even to negative symbols or harmful symbolic activities needs to be marked by some form of expressive event. The occasion should help people let go of old ways and offer something new that they can grasp to move ahead.

Owen (1987) vividly documents these issues in his description of change at "Delta Corporation." An entrepreneur named Harry invented a product that created enough demand to support a company of thirty-five hundred people. After a successful initial public stock offering, the company soon experienced soaring costs, flattened sales, and a dearth of new products. Facing stockholder dissatisfaction and charges of mismanagement, Harry passed the torch to a new leader.

Harry's replacement was very clear about her vision: she wanted "engineers who could fly." But her vision was juxtaposed against a history of "going downhill." Another problem was that various parts of the company were governed by a complicated array of stories, each representing a different Delta theme. Finance division stories exemplified the new breed of executives brought in following Harry's departure. Research and development stories varied by organizational level. At the executive level, "Old Harry" stories extolled the creative accomplishments of the former CEO. Middle management stories focused on the Golden Fleece award given monthly behind the scenes to the researcher who developed the idea with the least bottom-line potential. On the production benches, workers told of Serendipity Sam, winner of more Golden Fleece awards than anyone else, exemplar of the excitement and innovation of Harry's regime.

Instead of a company sharing a common story, Delta was a collection of independent cells, each with its own story. Across the levels and divisions, the stories clustered into two competing themes: the newcomers' focus on management versus the company's tradition of innovation. The new CEO recognized the importance of blending old and new to build a company where "engineers could fly." She brought thirty-five people from across the company to a management retreat where she surprised everyone:

> She opened with some stories of the early days, describing the intensity of Old Harry and the Garage Gang (now known as the Leper Colony). She even had one of the early models of Harry's machine out on a table. Most people had never seen one. It looked primitive, but during the coffee break, members of the Leper Colony surrounded the ancient artifact, and began swapping tales of the blind alleys, the late nights, and the breakthroughs. That dusty old machine became a magnet. Young shop floor folks went up and touched it, sort of snickering as they compared this prototype with the sleek creations they were manufacturing now. But even as they snickered, they stopped to listen as the Leper Colony recounted tales of accomplishment. It may have been just a 'prototype,' but that's where it all began. (Owen, 1987, p. 172)

After a coffee break, the CEO divided the group into subgroups to share their hopes for the company. When the participants returned, their chairs had been rearranged into a circle with Old Harry's prototype in the center. With everyone facing one another, the CEO led a discussion, linking the stories from the various subgroups. Serendipity Sam's account of a new product possibility came out in a torrent of technical jargon:

> The noise level was fierce, but the rest of the group was being left out. Taking Sam by the hand, the CEO led him to the center of the circle right next to the old prototype. There it was, the old and the new— the past, present, and potential. She whispered in Sam's ear that he ought to take a deep breath and start over in words of one syllable. He did so, and in ways less than elegant, the concept emerged. He guessed about applications, competitors, market shares, and before long the old VP for finance was drawn in. No longer was he thinking about selling [tax] losses, but rather thinking out loud about how he was going to develop the capital to support the new project. The group from the shop floor . . . began to spin a likely tale as to how they might transform

the assembly lines in order to make Sam's new machine. Even the Golden Fleece crowd became excited, telling each other how they always knew that Serendipity Sam could pull it off. They conveniently forgot that Sam had been the recipient of a record number of their awards, to say nothing of the fact that this new idea had emerged in spite of all their rules. (Owen, 1987, pp. 173–174)

In one intense event, part of the past was buried, yet its spirit was resurrected and revised to fit the new circumstances. Disparaging themes and stories were merged into a company where "engineers could fly" profitably.

CHANGE STRATEGY

The frames constitute a comprehensive checklist of issues that change agents must recognize and respond to. But how can they be combined into an integrated model? How does the change process move through time? John Kotter, an influential student of leadership and change, has studied both successful and unsuccessful change efforts in organizations around the world. In his book *The Heart of Change* (2002, written with Dan S. Cohen), he summarizes what he has learned. His basic message is very much like ours. Too many change initiatives fail because they rely too much on "data gathering, analysis, report writing, and presentations" instead of a more creative approach aimed at grabbing the "feelings that motivate useful action." In other words, change agents fail when they rely almost entirely on reason and structure and neglect human, political, and symbolic elements.

Kotter describes eight stages that he repeatedly found in successful change initiatives:

1. Creating a sense of urgency
2. Pulling together a guiding team with the needed skills, credibility, connections, and authority to move things along
3. Creating an uplifting vision and strategy
4. Communicating the vision and strategy through a combination of words, deeds, and symbols
5. Removing obstacles, or empowering people to move ahead
6. Producing visible signs of progress through short-term victories

7. Sticking with the process and refusing to quit when things get tough

8. Nurturing and shaping a new culture to support the emerging innovative ways

Kotter's stages are a model of a change process moving through time, though not necessarily unfolding in a linear sequence. In the real world, stages overlap, and change agents sometimes need to cycle back to earlier phases.

Consider, for example, Kotter's first stage, developing a sense of urgency. Strategies from the human resource, political, and symbolic strategies all contribute. Symbolically, leaders can construct a persuasive story by painting a picture of the current challenge or crisis and why failure to act would be catastrophic. Human resource techniques of participation and open meetings would help to get the story out and gauge audience reaction. Behind the scenes, leaders could meet with key players, assess their interests, and negotiate or use power as necessary to get people on board.

As another example, Kotter's fifth step calls for removing obstacles and empowering people to move forward. Structurally, this is a matter of identifying rules, roles, procedures, and patterns blocking progress and then working to realign them. Meanwhile, the human resource frame counsels training and providing support and resources to enable people to master new behaviors. Symbolically, a few "public hangings" (for example, firing, demoting, or exiling prominent opponents) could reinforce the message. Every situation and change effort is unique. Creative change agents can use the ideas to stimulate thinking and spur imagination as they develop an approach that fits local circumstances.

TEAM ZEBRA

A look at the successful restructuring of Kodak's Black-and-White Film Division might attribute much of the division's success to structural improvements: integrated flows, performance measures and standards, cross-functional teams, lateral coordination, and local decision making. These changes contributed substantially to the division's ability to reduce inventory, cut waste, improve relations with suppliers, and speed delivery time. All improvements paved the way for the division's transformation and return to profitability.

There is more to the story. Structural changes were necessary but not sufficient. Reengineering guru Michael Hammer, noting the disappointing outcomes of many restructuring efforts, acknowledged that there is more to change than redesigning process and structure. Team Zebra exemplifies an integrated multiframe approach to change.

Top-down, Bottom-up Structural Design

The division's first structural overhaul in a century was announced at a meeting for all employees. The shock was lessened by assurances that the initial changes were experimental, and that more substantive changes would appear gradually over a six-month period. This gave employees an opportunity to shape the initiative to fit local working conditions. Reasons for the change were clearly explained and reinforced by management, which had earlier learned in very graphic terms of the division's poor performance record from Jim Frangos, the divisional manager:

> During a special meeting convened one warm day in September, I rattled off my list of performance shockers to the Zebra managers. The reaction was one of disbelief and anger. "How could we have been kept in the dark so long?" People demanded to know. During my talk I boiled the issue down to the bitter problems that deeply eroded profit margins and made us dinosaurs in the marketplace.
>
> "You know about all the waste problems," I said. "But did you know we can't sell one-third of everything we make? We load up 1,000 dump trucks with wasted products every year."
>
> A whistle of disbelief broke the ensuing silence.
>
> "Imagine a consumer product company or automobile manufacturer tossing out one-third of its product—they'd be out of business in no time flat! Can you think of *any* organization that can survive that level of waste?" "Yeah, the federal government," someone called out from the back of the room.
>
> That started a spate of laughter, and took the edge off the meeting. I wanted people to feel concerned, but not personally threatened. (Frangos, 1996, pp. 65–66)

This opening round is a good example of the first stage in Kotter's model of change: building a sense of urgency. The managers learned that half their finished product sat in inventory, only 10 percent of their products were improved each year, the percentage of work performed during the manufacturing process was about one percent, and they were able to deliver products on time in only 66 percent of the cases. At the end of the meeting, some one asked angrily, "How have we managed to stay afloat so long?" (Frangos, 1996, p. 67).

The shared sense of crisis, combined with an opportunity for everyone to fine-tune and tinker with the radical new design, helped to realign roles and relationships so the new structure worked for, rather than against, people's efforts. Responsibility for shaping and implementing change was widely shared: "Mary Cutcliffe, an emulsion-making operator, went to have her foot x-rayed and discovered her physician was not using Kodak film. She asked him why. He said he didn't think a company the size of Kodak would care about a small town physician like himself. On returning to work she asked 'why not'? Her question led to a plan to focus aggressively on doctors with in-house labs" (Frangos, 1996, p. 120).

Zack Potter, on a family vacation, overheard a photographer complain about Kodak's poor service. When he returned, he spent his morning break and lunch hour trying to find out who was responsible. That afternoon the photographer received a call with the needed information (Frangos, 1996, pp. 120–121).

Learning and Training

The division made available several kinds of training. Technical training helped people master new skills needed for changing work patterns. Supervisors, the often overlooked linchpin in any transition from old to new, found ample opportunity to meet with colleagues for training and "peer learning": "In our case we had a hundred year heritage of the drill sergeant model, and many of our first-line supervisors were 20–25 year veterans of the company. We took into account that asking people to adopt new ways of doing their jobs is a threatening proposition, and asking them to relinquish the authority they have 'earned' can seem downright outrageous—unless you can offer them something better. In our case, the 'something better' was a set of unprecedented opportunities: the opportunity to have a greater influence over people through enlightened coaching and teaching" (Frangos, 1996, p. 200).

Supervisors and other employees were given the opportunity to learn new skills in a supportive, psychologically safe environment: "Peer learning is critical, because everyone makes faster gains when they learn from one another. There's also a critical mass phenomenon—when enough first-line supervisors are reporting about their acts of coaching and facilitating, others will feel safe trying the 'new style'" (Frangos, 1996, p. 200).

First-time supervisors and other were included with the management team in Pecos River experimental learning—training in team building: "The Pecos course turned out to be an ingenious blend of talk, music, and high energy exercises, offered in an upbeat and emotionally charged atmosphere. Through experiential learning, the Pecos program helps people to uncover buried layers of creativity, and to relate in new ways to others with whom they might have worked side by side for many years but never have really come to know" (Frangos, 1996, p. 169).

Apart from formal training, the idea that people can learn new skills from their own experience on the job and from others looms as one of Team Zebra's greatest human resource insights. Informal learning groups become unofficial resources anyone can turn to for suggestions on how to improve their performance. As people mastered a particular aspect of the new order of things, a premium was put on sharing (or even stealing) new ideas from others: "Our catch phrase for this sharing of knowledge was to 'steal shamelessly but to remember to say thank you.' Through B&W Views [a division newsletter] and informal seminars put on by [employees], the flow management made a concerted effort to broadcast our success stories. At the same time, people were encouraged to aggressively seek innovative solutions in one part of the flow and then employ them in their own" (Frangos, 1996, p. 182).

Arenas for Venting Conflict

From the early launching of the project, a variety of occasions created arenas or forums for airing people's concerns and grievances. The initiatives changed people's roles, relationships, titles, locations, and working conditions. They threatened a long Kodak tradition of job security. In 1989, even before anything became operational, Jim Frangos convened a series of town meetings to hear all employees' reactions to the planned changes:

> The first of the town meetings was closer to the terrible end of the spectrum than I had hoped. Although I had steeled myself for the worst, I was still taken by surprise by the amount of anger and hostility that erupted like a furious volcano. . . . In hindsight my straight talk

sessions were the first opportunity for the shop floor folks to speak their minds since the company began taking a battering in the Spring. Many were suspicious and completely distrustful of another desperate attempt on management's part to save the company. Some were convinced that they were going to be scapegoats for top management's poor judgment. So for the first month of straight talks I just resigned myself to getting skinned alive as I tried to sell the flow and the improvements it would bring. (Frangos, 1996, pp. 68–69)

The employees' negativity continued even though they were encouraged to get everything off their chest. Reactions to Frangos after the meetings included "The dude is nuts." "What's he been smoking?" "Turnaround? He probably can't even parallel park." "Does he think we're drunk or something?" "What's this 'fun' crap he keeps talking about? Glad I don't have to spend *my* fun off with him" (Frangos, 1996, p. 69).

Later, in 1990, Frangos scheduled a second round of what were now officially labeled Straight Talks. His wife asked him if he was a glutton for punishment. But Frangos knew that, even though the changes were moving along, anger remained. He was putting Kotter's stage seven into practice: he kept going when the going got tough. In the twenty-five or so sessions for all fifteen hundred B&W employees, he found people far less concerned about venting and more interested in "how things were going and what they could do to become part of the solution to our problems" (Frangos, 1996, p. 130).

In the second round, sessions moved beyond politics to encompass the social value of B&W's efforts. As Frangos put it, "I worked hard to reinforce the theme that we were making products important to society. At one meeting, I described Kodak CFT Film, which is used to determine if a patient needs bypass surgery, and Kodak MIN-RH Film, used in the detection of breast cancer. . . . At another I talked about Kodak WL Surveillance Film. Guess what? Every time you use your ATM card, you're being photographed with a camera loaded with 2210 film. Same if you're robbing the bank. Smile for the cameras" (Frangos, 1996, p. 130).

Occasions for Letting Go and Celebrating

Frangos's appeal to the deep purpose of B&W's operation highlights another impressive aspect of the division's turnaround: attention to symbols and culture. A change in physical arrangements was used to symbolize the management team's openness to dialogue: "I think we'd send a strong message to everyone if we got rid of the planning walls and used partitions instead. . . . We've been talking about a cross functional team—why not make the office a symbol of an organization without walls?" (Frangos, 1996, p. 71).

A central symbolic challenge in any transformation is helping people let go of old ways. Team Zebra's mourning rituals centered on humor and fun. Yet the subtext of outwardly zany occasions allowed sadness as well as playfulness. Humor is a powerful tool in making transitions. The line between laughing and crying is often subtle. Frangos understood that people would not let go until they could attach themselves to other symbols.

In the liminal state between release and capture, celebration can serve dual purposes: mourning and meaning making. Team Zebra presents several poignant examples of how symbols and symbolic activity ease the passage from old to new.

KEEPING AN EYE ON CORE VALUES. "Attitudes and morale can't change unless people believe what they're doing has intrinsic worth to the market place, and makes a contribution to other people's lives" (Frangos, 1996, p. 70).

ENCOURAGING RITUAL. Forum meetings, Breakfast Clubs, and other regular gatherings were opportunities for bonding: "The Breakfast Club had become one of the most exciting aspects of the flow. But Team Zebra still needed some kind of 'glue' that would bind the flow together and create a strong feeling of unity. That 'glue' came in the form of a shared vision and the articulation of a set of values and principles to live and work by" (Frangos, 1996, p. 84).

ANCHORING VISION EMBODIED IN METAPHOR AND SYMBOLS. In one meeting the management team chose animals as metaphoric representatives of B&W's unity. One manager chose the mongoose: "One of its claims to fame is being able to defeat and devour poisonous snakes. In fact, I've thrown a few of our competitors down here . . . those snakes in the corner . . . the mongoose is extremely quick . . . tenacious, too. They just keep chipping away at whatever they're working on, just like us" (Frangos, 1996, p. 86).

Visioning experiences led to development of a division logo, "Images of Excellence": a black diamond on one edge with lines passing throughout it. But the superglue, the galvanizing symbol that pulled B&W's fifteen hundred people together, was the zebra. The idea of making the zebra the division mascot crystallized in 1990 during a Secretary's Day excursion to the zoo. As the visitors were admiring two adults and a baby, the zoo director told them: "Every zebra is unique. No two zebras' stripes are the same—kind of like fingerprints. They also run in herds. Being animals that are preyed on, they understand that to the extent they can stay together, they can defend themselves from lions and other predators. In fact, predators probably have a hard time distinguishing the individuals from the mass of black and white stripes" (Frangos, 1996, p. 126).

The visitors picked up on the analogy, observing that each B&W employee brings something unique to the herd. "We need to band together as part of a team—when we're operating as such we 'baffle the competition'" (Frangos, 1996, p. 126). The B&W group became Team Zebra, and in following years the zebra was everywhere.

INVENTING CEREMONIES TO KEEP TEAM SPIRIT HIGH. Numerous skits and awards ceremonies were playful occasions featuring music and merriment. The Whirling Dervish award, for example, honored the group with the best success each month in reducing inventory. The award and trophy (a toy pinwheel mounted on a block of wood) were both invented by employees. "Each month, after reviewing the inventory figures, Bill would announce the team with the best improvement and present the pinwheel. After one group won it three times in a row, the group's managers decided not to 'hog the wheel.' He had the machine shop make a permanent, windmill-like whirling dervish, complete with a plaque. He then relinquished the award for others to enjoy (Frangos, 1996, p. 134).

Another example was a meeting of Zebra's leadership group to review the first year's progress: "The entire workshop was dotted with songs and skits commemorating the first year. Marty, Tim, and Chip had written a number of skits and songs, with Marty playing the keyboard and Rick accompanying her on the banjo. We poked fun at ourselves in a playful way about moving from being victims to being accountable for the results we generated. And as a cap for the event, we donned sweatshirts bearing our new logo and took a team picture. We then had a funeral for the ways of the past" (Frangos, 1996, p. 17).

CONCLUSION

Major organizational change inevitably generates four categories of issues. First, it affects individuals' ability to feel effective, valued, and in control. Without support, training, and a chance to participate in the process, people become a powerful anchor, making forward motion almost impossible. Second, change disrupts existing patterns of roles and relationships, producing confusion and uncertainty. Structural patterns need to be revised and realigned to support the new direction.

Third, change creates conflict between winners and losers—those who benefit from the new direction and those who do not. This conflict requires creation of arenas where the issues can be renegotiated and the political map redrawn. Finally, change creates loss of meaning for recipients rather than owners of the change. Transition rituals, mourning the past, and celebrating the future help people let go of old attachments and embrace new ways of doing things.

CHAPTER TWENTY-THREE

What Constitutes an Effective Internal Consultant?

Alan Weiss

A consultant is someone who provides expertise for a client for a particular issue, concern, opportunity, or problem. That expertise may include knowledge, experiences, processes, models, behaviors, technology, or other assets. An external and an internal consultant both provide this expertise in return for remuneration for the value provided. For an internal consultant, that remuneration is usually a job (and the continuance thereof).

The consultant has a basic, overarching role, which guides all subordinate roles: That role is to improve the client's condition. Just as the doctors say, "First, do no harm," the consultant is only successful if the client is better off after the engagement than before. That improvement may be in the form of a problem fixed, an opportunity exploited, a disaster averted, confidence validated, or any number of other salutary results. But if you haven't improved the client's condition, then you haven't been successful.

Consulting is a relationship business. That means we must develop trusting relationships with internal partners and clients. To me, trust means that both parties have the underlying conviction that the other person has the partner's absolute best interests in mind. Ten ways to develop, nurture, and/or recover trust with line partners include:

1. Learn their issues and understand the realities of their business objectives.
2. Don't approach with a boxed solution, but listen and customize your response.
3. Overcommunicate, and be proactive in your communications.
4. Seek personal interactions over e-mail and voice messages.
5. Proactively suggest approaches to improve their operation; don't wait for pain.
6. Eschew all jargon; "left brain/right brain" thinkers or "driver expressives" really don't matter.
7. Use only validated tools and bury the fads. There aren't many people today using "open meetings" or "future search," or any other nonsense that has no valid base.
8. Spend time doing the work. Don't spend a career in HR or training; work in sales, service, information technology (IT), finance, or wherever you can make a contribution and learn the business.
9. Use metrics that demonstrate progress directly related to your intervention.
10. Share credit, but also take credit. Develop a network of supporters, testimonials, and a history of success.

One of the key problems in internal consulting is a lack of trust. We all know that a lack of credibility attached to a department or function also attaches itself to individuals representing that department or function. When that's the case, it's far easier to build individual trust and credibility than it is to change an entire department's reputation. When enough individuals have made the change, the department will benefit. But functions do not change perceptions; people do. Departments don't earn trust; individuals do.

The role of an internal consultant should place an emphasis on anticipation, improvement, and innovation. There has been an inordinate concentration on problem solving. While always important, problem solving has become a fairly mechanized routine and therefore of less value, despite its frequency. Problem solving basically restores performance to past levels.

But innovation raises the bar and is of much higher value. Since most managers have their noses pressed tightly to the glass of their own operations, they often fail to see the opportunity surrounding them. Catching up with the competition is important, but creating a gap between yourself and the next closest competitor is invaluable.

As a rule, internal consultants have been far too reactive and not nearly proactive enough.

Finally, an important part of the role is to disagree. We're often swept along in the fervor of an executive's bright idea, but no one has had the fortitude to point out that no one is wearing any clothes. Outstanding (and trustworthy) consultants push back. They consider legality, ethics, pragmatics, risks, and costs to other parties. They don't blindly implement.

We have an excellent plumber. He arrives on time, fixes the leaks, and charges according to his efforts. But we would never ask him to come in and discuss the way the kitchen is decorated or the location of the bathrooms.

THE KEY PLAYERS

The most important person in the consultant's universe is the *economic buyer*. The economic buyer is that person who can actually pay for your services. If there's a charge back system, then the economic buyer's budget is the one charged. In any case, he or she is the one whose project is involved.

Other hallmarks of the economic buyer:

- They specify the results that are required.
- They can allocate resources.
- They are the clearly perceived sponsor or champion.
- They will evaluate results.
- Their unit or function is the target of the improved condition.
- They are taking the risk and reaping the rewards.
- The buck stops there.

The economic buyer, in effect, writes the check. There is not a direct hierarchical corollary. Division managers and department heads are often economic buyers (as are always CEOs, CFOs, and so on), but the critical element is the ability to fund the project without further approval. My key buyer in Merck for years was a man with the title of manager of international development, and in Hewlett-Packard a woman who held the position of director of knowledge management.

Many internal consultants try to avoid the economic buyer. Often intimidating and usually influential, the economic buyer presents a problem in some cases, especially in an organization setting in which you've each had your roles defined for a long time. You may well have separate colleagues, never attend the same meetings, and even eat lunch in different settings.

No matter. As a consultant, you need to be a partner of the buyer for the project. If you treat the buyer with deference due the position, or imbue him with Gnostic wisdom because of his rank, or refuse to oppose her because of fear of retribution, then you're a sycophant, not a consultant.

Most projects also have *critical sponsors.* These are people whose support can enlist others to the cause but whose opposition—even quietly—can undermine the entire endeavor. A critical sponsor may be:

- An influential direct report of the buyer
- A union officer
- A highly successful salesperson
- A major customer
- An informal, respected leader

It's important to co-opt the critical sponsors. That means that you and the buyer (hence, one more reason for a trusting partnership there) devise a strategy to convert key sponsors to the cause. This may be an appeal by the buyer, an appeal by you, careful relationship building, the identification of their self-interests, and so on. It may be different for each sponsor. The important thing is to bring them aboard before they scuttle the boat.

Implementers are those people who will have a responsibility for executing the appropriate actions and/or adopting the required behaviors. They may well be resistant, since the present is usually comfortable and the future is problematic. But they must be made situationally uncomfortable, so that maintaining the status quo is not possible.

It's not important that implementers like you; it's simply important that they change in the manner desired. A sales team might not like cross-selling several products when it was accustomed to specializing in a single product, but that's the direction in which they must be driven. The ideal agents for persuading implementers, in order of quality, are:

1. Appeal to enlightened self-interest. Persuade the implementer that he or she is better off by indulging in the new behaviors. For example, demonstrate a higher potential income, or more latitude of action, or greater learning potential.

2. Peer pressure. Develop a sufficient critical mass of converts so that any holdouts seem unenlightened and left in the dust. (The psychologists call this "normative pressure.") If enough people seem happy to make the changes requested, a momentum will be created that will affect the onlookers.

3. Coercion. Make it unbearably painful to continue to resist. The buyer might use the financial pressure inherent in evaluations, incentive compensation, and bonuses; job assignments might be increasingly unpleasant; status may be reduced; there can even be threats about retaining one's position. This is a tactic solely within the purview of the buyer, because the consultant wields no such power.

Move the implementers by whatever means necessary, but move them.

Finally, there are *stakeholders* of various types and varying degrees. These are people whose work or results will be impacted by the project. They may be employees, customers, vendors, management, shareholders, and so on. They have some stake in the quality of the outcomes.

It's a good idea to sample stakeholders early to determine their perceptions of their roles, interests, and impact in terms of the success of the project. It's crazy, for example, to introduce a new incentive system without sampling the sales force or a new pricing policy without talking to customers.

The ideal project will include a partnering relationship with the economic buyer; a strategy that successfully persuades all key sponsors to back you; focused and relatively rapid movement of implementers to execute the plan; and stakeholders who can recognize and support their own improved conditions due to the project.

Having said all that, if you don't have a relationship with the economic buyer, the odds are stacked greatly against you.

THE BASIC DYNAMICS

There are interpersonal and cultural dynamics that occur in virtually every consulting project. Four of these constants are important to master:

1. Resistance to change.

2. Process versus content.

3. The role of culture.

4. We've heard every objection.

1. Resistance to Change

There is a generally accepted myth that holds that people resist change. I've found that to be totally untrue. Every day, people adapt to, adjust for, and anticipate change in the form of roads closed, surprises from their family (good or bad), organizational shifting of priorities, cancellations, abrupt requests, and so on. If people were reluctant to change, we'd all be on heavy medication. Change is the universal norm, and it is both omnipresent and accepted.

What people do resist, however, is ambiguity. Some changes do not involve ambiguity, such as a highway detour that puts one on familiar, though less-traveled streets, or a work shift that involves a sudden trip, but to a site often visited. Other changes produce significant ambiguities: a road detour that takes one to completely unfamiliar territory or a sudden trip to a new country, new client, or new problem.

In organizational change work, most people can relate to the picture painted of the future organization, and all people are intimately familiar with where they are today. But the journey to that new future is likely to be highly ambiguous and unclear.

Work with your client to establish not only the future state desired, but also the details of the journey. For example, delineate the details of the transition, the numbers of people affected, what the universe of stakeholders looks like, likely obstacles, and so on. You'll find that the implementers are far more comfortable following a game plan—and even deviating from it, if necessary—than proceeding with no game plan at all.

2. Process Versus Content

Almost everyone reading this is a *process* consultant. By that I mean that the work you do (in negotiating, facilitating, training, conflict resolution, retention, succession planning, strategy, career development, ad infinitum) is applicable over vast acres of the corporate landscape. Just as good external consultants can readily work cross-industrially and cross-culturally, good internal consultants can readily work cross-functionally and cross-culturally.

In other words, "You don't know our business" is never an applicable phrase!

Processes are applicable in any environment with any content. While it's important to be conversant in the organization's content, it's not important to be expert in it.

Now here's the beauty of the internal consultant: At least you are living in the environment and, the longer you are there, presumably, the more you do become a content expert in the organization's work, to a greater degree than an outsider like me ever could. But don't be tripped up internally. Just because you've worked primarily for sales doesn't mean you can't work for finance, and merely because you've been working domestically doesn't mean you can't provide your expertise internationally.

Many internal consultants make the mistake of believing that they must become as expert as the people they are trying to help, and that's just crazy. Consultants who work with medical practices cannot perform surgery, and jury consultants don't attempt to try cases themselves in court (because they can't). In fact, the very power that you bring is that of someone untainted by the content and able to bring the best practices from a diverse array of internal units and operations. Whatever you do, don't become the content expert for actuarial services, or call center response, or building security.

The more processes you master, and the more agility with which you can apply them, the more potential customers you gain.

3. The Role of Culture

This is one of the greatest red herrings to land in the boat. If I can change culture from the outside, you can transmogrify it from the inside.

What is culture? I'll give you my quick definition, which has made more than one executive stop short.

Culture is simply that set of beliefs that governs behavior.

My point is not to allow the dreaded cultural gambit to thwart, undo, or sabotage you. "It's just our culture in this department" really means that the current belief system leads to those behaviors, and not that the behaviors are ingrained from the middle of an obscure reptilian brain of 30 million years' development hidden deep in our cerebral cortex. My response is always, "Well, what do you say we change it tomorrow?"

Culture is changed when belief systems change, and belief systems change when *key exemplars establish a different set of beliefs through their behavior.* If you want to change behavior, culture notwithstanding, then change the beliefs of the most visible and respected exemplars.

Don't feel handcuffed by "culture." Cultures change all the time (if you don't believe that, look at Continental Airlines before and after CEO Gordon Bethune), based on the actions of leaders. As a consultant, don't try to change behavior from the ground up. It usually doesn't work. Start at the top. That's why I stressed earlier the need to establish partnering relationships with the economic buyer.

4. We've Heard Every Objection

There is no objection you haven't heard, assuming you've been on the job for longer than twenty minutes. I'm serious. It is absolutely negligent to be thrown by an objection from one of your buyers, implementers, sponsors, or other stakeholders. You should be prepared to deal with the objections overwhelmingly.

Here are typical client objections, pre- and post-implementation, which you'd better be able to handle immediately and forcefully. How many are you comfortable spontaneously rebutting?

• We don't have the time.

• The operation can't absorb the disruption right now.

- HR (or whoever) doesn't have credibility with the sales force (or whomever).
- I can't afford the resource commitment.
- We don't have the money.
- The clients will hate it.
- We tried it before and it didn't work.
- I won't proceed unless you give me some guarantees.
- You don't have the expertise to do this internally.
- In retrospect, I promised too much support and have to withdraw.
- We need to delay this for a while due to other priorities.
- Things aren't happening as rapidly as I had hoped.
- We're experiencing more resistance from our people than I'd anticipated.
- Let's see how things work out at this stage before moving forward.
- My priorities have just changed.

Sound familiar? You need a response to every one, and others like them.

Finally, there is the classic "fish for" versus "teach to fish" dynamic. The ideal means that you are maximizing the importance of the issues on which you are working for clients as well as maximally transferring skills to the client to address such issues in the future. Again, this is an inherent advantage for the internal consultant. But too many internal people content themselves with far less valuable extremes, such as independent expert, analyst, or trainer.

These have been what I call the "basic dynamics" of consulting at the ground level. They aren't complicated and perhaps aren't elegant. But once you are both comfortable and conversant in the use of resistance to change, process versus content, the role of culture, and rebutting objections, you'll be a force to be reckoned with.

THE NATURE OF THE WORK

I want to conclude this initial discussion of the internal consulting role with some observations about the very nature of what we do as consultants. The job involves three basic areas or dimensions: physical ability, skills, and behavior.

Physically, we probably need some measure of mobility, the ability to use a keyboard, powers of observation, and so on. There is no heavy lifting. And many physical shortcomings can be compensated for with technology, assistance, and so forth. From a skills (knowledge and experiences) standpoint, we need to master the elements of various consulting methodologies, communications skills, and so forth. So we should be able to facilitate a meeting, moderate a focus group, interview people, create survey instruments, and so on.

Behaviors, however, often get short shrift. Few of us studied to be consultants, or had a lifelong passion to enter consulting. The behaviors an internal consultant needs include:

- Perseverance: the willingness and resiliency to rebound from setbacks, to remove roadblocks, and to stay the course, even in the face of criticism and skepticism.

- High self-esteem: the ability to refuse to take rejection personally, and to disassociate one's own worth from scorn or negativism directed at one's department or colleagues.

- Well-developed sense of humor: Call this one perspective if you wish, but the truth is that nothing you or I do, no matter how successfully or unsuccessfully, is likely to change the course of civilization as we know it. We need to keep our wits about us.

- Willingness to take risks: no risk, no reward. "A highly conservative, successful consultant" is an oxymoron. Consultants aren't around to protect the status quo, although too many internal people seem to take that position. We're not here to stick our toes into the water. We're here to make waves.

- Creativity and innovation: This goes with the raising of the bar. The real value is in improving standards and raising performance. We need to be able to generate new ideas and better ways for our clients to adapt and implement.

Basically, the successful internal consultant will be at the confluence of these three factors: *market need, competence,* and *passion.*

You need to be able to see (or create) the needs within the organization for the value you can provide; you must develop and demonstrate the competency to meet those needs; and you must be passionate about the prospect of being the key link in that process. You also need to be seen as a valuable peer.

TAKING THE ROLE OF A PEER

Remember that the primary drivers of dramatic internal consulting success are credibility, trust, and relationship building with line partners. Easier said than done, right?

Here's how you play the role of a peer. That is, here's how you become a colleague and not someone else's subordinate, despite job titles, office size, and amounts vested in the retirement plan.

Ten Steps to Peer Relationships

1. *Learn generic business terms and principles.*

Most human resources people seem to have trouble reading their own company's balance sheet, which is Accounting 101 and readily learnable. Understand what the P/E ratio means. Differentiate between earned and unearned income. Do you know what GAAP stands for, or cash vs. accrual? Are you familiar with cycle time, time-to-market, and just-in-time? Take a course or two if your company doesn't offer this very basic skills training. You need to talk the talk before you can walk the walk.

2. *Learn your organization's business terms and principles.*

Every organization has its own nomenclature and jargon. Amazingly, external consultants (at least the good ones) learn to master this quickly. Internal people should understand the terms that sales, IT, research, finance, manufacturing, and other areas use to communicate. There's nothing worse than to sit at a meeting and suddenly have a senior vice president turn to you and ask, "So how can you help us with our ASAC needs when customers are building straw men because of their own *just in time* demands?" Try to tap dance around that one. (Yes, I confronted that once. . . .)

3. *Never be defensive.*

Accept all feedback as constructively intentioned and potentially valid unless demonstrably proven otherwise. I've watched an executive state matter-of-factly, "We tried to improve delegation last year only to find that people were cynical of our intent," only to have one of the people responsible shoot back, "But that was because the senior people refused to go through the program first and we were refused the original budget request." People who see themselves as inferiors get very defensive; people who see themselves as peers seek constructive improvement: "You're right, and I'm concerned about that, too. I've developed three safeguards to prevent that from recurring, but I'd like your feedback and participation to make them most effective."

4. *When you speak, have something to say.*

People who feel insecure are often made highly uncomfortable when they're forced into silence, or haven't been able to contribute. As a result, they often blurt out nonsense or seek to fill silences with platitudes. By no means should you be unheard, but you must be heard saying something cogent and coherent. One of the worst scenarios is attempted humor that fails to amuse. Do some homework before a meeting, and have four or five key points you want to offer. You don't have to make them all, and one or two might be offered by someone else, since great minds think alike. But don't count on the extemporaneous or the sudden, blinding epiphany. Prepare in advance so that when you speak, people listen.

5. *Establish collaborations, not leg work.*

Whenever there's the opportunity for you to contribute, don't just run off and come back with your class project in a week, hoping for an A. Ask to sit down and compare some ideas. Request some conversation and brainstorming time. Play to ego: Tell them that it's not going to be very valuable if it's the result of you isolated in an office generating theoretical models. Start to educate your line partners that this is a collaboration, not an assignment.

6. *Judiciously push back.*

I have to laugh when I hear an internal consultant return from a meeting and say something like, "You won't believe what they've just decided to do!" Who was the consultant, an invisible fly on the wall? You must engage in what I call "push back," which is a gentle form of devil's advocacy. Here are the useful phrases:

- I'm sorry, but I need to challenge that basic assumption.
- What evidence do we have that this has ever worked at all?
- Why do you feel that way?
- Have you considered these risks even if we're successful?

These are all intelligent reactions to questionable logic and faulty premises. The people who raise them are inevitably appreciated by strong buyers.

7. *Don't go changing to try to please me (with apologies to Billy Joel).*

A sycophant is detectable three miles away by a stone. Sentient life is detectable even farther. Never cavil, bow, stoop, or otherwise genuflect to the management team. Don't go along for the ride if the idea is bad, but don't overly praise even good ideas. I actually saw a human resources guy tell the division general manager that he had better choices of shirts on casual Friday than any other man in the place. Two women in the room actually managed to roll their eyes up above their eyebrows, like cartoon characters. And those two women were potential line buyers.

8. *Accept the blame and share the credit.*

This is what great leaders do. If something goes wrong, don't blame a lack of support from a key manager, or poor materials purchased from the outside, or the particular phase of the moon. Simply state that you hadn't anticipated correctly the degree of difficulty in implementing this uniformly across the field force, and here is the contingency plan you've developed to correct things. Conversely, when things are going well, readily share the credit (don't abdicate the credit, which is different) with the buyer's subordinates and peers. Demonstrate that this was a team and collegial approach.

9. *Engage in lifelong learning.*

While you should eschew the fads, don't overlook the need to continually improve. For example, it was recently documented that heterogeneous teams are more productive than homogeneous teams, which makes a strong case for the utility and pragmatism of diversity (and shows why the subject belongs in the general domain of organization development). There have been even more recent studies that begin to show a clear productivity improvement as a result of executive coaching, demonstrating that it's not a fad but rather a practical aspect of career development. If I know about this, shouldn't you?

10. *Use superb communications skills.*

Finally and most grandly, learn to command a room. Never dumb down your vocabulary. Speak with expression. Listen with discernment. Use metaphors and analogies to support your points. Include judicious humor and always have a plethora of examples ready to bolster your arguments. We're all in the communications business these days, and we'd better get good at it. My observation is that people immediately respect others who can use the language well and color-fully. That's a learnable skill.

Most of all, you can't allow your self-esteem to become a roller coaster, as high as your last victory and as low as your last defeat. Your self-esteem must be constant, because you are confident about your skills and your role.

PROACTIVE VERSUS REACTIVE ADVICE

One of the secrets of internal consulting is to be proactive. Most HR people, for example, content themselves to sit back and wait for line management requests, which they fulfill with pride. The true calling of the internal consultant is not to respond but to anticipate. External consulting firms don't wait around to be called; they try to create need. Internal consulting operations are no different in that regard, yet have a potentially much more powerful asset—they know the organization intimately and should, therefore, be able to project need much more accurately.

Every internal consultant should be examining the following strategic considerations on a frequent basis:

• *How to make the best operations better.*

A common mistake is to focus on poorer operations. In fact, about 80 percent or more of all corporate developmental investment goes toward improving poor performers, rather than further exploiting strong performers. Consequently, the focus on internal consultants should be on raising the bar even higher for strong performers. If you'll forgive a baseball analogy, the benefits of improving a .310 hitter to .335 is far more beneficial than increasing a .210 hitter to .235. Don't fall into the trap of trying to analyze and improve poor operations. Instead, focus on the unusual: Make strong operations even stronger. The corporate contribution will be huge.

• *Break paradigms.*

Early in my career I was asked to chair a task force to determine which rental car company was best for our company's needs. In the midst of an arduous debate on frequency of use, the benefits of taking insurance coverage, and numbers of outlets, I suggested that we look at the alternative of requiring people to use taxis. After a nearly acrimonious debate, a test was approved and, what do you know, the people using taxis exclusively had lower travel costs than people renting cars. Find better ways to do things, which may involve challenging existing beliefs and questioning present values.

- *Look outside the company at the environment.*

Organizations tend to be extremely introspective and self-centered. They fail to consider the competition, consumer trends, economic developments, technological improvements, and so on. Find those outside influences that may have the greatest effect on the success or failure of current strategy and offer suggestions on how to avoid, escape, tolerate, or exploit such external factors. In the United States, especially, consumer trends tend to accelerate or undermine even the best corporate strategies.

- *Take risks.*

Staff functions are decidedly conservative. The legal people eschew anything that smacks of change, and the financial people want to eliminate risk altogether. This is not the formula of successful organizations (or careers). Seek dramatic ways to leverage sales, market share, time-to-market, and related high-impact areas. Become adept at risk/reward analyses. The key is to be able to demonstrate to management legitimate and attractive rewards while undergoing prudent and manageable risk.

In summary, the best internal consultants act as if they have just landed on the planet, unaccustomed to the culture, the conventional, and the consistent. They examine alternatives, options, and the unprecedented.

CHAPTER TWENTY-FOUR

Reversing the Lens

Dealing with Different Styles
When You Are the Boss

Gene Boccialetti

———

Managing your subordinate managers with sensitivity to their style, your style, and the tasks you face can help enhance organizational effectiveness and efficiency. On the other hand, ignoring these relationships, or reflexively adopting a comfortable style, can have many negative results, including poor decisions, the loss of talent, and derailing your own career.

DEFERENCE AND CONFLICT AT FORD

An example of the negative effects of a poorly managed boss-subordinate relationship—and also a rare and powerful glimpse of life at the top of an organization—is found in David Halberstam's book *The Reckoning* (1986), which describes the battle between Henry Ford II on one side and Lee Iacocca and Hal Sperlich on the other over the decision to downsize Ford cars in 1976. Ford, of course, was chairman of the Ford Motor Company, Iacocca was the head of Ford-U.S., and Sperlich was Iacocca's deputy for product design. Iacocca and Sperlich had what was sometimes described as a father-son relationship, and they were of one mind in advocating smaller, more fuel efficient cars to compete with foreign imports. They were sure they knew where the company needed to go; Henry Ford, unfortunately, disagreed.

Sperlich was notorious for his exuberant defiance of authority when he found himself in conflict with it. When Iacocca swallowed hard and deferred to the chairman, Sperlich refused to do the same. The battle between Sperlich and Henry Ford not only consumed and wasted their energies and talents for months but polarized the entire organization.

The conflict became a distraction for everyone, including Iacocca; it stopped progress on other fronts and so polarized thinking in the problem-solving process that no middle-range solutions were considered, much less proposed. The outcome was something that Sperlich neither wanted nor expected. Nor was it an outcome that benefited the Ford Motor Company.

Henry Ford announced there would be no Honda engines in Ford cars and no small cars. "Small cars mean small profits," he declared. Ford was interested in profit margins. Sperlich countered that the Packard company had the highest profit margin per car in the industry the year it went out of business. Furthermore, Ford did not like the idea of Japanese engines in American cars. Sperlich was convinced the market was changing and smaller cars were what the American public wanted. Ford was adamant, and Sperlich completely failed in his efforts to influence him. Iacocca warned Sperlich to back off. Time would prove Iacocca and Sperlich right, but Ford, a manager not known for his openness to influence, refused to budge. As Sperlich grew more insistent, Ford became angrier and angrier. The hopelessness of the struggle, in its last few months, seemed to intensify Sperlich's aggressiveness toward all who disagreed. He was relentless, combative, insistent. He let nothing pass unchallenged. Watching him, one friend thought, was like watching someone commit corporate suicide. He bowed to no one, not even Henry Ford II.

For his part, Ford had shown little affection for Sperlich, who seemed less polished than the new, smoother M.B.A.'s that Ford had hired. Sperlich lacked their panache. Now, as Sperlich argued with him regularly, almost as an equal, Ford's distaste grew. At one point Iacocca took Sperlich aside. "Hal," he counseled, "I know you don't think you're telling the chairman that he's full of shit, but it sounds to him— because of your tone and what he's accustomed to—like you're telling him he's full of shit" (Halberstam, 1986, p. 544).

Later, when Ford ordered Sperlich fired, Sperlich was stunned and astonished. He insisted that he had never done anything he was not supposed to do. Henry Ford II and the entire company would receive their punishment later from the American car buyer.

Like many managers, Ford made the error of not listening. He made this mistake, at least in part, because he did not like to be challenged. Ford's need to be deferred to got in the way of a good decision. Because innovation and change were the task, the challenge and push from Sperlich made sense. Although more skill in pushing might have helped Sperlich's case, the time had come for Ford to open his own thinking. A boss manager with high control needs bumped against a subordinate manager with a very low-deference (and probably high-divergence) orientation. Their clash in style obscured the demands of the task. Everyone lost.

WORKING WITH MANAGERS OF VARIOUS STYLES

In the next section, I will discuss effective approaches to the different styles of managers. I will pay particular attention to the implications for how you manage and how you encourage your subordinate managers to relate to you. Remember that all style approaches have value and are useful in one way or another. The boss manager's challenge is to help subordinate managers hold onto the strengths of a style while avoiding its weaknesses. The ideal is for a subordinate manager to learn how to deploy, at least some of the time, elements of the other styles. The task for you as a boss is to help your subordinates (managers or otherwise) complement or add to their styles, not correct them.

Military, Helper, Diplomat, Partisan: Working with the Accommodative Styles

Subordinates in the accommodative styles are generally cooperative and good at implementation, but are not likely to push their expertise or operate independently of you, the boss. They tend to avoid taking opposing points of view or promoting controversy. Further, they tend to withhold themselves personally, which can deprive the boss of information that might be useful in their development or in enhancing their motivational climate. Keep in mind that most organizations and bosses have conditioned and rewarded subordinate managers for being accommodative, even though it has often not been in their interests to do so.

In general subordinates with the accommodative styles will need some prodding if they are to develop and introduce their own ideas, particularly if this might lead to disagreement with you. You will probably need to go beyond just encouraging these subordinates; you will also need to acknowledge the ideas they do bring forward. Make sure they know you appreciate their thoughts. Tell them when and how their ideas have spurred you to some insight into a problem or helped you contemplate a solution. It is important that such feedback be explicit and somewhat detailed, not general.

On the other hand, if you choose not to follow or incorporate their thoughts, ideas, suggestions, or advice, be sure to get back to them and explain why. If you do not, the next time you want their input, it will be that much harder to get. They will be likely to see your encouragement as nothing more than a calculated technique, a kind of managerial political correctness. This could cause them to devalue their own ideas that much more.

You need to strike a balance with the accommodative styles: Value their "solid citizen" character and loyalty but get them to wake up a little. Push them to be more disciplined in their thinking and analysis, especially the Helper. This will help provide a better foundation for self-assertion. Put them into situations where they are required to think more for themselves. Perhaps have them lead a project team with only light monitoring. They will need to feel you as the boss behind them, interested and supportive, but not crowding or micromanaging. Development might also include deliberate exposure to new trends and ideas and a role in keeping others in the organization up to date on these changes.

For the most part expect subordinates in the accommodative styles to be reluctant to disclose their inner thoughts. They are inclined (except for the Helper) to keep to themselves or be cautious. You might be able to bring them out through occasional relaxed conversations. Offer some of your own thoughts about things that interest or puzzle you. Ask for their ideas, even prod a little, but do not push. Remember to keep a balance. Do not set about changing them or their preferred mode of operating. Instead, recognize their preference for structure and direction and then gradually help them develop their risk taking. Help them complement, or add to, their skill set.

One exception to this general advice on the accommodative styles occurs in the case of the Partisan. These subordinates are especially eager to please the boss, and their enthusiasm may cause them to go overboard. Just as Sperlich was attached to Iacocca in the Ford example, they may be more attached to you, their boss, than to the organization and end up doing things that are in neither's long-term interest.

Be perfectly clear about the tasks you are assigning to Partisan subordinates. Make sure they understand the limits to their discretion by having them confirm their instructions. In addition, try to convey more than the tasks you want completed. Work to get across your intentions and the values you want to maintain throughout the process of working together. Agree on check-in points, and make sure you know what they are doing through discreet inquiries. Again, this is a balancing act. You do not want to squash their gung-ho enthusiasm, but you do want to help them get their internal gyroscope functioning so that they can develop a better balance between exercising judgment and being advocates.

Independent, Counselor: Working with the Autonomous Styles

Subordinates in the autonomous styles are good at self-guided activity with minimal supervision. People with these styles are generally happiest when working independently on defined tasks that allow them, once they have their instructions, to operate with relative freedom and almost total discretion. The downside of this ability to operate independently is that they are often not well aligned with (or even aware of) larger goals. Furthermore, subordinates in the autonomous styles often resist even appropriate monitoring by authority.

They can be a great assist in cross-functional activities, since many seem to be natural boundary spanners who resist seeing their organizational world exclusively through the lens of their home function.

Subordinates with these styles need to get recognized for their work. They often feel their efforts are overlooked and underappreciated. They tend to mistrust upper-management support, which means they might mistrust your support.

In general, autonomous subordinates will need to learn how to cooperate in a context larger than their own interests. Although they are usually excellent individual contributors and are often good team leaders, they can lose sight of larger agendas and priorities and the need for cooperative synergies. Working in cooperative structures (and constraints) is not something that comes naturally to them, as it does to more accommodative subordinates.

Their most consistent feature is their low-deference orientation. These subordinates need to have influence with you, and it would be wise to allow them this influence. In return, you can insist that they meet three criteria:

1. They must be supremely knowledgeable in their task domain. You will, of course, need to provide the resources for them to develop this level of expertise.

2. They must maintain an alertness and sensitivity to larger goals and priorities. Make certain they hear and take in news about shifting priorities and goals. Discuss how their work might be affected.

3. They must agree to periodic reports and check-ins. These are necessary so that you can channel necessary resources and information to them and so that you will not be surprised from elsewhere by news of their activities. In those check-ins, become an excellent questioner. Pose questions such as, "How do you plan to handle . . . ?" "Did you know about . . . ?" "What do you need from me?" and "I am concerned about X. Are you?"

Be careful not to let any conflicts get heated, since these subordinates are likely to go to great lengths to get their way. To repeat, be especially certain that autonomous subordinates receive all due credit for their work and their contributions. If you are not effective politically, this can be a very difficult relationship to manage.

Women tend to fall more often into the autonomous styles and usually score low on deference. They are more inner-directed than their male counterparts and often mistrusting and self-protective because of a shared common experience of harassment and discrimination. They tend to be wary of developmental contact for fear of exploitation and their trust being abused.

Managers of women managers should take care in asking for their input. When their advice is not taken, make especially certain to get back to them with fuller explanations. This can enhance trust and promote development of the subordinate managers' thinking. Be careful also to establish the developmental intimacy that is necessary for mentoring, sponsoring, and development. Do not avoid appropriate personal dialogue, but draw a clear line for yourself that at all times precludes your actions from being interpreted as romantic or overly familiar.

Gamesman, Rebel, Whistleblower: Working with the Adversarial Styles

Subordinates in the adversarial styles are generally good at brainstorming, creativity, and innovation. They also serve quite easily in the devil's advocate role and can act as a sort of moral compass for the organization. They are effective organizational "outriders." Since they can easily separate themselves from you and their colleagues, they can easily become isolated and suffer large losses in influence and connection. With an unalert boss, their more contentious styles can also lead to escalated, distracting, and ultimately unproductive conflicts.

Working with subordinates in this group of styles is not as difficult as the adversarial label implies. Do not assume that your best approach is to counter their adversarial tendencies and civilize these subordinates. Also, do not make the opposite mistake of putting them in the devil's advocate role all the time. Instead, your task is to balance their strengths by making sure that they maintain the threads of connection to the organizational mainstream.

Organizations would probably be well served by having more of these types at higher levels, particularly in forming plans and strategies as well as innovation. As the boss, you will need to help sponsor their projects and channel their energies.

Like the Partisan in the accommodative group, the Gamesman is a special case in the adversarial group. Discreetly cultivate your own peer sources to keep abreast of the maneuvering of these subordinate managers. You might even casually let slip that you are aware of their activities.

Gamesmen are generally committed to the view of the organization-as-jungle. Convince them that the two of you can create an island of safety to be more effective. Failing this, convince them that, with you as an ally, they are likely to win more often. They can get further with you than without you. Where possible, try to bring them into discussions on larger purposes, goals, and priorities. This can help move some of their backstage activities to front stage and create at least an island of trust. Gamesmen are most often technically solid subordinates. Take advantage of their expertise and try to help them learn how to balance it by incorporating other decision criteria.

In the case of the Rebels, the danger for you as boss is letting their demonstrative style distract you from their value. Their contentiousness is usually harmless, and sometimes quite useful. Some bosses may view the Rebel's actions as a challenge to upper-level authority. This can lead to ill-advised attempts by you to reassert control. But because Rebels tend to be impatient and become easily frustrated, a more productive way to view them is as people who are merely testing their skill and exhibiting some impatience for more responsibility. It is also possible that they feel passion for the issues at hand and you are seeing their commitment to be involved.

Rebels are usually younger middle managers. Although they struggle against structure and direction, their fight is most often over the means and methods to obtain largely acceptable outcomes. Take comfort in the fact that they usually buy into the overall goals and are arguing over better or best ways to get there. Self-esteem and confidence are very much at stake for Rebels. Because Rebels have a low-distance orientation (more personal), you will find that acting the part of kindly uncle or aunt, and not taking their arguments personally, will get better results than assertions of managerial authority.

The Whistleblower has a very strong internal gyroscope that senses inappropriate or unethical behavior. Unlike the Rebel, this subordinate manager's problems with the organization go beyond conflicts over methods and concern basic goals and purposes. Conflicts with this subordinate are likely to involve much deeper questions than those that are raised by the Rebel. The Whistleblower's more withdrawn personal orientation makes it more difficult for both of you to negotiate difficulties.

Whistleblowers, who are often technical experts, are constantly wary and vigilant for incongruities between what the organization professes to value, what you are directing them to do, and what they consider acceptable. They are more likely to see their ultimate responsibility as being to their profession or to society in general. Their organization's goals come next on their list of priorities, and then their own personal sense of values. The boss's wishes tend to come last (unlike the Partisan, for whom they come first). Stay in good contact with Whistleblowers. They tend to be reluctant to express their views; by the time they come to you, the problem will be looming.

Whistleblowers do not need to be a problem as long as the organization and you are acting congruently. But their generally agreeable exterior (they are mostly deferential) masks a sharply defined set of convictions about what is right, proper, and congruent with larger values. For the ethical boss manager, they can be a useful sort of conscience and guide, alert to questionable behavior. The best option would be to take them into your confidence. Stay alert to and consider seriously any qualms they express about plans or activities.

For the boss manager inclined to cut corners, Whistleblowers may appear to go along, or go along for a while, until they become convinced that activities they are aware of, or are involved in, are wrong. They will then sound an alarm, going around or through you in order to have their concerns addressed. Ignoring, threatening, or dismissing their concerns will, in the final analysis, only make it worse for you, the boss.

THE BOSS'S ROLE IN DEVELOPING FLEXIBILITY IN SUBORDINATE STYLE

Subordinate managers learn to become flexible in their approach to the boss-subordinate relationship. This adapting by subordinate managers needs to be complemented by adaptations from their bosses. Attempts to change organizational leadership styles have been hampered by the failure to address commensurate "followership" changes. Likewise, attempts to change subordinate approaches requires complementary changes by their bosses.

It is a partnership. It takes two. The failure to address this dooms many organizations to ineffective change processes. You cannot change the boss-subordinate relationship by changing the subordinate alone. The boss also has a role to play and will also be required to change to make the relationship effective.

Here are several recommendations for you as a boss. Even as you are making changes as a subordinate manager, you will need to think about doing these things in your relationship with your own subordinates.

Assess Your Managerial Style

Many bosses, like subordinates, have built-in reflexive responses to certain situations. I am often surprised by how many managers find it easy to describe their managerial style independent of the tasks they face. Many managers will assert that they are participative or that they lean toward more autocratic methods. They make the error of thinking of their style as some innate quality of their personality that ends up being applied across the board in all situations. They do not see it as a tool to be adjusted to the many different circumstances they face. As a result, they can fail to see that certain contrary responses from their subordinates are useful or appropriate.

Many managers, for example, are prone to seeing challenges from their subordinate managers as challenges to their own authority, competence, or personal expertise. Their reflexive reaction is to attempt to reassert control. Other bosses reflexively wait and check with subordinates before making decisions, even when decisive unilateral action may be what is most effective. These are the kinds of reflex responses that you as a boss need to learn to check yourself on. What changes in your reactions as a boss must be made to complement the changes your subordinates are making?

As a boss, you need to develop a clear and preferably fact-based understanding of the facets of your own management style. How do you attempt to influence others? What is your learning style? Your communication style? Your approach to managing conflict? Do you tend to be autocratic in your decision making? Consultative? More group-centered? What assumptions do you hold about motivation? How do those assumptions fit with, or miss, your subordinates' interests and needs? The list could go on and on.

There are many useful assessment tools to help you gain some reliable views on these issues, and it is wise to use them. Your view about yourself is important, but try to find external sources of data to support, expand, and in some cases, contradict it. It is important that this self-assessment be accurate and consensually validated.

Managers find it tempting in the absence of information to make certain socially desirable assumptions about their managerial style. But as is the case in other arenas of human activity, how we see ourselves is often not how others see us. I may think I am principled and decisive. Someone else may see the same behavior as close-minded and rigid. Remember, others' responses to us are guided not by how we think we are, but how they think we are. To understand our relationships, we must find out how closely our self-perception aligns with others' perceptions of us.

When we discover how our behavior as managers are patterned, we can then learn how to complement our own preferences in relationship with subordinates. Modern demands on organizations make clear the need for that managers and leaders to learn to operate in multifaceted ways.

Organizational needs are changing along with the boss manager's role. I believe that there will always be a role for decisive, take-charge skills in managers. Not everything is, or should be, a group decision. Group decisions take more time and can be expensive as a strategy. In situations where expertise is concentrated in the minds of a few individuals, groups can reduce decision quality. However, demands for innovation, quality, lowered costs, and leaner staffs are driving a need for more frequent use of empowering, bottom-up strategies. Boss managers need to operate less frequently from a fixed or preferred style and become more flexible and versatile.

Any style you have operated from is likely to have promoted a reactionary style from your subordinates. If you have had an autocratic leaning, you may have inadvertently trained your subordinates to be seducers. Be alert to your own seduction by a subordinate who caters to your need for control. He or she may be colluding with you in being ineffective.

If your task is a creative one, for example, being deferred to means you will not have two (or more) minds working on a problem. You will have one, your own. The subordinate manager will be trying to scope out what you want, so he can appear to support your ideas. It has been demonstrated that boss managers tend to rate highly, and get along better with, subordinate managers in the accommodating group. These are mostly high-deference and low-divergence subordinates.

The subordinate manager who takes issue with you and fights for a point of view may be less easy for you to handle but might be providing you with a more valuable service. Watch out for your own negative emotional response. Other subordinates will read it (perhaps already have read it) and will be disinclined to support you through independent thought and pushing back.

Such subordinate contentiousness is not always best seen as a challenge to you. It may also indicate a higher state of readiness on the part of the subordinates for more advanced responsibilities, an impatience to assume leadership. Their voice and the questions they raise can prompt rethinking by everyone and can ensure that all problem and solution sets are examined. Besides, in addition to promoting more careful analysis by everyone, the pushy ones (like Hal Sperlich and Lee Iacocca) may be right.

Be careful that any conflict that arises is focused on the task. If you like to be deferred to, challenge yourself to accept and reward managers who push back. You can, and probably should, insist that managers base their views on real data and reasoned analysis. Explain where you are trying to go, get agreement on overall targets, but open yourself as much as possible and support controversial viewpoints. Point out the weaknesses in your own arguments. Explicitly and publicly thank those who raise contrary viewpoints to your own.

And, if you are a reflexive participator (or even a so-called abdicrat), consider that you may not provide enough structure for your subordinate managers or help promote their growth. In addition, you could be wasting valuable time when it is you who should be making the decision. Many managers who are uncomfortable with managerial authority welcome the current trends in autonomous teams and empowerment. However, they still need to exercise their authority when it is appropriate to do so. In those situations, boss managers should be decisive and directive. Subordinate managers used to offering input may need to just get their instructions and implement them. For many types of decisions, explaining your thought process afterward can serve to gain the commitment of subordinates just as well as their participation in the process of making the decision. Both parties adjust to the situational demands.

Assess the Tasks You and Your Subordinates Face

After you have developed an awareness of your own leanings as a manager, the next step is to begin to move from operating out of a set style toward operating in ways and relationship patterns that best serve the tasks at hand.

This means you must talk about these tasks with your subordinates; you will not be able to determine an appropriate relationship without having this kind of discussion. For most boss-subordinate pairs, many of the tasks that are faced can be predicted. Discuss those tasks and determine what is the best relationship strategy for each. Where does it make sense for your subordinate manager to operate in each of the different modes?

When the task requires a directive, telling approach by the boss (when the boss's expertise is obviously superior and decisive, the decision is structured, or it is a crisis demanding a quick response), the subordinate manager is advised to operate in an accommodative mode.

When the task is creative or innovative, the decision is not structured, and expertise or information is widely shared, then the boss-manager needs to flatten the authority structure and subordinate managers may need to push back more aggressively. When normal work is the priority, personalizing the relationship is less of a concern than when development is at issue or when the decision situation suggests managers clarify their respective value systems. When goals are in debate or the mission is unclear, consider the issue of alignment. Alignment requires considering goals first and then the methods used to achieve them. You can live with disagreement on methods, but not on goals. If the overall goals of the boss manager and the subordinate manager are at odds, resolve it before you try to get your work done.

Changing the way you relate to subordinates from task situation to task situation may be new for you and will probably be uncomfortable at first. But over time it will become natural.

Do not fall into the trap of meshing your styles so that you can be comfortable. Do not make comfort your highest priority. Effective work together may (and probably will) require both of you to be uncomfortable at least some of the time. Each of you will need to learn how to sometimes operate "out of style."

For example, suppose you, as a boss, prefer to be in control in most situations and you have accommodating subordinate managers. A match? Yes. Comfortable? Probably. Effective? Not if you are charged with creative tasks, innovation, or some kind of organizational change. Or, on the other hand, suppose you are a participative manager with low-deference, autonomous subordinates who like to provide input. A match? Yes. Comfortable? Sure. Effective? Not in certain situations, such as those involving routine tasks, structured problems, or some crises. In these cases, this pair will likely suffer from several kinds of ineffectiveness: excessive time and delay making decisions, opportunity costs, higher decision-making costs, possible lower decision quality, and poor modeling of management behavior.

Most organizations these days are trying to innovate, raise quality, and keep costs down. You have fewer resources, including time. Even if you are prone to close management of your subordinate managers, new trends in organizing (like increased spans of control and your broadened task responsibilities) will not allow you to indulge this preference. It suggests your subordinates will need to take more initiative and engage in more autonomous action within broad guidelines. This means you have to communicate goals and the pathways to those goals to your subordinate managers. You provide resources, offer consultation, and rely on them getting back to you, with agreed on check-in and data reporting.

The subordinate managers who have adapted well to autocratic managerial styles and have come to require structure and guidance (accommodating styles) will certainly need to make substantial adjustments in these newer work situations. Autonomous managers need to make sure their efforts tie in to the work of others. And adversarial managers will need to temper and channel their impulses to achieve positive task results and reduce their own alienation.

Innovative tasks require certain kinds of interactions that are different from routine tasks, developmental tasks, or crisis situations. Figure out where these different kinds of tasks fit together in your work, and how you both might need to adapt. In this adaptation, consider subordinate manager readiness and expertise. Is training needed for either or both of you?

Identify arenas for pushing back and task situations where the subordinate manager needs to just make it happen. Decide when to discuss more personal, developmental matters. Discuss what goals you are trying to serve. Get agreement, or at least acknowledge divergence. Divergence is a powerful force in this relationship. We know that when a boss-subordinate pair is out of alignment, disagreeing on goals or methods, they are often ineffective and waste energy.

Assess the Styles of Your Subordinates and Work Toward Flexibility

As a boss manager, you have considered your own preferences, particularly on the issues of control, making personal contact, and understanding and getting across overall goals to your subordinate managers. Next you have discussed with your subordinate managers what relationship approaches your tasks require. This discussion is an exchange of views; be careful not to announce or dictate what is required. Probe, ask, and listen. Remember that effective communication is two-way communication.

Now, have a discussion with your subordinates about their style. As we saw earlier, there are some general directions, given current organizational trends, for different subordinate styles to move to develop themselves. You can make this developmental interaction a regular part of performance appraisal, but I would recommend you do it more often than the periodic appraisal sessions.

What is your view of their leaning, their reflex? And how should that be rounded out? What is the subordinate's view of their style? Is it the same as your view? Reconcile any different views. The subordinate manager's view of themself should weigh heavily here. But it is important to develop a complex and consensual view.

I developed a version of the authority relations inventory (which forms the basis of this work) for bosses to fill out. In it, bosses answered questions based on how they saw their subordinate managers' style in relating to them. It was scored by the subordinate managers after they completed work on their own view of themselves. Most of the time there was significant difference on the deference scale. As mentioned earlier, most boss managers saw their subordinates as being more deferential (less pushy) than the subordinates saw themselves. In the small group I studied, no systematic differences were apparent on the other two aspects of style.

Once you figure out a consensual view, both of you should discuss how to incorporate other approaches to the subordinate manager's style to increase their overall effectiveness.

Provide Feedback and Training

Subordinate styles are not easily changed but they can change. And even if basic preferences do not change, subordinate managers can, with moderate effort and some help, learn how on a behavioral level to complement their preferred style with other approaches when those make sense. This change is all the more likely when you, their boss, is an active partner in the change process.

Such an adaptive competence is an achievable goal, but it requires some assistance and structure for practice and change. Getting accurate feedback on style and how the subordinate manager needs to develop are key first steps. Appreciating the general directions for change (becoming more adaptable, depending on the task) as well as their personal directions (where do I, as a subordinate manager, start from?) are both important first tasks.

Next comes some form of structured training. Training should be behaviorally based so that managers do not end up learning a new language without a chance to practice it. It is also important that managers be able to get direct personal feedback in this process. What is their individual orientation to the relationship with their bosses and how should they complement it to be more effective?

There also needs to be structures that support change. The issue of the boss-subordinate relationship needs to be part of performance evaluation and the reward system as well. Conduct periodic debriefings with you as their manager and with competent, professional educators. Establish behavioral objectives for both parties to the relationship. Very little will result if it is left as an informal "let's do better" form of resolve.

Walk the Talk

Challenge yourself to implement these ideas in your daily behavior. This is what finally matters. Give yourself time to work into new relationship arrangements, but check from time to time whether you can see a difference. The purpose of this learning is to apply it, to have it make a discernible difference in how the relationship functions.

Any new behavior is likely to feel somewhat awkward and uncomfortable for a bit. That can be a sign that you are making progress.

Review, Reward, and Reevaluate

Make this deliberate and scheduled. Set aside time for a discussion. Get outside third-party assistance or use your human resources staff if you are not sure how to go about this. Look at the work you have been doing as a pair as well as your experience of your interactions. Return to specific exchanges to point to the things you have been doing well as well as the things that you have not been doing well.

Make sure you recognize and reward progress in changing the range of your interactions. Measure what you are doing against the behavioral objectives you created. Recognize change, and reward it with a compliment, a short letter to your subordinate manager and to the file, or perhaps a lunch. Recognition does not need to be extravagant to have a very significant and positive motivational result.

Get feedback yourself and decide on effectiveness criteria that you will use with your managers in figuring out if you are working well together. Do not leave this criteria at "we seem to get along well." That does not always indicate you are being effective. Consider whether you want to stay on the course you have been on or make some adjustments in light of learning or new task demands.

Relationship structures should support your work, and as things change in your work, so should the relationship. Not all things can be foreseen, but reevaluate where you are heading.

CHAPTER TWENTY-FIVE

Relations with Superiors

The Challenge of "Managing" a Boss

John Kotter

E ffectively managing relationships with subordinates and with those outside one's chain of command is almost impossible without the support and assistance of key bosses. Because of their formal power position, bosses can play a critical role in linking subordinates to the rest of the organization, in securing key resources for them, in making sure their priorities are consistent with organizational needs, and in seeing that they are rewarded fairly for their performance. Providing the kind of leadership needed in so many jobs today is enormously difficult when one's bosses don't play these roles well.

Of course, if everyone in supervisory positions performed with great effectiveness all of the time, then relationships to bosses would not be an issue for us. But such a state is far removed from today's reality. Unfortunately, all too often today, relationships to bosses are a source of conflict and problems instead of a source of resources and help. And that means still another set of relationship-management challenges for people who are trying to provide leadership and to make a difference in their organizations—a set of challenges that are not at all well understood.

Few would argue that bosses are unimportant. Yet many people naïvely underestimate what a crucial role bosses can play in helping them to perform well and enabling them to provide the leadership necessary in so many of today's jobs. For a good detailed example of how a talented and successful young person can find himself having great difficulty with a boss, see Gerttula (1993).

The case of John Reed, Citicorp's new chairman, is instructive in this regard. (For a more detailed description of the situation, see First National City Bank Operating Group (A) and (B) by John Seeger, Jay Lorsch, and Cyrus Gibson, Case 7–1, in Kotter, Schlesinger, and Sathe [1986]). In 1970, Reed was put in charge of the Operating Group, that part of the bank that performed the physical work of processing business transactions—transferring money, handling checks, and so on. He had 8,000 people on his payroll, and a budget of over $100 million, despite the fact that he was only thirty-one years old at the time. He also had a big problem facing him: although the volume of transactions handled by his group had recently been increasing at an annual rate of 5 percent, the group's expenditures had been growing at 18 percent per year for almost a decade. Because his department was still using methods and procedures designed decades earlier, when the bank was smaller and times were very different, expenses had gotten completely out of control. The rising costs threatened the bank's ability to meet its obligation to shareholders, customers, and employees. Something had to be done. Reed was given this big leadership challenge, despite his lack of experience in either banking or in banking operations, because those running the bank felt that someone with a new and different perspective was needed to solve this most difficult problem.

Between 1970 and 1972, Reed and a team of managers that he assembled introduced huge innovative changes within the Operating Group. They reorganized, implemented new information and control systems, altered hiring and compensation practices, and generally implemented a whole new system of management. It was a difficult three years, because they ran into dozens of problems, including a lot of resistance to change, both from within the Operating Group and from the bank's other divisions (who had to rely on the Operating Group to process their transactions). Nevertheless, they managed to overcome these barriers and to get their costs well under control. It has been estimated that in 1976 the cost savings from Reed's leadership accounted for 25 percent of Citicorp's after-tax income! These spectacular results literally set a new norm for the banking industry. Even today, as I write this, some banks are studying what Citicorp did over a decade ago in order to apply those ideas to their operating departments.

Many factors contributed to this success story, the most important of which was John Reed himself. But also extremely important was the support Reed received from the bank's president, Bill Spencer, and its chairman, Walter Wriston.

At varying times during the change process, Reed and his team of managers ran into massive resistance from people who were being inconvenienced in the short run by the changes, from people who were skeptical about the direction in which Reed was moving, and from people who did not like the way their jobs were changing. Altogether, these individuals could have slowed Reed down and even stopped him in some areas, as often happens in corporate change efforts. But Reed was able to overcome the resistance, largely because of his bosses' ongoing and very visible support.

Reed has acknowledged publicly that any number of times "when the sharks saw blood in the water and wanted to strike," Spencer and Wriston moved in and saved the day. The ultimate example of this occurred immediately after the biggest crisis caused by all the changes. In September 1971, a reorganization ran into serious problems, and the "money pipeline" that the Operating Group managed "burst" (something that just does not happen in the banking industry!). The crisis that followed, which took a few weeks to correct, created major problems not only for the Operating Group, but for the other parts of the bank. Just when everyone with a complaint was ready to come down hard on the Operating Group management, Spencer and Wriston found a beautiful way to signal unambiguously that they still supported Reed completely and that they expected others to do so also. In October 1971, when some of the problems caused by this very visible crisis were still unsolved, they announced that Reed's two key subordinates, John White and Larry Small, would be promoted in rank to senior vice-president!

The kind of relationship Reed had with his bosses is not the norm in industry or government today. All too often, problems exist in boss-subordinate relationships, which undermine capable people's capacity to provide leadership in their jobs, and which often hurt the organizations and the individuals involved.

The case of Frank Gibbons and Philip Bonnevie is a perfect example of this. Gibbons was an acknowledged manufacturing genius in his industry and was, by any profitability standard, a very effective executive. (Names are described. This information comes from interviews with some of the people involved.) In 1973, his strengths propelled him into the position of vice-president of manufacturing for the second largest and most profitable company in that industry. Gibbons was not, however, a good manager of people. He knew this, as did many others. Recognizing this weakness, the president made sure that those who reported to Gibbons were good at working with people and could compensate for his limitations. The arrangement worked well.

In 1975, Philip Bonnevie was promoted into a position reporting to Gibbons. In keeping with the previous pattern, the president selected Bonnevie because he had an excellent track record and a reputation for being good with people. In making that selection, however, the president did not notice that, in his rapid rise through the organization, Bonnevie himself had never reported to anyone who was poor at managing subordinates. Bonnevie had always had good-to-excellent superiors and had never been forced to manage a relationship with a difficult boss. In retrospect, Bonnevie admits he had never thought about "managing his boss."

Gibbons began supervising Bonnevie the same way he treated all new people under his direct supervision. He was vague and sometimes inconsistent with his directions. He was slow to praise and quick to criticize. When Bonnevie wanted him, he was nowhere to be found. When Bonnevie did not need him, he always seemed to be getting into things.

Bonnevie responded to Gibbons first with frustration and anger, then with withdrawal. Because Bonnevie was convinced he knew what was required in his new job, he decided to get on with it and pretty much avoided Gibbons except when he really needed something from him. He realized that Gibbons might not like this approach at first but hoped that eventually he would be won over. After all, he thought to himself, good performance speaks for itself.

Fourteen months after he started working for Gibbons, Bonnevie was fired. During that same quarter, the company reported a net loss for the first time in seven years. Many of those who were close to these events say that they don't entirely understand what happened. This much is known, however: while the company was bringing out a major new product—a process that required its sales, engineering, and manufacturing groups to coordinate their decisions very carefully—a whole series of misunderstandings and bad feelings developed between Gibbons and Bonnevie. For example, Bonnevie claims Gibbons was aware of and had accepted Bonnevie's decision to use a new type of machinery to make the new product; Gibbons swears he was not. Furthermore, Gibbons claims he made it clear to Bonnevie that introduction of the product was too important to the company in the short run to take any major risks.

Because of such misunderstandings, planning went awry: a new manufacturing plant was built that could not produce the new product designed by engineering, in the volume desired by sales, at a cost agreed on by the executive committee. As a result, the company lost somewhere between $2 and $5 million.

The tragic thing about this situation—and thousands of less dramatic but similar episodes that occur every year—is that it probably could have been avoided. The cost to the company and the high personal price paid by Bonnevie—being fired and having his reputation damaged—were not inevitable, even taking into account Gibbons's ineptness at managing subordinates.

Situations like this can be dealt with effectively if the subordinate involved recognizes and acts on some basic organizational realities. (See, for example, Gabarro [1979] and Kotter [1979].) First, a relationship with a boss involves mutual dependence between people who have different backgrounds and different pressures on them; thus, if it is not managed well, neither can be effective in his job. Second because the boss-subordinate relationship is not like the one between a parent and a child, the burden for managing the relationship should not and cannot fall entirely on the boss. Bosses are only human; their wisdom and maturity are not always greater than their subordinates'. Third, because of this, managing the relationship with the boss is a necessary and legitimate part of a job in a modern organization, especially in a difficult leadership job. Finally, to do this requires that one take the time and energy to develop a relationship that is consonant with both people's styles, assets, and expectations and that meets the most critical needs of each.

This aspect of work, essential though it is to survival and advancement, is sometimes ignored by otherwise talented and aggressive people. Indeed, I have known dozens of people like Bonnevie, who actively and effectively manage subordinates, products, markets, and technologies, but who nevertheless naïvely take an almost passively reactive stance vis-à-vis their bosses. Such a stance practically always hurts these people and their companies.

———ᴧᴧ᷉—

To get the support, information, resources, and help needed from a boss to perform a difficult leadership job in an effective and responsible manner, it is essential to develop and maintain a good working relationship with that boss. People who are successful in this regard typically do the following:

1. First, they find ways to learn about the boss's goals, pressures, strengths, weaknesses, and working style.
2. They are sensitive to their own needs, objectives, strengths, weak spots, and personal styles.
3. They use all this information to help create a relationship that fits both their needs and styles and that is characterized by unambiguous mutual expectations.
4. Finally, they work to maintain that good relationship by keeping the boss informed, by behaving dependably and honestly, and by using their boss's time and other resources selectively.

In a sense, developing a good working relationship with anybody involves these same steps. But nowhere is it more important than with respect to a boss, because no one typically has more power over you than a boss. When successful, the relationship becomes a form of countervailing power that helps insure that you get the information, support, and resources that you need.

The first step in this process—getting sufficient information on the boss's goals, strengths, weaknesses, working style—seems obvious enough. But people all too often do not do this. And it creates problems for them.

Consider, for example, the situation in which a top-notch marketing manager with a superior performance record was hired into a company as a vice president "to straighten out the marketing and sales problems" (Gabarro & Norman, 1975). The company, which was having financial difficulties, had been recently acquired by a larger corporation. The president was eager to turn it around and gave the new marketing vice president free rein—at least initially. Based on his previous experience, the new vice president correctly diagnosed that the company needed to gain a greater share of the market and that strong product management was required to bring that about. As a result, he made a number of pricing decisions aimed at increasing high-volume business.

When margins declined and the financial situation did not improve, the president increased pressure on the new vice president. Believing that the situation would eventually correct itself as the company's share of the market increased, the vice president resisted the pressure. When by the second quarter margins and profits had still failed to improve, the president took direct control over all pricing decisions and put all items on a set level of margin, regardless of volume. The new vice president began to find himself shut out by the president, and their relationship deteriorated. In fact, the vice president found the president's behavior bizarre. Unfortunately, the president's new pricing scheme also failed to increase margins, and by the fourth quarter both the president and the vice president were fired.

What the new vice president had not known until it was too late was that improving marketing and sales had been only one of the president's goals. His most immediate goal had been to make the company more profitable—quickly. Nor had the new vice president known that his boss was invested in this short-term priority for personal as well as business reasons. The president had been a strong advocate of the acquisition within the parent company, and his personal credibility was at stake.

The vice president in this case made at least three basic errors—errors that are not at all uncommon. He took information supplied to him at face value, he made assumptions in areas where he had no information, and—most damaging—he never actively tried to clarify what his boss's objectives were. As a result, he ended up taking actions that were actually at odds with the president's priorities and objectives.

This kind of problem can be avoided. It simply requires that one *actively* seek out information about a boss's goals and problems and pressures. It demands that one be alert for opportunities to question the boss and others around him or her to test one's assumptions. It suggests that one pay attention to clues in the boss's behavior. Although it is imperative that one do this when beginning to work with a new boss, it is also important to do so on an ongoing basis because priorities and concerns change.

Being sensitive to a boss's work style can be especially crucial when the boss is new. My colleague, Professor Jack Gabarro, once encountered an excellent example of this. It seems a very organized and formal executive replaced a man who was informal and intuitive. The new executive worked best when he had written reports. He also preferred formal meetings with set agendas. One of his subordinates realized this need and worked with the new executive to identify the kinds and frequency of information and reports the executive wanted. This subordinate also made a point of sending the executive written background information and brief agendas for their discussions. He found that with this type of preparation, their meetings were very useful. Moreover, he found that with adequate preparation, his new boss was even more effective at brainstorming problems than his more informal and intuitive predecessor had been.

In contrast, another subordinate never fully understood how the new boss's work style differed from that of his predecessor. To the degree that he did sense it, he experienced it as too much control. As a result, he seldom sent the new executive the background information he needed, and the executive never felt fully prepared for meetings with this subordinate. In fact, the executive spent much of his time when they met trying to get information that he felt he should have had before his arrival. The boss experienced these meetings as frustrating and inefficient, and the subordinate often found himself thrown off guard by the questions that the executive asked.

The difference between the two subordinates just described was not so much one of ability or even adaptability. Rather, the difference was that one of the men was more sensitive to his boss's work style than the other and to the implications of his boss's needs. That is, he was more sensitive to issues such as how the boss liked to get information (through memos, formal meetings, or phone calls), whether the boss thrived on conflict or tried to minimize it, how he liked to approach problems, and what kind of language and concepts the boss preferred to employ in problem-solving situations.

Some people find it a burden or even distasteful to have to worry about these kinds of issues. But effective and responsible performance in most organizations today absolutely requires this kind of sensitivity.

—⁓—

The boss is only one half of the relationship. The subordinate is the other half. Developing an effective working relationship with a boss requires that the subordinate also know his or her own needs, strengths and weaknesses, and personal style.

In terms of self-awareness, nothing is more important for a subordinate than to know his or her temperamental reaction to a position of dependence on an authority figure. Although a superior-subordinate relationship is one of mutual dependence, it is also one in which the subordinate is typically more dependent on the boss than the other way around. This dependence inevitably results in the subordinate feeling a certain degree of frustration, sometimes anger, when actions or options are constrained by a boss's decisions. This is a normal part of life and occurs in the best of relationships. The way in which a person handles these frustrations depends largely on his or her predisposition towards dependence on authority figures.

Some people's instinctive reaction under these circumstances is to resent the boss's authority and to rebel against the boss's decisions. Sometimes a person will escalate a conflict far beyond what is appropriate. Seeing the boss almost as an institutional enemy, such people will often, without being conscious of it, fight with the boss just for the sake of fighting. Their reactions to being constrained are usually strong and sometimes impulsive. They see the boss as someone who, by virtue of his or her role, is a hindrance to progress, an obstacle to be circumvented or, at best, tolerated.

Psychologists call this pattern of reactions counterdependent behavior. Although a counterdependent person is difficult for most superiors to manage and usually has a history of strained relationships with superiors, this sort of person is apt to have even more trouble with a boss who tends to be directive or authoritarian. When such a person acts on his or her negative feelings, often in subtle and non-verbal ways, the boss sometimes does become the enemy. Sensing the subordinate's latent hostility, the boss will lose trust in the subordinate or the subordinate's judgment and will behave less openly.

Paradoxically, individuals with this type of predisposition are often good managers of their own people. They will often go out of their way to get support for subordinates and will not hesitate to go to bat for them.

At the other extreme are people who swallow their anger and behave in a very compliant fashion when the boss makes what they know to be a poor decision. Such individuals will agree with the boss even when a disagreement might be welcome or when the boss would easily alter a decision if given more information. Because their responses bear no relationship to the specific situation at hand, they are as much an overreaction as those of counterdependent people.

Instead of seeing the boss as an enemy, these people deny their anger—the other extreme—and tend to see the boss as if he or she were a wise parent who should know best, take responsibility for their careers, train them in all they need to know, and protect them from overly ambitious peers.

Both counterdependence and overdependence lead people to hold unrealistic views of what a boss is. Both views ignore that most bosses, like everyone else, are imperfect and fallible. They don't have unlimited time, encyclopedic knowledge, or extrasensory perception; nor are they evil enemies. They have their own pressures and concerns, and these are sometimes at odds with the wishes of the subordinate—often for good reasons.

Altering predispositions toward authority, especially at the extremes, is almost impossible without intensive psychotherapy (psychoanalytic theory and research suggest that such predispositions are deeply rooted in a person's personality and upbringing). However, an awareness of these extremes and the range between them can be very useful in helping one to identify where one's own predispositions fall and then to understand the implications of that assessment. In some cases, especially regarding career choice, the implications can be extremely important (for example, highly counterdependent people tend to be happier and more successful in careers as independent businesspeople or professionals, where they do not have a conventional boss). And in virtually all cases, understanding the implications can improve a person's effectiveness.

Take, for example, the case of an individual and her superior who ran into problems whenever they disagreed. The boss's typical response was to harden his position and overstate it. The individual's reaction was then to raise the ante and intensify the forcefulness of her argument. In doing this, she channeled her anger into sharpening her attacks on the logical fallacies in her boss's assumptions. Her boss, in turn, would become even more adamant about holding his original position. Predictably, this escalating cycle eventually resulted in the subordinate avoiding, whenever possible, any topic of potential conflict with her boss.

In discussing this problem with her peers, this person discovered that her reaction to her boss was typical of the way she generally reacted to counterarguments, especially from authority figures. Because her attempts to discuss this problem with her boss were unsuccessful, she concluded that the only way to change the situation was to deal with her own instinctive reactions. So she did the following. Whenever she and her boss reached an impasse, she would check her own impatience and suggest that they take a break and think about it before getting together again. This small change in her approach helped considerably, because when they renewed their discussion, they usually had digested their differences and were more able to work them through in a creative and productive way.

—*/\/\/*—

As this last example suggests, using a clear understanding of both parties to create a good working relationship with a boss means developing an approach, goals, and expectations that fit both of these parties.

Above all else, a good working relationship with a boss accommodates differences in work style. A good example of this can be seen in the case of an individual who had a relatively good, but not excellent, relationship with his superior. About three months after starting to work for this person, he realized that during meetings his boss would often become inattentive and sometimes brusque. The subordinate's own style tended to be discursive and exploratory. He would often digress from the topic at hand to deal with background factors, alternative approaches, and so forth. His boss, instead, preferred to discuss problems with a minimum of background detail and became impatient and distracted whenever her subordinate digressed from the immediate issue.

Recognizing the difference in style, this person became terser and more direct during meetings with his boss. To help himself do this, before meetings with the boss he would develop brief agendas that he used as a guide. Whenever he felt that a digression was needed, he explained why. This small shift in his own style made these meetings more effective and far less frustrating for both of them and, in the process, improved his relationship with his boss.

Subordinates can also sometimes profitably adjust their styles in response to their bosses' preferred method for receiving information. Peter Drucker (1967) divides bosses into "listeners" and "readers." He points out that some bosses like to get information in report form so that they can read and study it. Others work better with information and reports presented in person so that they can ask questions. As Drucker notes, the implications are obvious. If your boss is a listener, you brief him or her in person and then follow it up with a memo. If your boss is a reader, you cover important items or proposals in a memo or report and then discuss them.

Other useful adjustments can often be made according to a boss's decision-making style. Some bosses prefer to be involved in decisions and problems as they arise. These are high-involvement managers who like to keep their finger on the pulse of the operation. Usually their needs are best satisfied if subordinates touch base with them on an ad hoc basis. A boss who has a need to be involved will become involved one way or another, so there are advantages to including him or her at your initiative. Other bosses prefer to delegate—they don't want to be involved. They expect subordinates to come to them only with major problems and to inform them of important changes.

Making adjustments which draw on each party's strengths and make up for each party's weaknesses can also be important. For example, because he knew that his boss—the vice president of engineering—was not very good at monitoring his employees' problems, one manager made a point of doing so himself. The stakes were high: the engineers and technicians were all union members, the company worked on a customer-contract basis, and the company had recently experienced a serious strike. The manager worked closely with his boss, the scheduling department, and the personnel office to ensure that potential problems were avoided. He also developed an informal arrangement through which his boss would review with him any proposed changes in personnel or assignment policies before they were put into effect. The boss valued his subordinate's advice and credited him with improving both the performance of the division and the labor-management climate.

Finally, developing effective relationships with bosses demands that one make adjustments so as to establish mutual expectations around key issues. Many factors can produce differences in expectations, and those differences can create serious conflicts and other problems.

The subordinate who passively assumes that he or she knows what the boss expects is in for trouble. Of course, some superiors will spell out their expectations very explicitly and in great detail. But most do not. And although many corporations have systems that provide a basis for communicating expectations (such as formal planning processes, career planning reviews, and performance appraisal reviews), these systems never work perfectly. Also, between these formal reviews, expectations invariably change.

Ultimately, it is up to the subordinate to find out what the boss's expectations are, both broad expectations (regarding, for example, what kinds of problems the boss wishes to be informed about and when) as well as very specific ones (regarding such things as when a particular project should be completed and what kinds of information the boss needs in the interim). Getting a boss who tends to be vague or inexplicit to express his or her expectations can be difficult, but it is possible. One can periodically draft detailed memos covering key aspects of work, send it to the boss for approval, and then follow this up with a face-to-face discussion in which each item in the memo is discussed. Such discussions can bring to the surface many of the boss's relevant expectations. Or one can deal with an inexplicit boss by initiating an ongoing series of informal discussions about "good management" and "our objectives." Or one can sometimes get useful information more indirectly through those who used to work for the boss and through the formal planning systems in which the boss makes commitments to superiors. Which approach works best, of course, depends upon each boss's style.

Developing a workable set of mutual expectations also requires communicating your own expectations to the boss, finding out if they are realistic, and influencing the boss to accept the ones that are important to you. The key here is to be demanding without being seen as uncooperative or troublesome. Being able to influence the boss to value one's expectations can be particularly important if the boss is an overachiever. Such a boss will often set unrealistically high standards that need to be brought into line with reality.

—◦◦◦—

Maintaining a good relationship with a boss, once it has been established, requires a variety of additional actions. Foremost among these are keeping bosses informed, behaving dependably and honestly, and using bosses' time and resources very selectively.

How much information a boss needs about what a subordinate is doing will vary significantly depending on the boss's style, the situation, and the confidence the boss has in the subordinate. But it is not uncommon for a boss to need more information than a subordinate would naturally supply, or for a subordinate to think the boss knows more than he or she really does.

Young employees, in particular, often naïvely assume that "good performance speaks for itself," which then leads them to undercommunicate with their superiors. That is, as long as they think they are doing a good job and that there are really no problems, they tend to communicate little with their bosses. But for "good performance to speak for itself," a boss and subordinate must have 100 percent agreement on what tasks constitute the subordinate's job, on the relative importance of those tasks, and on unambiguous ways to measure the performance of the tasks. And then the boss must easily be able to see how well the subordinate's performance measures up. Few situations in reality meet these requirements.

When there are problems, managing the flow of information upward is particularly difficult if the boss does not like to hear about problems. Although many would deny it, bosses often give off signals that they want to hear only good news. They show great displeasure—usually nonverbally—when someone tells them about a problem. Ignoring individual achievement, they may even evaluate more favorably subordinates who do not bring problems to them. Nevertheless—for the good of the organization, boss, and subordinate—a superior needs to hear about failures as well as successes. And it is possible to pass on this information in ways that are not self-destructive. One can sometimes deal with a good-news-only boss by finding indirect ways to send the necessary information, such as a management information system in which there is no messenger to be killed. In other circumstances, one can see to it that potential problems, whether in the form of good surprises or bad news, are communicated immediately, before they have grown into big and difficult issues.

Few things are more disabling to a boss and will sour a relationship faster than a subordinate on whom one cannot depend, whose work cannot be trusted. Almost no one is intentionally undependable, but many people are inadvertently so because of errors of omission or uncertainty about the boss's priorities. A commitment to an optimistic delivery date may please a superior in the short term but be a source of displeasure if not honored.

Nor are many people intentionally dishonest with their bosses. But it is so easy to shade the truth a bit and play down concerns. Current concerns often become future surprise problems. It's almost impossible for bosses to work effectively if they cannot rely on fairly accurate readings from their subordinates. Because it undermines credibility, dishonesty is perhaps the most troubling trait a subordinate can have. Without a basic level of trust in a subordinate's word, a boss feels he or she has to check all of the subordinate's decisions, and this makes it difficult to delegate.

Subordinates who waste their boss's limited time and energy undermine a good relationship almost as much as those who are undependable. Because every request a subordinate makes of a boss uses some of the boss's limited resources, common sense suggests drawing on these resources with some selectivity. This may sound obvious, but it is surprising how many people use their boss's time to deal with relatively trivial issues. They do so without stopping to think of the consequences.

The point is this: maintaining a good relationship takes effort. For many people, just pausing occasionally to think about the issues raised in this chapter can help a great deal. This means reflecting on these kinds of questions:

- Do I really know what my boss expects of me, both in general and in terms of specific activities in the next week? In the next month? Am I satisfied that these expectations are sensible and fair?

- Does my boss really know what I expect in return? Does he or she know what resources, information, support, and help I need? In the longer run does my boss know my career expectations? Does he or she accept them and thus work on my behalf?

- How well do we get along on a daily basis? Are there many unpleasant conflicts or problems? If there are, what exactly creates these problems? What can I realistically do to help the situation?

- What demands have I made of my boss in the past month or two? How important were the issues involved to the organization, to my boss, and to me? Were any of these instances a waste of time for the boss?

- Of the various dimensions of trust in a relationship, which ones are particularly important to my boss? Have I been particularly trustworthy on these dimensions recently?

- How well does my boss know what I've been doing for the past few months? If he or she is uninformed about certain activities, could this create a problem? If so, what can I do to correct the situation?

—∿∿—

Developing and maintaining a really good working relationship with a boss is often challenging. But there are a number of conditions that can make the establishment of such a relationship particularly difficult. They are (1) the existence of very large differences in age, educational background, and values between the boss and the subordinate, (2) incompetence on the part of the boss, (3) powerlessness on the part of the boss, (4) serious differences and conflicts between the boss and others above him or her in management, or (5) the existence of multiple bosses who have serious differences and conflicts.

Bosses and subordinates are always different in some ways. But occasionally the differences will be so large that they create a significant barrier to building and maintaining a good working relationship. Take, for example, the case of a fifty-year-old boss with a high school education, thirty years of experience, and little chance of further advancement, and his new twenty-four-year-old highly ambitious, MBA-educated subordinate. Or consider the case of a middle-aged female American manager who is assigned to work for a young Saudi.

Serious barriers to developing a good working relationship also exist when the boss is not fully qualified for the job. All organizations have at least a few incompetent bosses. Some have quite a few, and most are not very good at coming to grips with this problem. Feelings of guilt often overcome the decision makers involved. Instead of quickly identifying bosses that are over their heads and correcting the situation, many firms tend to do nothing. These kind of bosses create relationship problems for subordinates in two ways. First, adapting to their styles, especially if they are really in over their heads, can be extraordinarily frustrating. Second, developing mutual expectations becomes complicated by the fact that what they think is needed and what in fact may truly be needed by the organization may be two different things.

Related to this last problem, one sometimes finds bosses who are essentially impotent. For whatever historical reasons, often having to do with incompetence, they simply wield very little power. Such bosses create relationship problems for subordinates because they often cannot deliver on their promises. And because their peers and bosses can so easily pressure them into shifting their goals, their expectations of their subordinates can change constantly.

Serious conflicts between a boss and others in top management create still another barrier to good relations between that boss and his or her subordinates. Such conflicts can manifest themselves in many ways. Sometimes the people involved are rivals. Sometimes they have strong and yet different opinions about key company policies. Sometimes they are just very different—in age, background, and so on—and have trouble relating to each other. Whatever the case, these problems can make life all the more difficult for the lower-level subordinate.

In attempting to establish a really good relationship with his or her immediate boss, the subordinate can sometimes inadvertently alienate other people. If the subordinate then tries to patch up the problem with these other people, he or she can just as easily alienate the immediate boss.

Another form of the same problem occurs when someone has multiple bosses who have highly diverse goals or who strongly dislike one another. This can occur in matrix-type organizations or in jobs (such as the chief executive officer) where the incumbent reports to a board.

All five of these situations are best handled by minimizing their existence in the first place. This means before accepting a job offer, a promotion, or any change in bosses, it is useful to consider (1) the extent of the differences between yourself and the person who will be your boss (is it possible that they are hopelessly large?); (2) whether the boss is at least as competent and powerful as his or her peers, and if not, what kinds of problems that could create for you; and (3) if there is more than one relevant boss involved, how well they agree on goals and policies, how well they get along, and whether there are any really strong animosities.

Of course, there will be some cases in which these problems cannot be eliminated by prior analysis—such as when a boss is promoted and someone else is brought in, or when a job is just so attractive that you feel it cannot be turned down. Then the burden falls on you as the subordinate to do the best you can. And if that doesn't work, the challenge becomes one of developing a sufficient power base independent of the boss or bosses so that you can avoid being arbitrarily pushed around or exploited.

Although it is far from easy, it is possible to perform admirably in a difficult leadership job despite any of the five problem situations described above. But it requires operating from a position of strength, a position that far too few people are in today.

CHAPTER TWENTY-SIX

Enlist Others

James Kouzes
Barry Posner

In the personal-best cases that we have collected over time, people frequently talked about the need to get buy-in on the vision, to enlist others in the dream. People talked about how they had to communicate the purpose and build support for the direction. They found that it's not enough for a leader to have a vision. The members of the organization must understand, accept, and commit to the vision. When they do, the organization's ability to change and reach its potential soars.

Simply put, you have to teach others your vision. Teaching a vision—and confirming that the vision is shared—is a process of engaging constituents in conversations about their lives, about their hopes and dreams. Remember that leadership is a dialogue, not a monologue. Leadership isn't about imposing the leader's solo dream; it's about developing a shared sense of destiny. It's about enrolling others so that they can see how their own interests and aspirations are aligned with the vision and can thereby become mobilized to commit their individual energies to its realization. A vision is inclusive of constituents' aspirations; it's an ideal and unique image of the future for the *common* good. Whether they're trying to mobilize a crowd in the grandstand or one person in the office, leaders must practice these three essentials to enlist others:

- Listen deeply to others
- Discover and appeal to a common purpose
- Give life to a vision by communicating expressively, so that people can see themselves in it

LISTEN DEEPLY TO OTHERS

The first task in enlisting others is to identify our constituents and find out what their common aspirations are. No matter how grand the dream of an individual visionary, if others don't see in it the possibility of realizing their own hopes and desires, they won't follow. Leaders must show others how they, too, will be served by the long-term vision of the future, how their specific needs can be satisfied.

One talent leaders need to strengthen is the ability to sense the purpose in others. By knowing their constituents, by listening to them, and by taking their advice, leaders are able to give voice to constituents' feelings. They're able to stand before others and say with assurance, "Here's what I heard you say that you want for yourselves. Here's how your own needs and interests will be served by enlisting in a common cause." In a sense, leaders hold up a mirror and reflect back to their constituents what they say they most desire. When the constituents see that reflection, they recognize it and are immediately attracted to it.

Irwin Federman was the chief financial officer at Monolithic Memories when the board of directors decided to replace the CEO and urged Irwin to take on this position. The company was bleeding money badly, it wasn't clear how it was going to be able to survive in this very competitive industry, and they had neither the time nor the resources to search for a new CEO. Irwin's not an engineer, not even a very technical sort of person, he says, and he questioned the wisdom of putting someone like him at the top of this technology-dominated company (and industry). Still, within several months, with Irwin at the helm, the company turned itself around, going from negative to positive cash flows. The lesson, according to Irwin: "Good leaders listen, take advice, lose arguments, and follow." Irwin listened very carefully to what people were saying. Since he didn't have an engineering background, he had to take the advice of others (and, in the process, make them, and not just him, responsible). He had to ask good (and tough) questions and be willing to lose arguments. In the end, he says, "I couldn't ask them to follow me, if I wasn't willing to follow them in return."

Understanding leadership as a reciprocal relationship puts listening in its proper perspective. Leaders know that they can't do it alone. Leaders know that they don't have to have all the ideas or know all of the answers. One of the key characteristics of the leaders of companies who have been honored with America's highest award for quality is that they have impressive listening skills. As one senior executive explained, winning the Malcolm Baldrige Award required "10,000 leaders, and I needed to listen to every one of them" (Garvin, 1991).

Leaders know very well that the seeds of any vision arise not from crystal ball–gazing in upper levels of the organization's stratosphere but from images passed on from volunteers or frontline personnel about what the clients or customers really want or from manufacturing's mumblings about poor product quality. The best leaders, like Irwin Federman, are the best followers. They pay attention to weak signals and quickly respond to changes in the marketplace, whether overseas or just around the corner (Deering, Dilts, & Russell, 2002).

Leaders find the common thread that weaves the fabric of human needs into a colorful tapestry. They develop a deep understanding of collective yearnings; they seek out the brewing consensus among those they would lead. They listen carefully for quiet whisperings and attend to subtle cues. They get a sense of what people want, what they value, what they dream about. Sensitivity to others is no trivial skill; rather, it is a truly precious human ability. But it isn't complex: it requires only receptiveness to other people and a willingness to listen. It means getting out of the office and spending time with people out in the field or on the factory floor or in the showroom or warehouse or back room. It means being delicately aware of the attitudes and feelings of others and the nuances of their communication.

To truly hear what constituents want—what they desperately hope to make you understand, appreciate, and include within the vision— requires periodically suspending regular activities and spending time listening to others. This means having coffee, breakfast, lunch, afternoon breaks—some unstructured time—with constituent groups (employees, associates, peers, advisers, shareholders, customers, and so on) and finding out what's going on with them and what they are hoping to achieve from their relationship with you (your product, your company, yourself). Some leaders put their desks right out on the office or factory floor to be close to the action and to the conversation. "I always refused to move into the executive office building," says Bill Flanagan, Technology Group president for Amdahl, "because then I wouldn't be able to hear what was going on firsthand. I always ate in the same cafeteria, washed my hands in the same rest rooms, used the same entrances, often copied my own materials, just so that I would be available if anyone had something they wanted to share. This gave me lots of opportunities to share ideas with others, my constituents, to make certain we were all on the same page."

Doug Podzilni, president of Gourmet Source Food Brokers, makes a point of finding off-line time with people, often spontaneously, as in the example he describes here:

> As a business manager traveling on the road with salespeople, I've found it's easy to fall into the trap of trying to fit more meetings into the day than the time allows. Recently, I surprised one salesperson by saying, "Let's stop and do something fun." We decided to go to a local ice cream parlor for a midafternoon snack. In that relaxed atmosphere, we talked about all sorts of things. As it turns out, this particular salesman had some serious personal issues on his mind. He took this opportunity to ask a few sensitive questions about his compensation, his future with the company, and the future of our division. He had been thinking about all of these questions for some time but had either not found the opportunity or had not felt comfortable in asking. I'm sure they were affecting his productivity and morale.

By taking the time to listen, Doug was able to find out information that this salesperson would never have revealed through formal communication channels. "Over chocolate sundaes," says Doug with a smile, "we addressed his concerns and strengthened the alignment between what he and the company were trying to achieve."

DISCOVER AND APPEAL TO A COMMON PURPOSE

Do you ask people why they stay? More likely, you worry about turnover and retention rates and why people leave the organization. But think about the vast majority of those who stay. Why do they?

Why do you? The most important reason people give is that they like the work they are doing, that they find it challenging, meaningful, and purposeful (Kaye & Jordan-Evans, 1999). Indeed, when we listen with sensitivity to the aspirations of others we discover that there are common values that link everyone together (Berlew, personal communication, November 14, 1994) (see also Berlew, 1974):

- A chance to be tested, to make it on one's own
- A chance to take part in a social experiment
- A chance to do something well
- A chance to do something good
- A chance to change the way things are

Aren't these the essence of what most leadership challenges, as well as opportunities, are all about?

What people want has not changed very dramatically through the years. Even though job security is increasingly tenuous, regardless of industry or location, workers rank "interesting work" well above "high income." And quality of leadership ("working for a leader with vision and values") is more motivating than dollars. The most frequently mentioned measure of success in worklife? Would it surprise you to learn that "personal satisfaction for doing a good job" is cited between three and four times as often as "getting ahead" or "making a good living" (Caggiano, 1992; Caudron, 1993; Galinsky, Bond, & Friedman, 1993)?

These findings suggest that there's more to work than is commonly assumed. There's rich opportunity for leaders to appeal to more than just the material rewards. Great leaders, like great companies and countries, create meaning and not just money. The values and interests of freedom, self-actualization, learning, community, excellence, uniqueness, service, and social responsibility truly attract people to a common cause.

There is a deep human yearning to make a difference. We want to know that we've done something on this earth, that there's a purpose to our existence. Work can provide that purpose, and increasingly work is where men and women seek it. Work has become a place where people pursue meaning and identity (Novak, 1996; Leider & Shapiro, 2001; Palmer, 2000). The best organizational leaders are able to bring out and make use of this human longing by communicating the meaning and significance of the organization's work so that people understand their own important role in creating it. When leaders clearly communicate a shared vision of an organization, they ennoble those who work on its behalf. They elevate the human spirit.

Leaders speak to people's hearts and listen to their heartbeats because, in the final analysis, common caring is the way in which shared visions get enacted. That's how David Clancy explained what Westpac's Commercial Banking organization in Australia was trying to accomplish by focusing on the question, "What does it mean to work here?" As head of that organization's Learning Resource Centre—which used to be called the Corporate Training Department—David had a vision: he and his colleagues had the job of making it possible for individuals to take responsibility for their own learning requirements and, in so doing, to discover what it is that they really care about—individually, as a team, and as an organization. John Evans, a partner in Cultural Imprint and an outside consultant with Westpac, studied a vast array of corporate "statements of vision" and found that they generally failed to compel people to action or personal responsibility. He contends that if people are to become committed to their organizations they need a cause to work for and a clear picture of what it means to work at their organization. Our research on what people expect from their leaders echoes this perspective: leaders uplift people's spirits.

Visions are not strategic plans. Contemporary management scholars all agree that strategic planning is not strategic thinking (Mintzberg & Norman, 2001; Handy, 1999; Hamel, 2000). Strategic planning often spoils strategic thinking because it causes managers to believe that the manipulation of numbers creates imaginative insight into the future and vision. This confusion lies at the heart of the issue: the most successful strategies are visions; they are not plans. McGill University professor Harry Mintzberg explains that planning represents a "calculating" style, while leaders employ a "committing" style—one that "engage[s] people in a journey. They lead in such a way that everyone on the journey helps shape its course. As a result, enthusiasm inevitably builds along the way. Those with a calculating style fix on a destination and calculate what the group must do to get there, with no concern for the members' preferences. But calculated strategies have no value in and of themselves. . . . Strategies take on value only as committed people infuse them with energy" (Mintzberg, 1994, p. 109).

Leadership that focuses on a committing style is what leadership scholars have called transformational leadership. Transformational leadership occurs when, in their interactions, people "raise one another to higher levels of motivation and morality. Their purposes, which might have started out as separate but related, as in the case of transactional leadership, become fused. . . . But transforming leadership ultimately becomes moral in that it raises the level of human conduct and ethical aspiration of both the leader and the led, and thus it has a transforming effect on both" (Burns, 1978, p. 20).

The most admired leaders speak unhesitatingly and proudly of mutual ethical aspirations. They know that people aspire to live up to the highest moral standards. So the first essential for enlisting others is to find and focus on the very best that the culture—group, unit, project, program, agency, community, organization, government, or nation—shares in common and what that means to its members. This communion of purpose, this commemoration of our dreams, helps to bind us together. It reminds us of what it means to be a part of this collective effort. It joins us together in the human family.

This sense of belonging is particularly key in tumultuous times, whatever the cause of the tumult. In the 1990s, the telecommunications industry took a quantum technological leap forward. As a consequence, competition became more fierce, downsizings more common, and customer needs changed dramatically. It was far from business as usual: people's talents had to drastically expand to meet the new demands. This was the situation facing AT&T branch manager Jack Schiefer and his leadership team as they set forth to grow their business throughout the Rocky Mountain states.

As Jack tells it, "We knew we had a problem as a team because we weren't a team. But none of us knew what to do to become one. We were too close to it." They began their quest to become a world-class sales organization with a leadership team offsite workshop based on The Leadership Challenge. A decade later, Jack still acknowledges and confirms that the team was acquiescent, but not totally committed. Then, as the discussion moved to the idea of a shared vision, "you could feel the energy change in the room from a very casual attitude to—all of a sudden—becoming electric." The difference came when the members of the group "became committed to a journey to find out what to do to become more effective as leaders and help our associates grow."

At first, "the horizon that we were looking at was maybe a month to three months." In looking up into space, they quickly saw that they needed a vision that would work, no matter what change was occurring, something that would stand the test of time. To get there, they shared with each other the heartfelt desires they each had for their Sales Center and for the kind of leaders they wanted to become. From that initial groundbreaking, the vision of a world-class sales organization, grounded in quality and reflecting a renewed commitment to their customers, their families, and each other, was born.

Theirs was much more than a one-time exercise to craft a slick-sounding statement; it was the creation of a new culture of success built on superior results and "value-based leadership." Has their vision work been helpful? In an industry where pricing has dropped through the floor, annual associate turnover has averaged 30 percent, and massive, gut-wrenching business-unit-wide reorganizations have occurred almost every year, Jack's team has continued to put up astonishing results. Jack feels so strongly about the sales center's vision and their continuing attention to it that he says, "you have nothing to lose and everything to gain by accepting the possibility that a shared vision and a commitment to it will allow your professional life and your personal life to be richer than they are today." With the zealousness of a converted skeptic (and a businessman interested in delivering results as cost-effectively as possible), he says, "inspiring a shared vision is the most efficient way to produce outstanding results."

GIVE LIFE TO A VISION

Clearly, shared vision is key—and to enlist others, leaders need to bring that vision to life. Leaders animate the vision and make manifest the purpose so that others can see it, hear it, taste it, touch it, feel it. In making the intangible vision tangible, leaders ignite constituents' flames of passion. By using powerful language, positive communication style, and nonverbal expressiveness, leaders breathe life (the literal definition of the word inspire) into a vision.

Use Powerful Language

Leaders make full use of the power of language to communicate a shared identity and give life to visions. Successful leaders use metaphors and other figures of speech; they give examples, tell stories, and relate anecdotes; they draw word pictures; and they offer quotations and recite slogans.

Review the words of Dr. Martin Luther King Jr. Notice his use of visual and aural images: "the red hills of Georgia," "the prodigious hilltops of New Hampshire," "the heightening Alleghenies of Pennsylvania," "the jangling discords of our nation," and "a beautiful symphony of brotherhood." Read the specific examples: "where little black boys and black girls will be able to join hands with little white boys and white girls and walk together as sisters and brothers" and "a dream that my four little children will one day live in a nation where they will not be judged by the color of their skin but by the content of their character" (King, 1983, pp. 95–98). Notice the references to the Constitution and the quotations from anthems and spirituals. All these skillful uses of language give the listener a visceral feel for King's dream. They enable us to picture the future, to hear it, to sense it, to recognize it.

All of us can enrich language with stories, references, and figures of speech; in fact, doing so is a natural way of communicating. You need only think of how children tell each other stories, how they love to have stories told to them. Or consider the days before television, when people loved to imagine scenes described by a radio announcer. Even today's most popular video games take the players through stories or adventures.

Metaphors are plentiful in our daily conversations. We talk of computers as having memory, of time as money and knowledge as power. We talk about business as a game. Military metaphors are used in corporate strategy and sports vernacular in meetings. Metaphors and analogies are as common as numbers in organizations. Leaders make conscious use of metaphorical expressions to give vividness and tangibility to abstract ideas.

In all our discussions of leadership, we use the journey metaphor to express our understanding of leadership. We talk about leaders as pioneers and trailblazers who take people on expeditions to places they've never been. We talk about vision as the beckoning summit. We talk about climbing to the top and about milestones and signposts. All of these metaphorical expressions are our way of communicating the active, pioneering nature of leadership.

Language is a powerful tool. Remember the contrast between the bank officer rallying his managers to take on the hostile competition and Anita Roddick joyfully liberating her people to make a difference at The Body Shop. Ken Wilcox, president and CEO for Silicon Valley Bank, which provides start-up funding to thousands of new ventures, explained how he learned about the power of language. An early vision statement for the bank was "50 in 5" and was meant to capture the drive to move the share price to $50 million within five years. "While it was a compelling rallying cry for our employees," he told us, "its problem was that it had very little relevance for our clients." For that reason, former president and CEO John Dean introduced a new vision statement: "Bringing our clients' vision to life by providing exceptional business solutions." As Ken puts it, "This brings us close to our customers, and makes our purpose and theirs one and the same." Leaders learn to master the richness of figurative speech so that they can paint the word pictures that best portray the meaning of their visions.

The shift in statements of vision and purpose for Silicon Valley Bank is one dramatic example of the difference in perspective between mercenaries and missionaries, a difference that was evident in the dot-com implosion at the start of this century. Those organizations and leaders who were driven only by money and revenue (and greed) were left behind in the marketplace by those companies compelled by a sense of purpose and a view, literally, of changing the landscape.

Practice Positive Communication

We want leaders with enthusiasm, with a bounce in their step, with a positive attitude. We want to believe that we'll be part of an invigorating journey. We follow people with a can-do attitude, not those who give sixty-seven reasons why something can't be done or who don't make us feel good about ourselves or what we're doing.

The leaders people most admire are electric, vigorous, active, full of life. We're reminded of our colleague Randi DuBois, one of the founders of Pro-Action, who gets people to stretch themselves by engaging in challenging physical tasks. Typically, her clients are nervous, even a bit scared at first. But people of all ages, all sizes, and all physical abilities have successfully completed the Pro-Action outdoor challenge courses. How does Randi succeed in leading these people? Her secret is very simple: she's always positive that people can do the course, and she never says never. She conveys very clearly that people have the power within themselves to accomplish whatever they desire. (Both authors know this from personal experience. We've been forty feet above the ground leaping off a small platform for an iron ring while Randi cheered us on.)

Less dramatic, and every bit as effective, is the positive attitude and communication style that Joan Carter exhibited when she took over as general manager and executive chef of the Faculty Club at Santa

Clara University. Before Joan's arrival, both membership and sales had been seriously declining for several years, remaining customers were unhappy, the restaurant's balance sheet was "scary," and the staff was divided into factions.

Joan took all this in, and what she saw was a dusty diamond. "I saw a beautiful and historic building full of mission-era flavor and character that should be, could be, would be the place on campus." In her mind's eye, she saw the club bustling. She saw professors and university staff chatting on the lovely enclosed patio and enjoying high-quality, appealing yet inexpensive meals. She smiled as she envisioned the club assisting alumni in planning wonderful, personal, and professionally catered wedding receptions and anniversary celebrations. Joan could see a happy staff whose primary concern was customer satisfaction, a kitchen that produced a product far superior to "banquet food," and a catering staff that did whatever it took to make an event exceptional. She wasn't quite sure how the club had deteriorated to the extent it had, but that really didn't matter. She decided to ignore the quick fix and set out to teach everyone how unique and wonderful the club could be.

Over the next two years, as she talked with customers and worked with her staff, she instilled a vision of the club as a restaurant that celebrated good food and good company. As food and service quality began to improve, smiles became more prevalent among customers and staff and sales began to rise: 20 percent the first year and 30 percent again the next. When a top financial manager of the university asked how she had managed to turn the finances around so quickly and dramatically, Joan responded, "You can't turn around numbers. The balance sheet is just a reflection of what's happening here, every day, in the restaurant. I just helped the staff realize what we're really all about. It was always here," she said, "only perhaps a little dusty, a little ignored, and a little unloved. I just helped them see it."

Tap into Nonverbal Expressiveness

In explaining why particular leaders have a magnetic effect, people often describe them as charismatic. But charisma has become such an overused and misused term that it's almost useless as a descriptor of leaders. "In the popular media," notes leadership scholar Bernard Bass (1985), "charisma has come to mean anything ranging from chutzpah to Pied Piperism, from celebrity to superman status. It has become an overworked cliché for strong, attractive, and inspiring personality" (p. 35).

Social scientists have attempted to investigate this elusive quality in terms of observable behavior (see, for example, Friedman, Prince, Riggio, & DiMatteo, 1980; Goleman, Boyatzis, & McKee, 2002; Conger, 1998). What they've found is that people who are perceived to be charismatic are simply more animated than others. They smile more, speak faster, pronounce words more clearly, and move their heads and bodies more often. They are also more likely to reach out and touch or make some physical contact with others during greetings. What we call charisma, then, can better be understood as nonverbal (and very human) expressiveness.

Similar reactions to nonverbal behavior are seen in the gestural language of children. The way children relate to each other nonverbally can be divided into five categories of interpersonal behavior: attractive actions, threatening actions, aggressive actions, gestures of fear and retreat, and actions that produce isolation (Pines, 1984). Children who become the leaders in their groups use attractive actions, not aggressive actions. At least in the world of the very young, real leaders—those who are naturally followed—aren't the young Rambos. The natural leaders are those who offer toys to others, lightly touch or caress, clap hands, smile, extend a hand, lean in to listen; they don't scratch, hit, or pull. Adults can learn much about leading from children: it's not aggression that attracts; it's warmth and friendship.

ENLIST OTHERS IN A COMMON VISION BY APPEALING TO SHARED ASPIRATIONS

Leaders breathe life into visions. They communicate their hopes and dreams so that others clearly understand and accept them as their own. Leaders know what motivates their constituents. They show others how their values and interests will be served by a particular long-term vision of the future. Above all, they're convinced of the value of that vision themselves and share that genuine belief with others.

Leaders use a variety of modes of expression to make their abstract visions concrete. Through skillful use of metaphors, symbols, positive language, and personal energy, they generate enthusiasm and excitement for the common vision. In this commitment, we provide some action steps that you can take to increase your ability to enlist the support of others.

- *Get to know your constituents.*

Identify your constituents. Make a list of all the individuals or groups of individuals you want to enlist in your vision of the future. Your organizational managers and any direct reports are obviously on the list. In all probability, you'll also want your peers, customers, and suppliers to buy into your dream. Perhaps you'll want the support of the citizens of your local community. There are bound to be elements of your vision that will be of interest to the state and the nation in which you do business. You may even have a global vision. And don't limit your list to present constituents only. As your organization grows and develops, it will want to attract new people to it. You'll want future generations to take an active interest in what you want to accomplish, so consider their needs and values. Today's students are tomorrow's employees, customers, and investors. They may be the ones who actually help you to realize what you only dream of today. The point is this: identify those who have a stake today and will have a stake tomorrow in the outcomes of what you envision.

Then, once you've identified your constituents, conduct what the marketing folks call "focus groups" with your key constituencies. On a regular basis, ask your constituents to tell you about what they like and don't like about your product, services, programs, policies, leadership practices, and so on. The important points are that you value their opinions, and that you listen carefully to their opinions. What's more, in focus group or forum settings you benefit from the way people bounce ideas off one another. You also get a chance to test whether one person's or group's needs are idiosyncratic or commonly held. Everyone learns in this process about what it takes to work together to achieve common objectives.

At the Ritz-Carlton, the only hotel company to receive the coveted Malcolm Baldrige National Quality Award, they take this process one step further. Every morning at 9:00, about eighty of the company's top executives gather for The Daily Lineup, a ten-minute meeting in the hallway outside the president's office. Just as important, within twenty-four hours, at every hotel from Boston to Bali, the rest of the company's employees get the same concentrated dose of the Ritz credo at their daily shift meetings. The lineup is run by a volunteer facilitator, and the meeting is split into three parts. First, they introduce the topic of the week. Second, they revisit one of their "customer service basics." Finally, they run through operational issues that are specific to each department: anything from the specials on the menu to an upcoming meeting with an investor. Ten minutes after the meeting begins, everyone is back at work. Leonardo Inghilleri, senior vice president of human resources, explained that the lineup "establishes an emotional tie with rest of the company. For one critical moment every day, the entire organization is aligned behind the same issue" (Olofson, 1998, p. 62).

Your forum need not be as formal as that of the Ritz. You might simply devise a regular scheme of having a morning or afternoon break with a random group of people in your organization to talk about whatever they want to talk about. Barry Posner does exactly that as dean at Santa Clara University's Leavey School of Business. One year Barry simply randomly divided the entire faculty into equal-size groups and took those people out to lunch (and conversation) during the month. The next year, he organized the groups by department or function; another year, by representative groups (relatively new and senior, tenured and untenured, assistant, associate, or full professors). As Posner says, "While there are lots of things that I hope my lunch guests, and constituents, get out of these conversations, I know that I always come away with new ideas and insights. They remind me how easy it is to get out of touch with people, even in a relatively small organization."

• *Find the common ground.*

Finding common ground is ever more important with the increase in diversity, both in workforce and customers and with the influence of the Internet. Virtual isn't enough. To attract people from divergent backgrounds and interests, you must discover what aspirations, goals, needs, and dreams they have in common. People are bound to differ in much of what they value; you must work through the differences to find what can bring them together. Your ability to enlist people depends on how effective you are at detecting the tie that binds.

There are numerous ways you can find out what people want, from sophisticated market research techniques (including gathering customer information via the Internet) to simple surveys. Each has its usefulness. But no technique can substitute for face-to-face human interaction. The very best way to get to know what other people want is to sit down and talk with them on their turf. If you feel that you don't really understand people in the factory, move your desk onto the floor for the next few weeks. If you feel that you don't know much about the store owners who buy your packaged goods, ride the route trucks once a week for a year. Get out there and make contact. Ask one simple question: "What do you most want from this organization?"

Then, when you've gathered the data and have a true feel for your constituents, sit down and see what patterns and themes emerge. There are bound to be several. For example, Tom Melohn found out that customers of North American Tool and Die (NATD) wanted "quality, service, price"—in that order. At first, Tom was surprised by this. He had spent twenty-five years in the packaged goods industry, where a fraction of a cent made a major difference. So he kept on asking, and the customers kept on telling him: first quality, then service, then price. Not surprisingly, the focus of NATD today is first and foremost on quality.

One other hint about finding the common ground: avoid being too specific. Vision statements aren't job descriptions. They're not product or service specifications. To have the broadest appeal, visions must be encompassing. They should transcend the day-to-day work (voluntary or paid) and find expression in higher-order human needs. Visions should uplift and ennoble.

• *Draft a collective vision statement.*

Leadership is not a monologue, nor should the creation of a vision statement be done individually and without the active involvement of others who must attend to these operations. The process of finding common ground, often through the creation of a statement of shared values and vision, is as important as the content itself, and sometimes even more so. Soliciting people's ideas and listening to their concerns is critical at the early stages. Look for feedback through such questions as, What interests of yours are not well represented? In what respect is it not fair? How would you improve upon it? If people resist giving you their ideas or giving you feedback on yours, try to involve them by offering a choice or list of alternatives. Once an alternative is selected, it becomes their idea. Remembering this Chinese proverb is useful in this regard: "Tell me, I may listen. Teach me, I may remember. Involve me, I will do it."

Once you've elicited everyone's ideas, circulate draft versions of the vision statement incorporating those ideas. Revise the draft, and as necessary ask for more input or criticism. Gradually you will build consensus because as people get involved, they begin to think of the draft as their own. And it will be!

Yet the process of developing a common vision can seem overwhelming even in small organizations. In larger ones, it requires serious ongoing effort. Imagine the effort involved in aligning over thirteen thousand employees—simultaneously. Victoria Sandvig, vice president of the Event and Production Services Department of Corporate

Communications at Charles Schwab & Co., Inc., spoke with us about the process used to align people and the long-term direction of Schwab. By 1999, nearly half of Schwab's employees were new since the vision and values had last been spread, company-wide. The beginnings of VisionQuest stirred when a group called Root Learning, Inc., started creating some maps of vision and values, originally for the executive committee. As Victoria puts it, "One of these maps addressed questions of who the company is, its vision, and values. The second one was very much about where we want to go, who our competition is, who our clients are, the profile of our customers." After the executive committee, the maps were presented to the senior management team, where their power became obvious to the larger group. Then began the process of involving the company at large. "We first thought of cascading it down through the organization. But," Victoria continues, "the idea of rolling it out to everyone at once took hold. We knew there was an incredible opportunity: we could create an event around it, and build in some elements that would touch the heart and the soul of every employee."

And so, across the United States and across the world, Schwab employees gathered on a Saturday in March 1999. The six-hour event kicked off in San Francisco's Moscone Center at 8:30 A.M., with six thousand people there. Other locations had fewer people—and they were all hooked up via satellite. "Whatever the locale," Victoria says, "everyone was seated in groups of ten, with a trained facilitator at each table. People were assigned seats so that they were mixed up by tenure, by enterprise, and by titles: we tried to get as much cross-pollenization as possible. The impact was incredible. It kept people renewed in the vision, committed to it, and absolutely aligned with who we are as a company and where we're going."

And, big as it was, VisionQuest was no one-shot deal. Schwab reenacted the event days later for the five hundred people in the crew that had kept the company up and running during the Saturday event. And it continued with a series of mini-VisionQuests for new employees who came on board subsequently.

As the people at Schwab understood, renewing community and commitment to shared values and common purpose is essential if we are to keep from being blinded by rigid adherence to a set of principles and aspirations that no longer make sense. Finding common ground is a dynamic rather than a stable process, and leaders are constantly vigilant in understanding how the ground beneath them may be shifting.

• *Expand your communication skills.*

If your communication abilities have room for improvement (and whose don't?), take advantage of training opportunities. Every leader ought to know how to paraphrase, summarize, express feelings, disclose personal information, admit mistakes, respond nondefensively, ask for clarification, solicit different views, and so on.

It is an absolute that the higher you advance in an organization, the more presentations you will give to an ever-widening audience. A course in presentation skills will benefit you greatly. Don't wait until your next promotion to improve your communication skills. If you haven't taken a public speaking course yet, sign up for the next available class. Presentation workshops can help you learn effective techniques for getting your ideas across. They can also help you gain confidence in yourself. If giving a speech makes you nervous, you're neither unusual nor alone. According to research done by a nationwide communication training and consulting firm, many people are more afraid of having to give a speech than they are of dying (Decker, 1993). Overcome the anxiety of public speaking and an enormous weight may be lifted from your shoulders.

Speak positively. When talking about mutual aspirations, don't say try, say will and are. There's no room for tentativeness or qualifiers in statements of vision. Sure, there are lots of contingencies and reasons why something might not happen. But citing eighty-three potential obstacles and thirty-three conditions that must be met will only discourage people from joining the cause. You need not be a Pollyanna: talk realistically about the hardships and difficult conditions—just don't dwell on them.

Reasonable people know that great achievements require hard work. Let people know that you have the utmost confidence in their ability to succeed. Tell them that you're certain that they'll prevail. Tell them that you have faith in them.

Furthermore, enthusiasm and emotions are catching, so let yours show. Smile. Use gestures and move your body. Speak clearly and quickly. Make eye contact. All of these signals are cues to others that you're personally excited about what you're saying. If you don't perceive yourself as an expressive person, begin to practice expressiveness by talking to a favorite friend about what most excites you in life. As you do this, pay attention to your verbal and nonverbal behavior. If possible, turn on a video camera so that you can watch yourself later.

We bet that you'll discover that when you talk about things that excite you, you do a lot of the things we've just described.

• *Breathe life into your vision.*

Write a vision statement for your current organization. Critique it and look for places where you can breathe life into it (add inspiration) to make it come alive for your audience. Prepare yourself now to make the vision sing.

Because visions exist in the future, leaders have to get others in the present to imagine what that future will look like, feel like, sound like, even smell like. In short, just as attributes such as quality, service, and responsiveness don't exist in nature but must be defined in concrete terms, your vision—an intangible—must be made tangible. Use as many forms of expression as you can to transform the vision's intangibles into tangibles. Make any abstractions—such as freedom, service, respect, quality, or innovation—concrete so that others can recognize what you imagine. When it comes to visions, we're all from Missouri: we need to be shown. So enrich your language with stories, metaphors, analogies, and examples; use slogans, theme songs, poetry, quotations, and humor. Think of ways to incorporate symbols, banners, posters, and other visual aids in your presentations. Remember that symbols, not acronyms, capture the imagination. The eagle is a symbol of strength, the olive branch a symbol of peace, and the lion a symbol of courage. The Statue of Liberty is a symbol of America as the land of freedom of opportunity. Wells Fargo Bank uses the stagecoach to symbolize its pioneering spirit. Mary Kay Cosmetics uses the bumblebee as a symbol for doing what others say can't be done.

Think you can't give an inspiring speech? Remember that most famous speeches were not extemporaneous. They had been tested before, on other events and in other conversations. For example, Martin Luther King Jr. tried out versions of his famous "I Have a Dream" speech on several occasions, refining it before its seemingly spontaneous presentation before the crowd at the Lincoln Memorial. Be prepared to take your first draft (or latest draft, whatever its number) and continue to revise, hone, edit, and revise again until you think it expresses your ideas just right.

If you need some help in adding tangibility to your presentations, spend a little time studying advertising and the performing arts. Those in theater and advertising have to get their audiences to experience something vicariously. Both fields are rich sources of creative ideas on how to convey abstract concepts and how to appeal to human emotions.

- *Speak from the heart.*

None of these suggestions will be of any value whatsoever if you don't believe in what you're saying. If the vision is someone else's, and you don't own it, it will be very difficult for you to enlist others in it. If you have trouble imagining yourself actually living the future described in the vision, you'll certainly not be able to convince others that they ought to enlist in making it a reality. If you're not excited about the possibilities, how can you expect others to be? The prerequisite to enlisting others in a shared vision is genuineness. The first place to look before making that speech is in your heart.

When asked how she was able to lead the development team for the PCnet family of Advanced Micro Devices, breaking all barriers and launching this extremely successful family of products, Laila Razouk replied simply, "I believed. Believing is a very important part of the action. You have to have faith. If you don't have that, then you're lost even before you get started." It's easy to understand why people are eager to follow Laila: "If I believe in something badly enough, and if I have the conviction, then I start picturing and envisioning how it will look if we did this or if we did that. By sharing these thoughts with other people, the excitement grows and people become part of that picture. Without much effort—with energy, but not much effort—the magic starts to happen. People start to bounce ideas back and forth, they get involved, brainstorm, and share ideas. Then I know I don't have to worry about it."

How successful would the project have been if instead Laila had thought, "This project will never work. The person who thought this up doesn't understand the details. I'm doing this because I'm forced to, but I really think this project is a stupid idea!" For Laila, the net effect of speaking from the heart, as she explains it, is that "by openly sharing what I saw, what I knew, and what I believed—not by dictating it, but by being willing to iterate and adjust things—I got other people involved."

- *Listen first—and often.*

Listening is one of the key characteristics of exemplary leaders. To truly hear what your constituents want—what they desperately hope to make you understand, appreciate, and include within the vision—requires that you periodically suspend your regular activity and spend time listening to others. Note the ratio between the number of your ears and your mouth, and make certain that you listen twice as often as you talk.

In listening we not only hear, but we are forced to pay attention. Leaders listen for more than just information; they listen to communicate how seriously they consider the feelings and thoughts of others. The Journal of the American Medical Association reported on a five-year investigation of why some doctors were sued, and others not, by parents who had all experienced the same tragedy (the death of their child during childbirth). The researchers report, "Physicians who had been sued frequently were perceived by their patients as unavailable, rushed, unconcerned, and poor communicators, while physicians with no malpractice claims were perceived as most available, interested, thorough, and willing to provide information and answer questions fully" (Hickson et al., 1994). Clearly, listening deeply makes a difference.

And being a good listener has the side benefit of making you more flexible and capable of functioning in a wide range of cultures and environments. If you get feedback that you're too one-dimensional in your approach to situations, consider becoming a better listener. For example, if you're planning a trip to another country, be sure to study the culture. Read about that culture, its history, politics, and religion. Listen to the music and sounds of that people, group, or community. Watch films. Visit art galleries. Sample the food. Your international colleagues will feel more comfortable around you (and you around them). The same principles apply closer to home when you step outside your cultural experience. One way to become a more skillful listener is by seeking the assistance of an "interpreter," someone who can answer your questions and who can show you around and help you learn outside your realm of experience. In this interchange, both parties often learn more about each other's culture and gain insight into the subtleties and unexamined aspects of their own.

• *Hang out.*

Gretchen Kaffer, a human resource administrator with Honeywell-Measurex, had gotten so busy that she stopped spending time in the cafeteria and the patio chatting with her coworkers during lunch and started eating at her desk, instead. A reorganization brought her group into a refurbished building with a spacious new break room where, as Gretchen noticed, people began to hang out for lunch. So she decided to make lunch a regularly scheduled part of her day again and join her colleagues.

"The first couple of times I popped in," she reports, "everyone looked up at me as if I were coming to ask someone a work-related question. They were surprised that I was joining them for lunch.

I think some people may have thought that I didn't want to spend time with them, or even didn't like them, since I had started eating lunch at my desk." It didn't take long before Gretchen learned all sorts of things about her colleagues, and the organization, things she'd been missing out on.

"It also opened up some good conversations about work and non-work-related issues and events," says Gretchen. "It has really allowed us to hash over some changes and procedures that we wouldn't normally get to discuss in such a large group, because we rarely have time to discuss even the big stuff in groups of more than two or three. I think this has allowed my coworkers access to what I am doing. It gives them the opportunity to ask me questions, make suggestions, and fill me in on the not-so-important, but interesting and possibly telling, employee relations and interactions that I have been missing while cooped up in my office."

There's another side benefit to the "lunch club thing," as they call it. Employees "from other departments seem pleasantly surprised by the laughter coming out of our break room. They walk by, or purposely seek us out. Sometimes they stop and ask if we're having a party. We often invite them to join us . . . I think this has definitely improved our image as a team, given us greater visibility and allowed us more contact with other employees in our building." And since the gang's gotten used to Gretchen's hanging out with them, they now expect to see her. "Around 12 or 12:15 there's usually a face in my doorway asking if I'm 'doing the lunch club thing.'"

Another way to hang out, get your ear to the ground, and be in a position to listen to others is to change places for some period of time with one of your key constituents or stakeholders. Many companies invite their employees to step into the shoes of their managers for a day and learn about the demands and responsibilities of management. But isn't what is good for the goose also good for the gander? Why not have your management team take over the jobs of their nonmanagerial associates? That's the way they worked at the Florence, Kentucky, distribution center of Levi Strauss & Co. The plant's general manager told us that he learned a great deal about how hard people work in getting pants out the door. "Spending time on the plant floor actually packing jeans and carting boxes around gives me a much greater appreciation for the talents required and pressures we place on people than anything I learn from reading reports generated by our human resources department. I also get to meet lots of people on an informal and first-name basis. Of course, they get to meet me on the same basis." Learn about what other people do in your organization by periodically working alongside them for a day (or more).

Whether it's joining the lunch club or walking the plant floor, being present, paying attention, and listening to the concerns and accomplishments of others allows leaders to gather critical information about what people care about and how well they understand what's going on in the organization. You've got to be there to know what's happening. And when you hang out and spend time listening, people know you're interested in them, and they want to see and talk with you.

PART SIX

OD Focus

Organizational Intervention Targets

C hanges in the environment, context, and knowledge base for OD over the last half century have expanded the range of points of system entry and targets for intervention. Enhancing organizational effectiveness and health requires attention to a wide range of organizational dynamics, areas, and processes. OD stays true to its core purpose—and strengthens its reputation and impact—when it does just that. OD began with a focus on meeting the needs of mature adults in organizations. Those roots initially took the field down a path emphasizing people processes and relationships at work. OD's early charter, however, was never intended to limit the field's own growth and development. Beckhard and Burke tell us that in Part One. And Edgar H. Schein reminds us in the Foreword to this volume that diversity in approach and method has characterized organization development from its inception. OD has an important role to play in aligning the full range of organizational elements, including mission, people, strategy, structure, work forms, culture, physical setting, and more. OD practitioners need the knowledge and versatility in content and process to play that role. Whatever the focus, OD stays true to its core when it approaches the work with strategies that mobilize the involvement, contributions, and commitment of people throughout the organization. OD methods have always been informed by a basic truth: two heads are better than one.

The chapters in Part Six carry readers on a journey to many of the more significant locales where OD can apply its methods and meaningfully involve people in critical choices. They offer change agents a map for exploring these different terrains. OD practitioners who understand where, why, and how to intervene in a broad array of circumstances are more likely to have the tools that fit the needs of different client systems.

Edward E. Lawler examines the role and function of strategy in organizational effectiveness in an excerpt from his book, *From the Ground Up: Six Principles for Building the New Logic Corporation.* A good strategy drives organizational structure, according to Lawler. It links mission, the core competencies and organizational capabilities needed to perform the work, a realistic understanding of the environment, and strong leadership. Jay Galbraith tackles the issue of organizational design in excerpts from *Designing Organizations: An Executive Guide to Strategy, Structure, and Process.* His model for matching strategy and structure complements the Lawler chapter. Next, Marvin Weisbord explores the design and meaning of work in contemporary organizations in a chapter from *Productive Workplaces Revisited: Dignity, Meaning, and Community in the 21st Century.* His work-design methodology promotes involving people in the redesign of their own jobs. The linkages to OD's core values and methods are obvious. Franklin Becker and Fritz Steele examine the impact of physical settings, workspace, and organizational ecology on productivity and effectiveness. Their chapter, "Making It Happen: Turning Workplace Vision into Reality," from *Workplace by Design: Mapping the High Performance Workscape,* is a practical guide for linking workplace design issues with organizational goals, culture, leadership, and learning.

Edgar Schein has written extensively on the issue of organizational culture. In an excerpt from *The Corporate Culture Survival Guide,* he provides strategies for how to assess a corporate culture, as well as case examples that illustrate application and uses for his methodology. Next, Edward E. Lawler makes a second contribution to Part Six. He offers both a helpful analysis of what makes people effective at work and suggestions for workforce development in a chapter from *Treat People Right! How Organizations and Employees Can Create a Win/Win Relationship to Achieve High Performance at All Levels.* As the title indicates, the consistency with OD's legacy and values is obvious. Teamwork is a given in organizations, and team building is a pillar in organization development work. Glenn M. Parker analyzes the causes of effective and ineffective teams and provides a framework for team development in excerpts from his book, *Team Players and Teamwork*.

Leadership development has had an on again-off again history with OD. The early days of the OD field focused heavily on the use of laboratory education to increase individual effectiveness and agency, thereby strengthening organizational productivity. Leaders were expected to take their personal learnings and insights into the workplace, model alternative behaviors, and lead others to more effective ways of functioning. Once the field's methods moved beyond T-groups and laboratory training, however, leaders were given a different role. Their new job was to launch and support OD efforts—and they were trained in how to do that appropriately. General leadership development, in contrast, fell largely outside the parameters of OD, even as workforce and team development continued to be intervention mainstays. The logic was that OD aims its intervention at groups and systems, not individuals. Leadership development came to be seen as an individual, not a system, benefit. This perspective, however, neglects the growing importance of leadership at all levels of an organization, as well as every organization's responsibility to foster leadership development across its ranks. The strength and success of a client organization's leadership development system shape that organization's present and future. For this reason, leadership development is a key organizational component and legitimate point of entry for intervention. Part Six ends with a chapter by Jay Conger and Beth Benjamin from *Building Leaders: How Successful Companies Develop the Next Generation* that examines both content and processes for effective organization-wide leadership development programs.

Business Strategy

Creating the Winning Formula

Edward E. Lawler

An effective business strategy provides the formula an organization needs in order to win. It should state the organization's purpose, direction, goals, and objectives and, in most cases, specify the tasks it must accomplish to succeed.

To be effective, an organization needs to develop the appropriate performance capabilities and to use them to do the right things. The process is not unlike preparing an athlete for the track and field competition of the decathlon, where an athlete must perform effectively in ten events. Athletes cannot work on one event, perform it, and then practice the next event before performing it. All the performance capabilities have to be present simultaneously. That is only possible if the athlete knows what capabilities are needed. In the decathlon, this is rather obvious; the events and the skills needed have been identified for decades. With organizational performance, the necessary capabilities and competencies are not always easily determined, nor is it always clear when different kinds of performance will be needed.

It is up to the leaders in the organization to develop a strategy that identifies the kinds of performances that are needed, to communicate the need for them through mission and values statements, and to

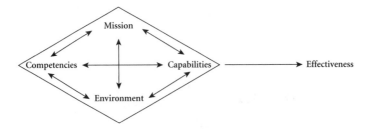

Figure 27.1.   The Diamond Model.

develop the competencies and capabilities needed to perform them. They can only do this well if they have a good understanding of the environment the organization faces and how business strategies and performance are related to competencies and capabilities. This relationship is shown in the Diamond Model (Figure 27.1), which shows that organizational effectiveness, and therefore a good strategy, results when there is a fit among four points: mission, competencies, capabilities, and the environment.

This chapter begins with a brief discussion of the way companies have historically developed strategy and why and how strategy development must change in the new logic. The focus will then shift to how mission and values statements, core competencies, and organizational capabilities are the key components of winning business strategies.

THE OLD WAY: FORMAL STRATEGIC PLANNING

In the old logic, a large corporate staff of strategic planners and futurists was responsible for developing and communicating corporate strategy to the rest of the organization. These experts, who usually were not involved in producing the organization's services or products, carefully studied them and their positions in the market. They then created one-year and longer-term strategic plans that were regularly updated with new numbers and new planning targets and objectives.

A classic example is General Electric of the 1970s and early 1980s. Once the strategic direction for the corporation was set, managers from the different business units were asked to produce plans for their units that supported the corporate plan. They were also required to produce large amounts of data to support their business plans, to present them to corporate strategic planners, and to convince the planners that their plans should be accepted.

To say that the old logic of strategic planning has fallen on hard times would be an understatement. Henry Mintzberg, a well-known organization theorist and professor, has argued in his book *The Rise and Fall of Strategic Planning* that strategic planning is an oxymoron, because planning is about analysis, and strategy is about synthesis (Mintzberg, 1994). Planning is about facts, operations, and budgets, whereas strategy requires creative thinking about mission and how to gain competitive advantage.

Recently, organization after organization has decided to abandon traditional strategic planning, because it simply has not produced the kinds of results that justify either the costs of having a central staff or the tremendous amounts of work generated throughout the organization. As Mintzberg notes, there are a number of reasons that strategic planning has delivered disappointing results, but perhaps the primary one is the difficulty of predicting the future in an increasingly turbulent world.

During the period when strategic planning was popular, some organizations spent considerable time and money trying to get good at predicting the future. They hired experts who studied the future through technologies like the delphi approach, which integrates the predictions of many experts. Universities such as my own created centers that focused on predicting future trends in world hunger, oil prices, and other areas. Companies contributed money to these centers in the hope of improving their strategic planning process and gaining an advantage over their competitors.

Unfortunately, most attempts at prediction proved faulty, particularly with respect to long-term trends. In the 1970s, for example, there were predictions that oil would be at $100 a barrel by the early 1990s; none of the experts dreamed that oil prices would fall steadily through the 1980s and stay at around $20 a barrel during the first half of the 1990s.

The demise of strategic planning has led some organizations to say that their strategic objective is simply to make money. Managers are then given annual budgets, financial targets, market share objectives, and new product introduction dates. But this approach goes too far in the opposite direction and is clearly incongruent with the new logic.

The new logic requires much more. It requires that individuals throughout the organization have a sense of purpose and mission as well as values that guide their behavior. Without many of the traditional bureaucratic controls to direct their efforts, employees must understand what the organization is trying to accomplish and what values should guide them. Their understanding is critical to their ability to make decisions and to manage themselves and their work. A simple statement such as "we exist in order to make money for our shareholders" is just not enough to allow the members of an organization to understand what they should be doing, why they should do it, and how they should do it.

James Collins and Jerry Porras (1994) present evidence to show that companies that have a strong sense of mission, values, and culture have outperformed their competitors in virtually every instance. They compare what they call built-to-last companies such as Merck, General Electric, and Boeing with companies that lack a sense of mission, such as Bristol-Meyers, Westinghouse, and McDonnell Douglas. The difference in performance between the two types of companies is dramatic. The built-to-last companies clearly have outperformed those that simply emphasize financial returns as their reason for being in business. This supports the new logic argument that organizations and individuals are most effective when they are guided by a sense of mission and values rather than by attention simply to the bottom line and controls.

Westinghouse is a clear example of a company that has had and continues to have difficulty defining its mission. It is one of the oldest and largest corporations in the United States. It was founded in 1886 and has had a number of successes, but it has also been unfavorably compared with General Electric by Collins and Porras as well as others. Incidentally, General Electric was founded about the same time as Westinghouse. General Electric and Westinghouse immediately became competitors, because they both focused on the generation of electricity. Westinghouse has entered and exited many businesses (recently it sold its newly acquired furniture business and its defense electronics business and bought CBS Broadcasting), and its history has been marked by several significant financial crises.

In order to better develop a sense of strategy and mission for the organization, Westinghouse issued a vision statement in 1989. According to this statement, Westinghouse stands for "total quality, market leadership, technology driven, global, focused growth, diversified." Needless to say, this jumble of pop management terms did not get the job done.

Today hardly anyone knows what businesses Westinghouse is in and what it stands for. People remember that they made home appliances, but they have not been in that business for decades. In fact, they own a constantly changing, rather eclectic mix of businesses. This is not necessarily a fatal flaw, if it is part of a well-developed strategy and the organization is managed accordingly. General Electric, for example, also has a diverse set of businesses, but it has managed to create a well-developed and very effective strategy for how to act as a corporation and, as a result, has consistently outperformed Westinghouse.

Today, effective organizational performance depends upon devising and implementing a strategy that fits the new logic. Key to such a strategy is how mission and values statements define purpose and strategic intent, how organizations identify and develop crucial core competencies, and how organizational capabilities support critical business processes. Leadership is also important, both in involving members of an organization in the process of creating strategy and in communicating strategic intent to everyone.

THE MISSION STATEMENT: WHAT ARE OUR GOALS?

More and more companies are developing mission statements that are designed to be the cornerstone of setting and communicating their corporate purpose. These often brief and very simple statements provide a broad sense of guidance and mission for the organization. Among the more visible ones: Xerox's statement that it is "the document company," and the British Airways' statement that it is in business "to fly and serve."

A new logic mission statement is neither a strategic plan nor a method of controlling the organization, nor does it lay out in any great detail how the company will market and price its products or services or how it will add value. Instead, it provides a broad sense of what the organization does and wants to be.

Of course, mission statements need to go beyond a few simple words if they are to provide meaningful guidance in the creation of an organization design that covers all critical business elements. They must talk about markets to be served, value provided to customers, and the competitive advantages on which the organization hopes to capitalize.

It is very important for organizations to develop and communicate their mission in the form of a statement that management professors Gary Hamel and C. K. Prahalad (1989) describe as expressing "strategic intent"—that is, the animating dream or "stretch" goal that energizes a company. For example, British Airways stated in 1987 that its goal was to become "the world's favorite airline," a bold quest given its history. Appleton Papers, a firm with more than four thousand employees that operates throughout North America, has a somewhat more specific strategic intent: "to be a world leader in specialty coated paper technologies, high value-added customer applications and customer focused quality."

Why are goals that represent a sizable stretch for the organization important? Considerable research in psychology on goal setting shows that the highest performance comes when individuals are committed to reaching such goals (Locke & Latham, 1990). It also shows that individuals are more likely to be committed to those goals when there are rewards that are attached to achieving them and when individuals believe that the goals agree with their value systems and contribute to objectives they share.

Hamel and Prahalad (1994) suggest that organizations need, in addition to strategic intent, a shared understanding of the future to help them identify what new products they need to pioneer, what alliances they need to make, and what product development programs they should support. This shared understanding needs to focus on such issues as what competitors are likely to do, what new markets exist, and how new markets can be entered and created. Hamel and Prahalad go on to argue that senior management should bear the major responsibility for continually updating this shared corporate perspective on the future.

I cannot agree more. As far as developing corporate strategy is concerned, nothing is so potentially dangerous as today's view of the world because it will soon be outdated. In successful firms it can lead to complacency and doing the old "right thing" long after it ceases to be the right thing (Lawler & Galbraith, 1994). General Motors, for example, committed just this mistake when it failed to recognize the seriousness of the Japanese threat to its dominance of the U.S. car market.

One way to develop a shared understanding of the future is to use scenario planning to help sensitize the organization to the need for change. In scenario planning, a group prepares several possible scenarios (or paths) for the business. Royal Dutch Shell, for example, at a time when industry mavens were forecasting $100-per-barrel oil, outlined an unthinkable scenario: a decline in the price of oil. When the price actually declined, Shell was prepared.

Each scenario should have some leading indicators to identify that it is indeed unfolding. The planning process then provides managers with mental maps to think differently. It prepares them to see facts as they occur in a new light. Scenarios can be great vehicles for preparing for a nontraditional competitor. Shell, for example, still regards Exxon and Mobil as key competitors, but the company is also keeping an eye on Schlumberger, the seismographic tester. After all, who knows more about where oil is?

Mission statements that focus on strategic intent present an interesting contrast to the traditional strategic planning document. They tend to have a much longer life expectancy and require much less maintenance because they are much less specific. As the business environment has become more and more turbulent, strategic intent documents have become a more and more obvious choice. Careful formal strategic planning, even when done well, can rapidly become obsolete with changes in the environment.

VALUES AND STRATEGY: HOW DO WE DO WHAT WE DO?

As part of their effort to provide meaning and direction to their activities, some organizations focus on defining and stating their values—that is, the kinds of activities, behaviors, and performance that are desirable. Such written statements of values are important because they can support a mission statement, guide the day-to-day operations of a company, and help an organization develop a sense of direction and purpose among its employees—all of which are critical to the successful implementation of the new logic principles. They can, in essence, be an effective substitute for the bureaucracy and control systems of traditional organizations because when combined with goals, they specify how individuals should behave and provide meaning to the work that individuals do.

Values statements can cover anything that has to do with how an organization operates—from how it treats customers and employees to what kinds of organizational processes are important. For example, a values statement can stress openness in communication, trust in dealings with internal and external groups, fair treatment for employees, social responsibility, concern for the environment, and consistently high-quality products or services.

Jim O'Toole, who writes about the importance of mission and values, has emphasized that company statements should combine high purpose and high aim (O'Toole, 1993). They need to stress critical values that are important to employees and that organizations can use to succeed—values such as community, liberty, fairness, and the dignity of individuals.

One of the most famous values statements—and one that is decades old—belongs to Johnson & Johnson, the large pharmaceutical and personal-care products firm. Johnson & Johnson's first core value in their credo is "Our first responsibility is to our customers." This strong emphasis on serving customers and protecting their health and well-being got a lot of attention during the Tylenol poisoning crisis, when, fearing that their product had been tampered with, they immediately withdrew all of their Tylenol products from store shelves in order to protect their customers.

Johnson & Johnson is not the only company to emphasize values and to work on developing a values-driven culture. Such companies as Patagonia, Herman Miller, and Motorola have, for a long time, emphasized values as an important part of their corporate identity. Years ago, sociologist Philip Selznick argued that organizations become enduring institutions only when they become infused with values that go beyond the bottom line (Selznick, 1957). He further argued that when an organization's values appeal to prospective members, it gives it competitive advantages: greater employee loyalty and more adaptability to a changing environment.

The impact of values and missions on organizational effectiveness has always been evident in volunteer organizations. Individuals work for them simply to contribute to achieving the organizations' missions because they identify with their goals and values. Individuals who do volunteer work at hospitals often will do cleanup and other menial tasks that they do not do around their own home and would never consider doing in any other situation.

Even less glamorous businesses that do not lend themselves to a mission such as improving the environment or reducing hunger can have values statements that include high standards and goals that are motivating, if not inspiring. For example, any company can aspire to be the best at what it does, to offer the highest-quality products, or to treat its customers and employees in a special way.

Levi Strauss is one of the most visible examples of a company that emphasizes the values approach to management. Since 1987 it has had a clearly stated set of values and aspirations concerning diversity, empowerment, communication, and ethical management practices. Its written mission statement is a simple and straightforward one: "To sustain profitable and responsible commercial success by marketing jeans and casual apparel." Not a terribly exciting statement, but when combined with the goals that Levi Strauss sets for itself—profitable return on investment, market leadership, products with superior profitability and service—it begins to take on the sense of a mission that shows not only what the company wants to do but also how it will be measured on what it does.

To me, the most interesting part of the Levi Strauss statement is where it addresses values and aspirations. It states: "We want a company that our people are proud of and committed to, where all employees have an opportunity to contribute, learn, grow, and advance based on merit, not politics or background. We want our people to feel respected, treated fairly, and listened to, and involved. Above all, we want satisfaction from accomplishments and friendships, balanced personal and professional lives, and to have fun in our endeavors." It goes on to talk about the type of leadership that can turn this dream into reality.

CEO Robert Haas, the great-great-nephew of founder Levi Strauss, is clearly committed to implementing the values that the corporation has stated. The mission and values statements, which were crafted by top management in 1987 (not by consultants or the human resource department), are posted on office and factory walls throughout Levi Strauss. Attention to its corporate aspirations has clearly helped Levi Strauss in a number of respects. It has produced loyal employees, and Levi is regularly listed as one of the best companies in the United States to work for.

It has also led Levi Strauss to do some things that have hurt its short-term profitability. For example, it will not do business with countries where the labor conditions are unsatisfactory. Thus it does not use suppliers in mainland China, an expensive decision in a business where manufacturing cost is critical. It has shifted some work to Mexico, however—a shift that has produced charges of hypocrisy and considerable criticism because of the loss of U.S. jobs and the low wage rates in Mexico.

Like most large-scale organizational transformations, Levi's strong emphasis on using values to direct behavior and focus efforts is and always will be a work in process, but it is one that seems to be heading in the right direction. Levi Strauss has reduced its overhead, adapted more rapidly to market changes, and improved its financial performance since it developed its values statement. It thus provides an interesting example of how mission and values statements can play an important role in a new logic corporation.

There is great variation from industry to industry in terms of how easy it is to get individuals to identify with an organization's mission and values. However, as was mentioned earlier, even organizations in industries that do not lend themselves to an appealing mission statement can still state values that will motivate people to work for them and to develop a sense of loyalty and identification with the organization. Levi Strauss provides an example of this, as does another clothing manufacturer, Patagonia, which has strong values about the treatment of employees and the environment.

THE BOTTOM LINE: PUTTING MISSION AND VALUES STATEMENTS TO WORK

The sudden popularity of mission and values statements (one estimate is that six out of ten U.S. corporations have one; a recent how-to-do-it book contains 301 mission statements from "America's top companies") has led to the charge that they are a fad and that in many companies they are worthless words on paper. The criticism is not of their content— they usually sound good—but of their lack of impact on organizational behavior. The effectiveness of a mission statement is only as great as the commitment to putting it to work. And quite simply stated, there is good reason to believe that often the commitment is missing.

An ineffective mission and values statement is not just a waste of time and paper. An organization can be worse off because of its values statement. This is likely to result if the actual behavior of the people in the organization does not match the values statement. A large discrepancy causes individuals to trust the organization less than if there were no values statement. They are understandably disillusioned when they see that the values statement and the behavior do not agree.

For me the issue is not whether to have a statement of mission and values; it is an important tool that organizations should have. The key question is, how can an organization turn a mission and values statement into a meaningful, realized, living element of an organization's behavior and its systems?

One thing that can be done is to wed the corporate values in the mission statement to every human resource management system. Beginning with the hiring process, every job applicant must be treated as the values statement says employees and customers should be.

It is critical that there be a fit between the types of employees who are hired and the values that the organization espouses in its mission and values statement. Southwest Airlines, which says work should be fun, hires employees who have a good sense of humor. Rather than punish employees when they demonstrate a sense of humor on the job, Southwest rewards them. In much the same way, one restaurant that wants employees to help customers have fun has job applicants go on stage and do something "entertaining" as part of its selection process.

Similarly, individuals must be rewarded for the kinds of behavior that the values statement says the organization believes in. At Levi Strauss, one third of an employee's performance evaluation is based on what Levi Strauss calls "aspirational behavior," that is, behavior that supports the mission and values of the company. Employees who ignore values such as diversity and empowerment, for example, do not get a raise. Another example of a company that weds its values statement to its reward system is General Mills, which says it values community involvement and volunteer activity and explicitly recognizes them in its performance appraisal system. NICE!

Often what distinguishes a mission statement that works from one that is ineffective is not how it phrases the ideas and the values it espouses but how the leadership develops the mission statement. Senior management must put in place a process that will not only lead to the development of an effective strategy but ensure that it is widely understood and accepted in the organization. Getting this accomplished, particularly getting it accepted, often requires more from senior management than simply preparing a mission and values statement.

All too often I have seen senior managers do just the opposite of what the Levi Strauss executives did in producing their statement. Too many companies send their top managers away for several days to "draft" a mission and values statement. They then present it to the organization, congratulate themselves for having done the necessary activities, declare victory, and go back to their offices. In most cases, when the process is over, everyone in the organization (including top management) simply disregards the statement.

Even worse, some senior management groups hire consultants to produce a mission and values statement for their organization. Indeed, a small cottage industry has grown up around the United States that specializes in developing these statements. They are then printed on wallet-sized cards and posters and liberally distributed throughout the organization. Too often, the implicit assumption is that simply creating them and distributing them will influence behavior. It almost never works. In fact, often all that has happened as a result of this exercise is that the organization has wasted time, money, effort, and paper.

How can the strategic planning process of developing a mission statement and corporate values be made more meaningful? The principles of the new logic provide a clear answer: involvement.

In a relatively small organization, it is possible to get most of the employees in the organization involved in the strategic planning process. Some small organizations have effectively held several day "community meetings" in which the elements of a mission and values statement are hammered out through a process that includes working in small groups, with the whole organization debating issues and ultimately fashioning a document (Weisbord, 1992). This type of participation is ideal because it captures input from a wide variety of organization members, thereby enriching the final product, and because everyone in the organization develops an understanding and acceptance of what is produced.

In large organizations it may not be possible to have broad-scale participation in developing or updating an organization's strategy. It should be possible, however, to select individuals from different parts of the organization to participate in the process.

In 1984, for example, Eaton Corporation, a fifty-thousand-employee organization that manufactures auto, truck, and electronic parts worldwide, put together a task force representing employees from different levels in the organization to develop a mission statement, known today as "Excellence Through People," that includes a number of important statements about how employees should be treated.

To introduce the philosophy, they did all of the usual things, such as producing a video and passing out brochures that described the philosophy. They did not stop there, however. In 1988, Eaton executive John Wendenhof and Gerry Ledford, a USC colleague of mine, developed an innovative process for monitoring how the philosophy was being implemented throughout the firm (Ledford, Wendenhof, & Strahley, 1995). Employee teams composed of a cross-section of managers from throughout the corporation made visits to Eaton locations to help the site employees implement the Eaton philosophy. The implementation teams were trained in organizational diagnosis and given the mandate to gather data from the site. They then gave feedback to the site members on how well the implementation process was going and how it could be improved.

So far this process is working well. Eaton managers who have been on the visiting teams have developed a better understanding of management processes. It also has helped stress to them and the plants they visit the importance of implementing the philosophy. Eaton's commitment to the site visits has also helped demonstrate the importance that it puts on the mission statement.

The Eaton case is just one of many examples that show that involvement is a key to the success of a corporate statement of mission and values. In company after company, the same thing happens: when people throughout the organization are involved in developing the document and in assessing how well it is being used, it has impact.

Involvement can take many forms. After a small group of individuals has done some initial development work, electronic mail can be used to help develop and perfect mission-vision-values statements for companies. A proposed mission and values statement can be put on the computer network with the invitation for all to give their thoughts and reactions. Successive iterations of the work can be edited throughout the organization, thus giving everyone an opportunity to have a say in the final document.

EDS, the large, very successful computer services firm based in Plano, Texas, recently went through a highly involving process in developing their strategic view of the future. Although very successful during the first half of the 1990s, EDS began to be concerned that its market was changing so rapidly that a new strategy was in order. New competitors were appearing, old customers were asking for greater discounts, and whole new markets were appearing, particularly as companies began to outsource their information services activities.

EDS created a corporate change team that used a broad-involvement approach. From across the company, 150 EDS managers who were known to be challenging and bright gathered in Dallas to begin developing their shared view of the future. Five groups of thirty worked on somewhat different issues and gathered data after their initial meeting in Dallas. Other groups, senior management, and the overall change management team analyzed and debated the final outputs from each group. Finally, a team composed of members from all of the groups produced a draft corporate strategy that was debated throughout the company. In all, more than two thousand people participated in the creation of EDS's new strategy.

This process lasted about a year, and it produced both a high level of understanding of the challenges EDS faces and a high level of commitment to the new strategy. That strategy can best be summarized as global and dedicated to giving customer organizations the kinds of information resources they need to gain competitive advantage. It also stresses individualizing information resources to fit the needs of each customer. In many respects, it is a mass-customization approach to information system management. The effects of this effort can only be measured in the long term, but in the short term, it is clear that the process led to a high level of debate, discussion, and, ultimately, commitment to the new strategy.

The challenge in a new logic organization is to make the mission and values of the organization a living piece of the corporate culture that helps to guide and direct behavior. It is also important that the mission and values statement reflect changes in the external environment and the organization's view of the future. Changes in the statement represent a key opportunity for involvement. People throughout the organization can participate in "town meetings" that review and update the mission, and they can work on task forces that help develop the changes and assess the environment.

CORE COMPETENCIES AND STRATEGY

In their influential 1990 *Harvard Business Review* article, Gary Hamel and C. K. Prahalad emphasized the importance of core competencies—which they define as a combination of technology and production skills that underlie various product lines and services—in the development of a corporate strategy.

For the purpose of developing and implementing strategy, organizations need to know what core competencies are critical to success in their business or businesses. If they succeed in developing the core competencies that support their mission, they can gain a competitive advantage over other organizations because they can produce superior products and services.

Sony's core competency in miniaturization technology allows them to make the Walkman, video cameras, notebook computers, and a host of other products. Honda's ability to produce gasoline motors is critical to their success in selling motorcycles, lawn mowers, outboard motors, and automobiles. 3M Corporation's competency in understanding chemical processes and materials has helped them to develop a vast range of products, from a variety of Scotch tape products and Post-it notes to exotic bonding materials for the aerospace industry.

In the service sector, American Airlines developed a core competency in computer information systems that for a long time gave it a significant advantage over its competitors because it could offer innovative prices and frequent-flier programs that its competitors could not match. Ultimately, American got so good at information management that it created a reservation service for all airlines.

Organizations must ask themselves two questions about their core competencies: Which core competencies do we need in order to reach our goals? How easily can other organizations duplicate our core competencies?

The challenge is to create core competencies that are hard to duplicate or, at the very least, can lead the organization to other competencies that can keep them ahead of the competition. As noted earlier, it is getting easier for organizations all over the world to develop competencies, because technology often moves across international and company boundaries through alliances and a host of other organizational approaches that will be discussed later.

ORGANIZATIONAL CAPABILITIES AND STRATEGY

Distinctly different from core competencies—yet, at the same time, very related to them—are organizational capabilities. They can be a particularly powerful source of competitive advantage because they are difficult to duplicate, and, when combined with appropriate core competencies, they can allow an organization to perform significantly better than its competition. Like core competencies, their development is key to the successful implementation of strategy; thus, they need to be part of the strategy development process.

What distinguishes organizational capabilities from core competencies? Organizational capabilities rest in the systems, culture, and overall design of the organization, not in laboratory research, in the heads of a few technology gurus, or in a set of patents. They represent shared knowledge that enables an organization to perform in ways that go beyond the skill of any one individual or set of individuals.

ABB, the Swiss-Swedish manufacturer of rail cars and electrical generating equipment, is a classic example of an organization that has developed the capability to operate both globally and locally simultaneously. Their products such as rail cars need to be sold to a large global market (because of high development costs), but at the same time they need to be built locally and contain some local parts. To achieve this, ABB has a multinational management team that coordinates technological activities in different countries—ensuring that it can develop its corporate core competencies in rail equipment design.

An engineering firm with which I have consulted, CH2M Hill, calls their organizational capabilities "critical success factors." In the late 1980s they identified the following critical success factors as part of a strategic planning effort targeted at understanding what they needed to be good at in order to continue the growth of the company:

- Becoming more client focused
- Devising market-driven strategies
- Integrating strengths
- Fostering creativity and innovation
- Becoming responsive, flexible, and adaptable
- Providing value for clients in all we do

So far, these organizational capabilities have provided a focus for their organizational improvement efforts that seems to be paying off, as the company is continuing to grow and gain market share.

As you may recall, earlier I mentioned 3M's organizational capability to innovate. I believe that its continued growth and success are only partially due to its core competency in the chemical properties of a variety of materials. An important part of its success has to do with its capability to innovate and to develop and market new products.

Norwest, the large Midwestern bank, has developed an outstanding capability in the area of customer focus. They have made it the key to their personal-touch approach to banking. Whereas other large banks have emphasized electronic banking and ATMs, Norwest has decided to emphasize getting close to the customer. They have developed this capability through a number of very specific practices that include cross-training tellers and all branch employees so that they are flexible and can sell many products. They also have developed a number of events to bring people into their branches and encourage interaction with employees. Their strategy is no secret; as one of their executives commented, "I could leave our strategic plan on a plane and it would not make any difference. No one could execute it; our success has nothing to do with planning—it has to do with execution." Execution is made possible because they have the capability to get close to their customers.

A single organizational capability may not be sufficient for success. It may take two or three that are exceptional and a number of others that are at least at the world-class level, because that is the nature of today's competitive environment. The success of Motorola, for example, is only partially based on its organizational capability in quality. As I mentioned earlier, they are also excellent at getting products quickly to market and at technological innovation.

I could go on listing examples, but at this point it is sufficient to repeat that the challenge for any organization is to develop a set of capabilities that support or fit its strategy. It is not enough for an organization to say it will be the world's favorite airline; it must also develop the appropriate capabilities—in this case, those that have to do with giving great service and understanding customers.

CREATING A SUCCESSFUL STRATEGY: THE ROLE OF LEADERSHIP

The old logic of organizing clearly places the responsibility for developing a business strategy in the hands of senior management. One of their major managerial responsibilities is to design, develop, and communicate the organization's business strategy. Indeed, it is one of the major ways that they are expected to add value to the corporation and to justify their high reward levels. In addition, they are responsible for overseeing the implementation of the strategy and for making strategy changes as the environment evolves.

In the new logic, too, senior management needs to play a leadership role in strategy development and implementation. Note, however, that the emphasis here is on leading rather than on managing. Senior management must lead a process that will not only develop an effective strategy but ensure that it is widely understood and accepted in the organization. Getting this accomplished—particularly, getting it accepted—requires senior management to actively communicate and live the strategy. There are many ways to do it: for example, through personal meetings, videotapes, e-mail, and interactive video broadcasts. But only senior management can do it.

Of all the approaches to communication, I believe personal contact with a charismatic leader is by far the best. I have seen a number of senior managers who are quite skilled at doing this. Among my personal favorites are Bob Galvin of Motorola; Kingman Brewster, the former president of Yale University; and Max De Pree of Herman Miller. They all have the ability to mix high purpose with high aim in their talks and interactions with organization members.

Rich Teerlink, the CEO of Harley-Davidson, is another good example of a CEO who understands how to infuse his company with a sense of direction by making the mission statement an integral part of the organization. Not too many years ago, Harley-Davidson was in serious trouble because of its terrible relationships with its customers, employees, and dealers. Teerlink realized that there was a tremendous need for the company to improve the quality of its products as well as its stakeholder relationships. He began to continually emphasize the theme of "Creating a Competitive Organization Through People and Processes Centered on Learning." Whenever he talked to managers at Harley, he asked questions focused on learning, the involvement of employees, and the reactions of customers. The business turnaround of Harley has been nothing short of amazing. It is one of the few U.S. organizations to regain market share from its Japanese competitors. Xerox, incidentally, is another, at least in part as a result of the leadership it has received from its last two CEOs, David Kearns and Paul Allaire.

Successful leaders are able to communicate not only strategic intent but also how the goals of the organization are relevant to the personal values and desires of the members of the organization. In short, they communicate what can happen and what it means to individuals if the organization succeeds. This step in the development of the strategic agenda of an organization is without question the most difficult to accomplish. It requires that senior managers act as leaders and motivate and inspire others throughout the organization.

I have a small confession to make at this point. For years I have been a skeptic about the importance of leaders because of the difficulty of defining and describing leadership. All too often, leadership falls into the "I cannot define it, but I know it when I see it" category. Once you get beyond gross generalizations, such as "leaders inspire others" and "leaders define the agenda," there is often very little substance that allows us to identify how successful leaders behave. Further, major change in traditional organizations often occurs not because a leader has galvanized the organization but because the environment threatens the organization's continued existence—which causes the organization, often under the direction of a new group of senior managers, to restructure, change products, or introduce other changes.

Sometimes it seems that the qualities of effective management in a traditional organization are captured in Antoine de Saint-Exupéry's fable *The Little Prince.* In this story, the Little Prince points out that he is the absolute ruler of his planet because everyone does exactly what he tells them to do. The secret of his success is simple: he only tells people to do things that they want to do. The Little Prince clearly is a leader who believes in the saying that "a good leader has to hurry to keep ahead of his followers." In an effective traditional organization, of course, individuals head in the direction they do because of well-designed reward systems, job descriptions, organization structures, and so on, not because of leadership.

I have come to believe that leadership is a key ingredient in shaping high-performance organizations. I have seen Jack Welch of General Electric, Bob Galvin of Motorola, Larry Bossidy of AlliedSignal, and a host of other leaders produce significant change in the way their very large organizations operate. Thus I am convinced that effective leadership at the top accounts for an important amount of the success of high-performance organizations, because leadership is so critical in defining the agenda of an organization, shaping its values, and determining its competencies and capabilities.

In a high-performance organization, effective leaders need to be able to create strategic goals that people want to head toward. They add enormous value when they get individuals to take new types of actions and move in new directions. And they do this not by creating bureaucratic controls and procedures but by creating a view of what can be and should be that is attractive to individuals and that fits with their values and goals.

KEYS TO DEVELOPING AN EFFECTIVE STRATEGY

In summary, here is what we have said about the development of an organization strategy:

- Senior managers need to take the lead in developing strategy, but they cannot and should not do it by themselves. The members of the organization need to be involved.

- Strategies should fit the unique situation of the organization; they cannot be copied or borrowed from others.

- Strategies need to set high aspirations for the organization so that members, individually and collectively, will feel that they have challenging but reachable goals.

- Strategies need to focus on how an organization will win in the future, what its outstanding products and services will be, and how those products and services will satisfy the customer.

- Strategies need to reflect the values that will guide how the organization accomplishes its goals and mission.

- Strategies need to appeal to values that will allow employees to identify with the way the organization operates.

- Strategies must communicate a sense of direction and stimulate discovery of what the organization can do and what works in particular business environments.

- Strategies must provide employees at all levels of the organization with a sense of what the company is trying to do and where it is trying to go.

- Strategies need to present a way to the future and provide emotional and intellectual energy for the journey.

- It is up to the leaders in the organization to identify the kinds of capabilities that are needed, communicate them through mission and values statements, and develop commitment to them throughout the organization.

When their strategy is developed, organizations need to create organization structures, reward systems, communication systems, and human resource management systems that support the strategy by creating the right competencies and capabilities and that drive performance effectiveness.

CHAPTER TWENTY-EIGHT

Matching Strategy and Structure

Jay Galbraith

————

S trategy is the company's formula for winning. The company's strategy specifies the goals and objectives to be achieved as well as the values and missions to be pursued; it sets out the basic direction of the company. The strategy specifically delineates the products or services to be provided, the markets to be served, and the value to be offered to the customer. It also specifies sources of competitive advantage and strives to provide superior value.

Traditionally, strategy is the first component of the star model to be addressed. It is important in the organization design process because it establishes the criteria for choosing among alternative organizational forms. Each organizational form enables some activities to be performed well while hindering others. Choosing organizational alternatives inevitably involves making trade-offs. Strategy dictates which activities are most necessary, thereby providing the basis for making the best trade-offs in the organization design.

Once the strategy is established, the structure of the organization sets the framework for the other organization design decisions. The traditional hierarchical structure of organizations—with its dysfunctional effects—continues to fall under harsher and harsher criticism.

At the same time, more and more structural design alternatives have begun to appear. There is an appropriate trend away from authoritarian management styles and the separatist titles and privileges of a multilevel hierarchy. Most companies have fewer hierarchical levels. Automation and information technology permit wider spans and therefore flatter structures (fewer hierarchical levels).

THE DIMENSIONS OF STRUCTURE

Hierarchies, albeit flatter ones, will still be around for some time. They are useful for reaching decisions among large numbers of people in a timely fashion. They provide a basis for an appeals process for conflict resolution. But they are being implemented much more sparingly and in conjunction with alternative structures. Before we turn our attention to these alternatives, it is important to become familiar with the four policy areas that determine the structure of an organization. These policy areas, or dimensions, are the following:

- Specialization
- Shape
- Distribution of power
- Departmentalization

These policy areas are not listed in order of importance. Rather, departmentalization—with its far-reaching ramifications and attendant complexities—is saved for last.

Specialization

Specialization refers to the types and numbers of specialties to be used in performing the work. In general, the greater the number of specialties, the better the subtask performance. But specialization also makes it difficult to integrate subtasks into the performance of the whole task. Today, the trend is toward less specialization and more job rotation in low- to moderate-skill tasks in order to allow speed and ease of coordination, while in high-skill tasks the trend is toward greater specialization in order to allow pursuit of in-depth knowledge.

The old rules of the division of labor were to break tasks into subtasks and have people specialize in small pieces of the work. For complex tasks, the work could be divided so that an expert could bring in-depth knowledge to bear on difficult issues. Electrical engineering work was broken into electromechanical and electronics segments. The electronics segment could be further divided, down to the role of circuit designer for digital signal processing.

A different logic applied to the subdivision of low-skill tasks. Work was divided to create simple tasks so that uneducated workers could perform them at low wages. Such workers were easy to find and little training was needed. If turnover was high, new workers could be found and made productive at little expense. This thinking still applies in developing countries.

But in developed countries, the old logic applies only for complex, high-technology work. Companies in electronics, genetics, and pharmaceuticals all search for experts in specialized fields to push the limits of technology. The level of specialization is actually increasing as new specialties are created every day. Specialization of high-skill workers allows talented employees to gain greater expertise in their specific areas. The expertise can often be accumulated into databases and delivered to the teams by new information devices. These devices provide text, graphics, photos, and video to teach multiskilled workers. Thus, the expertise not only serves its primary purpose of allowing the specialist to gain in-depth knowledge but also can be disseminated to educate and inform generalists.

In contrast, at the low- and medium-skill levels, several forces are combining to eliminate highly fragmented tasks. Simple low-skill tasks are being automated (machines can do the tasks more cheaply and reliably than people can) or exported to developing countries. In addition, the costs of coordinating fragmented, interdependent tasks are too high in rapidly changing situations; a large amount of communication is needed to combine the work when hundreds of subtasks are involved. The remaining low- and moderate-skill work is being handled by multiskilled teams of educated workers. These teams are given end-to-end responsibility to make decisions for an entire piece of work, providing a more rapid and effective work flow.

These new work arrangements offer the benefits of greater speed and motivation and lower coordination costs (see Lawler, 1996).

Shape

Shape is determined by the number of people forming departments at each hierarchical level. The more people per department, the fewer the levels. The number of people in a department is usually referred to as the *span of control*—or span of supervision—of the department manager.

The trend today is to wider spans and flatter structures, as shown in Figure 28.1. As we move away from command-and-control styles of leadership, managers can lead larger numbers. Thus the hierarchy becomes flatter. Fewer people are needed to supervise others. The flatter hierarchies lead to faster decisions, leaders who are in touch with organizational members, and lower overhead costs. But what is the best number for leaders to be able to provide help and training and make judgments about the work?

The Conference Board, a group that conducts research on organization structures, recently conducted a survey of spans of supervision among its members. With thousands of observations from work groups, the distribution ranged from 0 to 127 people. The distribution was trimodal, with modes at 7, 17, and 75. (The *mode*—as distinguished from *mean* and *median* as descriptors of central tendency—is the value that occurs most frequently. In this case, three numbers frequently occurred; hence, there was a trimodal distribution.) How could this happen?

The traditional organizational model typically used spans of about seven people (and a number of companies still do so). To communicate with subordinates and evaluate them, managers had the time for only about seven people. The traditional span can be increased or decreased based on several factors.

- The leader and group members are all experienced (so less communication and coaching are needed).

- Employees all do the same work.

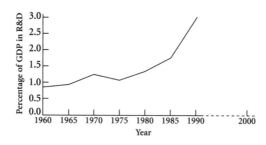

Figure 28.1.   Trends in Organization Shape.

• Each employee's task is independent of the others.
• The task is easily measured.

Thus groups of salespeople may include fifteen to twenty people while software design groups may consist of only five.

Delegation of work by the leader to the group also results in wider spans. Indeed, some organizations widen spans to encourage more delegation. Some organizations today monitor spans in organizational units and set goals to widen them progressively. They train their managers to adopt more of a coaching style and less of a controlling style. So spans of about seventeen are very possible.

A different kind of organization is needed for spans of seventy-five people. An example is a factory with a plant manager and seventy-five blue-collar workers. The workers are organized into three teams of twenty-five people, with a team for each of the three shifts. Each team is self-managing. It selects, trains, disciplines, and rewards all its own members. The teams schedule the work and propose capital investments. The plant manager advises the teams and spends most of the working day communicating with people outside the plant. Thus the more the managerial work is delegated to work teams, the less the need for direct supervision. These kinds of teams lead to the elimination of levels of supervision and the complete elimination of command-and-control styles.

In sum, it is quite possible to observe companies following the traditional management model, choosing spans of about seven. More delegation and goal setting can lead to spans of around seventeen. For companies with policies of self-managing teams, spans of around seventy-five are possible. It is important to follow all the policies on the star model to create these teams (see Lawler, 1996).

When looking at the shape of an organization with the purpose of creating a flatter structure, the spans of supervision, rather than hierarchical levels, are examined. This is because spans are more easily analyzed and changed; it is harder to eliminate levels. The redundant level may be different in different departments: the first level may be easiest to eliminate in one function, the third level easiest in another. Span analysis would lead to a reduction of levels and would account for differences among departments. So when reducing levels, an approach that widens spans is easier to implement than one that focuses on levels.

Distribution of Power

Distribution of power in an organization refers to two concepts. The first is the vertical distribution of decision-making power and authority. This is called *centralization* or *decentralization.* There are pros and cons attached to changes in centralization. These should be weighed and tested against the strategy when choosing. The second concept is the horizontal distribution of power. The leader needs to shift power to the department dealing with mission-critical issues. Today in many competitive industries, the power to influence prices or terms and conditions is shifting to the knowledgeable customer. So inside the organization, the decision-making power is shifting to units with direct customer contact. In industries where contracting out has raised purchased goods and services to 80 percent of cost of goods sold, the purchasing function is being given increased decision-making power. A task of the leader is to weigh the business situation continuously and tilt the balance of power when change is required.

Departmentalization

The activities of organizations involving more than two dozen people are grouped together to form departments. *Departmentalization* refers to the choice of departments to integrate the specialized work and form a hierarchy of departments. The choice of type of department is made at each hierarchical level. Departments are usually formed to include people working in one of the following areas:

- A function or specialty
- A product line
- A customer segment
- A geographical area
- A work flow process

Each department type is appropriate for certain situations. The strategy and the size of the organization determines the choice.

FUNCTIONAL STRUCTURES. Most companies start by organizing around activities or functions. Companies of modest size usually adopt the functional structure shown in Figure 28.2. The figure shows a typical Hewlett-Packard division.

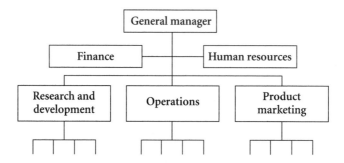

Figure 28.2. **Functional Organization Structure.**

The functional organization provides several advantages. First, gathering together all workers of one type—the R&D people, for example—allows them to transfer ideas, knowledge, and contacts among themselves. Second, it allows them to achieve a greater level of specialization. When two hundred or so engineers are pooled, they can afford to dedicate some to such specialties as circuit designers for gallium arsenide semiconductors. Third, using the example of a single purchasing function in operations, pooling the workers allows the company to present a single face to vendors and exercise buying leverage. Fourth, taking the example of using one manufacturing function to perform all production work, the company can afford to buy an expensive piece of test equipment and share it across product lines. Thus the functional structure permits more scale and specialization than other structural alternatives for companies of a certain size.

Organizations with functional departments also promote standardization and reduce duplication. An activity that is organized functionally is performed in the same way and (presumably) in the best way throughout the company. The functions adopt one system or one policy for everyone rather than have each department invent its own. The functions adopt a single computer system, inventory control policy, absenteeism policy, and so on. Companies often revert to the functional structure to reduce the proliferation and duplication of systems, standards, and policies that result when independent units don't manage to share or cooperate.

The functional organization has two weaknesses that frequently lead to the adoption of alternative structures. The first becomes apparent if a company has a variety of products, services, channels, and customers. The situation is illustrated in Figure 28.3. Apple Computer, for example, used the functional organization to great advantage when it produced only Macintosh computers and sold them through computer dealers. However, the product line expanded to include desktops, laptops, and palmtops, and the sales channels expanded to include direct sales, direct marketing, and mass merchandisers as well as computer dealers. This kind of variety overwhelms the decision-making capacity of the general manager and the functional leadership team. Thus Apple, like other companies in similar situations, abandoned the single functional structure. Interestingly, when Steve Jobs returned to Apple, he simplified the product lines and channels and brought back the functional structure.

The functional organization is best at managing a single product or service line. When strategies involve product or service diversification and market segmentation, the functional organization is either changed by organizing departments around products and markets or enhanced by introducing lateral processes.

The other weakness of the functional structure is the barriers created between different functions, inhibiting cross-functional processes such as new product development. When a company has only one product line (which does not change often) and when long product development cycles are feasible, the functional organization can manage the cross-functional processes and simultaneously deliver scale, expertise, and efficiency. But mass customization, short product life cycles, and rapid product development times overwhelm the functional structure. Thus today this structure is being replaced by product, market, or process structures and by lateral cross-functional processes.

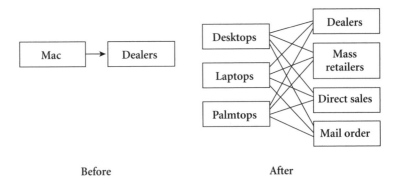

Figure 28.3.   Apple: Before and After Reorganization.

Thus the functional organization is appropriate for small companies and for those that need proprietary expertise and scale. It is appropriate if product and market variety is small, and if product life and development cycles are long. It is declining in popularity because in many industries speed is more important than scale, and responsiveness to variety from any source is a condition for survival.

PRODUCT STRUCTURES. The functional structure is usually superseded by a product structure. When a company diversifies its product lines and those lines achieve minimum efficient scale for their own manufacturing, the company creates multiple functional organizations, each with its own product line, as illustrated in Figure 28.4.

Hewlett-Packard and 3M became famous for continually subdividing divisions and product lines when scale permitted. Each division focused on a single product line and new product development. Forming departments or divisions around products is the best way to compress the product development cycle. So product structures became the standard method for managing strategies of product diversification and new product development. To create a new product, management created a new division.

But product structures have their own weaknesses. Product general managers all want autonomy. Each product division then reinvents the wheel, duplicating resources and generally missing opportunities for sharing. These features are the strengths of the functional structure. Therefore, companies usually augment product structures with lateral functional processes.

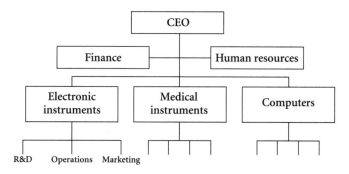

Figure 28.4. Product Structure.

Another weakness of product structures is the possible loss of economies of scale. Not all functions can be divided into product units without a scale loss. These functions are often kept centralized and shared. This situation creates hybrid structures that are mostly product but have a central shared function.

At Boeing's commercial aircraft group, the design and manufacture of planes is divided into product lines of narrow bodies (737, 757) and wide bodies (747, 767, and 777). However, the fabrication of major structural components requires very large and expensive computer-controlled machine tools. These would be too expensive to duplicate in each product line. Instead, a central fabrication unit is created and all manufacturing activities requiring scale and skill are placed in it and shared across product lines. The structure, shown in Figure 28.5, is a hybrid of products and functions. A similar situation can occur with the purchasing function. Today many companies are contracting out their component manufacturing. Purchased material can become as much as 80 percent of the cost of goods sold. In that situation, purchasing and procurement becomes an attractive candidate for a central shared function.

The biggest challenge to the product structure comes from customers who buy from more than one product division. In the past, a central sales function was created to handle all products. But today customers want sourcing relationships, solutions rather than stand-alone products, information exchange, a personalized Web site, single point of contact, and one invoice. These demands are forcing companies to create customer or market segment structures as a front end of the business to complement a product-focused back end.

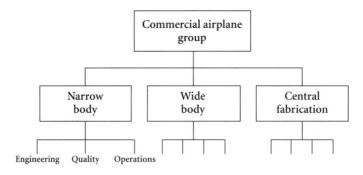

Figure 28.5.   Hybrid Product and Function Structure.

In summary, the product structure was, and in some cases still is, the organization structure of choice for manufacturing companies, allowing them to manage strategies of product diversification and rapid development. The negative features of this structure may be compensated for by functional lateral processes, by central functions, and, increasingly, by the front/back model.

MARKET STRUCTURES. The most rapidly increasing type of structure is the one based on customers, markets, or industries. There are several reasons for the popularity.

The first reason is the shift in power in many industries to the buyer. Increased global competition has created more capacity than demand in many industries, thereby giving the buyer more choices. The buyer is aware of the choice and is learning how to use this new-found buying power. In many cases, buyers are insisting on dedicated units to serve their needs.

Second, the decline of scale in manufacturing—combined with higher-volume, single-sourcing arrangements—makes it economical for a supplier to dedicate a unit to serve a customer. For example, 7-Eleven of Japan has chosen Ajinomoto as the sole supplier of some food products and given it a large volume of business. Ajinomoto, in return, has created a unit to manufacture and sell products exclusively to 7-Eleven stores in Japan.

Third, the shift to market structures is enabled by the increased trend toward and willingness to contract out. Previously, a function that required scale might have forced the company into a functional or hybrid structure. Today, if the scale function is not a source of competitive advantage, it can be contracted out. For example, recording companies can form labels around small, fast-moving market segment units that perform all functions and contract out the essential but not critical compact disc manufacturing. (Actually, contracting out could enable any of the nonfunctional structures to be adopted.)

Fourth, there is a shift of competitive advantage to those companies with superior knowledge and information about market segments. Inexpensive information technology, access to databases and networks, bar code data, a dedicated Web site like MyAmex.com at American Express, and so on, allow a company organized by market segment to gain superior knowledge about the preferences, buying habits, and lifestyles of customers in those segments. It can then create products and services that offer superior value to those customers.

In the music business, a company usually organizes around market segments—classical, rock, country, rap, and so on. Recording companies create a label for each segment. The segment focuses on its customers and artists. The winners are the ones that attract the top talent and know the customers best.

The final reason for the increased popularity of the customer structure is the increasing proportion of service businesses in operation today. Service businesses usually focus on—and organize around—market segments. Services are usually customized and personalized for various segments of the population or industry. Banks, telecommunications firms like MCI, hotels like Marriott, and engineering and construction firms focus on market segments and industries for their divisions.

Market structures have negatives that are similar to those of product structures. Market divisions have a tendency to duplicate activities and develop incompatible systems. They may reduce scale if there is no contracting out. (Hybrid structures that centralize and share purchasing or central telecom networks, like the ones at the former regional Bell companies such as Verizon or SBC, can achieve market focus and efficient scale simultaneously.) They also have difficulty sharing common products or services, which may go to several market segments. Banks may provide a cash management service to customer segments based on their size, such as multinational firms, large corporations, and medium-size companies. Banks would like the segments to share the expensive cash management system bought by all segments and not duplicate it in each market unit.

Thus organizations structured upon market or customer divisions are the fastest-growing kind. Their popularity reflects their compatibility with increasing buyer power, sourcing arrangements, declining scale, contracting out, the shift to the service economy, and especially the increasing competitive advantage of superior market segment knowledge and information.

GEOGRAPHICAL STRUCTURES. Geographical structures traditionally developed as companies expanded their offerings across territories. There was usually a need to be close to the customer and to minimize the costs of travel and distribution. Sometimes industries, like timber and coal, needed to locate near sources of supply. Today, the economics of location is important—but information technology is making it less important in certain industries. The use of geographical structure depends entirely on the industry.

In service industries where the service is provided on site, geography continues to be a structural basis for many companies. Service businesses and sales and service functions have always been geographically organized around districts, regions, and areas. McDonald's and Pizza Hut have geographical structures; the regions are influenced by span-of-control choices and the economics of distribution of food ingredients. Food service companies are likely to have flatter structures in the future, but they will still be geographical.

Geography is becoming less important in other sales and service activities. Sales forces and knowledge services—like consulting—were traditionally managed out of local offices, based on personal relationships and knowledge of the region. Relationships are still important, but industry knowledge and expertise are becoming more important: to sell to banks, one must be well-versed in the banking industry. As a result, industry or market segment structures are being adopted. Sales are also being made through electronic markets, direct computer access by a customer, 800 numbers, and catalogues. Selling today requires fewer office calls by expensive direct sales forces.

However, changes to the geographical structure are occurring in industries where the technology is creating smaller efficient scale and flexible plants and where customers demand just-in-time delivery. Functional organizations are being replaced by multiple small, fast profit centers. Smaller factories can be located close to the customer and produce a variety of products to serve all the needs of their customers. For example, Frito-Lay moved to a geographical structure recently. The company capitalizes on information captured by bar code scanners to move product with limited shelf life rapidly and frequently, and to move quickly on promotions.

The role of geography in manufacturing is complex, with a relationship between the ratio of product value to transport cost, and attention to the minimum efficient scale of a factory. Cement and paper are low-cost commodities with high transport costs. Such companies use regional profit centers. In contrast, semiconductors and pharmaceuticals are high-value items with low transport costs. They are global products and geography is less important and product more important in determining the organization structures of these firms.

Service companies that provide information and knowledge processing are increasingly becoming location-free. The engineering and construction industries can gain an edge with effective geographical structure. At an oil company's new Asian refinery, the initial high-skilled work is performed at the company's North American offices, where the leading design skills are located. Most of this work is located in Los Angeles, but the Calgary and Houston offices have excess capacity and need work. So some design activities are moved electronically to these offices and coordinated through a common computer system. At the completion of the high-level design, the work is beamed over satellite to a group of three hundred Filipino engineers. They generate the fifteen thousand drawings to guide the construction work. This lower-skilled work is more cost effective when performed in the Philippines at Filipino wages.

Companies are seeking the best global location because they can move the work anywhere. Insurance companies send claims forms overnight to Ireland to be processed and returned by satellite the next day. With the new information technology, much service work can be moved anywhere in this way, creating the location-free organization.

Many other service activities are becoming location-free. The elevator business was one in which companies made their money on the service contract and spare parts. A worldwide, geographically structured service organization was a competitive advantage. However, things have changed; today, elevators are designed not to fail. Electronic components mean fewer moving parts and less need for timely, nearby service calls. There is also a large component of software in elevator controls, which can be monitored and repaired from any remote location. Sensors can be installed in critical areas of potential failure. When monitors at a remote location report a likely failure, repair crews can be dispatched from their bases.

The monitoring and repair crews can be located in the most cost-effective areas of the world, provided those locations have skilled people and good telecom and airport infrastructures. In the future, as distance learning and remote medicine become feasible and popular, education and health will likewise become less location based.

PROCESS STRUCTURES. The newest generic organization structure is the process structure. There is considerable variation in what people are calling a process organization, however. In general, a process structure is based on a complete flow of work, such as that of the order fulfillment process. This process flows from initiation by a customer order through the functions to delivery to the customer. Currently, each function performs a part of the work along the sequential flow. The advocates of the process organization—sometimes also called the horizontal organization—suggest that the people from each function who work on the process should be gathered into a process team and given end-to-end responsibility for the overall process. The process team reports to a process leader. The structure is thereby converted from a vertical functional structure to a horizontal process structure, as shown in Figure 28.6.

The process structure is the culmination of three strategic initiatives that all focused on work flow processes and fought against the barriers of the functional structure. The first was total quality (TQ). TQ efforts all promote understanding processes, controlling processes, and improving processes to meet criteria defined by the customer. Cross-functional coordination is essential. The second initiative was cycle-time reduction. The attainment of speed requires tight coordination across functions. Finally, reengineering brought the new information technology to bear on the redesign of the processes themselves. Clearly, the momentum for a process orientation has been building for some time.

The process structure has been offered as an alternative to the functional structure. And there is much to recommend it. Perhaps the greatest benefit is a fresh look, from end to end, at the whole process. When combined with new information technologies, there is considerable opportunity for redesign of an entire process. A change in one function's piece may make an enormous difference in the pieces of the other functions. By having one manager in charge of the whole process rather than individual managers for each function, the resistance to process change can be overcome.

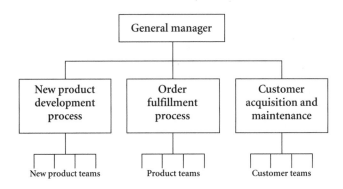

Figure 28.6. Process Organization Structure.

A process with end-to-end coverage also lends itself to measurement more easily than a group of functions does. Each function is responsible for a piece of the process. A unit responsible for the entire process is responsible for a reasonably self-contained piece of work. The unit can control most of the variables that influence the performance of the process. Hence, the unit can be held accountable.

A process orientation leads to cycle-time reduction by doing a good job of coordinating work across functions. Thus companies competing on time-to-market and fast-delivery bases will find a process organization far superior to a functional structure.

In addition, some costs are reduced with a process organization. The faster time cycles mean reduced inventories and faster receipt of cash. The reduced working capital translates into reduced costs of carrying inventory and cash. Other costs are reduced because duplication of work across functions is eliminated. With a functional structure, often one division will not trust the input of another and will check and rework information to its own satisfaction. A process organization eliminates such redundant activities, verifying input once for all functions.

The process organization is therefore superior to the functional organization in businesses with short product life and development cycles. It is also superior when the redesign of processes has great potential for reducing costs and satisfying the customer. In contrast, the functional organization is superior for companies with long cycles and where scale and expertise are important. Yet the benefits of a process orientation can still be obtained by creating lateral process teams that coordinate across the functional structure.

When compared with the functional organization, the process organization can break down barriers and achieve significant savings. However, the structure should be adopted with care. It is currently fashionable, which means the weaknesses associated with it get suppressed. When compared with product or market segment structures, it is not yet clear how the process structure stacks up. Product and market structures have themselves knocked down functional barriers and achieved end-to-end focus on products and customers. And the process structure creates its own barriers—for example, a handoff between the new product process group and the order fulfillment process group, as a product moves from new to existing status. In contrast, the product organization would be seamless on this issue.

The permanent process organization seems to be disappearing. Companies like Cisco have automated processes like order entry and moved them to the Web. There are no people involved. So as process activities move into software and the software process moves to the Web and is even outsourced, the need for permanent process structures disappears. However, a strong process team is needed to design the process before it is automated. This team is a temporary process structure.

Ultimately, combining a process focus within a product or market structure should prove to be a powerful productivity enhancer. It is probable that product, market, or geographical divisions will be the basic profit centers. The subunits within these profit centers will be divided into functions or processes that are useful within product or customer structures.

CHOOSING STRUCTURES

The leader's first organization design choice is the basic structure. This choice process begins with an understanding of the business's strategy. By matching what is required by the strategy to what is done best by the various structures, the leader can optimize the decision. The kinds of strategies executed best by the basic structures are listed as follows:

Functional Structure

- Small-size, single-product line
- Undifferentiated market
- Scale or expertise within the function
- Long product development and life cycles
- Common standards

Product Structure

- Product focus
- Multiple products for separate customers
- Short product development and life cycle
- Minimum efficient scale for functions or outsourcing

Market Structure

- Important market segments
- Product or service unique to segment

- Buyer strength
- Customer knowledge advantage
- Rapid customer service and product cycles
- Minimum efficient scale in functions or outsourcing

Geographical Structure
- Low value-to-transport cost ratio
- Service delivery on site
- Closeness to customer for delivery or support
- Perception of the organization as local
- Geographical market segments needed

Process Structure
- Best seen as an alternative to the functional structure
- Potential for new processes and radical change to processes
- Reduced working capital
- Need for reducing process cycle times

Unfortunately, in the typical situation no one type of structure best fits the business strategy. The decision maker should list the strengths and weaknesses of each structural alternative. The decision maker must also develop priorities for strategic attributes, such as cycle-time reduction or scale of manufacturing. Then the choice of structure can be made for the top priorities. The structural alternatives that are runners-up become candidates for hybrid structures or for lateral coordination processes.

Although the traditional hierarchy is losing favor, flatter hierarchies will be with us for some time. The functional, product, market, geographical, and process alternatives all have their own strengths and weaknesses. For some structures, the weaknesses can be overcome with hybrid structures. For others, lateral processes can augment the basic structures. Indeed, to be responsive on multiple dimensions, lateral processes are key.

CHAPTER TWENTY-NINE

Designing Work

Structure and Process for Learning and Self-Control

Marvin Weisbord

T he quickest way to increase dignity, meaning, and community in a workplace is to involve people in redesigning their own work. That is also the shortest route—in the long run—to lower costs, higher quality, and more satisfied customers. I learned that lesson first in my own business in the 1960s. Having repeated that experience in factories and offices, large and small, union and nonunion, in chemical, pharmaceutical, steel, printing, banking, and many other businesses, I'm more dedicated than ever to this mode of workplace improvement. The simplest way to get started is to have workers, technical experts, and managers sit down together and look at how the whole system works. If they listen to each other and hang in long enough, they can create satisfying and effective workplaces beyond Taylor's most extravagant dreams.

Work-Design Protocols

Work-design methodology is relatively simple. The values behind it, however, challenge more than a century of reductionist practice. A protocol of strategy, structure, and procedure has emerged. Relevant stakeholders form a steering group. It includes at minimum top management and union leaders. It formulates or reiterates the values and philosophy—the new-paradigm thinking—that have led them to a design effort. It makes people aware of the meaning of the effort. It also chooses one or more design teams to analyze work systems and recommend options. Regular progress reviews are set up.

Design team membership cuts across levels and functions. Teams differ from traditional task forces in major ways. First, line workers and engineers, top executives and staff supervisors serve together. Second, they look at the whole business together, seeking Emery's "joint optimization" of technical and social systems. This form of social learning, unavailable in traditional systems, changes management and worker perceptions of the problem and the nature of the solutions.

The perceptual shift can't be overemphasized. All parties see aspects of their business they have never seen before. To do it, they must get past strange feelings born of invisible walls between jobs and levels. Nobody quite knows how to work together in this odd mixture of status, role, level, gender, knowledge, skill, and authority sitting around the same table. It can be very uncomfortable at first.

Orientation seminars help. Going through a joint simulation exercise, reading cases, and visiting other companies are good team-building tasks for new work-design teams. Low-key group and interpersonal process work can help. A few hours with a simple personal-style instrument (for example, the Work-Style Preference Inventory [McFletcher, 1983]) may accelerate mutual acceptance and support. Brainstorming lists of appropriate behavior for group members and leader can set useful norms. Teams are best focused at this stage on tasks—learning about their own system and how to redesign it. If they get into fights, run away from the task, or insist that the consultant "give us the plan," they may need more explicit discussions of norms, processes, and styles to get back on track.

The Generic Menu

Here is a generic menu of typical tasks work designers do. I have derived it from managing or consulting in organizations seeking to translate into action the principles first articulated by Emery and Trist.

- A person who has formal authority *usually*:

  1. Identifies the window of opportunity, the compelling business need, and invites outside or internal help.

2. Encourages others to visit innovative sites, attend workshops, read up on what's happening.

3. Convenes a steering group.

- The steering group *usually*:

1. Restates the organization's purposes and the objectives of the design effort.

2. Begins articulating values and philosophies a new design should embody.

3. Selects design team members or criteria for self-selection.

4. Reviews design team progress regularly.

5. Validates new designs and implementation plans.

6. Manages the implementation.

- A design team *usually*:

1. Examines outside forces to which the organization must respond: customers, regulators, suppliers, government, and so on.

2. Specifies the most desirable responses.

3. Does two analyses of how the system works now:

   a. Technical: linear layout, what "steady state" means, where and why errors or upsets ("variances") occur.

   b. Social: what constitutes "good jobs," what skills are required to operate the system in a steady state, handle upsets, and do administrative work, who has which skills, and who needs training.

4. Educates itself about innovative solutions (visits to other sites, reading, seminars).

5. Drafts one or more new scenarios.

6. Presents emerging scenarios to the steering group and (in redesigns) to other departments to let people know the changes being contemplated, and to get feedback on feasibility.

7. Prepares a design plan and implementation proposal.

8. Discusses the plan and proposal with all affected parties *before* its approval by the steering committee.

The design team nearly always includes one or more members of the steering group, a very practical application of Likert's "link pin" in action. A useful detailed guide for getting started is William O. Lytle's (1997).

Implementation follows a learning curve. It doesn't happen all at once. Consider a graphic illustration of the ups and downs of order processing in a redesigned customer service department, which once needed nineteen days to process new orders. A design team estimated the job could be done in three days. A multiskilled customer team achieved this standard as jobs were learned. In seven months the teams had reached a new level dramatically better than the old.

Design Contingencies

The best-known innovative workplaces have been startups ("greenfields") like the Gaines Foods pet food plant in Topeka, Kansas (Walton, 1982), and the Shell Sarnia oil refinery in Ontario, Canada (Davis & Sullivan, 1980). However, a great many organizations are now undertaking redesigns, reorganizing work in ongoing operations.

Based on physical work in mines, mills, and factories, work-design principles for both startups and redesigns have been found applicable to offices, research laboratories, government agencies, and service businesses. Their spread into new settings mirrors that of scientific management in the early 1900s from machine shops to government offices. This new revolution, however, differs significantly from that earlier one. Work-design techniques now have been put directly into the hands of those who do the work. They have been used with equal success (and failure) in union and nonunion settings, with young and old, men and women, blacks, whites, and many other ethnic groups. Multiethnic workplaces present special problems of language and culture. Yet the principles hold for those able to see work design as an action-research process rather than implementing a predetermined structure.

The "right answer" is best worked out by local teams from all levels, functions, degrees of expertise. This is called learning. Although a lot of folks tried and a lot of folks died, nobody has found economic or technical substitutes for people learning together what to do and how to do it.

Three Analytic Tasks

Design teams do three analyses. One is a map of "environmental demands"—what the customers, regulators, suppliers, and the community want from the organization and how it responds now. Another is the technical analysis, a flow chart of how the system functions, and where and how often errors occur. This is done against a growing understanding of raw materials, conversion steps, and what customers consider to be high quality. The group analysis of key variances always excites and stimulates people. A third is a social analysis, looking at how satisfying each job is now and how to build a system where every job is a good one.

There are many wrinkles at each step. The classic procedures originally formulated by Emery (1980) can be found in many places. Consultants have invented endless variations. Appliers as quickly modify them, a sign of "ownership" heartening to those of us who like to see their ideas implemented. The classic procedure is to scan the environment before doing anything else. My preference is to start with technology and flow charts, because the product or service itself is often the only thing the diverse people around the table have in common, besides membership in the human race. Each analysis is needed to fully understand the others, a chicken-egg paradox that leads to iteration—going around the same mulberry bush several times. Inevitably people discover deeper meanings in what they do, and modify the work accordingly.

The exercise starts slowly. This unprecedented task baffles groups at first. If you start a design team, expect some frustrating "why are we here?" meetings. Some managers see this as a defect in the process, a waste of time, which efficient techniques should cure. Why doesn't the consultant just give them the "right" structure and get on with it? In fact, everything we have learned about group development since Lewin supports the view that floundering around is an essential precondition to learning and high output. No championship football team ever became a winning combination on the first day of practice. Neither do steering committees or design teams. They have to discover their own potential by playing the game.

Laying Out a New Work System

Eventually every design team arrives at a new analysis of how things currently work. They then try out some alternative designs. They seek to create systems that (1) eliminate errors and (2) have no crummy jobs.

The boundaries among functions, departments, and tasks are redrawn. Jobs become larger. Departments take on more responsibility. Supervisory and staff functions are redefined.

Every important traditional factor must be accounted for in a new system: hiring, firing, training, controlling, planning, scheduling, compensating, repairing, filing, reporting, and so on. In unionized places, task force members try to distinguish between problem-solving issues and collective bargaining issues. That is not possible in work design. The contract specifies work rules, division of labor, and compensation—exactly the issues a redesign brings into focus more sharply, the same way that scientific management did over eighty years ago. To maintain union-management cooperation in such an effort requires considerable behind-the-scenes negotiating and political skill of team members. Visible outcomes tend to be embodied in new contracts guaranteeing secure jobs, for example, in return for task flexibility.

Designers eventually devise a new supervisory pattern. Sometimes that means fewer supervisors, and nearly always the title changes to "coordinator" or "team leader" or some other nontraditional name. In every case—a new design cannot succeed otherwise—the supervisory role changes. Control shifts to workers when skills and knowledge are enlarged. Leaders manage resources, training, and relations with other departments. Since few of us know how to do that, we need to learn how, something teams must constantly be reminded about.

However, the job does not stop there. In new sites, we must draw up hiring and training plans. In redesigns, we need a plan to secure employment and use the skills and experience of every person, regardless of the staffing called for by the ideal design. We must offer choices to workers who are not needed, interim methods (and incentives) devised for the transfer of people's skill and knowledge, new coordinating procedures, and new supervisory activities.

None of this is quick or easy. Taylor estimated two to four years to install scientific management. That estimate held good for sociotechnical redesigns too until the late 20th century. In the 1980s design teams might work from three months to a year to come up with plans they had confidence in. By the turn of the century, though, the rate of change outran the ability of design teams to keep up. This called for quicker ways to do the job. It also made obvious that the solution was not a one-time fix but a work system in which people continually updated what they were doing. The process is analogous to the annual software update every computer user accepts as a cost of higher productivity. You'd better do it even if you'd rather not. Many ideas have emerged for accelerating work systems design (Lytle, 2002). In new designs people worry continually about whether "it" will work, whether they can get competent people in, whether they will start on time. When a team takes its time and does things right, startups can be accelerated dramatically.

Special Problems of Redesigns

Redesigns involve more ambiguity and anxiety than startups. The biggest worry among designers and steerers alike is "What happens to me?" This is a legitimate concern. Evidence from many projects confirms that a design done right alters every job, from janitor to president. Functions are combined, eliminated, farmed out. Supervisory functions don't disappear; they are managed differently by different people. This often reduces the number of formal leader positions and changes the nature of those left. It is very common for all members of a self-managing team, for example, to acquire more skill, knowledge, and responsibility than their former supervisors used to have. That is what makes teams so flexible, cost-effective, and challenging. It also reinforces the threat to middle managers and supervisors.

This reality requires additional principles in redesigns:

1. It is wrong and impractical to ask people to design themselves out of work. A way must be found to assure employment for people, even as their jobs change. This means gains cannot be taken through unilateral layoffs. They accumulate instead through attrition (not replacing dropouts), doing more work with the same work force, offering early retirements, transfers, retraining, career counseling, and help in starting their own businesses for those displaced by redesign. There are creative options—new technology and market teams, special proj-ects, ad hoc training groups—that add value not accessible before. As new technologies arise, a great many more people will be displaced. We cannot apply sociotechnical redesign without also imagining new forms of economic activity.

Displacement also is a two-way street. Many people who could and would be employed in a new design find, like some of my supervisors in the 1960s, that they don't want to work this way. That leads to the second principle.

2. Choices should be offered. In many redesign situations jobs are rebid, and leadership roles are opened up to all who think they meet

the criteria. Those who are not selected for their first choice retain their former pay and benefits until equitable arrangements can be made.

3. Displaced people need influence over their own futures. Displacement is a joint problem, caused by economics and technology. If it is to be solved in socially viable ways, management should not assume unilateral responsibility for redeploying people. That means enacting a policy decision that problem solving should include those most affected, who will be treated as adults.

These principles alter the old authority-dependency games between labor and management. One practical observer has gone further and suggested that management and labor reverse their traditional roles: management should take responsibility for job security, labor for productivity (Hickey, 1986). Later, these principles were built into several innovative labor-management contracts, notably one between the United Steel Workers and National Steel Corporation.

Supervisory and Staff Roles

The last things to be designed are leadership roles. These are best considered after all other aspects of the work have been figured out. Unless this practice is observed, people tend to reinvent traditional supervision, defeating their own new design. One sign that learning is taking place is when a supervisor on the design team says, usually with ambivalence, "Well, I do that now. But with what we're talking about, you don't need a special person."

Special Problems of Professional and Managerial Work

In a routine technical analysis, the system is flow-charted and errors pinpointed. In a routine social analysis, tasks are merged and blended to create "whole" jobs that better match the technology. Anyone who tries to clone this procedure for project management, product development, or planning quickly discovers that knowledge work happens differently from repetitive production work (a continuing source of irritation between scientists and cost accountants). The flow chart spills in all directions. People already have multiskilled jobs, with considerable decision latitude. What they lack is a map of the informal processes— apparently random—most likely to produce optimal results.

One sociotechnical design scheme to account for this reality uses a map of a nonlinear system's tasks in terms of the discussions that must take place on the road to a solution, invention, discovery, decision, or plan (Pava, 1983). Pava calls these "deliberations," a word that covers everything from new-product development to sales and service policy. The places where deliberations happen Pava calls "forums." These might involve anything from doodling on the backs of envelopes over coffee to long offsite meetings.

A map of required deliberations compared to actual reveals the kinds of teamwork needed among individual contributors, already multiskilled, for whom the classic work team would be inappropriate. To enhance the social side, Pava specifies the shifting cast of characters who come in and out of the deliberations as they progress. These he calls "coalitions," formal or informal allies thrown together by mutual need to carry out individual and common tasks.

A nonroutine design team's technical analysis, then, consists of mapping necessary versus actual deliberations and coalitions, then designing a realignment of forums which people predict will produce more satisfying outcomes. Sociotechnical principles remain intact. The methodology changes with the nature of the problem: equifinality in action again. John Dupre and I modified Pava's procedures and applied them during 1986 to the reorganization of McCormack & Dodge, a 1,200-person software development firm. One innovation that emerged was each staff vice-president taking on a product or customer service responsibility in addition to support functions like human resources, finance, or information systems. The top team also devised a dozen corporate-policy forums in each function. Each included specialists from business units and field offices, so that those most affected directly influenced what happens. They rejected the alternatives—building large corporate staffs or having a full-scale matrix organization—as (a) too expensive and (b) contrary to people's aspirations for broader career paths.

IMPLEMENTING NEW WORK DESIGNS

Events to Ponder Department: Thomas Edison, the inventor, spent ten years on the nickel-iron-alkaline battery. After 8,000 experiments, an assistant suggested giving up, seeing as there were no results. "Results?" said Edison. "We have lots of results. We know 8,000 things that don't work!"

—Popular Story

When a design team draws up a new plan, you can bet your last nickel that the designers have concluded that many old practices will not work. You can be equally sure that they do not know which of the new ones will. Uncertainty abounds. Nobody has gone down this road before. In the interim between design and new reality, ad hoc structures are required to help with learning. People who have been doing one task for years don't suddenly become multiskilled. Supervisors used to handling daily problems themselves don't suddenly become "boundary managers." It can take months or years to build new capabilities. Work must go on in the meantime.

So companies need transition structures. In one case, for example, newly created multiskilled work teams were complemented for nine months by a temporary technical team, which included former supervisors and staff experts. It had two tasks: (1) transfer its skills and knowledge to the other teams and (2) explore and develop new roles for its own members.

There are some useful guiding principles. An obvious one is "Try it out." One steering committee was skeptical of a design team's plan to put orders into the shop in three days instead of two weeks. They gave five design-group volunteers a room of their own and began feeding them orders. In a week the team got the cycle down to three days. They also learned new wrinkles that were incorporated into the emerging plan.

Minimum Critical Specs

Another basic is minimum critical specification, a breakthrough concept devised by David (P. G.) Herbst (1974) during the redesign of Norwegian merchant ships. It is a central principle of work design, wholly contradicting the old-paradigm notion of several contingency plans worked out in advance. Minimum critical specification means not making decisions for another group that its members ought to be making for themselves. By this principle, a steering group passes along "boundary conditions"—values, philosophy, and limits of space and money. The design team recommends basic structure, quality, output, and safety requirements, legal and ethical considerations, a process for member and leader selection, a training plan, and such personnel policies as the steering committee may require. Many problems people actually encounter, as the Three Mile Island disaster showed, often cannot be foreseen.

So details like housekeeping, job rotation, relief schedules, and monitoring safety are best left to those closest to the work. Specialists or supervisors may need to remain in ad hoc support roles, gradually transferring what they know to the work teams. Creative companies offer staff and line people promotions if they serve well in this role for a time.

Teams and management evolve an ongoing negotiation over skill acquisition, tasks, and responsibilities. Much experimenting takes place. Which skills and tasks will be acquired by people on the line? That is a design question, to be solved through ad hoc teams, teachers, or other arrangements. One company invited retirees back part-time to teach its new plant teams special technical skills, a creative arrangement that met everybody's needs without adding to permanent payroll. Certain kinds of outside expertise will always be needed, especially for new product and technology development. In new-design sites, however, engineers, scientists, and marketing specialists tend to interact with line operators regularly, a practice unheard of in traditional places.

Many how-to-do-it treatises exist on sociotechnical systems design. Case studies abound. Find them in the library or by keying "sociotechnical systems" into any business publications database through your computer. A common thread of these cases is that each site writes its own textbook, a thick binder of philosophy, mission, values, assumptions, and specific solutions for its problems. Each organization reinvents the process and adds its own twists. Sometimes it invents new analytic tools. There are so many ways to skin this cat nobody can imagine all of them. The only constant is a repeated question: "Which principles do we want to preserve?"

Perhaps five hundred factories had been designed in North America by new-paradigm principles from 1975 to 1985, and hundreds more since. Nearly all have features similar to what my customer service teams worked out in the 1960s. They integrate work and learning, pay skill-based salaries, organize around natural production segments, include maintenance, safety, and clerical tasks in work teams, have workers train one another and rotate jobs to acquire skills, have joint team-manager evaluations for pay raises, and coordinate through a committee or task force system. The most successful ones treat their own culture as a unique feature requiring constant attention. Many install a process review board to keep their norms and principles intact (Hirschhorn, 1984).

Implementation: Possible Pitfalls

People can mess up new-design implementations too. The reasons, broadly put, are too much structure or too little. In some cases management panics when production curves drop during early stages. In one innovative plant the management initiated ad hoc "assistant coordinators" to shore up slow-learning teams, angering team members who were not consulted. Although the decision was necessary, the process was seen as contrary to espoused principles of participation (Hirschhorn, 1984). Anxious managers are prone to recreate features of traditional supervision at the slightest hint of variance. This works against learning. It becomes a self-fulfilling prophecy.

Managers may also abdicate responsibility, leaving people too much on their own, without clear goals or enough skill to proceed. Some avoid direct statements for fear of being labeled authoritarian. They defer to participation, imagining a collective magic born of good intentions that absolves them from making tough choices. Laissez-faire management, as Lippitt and White showed years ago in Iowa, creates as many problems as capricious authoritarianism. Too little structure is as bad as too much.

Managers everywhere discover, as Lewin pointed out years ago, that while authoritarianism is everybody's old friend, democratic methods can be alien indeed. Effective managers learn to provide goal focus and instruction, and not to overload people with too many tasks in the early stages of a new design. Effective participation requires leaders to take a stand without becoming authoritarian. They learn to give over responsibility gradually to teams, a trick mastered only by doing it.

Relearning to Manage

This calls for a form of leadership training still not well defined. All of us, no matter how good our intentions, grew up with one foot planted in the old paradigm. How do you learn and lead at the same time? How do you walk the tightrope between taking over and leaving people alone in emergencies? How do you speak for your own goals and visions without preempting other people's? How do you lead and simultaneously develop other leaders? How will you reassure people when you don't have answers? How do you maintain the short-run economic integrity of an enterprise so that people can learn to keep it viable for the long haul? These are challenges the new paradigm poses. There are no textbook answers. Each company writes its own treatise.

Experiments founder on two other kinds of shoals. One is a change in leadership. The new leader does not know how to leave a self-managing system alone and inadvertently, or deliberately, recreates traditional supervision to reduce his or her anxiety. My own 1960s experiment lasted about three months longer than I did, because the managers who followed me had not been involved in the design and could not understand results based on self-control. They settled for less output and more turnover as the price of lower anxiety.

A more common situation is the boundary that can't be bridged. This happens especially to experiments contained within one department or division of a large company. The other departments continue business as usual. Eventually the maverick is swallowed up and digested. One large corporation fostered sixty self-managing team experiments, only one of which survived into the late 1970s. The others sunk without a trace, leading researchers to observe that the umbrella of values and commitment must be particularly strong from top to bottom for these innovations to survive (Trist & Dwyer, 1982).

What about workers who refuse responsibility? A few years ago the United Auto Workers sent a delegation to Volvo in Sweden to study alternatives to the assembly line. These factory hands concluded they would rather have high wages and machine-paced work than assume the responsibility the Swedish system entailed. They could not imagine a system where control was turned inside out.

Eric Trist observed that management commitment and learning over time are likely to convert resisters (an observation also made by Taylor about scientific management a century ago). The design of such auto factories as the joint Toyota-GM venture in California and the General Motors Saturn factory in Tennessee suggest that this is happening even in the highly traditional auto industry. Management is learning how to offer job security, unions to offer greater flexibility and focus on output. These unprecedented arrangements lead both parties down a path fraught with unknown pitfalls—and exciting possibilities. (At General Motors, the United Auto Workers' Irving Bluestone injected QWL into contract negotiations as early as 1973.)

The only safe work-design strategy, in this fast-changing world, is to build up workers' ability to learn how the "black box" works so they can detect errors no one has seen before. We are in a tug-of-war as never before between output and learning, what Larry Hirschhorn calls "developmental tension." People fail if there is too much to learn too quickly. Managers who rush into the gap with more structure may cut out future learning essential to success. External controls are self-perpetuating; the more you have the more you need.

People also fail if management does nothing to support them over the hump. People become demoralized when they lose faith in their ability to learn. People can also fail where there are too few product, market, and technology changes to sustain worker interest over time. Boredom and alienation can overtake a new design plant, too. Novelty is needed at intervals.

Another dilemma is the multi-skill system itself, by means of which everybody can eventually reach the top rate. Designers are learning to plan job progression so that people don't move too fast, compromising safety, quality, and learning. The emphasis must be on knowledge and skill, not rapid advancement. Even so, teams could experience malaise when everything becomes routine and everybody has mastered all skills. Introducing new products or equipment and systems is one way to keep work teams fresh. Another solution is continually providing new learning opportunities, inside or outside the system. Some companies pay for job-related college courses for workers. Others encourage community service or transfers.

The problem is a relatively new one in the world. It is likely to get worse. The more successful a new design, the quicker the demand for novelty, stimulation, and new challenges. (Managers and staff specialists, bored out of their socks when work becomes routine, register surprise when hourly workers mirror their aspirations. Taylorist assumptions die hard.) In my own 1960s experiment, people began prowling the office like restless cats after the day's order processing crunch was over, looking for excitement. I know of another case where one work team stole another team's work just to keep busy! Compared to boredom and alienation, those are good problems to have. However, it takes constant attention to devise novel solutions.

Finally, people resist peer salary reviews. It takes a mature, experienced work team to make peer review work without any input from management or the human resource department. In practice, skill-based evaluation responsibility seems to work best when shared between teams and management.

Changing Consultant Roles

If workers, managers, and supervisors move toward new learning, can consultants do less? It is one thing to advocate new paradigms from the sidelines and skewer those who fall short (the old paradigm in spades). It is quite another to get into the ballgame, which means joining in the vulnerability, risk, and egg-on-the-face messiness that attends jumping off the edge into the unknown. Can consultants keep up their old ways and expect to succeed? An early answer from Norway, where they had been thinking about these matters for a quarter of a century, was "No way." Max Elden (1978), at the Institute for Industrial Social Research in Trondheim, wrote about third-generation work democracy as a synthesis of sociotechnical thinking and participative change.

Elden's first generation in the 1960s aimed to prove that industrial self-managing teams, of the sort discovered spontaneously in the mines, were feasible elsewhere. Sociotechnical experts did the diagnosing, designing, and implementing. In this period the process side of sociotechnical redesign eroded, the mechanics of work analysis overriding change skills derived from Lewinian thinking. Experts sought to get the "right" merger of technology and social psychology.

In the second generation (late 1960s, early 1970s) the goal broadened—to change the pay scheme, to alter middle-management and supervisory roles, to apply new concepts to service and educational organizations. The expert became a consultant, contracting for a limited number of days to help organizations redesign their work. In this evolution, the influence of the NTL Institute, group dynamics, and the consulting practice that flowed from them became more important.

While consultants involved clients more in diagnosing and prescribing, they still directed and often performed the search. They also devised an ever-growing repertoire of models for new techniques like environmental scanning, variance analysis, role analysis, demand systems, and core transformation processes. It became hard for people to "own" their daily lives reinterpreted through so many unfamiliar frameworks.

What coal miners had invented spontaneously now became a grueling process. Groups started and could not finish. Just as Taylor built scientific management from pieces tried out in different places, consultants imagined comprehensive change strategies manufactured the same way, incorporating all of social science "knowledge," but leaving out common sense—like the fact that people can remember only a few things at once, that short-term problems drive out long-range thinking, that people in Contentment or Denial are not ready to change, that dogged leadership is required to finish anything.

In the third generation—there are more than fifty examples of employee-managed redesigns in Norway (and a growing number in the United States)—we are moving even further away, paradoxically from outside experts. I say "paradoxically" because more knowledge exists, thanks to Lewin, Emery and Trist, and their followers, than ever before. Hundreds, perhaps thousands, of managers have now had the sort of firsthand experience I did in the 1960s. Many now understand how to find novel, workable solutions to unprecedented problems by turning them over to players once considered ineligible for the game.

Fred Emery, in particular, devised some simple methods for transferring sociotechnical knowledge (Emery, 1982). He invented the participative design conference working with the Royal Australian Airforce in 1971, simplifying the methods to reduce dependency and extend his own efforts. He introduced the procedure into Norway in 1973. It requires that natural work groups, given a few simple inputs, then assist each other in doing redesigns, a procedure I find less workable as technologies grow more complex and a wider range of skills is called for. My firm has used variations in the United States in printing, textiles, contact lens manufacturing, and in steel mills. We have found ways to make useful contributions throughout the design phase and into implementation without doing the work for people. By economic and technical standards, results have been dramatic.

Two Important Lessons

Sociotechnical experts have learned two profound lessons from all this work.

First, given some minimal guidance, most work groups produce designs 85 to 90 percent congruent with what the best outside pros can do—with vastly more commitment to implement. Nobody can implement commitment for you.

Second, a work design is not an all-at-once activity to be finalized, the way plans for a house might be. Rather than try to do it all, managers and designers must learn to do as little as possible for others who will be involved. Herbst's "minimum critical specification" is a key new-paradigm design principle. It means, bluntly, don't try to figure out every contingency in advance. The best engineers can't do it, as Hirschhorn's (1984) studies of Three Mile Island show, and neither can you or I. Even if we could, doing it would cut down others' chances for learning, self-control, and ownership. Paradoxically, in the work-design business, slow is fast, less is more.

Under suitable conditions, people often invent the self-managing work team as I did in the 1960s. This happens enough that some folks believe work design means, by definition, work teams. That is an understandable mistake. The defining factors of work design, in my opinion, are (1) participation in the analysis and problem solving by all relevant players and (2) changing the supervisory role to managing boundaries instead of the work itself so people can learn self-control.

For routine and repetitive work, multiskilled teams are an excellent solution, socially, technically, and economically. It should be obvious, though, that such work teams do not fit all work, especially the individual contributor kind like computer programming. In one study of 134 projects, multiskilled teams showed up in 53 percent of the cases (Pasmore, Francis, Haldeman, & Shani, 1982). People who do nonroutine work tend to invent different kinds of solutions. They are most likely to be helped by the form of analysis recommended by Cal Pava (1983). You also can find excellent guidance in William O. Lytle's (1998) comprehensive work design textbook and in the team-based organization book by Mohrman, Cohen, and Mohrman (1995).

Back to Group Dynamics

In our effort to understand what it takes to do complex work under conditions of continual change, we come at last, in an age of cybernetics, robotics, and sophisticated process controls, back to group dynamics, Lewin, Lippitt, and the Iowa studies in authority/democracy and participation. How important is group skills training? What kind? When?

I am attracted to a classic piece of action research showing that a balanced use of leadership and authority is the key to effective self-managing work teams. Videotapes by Beth Atkinson reveal people using information, expertise, connections, communications skills, and charisma to exercise influence in positive and negative ways (Hirschhorn, 1984). People willing to risk disclosure of feelings and ideas and to confront differences created a better power balance and more effective teams.

Atkinson changed the climate of self-managing groups by teaching people to use, not abuse, power, and to recognize abuses by literally raising little red flags in meetings. Not surprisingly, she also found that pep talks and exhortation, such as "win one for the Gipper," had little value in motivating quality or output. "People who use charisma as a base," notes Atkinson, "produce the most stifling group climate" (Hirschhorn, 1984, p. 146). They abuse others, and powerless people (as Lippitt and White showed long ago) cease to act.

This confirms for me that the T-group, which put these issues in stark relief, is an important learning structure. It became problematical when enthusiasts tried to transfer its learning as pure process, leaving out an organization's extended social field. The self-managing team, focused on customers and externally driven tasks, can, paradoxically, improve its performance enormously through a deeper appreciation of its own process. But only when its members accept their common task.

We have discovered, as the British coal miners did in the 1940s, that higher levels of technology offer a chance for more humane work relationships. Technology, however, doesn't care what we do with it. So we can easily fall into the trap of creating "electronic sweatshops" too (Garson, 1989). To gain the full benefits of new technologies, we should consider new structural arrangements, involving those who do the work in its design, coordination, and control. In summary, feelings, trust, and openness need structures neither too tight nor too loose; and new structures are likely to bog down if people cannot achieve the necessary group and interpersonal skills.

I conclude that cross-functional teams from three or more levels can invent innovative systems with minimal direction. To operate them over time, however, they need help to learn. In team settings, people need to build up their power bases, to talk to one another on an equal footing. Most of us cannot do this without greater skills in supporting and confronting others, and in taking and yielding leadership in groups (Weisbord & Maselko, 1981). For practical guidelines in developing personal power in large corporations, I recommend Peter Block's book (2004) on constructive politics.

It is worth noting here that the Emerys, working in a highly unionized country, Australia, believed that gaining the legal right to control and coordinate your work renders group, interpersonal, and communications techniques unnecessary. In the United States, given our enormous diversity and political pressures, I find that attractive hypothesis hard to test. I take it seriously because of my 1960s experience with self-managing teams. If I could go back to the 1960s again, I would certainly figure out how to transfer whatever knowledge and skill in managing the task-process relationship I now have. The dilemma, I think, is not whether but rather when and how to do it so that we do not deprive people of choice and control.

We have come full circle—from early group and leadership experiments to T-groups to coal mines to textile mills to nuclear power plants to a merger of technical and group processes drawn from all these settings. Such is the convergence of OD and STS, two social learning traditions, one dug out of the British coalfields, the other stumbled upon in a Connecticut race relations conference, each concerned with the subtle interplay of work and feelings, the one highlighting structure, the other relationships, one developed by the Tavistock Institute, the other by the NTL Institute, both influenced by that "funny little man with the German accent."

CHAPTER THIRTY

Making It Happen

Turning Workplace Vision into Reality

Franklin Becker
Fritz Steele

———

Creating workplaces that serve the organization well requires leaders who recognize the impact of work settings and policies on organizational health, question traditional assumptions about how to create and use work settings, and pay attention to issues of organizational ecology as a continuous part of their roles. This chapter summarizes a number of practical approaches and guidelines that experience suggests will tend to create a healthy pattern—that is, an effective and efficient organization that provides a high-quality, adaptive work environment for its members. We have grouped these principles, or rules of thumb, into four broad topics: aspects of work-setting design, processes for making and managing workplaces, dealing with organizational culture, and leadership roles in continuous learning.

ASPECTS OF WORK-SETTING DESIGN

• *Use visibility as a communications tool.* If you want people to know what is going on in the organization and who is doing what, create settings that make as much activity visible as possible. This may sound like a meaningless statement, or even circular, but it is definitely not the norm today. Most layouts tend to wall off activities into neat compartments that bear no relation to each other, and therefore tend to have little effect on each other except when a special effort is made to "communicate."

We are suggesting that if space is deliberately designed to "display thinking" by making the daily activities of the organization more visible, communication among employees and awareness of what is going on in the organization will naturally increase, generating energy and interest throughout the firm. The other piece of this strategy is to encourage groups to show "work in progress" rather than letting information out only when they have finished something. When others see it in progress, they can provide much more interesting and helpful comments, if not always comfortable ones. Without this visibility, most reactions are after the fact, when they can't make much difference.

• *Use what you've got better.* In general, you can gain valuable resources by simply using better what you already have in your workplace. You need to be able to really see what you have, and the different ways that it potentially can be used. This usually requires letting go of labels or names for places (the boardroom, the presentation room, and so forth) and seeing instead the qualities that they possess (a large space that can accommodate twenty people seated, good task lighting, a handy location next to the entry to the building).

You can accommodate a greater variety of activities simply by using current facilities in looser ways, with little or no out-of-pocket costs at all. The only cost is the energy required to look for attributes instead of labels, and to alter policies to allow such places to be used in unorthodox ways.

• *Locate facilities where people want to be.* If you are choosing a location for a startup company or for a new facility for an existing one, try to put it in a location that is attractive to the people who will work there. Again this sounds so obvious as not to be worth mentioning, and yet it is violated more times than it is followed. As long as companies have been created, leaders have tended to physically locate them in spots that make economic or logistical sense but not necessarily social-system sense.

This is changing today, as many new companies locate in highly attractive areas of the country such as the foothills of the Rockies, and in places such as North Carolina and Texas where the sun not only shines but housing is affordable. With today's electronic communications tools, physical location has become much less of a constraint for a knowledge-based company than it once was. Even for manufacturing operations, leaders are finding that locating them in attractive spots puts them ahead of the game in terms of recruiting high-quality staff.

• *Build for function, not form or image.* By simplifying or eliminating status as a determinant of workplace form, you can create settings that truly support what the users are trying to accomplish and be free to change it when needs have changed. The same holds for building to express a particular image of the system or its occupants—it's too rigid and costly in terms of inertia. Create the best place for what you do, and trust that this will be a positive image. If it's not, change what you do.

• *Build for change and expect to change it.* As much as possible try to create loose-fit settings, those that are not rigidly constructed for only one use in one style. The world will not stand still, and organizations that do will tend to drop out.

• *Build in some slack for spontaneity.* Just as it's hard to predict changes in work style or tasks ahead of time, it's hard to predict the spur-of-the-moment needs that people will have for work settings. Unless you never have any need for spontaneous activities such as meetings, don't build facilities that are so lean and efficient that there is no place for any activity that wasn't already programmed into them. Reduce the inertia cost of people putting off a good idea because there's no place to follow through on it.

• *Make some great places for informal contact during the workday.* Just as people need time by themselves, they also need to have high-quality interchanges with other people. In many organizations there are no good spots to do this, or if there are they tend to be in locations that make them unlikely to be used (too far off the beaten track, out of the way, in the way of traffic flow).

Every work setting should have a few very good interaction spots, such as small, cheery rooms with sofas, armchairs, coffee table, softer lighting, or whatever appeals to the people who will be using such spaces. If there is conscious attention to creating great interaction spots, that communicates a message to everyone that the leadership really values such exchanges and wants to encourage them. It also improves the quality of life for the users.

• *Speed up group development by giving teams a place.* Workspace design can be a very effective tool in helping to create a sense of identity and teamwork in new groupings. In general, if you create a new, hybrid work entity or group, give it some concrete reality by also giving it a place of its own. This accomplishes a couple of things: it makes a clear commitment to the success of the new group; and it helps change the interaction patterns of the group, making it more likely that they will see and get to know one another and therefore begin to really think of themselves as a group. This should be done consistently as new groupings are created, so that it is expected and simply treated as part of business as usual.

• *Create a true center for a facility.* In a workplace that is a collection of individual and group spaces, work hard to create an inviting place near the actual center with good things that draw people—services, displays, entertainment, food and drink, and so forth—and make it the crossroads for coming and going through the system. This center will help provide the glue that holds the system together, by helping members be aware of the community as a whole, not just their own part.

• *Make a big deal out of having food and beverages available in central spots.* In our experience, having good food and drinks available in central spots is also a terrific community builder. Food draws people together just as it has throughout human history, and provides a kind of glue for the system. We have several clients who provide snacks such as fruit, bagels, donuts, and chips throughout the day, along with tea, coffee, soft drinks, and juices. Being generous with this sort of thing has big paybacks in terms of the climate that it helps to foster. People naturally feel a bit more relaxed when they are sharing something, and there is an almost festive quality to just being together in the café area.

• *Encourage workplaces that are more like home.* If you still have most people coming to the office, encourage them to add as many of the qualities of home as they would like it to have. This means having a variety of kinds of spaces, having artifacts that people like, and having spots for changes of pace and fun as well as for serious work. Sometimes these will in fact be the same spots used in different ways or by different people. We gave several examples of this in earlier chapters, and it may be one of the most important new directions. The point is to provide a rich setting that people feel at home in, so that they manage their time and pace to be both productive and creative over the long haul.

• *If you have people who travel a lot, create a great home base.* Many of today's service organizations (consulting firms, accountants, engineers, and the like) have a large percentage of professionals who work where the clients or customers are located, then come back to the firm to reconnect and do their own office work. Such return centers should be very carefully designed. They need to provide opportunities to relieve the stress of being "on stage" and on the road a lot. They also need to enhance connections with other people at the center. That suggests a mix of good personal work spots (not necessarily dedicated, though, as we have discussed earlier) and good mixing spots that allow people to see who's in the office and to talk to one another without the formality of appointments.

• *Pay special attention to entrances and exits.* Entrance design is very important in a work setting, since it shapes the first experiences people have when they enter it. Bad designs start people off on the wrong foot. Similarly, an awkward or hard-to-find exit can leave a bad taste as the lasting impression one has of a place. Poor design of either makes people feel that the owners don't care about the experiences of visitors.

PROCESSES FOR MAKING AND MANAGING WORKPLACES

• *Get employees involved.* The payoffs for involving users include better fit between the workplace and the users' needs, more excitement about the work, higher commitment to making the setting work, and better information about what fits and what needs changing. Designing the physical setting, when done right, is an invaluable form of organizational development.

• *Take care to do up-front direction setting.* Workplace choices are much more effective when they are based on clear notions of the organization's mission, values, key challenges, expected growth patterns, future ways of working, and the like. Leaders must drive the processes of inquiry that will keep these current and keep them matched to facilities choices.

• *If you have strategic business units, let them control their workplaces.* The notion behind the strategic business unit (SBU) is to give the pieces of a larger organization the tools and freedom to do a job, then hold them accountable for their results. The principles of organizational ecology should be applied here as in other situations. Within budget parameters, the SBU leaders should be free to follow their own space strategy as part of managing their business for results.

Controlling their space from the corporate facilities function sends a very contradictory message about whether they are really managing their business.

• *For space policies, just have a few good rules.* Whether as members of SBUs or not, people in the organization should be as free as possible to use settings in ways that suit their needs, moods, and work styles. This suggests keeping overall facilities policies to a bare minimum, using only those that are essential to the overall direction you are trying to set. For example, a rule about coordinating space changes with adjacent groups helps maintain an integrated choice process, while lots of specific rules about what can or can't be changed tend to demoralize people. It turns them off to problem solving about the workplace, and they defer and treat it as someone else's problem.

• *Encourage and support local influence.* "Tinkering" is an activity that can keep workplaces relevant to current demands. It does it more efficiently than having all decisions driven and controlled by a central facilities function. Tinkering should be actively supported with information and resources, not merely tolerated.

• *Be wary of adding space as an automatic solution for feeling cramped.* Always test whether you feel you're out of space because there really are no places to accommodate new people or activities, or because the space you have is allocated too rigidly or unevenly. What are the actual occupancy levels of offices over the course of a day or week? Are the largest offices the least often occupied? Seek ways to use the same square footage more effectively. For instance, we have recently helped a couple of clients turn grand lobbies into activity centers for employees rather than sterile sitting areas waiting for the occasional visitor who needs somewhere to be for a few minutes (a very poor use of what is usually a very visible central spot in the organization).

There are a number of approaches to this way of thinking today: the free-address system, just-in-time scheduling, office "hoteling," and other forms of nonterritorial offices are aimed at better use of scarce space.

• *Establish a responsive change-management process.* For those changes to personal or group workspaces that do require professional or technical support, provide the resources to users in a timely manner, so they don't make do with inadequate facilities for long periods while waiting their turn. This also helps combat a climate of cynicism, which can develop if big delays are standard. People tend to give up on trying to get changes made, and just make do.

- *Integrate support services.* Encourage the various building support services—food service, mail, information technology, maintenance, security, and so on—to think of themselves as one team in providing a high-quality environment for the occupants. The focus then becomes customer satisfaction and organizational effectiveness rather than the smooth operation of each individual unit.

- *Create policies to seek gains, not avoid losses.* Space-use policies should be simple and encourage positive behavior patterns (teamwork, communication, adaptability) rather than being driven by a failsafe mentality of trying to avoid possible aberrations in place use. If you focus on the positives there will still be some misfires, but they will tend to be inconsequential and worthwhile as learning experiences.

- *Define the problem before jumping to solutions.* Carefully describe the situation and identify what doesn't work about it, plus what you would like to have happening instead. Then it is possible to look at alternative ways to achieve the goal. Don't state the problem with an implied solution ("our problem is that we need to have more space"), but with what's missing, doesn't work, or needs to be done ("we need to be able to have forty new people work here within three months"). If you can stick to the problem, you are free to consider a range of alternatives (lease more space, have them work somewhere else, change the way workspaces are assigned, create new group work areas).

DEALING WITH ORGANIZATIONAL CULTURE

- *Make conscious choices about the impact of culture when doing a facilities project.* Do a diagnosis of the current organizational culture when working on mission, values, key success factors, and project goals. Assess basic assumptions to test which ones need to be changed to match projected use of the new facility and which ones are unlikely to be changeable. The top leaders have to lead the way in being willing to openly test their cultural assumptions.

- *Change the culture through concrete experiences.* You can create events and experiences that can loosen up the traditional assumptions about how things have to work. For example, if no one will use the boardroom for meetings, even though it is intended to be available for such use, design a specific event to be held there, to get people comfortable with it, and follow with a clear message from the top that it is intended to be used as a resource for meetings but is currently underutilized.

• *Promote a more inclusive definition of "real work" in the system.* Help people accept and value the whole range of activities that can be used to accomplish tasks, get new ideas, and solve problems: writing, thinking, talking to others, moving around, staring into space, eating, drinking, and so on. Anything can be useful in the right moment, and trust should be placed in the members to be able to decide what they should do next (including taking time out to regenerate their energy).

LEADERSHIP ROLES AND CONTINUOUS LEARNING

• *Work at developing explicit models of the different roles you should play in the management of your organization's settings.* There is no substitute for having thought about what you should get involved in and (just as important) what you should not. Get your role clear in your own mind and discuss it with others. Share expectations for your and others' roles, and negotiate them periodically so that others know what they should be doing and what they can expect from you.

• *Encourage feedback from a variety of sources and levels about how well the workplace is supporting your organization and its mission.* There is no substitute for feedback from occupants of different parts of th system, and you must beware of thinking that your own experience is representative of others. As a company president once told us, "I don't see why people feel that my office is cold and intimidating; it's a very homey place." And it was—to him, since it was his home. Others saw it as imposing, hidden away, and threatening since their experiences there were of being chewed out by the president in one-way performance reviews. If you create conditions where people will tell you how they see the place working, you'll be surprised at some of what you hear.

One way to maintain this feedback is to create some sort of sounding board that cuts across functional, operational, and hierarchical lines to give you a cross-section of experiences. It also helps to involve people who are really interested in the area of workplace design and impact.

• *Look for articles, videos, and other forms of information that will help you learn more about organizational ecology and its impact on your organization.* The more you take in new ideas and trends in the field, the more that useful questions will be raised about how your own places might be improved. Not all experiments will represent ideas you should try yourself, but they will raise interesting questions about what the people were trying to do and the new options they perceived for how to do it. Also look at architecture, interior design, and house magazines occasionally, just to get a feel for the new ideas in the field of space design. It's good to read outside your field of expertise anyway, as a means to making new connections and keeping loose about your assumptions about the world today.

• *Get out and look at examples of what has been done with space in other organizations.* Take the trouble to visit other organizations you have heard are doing something interesting with their workplace. Look at what they have done, and talk with those who did it about how they did it and what they were trying to accomplish. Take other people with you so that you are building a cadre of people who think about alternative workplace strategies in a looser way. To this end, you can also hire consultants to do workshops on organizational ecology and trends in design and management of settings.

Look at settings other than offices, too: public spaces, trade shows, expositions, museums (which often devote tremendous attention to detail and desired effect in their layout), and so on.

• *Get out and explore areas in your own organization.* Go see for yourself what different workplaces are like in your system, and talk to the people there about what work life is like for them. You never know what you will see and hear unless you take the trouble to do this periodically. We guarantee there will be surprises: conditions you wouldn't wish on anyone; areas where great things have been done with few resources and no fanfare—which could be applied around the system.

Getting around is good for your health, helps you to connect with others in the organization, and generates new ideas that can be followed up from your own vantage point. It also sends a message about your general interest and concern for people's working conditions.

• *Manage organizational ecology by doing a good job in the basic role of organizational leader.* Lastly, there are the basic leadership roles discussed earlier that are vital to developing and maintaining an effective workplace. These include:

- Keeping the vision, values, and mission of the system in focus, and testing for agreement
- Identifying change goals for business, culture, structure, and the like

- Setting overall standards for measuring the health of the organization

- Structuring data-collection processes for monitoring all of the above

- Structuring a workplace management process, including change management and the running of major projects; structuring ways to involve others in the process

- Modeling effective use of workplaces in your own behaviors, so that you set a tone of thoughtfulness and conscious choice making

CREATING NEW PLACES VERSUS RENOVATING EXISTING FACILITIES

We would like to consider a recurring issue that contains many of the issues of organizational ecology, in terms of both content and process. To produce a better match between desired ways of working and the organization's work settings, is it necessary to build a completely new place?

We have a bias toward creative reuse of existing facilities if this is at all feasible. Even when there is considerable dissatisfaction with the current facility, there is a kind of embedded energy in the place that is lost if it is simply abandoned. In many cases the perceived constraints are caused by the assumptions that are made about how space can be shaped, allocated, and used, rather than by inherent properties of the setting itself. If a diagnosis suggests that this is indeed the case, you may be able to free up the work possibilities by changing standards, policies, and other constraints on use, rather than throwing time and money into a new project. In fact, new projects often don't solve the problem anyway, because basic assumptions about how work is done and space is used have not changed.

Our rule of thumb here is simple: be very wary of getting into large-scale new projects unless they are absolutely necessary, such as when the existing setting is so confining or constraining that it will not be possible to function there in the ways that are needed for the future health of the organization.

The other key factor to consider is the accelerated rate of change in the environment of most organizations today. Driven by increasing uncertainty about markets, competitors, government regulations, environmental impact issues, technological advances, and the like, this turbulence makes it difficult to create brand-new work settings that are sized and equipped for the next change. In some cases, new facilities are obsolete before they are occupied, and in others it's even hard to know whether the place will be needed at all. Conceptions of what a corporate "headquarters" is are changing, and there are those who say that as a physical entity it may no longer be very useful in many enterprises.

All of this suggests to us that this is a time to be conservative about investing in major new office facilities, and progressive about experimenting with ways to use the facilities you already have. This not only saves potentially unnecessary investments, it takes advantage of the symbolic effects of working in a setting that has embedded in it the history of the enterprise and its people.

Having said this, we must also admit that analysis will sometimes show that the current setting just cannot support the level or variety of activities needed in the future. The flip side of the symbolic messages in the current setting is that if you want to truly change the culture and the way that people work, you may be fighting too much of an uphill battle to do it in the old setting. In some cultures the boardroom will always be the boardroom, a shrine to history and hierarchy, and you have to create an entirely new space if you want people to use it in different ways.

Between a renovation and creating a totally new place, there are obviously a number of other options. As a general strategy, we feel that it is best to first ask questions about policies and use patterns when sensing the need for workplace improvement, simply because these can be changed without a major capital expense. When you do choose to do some renovations, they should occur in the context of a relatively continuous process of space management, rather than only when there is an unavoidable space crisis.

You are ahead of the game if you have regularly gathered information about basic questions such as:

- What are we trying to do here?
- How is this changing and how quickly?
- What aspects of the setting are hindering us in changing?
- Are we making assumptions that are limiting the ways we are using our work settings?
- What alterations do we need to make to fit our changing needs to gain us the most flexibility for the money and time involved?

The point is to be assessing the match between settings and ways of working as you go along, so that changes become less abrupt and more part of business as usual. It is also important that this assessment include data from a range of types of users, so that the answers are not projections of what things look like from the top of the system.

Many of the physical changes that would be useful are low-cost interventions—rearranging some work stations, improving lighting, hanging some graphics in strategic spots, painting dingy hallways or stairwells so they don't feel so demoralizing, giving a group more latitude to rearrange common workspaces and include team-type furniture, and so on.

If you have good notions about how ways of working need to change, these will have a big return for a modest investment. If you don't have such concepts, spending major dollars on a totally new work setting carries the risk of not making very much practical difference in the long run. Being creative about organizational ecology doesn't necessarily require a large budget, but it does require a regular investment of time and attention in checking how you're doing and setting updated goals about how you want the members of the organization to be able to work.

CHAPTER THIRTY-ONE

So How Can You Assess Your Corporate Culture?

Edgar H. Schein

———

Culture assessment comes into play when an organization identifies problems in how it operates or as a part of a strategic self-assessment relating to merger, acquisition, joint venture, or partnership. But your ability to decipher your own culture is still limited. What other techniques are available to you?

SHOULD YOU USE A SURVEY?

Most managers are measurement-oriented. It is part of the culture of management. You probably want to know right away whether there are surveys available that allow you to measure your culture and put numbers on all of the dimensions reviewed in this chapter. There are survey instruments and questionnaires that claim to measure culture, but in terms of the culture model that I present, they only unearth some of the artifacts, some espoused values, and maybe one or two underlying assumptions. They do not reach the tacit shared assumptions that may be of importance in your organization. Why is this so? Why has no one developed a reliable and valid culture survey?

WHY CULTURE SURVEYS DO NOT AND CANNOT MEASURE CULTURE

There are several reasons why culture questionnaires do not reveal cultural assumptions—and why, in fact, they cannot do so.

You Don't Know What to Ask

First, *you don't know what to ask about, or what questions to design.* Remember that culture covers all aspects of what an organization learns over its history. To design a questionnaire that grapples with all of the relevant external and internal dimensions, you would have to write several hundred questions but still have no way of knowing which dimensions are the important ones in your organization. Some culture analysts claim they have isolated a limited set of relevant dimensions and designed surveys dealing with those dimensions; all of my experience tells me, though, that every organization has a unique profile of cultural assumptions that any questionnaire inevitably misses (see Hofstede, 1980, 1991; Cameron & Quinn, 1999; Goffee & Jones, 1998).

Surveys almost invariably deal with espoused values concerning working relationships. Do employees feel involved? Are communications open enough? Do employees feel they understand the company strategy? And so on. These may be important dimensions of the company's *climate,* and so they should be measured. The danger is that they become confused with culture. What if the important elements of the culture are instead the tacit assumptions about strategy, customers and markets, use of money, and other matters that may have little to do with human relations in the workplace and are completely overlooked by the survey? For example, if a company has always operated without much debt and been successful, it may now assume that keeping debt low and cash balance high is the correct way to manage its finances. This assumption about managing finances can become a crucial part of its culture and hence shape all kinds of strategic and operational decisions. But there is no way of knowing ahead of time whether one should design finance-type questions into one's culture survey.

Asking About Shared Processes Is Ineffective

Second, *asking individuals about a shared phenomenon is inefficient, and possibly invalid.* It is not easy for anyone to access shared tacit assumptions, so the idea of using a questionnaire is based on faulty logic in the first place. Inasmuch as culture is a group phenomenon, it is far easier to elicit information in groups by asking broad questions about different areas of organizational functioning and seeing where there is obvious consensus among the members of the group. In the group, one learns not only what the areas of concern are but also the intensity of feeling about them, and thereby the centrality of different shared assumptions in the total cultural profile.

Furthermore, there is no way of knowing what a person answering a questionnaire reads into the questions, nor the attitude elicited by the usual promises of anonymity and privacy. Ironically, having to give employees an anonymous survey surrounded by all kinds of procedures to ensure that no one is identified says more about the deep assumptions of the organization's culture than any statistical analysis of the responses. Consider what is implied by the need to keep things anonymous, the threat of punishment if an employee gives negative information, and the secrecy surrounding the whole project. In contrast, doing a culture study by bringing focus groups together openly to discuss the values and shared assumptions operating in the organization sends a completely different signal.

What Employees Complain About May Be Unchangeable

Third, *the things employees complain about may not be changeable* because they are embedded in the culture. The survey does have some value in identifying whether the espoused values are being met or not, and in most cases the survey data can show areas where they are not being met. But to make the changes the employees desire, one then has to do a "real" culture study to see why the values are not being met and what has to change in the culture for them to be met.

For example, as has been pointed out, it is common for companies to espouse teamwork; surveys often reveal that employees wish there were more teamwork, more trust among employees, and so on. However, examining the artifacts typically shows reward-and-incentive systems that put a premium on individual accomplishment and competition among employees for the scarce promotional opportunities that are available. If the company really wants to become team-based, it has to replace those individualistic systems that have worked in the past and are deeply embedded in people's thinking. If it cannot or will not do that, the end result could well be a *drop* in morale as employees discover that what they hoped for is not happening.

In other words, what is often labeled the "desired culture" is a set of espoused values that may simply not be tenable in the existing culture. We can espouse teamwork, openness of communication, empowered employees who make responsible decisions, high levels of trust, and consensus-based decision making in flat and lean organizations until we are blue in the face. But the harsh reality is that in most corporate cultures these practices don't exist because the cultures were built on deep assumptions of hierarchy, tight controls, managerial prerogatives, limited communication to employees, and the assumption that management and employees are basically in conflict anyway—a truth symbolized by the presence of unions, grievance procedures, the right to strike, and other artifacts that tell us what the cultural assumptions really are. These assumptions are likely to be deeply embedded and do not change just because a new management group announces a "new culture." As we see later, if such assumptions really are to change, we need a major organizational transformation effort.

HOW TO GET AT YOUR OWN CULTURE

Another way to put this is to ask yourself, *Am I a unique personality, or just an example of my culture?*

This question has preoccupied psychologists and sociologists for a long time. The answer is that you are unique, the product of your own genetic makeup and particular experience of growing up. But in the process of growing up, you also become a member of cultural units that leave their residue in your personality and mental outlook. The most obvious manifestation is the language or languages you speak, which clearly you learn (they are not genetic) and which determine to a great degree your thought process and how you perceive the world. Beyond language are the many attitudes and values you pick up in your family, school, and peer group. It has been shown over and over again that kids show patterns of attitudes and values that are *systematically* different according to the community and socioeconomic strata in which they grow up.

So how do you access your cultural side? The most useful exercise is to ask yourself now, as an adult, what groups and communities you belong to and identify yourself with. Pay special attention to your occupational community (Van Maanen & Barley, 1984). If you are an engineer doing engineering work, chances are you have a whole set of assumptions about the nature of the world that you learned as part of your formal education and in your early job experiences. On the other hand, if you have always been interested in selling, took a business course in school, and are working your way along in a sales and marketing career, you probably hold assumptions reflecting that occupational community. Notice that as a salesperson you often disagree with engineers and may even get angry at their outlook, forgetting that you and they see the world through the differing lenses of your own cultural educations.

Your political beliefs, your spirituality or religion, and your personal tastes and hobbies all reflect the kinds of groups you grew up in and belong to in the present. We know this intuitively and realize that we are a product of our environments. What a cultural perspective adds to this insight, however, is recognition that your current outlook, attitudes, and assumptions are also a reflection of *present* group and community memberships, and that one of the reasons you and others cling to your culture is that you do not want to be a deviant in the groups that you value. In other words, one source of strength for cultural assumptions is that they are shared and that the need to remain in the group keeps them active. To look ahead, let me say that when we advocate changing culture, we are, in effect, asking that entire groups and communities alter one of their shared characteristics. No wonder it is so difficult; no wonder people resist change so much.

DECIPHERING YOUR COMPANY'S CULTURE: A FOUR-HOUR EXERCISE

Remember that cultural assumptions are tacit and out of awareness. Even so, this does not mean they are repressed or unavailable. If you want to access your organization's culture, get together with several colleagues (and maybe some newcomers to the organization), bring in a facilitator who knows a little about the concept of culture along the lines described here, and interview yourselves about those areas that seem to matter to the continuing success of your organization. The steps are as follows.

Define the "Business Problem"

Meet in a room with lots of wall space and a bunch of flipcharts. Start with a "business problem": something you would like to fix, something that could work better, or some new strategic intent. Focus on concrete areas of improvement, or else the culture analysis may seem pointless and stale.

Review the Concept of Culture

Once you agree on the strategic or tactical goals—the thing you want to change or improve—review the concept of culture as existing at the three levels of visible artifacts, espoused values, and shared tacit assumptions. Make sure that all the members of the working group understand this model.

Identify Artifacts

Start with identifying lots of the artifacts that characterize your organization. Ask the new members of the organization what it is like to come to work there. What artifacts do they notice? Write down all the items that come up. Use Exhibit 31.1 as a thought starter to make sure you cover all of the areas in which cultural artifacts are visible. You will find that as the group gets started, all the participants chime in with things they notice. You might fill five to ten pages of chart paper. Tape them up so that the culture's manifestations are symbolically surrounding you.

- Dress code
- Level of formality in authority relationships
- Working hours
- Meetings (how often, how run, timing)
- How are decisions made?
- Communications: How do you learn stuff?
- Social events
- Jargon, uniforms, identity symbols
- Rites and rituals
- Disagreements and conflicts: How handled?
- Balance between work and family

Exhibit 31.1. Some Categories for Identifying Artifacts.

Identify Your Organization's Values

After an hour or so, shift gears and ask the group to list some of the espoused values that the organization holds. Some of these may have already been mentioned, but list them on pages separate from the artifacts. Often these have been written down and published. Sometimes they have been reiterated as part of the "vision" of how the organization should be operating in the future to remain viable and competitive.

Compare Values with Artifacts

Next, compare the espoused values with the artifacts in those same areas. For example, if customer focus is espoused as a value, see what systems of rewards or accountability you have identified as artifacts and whether they support customer focus. If they do not, you have identified an area where a deeper tacit assumption is operating and driving the systems. You now have to search for that deeper assumption.

To use another example, you may espouse the value of open communication and open-door policies with respect to bosses, yet you may find that whistle-blowers and employees who bring bad news are punished. You may have detected, among your artifacts, that employees are not supposed to mention problems unless they have a solution in mind. These inconsistencies tell you that at the level of shared tacit assumption your culture is really closed, that only positive communications are valued, and that if you cannot come up with a solution you should keep your mouth shut.

As a general principle, the way to deeper cultural levels is through identifying the inconsistencies and conflicts you observe between overt behavior, policies, rules, and practices (the artifacts) and the espoused values as formulated in vision statements, policies, and other managerial communications. You must then identify what is driving the overt behavior and other artifacts. This is where the important elements of the culture are embedded. As you uncover deep shared assumptions, write them down on a separate page. You will begin to see what the patterns are among those assumptions, and which ones seem to really drive the system in the sense that they explain the presence of most of the artifacts that you have listed.

Repeat the Process with Other Groups

If the picture formed from this meeting is incomplete or muddy, repeat the process with one or more other groups. If you think there might be subgroups with their own shared assumptions, test your thought by bringing together groups that reflect those possible differences. If you need to repeat this process several times (using about three hours each time), you are still far ahead of the game in terms of time and energy invested relative to doing a major survey by either questionnaire or individual interviews. The data you obtain are also more meaningful and valid.

Assess the Shared Assumptions

It is now time to assess the pattern of shared basic assumptions you have identified in terms of how they aid or hinder you in accomplishing the goals you set out in the first step of this process (defining the business problem). Since culture is very difficult to change, focus most of your energy on identifying the assumptions that can help you. Try to see your culture as a positive force to be used rather than a constraint to be overcome. If you see specific assumptions that are real constraints, then you must make a plan to change those elements of the culture. These changes can best be made by taking advantage of the positive, supportive elements of your culture.

DO YOU NEED AN OUTSIDE CONSULTANT TO DO THE ASSESSMENT?

In my experience, the group that is deciphering the culture needs a facilitator who understands the concept of culture as I have laid it out here, and who is not a member of the group or department doing the culture self-study. This can be an outside consultant, but it does not have to be. Many organizations have internal organization development professionals who can play the outsider role effectively. Sometimes an organization hires me to train the insiders on this process and then does the self-study with its own trained staff. The facilitator must be someone who can create the setting, provide the model, and keep asking provocative questions to keep the self-study group moving forward until some important shared tacit assumptions of the culture are brought to consciousness. This process is illustrated in the next few cases.

Four Case Examples and Analyses

If you are a "one minute" manager, and if you think you now understand this process, you can skip the cases but be careful. In my experience, it is the concrete examples and cases that really give you the insight into what culture is all about. As you read the cases, imagine yourself in one of several roles:

- You are the change agent who decides that your organization needs some self-assessment.
- You are a member of one of the assessment groups going through the process.
- You are a facilitator who is running this exercise for another organization, or for some part of your own organization in an outsider role.

Imagine how this exercise feels from all these points of view.

—◦◦◦—

"Beta Oil"

This case illustrates the culture-deciphering process in a project that did not initially involve the total corporate culture directly but instead required that we clarify the culture to accomplish the goals of the project.

Beta Oil restructured its internal engineering operations by combining all of engineering into a single service group. Previously, the eight hundred engineers involved had been working for various business units, refineries, and exploration and production units as members of those organizations. In the new, centralized organization, they would work as consultants to those organizations and charge for their services. The formal rules were that all engineering services would be charged for, with the fees to the various internal customers sufficient to cover the costs of running the eight-hundred-person engineering unit. The business units that would "hire" engineers to build and maintain the exploration, production, refining, and marketing activities could either use the internal central group or go outside for those services. However, the engineering services unit could only sell its services internally.

I learned all of this from the internal OD manager assigned to this central services group, whom we will call Mary. She was charged by the manager of the unit with forming a "culture committee," whose mission was to define the so-called new culture of this unit as it evolved into its new role. It was recognized that the individual engineers faced a major change, from being members of a business unit to being freelance consultants who now had to sell themselves and their services, and who had to bill for their time according to a preset rate. Mary recognized that creating a new culture in this unit was intimately connected to the existing culture in the larger company, since both the engineers and their customers were long-time employees of Beta Oil. It was also recognized that the engineers were coming from subcultures, and one problem was to create a single culture for the new unit.

After several hours of conversation with Mary to plan how the culture committee could function effectively and what kinds of intervention might be needed, we decided that we had to do an assessment of Beta's *corporate* culture. I was to be the facilitator, and she would bring together a group of fifteen or so engineers and managers from the unit. The workshop devoted four hours to a discussion along the lines described above:

1. Polling the group to get consensus on the business problem: the evolution of a new way of working and new values for the service unit in the context of the realities of the Beta culture

2. Explanation of the culture model

3. An hour or so on artifacts

4. Focusing on the espoused values

5. Exploration to identify the underlying shared tacit assumptions

6. Exploration of which of these assumptions would help or hinder the evolution of a new way of working in this unit

The meeting was successful in identifying a number of important assumptions. Mary, some of her colleagues on the culture committee, and I all felt that one or more additional groups should be run to flesh out the picture and check our perceptions of what we were hearing. Over the next several months, two more groups were brought together for half-day meetings, leading to a coherent picture of the present corporate culture.

The motivation for defining this picture was that the senior management committee of the unit needed to be involved if new ways of working and values were to be promulgated. Giving them feedback on the culture as we were beginning to see it provided the agenda for a working session with this group. They would elaborate the culture assessment and then make some decisions on what action steps they needed to take to define a new way of working, consistent with their new values.

I decided to give the cultural feedback as much as possible in terms of the language that the assessment groups had used. I also decided at this stage to present "themes" rather than trying to generalize to very abstract concepts, because we wanted the management group to become involved in the assessment process as well and felt that giving them themes would be more concrete. Higher-order generalizations could then be arrived at together during the meeting. Exhibit 31.2 presents the document that was shared with the management group. I commented briefly on each theme during the meeting and encouraged members of the group to comment on how accurate this was in their own experience.

I. Assumptions about the nature of the work to be done

- The organization is energized by identifying problems and developing fixes.
- It works by quick fixes of whatever problems are identified ("fire, ready, aim").
- It is assumed that if you break a problem down into small enough pieces and fix each piece, the big problem gets solved (blindness to interdependencies).
- Problems are recognized and named once variances get high enough. Management then steps in with a quick diagnosis and fix, sets up a new structure or remedial process, and then relaxes and does not follow through on implementation (for example, shortfall on cost recovery).
- We have a "hero" culture: waiting for problems to get serious, then fire fighting and rewarding the successful fire fighters ("But remember, a culture that rewards firefighters breeds arsonists").
- Quick fixes are always new structures and processes, and once a new structure or process has been put in place the job is done. Implementation is someone else's problem.
- All dilemmas and predicaments are viewed as problems to be solved and are thus subject to the quick structural-fix response. No sensitivity to the complexity of "soft" issues or the difficulties of implementation after a new structure or process is announced.
- Fixes are often the creation of teams or groups, and once a team is formed it is assumed that the job is done (but the culture is basically individualistic; hence teams may not function well).
- Getting involved with implementation is avoided because it exposes you to failure.
- It is assumed that fixes will sell themselves.

II. Assumptions about people and their motivation

- It is assumed that people can and will work on their own, that they are highly motivated and dedicated (that is, management does not have to micromanage).
- It is assumed that people will be successful; success is expected and taken for granted.
- It is assumed that people have no ego or social needs on the job.
- You must be willing to sacrifice for the company by working long hours, taking two briefcases home, etc. Nowadays, everyone has two jobs and is expected to be able to do them.
- It is assumed that groups can work on their own and set their own priorities (but there is a sense of lack of direction by management).

III. Assumptions about the management process

- The organization is procedure- and numbers-driven.
- It is all about dollars and costs.
- Surfacing costs is a good thing.
- The organization is numbers-oriented (for example, numerical target for how many people to have in the organization).
- The organization operates with a command-and-control mentality.
- It is assumed that "management decides; others do" (example: when there are jobs to be filled, management just decides who will fill the jobs, with little or no consultation).

**Exhibit 31.2.   Culture Themes Identified in
the "Beta Oil" Assessment Workshops.**

- There is very little accountability and great latitude, especially in the intangible or soft areas that are harder to measure.
- Teamwork is espoused but the reward system (forced ranking) is highly individualistic, with emphasis on rewarding "heroes."
- Engineers run the company. You know who is an engineer right away; they are the golden boys who are white, male, tall, clean-cut, and aggressive but not combative.
- Company is an autocratic/paternalistic family that takes good care of its children (pays well and has generous—but not portable—retirement), provided they are loyal, hardworking, and successful. If they are somewhat anxious, that is normal and OK.
- A done deal is irreversible.

IV. The organizational "climate"

- Climate is egalitarian, friendly, low-key, and polite, but possibly vicious and blaming when backs are turned.
- We are a punitive, blaming culture.
- You never say you don't know or admit that you made a mistake.
- No one wants to admit to bad things, but people talk about bad things that happened to others.
- When mistakes or failures are identified, blame is assigned quickly and without much systemic analysis; the guilty are named, badmouthed, and labeled, which affects their assignments, but no formal consequences follow.
- There are not many incentives to work together.
- A single mistake for which you are blamed can offset many successes and result in your being labeled and limited in future assignments and promotions.
- If you are labeled as having made a mistake, it affects whom you can work with in the future, so being negatively labeled can be very destructive to the career.
- Once you are labeled, it is forever; examples are "superior performer," "dinosaur," "not a team player," "high-potential," "low-potential," "not management material."
- Working overtime is the norm.
- Work is done through relationships, and you work with those people whom you know; you use the Old Boy network.
- The best strategy for self-protection is building a network of supporters.
- You stay because of the good pay and retirement program (golden handcuffs).
- There is now a climate of fear; the future is uncertain.
- Company used to be a gentle, lifetime employer, but it has had as many as ten rounds of layoffs and downsizings in various divisions.
- As a consequence, there is a real atmosphere of fear, reluctance to confront or complain, and avoidance or suppression of conflict.
- Combination of the shift to centralized service with downsizing exacerbates these feelings.
- In a restructuring you can lose scope, rank, or face—but not pay.
- The organization has no obvious supporters.
- Job security is not linked to individual competency.

Exhibit 31.2. Culture Themes Identified in the "Beta Oil" Assessment Workshops. *(continued)*

The management group basically bought this picture and confirmed with their own examples that the themes were accurately depicted. This reflection on their own culture allowed the senior management members to think through their own role. They recognized that the most difficult aspect of the Beta culture was the basic fear of being associated with any failure, or of being blamed for anything that went wrong. Furthermore, from the point of view of an engineering culture, they realized how hard it is for engineers to convert themselves into consultants selling themselves and charging clients by the hour.

These insights made it clear that the top priority for the project was to develop a new image of how to work that was consistent with the self-image they had. The culture committee was charged with coming up with a new set of values and practices—the *new way of working,* which would then be promulgated throughout the organization. Whereas in the past "new culture" was thought of as a set of general values such as teamwork, this new way of working was to be *a concrete description based on the culture assessment and the business realities that Beta faced.* The new way of working had to deal with the structural realities of how the engineering job was now defined, but at the same time it had to fit the larger "blaming culture" in which the entire organization was embedded.

To illustrate the power of an assumption like "You must never be associated with any failure because it can be career-threatening," a promising joint venture hit a major snag when it was discovered that the actual project structures would put Beta engineers into situations where they were subordinate to project managers from the other member of the joint venture. The whole planning process unraveled because Beta engineers refused to work for someone from another company. They pointed out that if a project failed, the manager from the other company could simply disappear, while their association with the failure would be negatively viewed within Beta. The fact that the manager was from the other company would not be viewed as a valid excuse.

The impact of the cultural assessment was twofold. It made the senior leaders of the organization aware of the magnitude of the change task they faced, and it made them aware that just announcing a new set of values and goals would not produce the change they desired. Unless they could specify concretely what the new way of working was, they could not expect the engineers in the unit to adapt effectively to the new structural conditions imposed on them.

"Circle Healthcare" Headquarters

This case illustrates how the assessment process reveals some of the critical elements in an organization's subcultures. Note also that we are dealing here with a different kind of organization, a very large health maintenance organization. I was originally called by the HMO's internal OD manager, Robert, to discuss with him some organizational changes that were going to happen. He felt that the Circle culture would be an important factor but was not sure that anyone was paying attention to this element. I functioned as a process consultant (Schein, 1987, 1999), helping Robert decide what kind of intervention would bring awareness of cultural issues to management.

We recognized from the outset that one part of Circle (in terms of historical evolution) was an insurance company driven by typical corporate cultural assumptions, but another part was a doctors' organization run by doctors much more democratically. For example, department chiefs were elected by the other physicians not appointed by senior management. The major question was whether the corporate restructuring would lead to one of these subcultures being taken over, so to speak— or would they blend, or continue to coexist?

In any case, it was important to understand some of the key elements of each subculture. A "diagonal" slice of people representing several ranks from the organization development and human resource departments were brought together to go through the assessment exercise. I followed the same model of explaining the levels of culture and then working from artifacts to values to shared tacit assumptions. However, we added a block of time for the members of the two subgroups to meet to develop their own subculture pictures and to share them with one another.

Following the exercise, which lasted a full day, I took all of the flipcharts and abstracted the key assumptions that surfaced across the entire organization. I inserted parenthetically the editorial comments and questions that occurred to me in my role as the outside consultant. I also appended some "issues and questions," observations about artifacts and observed behavior where the underlying assumptions had not been surfaced (Exhibit 31.3).

This report was mailed to Robert, to be used as he saw fit. Robert and I met several more times over the next few months, but the culture assessment did not lead to any changes in how executive managers moved forward with their own strategy consultants to restructure the organization.

They thought the insights were useful but not really relevant to the overall restructuring. I learned later that the "bureaucratic" management subculture of the insurance side of Circle had asserted itself and made changes that were primarily consistent with its own assumptions. The OD function was scaled back and Robert left Circle to become an independent consultant.

The "Delta" Sales Organization

Delta is the U.S. subsidiary of a large European pharmaceutical company. The vice president of sales had been in his job for thirty years and was widely credited with having built up a very successful sales organization. The culture issue came up around the question of whether to replace him after his retirement with an inside candidate, thereby reinforcing the culture that had been built over a long time, or to bring in an outsider, thereby setting in motion cultural changes toward another type of sales organization. In this case, the goal of the assessment was not only to understand the present culture of the sales organization but also to evaluate it to see whether it should be perpetuated or changed.

I. **Key Assumptions**

- *We are data-driven.*
  We must at all times appear to be data-driven and rational, though "data" are often opinions and/or past experience, not hard data.

- *We are superior.*
  We must not look too lavish, and we must always appear humble in public, though we know we are "superior." Many highly paid physicians drive inexpensive cars and in other ways present themselves in public in a more humble fashion. (Is there a need to manage the public image, to present oneself as an organization that watches its costs carefully? Would a physician who displayed wealth be "coached" not to do this?—*E.S.*)

- *We are unique.*
  Therefore, we are the only ones who really know what we can and must do. We are the wave of the future. This leads to self-centeredness and indifference to learning from others. (Reliance on consultants, and on having consultants provide alternatives or recommendations rather than struggling with one's own data, is anomalous here and requires further digging; what is the significance of the fact that the group did not want its own data to work with but was willing to let me go off with it and do my own analysis?—*E.S.*)

- *We are hierarchic.*
  Decisions are made at the top. (The group asked Michael, their boss, whether another meeting was possible, rather than asserting that they needed to meet again to resolve some of the issues that came up.—*E.S.*)

- *We are bureaucratic.*
  We have too much paper and too many signatures to get anything done, and we have an "incapacity to act." (I experienced this in the group more as a fact to be lived with than a problem to be addressed.—*E.S.*) You don't deal laterally, only through the hierarchy.

- *We have two strong subcultures.*
  They coexist in a complex symbiosis (my word—*E.S.*). First is the physician subculture, which is organizationally a professional partnership (a layered hierarchy—*E.S.*) consisting of many specialties and short career ladders. Second is a managerial bureaucratic subculture in which work, pay, status, and career lines are defined by rising in the hierarchy. In the professional subculture, one can move up into management and back down into one's specialty; in the managerial subculture one can only move up. In the professional subculture, employees can earn more than their managers, that is, physicians-in-chief; in the managerial one, the managers must always earn more than their subordinates. For example, a nursing supervisor renegotiated the contract with the nurses union when she discovered that some nurses were making more than she was.
  Status is clearly associated with being a physician, and only they are called professionals. The other functions are support and ancillary. Rage toward physicians is publicly suppressed, but physician bashing is a fine art. Physicians are a sacred cow, but paradoxically they feel quite powerless. They are often the most stable group in the system in terms of turnover.

- *We are action oriented.*
  Whatever is worth doing can and should be done quickly. Important things should not take too long. (Is the reverse true? If it cannot be done quickly, it is not worth doing? That is, if we cannot decipher our culture in a few hours then let's forget about that task, or let someone else worry about it and bring back some "answers."—*E.S.*)

Exhibit 31.3.   Shared Assumptions in the "Circle Healthcare" Headquarters Organization.

II. Additional Observations

The next few points are observations made by the group, but the assumptions behind them are not clear and we did not have time to explore them.

- There are tensions between headquarters ("region") and facilities (medical centers), especially around the feeling that the centers have cut costs while region continues to live high on the hog. Regional is seen as having cushier facilities, getting more money relative to the centers, always asking for more than they need. There is no cost accounting and no performance measurement.
- People come to meetings late, walk in and out, and leave when they feel like it (this happened in our meeting—E.S.).
- There is always food (is this a reflection of a nurturing paternalism?—E.S.).
- We value commitment and loyalty to the organization.
- There is a strong sense of a Protestant work ethic. The more work you do, the more work you get. Time for reflection or thinking is not sanctioned.
- Dress is generally informal, but at casual functions nurses dress up more.
- Physicians' salaries are officially secret and to be kept so.
- Education and training are highly available and highly valued.
- You cannot get fired, except for stealing or possibly breaking confidences.
- Satisfactory ratings are provided even for marginal employees; there is very little negative feedback, and also few rewards for quality performance. Good attendance and longevity are valued, not long hours. Long hours only get you more work.
- There are lots of meetings, and political consensus is built up there. Lots of use of e-mail, phones, fax.

III. Issues and Questions

- Is the "incapacity to act" a reflection of bureaucratic barriers, or complacency based on some deep level of self-satisfaction and feeling of superiority and invulnerability?
- How much of the above description is a function of the subculture of organization development (and not reflective of the "Circle Healthcare" culture)?
- Where are the forces toward the desired strategic changes of innovation, cost reduction, and more employee involvement? (The only place I see it is in the physician subculture, which is based more on partnership than managerial or bureaucratic principles.—E.S.)
- How can a dialogue be created that permits deciphering the best elements of each subculture so that the future can be built on a set of assumptions that represents an optimum integration of the professional and hierarchical subcultures? This process must begin with valuing both subcultures based upon the insight that both have some elements that are functional, but also some that are dysfunctional. That is, how do you reduce costs and remain affordable without compromising the quantity and quality of health care? The danger is that the managerial subculture will attempt to overwhelm the physician subculture, and this will lead either to paralysis because of resistance on the part of the physicians or a cutback in quantity and quality of health care.

Exhibit 31.3.   Shared Assumptions in the "Circle Healthcare" Headquarters Organization. *(continued)*

I met with the top executive team and determined that they were indeed open to either alternative. What they wanted was an effective sales organization; they would measure this effectiveness by determining first of all how they felt about the culture we would uncover, and second, how the members of the sales organization felt about their own culture. The basic assessment plan was for me to work my way down through the organization, doing individual or group interviews as seemed appropriate.

During our planning process, an important issue came up. The current VP of sales expected me to do extensive individual interviews to decipher the culture. I had to convince him that it was not only more valid but far more efficient to work with groups, unless there was reason to believe that group members would be inhibited in talking about the culture in front of others. The result was that I interviewed individuals at the top level of the organization, where inhibition might operate; but as I got to the regional and district organizations I ran group meetings along the lines described above.

Exhibit 31.4 gives some excerpts from my report, which led eventually to appointment of the inside candidate and reflected the decision to preserve and reinforce the existing culture. Notice that in this case the artifacts and values are more salient and the tacit assumptions are implied but not made explicit.

The report illustrates how a culture assessment can be used to deal with a very specific question—in this case, a decision on senior management succession. If there had been more conflict or discord in the culture, the decision would have been more complex, but, as it turned out, throughout the organization there was unanimity that the present culture was well adapted to the business situation and should therefore be preserved and enhanced.

—〰—

Naval Research Labs

The fourth and last case illustrates how the decision to assess the culture of an organization because of presumed geographic subculture issues led to a completely unexpected set of insights about other subcultural dynamics that were operating.

The initial goal was to determine how the geographical and structural differences between the Naval Research Lab unit that was located in New England and its administrative-political unit in Washington, D.C., might have created subcultures. The two units had different populations and tasks, so it was anticipated that there would be important subcultural differences that would create communication problems.

I was contacted by an MIT alumnus who worked in the labs and knew about my work on culture. He introduced me to senior management, and we decided to create a one-day assessment workshop in which we would explore the geographic subcultures, using my methodology. The assessment was done by senior managers representing both the research and administrative units. As we proceeded, it was revealed that an important set of structural differences not previously noticed had to be taken into

- There is a very strong sales culture that was largely created over the last several decades by the present vice president, who is about to retire.
- This sales culture is credited with being the reason why the company has been as successful as it is.
- The present sales culture is perceived to be the company's best hope for the future. The sales organization feels strongly that it should not be tampered with.
- The key elements of the sales culture—its strengths—are:

  1. The high morale, dedication, and loyalty of the sales reps
  2. The high degree of flexibility of the reps in responding to changing management demands in marketing existing products
  3. The high degree of openness of communication, which permits rapid problem solving, collaboration, and the shifting of strategy when needed
  4. Good communication and collaboration between district managers and reps
  5. A strong family feeling, informal relationships up and down the hierarchy; everyone is known to management on a first-name basis and employees trust management
  6. There is a strong development program that gives sales reps multiple career options according to their talents and needs
  7. High ethical and professional standards in selling; focus on educating doctors, not just pushing individual products
  8. High degree of discipline in following company directives in how to position products; feeling that "management showed us how to do it, and it worked"

- There was a strong feeling that only an insider would understand the culture they had built. Bringing in an outsider would be very risky because he or she might undermine or destroy the very things they felt made them effective.
- Though the culture is authoritarian and hierarchic, it works very well because top management gets across the message that it is the reps and the districts who make the system go, and that what management is doing is in support of the front lines. It is a very people-oriented culture that allows for both flexibility and discipline. For example, every district follows the sales and marketing plan, but every district manager allows the reps to use their own skills and biases to their own best advantage and does not impose arbitrary methods to be used in every case. Reps feel they have some autonomy but feel obligated and committed to company plans.
- The individual and group incentive and bonus systems are working well in keeping an optimum balance between individual competition and teamwork. The management system is very sensitive to the need to balance these forces, and it does so at the higher level as well between the sales and marketing organizations.
- The wider company culture is very people-oriented and makes multiple career paths available. The emphasis on personal growth and development, supplemented by thorough training, emanates from the top of the company and is perceived as the reason why people are so motivated.

Exhibit 31.4. Excerpts from the "Delta" Sales Culture Report.

account. The Naval Research Labs worked in terms of projects, and each project had particular financial sponsorship. Therefore, every project had its own administrative staff working in Washington to develop budgets, keep sponsors informed, and generally manage all of the external political issues that might come up.

What was originally perceived as two units, one in Washington and one in New England, turned out to be *nine*—each of which had both a New England and Washington subunit! However, because it was so critical for each project to work smoothly, the geographic factor was overcome in all nine projects, through multiple meetings and constant communication. Each project thus developed a subculture based on the nature of its work and its people, and there were indeed subcultural differences among the projects. But the original notion that there was a geographic problem had to be dropped completely.

The important learning from this exercise was that the focus on culture revealed some structures in the organization that had not really been thought significant before. Where geographic separation mattered, each project had already done a great deal to ameliorate the potential negative consequences. As in the Delta case, the assessment revealed that the subcultures should be preserved rather than changed.

—ᴧᴧᴧ—

THE BOTTOM LINE

I have tried in this chapter to convince you of several things:

- Culture *can* be assessed by means of individual and group interview processes, with group interviews being by far the better method both in terms of validity and efficiency. Such assessments can be usefully made in as little as half a day.

- Culture *cannot* be assessed by means of surveys or questionnaires because one does not know what to ask and cannot judge the reliability and validity of the responses. Survey responses can be viewed as cultural artifacts and as reflections of the organization's climate, but they do not say anything about the deeper values or shared assumptions that are operating.

- A culture assessment is of little value unless it is tied to some organizational problem or issue. In other words, diagnosing a culture for its own sake is not only too vast a problem but also may be viewed as boring and useless. On the other hand, if the organization has a purpose, a new strategy, or a problem to be solved, then to determine how the culture impacts the issue is not only useful but in most cases necessary. The issue should be related to the organization's effectiveness and stated as concretely as possible. One cannot say that "the culture" is an issue or problem. The culture has an impact on how the organization performs, and the focus should initially be on where performance needs to be improved.

- The assessment process should first identify cultural assumptions and then assess them in terms of whether they are strengths or constraints on what the organization is trying to do. In most organizational change efforts, it is much easier to draw on the strengths of the culture than to overcome the constraints by changing the culture.

- In any cultural assessment process, one should be sensitive to the presence of subcultures and prepared to do separate assessments of them to determine their relevance to what the organization is trying to do.

- Culture can be described and assessed at the levels of artifacts, espoused values, and shared tacit assumptions. The importance of getting to the assumption level derives from the insight that unless you understand the shared tacit assumptions, you cannot explain the discrepancies that almost always surface between espoused values and observed behavioral artifacts.

CHAPTER THIRTY-TWO

What Makes People Effective?

Edward E. Lawler

W hat makes people effective contributors to organizational performance? After all, if organizations are going to treat people right, they need to know what motivates them and what determines how well they can perform. A virtuous spiral can exist only if people are willing and able to take responsibility for providing the upward momentum.

The fact is, people influence all the important aspects of organizational performance in one way or another. People conceive and implement the strategy. An organization's capabilities are contained in the mix of its people and its systems. Competencies are primarily a function of the skills and knowledge of an organization's human capital. And a major feature of the environment is its ability to supply qualified high performers who can implement strategy.

In short, organizations can accomplish little without capable people. To be successful, they must commit themselves to attracting, retaining, and motivating the best and the brightest.

But who are the best and the brightest? What makes some people capable of performing at high levels while others do not? What motivates people to perform well and be committed to organizations?

Answering these questions requires us to delve briefly into the psychological literature on motivation and performance capability. There are numerous conflicting theories that attempt to explain why people make certain choices concerning their work, why they seek particular rewards, and why they are satisfied or dissatisfied with their work and rewards. But there are also some commonly accepted truths.

I will summarize what most modern researchers in psychology and human resources generally accept about motivation and the development of knowledge, skills, abilities, and personality. Some academic researchers, like myself, have written entire books on the topics I will cover in this chapter. By summarizing, I run the risks of being accused of oversimplifying a complex topic and of falling completely out of favor with my academic colleagues.

I think they are risks worth taking. Although not every theorist will endorse my summary, I believe it represents a useful and valid overview of the thousands of research studies available. I am also confident that it can help you understand the causes of human performance so that your organization can design strategies, structures, rewards, and processes that treat people right and contribute to creating a virtuous spiral.

THE CAUSES OF PERFORMANCE

People's performance is captured by the equation

$$\text{PERFORMANCE} = \text{MOTIVATION} \times \text{ABILITY}$$

Of course, this equation oversimplifies some very complex issues, but it reinforces a fundamental truth that performance depends on two factors, not one. People need both motivation and ability. Highly motivated workers will not achieve results if they do not have the skills, expertise, and personality the organization needs. Similarly, expertise, knowledge, and skills will not produce great results if employees are unmotivated.

That being true, we need to explore each of these factors to understand what makes for effective, high-performing people.

PEOPLE AND MOTIVATION

The most widely accepted explanation of why people are motivated to work and perform is rooted in what psychologists call *expectancy theory* (Lawler, 1973). Expectancy theory argues that people are mostly rational decision makers who think about their actions and act in ways that satisfy their needs and help them reach their goals. The theory recognizes that we sometimes have misperceptions about reality, make mistakes in our assessment of the likelihood that something might happen, and badly misread situations.

But overall, the core of the theory states that people generally try to deal rationally with the world as they see it and to direct their behavior in productive ways. The theory views people as proactive, future-oriented, and motivated to behave in ways that they believe will lead to valued rewards.

Expectancy theory is popular because it is useful for understanding how people are motivated in many aspects of their lives, including relationships, family, and work. The theory accepts the view that there are large differences among people in their needs and as a result in the importance they attach to rewards.

As the name implies, expectancy theory points to the fact that people are motivated by the promise of rewards. This has not escaped the attention of most organizations and managers. They constantly experiment with offering a wide range of rewards in the hope of finding those that motivate employees the most.

In fact, the rewards offered by corporations in recent years have become truly diverse, if not downright amusing. In addition to the usual ho-hum rewards of interesting work, recognition, fringe benefits, cash, stock options, and big offices, some corporations have given out trips to private rodeos with mechanical bulls, fly fishing vacations on western ranches, flights in a fighter plane, river rafting, sabbaticals, forty-two different free drinks, and a lifetime supply of Ben and Jerry's ice cream. The book *1001 Ways to Reward Employees* even became a best-seller in the 1990s (Nelson, 1994).

Which rewards truly matter when it comes to motivating performance? That depends on reward attractiveness, which is a large discussion in itself.

WHAT MAKES A REWARD ATTRACTIVE?

Research has shown that the attractiveness of a reward depends on at least two major determinants: (1) how much of it is being offered and (2) how much the individual values the particular type of reward being offered. The more an individual values the type of reward and the more of it that is offered, the more motivational potential there is.

If you live in a state with a lottery, you can readily understand what I mean about the amount of a reward being a significant factor. Think about what happens when your state lottery prize goes up. A $100 million payoff attracts many more players than a $1 million payoff. When the prize is big enough, a surprising number of people are willing to endure traffic jams and standing in line for hours just for a minuscule chance to be the next big winner.

Regarding the second determinant of attractiveness, research shows that the perceived value of a reward is related to a person's needs. The noted psychologist Abraham Maslow, whose theories are still well accepted, established that most of us have the same basic needs and that these arrange themselves into a hierarchy of importance. At the bottom, we all have fundamental physiological survival needs (food, water, shelter, security), followed by the need for social interaction, then respect from others, then self-esteem, and finally a need for personal growth and development (Maslow, 1954, 1968).

People's feelings of satisfaction or dissatisfaction are largely the result of the rewards they receive. The more dissatisfaction people feel with respect to a given need, the greater the importance they place on rewards that satisfy that need. As a need becomes satisfied, it tends to weaken. For example, people seem to need only so much food, water, and social interaction. However, the same may not be true at the highest level of needs: self-development. The more people experience it, the more they want of it.

According to Maslow, people first aim to satisfy their most basic, lowest-level needs for security, food, and water. Only after they satisfy them are the needs higher up in the hierarchy (social interaction, esteem, personal development) likely to come into play.

Satisfying needs is a constant. When one need is partially or fully satisfied, it is replaced by a new need, so people always want to obtain rewards. They may want more of a reward to satisfy the same need or one that satisfies a newly important need. This reality means that in order to experience a virtuous career spiral, people need to receive more of certain rewards and to receive new kinds of rewards over the course of their careers.

I need to mention that Maslow's theory does not include a need for spirituality and meaning in one's life. The closest he came to this was his statement about the need for personal growth and development. However, recent thinking suggests that the neglect of spirituality is a significant oversight in Maslow's work. It seems clear that many people want to understand their life experiences in the context of a supreme deity or another set of beliefs about their lives and that these beliefs are an important determinant of their behavior.

Intrinsic rewards count too. Maslow's higher-level needs remind us that people can also give themselves rewards in the form of self-esteem as well as feelings of achievement and growth. Individuals can literally reward themselves for certain kinds of behavior because they feel they have accomplished something worthwhile, achieved a personal goal, learned a new skill, or experienced excitement or intellectual stimulation.

Furthermore, there does not seem to be any canceling out or interference effect between intrinsic rewards and key extrinsic rewards such as money. That is to say, if performance is tied to extrinsic rewards, as in a pay-for-performance plan, any intrinsic rewards individuals may give themselves for performing well will not disappear. In fact, it seems that the greatest amount of motivation is present when people perform tasks that are both extrinsically and intrinsically rewarding. This argues for designing organizations in which high performance leads to both types of rewards.

Two Other Factors Affecting Reward Attractiveness

In addition to Maslow's hierarchy of needs, several other factors seem to influence how strongly a person is attracted to a reward. Two of these are the environmental and cultural conditions that color an individual's experience.

Maslow did not focus on the ability of external stimulation to increase the strength of needs. However, there is good reason to believe that one's environment, at least temporarily, can have a strong influence on the attractiveness of a reward. Just as the smell of food can stimulate the desire for food and viewing attractive pictures of the opposite sex can increase the desire for a relationship or for sex, watching somebody achieve something significant or talking about achievement can increase the need for achievement. This explains in large part the success of "motivational speakers" who are able to stimulate people's desire to develop and achieve.

Cultural conditioning can also play a role in determining the attractiveness of rewards. That is why international companies have learned that they may need to use different reward systems in the various countries in which they have employees. The same reward systems that work for American workers are not necessarily respected or appreciated by non-American workers because their cultural upbringing is infused with different values. As a result, workers in different countries may view a reward that is highly valued by most Americans (such as tickets to a sports event or a company golf outing) as not particularly attractive, preferring a reward that fits their culture (for example, a day off or a plaque of honor).

Gender and Age in Connection with Reward Attractiveness

Finally, research shows that gender, age, and maturity can also be factors in determining the strength of people's needs. A whole industry has grown up around studying the importance that people of various ages place on different kinds of rewards. There are an ever-increasing plethora of research reports that attempt to explain how generations differ in what they value.

For instance, some studies have claimed that the members of Generations X and Y are different from baby boomers in what they value and appreciate. In my view, such differences exist, but they are minor. In analyzing any generation, it seems more accurate to say that the differences between generations are less important than the similarities among them. You should also remember that people who are in their fifties and sixties are different from those in their twenties not necessarily because they grew up in different eras but because aging simply changes people and their needs.

Large Individual Differences

Perhaps the best general conclusion that can be reached about how people value rewards is that organizations must recognize that tremendous individual differences exist. These differences are the result of their environment, culture, age, generation, and many other factors. This explains why different people attach different degrees of importance to rewards such as money, recognition from a supervisor, and a ride on a mechanical bull.

The importance of individual differences should not escape those in organizations who design reward systems. When it comes to rewards, a manager who wishes to respond accurately to what his or her employees value must take individual differences into account.

This is particularly true when the workforce is diverse and global or when different kinds of employment relationships exist within the organization, such as temporary workers versus key technical "hot talent."

WHY NOT JUST ASK?

The most obvious way to find out what people want would seem to be simply to ask them what rewards they value. And indeed, many companies administer surveys that do just that.

Unfortunately, people's answers to questions assessing reward importance are often misleading. For a variety of reasons, it is difficult for most people to state what is important to them.

First, they may not know themselves well enough to respond accurately. Often they do not know how they will feel about something until they have experienced it.

Second, in some cases, social desirability, peer pressure, and modesty can prevent people from reporting their feelings accurately. This is particularly true in discussing money. In many societies and organizations, it simply does not make a good impression to admit, "I work for the money." As a result, people sometimes understate its true importance to them. Some employees also fudge their answers because they are trying to send a self-serving or self-enhancing message to the organization.

Another reason that surveys aren't good indicators is that they usually obtain different results depending just on the wording used in the questions. For example, studies that ask about the importance of "fair pay" often confirm that pay is indeed rated as one of the most important features of jobs, if not the most important one. However, studies that ask about the importance of "getting rich" or having "high pay" often report that the importance of pay is lower than the importance of career opportunities, the challenge that a job offers, and other features of work.

Recent research by three of my colleagues from the University of Southern California illustrates that serious incongruities can arise in using surveys to assess what people truly value. It also highlights the point that people are complex. Whatever they may say about the importance of various rewards found in the workplace, their behavior at work, commitment, and willingness to stay with a company (called retention) often prove otherwise.

In a study of knowledge workers in a variety of American companies, my colleagues Susan Mohrman, David Finegold, and Gretchen Spreitzer asked about the importance of a variety of factors (Feingold, Mohrman, & Spreitzer, 2002). As you might expect, there were clear age differences in the answers. For example, career advancement was much more important to people under thirty years of age than it was for employees over fifty. They found one strong point of agreement among all age groups, however: all said that work-life balance was the most important feature of the workplace to them.

Despite this answer, there was very little correlation between satisfaction with work-life balance and the indicators of employee commitment and retention. Workers who said they were satisfied with their work-life balance often had high levels of turnover. Actually, the best predictor of retention for the under-thirty crowd was satisfaction with career advancement. In second place was satisfaction with pay for organizational performance. Satisfaction with pay for performance also showed up as a strong predictor of commitment to the organization even though it was not rated as highly important. Job security was highly rated, but those satisfied with their job security did not show higher levels of either retention or commitment.

Finally, there was little relationship between age and what type of satisfaction best predicted retention and commitment; it was the same for all age groups. This, of course, supports my argument that generational differences are often given more importance than they deserve. Overall, the data for all age groups clearly reinforce the idea that what individuals say about reward importance is often not a good predictor of critical behaviors such as remaining with an organization and behaving in a committed way.

I highly recommend that you avoid acting on the latest study that touts a specific reward as the most important. Whether it identifies pay, career, family time, interesting work, or having a good boss, most of this research suffers from fatal methodological problems and should not be taken seriously. Problems with the ability of people to accurately report on what is important to them also argues against taking seriously studies that attempt to rank the importance of such working conditions as supportive supervision, interesting work, high pay, job security, and development opportunities. You will be better off if you simply accept that these rewards are likely to be important to most individuals, but not all, and that their attractiveness to particular individuals is likely to change over time.

WHAT DETERMINES SATISFACTION

As mentioned earlier, a reward is more attractive when there is more of it. The quantity of a reward is also a key factor in determining whether people are satisfied with the rewards they receive. As you might imagine, the general rule is, the more of a reward people receive, the more satisfied they are.

However, some funny quirks of human nature come into play here. People can be unpredictable and change rapidly when it comes to being satisfied with their rewards. For example, a basketball player who signs a record-setting contract of x million dollars may be very satisfied until another player signs one for $x + y$ million dollars. Suddenly, x million does not look as good.

A key aspect of satisfaction is how a reward amount compares to a hypothetical "standard" that people develop in their mind about what amount is fair. If their reward amount meets that standard, they are satisfied; if it falls short, they are dissatisfied and look for ways to increase the amount.

On the few occasions when a reward exceeds their standard, people can even end up feeling guilty about being overrewarded. However, it appears that feelings of being overrewarded are short-lived. People seem to quickly rationalize the excess and decide that they are in fact fairly rewarded or even underrewarded.

On rare occasions when even after reflection people still feel overrewarded, they may actually reduce their reward level by declining rewards or giving them away. But the important point to keep in mind is that when individuals feel underrewarded, they try to obtain additional rewards and to improve their situation, thus reducing their feelings of dissatisfaction.

Rational and Irrational Comparisons

How can organizations understand and assess the standards against which their employees measure rewards? The answer comes from research indicating that people set up standards by comparing what others who are similar to them receive. These "similar others" are selected according to a variety of factors: performance, training, background, and other personal characteristics. For comparison purposes, people are likely to choose the characteristics of themselves that they think are particularly outstanding and to think that these same characteristics should be the basis on which they are rewarded.

For example, if they are well educated, they compare themselves to people with similar education levels, and they think that education should be a major criterion in determining reward levels. If they perceive themselves to be high performers, as most do, they tend to compare their rewards with the rewards of other high performers and of course are strong advocates of basing rewards on performance.

The reward comparisons that individuals make can sometimes be irrational, especially as they move up the chain of command. For example, executives who are highly paid compared to others in their organization often look outside at other organizations for their comparisons in order to find people who are paid more. And if they can't find other executives who are paid more, they look elsewhere. I have heard CEOs compare their reward levels to those of star athletes and entertainers. Time and time again, I have heard CEOs and senior executives say, "Well, I'm worth at least as much as Michael Jordan or Tom Cruise."

To say the least, this is an apples and oranges comparison. A more valid comparison would be to contrast their pay with that of Michael Jordan's coach when he was a player with the Bulls or with that of the president of the Bulls or with that of Tom Cruise's business manager. These would be much better comparisons from a work content and skills perspective. These lower-paid individuals are doing administrative, leadership, and coaching activities that are more similar to what CEOs do than what Jordan and Cruise do. But the reason CEOs and other executives often compare themselves to Jordan and Cruise is not because of the similarity of their work or skills but because they are using "high rates of compensation" as their comparison factor.

Even though some individuals make irrational comparisons, not all do. Production workers typically do not compare themselves with CEOs, and sales representatives typically do not compare themselves with vice presidents of human resources. It is perfectly possible to find sales representatives and production workers who are just as satisfied with their rewards as CEOs and vice presidents of human resources are, even though they are paid much less. Because of this, it is very possible for organizations to satisfy most, if not all, of their employees if they treat them right.

The Perception of Fairness

Another factor that influences whether people are satisfied with their rewards has to do with the perceived fairness of the method of distribution. It is difficult to state exactly what makes people believe that "procedural justice" in reward distribution has occurred, but several factors usually contribute to the perception of fairness and feelings of satisfaction.

First, openness about the decision-making process is one way to build trust and a perception of a fair process. A second key is believing that the "right" individuals were involved in the decision-making process. The process must include people who are viewed as trustworthy and who have integrity and valid information on which to make reward distribution decisions. Third, reward distribution is more likely to be seen as fair when clear criteria are stated in advance and are used for the distribution. Fourth, people are more likely to feel fairly treated when they have had a chance to participate in the decision-making process. And finally, fairness is more likely when an appeal process exists that allows individuals to safely challenge decisions that they think were unfair, uninformed, or unreasonable.

HOW TO MAKE REWARDS MOTIVATE PERFORMANCE

Now that you understand how people value rewards and what makes them satisfied, the next issue we need to tackle is how rewards actually motivate people to perform well.

Expectancy theory points to the fact that the promise of future rewards is what motivates people to behave in ways that support an organization's business strategy and performance needs. As a result, a critical issue in developing a virtuous spiral is the need to establish what is often called a clear line of sight. This means that organizations must clearly make a connection between the promise of a reward and the behavior required to obtain it.

I prefer to think of this as a line of influence because it highlights the fact that to be motivated in a work situation, people must see how their behavior influences a performance measure that in turn drives the allocation of a reward, or rewards, they value.

Whichever term we use, the concept is simple: if people see valued rewards as being tied to a particular performance or behavior, the organization is likely to get more of that behavior. The complement is equally true: if a particular behavior is not rewarded, the organization is likely to get less of it.

Expectancy theory also helps explain people's job choices. In fact, it is particularly useful because it leads to another simple conclusion: people choose to join and remain members of organizations that offer them the best mix of the rewards they value.

Given this conclusion, the issue of attracting and retaining employees becomes quite straightforward and can be reduced to a simple principle: organizations that offer a very attractive mix of rewards will find that many individuals want to work for them. This explains why organizations that create virtuous spirals can increasingly attract and retain the people they need.

BECOMING AN OBSERVER OF BEHAVIOR

An important implication of what we have said so far about motivation is that there is much to learn by looking at people's behavior concerning rewards. The skillful manager needs to be a careful observer of how individuals respond to the opportunity to receive various rewards. By watching behavior, it is possible to develop a rewards value profile for anyone.

It is particularly useful to provide people with a choice between two or more rewards. Providing choice yields two useful benefits. It avoids giving individuals a reward that they don't particularly value—a common error in organizations—and it provides information about what individuals really value so that in the future, you can better target the rewards that are offered.

For example, instead of giving an employee a vacation to Hawaii without questioning whether such a trip is the best use of incentive money, it might be better to offer a choice between the vacation and the cost of the vacation. This not only provides important clues about what will motivate that employee's behavior in the future, but it also avoids giving the person a reward that may in fact be valued less than it costs the organization to purchase.

All too often, managers are not skillful at choosing the right rewards for their reports, so organizations end up spending far more to buy a reward than it is worth to the person who receives it. This is particularly true today with the very heterogeneous workforces that exist in most organizations. It is often true, for example, that many of the symbolic rewards that organizations give, such as clocks or plaques, are not valued in proportion to what they cost.

Finally, it is critical that managers be keen observers of how people respond to situations where rewards are tied to performance. When people are not motivated in these situations, it may very well be because they do not see a line of sight. An effective manager needs to determine why this has happened and figure out how to change the situation. Sometimes it is simply an information problem, because people have not been told about how they will be rewarded. Other times, people may see obstacles that will prevent them from being rewarded even if they perform well.

THE IMPACT OF GOALS ON MOTIVATION

Expectancy theory places great emphasis on the importance of goals in motivating people. Research backs this up by showing that when individuals commit themselves to a goal, they are highly motivated to achieve it (Locke & Latham, 1990). One reason is often that their self-esteem and sense of self-worth are tied to accomplishing the goal. People may also be motivated to achieve goals because there are financial or other extrinsic rewards tied to them.

A perennial question exists about goals: can they can be set too high and become too difficult for people to meet? Expectancy theory provides an interesting way of thinking about this. It argues that if the goal difficulty gets too high, people may see a low probability of achieving it. This in turn weakens or destroys their motivation to work toward the goal, since the receipt of a reward becomes very unlikely.

However, this is not to suggest that people never try to achieve very hard goals. As long as two conditions exist, people may still be motivated to reach a difficult goal. First, the connection between achieving the goal and the rewards is clear; in other words, the line of sight or line of influence is strong. Second, the amount of reward associated with accomplishing the goal is very large. Conversely, if there is a low probability of achieving a goal and the rewards are small, it is almost certain that individuals will not put forth the effort that is needed to achieve it.

The research on goal difficulty leads to a somewhat contradictory and paradoxical conclusion related to the impact of intrinsic rewards. Some evidence suggests that as goal difficulty rises, people end up feeling a greater sense of accomplishment and achievement when they achieve a goal. Under certain conditions, they become more motivated to achieve difficult rather than easy goals, even though the probability of achieving them is low. In essence, what may be happening is that the intrinsic rewards associated with accomplishing something significant and difficult become so large that people are willing to put out extraordinary effort to achieve them.

Finally, I need to raise a caution flag about very difficult goals. When very difficult goals are combined with very large rewards for achieving them, some people will do whatever it takes to reach them. Unfortunately, "whatever it takes" sometimes includes cheating, unethical behaviors, and falsifying performance measures.

Consider the scandals that have enveloped Enron, WorldCom, Global Crossing, Adelphi, and other companies where corporate fraud has occurred. In these companies, the executives had extraordinarily large stock option grants whose worth depended on their producing increasingly higher levels of corporate performance. When for a number of reasons these levels became unachievable, instead of forgoing the rewards, the executives chose to falsify the books, cash in their stock options, and reap millions of dollars of rewards. Obviously, organizations need to show increasing vigilance in ensuring that such events do not happen when high goals and high rewards are at stake.

JOB SATISFACTION AND PERFORMANCE

Many managers believe that job satisfaction is an important determinant of motivation and performance. This is more a myth than a truth. In fact, the opposite may be true.

In the view of expectancy theory, motivation is based on anticipated rewards and future satisfaction, not on present satisfaction. Anticipated satisfaction causes rewards to be viewed as important and a potential source of motivation. Job satisfaction may be the result of performance when performance leads to rewards that in turn fulfill needs, but job satisfaction does not directly cause motivation or performance.

Nevertheless, there are several points about the impact of job satisfaction that are important to remember. First, job satisfaction is a function of rewards, in that it is actually determined by how satisfied individuals are with the total package of rewards they receive as a result of working for an organization.

Second, as we have seen, what is satisfying for one person may not be so for another. Given the existence of large individual differences in what people value, it is futile to debate whether, for example, money, recognition, interesting work, or promotion opportunities is the most important determinant of job satisfaction. For some people there is little doubt that money is the most important; for others the work itself is key. For still others it is the social relationships or maybe the opportunity to learn new skills that is the most important determinant of job satisfaction.

Third, over time, people tend to gravitate to work situations that meet their needs, and as a result, their overall job satisfaction goes up. This bodes well for organizations that try to retain their people and develop a virtuous spiral relationship. The longer people stay with the company, the more satisfied they are likely to be.

Fourth, increasing job satisfaction is unlikely to have a positive effect on performance. In fact, it may have a negative effect because, at least temporarily, people will cease to seek additional rewards because they will be satisfied with their reward level. In most cases, the effect is temporary, however, because they either try to satisfy other newly important needs or they decide they want more of the reward they thought they had enough of!

THE IMPORTANCE OF SATISFACTION

The fact that satisfaction does not drive individual motivation and performance does not mean that it does not influence organizational performance. When employees are not satisfied with their jobs, they are saying that they do not see positive consequences associated with coming to work and remaining part of an organization. Their current dissatisfaction is thus an indicator of their anticipated state of dissatisfaction in the future.

It is therefore hardly surprising that dissatisfied employees typically begin to look elsewhere for employment and ultimately leave when they find a situation that offers a better mix of rewards. If they do not leave, they become disgruntled employees who often seek to change their current situation by organizing and voting for a union, becoming activists, filing lawsuits, or engaging in other actions that they think will improve their lot.

In addition, while job satisfaction does not have a direct impact on the job performance of most individuals, job dissatisfaction can have a serious impact on absenteeism and turnover. Turnover can be a particularly costly item for organizations. While it is relatively inexpensive to replace unskilled labor, knowledge workers and highly skilled employees can be very costly to replace, particularly when qualified replacements are scarce.

Estimates vary considerably, but most studies put the cost of replacing skilled employees at six to twenty times their monthly salary (Cascio, 2000). Costs increase as the level of complexity of the work rises and as the scarcity of workers with the right skills increases. Because turnover destroys the social fabric that enables people to effectively work together, costs are particularly high when work is interdependent and people need to work in teams.

Job satisfaction is also quite important in the case of relationship-oriented service employees, such as stockbrokers, real estate agents, hair stylists, and most others in personal and professional service situations. Customers end up feeling a sense of commitment to a particular service provider and have confidence in that person. As a result, job dissatisfaction–caused turnover can lead to a loss of customers. What is more, research has shown that people prefer to do business with organizations that have satisfied employees because their customer experience is more enjoyable. Customers would rather deal with employees who are satisfied and are not complaining about how they are treated by their organization.

Part of the success of the Nordstrom department store chain is due to its emphasis on building relationships between the sales staff and customers. Nordstrom does a number of things to be sure this happens. It pays its employees well in order to keep turnover low, and it tracks customer and employee satisfaction so that it can identify and resolve problems.

In service situations that are primarily transaction-oriented (as opposed to relationship-oriented), job satisfaction may be less important. For example, customers going into a 7-Eleven do not particularly want to make friends with the cashier; they simply want to be served by a person who quickly completes their transaction, with or without a smile. The same applies to many fast-food restaurants, as well as to toll takers, parking lot attendants, and a host of other transaction-oriented sales situations.

In the long run, though, because dissatisfaction leads to turnover, customer loss, and a host of other negative impacts on organizational performance, it is almost always important to pay attention to employee job satisfaction.

A RECAP OF REWARDS

Motivation and satisfaction are at the same time both complicated and simple topics—complicated because of the enormous individual differences that exist and the complexity of human beings. They are simple in that there are some key "truths" that can be used to guide the design of effective organizations when it comes to treating people right. These are worth repeating here because they are fundamental to the remainder of the book:

- Rewards must be important to be motivators.
- Individuals differ in the relative importance they attach to rewards.
- People value both extrinsic and intrinsic rewards.
- People give themselves intrinsic rewards.
- People may not know how important something is to them until they have experienced it.
- People may not be willing or able to accurately report on what is important to them.
- People are motivated to perform when they believe they can obtain rewards they value by performing well.
- People are attracted to jobs and organizations that offer the best mix of the rewards they value.
- Job satisfaction is determined by how the rewards individuals receive compare to what they feel they should receive and how the rewards are distributed.
- Satisfied employees are unlikely to quit or be absent.
- Customers prefer to deal with satisfied employees.

ABILITY: THE OTHER HALF OF PERFORMANCE EFFECTIVENESS

The other half of the equation that produces effective individual performance deals with ability, which refers to the knowledge, skills, competencies, and personality a person brings to the table. The research on what determines whether an individual can actually perform a task is vast and complex. A great deal of it makes the important distinction between the underlying characteristics of people that enable them to learn and perform and the specific skills and knowledge they have developed during their lives.

If we were to compare a person's ability to perform a task to an iceberg, specific skills and knowledge are the above-water portion. When a task is performed, specific skills and knowledge are relatively easily measured and addressed because they are visible. Below the water, though, are the underlying competencies that individuals have. These are harder to measure, but they have a big impact on what skills and knowledge people can develop.

In today's complex and rapidly changing business world, competencies are often as important to maintaining virtuous spirals as the skills and knowledge that people bring to their jobs. In fact, they are becoming even more critical since they are the foundation that enables new skills and knowledge to develop. If an organization's employees are regularly expected to learn new skills and knowledge, what they can learn and how quickly they can learn it may ultimately be more important than what they can do at any point in time.

Competencies can be categorized into a relatively small number of categories. The major ones are cognitive (thinking), motor (physical), and perceptual (recognizing patterns). Each of these contains a number of similar competencies (for example, cognitive competency includes memory, reasoning, logic, and so on). It often takes all three types of competencies for an individual to learn and perform a skill.

Furthermore, people who have a high level of one type of competency (such as cognition) tend to have high amounts of all the various competencies of that type (memory, reasoning, and so on). In other words, people seem to have either good or bad cognitive competencies in general. The same thing tends to hold true for motor competencies and perceptual competencies.

Other Factors That Influence Ability

In addition to the difference between competencies and learned knowledge and skills, here are some other parameters that organizations need to consider in understanding the ability of individuals to perform:

EARLY ENVIRONMENT. There is a never-ending debate about the degree to which people's abilities are determined by heredity (passed down genetically from their parents) or by the environment (formed by their family upbringing, education, friends, and other external influences). Researchers have never reached a definitive conclusion other than to assert that both heredity and environment are important.

One precept that is widely accepted, however, is that people's competencies are generally well established by the time they reach adulthood. This means that by the time someone enters the workforce, their competencies are relatively fixed and difficult to change. This is particularly true in the cognitive area.

INDIVIDUAL DIFFERENCES. From the early days of IQ testing to the present, study after study has found that individuals differ enormously in their cognitive, motor, and perceptual competencies. Some individuals simply move more quickly, learn faster, solve problems quicker, think faster, paint better, and so on, than others do.

Because of the large individual differences that exist, organizations need to place a great deal of emphasis on determining which people to hire and which tasks to assign them to work on. Not only do organizations need to select people who are competent and able to learn new skills, but they also need to be sure that there is a good fit between the tasks that individuals are assigned and their skills and competencies. Skill deficits can be made up by training classes and other training experience, but deficits in competencies usually cannot. For this reason, the selection and placement of people is crucial in creating a high-performance organization.

As I mentioned earlier, in traditional companies that have well-designed, relatively simple jobs, the differences between good performers and poor performers may be relatively small, even if ability differences are large. For example, a good performer may produce only 20 or 30 percent more than a poor performer.

However, in work situations that are ambiguous, creative, and self-managing and where large amounts of ability are needed, the difference between an average performer and an outstanding one can be enormous. For example, in writing software code, doing research and development, or solving complex business strategy issues, top performers are often many times more effective than poor performers.

Because individual differences in abilities can make a vast difference in performance, organizations need to focus on finding individuals who can perform their critical tasks at the highest level.

TRAINING AND DEVELOPMENT. Although people's underlying competencies are crucial in determining what they can do, it is also true that organizations can have a significant impact on the knowledge and skills of their employees, particularly through on-the-job training and formal training programs that teach a variety of skills (motor, intellectual, and conceptual). Employee training of all kinds is becoming increasingly easier to accomplish, due to the many programs offered via the Internet and in classroom settings.

Perhaps the most prevalent form of training is on-the-job mentoring. A knowledgeable coworker or manager can often do an excellent job of helping individuals develop the kind of task-specific knowledge that is needed to perform a particular job. As for management and leadership training, a great deal of evidence indicates that the most effective training results from assigning people challenging work that forces them to stretch themselves (McCall, Lombardo, & Morrison, 1988).

Some organizations take the position that they can hire people with the skills and knowledge that are needed to perform a job. Obviously, this may be a very cost-effective solution to staffing jobs because it means that someone else has paid the cost of training individuals to do the tasks required, but the proposition can be risky.

The danger with relying on this solution is that many people may not be as qualified as expected, and the organization may have to pay very high premiums in order to attract skilled people. However, hiring pretrained talent is certainly an important option that organizations need to increasingly consider given the speed with which business moves and the time it can take for people to develop the right job-related skills and expertise.

PERSONALITY AND PERFORMANCE. Personality traits predispose people to feel certain emotions, experience different types of reactions to situations, and behave and perform differently on the job. A large body of research indicates that five dominant personality traits have an important influence on behavior:

- Degree of extroversion or introversion
- Emotional stability
- Agreeableness
- Conscientiousness
- Openness to experience

Personality traits can determine many aspects of job performance, from the ability to learn to job satisfaction to the type of customer interactions that occur. Just as with competencies, large individual differences exist in personality, and an individual's personality is determined long before joining the workforce.

It may be even harder to change a person's personality than to change his or her competencies. Whereas training can often alter people's knowledge and skills, it is unclear that training can significantly influence people's personalities. As a result, organizations need to focus on assessing personality traits as part of the process of selecting people and determining what types of jobs to place them in.

THE RIGHT PEOPLE

As with motivation and satisfaction, ability and competency are both complicated and simple topics. They are complicated because of the enormous individual differences that exist and the complexity of human beings. And they are simple in that there are some key truths that can be used to guide the design of effective organizations. These truths are worth repeating here because they are fundamental to the remainder of the book:

- It is important to distinguish between the underlying competencies of individuals and the skills and knowledge they have.

- Skills and knowledge are usually more on the surface and therefore more easily identified and measured.

- Underlying competencies are harder to observe but critical to performance and learning.

- Individuals have a variety of competencies, but they can be grouped into three general types: cognitive, perceptual, and motor. By the time individuals enter the workforce, their competencies are relatively fixed.

- Organizations facing rapid change need to select individuals who have the ability to learn new skills and knowledge; this often means that cognitive competencies are critical.

- Organizations can influence the skills and knowledge that individuals have through both formal training and job experiences.

- Often individuals can, and perhaps should, be hired based on their existing skills and knowledge because they can be immediately productive contributors to the organization's success.

- People have wide-ranging differences in how much of the five dominant personality traits they have.
- Personality traits have an influence on how people perform their jobs.
- Because personality traits are very difficult to change, it is important to select individuals with the right personality.

CHAPTER THIRTY-THREE

What Makes a Team Effective or Ineffective?

Glenn M. Parker

Twelve characteristics or behaviors distinguish effective teams from ineffective teams. You get a certain feeling when you are part of a solid team. You enjoy being around the people, you look forward to all meetings, you learn new things, you laugh more, you find yourself putting the team's assignments ahead of other work, and you feel a real sense of progress and accomplishment. In the final analysis, effective teams are composed of effective team players. In this chapter, we outline the characteristics of an effective team and the role of team players.

Clear Sense of Purpose

Call it a mission, goal, charter, or task, but a team must know why it exists and what it should be doing at the end of a day's meeting, by the end of the quarter, at year's end, or perhaps five years from now. There are few more frustrating activities than being part of a group (masquerading as a team) that meets with no sense of why they have come together. In some organizations, employees are part of a unit because of what I call "administrative convenience." Everyone has to be somewhere in the company's hierarchy, but sometimes the rationale for the placement is not clear.

In a recent team-building session, a division management team spent three days formulating their mission—a statement outlining their basic products and services and their principal customers. While the meetings that led to the mission statement were difficult and tiring, operating without a shared understanding of the team's purpose was significantly more frustrating. No one likes to be part of something that is not going anywhere.

In my experience, teams that have existed for years often operate as if there were a common agreement on purpose. When the question "Why do we exist?" is raised and discussed, usually the quick answer is "To share information." However, there is often a lack of unity on such issues as overall purpose and role expectations and on procedural questions such as decision making, communication methods, and interfaces with other teams.

Teams often find it useful to create a shared vision. The visioning process, mentioned earlier, involves defining your preferred future. This is significantly different from your prediction of the future—what you think it will be.

Creating a vision is somewhat like brainstorming—a no-holds-barred, free-form, creative thinking process. In one exercise, I ask team members to close their eyes to imagine it is five years from now and they are in a helicopter hovering over their organization. Then I ask them to look down and get a picture of what they would like to see—not what they expect to see. Each person writes down or draws a picture of the elements of his or her vision. The team then prepares a shared vision drawn from outputs of the exercise. The vision becomes the focus of all succeeding efforts—mission statement, goals, objectives, and action plans.

Effective teams are clear about their daily tasks and about agenda items for meetings. Although it is important to create a shared vision and mission, the success of most teams is dependent upon their ability to focus on the task at hand. Therefore, every meeting must have a detailed agenda, and members should be prepared with the information necessary to discuss all agenda items. Team members should help to control the time of the meeting, and only emergency interruptions should be allowed. And, of course, minutes should be kept to record decisions and assignments.

Team players play an important role in creating a clear sense of purpose by

- Insisting that the team have a vision of the future, develop a mission, prepare goals and objectives, and then periodically revisit them
- Creating milestone charts and task assignments
- Ensuring the involvement of all members in development of the team's purpose
- Pushing the team to reach for "stretch" goals and objectives

Informal Climate

The atmosphere tends to be informal, comfortable, and relaxed. There are no obvious signs of boredom or tension.

One signal that your team is effective is that you enjoy being around the people. You want to come to the team meetings. You look forward to all associations and contacts with other team members. You know the feeling because you have had the opposite feeling so many times. When you are part of a poorly functioning team, your reaction to receiving the meeting notice is usually something like "ugh." You dread the team get-togethers and find yourself looking for excuses to avoid the meetings and other contacts with team members.

A team with a positive climate bypasses the formal trappings such as rigid voting rules and raising hands before speaking. Rather, an obvious ease of interaction and communication relaxes team members and enhances their contributions. Members feel comfortable speaking with each other regardless of position, age, sex, or race.

Humor seems to be an integral part of successful teams. Members talk about team meetings as "enjoyable," and "fun," and even "a lot of laughs." When the environment is relaxed and informal, people feel free to engage in good-natured kidding, social banter about events unrelated to work, and anecdotes regarding recent company business.

Look around at some of your best teams and assess the degree of formality. You will notice that team members often come early to the meetings because they enjoy the informal chatting over coffee prior to the meeting. And the pleasant looks on members' faces are indicators that they enjoy being there. After the meeting, they will usually stay for a while to continue the discussion or just to trade stories.

I have noticed that effective teams schedule meetings at times that facilitate the informal aspects. For example,

- First thing in the morning, beginning with time for coffee and socializing
- Just prior to noon, followed by a lunch together
- At the end of the day, backed up by a cocktail party or an informal get-together at a nearby restaurant

Team players help create an informal climate by

- Offering to provide the team with the necessary resources without waiting for a formal request
- Being willing to share the limelight with other members when the team is successful
- Helping members to get to know and feel comfortable with each other
- Using humor and discussions of subjects other than work to relieve tension and smooth over awkward moments

Participation

Team membership based upon the demands of the group's task will result in extensive member involvement in the group's discussions and activities. In short, everyone participates.

Although effective teams will have all team members actively participating, participation will vary; that is, not everyone will participate equally or in the same manner. I have observed and charted the participation levels of many teams. As a result, I am a firm believer in the concept of *weighted participation.* This concept holds that it is the quality and, more important, the impact of the participation that must be calculated. While clearly this is a subjective measurement (as opposed to the simple counting of the number of times a team member speaks), a trained observer can easily make a judgment about contributions.

I have observed one business team for many years, and one member comes to mind who reflects weighted participation in its purest sense. Jack is economical in his communication. He speaks only four or five times in a two-hour meeting. He wastes few words, gets to the point, and does not repeat himself. Jack's participation usually has impact because he provides useful information the team needs at the time, summarizes the key points, conclusions, or tentative decisions, or simply points out how the group has been wasting time and needs to move on.

Other team members participate extensively but not always in the verbal discussions. You can tell they are involved because they participate nonverbally by nodding, leaning forward, and taking notes. Some team members will prepare reports, handouts, and presentations while others will set up the meeting room, get the necessary equipment, or arrange for an outside speaker or tape.

The type of participation may vary, and it is important to measure both the manner and impact to determine if your team meets the test of extensive participation. The objective of effective participation is to encourage all team members to participate. Another key participation indicator, therefore, is opportunity. Effective teams provide all members with an opportunity to participate. Conversely, we have all known teams in which a few people dominated the action and limited the participation of other team members.

Participation can be enhanced by team players who

- Limit their participation to the agenda item under consideration
- Intervene when the participation is not relevant to the task
- Encourage silent members to participate in the discussion
- Speak out even when their views are contrary to the majority

Participation should be relevant to the goal or task of the team. Teams often engage in a great deal of talk, but much of it is off the mark. I have worked with a number of teams in which there was a great deal of good-natured kidding, story telling, and discussions of personal life. The members genuinely enjoyed each other and looked forward to the interaction that accompanied team meetings. Unfortunately, very little work was accomplished, few decisions were reached, and progress toward organizational goals was minimal. And my interventions, which were directed toward making the discussions more task relevant, were met with strong objections. They resented my implication that they are not an effective team. "We're communicating, aren't we?" was a typical team-member response. Beneath the surface was the belief that any changes in the team would destroy the delicate balance that was keeping the group from coming apart. Often, there were deep divisions that were being covered by the humor and trivial discussions.

Dealing with nonrelevant participation can be tricky. We want an informal, relaxed climate, but it must be combined with a focus on goals and tasks at hand. My approach has been to get the team to address their degree of satisfaction with accomplishments or progress toward goals. Interviews, surveys, or guided group discussions are simple but effective techniques for collecting data about participation and its relationship to team effectiveness.

Listening

The single most important factor distinguishing effective from ineffective teams is the ability of team members to listen to each other. It is a skill that serves as an underpinning for all the other determinants of effectiveness. Sadly, this is one area that gets more lip service than action. While everyone agrees that listening skills are important, little is done to develop that capacity in team members.

There are four communication skills: (1) reading, (2) writing, (3) speaking, and (4) listening. This list presents the four skills in a rank order based upon the amount of time the average person spends in training to develop the skill. Unfortunately, this list is an inverse ranking of the degree to which adults need to use the skills in the business world. In other words, listening and speaking are more widely used and more valuable capabilities than are writing and reading. Therefore, we have the problem and unfortunate situation of the communication skills in greatest demand receiving the fewest resources for training and development.

The principal listening skill is the ability to sit back, be attentive, and take in what is said while reserving judgment. We can absorb and process words spoken by other people much faster than they can verbalize the information. This leaves us lots of time to analyze, evaluate, and even anticipate their thoughts. But this extra time can be a disadvantage since we tend to concentrate minimally on what is being said and often discount comments before they are completed. The ability to listen and reserve judgment is critical if all ideas are to be given adequate consideration. This skill is especially important for team problem solving and decision making.

Another important listening skill is the capacity for active listening. Active listening takes a variety of forms. In its most basic and perhaps most powerful manifestation, team members react non-verbally to the contributions of others by nodding, maintaining eye contact, and leaning forward. They may add short verbal acknowledgments such as "I see" and "uh huh." Active listening is all the more powerful because it so rarely happens. Therefore, when someone really listens, you are doubly impressed—with yourself and with the other person. The person is saying "I'm interested in what you have to say."

An ancillary active listening skill is paraphrasing expressed facts and feelings. Sometimes called *reflecting,* the classic response begins, "What I hear you saying is . . ." Or "You seem upset about . . ." The goal of paraphrasing or reflecting is (1) to make sure you are clear about what is intended by the other team member and (2) to let the other person know you care about what he or she is communicating.

We have all had the experience of using words that we knew were not really communicating to other team members what we were feeling or thinking. The techniques of active listening are strong tools for help-ing all team members find the right words to express their thoughts or feelings and to maximize their contributions to the team effort.

In another sense, active listening helps team players develop self-understanding. In the process of explaining their thoughts, the team members often come to a better understanding of the issue. In short, we are providing them with a chance to alter their thoughts and feel-ings. Table 33.1 provides some examples of the uses of active listening.

Team players can support the norm of high-level listening by

- Reserving judgment on a presentation until all the data are pre-sented and analyzed

- Being willing to learn and act on opinions and facts that may alter the team mission or goals

- Modeling the effective listening skills (for example, paraphras-ing) for other team members

- Summarizing and acknowledging when their views differ from those of other team members

Use of Active Learning	Examples
1. To convey interest in what the other person is saying	I see!
2. To encourage the individual to expand further on his or her thinking	Yes, go on. Tell us more.
3. To help the individual clarify the problem in his or her own thinking	Then the problem as you see it is . . .
4. To get the individual to hear what he or she has said in the way it sounded to others	This is your decision then, and the reasons are . . . If I understand you correctly, you are saying that we should . . .
5. To pull out the key ideas from a long statement or discussion	Your major point is . . . You feel that we should . . .
6. To respond to a person's feelings more than to his or her words	You feel strongly that . . . You do not believe that . . .
7. To summarize specific points of agreement and disagreement as a basis for further discussion	We seem to be agreed on the following points . . . , but we seem to need further clarification on these points . . .
8. To express a consensus of group feeling	As a result of this discussion, we as a group seem to feel that . . .

Table 33.1.   Active Listening.

Civilized Disagreement

Disagreement is, of course, a euphemism for conflict. We tend to shy away from the word *conflict* because it connotes negative behavior or, at the very least, an unpleasant relationship. We have developed many of our feelings about the word because of media headlines such as the "Middle-East conflict," "labor-management conflict," and "conflict between city hall and the gay community." Therefore, conflict is portrayed as war and, as a result, a situation to be avoided. In terms of effective teamwork, nothing could be further from the truth. Conflicts will occur. The problem is that these conflicts usually are not resolved satisfactorily; most groups have not learned the requisite conflict-resolution skills.

Disagreements are to be encouraged and accepted as a natural consequence of a dynamic, active organization. Effective teams create a climate in which people feel free to express their opinions even when those opinions are at odds with those of other team members.

Problems often arise from the manner in which an opinion is expressed. Attacking another team member, denigrating the opposite position, a hostile tone or voice, or an aggressive hand gesture can all lead to destructive conflict. In short, we get uncivilized disagreement.

Effective teams want differences to be expressed, and members use their communication and listening skills to ensure that all points surface. They see diversity as a strength of the team. As a result, team members are supported in their efforts to articulate their ideas, to come forth with contrary information, and to discuss their feelings in a positive manner.

Conflict, therefore, has become a dirty word because differences often linger unresolved, leading the parties to become contentious, or because the outcome is arrived at in such a manner that no one feels satisfied.

I have encountered five different methods of resolving conflicts: denial, smoothing over, power, compromise, and problem solving.

When *denial* is operating, team members simply do not recognize or, more accurately, do not acknowledge the existence of any dissension. They simply go about their business, often going on to the next agenda item without blinking an eye. If someone on the team asks about the "problem," other team members will refer to the matter as a "healthy discussion" or "good exchange of ideas" and then move on.

Smoothing over is the first cousin of denial, although here the conflict or difference of opinion is admitted but characterized as "trivial." Team members are advised not to worry about it, but, of course, everybody secretly wishes that it would go away. There is a strong feeling among some people that talking about problems, feelings, and conflicts only makes them worse. A favorite ploy to smother conflict is the use of humor. Tension among colleagues may make other team members uncomfortable, and joking relieves the tension. But it can lead to avoidance of any serious consideration of the issues. Humor is important to the success of a team, but in excess, it can detract from the group's mission, and when misused, it can deter discussion of important problems.

The third method of resolving conflicts is use of *power*. The simplest, cleanest, and easiest way is for one person to decide the outcome.

One team member may be the boss or in some other way may have control over the behavior of the others. Therefore, when conflicts arise, members of the team turn to this person for "the word." In a more subtle version of the power game, team members discuss their differences, and it may appear that some real team problem solving is taking place. Then, when a deadline approaches or the meeting is about to end, the "power" steps in with a decision to "save time" or "move things along."

Compromise is the most deceptive and seductive method of conflict resolution. Like cotton candy, it looks filling on the outside, but when you are finished, it is not very satisfying. Compromise, in its crudest form, is "splitting the differences." In other words, you believe the team should meet six times a year while I think four meetings are sufficient. After some discussion, we settle on five meetings, and on the surface, this decision looks great. However, neither of us is satisfied; we have just minimized our dissatisfaction. More important, we have not worked toward a decision that is best for our team; rather, we have worked toward a decision that is acceptable. Compromise is used when team members want to reduce the extent of the conflict and avoid the work associated with problem solving.

Problem solving, sometimes called collaborative conflict resolution, is the most difficult but potentially the most satisfying method. This approach requires that team members acknowledge that some differences exist, agree to deal with the issues and not smooth them over, forgo power as a quick and easy alternative, and avoid simple compromises when the problems are complex and important.

Effective problem solving begins with a discussion leading ultimately to an agreement on a problem statement. This discussion may involve an examination of where we are now versus where we want to be. In other contexts, we talk about degree of nonconformance, plan versus actual, or current condition against standard. Sometimes the development of a problem statement involves constructing the ideal or desired state, as in "How would it look if there were no communications problems?"

The next step is problem analysis. This is when we want the participation of team members who have data and opinions. Research and study by team members may also be necessary.

Generating alternative solutions is an important step that is often overlooked. Too often, teams jump to the first available answer without considering other possibilities. Few problems have only one possible solution. Solution selection should involve as many team members as possible. While the team needs a diversity of ideas, the team's commitment to the ultimate solution is equally important. Participation in the decision process will help ensure the team's support for the implementation of the solution.

This collaborative approach to conflict resolution moves a team toward a search for the best response to a problem. Successful application of this method also leads to strengthening the team and increasing group cohesion. Team players can establish a climate for civilized disagreement by

- Maintaining an objective, analytical approach to the differences
- Being flexible and open to all points of view
- Diffusing overt hostility through the use of humor
- Backing off when their views are not being accepted by the rest of the team

Consensus

A centerpiece of the effective team is the use of the consensus method for making key decisions. A consensus requires unity but not unanimity, and concurrence but not consistency. The problem-solving approach to conflict resolution implies differences among team members, and consensus is the technique to reach agreement about the problem statement and the recommended solution. Here is how it works:

> In a steering committee meeting, the group had to decide on the format for an upcoming company conference. Bruce argued strongly for an overnight session because it would allow sufficient social time after the meetings to facilitate informal get-togethers, which he felt were important for improving intergroup communication. The other committee members agreed with the need for the social aspect but felt the lodging costs would not be viewed positively by upper management. As an alternative, they proposed a one-day conference ending at 4:00 P.M. followed by a two-hour cocktail party. Bruce still felt the overnight was preferable but went along with the one-day alternative as "the best approach, given the current cost containment environment." A consensus had been reached.

A consensus is reached when all members can say they either agree with the decision or have had their "day in court" and were unable to convince the others of their viewpoint. In the final analysis, everyone agrees to support the outcome. It is not a majority because that implies a vote, and voting is verboten for teams using the consensus method. Voting tends to split the group into winners and losers, thereby creating needless divisions. Consensus does not require unanimity since members may still disagree with the final result but are willing to work toward its success. This is the hallmark of a team player.

Horse-trading is a variation of the compromise approach to conflict resolution. It means that I got something that was important to me on the last round, so this time I will go along with your pet project. To get the best decisions, teams must avoid even subtle horse-trading.

One of the major arguments against the consensus method is that it is too time-consuming. It is true that it takes longer than the autocratic (one person decides) and democratic (majority vote) systems. However, autocratic and democratic decisions often unravel because the team does not truly support the outcome, so members are unwilling to put forth the effort required for successful implementation.

The consensus approach has its place even in difficult situations, but it is not always appropriate. It must be used judiciously. Your team should use the consensus technique when

- There is no clear answer
- There is no single expert in the group
- Commitment to the decision is essential
- Sufficient time is available

Consensus decisions can be facilitated by team players who press for reasons and data to support decisions. They

- Discourage the use of other decision-making tactics (for example, voting and one-person rule)
- Periodically summarize and test possible decisions with the group
- Are willing to go along with the team's consensus even though they may disagree with it

Open Communication

A company president complained to me that all his management board meetings were too cheerful. "Everyone is so polite to each other," he remarked. Conflicts existed among the vice presidents but were never addressed. There was a low level of trust among members of the group resulting in a reluctance to discuss openly key issues. Individual vice presidents talked to the president about their problems with other VPs and hoped the president would handle them (meaning that he would talk to the other person).

Trust is clearly the avenue to open communication. Members must have confidence that they can reveal aspects of themselves and their work without fear of reprisals or embarrassment. The higher the level of trust, the more risks team members are willing to take.

When a new team forms, typically the level of trust among all members is low. They are defensive and interact with each other from their formal role positions. They are testing each other, norms of acceptable behavior are forming, and safety in interpersonal relations is the goal. The formal leader tends to be more controlling as he or she exercises considerable leadership authority.

Initially, the flow of communication is distorted as team members "play their cards close to the vest." As the team matures, trust increases with a corresponding increase in openness, in confrontation of issues, and in the use of influence skills. At the outset, goal setting and planning are often competitive activities as team members are intent on winning a game of wits. Later, as they are able to level with each other, the team adopts a problem-solving mode in which members are open to learning from each other.

Team players can encourage open communication and trust by

- Being dependable—someone on whom the team can rely to deliver on commitments
- Pitching in and helping other team members who need assistance
- Reading and responding to nonverbal cues that suggest a lack of openness
- Candidly sharing views and encouraging others to do the same

The leader's behavior is crucial in building trust and opening communication. First, the leader must encourage discussion of problems and key issues and then model a response that is nonjudgmental. It must be seen as OK to ask for help or to seek the advice of other team members. Second, the leader should support (and feel comfortable with) the concept of subgroups of team members working together. This decontrolling is critical for group growth. The goal is shared leadership whereby all members take responsibility for ensuring the success of the team by performing leadership functions on an as-needed basis. This process relieves the formal leader of the burden of doing it all and empowers the team.

Clear Roles and Work Assignments

Every team member has a formal job with a series of functions often defined in a job description or specification. The concept of *role* goes beyond a listing of tasks to the expectations a specific team member has about his or her job and to the expectations that other team members have about that job. Because effective teamwork involves task interdependence, agreement on these expectations is extremely important. The work of the team will not be optimized if team members do not know what others expect of them or if there is a conflict in expectations.

During interviews in preparation for team building with a group of health professionals, it became clear to me that role conflict was the problem. I asked all team members how they viewed the critical jobs on the team. In summarizing the interview data, it became clear that there were widely varying expectations of several of the key players. A number of techniques for clarifying expectations were available, but I elected to use a brief version of role negotiations (Harrison, 1971) in which each team member enlists the aid of other members in doing his or her job more effectively. These requests brought out some expectations that had not been communicated previously and some other expectations that were conflicting or difficult to implement. A process of clarification, exploring alternatives, and agreement culminated in a series of "contracts" among team members. In the final analysis, conflicts that were surfacing as personality differences turned out to be conflicts in role expectations.

Awareness of the importance of roles is essential to the success of a team. Teams often see conflicts among their members on the emotional (feelings) level when, in fact, the conflict is substantive (roles, procedures). Role conflict and ambiguity can cause considerable stress on the team and can result in lost productivity, dissatisfaction, and a tendency of members to leave the team.

Role clarification is important at any time. It is useful when (1) as in this case, data collection reveals a diagnosis of role conflict or ambiguity, (2) a new team is forming, or (3) a new member joins the team.

A great deal of teamwork takes place outside of team meetings. In order for teams to be effective, they must make clear-cut decisions and plan necessary follow-up actions.

In my experience, the most successful teams are those in which team members take responsibility for work assignments critical to the achievement of the team's mission. They volunteer for jobs such as data collection, drafting reports, preparing presentations, and setting up meetings.

Assignments must also be completed on time. Effective team players are committed to the team, and as a result, they would not dare come unprepared to a meeting. In fact, one of the best teams I have experienced has a norm that strongly encourages team members to send all reports, background materials, and other relevant information out to the team in advance of the next meeting. This procedure helps the team save time during the meetings and allows members to be prepared for team decisions.

One key test for team effectiveness is the extent to which task assignments are distributed among team members. The negative effects of a team in which a few people carry the load quickly become obvious. At first, things seem very efficient, and a great deal of work gets done. Soon, however, these people experience burnout or, worse, resentment toward other team members. Eventually, this kind of team deteriorates into a loose group with a small core of workers and others who are members in name only.

Members of effective teams never say, "That's not my job." When team members realize that one of their colleagues has an especially difficult or time-consuming assignment, they offer to pitch in and help. One situation that illustrated this point was an assignment to locate an appropriate conference facility for an off-site company meeting. This assignment was difficult because of certain location, facility, and budget constraints. One team member volunteered to conduct the basic research of contacting a number of potential conference centers and collecting information. She then turned over the information to the responsible team member who used the data for analysis and subsequent negotiations.

Another team I know of does not allow team members to send substitutes to the meetings. This rule tends to ensure that all assignments are completed on time because team members cannot skip a meeting if they have not done their homework.

Effective role clarification and assignments occur when team players

- Push the team to set high quality standards for work contributed by members
- Are willing to work outside their defined roles when necessary
- Ensure that assignments are evenly distributed among team members
- Openly discuss and negotiate their expectations of each team member's role

Shared Leadership

All teams have a formal leader. A variety of titles are used to designate the position: manager, supervisor, coach, chairperson, coordinator, captain, director, or, simply, the boss. Traditionally, we give a great deal of authority and, accordingly, much responsibility to the leader for the success of the team. This is just plain wrong. Over the long haul, a team will not be successful if the leader carries the sole responsibility for ensuring that the team reaches its goals. Leadership of a team must be shared among team members. Everyone must feel and take responsibility for meeting the task and process needs of the team. If the team fails, everybody fails. This is one of the most important concepts of team effectiveness, but it is also the most difficult to teach.

Clearly, it is easier and, for many people, more desirable to have someone who will tell us what to do, when to do it, and how to do it. And it is convenient to have someone to blame! One of the most frustrating things for me is to leave a team meeting and meet a member in the hall who says, "Well, wasn't that a waste of time?" My response is always the same: "Don't bring it up to me after the meeting. This does no good at all. Next time, say something during the meeting when it counts. It is your team, your meeting, your valuable time, and, therefore, your responsibility to do whatever it takes (for example, ask the group to stick to the agenda) to help ensure it is not a waste of time."

In many situations, the formal leader is either unaware of or unable to exercise the required leadership function at the time it is needed. And I did use the word *leadership* to describe the activity. In its most basic form, leadership is any action that helps a team reach its goals.

Members of successful teams use words such as *our* and *we* when referring to their teams.

In successful teams, leadership is shared. While the formal leader has certain administrative, legal, and bureaucratic responsibilities, leadership functions shift from time to time among team members, depending upon the needs of the group and the skills of the members. Behavioral scientists have categorized these functions as task responsibilities and process responsibilities.

As the name implies, *task responsibilities* are actions that help the team reach its goal, accomplish an immediate task, make a decision, or solve a problem. Teams tend to be most effective in this area because, by training and temperament, people are more task oriented. Most role models and most training in education and business settings focus on what to do to accomplish a task. Consider all the books and workshops on such topics as time management, meeting planning, and goal setting.

For *process responsibilities,* the emphasis is on how we go about accomplishing our task. It is the interpersonal glue that helps maintain or, better yet, exploit all our team's resources. On the whole, teams tend to be less process oriented because traditional training stresses such axioms as "The end justifies the means" and "Winning is everything." Effective teams, however, know that the quality of their decisions is impacted by the manner in which they make their judgments.

Team players can help establish the norm of shared leadership by ensuring that both the task and process functions are addressed by the team. Some examples are found in Table 33.2.

External Relations

In *The Superteam Solution,* Hastings, Bixby, and Chaudhry-Lawton (1987) made us aware of the "importance of the invisible team"—customers, clients, users, and sponsors. These other players make demands on the team, provide access to needed resources, and are a source of valuable feedback on team performance.

The resources of customers and clients are important indicators of success. Tom Peters has provided many examples of companies that regularly ask customers, "How are we doing?" (Peters, 1987). In the data processing field, there are many user groups and joint developer-user committees.

Task	Process
1. Initiating: proposing tasks, goals, or actions; defining group problems; suggesting a procedure	1. Harmonizing: attempting to reconcile disagreements; reducing tension; getting people to explore differences
2. Offering Facts: giving expression of feeling; giving an opinion	2. Gatekeeping: helping others to participate; keeping communication channels open; facilitating the participation of others
3. Seeking Information: asking for opinions, facts, feelings	3. Consensus Testing: asking if a group is nearing a decision; sending up a trial balloon to test a possible conclusion
4. Clarifying: interpreting or elaborating ideas; asking questions in an effort to understand or promote understanding	4. Encouraging: being friendly, warm, and responsive to others; indicating (by facial expression or remark) an interest in others' contributions
5. Coordinating/Summarizing: pulling together related ideas; restating suggestions; offering a decision or conclusion for the group to consider	5. Compromising: when one's own idea or status is involved in a conflict, offering a compromise that yields status; modifying in the interest of group cohesion or growth
6. Reality Testing: making a critical analysis of an idea; testing an idea against some data; trying to see if the idea would work	

Table 33.2.   Leadership Responsibilities.

Teams usually need a sponsor who can serve as godfather, mentor, and promoter. A good sponsor can increase the life of a team and provide access to needed resources (budget, staff, publicity).

Multidisciplinary teams need the cooperation of the functional departments from which team members are drawn. The managers of the functional departments can support the team by encouraging their people to give all assignments a high priority. In addition, service departments can provide information, staff, expertise, facilities, and equipment that can be vital to the success of the team.

The effective team builds key relationships with people outside the team. The team leader is usually the person with the responsibility for external relations, but the leader may not always be the best person to handle every contact. Even the person from the same discipline or with the requisite expertise may not be the most appropriate to handle the interface. Managing the "boundary" is an important aspect of teamwork, and selecting the best person is the key decision. For example, teams may elect to have a person who lacks the technical expertise but who possesses high-level negotiating skills to manage the budget process and good communications skills to facilitate a users' meeting.

Managing the "outside" often involves the creation of a positive image. Teams find that doing a good job is not enough; they must find ways to communicate their successes to significant others on the invisible team. Many teams create a newsletter, others resort to presentations at meetings, and still others focus on personal contact by team members. Lack of information about the team can lead to a lack of credibility. Ultimately, poor image can hamper success.

External relations also involve building a network of contacts who can assist the team. This network can help the team get an approval quickly through the bureaucracy, obtain funds for a special project, locate an expert to solve a team problem, smooth out a conflict with another organization, or find new product and service ideas.

All of this network building is geared to the mobilization of resources. Teams need help, and the effective teams get the resources they need when they need them. Effective teams lay the groundwork by building a positive image, confidence, and active support for their efforts.

Building support for a team is especially crucial for a new team or for a team with a new idea. It is important for members to be "engaged in a process of informing others, understanding and overcoming their objections, understanding the factions and motives of the different parties involved, lobbying and persuading these key figures how the idea can benefit the organization" (Hastings, Bixby, & Chaudhry-Lawton, 1987, p. 49).

The results of this networking can be some fascinating interpersonal dynamics. Effective teams are often seen as a "pain in the butt." The use of this phrase implies both good-natured kidding and healthy respect. Sponsors, customers, and others would sometimes just as soon avoid dealing with the team but are often impressed with the team's fervor and tenacity.

Effective image building with the invisible team also has a salutary effect on team members. As Hastings and his associates (p. 50) note, "[effective] publicity breeds pride and pride reinforces commitment."

Team players help the team build effective external relations by

- Completing all work assignments in their functional department
- Sharing the credit for team successes with members of the invisible team
- Informing members of the invisible team of important actions that may impact their interactions with the team
- Encouraging honest feedback from clients, customers, and sponsors

Style Diversity

Most of the thinking and writing about teamwork has focused on the group dynamics of an effective team and on management and leadership skills. Very little attention has been given to the composition of the team as a determinant of success or to the concept of *team player*. This means that a team increases its chances for success if it includes a mix of members who are concerned about high-quality task accomplishments, push the team to set goals and objectives, work hard to ensure a positive team process, and raise questions about the team's operations.

We have seen the effects of teams without style diversity. For example, one team of systems developers seemed very busy. In fact, they did work very hard, spending long hours and weekends on their project. They were very bright and set high standards for their work, and they expected high quality from their colleagues. But then, at a project meeting, the frustration that had been building surfaced in an avalanche of self-criticism:

- "We've lost sight of the big picture."
- "This isn't fun anymore."
- "I'm not sure we're doing things right."
- "Are we all in agreement on where we want to be by the end of the year?"

With some help, they began to see their team as being task oriented to the exclusion of other styles. Members of the team were encouraged to expand their repertoire to (1) emphasize the big picture—specifically, to focus on where the project was going and where it fit into other organization efforts in the systems area, (2) take the time to address the process needs of the team—specifically, to emphasize interpersonal relationships among team members, and (3) regularly take a hard look at project outcomes and team effectiveness.

By the way, it is quite easy and almost natural for teams to be composed of members with similar orientations. When a team is being organized or when new members are added to an existing team, we look for variety in knowledge and skills to match the team's function. However, when it comes to deciding which engineer or computer programmer we will select, we look for similarity, not diversity. We look for "someone who will fit in," "my kind of guy," "a person who thinks the way we do," or "someone I can relate to."

People simply feel more comfortable around other people with similar styles. It is an effort to appreciate another person with a different way of getting things done. And yet, we know that diversity in both substance and style strengthens a team.

Self-Assessment

Periodically, teams should stop to examine how well they are functioning and what may be interfering with their effectiveness. This self-assessment may be formal or informal. Informal assessments may take the form of a team member simply asking, "How are we doing?" A good group discussion can be a quick and effective exercise for a team. Some good questions for such an exercise are the following: What are our strengths? What are we doing well? What things should we stop doing because they are reducing our effectiveness? What should we begin doing that would increase our effectiveness? Or, to simplify matters even more, we could just ask, "How can we improve our team?" An assessment can also have more structure and depth, and use our twelve team characteristics as the criteria against which the team is evaluated.

THE INEFFECTIVE TEAM

Poorly functioning teams are not just the mirror image of effective teams. A team may rank high on some of the dimensions but may not be addressing several critical areas. The stage of development determines the critical needs of the team, and if those needs are not met, the team will not be successful.

For example, in the early stages, a team needs direction and agreement on mission and goals. Therefore, while there may be an informal climate, open communication, and good listening among members, the team will still be considered ineffective if it lacks a clear mission and clear goals. In a later stage when conflicts arise, a set of goals buttressed by hard-working, task-oriented members may not be sufficient. The team may fail because they lack good process skills to successfully resolve differences among the members. A number of warning signs indicate the potential for team difficulties.

SIGNS OF TROUBLE

You Cannot Easily Describe the Team's Mission

Describing the mission is especially important in the early stages of a team's history. However, it also may be a problem when the team has been together for many years and they have lost their focus. One other test: if you can come up with a mission statement, would other team members agree with you?

The Meetings Are Formal, Stuffy, or Tense

People do not do their best work in an uncomfortable atmosphere. While people may be somewhat reserved during the first few meetings as they assess the situation, be wary if things do not relax after a reasonable period of time. And you might ask yourself whether anyone on the team is making an effort to develop an informal climate.

There Is a Great Deal of Participation but Little Accomplishment

Some teams exhibit a lot of talk but not much action; they simply seem to enjoy the interaction that a group provides. If you are a member of a team that has a high level of involvement, ask yourself whether you are satisfied with the amount of tangible output or progress toward goals in the last three weeks.

There Is Talk but Not Much Communication

Many teams are composed of very talented people who enjoy talking but do not listen to the contributions of others. Listening is the key to effective planning, problem solving, conflict resolution, and decision making. Think about your last team meeting. Did you notice team members asking questions for clarification, paraphrasing to ensure understanding, or summarizing other members' ideas?

Disagreements Are Aired in Private Conversations After the Meeting

Although occasionally there are flare-ups in public, rarely are organizational differences brought out into the open. Healthy teams have open discussions of professional differences. Reflect for a moment. Are you aware of important differences among team members that are not being openly addressed?

Decisions Tend to Be Made by the Formal Leader with Little Meaningful Involvement of Other Team Members

Because many modern managers are aware of the emphasis on participation, there is a greater use today of meetings, surveys, and other methods to obtain team-member involvement in decision making. However, the real test is whether important team discussions and everyone's ideas are seriously considered in an effort to reach a true consensus.

Members Are Not Open with Each Other Because Trust Is Low

In the early stages, a low level of trust is expected as members get to know each other. However, if your team has been together for some time, it would be appropriate to ask whether you feel comfortable airing your true feelings about issues that come up.

There Is Confusion or Disagreement About Roles or Work Assignments

Conflicts usually surface as interpersonal, emotional issues. In other words, people are just plain mad because another team member has done something or failed to do something. Role conflicts are difficult to see. It may require you to sit down with the other team members and ask whether all members think and act as if it is "our" team.

People in Other Parts of the Organization Who Are Critical to the Success of the Team Are Not Cooperating

Teams usually require the assistance of external people who provide funds, equipment, staff, and intangible support. There is rarely a period in a team's history when good external relations are not important. At any point, it would be important to ask whether there are significant people out there who do not know what you are doing or who are aware of your work but are not supportive.

The Team Is Overloaded with People Who Have the Same Team-Player Style

Although there may be diversity in technical expertise, there is often a similarity in approach to teamwork. Style diversity leads to looking at all aspects of team effectiveness. If you suspect a lack of style diversity on your team, consider whether members are equally concerned about completing tasks in a highly professional manner, setting goals and ensuring all work is directed toward those goals, developing and maintaining the group as a team, and candidly questioning goals and methods.

The Team Has Been in Existence for at Least Three Months and Has Never Assessed Its Functioning

Periodically, teams need to assess progress toward goals and to evaluate team process. Look around at your team and ask, "When was the last time we took a hard look at ourselves?"

BUILDING YOUR TEAM

The first step in the process of increasing the effectiveness of your team is to assess the current state of the team. The twelve dimensions of team effectiveness provide the framework.

Team development requires taking a hard look at the current effectiveness of your organization. Our twelve characteristics provide a framework to direct the effort.

The effective team is equally concerned with getting the job done and how the job gets done—both the means and the end. A team needs to think strategically about the future and about its role in the organization. At the same time, the effective team is building and maintaining a positive internal climate.

Effective teams require effective team players. Each of the dimensions of the effective team is furthered by the actions of effective team players.

CHAPTER THIRTY-FOUR

Developing the Individual Leader

Jay Conger
Beth Benjamin

There are a number of reasons why organizations design so many programs aimed solely at developing the individual. The most obvious is to improve leader effectiveness. To the extent that budding leaders become more proficient, they presumably will be more effective in their jobs and provide greater benefit to the organization. Another reason, however, is to personalize the development experience to the leader's individual capabilities. Adult learning theory tells us that adults learn best when topics are relevant to what they need and want to know and thus fit their learning style. Programs aimed at individual development can facilitate the learning process by highlighting the relevance of particular concepts and by tailoring a program's pace and content to specific needs. Finally, as leadership experts James Kouzes and Barry Posner (1987) point out, leadership development is very much about "finding your own voice." Because credibility and authenticity lie at the heart of leadership, determining and defining one's own guiding beliefs and assumptions lie at the heart of becoming a good leader. By focusing on the individual, providing structured feedback, and prompting reflection, individual development programs can stimulate an important self-discovery process.

The best programs accomplish these objectives using a number of strategies. Most offer a mix of learning experiences, including lectures, case studies, experiential exercises, simulations, and other practices. Lectures, for example, convey models and theories that provide frameworks for thinking about leadership and the actions and behaviors that go into it. Case studies illustrate these concepts by describing applications within actual corporate settings. Simulations and exercises allow participants to experiment with typical leadership challenges, which in turn may help them to develop a feel for leadership behavior and hone particular skills. Perhaps most important, feedback from course members, trainers, and coworkers can provide opportunities for developing leaders to assess and reflect on their own leadership style.

Leadership programs emphasizing individual development create a number of benefits. For the individual, they provide knowledge, awareness, and greater insight into one's own leadership abilities. Because most organizations continue to leave leadership development largely to chance, few if any opportunities exist on the job to learn concepts and frameworks that may guide a manager in becoming a better leader. Formal programs can accelerate and improve learning by structuring and guiding a manager's experience in ways that facilitate the interpretation of complex relationships. Programs aimed at the individual can also increase awareness. They can provide exposure to a range of experiences that a leader has yet to encounter. Moreover, case studies of successful—as well as not-so-successful—leadership illustrate how leaders good and bad can influence an organization and its outcomes. This gives managers a greater appreciation of the importance of leader behavior and may motivate some individuals to actively seek out opportunities to improve their capabilities. Finally, formal programs can provide one of the few windows that managers can use to look objectively at their own leadership style. Well-designed programs afford opportunities for detailed feedback from facilitators and other participants, giving leaders a chance to reflect on their strengths and weaknesses. Interestingly, studies have shown that development programs can actually change self-perceptions even with very little feedback. It appears that participation alone can encourage self-evaluation and insight (Schmitt, Ford, & Stults, 1986)—factors that in turn may lead to improved performance.

Programs aimed at individual development can also provide benefits to the organization. First, these programs can identify strengths and development areas that can subsequently be used to formulate development plans or training programs. Development plans may be tailored to the needs of a particular individual or, to the extent that similar issues emerge for a number of individuals, programs may be developed as formal offerings to all managers at a certain level or those facing certain challenges. Second, individual development programs can help in the early identification of managerial talent. Identifying high-potential individuals allows the organization to channel these developing leaders into positions where their talents can best be utilized. It also allows the organization to conduct effective succession planning that subsequently improves the long-term strength of the firm, as well as its ability to retain talent. Third, training at the individual level can, in fact, improve group-level processes. Research has shown that training managers to improve their problem-solving skills actually helps teams solve problems more effectively. Last, individually oriented programs benefit the organization by allowing greater visibility into the workforce as a whole. Valid information about the leadership capabilities of managers at different levels throughout the organization can help guide the allocation of limited development dollars and other resources, and may even affect strategic business decisions. For all of these reasons, leadership development programs tailored to the individual will continue to enjoy great popularity.

Given the continued importance of these programs, our purpose in this chapter is to provide a set of best practices to guide those hoping to build even better programs in the future.

A TYPICAL DESIGN

To illustrate a program focused on individual development, we use the example of a leadership course designed for a manufacturing company. The company had a long history of promoting leadership development and had recently become concerned about building a cadre of "change-agent" leaders capable of coping with the accelerating pace of innovation in the industry. Two professors from a leading business school, experts in leadership, were called in to design a program around the leadership competencies required to effect organizational change. Together the professors and company sponsors produced and delivered a four-day learning experience structured around three distinct modules: the leader's role in change, skills for implementing change, and motivational and empowerment practices.

At the start of day one, participants received survey feedback from a dozen of their workplace colleagues (superiors, peers, and subordinates). This feedback was structured so that the competency categories that were reported corresponded with each of the course's three themes. This ensured that participants could personally gauge their strengths and weaknesses against the competencies described in the modules about to be taught. It was assumed that feedback early in the course would stimulate the participants' desire to learn.

Following this feedback and a personal review session with an on-site coach, the program began with a module on leadership vision and change. Using a series of case studies from companies such as General Electric, Microsoft, and the Virgin Group, participants learned lessons about core leadership concepts such as strategic vision, unconventional market perspectives, and environmental scanning for opportunities. During course discussions, the professors encouraged participants to share their own experiences. This created dialogue that allowed the core concepts to be applied to the individuals' own leadership challenges and personal work situations.

A second module was presented in days two and three that emphasized skills required for implementing change. Another series of case studies illustrated how effective leaders at several companies had successfully orchestrated large-scale organizational change. For example, participants explored the successful turnaround of the international advertising agency Ogilvy & Mather by its senior leader Charlotte Beers. This case study taught lessons about the process of developing a strategic vision and ways to implement the vision once it was defined. Experiential exercises were used to teach communications and influence skills. A portion of day three and all of day four explored the remaining themes of motivation and empowerment—again using experiential exercises and case discussions as the principal vehicles for conveying lessons and insight. Participants learned about the personal philosophies that leaders often draw on in their efforts to empower others, and about the importance of leaders demonstrating their values and beliefs in day-to-day actions. Throughout the program, participants were continually required to reflect on their own actions. They were encouraged to think about the extent to which they embody the skills and worldviews they were being taught, and they were asked to discuss their own personal challenges. There were also opportunities to practice some of the skills and to receive performance feedback.

Such is the design of a fairly typical in-company program aimed at developing individual leadership capabilities. A carefully tailored assessment tool gathers feedback from colleagues prior to the course and provides detailed input on the developing leader's effectiveness along course dimensions. This gives the individual a good sense of specific strengths and weaknesses and motivates the need to learn. Case studies, practice sessions, and reflective exercises convey and teach essential ideas, frameworks, and techniques. In the end, participants learn about the characteristics of effective leaders and learn what these leaders actually do. Individuals are compelled to contemplate these leadership characteristics in light of the beliefs and behavior they demonstrate in their own jobs. With this knowledge, it is presumed that participants will return to their workplaces and implement the skills and worldviews they have learned.

Though the course meets a larger organizational need around change leadership, the experience is geared toward the individual learner. There may be limited attempts to address some of the leadership challenges facing the organization itself, but the emphasis remains on the individual. Moreover, participants may or may not attend the development program with colleagues they work with on a regular basis (in this example, they did not). In programs where participants attend individually from different parts of the organization, they are likely to have greater difficulty applying their learning when back on the job due to a lack of common understanding and support among the members of their work group. As a result, learning often remains an individual experience built around the one-time learning event. This is particularly true with open-enrollment university programs where participants may be the sole representative from their company.

BEST PRACTICES FOR EFFECTIVE PROGRAMS IN INDIVIDUAL DEVELOPMENT

Based on our research, a number of design features can heighten the impact of programs aimed at individual development. These "best practices" significantly enhance an individual's learning experience and hold great potential for improving the effectiveness of leader behavior back on the job. In the ideal world, optimal learning environments would incorporate as many of the following design elements as possible.

1. Build Around a Single Well-Delineated Leadership Model

In order to improve one's leadership ability, it is important first to have a clear understanding of what leadership is and what effective leaders do. One of the biggest problems that many development programs must overcome is a vague concept of what they are trying to accomplish. In many cases, a lack of consensus about what leadership entails results in program designers incorporating as many leadership dimensions as they can into the learning plan. This tends to overwhelm participants, and it diminishes the emphasis placed on those skills and characteristics most relevant to the individuals and organization at hand.

It is clear from our research that a single well-defined model or framework of leadership improves participants' learning. In contrast, multiple models increase the probability that participants will forget essential components or find themselves confused about differing frameworks. Having a well-defined model allows more opportunities to explore in depth the various dimensions of a given framework—an important consideration when one considers how short most programs are. In programs where we saw multiple leadership models being emphasized, participants typically received only a brief, singular exposure to an individual dimension of each model. This caused participants to have problems discerning which dimensions were most important and resulted in them forgetting many of the dimensions that had been presented.

Having a single model of leadership, however, does not mean that the same aspects of leadership are taught across all levels of the organization. On the contrary, many of the best organizations we observed emphasized different facets of leadership for individuals at different levels of development or in different functions or domains. Federal Express, for example, provides leadership development at three distinct levels of management through three separate but mandatory core courses. Similarly, the U.S. Army also believes in differentiating development experiences by level even while adhering to a common leadership framework throughout. "There are some aspects of leadership that apply to everyone, regardless of rank. On the other hand, leadership in some ways is not the same for the sergeant as it is for the colonel. [There are] unique aspects of leadership that exist at the specific levels of leadership" (Army Leadership, 1997, p. iii). Because leaders at each level differ in the types of tasks they are responsible for, the spans of control they oversee, their level of operations, planning horizons, and the like, the Army tailors its development programs to the responsibilities required at each successive level. Although the Army adheres to a single leadership framework across its entire military workforce, it recognizes that leadership progresses along a continuum of roles and responsibilities and requires different skills and abilities as the leader advances.

In recent years, most programs have moved toward the use of a single model or framework. These are often built around a set of competencies—that is, bundle of desirable skills. Competencies, in turn, form the skill categories that participants learn in exercises and on which they receive personalized feedback. Later in this chapter we discuss the distinct advantages and disadvantages of these competency-based programs.

2. Use a Participant Selection Process with Clear Criteria

Who is selected to attend a development program depends primarily on what the program is intended to accomplish in the first place. As a result, criteria for selection can range widely from firm to firm and from program to program. Some programs, for example, are designed to provide accelerated development experiences for individuals who are essentially candidates for the company's next generation of senior leaders. These "high-potential" individuals may be selected through a formal succession system or may be nominated by senior management. Other programs are designed to provide skills that may be needed when assuming a new position. Selection for these programs may be based on promotion to a certain level—maybe the person's first management role—or else on a sizable jump in scale and scope from prior responsibilities. Other programs are designed to build leadership strength in a particular functional area or division. These programs may be intended to improve leadership capabilities in a unit that is performing below par, or they may be designed to strengthen capabilities in an area that is extremely important to the firm from a strategic standpoint. Selection into these programs would obviously be based on belonging to the particular unit. Finally, some programs are designed to enhance the leadership strength of an organization overall. Selection into these programs is usually based on an individual's performance. In some cases, programs may be designed to reward and improve the skills of those who have done particularly well. In other cases, programs may be more remedial, aimed at improving interpersonal skills, teaming, or other factors that hamper an individual's ability to lead effectively.

It is nice to think that selection into a development program will be based on the program's defined purpose, but the reality is usually quite different. In many cases, selection criteria are either undefined or poorly enforced. It is clear from many of the programs we observed that organizations have difficulty maintaining consistent selection processes over time. In most instances, selection becomes muddied as programs begin to develop a reputation. People watch who attends a program, what opportunities they are allowed, and what transpires when they return to the workplace. Often, attendance is viewed as a form of recognition and becomes associated with advancement and success. Other times, misleading rumors arise that distort a program's intended purpose and potentially taint it in the eyes of future participants. Programs may be viewed as the fad of the week, a waste of time, or the only way to get ahead in the organization. To minimize misleading rumors, it is important to be clear and up-front about selection criteria, to publicize requirements, and to push for adherence. When these steps are overlooked, selection can easily become politicized, thereby undermining the program's credibility. Maintaining a focused selection process means that those responsible for nominating and selecting participants must clearly understand the selection criteria and the rationale behind them. They must also be able to apply these criteria reliably when making judgments about potential candidates.

In one program we encountered, designers had decided that participants should represent a mix of levels, business units, functions, and geography in order to ensure that information from the program flowed throughout the organization. Beyond this mix, the program's designers had also established another set of criteria. Because the program sought to focus on the company's future leaders, participants were also to be selected according to their demonstration of leadership. The selection criteria, along with a description of the program and its purpose, were sent to the senior executives of each of the company's operating groups. These executives were then responsible for nominating a list of candidates that would be sent to the human resources group for the final selection cut. It is important to note that nominations were based solely on the judgment of the executives.

However, the extent to which these senior officials had the expertise and motivation to select appropriate candidates was at times in question. Many of the executives were, in fact, part of the "old guard" and represented the type of leadership that the firm wanted to move away from. To the extent that these executives selected (consciously or otherwise) nominees in their own image, the nomination process fell into question.

Maintaining a valid selection process also means ensuring that selection criteria are adhered to as the program matures and develops a reputation. This can be particularly difficult because, in many ways, the program begins to take on a life of its own and may become politicized. In the first year of the program just described, very little was known about its merit or the implications of participating. In the intervening years, however, the program garnered greater and greater prestige. The program's status was in part fueled by the support that it received from the organization's senior management. As a result, inclusion in the program is now well regarded, and exclusion from the program is often viewed as a signal that an individual does not belong to the "new world order." This, in turn, has created a strong feeling with many in the organization that the program is the pathway to promotion and success at the firm. As a result, strong political pressures have arisen to extend nominations that are not necessarily based on the designers' original set of leadership criteria but rather on the personal ambitions of the participants.

3. Conduct Precourse Preparation

Based on our interviews with program participants, precourse preparation can be very helpful in getting individuals to carefully contemplate their own leadership style and the potential applications of course knowledge back in the workplace. By sending out exercises and materials that encourage participants to reflect on their styles and those of others in their organization, precourse preparation can heighten an appreciation for the upcoming learning experience and its importance. It may also allow participants to see potential links between their own daily challenges and the training program that lies ahead. This may further increase their motivation for learning.

The Army relies heavily on precourse preparation. In light of military downsizing and budget cuts, the Army's Training and Doctrine Command increasingly seeks ways to squeeze more out of its training dollar. As many programs have become shorter, it is paramount that the Army takes every available step to increase each program's impact on the individual. By sending program participants materials several weeks before a program commences, instructors and participants are able to hit the ground running. Participants enter the program with a common understanding of some of the themes of the course and have already begun to grapple with difficult topics.

The National Australia Bank is another excellent example of using prework to jump-start the learning process and stimulate motivation. About three to four weeks before the program begins, participants receive a package of materials: articles on the leadership and team-work topics to be presented at the seminar, video overviews on the concept of leadership, and questions to reflect on. The questions in particular are designed to encourage participants to think about their own leadership and teaming styles. Course lessons build directly on the issues raised by these questions and the other prework material.

4. Use Personalized 360-Degree Feedback to Reinforce Learnings

Extensive research on learning and education has shown that feedback is a critical part of any learning process. Feedback is particularly important in the leadership development process because as leaders progress in the organization they have fewer opportunities to get direct and objective input on how they are perceived by others. Rewards may depend more on the performance of one's unit or division and less on one's method or style for achieving results. Moreover, as one moves up in the hierarchy, others may be less likely to offer constructive criticism or provide other feedback that may facilitate a superior's development.

From research on training, we know that feedback facilitates the development of leadership skills (Conger, 1992; McCauley, Moxley, & Van Velsor, 1998; Wexley & Thornton, 1972). Better-designed programs tend to employ more comprehensive forms of feedback such as structured 360-degree assessments based on input provided by colleagues. They utilize these assessment tools in a manner that tightly aligns feedback to course material, focusing on the very dimensions of leadership that participants will soon be taught.

Feedback in the form of 360-degree surveys is increasingly a standard component of many leadership training programs. In certain ways, this comprehensive feedback is a surrogate for the sensitivity or T-group experience of the 1960s where relative strangers in one's group provided their observations of an individual's style. Today feedback comes in a more packaged form along a set of specific dimensions and directly from one's coworkers.

Given its growing use over the last several years, it is important that we discuss what we know about the use and effectiveness of 360-degree feedback. We draw heavily upon the conclusions of Hollenbeck and McCall (1999), who have summarized current thinking. As they point out, few human resources tools have achieved as much popularity as quickly as the 360-degree evaluation method. Essentially, 360-degree assessment involves enlisting multiple raters, often including a self-rating, in assessing an individual along a series of dimensions that are behaviorally specific and related to valued performance measures. Typically, in educational initiatives the feedback is derived from the competencies associated with the course's leadership model. In the ideal situation, this model reflects a set of competencies for the future of the firm and usually describes actions and behaviors that support change and strategic vision within the organization.

Assessments are usually gathered from a minimum of three to as many as twenty or more colleagues of the individual. These colleagues typically include subordinates, peers, and bosses—and in some cases customers—who fill out an assessment in the form of a questionnaire with a rating scale. In addition, there may be open-ended questions where respondents can write further comments about the individual. Once completed by raters, the questionnaires are returned to a central location where summaries are compiled for presentation to the assessee. Normally the identity of raters is not revealed. It is assumed that confidentiality for the assessor increases the chances of greater candor. When used in conjunction with leadership development programs, the intention of 360-degree feedback is typically developmental rather than evaluative (in the sense of a performance appraisal). As such, there are no direct rewards or punishments, and feedback is entirely for the participants' benefit.

As Conger (1992) discovered in his examination of feedback-based training programs, the impact of these types of formal surveys varies dramatically. Some individuals are prepared to use them as a source of real learning and insight; others react more defensively. It basically depends on the person. However, to have impact potential, as Dalton and Hollenbeck (1996) point out, feedback in any form must meet certain criteria. First, the sources of feedback need to be perceived as credible and competent. In other words, the individual must believe that his or her evaluators—subordinates, peers, and bosses—are in a position to make realistic and objective assessments. Second, the information must be seen as meaningful and in a form that makes sense. Measured dimensions must be useful. They should be easily translated into tangible behaviors and actions, and they should be presented in a manner that makes interpretation straightforward and reliable. Third, the confidentiality of evaluators must be maintained. Feedback should not be attributed to any individual or group of individuals to ensure that evaluations remain as candid as possible. Finally, feedback should be timely, reflecting recent assessments. If not, those being evaluated may feel that the information is dated and therefore does not accurately depict their current situation—in which case they may simply choose to ignore it.

Despite the popularity of 360-degree feedback, there have been criticisms of the approach (Waldman, Atwater, & Antonioni, 1998). First of all, it can be very time-consuming. A boss might have to fill out one or two dozen forms for her peers and subordinates. Technology can alleviate some of this burden by placing assessment forms on a company intranet or other platform; however, even technology does little to reduce the burden of evaluating numerous colleagues who may be at different levels and performing different jobs.

Given that behavior is driven by what gets measured and rewarded, organizations must be very clear about the behaviors they are seeking to reinforce—as well as discourage—and how these relate to company goals. Raters themselves may not see a link between an individual's behavior and problems facing the organization. For example, at one organization we examined, the company was experiencing a significant downturn in market share due to its failure to understand changing customer needs. At the same time, 360-degree feedback surveys of the company's managers showed high ratings across the organization on dimensions pertaining to managers' understanding of and sensitivity to customer needs. Clearly, there was a critical and misleading disconnect between reality and the results of the survey instrument. Other potential shortcomings with these assessments include poor follow-up and coaching, feedback that is too vague or imprecise to motivate change, and the use of a "one-size-fits-all" approach that uses a universal set of dimensions for all levels and all jobs.

We also know from research (Waldman, Atwater, & Antonioni, 1998) that raters themselves may commit a host of common rating errors. They may rate too harshly or too leniently or simply play it safe by using mid-point scores. So it is important that raters receive some form of guidance beforehand to avoid such errors. In addition, certain organizational cultures that are highly autocratic or conflict-averse may inhibit respondent candor and thereby produce feedback that is, on average, more positive than it should be.

In answering the all-important question of whether 360-degree is truly an effective feedback mechanism, there has been a surprising absence of sound research. We believe, however, that its selective use is appropriate on the grounds that research in other contexts has shown that feedback in itself can be of developmental value when it is detailed and behaviorally specific (Boehm, 1985). Moreover, to the extent that 360-degree assessment highlights expected performance dimensions and places all employees in the role of a potential evaluator, it increases the attention paid to desired competencies and produces subtle peer pressure to perform accordingly. As a result, participants may gauge the extent to which they need to focus their energies on developing weaker competencies or at a minimum be more aware of their shortcomings and find ways to compensate. In the end, however, the potential for 360-degree assessment as a developmental tool depends on how tightly linked its performance dimensions are to the themes emphasized in development programs. The better aligned they are, the more they will enhance the individual's overall learning experience.

5. Use Multiple Learning Methods

Multiple learning methods are essential to a well-designed leadership program (Conger, 1992). Adult learning theory suggests that individuals differ in their learning styles. Some people learn best from lectures, others from structured exercises, and still others from direct experience. There are numerous ways by which we learn. Multiple instructional techniques increase the likelihood that at least one, if not several, methods will be compatible with an individual participant's style. Also, learning occurs at several levels. For example, it helps to have an intellectual or conceptual understanding of the basic roles and activities of leadership as it contrasts to management. At the same time, there are behavioral skills that the learner can acquire through actual practice and experimentation. As we noted in the prior section, personalized feedback is useful to target the learner's attention and awareness. Learning that taps into the psychological and emotional needs of the learner may also be necessary to stimulate interest in seeking out developmental opportunities after classroom experiences. The more a learning environment can touch upon these multiple dimensions, the higher its probability of success.

We can categorize most training approaches to leadership into four fundamental pedagogies (Conger, 1992), each with distinct assumptions about how leadership is learned as well as distinct instructional methods. These four approaches are conceptual awareness, feedback, skill building, and personal growth. A training program may contain elements of all four, but there is a tendency for one approach to dominate at the expense of the others. In other words, each program has a dominant paradigm or methodology. This occurs largely because of differences in the backgrounds of program designers. Their orientations can produce sharp differences in actual designs.

The first of the approaches—*conceptual awareness*—is built around the notion that individuals need to understand leadership from a conceptual or cognitive vantage point. In other words, participants require mental models and frameworks that will help them grasp the many dimensions of leadership. With this awareness in place, they can seek out developmental experiences after the course has ended. Not so surprisingly, this approach has been influenced primarily by the work of academic researchers (such as Bass, 1985; Bennis & Nanus, 1985; Conger, 1989; Kotter, 1990; Tichy & Devanna, 1986), whose models become the centerpiece of instructional designs. As a result, we find that this more analytical approach to training leadership has long been the domain of business school executive education and MBA programs. Theory oriented by nature, business schools use the traditional tools of conceptual learning—case studies, lectures, films, and discussions—to convey knowledge to participants. They often rely on contrasting ideas to build conceptual understanding—for example, contrasting leadership with management to distinguish their unique qualities, activities, and characteristics. Participants might, for example, learn that leaders rely on strategic visions to set direction for their organizations, whereas managers direct through formal planning systems and a focus on shorter-term operating targets. Written and video case studies illustrating these differences are typically employed along with discussions and lectures to teach fundamental ideas.

The principal advantage of this more cognitive approach to learning about leadership is that it helps participants understand intellectually the important differences in the behaviors and worldviews of leaders versus managers. In addition, if programs are of limited duration, it is an efficient approach. It is far more realistic for an individual to develop a mental model of leadership in two days than to successfully acquire new behaviors in the same period. The hope of such programs, of course, is that after exposure to essential ideas about leadership the learners will be motivated to seek out opportunities to develop their leadership capabilities.

The most serious limitation of this approach, however, is that concepts about leadership are insufficient by themselves to develop an individual's leadership ability in behavioral terms. Understanding something intellectually often has little to do with our ability to implement the behavior ourselves. If it did, we would certainly see many more young Jack Welches (chairman of General Electric) given that most managers and MBA students today read case studies and watch videos on his leadership style. As such, it is important to see conceptual learning as only a first step in the process of learning about leadership. It is a critical one, however, because we require mental models to orient ourselves in understanding any phenomenon. They also sensitize us to where our own developmental needs may lie and the skills one needs to acquire.

The second approach—*feedback*—is based on the premise that learners need behavioral feedback in order to attend to deficiencies as well as to build self-confidence in their areas of strength. This approach assumes correctly that most of us cannot completely see our behavioral selves. Due to psychological defenses and biases, we have only a partial picture of what we do and how we are perceived. Therefore we require a mirror of some form to discern more fully our strengths and weaknesses as leaders. The mirror in the feedback approaches comes in the form of outside observers. In addition to 360-degree assessment tools, feedback designs employ in-class simulations and fishbowl exercises where participants conduct tasks under the watchful eyes of trained observers and fellow participants. After completion of an exercise, the numerous observers provide survey or direct feedback concerning each other's behavior in the exercise. More comprehensive programs such as those run at the Center for Creative Leadership also provide interviews with staff psychologists so that participants are able to develop an integrated understanding of the many sources of feedback they have received.

As we noted in the previous section, there are several advantages to feedback approaches. For one, feedback is essential in any learning process especially as it applies to the acquisition and improvement of behavioral skills. They help learners clearly identify important strengths and weaknesses in skill areas and help them gauge progress. For motivated learners, they serve to focus their efforts on specific developmental areas. For younger managers, positive feedback can boost confidence, which in turn enhances their leadership back on the job (Conger, 1992).

Beyond these advantages, however, are several drawbacks. Programs built largely around feedback have a tendency to overwhelm participants with information. Individuals might receive data on two or three hundred different dimensions of their behavior—their coaching style, conflict approaches, orientation to innovation, decision making, communications, and so on. As a result, information overload and selective recall may occur. To compensate, participants tend to actively remember and focus on only two or three areas as developmental goals (Conger, 1992). On occasion, some of these might include behavioral changes that involve a fundamental shift in the individual's psychological makeup. But such outcomes are rare. Because the training environment is limited in its ability to help participants make profound adjustments, participants tend instead to gravitate to changes that are more superficial in terms of dispositional traits (Conger, 1992). Yet these dimensions may be the ones that are the least significant for developing the individual's leadership potential.

The greatest shortcoming of these programs, however, is the limited opportunity to experiment with new behaviors that may remedy competency deficiencies or reduce dysfunctional behavior. For example, a participant might discover from a simulation that his interpersonal influence skills or ability to communicate compelling goals are in need of greater development. In theory, this should be followed up immediately with opportunities to improve these skills through practice and experimentation. In many programs, however, participants simply move on to the next feedback exercise, with limited time for skill development. In addition, given the number of participants in a given program and the time demands on instructors, there are few windows of sufficient time for personalized coaching. Therefore, although feedback should be an essential element of any program, it needs to be modified and complemented extensively by other approaches.

This brings us to the third approach—*skill building.* This approach focuses on visible, behavioral skill development. It is the "tennis clinic" of leadership development, where participants go and literally practice certain basic competencies associated with effective leadership. For example, program designers might construct a learning module around inspirational speaking skills. Participants would be introduced to a list of behaviors associated with inspirational communications. An exercise would follow where each participant devises a five-minute presentation employing these inspirational behaviors. In small groups, they deliver their presentations and then are rated by teammates and instructors on their effective use of the new behaviors.

The principal advantage of this approach is that it attempts to turn leadership into a set of teachable behavioral skills. As such, participants are given opportunities to learn from behavioral models and to experiment with the behaviors themselves. Generally, immediate feedback on the participant's demonstration of the skill is provided after each exercise. In many ways, this approach is similar to how recreational sports such as tennis or golf are taught. The instructor explains and demonstrates the skill. Then the participant practices the skill as demonstrated and afterward receives feedback on her performance from the instructor and others. In more effective programs, there are further opportunities to practice.

To a great extent, the success of skill-building approaches depends on how teachable a particular leadership competency is. For example, by following a series of practice exercises an individual might indeed improve certain communication skills. But complex competencies such as strategic vision may not be easily taught. We know from research on visionary leaders (Conger, 1989; Westley, 1992) that such competencies often have a long gestation period and involve a multiplicity of skills. Moreover, timing and luck play a role. Given the complexity of forces behind vision, it is unlikely that an individual could be taught to be more "visionary" in three days. However, an appreciation for the importance of vision could be taught in a three-day workshop. Similarly, receiving advice on the work experiences that might facilitate one's future vision is also feasible.

Skill-building programs face a second dilemma concerning time. To truly develop expertise in a skill, an individual needs multiple and varied experiences—studying the basic characteristics of the skill, experimenting with it, getting coached, and then making improvements and refinements (Ericsson & Smith, 1991). Yet many programs attempt to cover a wide range of leadership skills within just a few days. A half-day might be spent on motivation, an afternoon on inspirational speaking skills, and a morning on empowerment. In the course of three days, as many as ten or fifteen skill categories might be covered. By analogy, this experience would be similar to an individual attempting to learn golf, basketball, tennis, and racketball in a three-day program. As a result, participants often receive only a single opportunity to practice a particular skill and receive feedback. With so little exposure, the experience simply builds awareness rather than true understanding and skill development.

Finally, the exercises employed by the skill-building approaches may be flawed. They often attempt to simulate work environments, but may be far different from actual workplace realities. For example, to simulate task demands on the job participants might be asked to lead a team of counterparts in assembling toy trucks. But unlike one's real workplace, there are no career consequences, no political issues, no investment risks, and no post-task implications involved. Yet all these profoundly shape behavior at work. Their absence in the simulation renders it a make-believe exercise with few of the consequences that would be encountered at work.

The final of our four training approaches is *personal growth.* This approach has its origins in outdoor adventure programs such as Outward Bound and in personal development seminars from the 1970s such as EST or "new age" psychotherapies such as Gestalt. Adopting their interventions to the business world, trainers and psychotherapists from these programs developed management education programs in the 1980s, bringing with them their humanistic orientations to leadership development. Personal growth approaches typically employ emotional and physical challenges that provoke reflection on one's behavior and life choices. These experiences are intended to help trainees ascertain their natural tendencies around risk and teamwork, their career ambitions in contrast to their current career status, and their choice of priorities between work and personal life. In the end, most of these programs attempt to create experiences whereby participants take greater responsibility for the destiny of their lives through clear personal goals and behavioral changes.

Underlying these programs—particularly the psychologically based ones—is a singular premise that effective leaders are in touch with their personal dreams and are confident enough in themselves to realize them. In addition, we often find a second premise: leaders are balanced human beings in terms of their work and personal lives. These programs argue that most participants are some distance from these two states of being. Instead, they have chosen to ignore their inner callings and personal priorities. To direct participants' attention to these contradictions, the personal growth approach relies on "upending" emotional experiences—adventures that become metaphors for the issues they wish participants to learn from. So, for example, a rafting trip down a difficult-to-navigate river might teach participants about the necessity of teamwork and the pleasures of risk taking.

There are several advantages to personal growth approaches. They do offer opportunities to experience risk taking, emotional expressiveness, highly cooperative teamwork, and empowerment. As well, we know from research in adult education that the more levels a learning experience engages, the more powerful the learning will be. The personal growth approach engages a wide variety—emotional, imaginative, cognitive, and behavioral. Learning can also be magnified by experiences that are perceived as risky and that challenge us to act in new ways or to see the world vividly with a new set of eyes (Conger, 1992).

In terms of drawbacks, personal growth programs fall short on several dimensions. Like skill building exercises, the actual character of an exercise may not truly reflect workplace realities. For example, one might jump from a cliff wearing a harness tethered to a safety line. This experience is used to teach risk taking. Yet how comparable is this to a manager making a multimillion-dollar product investment at work? Both entail risk. But the cliff-jump exercise offers the participant no real guidelines for taking thoughtful risks when back at the office. Instead, much like a pep talk from a motivational speaker, the cliff-jumping participant leaves emotionally excited about taking risks but with no gauge for measuring them back at work. When the participant faces the product investment decision at the office, there are other dynamics at play. First, the risk is shared by the management team. Second, it depends on a rigorous analytical process. Third, there are potentially important career consequences with few figurative "safety harnesses."

A second problem with personal growth approaches is a higher probability of learner disappointment or letdown upon return to the workplace. These programs create an emotional high that generally cannot be sustained as risk-averse bosses and bureaucratic inertia undermine the trainee's newfound zeal to exhibit leadership.

The underlying premise of personal growth approaches—that within each of us lie important passions and values that will help us lead—may also be faulty. Younger managers, for example, may be lacking in sufficient experience to ascertain their potential talents, interests, and passions. Moreover, a few days of training cannot substitute for the insights and opportunities that multiple work experiences can provide. As well, getting in touch with one's talents and interests is no guarantee of leadership. For example, a manager may discover that her real interests lie in acting or photography. Quite simply, many passions have little to do with leadership.

With their emphasis on work-life balance, these programs tend to improve participants' personal lives far more than their work lives (Conger, 1992). In various exercises, trainees might confront the personal trade-offs they have made with their families. With a strong emphasis on our emotional dynamics, it is not surprising that we turn to our private lives. The family allows us to live out our deeper emotional needs that the workplace cannot hope to fulfill. Unfortunately, the premise itself that leaders are well balanced is not borne out by actual biographical evidence on leaders. Instead, many leaders have devoted their lives largely to their work.

6. Conduct Extended Learning Periods and Multiple Sessions

We know from research on the transfer of learning from training that information learned under distributed periods of training is generally retained longer than in a one-time program (Briggs & Naylor, 1962; Naylor & Briggs, 1963). As well, feedback-oriented programs that span multiple periods appear to move participants from awareness to an enhanced probability of effecting change in their behaviors and perspectives (Young & Dixon, 1996). Our case study of the National Australia Bank exemplifies this idea of spreading learning out over an extended time. Consisting of several stages, it provided multiple opportunities to reflect on and revisit key learnings.

The research that perhaps sheds the greatest light on why extended and multiple periods of learning are required for learning leadership comes from a growing body of knowledge on expertise—on how individuals become experts. The topic has been explored extensively in a great variety of domains, including art, chess, medicine, music, physics, and sports. Although each domain shapes how expertise is acquired, it is possible to draw generalizations that are fundamental to the acquisition of expertise across many fields, including leadership.

First, becoming an expert takes time. In studies of experts who attain international levels of performance across diverse fields, ten years of preparation appears to be the norm and often the period is substantially longer. For example, in a review of the existing research, Ericsson, Krampe, and Tesch-Romer (1993) found that this ten-year rule was remarkably accurate.

During this extended time, a second developmental experience must take place: deliberate, focused, and repeated practice (Ericsson & Charness, 1994). Practice during this period results in the acquisition of tacit knowledge. Tacit knowledge—knowledge that is not formally transferable or describable—is a key part of expertise and is therefore difficult to train per se. It must be learned through multiple and varied exposures to the area in which one wishes to become an expert. Finally, training and coaching play a key role during this period of practice. It is clear that to reach exceptional levels of performance individuals must undergo a very extended period of active learning, where they continually refine and improve their skills under the supervision of a teacher, coach, or mentor (Ericsson & Charness, 1994).

This literature makes an important distinction between exposure and deliberate practice (Ericsson & Smith, 1991). Simple exposure to an area does not suffice; rather the efforts put forth toward learning must be deliberate, focused, and repeated. Deliberate practice is defined as an activity involving effort that is motivated by the goal of improving performance (Ericsson & Charness, 1994). This insight applies to both executive training and on-the-job learning. Training built around a few days of practice is clearly insufficient; it takes a longer-term orientation with multiple, focused sessions, ultimately over several years. Similarly, on-the-job experiences would need to deepen learning in a particular domain through deliberate practice accompanied by immediate and specific feedback. At the same time, on-the-job learning may not necessarily occur if it is not focused and continual feedback is largely absent. This is especially the case for complex skills such as leadership. The expertise literature would argue that leadership, like any form of expertise, requires intensive, focused learning over extended periods of time to be developed.

7. Put Organizational Support Systems in Place

One of the core dilemmas facing individuals who return from these programs is a lack of reinforcement for the leadership behaviors they have learned. For example, it is rare that an organization's performance appraisals and rewards have been altered to reflect incentives for leadership behavior. In addition, the participants' superiors may not have attended the program and so are in no position to coach their subordinates on the new skills they have learned. Even the newly acquired program vocabularies may sound foreign to a participant's superior. Yet research (Huczynski & Lewis, 1980) shows that the attitudes and management styles of trainees' bosses are the most important factors in the transfer of management training back to the job. In fact, studies that specifically examine the factors that either inhibit or facilitate learning discovered that a trainee's application of new learnings on the job was largely dependent on his or her superior's support. In significant part, this is due to the boss being the principal source of a subordinate's rewards. Through praise, promotions, pay, and challenging assignments, the supervisor can reinforce the use of new skills or similarly discourage them. Simple encouragement itself can have a significant influence. In one recent study (Facteau, Dobbins, Russell, Ladd, & Kudisch 1995), it was discovered that managers who perceive a greater measure of support from their immediate bosses report a higher degree of motivation to both attend and learn from training. Similarly, a boss may choose to ignore or even punish the leadership initiatives of their subordinates, which in turn will stunt their development.

The supervisorial behavior required to support a subordinate's development following training can take many forms (Baldwin & Ford, 1988): encouragement, goal-setting activities, modeling, and reinforcement. For example, supervisors can encourage subordinates to attend a leadership development program in the first place. (They discourage attendance by showing disinterest or by not providing time off for education.)

To further motivate learning, bosses can discuss program learnings and benefits both beforehand and afterward and set action goals for the individual to learn and implement specific behaviors or actions. The boss's own role modeling also influences subordinate behavior (Sims & Manz, 1982). For example, staff will imitate their supervisors in order to obtain rewards. In the ideal case, supervisors would model behavior that is congruent with the training objectives and what is being taught. Finally, supervisors can support new behaviors through rewards and by providing opportunities to practice new skills. For example, they may place subordinates on special projects or provide them with new responsibilities that require leadership to succeed. The greater the number of opportunities that trainees have to practice and experiment with their new skills, the higher the probability that the skills will be developed and behavior change will occur (Noe, 1986). As such, work assignments following training experiences can reinforce and deepen learnings. Yet rarely is such a connection made.

In conclusion, we see that leadership development programs geared toward the individual hold the promise of helping participants learn more about their leadership abilities as well as fostering an understanding of the essential basics of effective leadership. In the best of cases, these experiences also provide a motivational stimulus for managers to seek out developmental opportunities that will deepen their skill set. They may also encourage a greater reflective capacity—helping managers to be more alert to their strengths and weaknesses as leaders and the implications of these.

PART SEVEN

OD Purpose and Possibilities

Seeing the Forest for the Trees

O
D has come under fire in recent years. Critics claim that it has lost its way and become too technique driven, splintered, piecemeal, antiquated, and marginal in its impact. Many OD professionals are involved in a host of training, coaching, facilitating, and consulting activities. Far fewer employ their skills in the kind of large, systematic, planned change efforts that characterized the field in its heyday. There are many explanations for all this. Some sources of OD's problem come from broader social and organizational trends that have led to misconceptions about OD and its processes, a narrow focus on the short term and the bottom line, and widespread indifference to the human side of enterprise.

But other explanations are internal to the field and its practices. These include the following:

1. A narrow definition of OD's boundaries and applications

2. Parochial possessiveness of its name and methods

3. Overemphasis on social processes and neglect of more substantive and strategic client needs

4. Limited collaboration with other management areas and disciplines

5. A shortage of new theory, concepts, and methods to energize the field

6. Confusion between applying OD's tools and preaching its values

7. Failure to take full advantage of leadership possibilities in the change agent's role

8. Limited understandings of business and management realities

9. Lack of an integrated agenda for the field in the twenty-first century

Much has been written detailing OD's current challenges. The intention in this volume is to strengthen a powerful comeback.

The chapters in Part Seven suggest an expanded future for organization development. The field's potential is constrained only by the limits of its creativity and vision. OD's core purpose is to improve organizational health and effectiveness. A creative vision of what a healthy and effective organization looks like in the twenty-first century is vital. The chapters here suggest a range of possibilities: widespread collaboration and deep connections within and across boundaries; organizations as communities of leaders; multinational organizations that foster productivity, profit, and social activism; passion and commitment to shared purpose; well-integrated systems that withstand global competitive pressures; learning organizations; compassionate workplaces; systems that celebrate and leverage diversity well; organizations that foster concurrent personal, team, and organizational transformation.

The possibilities are exciting. A powerful vision is the antidote for a splintered field that has lost its way. OD professionals are centered and empowered when they can see a beautiful forest instead of scraggly individual trees.

The first chapter in Part Seven examines creative interventions designed to foster a renewed sense of leadership, community, responsibility, and shared purpose in a multinational corporation. Philip H. Mirvis and Louis "Tex" Gunning, an OD consultant and CEO, respectively, collaborated on the projects and the chapter, "Creating a Community of Leaders." Their strategies and experiences bear witness to the challenges and importance of community building in an increasingly global world. David A. Nadler and Marc S. Gerstein follow with "Designing High-Performance Work Systems: Organizing People, Work, Technology, and Information." Their work builds on one of the early influences in the field—the sociotechnical systems movement in England in the 1940s and 1950s—and suggests updated ways to understand and practice OD's classic commitment to a good fit between people and their organization. David A. Thomas, in "Diversity as Strategy," examines IBM's success in expanding its minority markets by expanding the diversity of its workforce. The case offers a model for translating espoused commitments to workplace diversity into strategy.

OD has fostered the concept of a learning organization from its inception. Peter M. Senge, in "The Leader's New Work: Building Learning Organizations," provides a vision of the learning organization and describes the leadership necessary for developing and sustaining that vision. Senge's ideas are a direct extension of the work of Chris Argyris, a founder and significant contributor to the field of OD. Next, Jason M. Kanov, Sally Maitlis, Monica C. Worline, Jane E. Dutton, Peter J. Frost, and Jacoba M. Lilius explore the meaning of a humane workplace in their chapter, "Compassion in Organizational Life." Humane workplaces are compassionate organizations where members minister to each other in the face of workplace pain, disappointment, and loss. The authors suggest strategies for creating caring organizations and examine the consequences for organizational effectiveness and health. Part Seven ends with a chapter by William R. Torbert written for this volume, "Generating Simultaneous Personal, Team, and Organization Development." The chapter explores the tight linkages among human development, team development, and organization development. Torbert provides a developmental framework for diagnosing individuals and organizations, and offers solid references for those new to developmental theory and thinking. Two case examples illustrate application of Torbert's framework and remind readers that organization development is transformational when it incorporates strategies for individual and team growth into its efforts.

CHAPTER THIRTY-FIVE

Creating a Community of Leaders

Philip H. Mirvis
Louis "Tex" Gunning

P icture the two hundred and fifty company leaders, ranging from top corporate officers to local brand managers, spending two to three days in India visiting ashrams, hospitals, schools, micro-enterprises, and charities. They tend to the needy, offer service and support, and ponder how spiritual leaders, caregivers, and community entrepreneurs can accomplish so much with so few resources. In a desert campsite, for three days thereafter, they reflect on the meaning of their experiences, talk over its relevance for them, and rediscover what a true mission is—and what a new form of leadership could mean.

Said one leader, "Looking at the Sikh community, I cannot overstate the power of common values. People can simply work together in perfect harmony without a formal organization." Said another, after visiting the charity of Mother Teresa, "The sisters and volunteers really inspired me with their humility, selflessness, courage, and mostly their faith. The energy they have to serve the poor, disabled, and left-over really touched me and honestly I cried during the visit."

Although such experiences deepened understanding of the people and communities in India, there was more to this than benchmarking or lending a hand. Tex Gunning, then president of Unilever Foods

Asia (UFA), posed this to the assembled leaders: "We confront ourselves with the questions: What life do I want to live? Do I want to live my own dream? And, can we as a leadership community create a common dream, and take it into our hands and realize it?"

These questions provoked deeper considerations. An Indonesian recalled, "A new challenge arose for me: How could I be worried about my job and 'how much tea we sold last week' when thinking of all those that are giving their lives to care for people for whom life seems so unfair. This was a gap I could not bridge, and I struggled with the rest of the group to see the link between those communities and our business driven environment."

To bridge this gap, the two hundred and fifty leaders came to the conclusion that they would have to reexamine their own community and reconsider their corporate purpose.

BRINGING LIFE TO MISSION

The idea that vision, mission, and values can guide a business and give meaning to its people is well established. Practitioners and professors alike agree that clarifying and committing to one's own aspirations create a strong personal sense of purpose, and that a strong personal sense of purpose can energize organizations and make them more effective in the long run. Yet, in so many cases (including Unilever's), company mission statements merely hang on the walls of offices or appear on mugs and plaques without carrying any real meaning for employees who don't—either individually or collectively—embody the mission. The results: empty rhetoric and uninspired people.

To build a sustainable, profitable foods-and-beverage business in Asia, we are experimenting with a new way to create a genuine mission and infuse it with personal values. A starting point in 2002 was to connect senior leaders of seventeen national companies in the Asia Pacific region—which operated independently—and to include the next layers of country marketers, supply chain managers, and corporate staff in setting strategy and reviewing performance for the whole of the regional business. Behind this was a desire to build the capacity of this entire leadership body to think, feel, and work together— that is, to operate as a *community of leaders*.

This is where Phil Mirvis came in. We two first met in 1998 on the basis of our mutual interest in the work of M. Scott Peck, who pioneered an approach to community building that brings large numbers of people together to talk openly and authentically about their lives and circumstances. The intent is for the assembled group to develop deeper connections and ultimately find common ground. Tex had used these methods, along with other group development and learning tools, to join together one hundred and eighty business team leaders and turn around Unilever's foods business in Holland—reversing years of losses and achieving double-digit growth. He brought this philosophy with him to Asia when he took charge of the foods-and-beverage business in 2002.

But it is one thing to unite people from a single country with a relatively egalitarian culture, and quite another to bond leaders of so many different nationalities and ethnic cultures that in some cases favor hierarchy and social distance. Furthermore, the UFA leaders were based in the business units of historically independent countries and, to this point, had progressed through single-country career paths. The new model called for the creation of pan-Asian business models and managers. The challenge: UFA leaders would have to find common cause and learn to work together.

BUILDING A LEADERSHIP COMMUNITY

What comes to mind when you hear the word *leadership?* Most often the image is of the heroic individual, often charismatic, whose positional power, intellectual strength, and persuasive gifts motivate followers. But this is not necessarily the ideal in Asia, nor does it match the requirements of large global corporations where forms of distributed and shared leadership are needed to address complex, interlocking problems. The case for connecting leaders across units and levels in UFA also hinges on a simple proposition: *none of us is as smart as all of us.* Some companies enlist collective brainpower through multilevel teams or tiers of committees. We prefer the more inclusive image of a community where leaders truly share responsibility and value being together.

The process of building such a leadership community cycles back and forth from the individual to the collective. The foundation is individuals who understand *"who I am"* and make a conscious choice to lead with others. Self-consciousness is crucial, as only those who can "lead from within" are able to connect fully to others and forge mutual, reciprocal ties. Efforts to deepen person-to-person relationships, in turn, create a sense of trust and unity that brings a collection of individuals into community.

Getting there, as in all kinds of personal and group development processes, is marked by conflict and paradoxes. Thus UFA leaders spend collective time looking at their differences and trying to understand each other's emotional and cultural makeup. The intent is not to "work through" differences by confronting them directly—as in so much human relations and diversity training. Instead, the leadership body serves as a "container" that holds up differences and conflicts for ongoing exploration. Thoughtful, if sometimes heated, reflection on *"who we are"* yields a collective identity and oneness that, at the same time, preserves individuality and diversity in the community.

The next layers of community building engage collective consciousness and enrich it with new perspectives, challenges, and inspiration from the world around us. Here is where experiences such as those in India tap into the emotional and spiritual as well as cognitive character of a leadership body and bring to the surface questions of purpose and values. The practical work of the leadership community is then to tackle these questions and other complex business problems in such a way that every individual thinks and acts mindful of the "whole"—themselves, fellow leaders and employees, the enterprise, and, of course, customers, shareholders, and other relevant interests.

BUILDING COMMUNITY THROUGH LEARNING JOURNEYS

During the first year of forming the business, UFA leaders spent many months in varied forums sharing market information, consumer insights, and competitive analyses to develop a holistic picture of the region and to decide where to use local products and processes and where to reach across country lines. The cultural challenge, less clear and more daunting, would be to unlock barriers to connecting and bridging the diversity in the region.

Communication is integral to building community, which is not surprising considering that they have the same root word, *communus,* "to share." To build a sense of community, leaders in the region would be asked to open up about their life experiences, values, and dreams; talk frankly about their own leadership, national culture, and business; and listen thoughtfully to one another in search of commonality and differences. It would take time to create an environment of candor and trust. "If we as leaders live in denial about our fears, doubts, and anxieties, and about the differences of opinions amongst ourselves," Tex said when the top two hundred and fifty leaders first met together, "we will never get convergence; we will never get the sense of a powerful group pushing in the right direction." He then explained, "Community is important. It stands for a safe environment to share."

In principle, this kind of sharing can take place in meeting rooms and in the course of everyday business. And it has. But UFA has created deeper bonds through a series of annual "learning journeys" where all its leaders come together to see the region and themselves with fresh eyes. (See Exhibit 35.1 for a list of the characteristics of learning journeys.) We have together traveled to locales of historic and cultural significance; hiked through mountains and deserts; met with schoolchildren, indigenous peoples, everyday consumers, and the poor; learned from leaders in business, government, and community organizations; and talked deeply with one another about our personal and business lives.

The journeys, lasting up to a week, are multilayered, multisensory experiences that engage the head, heart, body, and spirit. They are tribal gatherings in that we typically wake at dawn, dress in local garb, exercise or meditate together, hike from place to place, eat communally, swap stories by the campfire, and sleep alongside one another in tents. In our daily experiences, we might meet monks or a martial arts master, talk with local children or village elders, or simply revel in the sounds and sights of nature. We spend considerable time along the way in personal and collective reflections about who we are as a community, what we are seeing, and what this could mean for our work together. Throughout each journey, a team of researchers prepares a "learning history" that documents key insights for continued reflection. (Quotations used in this chapter come from these learning histories.)

- Led by senior executives: leaders as teachers
- Intent: build a leadership community
- Travel into nature; camp-style living
- Locales of historic, cultural, or spiritual significance
- Meet local leaders and people
- Community service
- Multilevel activities: individual, small group, and collective
- Multisensory experiences: engage mind, heart, body, and soul
- Action learning: practice, then theory
- Continuous personal reflection
- Dialogue to share and apply insights
- Document as a learning history

Exhibit 35.1. Learning Journey Characteristics.

It is important to note that Unilever people don't take these journeys to get away from business. On the contrary, the journeys help them see how their business can connect better to the larger world. Community service is an integral part of this. In India, for instance, we formed into seventeen "study groups" that lived in several communities, including Mother Teresa's hospital, the Dalai Lama's monastery in Dharmashala, the Brahma Kumaris's retreat in Mt. Abu, and Ravi Shankar's Art of Living foundation, as well as cloth-spinning communes, the Self-Employed Women's Association, schools and colleges, and so forth. Leaders were asked to use their fives senses to work through a study guide on how these communities functioned and to rely on their sixth sense—intuition—to connect to the more tacit rhythms of human and community life. In so doing, they were prepared to be aware of preconceived assumptions, to be open to what they might experience, and to reflect on the lessons for themselves and the business.

Many were surprised at what they saw, and found some aspects dispiriting and others delightful. Most connected deeply with the people they met:

> You go into Mother Teresa's place and it is full of sick and dying people, but the atmosphere is not that of misery but of joy and love. [My coworker] and I were told to massage some who were just flesh and bones. And this volunteer, who had been there for 14 years, came to us and said: "Look, this is how you've got to do it. It improves their blood circulation and bedsores. But most importantly, it's the human touch that they've missed for years that you give them." We saw so much love in that place. You start doing things that you thought were impossible for you to do.

Beyond personal enrichment and communal bonding, such encounters stimulated thinking about leadership and how to lead the UFA business. Tex's field notes exemplify one such lesson:

> The core insight about great leadership comes down to service. Somehow it humanizes us. One of our problems, especially as we advance in positions of leadership, is that our egos get bigger and bigger, we suppress our human sides, and we don't listen to people—employees, customers, and others—whose needs should shape our business agenda. Face-to-face with great need, a leader is compelled to listen to the one in need.

The reflections of a supply chain manager illustrate another takeaway:

> We met the principal of the Ramakrishna College. He quoted from Jim Collins's *Good to Great*. A monk talking about Collins's greatness concepts! He said: "Look, whether as an individual or as a corporation, we waste 90 percent of our energy in creating an image that is not our real self. If that energy is actually spent in exploring your own uniqueness, the greatness that is there inside you, then you will be really on a journey to greatness. Otherwise you're just wasting your time.

These reflections, in turn, fold into business talk during a journey. Country teams typically meet separately to digest lessons and consider the implications in their national business environments. Then we meet as a whole community to reflect on and review our collective intent. This open and inclusive forum aims to sharpen the regional strategy and build emotional commitment to delivering on it. It can also spark tough questions about strategic direction and the corporate mission.

Although learning journeys of this sort may be beyond the scale or interests of some business leaders, we believe that the components are relevant to every organization that wants to build new leadership capacity and bring its mission to life. Here we describe in brief the Asian journeys and how they help UFA build its community of leaders. The first Asian gathering of two hundred and fifty was held in Guilin, China, in 2003. The next took us throughout India in 2004. The most recent, to Sri Lanka in 2005, had us offer service to survivors of the tsunami. In addition, journeys with smaller groups—of senior regional executives and emerging future leaders—have led us to the jungles of Sarawak, islands of Thailand, and shores of Vietnam. Here are the key elements.

Self-Knowledge: Leadership Is a Choice

UFA has adopted the mantra "leadership is a choice" and encouraged its leaders to inquire into their motives, ambitions, and personal strengths and weaknesses. Like many companies, Unilever uses personality tests, 360-degree feedback, coaching, and the like to enhance self-awareness. And although these methods have their place in personal development programs, we use less formal, more timeless means to promote self-awareness in the full community of leaders.

One such approach involves personal reflection and storytelling about one's life history and lessons. Tex, for instance, has shared his own "lifeline," traced from early childhood to the present, with attention to emotional highs and lows. The first time he did this, while he was in the Dutch foods business, was not easy. In a torch-lit cavern in an abandoned monastery in the Ardennes forest, he talked hesitantly about his abusive stepfather, scraps with authority figures in childhood and military service, and assorted ups and downs over his life course. Subsequently, all the Dutch leaders shared lifelines with one another. During a later collective reflection, one recalled how "moments of silence became tangible." The combination of emotional openness and vulnerability seemed to touch people's hearts.

In Asia, self-reflection and storytelling are part of every leader's work. In a future leaders' forum, for example, younger execs have written and shared their life stories with one another. "It's like a surgery of the soul, you begin to see the roots and patterns," said one young leader about this self-reflection, "and you understand what truly moves you." Biographical studies by psychologist Howard Gardner underscore this point by showing that formative experiences shape the beliefs and practices of leaders in almost every culture. They make up the leader's identity. UFA has also encouraged its current senior leaders to delve into their roots and convey their life lessons to their people. The telling of identity stories, Gardner finds, builds deep connections between leaders and followers and, in particular, informs the identities of younger leaders.

During the China trip, after a hike into the mountains, Asian leaders wrote letters to "mom and dad" that surfaced heartfelt discussion about the emotional sides of leadership. Some ten or twelve leaders read their letters aloud, many striking the same themes:

> While writing to my parents, I nearly choked with emotion as I realized how much I loved them. But I had never shared my feelings with them. I had always been taught that open display of emotions was a sign of weakness. The credo of my clan is that "Men are born to face the challenges of this world. They do not cry. They lead. They are the pride of their family and must not fail." This was drummed into me since I was a little boy.
>
> Till now I had been trying to live up to this myth of invincibility even though I knew that I didn't have all the answers. I could not share my emotions and my fears with even my family as this, I thought,

would be perceived as a sign of weakness. Now I realize how much more I could have done if only I had sought the emotional support that I knew was there all along.

This kind of introspection has helped develop the emotional intelligence and vocabulary of UFA leaders. At a subsequent gathering, we heard a young marketer from Hong Kong—a modern woman raised by a traditional mother—talk movingly about what she and her mother have found in common. In turn, an Australian—deeply disappointed by his failings in the family business—spoke of becoming a parent and reconciling with his father. Through sharing life stories, the leadership body came to see commonality in everyone's life experiences and talked together about how these experiences, good and bad, shape who we are as leaders and who we hope to become.

From Me to You: Connecting to "Other"

A second stratum of community has people strive to understand and connect to others. It is well established that human relationships develop and deepen as people begin to see themselves in another person and see another in themselves. "In listening to other people's stories, you hear your own story," remarked one leader. "Other people's stories often clarify things in your own mind—what your past is and what drives you." Sharing such stories also establishes bonds of mutual understanding and empathy.

"This is really about connecting to a group of people," said a leader from Taiwan, "so we really know the people, and have a feeling about who they are. That's the only way we can really commit ourselves to build a great Unilever Asia together."

"In Chinese we always say it's quite easy to break one chopstick," added another. "But if you put the whole bunch of chopsticks together, it's unbreakable."

In the competitive business culture, it is difficult to "lower the guard," as one senior leader put it. "The initial step of sharing personal information was difficult," he recalled, "but once you sense the value of truly connecting, building on it seemed relatively easy."

"I have understood myself, and I have understood my team," added a Filipino. "I also feel that the emotional bonding within the team has now developed even more. It's great to hear everyone's view and aspiration, and also to see our willingness to put the entire burden on the table to discuss, all to speak up and honestly share."

Connecting to others extends beyond the boundaries of the UFA leadership group. In the journey to China, for instance, we spent time "getting into the skin" of villagers in the ancient hamlet of Xin Ping. The leaders worked alongside local people in their daily lives—sweeping streets, herding buffalo, forming cement blocks, cooking noodles, and teaching school. One commented, "We spent the day with a family who made ropes from the dried grass and pine tree skin. The grand old man in the family—the way he taught us to make ropes, the way he kept his cool despite our silly mistakes—made me think about my style of management when teaching the new managers at the factory."

A Pakistani added, "We met villagers in rural China whose income was less than 125 USD per annum. Seventy percent of my country's 140 million population is similar to the family of the man I met today, while only 5 percent have a lifestyle similar to mine. I respect and value these villagers for who they are and what they deliver to all of us."

The power of connecting person-to-person has had a palpable effect on UFA. The leaders, for example, no longer refer to each other as colleagues; instead they call each other friends. "I feel as if strong ties of friendship bind us," said a Vietnamese. "[It is] absolute friendship, rather than a dry 'network,' that helps you when you need it." A young Thai's comments to a top European executive exemplify the benefits:

> Getting to know you as a person was very valuable. I never thought I would have the opportunity to meet you, let alone hear your real story. In Thailand, we don't get to see our chairman. If he's around, we are too scared to meet him. But, with you now, I feel different. Whenever you come to Thailand, I hope you will visit us. Now it feels like we know each other, not that you are "Mr. Chairman." It feels good to know that, even in a big position, you are a real person.

Collective Dialogue: Developing "Us"

Group consciousness is the next layer of community. It concerns the creation of a collective "us." The community-building process engages what M. Scott Peck calls a "group mind"—the ability of a collective to see both its constituent parts and the whole. This mindfulness develops through free-flowing conversation as people pay close attention to both their own thoughts and feelings and to what is happening in the group overall.

In UFA, we use a large-group discussion methodology called "dialogue" to help develop collective intelligence. We sometimes talk in smaller, fifteen- to twenty-person groups, and sometimes as a full community of two hundred plus, all sitting in a circle, with everyone given the opportunity to speak, irrespective of rank or tenure. The expectation is set to speak openly and frankly, and to deal with the "difficult issues" that would otherwise be avoided or denied. There is also space for "process comments"—observations about how the collective is operating—and periodic moments of silence so that leaders can reflect quietly on what's been said and what they next want to say.

UFA leader's first experiences with dialogue were mixed at best. The Indians and Pakistanis, already heated up by their two nations' cricket match, dominated conversation with long-winded, albeit elegant, philosophical commentary on leadership in their lands. Meanwhile, the Chinese and Southeast Asian leaders were silent. One commented, "The first dialogue was very frustrating, despite my own pitiful efforts at involvement. In an Asian culture, it's not easy to speak out. The risk is very high to stand up and say something. It must be the right thing."

"I was one of those who didn't stand up to talk," added another. "Why? Well, truthfully, I was scared. Nervous about standing up in front of two hundred people to express how I feel. Not knowing if I could trust them." But then, he said, "It finally dawned on me that everything must come from the 'heart.' That is where it all begins."

A third chimed in, "The experience drove me and a colleague, with whom I had never had a discussion before, to open up. We shared deeply our thoughts and difficulties. It was worth the pain!"

To learn to dialogue among so many people across so many different cultures takes time and patience. At the communal gathering in India, one year later, leaders, irrespective of nationality, spoke easily and naturally to the collective, built on each other's comments, challenged gracefully, and encouraged new voices to emerge. Said one, "It was great to see that words just poured out from everyone. We are starting to see the connections with each other."

What helped the process mature? More time together, familiarity with one another, and a degree of psychological safety established from our past encounters all helped. In addition, some practices of community building, such as speaking personally, raising difficult issues, and talking from the heart, though originally "foreign" to these Asian leaders, were proving more agreeable.

The leadership community has now evolved to a stage where leaders can talk about sensitive and emotional subjects, such as "saving face," and confront the assumptions and cultural values behind each other's points of views. "Whilst there are differences in our appearance, speech, and food," said an Indian manager, "sharing innermost feelings and fears so openly has bonded us emotionally." The leaders have also come to realize that intellect, wisdom, and virtues are not the heritage or property of any particular nation or a group of people. Noted an Indonesian, "We have different backgrounds. I have to look into that deeply, open my mind up, and be big enough to accept each of you in my heart so we can have some sort of the same understanding and then become more united."

Reaching Out: From Us to the Larger World

What do the UFA leaders talk about collectively? They discuss what all business leaders have to talk about: profit margins, market shares, trends, budgets, targets, and the like. However, we typically address these matters at regular strategy sessions and operating reviews. On our journeys, we talk more about leadership, culture, and purpose.

The next stratum of community is the connection between people and the larger world. On our trip to China, we spent a playful day with schoolchildren in a mountain village. There was a dragon dance that wound through and around the schoolyard, volleyball games, and jump rope. The happiness of kids, their purity, innocence, energy, smiles, spontaneity, and eagerness, really touched the UFA leaders. "Watching kids, I asked myself if I really live my life innocently enough," said one. "The passion for life that I saw in the children we met was amazing."

"I have always been caught up between the past and future," said another. "I have brought back with me this wonderful gift of living in the moment."

After celebrating a birthday party with all the children, the leaders hiked off toward a campsite and reflected on this encounter. At a stop along the way, the leaders were asked for "words" to describe the kids, and they shouted out:

Friendly, fun, simplicity, inquisitive, sincere, love, unpretentious, celebration, courage, sharing, smiles, curious, honest, naïve, sparkling, real, generous, joy, full of life, unbiased, genuine, creative, ambitious, spontaneous . . .

Next they were asked for words to describe UFA company culture:

Aggressive, control, competitive, complex, scared, rigid, pretentious, hierarchy, ambitious, judgmental, growing, defensive, political, compassionate, challenging, connecting, reactive, structured, demanding, family . . .

The contrast between our corporate world and the children's was sharp, and provoked lots of talk about energizing the UFA culture. "I heard a comedian say that as children, we laugh between 100 to 200 times a day. And as adults, this drops to 11," observed one leader. "We should remember to have fun; laughter can be very energizing and we should not underestimate it."

"We need to consciously and constantly remind ourselves to take off the professional masks that we put on, communicate from our heart, and enjoy life as a kid sometimes," said another.

At a meeting in Sarawak (once part of Borneo), attention turned to the natural environment. The Southeast Asian leaders encountered the terrible costs incurred in the clear-cutting of tropical rainforests. We heard a talk by an expert from a natural resources group; then, to get physically involved and symbolically lend a hand, we cleaned a nearby beach of industrial flotsam and tourist trash. A trip upriver in hollowed-out wooden canoes took us to the village of the Penan people, where we met their chief, medicine man, and tribe, and took a long walk with them through their clear-cut forests. The experience led to earnest discussion of the benefits and costs of economic growth in the region. This in turn led to calls to incorporate criteria of environmental sustainability into strategic and operating plans.

In principle, knowledge about environmental and social conditions can be gleaned from text, talks, and conversations in any forum. But the experience of being there and seeing firsthand adds texture and has greater potential to raise collective consciousness. The community visits in India illustrate that. There was real inspiration in applying insights from our visits to the mission of UFA. Said one, "I started getting the feeling that my work need not be confined to producing and selling as efficiently as possible but has a higher purpose of community service to the people of Asia." Said another, "In the context of the larger things in the world, I feel I can do a more fulfilling job. Something bold that I will be proud of, something that has the humanity that I have valued."

Ongoing dialogue brought the leaders closer to the conclusion that organizations have to be driven by their missions rather than by numbers and processes. "This changes the paradigm of thinking that we are selling to consumers," said one. "Instead we are serving our communities." Other reflections carry the same theme:

> Connecting with poverty in India reminds us that UFA, as a member in Asia, has strong social responsibility. We need to build our business success while taking on social responsibilities—to help to protect the environment, to relieve poverty. . . . At the same time these actions will help our business grow.

> I was struggling with the concept of community in a business corporation such as ours but the layers unpeeled over the days slowly. It is a very powerful thought and I am still trying to soak it in. The contact with Indian communities really touched me as I saw voluntary work, devotion, sacrifice, purity, truth, belonging, affiliation, caring, working together in a responsible and dedicated fashion like a family. While family is so central to me in personal life, I feel that similar core thoughts need to be internalized and become a way of life in work life.

An imperative emerged: the leaders had to put flesh onto these caring aspirations and translate them into a mission that would emphasize the healthy, nourishing aspects of food. We pledged to become responsible partners with the people of Asia and to address the health, vitality, and development of the children and families through better food and beverages. We also pledged to be actively involved in communities, and especially to understand and respond to the needs of the economically underprivileged and children.

BRINGING MISSION TO LIFE

Passion. Purpose. Community. Fine words and uplifting sentiments, but what meaning do they have in business? In sharing their final thoughts and feelings about the challenge, some found the prospect energizing. Said a country manager, "We had put together aspirations for our country and where we want to go. But we found out, actually, it was very superficial. We were not truly listening nor truly talking from our heart. So this morning, we started to be truly open. Of course we know that there will be stormy periods. We will have debates and arguments. But at least it has started. It's just the beginning of our journey."

On a more personal note, another added, "I am excited with the idea of creating something magical and I am committed—realizing fully well the newly found meaning of this word community—to making this happen."

Others were more daunted: "What still concerns me is how I will make this transition with my own selfish interests—of career growth, financial security, being in good books of my bosses, saying the politically acceptable things, taking shortcuts, putting myself ahead of others, etc." Or, as another remarked, "This mission cannot co-exist with bad business performance or in the absence of immediate action to bring it alive."

Will this community of leaders be able to deliver on the promise of their mission? The jury is out and will be for a while. A shared aspiration and declaration of intent are not enough to bring the mission alive. To truly care for the needy in Asia will require tough business decisions that might threaten the core business. Even so, UFA has begun making major investments in children's nutrition to fortify its offerings to enhance children's mental and physical performance. It is also reaching out to the poorest of the poor with enriched inexpensive foods and community-based distribution systems—broadening Unilever's bottom-of-the-pyramid portfolio.

UFA is also partnering with development agencies and working with local companies to enlarge its own community of leaders and expand its definition of itself as a socially responsive company: "With the kind of community and mission driven approach that we have in UFA, it is possible for us to make a difference to our society and still be in business," said one leader. "And it is important for us to be in business because that is the only way we will continue to make a difference to society."

Reaching Beyond: A Higher Purpose

A final stratum of community is reached when people connect to something larger than themselves. "Truly, this is a soul searching journey," said one leader about our times together. "It is a journey of self-connecting, connecting with others, connecting with the universe and certainly connecting with God." UFA is by no means a church or cult, but its leaders have reached a level of comfort and candor where they can talk openly about their spiritual beliefs and about the importance of a higher power and higher purpose in their lives.

The journeys provide many opportunities for this sort of contemplation. We often begin the day with yoga, meditation, or tai chi. In China, for example, we awoke daily at dawn, dressed in red-and-black silk outfits, and walked to a large field where a tai chi master led us through the fighting and dancing styles of this martial art. He told us that a master must be aware of himself, his opponent (or partner), and the situation around him, and then forget it all when fighting (or dancing). This opened up deep conversation among the leaders about how to integrate consciousness of the self, other, and the world when taking action. And the fact that our teacher, nearly eighty and revered around in the world for his skill, did not yet consider himself a true master provoked a new appreciation of the importance of discipline, persistence, and especially humility on a leader's journey.

Nature is another of our teachers. The majestic mountains of Guilin, for instance, informed our deliberations. "This is not scenery," said one of our leaders, pointing to a lush valley. "This brings us food. It gives us air. It gives us water. It gives us light. When we die, we become this," he said, the sweep of his arm drawing gazes to the magnificent setting in which we were trekking, reflecting, sharing. The impact of nature was beginning to sink in: "One night in front of the camp fire, I imagined that we were looked upon from a satellite. I saw a small campfire light in the middle of vast land on the earth. I felt how small we were and how small I was."

"Great nature raises people," said another. "One can only reflect on it with honesty and purity."

This connection to a force or field larger than ourselves goes by many names: the religious call it karma, grace, or God. The more secular terms used are transcendence or connecting to universal consciousness. Such larger-than-life themes were palpable on the recent journey to Sri Lanka, where UFA leaders offered service to people and villages ravaged by the tsunami.

As we progressed on this mind-opening and heart-rending journey, we saw ever-increasing signs of the tsunami's destruction: the wreckage of small whitewashed homes, their former inhabitants living alongside in pup tents; boats, cars, and trains pitched on barren beaches and ravaged roads; and then a large tent city constructed to shelter survivors. One leader reported, "We felt the tension in our bones. The place was pregnant with disaster and it was racing towards us in all its ferocity. The community had lost its will to survive, let alone live. What was the contribution we were going to make? These thoughts screamed through our brains."

Several days were spent cleaning up debris in a school, helping local merchants assess inventory and reconnect with suppliers, and talking with Sri Lankans, individually and in large gatherings. Two leaders reflected on the connections made:

> Walking through the village, a young father gestured a friendly "hello" towards me. Before I could say anything, he started to tell his tragic story of how he lost his four children and his home. He led me to his wooden cabin where his wife was waiting for him and she looked pleased to meet a new face. They showed me photographs of their lost kids which left me in tears. They made me feel at home right away; grief became our mutual language.

> This man who had lost two of his family members told me how God has been kind to him—his neighbor had lost all of his five family members. He made me realize that there is such goodness in simple lives—where I have never bothered to look.

We had an ennobling experience sitting with a whole village that had lost so much from the tsunami. One by one, the women of the village told their stories, and we witnessed their trials and courage. A leader reflected on its impact: "We were all crying listening to their stories, but it brought them together, and it brought us together. We stood there with these people we had met only one hour ago, hand in hand, in silence, tears pouring out our eyes in togetherness."

Through personal reflections long into the night and on a solo journey to a quiet place, the leaders gave voice to our sense of being a part of something larger than ourselves. "We listened to the fears and hopes of the mothers, fathers, and children left behind in this beautiful but devastated country. We shed tears of pain, hope, and love," recalled one, adding, "We shed even more tears when we realized that by simply sharing our spirit with them, we made an incredible difference not only to their lives but also to our own. It continues to surprise me how care and service for others help me discover my own love."

"For me spirituality is about the interconnectedness between each and every one of us," reflected another leader. "What connects me with the tsunami victims in Sri Lanka goes beyond emotion, it is our shared humanity."

A third said, "We are all souls whether we are born in one religious family or another. This goes beyond body, birth, nationality, color, caste, religion, culture, etc. The original nature of soul is love, peace, happiness, mercy, tolerance, patience. That's who we really are."

These profound reflections also apply to what UFA is striving to create as a leadership community:

> I realize that words like emotions, feeling, moods may not sound businesslike; however, once used in their best and sincere form, they have real consequences for getting work done. I am beginning to understand that building a resonant culture, one where all of us can bring out the best in us, will bring us to greatness.
>
> I feel very close to the Asia group. There is some weird sense of bonding that has developed even though I didn't know more than half of the people. I really can't explain it well but it is a sense of oneness or being together. It is strange because I felt this when we weren't even talking. It was a nice feeling. For the first time, I experienced it outside my family. Maybe this is what we call community feeling.

It is uncertain whether this community of leaders will be sustained. No doubt its continuity will be challenged by personnel moves and restructuring. And surely UFA's efforts to meet its new mission—to be responsible partners with the people of Asia; to promote health, vitality, and the development of children and families through food and beverage—will have its ups and downs. All agree that this means earning the trust of consumers, having authentic standards for food health and production, and being at the leading edge of nutrition science and technology. They also say it means being actively involved in communities and applying business acumen to their human needs.

Tex closed the journey to Sri Lanka with these remarks to the community of leaders:

> As leaders, we need a whole new level of consciousness about the functioning of organizations, deeply recognizing that ours is a living and therefore continuously changing organism, adjusting itself to its new circumstances and to the humans that make it up. You cannot force human beings to adjust themselves to organizational logics. You can

only let the organization adjust itself to the universal needs of all human beings. People want to live meaningful lives; they want to live in service and care for others; they want the freedom and space to be creative; they want to grow and they want to be part of an organization that helps them to contribute to something that is far bigger than they could ever be on their own.

Caring for community needs to be in the heart of all our actions. I think once we get this right, then the rest will come into place. The profits will be there because we are heading in the right direction. If our competitors start doing things similar to us, we should not be mad at them. In fact we should be happy, because they will also help people and grow the marketplace. And with that in mind we will have a very strong foundation to bring value into this world.

Reflections on the Journeys—Tex Gunning

Our journeys have been all about the "How?"—How do we bring our mission to life? How do we become great leaders? How do we create a great business and culture?

Great businesses have great leaders at all levels of the organization. They take care of the needs of all their stakeholders and want to make this world a better place for all of us. Great businesses have great cultures. They understand that business beings are human beings that want to belong, live meaningful lives. They want to have space to create, grow, and contribute to a better world. It is, therefore, no surprise that business leaders of great companies are first and foremost great human beings. They care and live in service, and they commit to a lifelong journey of personal mastery, developing all the necessary skills and competencies and all of their intelligences—PQ (physical intelligence), IQ (intellectual intelligence), EQ (emotional intelligence), and SQ (spiritual intelligence).

In Unilever Asia Foods, we have through our various journeys attempted to become great human beings, understanding deeply that it would make us more effective as business leaders.

To help develop our EQ and SQ, we confront community service and take care of the underprivileged and destitute. We experienced that it humanizes our characters. It reminds us that we have a soul and qualities of love and compassion—all innate qualities of great leaders. It also reminds us that leadership is not a position but a responsibility to act: it's not a noun but a verb.

So, we went to Sri Lanka to help the tsunami victims, as we had committed ourselves never to close our eyes again to the misery around us.

We worked, cried, played with the beautiful people of Sri Lanka, who taught us again that greatness has many faces and has all to do with compassion, service, and care for others.

The profound lesson was that while we can give people in need assets like shelter and even food, what they need most is love and a rekindling of their spirits. They taught us that in times of despair and total destruction, the only thing that we human beings can rely on to persevere is the human spirit.

It's our spirits that ignite our souls. It's our souls that give us guidance and wisdom, and it is our souls that animate human qualities of love, compassion, and humility. To be conscious of these innate qualities is essential for leaders, as it will help us to have the faith, courage, and wisdom to persevere in complex situations of flux and adversity, and to stay truthful to our mission to make this world a better place for all of us. . . . The journey continues.

SELECTED BIBLIOGRAPHY

M. Scott Peck's approach to community building draws on an amalgam of methods from human relations training, twelve-step programs, and Quakerism. The community-building process has people "empty" themselves of barriers to others by sharing reflections on their own life and listening deeply to others' stories. The result of this emptying and empathizing is the emergence of group consciousness whereby a group begins to think, feel, and operate as a "whole." In Peck's model, this has a spiritual dimension in that the process often opens a sense of wonder about human purpose and the presence of a higher power. See M. Scott Peck's *A World Waiting to Be Born: Civility Rediscovered* (New York: Doubleday, 1993) and *The Different Drum* (New York: Simon & Schuster, 1987).

Leaders use their own "identity stories" to help followers develop their own sense of self. Howard Gardner's *Leading Minds: An Anatomy of Leadership* (New York: Basic Books, 1995) lays out the theory. For illustrations of such storytelling in business, see *The Leadership Engine: How Winning Companies Build Leaders at Every Level,* by Noel Tichy and Eli Cohen (New York: HarperInformation, 1997), and *The Three Faces of Leadership: Manager, Artist, Priest,* by Mary Jo Hatch, Monika Kostera, and Andrzej K. Komiski (London: Blackwell, 2005).

For background on dialogue and the development of a "group mind," see *Dialogue and the Art of Thinking Together: A Pioneering Approach to Communicating in Business and Life,* by William Isaacs (New York: Doubleday, 1999), and *Wholeness and the Implicate Order,* by David Bohm (London: Ark, 1986).

There are several writings about the community-building process with Gunning and his leaders. A "learning history" recounts the work in Holland from 1995 to 2000: *To the Desert and Back: The Story of One of the Most Dramatic Business Transformations on Record,* by Philip H. Mirvis, Karen Ayas, and George Roth (San Francisco: Jossey-Bass, 2003). For more on the leadership community and young leaders' forum by Karen Ayas and Philip H. Mirvis, see "Young Leaders' Forum in Asia: Learning About Leadership, Abundance, and Growth" (*Reflections,* April 1, 2002, pp. 33–42) and "Bringing 'Mission' to Life: Corporate Inspiration from Indian Communities" (*Reflections,* May 10, 2004, pp. 1–12).

CHAPTER THIRTY-SIX

Designing High-Performance Work Systems

Organizing People, Work, Technology, and Information

David A. Nadler
Marc S. Gerstein

————

Two black swans, aptly named Dream and Vision, serenely oversee the duck pond in front of American Transtech's Jacksonville, Florida, headquarters. Since 1983, when the company was established by AT&T to handle the dramatic increase in shareholder activity resulting from the creation of the Regional Bell Operating Companies, American Transtech has become a leader in work redesign in the United States.

Employing self-directed teams, a redesigned work process, and a virtually flat, three-level hierarchy in the operating business, the company has improved productivity from 100 to 300 percent and reduced its costs and staff in the core stock transfer area by more than 50 percent. American Transtech has taken in outside customers such as American Express to use the excess capacity necessitated by the cyclical nature of dividend payments and exploited its skills in phone customer contact to build a significant telemarketing business.

Employees monitor the performance and costs of their operations on a continuous basis and know their operations inside-out. In addition to their work redesign and operations responsibilities, they participate in hiring, career progression, and compensation decisions.

Outsiders are universally surprised by the depth of employee knowledge, candor, and willingness to change. Although life is not perfect at American Transtech, as everyone is quick to admit, they are working on it.

A revolution is under way in the workplaces of America. It is a quiet revolution; there are few banners, no great battles, and relatively little publicity. It involves innovative thinking about how people, work, technology, and information can be brought together in new forms of organization capable of achieving significantly higher levels of sustained performance. The quiet beginnings of this revolution are setting the stage for profound changes in the way we think about the organization of work in the 1990s.

In fact, these efforts to develop new and better ways to organize human effort have been going on for some time. Since the late 1960s, innovation and learning about the organization of work has proceeded in a number of different companies under a variety of different names. Companies have experimented with autonomous work teams, sociotechnical systems, open systems planning, new plant designs, and other similar innovations. These efforts, however, have gone far beyond experimentation and pilots. In such corporations as Procter & Gamble, Digital Equipment Corporation (DEC), Corning, Inc., and AT&T, these new approaches to organizing have been implemented and have achieved sustained superior results.

In recent times, a term has emerged to describe these different innovations. The concept of *high-performance work systems* has been used as an integrating concept and a label to describe a variety of different specific innovations that all draw from a common set of principles and practices. The purpose of this chapter is to provide a perspective on high-performance work systems (HPWS), as a reference point for managers who are considering HPWS initiatives. This chapter is an attempt to integrate a number of different perspectives on this topic, with a focus toward practice and application. We begin with a short historical perspective to provide a sense of how this approach to organizing developed. We then describe what we believe HPWS means today. Next we focus on two core elements of HPWS. First, we identify principles of HPWS design and contrast them with traditional approaches to organization design. Second, we describe the basic HPWS design process, the steps involved in implementing the design principles. In a final section, we discuss the relationship of HPWS to some other organizational improvement strategies.

HISTORICAL PERSPECTIVE
Traditional Models

Most of the conventional wisdom about how to organize dates back to two approaches developed close to a century ago. At the turn of the century, F. W. Taylor, an American, developed a "scientific" model of organization using the machines of the Industrial Revolution as his model (Taylor, 1911). Taylor believed in careful and comprehensive analysis of the work system and the removal of any possible cause of variation. At the core of his approach to organizing, called *scientific management,* were some design principles including specialization of work into the narrowest possible jobs, careful specification of work tasks in detail, repetition of activity with little (or no) variety, and removal of all discretion and "brain work" from operational personnel.

At approximately the same time, the German sociologist Max Weber, observing the organizational innovations of the German leader Bismarck, articulated a management model called *bureaucracy* (Weber, 1947). Weber's bureaucracy was a coherent and well thought out theory of organizing containing the following important elements:

- Organizations should be built around a clear system of hierarchical relationships, with greater discretion in decision making as one moves up the hierarchy and with an established chain of command as the primary mechanism for coordination.

- Organizations should be governed by a clear and consistent set of written rules and procedures covering all positions, both operational and managerial.

- Job holders should be qualified to perform their assignments; therefore, technical competence should be the basis for filling jobs and for promotion.

Today it is difficult to understand the tremendous leap forward that these approaches to organizing represented compared with earlier feudal or tribal models. The "machine bureaucracy" that emerged from the fusion of Taylor's and Weber's ideas achieved previously unattainable levels of performance through enhanced individual performance and vast improvements in coordination between organizational units. As this model of organization-as-machine matured in the early part of the twentieth century, it established a template for industrial organization that persists to this day. Though the basic principles of Taylor's and Weber's works may seem obvious and perhaps dated as they are read today, they clearly laid the foundation for an enormous increase in industrial productivity and established a pattern of beliefs about the right way to structure a productive enterprise. In fact, this approach has become so pervasive that we unconsciously equate the machine bureaucracy model with the process of organizing; it is hard for us to think of any other way of structuring work enterprises.

Human Relations Approaches

Despite the dramatic successes of the model of organization-as-machine, productivity came at enormous costs. The enterprise was frequently shortchanged of people's motivation and creativity, which could not be harnessed as a result of narrow, repetitious jobs that had little discretion. Coordination between units was difficult, despite attempts to systematize interactions with rules and procedures. The bureaucratic system itself had a number of serious unintended consequences, such as communications bottlenecks, decision making in the absence of the information necessary to make decisions, and an incapacity to act brought about by layer upon layer of rules and managerial approvals.

In summary, the machine bureaucracy model, while tremendously successful at first, ultimately suffered from three significant problems, which became apparent by the middle of the twentieth century (see, for example, Roethlisberger & Dickson, 1939; Argyris, 1957).

1. The model was built for the management of relatively stable and predictable situations. It broke down under conditions of uncertainty and instability because of the inability to reconfigure and the lack of emphasis on discretion by individuals. As rates of change increased, organizations based on this model became less effective.

2. The model was built on the assumption that the work force was relatively uneducated, had little mobility, and was driven almost exclusively by economic needs. As more educated workers with greater mobility and a desire for noneconomic returns from their employment (pride, a feeling of worth and accomplishment, challenge, and growth) came into the work force, the

organizations built on this model had a more difficult time motivating and satisfying workers.

3. Over time, organizations based on this model experienced their own entropy: they tended to become more complex, less responsive, more inwardly oriented, and more unwieldy.

Starting in the 1940s and continuing well into the 1970s, management theorists and practitioners responded with a variety of techniques to compensate for the inherent limitations of the machine bureaucracy (Argyris, 1957; Likert, 1961). These theorists worked from a very different set of assumptions based on the beliefs that people wanted to work and produce quality products; that through participation, people's energies could be enlisted in the service of organizational goals; and that there was potential power in groups or teams of people working together collaboratively. Such techniques included participative management, management style training, team building, job enrichment and enlargement, and other similar approaches. Despite the initial reports of the success of such innovations, in many cases their impact was short-lived. Frequently, these new approaches were "pasted on" the existing organization, which had been designed using the machine bureaucracy model. Two conflicting models of design were being employed, and these approaches had fundamentally different underlying values and design principles. Over time, these "paste ons" tended to have little positive impact.

Origins of High-Performance Work Systems

High-performance work systems can be traced back to a series of experiments conducted in the United Kingdom during the late 1940s. Researchers from the Tavistock Institute, studying the introduction of new technology in British coal mines (and later in the weaving industry in India), discovered that technological innovation alone could not explain differences in performance (Trist & Bamforth, 1951; Rice, 1958). In fact, certain technological changes that were intended to increase performance resulted, instead, in performance declines. Research revealed that high performance resulted when the design of the technical system and the design of the social system of work were congruent. Building on group dynamics and general systems theory, the Tavistock researchers demonstrated that high performance required that the needs of the organization's social system and the needs of the technical system be considered equally and simultaneously in the design process. They argued that a set of design principles different from the classical "one man/one job" approach be used to construct work systems. Rather than fitting jobs (and thus people) to the optimum technical system, the joint optimization of both the social and technical systems would be required.

Research over subsequent years led to the development of an approach to work design called *sociotechnical systems* (Cherns, 1976). At the core of the sociotechnical model is the concept of two work system elements—social and technical—designed deliberately to fit each other. Where a high degree of sociotechnical fit was achieved, performance increased. By the late 1960s, a large amount of experience (largely outside of the United States) had begun to accrue so that the principles of sociotechnical work design could be articulated. At the core of the approach are five principles (Hanna, 1988; Cherns, 1976):

1. Although rules and work processes critical to overall success should be identified, no more rules should be specified than are absolutely essential.

2. Variances, or deviations, from the ideal process should be controlled at the point of origin.

3. Each member of the system should be skilled in more than one function so that the work system is flexible and adaptive.

4. Roles that are interdependent should be within the same departmental boundaries.

5. Information systems should be designed primarily to provide information to the point of action and problem solving.

In practice, sociotechnical design also led to the heavy use of teams to manage interdependent work, with those teams empowered to manage their own work processes and flows. This approach therefore became known as "autonomous work teams" and was prevalent in Europe during the 1970s. During the 1960s and 1970s, an additional element was added to the concept of sociotechnical design. A number of designers pointed out that most of the sociotechnical design work had been done with an internal focus. They argued that effective work system design needed to start with an external or "open systems" perspective, starting with the external stakeholders (customers, suppliers, competitors). Work system design would thus start with an understanding of environmental requirements, demands, and opportunities and then move to the design of specific elements of the social and technical systems (Lawrence & Lorsch, 1967).

At the same time, other experimenters were seeking to extend some of the concepts of sociotechnical design by applying them to larger work systems, in particular, to complete manufacturing installations. The greatest success was gained in new plants that were designed from the ground up using sociotechnical principles. Notable examples were the General Foods Topeka dog food plant and the Volvo Kalmar assembly plant in Sweden. By the late 1970s, several hundred new plant designs had been implemented in the United States with a very high success rate (Lawler, 1978). These new plant designs used sociotechnical principles but went beyond them. The new plants also reflected significant changes in the design of the organizational architecture—the formal and informal structures and processes—that formed the context for the core work process (Lawler, 1986):

> *Employee selection.* Peer selection and information sharing enable workers to select the new type of work environment.
>
> *Design of physical layout.* Employees participate in the design of the physical setting and the work configurations that support team designs, team planning, and meeting areas.
>
> *Job design.* Individual jobs within the context of the teams are designed to increase autonomy, variety of tasks, feedback, and the sense of completing a piece of work.
>
> *Pay system.* Rewards are tied to skill acquisition for individuals, to encourage multiskill acquisition. Gain-sharing plans motivate improved performance.
>
> *Organizational structure.* These plants typically are designed with fewer levels of hierarchy, with more self-contained or autonomous units, and in support of self-managing teams.
>
> *Training.* The plants invest heavily in intensive training in skills, as well as training to provide the broad background knowledge that supports participation in decision making.
>
> *Management philosophy.* These plants are run with an explicit philosophy of partnership between management and the work force, aimed at a common vision.

These new plant designs continue to be employed. Some notable examples are the Digital Equipment facility in Enfield, Connecticut, and the Procter & Gamble technician plant in Lima, Ohio. During the 1980s, as more experience was gained with different design approaches, a growing number of companies began to integrate the sociotechnical, open systems, and new plant design concepts into an approach called high-performance work systems. It was a logical extension of the earlier frameworks.

DEFINITION

The *high-performance work systems* (HPWS) approach to the design of human work organizations, in its simplest form, is an organizational architecture that brings together work, people, technology, and information in a manner that optimizes the congruence or "fit" among them in order to produce high performance in terms of the effective response to customer requirements and other environmental demands and opportunities (Hanna, 1988; Sherwood, 1988; Nadler & Tushman, 1988; Tushman & Nadler, 1978; Brown, 1989; Nadler, 1989). High-performance work systems can be characterized as follows:

> *A way of thinking about organization.* Instead of fitting people to the requirements of the technical system with a focus on internal efficiency, the HPWS approach emphasizes the fit among work, people, technology, and information with an external focus on the effectiveness of the system in meeting the changing requirements of the environment.
>
> *A set of principles for designing organizations.* The HPWS approach comprises very specific design principles that guide the designer in making choices. These principles reflect a set of values about people and work.
>
> *A process for applying those design principles.* The HPWS approach also includes a design process—a series of generic steps for the design (or redesign) of work systems and organizations.
>
> *A variety of specific organizational design features.* Very specific design devices or features, such as autonomous work teams, enriched jobs, and flat hierarchies, are employed as a consequence of using the design principles.

The historical view provided above described the evolution of the HPWS approach. Now, we focus on what we see as the two core elements of HPWS: the design principles and the design process.

DESIGN PRINCIPLES

The HPWS approach is not a specific design or even a particular design feature (such as autonomous work teams) any more than machine bureaucracy could be equated to a seven-level hierarchy. HPWS is a set of design principles that are applied to particular organizational situations. Looking at a range of projects and initiatives, we see ten principles:

1. *Customer- and environmentally focused design.* Design must, over time, be driven by environmental requirements and conditions if an organization is to be successful. The primary environmental factor is the customer of the product or service that the organization produces. Therefore, design starts from outside of the organization (or unit), beginning with customers and their requirements, and then moves back to the work and organizational processes. The core purpose of HPWS design is to enable sets of people working together to produce and deliver products and services that meet customer requirements in the context of changing environments.

2. *Empowered and autonomous units.* Organizational units should be designed around whole pieces of work—complete products, services, or processes. The goal is to maximize interdependence within the work unit and minimize interdependence among work units. Obviously, there is still some need for coordination among different units, but the aim is to create loosely coupled units with the ability to manage their relationships with each other. Teams, as opposed to individuals are the basic organizational building blocks. Rather than focus on how to break down work into the smallest units that can be performed by an individual, the HPWS approach emphasizes complete units of work that can be performed by sets of individuals who are empowered to determine how they will do the work. Within the context of very stringent customer requirements, great freedom is provided to those doing the work to design and manage their own work processes. This implies minimum specification of the work and resources to enable empowerment, such as time, money, information, and decision-making authority.

3. *Clear direction and goals.* Although there is great latitude in determining how the work will be done, there is a great need for clarity about the requirements of the output. Therefore, the empowered autonomous work unit needs to have a very clear mission, defined output requirements, and agreed-on measures of performance. Clear direction and goals provide the work unit with the information needed to design and manage its own work structure and process.

4. *Control of variance at the source.* Work processes and units should be designed so that variances (errors) can be detected and controlled at the source, as opposed to outside the work unit. It is much less costly to detect and correct variance at the point of creation than later on. This implies that the work unit is provided with the information and tools to detect and prevent error.

5. *Socio-technical integration.* The social and technical systems are seen as inexorably interlinked. The purpose of design is to achieve effective integration between the two. The technical system includes the work flow, the specific technologies employed, the movement of information, and the work processes. Rather than design the technical system for the people or select the people with respect to the technical system, the goal is to achieve joint optimization to create an integrated work system capable of responding to customer and environmental requirements.

6. *Accessible information flow.* As implied by many of the principles already articulated, information is critical to the effective functioning of an HPWS design. Members of the empowered autonomous unit need to have access to information about the environment, about the output, about the work process, about variances, and so on. The flow of information (as opposed to the flow of data) must be designed so that work unit members can create, receive, and transmit information as needed.

7. *Enriched and shared jobs.* The capacity of the empowered autonomous work unit is enhanced if people in the unit are cross-trained in a variety of skills. Broader jobs increase individual autonomy, learning, and internal motivation (Hackman & Oldham, 1980). The work unit's ability to reconfigure is enhanced. As individuals understand the nature of the work performed by others, their ability to participate in the design and management of the entire work process is also enhanced. Learning, as well as performance, becomes an important driver for individuals.

8. *Empowering human resources practices.* Many of the human resources policies and practices in organizations reflect the machine bureaucracy model. The emphasis is on control, uniformity, and inspection of variance outside the unit. HPWS design implies the need to create human resources practices that are consistent with autonomous empowered units, such as local selection, skill-based pay, peer feedback, team bonuses, minimization of rank and hierarchy, and gain sharing.

9. *Empowering management structure, process, and culture.* HPWS units placed in the context of machine bureaucracies are like hostile, alien life forms. The larger system detects their presence and attempts to destroy or expel them. The literature on organizational change is abundant with examples of this phenomenon (Walton, 1977). The design principle is to ensure that the "host system" is consistent with and supportive of the empowered autonomous unit. In the early stages of HPWS design, this may mean the creation of a protective shield of sponsorship, but ultimately it will require redesign of the larger system according to principles consistent with HPWS: different modes of structure and coordination (for example, thinking about work units as linked together in sets of customer-supplier relationships), different approaches to planning and budgeting, different modes of decision making, different management styles, different types of information systems, and, ultimately, radically different management processes.

10. *Capacity to reconfigure.* The final design principle is in some ways an outcome of the application of the other principles. The work unit (or sets of work units) should have the capacity to reconfigure as required. An assumption is that organizations are designed to anticipate or respond to environmental requirements and conditions. If the environment is changing at an increasing rate, there is a competitive advantage for those who can anticipate and respond to those changes more quickly. This involves the creation of units that are able to learn—to collect information, to reflect on the consequences of their actions, and to gain insight. It requires units that have the ability to act on their learning, either through continuous improvement or through large "leaps" of redesign.

These ten design principles constitute an interrelated set of concepts for design. When combined, they lead the designer to create organizations very different from the traditional machine bureaucracy model. To highlight this difference, we can contrast the principles of the two approaches (Table 36.1). It becomes apparent that HPWS is a fundamentally different paradigm for organizing.

Traditional	HPWS
Internally driven design	Customer- and environmentally focused design
Highly controlled fractionated units	Empowered and autonomous units
Ambiguous requirements	Clear direction and goals
Inspection of errors	Control of variance at the source
Technical system dominance	Sociotechnical integration
Limited information flow	Accessible information flow
Fractionated, narrow jobs	Enriched and shared jobs
Controlling and restrictive human resources practices	Empowering human resources practices
Controlling management structure, process, and culture	Empowering management structure, process, and culture
Static designs dependent on senior management redesign	Capacity to reconfigure

Table 36.1.   Comparison of Traditional and High-Performance Work Systems Design Principles.

PERFORMANCE

Research and experience with HPWS have now yielded more than two decades of consistent evidence of the performance of units designed with HPWS principles as compared with those designed using traditional principles. In general, the data suggest that HPWS units produce the following results:

Reduced cost. HPWS units appear to be able to produce comparable products, with the same base technology, at significantly reduced cost, in general, 40 to 50 percent less than traditional analogs.

Increased quality. Many of the principles of HPWS are consistent with those of total quality. It is therefore not surprising that HPWS units have lower error rates and higher overall quality of service and product.

Enhanced internal motivation. The creation of high levels of ownership from this approach to design appears to lead to higher levels of commitment and higher internal (or "intrinsic") motivation. Employees feel that the work, the product, and the process are theirs, and they therefore feel internally driven to do well. They display increased feelings of pride and accomplishment.

Lower turnover and absenteeism. Feelings of involvement in and commitment to the team appear to lead to longer tenure, and lower levels of absenteeism and tardiness.

Increased learning. The emphasis on individual skill acquisition and the creation of responsibility for teams for the entire product and process lead to more openness to new ideas and, in fact, increased emphasis on the value of learning.

Increased capacity to adapt. As those close to the work and the customer have the ability to reconfigure or redesign the work process, these units appear to be able to respond to change more quickly and to adapt to shifts in environment, technology, or customer needs, which lead to a significant competitive advantage.

Although these benefits are impressive, there are some systems that seem to do significantly better than others. It appears that part of the explanation comes from the way in which the new design approach is introduced. The process of HPWS design can be as critical an element as the design principles themselves.

DESIGN PROCESS
Approach

The HPWS approach is more than simply a set of design principles. Inherent in the approach is a way of thinking about the process of design. Several assumptions underlie the design process.

The design process should be diagnostically driven. HPWS is not a universal solution; rather, it is a way of using organizational design to enhance organizational performance or to solve business problems. HPWS is not necessarily the solution of choice in all situations; therefore the design process needs to include a diagnostic phase in which the current system, its performance, and its problems are examined with an emphasis on understanding causes.

The design process must include data collection on both the social and technical systems. If sociotechnical integration is one of the core design principles, then the design process must include collection of data and analysis of those two systems and the nature of their interdependence before the design of new structures and processes begins.

The design process should be participative. The people who frequently have the best and most complete data on the true nature of the social and technical systems are those who work in them. It is therefore difficult, if not impossible, for outsiders to develop effective HPWS designs. The design process should mirror the values of the HPWS approach itself and, therefore, should empower and enable members of the work system to do the designing. Typically, this is done by creating a design team that includes members of the target work system as well as subject matter and technical resources. At the same time, because new tools and concepts are to be used in the design work, there is a role for a design consultant (either external or internal) to help teach design concepts and facilitate the design team.

Steps

High-performance work systems designers have developed a number of different design processes, but most of them follow a relatively consistent logic, as displayed in Figure 36.1. The process begins with an analysis of customer, environmental, and strategic requirements. If the design is to be done "outside-in," then the nature of external requirements is critical. Typically, this step also includes some diagnostic work, focusing on the degree to which the organization is meeting environmental and customer requirements, with an emphasis on understanding the root causes of any problems.

The second step is analysis of the work process. This includes examination and description of the flow of work, the elements of the technical system, and the current formal organizational structures and processes used to manage the work. During this step, it is important to understand the inherent requirements of the work, as opposed to the steps in the work flow that reflect how the work is currently organized.

Concurrent with the work process analysis is the third step, analysis of the social system. This involves data collection on patterns of communication, emergent group structures, values, work practices, informal leadership patterns, norms, and other items.

The fourth step is to design the new organization. This involves application of the ten design principles (mentioned above) to the particular work unit(s). Perhaps the most critical activity in this step is determining what the new work flow will be and identifying the major pieces of work around which groups or teams will be constructed.

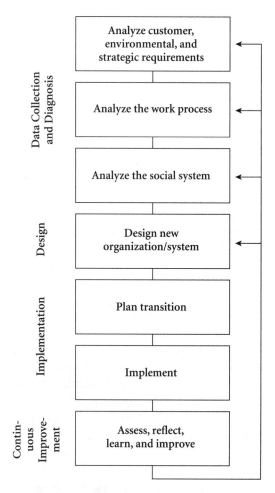

Figure 36.1. The High-Performance Work Systems Design Process.

The fifth and sixth steps involve implementation. In step 5, a transition plan is developed that accounts for both the technical and social/organizational issues involved in managing the change to the new organizational design (see Nadler, 1981). The change strategy needs to understand, account for, and manage the predictable issues of power, anxiety, and control that arise any time a significant organizational change is implemented. In step 6, the transition plans are executed.

An important feature of the design process is a seventh step, which is continuous. Once the design is in place, there needs to be some form of assessment to determine how well the new work system is functioning. Even a new and innovative work system design can become rigid and unresponsive to change over time. There is a tendency to institutionalize practices and processes that have succeeded, and this institutionalization makes the work system less responsive to change. The key is to create some mechanism to ensure renewal and to build in the capacity to reconfigure the work design as the environment, customer requirements, or work technology changes. Periodic assessment can serve as a catalyst for renewal. Assessment, reflection, learning, and improvement activities provide the HPWS units with the ability to reshape themselves over time.

Design and Redesign

So far, we have talked about design as a generic activity, ignoring whether the design is of a new or an existing organization. Although the same basic process would be used in both situations, some significant differences should be noted. The most critical point is that it is much easier to design a new setting than it is to redesign an existing work system. In fact, the success rate for HPWS design of new "greenfield" organizations is much higher than the success rate for the redesign of existing organizations. Most of this difference can be attributed to problems of change management—the natural resistance to change by those who have a vested interest in the existing organization. People outside the work units, such as middle-level managers and staff specialists, may feel threatened by HPWS, particularly because it reduces their day-to-day control. In addition, there are the costs associated with redesign, including downtime for transition, capital investment, and disruption of the work process.

The implication is that in redesign (versus design) initiatives, the change management issues require extra attention, particularly in the early stages. It is usually necessary to invest in education of those outside the work unit who will be impacted by the change and to develop a support system that can help manage the political dynamics associated with the redesign.

OTHER ORGANIZATIONAL IMPROVEMENT STRATEGIES

High-performance work systems is one of a number of organizational improvement strategies and approaches that have come into broad use in recent years and will be increasingly employed in the years to come (Nadler, 1989). Of course, many other different improvement strategies are being discovered and employed by organizations, and to avoid confusion, it may be useful to briefly discuss the relationship between HPWS and some of these other approaches.

High-performance work systems is perhaps most directly linked with what might be called *strategic organizational design,* or the design of complex organizations starting from the top down. The focus of strategic design is on the architecture of major organizational units and the methods of linking those units together. Innovative strategic designs have begun to focus on new ways of structuring and linking groups through network organizations, joint ventures, alliances, flat hierarchies, and so on. HPWS is, in contrast, a "bottom-up" design process, starting with the work and the external requirements. HPWS and strategic organizational design are complementary. Although there are many examples of highly successful HPWS design efforts focusing only on a particular part or level of the organization (for example, manufacturing plants), HPWS units are likely to be more successful when the design of the larger organization is consistent with HPWS principles and is oriented toward responding to the same customer and environmental requirements. Similarly, strategic designs are more likely to be successful when they do more than just "move around the boxes" but rather lead to subsequent reconfiguration of the real work and how that work is managed.

Another organizational improvement strategy, *employee involvement,* is based on the research finding that when employees are involved they are more motivated to perform, their commitment to the organization increases, quality increases, and they contribute to better decision making. More and more organizations have moved toward adopting high-involvement management as a core principle (Lawler, 1986). In that context, HPWS is an intensive form of high-involvement management. It takes involvement to its extreme, by creating self-managed organizations.

In many organizations, HPWS work has occurred in the context of unionized environments. HPWS has thus been related to some form of labor-management collaboration. Indeed, the flexibility and ambiguity inherent in HPWS design run counter to the traditional orientation of the labor contract toward work rules, clear job specifications, and similar devices aimed at clarifying roles and responsibilities in the workplace. Where organized labor is involved, the more successful companies have therefore engaged the union as a valued partner in the work redesign effort.

Many other organizations have begun major drives toward *total quality management.* This strategy is based on the concepts of quality improvement, including fulfillment of customer requirements, statistical process control, management by prevention, and continuous improvement. Total quality management involves the systematic application of quality principles to the entire enterprise in a planned process of change over years. HPWS is highly consistent with total quality; in fact, many of the organizations that have pioneered HPWS have also been pioneers in total quality. Many of the principles of HPWS (for example, customer-driven design and control of variance at the source) are identical to principles of total quality. HPWS, however, does fill a potential void in many total quality approaches. Most total quality processes include a step where the work process is designed (or redesigned). Although methods to control the work process are specified, in practice there is little guidance as to how to design or configure these work processes. Therefore, people tend to fall back on their unconscious models of design (machine bureaucracy) and end up creating work processes in the one man/one job mode. HPWS provides the tools to aid in the application of total quality to major work processes.

CHAPTER THIRTY-SEVEN

Diversity as Strategy

David A. Thomas

When most of us think of Lou Gerstner and the turnaround of IBM, we see a great business story. A less-told but integral part of that success is a people story—one that has dramatically altered the composition of an already diverse corporation and created millions of dollars in new business.

By the time Gerstner took the helm in 1993, IBM already had a long history of progressive management when it came to civil rights and equal employment. Indeed, few of the company's executives would have identified workforce diversity as an area of strategic focus. But when Gerstner took a look at his senior executive team, he felt it didn't reflect the diversity of the market for talent or IBM's customers and employees. To rectify the imbalance, in 1995 Gerstner launched a diversity task-force initiative that became a cornerstone of IBM's HR strategy. The effort continued through Gerstner's tenure and remains today under current CEO Sam Palmisano. Rather than attempt to eliminate discrimination by deliberately ignoring differences among employees, IBM created eight task forces, each focused on a different group such as Asians, gays and lesbians, and women. The goal of the initiative was to uncover and understand differences among the groups and find ways to appeal to a broader set of employees and customers.

The initiative required a lot of work, and it didn't happen overnight—the first task force convened almost two years after Gerstner's arrival. But the IBM of today looks very different from the IBM of 1995. The number of female executives worldwide has increased by 370 percent. The number of ethnic minority executives born in the United States has increased by 233 percent. Fifty-two percent of IBM's Worldwide Management Council (WMC), the top fifty-two executives who determine corporate strategy, is composed of women, ethnic minorities born in the United States, and non-U.S. citizens. The organization has seen the number of self-identified gay, lesbian, bisexual, and transgender executives increase by 733 percent and the number of executives with disabilities more than triple.

But diversity at IBM is about more than expanding the talent pool. When I asked Gerstner what had driven the success of the task forces, he said, "We made diversity a market-based issue. . . . It's about understanding our markets, which are diverse and multicultural." By deliberately seeking ways to more effectively reach a broader range of customers, IBM has seen significant bottom-line results. For example, the work of the women's task force and other constituencies led IBM to establish its Market Development organization, a group focused on growing the market of multicultural and women-owned businesses in the United States. One tactic: partnering with vendors to provide much-needed sales and service support to small and midsize businesses, a niche well populated with minority and female buyers. In 2001, the organization's activities accounted for more than $300 million in revenue compared with $10 million in 1998. Based on a recommendation from the people with disabilities task force, in October 2001 IBM launched an initiative focused on making all of its products more broadly accessible to take advantage of new legislation—an amendment to the federal Rehabilitation Act requiring that government agencies make accessibility a criterion for awarding federal contracts. IBM executives estimate this effort will produce more than a billion dollars in revenue during the next five to ten years.

Over the past two years, I have interviewed more than fifty IBM employees—ranging from midlevel managers all the way up to Gerstner and Palmisano—about the task force effort and spent a great deal of time with Ted Childs, IBM's vice president of Global Workforce Diversity and Gerstner's primary partner in guiding this change process. What they described was a significant philosophical shift—from a long tradition of minimizing differences to amplifying them and seizing on the business opportunities they present.

CONSTRUCTIVE DISRUPTION

Gerstner knew he needed to signal that diversity was a strategic goal, and he knew that establishing task forces would make a powerful impression on employees. Early in his tenure, Gerstner had convened various task forces to resolve a range of strategic choices and issues. He used the same structure to refine and achieve IBM's diversity-related objectives.

Gerstner and Childs wanted people to understand that this was truly something new. IBM had a long practice of being blind to differences and gathering demographic information only to ensure that hiring and promotion decisions didn't favor any particular group. So this new approach of calling attention to differences, with the hope of learning from them and making improvements to the business, was a radical departure. To effectively deliver the message and signal dramatic change, IBM kicked off the task forces on Bastille Day, July 14, 1995. "We chose Bastille Day . . . because it's considered to be a historic day of social disruption," Childs told me. "We were looking for some constructive disruption."

Each task force comprised fifteen to twenty senior managers, cutting across the company's business units, from one of the following demographic employee constituencies: Asians; blacks (African-American and of African descent); gays/lesbians/bisexuals/transgender individuals (GLBT); Hispanics; white men; Native Americans; people with disabilities; and women. To be eligible, members had to meet two criteria: executive rank and member of the constituency. (Three of the groups—people with disabilities, Native Americans, and GLBT—didn't have enough representation in the executive ranks to fill the task forces, so membership also included midlevel managers.) Members were chosen by Ted Childs and Tom Bouchard, then senior vice president of human resources, based on their knowledge of and experiences with the top executive team. In particular, Childs sought executives who had spoken to him or to a colleague in his office about their own experiences and perceptions that diversity was an untapped business resource; he persuaded those individuals to participate by describing the effort as a chance to make a difference and eliminate some of the roadblocks they may have faced in their careers.

Each task force also had two or more executive cochairs who were members of the constituency. For these roles, Childs and Bouchard recruited high-performing, well-respected senior managers and junior executives who were at least at the director level. Each task force was also assigned an executive sponsor from the WMC, who was charged with learning about the relevant constituency's concerns, opportunities, and strategies and with serving as a liaison to top management. The executive sponsors were senior vice presidents, and most reported directly to Gerstner. They were selected by Bouchard and Childs based on their willingness to support the change process and on the potential for synergies within their given business areas.

The first sponsor of the women's task force, for instance, was the senior vice president (SVP) of sales and marketing worldwide. Childs knew that the company's senior executives believed that potential buyers in many countries outside of the United States wouldn't work with female executives and that this could interfere with women's success in international assignments. By connecting this SVP with the women's task force, Bouchard and Childs hoped these barriers could be better understood—and that opportunities for women to advance in the sales organization might improve. Similarly, the SVP for research and development was asked to sponsor the people with disabilities task force, with the expectation that if he could get closer to the day-to-day experiences of people with disabilities in his own organization, he would gain new insights into the development of accessible products.

Sponsors were not necessarily constituents of their groups. The sponsor for the white men's task force was a woman; the sponsor for the women's task force, a man. Indeed, there was a certain advantage to having sponsors who didn't come from the groups they represented. It meant that they and the task force members would have to learn from their differences. A sponsor would have to dig deep into the issues of the task force to represent its views and interests to other WMC members.

In addition to having a sponsor, cochairs, and members, each task force was assigned one or two HR employees and a senior HR executive for administrative support, as well as a lawyer for legal guidance. The groups also received logistical and research support from Childs's

Global Workforce Diversity organization, which was responsible for all of IBM's equal employment and work/life balance programs.

Once the task forces had been set up and launched, Bouchard sent an e-mail to every U.S. employee detailing the task forces and their missions and underscoring how important the initiative was to the company. In his message, he acknowledged IBM's heritage of respecting diversity and defined the new effort in business terms. Here's an excerpt from the e-mail:

> To sustain [IBM's recognition for diversity leadership] and strengthen our competitive edge, we have launched eight executive-led task forces representing the following IBM employee constituencies. . . . We selected these communities because collectively they are IBM, and they reflect the diversity of our marketplace.

He also encouraged employees to respond with specific suggestions for how to make IBM a more inclusive environment. Childs then compiled more than 2,000 responses to the e-mail and channeled them to the appropriate task forces. As a result of these suggestions, the task forces focused on the following areas for evaluation and improvement: communications, staffing, employee benefits, workplace flexibility, training and education, advertising and marketplace opportunities, and external relations.

The initial charge of the task forces was to take six months to research and report back to the CEO and the WMC on four questions: What is necessary for your constituency to feel welcome and valued at IBM? What can the corporation do, in partnership with your group, to maximize your constituency's productivity? What can the corporation do to influence your constituency's buying decisions, so that IBM is seen as a preferred solution provider? And which external organizations should IBM form relationships with to better understand the needs of your constituency?

At first, skepticism prevailed. Here's what one white male executive told me:

> This whole idea of bringing together people in the workplace and letting them form these groups was really repugnant on its face to a lot of people, and of course IBM had been a nonunion company in the United States for a long, long time. I mean, having groups was like letting them into your living room.

And from a black executive:

> I was somewhat skeptical, and there was a level of reluctance in terms of how successful this would ultimately become in IBM, given some of the complex issues around the topic of diversity.

The groups faced other challenges as well. When the women's task force met for the first time, many members were relieved to hear that some of their colleagues were sharing similar struggles to balance work and family; at the same time, some of IBM's women believed strongly that female executives should choose between having children and having a career. The dissenting opinions made it more difficult to present a united front to the rest of senior management and secure support for the group's initiatives.

Task force members also disagreed on tactics. Some within the black task force, for instance, advocated for a conservative approach, fearing that putting a spotlight on the group would be perceived as asking for unearned preferences, and, even worse, might encourage the stereotype that blacks are less capable. But most in the group felt that more aggressive action would be needed to break down the barriers facing blacks at IBM.

In both cases, members engaged in lengthy dialogue to understand various points of view, and, in light of very real deadlines for reporting back, were forced to agree on concrete proposals for accomplishing sometimes competing goals. The women's group concluded that IBM needed to partner with its female employees in making work and family life more compatible. The black group decided it needed to clarify the link between its concerns and those of the company— making it clear that the members were raising business issues and that the task force effort was not intended to favor any group.

During the six months of the initial phase, Childs checked in with each group periodically and held monthly meetings to ensure that each was staying focused. The check-ins were also meant to facilitate information sharing across groups, especially if several were grappling with similar issues. The task forces' work involved collecting data from their constituencies, examining internal archival data to identify personnel trends, and reviewing external data to understand IBM's labor and customer markets. Their most critical task was to interpret the data as a means of identifying solutions and opportunities for IBM. Task forces met several times a month, in subcommittees or in their entirety, and at the end of the research period, Childs met with each group to determine its top issues—or the "vital few." (See Exhibit 37.1.) These were defined as the issues that were of greatest importance to the group and would have the most impact if addressed. Childs and the task force cochairs also realized that not addressing these concerns would hamper the credibility of the initiative with frontline employees.

Charged with getting to know their constituencies' needs and concerns, IBM's eight diversity task forces gathered data on personnel trends as well as labor and customer markets for their respective groups. Interpreting that information led to the list of issues below—what IBM calls the "vital few," as identified by each of the task forces. The task force members then used the vital few to shape their thinking about possible business and development opportunities.

Asians
Stereotyping
Networking and Mentoring
Employee Development and Talent Pipelines
Target Advertising and Marketing

Blacks
Representation, Retention, and Networking
Education and Training
Target Advertising and Marketing

People with Disabilities
Recruiting
Target Advertising and Marketing
Centralized Fund for Accommodations
Benefits Review
New World HQ Building (Accessibility)
Online Help for Self-Identification

White Men
Executive Accountability
Education and Awareness
Aging
Work/Life Balance

Women
Networking
Career Advancement
Succession Planning
Work/Life Balance
Flexibility as a Business Strategy
Executives' Personal Commitment to Advancing Women
Target Advertising and Marketing

Gays/Lesbians/Bisexuals/Transgender Individuals
Domestic Partner Benefits
Education and Training
Networking
Target Advertising and Marketing
Online Help for Self-Identification

Hispanics
Recruiting
Employee Development and Talent Pipelines
Target Advertising and Marketing

Native Americans
Recruiting
Community Outreach
Networking

Exhibit 37.1.   The Vital Few Issues: Employees' Biggest Diversity Concerns.

On December 1, 1995, the task forces met to share their initial findings. Again, the date was chosen with the idea of sending a message to employees: it was the fortieth anniversary of Rosa Parks's refusal to give up her seat on a bus in Montgomery, Alabama, to a white passenger. That act, of course, led to her arrest and ignited the Montgomery bus boycotts that ushered in the modern U.S. civil rights movement. Just as the Bastille Day launch signaled a release from old ways of thinking, the timing of this meeting indicated a desire for a radically new approach to diversity.

Several of the task forces shared many of the same issues, such as development and promotion, senior management's communication of its commitment to diversity, and the need to focus on recruiting a diverse pool of employees, especially in engineering and science-related positions. Other concerns were specific to particular groups, including domestic partner benefits (identified by the GLBT task force) and issues of access to buildings and technology (raised by the people with disabilities task force). Overall, the findings made it clear that workforce diversity was the bridge between the workplace and the marketplace—in other words, greater diversity in the workplace could help IBM attract a more diverse customer set. A focus on diversity was, in short, a major business opportunity.

All eight task forces recommended that the company create diversity groups beyond those at the executive level. In response, IBM in 1997 formed employee network groups as a way for others in the company to participate. The network groups today run across constituencies, offering a variety of perspectives on issues that are local or unique to particular units. They offer a forum for employees to interact electronically and in person to discuss issues specific to their constituencies. (For more on these groups, see the case "Engage Employees.")

ENGAGE EMPLOYEES

IBM's diversity task forces asked that the company allow employees who were not at the executive level to get more involved in the effort. The company did, and diversity councils and employee network groups were born.

The diversity councils, groups of employees across diverse constituencies, were created specifically to address local or unique diversity issues. Through these seventy-two councils, IBM seeks to ensure that its workforce represents an environment that visibly encourages and values the contributions and differences of employees from various backgrounds. The objectives include heightening employee awareness, increasing management sensitivity, and making the most out of a diverse workforce. For example, within IBM's R&D and engineering units, specific efforts have focused on women and minority retention and development in technology-related jobs.

The network groups came out of a grassroots initiative driven by employees and have a broader scope than the task forces or councils. IBM has 160 such groups, in which employees interact electronically and in person to discuss issues specific to their constituency. The black networks, for instance, have been helpful in connecting employees who are working in areas of the company where there are few blacks. Those who are part of the networks, especially at facilities located far from urban areas, feel less isolated and report greater job satisfaction.

Although diversity councils and employee network groups are independent from the task forces, all three frequently collaborate. The women's task force has started diversity councils and employee network groups globally, all of them in close communication with the task force. One area of focus has been the importance of mentoring women globally. IBM regions have tailored programs to the needs of women in various locations. The goal is to ensure that they receive advice, guidance, and support and share knowledge that is relevant to other constituencies. This has been accomplished via Web-based mentoring, job shadowing, and group mentoring. Additionally, material is available on IBM's intranet on how to have effective mentoring relationships. Several Web lectures have also been developed on this topic.

Another recommendation, this time put forth by the women's group, aimed to rectify a shortage in the talent pipeline of women in technology, identifying young girls' tendency to opt out of science and math in school as one of the causes. To encourage girls' interest in these disciplines, in 1999 a group of women engineers and scientists in Endicott, New York, ran a pilot "EXITE" (Exploring Interests in Technology and Engineering) camp. The program brought together 30 middle-school girls for a week that summer to learn about science and math in a fun, interactive way from female IBM employees. In 2000, the women's task force replicated the program in five other locations throughout the United States, reaching 400 girls, and in 2001 the program expanded internationally. In 2004, IBM will have a total of thirty-seven EXITE camps worldwide—fifteen in the United States, one in Canada, eight in Asia-Pacific, six in Europe, and seven in Latin America. After the girls attend camp, they are assigned an IBM female scientist or engineer as a mentor for one year.

Since 1999, IBM has reached 3,000 girls through EXITE camps. In 2003 alone, 900 girls attended, and in 2004, 1,100 will have gone through the program. In collaboration with IBM's technology group, the women's task force also created a steering committee focused on retaining women in technology currently at IBM and attracting female scientists from universities.

As for external initiatives that arose from the task forces, IBM's Market Development (MD) unit came directly out of the groups' responses to the third question: What can IBM do to influence your constituency's buying decisions, so that the company is seen as a preferred solution provider? It became clear that IBM wasn't well positioned in relation to the market's fastest growing entrepreneurial segments—female- and minority-owned businesses. The MD was formed as a unit of the Small and Medium-Sized Business Sales and Marketing organization. Initially, the group helped IBM revamp its communications strategy for reaching female- and minority-owned companies. Its role has since evolved into identifying and supporting sales and marketing strategies aimed at these important segments.

The MD's efforts have directly translated into hundreds of millions of dollars in new revenue. More important to IBM's senior executives, the MD is elevating the company's overall level of cultural competence as it responds to the needs of IBM's diverse customer base. A case in point is advertising, where the MD convened teams from the task forces and the advertising department to create constituency casting guidelines and other communications. These changes have helped ensure appropriate representation of constituencies in all aspects of the company's marketing, with the guidelines forming the basis for ongoing discussions about how to reach and relate effectively to IBM's diverse customer base.

The people with disabilities task force (PWD), which initially focused on compliance with accessibility laws, began in 2001 to think about making the leap from compliance to market initiatives. That same year, Ted Childs arranged for each task force to meet with senior management, including Sam Palmisano, then IBM's president. The PWD task force leaders took the opportunity to point out the tremendous market potential in government contracts if IBM made its products more accessible. Palmisano agreed, and PWD received the green light it needed to advance its projects.

One reason for the increased focus on accessible technology was that in June 2001, the U.S. Congress implemented legislation mandating that all new IT equipment and services purchased by federal agencies must be accessible. This legislation—known as Section 508—makes accessibility a more important decision criterion than price in many bid situations, thus creating an opportunity for accessibility IT leaders to gain market share, charge a price premium, or both, from federal buyers. In addition to legislation, other indicators made it clear that the demand for accessibility was growing: a World Health Organization estimate of more than 750 million disabled people across the globe, with a collective buying power of $461 billion, and an increase in the number of aging baby boomers in need of accessible technology.

IBM believes that business opportunities will grow as countries around the world implement similar legislation. Furthermore, the private-sector opportunity for accessible technology could be far greater than that of the government as companies address a growing aging population. IBM's worldwide Accessibility Centers comprise special teams that evaluate existing or future IBM technologies for their possible use in making products accessible. There are now a total of six IBM Accessibility Centers, in the United States, Europe, and Japan.

PILLARS OF CHANGE

Any major corporate change will succeed only if a few key factors are in place: strong support from company leaders, an employee base that is fully engaged with the initiative, management practices that are integrated and aligned with the effort, and a strong and well-articulated business case for action. IBM's diversity task forces benefited from all four.

Demonstrate Leadership Support

It's become a cliché to say that leadership matters, but the issue merits discussion here because diversity is one of the areas in which executive leadership is often ineffectual. Executives' espoused beliefs are frequently inconsistent with their behavior, and they typically underestimate how much the corporation really needs to change to achieve its diversity goals. That's because diversity strategies tend to lay out lofty goals without providing the structures to educate senior executives in the specific challenges faced by various constituencies. In addition, these strategies often don't provide models that teach or encourage new behaviors.

IBM has taken several approaches to helping executives deepen their awareness and understanding. To begin with, the structure of the task forces—how they operate and who is on them—immerses executive sponsors in the specific challenges faced by the employee constituency groups. The groups are a formal mechanism for learning, endorsed at the highest levels of the company.

Second, the chief diversity officer, Ted Childs, acts as a partner with the CEO as well as coach and adviser to other executives. In addition to educating them on specific issues, as he did when the company decided to offer domestic partner benefits, Childs also works to ensure that they behave in ways that are consistent with the company's diversity strategy. A senior executive described Childs's role as a coach and teacher:

> I know that he's had a number of conversations with very senior people in the company where he's just sat down with them and said, "Listen, you don't get it, and you need to get it. And I care about you, and I care about this company. I care about the people who are affected by the way you're behaving, and so I owe it to you to tell you that. And here's how you don't get it. Here's what you need to do to change."

And third, Gerstner and later Palmisano not only sanctioned the task force process but actively sought to be role models themselves. A number of the executives I interviewed were struck by Gerstner's interest and active involvement in the development of high-potential minority and female senior managers and junior executives; he took a personal interest in how they were being mentored and what their next jobs would be. He also challenged assumptions about when people could be ready for general management assignments. In one case, Gerstner and his team were discussing the next job for a high-potential female executive. Most felt that she needed a bigger job in her functional area, but Gerstner felt that the proposed job, while involving more responsibility, would add little to the candidate's development. Instead she was given a general management assignment—and the team got a signal from the CEO about his commitment to diversity. His behavior communicated a sense of appreciation and accountability for people development. Indeed, accountability for results became as critical in this domain as it was for all business goals.

Gerstner also modeled desired behaviors in his interactions with his direct reports. One of them told me this story:

> During a board of directors' dinner, I had to go to [my daughter's] "back-to-school night," the one night a year when you meet the

teachers. I had been at the board meeting that day. I was going to be at the board meeting the next day. But it was the dinner that posed a problem, and I said, "Lou, I'll do whatever you want, but this is the position I am in," and . . . he didn't even blink. He said, "Go to back-to-school night. That is more important." And then . . . he told the board at dinner why I wasn't there and why it was so important . . . to make it possible for working parents to have very big jobs but still be involved parents. He never told me that he told the board. But the board told me the next day. They . . . said, "You should know that Lou not only said where you were but gave a couple minute talk about how important it was for IBM to act in this way."

CEO leadership and modeling didn't stop when Gerstner left. One senior executive who is a more recent arrival to the WMC described how Palmisano communicates the importance of the diversity initiative:

Executive involvement and buy-in are critical. Sam has played a personal and very important role. He personally asked each task force to come and report its progress and agenda to him. He spent time with the [task force that I sponsor] and had a detailed review of what we are doing on the customer set. What are we focused on internally? How can he help in his role as CEO? He's really made it clear to the senior-level executives that being good at [leading the diversity initiative] is part of our job.

Engage Employees as Partners

Although the six-month task force effort was consistent with IBM's history of promoting equal opportunity, the use of the task force structure to address issues of diversity represented a significant culture shift. IBM was an organization that had discouraged employees from organizing around any interest not specifically defined by the requirements of their jobs. The idea of employees organizing to advocate was anathema. One white male executive said, "Does this mean that we can have a communist cell here? Are we going to have hundreds and hundreds of these?" The skepticism reached up to the highest levels: When Childs first proposed the task force strategy, Gerstner asked him one question: "Why?"

But in the end, IBM's task force structure paved the way for employee buy-in because executives then had to invite constituent groups to partner with them in addressing the diversity challenge. The partnerships worked because three essential components were in place: mutual expectations, mutual influence, and trust.

When the task forces were commissioned, Childs and Gerstner set expectations and made sure that roles and responsibilities were unambiguous. Initially, the task forces' charters were short, only six months (the groups are still active today), and their mission was clear: to explore the issues, opportunities, and strategies affecting their constituencies and customers. Once this work was done, it fell to the corporation's senior executives to respond and to report on the task forces' progress at various junctures to the WMC. Gerstner and Childs followed up with the task force sponsors to ensure that the groups were gathering meaningful information and connecting it to the business.

The task forces' work has evolved to focus on more tactical issues, and the organization has demonstrated its willingness to be influenced, committing significant resources to efforts suggested by the groups. Trust was also built as the task force structure allowed employees more face time with executives—executives they would likely not have had a chance to meet—and provided new opportunities for mentoring. According to one task force participant:

> What got me to trust that this was a real commitment by the WMC was when I saw them ask for our advice, engage us in dialogue, and then take action. They didn't just do whatever we said, but the rationale for actions was always shared. It made me feel like our opinions were respected as businesspeople who bring a particular perspective to business challenges.

The task force structure has been copied on a smaller scale within specific business units. Even without a mandate from corporate brass, most units have created their own diversity councils, offering local support for achieving each unit's specific diversity goals. Here, too, the employee partnership model prevails.

Integrate Diversity with Management Practices

Sustaining change requires that diversity become an integrated part of the company's management practices. This was a priority for Gerstner, who told me:

> If you were to go back and look at ten years' worth of executive committee discussions, you would find two subjects, and only two, that

appeared on every one of the agendas. One was the financial performance, led by our CFO. The second was a discussion of management changes, promotions, moves, and so on, led by our HR person.

In my interviews, among the most frequently mentioned diversity-related HR practices was the five-minute drill, which began with Gerstner's top team and has cascaded down from the chairman to two levels down from the CEO. The five-minute drill takes place during the discussion of management talent at the corporate and business unit levels. During meetings of the senior team, executives are expected at any moment to be able to discuss any high-potential manager. According to interviewees, an explicit effort is made to ensure that minorities and females are discussed along with white males. The result has been to make the executives more accountable for spotting and grooming high-potential minority managers both in their own areas and across the business. Now that it's been made explicit that IBM executives need to watch for female and minority talent, they are more open to considering and promoting these individuals when looking to fill executive jobs.

Managing diversity is also one of the core competencies used to assess managers' performance, and it's included in the mandatory training and orientation of new managers. As one executive responsible for designing parts of this leadership curriculum commented, "We want people to understand that effectively managing and developing a diverse workforce is an integral part of what it means to manage at IBM."

Both Gerstner and Palmisano have been clear that holding managers accountable for diversity-related results is key. Gerstner noted, "We did not set quotas, but we did set goals and made people aware of the people in their units who they needed to be accountable for developing." And Palmisano said, "I reinforce to our executives that this is not HR's responsibility; it is up to us to make sure that we are developing our talent. There is a problem if, at the end of the day, that pool of talent is not diverse."

Link Diversity Goals to Business Goals

From the beginning, Gerstner and Childs insisted that the task force effort create a link between IBM's diversity goals and its business goals—that this would be good business, not good philanthropy. The task force efforts have led to a series of significant accomplishments.

For instance, IBM's efforts to develop the client base among women-owned businesses have quickly expanded to include a focus on Asian, black, Hispanic, mature (senior citizens), and Native American markets. The Market Development organization has grown revenue in the company's Small and Medium-Sized Business Sales and Marketing organization from $10 million in 1998 to hundreds of millions of dollars in 2003.

Another result of the task forces' work has been to create executive partner programs targeting demographic customer segments. In 2001, IBM began assigning executives to develop relationships with the largest women- and minority-owned businesses in the United States. This was important not only because these business sectors are growing fast but because their leaders are often highly visible role models, and their IT needs will grow and become increasingly more sophisticated. Already, these assignments have yielded impressive revenue streams with several of these companies.

The task force effort has also affected IBM's approach to supplier diversity. Although the company has for decades fostered relationships with minority-owned businesses as well as businesses owned by the disabled, the work of the task forces has expanded the focus of IBM's supplier diversity program to a broader set of constituencies and provided new insights on the particular challenges each faced. The purpose of the supplier diversity program is to create a level playing field. It's important to note, though, that procurement contracts are awarded on the merits of the bid—including price and quality—not on the diversity of the vendor. In 2003, IBM did business worth more than $1.5 billion with over 500 diverse suppliers, up from $370 million in 1998.

The cynics have come around. One black executive said, "Yes, I think [the initiative] has been extremely effective if you look at where we started back in the mid-nineties. I can tell you that I was somewhat skeptical [at first]." Another commented on the growing acceptance of the effort across IBM: "You can see that support actually changed over time from 'I'm not sure what this is about' to . . . a complete understanding that diversity and the focus on diversity make good business sense."

Perhaps the best evidence of the task forces' success is that the initiative not only continues but has spread and has had lasting impact. In more than one instance, after an executive became a task force sponsor, his or her division or business unit made significant progress on its own diversity goals. Leaders of some of the task forces described seeing their sponsors grow in their ability to understand, articulate, and take action on the issues identified by their groups. One executive described how the task force sponsor experience had been important for him as a business leader and personally, as well as for IBM:

> There is no doubt that this is critical for how we manage the research organization, because of the need for diverse thought. It has affected me substantially because . . . I became involved with diverse populations outside of IBM that I may well not have been connected with if it hadn't been for my involvement with the task force. I'm on the Gallaudet University [school for the deaf] board. Without the task force, I would have never thought of it. And so this has been a terrific awakening, a personal awakening. . . . Since it's focusing particularly on accessibility, we can help in a lot of ways with technology for accessibility, and Gallaudet turns out to be, for the subset of people who are hearing impaired, a terrific place to prototype solutions in this space.

Such comments were not atypical. In many instances, the sponsorship experience was developmental in important and unexpected ways. Having eight task forces means that in a group of fifty-two top leaders, there is always a critical mass strategically connected to the issues. Today, more than half of the WMC members have been engaged with the task forces in the role of sponsor or task force leader prior to being promoted to the senior executive level.

For IBM, that makes good business sense. The entire effort was designed to help the company develop deeper insights into its major markets, with a direct tie to two of Gerstner's central dictates. One: IBM needed to get closer to its customers and become more externally focused. Two: it needed to focus on talent—attracting, retaining, developing, and promoting the best people. On both measures, the company has come a long way.

CHAPTER THIRTY-EIGHT

The Leader's New Work

Building Learning Organizations

Peter M. Senge

H uman beings are designed for learning. No one has to teach an infant to walk, or talk, or master the spatial relationships needed to stack eight building blocks that don't topple. Children come fully equipped with an insatiable drive to explore and experiment. Unfortunately, the primary institutions of our society are oriented predominantly toward controlling rather than learning, rewarding individuals for performing for others rather than for cultivating their natural curiosity and impulse to learn. The young child entering school discovers quickly that the name of the game is getting the right answer and avoiding mistakes—a mandate no less compelling to the aspiring manager.

"Our prevailing system of management has destroyed our people," writes W. Edwards Deming, leader in the quality movement (Senge, 1990). "People are born with intrinsic motivation, self-esteem, dignity, curiosity to learn, joy in learning. The forces of destruction begin with toddlers—a prize for the best Halloween costume, grades in school, gold stars, and on up through the university. On the job, people, teams, divisions are ranked—reward for the one at the top, punishment at the bottom. MBO quotas, incentive pay, business plans, put together separately, division by division, cause further loss, unknown and unknowable."

Ironically, by focusing on performing for someone else's approval, corporations create the very conditions that predestine them to mediocre performance. Over the long run, superior performance depends on superior learning. A Shell study showed that, according to former planning director Arie de Geus, "a full one-third of the Fortune '500' industrials listed in 1970 had vanished by 1983" (de Geus, 1988). Today, the average lifetime of the largest industrial enterprises is probably less than *half* the average lifetime of a person in an industrial society. On the other hand, de Geus and his colleagues at Shell also found a small number of companies that survived for seventy-five years or longer. Interestingly, the key to their survival was the ability to run "experiments in the margin," to continually explore new business and organizational opportunities that create potential new sources of growth.

If anything, the need for understanding how organizations learn and accelerating that learning is greater today than ever before. The old days when a Henry Ford, Alfred Sloan, or Tom Watson *learned for the organization* are gone. In an increasingly dynamic, interdependent, and unpredictable world, it is simply no longer possible for anyone to "figure it all out at the top." The old model, "the top thinks and the local acts," must now give way to integrating thinking and acting at all levels. While the challenge is great, so is the potential payoff. "The person who figures out how to harness the collective genius of the people in his or her organization," according to former Citibank CEO Walter Wriston, "is going to blow the competition away."

ADAPTIVE LEARNING AND GENERATIVE LEARNING

The prevailing view of learning organizations emphasizes increased adaptability. Given the accelerating pace of change, or so the standard view goes, "the most successful corporation of the 1990s," according to *Fortune* magazine, "will be something called a learning organization, a consummately adaptive enterprise" (Dumaine, 1989). As the Shell study shows, examples of traditional authoritarian bureaucracies that responded too slowly to survive in changing business environments are legion.

But increasing adaptiveness is only the first stage in moving toward learning organizations. The impulse to learn in children goes deeper than desires to respond and adapt more effectively to environmental change. The impulse to learn, at its heart, is an impulse to be generative, to expand our capability. This is why leading corporations are focusing on *generative* learning, which is about creating, as well as *adaptive* learning, which is about coping. The distinction between adaptive and generative learning has its roots in the distinction between what Argyris and Schön have called their "single-loop" learning, in which individuals or groups adjust their behavior relative to fixed goals, norms, and assumptions, and "double-loop" learning, in which goals, norms, and assumptions, as well as behavior, are open to change (for example, see Argyris & Schön, 1978).

The total quality movement in Japan illustrates the evolution from adaptive to generative learning. With its emphasis on continuous experimentation and feedback, the total quality movement has been the first wave in building learning organizations. But Japanese firms' view of serving the customer has evolved. In the early years of total quality, the focus was on "fitness to standard," making a product reliably so that it would do what its designers intended it to do and what the firm told its customers it would do. Then came a focus on "fitness to need," understanding better what the customer wanted and then providing products that reliably met those needs. Today, leading edge firms seek to understand and meet the "latent need" of the customer—what customers might truly value but have never experienced or would never think to ask for. As one Detroit executive commented recently, "You could never produce the Mazda Miata solely from market research. It required a leap of imagination to see what the customer *might* want."[1]

Generative learning, unlike adaptive learning, requires new ways of looking at the world, whether in understanding customers or in understanding how to better manage a business. For years, U.S. manufacturers sought competitive advantage in aggressive controls on inventories, incentives against overproduction, and rigid adherence to production forecasts. Despite these incentives, their performance was eventually eclipsed by Japanese firms who saw the challenges of manufacturing differently. They realized that eliminating delays in the

---

[1]All unattributed quotes are from personal communications with the author.

production process was the key to reducing instability and improving cost, productivity, and service. They worked to build networks of relationships with trusted suppliers and to redesign physical production processes so as to reduce delays in materials procurement, production set up, and in-process inventory—a much higher-leverage approach to improving both cost and customer loyalty.

As Boston Consulting Group's George Stalk has observed, the Japanese saw the significance of delays because they saw the process of order entry, production scheduling, materials procurement, production, and distribution *as an integrated system.* "What distorts the system so badly is time," observed Stalk—the multiple delays between events and responses. "These distortions reverberate throughout the system, producing disruptions, waste, and inefficiency" (Stalk, 1988). Generative learning requires seeing the systems that control events. When we fail to grasp the systemic source of problems, we are left to "push on" symptoms rather than eliminate underlying causes. The best we can ever do is adaptive learning.

THE LEADER'S NEW WORK

"I talk with people all over the country about learning organizations, and the response is always very positive," says William O'Brien, CEO of the Hanover Insurance companies. "If this type of organization is so widely preferred, why don't people create such organizations? I think the answer is leadership. People have no real comprehension of the type of commitment it requires to build such an organization" (Senge, 1990).

Our traditional view of leaders—as special people who set the direction, make the key decisions, and energize the troops—is deeply rooted in an individualistic and nonsystemic worldview. Especially in the West, leaders are *heroes*—great men (and occasionally women) who rise to the fore in times of crisis. So long as such myths prevail, they reinforce a focus on short-term events and charismatic heroes rather than on systemic forces and collective learning.

Leadership in learning organizations centers on subtler and ultimately more important work. In a learning organization, leaders' roles differ dramatically from that of the charismatic decision maker. Leaders are designers, teachers, and stewards. These roles require new skills: the ability to build shared vision, to bring to the surface and challenge prevailing mental models, and to foster more systemic patterns of thinking. In short, leaders in learning organizations are responsible for *building organizations* where people are continually expanding their capabilities to shape their future—that is, leaders are responsible for learning.

CREATIVE TENSION: THE INTEGRATING PRINCIPLE

Leadership in a learning organization starts with the principle of creative tension (Fritz, 1989, 1990). Creative tension comes from seeing clearly where we want to be, our "vision," and telling the truth about where we are, our "current reality." The gap between the two generates a natural tension (see Figure 38.1).

Creative tension can be resolved in two basic ways: by raising current reality toward the vision, or by lowering the vision toward current reality. Individuals, groups, and organizations who learn how to work with creative tension learn how to use the energy it generates to move reality more reliably toward their visions.

The principle of creative tension has long been recognized by leaders. Martin Luther King Jr. once said, "Just as Socrates felt that it was necessary to create a tension in the mind, so that individuals could rise from the bondage of myths and half truths . . . so must we . . . create the kind of tension in society that will help men rise from the dark depths of prejudice and racism" (King, 1986).

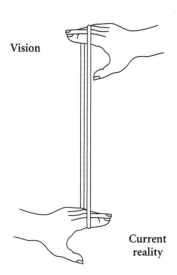

Vision

Current reality

Figure 38.1. The Principle of Creative Tension.

Without vision there is no creative tension. Creative tension cannot be generated from current reality alone. All the analysis in the world will never generate a vision. Many who are otherwise qualified to lead fail to do so because they try to substitute analysis for vision. They believe that, if only people understood current reality, they would surely feel the motivation to change. They are then disappointed to discover that people "resist" the personal and organizational changes that must be made to alter reality. What they never grasp is that the natural energy for changing reality comes from holding a picture of what might be that is more important to people than what is.

But creative tension cannot be generated from vision alone; it demands an accurate picture of current reality as well. Just as King had a dream, so too did he continually strive to "dramatize the shameful conditions" of racism and prejudice so that they could no longer be ignored. Vision without an understanding of current reality will more likely foster cynicism than creativity. The principle of creative tension teaches that *an accurate picture of current reality is just as important as a compelling picture of a desired future.*

Leading through creative tension is different from solving problems. In problem solving, the energy for change comes from attempting to get away from an aspect of current reality that is undesirable. With creative tension, the energy for change comes from the vision, from what we want to create, juxtaposed with current reality. Although the distinction may seem small, the consequences are not. Many people and organizations find themselves motivated to change only when their problems are bad enough to cause them to change. This works for a while, but the change process runs out of steam as soon as the problems driving the change become less pressing. With problem solving, the motivation for change is extrinsic. With creative tension, the motivation is intrinsic. This distinction mirrors the distinction between adaptive and generative learning.

NEW ROLES

The traditional authoritarian image of the leader as "the boss calling the shots" has been recognized as oversimplified and inadequate for some time. According to Edgar Schein, "Leadership is intertwined with culture formation." Building an organization's culture and shaping its evolution is the "unique and essential function" of leadership (see Schein, 1985; Selznick, 1957; Bennis & Nanus, 1985; Tichy & Devanna, 1986).

In a learning organization, the critical roles of leadership—designer, teacher, and steward—have antecedents in the ways leaders have contributed to building organizations in the past. But each role takes on new meaning in the learning organization and, as will be seen in the following sections, demands new skills and tools.

Leader as Designer

Imagine that your organization is an ocean liner and that you are "the leader." What is your role?

I have asked this question of groups of managers many times. The most common answer, not surprisingly, is "the captain." Others say, "The navigator, setting the direction." Still others say, "The helmsman, actually controlling the direction," or, "The engineer down there stoking the fire, providing energy," or, "The social director, making sure everybody's enrolled, involved, and communicating." Although these are legitimate leadership roles, there is another which, in many ways, eclipses them all in importance. Yet rarely does anyone mention it.

The neglected leadership role is the *designer* of the ship. No one has a more sweeping influence than the designer. What good does it do for the captain to say, "Turn starboard 30 degrees," when the designer has built a rudder that will only turn to port, or which takes six hours to turn to starboard? It's fruitless to be the leader in an organization that is poorly designed.

The functions of design, or what some have called *social architecture,* are rarely visible; they take place behind the scenes. The consequences that appear today are the result of work done long in the past, and work today will show its benefits far in the future. Those who aspire to lead out of a desire to control, or gain fame, or simply to be at the center of the action, will find little to attract them to the quiet design work of leadership.

But what, specifically, is involved in organizational design? "Organization design is widely misconstrued as moving around boxes and lines," says Hanover's O'Brien. "The first task of organization design concerns designing the governing ideas of purpose, vision, and core values by which people will live." Few acts of leadership have a more enduring impact on an organization than building a foundation of purpose and core values.

In 1982, Johnson & Johnson found itself facing a corporate nightmare when bottles of its best-selling Tylenol were tampered with, resulting in several deaths. The corporation's immediate response was to pull all Tylenol off the shelves of retail outlets. Thirty-one million capsules were destroyed, even though they were tested and found safe. Although the immediate cost was significant, no other action was possible given the firm's credo. Authored almost forty years earlier by president Robert Wood Johnson, Johnson & Johnson's credo states that permanent success is possible only when modern industry realizes that:

- Service to its customers comes first
- Service to its employees and management comes second
- Service to the community comes third
- Service to its stockholders, last

Such statements might seem like motherhood and apple pie to those who have not seen the way a clear sense of purpose and values can affect key business decisions. Johnson & Johnson's crisis management in this case was based on that credo. It was simple, it was right, and it worked.

If governing ideas constitute the first design task of leadership, the second design task involves the policies, strategies, and structures that translate guiding ideas into business decisions. Leadership theorist Philip Selznick calls policy and structure the "institutional embodiment of purpose" (Selznick, 1957). "Policy making (the rules that guide decisions) ought to be separated from decision making," says Jay Forrester (1965). "Otherwise, short-term pressures will usurp time from policy creation."

Traditionally, writers like Selznick and Forrester have tended to see policy making and implementation as the work of a small number of senior managers. But that view is changing. Both the dynamic business environment and the mandate of the learning organization to engage people at all levels now make it clear that this second design task is more subtle. Henry Mintzberg has argued that strategy is less a rational plan arrived at in the abstract and implemented throughout the organization than an "emergent phenomenon." Successful organizations "craft strategy" according to Mintzberg (1987), as they continually learn about shifting business conditions and balance what is desired and what is possible. The key is not getting the right strategy but fostering strategic thinking. "The choice of individual action is only part of . . . the policymaker's need," according to Mason and Mitroff (1981, p. 16). "More important is the need to achieve insight into the nature of the complexity and to formulate concepts and world views for coping with it."

Behind appropriate policies, strategies, and structures are effective learning processes; their creation is the third key design responsibility in learning organizations. This does not absolve senior managers of their strategic responsibilities. Actually, it deepens and extends those responsibilities. Now, they are not only responsible for ensuring that an organization have well-developed strategies and policies, but also for ensuring that processes exist whereby these are continually improved.

In the early 1970s, Shell was the weakest of the big seven oil companies. Today, Shell and Exxon are arguably the strongest, both in size and financial health. Shell's ascendance began with frustration. Around 1971 members of Shell's "Group Planning" in London began to foresee dramatic change and unpredictability in world oil markets. However, it proved impossible to persuade managers that the stable world of steady growth in oil demand and supply they had known for twenty years was about to change. Despite brilliant analysis and artful presentation, Shell's planners realized, in the words of Pierre Wack, that they "had failed to change behavior in much of the Shell organization" (Wack, 1985). Progress would probably have ended there, had the frustration not given way to a radically new view of corporate planning.

As they pondered this failure, the planners' view of their basic task shifted: "We no longer saw our task as producing a documented view of the future business environment five or ten years ahead. Our real target was the microcosm (the 'mental model') of our decision makers." Only when the planners reconceptualized their basic task as fostering learning rather than devising plans did their insights begin to have an impact. The initial tool used was "scenario analysis," through which planners encouraged operating managers to think through how they would manage in the future under different possible scenarios. It mattered not that the managers believed the planners' scenarios absolutely, only that they became engaged in ferreting out the implications. In this way, Shell's planners conditioned managers to be mentally prepared for a shift from low prices to high prices and from stability to instability. The results were significant. When OPEC became a reality, Shell quickly responded by increasing local operating company control (to enhance maneuverability in the new political environment), building buffer stocks, and accelerating development of non-OPEC sources—actions that its competitors took much more slowly or not at all.

Somewhat inadvertently, Shell planners had discovered the leverage of designing institutional learning processes, whereby, in the words of former planning director de Geus, "Management teams change their shared mental models of their company, their markets, and their competitors" (de Geus, 1988). Since then, "planning as learning" has become a byword at Shell, and Group Planning has continually sought out new learning tools that can be integrated into the planning process. Some of these are described below.

Leader as Teacher

"The first responsibility of a leader," writes retired Herman Miller CEO Max de Pree, "is to define reality" (de Pree, 1989, p. 9). Much of the leverage leaders can actually exert lies in helping people achieve more accurate, more insightful, and more *empowering* views of reality.

Leader as teacher does *not* mean leader as authoritarian expert whose job it is to teach people the "correct" view of reality. Rather, it is about helping everyone in the organization, oneself included, to gain more insightful views of current reality. This is in line with a popular emerging view of leaders as coaches, guides, or facilitators (Peters & Austin, 1985; Kouzes & Posner, 1987). In learning organizations, this teaching role is developed further by virtue of explicit attention to people's mental models and by the influence of the systems perspective.

The role of leader as teacher starts with bringing to the surface people's mental models of important issues. No one carries an organization, a market, or a state of technology in his or her head. What we carry in our heads are assumptions. These mental pictures of how the world works have a significant influence on how we perceive problems and opportunities, identify courses of action, and make choices.

One reason that mental models are so deeply entrenched is that they are largely tacit. Ian Mitroff (1988), in his study of General Motors, argues that an assumption that prevailed for years was that, in the United States, "Cars are status symbols. Styling is therefore more important than quality." The Detroit automakers didn't say, "We have a *mental model* that all people care about is styling" (pp. 66–67). Few actual managers would even say publicly that all people care about is styling. So long as the view remained unexpressed, there was little possibility of challenging its validity or forming more accurate assumptions.

But working with mental models goes beyond revealing hidden assumptions. "Reality," as perceived by most people in most organizations, means pressures that must be borne, crises that must be reacted to, and limitations that must be accepted. Leaders as teachers help people *restructure their views of reality* to see beyond the superficial conditions and events into the underlying causes of problems— and therefore to see new possibilities for shaping the future.

Specifically, leaders can influence people to view reality at three distinct levels: events, patterns of behavior, and systemic structure.

Systemic Structure
(Generative)
↓
Patterns of Behavior
(Responsive)
↓
Events
(Reactive)

The key question becomes, *where do leaders predominantly focus their own and their organization's attention?*

Contemporary society focuses predominantly on events. The media reinforces this perspective, with almost exclusive attention to short-term, dramatic events. This focus leads naturally to explaining what happens in terms of those events: "The Dow Jones average went up sixteen points because high fourth-quarter profits were announced yesterday."

Pattern-of-behavior explanations are rarer, in contemporary culture, than event explanations, but they do occur. "Trend analysis" is an example of seeing patterns of behavior. A good editorial that interprets a set of current events in the context of long-term historical changes is another example. Systemic, structural explanations go even further by addressing the question, "What causes the patterns of behavior?"

In some sense, all three levels of explanation are equally true. But their usefulness is quite different. Event explanations—who did what to whom—doom their holders to a reactive stance toward change. Pattern-of-behavior explanations focus on identifying long-term trends and assessing their implications. They at least suggest how, over time, we can respond to shifting conditions. Structural explanations are the most powerful. Only they address the underlying causes of behavior at a level such that patterns of behavior can be changed.

By and large, leaders of our current institutions focus their attention on events and patterns of behavior, and, under their influence, their organizations do likewise. That is why contemporary organizations are predominantly reactive, or at best responsive—rarely generative. On the other hand, leaders in learning organizations pay attention to all three levels, but focus especially on systemic structure; largely by example, they teach people throughout the organization to do likewise.

Leader as Steward

This is the subtlest role of leadership. Unlike the roles of designer and teacher, it is almost solely a matter of attitude. It is an attitude critical to learning organizations.

Although stewardship has long been recognized as an aspect of leadership, its source is still not widely understood. I believe Robert Greenleaf (1977) came closest to explaining real stewardship, in his seminal book *Servant Leadership*. There, Greenleaf argues that "The servant leader *is* servant first. . . . It begins with the natural feeling that one wants to serve, to serve *first*. This conscious choice brings one to aspire to lead. That person is sharply different from one who is leader first, perhaps because of the need to assuage an unusual power drive or to acquire material possessions."

Leaders' sense of stewardship operates on two levels: stewardship for the people they lead and stewardship for the larger purpose or mission that underlies the enterprise. The first type arises from a keen appreciation of the impact one's leadership can have on others. People can suffer economically, emotionally, and spiritually under inept leadership. If anything, people in a learning organization are more vulnerable because of their commitment and sense of shared ownership. Appreciating this naturally instills a sense of responsibility in leaders. The second type of stewardship arises from a leader's sense of personal purpose and commitment to the organization's larger mission. People's natural impulse to learn is unleashed when they are engaged in an endeavor they consider worthy of their fullest commitment. Or, as Lawrence Miller (1984) puts it, "Achieving return on equity does not, as a goal, mobilize the most noble forces of our soul" (p. 15).

Leaders engaged in building learning organizations naturally feel part of a larger purpose that goes beyond their organization. They are part of changing the way businesses operate, not from a vague philanthropic urge, but from a conviction that their efforts will produce more productive organizations, capable of achieving higher levels of organizational success and personal satisfaction than more traditional organizations. Their sense of stewardship was succinctly captured by George Bernard Shaw when he said,

> This is the true joy in life, the being used for a purpose you consider a mighty one, the being a force of nature rather than a feverish, selfish clod of ailments and grievances complaining that the world will not devote itself to making you happy.

NEW SKILLS

New leadership roles require new leadership skills. These skills can only be developed, in my judgment, through a lifelong commitment. It is not enough for one or two individuals to develop these skills. They must be distributed widely throughout the organization. This is one reason that understanding the *disciplines* of a learning organization is so important. These disciplines embody the principles and practices that can widely foster leadership development.

Three critical areas of skills (disciplines) are building shared vision, surfacing and challenging mental models, and engaging in systems thinking. (These points are condensed from the practices of the five disciplines examined in Senge, 1990.)

Building Shared Vision

How do individual visions come together to create shared visions? A useful metaphor is the hologram, the three-dimensional image created by interacting light sources.

If you cut a photograph in half, each half shows only part of the whole image. But if you divide a hologram, each part, no matter how small, shows the whole image intact. Likewise, when a group of people come to share a vision for an organization, each person sees an individual picture of the organization at its best. Each shares responsibility for the whole, not just for one piece. But the component pieces of the hologram are not identical. Each represents the whole image from a different point of view. It's something like poking holes in a window shade; each hole offers a unique angle for viewing the whole image. So, too, is each individual's vision unique.

When you add up the pieces of a hologram, something interesting happens. The image becomes more intense, more lifelike. When more people come to share a vision, the vision becomes more real in the sense of a mental reality that people can truly imagine achieving. They now have partners, co-creators; the vision no longer rests on their shoulders alone. Early on, when they are nurturing an individual vision, people may say it is "my vision." But, as the shared vision develops, it becomes both "my vision" and "our vision."

The skills involved in building shared vision include the following:

• *Encouraging Personal Vision.* Shared visions emerge from personal visions. It is not that people only care about their own self-interest—in fact, people's values usually include dimensions that concern family, organization, community, and even the world. Rather, it is that people's capacity for caring is *personal.*

• *Communicating and Asking for Support.* Leaders must be willing to continually share their own vision, rather than being the official representative of the corporate vision. They also must be prepared to ask, "Is this vision worthy of your commitment?" This can be difficult for a person used to setting goals and presuming compliance.

• *Visioning as an Ongoing Process.* Building shared vision is a never-ending process. At any one point there will be a particular image of the future that is predominant, but that image will evolve. Today, too many managers want to dispense with the "vision business" by going off and writing the Official Vision Statement. Such statements almost always lack the vitality, freshness, and excitement of a genuine vision that comes from people asking, "What do we really want to achieve?"

• *Blending Extrinsic and Intrinsic Visions.* Many energizing visions are extrinsic—that is, they focus on achieving something relative to an outsider, such as competitor. But a goal that is limited to defeating an opponent can, once the vision is achieved, easily become a defensive posture. In contrast, intrinsic goals like creating a new type of product, taking an established product to a new level, or setting a new standard for customer satisfaction can call forth a new level of creativity and innovation. Intrinsic and extrinsic visions need to coexist; a vision solely predicated on defeating an adversary will eventually weaken an organization.

• *Distinguishing Positive from Negative Visions.* Many organizations only truly pull together when their survival is threatened. Similarly, most social movements aim at eliminating what people don't want: for example, anti-drugs, anti-smoking, or anti-nuclear arms movements. Negative visions carry a subtle message of powerlessness: people will only pull together when there is sufficient threat. Negative visions also tend to be short term. Two fundamental sources of energy can motivate organizations: fear and aspiration. Fear, the energy source behind negative visions, can produce extraordinary changes in short periods, but aspiration endures as a continuing source of learning and growth.

Surfacing and Testing Mental Models

Many of the best ideas in organizations never get put into practice. One reason is that new insights and initiatives often conflict with established mental models. The leadership task of challenging assumptions without invoking defensiveness requires reflection and inquiry skills possessed by few leaders in traditional controlling organizations. These ideas are based to a considerable extent on the work of Chris Argyris, Donald Schön, and their Action Science colleagues (Argyris & Schön, 1978; Argyris, Putnam, & Smith, 1985; Argyris, 1990).

• *Seeing Leaps of Abstraction.* Our minds literally move at lightning speed. Ironically, this often slows our learning, because we leap to generalizations so quickly that we never think to test them. We then confuse our generalizations with the observable data upon which they are based, treating the generalizations *as if they were data.* The frustrated sales rep reports to the home office that "customers don't really care about quality, price is what matters," when what actually happened was that three consecutive large customers refused to place an order unless a larger discount was offered. The sales rep treats her generalization, "customers care only about price," as if it were absolute fact rather than an assumption (very likely an assumption reflecting her own views of customers and the market). This thwarts future learning because she starts to focus on how to offer attractive discounts rather than probing behind the customers' statements. For example, the customers may have been so disgruntled with the firm's delivery or customer service that they are unwilling to purchase again without larger discounts.

• *Balancing Inquiry and Advocacy.* Most managers are skilled at articulating their views and presenting them persuasively. Although important, advocacy skills can become counterproductive as managers rise in responsibility and confront increasingly complex issues that require collaborative learning among different, equally knowledgeable people. Leaders in learning organizations need to have both inquiry and advocacy skills.[2]

Specifically, when advocating a view, they need to be able to

- Explain the reasoning and data that led to their view
- Encourage others to test their view (for example, Do you see gaps in my reasoning? Do you disagree with the data upon which my view is based?)
- Encourage others to provide different views (for example, Do you have either different data, different conclusions, or both?)

When inquiring into another's views, they need to

- Actively seek to understand the other's view, rather than simply restating their own view and how it differs from the other's view
- Make their attributions about the other and the other's view explicit (for example, Based on your statement that . . . ; I am assuming that you believe . . . ; Am I representing your views fairly?)

If they reach an impasse (others no longer appear open to inquiry), they need to

- Ask what data or logic might unfreeze the impasse, or if an experiment (or some other inquiry) might be designed to provide new information

- *Distinguishing Espoused Theory from Theory in Use.* We all like to think that we hold certain views, but often our actions reveal deeper views. For example, I may proclaim that people are trustworthy, but never lend friends money and jealously guard my possessions. Obviously, my deeper mental model (my theory in use) differs from my espoused theory. Recognizing gaps between espoused views and theories in use (which often requires the help of others) can be pivotal to deeper learning.

---

[2]I am indebted to Diana Smith for the summary points here.

• *Recognizing and Defusing Defensive Routines.* As one CEO in our research program puts it, "Nobody ever talks about an issue at the 8:00 business meeting exactly the same way they talk about it at home that evening or over drinks at the end of the day." The reason is what Chris Argyris calls *defensive routines,* entrenched habits used to protect ourselves from the embarrassment and threat that come with exposing our thinking. For most of us, such defenses began to build early in life in response to pressures to have the right answers in school or at home. Organizations add new levels of performance anxiety and thereby amplify and exacerbate this defensiveness. Ironically, this makes it even more difficult to expose hidden mental models, and thereby lessens learning.

The first challenge is to recognize defensive routines, then to inquire into their operation. Those who are best at revealing and defusing defensive routines operate with a high degree of self-disclosure regarding their own defensiveness (for example, I notice that I am feeling uneasy about how this conversation is going. Perhaps I don't understand it or it is threatening to me in ways I don't yet see. Can you help me see this better?)

Systems Thinking

We all know that leaders should help people see the big picture. But the actual skills whereby leaders are supposed to achieve this are not well understood. In my experience, successful leaders often *are* "systems thinkers" to a considerable extent. They focus less on day-to-day events and more on underlying trends and forces of change. But they do this almost completely intuitively. The consequence is that they are often unable to explain their intuitions to others and feel frustrated that others cannot see the world the way they do.

One of the most significant developments in management science today is the gradual coalescence of managerial systems thinking as a field of study and practice. This field suggests some key skills for future leaders:

• *Seeing Interrelationships, Not Things, and Processes, Not Snapshots.* Most of us have been conditioned throughout our lives to focus on things and to see the world in static images. This leads us to linear explanations of systemic phenomenon. For instance, in an arms race each party is convinced that the other is *the cause* of problems. They react to each new move as an isolated event, not as part of a process.

So long as they fail to see the interrelationships of these actions, they are trapped.

• *Moving beyond Blame.* We tend to blame each other or outside circumstances for our problems. But it is poorly designed systems, not incompetent or unmotivated individuals, that cause most organizational problems. Systems thinking shows us that there is no outside—that you and the cause of your problems are part of a single system.

• *Distinguishing Detail Complexity from Dynamic Complexity.* Some types of complexity are more important strategically than others. Detail complexity arises when there are many variables. Dynamic complexity arises when cause and effect are distant in time and space, and when the consequences over time of interventions are subtle and not obvious to many participants in the system. The leverage in most management situations lies in understanding dynamic complexity, not detail complexity.

• *Focusing on Areas of High Leverage.* Some have called systems thinking the "new dismal science" because it teaches that most obvious solutions don't work—at best, they improve matters in the short run, only to make things worse in the long run. But there is another side to the story. Systems thinking also shows that small, well-focused actions can produce significant, enduring improvements, if they are in the right place. Systems thinkers refer to this idea as the principle of "leverage." Tackling a difficult problem is often a matter of seeing where the high leverage lies, where a change—with a minimum of effort—would lead to lasting, significant improvement.

• *Avoiding Symptomatic Solutions.* The pressures to intervene in management systems that are going awry can be overwhelming. Unfortunately, given the linear thinking that predominates in most organizations, interventions usually focus on symptomatic fixes, not underlying causes. This results in only temporary relief, and it tends to create still more pressures later on for further, low-leverage intervention. If leaders acquiesce to these pressures, they can be sucked into an endless spiral of increasing intervention. Sometimes the most difficult leadership acts are to refrain from intervening through popular quick fixes and to keep the pressure on everyone to identify more enduring solutions.

Although leaders who can articulate systemic explanations are rare, those who *can* will leave their stamp on an organization. One person who had this gift was Bill Gore, the founder and long-time CEO of W.L. Gore and Associates (makers of GoreTex and other synthetic fiber products). Bill Gore was adept at telling stories that showed how the organization's core values of freedom and individual responsibility required particular operating policies. He was proud of his egalitarian organization, in which there were (and still are) no "employees," only "associates," all of whom own shares in the company and participate in its management. At one talk, he explained the company's policy of controlled growth: "Our limitation is not financial resources. Our limitation is the rate at which we can bring in new associates. Our experience has been that if we try to bring in more than a 25 percent per year increase, we begin to bog down. Twenty-five percent per year growth is a real limitation; you can do much better than that with an authoritarian organization." As Gore tells the story, one of the associates, Esther Baum, went home after this talk and reported the limitation to her husband. As it happened, he was an astronomer and mathematician at Lowell Observatory. He said, "That's a very interesting figure." He took out a pencil and paper and calculated and said, "Do you realize that in only fifty-seven and a half years, everyone in the world will be working for Gore?"

Through this story, Gore explains the systemic rationale behind a key policy, limited growth rate—a policy that undoubtedly caused a lot of stress in the organization. He suggests that, at larger rates of growth, the adverse effects of attempting to integrate too many new people too rapidly would begin to dominate. (This is the "limits to growth" systems archetype explained below.) The story also reaffirms the organization's commitment to creating a unique environment for its associates and illustrates the types of sacrifices that the firm is prepared to make in order to remain true to its vision. The last part of the story shows that, despite the self-imposed limit, the company is still very much a growth company.

The consequences of leaders who lack systems thinking skills can be devastating. Many charismatic leaders manage almost exclusively at the level of events. They deal in visions and in crises, and little in between. Under their leadership, an organization hurtles from crisis to crisis. Eventually, the worldview of people in the organization becomes dominated by events and reactiveness. Many, especially those who are deeply committed, become burned out. Eventually, cynicism comes to pervade the organization. People have no control over their time, let alone their destiny.

Similar problems arise with the "visionary strategist," the leader with vision who sees both patterns of change and events. This leader is better prepared to manage change. He or she can explain strategies in terms of emerging trends, and thereby foster a climate that is less reactive. But such leaders still impart a responsive orientation rather than a generative one.

Many talented leaders have rich, highly systemic intuitions but cannot explain those intuitions to others. Ironically, they often end up being authoritarian leaders, even if they don't want to, because only they see the decisions that need to be made. They are unable to conceptualize their strategic insights so that these can become public knowledge, open to challenge and further improvement.

NEW TOOLS

Developing the skills above requires new tools—tools that will enhance leaders' conceptual abilities and foster communication and collaborative inquiry. What follows is a sampling of tools starting to find use in learning organizations.

Systems Archetypes

One of the insights of the budding, managerial systems-thinking field is that certain types of systemic structures recur again and again. Countless systems grow for a period, then encounter problems and cease to grow (or even collapse) well before they have reached intrinsic limits to growth. Many other systems get locked in runaway vicious spirals where every actor has to run faster and faster to say in the same place. Still others lure individual actors into doing what seems right locally, yet which eventually causes suffering for all. The system archetypes are one of several systems diagramming and communication tools. See Kim (1989).

Some of the system archetypes that have the broadest relevance include:

• *Balancing Process with Delay.* In this archetype, decision makers fail to appreciate the time delays involved as they move toward a goal. As a result, they overshoot the goal and may even produce recurring cycles. Classic example: real estate developers who keep starting new projects until the market has gone soft, by which time an eventual glut is guaranteed by the properties still under construction.

• *Limits to Growth.* A reinforcing cycle of growth grinds to a halt, and may even reverse itself, as limits are approached. The limits can be resource constraints, or external or internal responses to growth.

Classic examples: product life cycles that peak prematurely due to poor quality or service, the growth and decline of communication in a management team, and the spread of a new movement.

• *Shifting the Burden.* A short-term "solution" is used to correct a problem, with seemingly happy immediate results. As this correction is used more and more, fundamental long-term corrective measures are used less. Over time, the mechanisms of the fundamental solution may atrophy or become disabled, leading to even greater reliance on the symptomatic solution. Classic example: using corporate human resource staff to solve local personnel problems, thereby keeping managers from developing their own interpersonal skills.

• *Eroding Goals.* When all else fails, lower your standards. This is like "shifting the burden," except that the short-term solution involves letting a fundamental goal, such as quality standards or employee morale standards, atrophy. Classic example: a company that responds to delivery problems by continually upping its quoted delivery times.

• *Escalation.* Two people or two organizations, who each see their welfare as depending on a relative advantage over the other, continually react to the other's advances. Whenever one side gets ahead, the other is threatened, leading it to act more aggressively to reestablish its advantage, which threatens the first, and so on. Classic examples: arms race, gang warfare, price wars.

• *Tragedy of the Commons.*[3] Individuals keep intensifying their use of a commonly available but limited resource until all individuals start to experience severely diminishing returns. Classic examples: sheepherders who keep increasing their flocks until they overgraze the common pasture; divisions in a firm that share a common salesforce and compete for the use of sales reps by upping their sales targets, until the salesforce burns out from overextension.

• *Growth and Underinvestment.* Rapid growth approaches a limit that could be eliminated or pushed into the future, but only by aggressive investment in physical and human capacity. Eroding goals or standards cause investment that is too weak, or too slow, and customers get increasingly unhappy, slowing demand growth and thereby making the needed investment (apparently) unnecessary or impossible. Classic example: countless once-successful growth firms that allowed product or service quality to erode, and were unable to generate enough revenues to invest in remedies.

---

[3]This archetype is closely associated with the work of ecologist Garrett Hardin, who coined its label (Hardin, 1968).

The archetype template is a specific tool that is helping managers identify archetypes operating in their own strategic areas (see Figure 38.2). The template shows the basic structural form of the archetype but lets managers fill in the variables of their own situation. For example, the shifting the burden template involves two balancing processes ("B") that compete for control of a problem symptom. The upper, symptomatic solution provides a short-term fix that will make the problem symptom go away for a while. The lower, fundamental solution provides a more enduring solution. The side effect feedback ("R") around the outside of the diagram identifies unintended exacerbating effects of the symptomatic solution, which, over time, make it more and more difficult to invoke the fundamental solution.

Several years ago, a team of managers from a leading consumer goods producer used the shifting the burden archetype in a revealing way. The problem they focused on was financial stress, which could be dealt with in two different ways: by running marketing promotions (the symptomatic solution) or by product innovation (the fundamental solution). Marketing promotions were fast. The company was expert in

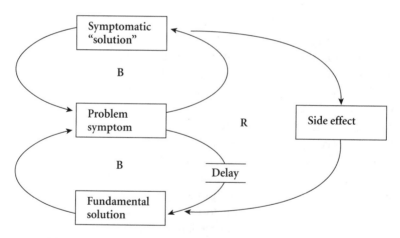

Figure 38.2. "Shifting the Burden" Archetype Template.

In the "shifting the burden" template, two balancing processes (B) compete for control of a problem symptom. Both solutions affect the symptom, but only the fundamental solution treats the cause. The symptomatic "solution" creates the additional side effect (R) of deferring the fundamental solution, making it harder and harder to achieve.

These templates were originally developed by Jennifer Kemeny, Charles Kiefer, and Michael Goodman of Innovation Associates, Inc., Framingham, MA.

their design and implementation. The results were highly predictable. Product innovation was slow and much less predictable, and the company had a history over the past ten years of product-innovation mismanagement. Yet only through innovation could they retain a leadership position in their industry, which had slid over the past ten to twenty years. What the managers saw clearly was that the more skillful they became at promotions, the more they shifted the burden away from product innovation. But what really struck home was when one member identified the unintended side effect: the last three CEOs had all come from advertising function, which had become the politically dominant function in the corporation, thereby institutionalizing the symptomatic solution. Unless the political values shifted back toward product and process innovation, the managers realized, the firm's decline would accelerate—which is just the shift that has happened over the past several years.

Charting Strategic Dilemmas

Management teams typically come unglued when confronted with core dilemmas. A classic example was the way U.S. manufacturers faced the low cost-high quality choice. For years, most assumed that it was necessary to choose between the two. Not surprisingly, given the short-term pressures perceived by most managements, the prevailing choice was low cost. Firms that chose high quality usually perceived themselves as aiming exclusively for a high quality, high price market niche. The consequences of this perceived either-or choice have been disastrous, even fatal, as U.S. manufacturers have encountered increasing international competition from firms that have chosen to consistently improve quality *and* cost.

Charles Hampden-Turner (1990) presented a variety of tools for helping management teams confront strategic dilemmas creatively. He summarizes the process in seven steps:

• *Eliciting the Dilemmas.* Identifying the opposed values that form the "horns" of the dilemma, such as cost as opposed to quality, or local initiative as opposed to central coordination and control. Hampden-Turner suggests that humor can be a distinct asset in this process because "the admission that dilemmas even exist tends to be difficult for some companies."

• *Mapping.* Locating the opposing values as two axes and helping managers identify where they see themselves, or their organization, along the axes.

• *Processing*. Getting rid of nouns to describe the axes of the dilemma. Present participles formed by adding "ing" convert rigid nouns into processes that imply movement. For example, central control versus local control becomes "strengthening national office" and "growing local initiatives." This loosens the bond of implied opposition between the two values. For example, it becomes possible to think of "strengthening national services from which local branches can benefit."

• *Framing/Contextualizing*. Further softening the adversarial structure among different values by letting "each side in turn be the frame or context for the other." This shifting of the "figure-ground" relationship undermines any implicit attempts to hold one value as intrinsically superior to the other, and thereby to become mentally closed to creative strategies for continuous improvement of both.

• *Sequencing*. Breaking the hold of static thinking. Very often, values like low cost and high quality appear to be in opposition because we think in terms of a point in time, not in terms of an ongoing process. For example, a strategy of investing in new process technology and developing a new production-floor culture of worker responsibility may take time and money in the near term, yet reap significant long-term financial rewards.

• *Waving/Cycling*. Sometimes the strategic path toward improving both values involves cycles where both values will get "worse" for a time. Yet, at a deeper level, learning is occurring that will cause the next cycle to be at a higher plateau for both values.

• *Synergizing*. Achieving synergy where significant improvement is occurring along all axes of all relevant dilemmas. (This is the ultimate goal, of course.) Synergy, as Hampden-Turner points out, is a uniquely systemic notion, coming from the Greek *syn-ergo* or "work together."

"The Left-Hand Column": Surfacing Mental Models

The idea that mental models can dominate business decisions and that these models are often tacit and even contradictory to what people espouse can be very threatening to managers who pride themselves on rationality and judicious decision making. It is important to have tools to help managers discover for themselves how their mental models operate to undermine their own intentions.

One tool that has worked consistently to help managers see their own mental models in action is the "left-hand column" exercise developed by Chris Argyris and his colleagues. This tool is especially helpful in showing how we leap from data to generalization without testing the validity of our generalizations.

When working with managers, I start this exercise by selecting a specific situation in which I am interacting with other people in a way that is not working, that is not producing the learning that is needed. I write out a sample of the exchange, with the script on the right-hand side of the page. On the left-hand side, I write what I am thinking but not saying at each stage in the exchange (see Exhibit 38.1).

Imagine my exchange with a colleague, Bill, after he made a big presentation to our boss on a project we are doing together. I had to miss the presentation, but I've heard that it was poorly received.

Me: How did the presentation go?
Bill: Well, I don't know. It's really too early to say. Besides, we're breaking new ground here.
Me: Well, what do you think we should do? I believe that the issues you were raising are important.
Bill: I'm not so sure. Let's just wait and see what happens.
Me: You may be right, but I think we may need to do more than just wait.

Now, here is what the exchange looks like with my "left-hand column":

What I'm Thinking	What Is Said
Everyone says the presentation was a bomb.	**Me:** How did the presentation go?
Does he really not know how bad it was? Or is he not willing to face up to it?	**Bill:** Well, I don't know. It's too early to say. Besides, we're breaking new ground here.
	Me: Well, what do you think we should do? I believe that the issues you were raising are important.
He really is afraid to see the truth. If he only had more confidence, he could probably learn from a situation like this.	**Bill:** I'm not so sure. Let's just wait and see what happens.
I can't believe he doesn't realize how disastrous that presentation was to our moving ahead.	**Me:** You may be right, but I think we may need to do more than just wait.
I've got to find some way to light a fire under the guy.	

Exhibit 38.1.   The Left-Hand Column: An Exercise.

The left-hand column exercise not only brings hidden assumptions to the surface, it shows how they influence behavior. In the example, I make two key assumptions about Bill: he lacks confidence and he lacks initiative. Neither may be literally true, but both are evident in my internal dialogue, and both influence the way I handle the situation. Believing that he lacks confidence, I skirt the fact that I've heard that the presentation was a bomb. I'm afraid that if I say it directly, he will lose what little confidence he has, or he will see me as unsupportive. So I bring up the subject of the presentation obliquely. When I ask Bill what we should do next, he gives no specific course of action. Believing he lacks initiative, I take this as evidence of his laziness; he is content to do nothing when action is definitely required. I conclude that I will have to manufacture some form of pressure to motivate him, or else I will simply have to take matters into my own hands.

The exercise reveals the elaborate webs of assumptions we weave, within which we become our own victims. Rather than dealing directly with my assumptions about Bill and the situation, we talk around the subject. The reasons for my avoidance are self-evident: I assume that if I raised my doubts, I would provoke a defensive reaction that would only make matters worse. But the price of avoiding the issue is high. Instead of determining how to move forward to resolve our problems, we end our exchange with no clear course of action. My assumptions about Bill's limitations have been reinforced. I resort to a manipulative strategy to move things forward.

The exercise not only reveals the need for skills in surfacing assumptions, but that we are the ones most in need of help. There is no one right way to handle difficult situations like my exchange with Bill, but any productive strategy revolves around a high level of self-disclosure and willingness to have my views challenged. I need to recognize my own leaps of abstraction regarding Bill, share the events and reasoning that are leading to my concern over the project, and be open to Bill's views on both. The skills to carry on such conversations without invoking defensiveness take time to develop. But if both parties in a learning impasse start by doing their own left-hand column exercise and sharing them with each other, it is remarkable how quickly everyone recognizes their contribution to the impasse and progress starts to be made.

Learning Laboratories: Practice Fields
for Management Teams

One of the most promising new tools is the learning laboratory or "microworld": constructed microcosms of real-life settings in which management teams can learn how to learn together.

The rationale behind learning laboratories can best be explained by analogy. Although most management teams have great difficulty learning (enhancing their collective intelligence and capacity to create), in other domains team learning is the norm rather than the exception—team sports and the performing arts, for example. Great basketball teams do not start off great. They learn. But the process by which these teams learn is, by and large, absent from modern organizations. The process is a continual movement between practice and performance.

The vision guiding current research in management learning laboratories is to design and construct effective practice fields for management teams. Much remains to be done, but the broad outlines are emerging.

First, because team learning in organizations is an individual-to-individual and individual-to-system phenomenon, learning laboratories must combine meaningful business issues with meaningful interpersonal dynamics. Either alone is incomplete.

Second, the factors that thwart learning about complex business issues must be eliminated in the learning lab. Chief among these is the inability to experience the long-term, systemic consequences of key strategic decisions. We all learn best from experience, but we are unable to experience the consequences of many important organizational decisions. Learning laboratories remove this constraint through system dynamics simulation games that compress time and space.

Third, new learning skills must be developed. One constraint on learning is the inability of managers to reflect insightfully on their assumptions, and to inquire effectively into each other's assumptions. Both skills can be enhanced in a learning laboratory, where people can practice surfacing assumptions in a low-risk setting. A note of caution: it is far easier to design an entertaining learning laboratory than it is to have an impact on real management practices and firm traditions outside the learning lab. Research on management simulations has shown that they often have greater entertainment value than educational value. One of the reasons appears to be that many simulations do not offer deep insights into systemic structures causing business problems. Another reason is that they do not foster new learning skills. Also, there is no connection between experiments in the learning lab and real life experiments. These are significant problems that research on learning laboratory design is now addressing.

DEVELOPING LEADERS AND LEARNING ORGANIZATIONS

In a recently published retrospective on organization development in the 1980s, Marshall Sashkin and N. Warner Burke (1990a, 1990b) observe the return of an emphasis on developing leaders who can develop organizations. They also note Schein's critique that most top executives are not qualified for the task of developing culture (Schein, 1985). Learning organizations represent a potentially significant revolution of organizational culture. So it should come as no surprise that such organizations will remain a distant vision until the leadership capabilities they demand are developed. "The 1990s may be the period," suggest Sashkin and Burke, "during which organization development and [a new sort of] management development are reconnected."

I believe that this new sort of management development will focus on the roles, skills, and tools for leadership in learning organizations. Undoubtedly, the ideas offered above are only a rough approximation of this new territory. The sooner we begin seriously exploring the territory, the sooner the initial map can be improved—and the sooner we will realize an age-old vision of leadership:

> *The wicked leader is he who the people despise.*
> *The good leader is he who the people revere.*
> *The great leader is he who the people say, "We did it ourselves."*
>
> *—Lao Tsu*

CHAPTER THIRTY-NINE

Compassion in Organizational Life

Jason M. Kanov
Sally Maitlis
Monica C. Worline
Jane E. Dutton
Peter J. Frost
Jacoba M. Lilius

C ompassion occupies a prominent role in the history of modern society, implicated in the creation and sustenance of human community (Clark, 1997; Nussbaum, 1996, 2001). Seen as virtuous and contributing to personal and social good (Blum, 1980; Nussbaum, 2001; Solomon, 1998; Wuthnow, 1991), compassion lies at the core of what it means to be human (Himmelfarb, 2001; Wuthnow, 1991). Discussions about the meaning of compassion as a human experience date back over two thousand years, spanning disciplines such as religion, philosophy, and sociology. Through early philosophical accounts to more contemporary depictions, the notion of compassion has remained remarkably constant (Nussbaum, 1996). Similarly, despite fundamental differences in philosophy and tradition, all major religions emphasize the importance of compassion.

Judaism, for example, mandates to emulate God in his attribute of compassion (Sears, 1998), and Buddhist philosophy considers that the basic nature of human beings is to be compassionate (Dalai Lama, 1995). The Biblical tradition, too, teaches compassion as "a duty to divine law, as a response to divine love, and a sign of commitment to the Judeo-Christian ethic" (Wuthnow, 1991, p. 50). Compassion is a fundamental and timeless part of human existence.

Compassion is also an essential, yet often overlooked, aspect of life in organizations. Although organizations are frequently portrayed as sites of pain and suffering, they are also places of healing, where caring and compassion are both given and received (Frost, Dutton, Worline, & Wilson, 2000; Kahn, 1993). Compassionate acts can be found at all levels in an organization, from leaders who buffer and transform the pain of their employees, to office workers who listen and respond empathically to their colleagues' troubles (Frost, 2003). Compassion in organizations makes people feel seen and known; it also helps them feel less alone (Frost et al., 2000; Kahn, 1993). Moreover, compassion alters the "felt connection" between people at work (Frost et al., 2000) and is associated with a range of positive attitudes, behaviors, and feelings in organizations (Dutton, Frost, Worline, Lilius, & Kanov, 2002; Lilius et al., 2003). Research and writing on compassion in organizations reveals it as a positive and very powerful force.

We regard compassion in organizations as processual and relational. It is common to think of it as an individual characteristic, and a given individual as being either "compassionate" or "uncompassionate." Compassion is also seen as a state induced by another person's suffering, a "painful emotion" that one person experiences for another (Nussbaum, 1996). In contrast, we conceptualize compassion as a dynamic process, or a set of subprocesses, that may be found both in individuals and collectivities. Building on Clark (1997), we identify these subprocesses as "noticing," "feeling," and "responding," each contributing uniquely to the process of compassion. We argue that compassion and each of its subprocesses is relational in nature, occurring in and through interactions and connections between people (Dutton, 2003). By strengthening people's feelings of connectedness, the process of compassion builds and shapes the communities in which we live and work.

In this chapter, we explore the process of compassion in organizations. We do this in two stages. First we examine what it means for individuals in organizations to experience compassion. We identify the many sources of pain in organizations and discuss how individuals can heal one another by noticing another's suffering, experiencing an emotional reaction to his or her pain, and acting to help ease or alleviate it. Then we develop a conceptualization of "organizational compassion," which we argue is composed of these same processes operating at a collective level. Organizational compassion exists when members of a system collectively notice, feel, and respond to pain experienced by members of that system. We argue that these subprocesses become collective when they are legitimated within an organizational context and propagated among organizational members. For responding to become collective, it must also be coordinated across individuals. We then explore how legitimation, propagation, and coordination are enabled by a variety of systemic organizational features, such as values, practices, and routines. Examining organizational compassion thus allows us to see organizations as systems with the capacity for collective noticing, feeling, and responding.

By developing conceptualizations of compassion processes that exist at the individual and organizational levels, we contribute in important ways to understanding behavior in organizations, and to the emerging field of positive organizational scholarship. First, this work acknowledges both the human pain and the compassion present in organizational life. In general, the study of organizations tends to engage our minds but fails to engage our hearts. As a result, researchers typically have little to say about the humanity or aliveness of organizations (Dutton, 2003; Follet, 1995; Frost, 1999; Rozin, 2001; Sandelands, 1998, 2003; Weick, 1999). The study of compassion in organizations acknowledges the realities of pain, suffering, and healing that are part of the human experience, and in so doing, helps to fill in gaps in the organizational literature, which often fails to portray organizations as human institutions.

Second, extending the idea of compassion beyond the individual allows us to see how collective capacities for noticing, feeling, and responding to human suffering vary by organization. By highlighting the role of organizational systems, routines, and values in facilitating the enactment of collective compassion processes, our focus on organizational compassion thus contributes to the emerging field of positive organizational scholarship, showing how one form of virtuousness can be enabled in organizations (Cameron, 2003; Cameron, Dutton, & Quinn, 2003). Furthermore, this chapter begins to articulate the mechanisms through which organizational contexts enable the patterns of collective noticing, feeling, and responding that differentiate organizations as sites of human healing. For organizations in which dealing with human pain is a persistent and central part of the organization's mission (for example, hospitals and health care organizations, fire-fighting units, social services, and support organizations), this form of collective compassion capability may be particularly important for sustained organizational survival and effectiveness.

PAIN AND COMPASSION AT WORK

Given the amount of time people spend at work, it should come as no surprise that work organizations are fraught with pain and suffering (Frost, 1999, 2003; Frost et al., 2000). People often carry pain from their personal lives with them to work. For example, a family member being diagnosed with cancer, a single working mother leaving her sick child in someone else's care, or a failing personal relationship all affect how people feel at work. Equally, a vast number of work-related factors, such as hostile coworker interactions, an abusive boss, or having to deal with overly demanding clients, can lead people to experience intense and enduring pain. Pain can also result from organizational actions such as a merger that produces severe conflict, poorly handled change, or indiscriminate restructuring and downsizing. Hostile or unethical acts from other organizations can further contribute to the pain felt by employees in an organization. For instance, companies with deep economic pockets coming into communities can drive smaller or less wealthy competitors out of business, causing pain and suffering for many who are on the losing end of the competition. Finally, emotional pain stems from inevitable calamities, be they environmental (heavy pollution, earthquakes, floods), political (painful inter-group conflict or contests for power), or economic (jolts felt as the economy falters and one's livelihood is threatened). Whether organizations themselves directly cause pain and suffering, they are sites that harbor the emotional duress and anguish that stem from all aspects of members' lives (Dutton et al., 2002; Frost & Robinson, 1999; Frost et al., 2000).

Pain and suffering have serious implications for organizational performance and productivity. Employee grief, for example, costs work organizations upwards of 75 billion dollars annually (Zaslow, 2002). The costs also extend beyond financial losses to include a variety of psychological, physiological, and interpersonal outcomes such as a diminished sense of self-worth, a weakened immune system, and workplace sabotage (Frost, 2003; Ryff & Singer, 2001). Organizational members are often left without reliable opportunities to deal with their suffering, however, because of organizations' typically limited capacity to acknowledge and respond to it (Frost, 1999).

Given the pain present in the workplace and the dearth of resources available to handle it, compassion in organizations clearly has a critical and consequential role. The possibility for compassion as a part of organizational work is powerfully illustrated in the medical and nursing literatures, where clinicians and policy makers emphasize the importance of attending to patients' suffering (defined as an impairment or threat to the meaning of the self, Reich [1989]), as well as their physical illness. For instance, medical ethics discourse increasingly includes compassion (for example, Brody, 1992; Shelp, 1985, as cited in Brody, 1992), spurring interest in understanding what it means for medical professionals to be compassionate and how they can express compassion in interactions with their patients (for example, Connelly, 1999). The nursing literature similarly identifies compassion as a moral imperative that is an essential component of patient care (von Dietze & Orb, 2000).

Compassion brings medical practitioners closer to their patients, allows them to establish a connection with their patients, and enables them to achieve a deeper level of healing through their treatment of the "whole person" rather than just illness (Brody, 1992; Cassell, 2002). It heals by reducing the felt presence of pain through being noticed, through feeling cared for and understood, and through receiving responses that alleviate pain. To attend to a patient's suffering is to guard against "losing" the person in the medical process (Frank, 1992). Compassion provides comfort in a time of distress and disorientation, and serves as a reminder to professionals of the human dimension of practices that can easily become exclusively system, function, or technique driven. Recent work with dying people explores how insensitive communications by physicians can engender more suffering than the illness itself or an awareness that the condition is terminal (Kuhl, 2002). Findings from research on compassion in the caring professions parallel those on terminal experiences in the workplace, such as firings, layoffs, and downsizings, where the compassion with which painful acts are carried out has been shown to positively influence the perceptions and feelings of the target individuals (Cameron, 1994; Gittell & Cameron, 2003; Wanburg, Bunce, & Gavin, 1999).

ELEMENTS OF COMPASSION

In this section, we identify the key elements of the process of compassion as it is experienced among individuals. Following Clark (1997), we regard compassion as a process comprising three interrelated elements: "noticing" another's suffering, "feeling" the other's pain, and "responding" to that person's suffering. We discuss each of these below.

Noticing

A critical first step in the compassion process is noticing another person's suffering and becoming aware of the pain he or she is feeling. Noticing often requires an openness and receptivity to what is going on in those around us, paying attention to others' emotions, and reading subtle cues in our daily interactions with them (Frost, 2003). Noticing may take the form of a cognitive recognition of another's suffering, or may first be experienced through an unconscious physical or emotional reaction to that person's distress, which in turn creates in us an awareness of their suffering. Equally, we may notice the pain of others because people call our attention to it. In all cases, awareness of another's pain is a critical first step in the compassion process.

People's motivation and skill in noticing varies across individuals and situations: We tend to find noticing easiest when the person is similar to us and when we like him or her; we are also more likely to detect a person's suffering when we have experienced a similar kind of pain ourselves (Clark, 1997). When we are especially busy at work and preoccupied with our own deadlines and concerns, however, we are often unable to notice the pain that may be in front of us (Frost, 2003; Hallowell, 1999).

Feeling

All accounts of compassion from ancient Greek philosophy to the everyday vernacular recognize that people *feel* compassion. Compassion is a social emotion in that it is inherently other-regarding: people feel compassion for someone else (Cassell, 2002; Solomon, 1998). Moreover, the feeling of compassion implies that the object of one's compassion is experiencing some sort of pain or suffering (for example, Frost et al., 2000; Reich, 1989; Solomon, 1998). Compassion literally means *suffer with* (Solomon, 1998; von Dietze & Orb, 2000). Feelings of compassion thus connect one person to another's hurt, anguish, or worry. These feelings can be more or less intense, and may last over a long period, for example, toward a disadvantaged group of people, or be experienced only briefly in response to someone's short-lived misfortune. Feelings of compassion also vary in form: a person may simply feel concern for another, or she may experience a more complex set of emotions, for instance, simultaneously feeling concern as well as indignation on the person's behalf, or guilt at not having done more to prevent his distress (Clark, 1997).

Compassionate feelings resemble empathic concern (Batson, 1994; Davis, 1983), in which a person imagines or feels the condition of the person in pain or suffering. Nussbaum (2001, p. 327) talks of "the imaginative reconstruction of the experience of the sufferer," which allows someone to get a sense of what it means for a person to suffer, and to connect himself to that person's situation and prospects. These feelings also involve "taking the attitude" of the other person (Mead, 1962, p. 366; Shott, 1979), seeing the situation from her perspective, and taking her role (Clark, 1997). To feel empathic concern, we must therefore be able to appreciate the suffering person's pain from his or her perspective. Noticing another's pain does not, however, inevitably lead to the feeling of compassion: it is possible to acknowledge that a person is suffering, but feel nothing for her, or even feel that she deserves what has happened (Lerner, 1980).

Responding

In addition to connecting those who feel empathic concern with those who suffer, the experience of compassion also moves those feeling the concern to act toward easing or eliminating the other's suffering (Reich, 1989; von Dietze & Orb, 2000). As Rinpoche (1992) explains,

> [compassion] is not simply a sense of sympathy or caring for the person suffering, not simply a warmth of heart toward the person before you, or a sharp recognition of their needs and pain, it is also a sustained and practical determination to do whatever is possible and necessary to help alleviate their suffering. (p. 187)

Compassion is thus an empathic emotional response elicited by another person's suffering that moves people to act in a way that will ease the person's anguish or make it more tolerable (Frost et al., 2000; Reich, 1989).

We introduce the term *compassionate responding* to refer to any action or display that occurs in response to another's pain, with the aim of alleviating that pain or helping the sufferer to live through it (Reich, 1989). Compassionate responding may or may not be instrumental in fixing or correcting the immediate cause of one's suffering. For example, holding someone's hand as she talks about the painful process of caring for her terminally ill father can be just as compassionate as giving money to someone who incurs unexpected medical expenses. Both actions aim to make the experience of suffering more bearable. Such acts are only compassionate responses, however, if they occur together with feelings of compassion. Thus, commonly studied and valuable organizational behaviors such as general helping behavior, social support, and organizational citizenship behavior are not compassion unless they are accompanied by the noticing and feeling elements of the compassion process.

Acting compassionately does not necessarily follow from compassionate feelings, although we would likely reject the claims of a person who frequently expressed feelings of compassion but never acted on them (Blum, 1980; Solomon, 1998). There may, however, be times when compassionate feelings exist but no available course of action suggests itself or is possible in the circumstances (Nussbaum, 2001). For example, a newcomer at work learns her peer is undergoing radiation treatment from newly detected breast cancer, but, neither knowing her new colleague well nor the norms of the organization, does nothing despite feeling deeply for her coworker. She is feeling but not displaying compassion.

Although compassionate responding often follows feelings of compassion, it is also possible that these feelings may come as a result of compassionate responding. Just as the act of smiling has been found to generate positive affect in a person (Strack, Martin, & Stepper, 1988), so performing a compassionate act may, by connecting someone to a sufferer, give him an appreciation of that person's plight and evoke feelings of compassion for her (Clark, 1997). Compassionate responding is a critical piece of the process in that it alerts others to the fact that the person engaging in the action is indeed feeling compassion. An implication of this is that, although a feeling of compassion may have moral value in its own right, it is through compassionate responding that the feeling comes to be a "social force" that compels interaction and promotes social solidarity (Clark, 1997, pp. 56–57).

COMPASSION AND RELATED PROCESSES

Before moving on to discuss the process of compassion at the organizational level, we see value in distinguishing individual compassion from the related processes of empathy, sympathy, and caregiving. Comparing empathy and compassion, von Dietze and Orb (2000) have suggested that compassion is a deeper level of participation in another's suffering. In their account, compassion can involve empathy, but it also suggests a fuller connection to the sufferer, thereby taking on or participating in his or her suffering (see also Clark, 1997; Reich, 1989; Rinpoche, 1992). In other writing, empathy has been seen as synonymous with compassion, both being other-oriented emotional responses characterized by feelings of concern for the other person's welfare (for example, Batson, 1994; Batson & Oleson, 1991; Davis & Kraus, 1997). In such work, empathy is conceptualized as involving an appreciation or understanding of what someone else is going through as well as an emotional reaction to that person's condition.

Our conception of individual compassion places empathy as an important part of the feeling process, emotionally connecting with and taking the perspective of the sufferer. We argue, however, that compassion differs from empathy in that compassion also involves being moved to respond to a person's suffering. Although sympathy is sometimes treated as being one and the same with empathy (for example, Davis & Kraus, 1997; von Dietze & Orb, 2000), in this chapter, we draw on Clark's (1997) sophisticated account of sympathy, which is essentially synonymous with the present conceptualization of compassion (Nussbaum, 2001).

We also see a conceptual overlap between compassion and the process of caregiving, which is an "emotional act" involving the transfer of emotions from caregiver to caretaker (Kahn, 1993). Caregiving is composed of eight behavioral dimensions, several of which connect to compassion as conceptualized in this chapter. However, in contrast with the less tangible acts of noticing another's suffering and feelings of empathic concern that are so central to our understanding of compassion, caregiving emphasizes the enactment of a set of behaviors, such as inquiry, validation, and support. Furthermore, caregiving is seen as a way of replenishing a colleague who is emotionally drained or experiencing burnout from work. We regard compassion as a response to pain that might arise from a variety of sources inside and outside of work, and to suffering that may include, but is not restricted to, emotional exhaustion and burnout.

ORGANIZATIONAL COMPASSION

Our discussion to this point has focused on compassion among individuals. To more fully appreciate compassion in organizational life, however, we now shift our attention to examine it at the organizational level. We focus on organizational compassion as a process carried out by and directed toward the members of an organization. We argue that it is not a fixed or absolute quality, and we do not encourage distinguishing between "compassionate" and "uncompassionate" organizations. Rather, we believe that organizational compassion can be found in any kind of organization, although some kinds, such as nongovernmental aid organizations or certain community service organizations, may be more predisposed to compassion as a result of their mission and the centrality of organizational compassion to their viability and success. In this chapter, we seek to establish a way of thinking about organizational compassion that enables the identification of factors that reflect the relative compassion of all organizations.

In developing the present conceptualization of organizational compassion, we are not suggesting that organizations are entities that, like individuals, literally notice, feel, and respond to pain; nor are we suggesting that organizational compassion is a mere aggregation of compassion among individuals. Rather, organizational compassion involves a set of social processes in which noticing, feeling, and responding to pain are shared among a set of organizational members. To be shared, and so become collective within an organization, each of these processes must be legitimated and propagated, and responding must also be coordinated. These mechanisms are in turn enabled by a variety of systemic organizational factors, such as values, practices, and routines. Collective noticing, feeling, and responding also feed back into the system and influence how organizations and their members will respond to pain in the future (Nussbaum, 2001). Each of these collective processes will be discussed in more detail in the subsections below.

Collective Noticing

Collective noticing is the first of three subprocesses that compose organizational compassion. Collective noticing is not simply a matter of multiple people within a social system independently recognizing another person's pain. Rather, it refers to a collective acknowledgment of pain within a social system such that individuals within the system have a shared appreciation that pain is present. Understanding the role of individuals in this collective process is important because organizations themselves cannot notice pain. Rather, it is individual organizational members that are able to pick up on emotional cues and sense what is going on in those around them. Organizations play a critical role in this process by influencing, through certain structures, systems, and practices, what their members notice and attend to in their environments (Sutcliffe, 2000).

Organizational characteristics can both inhibit and enhance the extent to which members notice each other's pain, view it as legitimate and worthy of attention, and share their awareness with others. These characteristics include organizational policies and shared values that heighten members' vigilance for pain and provide a language with which to identify it, aspects of the organization's physical architecture that make members accessible to each other and make it easier for them to see suffering in the organization, and organizational systems and technologies that facilitate communication about the presence of pain in the system. Each of these has the potential to influence the extent to which organizational members will be receptive to the presence of pain in those around them and the degree to which this awareness will be legitimated in the organization. We describe organizations with such characteristics as having a capacity for collective noticing.

Cisco Systems offers an example of an organization with policies that create such a capacity. John Chambers, CEO, has a policy that he is to be notified (within 48 hours) of every instance in which a Cisco employee or an employee's immediate family member falls seriously ill or passes away. This policy increases individual members' vigilance by encouraging them to be on the lookout for pain: employees realize they need to be aware of a colleague's grief. The policy also expresses shared organizational values that indicate that people's family circumstances are legitimate foci of concern, thus making it more likely that members will share painful family news. It also clearly articulates what pain is (in this case, grief) so members appreciate what to look out for and know when they have seen it. Furthermore, Cisco also has a communication system called the Serious Health Notification System that enables such information to reach the CEO quickly. It is also used by employees to spread the word among members, thus alerting others to the presence of pain in the organization and allowing the collective acknowledgment of a colleague's pain. Together, this policy, and the communication system and technology that support it, serve to legitimate and propagate organizational members' awareness of pain and their appreciation of its significance. In so doing, they help to build the organization's capacity for collective noticing.

The Cisco example illustrates how features of an organization such as its policies, values, systems, and technology can enable collective noticing. We argue that this relationship is bidirectional: members of an organization who are engaged in collective noticing will also be more likely to promote further systems, policies, and work practices that increase the organization's capacity for collectively noticing pain. Developing this capacity is a critical first step in enabling organizational compassion.

Collective Feeling

Collective feeling is the second of three subprocesses that make up the process of organizational compassion. When people collectively feel concern, they not only compassionately share in the distress of a suffering colleague, they also share these feelings more widely with one another. Through narratives and emotionally expressive communication, members are able to develop a collective appreciation of the experiences of the sufferer in their midst. Feelings are also likely to become shared through the process of "emotional contagion" (Hatfield, Cacioppo, & Rapson, 1994), as people working together unconsciously "catch" each other's emotions. We argue that feelings of empathic concern come to be experienced more intensely through their social experience and expression in the organization (Kelly & Barsade, 2001; Parkinson, 1996).

Collective feeling is most likely to be found in organizations where members openly express their emotions, commonly talk about how they are feeling, and exchange emotionally laden stories about work and home life. These member behaviors will occur most readily in organizations that enable the propagation and legitimation of feelings of empathic concern. Key characteristics of such organizations include certain organizational practices and routines related to feeling (Huy, 1999), as well as aspects of the organization's culture, such as its values, norms, and the kinds of feeling language and stories encouraged at work. Leadership, and especially the feelings that leaders model and endorse in their members, also has a significant impact (Frost, 2003). In organizations that lack such practices, culture, and leadership, members must either suppress their personal feelings or express them privately in a way that is not acknowledged or endorsed by the organization and therefore is unlikely to influence other members or the organization itself.

One example of a practice in an organization with a capacity for collective feeling is a regular team meeting in which members are encouraged to talk not only about their task progress but also about how they are feeling about their work, and about nonwork issues. This mechanism allows members to reveal and talk openly about their pain as well as share their emotional responses to colleagues' suffering. As members develop a shared appreciation and acceptance of pain and the emotional reactions it evokes, collective feelings are likely to be generated and maintained (Meyerson, 1994).

Organizational culture can also play a major role in enabling collective feeling at work (Van Maanen & Kunda, 1989). In an organization with a culture that values the expression of suffering and the sharing of emotional reactions to others' pain, for example, members will be more likely to feel and express empathic concern for those in distress. Sharing these feelings in turn reinforces the organization's humane culture. "Feeling rules" (Hochschild, 1983) and "display rules" (Ekman, 1973) play an important part in the organizational culture of an organization with a capacity for collective feeling. These kinds of rules capture the emotion norms of an organization, conveying expectations about how people should feel, and what feelings they should express at work. A collective feeling of empathic concern is likely to develop and spread where feeling and display rules advocate the experience and expression of warmth and concern for those who are suffering.

For example, Cameron and colleagues have studied the pain-inducing processes of downsizing in a variety of organizational settings (Cameron, 1998, 2003; Cameron, Freeman, & Mishra, 1993). They find that human and financial recovery from downsizing happens more effectively in organizations in which stories of kindness and care

are accepted and reinforced, and where normal organizational language includes words like love, compassion, and hope (Cameron, 2003; Cameron, Bright, & Caza, 2004). In the terms we are proposing, these cultural features enable the expression of feelings of pain and feelings associated with forgiveness and care in the face of pain. As a result, these organizations have greater capacities for the collective feeling of pain, which in this case, translates into a more rapid and effective recovery.

Leadership represents another example of a key characteristic of an organization that can contribute to the enabling of collective feeling around pain. Where an organization's leader models the open expression of certain feelings and shows concern for members' pain, others in the organization are much more likely to experience compassionate feelings as legitimate and to share them openly with their colleagues (Dutton et al., 2002; Frost, 2003). For example, when a senior executive at a market research firm passed away suddenly, the CEO personally visited each member of his management team to express his grief and share in their sorrow (Dutton et al., 2002).

Thus, we see how organizational practices, cultural values, and leadership may legitimate and propagate feelings of compassion within organizations. Collective feeling is also part of a positive feedback loop. Organizational members who collectively feel compassion are more likely to interact with one another in ways that reinforce the organization's values and norms, and to enact practices through which collective feelings are likely to be further propagated and legitimated. When members experience others feeling as they do about an event or issue, these feelings will seem more legitimate, and they will feel encouraged to express their emotions more openly and to talk and act in ways that, by shaping the culture and practices of the organization, increase its collective capacity to feel compassion.

Collective Responding

The third subprocess of organizational compassion involves collective responding to pain and suffering. Although we might find individuals engaging in compassionate acts on an occasional basis in any number of organizations, the notion of collective responding refers to a coordinated behavioral response to pain within an organization. Collective compassionate responding, therefore, is partially enabled when members' responses to pain are propagated and legitimated in an organization, but only becomes truly collective when these responses are coordinated in some way. Coordination may come about through a centralized process in which members' responses to pain are coordinated by a particular person or group. Coordination may also occur through the spontaneous emergence and transformation of roles as people find ways to self-organize around the delivery of care (Dutton, Worline, Frost, & Lilius, 2003). Collective compassionate responding may take the form of heedful interrelating (Weick & Roberts, 1993), such that coordination is accomplished through members' appreciation of how to act with others in response to pain, and their understanding of how to interrelate their actions within the system. Just as Weick and Roberts (1993) argue that the intelligence of a collective mind is dependent on the heedfulness with which people act, so an organization's capacity for collective compassionate responding is dependent on its members' heedful interrelating in the face of pain.

Organizations vary in their capacity for collective responding, some reacting quickly and readily to trauma in members' lives, others failing to respond at all (Dutton et al., 2002, 2003). We argue that these variations in capacity result from differences in key organizational characteristics, including leadership and values, as well as structures and systems. These characteristics have the potential to help propagate and legitimate certain kinds of responses to pain, as well as enable the effective coordination of these actions.

Leadership and cultural values that publicly endorse compassionate acts play a key role in propagating and legitimating collective responding. In the wake of the violence of September 11, 2001, we saw, in sharp relief, the difference leadership values made in signaling what were appropriate acts of compassion. Although some leaders modeled caring through the actions they took with respect to employees, customers, and suppliers, other leaders stifled the healing momentum by denying people's need to process and respond to the pain of this day's event and its aftermath (Dutton et al., 2002).

Propagation and legitimation of compassionate responding may also happen through other organizational means. Policies and practices that explicitly acknowledge responding to pain with compassion as an organizational priority can help to promote a culture in which employees believe in working together to alleviate pain in their members. For example, a particular hospital encourages compassion by publicly rewarding employees for their compassionate behaviors. It also distributes a monthly "Caring Times" newsletter to all staff that is composed entirely of stories about hospital employees engaging in caring and compassionate acts. Organizations may also have mechanisms through which the collection of resources for a distressed employee can be centrally coordinated and the giving of collective gifts or memorials organized. For example, this same hospital also has a system that allows its employees to donate their paid vacation and personal days to others who are in need of time off as a result of painful or difficult circumstances (Dutton et al., 2002).

Coordination through heedful interrelating is most likely to occur where systems permit members to develop overlapping knowledge about how to respond to pain. They are then potentially able to take responsibility for all parts of the process to which they can contribute (Hutchins, 1990, p. 210). For example, in an organization where job roles are flexible, responsibilities are broad, and members are empowered, employees are more likely to see and act beyond the boundaries of their formal position and heedfully organize themselves in response to a trauma. When a *Newsweek* editor fell seriously ill, other staff members initiated a number of different responses, each focused on easing a specific aspect of the editor's condition. One employee organized a blood and platelet donation drive in which many staff members participated, another managed home chores for the editor's family, and someone else babysat his children (Dutton et al., 2002).

By propagating, legitimating, and coordinating members' acts in response to pain, an organization can increase its capacity for collective responding, and in turn the organizational compassion of the system. As with collective noticing and feeling, collective responding can produce a virtuous cycle in which members, through their actions, may highlight the need for and value of systems and policies, and reinforce a culture that supports the legitimation, propagation, and effective coordination of collective compassionate acts in the organization.

DYNAMICS OF ORGANIZATIONAL COMPASSION

Organizational compassion is the process in which organizational members collectively notice, feel, and respond to pain within their organization. Although examining the three subprocesses independently of one other allows for a clearer understanding of each of them, in reality, these collective processes are highly interconnected. Different processes often take place simultaneously in a set of organizational members, and any one process may feed into another. Moreover, the organizational characteristics that contribute to an organization's capacity for each process are likely to have a simultaneous impact on more than one collective capacity at a time. For instance, having a culture in which expressions of suffering and empathic concern for others' pain are legitimated can help organizations develop a capacity for collective feeling in the face of pain, as well as contributing to the organization's capacity for collective noticing. In such an organization, members would likely be more open about sharing their pain, making it both more easily felt by others, and more noticeable to them.

Organizational compassion thus involves the interconnection of different people and processes, operating in a way that suggests a "transactive memory system" or "collective mind" (Moreland & Myaskovsky, 2000; Wegner, 1987, 1995; Weick & Roberts, 1993), such that members think, feel, and act not only with an appreciation of the sufferer but with an awareness of how their activities interrelate with those of others. An organization's capacity for collective noticing, feeling, and responding thus derives from its "mindfulness" (Weick, Sutcliffe, & Obstfeld, 1999), or perhaps "carefulness," which is an enriched awareness reflected in the way members notice, feel, and respond to pain in the organization.

Despite the apparently holistic notion of "collective mind," we are not arguing that most organizations' capacities for collective noticing, feeling, and acting will be spread evenly throughout the organization. Instead, we can imagine the existence of pockets of compassion in an organization, such that some departments or divisions exhibit more compassion than others, this often varying over time and across situations. We suggest that the processes of compassion found in these pockets, and the extent to which they are preserved and extended, are significantly shaped by aspects of the organizational context. For example, the physical architecture of a particular department may engender a considerable capacity for collective noticing, feeling, and responding (for example, an open plan unit, where members can typically see other members and often overhear each others' interactions) and at the same time may isolate these collective processes so they remain largely confined to this pocket (such as, if the unit is in a separate building from other parts of the organization). Thus organizational compassion may not be dependent on an organization-wide capacity for collective noticing, feeling, and responding, but, rather, be constituted by the capacities of different organizational areas.

Our conceptualization of organizational compassion reveals it as a complex and potentially time and energy-consuming process. This raises questions about its longer-term impact on an organization, particularly the extent to which it could drain the organization's capacity in other areas and organizational members themselves. Previous research suggests that individuals who engage in compassion and other forms of emotional work may experience emotional exhaustion and burnout, that in turn are costly for the organization (Frost, 2003; Frost et al., 2000; Frost & Robinson, 1999; Kahn, 1993; Meyerson, 2000). Thus, although compassion is healing for those in pain, it has the potential to negatively impact the organizations through its demands on those who "give" it. These effects are especially damaging when an individual acts alone in giving compassion (Frost, 2003). Organizations that support and encourage individual expressions of compassion, however, build capacities for collectively noticing, feeling, and responding to pain, which can be instrumental in replenishing and strengthening individuals' emotional resources (Frost, 2003; Worline et al., 2003). Given the inevitability of pain in organizational life, we expect that developing a capacity for the processes of organizational compassion is likely to increase, rather than reduce, an organization's resilience (Gittell & Cameron, 2003; Worline et al., 2003).

LOOKING FORWARD: POSITIVE ORGANIZATIONAL SCHOLARSHIP RESEARCH IN THE FUTURE

In this chapter, we have explored the process of compassion in organizations. We first examined the three subprocesses of which compassion among individuals is composed, and then developed a conceptualization of "organizational compassion," which exists when members of a system collectively notice, feel, and respond to pain experienced by members of that system. Furthermore, we have examined the role of certain organizational characteristics in the legitimation, propagation, and coordination of these processes.

This chapter makes a number of contributions and has some important implications for our understanding of compassion in organizations and for positive organizational scholarship more generally. Studies of compassion at work have revealed both the prevalence of pain in organizations, but also the great variety of ways in which individuals spontaneously reach out to others who are suffering (Dutton et al., 2002; Frost, 2003; Frost et al., 2000). This chapter adds to the compassion literature by allowing us to see the process of compassion as more than an individual experience or as a process in which a number of people individually engage in an organization. It builds on our understanding of individual compassion in the workplace to identify how organizational members can *collectively* notice, feel, and respond to pain. A valuable avenue for future research would be to examine how members of organizations can, through their co-construction of meaning, their sharing of emotion, and their heedful responding, create pockets of collective compassion within an organization.

This chapter also contributes to the growing field of positive organizational scholarship, which has demonstrated the uniquely important role of positive human processes and dynamics in organizations (Cameron, Dutton, & Quinn, 2003). In particular, such research has highlighted the value to individuals and organizations of institutionalized virtuousness, defined as an orientation toward human fulfillment and social betterment, and characterized by ennobling human behaviors. Although we have evidence of relationships between individual expressions of virtuousness and individual performance (Cameron, 2003) and health (Ryff & Singer, 1998), we have only scratched the surface in understanding how these same dynamics occur in organizations (Cameron, Dutton, Quinn, & Wrzesniewski, 2003). Certainly we cannot assume that individual processes will unfold in the same way as collective ones, and understanding virtuousness at the organizational level represents an important challenge for the field. Our chapter suggests some important processes— propagation, legitimation, and coordination—which we believe may have significance for the development of many positive outcomes in organizations. These processes, which enable the transformation of compassion into a collective phenomenon, have the potential to similarly make other virtues collective (such as the collective processes of forgiveness, integrity, wisdom).

This chapter further contributes to positive organizational scholarship by identifying a variety of systemic features through which organizations can increase their capacity for organizational compassion. Research in positive organizational scholarship raises questions about the "enablement of positivity," or the factors in organizations that enable positive outcomes (Cameron, Dutton, Quinn, & Wrzesniewski, 2003). In the present chapter, we have identified a range of characteristics, including culture, systems, leadership, and technology, that appear to enable the collective processes of noticing, feeling, and responding, and therefore of organizational compassion. An empirical investigation that examines the combinations of organizational features most important in propagating, legitimating, and coordinating different subprocesses of compassion would make a valuable contribution to our understanding of the positive dynamics in organizational life.

By their very nature, the processes described in this chapter lend themselves to certain methodological approaches. Our interest in the process of organizational compassion suggests the use of interpretive methods, which allow the investigation of noticing, feeling, and responding as experienced and understood by organizational members. In particular, we believe that the three subprocesses of organizational compassion might be usefully examined through methods that allow the observation of and engagement with organizational members at close quarters and over time (for example, Fineman, 2000; Huy, 2002). Although the study of positive organizational dynamics, including compassion, can gain from a variety of different research methodologies, qualitative methods are particularly well-suited to the study of collective processes in organizations.

To conclude, we want to suggest that the study of organizational compassion and other positive organizational processes presents an exciting opportunity for organizational researchers not only to investigate a set of fascinating phenomena, but also to raise awareness of the positive potential inherent in human organization and in human organizing processes. The set of processes we have described here as constituting organizational compassion—collective noticing, feeling, and responding—require rich and systematic investigation if their dynamics and impact are to be understood and their promise realized.

CHAPTER FORTY

Generating Simultaneous Personal, Team, and Organization Development

William R. Torbert

——ᴡᴡ— T his chapter illustrates how developmental theory can be used both to assess and transform leaders, teams, and organizations simultaneously. The chapter first briefly introduces developmental theory as it applies to individuals, interpersonal processes, and organizations, including references to quantitative empirical research that supports the theoretical claims. Next, it offers two case studies of interventions that support simultaneous individual, interpersonal, and organizational transformation. The chapter concludes with the argument that interweaving first-, second-, and third-person research into practice generates both transforming action and valid knowledge.

PERSONAL, INTERPERSONAL, AND ORGANIZATION DEVELOPMENT

Table 40.1 offers a brief overview of individual and organizational development action-logics. These have been described in much greater detail elsewhere, and if you are new to these issues, you may wish to review other sources (Kegan, 1982, 1994; Kohlberg, 1984; Torbert, 1976, 1987; 1989; Torbert & Associates, 2004; Wilber, 1999). In this chapter, you can get a first impression of the theory by scanning Table 40.1, and will gain a greater intuitive sense of these action-logics by referring backwards and forwards from Table 40.1 to the case studies offered.

At the outset, however, let me highlight a few key points about the overall theory. First, development is sequential: each later personal and organizational action-logic includes all the options and capacities of the earlier logics, plus new ones. Second, the personal action-logics alternate between those that are more agency-focused (Opportunist, Expert, Individualist . . .) and those that are more relationally focused (Diplomat, Achiever, Strategist . . .). Likewise, the organizational action-logics alternate between those that tend toward centralization (Incorporation, Systematic Productivity, Collaborative Inquiry . . .) and those that tend toward decentralization (Investments, Experiments, Social Network . . .). In the case of both individuals and organizations, the tension of these opposites declines at the later action-logics, which are increasingly win-win; both-and; paradox welcoming; difference friendly; and transformational, not static.

Third, people and organizations do not necessarily develop to later action-logics. Many cease evolving when they reach the Diplomat/ Incorporation action-logic. Less than half of all people and organizations develop beyond the Expert/Experiments action-logic, and fewer than 5 percent develop beyond the next. A fourth quality of this analogical developmental model is that the early action-logics up through Achiever/Systematic Productivity do not recognize themselves as assumed and transformable frames of activity and thought, but rather treat their (unrecognized) assumptions as the very bedrock of reality (Torbert, 1991). These early action-logics assume that everyone shares the same "reality" and that significant deviations from one's own judgment represent lack of proper training, incompetence, or evil. In other words, the early action-logics do not recognize that different people or organizations frame reality differently. Nor do they understand the common potential in them for questioning and transforming our assumptions if events and constructive feedback suggest significant anomalies.

A final point is that each developmental transformation represents a significant qualitative enhancement of the person or organization's systemic agentic and relational capacities. For example, the great victory of the Achiever/Systematic Productivity action-logic is that it welcomes single-loop feedback, permitting the person or organization to improve in the ability to reach a set goal. But this action-logic is not

Personal Development	Organizational Development
1. Impulsive Impulses rule behavior	1. Conception Dreams about creating a new organization
Multiple, distinctive impulses gradually resolve into characteristic approach (for example, many fantasies resolve into a particular dream for a new organization)	
2. Opportunist Needs rule impulses	2. Investments Spiritual, social network, and financial investments
Dominant task: gain power (for example, bike-riding skill, capital) to have desired effects on outside world	
3. Diplomat Norms rule needs	3. Incorporation Products or services actually rendered
Looking-glass self: understanding others' culture/expectations and molding own actions to succeed on their terms (for example, a marketable product)	
4. Expert "Craft logic" rules norms	4. Experiments Alternative strategies and structures tested
Intellectual mastery of outside-self systems (such that actions experiments that generate new ways of doing business)	
5. Achiever System effectiveness rules "craft logic"	5. Systematic Productivity Single structure/strategy institutionalized
Pragmatic triangulation among plan/theory, operation/implementation, and outcome/evaluation—single-loop feedback acted on unsystematically but regularly	
6. Individualist Reflexive awareness rules effectiveness	6. Social Network Portfolio of distinctive organizational structures
Experimental awareness that diverse assumptions may complement one another both for inquiry and for productivity	
7. Strategist Self-amending principle rules reflexive awareness	7. Collaborative Inquiry Self-amending structure matches dream/mission
Self-conscious mission/philosophy; sense of time/place; invites conversation among multiple voices and reframing of boundaries—double-loop feedback occasionally acted on	
8. Alchemist Mutual process (interplay of principle/action) rules principle	8. Foundational Community of Inquiry Structure fails, spirit sustains wider community
Life/science = a mind/matter, love/death/transformation praxis among others; cultivating interplay, reattunement, and continual triple-loop feedback among purpose, strategy, practice, and outcomes	
9. Ironist Intergenerational development rules mutual process	9. Liberating Disciplines Structures encourage productivity and transformational learning through manageable conflict and vulnerable power

Table 40.1.   Parallels Between Personal and Organizational Stages of Development.

Source: Adapted from Torbert & Associates, 2004.

yet open to seeking out and testing the validity of double-loop feedback, which questions whether current goals, structures, and assumptions about reality deserve to be examined and transformed over time (Merron, Fisher, & Torbert, 1987; Fisher & Torbert, 1991). And it is also not yet capable of cultivating triple-loop feedback, which tests the timeliness of one's own and others' assumptions, strategies, actions, and outcomes from moment to moment (Torbert, 1996). This will be the victory in transforming to the Alchemist action-logic.

According to this theoretical distinction, we would expect that organizational leaders and consultants who measure at the later action-logics (for example, Strategist, Alchemist) will be more likely to succeed in supporting individual, interpersonal, and organizational transformation than leaders and consultants at the earlier action-logics. And indeed several empirical studies statistically support this (Bushe & Gibbs, 1990; Rooke & Torbert, 1998; Foster & Torbert, 2005). Likewise, we would expect that organizations exhibiting later action-logic qualities (for example, Collaborative Inquiry, Liberating Disciplines) would be more likely to support individual transformation among their members than organizations at earlier action-logics. Once again, several statistical studies support this (Manners, Durkin, & Nesdale, 2004; Torbert, 1991, 1994; Torbert & Fisher, 1992).

If we ask how these analogical theories of individual and organization development manifest themselves in the interpersonal realm of conversations and teams, we find that the work of Chris Argyris sheds light on the question. Undisputedly the leading theoretician among management scholars of individual and organization development over the past fifty years, Argyris (1957, 1962, 1965, 1970, 1980, 1981, 1994) has been articulating a theory and researching a practice of transformational learning and change with particular emphasis on the interpersonal scale. He has developed two models of interpersonal processes that he calls Models I and II (Argyris & Schön, 1974). Model I characterizes virtually all observable managerial practice and includes four key assumptions, or "governing variables" in Argyris's terms, that make norms and power dynamics undiscussable, reduce ongoing inquiry, and inhibit trust and the possibilities for transformational change in groups. These four governing variables correspond with the frames of the early action-logics (Opportunist through Achiever) that constitute the framing assumptions of some 95 percent of the general population and 85 percent of corporate managers and executives (Kegan, 1994; Rooke & Torbert, 2005; Torbert, 1991).

Argyris (1994, p. 55) names Model II governing variables "valid information, informed choice, and vigilant monitoring of the implementation of the choice in order to detect and correct error." Earlier, these variables were named "valid information, free and informed choice, and internal commitment to the choice and constant monitoring of its implementation" (Argyris & Schön, 1974, p. 87). Exhibit 40.1 shows how these Model I and Model II governing variables correspond to preeminent concerns of the four post-Achiever action-logics.

In short, we see that Argyris's Model II governing variables are included among the interpersonal concerns of the post-Achiever action-logics. These concerns also relate to issues of (1) developing a shared vision (an issue rife with dilemma when worldviews differ widely); (2) exercising power in ways that increasingly enhance mutuality (another major dilemma when all early action-logics treat power as a unilateral phenomenon); and (3) achieving timely action in both the short and the long terms (a third major challenge, given the varying time horizons of different action-logics). The first case study offered in this chapter illustrates these concerns in action: it shows how a consultant measured at the Alchemist action-logic works through these issues with an Achiever/Individualist president, an Expert/Achiever vice president, and a software company spread-eagled across the Investments/Incorporation/Experiments action-logics.

Model I—Mystery-Mastery

1. Maximize winning, minimize losing	Opportunist
2. Minimize eliciting negative emotions	Diplomat
3. Maximize rationality in presentation	Expert
4. Achieve own self-defined goals	Achiever

Model II—Collaborative Inquiry

1. Maximize inquiry and valid information about actual performance vs. espoused values	Individualist
2. Maximize internal commitment of partners to shared vision	Strategist
3. Maximize mutual influence and positive freedom of choice	Alchemist
4. Maximize timely action and intergenerational sustainability	Ironist

Exhibit 40.1.   Two Models of Interpersonal Process.

The case study will be more meaningful to readers armed with some sense of what senior management teams at several different action-logics look like. The brief archetypal illustrations, adapted from work by Rooke & Torbert (2005), provide a more concrete image of developmental positions at the interpersonal scale.

Senior teams, for example, operating at the Diplomat/Incorporation action-logic are typically dysfunctional in generating organizational efficacy. They are characterized by deference to the leader, strong status differences, undiscussable norms, jokes and nervous laughter, irregular meetings where little real work is done, and ritual "court" ceremonies that are carefully staged and managed.

In Expert/Experiments senior management teams, vice presidents typically see themselves as chiefs of their own divisions and see the senior "team" as an information-reporting formality or political gauntlet. Team "life" is bereft of shared problem-solving, decision-making, or strategy-formulating efforts, and is sometimes characterized by outside-the-meeting politicking.

Many senior manager teams in Fortune 500 corporations operate at the Achiever/Systematic Productivity level. They prefer unambiguous targets and deadlines; work best with clear strategies, tactics, plans, and tight deadlines; thrive in a climate of adversity; and derive great pleasure from pulling together and delivering. Their shadow side is that members are typically impatient at slowing down to reflect, are apt to dismiss questions about goals and assumptions as "endless philosophizing," and typically respond with hostile humor to creative exercises that seem like "off the wall" diversions to them. These behaviors limit the team's ability to transform or sustain any creative reinvention of the company.

Individualist/Social Network senior teams are rare and more likely to be found in creative, consulting, and not-for-profit organizations. They may be strongly reflective. In fact, excessive time may be spent in creative brainstorming and in reviewing and reexamining goals, assumptions, and work practices. Rapid decision making can be difficult, but decision quality is high.

Over the long term, teams with a Strategist/Collaborative Inquiry culture are more effective than those with earlier action-logics. They see business challenges as opportunities for growth, learning, and transformation of themselves and others, as well as for efficient and effective productivity. A leadership team at one of the companies that we worked with, for example, decided to invite managers from across departments to participate in time-to-market new product teams. Seeing the teams as a risky distraction, few managers volunteered, except for a few Individualists and budding Strategists. Senior management provided sufficient support and feedback that led to the teams' early successes. Soon the first participants were promoted and leading their own cross-departmental teams. Achievers in the organization, seeing that others were being promoted, started volunteering for these new product teams. Gradually, more people within the organization were experiencing shared leadership, mutual testing of one another's assumptions and practices, and the individual challenges that supported their leadership development and growth to later action-logics.

CASE STUDY: AN ALCHEMIST CONSULTANT IN AN EARLY ACTION-LOGIC SOFTWARE COMPANY

Multiple developmental processes on different levels and scales (personal, interpersonal, team, organizational, national) influence one another. They can interrupt, inhibit, or encourage developmental progress. Consultants' contributions are enhanced when they learn to see these interweaving developmental processes in action and intervene to help whole organizations transform from one developmental action-logic to another. The case of a small software company stuck spread-eagled across the Investments, Incorporation, and Experiments action-logics illustrates the power of this. Adapted from Torbert & Associates (2004), this case explores how a consultant's intervention can encourage an organizational transformation by creating a temporary Collaborative Inquiry action-logic learning organization within the larger company. The temporary state encourages a great deal of feedback and creative, collaborative decision-making processes in the short run and offers significant aftereffects as well.

———〰———

The company in this case has burned through its initial round of venture financing. It is seeking a second round (Investments), has produced a large number of high-quality products (Experiments), and has thirty-five employees (Incorporation), but there are no net revenues on the horizon. The organizational consultant, who takes a developmental approach in his work, is invited to help the company over a two-day period. He approaches the assignment believing that he must engage in an interviewing and meeting process to discover how disharmonies among the corporate dream, leadership's strategies, and the day-to-day operations account for the company's continuing losses. Further, he believes that the research and intervention processes must discover a positive way to reframe or restructure the situation with the senior leadership team so that they can enact vision, strategy, and operations more harmoniously.

On the first day, the consultant interviews top management (the president and the vice presidents for production, marketing, and sales). He discovers that everybody knows that the company must make a breakthrough in marketing and sales. Yet this "bottom-line," relatively objective negative feedback is not enough to propel the company into a new operating pattern. The president is a generation older than the three VPs, and the company is a partnership between the president and the VP for production. Together, the two had developed the company's initial product.

The consultant discovers numerous problems that have remained unresolved for a long time. Neither mission nor market is well defined. Pricing is a subject of acrimonious controversy. Employee morale is fragile. It is unclear whether competence or nepotism is the basis for rewards: one partner's daughter is the VP for sales and the other's best friend is an employee. Decisions are not driven by any internal sense of mission: they are only made when situations deteriorate into external emergencies.

The bottleneck in decision making appears to be the relationship between the two partners. They respect one another and attempt to share responsibility as equals; however, they repeatedly fall prey to differences in age, formal role, and managerial style. The president plays the role of an optimistic, appreciative, absentminded father. The VP plays the role of the pessimistic, rebellious son.

Having interviewed the senior managers individually, the consultant is slated to meet with the two partners to set the agenda for the next day's senior management retreat. Based on what he has heard, the consultant fears that the agenda-setting session and the retreat may fall prey to the partners' wrangling and habitual indecisiveness. In a ten-minute walk around the building prior to his meeting with the partners, the consultant engages in first-person action inquiry: he intentionally focuses on his breathing; following that, he moves his attention to the vividness of the outside world; he then turns to his feelings; only when he has established this triple-loop, ongoing circulation of attention does he focus on what he knows about the company. Maintaining this wider attention and taking seriously his feeling of fear and crisis in regard to his imminent meeting with the partners, the consultant decides that the partners' pattern of behavior will need to change before any other productive decisions are likely. He decides that he should invent an initiative to launch this learning process for the partners immediately if possible. To help him generate design ideas for the meeting that is only moments away, the consultant quickly, analogically, and heuristically applies developmental theory to the company as a whole, to the individual partners, and to his two-day intervention.

Looking developmentally at the company as a whole, the consultant sees the organization as spread-eagled across the fluid, decentralized Investments and Experiments stages. It still lives off venture capital, but is experimenting with a whole line of products. At the same time, the company is failing to "bite the bullet" and meet the limiting, centralizing, differentiating demands of the Incorporation stage—the demand, in short, for net revenues.

Applying developmental theory to each of the partners, the consultant wonders whether the junior partner is an Opportunist, given his seeming self-centeredness and irritability, or an Expert, given his technical creativity in designing new software products and his doctoral degree. Recognizing that he is working with scant data, the consultant chooses to err on the upside. (Erring on the downside can insult the client and hurt the relationship, whereas the client will typically not even recognize an upside developmental error, allowing the consultant to adjust with little loss.) In this case, the consultant then estimates that the VP is in transition from Expert to Achiever, both itching for and resisting the true executive responsibility that Achievers relish. Similarly, he wonders whether the president is a Diplomat, given his affable, conflict-avoiding style, or an Individualist, given his appreciation of individual differences and willingness to share power. The consultant estimates that the president is in transition from Achiever to Individualist, ready to give up day-to-day executive responsibility in favor of an elder statesman role of mentoring his junior partner and godfathering the company's research and development function. In fact, the president had spoken wistfully of his preference for the VP R&D position.

Applying developmental theory to the two-day visit, the consultant interprets his initial interviews as the Conception stage of the intervention. He sees the agenda-setting session with the two partners at the Investments stage. The question now is how to transform his consulting style from a more passive, receptive, relational interviewing process to a more active, agentic, intervening Incorporation process to model the very decisiveness that he believes the partners must be willing to enact in order to effect the rapid major changes needed in the organization as a whole.

The consultant decides to recommend at the agenda-setting session that only the partners and the consultant participate in tomorrow's retreat and that whatever decisions the partners reach be put in writing with definite implementation dates. The smaller retreat makes crisp decision making more likely, especially with regard to restructuring senior management, which the consultant now views as important. He believes that the VP for sales should be demoted. He already knows from his interviews that everyone, including the VP herself, agrees on this, but no one has discussed it with anyone else.

The consultant believes that the partners' roles need redefining and that the company needs a single decisive executive for its Incorporation stage. Interestingly, both partners have used ballot imagery during their initial interviews to describe their relative power within the company. The president, in referring to their equal salaries and his own style of consulting his partner on all significant decisions, spoke of their holding "ballots of the same size" on company decisions. The VP, however, sees the president as having the larger vote. It now occurs to the consultant to invite the two to switch roles as a role play for this one day. This "liberating discipline" may help each move onward developmentally, break the company's decision-making logjam, or both. The mere suggestion will alter their usual dynamics and put them (and the consultant!) into a posture of simultaneous learning and into performance conducive to Model II collaborative inquiry.

The consultant begins his feedback and agenda-setting session with the two partners by proposing that the VP resign or become president. Although quiet, the president seems ready to play this game. True to his customary opposing role, the VP objects: he sees this as "rehearsing" to be president. The VP probes the consultant's reasoning. The two senior officers finally agree to take the role-switch game seriously. This puts the VP in the action role right away, a switch from his usual role of combatively reacting to the president.

The VP, now in the role of the president, acts decisively. He and the consultant propose various changes, with the president in his subordinate role making constructive suggestions and raising questions. The two partners reach written agreement on six major organizational changes the next day, including resolving cost and pricing issues and focusing on only one of their innovative products. The first of these changes is implemented at lunch that day. The VP for sales (the president's daughter) is invited to join them. The partners discuss the major changes they are considering. They ask her to accept a demotion and work under the VP of marketing. She agrees, expressing both disappointment that she has not been able to help the company more and relief that her duties will be more circumscribed. Showing that they have retained confidence in her, the partners ask her to take the lead that afternoon in communicating the new reporting arrangement to the VP of marketing, as well as informally communicating the other two decisions made that morning to others in the company. She enthusiastically agrees.

The following Monday, the written agreement describing the six changes, signed by both partners, is in all company members' mailboxes when they arrive. A companywide meeting at the end of the following day confirms the partners' agreement and allows for questions and discussion of the implications. A month later, the changes have all been implemented. Two months later and six months ahead of schedule, the company completes a first-of-its-kind product for a large market. The company fails to get a second round of venture financing, but sales revenues exceed costs for the first time in the company's history.

In the meantime, the VP has decided not to become president, and the president stipulates that henceforward he will draw a higher salary and exercise the managerial authority of CEO on a day-to-day basis. Three months later, the VP decides he is ready to become president after all and negotiates the change with his partner.

—⁓—

This case illustrates how a simultaneous developmental analysis of an organization and its leaders and an ongoing intervention process can help bring the primary issues and priority decisions into focus. It also illustrates how the consultant as a late action-logic leader can interweave actions that lead to personal, interpersonal, and organizational trans-formations. On the personal scale, the consultant engages in actions and reflections that transform his perspectives at a critical moment: his triple-loop attention-clearing exercise, followed by his double-loop effort to integrate and translate everything he has learned about the company into a theory and strategy for redesigning the rest of the consulting engagement. Next, he generates an interpersonal action inquiry process among members of the company, particularly the partners and the sales VP. Over the next several months, the company as a whole transforms into a more centralized and successful Incorporation action-logic. Over time, the VP continued his own inquiry into the leadership role he wished to embody. His eventual choice to become president may be seen as his transformation from Expert to Achiever.

FIFTEEN YEARS LATER: ANOTHER ILLUSTRATIVE CASE

Fifteen years later, the same consultant and a number of colleagues began offering three-day "Leading Organizational Transformation" workshops for senior teams of sizeable organizations. The twenty-or-so participants in the workshops take the Leadership Development Profile (Cook-Greuter, 1999; Torbert & Associates, 2004) beforehand to discern their personal action-logics. They also write a short inter-personal case on a difficult conversation and unsatisfactory outcome that occurred with another member also attending the workshop (Argyris & Schön, 1974; Rudolph, Taylor, & Foldy, 2001). The consultants also interview participants prior to the workshop and use other data about their organization to estimate its developmental position. The workshop itself helps participants move along a developmental progression: from making personal developmental commitments, to learning new conversational strategies and practices, to generating strategies and commitments for organizational change.

———〜〜〜———

One such workshop was held with eighteen members of a new division in a major energy company. Diverging from the company's current strategy that supported its profitable production and distribution of oil, a number of upper-middle-level leaders had gained some executive support for exploring alternatives to oil. They commissioned the workshop because their own consensus about the importance of thinking "outside the industry box" on these questions was not shared within the rest of the company. A critical issue for them was how to influence the leadership culture of the organization as a whole. As might be predicted, these eighteen leaders scored, on average, at much later action-logics than our larger samples. Instead of 85 percent at the early action-logics and Achiever as the mode, 66 percent of this group scored at the post-Achiever action-logics, with Strategist as the mode. We had two Alchemists to boot!

Organizational-level data, however, which included an annual internal survey, suggested that the senior team of the organization was operating at the Systematic Productivity action-logic. They had also generated significant distrust in the organization because of perceived contradictions between the senior team's espoused and enacted values. Also, the lead consultant had spent an earlier day with the new "alternative" division members. He had diagnosed and shared with the group that it was operating in a decentralized, reflective, inconclusive Individualist/Social Network fashion that was inhibiting it from pursuing its own strategies and having impact on the larger organization. The team confirmed the diagnosis as accurate.

On the first day of the workshop, one participant became distressed that his Leadership Development Profile measured him at the Achiever action-logic when he had diagnosed himself as a Strategist. He asked for a public discussion of the validity and ethics of the measure. The staff and other participants agreed to the discussion. They scheduled it at the end of the second afternoon and after small-group work on each participant's "difficult conversation" case. The decision reflected a reasonable strategy for approaching a conflict between a third-person, relatively objective empirical measure (the Leadership Development Profile) and the participant's first-person, reflective subjective judgment. It seemed useful to work through a second-person methodology before the public discussion, giving opportunities during the discussion to triangulate among first-, second-, and third-person forms of research (Reason & Bradbury, 2001; Reason & Torbert, 2001; Chandler & Torbert, 2003).

The participant's "difficult conversation" case showed that he felt like a "lone ranger" committed to creativity in an organization that espoused, but did not reward, such creativity. He felt isolated and powerless at work, even with so many late action-logic colleagues, but gratified by the group's responsiveness to his request for public discussion of the instrument.

The participant's framing assumptions in the case did not seem Achiever-like, either to him or others. They also did not seem Strategist-like, but more Individualist. The participant and those with whom he was debriefing the case felt a strong emotional analogy between his attitude of isolation in the larger organization and the attitude of the team as a whole toward it. During the public conversation that occurred next, this initially distressed and disgruntled participant displayed humor, tears, and positive passion as he led a discussion about three important issues:

1. His personal transformation over the past day. He had changed his view of himself from Strategist to Individualist. It was still postconventional as he had initially believed, but now with an added and clear developmental agenda: learning to move beyond simple advocacy to the political skills involved in exercising mutuality-enhancing, transforming power.

2. The team's newly forming identity as a group that interweaves first-, second-, and third-person action and research in an artistic, compassionate, and timely manner and that uses this approach in its future scholarly, pedagogical, and business initiatives.

3. The need for the team to take a more proactive, strategic stance toward the organization's senior management.

The group continued its work together in the workshop at a new level. On the third day of the workshop, participants generated various organizational action initiatives; described the commitments to personal, team, and organizational development that each were prepared to make; and offered quantitative and qualitative assessments of the workshop. (Exhibit 40.2 shows the results of the anonymous, quantitative assessments.)

―∿∿―

Since the workshop, the new division has taken new and decisive steps toward intervening constructively in the larger organization. Subgroups have worked to (1) consult to the senior management team; (2) influence the organization's overall strategy; (3) hold further workshops with a wider array of organizational members to refine the division's strategic initiative and explore how others frame and consider the issue of alternative energy sources and products; and (4) develop a research project based on interweaving first-, second-, and third-person methods to find innovative organizations in related industries with whom to explore strategic alliances.

1. Compared to your expectations coming into this workshop, how much have you learned about developmental theory and instruments, as well as action inquiry practice and methods?

Much less than expected		About what expected		Much more than expected	
1	2	3	4	5	6
(Avg.: 4.47)		1	1 5	9	

2. In "absolute" terms, how much have you learned about these ideas and practices?

Virtually nothing		A moderate amount		An unusually great amount	
1	2	3	4	5	6
(Avg.: 4.74)			4	7	2

3. Compared to a typical month in your life this past year, how much personal double- and triple-loop learning has this three-day workshop catalyzed to date?

Much less		About the same		Much more		As much as in any other month in my life
1	2	3	4	5	6	7
(Avg.: 5.56)				2 10	2	1

4. Compared to a typical month at work this past year, how much double- and triple-loop learning and transformation in working relationships with individual colleagues and the group as a whole have you done these past three days?

Much less		About the same		Much more		As much as in any other month in my life
1	2	3	4	5	6	7
(Avg.: 5.38)		2	2	4	4	4

5. Compared to a typical month at work this past year, how much double- and triple-loop learning do you see occurring during this workshop as regards the relationship between this group and the organization as a whole?

Much less		About the same		Much more		As much as in any other month in my life
1	2	3	4	5	6	7
(Avg. 4.8)		2	4	4	5	

(1 "unable to answer" on last question)

Exhibit 40.2.   Quantitative Assessment of Developmental Action Inquiry Workshop.

DISCUSSION

The long-term power and efficacy of organization development (OD) has been severely compromised by a number of choices and forces. These include the field's lack of widespread and disciplined attention to

- Developmental theory.
- First- and second-person transformational practices. Developmental theory highlights these as essential for supporting double-loop change and movement from earlier to later action-logics for individuals, teams, and organizations.

- Third-person measures of development that can document the efficacy (or inefficacy) of transformational practices.

- Development of a paradigm of social science as an "action science" (Torbert, 1976; Argyris, Putnam, & Smith, 1985) that interweaves the first-, second-, and third-person theory, practice, and research necessary to support and document individual, team, and organizational transformation.

Despite these gaps in the OD literature, there are a number of related theories and measures of personal development in the psychological literature that can be used to advance understandings of the linkages between development and transformation (Kegan, 1982, 1994; Kohlberg, 1984; Loevinger, 1982; Wilber, 1999). There are also several developmental theories of organizations (Greiner, 1972; Lippitt & Schmidt, 1967; Torbert, 1976), although only one has been measured quantitatively (Rooke & Torbert, 1998; Leigh, 2002). In addition, the leadership and organizational studies that this chapter draws on make important contributions. They document profound differences in the capability of leaders and organizations at different developmental action-logics (Merron et al., 1987; Rooke & Torbert, 2005; Torbert, 1987, 1991). They identify which individual and organizational action-logics successfully generate and support personal and organizational transformations, offering both case studies and statistical evidence for the transformational efficacy of these efforts (Manners et al., 2004; Rooke & Torbert, 1998; Torbert, 1994; Torbert & Associates, 2004; Torbert & Fisher, 1992). They also reconceptualize social science itself as simultaneously operating through multiple developmental action-logics or paradigms, some of which seek to integrate theory, practice, and research and to invite inquiry into their own assumptions for their own potential transformation (Chandler & Torbert, 2003; Reason & Torbert, 2001; Sherman & Torbert, 2000; Torbert, 1991, 1998, 2000).

The two case studies presented in this chapter humanize and "give a face" to developmental theory and practice. You may be skeptical, however, about the validity and generalizability of such theory and practice—despite their consistency with Chris Argyris's large body of work and the references to various statistical studies provided in the chapter. Certainly, this theory and practice must be cultivated and tested widely before final judgments on their validity and transformational efficacy are made. The strength of the tests to date, however, deserve to be emphasized in closing.

For example, a study of five for-profit and five not-for-profit organizations (in six industries and in different countries) attempting organizational transformation with consulting help (Rooke & Torbert, 1998; Torbert & Associates, 2004) showed that the combination of the CEO's action-logic and the consultant's action-logic accounted for an extraordinarily high 59 percent of the variance (Spearman rank-order test, significant beyond the .01 level of probability; Cohen [1983] classifies 25 percent of the variance as a "large effect") in whether or not the organization successfully transformed (with .90 inter-rater reliability among three scorers on the organizational transformation measure). In that study, if both the CEO and the consultant measured at the Strategist action-logic or beyond, the organization successfully transformed in every case. However, if the CEO measured at a pre-Strategist action-logic, the organization successfully transformed only 40 percent of the time and then only if the consultant was measured at the Alchemist action-logic. A careful review of threats to internal and external validity in this study shows that the primary limitation is one of external validity: the ten organizations ranged from 10 to 1,019 employees, thus making the results generalizable to 95 percent of organizations, but not necessarily to the largest Fortune 500–type organizations.

In conclusion, developmental theory and practice have much to offer to OD. The OD field is invited to embrace both theory and practice seriously to increase its impact, its possibilities, and the real opportunity to make a transformational difference in social science and social action during the next generation.

OD and the Future

Embracing Change and New Directions

O D is at a crossroads. The public and private sectors need OD's skills, values, and experiences more than ever to deal with the increased complexity, competition, and pressures of modern organizational life. At the same time, too few organizations recognize all that OD can offer. The resulting opportunities are as exciting and daunting as those faced by the field's founders: developing and teaching new ways of organizing that meet the contemporary needs of people and organizations. Rising fully to this challenge, however, takes the field toward new theories, practices, markets, and applications. Doing this well requires (1) differentiating OD's core from its peripheral trappings and (2) creating a proactive strategy for identifying possibilities for OD's future.

Rob Kapilow, a composer, conductor, and National Public Radio commentator, travels the world on a mission to open new ears to music. His message is straightforward: listening is more than just hearing; individuals learn to understand and relate to a piece of music when they actively engage with it. For Kapilow, this means *listening for possibilities*—holding on to core themes in a piece while searching for variations, staying grounded in the familiar while relishing the unexpected, embracing the comfort of repetition while anticipating the energy in change, and celebrating the beauty and power in the mix.

Listening for possibilities is a deliberate commitment to search for new levels of understanding. It challenges the listener by asking for both focus and openness. It turns the old and distant into something personal and relevant. The process respects the past and transforms it at the same time: listening for possibilities embraces the paradoxical and liberating nature of tradition. Vibrant, creative artists respect and study the past because it is the platform for their next innovative leap. Stravinsky got it right almost three quarters of a century ago in his Charles Eliot Norton lectures at Harvard:

> Tradition is entirely different from habit, even from an excellent habit, since habit is by definition an unconscious acquisition and tends to be mechanical, whereas tradition results from a conscious and deliberate acceptance. A real tradition is not the relic of a past that is irretrievably gone; it is a living force that animates and informs the present. . . . Far from implying the repetition of what has been, tradition presupposes the reality of what endures. It appears as an heirloom, a heritage that one receives on condition of making it bear fruit before passing it on to one's descendants. . . . A tradition is carried forward in order to produce something new. Tradition thus assures the continuity of creation. (Stravinsky, 1970, pp. 56–57)

Kapilow developed his ideas to make classical music more accessible. The relevance of his message for a field like OD, however, should not be missed. OD's future rests in maintaining the complex balance between holding on and letting go. The OD field needs to celebrate and build on its distinct heritage—its focus on organizational effectiveness and health, growth and learning, and the essential contribution of people. But when OD gets trapped in its own history and traditions, it loses its competitive edge, alienates its audience, and falls behind the times. The way forward requires honoring the past while aggressively listening for possibilities.

There is irony in this. More than half a century ago, OD began as a field steeped in hope. Somewhere between then and now, things changed. A field that advocated the importance of staying connected, engaged, and cutting edge—actively listening and probing, attending to the particular needs of time and place, incorporating ideas from a range of sources and arenas, testing new theories and models, searching for new methods and practices—stopped following its own advice. As a result, OD has drifted off center stage and into the wings, but there is the possibility for a strong comeback.

Decades before *Dilbert*, OD's founders were well aware of the inefficiencies, discomforts, and tragedies in organizational life. But they were unquenchably optimistic—convinced that new ideas and tools were emerging that could produce revolutionary changes in current forms of managing and organizing. They were carriers of America's historic faith in the idea of progress and possibility. They believed in democracy, openness, and the worth of every individual. Above all, they believed in learning and experimentation. They knew they did not have all the answers, but they were confident that answers were waiting to be found, and they set out with others in bold pursuit to find them. Their faith and courage were, indeed, rewarded. Open minds and entrepreneurial spirits spawned an exciting intellectual movement—a paradigm shift—and changed how the world understood people, organizations, and change. They gave birth to the organizational and applied behavioral sciences, and OD developed a powerful array of ideas and practices for understanding and improving organizations, many of which have been discussed in earlier chapters of this volume.

Has the field lost its faith and courage along with its direction? The authors who have contributed to this volume provide a clear and hopeful response. OD will grow and thrive so long as there are scholars and practitioners who continue to search for possibilities—who scan the environment, grow markets, rethink preparation, expand applications, discover new techniques, identify opportunities, update old approaches, test and generate new concepts, foster collaborations between the academy and practice, and more. OD's proud tradition of engaging people and their expertise in the design and management of healthy and effective organizations can be carried forward to produce something new. The chapters in Part Eight point to possibilities.

Part Eight begins with two perspectives on the current state of the field. Robert J. Marshak, a distinguished practitioner, wrote "Emerging Directions: Is There a New OD?" for this volume. He identifies major philosophical shifts over time in the assumptions that underpin OD practices, and sees the field's future as dependent on a willingness to clarify the meaning and purpose of organization development work today. David L. Bradford and W. Warner Burke, faculty members at Stanford and Columbia University, respectively, bring the scholar's lens to the issue of OD's future in a chapter from their book, *Reinventing Organization Development: New Approaches to Change in Organizations.* They identify three areas for OD to address in its revitalization: the field's overemphasis on technique, human processes, and rigid values. They express hope that OD will rise to the challenge of the work.

Major changes in the external environment and the nature of work represent other areas for OD's attention (and expand possibilities identified by the authors in Part Seven of this volume). Technology, globalization, the growing knowledge economy, and environmental concerns are a few of the obvious. The next four chapters examine those issues.

In *Evolve! Succeeding in the Digital Culture of Tomorrow,* respected scholar and innovator Rosabeth Moss Kanter examines what she calls "e-culture"—a new way of living and working in the digital age. As should come as no surprise to advocates of OD, Kanter argues that an organization's soul and success in the Internet Age rest in the personal networks and relationships forged by its members. Her chapter offers six steps for building community in contemporary organizations. Next, Ron Ashkenas, Dave Ulrich, Todd Jick, and Steve Kerr explore the challenges of globalization and strategies for working across national, cultural, space, and time differences in an excerpt from *The Boundaryless Organization: Breaking the Chains of Organizational Structure.* The authors' discussion complements the provocative Mirvis and Gunning chapter in Part Seven.

"Knowledge-Worker Productivity: The Biggest Challenge," by the late Peter F. Drucker, explores the critical shift from manual work to knowledge work in contemporary organizations. Drucker provides background for understanding the implications of this change for individuals, the structure of work, organizational governance, and the larger economy. Next, Stuart L. Hart tackles the issues of organizational responsibilities and impact in his chapter, "Beyond Greening: Strategies for a Sustainable World," which first appeared as an article in *Harvard Business Review.* Developing a sustainable global economy entails more than just controlling pollution. It requires a special kind of organizational leadership that attends to its own values and internal decision making while working to affect consumer behavior and public policy.

This volume began with Richard Beckhard's early definition of organization development as an approach to planned change that fosters organizational effectiveness and health. It ends with his observation some thirty years later that OD has yet to agree on a definition of a healthy organization. Beckhard provides one that is workable and contemporary, yet respectful of all that OD could and should be.

Emerging Directions
Is There a New OD?

Robert J. Marshak

T here has been a great deal of commentary and controversy about the current state of organization development (OD). One ongoing concern is the underlying value system of OD and whether the traditional humanistic values espoused by the founders of the field are still relevant or whether they should be replaced by a set of more pragmatic business considerations as articulated by newer practitioners (Worley & Feyerherm, 2003). As I experienced in teaching a class titled "Values and Ethics in Organization Development," this set of issues reveals itself in stark terms. After reviewing several OD values and ethics statements (for example, Gellermann, Frankel, & Ladenson, 1990), I was asked if I really believed "all that stuff." I was then told that if anyone actually practiced that value system, they would not get any work. The controversy over OD's values continues today and is part of a larger set of concerns about the field's future, relevance, and continued viability (Bradford & Burke, 2004, 2005).

This chapter develops ideas originally published in R. J. Marshak, 2005, "Is There a New OD?" *Seasonings, 1*(1). Available: www.odnetwork.org/publications/seasonings/article_marshak.html.

Overlooked in these discussions, however, is a larger and more basic issue: OD may be facing a challenge from within the field—an emerging "new OD," not necessarily different in values so much as in ontology and epistemology. This emerging set of OD beliefs and practices is based on philosophical assumptions and methodologies about social phenomena and social reality that are widely different from the key assumptions of the field's founders. This chapter explores the possibilities of an emergent new OD and outlines potential implications for the field and its practitioners.

CLASSICAL ORGANIZATION DEVELOPMENT

The original formulation of OD included a strong positivist orientation based in mid-twentieth-century social science research methodologies. The whole idea of data-based change, like action research and survey research methods, presumes the existence and validity of an objective, discernible reality that can be investigated to produce valid data and information to influence change. One of Argyris's three core tasks for a change agent is the creation of valid data. "It has been accepted as axiomatic that valid and useful information is the foundation for effective intervention" (1973, p. 17). This theme is echoed by Chin and Benne (1976) in their classic discussion of general strategies for effecting change in human systems. "One element in all approaches to planned change is the conscious utilization and application of knowledge as an instrument or tool for modifying patterns and institutions of practice" (p. 22). Knowledge in this perspective is discovered through the scientific method, which historically assumed an objective, transcendent, and knowable reality. Blake and Mouton (1976) also reflect this in their five basic types of interventions, including catalytic interventions, which are closest to classical OD. "Catalytic interventions assist the client in collecting data and information to reintegrate his or her perceptions as to how things are" (p. 4).

In sum, classical OD is based explicitly or implicitly in an ontology and epistemology that assume an objective, transcendent, knowable world. The ideas are consistent with the central assumptions of mainstream mid-twentieth-century social, biological, and physical sciences. Methodologies based on these assumptions, such as action research, are then employed to discover and reveal this reality to client systems in order to correct distortions and misperceptions. The use of objective data in the process of social discovery, therefore, is a central foundation in classical OD's approach to change.

THE NEW ORGANIZATION DEVELOPMENT

In the 1980s, constructionist and postmodern approaches heavily influenced the social sciences with their ideas about multiple realities and the inherent subjectivity of experience (for example, Berger & Luckmann, 1966; Bergquist, 1993; Searle, 1995). Their notion of multiple realities implies that there can be no transcendent, objective truth to be discovered. Instead the issue is how immanent agreements about the reality of a situation are or could be most effectively negotiated among contending points of view. This framing raises issues of power and how it is used to create or impose a socially agreed-on or "privileged" version of things. In addition, ideas from the new sciences, including chaos theory and self-organizing systems, influenced how people thought about change in organizations, especially assumptions about and approaches to planned change (Wheatley, 1992).

These ideas naturally made their way into the OD world. They have been incorporated into theory and practice in recent years, although perhaps without a conscious intent to create a new OD. At least six contemporary OD-related theories and practices are based on these newer assumptions and will be explored in this chapter: appreciative inquiry; large group interventions; approaches to transformational change through individual mind-sets and consciousness; practices that address diversity and multicultural realities; approaches based on the new sciences, such as complex adaptive systems theory; and models of change that differ from the classical "unfreezing-movement-refreezing" paradigm.

Appreciative Inquiry

The development of appreciative inquiry is based on the social constructionist premise that reality is partially (if not completely) a result of one's mind-set. Watkins and Mohr (2001) assert that appreciative inquiry is postmodern in orientation and "is grounded in the theory of social constructionism" (p. 26). They contrast it with practices based on a "modernist," objectivist, and scientific orientation, and conclude, "Post-modernism, on the other hand, rejects the idea of an underlying structure and of an underlying truth. Post-modern thought embraces the idea of multiple and contextually determined realities. Social constructionism is a formative theory of the post-modern era" (p. 27).

The power of socially constructed mind-sets is also reflected in appreciative inquiry's concerns about the negative impact of the "deficit-focused thinking" of traditional action research. "Positive-focused thinking" is at the core of appreciative inquiry.

Common Ground and Social Agreements

Large group interventions seeking "common ground"—as opposed to objective common truth—are designed to achieve agreement among multiple constituencies, all of whose points of view are considered legitimate versions of reality (see, for example, Bunker & Alban, 2005). Although data are gathered and used in these approaches, data gathering is more for the purpose of presenting multiple possibilities and perspectives than for bringing "facts" to bear on the situation. Greater emphasis is on reaching social agreements and adopting new ways of seeing reality that will guide future actions. "Future Search is designed to help the group arrive at agreements about the future they want and actions to achieve it" (Lent, McCormick, & Pearce, 2005, p. 61). The underlying power and political dimensions in large group interventions are recognized by researchers, if not practitioners. In analyzing a case example of a search conference (SC), for example, Clarke (2005) comments that "it was found that the most important outcome from the SC was its predominately political effects" (p. 42). Tenkasi and Chesmore (2003) provide additional evidence for the impact of large group interventions on networks, connections, influence, politics, and power dynamics in organizations.

Changing Mind-Sets and Consciousness

Another stream of work related to multiple realities is the development of theories and models that promote changes in mind-sets and consciousness as the route to organizational transformation (for example, Anderson & Ackerman-Anderson, 2001). These have been developed by

OD consultants and academics in direct reaction to the perceived limitations of classical, Newtonian, Industrial Age views of change and are being used to think, talk about, and address contemporary and emerging change dynamics. For example, Ackerman-Anderson and Anderson (2001) assert, "We call the traditional leadership mindset, most prevalent today, the Industrial Mindset. This worldview contains the very blinders that prevent leaders from seeing the dynamics of transformation" (p. 7). Organizational transformation from this perspective requires shifts in individual consciousness, starting with the leadership and extending throughout the organization.

Diversity and Multicultural Realities

A third change in the field has been an increase of interest in diversity, multicultural realities, and explorations of how power is used to establish or reinforce exclusionary standards, practices, and paradigms. Miller and Katz (2002) capture the essence of the issues: "Most organizations are filled with barriers—rigid structures, poor training processes, outmoded equipment, misguided incentive programs, and discriminatory promotion and assignment practices that keep people from contributing the full breadth of their skills, ideas, and energies to the organization's success. Expressed in conscious and unconscious behaviors, as well as routine practices, procedures, and bylaws, these barriers are typically rooted in the very culture of an organization. They favor people who are most like the founders or senior leaders of the organization" (p. 7).

Most contemporary approaches to diversity and multicultural dynamics in organizations also include explicit recognition of the linkages between power dynamics and the version of reality that favors some groups and interests over others, and they have practices for addressing this kind of political asymmetry.

Applications of the New Sciences

Some OD practitioners have embraced ideas from the new sciences, such as complexity theory and self-organizing systems. Olson and Eoyang (2001), for example, see the need for a new OD change paradigm that incorporates these ideas. "The use of rational planned change approaches, driven by leaders with the help of change facilitators, has fallen short even when bolstered by formal (and expensive) programs such as TQM and re-engineering" (p. 19). They believe that "the emerging science of complex adaptive systems offers such a paradigm" (p. 19) and "establishes a foundation for a new theory of change" (p. 19).

Different Models of Change

Finally, these trends and changes in the contexts, technologies, and requirements of twenty-first-century organizations have raised questions about the theories and practices needed to address contemporary change dynamics and have led to the development of new change models. These include interests in cyclical change that flow from the new sciences as well as from some cultural traditions, and stand in contrast to classical OD's linear unfreezing-movement-refreezing model (Marshak, 1993); continuous, as opposed to episodic, approaches to change (Weick & Quinn, 1999); "spiral dynamics," which combine consciousness-changing with other nonlinear approaches to change (Beck & Cowan, 1996); and processes of continuous transformation (Marshak, 2004). For OD practitioners, these new models and approaches will require a conscious shift from the field's implicit bias for stability and "start-stop" models of change to alternative theories and assumptions that better support the concept of continuous, whole-system growth.

—◦◦◦—

All these changes and factors—emphases on socially constructing reality, transforming mind-sets and consciousness, operating from multicultural realities, exploring different models and assumptions about change, and creating common social perceptions and agreements—contribute to a contemporary OD whose theories, assumptions, and practices are vastly different from OD's classical roots. Table 41.1 summarizes classical OD and what I call the new OD.

IMPLICATIONS

If a new OD is emerging (or has emerged), there are important implications for theory and practice.

1. *We will need to do something about definitions and terminology.* When practitioners, academics, or managers talk about organization development, are they referring to classical OD, new OD, or something

Classical OD	New OD
Approach is influenced by classical science and modern thought and philosophy.	Approach is influenced by the new sciences and postmodern thought and philosophy.
Reality is an objective fact.	Reality is socially constructed.
There is a single reality.	There are multiple realities.
Truth is transcendent and discoverable.	Truth is immanent and emerges from the situation.
Reality is discovered by using rational and analytic processes.	Reality is negotiated and involves power and political processes.
Change results from collecting and applying valid data using objective problem-solving methods.	Change results from creating new social agreements through explicit or implicit negotiation.
Change can be created, planned, and managed.	Change is inherent and can be self-organizing.
Change is episodic and linear.	Change is continuous, cyclical, or both.
Emphasis is on changing behavior and what one does.	Emphasis is on changing mind-sets and how one thinks.

Table 41.1.   Classical OD and the New OD.

Source: Adapted from R. J. Marshak (2005).

else? We need better definitions and ways to know and to compare the variations of OD over time. In this chapter, two types of OD have been highlighted, but there may be more. Without additional philosophical and conceptual clarity, talking about the current state of the field is difficult. Witness the discussions in recent years about how and if organization development (OD) and organization transformation (OT) are different. Add to that the ongoing discussion about whether appreciative inquiry is revolutionary or simply another form of action research. Clarifying concepts, assumptions, and philosophy also brings benefits to clients and client systems. Now, practitioners of both classical OD and new OD claim they are doing "organization development," yet each offers different services and expertise often based on differing, but unarticulated, philosophical premises.

2. *We will need to explicitly identify philosophical differences when discussing and teaching OD and its practices.* Presently, OD practitioners and scholars discuss the theory and practice of OD as if it were a single entity and based on a single set of values and premises. This chapter raises questions about whether that is true. Differing perspectives can easily lead to cross-communication and confusion. Worse, those entrenched in one set of assumptions may question or challenge the practices of those in another. The two parties may never fully recognize that they are not talking about the same things at all.

Discussions about OD theory and practice are no longer univocal: they are plurivocal. The field must find ways to contend with its own multiple realities, philosophical differences, and competing discourses in order to advance theory and practice, as well as support all engaged in our shared efforts to enhance organizational effectiveness. By clarifying and differentiating premises and associated practices, we have the opportunity to develop new social technologies and approaches based on the field's well-established principles.

3. *We may need to purposefully articulate and legitimate the new OD.* A fully articulated and legitimated new OD needs a more self-conscious foundation in constructionist approaches to the social sciences and in the latest developments in the new sciences. The new OD might have an emphasis on affecting consciousness or mind-sets and on using social interaction in large and small groups to create or negotiate meaning and reality. Its core methods would be based on practices in constructionist social and symbolic interaction, not on objectivist action research focused on problem solving. It would explicitly recognize that reality is created and maintained through negotiations involving power. It would develop and advance values, theories, and methodologies for working effectively with these kinds of political dynamics.

Developing new premises and practices related to the role and uses of negotiation, for example, would be in order. So would new approaches to the power and political processes that establish and maintain socially constructed realities, agreements, and mind-sets that guide day-to-day behavior. All this may be challenging to the field given classical OD's seeming aversion to the positive possibilities of power and its preference for rational, objective, and fact-based processes. Many OD consultants treat power and political processes as if they were evil forces operating in organizations. At best, many have a profound ambivalence toward power and its manifestations (Marshak, 1992, 2001). Exactly when, how, and what kinds of power can be used in the new OD to facilitate social agreements among contending realities will be a critical and complex question for the field to confront and explore.

The new OD does not necessarily negate other classical OD practices. It would, however, ultimately require those practices to be consistent with the philosophical premises of the new approach. All this might also stimulate academics and practitioners to pursue additional approaches, innovative practices, and new social technologies for addressing change in human systems.

A CONCLUDING COMMENT

The jury is still out as to whether or not there is a distinctive new OD. Nonetheless, it is important to acknowledge that there have been ongoing developments and evolutions in the philosophy, values, theories, and practices of organization development since its origin. These need to be more clearly articulated, distinguished, and addressed by practitioners and scholars in the field. Absent clearer delineations and understandings, we continue to risk miscommunication, confusion, or worse.

CHAPTER FORTY-TWO

The Future of OD?

David L. Bradford
W. Warner Burke

W hat has happened to organization development? Is OD's heyday past? Should one pull the plug, as Jerry Harvey suggests, and let it die a graceful death? Is it barely kept alive by periodic transfusions of a new approach that rejuvenates the field for a short time, only then to relapse into a semi-comatose state?

Or has it been so successful that it is firmly integrated into many other change approaches, as Tichy and DeRose (2003) suggest? They assert that, rather than dying, it has been reborn and currently widely used but without the OD label. One example they cite is the actions by Jack Welch in transforming GE with workout and other OD-like approaches. Is it time for the field to declare victory and move on?

Whether one takes the pessimistic or optimistic view, the implications are that we should acknowledge that OD is over. Long live the king; the king is dead. But in this chapter, we are going to suggest that such an announcement of the field's demise may be premature and that OD has the potential still to play a vital role in organizations. However, to do so requires some tough decisions about how it operates. Before exploring those requirements, a slight digression is necessary to place the role of OD within the larger field of organization change and development.

As has been discussed elsewhere (Burke, 2002), OD is a subset of the larger field of organization change, which includes directive change as well as collaborative change; change in structure and systems as well as culture, values, and norms; and change in purpose as well as process, and technology as well as social factors. There is change constantly imposed by the organizational leaders, major consulting firms, and individual change agents.

This is not to minimize the potential importance of OD.

- In a world where change is constant, for organizations to be adaptive decisions must be pushed down the hierarchy and members must be aligned around the same strategic goals. OD practitioners know how to do this.

- This consistency of change means there is a decreasing probability that today's solutions will fit tomorrow's problems. Thus organizations need to learn how to learn. This is another area that OD practitioners have addressed.

- With organizations growing increasingly knowledge-based and staffed by employees with higher-level education and competence, OD practitioners can play a crucial role in knowing how to release and focus organizational members' abilities.

- With more than two-thirds of change efforts failing and an even greater number of mergers and acquisitions not achieving their financial promise, OD practitioners' expertise on implementation is crucial.

Mike Beer has made a persuasive argument about the importance of integrating the hard economic-based change strategies (E-change) with the softer organizational strategies (O-change) (Beer & Nohria, 2000). We fully subscribe to that proposition. Not only is such an integration more effective, it also moves away from the trap of the present either-or modes of thinking ("Are we concerned for people or are we concerned for profits?" "Are we concerned about today or are we building for tomorrow?"). *Or* needs to be replaced with *and* to see if it is possible to have both.

Such exploration leads to a much more interesting set of questions than those presently being asked. With these two major change fields separated, much of the exploration is at best around new approaches (how-to issues). Though of use, these are more pedestrian and less exciting than the sort of fundamental "under what conditions" type of question that would arise if the two change approaches were integrated. "When should one involve people in the change effort, and what are the conditions in which such actions might not be useful?" "What are the conditions under which the process should be transparent, and when should information be withheld?" "What is the sort of information that is crucial to share?" "When should the change agents play the expert role, and when should they primarily focus on process (and under what conditions can they be merged)?" Burke (2004b) has raised similar questions about what we need to know for the future.

It might appear that this integration would call for the end of OD as a separate field as it melds unobtrusively with other forms of organization change. But we suggest that taking this route is not advisable. Instead, there needs to be "differentiation before integration." Hard drives out soft. Today's concerns drive out tomorrow's. What can be easily measured drives out what is more difficult to quantify. A premature integration is likely to mean that e-change will overwhelm o-change approaches. Instead, OD practitioners need to work on developing their full voice before they can become an equal partner at the table with other forms of change. In doing so, their contributions are likely to be highly valued by organizational leaders who then will be more willing to include them when major change efforts are being developed.

HOW OD NEEDS TO CHANGE

If OD is to be a true partner with e-consulting and is to be listened to and respected by organizational leaders, OD practitioners must first confront and overcome its present barriers. Several authors in this volume have described various problems facing the field, and we have no argument with any of their points. However, there are three interrelated dimensions we wish to explore that are crucial to remedy if OD is to have a viable future:

1. Too little O in OD

2. Too exclusive an emphasis on human processes

3. The deleterious effects of humanistic values

Problem One: Where Is the O in OD?

"Where is the O in OD?" was a question that Richard Beckhard repeatedly asked. There is a difference between "using OD approaches" (for example, team building, survey research, appreciative inquiry) and "doing OD." We use this definition of OD: "Organization development is an effort (1) planned, (2) organizationwide, and (3) managed from the top, to (4) increase organization effectiveness and health through (5) planned interventions in the organization's 'processes,' using behavioral-science knowledge" (Beckhard, 1969, p. 9).

We assert that there are relatively few people who call themselves OD consultants who do OD as Beckhard and long-time consultant Tony Petrella define it. Most OD consultants "use OD techniques." In doing so, they have minimal impact and are seen by executives (and e-consultants) as providing only marginal value.

There are multiple reasons why so few OD consultants do OD. For many, it is not having the comprehensive systems view that is necessary. For others, they are caught in a chicken-and-egg dilemma. Because they are not involved in systemwide change, they are not selected to help with the large-scale interventions. Instead, they are only brought in periodically to use some OD techniques or to clean up an "implementation mess." We want to examine four important causes that keep so many OD consultants stuck in their limited role and prevented from putting the O in OD.

THE "REDUCTIONIST" TRAP. In an interview, Jerry I. Porras talks about the assumptions made by the early leaders in the field. They held a reductionist notion that it was first important to develop healthy individuals who would then be able to have functional relationships that would in turn lead to high-performing teams that could produce beneficial organizations that would build a better society.

But this kind of thinking crosses levels of analysis. There can be excellence at one level without it existing at others. All of us have seen dysfunctional teams comprising healthy individuals as well as destructive organizations that contain functional teams. Conversely, it is possible to have effective organizations comprising poor functioning teams as well as functional teams with deeply flawed individuals (because the social system can control and compensate for dysfunction at a lower level of analysis).

This reductionist thinking has led many consultants to start with the individual, interpersonal, and team level and get no further. The present craze with executive coaching is one example of this orientation. Instead, as Petrella argues, one needs to take a total system orientation. Start with the system and, if necessary, move downward.

LACK OF A BUSINESS PERSPECTIVE. Any organizational consultant would agree that it is difficult to be effective if one doesn't understand and appreciate the client's concerns. But to what extent is this true for the OD practitioner? As a partner in an organization consulting firm put it: "The problem with too many OD folks is that they are not business people. They don't think like business people, they don't talk like business people, and they don't behave like business people. E-consultants always have the business issue front and center, and all work done in an organization is in service of addressing these business issues (such as increasing profitability, opening new markets, developing competitive advantage, and so forth). In fact, not only are some OD consultants not business people, but they are proud of it! As though being a business person is somehow 'tainted'" (Carole Robin, personal communication, emphasis hers).

The need for a business perspective applies to the nonprofit sector as well. Museum directors, for example, need to be concerned about what "products" they offer, who their competitors are (in education or entertainment), and what value they are offering to justify grants and donations. Our point is that if OD consultants thought more like senior executives, they would then have to take on more of an organization perspective.

FAILURE TO INTEGRATE SOCIAL SYSTEMS WITH THE TECHNICAL SYSTEM. In the early years of OD, change work was done with a socio-technical systems perspective. This perspective sees the interrelationship between the technical aspects of the organization and the social. But this orientation has been largely lost in present-day OD. Most OD consultants focus exclusively on the social system factors because few are knowledgeable about the technical. There is often the assumption that what the organization does isn't relevant ("It doesn't make a difference if we are dealing with computer chips or potato chips; interpersonal, group, and change dynamics are the same"). But if change agents do not take account of the uniqueness of the industry within which the organization operates (specific competitors, technology used, crucial skills required, and so on), then it is very difficult, if not impossible, to take a system perspective.

STRUCTURAL LIMITATIONS. Most OD consultants work alone or with only a few colleagues. But it is not possible for two or three individuals, no matter how competent they are, to (1) understand the uniqueness of a particular industry; (2) be sufficiently knowledgeable about the company's technology; and (3) know enough about how IT, financial systems, strategic formulation, and other business processes affect the social system (and vice versa) to integrate these subsystems with the social change processes that they may be competent in. It is not by accident that the major consulting firms (who are able to gain the contracts to do systemwide change) are large enough to include these various competencies in a single consulting team.

There is a similar problem for the internal OD consultant. As Burke (2004a) points out, if one is stuck down in HR then one is structurally removed from the other central processes that are more likely to drive change in an organization.

Problem Two: Too Exclusive an Emphasis on Human Processes

Two of the mantras commonly heard from OD consultants are that "we never know the organization as well as the client does" and "if you have the right people at the table and the process is right, they will solve the problem; we don't have to be the task experts." This has led to an emphasis on *process consultation* (as contrasted with *expert consultation;* Schein, 1988), which has been one of the strengths of the field. This orientation has led to many useful ways to help clients feel empowered by discovering their own expertise without building dependency on the consultant. It has also led OD practitioners to avoid one of the common traps of the major consulting firms: an emphasis on finding the solution with less attention paid to implementation. But too rigid a focus on human processes has some significant costs and can seriously undermine the perceived value of the OD consultant in the client's eyes.

One of the problems with this focus is that it denies the possibility of task expertise (held by the OD consultant and desired by the client). A pure process stance might be appropriate for the neophyte starting out, but after years of experience the consultant will gradually acquire task expertise. Denying this knowledge can be extremely frustrating to the client.

Another problem with this emphasis on human processes is that it denies other forms of process expertise. As mentioned in the previous section, systemwide change can be successful only if all relevant systems are considered. This does not mean that OD practitioners must be fully qualified to design an IT intervention, revamp the financial or accounting systems, or be able to conduct a sophisticated strategic analysis. But OD practitioners need to know enough about these functions to be able to integrate relevant social processes. Most of the problems with mergers and acquisitions, for example, are not due to faulty initial financial analysis but to lack of integration of the two organizations' cultures. Difficulties with strategy are more likely to arise out of implementation than out of strategy formulation. But for OD consultants to be invited to the table when plans are being made in these areas, they have to be familiar enough with these processes to hold their own in the discussion.

Finally, such an exclusive focus on human processes distorts how situations are defined. Here is a story involving one of the authors that illustrates this problem.

IF YOU HAVE ONLY A HAMMER . . .

I was asked to teach a workshop on developing "high-performing teams" to a group of OD consultants who were presently enrolled or were alumni of a leading school that offers a master's in OD. Almost all of the participants were practicing consultants. As part of the program, I showed a video of a staff meeting. I told the participants, "Imagine that you are a consultant to Larry, the team leader. You have begun team building with that group and have built preliminary relationships with all the members. You are sitting in the corner of the room observing."

The video shows Larry starting the meeting by announcing that the only agenda item is whether the organization should purchase a new phone system. Dorothy, head of sales, knew about this plan and has come to the meeting prepared with a proposal. Hank, head of production, is surprised by this topic and raises all sorts of objections, saying that there is greater need for new machinery in the plant. Their argument escalates with some mutual name calling and ends with Dorothy rising from her seat and shouting, "With colleagues like you, who needs competitors!"

I then say to the participants, "Larry has now turned to you with the unspoken question, 'What should I do now?' As the consultant, what would you do?"

"Clearly they are not aligned around the same goals," one person responded.

"So what would you say as the consultant?" I ask.

"I would lead a discussion about what was our vision and what should be our major goals."

"No, no," broke in a second participant. "The problem is that they haven't agreed on their norms of interaction. What the consultant should do is stop their discussion of the phone system and have them talk about what norms they want to operate under."

A third jumped in, disagreeing with the previous two. "The problem is the relationship between Dorothy and Hank. They aren't appreciating the other's point of view, so I would have each of them state what is valuable about the other's position."

This went on with a couple of more suggestions of a similar nature, and finally one person tentatively raised his hand. "I'm new to this program and really don't know much about OD, but it seems to me that the team discussion is framed wrong. Shouldn't this be about what's the best ROI from various capital expenditures?"

—∿∿—

Bingo. Now, it is possible that members of this team aren't aligned around the same goals, that they aren't in full agreement as to their norms, and that Dorothy and Hank have a strained relationship. But those aren't the present problem. If they are frustrated because the agenda has been defined in a way that prevents them from having an objective discussion about the best payoff for a major capital expenditure, then they will be even more frustrated by our consultant doing the touchy-feely thing. Imagine the eye-rolling if our consultant makes any of the first three interventions. No wonder the field gets described as soft and irrelevant.

Problem Three: Deleterious Effects of Rigid Adherence to Humanistic Values

Again, one of OD's strengths is also a major weakness. A valuable contribution that OD has made is "democratizing" organizations and stressing the inherent value of the human component. The field has amounted to a useful counterbalance to overreliance on "experts," be they from outside the organization or represented by the top leadership. OD has pioneered numerous approaches that tap into the knowledge and competence that exist throughout the institution.

Another benefit from humanistic values is the emphasis on multiple stakeholders that an organization should respond to, rather than a sole focus on shareholders with their economic priority. Many, if not most, organizations have a culture that ignores the human side of the enterprise. Recently a client of ours described his company's culture as "hard and spikey." OD practitioners with a humanistic bias have confronted these attitudes, thereby making a significant contribution to organizational effectiveness and change.

However, there is a difference between having a humanistic bias and deifying these values as the only way to be. The latter can produce a limited mind-set that focuses only on human factors and is blind to a broader perspective that considers the needs of both the organization as well as the members. This emphasis on humanistic values has produced a series of negative consequences.

WHICH VALUES? OD practitioners also claim that they are applied behavioral scientists. But what happens when research findings from the behavioral sciences contradict the beliefs they hold from their humanistic values? For example, research shows that commitment can be built without involving people in the decision-making process, that there are times when coercive change is more effective than collaboration (in the long run as well as the short), that under some conditions individuals make superior decisions to groups, and that cohesive groups can hold down the high performers.

When such a contradiction occurs, it is the humanistic values that tend to trump the research findings. Recently in conversation a respected senior OD consultant made the astonishing claim that "there has been no successful change that hasn't been collaborative." Such a value-driven belief not only distorts reality and decreases the consultant's effectiveness but also opens that person (and the field) up to the charge of pseudoscience—of using only those results that fit their preconceptions.

WHOSE VALUES? When there is a strong belief that humanistic values are the "right ones," then the consultant moves from a helping role into an advocacy position. The goal shifts from helping the client achieve their goals to the client being the site for the consultant's need "to make a better world" as the consultant has defined it. When this is the case, OD changes from organization consulting to being on a social mission. The consultant has to accept the goals and purpose of the organization. Yet in a recent book by OD consultants, Meg Wheatley writes, "I believe that in the war of values, there has been a victory. Market values have won: individualism, competition, speed, and greed" (Wheatley, Tannenbaum, Griffin, & Quade, 2003, p. 9).

THE CLIENT AS ENEMY. There is a strong antileadership streak that runs through much of the OD community. It is unclear whether this comes from the humanistic values, counterdependency on the part of the practitioners, or carryover from the culture of the 1960s when the field was emerging. But one has only to overhear conversation at meetings or read e-mail in OD chatrooms to pick up the notion that it is the CEOs and senior executives who are the bad guys. They are charged with being concerned only with achieving quarterly results, propping up the stock price, and acquiescing to the Wall Street analysts. In doing so, they are willing to exploit employees and fire at will.

Several years ago at an annual OD Network meeting, there was a special one-day session where the leading OD consultants were invited to discuss how the field was doing. Much of the conversation was self-congratulatory, but there was a fair amount of criticism about the myopic economic focus of business leaders and their lack of concern for "human factors." One of us mused, "I wonder how CEOs would feel, listening to our conversation?" A leading OD consultant snapped back, "Why should we care what CEOs think!" Nobody else in the room expressed any dissent to that opinion.

In a recent article, Burke (2004b) raised the question, "Why is it that OD practitioners do not have a seat at the executive table in the organizations they work for or consult with as an external?" Fred Nichols, in an e-mail to the OD Network, gave two answers.

> For some ODers, OD is a social movement, aimed at changing the world around them. More important, it aims to change the world in ways that ODers value and approve of. Instead of helping execs and managers with the issues the managers and execs care about, the managers and execs become the bad guys and ODers draw a bead on them and their systems. In short, some ODers are working their own agenda through OD.
>
> [Second,] some ODers belong to what I call the "warm and fuzzy" school of OD, the "soft side" of OD. They seem convinced that improving interpersonal and intergroup relations, for example, will improve organizational performance. Like much of training, "warm and fuzzy" OD work is often an act of faith.
>
> Neither set of OD folks I've just stereotyped is likely to get a seat at the table.

WHAT'S A GIVEN, AND WHAT'S UP FOR EXAMINATION? When one holds a certain value position, it is difficult to question the underlying assumptions behind the belief system (the challenge of double-loop learning). If there is the belief that collaboration is always best, then the question is not asked, Under what conditions is that true and not true? Unfortunately, adherence to humanistic values has meant there are a range of issues that are not up for exploration. If it is true that the earth is the center of the universe, what is the use of looking through Galileo's telescope?

UNEXPLORED "DARK SIDE." Any approach has a dark side: unintended negative effects. Chris Argyris, for example, charges that one consequence of how humanistic values are used in OD is that it denies the ability to objectively assess the impact of an intervention. We would suggest that there is reticence among OD consultants to look at the dysfunctional effects of their interventions. For example, in the 1990s Levi Strauss made extensive use of OD throughout the organization. The activities did much to increase members' willingness to take initiative and feel empowered. However, one of the unintended consequences of the belief that "those affected by a decision should be involved in making it" was that members who weren't involved sometimes refused to abide by the decision, leading to significant barriers to producing change.

DEVALUATING ORGANIZATIONAL POLITICS. OD has often been accused of naïveté. Does the emphasis on openness, trust, self-disclosure, and the like lead to denial that organizations are basically political systems? We are not talking about sliminess, deception, and behind-the-back attacks but instead about the recognition that every organization has a history and an informal system. It is the realization that

- There are historic events in the organization that stigmatize certain approaches and support others.
- There are sacred cows that must be taken account of if any change is to be successful.
- There are some people who have more influence than their position on the organization chart would suggest and others who have less.
- There are some people who must be included in any change and others who can be ignored.
- There are some people who are the "rainmakers"; their approval will have a significant impact on others' acceptance.

The preceding section sounds as if we are opposed to humanistic values. That is not the case. As individuals, we subscribe to most of them. The distinction we are making is between values that individuals hold for themselves and values that underlie the field. All conceptual systems have underlying values, including the applied behavioral sciences (for example, the importance of data that can be objectively verified).

We are in support of individual consultants being clear on their own personal values and using them to determine which clients they work with and the nature of the consulting they do. Our concern is when these values are used to define the field itself. OD practitioners can't claim to be applied behavioral scientists and treat humanistic values as the underlying belief system of the field. They have to decide which is dominant.

WHAT OD COULD BECOME

We first need to clarify that this discussion does not apply to all OD consultants. There are some who do take an open systems approach, support the organization's goals, and integrate technical with social systems. But we argue they are a small minority. What we are discussing is the field as a whole. Nor are these concerns ours alone; recently the major OD organizations (OD Network, the OD Institute, and the International Organization Development Association) sponsored a study of the field. In a preliminary survey involving more than nine hundred OD consultants, many of the respondents expressed the same issues we have stated (Wirtenberg, Abrams, & Ott, 2004).

OD has much to offer today's organizations. Maybe the field is stuck in the mind-set of the late 1950s, when OD started. At that time, much work was routine, compliance was stressed, and initiative was frequently punished. It is not surprising that OD folks felt in moral combat to "humanize the organization" and saw themselves at odds with the existing leadership.

But much has changed in the past half-century. Computers, IT, and automation have replaced much of the routine work done before. The knowledge economy has become central, and the battle between centralized planning and market economy is over. Rather than bemoaning the values of "individualism, competition, speed and greed," why not embrace them? Does OD really want to be seen as the bastion of "sameness, routine, slowness, and failure?"

With this new orientation, couldn't OD practitioners say:

- "We believe in competing against one's own past performance, against standards of excellence, and against the market competitor. We have approaches that help you achieve that by learning how to cooperate with colleagues so all can compete better and so we hold each other accountable for high performance."
- "In your consideration of which company to acquire, we can help not only in assessing the cultural fit of the various possibilities but in assisting with the acquisition process itself to speed up integration and maximize profits. We agree that the acquisition will lead to layoffs, and we have approaches that can make that process fair and objective."
- "We know that organizations can't guarantee lifetime employment. But you can build employee loyalty and commitment through increasing their employability. We know how to build learning systems so that your people can perform better while increasing their competencies."
- "Given your thoughts about [moving into new markets, providing other products and services], we can help you develop the appropriate structures and systems. To do that, we need to be involved in the strategic planning process."
- "Time, not money, is the scarce resource today. Organizations waste incredible amounts of time avoiding issues and being indirect. We have approaches that will save you time and money by building organizations where directness is the norm."
- "You are losing time and money in your change efforts largely because differences and disagreements can't be productively raised and resolved. We know how to make yours a conflict-positive organization."
- "In the new IT system that you want to introduce, we can help in developing the process for determining the specific needs of the various divisions in a way that will produce the most valid data and decrease resistance."
- "The trouble is that your managers aren't tough enough. They either won't make the difficult decisions or they confuse toughness with punitiveness, but they aren't the same. Being tough is being willing to give honest feedback, confront issues rather

than manage around them, and make the hard decisions. We have approaches that can build that sort of toughness in your organizational culture."

With these changes in mind-set, OD practitioners will be better able to align their skills with the organization's goals (economic and developmental). Doing so increases the chance of the OD practitioner being included in the planning process in the business development, IT, and strategy departments as well as being invited to the executive table, where the crucial change decisions are made. This orientation can also build bridges to e-consultants because both groups now have complementary ways to reach the same objectives—a more developed organization better skilled in achieving its core performance and economic goals.

WILL THE PROMISE BE ACHIEVED?

When we started this project, we were relatively optimistic that OD could reinvent itself and be a major player in the change world. After eighteen months of work, discussions with colleagues, and our own reflection, we are less sanguine about this occurring. We see formidable barriers:

• *Few organizations can reinvent themselves.* The success rate of organizations basically changing their orientation is very low, be it in the profit or nonprofit sector. Just because OD deals with change doesn't mean it can apply those skills to itself. Too often the cobbler's children go without shoes.

• *Requirement of new competencies.* What has been laid out is not just a change in mind-set, which is challenging enough. But it demands learning new competencies. This may not require going back for an MBA, but it does require learning the various business functions that the degree covers. How many OD consultants will retool themselves? Also, how many will put in the effort to become competent in IT technology, finance, and strategy?

• *Needs presently being fulfilled.* When OD consultants talk about where they find personal satisfaction, it is rarely about how they increased ROI, cut cycle time, or reengineered the work flow. Instead, it tends to be around personal transformation on the part of the client or incidents of high self-disclosure and vulnerability in a team interaction. Developing the organization might actually be a secondary goal for most OD practitioners!

• *The hold of humanistic values.* A common lament when OD practitioners assemble is, "Have we lost our values?" (There is no corresponding worry of "Have we lost our relevance?") Will they be willing to objectively assess the situation and, when necessary, embrace downsizing, cost-cutting, reengineering, and the like?

• *Changes required in supporting systems.* For the changes that we have suggested, there has to be change in the role of the supporting systems. Books and articles on OD must become cross-disciplinary and deal with issues of technology, strategy, and the like. OD master's programs should modify their curriculum to be more concerned with organization change (as contrasted with the more limited organization development) and bring in other business functions now typically covered in a standard MBA program. The OD Network presently appears to be primarily concerned at its annual meeting with giving members what they want (tools, reassurance they are doing the right thing, and a chance for socioemotional bonding). Instead, will it be willing to build those sessions around what the members need (which may include confronting present complacency and lack of relevant competencies)?

• *The leadership void.* Most fundamental change requires a strong leader who is willing to wrench the organization in a new direction. The decision to change is rarely or ever produced by a committee. Yet this is where OD gets hoisted on its own petard. Being an advocate of inclusion (and dubious about directive leadership), will it tolerate a leader (or leaders) who demand this necessary change? (It is interesting to note that the change study referred to that was sponsored by the various OD organizations has set up an advisory committee of two hundred members!)

Our hope is that the field of OD will rise to the challenge and reinvent itself. One positive sign is the previously mentioned study sponsored by the major OD organizations. That they are willing to look at themselves is a hopeful sign. But are they willing to act on it? Our fear is that they will not, and that the future of OD will be just more of how it has been in the past. It will not change its basic orientation, and the field will comprise people who largely use OD tools and techniques but don't do OD. The consequences are that they will not be at the table where the significant change decisions are made. Instead, at that table will be representatives from the major consulting firms. Only the crumbs will be left for the OD practitioner.

Instead, what will emerge is a new field of organization change and development that will integrate the E and the O consulting that Mike Beer discusses. This will likely be housed in schools of business and see an integration of strategy with change theory. It would include imposed change with collaborative change, and it would truly be concerned with development of the organization's competencies, not just those of the individual members.

This new field will not be as strong as it could be because it will not have much substantive input from OD. Instead, there is the danger of pseudo-OD, where organization members are involved in change projects, not to tap into their knowledge but to gain their compliance. Furthermore, any member involvement will be on the safe, "cosmetic" issues, not on the crucial ones where their knowledge could make a significant difference. This would be a loss—to the development of an integrative theory of organizational change and to OD. Instead, let us hope that the leaders in the field will be willing to face this present crisis in OD so that its potential can be fully realized.

CHAPTER FORTY-THREE

From Cells to Communities

Deconstructing and Reconstructing the Organization

Rosabeth Moss Kanter

> *A community is like a ship. Everyone ought to be prepared to take the helm.*
>
> —Henrik Ibsen, An Enemy of the People, *Act I*

> *Management fighting for its God-given territory . . .*
>
> —CEO's response to interview question about the biggest barrier to change

The scene was a conference room on the California coast filled with twenty senior executives of a large multichain retailer I'll call Brand E. To open discussion of future business challenges, I posed my favorite icebreaker question: Describe the sport that most resembles running this company. The first woman up said, "Gymnastics. We are all really strong and talented people. We practice and perform alone." The man on her right changed the game to a relay race: "We each have to be fast but then hand the baton to the next one in line." Finally, the head of global distribution begged to differ, naming the Olympics: "All of us represent our flag to big audiences, with lots of competition, so we'd better pull together."

Brand E is successful and widely admired, known for aggressive marketing and strong financial performance, and even for early bricks-and-clicks achievements. Yet its leaders were uncertain about whether they were playing individual sports or coordinating a complex enterprise. Powerful external forces, from the Internet to globalization, are calling for a unified one-company response from Brand E. But getting every division to cede even a little bit of control seems nearly impossible. People are isolated in cells, the cells are stuck in silos, and it is hard for the cells to unite to become a powerful organism.

Like many others, this company embraced decentralization because of advice about how to be lean and speedy, focused and performance oriented. Less than two decades ago, management thinkers proposed a "new organizational paradigm." The outlines of the new model are familiar by now, even if less common in practice: flattened hierarchies, open boundaries, horizontal orientation, an emphasis on processes over structure. In the 1980s, that model encouraged a pendulum swing toward decentralization. Indeed, federations of nearly sovereign divisions were considered an improvement over centralized bureaucracies (Handy, 1992). Technology from the same era reinforced the decentralization thrust. A PC on every employee's desk was considered empowering, even if each set of silos had different systems and different information and could not communicate with each other.

Then along came the Internet as a revolutionary integrating force, and the problems of excessive decentralization became apparent. In a global, high-tech world, organizations need to be more fluid, inclusive, and responsive. They need to manage complex information flows, grasp new ideas quickly, and spread those ideas throughout the enterprise. What counts is not whether everybody uses e-mail but whether people quickly absorb the impact of information and respond to opportunity. The Web creates an expectation of being able to find everything easily in the same place. E-business cuts across every organizational process. It can touch every function, affect every product. It can magnify mistakes and turn them into opposition of unprecedented magnitude. For already-established companies, the Internet makes more urgent the need to present one face to the customer and link separate actors and actions for seamless integration. The Internet isn't just another channel; it is a medium that demands connections to all the other channels. When companies are embarrassed because they cannot accept returns from online sales in their physical stores, or when customer data residing in different corners of various silos cannot be retrieved to the frustration of those customers, it is clear that existing operations must be reconceived.

Companies pose organizational questions at two levels of sophistication. The narrow question is, How do we structure our e-business unit? And the broader question is, How do we change our whole organization? The first is oriented toward presenting the best face to outside audiences. The second recognizes that the biggest challenge is inside.

Companies that are successful on the Web operate differently from their laggard counterparts. On my global e-culture survey, those reporting that they are much better than their competitors in the use of the Internet tend to have flexible, empowering, collaborative organizations. The "best" are more likely than the "worst" to indicate, at statistically significant levels, that

- Departments collaborate (instead of sticking to themselves)
- Conflict is seen as creative (instead of disruptive)
- People can do anything not explicitly prohibited (instead of doing only what is explicitly permitted)
- Decisions are made by the people with the most knowledge (instead of the ones with the highest rank)

Pacesetters and laggards describe no differences in how hard they work (in response to a question about whether work was confined to traditional hours or spilled over into personal time), but they are very different in how *collaboratively* they work.

Working in e-culture mode requires organizations to be communities of purpose. A community makes people feel like members, not just employees—members with privileges but also responsibilities beyond the immediate job, extending to colleagues in other areas. Community means having things in common, a range of shared understandings transcending specific fields. Shared understandings permit relatively seamless processes, interchangeability among people, smooth formation of teams that know how to work together even if they have never previously met, and rapid transmission of information. In this chapter we will see how the principles of community apply inside organizations and workplaces, sometimes facilitated by technology but also independent of it. And I will examine the challenges that have to be overcome to create organizational communities.

The greater integration that is integral to e-culture is different from the centralization of earlier eras. Integration must be accompanied by flexibility and empowerment in order to achieve fast response, creativity, and innovation through improvisation. Web success involves operating more like a community than a bureaucracy. It is a subtle but important distinction. Bureaucracy implies rigid job descriptions, command-and-control hierarchies, and hoarding of information, which is doled out top-down on a need-to-know basis. Community implies a willingness to abide by standardized procedures governing the whole organization, yes, but also by voluntary collaboration, which is much richer and less programmed. Communities can be mapped in formal ways, but they also have an emotional meaning, a feeling of connection. Communities have both a structure and a soul.

In youthful dotcoms, the search for community finds its most important physical manifestation in the communal kitchen—a nice carryover from the traditional role that sharing food has always played in community spirit and religious rituals. But the barriers to community also have a physical symbol: the political and cultural walls that divide cells and silos in established organizations. Before reaching the ideal of community, people must tear down the walls of the past. And they must be careful not to erect new ones when they start e-ventures.

THE WALLS OF THE PAST: DIVISIONAL DOTCOMBAT

People unaccustomed to seeing the world outside their silos have a problem understanding that distinctions and separations appropriate for physical space disappear in cyberspace. Some companies get it; others don't.

For example, Kraft's products, such as coffee, cheese, or gelatin desserts, are lodged in separate divisions because of great differences in sourcing, processing, storing, marketing, handling, and consuming; only cheese bears the Kraft brand name. Yet, with the help of e-strategy marketing firm Digitas, Kraft linked all its brands on the Web using a Kraft Kitchen concept—over protests from some of the business units, whose autonomy was reduced. When a manager from Nestlé in Europe approached me to discuss how online grocery sales in Europe might affect Nestlé, I suggested an approach similar to the Kraft Kitchen, such as a Nestlé dessert boutique. "We could never do that," he replied. The divisions were too separate, they didn't talk to each other, and brand names for the same product differed across countries.

"Many, many organizations have independent business units not used to seeing the big picture," Digitas's Sheila Malkin observed. "People have various interests and they are unable to reach agreement. Time and again, deadlines get missed and action is prevented." Opponents do not even have to express overt hostility; they can nod politely in meetings and then engage in passive resistance through foot-dragging and minimal cooperation.

Decisions about e-business expose organizational fault lines, and their emergence can cause earthquakes. Joe Sweeney, a consultant with Gartner Group in Hong Kong who had run the "blue sky department" at Asia Online, felt that this was especially true of Chinese businesses: "E-business crosses so many boundaries. The business managers think that if they don't grab hold of it that they will lose their power position in the company. And to be honest, they're probably right. Greater China businesses are extremely political by nature. They're very deep hierarchies. E-business cuts through that so I think that they react with terror. Either control it or hide from it, there's no middle reaction."

But my e-culture team uncovered concerns about loss of power everywhere, even in some of the most innovative American companies. Almost 41 percent of the 108 big-company respondents to the global e-culture survey (those with over 20,000 employees) identify rivalry and conflict between divisions as a barrier to Internet effectiveness, and 26 percent of them indicate that "managers fear loss of privilege and status." The CEOs we interviewed noted repeatedly that a pervasive barrier to leading their companies to the Web is "management fighting for its God-given territory," as one put it.

Highly innovative companies that once thrived on decentralization and internal entrepreneurship find that the Internet forces an unfamiliar degree of integration and communal sharing. In 1997, Sun Microsystems was not yet fully using internally all the networks and Internet applications it sold to customers. But because of organizational silos, this success almost didn't happen. Let's dig deeper into this case.

It was Sun president Ed Zander's idea to create e-Sun out of the ashes of SunExpress, an after-market, tele-Web-based operation that had sold Sun products in direct competition with other Sun units. Market analysts as well as customers were asking Sun to follow Cisco's lead and walk the talk, to eat its own dog food by using Web technology itself. Albert Ormiston, who became vice president and general manager of e-Sun, recalled, "Our ads say 'We're the dot in dot-com' and customers are saying to us 'How are you dot-comming yourself?'" E-Sun was envisioned as a unified e-business portal—a partner to the rest of the organization, not a competitor. That was the theory, anyway.

Ormiston set to work to get "buy-in to integrate the whole front office, the back office, the supply chain, across all of the company." Because the new processes cut across traditional functions, everyone was affected, but it seemed (at first) that few wanted to change. An underlying reason was an absence of trust. "You find yourself right in the middle of some horrendous historical relationships across silos," observed Kenneth Sauter, Vice President of Sun Online, who worked with Ormiston. "Sales hates Operations. Finance doesn't talk straight to Sales. Finance doesn't talk straight to Operations. They all screw around with each other. They don't talk honestly with each other. And because the silos are driven so deep, they don't talk about the business anymore. When you move in with a change like this across the functions, you go in with a fresh message about the business, but that's totally foreign to a lot of these folks. They're like, 'What are you talking about? And who are you to come to me and talk about this?'"

It is not surprising that the sales force was the most resistant, but loss of commissions to the Internet channel wasn't the main reason. Sun could figure out how to compensate its sale force for online sales, just as partners such as Oracle had. Rather, e-Sun would force them to join the community, and there was little community spirit in sales. "There was a certain macho-ness about the sales organization," another Sun leader said. "We had always pushed the notion that you take care of yourself and make as much money as you can, and you will have served the company. Ten years ago, the direct sales organization was an independent entity. They could get things done without having any partners or anybody else involved. They could just push it through with brute force. In today's world, they can't do it. It's just impossible. You need internal support, from enterprise services, from the service organization, from professional services, from all the groups that are supporting our partners, our system integrators, resellers. And you need help from them on specific projects that we're dealing with in the commercial world."

Sun needed to develop greater internal cooperation so that it could mobilize quickly and efficiently to meet the needs of customers, and not just through the Web. The challenge for Ormiston and e-Sun was to get people to care about contributing to something that was not included in their immediate list of responsibilities. "We don't have any way to get anyone to pull together and say, 'Yes, we could get a major win with a new customer if we deliver a large server in five days, let's get it there in five.' Immediately the first 10 people step forward and say, 'We can't do that'—and by the way, they don't care. Because their job doesn't involve getting anything to that customer."

Sun's legacy of decentralization and entrepreneurship meant that it was impossible just to force change on the organization by top-down edict, as more hierarchical companies tried to do. It took a year of demonstration projects and constant communication, but Ormiston and his team eventually prevailed for a successful launch of Sun.com. To get people out of their cells and into a community, they borrowed techniques from community organizing: one-on-one persuasion, a lot of coalition building, and when there was enough evidence that this was the wave of the future, getting e-Sun mentioned at every top management meeting. The longer process of buy-in turned out to be a community-building activity, as more and more isolated Sun cells started thinking about their connections to the larger whole. And by 1999, Sun was an e-business star.

THE DANGER OF NEW WALLS:
NEWSTREAMS VERSUS MAINSTREAMS

The second issue in deconstructing and reconstructing the organization is relevant primarily to established companies: exactly how to organize around e-business itself. Should there be a unit dedicated to e-business? A venture or two focused on e-commerce or other new business opportunities? Where should they be located? How much independence should they have?

This is a classic problem of all new ventures in established companies—the tension between newstreams and the mainstream (Kanter, 1989). Once wannadots get beyond the cosmetic stage of part-time, casual attention to new e-ventures, they sometimes swing in the opposite direction, setting up an independent unit that has total autonomy and few synergies with the parent company. Until the devaluation of Internet stocks in the spring of 2000, some rushed to create quasi-independent dotcoms of their own in response to the capital markets in order to unlock valuation, raise cash for acquisitions, and compensate employees with stock options, just as the Internet pure plays did.

Tesco, a leading British grocery chain and online first mover, grappled with finding the right organization and the right degree of separation. In September 1999, Tesco combined Tesco Direct and a new business development unit which explored opportunities beyond groceries. This was one effort to move beyond the mainstream emphasis on groceries to become a broad portal for online shoppers. (Tesco was already an ISP and an e-mail provider.) Eight months later, Tesco announced the formation of Tesco.com as a separate, wholly owned subsidiary with its own P&L, accountability, and objectives. The separation would help Tesco.com focus as it competed with other strong brands seeking portal status, such as Virgin.net and FreeServe (a spinoff from Dixon's). But the advantages of staying close to the Tesco mainstream were also apparent, as an insider indicated: "We don't intend to be disintermediated from our customers . . . FreeServe could not offer Internet grocery shopping without partnering with someone else." The announcement of Tesco.com ended the debate about spinning off an organizationally separate venture. The opportunity to raise cash for investment that the bricks-and-mortar mainstream would never consider was appealing, but managers were also aware that "online is simply the next evolution of Tesco, and is integral to the whole company." One demonstration of the close ties: when there was a delivery problem one Christmas, e-commerce and mainstream employees packed baskets in stores, piled them in managers' cars, and delivered them personally on Christmas eve. The relationship between mainstream and newstream could not have been clearer.

Ironically, some e-business enthusiasts who want to unite the organization around the Web behave in ways that push the organization away or create new barriers between newstream and mainstream. Those in the newstream flaunt their differences in style or privileges, and then wonder why they engender resentment instead of support. When I am asked questions by embattled e-commerce heads in laggard companies that amount to "Why doesn't anyone like us?" I throw the question back at them: "Why don't you like any of them?" Convinced they are the vanguard of the revolution, they are scornful of the traditional business and isolate themselves from it, confining themselves to their own cells rather than helping other groups move out of theirs.

It has to be a two-way street. Managers on the traditional side must cede some control in order to attain the full potential of the Web. At the same time, those in new Internet ventures must build connections to the mainstream organization. To create an organizational community of purpose, both groups must let go of identities that divide rather than unite.

The problems on both sides are captured in the sad story of an internal Internet entrepreneur at a global bank in Hong Kong. I'll give him the pseudonym "Nigel Brown" and call his employer "Empire International Bank," because he was already punished enough for trying to do the right thing. Empire, a British-led Asian bank, had swung the pendulum toward decentralization in the early 1990s and now enjoyed all the power bases that ensued, spread across dozens of countries. Empire's Web presence was a Tower of Babel of hundreds of offerings that could not communicate with each other. In Asia alone, there was a Singapore consumer banking Internet product with little in common with a Singapore treasury Internet product and nothing in common with a Hong Kong consumer banking Internet product. Hong Kong had an e-mortgage service not used anywhere else in the bank. And experienced technology people were beginning to jump ship for dotcom startups.

In 1999, Nigel Brown was a temporary hero. His Hong Kong team had developed a successful Y2K website for international use. It was so user-friendly that it became the first step in a campaign Brown undertook to Internet-enable the bank. He created another project. He negotiated across territories and across power bases. Then a delegation from the central IT group in London came to audit him. Because he had started to work on Web projects against their wishes, they froze his budget. Brown suspected it was because he was successful, and "London" did not want to be seen as subordinate to him.

No sooner did he survive his suspension (he had other supporters and another source of funds) than his Web skunk works decided to flaunt tradition. The group spent endless time on how to distinguish itself from a buttoned-down British bank. "Part of the discussion we're having is how different do we make ourselves?" he remarked. "Do we come in wearing ponytails, jeans, and things like this? Or do we play the game and look like them? I honestly don't know. We spent a long time discussing how the bank needs to change. We color-coded it. So yellow is old world. Pink is today. Green is tomorrow." Brown was wearing a pink shirt the day of our interview. "I have a lot of bright pink, that's true. Kevin [a co-worker] thinks I'm very 'today' because I use politics and people to get my job done. But if I were truly 'green,'

I would come in wearing a pigtail, jeans, long hair, and stuff like that because I'd show that I don't care even a little bit about how we do this."

Although Brown's group had not decided how different they wanted their appearance to be, they signaled difference in their actions. Instead of holding meetings in the bank's usual style, complete with PowerPoint slide presentations, they turned the office into an art gallery to show visitors how they could move their functions onto the Internet. These creative thoughts made Brown's group feel good, but it remained to be seen whether members of the mainstream would become more open to change or just dig in their heels. Brown was walking a fine line that could easily widen into a cultural wall.

When the Wall Becomes Real

Sometimes imaginary walls turn into real ones. In the spring of 1999, construction workers arrived to erect a thick, unpenetrable wall of brick and plaster to permanently divide Arrow Electronics's new Internet group from a mainstream Arrow sales unit occupying the other side of the same building.

Here is what led to the wall. Arrow Electronics was the world's largest distributor of electronic components and computer products, with 175,000 big customers, sales of $9 billion, and a track record of profitability. Arrow was already connected electronically to its customers through proprietary electronic data interchange networks, but Marshall Industries had been the first distributor to move to the Internet. Other competitors such as Avnet were also rushing to the Web, along with over a dozen new dotcoms—all vying for a share of a market estimated to be $50 billion in the United States alone. CEO Steven Kaufman was determined to prevent Arrow Electronics from being disintermediated. If online distributors were going to eat into Arrow's business, then Kaufman wanted a part of his own company to be the one to enjoy the meal first.

After executive and board discussions, Kaufman mounted an internal new venture, Arrow.com. Tom Hallam, then Arrow's chief corporate HR officer, took on leadership of the Internet group first part-time and eventually as full-time president in November 1998. Hallam was an MIT-trained engineer who was a PC devotee in the mid-1980s and then became a Web aficionado. He assembled a core team, with a few of them coming from Arrow's MIS and marketing departments, and moved into a building in Hauppauge, Long Island, shared by a branch of Arrow's mainstream sales group.

Hallam believed that he needed to create a flexible, fast-acting culture distinct from the Arrow norm in order to attract dotcom talent and establish new media partnerships. "Steve told me, 'do it any way you want to, and we'll tell you when it causes some problem that we all have to talk about.'" So he emulated a youthful dotcom style.

Arrow.com's offices were open cubicles in a large warehouse-like square. Everyone—the president, the marketing team, the webmaster—was visible to everyone else from across the large room. Big windows stretched from the ceiling to the floor across the entire front wall to let in as much sunlight as possible. The walls were painted yellow, and there were only three or four offices with doors, for the occasional confidential meeting. One area on the side of the room was designated a meeting space, with big comfortable leather couches arranged in a circle. A big-screen TV, VCR, CD player, and an assortment of video tapes and music CDs were displayed at the head of the circle, with a glass coffee table in the middle. Behind the meeting space off toward the corner was a kitchen, with a cappuccino machine and cupboards worth at least $35,000. (I'm cataloging the furniture because it became a sore point.)

Arrow.com's hours of operation were loose. A requirement that every employee use a cell phone and a wireless hand-held e-mail pager kept the staff in constant communication. "We've erased the line between work life and home life," Hallam said. "In a traditional setting, you're either at work or you're not. For us, it's not obvious when we're working and when we're not." Anyone could assemble an informal cross-functional meeting or ask a question anytime. The Internet group even worked out the equivalent of a secret handshake—a series of hand gestures and codes to determine whether or not they were on the phone, busy at work, or available to be interrupted.

"That was about as left of Arrow as you could get," remarked Jim Heuther, VP of semiconductor product management. (He added, "The fact that the organization allowed it at all is a sign of how progressive the company is.") It was no surprise that the traditional Arrow branch sales and marketing employees on the other side of the building immediately resented the dotcom. They were quick to point out the drawbacks of the open offices and open style. One exclaimed combatively: "If I was a vice president over there, I would be sitting in a cube out on the floor. Guess what? I'm not going to do that. I don't care if it's old fashioned or not: I want a door. A door with an office, because I don't want it to be a big deal every time I want to have a private conversation and people speculating what I'm working on. I don't want to work out in the open. I don't care if that's the new model, I guess I'll go down as a dinosaur." Hallam retorted, "Our culture is created this way for communication. The fact that we don't have secretaries, we dress differently, we work different hours, frustrates the hell out of the traditional business group."

Kaufman felt that Arrow.com needed to operate by a different set of rules in order to attract dotcom talent. Other executives agreed that the Internet requires different programming skills and development cycles. But Kaufman also knew that the freedom could make it look like "they are the favored, chosen few." Rather than let the tensions spin out of control, Arrow leaders decided it was too "confusing" to have a door between newstream and mainstream. They erected the infamous wall instead.

Not only the neighbors—now conveniently walled off—were critical of the Internet group. Many mainstream senior leaders felt that Arrow.com was operating in a vacuum. Jan Salsgiver, president of Arrow's North American business, said: "We felt that they were going off doing whatever they wanted to do; and we were sitting here feeling very self-righteous about Arrow. We wanted to say, don't call it Arrow.com—because that's us. If you want to be something different, then go be something different, but name yourself something different." She confessed, "We got into these pissing contests."

Kaufman described the tensions between Arrow.com and the traditional business group as sibling rivalry stemming from different standards for mainstream and newstream: "If you had to wear a jacket and tie to eat dinner every night while your sibling could come in a sweatshirt—and then he went with one of your parents every night to the baseball game and you couldn't go, but you had to keep dressing up, and you had to keep getting A's, but they were allowed to get C's and they got praised, would you get jealous? Sure you'd get jealous."

But some of the concerns were not just emotional reactions to different degrees of freedom, they were business concerns about being left out of essential discussions—concerns that people in Arrow.com were not seeking the input of business units whose Web fate they might be controlling. The Internet group needed the support of the core business because they depended on the mainstream computer systems for raw data, order entry, and order processing; on the mainstream purchasing organization for access to inventory; and on the mainstream fulfillment operation for product shipments. Customers, of course, didn't recognize the wall that had been constructed between Arrow.com and the mainstream; they tried to use both channels. Arrow needed internal collaboration to sort out whether new customers registering on the Web really were new accounts for Arrow. And important synergies could benefit the entire business. Some of the processes Arrow.com developed for the Web, such as customer order changes or requests for authorization of returns, could be deployed for other customers through the mainstream sales organization.

Kaufman, an experienced leader under whose guidance Arrow reached new heights of profitability, was not rattled by the battles. "Arrow is a pretty open culture, and while people grumble a little bit, it is not horribly political," he said. "If it gets horribly political, if the time ever comes when the core group is actively working to hurt the Internet business, then I'll have to step in with a little more intervention. But at this point it is more the grumbling that, 'oh Christ, here they come again, they want something tomorrow, just like always, don't they know we have real work to do. Well, let's see if we can help them because if we don't, they are just going to go whining to Kaufman and he's going to come in and say why can't you help them, so let's just help them and get it over with.'" He felt there was too much to do to get bogged down in politics. His tactic was to stand firm and repeat his explanations of why Arrow.com was important, the strategy behind it, and why the Internet group needed to work differently.

Another executive said that the problem was "a feeling that the Internet business people thought they could do anything they wanted. And everybody else is abiding by the normal rules, the culture, the approvals. It was almost like they were thumbing their noses at all this. The same people who had been part of our organization who went over there, 'oh, they're so arrogant.' Now they are trying to work with the core business. Some of them are having to mend bridges that they may have burned." (I'll get to some of Arrow's solutions after we take a tour of one more set of walls.)

Arrow Electronics' wall divided newstream from mainstream, but embattled new ventures sometimes erect their own internal walls. Barnesandnoble.com's wall created cells and silos within the e-venture itself.

In late 1997, barnesandnoble.com moved to a giant warehouse floor in Chelsea, with something like 65,000 square feet of open space. In the middle was a loading dock converted into the network operations center. A window was put into that area to allow passers-by to peer in to observe the activity. Several informants described a similar first reaction: that this was a good symbol for an Internet company—the network at the center, visible to all. But when the renovations were completed, the technology group decided to put a rack mount up against the window. "So then you could see lights flashing but you couldn't see the people in there working on the technology," an insider recalled. "I thought, isn't this ironic? We put technology in the center, we built a window so we can all look at it, and then we put a wall up against it so that you can't really see what's going on. Putting that rack up against the window was a great metaphor for the network group trying to build walls around themselves. To be fair, they were bombarded with requests and demands. But they worked behind walls."

The company's main functions were located in separate quadrants of the building and were clearly demarcated, despite the open space. The rest of technology had one corner, editorial and merchandising was in another corner, the executive and business side was in a third corner, and marketing and customer service was in the fourth corner. People stuck to their own groups. A social wall divided them. "You didn't even know the people," a former manager commented. "So to get things done, you would follow this path up through your chain of command and down to their chain of command, even though the people you needed at the working level were only a few steps away. They were opposite us physically in the building, and we would never talk to them." One consequence of the separation was a disregard for the other functions, the manager said. "Marketing would be humming along a million miles an hour driving people to the website without any notion of what was actually going on there."

Unlike the physical barrier erected by the network operations group, the other walls were invisible, but there were still clear dividing lines. Another former employee described the visual and cultural separation, especially between technology and editorial: "Those two organizations were such polar opposites: the sneakers and jeans culture of programmers and developers versus the all-black clothes, granola, Soho-type culture of the book literati. Those people didn't speak the same language. What was important to one group didn't make any sense to the other, and vice versa. They butted heads."

CLIMBING OVER THE WALLS

It's a hard climb over all these walls unless there are ladders and bridges. Those are often human bridges. Barnesandnoble.com's solution was already common among strong dotcoms like Abuzz: to create a product development team with people who spoke both the language of marketing and the language of technology.

Arrow Electronics used several types of connectors. Its most powerful bridge was an Internet advisory board—in effect, a board of directors—linking mainstream and newstream through representatives of various traditional units. Informally, strong personal relationships helped give people ladders to get from mainstream to newstream. Because Arrow moved insiders to its Internet unit, mainstream employees knew people in the dotcom and could stay connected. Jim Heuther, for example, kept in touch with former colleagues Stephanie Baranak and Theresa Stanson. A formal integrating structure, personal relationships, and a shared belief in the importance of the Internet eventually healed Arrow's wounds of war. By mid-2000, Arrow was acknowledged as an Internet leader and had been named one of the top 100 online companies by major industry trade journals such as *Internet Week, Business 2.0,* and *Electronic Buyers News.*

Similar bridges helped Lucent Technology's New Venture Group avoid the classic problems of new ventures in established companies. NVG co-founder and vice president Steve Socolof recruited experienced Lucent people with ties back to the business units and corporate staffs. He made NVG participation part of a Lucent career path, rotating people through both newstream and mainstream assignments. He stressed communication about the NVG and its companies. An NVG-dedicated PR director placed a steady stream of stories in the media that would be seen inside the company as well as outside. NVG staff went on speaking tours through Lucent, and mainstream people were welcomed at NVG facilities. They kept enumerating benefits to both Lucent and the startups from their coexistence in the big organization.

Using ladders and bridges takes good balance—for example, balancing a clear identity and autonomy for a new venture to chart its own course with collaborative connections to the mainstream to tap synergies and exchange benefits. When she became president of CNBC.com in September 1999, Pamela Thomas-Graham was determined to get the balance right.

As a former McKinsey consultant, Thomas-Graham had observed the mistakes that retail and media companies made in their Web experiments, especially during the "lipstick on a bulldog" stage of cosmetic change. She shaped her job at CNBC.com to ensure that her new venture was neither starved by being treated too casually nor separated from corporate parents NBC and General Electric. She reports directly to the president of NBC as head of a distinct business. At the same time, as a close colleague of CNBC television and sharer of its brand, her dotcom is located in CNBC's Fort Lee, New Jersey, facility and engages in numerous forms of cooperation and collaborative planning. This helped CNBC.com get dozens of on-air mentions a day from CNBC, fast interchange with the MSNBC newswriters deployed to CNBC, and inclusion in the CNBC advertising sales bundle. These benefits came at a price: CNBC.com could not be fully autonomous, break rules, or avoid conformity with GE financial systems. So Thomas-Graham works with an internal NBC advisory board that helps her get what she needs from the rest of GE.

For Williams-Sonoma, formal integrators help link the new e-commerce division to the mainstream. Although the e-commerce group has its own functional teams for application development, merchandising, and marketing for each store brand, Shelley Nandkeolyar recognized the need for a diplomatic operations manager to create more legitimacy for e-commerce in the eyes of the rest of the company. It made sense that this person be an insider with a strong network of relationships throughout W-S. He chose Patricia Skerrett, who had worked both in inventory management and marketing. Her new role, officially called Operations Manager, marked the first time someone in upper management would be responsible for identifying and resolving conflicts across the separate channels of business.

"Two words summarize what I'm supposed to do. Seamless Integration," Skerrett said. "We needed somebody to tie together all of the channels and functional areas. So I deal very closely with the call center, the distribution center, store operations, inventory, and marketing, in order to make sure that first and foremost, people understand what [e-commerce's] direction is, what we're doing in the Internet and how that can potentially impact their areas." Skerrett and Nandkeolyar meet regularly with leaders in the retail and catalog divisions to maintain consistency across channels, ensure that items looked identical, and protect the customer experience. Interpersonal relationships are the key to bridging Williams-Sonoma's silos.

FROM "KNOWING TOGETHER" TO WORKING TOGETHER

Community doesn't just happen to organizations: leaders must explicitly promote it. They can lead by example, select people for collaborative instincts, head off any sign of territoriality, and coach people to work cooperatively.

Michael Robinson's distaste for workplace politics made him determined to lead renren.com as a unified community. Even the name promised inclusion; *renren* is the Chinese term for everybody. Renren.com is a growing Internet portal headquartered in Hong Kong that claims to be the first truly bilingual destination site for the global Chinese community. Founded in 1998 by ex-McKinsey consultants Robinson as CEO and Anthony Cheng as president, renren.com soon attracted name-brand Silicon Valley investors and partners and went live in May 1999, with seven employees. By January 2000, renren was up to 100 employees, and by May it had 200 employees spread across offices in Hong Kong, Beijing, Shanghai, Taipei, and California. The founders did not want dispersion to result in dysfunctional divisions.

Communication is at the heart of running renren.com as an organizational community. Language is one possible barrier, so it helps that senior people are trilingual in English, Mandarin, and Cantonese and can revert to English as a common international language. Robinson and Cheng look for people who are team players, they said, and remind them constantly that they want renren.com to be a politics-free zone. (A noble, if quixotic, aspiration.) Robinson said, "Everybody knows that Anthony and I are adamant about destruction of any political stuff. Politics leaves such a bad taste in my mouth because I've lived through it with academia. I just won't have any part of it."

Even so, cross-office communication posed a tough challenge that eventually led to a very unusual policy for an Internet company: no e-mail for disagreements or strategic decisions, only phone conferences. In early 2000, there was a heated e-mail argument going on between Shanghai and Hong Kong that really bothered Robinson. The person in Shanghai was upset that hardware equipment decisions were being made in Hong Kong, arguing that he should make that decision on the ground, but indicating in more subtle ways that he didn't want Shanghai to be subordinate to Hong Kong.

"It got to the point that one of them cc'd me on this e-mail thread," Robinson recalled. "I said, no more e-mails, get on the phone. Just settle it quickly. I told both the guys that things are done based on their business logic, not on any people hierarchy. That's just baloney, so don't go there. I know you're both nice guys and I know you both actually like each other, so just get on the phone. They got on the phone, and within 20 seconds, it was back to normal. They were very embarrassed afterwards." Getting over that hurdle became an oft-told war story—and the source of the "no e-mail for controversies" rule.

Robinson shifted his emphasis from better communication to higher levels of teamwork across offices. "We went from poor interoffice communication to great interoffice communication but poor interoffice working, so now the big theme is cross-working," he said. "We enforce weekly cross-office meetings by phone." For example, the marketing team might have a meeting in Hong Kong, then a meeting in Beijing, followed by a multioffice meeting by phone to make sure that everybody has the latest information, across functions as well as across offices. It became the norm to e-mail documents back and forth so that everybody knew what everybody else was doing. But even those moves were too passive. Just because people were better informed did not mean that they acted on the information or worked together effectively. "They weren't really working together," he said. "They were just knowing together."

The next step was to foster active exchange of knowledge so that groups could quickly move on opportunities presented by other groups. As the personal visits, conference calls, e-mail updates, and follow-up conference calls mounted, wider involvement became the norm. The ultimate sign of community at renren.com was when teamwork became spontaneous rather than directed from the top, and when groups started setting goals together rather than just responding to each other's goals. "Now people in different areas brainstorm tasks together," Robinson commented. "They work together to come up with the ideas. So everybody buys in and is motivated to get it done."

Acting as an organizational community quickly became self-reinforcing. It reduced frustration and made work more successful. Robinson said, "Satisfaction increases tremendously when people take ownership and are proud of something that millions of people will see on the Internet."

Abuzz is a little older than renren.com, and it is further along in internal teamwork, cross-functional collaboration, and frequent abundant communication. But new companies like these are still just the size of a small village. Can the same spirit of community pervade larger organizations? Let's move up to a thousand people. One pacesetter company responding to my e-culture survey attributed its ability to work as a unified community to having only a thousand employees. "Since we are a relatively nimble and small or tight organization, we are able to function as one big unit, with an underlying culture that embraces change," a leader said. "We have successfully launched a major extranet initiative seeking a wide audience. We took the time to set priorities upfront and create a consensus for a bottom-up focus that enables many participants to feel like stakeholders in the launching process. The enthusiasm for this initiative spurred us to go beyond our original bounds and seek broader scope."

The classic assumption in organization theory was that bureaucracy is inevitable. Theorists long held that coordination becomes more difficult and costly as organizations scale up. Indeed, classic studies showed that administrative overhead generally grows faster than productive capacity. But in the Internet Age, size does not have to limit communication, and a division of labor doesn't have to create permanent class distinctions. Cisco Systems's success is a prime example. Cisco didn't divide into too many rigid territories in the first place, and didn't turn particular technologies into a religion accompanied by priests to enforce orthodoxy. It did not create separate brands with their own pride of place. Cisco emphasizes rapid information dissemination and abundant communication. It has dazzling figures for sales per employee and remarkable feats of speed, such as the ability to close the books every twenty-four hours.

Cisco—which calls itself the world's largest e-commerce company—builds an internal electronic community. It uses its own networks to encourage very large numbers of people to head in the same direction. So does Cisco's key strategic partner, IBM, which could soon surpass Cisco in e-commerce size. But to get there, IBM had to undergo a massive organizational upheaval. The IBM case is complex, but behind the alphabet soup of titles and task forces, this story illustrates how even an $87 billion company can reconstruct its organization to support e-culture.

THE ROUTE TO E-BUSINESS LEADERSHIP: CONNECTING "ONE IBM"

In 1993, when the World Wide Web opened for business, IBM was an ailing giant out of synch with the market. Its complexity was overwhelming, and so were its silos: 3 million orders, 10 million invoices, 20 disparate business units, 5,000 hardware products, 20,000 software offerings, 1,000+ product announcements a year, 25 major fulfillment systems, 50+ manufacturing floor systems. "We were a beached whale. We couldn't get out of our own way. Wall Street was needling us to break into various Baby Blues," recalled Bruce Harreld, Senior Vice President of Strategy. "We had been taught that as things got complex we created new divisions and more general managers who thought they had a God-given right to create their own everything."

New CEO Louis V. Gerstner, Jr., wanted to go to market as "One IBM," an integrated, global organization, using technology as an enabler and customer focus as the stimulus for change. Two years of internal reengineering centralized HR, finance, and CIO functions. Then in 1995, the focus shifted to customers and suppliers. Recognizing the huge potential of the Internet, Gerstner began to reposition IBM as a world-class e-business. At first this was greeted skeptically by the media. But when Internet applications exploded in 1997, IBM was ready with IT solutions.

Inside the company, however, this very proliferation of its own e-business activities contributed to a fragmented and uncoordinated result. Consider these amazing numbers: by 1997, IBM ran the world's largest corporate website, with over half a million webpages, 50 million hits a week (half of them over the Internet), and a rising annual investment of over $120 million. Over 250 disparate content organizations contributed to webpages, nearly 1,000 people worked on webpage development, and 4,000 servers scattered throughout the company hosted the sites. Most of the sites were not very strategic, and multiple sites targeted the same audience with conflicting messages. Customers had to use different Web addresses to research several types of products. Worse yet, the sites were oriented toward selling to website visitors rather than supporting their buying decision. And even if the customer was interested in making a purchase over the Web, complex site navigation made this hard to do. The internal organization itself was becoming an obstacle to reaching customers.

By mid-1997, Gerstner was losing patience. Too much was still being spent on IT within IBM. Even more alarming as a sign of fragmentation, 128 different people across IBM held the title of Chief Information Officer. Then-corporate-CIO Dave Carlucci issued an edict that things must change. Silo-shattering structural changes were forced on a reluctant organization. Instead of 128 CIOs, there would be only one CIO for the corporation. All the hundred-plus functions these CIOs were running were consolidated into seven clusters. The former business-unit CIOs became BIEs (business information executives) to represent the data needs of their units to the corporate CIO organization. "There were big disagreements," recalled an insider close to the action. "Business unit heads wanted to keep their own CIO, wanted to maintain control of budgets and reporting relationships.

And to this day, almost three years later, some of the BIEs still loathe the people who took away their CIO title."

While back-room change was under way, IBM's top leaders embraced the e-business theme, and in 1998, IBM introduced a centralized e-business organization called Enterprise Web Management (EWM). EWM was a new Internet-focused unit that would integrate product development, the supply chain, and customer interfaces, as well as unite employees, in effect taking the reengineered business processes to the Web. Dick Anderson, an experienced IBM marketing executive, was appointed general manager, reporting to Steve Ward, who replaced Carlucci as CIO in early 1998.

Anderson's mandate was to move IBM to a new business model based on "Web governance," a third and more productive stage IBM consultants identified as the ultimate goal. The EWM group was expected to develop consistent, companywide business strategies and work with business units to create "One IBM" on the Web. This involved IT infrastructure tasks, of course, but it also included a significant organizational challenge: wresting control from business units accustomed to charting their own course for their own divisions, brands, and geographies. Losing a CIO was one thing; this next wave of change was even more threatening to the cells and silos.

EWM took immediate control of the Internet flagship, ibm.com, and began to centralize the numerous initiatives under the Web umbrella, including content approval and security standards. Though IBM was known for discipline, even conformity—it was only a few years beyond white-shirts-and-blue-suits-only policies—there were still many battles behind the scenes, insiders reported. But Anderson kept reminding people about Gerstner's focus on customers. Gerstner preached customer focus and modeled it in his own behavior, spending much of his own time visiting major customers. Since customer feedback drove the need for centralization—it would help customers access IBM products and services in faster and simpler ways—business heads had few grounds for resistance, although some tried the "my customers are different" argument. Loss of business unit sovereignty, they were told in response, would be more than balanced by access to new technology, skills, and infrastructure formerly scattered through disparate groups across the vast company and hard to find.

To design a new organizational structure, EWM convened a large, representative task force of senior people from the business units and corporate groups already engaged in various e-business activities (for example, e-procurement and e-commerce). The task force sought an operating structure that would combine the best of centralization ("One IBM") as well as decentralization (business unit–specific strategies). Their "One IBM" objective was met through directors for interactive marketing and ibm.com. Seven core processes were identified, and each was given the attention of a director and a cross-business Web Initiative Team: e-commerce, e-care for customers, e-care for business partners, e-care for influencers, e-procurement, e-care for employees, and e-marketing communications. Their "best of decentralization" goal was reflected in ownership by the business units of e-strategies that they developed in partnership with EWM but would execute themselves.

To oversee all of IBM's e-business activities, the task force created a two-level cross-functional management structure. At the top, an e-business executive steering committee provided the vision, clout, and final authority. At the next level, translating vision into action, an e-business management committee made corporatewide decisions. EWM teams facilitated workshops within each business unit and developed new tools to permit a common methodology. The "Web-Site-Go" process provided a streamlined way for business units to generate a new Web address or e-initiative, while also forcing them to justify the business case for their investments and initiatives. Unless business units were willing to cede some of their traditional authority, their initiatives could be denied funding.

Compensation tied to cooperation made the new direction real. "By linking individual incentives to IBM e-business success, Lou Gerstner established the motivation for collaboration across IBM—a tremendous lever for us," said Jamie Hewitt, Business Process VP. IBM created a new annual assessment process, called Personal Business Commitments, which included a bonus scheme that reached far down the hierarchy. An organizational assessment was added in 1998 to measure business units on accomplishment of targets for the top four corporate processes and to adjust the unit's compensation pool according to performance.

By the turn of 1999, the central group was gaining control. It had taken some time, but there was a common IBM look and feel on the Web. E-business was gaining momentum, although EWM was still fighting internal battles and running into organizational walls. A dramatic expansion of e-commerce—from around $3 billion in 1998 to a projection of over $20 billion for 2000—made acceleration of progress essential. One challenge was that the front end (the marketing of IBM as an e-business leader) was shooting ahead, but the back end (the capacity to deliver) was lagging. "In 1999, we were still not integrated, and we had to automate; rip and read wouldn't do," indicated Doug Swanson, a director in the business transformation office of the CIO, referring to the manual process of making hard copies of online orders. In short, one of the world's leading technology companies had still not integrated all of its own processes and was filling e-commerce orders the old-fashioned way. The good news was that there were 150 extranets for IBM's top industry accounts; the bad news was that it was still too slow to update them and add functions.

To create offline community to support online commerce, CIO Ward deployed Swanson to support the e-BT (business transformation) group, a biweekly meeting of BIEs (the former unit CIOs), BPEs (executives in charge of each of the four key business processes), and EWM staff, as they tried to hammer out a solution. The group decided they could make the needed improvements for about $65 million, but the question was where to find that money. "We didn't want to go to Lou [Gerstner]," an insider reported. "So we got the business units to re-set their own priorities and chip in." The prioritization exercise involved a common set of questions each business unit could use to make the business case for that project. Some were easy to justify, because they supported a customer. Others were more contentious, such as bets for the future about how much capacity to add. But after six months of large and small meetings every two weeks, using a common discipline and guided by the need to justify separate cells in terms of their contribution to the whole community, the deal was done. By mid-1999, there was for the first time "One IBM" in the technology organization—a set of shared priorities and a $65 million investment by separate silos in the common good.

Successful execution required the rest of the mainstream organization to get involved. To truly operate as "One IBM" required breadth as well as depth, soul as well as structure. Large numbers of people—outside as well as inside the corporation—would need to think and behave differently. That required extensive ongoing and focused communication. So the message was aimed at a large, diverse audience. This was a sales campaign as big as anything IBM had ever done, but what was being sold was an idea for change. People had to become believers.

The goal was to convey a consistent theme to everyone simultaneously through many different media and channels. "The 'One IBM' objective meant that IBMers everywhere had to understand why becoming an e-business was critical to our success, as well as what they needed to do—or not do—to help," said Will Runyon, communications director for EWM. "And for external influencers and the media, it was absolutely critical that we walked the talk when it came to being an e-business ourselves."

The message was broadcast well before all capabilities were in place to deliver on it, and even before top leaders knew what it would mean in practice. In the spirit of improvisational theater, setting the theme would force internal constituencies to make sure that they could deliver on the promises. "Certainly the most effective communication vehicle was Lou Gerstner himself, whether he was leading the e-business industry debates, setting the vision for IBM, or communicating to all employees," Dick Anderson observed.

A theme is one thing, but how would people know if they were headed in the right direction? EWM developed very specific companywide metrics for the seven clusters of e-business initiatives. For example, the goal for e-care for employees was to increase the use of self-service and distance learning applications. E-care for customers sought to increase web registrations, increase customer satisfaction, and reduce call center costs. Policies addressed three areas: content (for example, third-party links, acceptable employee use, brand and logo), context (for example, site navigation, user experience, site design), and infrastructure (for example, hosting, security, data management). Abundant communication was important here, too. Employees had to be made aware of the dangers of degrading the common look or of posting information that created legal liabilities.

Creating an IBM-wide content model was a critical, yet difficult, step in implementing the desired consistency, and it took nearly two years. Rory Read, vice president of E-Business Enablement, reported, "The ibm.com content model has now gone through ten major redesigns. And the redesigns grow as we learn more about our relationships with customers and stakeholders." Like the successive versions important to improvisation, each wave reduced costs, made development faster, and made the site easier to navigate. Nearly every function at IBM, not just IT and marketing, took some responsibility for Web content management. Content managers were trained in consistent frameworks that all business units would use and were given Web-based tools to assess themselves against global corporate requirements.

By 2000, IBM had become very effective at using its own experience in becoming the world's largest e-business to help educate its global customers. Indicators of change were impressive. IBM moved everything possible to the network, including big things such as the sales of PCs (no longer available except on the Web) and small things such as the sign-in process at headquarters in Armonk, New York (visitors type their name on an IBM ThinkPad and their name tag is printed automatically). Over 42 million service transactions and over 29 percent of all employee training are handled via the Web, and IBM is online with 14,000 business partners and $13 billion in e-procurement.

Inside IBM, the Web facilitates far-flung communities of interest, such as cybercafés, to share knowledge throughout the Global Services group. IBM's 300,000 people send about 2 million real-time instant messages a day. IBM's external community service was focused almost entirely on K–12 public education, and its massive Reinventing Education initiatives in twenty-one U.S. cities and states and seven other countries draw on fluid teams of experts throughout IBM to find technology-based solutions to education problems—in effect, helping schools become e-businesses too.

Elements of e-culture pop up everywhere: a looser style reflected in casual dress, reverse mentoring, improvisational theater, an orientation toward partnering, and an emphasis on speed and teamwork. "Our innovation centers are populated with people that IBMers of the past would never recognize as IBMers: jeans-wearing 'netgens' with long hair who work for the beauty of the finished product," exclaimed Cheryl Shearer, manager of European business partner channels for IBM Global Services in London. *Fast Company* magazine featured an IBM speed team in a spring 2000 issue. Because this New Economy–focused magazine scorned Old Economy companies, this was almost as good as a national prize for transformation. Stories such as the speed team are textbook examples of improvisational theater in action—dramatizing a message to accelerate creativity and innovation.

Sean Gresh, an executive speechwriter at IBM headquarters in Armonk, New York, exemplifies the new all-E employee. In December 1999, he went online to Monster.com to apply for a job at IBM and was called by a recruiter in Raleigh, North Carolina. After a three-day orientation called "Becoming One Voice," he began life as a virtual employee managing his work through the Web. Gresh reported: "I was struck with the fact that literally everything at IBM centered on the Web—registering for a Lotus Notes account, choosing medical and dental benefits, signing up and taking training programs. And the kicker is that I work at home in Massachusetts and travel to my office one day or so a week. Whenever I need help, I access the intranet. If I need a person to walk me through a process, I dial 1-800-IBM-HELP, and someone is there, 24/7."

As would be expected in one of the world's largest companies, there are still vestiges of the old lumbering bureaucracy (especially the closer one gets to Armonk) and too many examples of the right hand not knowing what the left hand was doing. But global teams working together across traditional business silos are more pervasive, and they use the Web to get things done faster. In June 2000, EWM declared victory and moved on. A reorganization dissolved the central group. Its activities were handed to a small set of functions (for example, Dick Anderson became VP of Internet sales and operations) while the two-tiered corporate committees ensured integrated governance. "I don't want to leave you with the impression that our transformation is over," Bruce Harreld said. "We continue to realize that e-business transformation is about looking deep into the soul of a company, deciding what needs to change, and then using the Web to make that transformation happen." Harreld is right to mention a company's soul. That takes longer to change than its structure.

The benefits of IBM's new-found sense of internal community extend to the external community in unusual and powerful ways, and they help reach the soul. After the refugee crises hit in Kosovo in 1999, a global cross-disciplinary, cross-business team of IBMers was mobilized to help reunite children with their parents in the refugee camps. The International Rescue Committee (IRC), which operated refugee assistance centers in the former Yugoslavian republic of Macedonia, needed the ability to set up a data system in the field. Stanley Litow, Corporate Community Relations VP, wanted to help. Reg Foster in New York and Celia Moore in London led a virtual team from Lotus, Global Services, a Minnesota plant, the European geographic unit, and the worldwide Government Industry Solutions Unit. Within three weeks, they developed customized disaster management database software, delivered servers and laptops, and trained local IRC staff. When word of IBM's contribution appeared on its website, hundreds of e-mails filled Litow's in-box, expressing great pride. Service to the external community throughout the world, using IBM's own tools, was starting to reinforce a feeling of membership in "One IBM."

CONSTRUCTING COMMUNITY

I said earlier that community has both a structure and a soul. As the IBM story shows, structure is the easy part. A few bold strokes such as Gerstner's and Carlucci's edict, and titles change; or a new centralized EWM group arrives to set policy, and Internet protocols and processes become must-use tools. Traditionally participatory Motorola enforced Web integration by top-down dictate. To put the Internet at the center of Motorola's new strategy, CEO Christopher Galvin closeted himself with his COO and emerged two weeks later with a new organization chart. He combined thirty business units (cell phones, wireless equipment, satellite, and cable modem products) into one large division, removed some managers' P&L responsibilities, and added an Internet group to coordinate all Web strategies.

So far, this doesn't look any different from old-fashioned centralization. But there's more to organizational community than compliance; it requires voluntary collaboration. E-culture derives from the soul of community, its human elements. And that's the hard part. Moving from policies and standards to ongoing collaboration takes time and attention—what Barry Stein and I call long marches (Kanter, Stein, & Jick, 1992).

Structure needs soul to produce effective work communities. Consider evidence from Harvard Business School Professor Jody Hofer Gittell's studies of flight crews and health care teams who coordinate complex activities. She found that the ideal combination for high quality and efficient operations is both programmed routines and human relationships. On the structure side, standard procedures and information systems provide a uniform infrastructure that improves communication accuracy and timeliness and problem-solving speed; without this precision, meetings are a waste of time. But technology and rules don't produce the feelings and emotions underlying strong relationships. It takes people communicating directly with each other to strengthen shared knowledge, shared goals, and mutual respect. Strong relationships, it turns out, are what turn efficient routines into high performance (Gittell, 2000).

Six elements contribute to building organizational community.

1. *A balanced governance structure.* Formal structures signal importance, clarify responsibilities, and include those whose input will

make a difference. Activities that touch every part of the company cannot be managed by committees—someone needs to be clearly in charge—but they can't work without input and linkages to the rest of the organization either. The best combination for the Web is a dedicated e-commerce unit that can operate as a venture with rights to pursue its own destiny balanced by a representative advisory board with the mandate to connect newstream to mainstream—Arrow Electronics's solution.

2. *Shared disciplines and routines.* Collaboration is nearly impossible without a common vocabulary and common language. It is facilitated by common tools and disciplines that make it easy to do routine things quickly. The extensive use of their own Web-based tools at Cisco or IBM helps any new group to know how to work together—for example, IBM's lightning-fast disaster relief team.

3. *Multichannel, multidirectional communication.* Communities are communication intensive. They spread more information to more people more regularly through every medium, from large gatherings to the external press. Despite Cisco's reliance on its networks for rapid, routine communication, the company considers face-to-face communication skills vital: top leaders must be capable of emulating John Chambers's ability to speak without notes to large groups. Then Cisco webcasts key events so the whole company can see them. iXL holds a weekly management call for its dozen worldwide offices. The call is backed up by data transmission, so everybody sees the same numbers; at Atlanta headquarters, the numbers are shown on a cinema-sized screen, observable by anyone who is interested. With many channels, people can use the right one for the occasion—such as renren.com's norm of voice-only communication for strategy or disputes, not e-mail. Abuzz convenes weekly meetings of the whole company, uses Abuzz TV to keep everyone informed of daily news, and welcomes visitors from other areas in functional meetings. A British Telecom manager renamed his IT group the IF unit, for information flow, to change the emphasis from technology to communication.

4. *Integrators.* Communities are built through networks of people who meet across areas to share knowledge. They can be structured and formal (the product development team at barnesandnoble.com) or loose and informal (diversity interest groups at FleetBoston). Unlike committees, networks are fluid and open ended, but not just spontaneously self-organizing; they work best when actively managed. Network champions hold people together. DuPont made an art of forming knowledge-sharing networks because Parry Norling in

central R&D served as network guru. He helped networks form, cataloged them (at one point he counted over 400 at a time), encouraged them, and passed on lessons about effectiveness. Norling-nurtured networks included resource groups on a particular technical topic, such as abrasion or adhesion; best-practice sharing; and task-oriented networks, such as the plant maintenance improvement network, which ultimately involved over 600 people and led to cost savings of several hundred million dollars a year.

Appointing official integrators—internal ambassadors and diplomats—ties cells and silos together. Patricia Skerrett at Williams-Sonoma was the first companywide operations manager, because e-commerce involved all functions and divisions. Ambassadors from one group to another are like wandering minstrels, traveling from place to place sprinkling seeds of knowledge—what's happening in Chicago, what's troubling Frankfurt, what's new in Singapore. They build community not just through tasks but through the folklore and war stories they convey. Just as the Web needs webmasters, e-culture communities need wandering minstrels.

5. *Cross-cutting relationships.* Personal relationships are vitally important. It helps to have people with strong social skills who are team oriented and collaborative; innovators at Sun Microsystems, such as Albert Ormiston and his e-Sun project, must build coalitions of supporters in order to lead significant change. But this is also something the organization encourages by convening people across territories on every relevant occasion—corporate conferences, training programs, celebrations. A base of goodwill derived from past encounters keeps communication and support flowing. That's why insiders with long service help build community. Williams-Sonoma and Honeywell's successful e-commerce units balanced new hires with insiders who had a history of good relationships throughout the mainstream. Tesco.com appointed a mainstream manager as its CEO. Arrow's wall was bridged because of relationships. Communities are built around people who know each other, understand each other, like each other, and have a shared history.

6. *Shared identity, shared fate.* Collaboration is not altruism; it stems in part from people identifying with each other and feeling that they share a fate. Incentives that induce cooperation are a starting point. Tesco executives felt that one of their early mistakes was to count dotcom sales outside of local store manager results, even though online orders were picked from the stores, because store managers

then had no incentive to promote the website. At IBM, Gerstner linked individual performance measures to corporate business success. A shared identity is fostered, too, by role switching and job exchanges. Career paths can carry people across silos. Task teams can routinely include people from many silos.

Collaboration works best when it is mutual: Each participant gets something out of it. Each feels good about his or her own part in the success of the whole. Pride in collective achievements reinforces a shared identity, as IBM's community service does. Service to the external community can unite the internal community. But that's not enough without pride in each other. Strong communities thrive on trust and mutual respect. People must respect each other's differences without using them to divide, unlike Nigel Brown's actions at Empire.

E-culture pacesetter companies behave more like communities offline and online. This doesn't mean they erase all distinctions or replace hierarchy with democracy—far from it, as the IBM case shows. Nor does it mean that they eliminate individuality and replace it with conformity. The community ideal is about *unity,* not uniformity; *inclusion,* not consensus; and *communication,* not decision rights.

Community occupies an intermediate position on a continuum from bureaucracy to democracy. It is an organizing principle that allows people to collaborate quickly and effectively, facilitated by technology. Formal systems and processes can certainly produce official integration, but community is the behavioral and emotional infrastructure that supports those other organizational processes and makes them effective. Community action and spirit permit speed and seamlessness, encourage creativity and collaboration, and release human energy and brainpower—the essence of e-culture.

CHAPTER FORTY-FOUR

Actions for Global Learners, Launchers, and Leaders

Ron Ashkenas
Dave Ulrich
Todd Jick
Steve Kerr

Like Marco Polo discovering new realms of trade, organizations today are exploring vast new markets. The process is nothing less than a revolution, breaking down once-sacrosanct boundaries of space, time, and nationality. Suddenly, we find ourselves in a global village, exchanging trade, business, and information so rapidly that the dichotomy between domestic and foreign has vanished. Global boundaries between companies, markets, and people have become irrevocably blurred.

But, it isn't enough to make a goal of loosening geographic boundaries—to adapt to a global world, you have to take action. This chapter presents a set of digital switches—specific geographic boundary–breaking techniques and practices—for tuning your organization's outermost boundaries, along with some thoughts on pitfalls to avoid in the process.

If well managed, the actions described here can help global learners become global launchers and global launchers become global leaders.

FROM GLOBAL LEARNER TO GLOBAL LAUNCHER

Most companies today would probably class themselves as global learners. That is, they are interested in developing some level of cross-border contacts or sites to expand their markets and resources, and may feel competitive pressure to do so. Yet they are inexperienced in international business. How can such learners transform themselves into launchers?

There's no one-size-fits-all solution, of course. Cross-border relationships and a truly global approach to business depend on many factors, including the industry, the level of competition, the trade-off between opportunities and costs, and the legal, social, and cultural hurdles of the specific locale. However, we can describe a wide range of actions that an organization may initiate to take its first steps into the global arena (see Exhibit 44.1).

HR Practices: Focus on Cultural Awareness and Diversity

The most basic task in any globalization effort must be to sensitize people to the vast landscape beyond their own doors. The place to start is with some degree of foreign language learning. Although English remains the international business language, most non-English speakers feel that Anglophones should not be immune to language training. At the least, people need the ability to speak basic phrases in the language of the locale where they do business and to follow light social conversation. Almost everyone appreciates any efforts businesspeople from other countries make along these lines.

Even more important, however, is cultural awareness training. People doing global business must become familiar with critical cultural differences, business practices, cultural attitudes and values, and socialization customs. The best global companies have extensive orientation programs, often including computer simulations of special cultural circumstances, especially ones likely to be perceived as problems. They also present factual information and discussions about cultural differences.

For many managers in U.S. companies, cultural awareness training is not a trivial issue—they often have, to put it mildly, a parochial outlook, little international exposure and experience, and a false sense that the world revolves around American habits. This is often due to

---

Human Resource Practices
- Supply language and cultural sensitivity training
- Standardize forms and procedures
- Set up an overseas presence via joint venture, modest acquisition, or establishment of a headquarters
- Engage in extensive cross-border relationship building

Organizational Structures
- Arrange short-term visits and international assignments
- Staff for more diversity in management and board of directors
- Use e-mail and video conferencing to maintain day-to-day contact

Organizational Processes and Systems
- Establish worldwide shared values, language, and operating principles
- Conduct fact-finding missions
- Design ad hoc transnational teams
- Hold global town meetings and best-practice exchanges of information

---

Exhibit 44.1.   Organizational Actions to Gain Entrance into a Global Arena.

the distance between the United States and other countries. To see the world in its true diversity—and to learn to understand, respect, and appreciate its cultural and traditional differences—is a challenge that requires commitment and an open frame of mind.

Home-country programs in foreign languages and cultural awareness training are the first step in preparing people for foreign travel and work with international counterparts. Next, short-term visits are the necessary spark for the beginnings of any globalization process: fact-finding missions, exploratory discussions, and setting up legal and financial arrangements. A bigger step, when the time is right, is to assign selected staff to live abroad for a year or two, establishing a permanent office or representative site. This longer time frame produces a much better acquaintance with the business methods and cultural values in the host country than do short-term visits. It also helps build personal relationships with local customers and suppliers. As an example of how far a company can go with this, Samsung once sent about four hundred of its brightest junior employees overseas for a year with a specific mission to goof off. Some went to the United States to hang out at the malls, watching American consumers. Others went to Russia to live, eat, and drink with the Russians for a year, study the language, and travel to every republic.

Beyond cultural training, the next most significant HR building block is the establishment of a set of global values and principles that will form the basis of a shared mindset for all members of the organization. This action can range from creating mission statements on corporate globalization goals to writing policy manuals that document standard operating procedures everywhere the company has business. Of course, mission statements tend to be dismissed as nothing more than pretty words unless they are truly backed up by action and frequent review (Donkin, 1994). Therefore, as ASEA Brown Boveri former CEO Percy Barnevik pointed out, these statements must relate directly to people's behavior:

> Our policy bible, which was produced at the inception of ABB and presented at our Cannes meeting for 250 managers, . . . describes our mission and values, where we want to be several years from now, and gives guidelines for overall behavior. It also describes how we should behave internally. To illustrate, one value is that it is better to be roughly right than exactly right with respect to speed. Then there are rules about minimizing overhead, about integrating newly acquired companies, about rewarding and promoting people. But the most important glue holding our group together is the customer-focus philosophy—how we want to be customer driven in all respects. The values describe how we want to create a global culture, what can be done to understand each other, the benefits of mixed nationality teams, and how to avoid being turf defenders. Our policy bible is not a glossy brochure with trivial and general statements, but practical advice on how we should treat each other and the outside world. (de Vries, 1994)

A second aspect of developing a shared mindset involves making sure that key administrative and corporate procedures are implemented in the same manner throughout the organization. Such standardization helps ensure a one-firm concept and has four additional beneficial results.

- *Efficiency.* People at each location should not be developing their own forms or procedures; this is both time-consuming and costly. All forms should be usable worldwide.

- *Common metrics.* The global firm will function better when people use measures that have meaning regardless of geography (for example, cash flow).

- *Common strategy and vision.* Standardized procedures reinforce the organization's shared goals and vision.

• *Consistent image to the marketplace.* A global company benefits from promoting a consistent image regardless of location.

All the actions just discussed point to many fundamental HR steps that can be taken to prepare an organization for doing business in different countries. Each clearly reflects the need to expose employees to other cultures and business practices—a prerequisite for avoiding debilitating stereotyping and misunderstandings.

Organizational Structures: The Dilemma for Learners

Most learner companies hesitate to overhaul their structure when planning their first expansion across borders. A fact-finding task force is therefore a useful way to open the organization to new information and to identify opportunities. The task force can carry out data collection and market research that familiarizes the company with the targeted territory. For example, the French public utility company Électricité de France (EDF) was once primarily a domestic provider of electrical energy and services. However, given the saturation of its domestic market, opportunities to export its technology to other countries, and increasing competition and privatization in utilities, EDF set out in the early 1990s to expand its exports. To identify opportunities and better understand the challenges of cross-border business, EDF took a very simple and modest first step: it set up an eight-person task force to study the international arena and to prepare a report for top management. The group served as a change catalyst by making recommendations as well. EDF began to expand modestly into the international arena as a result of the recommendations of the fact-finding exercise. Since that time, EDF has continued to grow its international operations, and today would be considered more of a global launcher than a learner.

Beyond this simple kind of exploration, the global learner must opt for some kind of first structural step. At a minimum, doing business globally requires the organization to initiate an overseas presence, if not an autonomous headquarters, moving part of itself away from its traditional base and closer to the new customers. On-site location is a powerful indicator of a firm's intent to participate in a foreign market, and management based on site rather than in the home country is a constant reminder that it must adapt to a new business climate and culture.

Alternatively, global learners can penetrate a geographic boundary using what we call a soft structure, meaning a structural change that is reversible and can be limited in length, commitment, and financial investment: a joint venture, for example, or a small acquisition. At this early point in a globalization effort, soft structures make sense because they keep options open while the firm explores markets and develops expertise. Soft-structure arrangements limit risk because they leave the main organizational structure intact. If the firm needs to rethink its plans or if a soft structure fails, the firm's core is not damaged.

A joint venture is perhaps one of the safest ways to get your feet wet. Its value is to combine expertise and capability from two firms, forming a more powerful and efficient operation than either could mount on its own. In the global context, a joint venture using the knowledge and on-site presence of a foreign firm may be one of the best strategies for a monocultural organization that wants to break out of its boundaries.

However, joint ventures do commonly disintegrate over time, as corporate differences emerge after the sparkle of the first meetings. One McKinsey study showed that fully 70 percent of all joint ventures (not just international ones) break up within three and a half years (Savona, 1992). Other studies have indicated that even the survivors do not achieve their participants' expectations. Of course, joint ventures with overseas companies are even more complex than domestic ones, given the language and cultural barriers to be crossed as well as the potential for substantive differences in operating style and strategy.

As a result, we suggest approaching international joint ventures without counting on big direct paybacks. You'll get most value from them as learning experiences: discovering the success factors in the new culture, making connections and contacts with industry leaders, obtaining benchmarking information and new technology to use in your own processes, and exploring new markets. And the significance of this learning process is not to be underestimated. Many studies have shown that the joint venture partner who learns the fastest can dominate the relationship and dictate the terms. Yet some show that Japanese organizations excel at learning from others while North American and European companies have more trouble with it (Main, 1990). That observation suggests that this is an area deserving an organization's close attention.

Two additional elements will enhance the success of an overseas joint venture. First, choose a compatible partner—one where you can develop a personal relationship based on trust and mutual respect. That's a critical part of the glue that holds partners together. Personal incompatibility is thought to cause more failures among joint ventures and alliances than any other factor. Second, take time to fully evaluate the venture and its goals. Do not rush headlong into a deal without clearly identifying the market opportunities, potential drawbacks, and long-term gains.

In some cases, acquiring a small company abroad can move an organization into the international arena more quickly than a joint venture. In theory, an acquisition also carries less risk. The company comes under your control and the chances of disagreement with its management are reduced. Nevertheless, the word modest should be emphasized when it comes to a foreign acquisition. Without experience in a culture or market, the global learner may wind up throwing resources away on improvements, restaffing, training, or accommodating constraints imposed by the foreign government. The keys to a successful acquisition, like the keys to a joint venture, are to ensure that the planning phase has covered every decision point in depth and to keep expectations and investment low. As is also true in joint ventures, an ability to learn from the experience is vital, as is the ability to adapt quickly if it becomes clear that the original plans are failing.

As the company gets deeper into foreign operations, its domestic structure should include increasingly diverse senior people. The global learner should begin to seek the involvement of top managers representing a range of nationalities, experience, and professional backgrounds in the geographic area of its globalization. We have seen the dynamics of companies change significantly with the arrival of a few foreign members. Managers with diverse experiences often yield different insights into the cultural impact of decisions. Diversity can be difficult to manage initially, but companies need to recognize that a long-term perspective is required when establishing a new global mindset.

In particular, adding foreign directors to the board yields many benefits. Knowledgeable foreign leaders can expand company perspective and open doors to new contacts. They can often improve negotiations in their home countries. Smaller companies, especially, can gain from the advice and intelligence a foreign director brings— advice that would cost far more if bought from an international consulting firm.

Organizational Processes and Systems: Global Colleagues and Meetings

More and more, the starting point for crossing borders effectively is getting to know your global colleagues. In many companies in the early stages of globalization, people literally do not know their counterparts from different countries. And even when they've met, they may still have distancing stereotypes that interfere with normal business processes. An important tuning action here is to give people intense, even if not frequent, opportunities to be together in both social and task situations. Both will socialize them, and a socialization process, says Paul Evans, builds a network of personal contacts that "becomes the nervous system of the organization. [Moreover] a network does not require everyone to know everyone else." This is the essence of what Evans calls "loose ties"—connections to one or another of a small set of gatekeepers who maintain connections to each other that are strong enough to keep the whole network functioning (Evans, 1992).

Consider the example of a multibusiness conglomerate with its central headquarters in London but much of its business in Asia. Every year, the company sent a group of managers—consisting of equal numbers of British managers and Chinese managers—to a month-long business school program specially designed to upgrade management capability for the company. Program faculty met with senior management to discuss each year's training. But training was not the program's sole or perhaps even its primary purpose, as the company chairman made clear when he reputedly instructed the faculty, "I don't really care what you do in the classroom as long as they are getting drunk every night together. That's the best way to break down cultural barriers and create a lasting bond!" Of course, a drinkfest isn't the only technique to accomplish this end, but intense socializing experiences do go a long way toward removing barriers between people and breaking down stereotypes.

Another global learner was the former Chemical Bank Europe, now JP Morgan-Chase. When Chemical originally merged with Manufacturer's Hanover Trust, its people had to get to know the other company, reaching across not only geographic but also corporate cultures. Despite the cost-cutting climate, the merged bank's European head decided to convene a three-day off-site workshop in which his top hundred marketing managers gathered to clarify common goals, work on serving the needs of common clients, and build mutual trust. The workshop combined intense work and intense play. Every meal table, every breakout discussion, and every sports and recreational activity was carefully designed to socialize a different group of people. Over the three days, each individual had the opportunity to meet virtually all the others. This workshop became an annual event and a valuable source of bonding, supplementing many of the bank's other global processes.

It is important to note, however, that the emerging trust that people build across national and organizational cultures may be fragile. Years later, after another merger, the bank tried the same off-site relationship-building approach that had worked so well before. The first two days were successful. Then at the final banquet, one of the speakers began making off-color jokes with sexual and culturally insensitive overtones. As a result, two days of building trust were undone in fifteen minutes. The bank learned that trust can take many years to build, and only an instant to lose.

A novel approach to building relationships between managers from different cultures is practiced by AXA, which set out to create a global insurance services company. It operates in a "multidomestic" fashion in multiple countries, but integrates these units through pursuing global synergies, best practice sharing, and personnel exchanges. AXA has grown through acquisitions over many years, and faces challenges of both cultural and organizational integration. The company's CEO is committed to creating an international, multicultural ethos that permeates the organization. One way he does this is through offsite conferences held every two or three years for the top management team, which represents all the acquired companies. Three things make these conferences unique:

- Each one is held in a different, exotic location where few if any participants have ever been before (on a boat in the Bosphorus, in the Sahara desert, in a remote village in the Amazon jungle). The location ensures that no culture or individual feels comfortable or conversant enough to dominate, and the group truly engages in the experience together.

- For each conference, participants are given uniform clothing to wear that is appropriate to the location and climate, but also creates a common look and feel.

• Content sessions are designed to raise awareness of multicultural issues while also emphasizing the organization's shared values, overall strategy, and emerging global brand platform. Participants represent sixteen languages, and the meeting is conducted in English and French with simultaneous translation available as required.

These conferences are immortalized in stories that symbolize AXA's multicultural value system, and are told again and again throughout the company. They also provide AXA's managers with firsthand experience of how to operate within and benefit from cultural diversity, while creating something larger than any one unit or culture.

The global learner must carefully balance universal and local needs in designing and developing new products or services. This makes ad hoc transnational teams useful as another action for global learners to develop projects that can benefit from a global perspective. Such teams used to be much harder to manage, but modern communications have essentially eliminated many of the barriers of time and distance that once interfered with their use. Both e-mail and videoconferencing have many advantages besides speed and cost-effectiveness. E-mail provides a real-time record and allows people from different cultures and with different language capabilities to communicate without having to cope with pronunciation or cultural conventions. Videoconferencing allows participants to see facial reactions and body language and perhaps gives a better picture of attitudes and behaviors.

Moreover, technology is essential to making managers' offices geographically boundaryless. As Philippe Chevaux, head of an AT&T business located near the French-Italian border, says (speaking of his ability to communicate with clients or his home office), "We are a global business, open twenty-four hours a day. My office is anywhere I am." That mentality must be part of the mindset for any global company.

Two final processes recommended for learners are global town meetings and best-practice exchanges. The global town meeting works very much like the domestic variety we described earlier. People from related functions among multiple worldwide locations come together for the purpose of identifying common problems or challenges that cross borders. For example, an international bank might conduct a town meeting to resolve conflicts over originating new products, addressing questions like these: Should the products be uniform for all markets or tailored to individual locales? Who owns the market intelligence that determines the decision—headquarters or the field? If one country develops products on its own, what mechanism does it use to share those ideas with other countries? As in any town meeting, people must feel able to exchange information honestly and openly and to resolve differences of opinion on the spot or in a timely fashion. They must go back to their home countries knowing that issues raised have been resolved.

The objective of the best-practice exchange, again, is to see whether what works in one territory might work in another. Too often, international borders reinforce a not-invented-here mindset. People want to reinvent the wheel each time a problem comes up, because that makes it their wheel. Best-practice exchanges counter this wasteful mindset. They are ultimately a form of sanctioned plagiarism of good ideas from any and all geographies and locations within the organization, and they should be explicitly encouraged through newsletters, e-mail, and conferences.

The Clifford Chance Experience

Clifford Chance, a law firm with roots in the United Kingdom, illustrates how one global learner became a global launcher (Gee, Jick, & Paine, 1993). It is a prototype for companies with long-standing reputations for domestic or regional success that then realize their marketplaces can be, or must be, far more expansive.

Traditionally, legal service firms were strictly local. However, the growth of the Euromarket in the 1970s, followed by the emergence of the global financial marketplace in the 1980s, prompted a few law firms from the advanced economies to consider global opportunities. In subsequent years, more and more law firms began restructuring and globalizing.

By no stretch of the imagination would the British-based law firms of Clifford Turner and Coward Chance have seemed likely candidates to become global players. But after the two merged in 1987 to become Clifford Chance, they worked hard at internationalization. By the beginning of the twenty-first century, Clifford Chance was the world's largest globally integrated law firm, with thousands of lawyers representing dozens of nationalities in offices throughout the world. Its strength— both strategic and organizational—catapulted it to a position of international renown. It now serves business clients worldwide in areas of corporate finance, banking, tax, property, and international law.

How did Clifford Chance make its transformation? What actions for change did it use? How did it move from being a global learner to a global launcher? And what lies ahead as it deepens its attempts to serve other multinational clients?

Some premerger history is relevant. The firm of Coward Chance, founded in 1881, had sixty-one partners in 1987. Its reputation was built on a combination of technical knowledge and understanding of the needs of fast-developing financial markets. In 1976, it had been one of the first law firms to enter the Middle East, and it had served the Southeast Asia financial markets from Hong Kong and Singapore offices from the early 1980s. Clifford Turner, founded in 1900, was slightly larger, with eighty-seven partners, and its strength was corporate finance. It served many large British retailers, but it had also established a practice in Japan in the late 1970s. It had several offices in continental Europe and, from 1986, an office in New York to specialize in transatlantic legal matters.

Thus both firms had been global learners, with a presence in several foreign locales, although both still largely operated as U.K.-minded law practices. One critical goal of their merger was to become more international. But the leadership of the new firm quickly discovered that achieving this goal would not happen by itself.

The newly merged company faced many real barriers to further globalization. Nearly 80 percent of the lawyers were in London, giving the firm a strictly English feel. Its potential clients and even its young recruits around the world thought of it as an English firm. Moreover, the older lawyers at the home office cherished their English traditions, personal independence, and lack of bureaucracy in operations. To themselves, they wondered why partners from high-earning offices should invest in less profitable operations in developing countries. As a result, international expansion required changes not only in structure, systems, and processes but also in mindset.

As a first step, Clifford Chance set out to establish a broader presence in several European cities. It could have done this by buying up established law firms. Instead, management opted for a more flexible structure. The firm set up its own offices in each location and slowly hired people according to the client needs that presented themselves. It then opened six additional offices—in Barcelona, Frankfurt, Rome, Warsaw, Budapest, and Shanghai—starting very small in each locale.

As the offices developed, management sent lawyers from London to temporary postings in these offices. "One of the ways you integrate cultures," said Geoffrey Howe, the senior managing partner, "is by moving around. Increasingly the people who make partner in Paris or Madrid will have spent a year or two in London and vice versa. There is a direct cost, but it is the best way you integrate the people: it is not done by statements or strategies on paper."

But new locations and international assignments were not enough, because people were still thinking in the old domestic ways. Many of the lawyers still thought of Clifford Chance as an English law firm with offices in foreign places. As a result, service to clients was not seamless across borders. One indication of the problem was the use of words and phrases that reinforced the old mindset. Management thus introduced another tuning switch: the "Unwords Campaign," for which the firm newsletter printed a set of linguistic rules—words that had to be removed from everyday parlance and the new words that would replace them:

UNWORD	GLOBAL WORD
City firm (British equivalent of "Wall Street firm")	Business and financial firm
English firm	International firm
U.K. firm	European-based international firm
Assistant solicitor	Lawyer
Overseas offices	International offices
The [Paris, Madrid, and so on] office	My colleagues in [Paris, Madrid, and so on]
Cross-selling	Integrated service

The technique of teaching employees a new vocabulary to encourage them to think in new ways is not unusual at all. Clifford Chance simply made it more explicit and more mandatory than in many companies.

Finally, to reinforce the global mindset, the firm redesigned its procedures and systems to instill more consistency across all offices and geographies. It asked secretaries worldwide to use the same typeface for all documents, right down to the cover sheets for faxes. It increased the use of standard templates to draft frequently used commercial documents such as leases, loan agreements, joint venture agreements, or board minutes. The clear signal sent to all employees at every level was, "We are one firm worldwide—with the same image to the marketplace and internally no matter where we are in the world."

The actions just described exemplify some of the steps that have moved Clifford Chance from a global learner to a global launcher. Given the firm's starting point, its progress was substantial. Nevertheless, senior partners still felt they had a long way to go, since their ultimate aspiration was to become, in our term, truly glocal, the hallmark of the global leaders. As one partner in Amsterdam said: "Each office should be a link in the international chain as well as having a focus in its national marketplace. Our strategy is to be recognized not only as part of a major international firm but also as a Dutch law firm in [our] own right."

In January 2000, Clifford Chance took another major step along the path to globalization, propelling itself from global launcher to global leader. It merged with two other law firms, Frankfurt-based Punder, Volhard, Weber & Axter, and U.S.-based Rogers and Wells, both of which had also been pioneers in international expansion. The result was the world's largest globally integrated law firm, with twenty-nine offices throughout Europe, Asia, the Americas, and the Middle East, and three thousand legal advisers representing more than fifty nationalities.

Beware of Learner Landmines

All globalization efforts carry risks. Experience tells us, however, that the following are the typical landmines lying in wait for global learners:

INDECISION. Jumping into the global waters demands a greater understanding of management, financial, geopolitical, and cultural issues than that required for a domestic operation. Many companies naturally become indecisive when attempting to determine how to dedicate time and resources when many options are available.

LACK OF PLANNING. Planning is an essential element of business when cultural and physical distances are involved. You must decide certain questions in advance, such as: How far do you want your company to go? How aggressive and ambitious is your global strategy? Do you intend to develop a business that will become 20 percent nondomestic, or 50 percent, or 80 percent? The answers to such questions have a direct impact on a firm's willingness to make investments of time and financial resources.

CULTURAL HYPERSENSITIVITY. In developing greater cultural awareness, global learners often go overboard and become hypersensitive to differences in work styles and management philosophies, causing them to excuse problems rather than face them. Recently, a senior manager, about to leave his post in France after two years, told us an anecdote that typifies the phenomenon. While reflecting on what he learned about doing business abroad, he recalled receiving extensive crosscultural sensitivity training at the beginning of his assignment. Although he originally felt this made him more understanding about performance problems, he now believed he had bent over too far to accommodate cultural differences when he should have followed universal principles of good management—holding all employees accountable for target dates they set for themselves, for example. In short, cultural awareness shouldn't supersede basic management principles, hard-core analysis, and market experience.

One of the best detection systems for many of the landmines learners face turns out to be an early mistake. We often find that organizations learn from mistakes that surface at the beginning of a venture and make adjustments rather painlessly compared to those that discover a mistake only after a significant investment of time and resources. The more effective way to avoid stepping on landmines, however, is to benchmark other companies that have recently traversed the same territory. For example, an Israeli company contemplating the acquisition of a privatized Hungarian firm closely studied GE Lighting's experience with Tungsram before making a decision.

Finally, the global learning organization requires a leader with exceptional personal courage and humility—as well as ambition—to support whatever stumbles happen among first steps. As in any infancy, the leader must encourage celebration of any early accomplishments with pride. Clifford Chance has had such leadership. Along with other decision makers in the firm, managing partner Geoffrey Howe has helped ensure the consistency, courage, and continuity to enable the firm's success. The importance of this leadership task to breaking down global barriers cannot be overestimated.

GLOBAL LAUNCHERS TO GLOBAL LEADERS

For organizations that have become global launchers, moving to the next stage of global leadership entails a new set of challenges. For the most part, a global launcher has developed a global strategy and vision. It has some experience under its belt at trying to remove geographic boundaries, and it appreciates how difficult the challenges will be. It has also seen the progress born of some of the steps described in the global learner section. What launchers must do next is to deepen commitment to removing geographic boundaries. They must also recalibrate their human resource practices, their organizational structures, and their systems and processes accordingly.

HR Practices: Make Human Resources More Fluid

Global launchers need to develop a more fluid workforce, so that they can pour it into whatever vessel they must fill (see Exhibit 44.2). The rationale for resource fluidity is that, in a completely globalized market, companies need to move people with flexible sets of skills from location to location or task to task to respond to customer needs. For example, ABB routinely moves its managers laterally to positions in other countries so they develop a wider understanding of local markets. Many professional service firms, such as McKinsey and Accenture, have also developed systems for rotating professionals to projects around the world for periods of three to six months, as their clients require.

Human Resource Practices
- See complete fluidity of human resources: recruit outside the domestic base; place foreign recruits within the domestic base; promote the best people to global assignments; rotate people internationally; use twinning
- Aim for a global structure
- Map global processes

Organizational Structures
- Provide continuing global leadership training and regular transnational training to reinforce the global mindset
- Remove or minimize country management, replace with global managers, and focus on global customers
- Routinize real-time global communications

Organizational Processes and Systems
- Use global reward systems
- Multiply ongoing transnational project teams
- Work for global integration (for example, total global sourcing, global design, global engineering, and global purchasing)

Exhibit 44.2. How Global Launchers Become Global Leaders.

To develop fluid human resources, the global launcher organization needs high-quality HR programs that attract the best people and assign them to top global positions, regardless of their country of origin. Such programs send out a clear message that international assignments are valued and critical positions, not career dead ends. As openings arise, HR must fill them with individuals who are recognized as among the most talented and successful in the company at working globally. Launchers benefit particularly by making good use of the different educational backgrounds and viewpoints of their personnel, demonstrating that the firm is able to do business from a multicultural perspective, without prejudice or ethnocentrism. In short, launchers moving to leaders must promote the free flow of individuals from country to country, without regard to national origin.

Launchers also progress globally by bringing recruits from operations abroad to work in the domestic base, as Gillette's international trainee program does. Several hundred trainees have passed through the program since the early 1980s. Begun originally as an internship operation, the program turned into a formal training tool when Gillette realized that many interns wanted to return to work in Gillette plants in their home countries. University graduates from business schools around the world begin by working for Gillette plants in their home countries for six months. The best and brightest of these people are then transferred to one of the three Gillette headquarters (in Boston, London, and Singapore) for more intensive work. Successful trainees are assigned to management positions back in their home countries or in other Gillette facilities. Many eventually become general managers or senior operating managers in their home countries.

Another critical element in making human resources more fluid is the same kind of regular rotation of people around the world that ABB and McKinsey engage in. Rotations give managers the experience and enlarged perspective to tackle a wide range of problems. International experience allows people to

- See local conditions firsthand and obtain direct exposure to markets and ways of doing business abroad.
- Live in others' shoes for a while to learn others' ways of thinking.
- Develop loyalties to multiple regions or segments of a business.

Another value of regular rotations is the development of alternative worldviews that boost the quality of decisions. We hear many U.S.

managers with global experience take a healthy contrary stance in discussions, saying, in effect, "We don't see it the same way as you do in the United States." Living and breathing a different culture has shown them new points of view. This is so desirable that many firms hesitate to have a local person run an important center unless that person has proved effective in another country as well as in a headquarters or central staff role. Ultimately, rotations help all members of the organization learn and grow.

Launchers moving to leaders also benefit from consistent transnational training that continues to develop a global mindset and shared values among all organizational members. PricewaterhouseCoopers periodically brings newly appointed partners from around the world together (at a new location each year) for education on the firm's basic values and principles. This serves both purposes of training and international socialization.

Another technique to foster continual training and learning is twinning, the process of assigning one local and one foreign person to the same job for a time. GE Lighting employed twinning at Tungsram so that GE managers would learn about global issues while Tungsram people learned about Western business practices.

Although perhaps more subtle than the actions just described, restructuring reward systems is another important adjustment that helps global launchers become leaders. Their new systems reward a broader view of performance than formerly and encourage managers to use their expertise more flexibly in such areas as improving market penetration worldwide or helping sister companies in other countries. For example, Goldman Sachs implemented a new compensation and organizational structure that promotes cooperation. In this system, "because compensation is based more on subjective criteria than on transaction count, officers in different departments don't constantly bicker over how much credit they should get for a particular deal. And unlike other firms that are organized by geographical region, Goldman brings in the firm's heaviest hitters . . . to pitch in on a transaction in any region" (Zweig, 1993).

Organizational Structure: Resolving Complexity

The global launcher is likely to have numerous sites or headquarters in countries around the world. To become a leader, the launcher must resolve the complexities this multidomestic approach entails. It must develop a structure that will balance the centralizing needed for pooling of resources and economies of scale at the global level with the decentralizing that allows catering to local preferences with speed and precision.

For many firms, the choice boils down to converting to a loose matrix that interlaces management by product, customer, and function with a continuing country or regional structure. This solution offers the advantages found in centralizing certain kinds of decision making and expertise with those of maintaining a strong product or local orientation. As the *Economist* summed it up, "In theory, this means that management can make decisions without regard for national borders—but only if they want to" ("The Discreet Charm . . .", 1994).

However, no one solution is guaranteed to fit the advanced stages of globalization for every company. The best answer for any given company most likely depends on a number of variables: type of product, number of markets, methods of distribution, and long-term strategy. Nevertheless, the active and ongoing search for a solution to complexity in the best global companies suggests a definite move away from a multidomestic structure and toward more product, customer, or brand-driven arrangements. For a number of years, Sony used a four-zone global operation—Japan, America, Europe, and the rest of the world—while maintaining product managers as well. It recently reorganized to focus on key strategic thrusts. This involved trimming its sprawling global network of seventy manufacturing companies down to fifty-five, placing all of its electronics businesses under a separate upper-management group, and establishing a new division to focus exclusively on mobile phones and strategy. IBM reorganized into fourteen worldwide industry groups—such as banking, retailing, and insurance—but also kept its geographic chieftains. It then refined its structure further, focusing on five overarching business segments. Having traditionally used a regional structure, Unilever now operates with two global divisions. Reporting to their divisional executive directors are the regional presidents, responsible for driving profitability in their regions. A third division is managed on a global basis.

Each of these is a solution that is somewhat unique to the industry, size of company, and individual leader preferences. However, they share the intention to achieve clout and focus, to find a balance between global synergy and local responsiveness, and to deal effectively with the tensions inherent in maintaining this balance.

Organizational Processes and Systems: Technological Solutions to Complexity

Successfully managing complexity in processes and systems is a major challenge for launchers who want to become global leaders. Launchers typically have extensive R&D, manufacturing, sourcing, purchasing, and distribution networks that cover wide territories and consumer needs. A key action for strengthening and globalizing these systems is process mapping. Examples of processes to be mapped include development of a new product from design through warehousing and fulfillment of an order from customer request to delivery. Global process mapping reveals the links and kinks in operations and where companies may be able to save time, money, or space.

For example, the global company at the launcher level may have orders from around the world going to a central order bank, which then transmits them to manufacturing or distribution centers at other locations. However, if a process map shows that most orders for certain products arrive from one region, the organization might decide to adjust warehousing and distribution to accommodate that regional pattern.

Launchers who want to become leaders make more use of technology than learners do, and at higher levels, to achieve real-time global communications. Dedicated trunk lines, intranets, e-mail, groupware, paging devices, and portable computers with fax and modem cards allow people to communicate at length and instantaneously across time zones, at any hour of the day or night, and with a common language.

Two organizations that emphasize the use of technology are PricewaterhouseCoopers and GlaxoSmithKline. PricewaterhouseCoopers, the largest professional service firm in the world, has increasingly focused its attention on serving multinational clients. This adjustment entailed abandoning the long-standing tradition of treating the local office as supreme in favor of a worldwide operating structure and decision-making process that could mobilize human resources, investment advice, and technical information from any office as needed. To accomplish this, it turned to groupware technology that connects everyone through an elaborate electronic system.

Groupware is particularly useful in the development of client proposals. Formerly, the originating office had to communicate with other parts of the firm by phone or fax across time zones, a process that was time-consuming and had a high rate of incomplete contacts. Today, the groupware system allows an office developing a proposal to collect data and information easily from any of the resources throughout the twenty-six offices worldwide. Within days rather than weeks, the lead partner can draft a proposal, send it electronically to others for review, receive feedback, and even recruit colleagues to help rewrite the proposal.

GlaxoSmithKline's "R&D Team Connect" groupware allows researchers throughout the company to hook their personal computers or terminals to a common set of databases for information sharing. Team members can also carry on electronic conversations to get comments and feedback about their experiments or clinical results.

In short, launchers becoming leaders recognize that technology supports their ability to be global. They track new technological developments and install the latest equipment if it can save time and contribute to gathering information and making decisions that otherwise would require unwieldy meetings, exorbitant travel costs, or excessive investments of time.

Finally, launchers becoming leaders must identify opportunities for global sourcing and purchasing, global design, and global engineering to reduce costs and maximize economies of scale. An additional common benefit from centralization of these processes is the transfer of learning across the organization.

The Alcatel Bell Experience

A leading supplier of telecommunications equipment, Alcatel Bell is moving from global launcher to leader in an industry that has seen intense competition in taking advantage of both emerging markets and the increasingly sophisticated needs of advanced economies. As a result, the challenge for Alcatel Bell has been to globalize as effectively and quickly as possible.

Alcatel Bell is a Belgium-based subsidiary of Alcatel Alsthom, an international producer of technologically advanced infrastructure equipment for the communication, energy, and transport sectors. Alcatel Alsthom ranks among the world's leaders in all its areas of activity. Highly aggressive and ambitious, it has dedicated itself to internationalization through growth and almost two hundred acquisitions.

At one time, Alcatel Bell was a very local business, with long-term secure contracts for serving the Belgian telephone company and a reliable revenue stream from its Belgian world of business. In the 1960s, 70 percent of its business was local. In the 1970s and 1980s, its business widened, becoming 50 percent global but largely through export and licensing agreements. However, in the 1980s and 1990s, it began globalizing substantially, attempting to become a global leader. Through joint ventures, start-ups, mergers, and acquisitions, Alcatel Bell sales today are only 30 percent Belgian; most of its attention is focused on the international world. (Alcatel Bell's global development is summarized in Table 44.1.)

What switches has Alcatel Bell used to enable the radical retuning of both its business mix and its business mindset? What did it take to transform this rather localized business into a leading world player?

One major step was to fill critical senior positions with people (insiders and outsiders) who had extensive international experience and orientation. The new players understood the structures, people, and systems required to build and sustain a global business. They shaped a new strategy and direction of deepening globalization in such places as Russia, China, and Turkey.

The new leaders also filled key slots in Belgium with people who were comfortable in an international context and who had lived as expatriates elsewhere. As joint ventures and acquisitions were made, the leaders relied on this select group to serve as managers in resident positions abroad. They also called on a cadre of functional specialists from engineering, finance, and technical operations—no functional specialty was excluded from international assignments. Specialists had to be prepared to go to any country in which Alcatel Bell operated.

In addition, Alcatel Bell invested heavily in ongoing people development. Employees from newly acquired subsidiaries spend three months to two years in Antwerp for technical training. New customers also are trained on equipment in Antwerp, while managers are familiarized with Alcatel Bell management techniques there. On any given day, the number of languages spoken at the training center mirrors the United Nations, even though the training is conducted in English. In addition, in China and Russia, people trained by Alcatel Bell train other people locally, in their local languages.

In these ways, Alcatel Bell has instituted many of the practices summarized at the beginning of this section, namely, HR practices that enable top talent from different parts of the world to work together regularly, processes and systems that integrate key functional areas and expertise, and many ongoing transnational project teams.

Period	Local Sales (Percent)	Global Sales (Percent)	Strategic Steps
1960s	70	30	Local manufacturing; exporting to international locations; first licensing agreement (Romania)
1970s	50	50	Multiple licensing agreements and turnkey contracts (for example, India, Taiwan, Yugoslavia)
1980s	50	50	Joint ventures in China, Mexico, Russia, Turkey; centralized engineering; exporting to seventy-two countries
1990s	30	70	Starting new companies (for example, in Russia and Colombia); making mergers and acquisitions; managing businesses worldwide

Table 44.1.   Alcatel Bell's Globalization.

To understand the progress of Alcatel Bell, we interviewed one of its key regional managers, Stan Abbeloos, at the time the Alcatel Bell general director in Russia. A Belgian by birth, Abbeloos has an engineering degree and speaks English, French, German, and some Russian in addition to his native Flemish. (Every one of the Alcatel Bell general directors speaks two or three additional languages.) In 1994, at forty-two years of age, he was completing his third year in Russia. Prior to that, he had worked for Alcatel Bell in China for four years. A glimpse into a month of his life is telling of the kind of energy and work needed by global leaders:

I started the month traveling to Anadyr, Russia, near Alaska. It took five days to get there because of the weather. But we signed a contract for $4 million by the end of the day. Then we waited two additional days to get the plane back. And you must fly Aeroflot—you have no choice! If you want, you could take the train, but it would take a lot longer to travel, often up to thirty-six hours between cities.

Then I next went to Novosibirsk, in the middle of Siberia, where we have one of our offices. It's actually a joint venture in which we have 75 percent control. I had to negotiate next year's delivery of product.

Then I went to Surgut, also in Siberia, where the temperature was minus twenty-six degrees centigrade, but I got final acceptance to sell a System 12 toll exchange, and they signed a maintenance agreement.

I then went back to St. Petersburg, where for one week I was managing the creation of a space for refurbishing our products. Then I went to Anadyr to finalize a contract, then on to Moscow for a steering committee meeting to coordinate international activities across Alcatel Alsthom, and finally I was sent to France for one week to attend a "High Potential Leaders" training program!

What does this hectic month of activity show? First, it is an excellent example of a glocal executive's focus. Although the better part of the month represented intense attention to local matters, the end of the month provided two global links—the corporate task force on global coordination and the leadership training with worldwide representation. Such agenda balancing is crucial if a company is to become a global leader.

Second, the example reveals the stress tolerance required of global leaders. Operating in this mobile, fluid fashion was not unusual for Abbeloos and the other general directors, especially in emerging marketplaces. It is the grueling, stressful life of a pioneer, albeit challenging and gratifying. Abbeloos found that "one of the major limiting factors [of operating this way] is family. You have to have a fluid family or give it up, especially in places like Russia and China." Although that principle by no means applies for all aspiring to be global leaders, there is no denying that people operating across the world stage must accept a heavy wear-and-tear factor.

Finally, the example reveals how Alcatel Bell created a multiplier effect as it expanded and integrated. It opted to create a roving team of global leaders such as Abbeloos, all willing to accept the sacrifices and stresses inherent in such assignments. The members of this transnational team could then learn from each other as they came to truly understand the cultural differences required to operate across the world. For example, owing to cultural differences, marketing in China is done by local Chinese. Alcatel Bell people are rarely involved. But in Russia, Alcatel Bell people do the marketing because Russians are not interested in selling. In Russia, then, knowing the language becomes more critical for foreigners doing business there.

Alcatel Bell's process of becoming a global leader is not over. It still needs better ways to integrate people with international experience back into their home countries and ways to hand new assignments to local talent. But Abbeloos is confident that Alcatel Bell has built global leadership: "In terms of operating in Europe, we have all [the] languages and capabilities required. Our real opportunity now is across the world. Here we have the flexibility required. . . . And we have marketing and sales people who can be deployed from throughout Alcatel Bell to be 'door-openers' and a full organization behind them able to serve customers wherever they are."

Beware of Launcher Landmines

Beyond the sheer complexity of running an international firm with a slew of variables including diversity of workforce cultures, varying raw material suppliers, currency fluctuations, political swings, and a multitude of other unpredictable factors, several specific landmines lurk in the ground that global launchers must cross to become leaders.

First, firms pursuing leadership often find themselves triggering unexpected—and unpleasant—domino effects. They solve one problem only to see the solution engender another. Sometimes they end up in seemingly no-win situations, such as growing so large they compete with themselves. For example, Matsushita now finds that its cost-effective and productive subsidiaries in southeast Asia produce so much and export so much to Japan so cheaply that Matsushita employees back home cannot keep up. The one-time slogan of Matsushita's Malaysian plants, "Let's catch up with Japan," is outmoded—these plants outperform the Japanese plants in both quality and efficiency. Similarly, Fuji Xerox, the Japanese affiliate of Fuji Film and Xerox, found itself embroiled with its parent company Xerox over sales territory and R&D independence.

A second landmine is sociopolitical and cultural embroilment. As launchers become players in more and more places, they automatically face a greater probability of encountering political, social, cultural, and ethical values that differ significantly from their own and lead to turbulence and moral dilemmas. For example, several global launchers have been fined for obtaining contracts in certain countries by using a form of bribery that in their view was acceptable if not required in those cultures. Meanwhile, companies such as Levi Strauss withdrew their initiatives to open up plants and operations in China because of continuing human rights violations that they viewed as contrary to their corporate values and principles.

Overall, global launchers require a perspective that guides them toward grand but realistic ambitions. Many companies look at China, for example, and imagine that if one billion people each bought a $1 product, they would produce $1 billion in revenues. Unfortunately, doing business in China today is far more difficult than the scenario suggests. A realistic ambition in this situation would recognize the market potential but at the same time plan to explore all the cultural and political differences in the Chinese market and to understand the complex arrangement of structures, processes, and systems that would support success in that market.

Similarly, at the individual level, the familiar adage "Think global, act local!" captures the required perspective. Managers in global launcher and leader companies must maintain a vision of the world that is complex and sophisticated but also simple from where they sit. It is analogous to playing chess. The players must be able to think strategically and continually about the overall course of the game, but must also be able to focus on one move at a time.

THE GLOBAL VILLAGE OF TOMORROW

As companies like AXA, PriceWaterhouseCoopers and many others will testify, becoming a global leader is a tough transition. Many tools are available, and we have described a good number of them here. But senior management must have the skill and foresight to use the right tools in the right way, at the right time, and in the right sequence. There are no magic bullets, no matter where you are in the global learning curve. Each stage requires structures that enable the crossing of boundaries, systems and processes that drive global behavior, and people who can extend their thinking beyond their present outlook. If these goals are consciously set and strongly pursued and achieved, the ultimate reward is an international organization rich in multicultural diversity, a complex and sophisticated management outlook, and successful global products and services.

CHAPTER FORTY-FIVE

Knowledge-Worker Productivity

The Biggest Challenge

Peter F. Drucker

T he most important, and indeed the truly unique, contribution of management in the twentieth century was the fifty-fold increase in the productivity of the *manual worker* in manufacturing. The most important contribution management needs to make in the twenty-first century is similarly to increase the productivity of *knowledge work* and *knowledge workers*. The most valuable assets of a twentieth-century company was its *production equipment*. The most valuable asset of a twenty-first-century institution (whether business or nonbusiness) will be its *knowledge workers* and their *productivity*.

THE PRODUCTIVITY OF THE MANUAL WORKER

First, we must take a look at where we are. It was only a little over a hundred years ago that for the first time an educated person actually *looked* at manual work and manual workers, and then began to study both. The Greek poet Hesiod (eighth century B.C.) and the Roman poet Virgil (700 years later) sang about the work of the farmer. Theirs are still among the finest poems in any language, but neither the work they sang about nor their farmers bear even the most remote resemblance

914

to reality, nor were they meant to have any. Neither Hesiod nor Virgil ever held a sickle in their hands, ever herded sheep, or even looked at the people who did either. When Karl Marx, 1900 years after Virgil, came to write about manual work and manual workers, he too never looked at either, nor had he ever as much as touched a machine. The first man to do both—that is, to work as a manual worker and then to study manual work—was Frederick Winslow Taylor (1856–1915).

Throughout history there have been steady advances in what we today call *productivity* (the term itself is barely fifty years old). They were the result of new tools, new methods, and new technologies; they were advances in what the economist calls *capital.* There were few advances throughout the ages in what the economist calls *labor*—that is, in the productivity of the worker. It was axiomatic throughout history that workers could produce more only by working harder or by working longer hours. The nineteenth-century economists disagreed about most things as much as economists do today. However, they all agreed—from David Ricardo through Karl Marx—that there are enormous differences in *skill* between workers, but there are none with respect to productivity other than between hard workers and lazy ones, or between physically strong workers and weak ones. Productivity did not exist. It still is an "extraneous factor" and not part of the equation in most contemporary economic theories (for example, in Keynes, but also in that of the Austrian School).

In the decade after Taylor first looked at work and studied it, the productivity of the manual worker began its unprecedented rise. Since then, it has been going up steadily at the rate of 3 percent per annum compound—which means it has risen fifty-fold since Taylor. On this achievement rest *all* of the economic and social gains of the twentieth century. The productivity of the manual worker has created what we now call *develope*d economies. Before Taylor, there was no such thing—all economies were equally "underdeveloped." An underdeveloped economy today—or even an "emerging" one—is one that has not, or at least has not yet, made the manual worker more productive.

THE PRINCIPLES OF MANUAL-WORK PRODUCTIVITY

Taylor's principles sound deceptively simple. The first step in making the manual worker more productive is to look at the task and to analyze its constituent motions. The next step is to record each motion, the physical effort it takes, and the time it takes. Then motions that are not needed can be eliminated; and whenever we have looked at manual work, we have found that a great many of the traditionally most-hallowed procedures turn out to be wastes and do not add anything. Then, each of the motions that remain as essential to obtaining the finished product is set up so as to be done the simplest way, the easiest way, the way that puts the least physical and mental strain on the operator, and the way that requires the least time. Next, these motions are put together again into a "job" that is in a logical sequence. Finally, the tools needed to do the motions are redesigned. Whenever we have looked at any job—no matter for how many thousands of years it has been performed—we have found that the traditional tools are wrong for the task. This was the case, for instance, with the shovel used to carry sand in a foundry (the first task Taylor studied). It was the wrong shape, the wrong size, and had the wrong handle. We found this to be equally true of the surgeon's traditional tools. Taylor's principles sound obvious—effective methods always do. However, it took Taylor twenty years of experimentation to work them out.

Over these last hundred years, there have been countless further changes, revisions, and refinements. The name by which the methodology goes has also changed over the past century. Taylor himself first called his method *task analysis* or *task management.* Twenty years later it was rechristened *scientific management.* Another twenty years later, after the First World War, it came to be known as *industrial engineering* in the U.S. and Japan, and as *rationalization* in Germany.

To proclaim that one's method "rejects" Taylor or "replaces" him is almost standard "public relations." For what made Taylor and his method so powerful has also made it unpopular. What Taylor *saw* when he actually looked at work violated everything poets and philosophers had said about work from Hesiod and Virgil to Karl Marx. They all celebrated "skill." Taylor showed that in manual work there is no such thing. There are only simple, repetitive motions. What makes them more productive is *knowledge,* that is, the way the simple, unskilled motions are put together, organized, and executed. In fact, Taylor was the first person to apply knowledge to work.[1] This also

---

[1]For work in the oldest knowledge profession—that is, in medicine—Taylor's close contemporary William Osier (1849–1919) did what Taylor did at the same time in his 1892 book *The Principles and Practice of Medicine* (arguably the best textbook since Euclid's *Geometry* in the third century B.C.). Osier's work has rightly been called the application of scientific management to medical diagnosis. Like Taylor, Osier preached that there is no "skill," there is only *method.*

earned Taylor the undying enmity of the labor unions of his time, all of which were craft unions and based on the *mystique* of craft skill and their monopoly on it. Moreover, Taylor advocated—and this is still anathema to a labor union—that workers be paid according to their productivity—that is, for their output, rather than for their input (that is, for hours worked). However, Taylor's definition of work as a series of operations also largely explains his rejection by the people who themselves do not do any manual work: the descendants of the poets and philosophers of old, the literati and intellectuals. Taylor destroyed the romance of work. Instead of a "noble skill," it becomes a series of simple motions.

Nevertheless, every method during these past hundred years that has had the slightest success in raising the productivity of manual workers—and with it their real wages—has been based on Taylor's principles, no matter how loudly his antagonists proclaimed their differences with Taylor. This is true of "work enlargement," "work enrichment," and "job rotation"—all of which use Taylor's methods to lessen the worker's fatigue and thereby increase the worker's productivity. It is also true of such extensions of Taylor's principles of task analysis and industrial engineering as Henry Ford's assembly line (developed after 1914, when Taylor himself was already sick, old, and retired). It is just as true of the Japanese "quality circle," "continuous improvement"(*Kaizen*), and "just-in-time delivery."

The best example, however, is W. Edward Deming's "total quality management." What Deming did—and what makes total quality management effective—is to analyze and organize the job exactly the way Taylor did. However, he also added quality control (around 1940) that was based on a statistical theory that was only developed ten years after Taylor's death. Finally, in the 1970s, Deming substituted closed-circuit television and computer simulation for Taylor's stopwatch and motion photos. Deming's quality control analysts are the spitting image of Taylor's efficiency engineers and function the same way.

Whatever his limitations and shortcomings—and he had many—no other American, not even Henry Ford, has had anything like Taylor's impact. Scientific management (and its successor industrial engineering) is the one American philosophy that has swept the world—more so even than the Constitution and the Federalist Papers. In the past century, there has been only one worldwide philosophy that could compete with Taylor's: namely, Marxism. In the end, Taylor has triumphed over Marx.

During the First World War, scientific management swept through the U.S. together with Ford's Taylor-based assembly line. In the 1920s, scientific management swept through Western Europe and began to be adopted in Japan.

During the Second World War, both the German achievement and the American achievement were squarely based on applying Taylor's principles to Training. The German General Staff, after having lost the First World War, applied "rationalization" (that is, Taylor's scientific management) to the job of the soldier and to military training. This enabled Hitler to create a superb fighting machine in the six short years between his coming to power and 1939. In the U.S., the same principles were applied to the training of an industrial work force, first tentatively during the First World War and then, with full power, during the Second World War. This enabled the Americans to outproduce the Germans, even though a larger proportion of the U.S. than the German male population was in uniform and thus not in industrial production. Then, training-based scientific management gave the U.S. civilian work force more than twice—if not three times—the productivity of the workers in Hitler's Germany and in Hitler-dominated Europe. Scientific management thus gave the U.S. the capacity to outnumber both Germans and Japanese on the battlefield and yet still outproduce both by several orders of magnitude.

Since 1950, economic development outside the Western World has largely been based on copying what the U.S. did in the Second World War, that is, on applying scientific management to making the manual worker more productive. All earlier economic development had been based on technological innovation—first in France in the eighteenth century, then in Great Britain from 1760 until 1850, and finally in the new economic Great Powers, Germany and the U.S., in the second half of the nineteenth century. The non-Western countries that developed after the Second World War, beginning with Japan, eschewed technological innovation. Instead, they imported the training that the U.S. had developed during the Second World War based on Taylor's principles and they used it to make highly productive, almost overnight, a still largely unskilled and preindustrial work force. (In Japan, for instance, almost two-thirds of the working population were still, in 1950, living on the land and unskilled in any work except cultivating rice.) However, although highly productive, this new work force was still—for a decade or more—paid preindustrial wages so that these countries—first Japan, then Korea, then Taiwan and Singapore—could produce the same manufactured products as the developed countries, but at a fraction of their labor costs.

THE FUTURE OF MANUAL-WORKER PRODUCTIVITY

Taylor's approach was designed for manual work in *manufacturing*, and at first applied only to it. Nevertheless, even within these traditional limitations, Taylor's approach still has enormous scope. It is still going to be the organizing principle in countries in which manual work, and especially manual work in manufacturing, is the growth sector of the society and economy—that is, "Third World" countries with very large and still growing numbers of young people with little education and little skill.

However, there is equal—or even greater—opportunity in the *developed* countries to organize nonmanufacturing production (that is, production work in services) on the production principles now being developed in manufacturing—and that means applying industrial engineering to the job and work of the individual service worker. There is equally a tremendous amount of knowledge work—including work requiring highly advanced and thoroughly theoretical knowledge— that includes *manual* operations. The productivity of these operations also requires industrial engineering.

Still, in developed countries, the central challenge is no longer to make manual work more productive—after all, we know how to do it. The central challenge will be to make knowledge workers more productive. Knowledge workers are rapidly becoming the largest single group in the work force of every developed country. They may already compose two-fifths of the U.S. work force—and a still smaller but rapidly growing proportion of the work force of all other developed countries. It is on their productivity, above all, that the future prosperity—and indeed the future survival—of the developed economies will increasingly depend.

WHAT WE KNOW ABOUT KNOWLEDGE-WORKER PRODUCTIVITY

Work on the productivity of the knowledge worker has barely begun. In terms of actual work on knowledge-worker productivity, we will be in the year 2000 roughly where we were in the year 1900 in terms of the productivity of the manual worker. Nevertheless, we already know infinitely more about the productivity of the knowledge worker than we did then about that of the manual worker. We even know a good many of the answers. We also know the challenges to which we do not yet know the answers, and on which we need to go to work.

Six major factors determine knowledge-worker productivity.

- Knowledge-worker productivity demands that we ask the question: *"What is the task?"*
- It demands that we impose the responsibility for their productivity on the individual knowledge workers themselves. Knowledge workers *have* to manage themselves. They have to have *autonomy.*
- Continuing innovation has to be part of the work, the task and the responsibility of knowledge workers.
- Knowledge work requires continuous learning on the part of the knowledge worker, but equally continuous teaching on the part of the knowledge worker.
- Productivity of the knowledge worker is not—at least not primarily—a matter of the *quantity* of output. *Quality* is at least as important.
- Finally, knowledge-worker productivity requires that the knowledge worker is both seen and treated as an "asset" rather than a "cost." It requires that knowledge workers *want* to work for the organization in preference to all other opportunities.

Each of these requirements (except perhaps the last one) is almost the exact opposite of what is needed to increase the productivity of the manual worker. In manual work, of course, quality also matters. However, lack of quality is a restraint. There has to be a certain minimum quality standard. The achievement of total quality management—that is, of the application of twentieth century statistical theory to manual work—is the ability to cut (though not entirely to eliminate) production that falls below this minimum standard.

In most knowledge work, quality is not a minimum and a restraint. Quality is the essence of the output. In judging the performance of a teacher, we do not ask how many students there can be in his or her class. We ask how many students learn anything—and that's a quality question. In appraising the performance of a medical laboratory, the question of how many tests it can run through its machines is quite secondary to the question of how many tests results are valid and reliable. This is true even for the work of the file clerk.

Productivity of knowledge work therefore has to aim first at obtaining quality—and not minimum quality but optimum if not maximum quality. Only then can one ask: "What is the volume, the quantity of work?" This not only means that we approach the task of making more productive the knowledge worker from the quality of the work rather than the quantity, it also means that we will have to learn to define quality.

What Is the Task?

The crucial question in knowledge-worker productivity is: *What is the task?* It is also the one most at odds with manual-worker productivity. In manual work, the key question is always: *How should the work be done?* In manual work, the task is always given. None of the people who work on manual-worker productivity ever asked: "What is the manual worker supposed to do?" Their only question was: "How does the manual worker best do the job?" This was just as true of Frederick W. Taylor's scientific management as it was true of the people at Sears Roebuck or the Ford Motor Company who first designed the assembly line, and as it is true of W. Edward Deming's total quality control.

Again, in knowledge work the key question is: What is the task? One reason for this is that knowledge work, unlike manual work, does not program the worker. The worker on the automobile assembly line who puts on a wheel is programmed by the simultaneous arrival of the car's chassis on one line and the wheel on the other line. The farmer who plows a field in preparation for planting does not climb out of his tractor to take a telephone call, to attend a meeting, or to write a memo. *What* is to be done is always obvious in manual work.

However, in knowledge work the task does not program the worker. A major crisis in a hospital, such as when a patient suddenly goes into coma, does of course control the nurse's task and programs her; but otherwise, it is largely the nurse's decision whether to spend time at the patient's bed or whether to spend time filling out papers. Engineers are constantly being pulled off their task by having to write a report or rewrite it, by being asked to attend a meeting, and so on. The job of the salesperson in the department store is to serve the customer and to provide the merchandise the customer is interested in or should become interested in. Instead, the salesperson spends an enormous amount of time on paperwork, on checking whether merchandise is in stock, on checking when and how it can be delivered, and so on—all things that take salespeople away from the customer and do not add anything to their productivity in doing what salespeople are being paid for, which is to sell and to satisfy the customer.

The first requirement in tackling knowledge work is to find out what the task is so as to make it possible to concentrate knowledge workers on the task and to eliminate everything else—at least as far as it can possibly be eliminated. This requires that the knowledge workers themselves define what the task is or should be—and only the knowledge workers themselves can do that. Work on knowledge-worker productivity therefore begins with asking the knowledge workers themselves: *What is your task? What should it be? What should you be expected to contribute?* and *What hampers you in doing your task and should be eliminated?*

Knowledge workers themselves almost always have thought through these questions and can answer them. Still, it then usually takes time and hard work to restructure their jobs so that they can actually make the contribution they are already being paid for. However, asking the questions and taking action on the answers usually doubles or triples knowledge-worker productivity, and quite fast.

Nurses in a major hospital were asked these questions. They were sharply divided as to what their task was, with one group saying "patient care" and another saying "satisfying the physicians." However, they were in complete agreement on the things that made them unproductive. They called them "chores"—paperwork, arranging flowers, answering the phone calls of patients' relatives, answering the patients' bells, and so on. All—or nearly all—of these could be turned over to a non-nurse floor clerk, paid a fraction of a nurse's pay. The productivity of the nurses on the floor immediately more than doubled, as measured by the time nurses spent at the patients' beds. Patient satisfaction more than doubled and turnover of nurses (which had been catastrophically high) almost disappeared—all within four months.

Once the task has been defined, the next requirements can be tackled, and they will be tackled by the knowledge workers themselves. These requirements are:

- Knowledge workers' *responsibility* for their own contribution. It is the knowledge worker's decision what he or she should be held accountable for in terms of quality and quantity with respect to time and with respect to cost. Knowledge workers have to have autonomy and that entails responsibility.
- Continuous innovation *has to be built into the knowledge worker's job.*
- *Continuous learning* and *continuous teaching* have to be built into the job.

One central requirement of knowledge-worker productivity remains. We have to answer the question: What is quality? In some knowledge work—and especially in some work requiring a high degree of knowledge—we already measure quality. Surgeons, for example, are routinely measured, especially by their colleagues, by their success rates in difficult and dangerous procedures (for example, by the survival rates of their open heart surgical patients or the full recovery rates of their orthopedic surgery patients). By and large, we mainly have judgments rather than measures regarding the quality of a great deal of knowledge work. The main trouble is, however, not the difficulty of measuring quality. It is the difficulty—and more particularly the sharp disagreements—in defining what the task is and what it should be.

The best example of this is the American school system. As everyone knows, public schools in the American inner city have become disaster areas. Next to them—in the same location and serving the same kind of children—are private (mostly Christian) schools in which the kids behave well and learn well. There is endless speculation to explain these enormous quality differences. A major reason is surely that the two kinds of schools define their tasks differently. The typical public school defines its task as "helping the underprivileged," while the typical private school (and especially the parochial schools of the Catholic church) define their task as "enabling those who want to learn, to learn." One therefore is governed by its scholastic failures, the other one by its scholastic successes.

Similarly, the research departments at two major pharmaceutical companies have totally different results because they define their tasks differently. One sees its task as not having failures, that is, in working steadily on fairly minor but predictable improvements in existing products and for established markets. The other one defines its task as producing "breakthroughs" and therefore courts risks. Both are considered fairly successful—by themselves, by their own top managements, and by outside analysts. Yet each operates quite differently and quite differently defines its own productivity and that of its research scientists. To define quality in knowledge work and to convert the definition into knowledge-worker productivity is thus to a large extent a matter of defining the task. It requires the difficult, risk-taking, and always controversial definition as to what "results" are for a given enterprise and a given activity. We therefore actually *know* how to do it. Nevertheless, the question is a completely new one for most organizations and also for most knowledge workers. To answer it *requires* controversy, *requires* dissent.

THE KNOWLEDGE WORKER AS CAPITAL ASSET

In no other area is the difference greater between manual-worker productivity and knowledge-worker productivity than in their respective *economics*. Economic theory and most business practices sees manual workers as a *cost*. To be productive, knowledge workers must be considered a *capital asset*. Costs need to be controlled and reduced. Assets need to be made to grow.

To be sure, in managing manual workers we learned fairly early that high turnover (that is, losing workers) is very costly. The Ford Motor Company, as is well known, increased the pay of skilled workers from eighty cents a day to $5.00 a day on January 1, 1914. It did so because its turnover had been so excessive as to make its labor costs prohibitively high; it had to hire 60,000 people a year to keep 10,000. Even so, everybody (including Henry Ford himself, who had at first been bitterly opposed to this increase) was convinced that the higher wages would greatly reduce the company's profits. Instead, in the very first year, profits almost doubled. Paid $5.00 a day, practically no workers left—in fact, the Ford Motor Company soon had a waiting list.

However, short of the costs of turnover, rehiring, retraining, and so on, the manual worker is still being seen as a cost. This is true even in Japan, despite the emphasis on lifetime employment and on building a "loyal," permanent work force. The management of people at work, based on millennia of work being almost totally manual work, still assumes that with few exceptions (for example, highly skilled people) one manual worker is like any other manual worker.

This is definitely not true for knowledge work. Employees who do manual work do not own the means of production. They may, and often do, have a lot of valuable experience, but that experience is valuable only at the place where they work. It is not portable. Knowledge workers, however, *own* the means of production. That knowledge between their ears is a totally portable and enormous capital asset. Because knowledge workers own their means of production, they are mobile. It may not be true for most of them that the organization needs them more than they need the organization. For most of them it is a symbiotic relationship in which they need each other in equal measure. It is not true, as it was for the manual worker in modern industry, that they need the job much more than the job needs them.

Management's job is to preserve the assets of the institution in its care. What does this mean when the knowledge of the individual knowledge worker becomes an asset—and, in more and more cases, the *main* asset—of an institution? What does this mean for personnel policy? What is needed to attract and to hold the highest producing knowledge workers? What is needed to increase their productivity and to convert their increased productivity into performance capacity for the organization?

THE TECHNOLOGISTS

A very large number of knowledge workers do both knowledge work *and* manual work. I call them *technologists.* This group includes people who apply knowledge of the highest order.

Surgeons preparing for an operation to correct a brain aneurysm before it produces a lethal brain hemorrhage spend hours in diagnosis *before* they cut—and that requires specialized knowledge of the highest order. Again, during the surgery, an unexpected complication may occur that calls for theoretical knowledge and judgment, both of the very highest order. However, the surgery itself is manual work— and manual work consisting of repetitive, manual operations in which the emphasis is on speed, accuracy, and uniformity. These operations are studied, organized, learned, and practiced exactly like any manual work—that is, by the same methods Taylor first developed for factory work.

The technologist group also contains large numbers of people in whose work knowledge is relatively subordinate—though it is always crucial. The file clerk's job—and that of the clerk's computer-operator successor—requires knowledge of the alphabet that no experience can teach. This knowledge is a small part of an otherwise manual task, but it is its foundation and is absolutely crucial.

Technologists may be the single biggest group of knowledge workers. They may also be the fastest-growing group. They include the great majority of health-care workers: lab technicians; rehabilitation technicians; technicians in imaging such as X-ray, ultrasound, magnetic-resonance imaging; and so on. They include dentists and all dental-support people. They include automobile mechanics and all kinds of repair and installation people. In fact, the technologist may be the true successor to the nineteenth and twentieth century skilled workers.

Technologists are also the one group in which developed countries can have a true and long-lasting competitive advantage. When it comes to truly high knowledge, no country can any longer have much of a lead the way nineteenth century Germany had through its university. Among theoretical physicists, mathematicians, economic theorists, and the like, there is no "nationality." Any country can, at fairly low cost, train a substantial number of high-knowledge people. India, for instance, despite her poverty, has been training fairly large numbers of first-rate physicians and first-rate computer programmers. Similarly, there is no "nationality" with respect to the productivity of manual labor. Training based on scientific management has made all countries capable of attaining—overnight—the manual-worker productivity of the most advanced country, industry, or company. Only by educating technologists can the developed countries still have a meaningful and lasting competitive edge.

The U.S. is so far the only country that has developed this advantage through its unique nationwide systems of community colleges. The community college was actually *designed* (beginning in the 1920s) to educate technologists who have *both* the needed theoretical knowledge *and* the manual skill. On this, I am convinced, rests both the still huge productivity advantage of the American economy and the (so far unique) American ability to create, almost overnight, new and different industries.

Currently, nothing quite like the American community college exists in any other nation. The famous Japanese school system produces either people prepared only for manual work or people prepared only for knowledge work. Not until the year 2003 is the first Japanese institution devoted to train technologists supposed to get started. The even more famous German apprenticeship system (started in the 1830s) was one of the main factors in Germany's becoming the world's leading manufacturer. However, it focused—and still focuses—primarily on manual skills and slights theoretical knowledge. It is thus in danger of becoming rapidly obsolete.

Other developed countries should be expected to catch up with the U.S. fairly fast. "Emerging" or "third world" countries are, however, likely to be decades behind—in part because educating technologists is expensive, in part because in these countries people of knowledge still look down with disdain, if not with contempt, on working with one's hands. "That's what we have servants for" is still their prevailing attitude. However, in developed countries—and again foremost in the U.S.—more and more manual workers are going to be technologists. To increase knowledge-worker productivity, increasing the productivity of technologists deserves to be given high priority.

The job was actually done more than seventy years ago by the American Telephone Company (AT&T) for its technologists, the people who install, maintain, and replace telephones. By the early 1920s, the technologists working outside the telephone office and at the customer's location had become a major cost center—and at the same time a major cause of customer unhappiness and dissatisfaction. It took about five years or so (from 1920 until 1925) for AT&T—which had by that time acquired a near monopoly on providing telephone service in the United States and in parts of Canada—to realize that the task was not installing, maintaining, repairing, and replacing telephones and telephone connections. *The task was to create a satisfied customer.* Once they realized this, it became fairly easy to organize the job. It meant, first, that the technicians themselves had to define what "satisfaction" meant. The results were standards that established that every order for a new telephone or an additional telephone connection would have to be satisfied within 48 hours, and that every request for repair would have to be satisfied the same day if made before noon, or by noon the following day. Then it became clear that the individual service people—in those days all men, of course—would have to be active participants in such decisions as whether to have one person installing and replacing telephones and another one maintaining and repairing them or whether the same people had to be able to do all jobs (which in the end turned out to be the right answer). Then these people had to be taught a very substantial amount of theoretical knowledge—and in those days few of them had more than six years of schooling. They had to understand how a telephone works. They had to understand how a switchboard works. They had to understand how the telephone system works. These people were not qualified engineers nor skilled craftsmen, but they had to know enough electronics to diagnose unexpected problems and be able to cope with them. Then they were trained in the repetitive manual operation or in the "one right way" (that is, through the methods of scientific management) and *they* made the decisions (such as where and how to connect the individual telephone to the system and what particular kind of telephone and service would be the most suitable for a given home or a given office). They had to become salesmen in addition to being servicemen.

Finally, the telephone company faced the problem how to define *quality.* The technologist had to work by himself. He could not be supervised. He, therefore, had to define quality, and he had to deliver it. It took another several years before that was answered. At first the telephone company thought that this meant a sample check, which had supervisors go out and look at a sample (maybe every twentieth or thirtieth job done by an individual service person) and check it for quality. This very soon turned out to be the wrong way of doing the job, annoying servicemen and customers alike. Then the telephone company defined quality as "no complaints"—and they soon found out that only extremely unhappy customers complained. It then had to redefine quality as "positive customer satisfaction." In the end, this then meant that the serviceman himself controlled quality (for example, by calling up a week or ten days after he had done a job and asking the customer whether the work was satisfactory and whether there was anything more the technician could possibly do to give the customer the best possible and most satisfactory service).

I have intentionally gone into considerable detail in describing this early example because it exemplifies the three elements for making the worker who is both a knowledge worker and a manual worker both effective and productive.

- First, there is the answer to the question "What is the task?"—
  the key question in making every knowledge worker more
  productive. As the example of the Bell System shows, this is not

an obvious answer. As the Bell System people learned, the only people who knew the answer to this were the technologists themselves. In fact, until they asked the technologists, they floundered. However, as soon as the technologists were asked, the answer came back loud and clear: "a satisfied customer."

- Then, the technologists had to take full responsibility for giving customer satisfaction, that is, for delivering quality. This showed what *formal knowledge* the technologist needed. Only then could the *manual* part of the job be organized for manual-worker productivity.

- Above all, this example shows that technologists have to be treated as *knowledge workers.* No matter how important the manual part of their work—and it may take as much time as it did in the case of the AT&T installers—the focus has to be on making the technologist knowledgeable, responsible, and productive as a knowledge worker.

KNOWLEDGE WORK AS A SYSTEM

Productivity of the knowledge worker will almost always require that the *work itself* be restructured and be made part of a *system.* One example is servicing expensive equipment, such as huge and expensive earth-moving machines. Traditionally, this had been seen as distinct and separate from the job of making and selling the machines. However, when the U.S. Caterpillar Company, the world's largest producer of such equipment, asked, "What are we getting paid for?" the answer was "We are not getting paid for machinery. We are getting paid for what the machinery does at the customer's place of business. That means keeping the equipment running, since even one hour during which the equipment is out of operation may cost the customer far more than the equipment itself." In other words, the answer to "What is our business?" was "Service." This then led to a total restructuring of operations all the way back to the factory in order that the customer could be guaranteed continuing operations and immediate repairs or replacements. The service representative, usually a technologist, has become the true "decision maker."

As another example, a group of about twenty-five orthopedic surgeons in a midwestern U.S. city have organized themselves as a "system" to produce the highest quality work, make optimal use of the limited and expensive resources of operating and recovery rooms, make optimal use of the supporting knowledge people such as anesthesiologists or surgical nurses, build continuous learning and continuous innovation into the work of the entire group and of every member thereof, and, finally, minimize costs. Each of the surgeons retains full control of his or her practice. He or she is fully responsible for obtaining and treating the individual patient. Traditionally, surgeons schedule surgeries early in the morning. Hence, operating rooms and recovery rooms are standing empty most of the time. The group now schedules the use of operating and recovery rooms for the entire group so that this scarce and extremely expensive resource is utilized ten hours a day. The group, as a group, decides on the standardization of tools and equipment so as to obtain the highest quality at the lowest cost. Finally, the group has also built quality control into its system. Every three months three surgeons are designated to scrutinize every operation done by each of the members—the diagnosis, the surgery, the after-treatment. They then sit down with the individual surgeons and discuss their performance. They suggest where there is need for improvement and they also may recommend that a certain surgeon be asked to leave the group when his or her work is not satisfactory. Each year, the quality standards that these supervising committees apply are discussed with the whole group and are raised, often substantially. As a result, this group now does almost four times as much work as it did before. It has cut the costs by 50 percent, half of it by cutting back on the waste of operating and recovery rooms and half by standardizing tools and equipment. In such measurable areas as success rates in knee or shoulder replacements and in recovery after sports injuries, it has greatly improved its results.

What to do about knowledge-worker productivity is thus largely known. So is *how* to do it.

HOW TO BEGIN?

Making knowledge workers more productive requires changes in basic attitude, whereas making the manual worker more productive only required telling the worker how to do the job. Furthermore, making knowledge workers more productive requires changes in attitude not only on the part of the individual knowledge worker, but on the part of the whole organization. It therefore has to be "piloted," as any major change should be. The first step is to find an area in the organization where there is a group of knowledge workers who are receptive. (The orthopedic surgeons, for instance, first had their new ideas tried out by four physicians who had long argued for radical changes.) The next step is to work consistently, patiently, and for a considerable length of time with this small group. The first attempts, even if greeted with great enthusiasm, will almost certainly run into all kinds of unexpected problems. It is only after the productivity of this small group of knowledge workers has been substantially increased that the new ways of doing the work can be extended to a larger area, if not to the entire organization. At this point, the main problems will be known, such as where resistance can be expected (such as from middle management) or what changes in task, organization, measurements, or attitudes are needed for full effectiveness. To bypass the pilot stage— and there is always pressure to do so—only means that the mistakes become public while the successes stay hidden. It only means discrediting the entire enterprise. If properly piloted, a great deal can be done to improve knowledge-worker productivity.

Knowledge-worker productivity is the biggest of the twenty-first-century management challenges. In the developed countries, it is their first *survival requirement.* In no other way can the developed countries hope to maintain themselves, let alone maintain their leadership and their standards of living. In the twentieth century, this leadership very largely depended on making the manual worker more productive. Any country, any industry, any business can do that today using the methods that the developed countries have worked out and put into practice in the 120 years since Frederick Winslow Taylor first looked at manual work. Anybody today, any place, can apply those policies to training, the organization of work, and the productivity of workers—even if they are barely literate, if not illiterate, and totally unskilled.

Above all, the supply of young people available for manual work will be rapidly shrinking in the developed countries—in the West and in Japan very fast, in the U.S. somewhat more slowly—whereas the supply of such people will still grow fast in the emerging and developing countries for at least another thirty or forty years. The only possible advantage developed countries can hope to have is in the supply of people prepared, educated, and trained for knowledge work. There, for another fifty years, the developed countries can expect to have substantial advantages, both in quality and in quantity. Whether this advantage will translate into performance depends on the ability of the developed countries—and of every industry in it, of every company in it, of every institution in it—to raise the productivity of the knowledge worker and to raise it as fast as the developed countries have raised the productivity of the manual worker in the last hundred years.

The countries and the industries that have emerged as the leaders in the last hundred years in the world are the countries and the industries that have led in raising the productivity of the manual worker—the U.S. first, Japan and Germany second. Fifty years from now, if not much sooner, leadership in the world economy will have moved to the countries and to the industries that have most systematically and most successfully raised knowledge-worker productivity.

THE GOVERNANCE OF THE CORPORATION

What does the emergence of the knowledge worker and of knowledge worker productivity mean for the *governance of the corporation?* What does it mean for the future and structure of the economic system?

In the last ten or fifteen years, pension funds and other institutional investors became the main share owners of the equity capital of publicly owned companies in all developed countries. In the U.S., this has triggered a furious debate on the governance of corporations. With the emergence of pension funds and mutual funds as the owners of publicly owned companies, power has shifted to these new owners. Similar shifts in both the definition of the purpose of economic organizations (such as the business corporation) and their governance can be expected to occur in all developed countries.

Within a fairly short period of time, we will face the problem of the governance of corporations again. We will have to redefine the purpose of the employing organization and of its management as *both* satisfying the legal owners (such as shareholders) and satisfying the owners of the human capital that gives the organization its wealth-producing power—that is, satisfying the knowledge workers. Increasingly, the ability of organizations—and not only of businesses—to survive will come to depend on their "comparative advantage" in making the knowledge worker more productive. The ability to attract and hold the best of the knowledge workers is the first and most fundamental precondition.

However, can this be *measured* or is it purely an "intangible"? This will surely be a central problem for management, for investors, and for capital markets. What does "capitalism" mean when knowledge governs rather than money? And what do "free markets" mean when knowledge workers—and no one else can "own" knowledge—are the true assets? Knowledge workers can neither be bought nor sold. They do not come with a merger or an acquisition. In fact, although they are the greatest "value," they have no "market value"—that means, of course, that they are not an "asset" in any sense of the term.

These questions go far beyond the scope of this chapter. However, it is certain that the emergence as *key questions* of the knowledge worker and of the knowledge-worker's productivity will, within a few decades, bring about fundamental changes in the very structure and nature of the economic system.

Beyond Greening

Strategies for a Sustainable World

Stuart L. Hart

T he environmental revolution has been almost three decades in the making, and it has changed forever how companies do business. In the 1960s and 1970s, corporations were in a state of denial regarding their impact on the environment. Then a series of highly visible ecological problems created a groundswell of support for strict government regulation. In the United States, Lake Erie was dead. In Europe, the Rhine was on fire. In Japan, people were dying of mercury poisoning.

Today many companies have accepted their responsibility to do no harm to the environment. Products and production processes are becoming cleaner; and where such change is under way, the environment is on the mend. In the industrialized nations, more and more companies are "going green" as they realize that they can reduce pollution and increase profits simultaneously. We have come a long way.

But the distance we've traveled will seem small when, in thirty years, we look back at the 1990s. Beyond greening lies an enormous challenge—and an enormous opportunity. The challenge is to develop a *sustainable global economy:* an economy that the planet is capable of supporting indefinitely. Although we may be approaching ecological recovery in the developed world, the planet as a whole remains on an unsustainable course. Those who think that sustainability is only a matter of pollution control are missing the bigger picture. Even if all the companies in the developed world were to achieve zero emissions by the year 2000, the earth would still be stressed beyond what biologists refer to as its carrying capacity. Increasingly, the scourges of the late twentieth century—depleted farmland, fisheries, and forests; choking urban pollution; poverty; infectious diseases; and migration—are spilling over geopolitical borders. The simple fact is this: in meeting our needs, we are destroying the ability of future generations to meet theirs.

The roots of the problem—explosive population growth and rapid economic development in the emerging economies—are political and social issues that exceed the mandate and the capabilities of any corporation. At the same time, corporations are the only organizations with the resources, technology, global reach, and, ultimately, motivation to achieve sustainability.

It is easy to state the case in the negative: faced with impoverished customers, degraded environments, failing political systems, and unraveling societies, it will be increasingly difficult for corporations to do business. But the positive case is even more powerful. The more we learn about the challenges of sustainability, the clearer it is that we are poised at the threshold of a historic moment in which many of the world's industries may be transformed.

To date, the business logic for greening has been largely operational or technical: bottom-up pollution-prevention programs have saved companies billions of dollars. However, few executives realize that environmental opportunities might actually become a major source of revenue growth. Greening has been framed in terms of risk reduction, reengineering, or cost cutting. Rarely is greening linked to strategy or technology development, and as a result, most companies fail to recognize opportunities of potentially staggering proportions.

WORLDS IN COLLISION

The achievement of sustainability will mean billions of dollars in products, services, and technologies that barely exist today. Whereas yesterday's businesses were often oblivious to their negative impact on the environment and today's responsible businesses strive for zero impact, tomorrow's businesses must learn to make a positive impact.

Increasingly, companies will be selling solutions to the world's environmental problems.

Envisioning tomorrow's businesses, therefore, requires a clear understanding of those problems. To move beyond greening to sustainability, we must first unravel a complex set of global interdependencies. In fact, the global economy is really three different, overlapping economies.

The *market economy* is the familiar world of commerce comprising both the developed nations and the emerging economies.* About a billion people—one-sixth of the world's population—live in the developed countries of the market economy. Those affluent societies account for more than 75 percent of the world's energy and resource consumption and create the bulk of industrial, toxic, and consumer waste. The developed economies thus leave large ecological footprints—defined as the amount of land required to meet a typical consumer's needs.

Despite such intense use of energy and materials, however, levels of pollution are relatively low in the developed economies. Three factors account for this seeming paradox: stringent environmental regulations, the greening of industry, and the relocation of the most polluting activities (such as commodity processing and heavy manufacturing) to the emerging market economies. Thus to some extent the greening of the developed world has been at the expense of the environments in emerging economies. Given the much larger population base in those countries, their rapid industrialization could easily offset the environmental gains made in the developed economies. Consider, for example, that the emerging economies in Asia and Latin America (and now Eastern Europe and the former Soviet Union) have added nearly 2 billion people to the market economy over the past forty years.

With economic growth comes urbanization. Today one of every three people in the world lives in a city. By 2025, it will be two out of three. Demographers predict that by that year there will be well over thirty megacities with populations exceeding 8 million and more than 500 cities with populations exceeding 1 million. Urbanization on this scale presents enormous infrastructural and environmental challenges.

---

*The terms *market economy, survival economy,* and *nature's economy* were suggested to me by Vandana Shiva in *Ecology and the Politics of Survival* (New Delhi: United Nations University Press, 1991).

Because industrialization has focused initially on commodities and heavy manufacturing, cities in many emerging economies suffer from oppressive levels of pollution. Acid rain is a growing problem, especially in places where coal combustion is unregulated. The World Bank estimates that by 2010 there will be more than 1 billion motor vehicles in the world. Concentrated in cities, they will double current levels of energy use, smog precursors, and emissions of greenhouse gases.

The second economy is the *survival economy:* the traditional, village-based way of life found in the rural parts of most developing countries. It is made up of 3 billion people, mainly Africans, Indians, and Chinese who are subsistence oriented and meet their basic needs directly from nature. Demographers generally agree that the world's population, currently growing by about 90 million people per year, will roughly double over the next forty years. The developing nations will account for 90 percent of that growth, and most of it will occur in the survival economy.

Owing in part to the rapid expansion of the market economy, existence in the survival economy is becoming increasingly precarious. Extractive industries and infrastructure development have, in many cases, degraded the ecosystems upon which the survival economy depends. Rural populations are driven further into poverty as they compete for scarce natural resources. Women and children now spend on average four to six hours per day searching for fuelwood and four to six hours per week drawing and carrying water. Ironically, those conditions encourage high fertility rates because, in the short run, children help the family to garner needed resources. But in the long run, population growth in the survival economy only reinforces a vicious cycle of resource depletion and poverty.

Short-term survival pressures often force these rapidly growing rural populations into practices that cause long-term damage to forests, soil, and water. When wood becomes scarce, people burn dung for fuel, one of the greatest—and least well-known—environmental hazards in the world today. Contaminated drinking water is an equally grave problem. The World Health Organization estimates that burning dung and drinking contaminated water together cause 8 million deaths per year.

As it becomes more and more difficult to live off the land, millions of desperate people migrate to already overcrowded cities. In China, for example, an estimated 120 million people now roam from city to city, landless and jobless, driven from their villages by deforestation, soil erosion, floods, or droughts. Worldwide, the number of such "environmental refugees" from the survival economy may be as high as 500 million people, and the figure is growing.

The third economy is *nature's economy,* which consists of the natural systems and resources that support the market and the survival economies. Nonrenewable resources, such as oil, metals, and other minerals, are finite. Renewable resources, such as soils and forests, will replenish themselves—as long as their use does not exceed critical thresholds.

Technological innovations have created substitutes for many commonly used nonrenewable resources; for example, optical fiber now replaces copper wire. And in the developed economies, demand for some virgin materials may actually diminish in the decades ahead because of reuse and recycling. Ironically, the greatest threat to sustainable development today is depletion of the world's *renewable* resources.

Forests, soil, water, and fisheries are all being pushed beyond their limits by human population growth and rapid industrial development. Insufficient fresh water may prove to be the most vexing problem in the developing world over the next decade, as agricultural, commercial, and residential uses increase. Water tables are being drawn down at an alarming rate, especially in the most heavily populated nations, such as China and India.

Soil is another resource at risk. More than 10 percent of the world's topsoil has been seriously eroded. Available cropland and rangeland are shrinking. Existing crop varieties are no longer responding to increased use of fertilizer. As a consequence, per capita world production of both grain and meat peaked and began to decline during the 1980s. Meanwhile, the world's eighteen major oceanic fisheries have now reached or actually exceeded their maximum sustainable yields.

By some estimates, humankind now uses more than 40 percent of the planet's net primary productivity. If, as projected, the population doubles over the next forty years, we may outcompete most other animal species for food, driving many to extinction. In short, human activity now exceeds sustainability on a global scale. (See Table 46.1.)

As we approach the twenty-first century, the interdependence of the three economic spheres is increasingly evident. In fact, the three economies have become worlds in collision, creating the major social and environmental challenges facing the planet: climate change, pollution, resource depletion, poverty, and inequality.

	Pollution	Depletion	Poverty
Developed economies	–greenhouse gases –use of toxic materials –contaminated sites	–scarcity of materials –insufficient reuse and recycling	–urban and minority unemployment
Emerging economies	–industrial emissions –contaminated water –lack of sewage treatment	–overexploitation of renewable resources –overuse of water for irrigation	–migration to cities –lack of skilled workers
Survival economies	–dung and wood burning –lack of sanitation –ecosystem destruction due to development	–deforestation –overgrazing –soil loss	–income inequality –population growth –low status of women –dislocation

Table 46.1.   Major Challenges to Sustainability.

Consider, for example, that the average American today consumes seventeen times more than his or her Mexican counterpart (emerging economy) and hundreds of times more than the average Ethiopian (survival economy). The levels of material and energy consumption in the United States require large quantities of raw materials and commodities, sourced increasingly from the survival economy and produced in emerging economies.

In the survival economy, massive infrastructure development (for example, dams, irrigation projects, highways, mining operations, and power generation projects), often aided by agencies, banks, and corporations in the developed countries, has provided access to raw materials. Unfortunately, such development has often had devastating consequences for nature's economy and has tended to strengthen existing political and economic elites, with little benefit to those in the survival economy.

At the same time, infrastructure development projects have contributed to a global glut of raw materials and hence to a long-term fall in commodity prices. And as commodity prices have fallen relative to the prices of manufactured goods, the currencies of developing countries have weakened and their terms of trade have become less favorable. Their purchasing power declines while their already substantial debt load becomes even larger. The net effect of this dynamic has been the transfer of vast amounts of wealth (estimated at $40 billion per year since 1985) from developing to developed countries, producing a vicious cycle of resource exploitation and pollution to service mounting debt. Today developing nations have a combined debt of more than $1.2 trillion, equal to nearly half of their collective gross national product.

STRATEGIES FOR A SUSTAINABLE WORLD

Nearly three decades ago, environmentalists such as Paul Ehrlich and Barry Commoner made this simple but powerful observation about sustainable development: the total environmental burden (EB) created by human activity is a function of three factors. They are population (P); affluence (A), which is a proxy for consumption; and technology (T), which is how wealth is created. The product of these three factors determines the total environmental burden. It can be expressed as a formula: $EB = P \times A \times T$.

Achieving sustainability will require stabilizing or reducing the environmental burden. That can be done by decreasing the human population, lowering the level of affluence (consumption), or changing fundamentally the technology used to create wealth. The first option, lowering the human population, does not appear feasible short of draconian political measures or the occurrence of a major public-health crisis that causes mass mortality.

The second option, decreasing the level of affluence, would only make the problem worse, because poverty and population growth go hand in hand: demographers have long known that birth rates are inversely correlated with level of education and standard of living. Thus stabilizing the human population will require improving the education and economic standing of the world's poor, particularly women of childbearing age. That can be accomplished only by creating wealth on a massive scale. Indeed, it may be necessary to grow the world economy as much as tenfold just to provide basic amenities to a population of 8 billion to 10 billion.

That leaves the third option: changing the technology used to create the goods and services that constitute the world's wealth. Although population and consumption may be societal issues, technology is the business of business.

If economic activity must increase tenfold over what it is today just to provide the bare essentials to a population double its current size, then technology will have to improve twentyfold merely to keep the planet at its current levels of environmental burden. Those who believe that ecological disaster will somehow be averted must also appreciate the commercial implications of such a belief: over the next decade or so, sustainable development will constitute one of the biggest opportunities in the history of commerce.

Nevertheless, as of today few companies have incorporated sustainability into their strategic thinking. Instead, environmental strategy consists largely of piecemeal projects aimed at controlling or preventing pollution. Focusing on sustainability requires putting business strategies to a new test. Taking the entire planet as the context in which they do business, companies must ask whether they are part of the solution to social and environmental problems or part of the problem. Only when a company thinks in those terms can it begin to develop a vision of sustainability—a shaping logic that goes beyond today's internal, operational focus on greening to a more external, strategic focus on sustainable development. Such a vision is needed to guide companies through three stages of environmental strategy.

Stage One: Pollution Prevention

The first step for most companies is to make the shift from pollution control to pollution prevention. Pollution control means cleaning up waste after it has been created. Pollution prevention focuses on minimizing or eliminating waste before it is created. Much like total quality management, pollution prevention strategies depend on continuous improvement efforts to reduce waste and energy use. This transformation is driven by a compelling logic: pollution prevention pays. Emerging global standards for environmental management systems (ISO 14,000, for example) also have created strong incentives for companies to develop such capabilities.

Over the past decade, companies have sought to avoid colliding with nature's economy (and incurring the associated added costs) through greening and prevention strategies. Aeroquip Corporation, a $2.5 billion manufacturer of hoses, fittings, and couplings, saw an opportunity here. Like most industrial suppliers, Aeroquip never thought of itself as a provider of environmental solutions. But in 1990, its executives realized that the company's products might be especially valuable in meeting the need to reduce waste and prevent pollution. Aeroquip has generated a $250 million business by focusing its attention on developing products that reduce emissions. As companies in emerging economies realize the competitive benefits of using raw materials and resources more productively, businesses like Aeroquip's will continue to grow.

The emerging economies cannot afford to repeat all the environmental mistakes of Western development. With the sustainability imperative in mind, BASF, the German chemical giant, is helping to design and build chemical industries in China, India, Indonesia, and Malaysia that are less polluting than in the past. By colocating facilities that in the West have been geographically dispersed, BASF is able to create industrial ecosystems in which the waste from one process becomes the raw material for another. Colocation solves a problem common in the West, where recycling waste is often infeasible because transporting it from one site to another is dangerous and costly.

Stage Two: Product Stewardship

Product stewardship focuses on minimizing not only pollution from manufacturing but also all environmental impacts associated with the full life cycle of a product. As companies in stage one move closer to zero emissions, reducing the use of materials and production of waste requires fundamental changes in underlying product and process design.

Design for environment (DFE), a tool for creating products that are easier to recover, reuse, or recycle, is becoming increasingly important. With DFE, all the effects that a product could have on the environment are examined during its design phase. Cradle-to-grave analysis begins and ends outside the boundaries of a company's operations— it includes a full assessment of all inputs to the product and examines how customers use and dispose of it. DFE thus captures a broad range of external perspectives by including technical staff, environmental experts, end customers, and even community representatives in the process. Dow Chemical Company has pioneered the use of a board-level advisory panel of environmental experts and external representatives to aid its product-stewardship efforts.

By reducing materials and energy consumption, DFE can be highly profitable. Consider Xerox Corporation's Asset Recycle Management (ARM) program, which uses leased Xerox copiers as sources of high-quality, low-cost parts and components for new machines. A well-developed infrastructure for taking back leased copiers combined with a sophisticated remanufacturing process allows parts and components to be reconditioned, tested, and then reassembled into "new" machines.

Xerox estimates that ARM savings in raw materials, labor, and waste disposal in 1995 alone were in the $300 million to $400 million range. In taking recycling to this level, Xerox has reconceptualized its business. By redefining the product-in-use as part of the company's asset base, Xerox has discovered a way to add value and lower costs. It can continually provide its lease customers with the latest product upgrades, giving them state-of-the-art functionality with minimal environmental impact.

Product stewardship is thus one way to reduce consumption in the developed economies. It may also aid the quest for sustainability because developing nations often try to emulate what they see happening in the developed nations. Properly executed, product stewardship also offers the potential for revenue growth through product differentiation. For example, Dunlop Tire Corporation and Akzo Nobel recently announced a new radial tire that makes use of an aramid fiber belt rather than the conventional steel belt. The new design makes recycling easier because it eliminates the expensive cryogenic crushing required to separate the steel belts from the tire's other materials. Because the new fiber-belt tire is 30 percent lighter, it dramatically improves gas mileage. Moreover, it is a safer tire because it improves the traction control of antilock braking systems.

The evolution from pollution prevention to product stewardship is now happening in multinational companies such as Dow, DuPont, Monsanto, Xerox, ABB, Philips, and Sony. For example, as part of a larger sustainability strategy dubbed A Growing Partnership with Nature, DuPont's agricultural-products business developed a new type of herbicide that has helped farmers around the world reduce their annual use of chemicals by more than 45 million pounds. The new Sulfonylurea herbicides have also led to a 1-billion-pound reduction in the amount of chemical waste produced in the manufacture of agricultural chemicals. These herbicides are effective at 1 percent to 5 percent of the application rates of traditional chemicals, are nontoxic to animals and nontarget species, and biodegrade in the soil, leaving virtually no residue on crops. Because they require so much less material in their manufacture, they are also highly profitable.

Stage Three: Clean Technology

Companies with their eye on the future can begin to plan for and invest in tomorrow's technologies. The simple fact is that the existing technology base in many industries is not environmentally sustainable. The chemical industry, for example, while having made substantial headway over the past decade in pollution prevention and product stewardship, is still limited by its dependence on the chlorine molecule. (Many organochlorides are toxic or persistent or bioaccumulative.) As long as the industry relies on its historical competencies in chlorine chemistry, it will have trouble making major progress toward sustainability.

Monsanto is one company that is consciously developing new competencies. It is shifting the technology base for its agriculture business from bulk chemicals to biotechnology. It is betting that the bioengineering of crops rather than the application of chemical pesticides or fertilizers represents a sustainable path to increased agricultural yields.

Clean technologies are desperately needed in the emerging economies of Asia. Urban pollution there has reached oppressive levels. But precisely because manufacturing growth is so high—capital stock doubles every six years—there is an unprecedented opportunity to replace current product and process technologies with new, cleaner ones.

Japan's Research Institute for Innovative Technology for the Earth is one of several new research and technology consortia focusing on the development and commercialization of clean technologies for the developing world. Having been provided with funding and staff by the Japanese government and more than forty corporations, RITE has set forth an ambitious 100-year plan to create the next generation of power technology, which will eliminate or neutralize greenhouse gas emissions.

SUSTAINABILITY VISION

Pollution prevention, product stewardship, and clean technology all move a company toward sustainability. But without a framework to give direction to those activities, their impact will dissipate. A vision of sustainability for an industry or a company is like a road map to the future, showing the way products and services must evolve and what new competencies will be needed to get there. Few companies today have such a road map. Ironically, chemical companies, regarded only a decade ago as the worst environmental villains, are among the few large corporations to have engaged the challenge of sustainable development seriously.

Companies can begin by taking stock of each component of what I call their *sustainability portfolio*. (See Table 46.2.) Is there an overarching vision of sustainability that gives direction to the company's activities?

	Internal	External
Tomorrow	**Clean technology** Is the environmental performance of our products limited by our existing competency base? Is there potential to realize major improvements through new technology?	**Sustainability vision** Does our corporate vision direct us toward the solution of social and environmental problems? Does our vision guide the development of new technologies, markets, products, and processes?
Today	**Pollution prevention** Where are the most significant waste and emission streams from our current operations? Can we lower costs and risks by eliminating waste at the source or by using it as useful input?	**Product stewardship** What are the implications for product design and development if we assume responsibility for a product's entire life cycle? Can we add value or lower costs while simultaneously reducing the impact of our products?

Internal

This simple diagnostic tool can help any company determine whether its strategy is consistent with sustainability. First, assess your company's capability in each of the four quadrants by answering the questions in each box. Then rate yourself on the following scale for each quadrant: 1=nonexistent; 2=emerging; 3=established; or 4=institutionalized.

Most companies will be heavily skewed toward the lower left-hand quadrant, reflecting investment in pollution prevention. However, without investments in future technologies and markets (the upper half of the portfolio), the company's environmental strategy will not meet evolving needs.

External

Unbalanced portfolios spell trouble: a bottom-heavy portfolio suggests a good position today but future vulnerability. A top-heavy portfolio indicates a vision of sustainability without the operational or analytical skills needed to implement it. A portfolio skewed to the left side of the chart indicates a preoccupation with handling the environmental challenge through internal process improvements and technology-development initiatives. Finally, a portfolio skewed to the right side, although highly open and public, runs the risk of being labeled a "greenwash" because the underlying plant operations and core technology still cause significant environmental harm.

Table 46.2.   The Sustainable Portfolio.

To what extent has the company progressed through the three stages of environmental strategy—from pollution prevention to product stewardship to clean technology?

Consider the auto industry. During the 1970s, government regulation of tailpipe emissions forced the industry to focus on pollution control. In the 1980s, the industry began to tackle pollution prevention. Initiatives such as the Corporate Average Fuel Efficiency requirement and the Toxic Release Inventory led auto companies to examine their product designs and manufacturing processes in order to improve fuel economy and lower emissions from their plants.

The 1990s are witnessing the first signs of product stewardship. In Germany, the 1990 "take-back" law required auto manufacturers to take responsibility for their vehicles at the end of their useful lives. Innovators such as BMW have influenced the design of new cars with their design for disassembly efforts. Industry-level consortia such as the Partnership for a New Generation of Vehicles are driven largely by the product stewardship logic of lowering the environmental impact of automobiles throughout their life cycle.

Early attempts to promote clean technology include such initiatives as California's zero-emission vehicle law and the U.N. Climate Change Convention, which ultimately will limit greenhouse gases on a global scale. But early efforts by industry incumbents have been either incremental—for example, natural-gas vehicles—or defensive in nature. Electric-vehicle programs, for instance, have been used to demonstrate the infeasibility of this technology rather than to lead the industry to a fundamentally cleaner technology.

Although the auto industry has made progress, it falls far short of sustainability. For the vast majority of auto companies, pollution prevention and product stewardship are the end of the road. Most auto executives assume that if they close the loop in both production and design, they will have accomplished all the necessary environmental objectives.

But step back and try to imagine a sustainable vision for the industry. Growth in the emerging markets will generate massive transportation needs in the coming decades. Already the rush is on to stake out positions in China, India, and Latin America. But what form will this opportunity take?

Consider the potential impact of automobiles on China alone. Today there are fewer than 1 million cars on the road in China.

However, with a population of more than 1 billion, it would take less than 30 percent market penetration to equal the current size of the U.S. car market (12 million to 15 million units sold per year). Ultimately, China might demand 50 million or more units annually. Because China's energy and transportation infrastructures are still being defined, there is an opportunity to develop a clean technology yielding important environmental and competitive benefits.

Amory Lovins of the Rocky Mountain Institute has demonstrated the feasibility of building hypercars—vehicles that are fully recyclable, twenty times more energy efficient, 100 times cleaner, and cheaper than existing cars. These vehicles retain the safety and performance of conventional cars but achieve radical simplification through the use of lightweight, composite materials, fewer parts, virtual prototyping, regenerative braking, and very small, hybrid engines. Hypercars, which are more akin to computers on wheels than to cars with microchips, may render obsolete most of the competencies associated with today's auto manufacturing—for example, metal stamping, tool and die making, and the internal combustion engine.

Assume for a minute that clean technology like the hypercar or Mazda's soon-to-be-released hydrogen rotary engine can be developed for a market such as China's. Now try to envision a transportation infrastructure capable of accommodating so many cars. How long will it take before gridlock and traffic jams force the auto industry to a halt? Sustainability will require new transportation solutions for the needs of emerging economies with huge populations. Will the giants in the auto industry be prepared for such radical change, or will they leave the field to new ventures that are not encumbered by the competencies of the past?

A clear and fully integrated environmental strategy should not only guide competency development, it should also shape the company's relationship to customers, suppliers, other companies, policymakers, and all its stakeholders. Companies can and must change the way customers think by creating preferences for products and services consistent with sustainability. Companies must become educators rather than mere marketers of products. (See Figure 46.1.)

For senior executives, embracing the quest for sustainability may well require a leap of faith. Some may feel that the risks associated with investing in unstable and unfamiliar markets outweigh the potential benefits. Others will recognize the power of such a positive mission to galvanize people in their organizations.

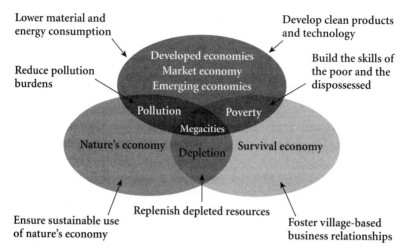

Lower material and
energy consumption

Develop clean products
and technology

Reduce pollution
burdens

Build the skills of
the poor and the
dispossessed

Developed economies
Market economy
Emerging economies

Pollution   Poverty

Megacities

Nature's economy   Depletion   Survival economy

Ensure sustainable use
of nature's economy

Replenish depleted resources

Foster village-based
business relationships

Figure 46.1.   Building Sustainable Business Strategies.

Regardless of their opinions on sustainability, executives will not be able to keep their heads in the sand for long. Since 1980, foreign direct investment by multinational corporations has increased from $500 billion to nearly $3 trillion per year. In fact, it now exceeds official development-assistance aid in developing countries. With free trade on the rise, the next decade may see the figure increase by another order of magnitude. The challenges presented by emerging markets in Asia and Latin America demand a new way of conceptualizing business opportunities. The rapid growth in emerging economies cannot be sustained in the face of mounting environmental deterioration, poverty, and resource depletion. In the coming decade, companies will be challenged to develop clean technologies and to implement strategies that drastically reduce the environmental burden in the developing world while simultaneously increasing its wealth and standard of living.

Like it or not, the responsibility for ensuring a sustainable world falls largely on the shoulders of the world's enterprises, the economic engines of the future. Clearly, public policy innovations (at both the national and international levels) and changes in individual consumption patterns will be needed to move toward sustainability. But corporations can and should lead the way, helping to shape public policy and driving change in consumers' behavior. In the final analysis, it makes good business sense to pursue strategies for a sustainable world.

—*∿∿*—

ARACRUZ CELULOSE: A STRATEGY FOR THE SURVIVAL ECONOMY

"Poverty is one of the world's leading polluters," notes Erling Lorentzen, founder and chairman of Aracruz Celulose. The $2 billion Brazilian company is the world's largest producer of eucalyptus pulp. "You can't expect people who don't eat a proper meal to be concerned about the environment" (Rigoglioso, 1996, p. 55).

From the very start, Aracruz has been built around a vision of sustainable development. Lorentzen understood that building a viable forest-products business in Brazil's impoverished and deforested state of Espirito Santo would require the simultaneous improvement of nature's economy and the survival economy.

First, to restore nature's economy, the company took advantage of a tax incentive for tree planting in the late 1960s and began buying and reforesting cut-over land. By 1992, the company had acquired over 200,000 hectares and planted 130,000 hectares with managed eucalyptus; the rest was restored as conservation land. By reforesting what had become highly degraded land, unsuitable for agriculture, the company addressed a fundamental environmental problem. At the same time, it created a first-rate source of fiber for its pulping operations. Aracruz's forest practices and its ability to clone seedlings have given the company advantages in both cost and quality.

Aracruz has tackled the problem of poverty head-on. Every year, the company gives away millions of eucalyptus seedlings to local farmers. It is a preemptive strategy, aimed at reducing the farmers' need to deplete the natural forests for fuel or lumber. Aracruz also has a long-term commitment to capability building. In the early years, Aracruz was able to hire local people for very low wages because of their desperate situation. But instead of simply exploiting the abundant supply of cheap labor, the company embarked on an aggressive social-investment strategy, spending $125 million to support the creation of hospitals, schools, housing, and a training center for employees. In fact, until recently, Aracruz spent more on its social investments than it did on wages (about $1.20 for every $1 in wages). Since that time, the standard of living has improved dramatically, as has productivity. The company no longer needs to invest so heavily in social infrastructure.

CHAPTER FORTY-SEVEN

The Healthy Organization

Richard Beckhard

W e are living in a world that is the most unstable, dynamic, exciting, and frustrating in modern history. Technology is exploding. We can contact anyone in the world in milliseconds. Surviving organizations, particularly in the private sector, are increasingly global entities.

Paradoxically, the need for local and community power is growing. The sectors of society are changing places. As the social sector becomes more powerful in influencing the direction of national policy, governments are devolving from national to local. Soon, the private sector will no longer be the only source of wealth. The public sector will need to reexamine its role of serving the people. The social, or volunteer, sector is exponentially increasing in importance.

Throughout history, the "world's work" has been done through institutions and organizations. As our global society tries to cope with the differences between rich and poor, North and South, developed and developing countries, and global and local issues, organizations increasingly serve as the bridges between issues and people. But just as individuals have personalities, which are a function of both heredity and environment, so organizations have personalities with the same causes.

Many individuals spend major amounts of energy in trying to understand and manage their behavior in an ever-changing environment. Increasingly, organizations and their leaders are engaged in the same inquiries. Look at the recent explosion of interest in the learning organization. Listen to executives struggling with managing dilemmas, rather than being faced with simple choices. Organizations are no longer stand-alone entities that can operate autonomously in a relatively stable environment. They are part of a system of relationships and interactions that is in a constantly dynamic state.

We can describe healthy people in a number of ways, from "not sick" to "moving toward highest potential" to "having it all together." There is no consensus, however, on how to define healthy organizations. I have spent a major part of my professional life exploring the nature of the health of organizations, and I have come to the conclusion that, although every aspect of our environment is in a turbulent and rapidly changing condition, both individual and organizational health can be measured now and in the future by the same criteria.

PROFILE OF A HEALTHY ORGANIZATION

- A healthy organization defines itself as a system, and the organization's work is to take in needs and raw materials and to transform them into goods and services. The organization's stakeholders include its owners and staff, its suppliers, intermediate customers, the ultimate consumers of the product or service, the media, and the communities in which the organization operates.

- It has a strong sensing system for receiving current information on all parts of the system and their interactions (systems dynamics thinking).

- It has a strong sense of purpose. It is managed against visions of its future.

- It operates in a "form follows function" mode. The work to be done determines the structures and mechanisms to do it. As a result, it uses multiple structures: the formal pyramidal structure, horizontal structures and teams, project structures, and temporary structures (as when managing a major change).

- It employs team management as the dominant mode. There is an executive team at the top; teams manage divisions and functions and also manage projects; there are interfunctional councils; and the professional development teams are composed of both specialists and users of services.

- It respects customer service—both to outside customers and to others within the organization—as a principle.

- Its management is information-driven. Large amounts of information can be received and processed in seconds. Access to information is widely shared across geographic areas, functions, and organization levels.

- It encourages and allows decisions to be made at the level closest to the customer, where all the necessary information is available.

- It keeps communication relatively open throughout the system.

- Its reward systems are designed to be congruent with the work and to support individual development. Managers and work teams are appraised against both performance and improvement goals.

- The organization operates in a learning mode. Identifying learning points is part of the process of all decision making.

- It makes explicit recognition for innovation and creativity and has a high tolerance for different styles of thinking and for ambiguity in all things.

- Its policies reflect respect for the tensions between work and family demands. Work at home is encouraged where appropriate. Job sharing is supported. Parental leave and child care are seen as responsibilities of the firm.

- It keeps an explicit social agenda. Community citizenship, protecting the environment, and supporting the arts are corporate policies, not isolated activities.

- It gives sufficient attention to efficient work, quality and safety awareness in operations, and identifying and managing change for a better future.

—∿— References

FOREWORD

Schein, E. H. (1969). *Process consultation: Its role in organization development.* Reading, MA: Addison-Wesley.

Schein, E. H. (1999). *Process consultation revisited: Building the helping relationship.* Reading, MA: Addison-Wesley.

Schein, E. H. (2003). *DEC is dead, long live DEC: The lasting legacy of Digital Equipment Corporation.* San Francisco: Berrett-Koehler.

Schein, E. H. (2004). *Organizational culture and leadership* (3rd ed.). Hoboken, NJ: Wiley.

Schein, E. H., Schneier, L., & Barker, C. (1961). *Coercive persuasion: A socio-psychological analysis of the "brainwashing" of the American civilian prisoners by the Chinese Communists.* New York: Norton.

CHAPTER ONE

Blake, R. R., & Mouton, J. S. (1968). *Corporate excellence through grid organization development.* Houston: Gulf Publishing.

Gardner, J. W. (1965, October). How to prevent organizational dry rot. *Harper's.*

Herzberg, F., Mausner, B., & Snyderman, B. (1959). *The motivation to work.* New York: John Wiley & Sons.

Lesieur, F. (1958). *The Scanlon plan: A frontier in labor-management cooperation.* New York: The Technology Press.

Miles, M. B., & others. (1966, August 27). Data feedback and organization change in a school system. Paper given at a meeting of the American Sociological Association.

Morse, L. H. (1968, June). Task-centered organization development. Master's Thesis, Cambridge, MA: Sloan School of Management.

Schein, E. H. (1965). *Organizational psychology.* Englewood Cliffs, NJ: Prentice-Hall.

CHAPTER TWO

Argyris, C. (1962). *Interpersonal competence and organizational effectiveness.* Homewood, IL: Dorsey Press.

Argyris, C. (1970). *Intervention theory and method.* Reading, MA: Addison-Wesley.

Argyris, C. (1971). *Management and organizational development.* New York: McGraw-Hill.

Argyris, C. (1973). The CEO's behavior: Key to organizational development. *Harvard Business Review, 51*(2), 55–64.

Argyris, C., & Schön, D. A. (1978). *Organizational learning: A theory of action perspective.* Reading, MA: Addison-Wesley.

Beckhard, R. (1969). *Organization development: Strategies and models.* Reading, MA: Addison-Wesley.

Bennis, W. G. (1966, November–December). The coming death of bureaucracy. *Think,* pp. 30–35.

Bennis, W. G. (1967, September–October). Organizations of the future. *Personnel Administration,* pp. 6–19.

Bennis, W. G. (1969). *Organization development: Its nature, origins, and prospects.* Reading, MA: Addison-Wesley.

Bennis, W. G. (1970). A funny thing happened on the way to the future. *American Psychologist, 25,* 595–608.

Bion, W. R. (1961). *Experiences in groups.* New York: Basic Books.

Blake, R. R., & Mouton, J. S. (1978). *The new managerial grid.* Houston: Gulf Publishing.

Burck, G. (1965, December). Union Carbide's patient schemers. *Fortune,* pp. 147–149.

French, W. L., & Bell, C. H., Jr. (1978). *Organization development* (2nd ed.). Englewood Cliffs, NJ: Prentice-Hall.

Hackman, J. R., & Oldham, G. R. (1975). Development of the job diagnostic survey. *Journal of Applied Psychology, 60,* 159-170.

Hackman, J. R., & Oldham, G. R. (1980). *Work redesign.* Reading, MA: Addison-Wesley.

Harvey, J. B. (1974, Summer). The Abilene paradox: The management of agreement. *Organizational Dynamics, 3,* 63–80.

Herzberg, F. (1966). *Work and the nature of man.* Cleveland: World.

Herzberg, F., B. Mausner, & B. Snyderman. (1959). *The motivation to work.* New York: Wiley.

Homans, G. C. (1950). *The human group.* New York: Harcourt, Brace.

Lawler, E. E., III. (1973). *Motivation in work organizations.* Monterey, CA: Brooks/Cole.

Lawrence, P. R., & Lorsch, J. W. (1967). *Organization and environment: Managing differentiation and integration.* Boston: Division of Research, Harvard Business School.

Lawrence, P. R., & Lorsch, J. W. (1969). *Developing organizations: Diagnosis and action.* Reading, MA: Addison-Wesley.

Levinson, H. (1972a). *Organizational diagnosis.* Cambridge, MA: Harvard University Press.

Levinson, H. (1972b). The clinical psychologist as organizational diagnostician. *Professional Psychology, 3,* 34–40.

Levinson, H. (1975). *Executive stress.* New York: Harper & Row.

Lewin, K. (1948). *Resolving social conflicts.* New York: Harper & Brothers.

Lewin, K. (1951). *Field theory in social science.* New York: Harper & Brothers.

Lewin, K. (1958). Group decision and social change. In E. E. Maccoby, T. M. Newcomb, & E. L. Hartley (Eds.), *Readings in social psychology* (pp. 197–211). New York: Holt, Rinehart, and Winston.

Likert, R. (1967). *The human organization: Its management and value.* New York: McGraw-Hill.

Mann, F. C. (1957). Studying and creating change: A means to understanding social organization. In *Research in industrial human relations* (publication no. 17). Champaign, IL: Industrial Relations Research Association.

Marrow, A. J. (1969). *The practical theorist.* New York: Basic Books.

Maslow, A. H. (1954). *Motivation and personality.* New York: Harper & Brothers.

Mayo, E. (1933). *The human problems of an industrial civilization.* Boston: Harvard University Graduate School of Business.

McGregor, D. (1960). *The human side of enterprise.* New York: McGraw-Hill.

McGregor, D. (1967). *The professional manager.* New York: McGraw-Hill.

Nadler, D. A. (1977). *Feedback and organization development: Using data-based methods.* Reading, MA: Addison-Wesley.

Rice, A. K. (1958). *Productivity and social organizations: The Ahmedabad experiment.* London: Tavistock.

Rioch, M. J. (1970). The work of Wilfred Bion on groups. *Psychiatry, 33,* 56–66.

Roethlisberger, F. J., & Dickson, W. J. (1939). *Management and the worker: An account of a research program conducted by the Western Electric Company.* Cambridge, MA: Harvard University Press.

Rogers, C. R. (1968). Interpersonal relationships: U.S.A. 2000. *Journal of Applied Behavioral Science, 4,* 265–280.

Schein, E. H. (1969). *Process consultation: Its role in organization development.* Reading, MA: Addison-Wesley.

Skinner, B. F. (1948). *Walden two.* New York: Macmillan.

Skinner, B. F. (1953). *Science and human behavior.* New York: Macmillan.

Skinner, B .F. (1971). *Beyond freedom and dignity.* New York: Knopf.

Trist, E. (1960). *Socio-technical systems.* London: Tavistock Institute of Human Relations.

Trist E., & Bamforth, K. (1951). Some social and psychological consequences of the long wall method of goal-setting. *Human Relations, 4*(1), 1–8.

Vroom, V. (1964). *Work and motivation.* New York: Wiley.

Walton, R. E. (1969). *Interpersonal peacemaking: Confrontations and third-party consultation.* Reading, MA: Addison-Wesley.

CHAPTER THREE

Abrahamson, E. (2004). *Change without pain.* Boston: Harvard Business School Press.

Ackerman, L. (1986, December). Development, transition, or transformation: The question of change in organizations. *OD Practitioner,* pp. 1–8.

Alderfer, C. P. (1977). Organization development. *Annual Review of Psychology, 28,* 197–223.

Alderfer, C. P., & Berg, D. N. (1977). Organization development: The profession and the practitioner. In P. H. Mirvis & D. N. Berg (Eds.), *Failures in organization development and change* (pp. 89–110). New York: Wiley-Interscience.

Argyris, C. (1957). *Personality and organization.* New York: HarperCollins.

Argyris, C. (1962). *Interpersonal competence and organizational effectiveness.* Homewood, IL: Irwin-Dorsey.

Argyris, C. (1964). *Integrating the individual and the organization.* New York: Wiley.

Argyris, C. (1970). *Intervention theory and method: A behavioral science view.* Reading, MA: Addison-Wesley.

Argyris, C. (1974). *Behind the front page.* San Francisco: Jossey-Bass.

Argyris, C. (1982). *Reasoning, learning, and action.* San Francisco: Jossey-Bass.

Argyris, C. (1988). Crafting a theory of practice. In R. E. Quinn & K. S. Cameron (Eds.), *Paradox and transformation: Towards a theory of change in organizations and management* (pp. 255–278). Boston: Ballinger.

Argyris, C., Putnam, R., & Smith, D. (1985). *Action science.* San Francisco: Jossey-Bass.

Argyris, C., & Schön, D. (1974). *Theory in practice.* San Francisco: Jossey-Bass.

Argyris, C., & Schön, D. (1978). *Organizational learning: A theory of action perspective.* Reading, MA: Addison-Wesley.

Ayas, K., & Mirvis, P. H. (2004). Bringing mission to life: Corporate inspiration from Indian communities. *Reflections, 5*(10), 1–12.

Ayas, K., & Mirvis, P. H. (2005). Educating managers through service learning projects. In C. Wankel & R. Defillippi (Eds.), *Educating managers through real-world projects* (pp. 93–114). Greenwich, CT: IAP.

Bacon, S. (1983). *The conscious use of metaphor in Outward Bound.* Denver: Outward Bound School.

Bales, R. F. (1951). *Interaction process analysis.* Chicago: University of Chicago Press.

Barrett, F. J., Thomas, G. F., & Hocevar, S. P. (1995). The central role of discourse in large-scale change: A social construction perspective. *Journal of Applied Behavioral Science, 31,* 352–372.

Bartunek, J. M., & Louis, M. (1988). The interplay of organization development and organizational transformation. In R. Woodman & W. Pasmore (Eds.), *Research in organizational change and development* (Vol. 2, pp. 97–134). Greenwich, CT: JAI Press.

Bartunek, J. M., & Moch, M. K. (1987). First-order, second-order, and third-order change and organization development interventions: A cognitive approach. *Journal of Applied Behavioral Science, 23,* 483–500.

Bateson, G. (1972). *Steps to an ecology of the mind.* New York: Ballantine.

Bateson, G. (1979). *Mind and nature: A necessary unity.* New York: Dutton.

Beckhard, R. (1969). *Organization development: Strategies and models.* Reading, MA: Addison-Wesley.

Beckhard, R. (1972, Summer). Optimizing team-building efforts. *Journal of Contemporary Business, 1,* 23–32.

Benne, K. (1964). History of the t-group in the laboratory setting. In L. Bradford, J. Gibb, & K. Benne (Eds.), *T-group theory and laboratory method: Innovation in re-education* (pp. 80–135). New York: Wiley.

Bennis, W. G. (1964). Patterns and vicissitudes in T-group development. In L. P. Bradford, J. R. Gibb, & K. W. Benne (Eds.), *T-group theory and laboratory method* (pp. 248–278). New York: Wiley.

Bennis, W. G. (1966). *Changing organizations: Essays on the development and evolution of human organizations.* New York: McGraw-Hill.

Bennis, W. G. (1969). *Organization development: Its nature, origins, and prospects.* Reading, MA: Addison-Wesley.

Bennis, W. G., Benne, K., & Chin, R. (Eds.). (1961). *The planning of change.* Austin, TX: Holt, Rinehart and Winston.

Bennis, W. G., & Slater, P. (1968). *The temporary society.* New York: Harper-Collins.

Berlew, D. (1974, Winter). Leadership and organizational excitement. *California Management Review, 17,* pp. 21–30.

Bion, W. R. (1961). *Experiences in groups.* London: Tavistock.

Blake, R. B., & Mouton, J. S. (1976). *Consultation.* Reading, MA: Addison-Wesley.

Blumenthal, B., & Haspeslagh, P. (1994, Spring). Towards a definition of corporate transformation. *Sloan Management Review, 35*(3), 101–106.

Bohm, D. (1986). *Wholeness and the implicate order.* London: Ark.

Bohm, D. (1989). *On dialogue.* Ojai, CA: David Bohm Seminars.

Bolman, L. G., & Deal, T. E. (1995). *Leading with soul: An uncommon journey of spirit.* San Francisco: Jossey-Bass.

Bradford, D. L., & Burke, W. W. (Eds.). (2004). Is organization development in crisis? *Journal of Applied Behavioral Science, 40,* 369–373.

Bradford, L. P., Gibb, J. R., & Benne, K. W. (Eds.). (1964). *T-group theory and laboratory method.* New York: Wiley.

Brown, L. D. (Ed.). (2001). *Practice research engagement for civil society in a globalizing world.* Cambridge, MA: Harvard University Hauser Center for Nonprofit Organizations and CIVICUS: World Alliance for Citizen Participation.

Brown, L. D., & Tandon, R. (1983). Ideology and political economy in inquiry: Action research and participatory research. *Journal of Applied Behavioral Science, 19,* 277–294.

Brown, S. L., & Eisenhardt, K. M. (1998). *Competing on the edge: Strategy as structured chaos.* Boston: Harvard Business School Press.

Bunker, B., & Alban, B. (1997). *Large group intervention.* San Francisco: Jossey-Bass.

Bunker, B., & Alban, B. (2005). Introduction to the special issue on large group interventions. *Journal of Applied Behavioral Science, 41*(1), 9–14.

Bunker, B., & Seashore, E. W. (1977). *Power, collusion, intimacy-sexuality, support.* In A. Sargent (Ed.), *Beyond sex roles* (pp. 356–370). St. Paul, MN: West.

Bushe, G. R. (1995). Advances in appreciative inquiry as an organization development intervention. *Organization Development Journal, 13*(3), 14–22.

Cameron, K., Dutton, J. E., & Quinn, R. E. (Eds.). (2003). *Positive organizational scholarship: Foundations of a new discipline.* San Francisco: Berrett-Koehler.

Capra, F. (1976). *The tao of physics: An exploration of the parallels between modern physics and eastern mysticism.* Boston: Shambhala.

Capra, F. (1982). *Turning point: Science, society, and the rising culture.* New York: Bantam.

Carlson, M. (1996). *Performance.* London: Routledge.

Carnegie, D. (1936). *How to win friends and influence people.* New York: Simon & Schuster.

Chin, R., & Benne, K. D. (1969). General strategies for effecting changes in human systems. In W. G. Bennis, K. D. Benne, & R. Chin (Eds.), *The planning of change* (2nd ed., pp. 32–59). Austin, TX: Holt, Rinehart and Winston.

Churchman, C. W. (1971). *The design of inquiring systems.* New York: Basic Books.

Collins, J. (2001). *Good to great: Why some companies make the leap—and others don't.* New York: HarperBusiness.

Companies hit the road less traveled. (1995, June 5). *Business Week,* pp. 82–85.

Conger, J. A., & Associates. (1994). *Spirit at work.* San Francisco: Jossey-Bass.

Cooperrider, D. L. (1990). Positive image, positive action: The affirmative basis of organizing. In S. Srivastva & D. L. Cooperrider (Eds.), *Appreciative management and leadership* (pp. 91–125). San Francisco: Jossey-Bass.

Cooperrider, D., & Srivastva, S. (1987). Appreciative inquiry in organization life. In R. Woodman & W. Pasmore (Eds.), *Research in organizational change and development* (Vol. 1, pp. 129–168). Greenwich, CT: JAI Press.

Cox, T. H., Jr. (1993). *Cultural diversity in organizations.* San Francisco: Berrett-Koehler.

Csikszentmihalyi, M. (1990). *Flow: The psychology of optimal experience.* New York: HarperCollins.

Czarniawska, B. (1997). *Narrating the organization: Dramas of institutional identity.* Chicago: University of Chicago Press.

Dannemiller, K., & Jacobs, R. W. (1992). Changing the way organizations change: A revolution in common sense. *Journal of Applied Behavioral Science, 28,* 480–498.

Darso, L. (2004). *Artful creation: Learning tales of arts-in-business.* Copenhagen: Learning Lab Denmark.

Davies, G., & Hancock, R. (1993). Drama as a learning medium. *Management Development Review, 6*(2), 11–13.

Davis, M. K. (1998). *Change management: Not your father's OD.* Presentation to the annual conference of OD Network. Available: www.odnetwork.org.

Davis, S. M. (1984). *Managing corporate culture.* Cambridge, MA: Ballinger.

Davis, S. M. (1987). *Future perfect.* Reading, MA: Addison-Wesley.

Deal, T., & Kennedy, A. (1982). *Corporate cultures.* Reading, MA: Addison-Wesley.

de Geus, A. P. (1991, March-April). Planning as learning. *Harvard Business Review,* pp. 129–134.

Dewey, J. (1933). *How we think.* New York: Heath.

Emery, F., & Trist, E. (1973). *Towards a social ecology: Contextual appreciation of the future in the present.* London: Plenum Press.

Emery, M., & Purser, R. E. (1996). *The search conference.* San Francisco: Jossey-Bass.

Evans, P.A.L., & Doz, Y. (1992). Dualities: A paradigm for human resource and organizational development in complex organizations. In V. Pucik, N. M. Tichy, & C. K. Barnett (Eds.), *Globalizing management* (pp. 187–205). New York: Wiley.

Fisher, D., Rooke, D., & Torbert, W. R. (2000). *Personal and organizational transformations through action inquiry.* Boston: Edge/Work Press.

Forisha-Kovach, B. (1984). *The flexible organization.* Upper Saddle River, NJ: Prentice Hall.

Freire, P. (1972). *Pedagogy of the oppressed.* New York: Penguin.

French, C., Bell, W., & Zawaki, R. A. (1994). *Organization development and transformation.* Chicago: Irwin.

Frohman, M., Sashkin, M., & Kavanaugh, M. (1976). Action research as applied to organization development. *Organization and Administrative Sciences, 1,* 129–161.

Fromm, E. (1955). *The sane society.* New York: Henry Holt.

Gagliardi, P. (1996). Exploring the aesthetic side of organizational life. In S. R. Clegg, C. Hardy, & W. R. Nord (Eds.), *Handbook of organization studies* (pp. 566–580). London: Sage.

Gardner, H. (1995). *Leading minds: An anatomy of leadership.* New York: Basic Books.

Gergen, K. (1982). *Toward transformation in social knowledge.* New York: Springer-Verlag.

Gibb, S. (2004). Imagination, creativity, and HRD: An aesthetic perspective. *Human Resource Development Review, 3*(1), 53–74.

God in business. (2001, July 9). *Fortune,* p. 78.

Goffman, E. (1959). *The presentation of self in everyday life.* New York: Doubleday.

Golembiewski, R., Billingsley, K., & Yaeger, S. (1976). Measuring change and persistence in human affairs: Types of change generated by OD designs. *Journal of Applied Behavioral Science, 12,* 133–154.

Gozdz, K. (Ed.). (1996). *Community building: Renewing spirit and learning in business.* San Francisco: New Leaders Press.

Gray, B. (1989). *Collaborating: Finding common ground for multiparty problems.* San Francisco: Jossey-Bass.

Greenwood, D. J., & Levin, M. (1998). *Introduction to action research: Social research for social change.* Thousand Oaks, CA: Sage.

Greiner, L. E. (1972). Evolution and revolution as organizations grow. *Harvard Business Review, 50,* 37–46.

Guskin, A. E., & Chesler, M. A. (1973). Partisan diagnosis of social problems. In G. Zaltman (Ed.), *Process and phenomena of social change.* New York: Wiley-Interscience.

Habermas, J. (1971). *Knowledge and human interests.* Boston: Beacon Press.

Hampden-Turner, C. (1990). *Charting the corporate mind: Graphic solutions to business conflicts.* New York: Free Press.

Harman, W. (1988). *Global mind change.* New York: Warner.

Harman, W., & Hormann, J. (1990). *Creative work.* Indianapolis: Knowledge Systems.

Hatch, M. J. (1993). The dynamics of organizational culture. *Academy of Management Review, 18,* 657–693.

Hatch, M. J. (1997). Jazzing up the theory of organizational improvisation. *Advances in Strategic Management, 14,* 181–191.

Hatch, M. J., Kostera, M., & Kozminski, A. K. (2005). *The three faces of leadership: Manager, artist, priest.* London: Blackwell.

Hernes, G. (1976). Structural change in social process. *American Journal of Sociology, 82,* 513–547.

Holland, J. H. (1995). *Hidden order.* Reading, MA: Helix.

Isaacs, W. (1999). *Dialogue and the art of thinking together: A pioneering approach to communicating in business and life.* New York: Doubleday.

Isenberg, D. J. (1984, November). How senior managers think. *Harvard Business Review,* pp. 81–90.

Jantsch, E. (1980). *The self-organizing universe.* Oxford: Pergamon.

Jones, L. B. (1995). *Jesus, CEO: Using ancient wisdom for visionary leadership.* New York: Hyperion.

Kahane, A. (2004). *Solving tough problems: An open way of talking, listening, and creating new realities.* San Francisco: Berrett-Koehler.

Kanter, D. L., & Mirvis, P. H. (1989). *The cynical Americans.* San Francisco: Jossey-Bass.

Kanter, R. M. (1977). *Men and women of the corporation.* New York: Basic Books.

Kauffman, S. (1995). *At home in the universe: The search for laws of complexity.* Harmondsworth, England: Penguin.

Kegan, R., & Lahey, L. (2002). *How the way we talk can change the way we work: Seven languages for transformation.* San Francisco: Jossey-Bass.

Kelly, S., & Allison, M. A. (1999). *The complexity advantage: How the science of complexity can help your business achieve peak performance.* New York: McGraw-Hill.

Khurana, R. (2002). *Searching for a corporate savior: The irrational quest for charismatic CEOs.* Princeton, NJ: Princeton University Press.

Kiefer, C. F., & Senge, P. M. (1984). Metanoic organization. In J. Adams (Ed.), *Transforming work.* Alexandria, VA: Miles River Press.

Kiefer, C. F., & Stroh, P. (1984). A new paradigm for developing organizations. In J. Adams (Ed.), *Transforming work* (pp. 171–184). Alexandria, VA: Miles River Press.

Kilmann, R. H., & Covin, T. J. (1988). Critical issues in large-scale change. *Journal of Organizational Change Management, 1*(2), 59–72.

Koestler, A. (1964). *The act of creation.* New York: Macmillan.

Kotter, J. P. (1996). *Leading change.* Boston: Harvard Business School Press.

Kuhn, T. (1970). *The structure of scientific revolutions.* Chicago: University of Chicago Press.

Lager, F. (1994). *Ben & Jerry's: The inside scoop.* New York: Crown.

Laue, J., & Cormick, G. (1978). The ethics of intervention in community disputes. In G. Bermant, H. C. Kelman, & D. P. Warwick (Eds.), *The ethics of social intervention.* New York: Hemisphere.

Lawler, E. E. (1986). *High-involvement management.* San Francisco: Jossey-Bass.

Levy, A. (1986). *Organizational transformation: Approaches, strategies, theories.* New York: Praeger.

Lewin, K. (1935). *A dynamic theory of personality.* New York: McGraw-Hill.

Lewin, K. (1936). *Principles of topological psychology.* New York: McGraw-Hill.

Lewin, K. (1948). *Resolving social conflicts.* New York: HarperCollins.

Lindbloom, C. (1959). The science of muddling through. *Public Administration Review, 21,* 78–88.

Lippitt, R., Watson, J., & Westley, B. (1958). *The dynamics of planned change.* New York: Harcourt.

Luft, J. (1963). *Group processes.* Palo Alto, CA: Mayfield.

Lukensmeyer, C. (2005). Taking democracy to scale: Large scale interventions for citizens. *Journal of Applied Behavioral Science, 41*(1), 47–60.

Mangham, I. L., & Overington, M. A. (1987). *Organisations as theatre: A social psychology of dramatic appearances.* Chichester, England: Wiley.

Marrow, A. (1969). *The practical theorist.* New York: Basic Books.

Maslow, A. H. (1954). *Motivation and personality.* New York: HarperCollins.

Mason, R. O., & Mitroff, I. I. (1981). *Challenging strategic planning assumptions.* New York: Wiley.

Maturana, H. R., & Varela, F. J. (1987). *The tree of knowledge.* Boston: Shambhala.

McGregor, D. (1960). *The human side of enterprise.* New York: McGraw-Hill.

McTaggart, L. (2002). *The field: The quest for the secret force of the universe.* New York: HarperCollins.

Meisiek, S. (2002). Situation drama in change management. *International Journal of Arts Management, 4,* 48–55.

Meyerson, D. (2001). *Tempered radicals: How people use difference to inspire change at work.* Boston: Harvard Business School Press.

Michael, D. N. (1973). *Learning to plan and planning to learn.* San Francisco: Jossey-Bass.

Michael, D. N., & Mirvis, P. H. (1977). Changing, erring, and learning. In P. H. Mirvis & D. N. Berg (Eds.), *Failures in organization development and change* (pp. 311–334). New York: Wiley-Interscience.

Mirvis, P. H. (1980). The art of assessing the quality of work life. In E. Lawler, D. Nadler, & C. Cammann (Eds.), *Organizational assessment* (pp. 471–489). New York: Wiley.

Mirvis, P. H. (1988). Organization development: Part 1. An evolutionary perspective. In R. W. Woodman & W. A. Pasmore (Eds.), *Research in organizational change and development* (Vol. 2, pp. 1–57). Greenwich, CT: JAI Press.

Mirvis, P. H. (1990). Organization development: Part 2. A revolutionary perspective. In R. W. Woodman & W. A. Pasmore (Eds.), *Research in organizational change and development* (Vol. 4, pp. 1–66). Greenwich, CT: JAI Press.

Mirvis, P. H. (1991). Ben & Jerry's: Team development intervention (A & B). In A. Glassman & T. Cummings (Eds.), *Cases in organization development* (pp. 213–234). Homewood, IL: Irwin.

Mirvis, P. H. (1996). Historical foundations of organizational learning. *Journal of Organization Change Management, 9*(1), 13–31.

Mirvis, P. H. (1997). "Soul work" in organizations. *Organization Science, 8*(2), 193–206.

Mirvis, P. H. (1998). Practice improvisation. *Organization Science, 9,* 586–592.

Mirvis, P. H., Ayas, K., & Roth, G. (2003). *To the desert and back: The story of one of the most dramatic business transformations on record.* San Francisco: Jossey-Bass.

Mirvis, P. H., & Gunning, L. (2006). Creating a community of leaders. *Organizational Dynamics, 35*(1), 69–82.

Mitroff, I. I. (1983). *Stakeholders of the organization mind.* San Francisco: Jossey-Bass.

Mitroff, I. I., & Kilmann, R. (1978). *Methodological approaches to social science.* San Francisco: Jossey-Bass.

Morgan, G. (1993). *Imagination: The art of creative management.* Thousand Oaks, CA: Sage.

Morgan, G. (1996). *Images of organization* (2nd ed.). Thousand Oaks, CA: Sage.

Nadler, D. A., Shaw, R. B., & Walton, A. (1995). *Discontinuous change: Leading organizational transformation.* San Francisco: Jossey-Bass.

Naisbitt, J. (1982). *Megatrends.* New York: Warner Books.

Nelson, L., & Burns, F. (1984). High-performance programming: A framework for transforming organizations. In J. Adams (Ed.), *Transforming work* (pp. 226–242). Alexandria, VA: Miles River Press.

Nissley, N. (2002). Arts-based learning in management education. In B. Defillippi & C. Wankel (Eds.), *Rethinking management education in the 21st century* (pp. 27–61). Greenwich, CT: Information Age Press.

Nissley, N., Taylor, S., & Houden, L. (2004). The politics of performance in organizational theatre-based training and interviews. *Organization Studies, 25,* 817–839.

Nonaka, I. (1988, Spring). Toward middle-up-down management: Accelerating information creation. *Sloan Management Review, 29,* 9–18.

Oshry, B. (1977). *Power and position.* Boston: Power and Systems.

Oshry, B. (1995). *Seeing systems: Unlocking the mysteries of organizational life.* San Francisco: Berrett-Koehler.

Oshry, B. (1999). *Leading systems: Lessons from the power lab.* San Francisco: Berrett-Koehler.

Owen, H. (1997). *Open space technology: A user's guide.* San Francisco: Berrett-Koehler.

Pascale, R., Millemann, M., & Gioja, L. (2000). *Surfing the edge of chaos.* New York: Crown Business.

Pasmore, W. (2001). Action research in the workplace: The socio-technical perspective. In P. Reason & H. Bradbury (Eds.), *The handbook of action research: Participative inquiry and practice.* London: Sage.

Peale, N. V. (1952). *The power of positive thinking.* Upper Saddle River, NJ: Prentice Hall.

Peck, M. S. (1987). *The different drum: Community making and peace.* New York: Simon & Schuster.

Peck, M. S. (1993). *A world waiting to be born: Civility rediscovered.* New York: Bantam Books.

Peters, T. J. (1987). *Thriving on chaos: Handbook for a management revolution.* New York: Knopf.

Peters, T. J., & Austin, N. (1985). *A passion for excellence.* New York: Random House.

Peters, T. J., & Waterman, R. H., Jr. (1982). *In search of excellence.* New York: HarperCollins.

Pfeffer, J. (1981). *Power in organizations.* Marshfield, MA: Pitman.

Pine, B. J., & Gilmore, J. H. (1999). *The experience economy.* Boston: Harvard Business School Press.

Polanyi, M., Prosch, H., & Prosch, K. (1977). *Meaning.* Chicago: University of Chicago Press.

Prigogine, I. (1984). *Order out of chaos.* New York: Random House.

Prochaska, J. O., Norcross, J. C., & DiClemente, C. C. (1994). *Changing for good.* New York: Morrow.

Purser, R. E., & Pasmore, W. A. (1992). Organizing for learning. In R. W. Woodman & W. A. Pasmore (Eds.), *Research in organizational change and development* (Vol. 6, pp. 37–114). Greenwich, CT: JAI Press.

Quinn, R. E. (1988). *Beyond rational management.* San Francisco: Jossey-Bass.

Quinn, R. E. (1996). *Deep change: Discovering the leader within.* San Francisco: Jossey-Bass.

Quinn, R. E. (2000). *Change the world: How ordinary people can accomplish extraordinary things.* San Francisco: Jossey-Bass.

Quinn, R. E., & Cameron, K. S. (Eds.). (1988). *Paradox and transformation: Toward a theory of change in organization and management.* Cambridge, MA: Ballinger.

Quinn, R. E., & Kimberly, J. R. (1984). Paradox, planning, and perseverance. In J. R. Kimberly & R. E. Quinn (Eds.), *The challenge of managing corporate transitions.* Homewood, IL: Dow Jones-Irwin.

Reason, P., & Bradbury, H. (Eds.). (2001). *Handbook of action research: Participative inquiry and practice.* London: Sage.

Reason, P., & McArdle, K. L. (2006). Action research and organization development. In T. C. Cummings (Ed.), *Handbook of organization development.* Thousand Oaks, CA: Sage.

Religion in the workplace. (1999, November 1). *Business Week,* pp. 151–158.

Rice, A. K. (1969). Individual, group, and intergroup processes. *Human Relations, 22,* 565–585.

Roethlisberger, F. J., & Dickson, W. J. (1939). *Management and the worker.* Cambridge, MA: Harvard University Press.

Rogers, C. R. (1969). *Freedom to learn.* Columbus, OH: Merrill.

Rogers, E. M. (1962). *Diffusion of innovations.* New York: Free Press.

Salk, J. (1972). *Man unfolding.* New York: HarperCollins.

Schein, E. (2001). The role of art and the artist. *Reflections, 4*(2), 81–83.

Schein, E. H. (1964). The mechanisms of change. In W. G. Bennis, E. H. Schein, F. Steele, & D. Berlew (Eds.), *Interpersonal dynamics.* Homewood, IL: Dorsey.

Schein, E. H. (1965). *Organizational psychology.* Upper Saddle River, NJ: Prentice-Hill.

Schein, E. H. (1985). *Organizational culture and leadership.* San Francisco: Jossey-Bass.

Schein, E. H. (1995). Kurt Lewin's change theory in the field and in the classroom: Notes toward a model of managed learning. Available: www.solonline.edu.

Schindler-Rainman, E., & Lippitt, R. (1980). *Building the collaborative community: Mobilizing citizens for action.* Irvine, CA: University of California Press.

Schön, D. (1983). *The reflective practitioner: How professionals think in action.* New York: Basic Books.

Schutz, W. (1958). *FIRO: A three dimensional theory of interpersonal behavior.* Austin, TX: Holt, Rinehart and Winston.

Schwartz, P. (1991). *The art of the long view.* New York: Doubleday.

Seashore, S. E., Lawler, E. E., Mirvis, P. H., & Cammann, C. (1983). *Assessing organizational change.* New York: Wiley-Interscience.

Seligman, M. P., & Csikszentmihalyi, M. (2000). Positive psychology: An introduction. *American Psychologist, 55*(1), 5–14.

Senge, P. (1990). *The fifth discipline: The art and practice of the learning organization.* New York: Doubleday/Currency.

Senge, P., Kleiner, A., Roberts, C., Ross, R., Roth, G., & Smith, B. (1999). *The dance of change: The challenges to sustaining momentum in learning organizations.* New York: Doubleday.

Senge, P., Roberts, C., Ross, R., Smith, B., & Kleiner, A. (1994). *The fifth discipline fieldbook.* New York: Doubleday.

Senge, P., Scharmer, P. O., Jaworski, J., & Flowers, B. S. (2004). *Presence: Human purpose and the field of the future.* Cambridge, MA: Society for Organizational Learning.

Shaw, P. (1997). Intervening in the shadow systems of organizations: Consulting from a complexity perspective. *Journal of Organizational Change Management, 10,* 235–250.

Shephard, H. A. (1975). Rules of thumb for change agents. *Organization Development Practitioner, 7*(3), 1–5.

Shlain, L. (1991). *Art and physics: Parallel visions in space, time and light.* New York: Morrow.

Smith, K. K. (1977). An intergroup perspective on individual behavior. In J. R. Hackman, E. E. Lawler, & L. W. Porter (Eds.), *Perspective on behavior in organizations.* New York: McGraw-Hill.

Smith, K. K. (1982a). Philosophical problems in thinking about organizational change. In P. S. Goodman & Associates (Eds.), *Change in organizations.* San Francisco: Jossey-Bass.

Smith, K. K. (1982b). *Groups in conflict.* Dubuque, IA: Kendall/Hunt.

Smith, K. K., & Berg, D. N. (1987). *Paradoxes of group life.* San Francisco: Jossey-Bass.

Stacey, R. (1996). *Complexity and creativity in organizations.* San Francisco: Berrett-Koehler.

Stent, G. S. (1972). Prematurity and uniqueness in scientific discovery. *Scientific American, 227,* 84–93.

Strati, A. (1992). Aesthetic understanding of organizational life. *Academy of Management Review, 17,* 568–581.

Susman, G., & Evered, R. (1978). An assessment of the scientific merits of action research. *Administrative Science Quarterly, 23,* 582–603.

Talbot, M. (1986). *Beyond the quantum.* New York: Bantam Books.

Tannenbaum, R., & Davis, S. (1969). Values, man, and organizations. *Industrial Management Review, 10,* 67–83.

Taylor, F. W. (1911). *The principles of scientific management.* New York: Norton.

Taylor, S., & Hansen, H. (2005). Finding form: Looking at the field of organizational aesthetics. *Journal of Management Studies, 42,* 1211–1231.

Tetenbaum, T. J. (1998, Spring). Shifting paradigms: From Newton to chaos. *Organizational Dynamics, 26,* 21–32.

Thomas, D. A., & Ely, R. J. (1996). Making differences matter. *Harvard Business Review, 74*(5), 79–90.

Thompson, V. (1976). Dramaturgy: The dramatical aspect of organizations. In J. E. Combs, & M. W. Mansfield (Eds.), *Drama in life* (pp. 329–337). New York: Hastings House.

Tichy, N. M., & Cardwell, N. (2002). *The cycle of leadership: How great leaders teach their companies to win.* New York: HarperBusiness.

Tichy, N. M., & Cohen, E. (1997). *The leadership engine: How winning companies build leaders at every level.* New York: HarperInformation.

Tichy, N. M., & Devanna, M. A. (1986). *The transformational leader.* New York: Wiley.

Tichy, N. M., & Sherman, S. (1993). *Control your destiny or someone else will.* New York: Doubleday/Currency.

Torbert, W. (1978). Empirical, behavioral, theoretical, and attentional skills necessary for collaborative inquiry. In R. Reason, & P. Rowan (Eds.), *Human inquiry: A sourcebook of new paradigm research*. London: Wiley.

Torbert, W. (1987). *Managing the corporate dream: Restructuring for long term success*. Homewood, IL: Dow Jones-Irwin.

Torbert, W. (1989). Leading organization transformation. In R. W. Woodman & W. A. Pasmore (Eds.), *Research in Organizational Change and Development* (Vol. 3, pp. 83–116). Greenwich, CT: JAI Press.

Torbert, W. (1991). *The power of balance: Transforming self, society, and scientific inquiry*. Thousand Oaks, CA: Sage.

Toulmin, S., & Gustavsen, B. (Eds.). (1996). *Beyond theory: Changing organizations through participation*. Amsterdam: John Benjamins.

Trist, E. (1979). New directions of hope: Recent innovations interconnecting organizational, industrial, community and personal development. *Regional Studies, 13*, 439–451.

Trist, E. (1981). *The evolution of socio-technical systems: A conceptual framework and action research program*. Toronto: Ontario Quality of Work Life Centre.

Turner, V. (1957). *Schism and continuity*. Manchester, England: Manchester University Press.

Vaill, P. B. (1982, Autumn). The purposing of high performing systems. *Organizational Dynamics, 111*, 23–39.

Vaill, P. B. (1984). Process wisdom in a new age. In J. Adams (Ed.), *Transforming work*. Alexandria, VA: Miles River Press.

Vaill, P. B. (1989). *Managing as a performing art: New ideas for a world of chaotic change*. San Francisco: Jossey-Bass.

Vaill, P. B. (1996). *Learning as a way of being*. San Francisco: Jossey-Bass.

Varela, F. J. (1976, Fall). Not one, not two. *Coevolution Quarterly, 12*, 62–67.

Vickers, G. (1965). *The art of judgment*. London: Chapman & Hall.

Wallace, A.F.C. (1956). Revitalization movement. *American Anthropologist, 22*, 264–281.

Walton, R. E., & Warwick, D. P. (1973). The ethics of organization development. *Journal of Applied Behavioral Science, 6*, 681–698.

Watkins, K. E., & Marsick, V. J. (1993). *Sculpting the learning organization: Lessons in the art and science of systemic change*. San Francisco: Jossey-Bass.

Watzlawick, P., Weakland, J., & Fisch, R. (1974). *Change: Principles of problem formation and problem resolution*. New York: Norton.

Weisbord, M. (1987). *Productive workplaces*. San Francisco: Jossey-Bass.

Weisbord, M. (1992). *Discovering common ground.* San Francisco: Berrett-Koehler.

Weisbord, M., & Janoff, F. (1995). *Future search: Finding common ground for action in organizations and communities.* San Francisco: Berrett-Koehler.

Wenger, E., McDermott, R., & Snyder, W. (2000). *Cultivating communities of practice.* Boston: Harvard Business School Press.

Wheatley, M. J. (1993). *Leadership and the new science: Learning about organization from an orderly universe.* San Francisco: Berrett-Koehler.

Wheatley, M. J., & Kellner-Rogers, M. (1996). *A simpler way.* San Francisco: Berrett-Koehler.

Whitney, D. (1995). *Spirituality as a global organizing potential.* Paper delivered at the Organizational Dimensions of Global Change conference. Cleveland: Case Western Reserve University.

Whyte, D. (1994). *The heart aroused: Poetry and the preservation of the soul in corporate America.* New York: Currency.

Whyte, W. H., Jr. (1956). *The organization man.* New York: Doubleday.

Wilber, K. (1984). *Quantum questions.* Boston: Shambhala.

Worley, C. G., & Feyerherm, A. E. (2003). Reflections on the future of organization development. *Journal of Applied Behavioral Science, 39*(2), 97–115.

Wuthnow, R. (1991). *Acts of compassion: Caring for others and helping ourselves.* Princeton, NJ: Princeton University Press.

Zander, R. S., & Zander, B. (2000). *The art of possibility.* Boston: Harvard Business School Press.

CHAPTER FOUR

Amabile, T. M., Conti, R., Coon, H., Lazenby, J., & Herron, M. (1996). Assessing the work environment for creativity. *Academy of Management Journal, 39,* 1154–1184.

Amburgey, T. L., Kelly, D., & Barnett, W. P. (1993). Resetting the clock: The dynamics of organizational change and failure. *Administrative Science Quarterly, 38,* 51–73.

Amburgey, T. L., & Miner, A. S. (1992). Strategic momentum: The effects of repetitive, positional, and contextual momentum on merger activity. *Strategic Management Journal, 13,* 335–348.

Argyris, C., Putnam, R., & Smith, D. M. (1985). *Action science: Concepts, methods and skills for research and intervention.* San Francisco: Jossey-Bass.

Argyris, C., & Schön, D. (1974). *Theory in practice: Increasing professional effectiveness.* San Francisco: Jossey-Bass.

Argyris, C., & Schön, D. (1978). *Organizational learning: A theory of action perspective.* Reading, MA: Addison-Wesley.

Armenakis, A. A., & Bedeian, A. G. (1999). Organizational change: A review of theory and research in the 1990s. *Journal of Management, 25,* 293–315.

Austin, J. R. (1997). A method for facilitating controversial social change in organizations: Branch Rickey and the Brooklyn Dodgers. *Journal of Applied Behavioral Science, 33*(1), 101–118.

Babüroglu, O., Topkaya, S., & Ates, O. (1996). Post-search follow-up: Assessing search conference based interventions in two different industries in Turkey. *Concepts and Transformation, 1,* 31–50.

Bacharach, S. B., Bamberger, P., & Sonnenstuhl, W. J. (1996). The organizational transformation process: The micropolitics of dissonance reduction and the alignment of logics of action. *Administrative Science Quarterly, 41*(3), 477–506.

Barley, S. J., & Tolbert, P. S. (1997). Institutionalization and structuration: Studying the links between action and institution. *Organization Studies, 18,* 93–117.

Barr, P. S., Stimpert, J. L., & Huff, A. S. (1992). Cognitive change, strategic action, and organizational renewal. *Strategic Management Journal, 27,* 489–510.

Barrett, F. J. (1995). Creating appreciative learning cultures. *Organizational Dynamics, 24,* 36–49.

Barrett, F. J., & Peterson, R. (2000). Appreciative learning cultures: Developing competencies for global organizing. *Organization Development Journal, 18*(2), 10–21.

Barrett, F. J., Thomas, G. F., & Hocevar, S. P. (1995). The central role of discourse in large-scale change: A social construction perspective. *Journal of Applied Behavioral Science, 31,* 352–372.

Barry, D. (1997). Telling changes: From narrative family therapy to organizational change and development. *Journal of Organizational Change Management, 10*(1), 30–46.

Bartunek, J. M. (1983). How organization development can develop organizational theory. *Group and Organization Studies, 8,* 303–318.

Bartunek, J. M. (1984). Changing interpretive schemes and organizational restructuring: The example of a religious order. *Administrative Science Quarterly, 36,* 187–218.

Bartunek, J. M., Foster-Fishman, P., & Keys, C. (1996). Using collaborative advocacy to foster intergroup collaboration: A joint insider/outsider investigation. *Human Relations, 49,* 701–732.

Bartunek, J. M., Krim, R., Necochea, R., & Humphries, M. (1999). Sense-making, sensegiving, and leadership in strategic organizational development. In J. Wagner (Ed.), *Advances in qualitative organizational research* (Vol. 4, pp. 37–71). Greenwich: JAI Press.

Bartunek, J. M., & Louis, M. R. (1996). *Insider-outsider team research.* Thousand Oaks, CA: Sage.

Bartunek, J. M., Walsh, K., & Lacey, C. A. (2000). Dynamics and dilemmas of women leading women. *Organization Science, 11,* 589–610.

Bass, B. M. (1985). *Leadership and performance beyond expectations.* New York: Free Press.

Bass, B. M., & Avolio, B. J. (1994). *Improving organizational effectiveness through transformational leadership.* Thousand Oaks, CA: Sage.

Bate, P., Khan, R., & Pye, A. (2000). Towards a culturally sensitive approach to organization structuring: Where organization design meets organization development. *Organization Science, 11*(2), 197–211.

Baxter, L. A., & Montgomery, B. M. (1996). *Relating: Dialogues and dialectics.* New York: Guilford Press.

Beer, M., & Nohria, N. (2000). Breaking the code of change. *Harvard Business Review, 78*(3), 122–141.

Bennis, W. G. (1966). *Changing organizations.* New York: McGraw-Hill.

Berger, P., & Luckmann, T. (1966). *The social construction of reality.* New York: Anchor Books.

Block, P. (1987). *The empowered manager: Positive political skills at work.* San Francisco: Jossey-Bass.

Bloodgood, J. M., & Morrow, J. L. (2000). Strategic organizational change within an institutional framework. *Journal of Managerial Issues, 12*(2), 208–226.

Boje, D. (1991). The storytelling organization: A study of story performance in an office-supply firm. *Administrative Science Quarterly, 36*(1), 106–126.

Bowen, D. E., & Lawler, E. E. (1992, Spring). The empowerment of service workers: What, why, how, and when. *Sloan Management Review,* pp. 31–39.

Boyce, M. E. (1995). Collective centering and collective sensemaking in the stories of one organization. *Organization Studies, 16*(1), 107–137.

Bradbury, H., & Clair, J. (1999). Promoting sustainable organizations with Sweden's natural step. *Academy of Management Executive, 13*(4), 63–74.

Brown, J. S., & Duguid, P. (1991). Organizational learning and communities-of-practice: Toward a unified view of working, learning, and innovation. *Organization Science, 2,* 40–57.

Brown, J. S., & Duguid, P. (1999). Organizing knowledge. *Reflections: The Sol Journal, 1*(2), 28–42.

Brown, S. L., & Eisenhardt, K. M. (1997). The art of continuous change: Linking complexity theory and time-paced evolution in relentlessly shifting organizations. *Administrative Science Quarterly, 42,* 1–34.

Brulin, G. (1998). The new task of Swedish universities: Knowledge formation in interactive cooperation with practitioners. *Concepts and Transformation, 3,* 113–128.

Bunker, B. B., & Alban, B. T. (1997). *Large group interventions.* San Francisco: Jossey-Bass.

Bushe, C., & Coetzer, G. (1995). Appreciative inquiry as a team development intervention. *Journal of Applied Behavioral Science, 31,* 13–30.

Cameron, K. S., & Quinn, R. E. (1999). *Diagnosing and changing organizational culture.* Reading, MA: Addison-Wesley.

Church, A. H., & Burke, W. W. (1995). Practitioner attitudes about the field of organization development. In W. A. Pasmore & R. W. Woodman (Eds.), *Research in organization development and change* (Vol. 8, pp. 1–46). Greenwich, CT: JAI Press.

Church, A. H., Waclawski, J., & Seigel, W. (1999). Will the real O.D. practitioner please stand up? *Organization Development Journal, 17*(2), 49–59.

Coghlan, D. (2001). Insider action research projects: Implications for practising managers. *Management Learning, 32,* 49–60.

Coghlan, D., & Brannick, T. (2001). *Doing action research in your own organization.* London: Sage.

Collier, J. (1945). United States Indian Administration as a laboratory of ethnic relations. *Social Research, 12,* 275–276.

Cook, S.D.N., & Brown, J. S. (1999). Bridging epistemologies: The generative dance between organizational knowledge and organizational knowing. *Organization Science, 10,* 381–400.

Cooper, D., Hinings, B., Greenwood, R., & Brown, J. (1996). Sedimentation and transformation in organizational change: The case of Canadian law firms. *Organization Studies, 17,* 623–647.

Cooperrider, D. L. (1997). Resources for getting appreciative inquiry started: An example OD proposal. *OD Practitioner, 28*(1), 28–33.

Cooperrider, D. L., & Srivastva, S. (1987). Appreciative inquiry in organizational life. In R. W. Woodman & W. A. Pasmore (Eds.), *Research in organization development* (Vol. 1, pp. 129–169). Greenwich, CT: JAI Press.

Creed, W.E.D., Scully, M., & Austin, J. R. (forthcoming). Clothes make the person? The tailoring of legitimating accounts and the social construction of identity. *Organization Science.*

Cummings, T., & Worley, C. (2000). *Organization development and change* (7th ed.). Cincinnati: Southwestern College Publishing.

Czarniawska, B., & Joerges, B. (1996). Travel of ideas. In B. Czarniawska & G. Sevon (Eds.), *Translating organizational change* (pp. 13–48). New York: Walter De Gruyter.

D'Aunno, T., Sutton, R. I., & Price, R. H. (1991). Isomorphism and external support in conflicting institutional environments: A study of drug abuse treatment units. *Academy of Management Journal, 34,* 636–661.

Denison, D. R., Hooijberg, R., & Quinn, R. E. (1995). Paradox and performance: Toward a theory of behavioral complexity in managerial leadership. *Organization Science, 6*(5), 524–540.

Dent, E. B., & Goldberg, S. G. (1999). Challenging resistance to change. *Journal of Applied Behavioral Science, 35,* 25–41.

DiMaggio, P. J., & Powell, W. W. (1991). The iron cage revisited: Institutional isomorphism and collective rationality in organizational fields. In W. W. Powell & P. J. DiMaggio (Eds.), *The new institution in organizational analysis* (pp. 63–82). Chicago: University of Chicago Press.

Doz, Y. L., & Prahalad, C. K. (1987). A process model of strategic redirection in large complex firms: The case of multinational corporations. In A. Pettigrew (Ed.), *The management of strategic change* (pp. 63–83). Oxford, UK: Blackwell.

Drazin, R., Glynn, M. A., & Kazanjian, R. K. (1999). Multilevel theorizing about creativity in organizations: A sensemaking perspective. *Academy of Management Review, 24,* 286–307.

Drazin, R., & Schoonhoven, C. B. (1996). Community, population, and organization effects on innovation: A multi-level perspective. *Academy of Management Journal, 39,* 1065–1083.

Dutton, J. E., & Dukerich, J. M. (1991). Keeping an eye on the mirror: Image and identity in organizational adaptation. *Academy of Management Journal, 34,* 517–554.

Dyck, B., & Starke, F. A. (1999). The formation of breakaway organizations: Observations and a process model. *Administrative Science Quarterly, 44*(4), 792–822.

Easterby-Smith, M. (1997). Disciplines of organizational learning: Contributions and critiques. *Human Relations, 50,* 1085–1113.

Ehin, C. (1995). The quest for empowering organizations: Some lessons from our foraging past. *Organization Science, 6,* 666–670.

Eisenhardt, K. M., & Brown, S. L. (1998a). Time pacing: Competing in markets that won't stand still. *Harvard Business Review, 76*(2), 59–69.

Eisenhardt, K. M., & Brown, S. L. (1998b). *Competing on the edge: Strategy as structured chaos.* Cambridge, MA: Harvard Business School Press.

Elsbach, K. D., & Sutton, R. I. (1992). Acquiring organizational legitimacy through illegitimate actions: A marriage of institutional and impression management theories. *Academy of Management Journal, 35,* 699–738.

Emery, F., & Trist, E. (1973). *Towards a social ecology.* New York: Plenum.

Emery, M. (1996). The influence of culture in search conferences. *Concepts and Transformation, 1,* 143–164.

Emery, M., & Purser, R. (1996). *The search conference.* San Francisco: Jossey-Bass.

Faber, B. (1998). Toward a rhetoric of change: Reconstructing image and narrative in distressed organizations. *Journal of Business and Technical Communication, 12*(2), 217–237.

Feldman, M. S. (2000). Organizational routines as a source of continuous change. *Organization Science, 11,* 611–629.

Filipczak, B. (1995, September). Critical mass: Putting whole systems thinking into practice. *Training,* pp. 33–41.

Fligstein, N. (1991). The structural transformation of American industry: An institutional account of the causes of diversification in the largest firms, 1919–1979. In W. W. Powell & P. J. DiMaggio (Eds.), *The new institution in organizational analysis* (pp. 311–336). Chicago: University of Chicago Press.

Fligstein, N. (1997). Social skill and institutional theory. *American Behavioral Scientist, 40*(4), 397–405.

Fombrun, C. J., & Ginsberg, A. (1990). Shifting gears: Enabling change in corporate aggressiveness. *Strategic Management Journal, 11,* 297–308.

Ford, C. M. (1996). A theory of individual creative action in multiple social domains. *Academy of Management Review, 21,* 1112–1142.

Ford, J. D. (1999a). Conversations and the epidemiology of change. In W. A. Pasmore & R. W. Woodman (Eds.), *Research in organizational change and development* (Vol. 12, pp. 1–39). Greenwich, CT: JAI Press.

Ford, J. D. (1999b). Organizational change as shifting conversations. *Journal of Organizational Change Management, 12,* 480–500.

Ford, J. D., & Ford, L. W. (1995). The role of conversations in producing intentional change in organizations. *Academy of Management Review, 20,* 541–570.

Foster, P. C. (2000, August). *Action learning and institutional change processes.* Paper presented at the Annual Academy of Management Meeting, Toronto, Ontario, Canada.

French, W. L., & Bell, C. H. (1999). *Organization Development* (6th ed.). Englewood Cliffs, NJ: Prentice-Hall.

Frost, P., & Egri, C. (1994). The shamanic perspective on organizational change and development. *Journal of Organizational Change Management, 7,* 7–23.

Garvin, D. A. (1993, July-August). Building a learning organization. *Harvard Business Review,* pp. 78–91.

Geertz, C. (1983). *Local knowledge: Further essays in interpretive anthropology.* New York: Basic Books.

Gergen, K., & Thatchenkery, T. (1996). Organization science as social construction: Postmodern potentials. *Journal of Applied Behavioral Science, 32,* 356–377.

Gersick, C.J.G. (1991). Revolutionary change theories: A multi-level exploration of the punctuated equilibrium paradigm. *Academy of Management Review, 16,* 10–36.

Giddens, A. (1984). *The constitution of society.* Berkeley: University of California Press.

Gilmore, T., Shea, G., & Useem, M. (1997). Side effects of corporate cultural transformations. *Journal of Applied Behavioral Science, 33,* 174–189.

Gioia, D. A., & Chittipeddi, K. (1991). Sensemaking and sensegiving in strategic change initiation. *Strategic Management Journal, 12,* 433–448.

Glynn, M. A. (1996). Innovative genius: A framework for relating individual and organizational intelligences to innovation. *Academy of Management Review, 21,* 1081–1111.

Golembiewski, R. T. (1998). Appreciating appreciative inquiry: Diagnosis and perspectives on how to do better. In R. W. Woodman & W. A. Pasmore (Eds.), *Research in organizational change and development* (Vol. 11, pp. 1–45). Greenwich, CT: JAI Press.

Greenwood, R., & Hinings, C. R. (1993). Understanding strategic change: The contributions of archetypes. *Academy of Management Journal, 36,* 1052–1081.

Greenwood, R., & Hinings, C. R. (1996). Understanding radical organizational change: Bringing together the old and the new institutionalism. *Academy of Management Review, 21*(4), 1022–1054.

Greiner, L. (1972, July-August). Evolution and revolution as organizations grow. *Harvard Business Review,* 37–46.

Greve, H. R. (1998). Managerial cognition and the mimetic adoption of market positions: What you see is what you do. *Strategic Management Journal, 19,* 967–988.

Hanks, S., Watson, C., Jansen, E., & Chandler, G. (1994). Tightening the life cycle construct: A taxonomic study of growth stage configurations in high-technology organizations. *Entrepreneurship Theory and Practice, 18,* 5–29.

Hannan, M. T., & Freeman, J. (1984). Structural inertia and organizational change. *American Sociological Review, 49,* 149–164.

Hardy, C., & Leiba-O'Sullivan, S. (1998). The power behind empowerment: Implications for research and practice. *Human Relations, 51,* 451–483.

Harrison, R. (1970). Choosing the depth of organizational intervention. *Journal of Applied Behavioral Science, 6,* 181–202.

Hazen, M. (1994). Multiplicity and change in persons and organizations. *Journal of Organizational Change Management, 6,* 72–81.

Head, T. C. (2000). Appreciative inquiry: Debunking the mythology behind resistance to change. *OD Practitioner, 32*(1), 27–32.

Holman, P., & Devane, T. (Eds.). (1999). *The change handbook: Group methods for shaping the future.* San Francisco: Berrett-Koehler.

Hooijberg, R., Hunt, J. G., & Dodge, G. (1997). Leadership complexity and development of the leaderplex model. *Journal of Management, 23,* 375–408.

Jansen, K. J. (2000, August). *A longitudinal examination of momentum during culture change.* Paper presented at the Annual Academy of Management Meeting, Toronto, Ontario, Canada.

Jelinek, M., & Litterer, J. A. (1988). Why OD must become strategic. In W. A. Pasmore & R. W. Woodman (Eds.), *Research in organizational change and development* (Vol. 2, pp. 135–162). Greenwich, CT: JAI Press.

Jick, T. D. (1995). Accelerating change for competitive advantage. *Organizational Dynamics, 24*(1), 77–82.

Johnson, G., Smith, S., & Codling, B. (2000). Microprocesses of institutional change in the context of privatization. *Academy of Management Review, 25,* 572–580.

Katzenbach, J. R. (1996). Real change leaders. *McKinsey Quarterly, 1,* 148–163.

Kelly, D., & Amburgey, T. L. (1991). Organizational inertia and momentum: A dynamic model of strategic change. *Academy of Management Journal, 34,* 591–612.

Kimberly, J. R., & Bouchikhi, J. (1995). The dynamics of organizational development and change: How the past shapes the present and constrains the future. *Organization Science, 6,* 9–18.

Kleiner, A., & Roth, G. (1997). How to make experience your company's best teacher. *Harvard Business Review, 75*(5), 172–177.

Kleiner, A., & Roth, G. (2000). *Oil change: Perspectives on corporate transformation.* New York: Oxford University Press.

Kostera, M., & Wicha, M. (1996). The "divided self" of Polish state-owned enterprises: The culture of organizing. *Organization Studies, 17*(1), 83–105.

Kotter, J. P. (1995). Leading change: Why transformation efforts fail. *Harvard Business Review, 73*(2), 59–67.

Kuwada, K. (1998). Strategic learning: The continuous side of discontinuous strategic change. *Organization Science, 9,* 719–736.

Labianca, G., Gray, B., & Brass, D. J. (2000). A grounded model of organizational schema change during empowerment. *Organization Science, 11,* 235–257.

Laughlin, R. C. (1991). Environmental disturbances and organizational transitions and transformations: Some alternative models. *Organization Studies, 12,* 209–232.

Levitt, B., & March, J. G. (1988). Organizational learning. *Annual Review of Psychology, 14,* 319–340.

Lewin, K. (1951). *Field theory in social science.* New York: Harper & Row.

Lichtenstein, B. B. (2000a). Self-organized transition: A pattern amid the chaos of transformative change. *Academy of Management Executive, 14*(4), 128–141.

Lichtenstein, B. B. (2000b). Emergence as a process of self-organizing: New assumptions and insights from the study of non-linear dynamic systems. *Journal of Organizational Change Management, 13,* 526–544.

Lippitt, R. (1980). *Choosing the future you prefer.* Washington, DC: Development Publishers.

Lipshitz, R., Popper, M., & Oz, S. (1996). Building learning organizations: The design and implementation of organizational learning mechanisms. *Journal of Applied Behavioral Science, 32,* 292–305.

Louis, M. R., & Sutton, R. I. (1991). Switching cognitive gears: From habits of mind to active thinking. *Human Relations, 44,* 55–76.

Mantel, J. M., & Ludema, J. D. (2000). From local conversations to global change: Experiencing the Worldwide Web effect of appreciative inquiry. *Organization Development Journal, 18*(2), 42–53.

Marks, M. L., & Mirvis, P. H. (2001). Making mergers and acquisitions work: Strategic and psychological preparation. *Academy of Management Executive, 15*(2), 80–92.

Meyer, J. W., & Rowan, B. (1977). Institutionalized organizations: Formal structure as myth and ceremony. *American Journal of Sociology, 82*, 340–363.

Mezias, S. J., & Glynn, M. A. (1993). The three faces of corporate renewal: Institution, revolution, and evolution. *Strategic Management Journal, 14*, 77–101.

Miller, D. (1996). A preliminary typology of organizational learning: Synthesizing the literature. *Journal of Management, 22*, 485–505.

Mirvis, P. H. (1988). Organizational development: Pt. 1. An evolutionary perspective. In W. A. Pasmore & R. W. Woodman (Eds.), *Research in organizational change and development* (Vol. 2, pp. 1–57). Greenwich, CT: JAI Press.

Mirvis, P. H. (1990). Organizational development: Pt. 2. A revolutionary perspective. In W. A. Pasmore & R. W. Woodman (Eds.), *Research in organizational change and development* (Vol. 4, pp. 1–66). Greenwich, CT: JAI Press.

Mitchell, T. R., & Beach, L. R. (1990). ". . . Do I love thee? Let me count . . ." toward an understanding of intuitive and automatic decision making. *Organizational Behavior and Human Decision Processes, 47*, 1–20.

Mohrman, S., Cohen, S., & Mohrman, A. (1995). *Designing team-based organizations.* San Francisco: Jossey-Bass.

Nadler, D. A., Shaw, R. B., & Walton, A. E. (1995). *Discontinuous change: Leading organizational transformation.* San Francisco: Jossey-Bass.

Nadler, D. A., & Tushman, M. L. (1989). Organizational frame bending: Principles for managing reorientation. *Academy of Management Executive, 3*, 194–204.

Nelson, R. R., & Winter, S. G. (1982). *An evolutionary theory of economic change.* Cambridge, MA: Belknap Press.

Neumann, J. E. (1989). Why people don't participate in organizational change. In R. W. Woodman & W. A. Pasmore (Eds.), *Research in organizational change and development* (Vol. 3, pp. 181–212). Greenwich, CT: JAI Press.

Nevis, E. C., DiBella, A. J., & Gould, J. M. (1995, Winter). Understanding organizations as learning systems. *Sloan Management Review, 36*, 73–85.

Nielsen, R. P. (1996). *The politics of ethics.* New York: Oxford University Press.

North, D. C. (1990). *Institutions, institutional change and economic performance.* New York: Cambridge University Press.

Nutt, P. C., & Backoff, R. W. (1997). Transforming organizations with second-order change. In W. A. Pasmore & R. W. Woodman (Eds.), *Research in organizational change and development* (Vol. 10, pp. 229–274). Greenwich, CT: JAI Press.

O'Connor, E. S. (2000). Plotting the organization: The embedded narrative as a construct for studying change. *Journal of Applied Behavioral Science, 36,* 174–192.

Oldham, G. R., & Cummings, A. (1996). Employee creativity: Personal and contextual factors at work. *Academy of Management Journal, 39,* 607–634.

Oliver, C. (1991). Strategic responses to institutional processes. *Academy of Management Review, 16,* 145–179.

Orlikowski, W. J., & Hofman, D. J. (1997). An improvisational model for change management: The case of groupware technologies. *Sloan Management Review, 38*(2), 11–21.

Pasmore, W. A., & Friedlander, F. (1982). An action-research program for increasing employee involvement in problem solving. *Administrative Science Quarterly, 27,* 343–362.

Porras, J. I., & Robertson, P. J. (1987). Organization development theory: A typology and evaluation. In R. W. Woodman & W. A. Pasmore (Eds.), *Research in organizational change and development* (Vol. 1, pp. 1–57). Greenwich, CT: JAI Press.

Porras, J. I., & Robertson, P. J. (1992). Organizational development: Theory, practice, research. In M. D. Dunnette & L. M. Hough (Eds.), *Handbook of organizational psychology* (Vol. 3, pp. 719–822). Palo Alto, CA: Psychology Press.

Quinn, R. E., & Cameron, K. (1983). Organizational life cycles and the shifting criteria of effectiveness. *Management Science, 29,* 33–51.

Quinn, R. E., & Cameron, K. S. (1988). *Paradox and transformation: Toward a theory of change in organization and management.* Cambridge, MA: Ballinger.

Quinn, R. E., Spreitzer, G. M., & Brown, M. V. (2000). Changing others through changing ourselves: The transformation of human systems. *Journal of Management Inquiry, 9,* 147–164.

Raelin, J. A. (1997). Action learning and action science: Are they different? *Organizational Dynamics, 26*(1), 21–44.

Rainey, M. A. (1996). An appreciative inquiry into the factors of cultural continuity during leadership transition. *OD Practitioner, 28*(1), 34–42.

Rajagopalan, N., & Spreitzer, G. M. (1996). Toward a theory of strategic change: A multi-lens perspective and integrative framework. *Academy of Management Review, 22,* 48–79.

Rapoport, R. N. (1970). Three dilemmas in action research. *Human Relations, 23,* 488–513.

Reason, P. (1999). Integrating action and reflection through cooperative inquiry. *Management Learning, 30,* 207–226.

Reger, R. K., Gustafson, L. T., DeMarie, S. M., & Mullane, J. V. (1994). Reframing the organization: Why implementing total quality is easier said than done. *Academy of Management Review, 19,* 565–584.

Revans, R. (1980). *Action Learning.* London: Blond and Briggs.

Rooke, D., & Torbert, W. R. (1998). Organizational transformation as a function of CEO's developmental stage. *Organization Development Journal, 16,* 11–28.

Roth, G., & Kleiner, A. (2000). *Car launch: The human side of managing change.* New York: Oxford University Press.

Rynes, S. L., Bartunek, J. M., & Daft, R. L. (2001). Across the great divide: Knowledge creation and transfer between practitioners and academics. *Academy of Management Journal, 44,* 340–356.

Sastry, M. A. (1997). Problems and paradoxes in a model of punctuated organizational change. *Administrative Science Quarterly, 42,* 237–275.

Schmuck, R. A., Runkel, P. J., Saturen, S. L., Martell, R. T., & Derr, C. B. (1972). *Handbook of organization development in schools.* Palo Alto, CA: National Press Books.

Senge, P. (1990). *The fifth discipline: The art and practice of the learning organization.* New York: Doubleday/Currency.

Senge, P., Kleiner, A., Roberts, C., Ross, R., & Smith, B. (1994). *The fifth discipline fieldbook: Strategies for building a learning organization.* New York: Doubleday/Currency.

Senge, P., Kleiner, A., Roberts, C., Roth, G., Ross, R., & Smith, B. (1999). *The dance of change: The challenges to sustaining momentum in learning organizations.* New York: Doubleday/Currency.

Seo, M., Putnam, L., & Bartunek, J. M. (2001). *Tensions and contradictions of planned organizational change.* Unpublished manuscript, Chestnut Hill, MA: Boston College.

Simons, R. (1994). How new top managers use control systems as levers of strategic renewal. *Strategic Management Journal, 15,* 169–189.

Sorenson, P. F., Yaeger, T. F., & Nicoll, D. (2000). Appreciative inquiry 2000: Fad or important new focus for OD? *OD Practitioner, 32*(1), 3–5.

Spreitzer, G. M. (1996). Social structural characteristics of psychological empowerment. *Academy of Management Journal, 39,* 483–504.

Spreitzer, G. M., & Quinn, R. E. (1996). Empowering middle managers to be transformational leaders. *Journal of Applied Behavioral Science, 32,* 237–261.

Srivastva, S., & Cooperrider, D. L. (1999). *Appreciative management and leadership* (Rev. ed.). Euclid, OH: Williams Custom Publishing.

Suchman, M. (1995). Managing legitimacy: Strategic and institutional approaches. *Academy of Management Review, 20,* 571–610.

Tenkasi, R. V. (2000). The dynamics of cultural knowledge and learning in creating viable theories of global change and action. *Organization Development Journal, 18*(2), 74–90.

Thomas, K. W., & Velthouse, B. A. (1990). Cognitive elements of empowerment: An "interpretive" model of intrinsic task motivation. *Academy of Management Review, 15,* 666–681.

Tichy, N. M., & Devanna, M. A. (1986). *The transformational leader.* New York: Wiley.

Torbert, W. R. (1989). Leading organizational transformation. In R. W. Woodman & W. A. Pasmore (Eds.), *Research in organizational change and development* (Vol. 3, pp. 83–116). Greenwich, CT: JAI Press.

Torbert, W. R. (1991). *The power of balance: Transforming self, society, and scientific inquiry.* Newbury Park, CA: Sage.

Torbert, W. R. (1999). The distinctive questions developmental action inquiry asks. *Management Learning, 30,* 189–206.

Tsang, E.W.K. (1997). Organizational learning and the learning organization. *Human Relations, 50,* 73–89.

Tushman, M. L., & Romanelli, E. (1985). Organizational evolution: A metamorphosis model of convergence and reorientation. In L. Cummings & B. M. Staw (Eds.), *Research in organizational behavior* (Vol. 7, pp. 171–222). Greenwich, CT: JAI Press.

Van de Ven, A. H., & Poole, M. S. (1995). Explaining development and change in organizations. *Academy of Management Review, 20,* 510–540.

Watkins, K. E., & Marsick, V. J. (1994). *Sculpting the learning organization.* San Francisco: Jossey-Bass.

Watzlawick, P., Weakland, J. H., & Fisch, R. (1974). *Change: Principles of problem formation and problem resolution.* New York: W. W. Norton.

Weber, P. S., & Manning, M. R. (1998). A comparative framework for large group organizational change interventions. In R. W. Woodman & W. A. Pasmore (Eds.), *Research in organizational change and development* (Vol. 11, pp. 225–252). Greenwich, CT: JAI Press.

Weick, K. (1979). *The social psychology of organizing* (2nd ed.). Reading, MA: Addison-Wesley.

Weick, K. (1995). *Sensemaking in organizations.* Thousand Oaks, CA: Sage.

Weick, K., & Quinn, R. E. (1999). Organizational change and development. *Annual Review of Psychology, 50,* 361–386.

Whyte, W. F. (Ed.). (1991). *Participatory action research.* Newbury Park, CA: Sage.

Worley, C. G., & Feyerherm, A. E. (2001, April). *Founders of the field reflect on the future of OD.* Paper presented at the Western Academy of Management Conference, Sun Valley, Idaho.

Worley, C., & Varney, G. (1998, winter). A search for a common body of knowledge for master's level organization development and change programs. *Academy of Management ODC Newsletter,* pp. 1–4.

Zucker, L. G. (1987). Institutional theories of organizations. *Annual Review of Sociology, 13,* 443–464.

CHAPTER FIVE

Allaire, Y., & Firsirotu, M. E. (1984). Theories of organizational culture. *Organization Studies, 5,* 3, 193–226.

Allport, G. W. (1948). Foreword. In G. W. Lewin (Ed.), *Resolving social conflict.* London: Harper & Row.

Argyris, C. (1990). *Overcoming organizational defenses.* Boston: Allyn and Bacon.

Argyris, C. (1992). *On organizational learning.* Oxford: Blackwell.

Argyris, C., Putnam, R., & McLain-Smith, D. (1985). *Action science: Concepts, methods, and skills for research and intervention.* San Francisco: Jossey-Bass.

Ash, M. G. (1992). Cultural contexts and scientific change in psychology— Kurt Lewin in Iowa. *American Psychologist, 47*(2), 198–207.

Back, K. W. (1992). This business of topology. *Journal of Social Issues, 48*(2), 51–66.

Bargal, D., & Bar, H. (1992). A Lewinian approach to intergroup workshops for Arab-Palestinian and Jewish Youth. *Journal of Social Issues, 48*(2), 139–154.

Bargal, D., Gold, M., & Lewin, M. (1992). The heritage of Kurt Lewin— Introduction. *Journal of Social Issues, 48*(2), 3–13.

Bechtold, B. L. (1997). Chaos theory as a model for strategy development. *Empowerment in Organizations, 5*(4), 193–202.

Beer, M., & Nohria, N. (2000, May–June). Cracking the code of change. *Harvard Business Review,* pp. 133–141.

Bennett, R. (1983). Management research. *Management Development Series, 20.* Geneva: International Labour Office.

Bernstein, L. (1968). *Management development.* London: Business Books.

Black, J. (2000). Fermenting change: Capitalizing on the inherent change found in dynamic nonlinear (or complex) systems. *Journal of Organizational Change Management, 13*(6), 520–525.

Boje, D. M. (2000). Phenomenal complexity theory and change at Disney: Response to Letiche. *Journal of Organizational Change Management, 13*(6), 558–566.

Brown, S. L., & Eisenhardt, K. M. (1997, March). The art of continuous change: Linking complexity theory and time-paced evolution in relentlessly shifting organizations. *Administrative Science Quarterly, 42,* 1–34.

Buchanan, D. A., & Storey, J. (1997). Role-taking and role-switching in organizational change: The four pluralities. In I. McLoughlin & M. Harris (Eds.), *Innovation, organizational change and technology.* London: International Thompson.

Burnes, B. (2000). *Managing change* (3rd ed.). London: Pearson Education.

Cartwright, D. (1951). Achieving change in people: Some applications of group dynamics theory. *Human Relations, 6*(4), 381–392.

Cartwright, D. (Ed.). (1952). *Field theory in social science.* London: Social Science Paperbacks.

Choi, T. Y., Dooley, K. J., & Rungtusanatham, M. (2001). Supply networks and complex adaptive systems: Control versus emergence. *Journal of Operations Management, 19*(3), 351–366.

Coch, L., & French, J.R.P., Jr. (1948). Overcoming resistance to change. *Human Relations, 1*(4), 512–532.

Collins, D. (1998). *Organizational change.* London: Routledge.

Conner, P. E. (1977). A critical enquiry into some assumptions and values characterizing OD. *Academy of Management Review, 2*(1), 635–644.

Cooke, B. (1999). Writing the left out of management theory: The historiography of the management of change. *Organization, 6*(1), 81–105.

Cummings, T. G., & Huse, E. F. (1989). *Organization development and change* (4th ed.). St Paul, MN: West Publishing.

Cummings, T. G., & Worley, C. G. (1997). *Organization development and change* (6th ed.). Cincinnati, OH: South-Western College Publishing.

Cyert, R. M., & March, J. G. (1963). *A behavioral theory of the firm.* Englewood Cliffs, NJ: Prentice-Hall.

Darwin, J., Johnson, P., & McAuley, J. (2002). *Developing strategies for change.* London: FT/Prentice-Hall.

Dawson, P. (1994). *Organizational change: A processual approach.* London: Paul Chapman Publishing.

Dent, E. B., & Goldberg, S. G. (1999). Challenging resistance to change. *Journal of Applied Behavioral Science, 35*(1), 25–41.

Dickens, L., & Watkins, K. (1999). Action research: Rethinking Lewin. *Management Learning, 30*(2), 127–140.

Dunphy, D. D., & Stace, D. A. (1992). *Under new management.* Sydney: McGraw-Hill.

Dunphy, D. D., & Stace, D. A. (1993). The strategic management of corporate change. *Human Relations, 46*(8), 905–918.

Eden, C., & Huxham, C. (1996). Action research for the study of organizations. In S. R. Clegg, C. Hardy, & W. R. Nord (Eds.), *Handbook of organization studies.* London: Sage.

Elden, M., & Chisholm, R. F. (1993). Emerging varieties of action research: Introduction to the Special Issue. *Human Relations, 46*(2), 121–142.

Elrod, P. D., II, & Tippett, D. D. (2002). The "Death Valley" of change. *Journal of Organizational Change Management, 15*(3), 273–291.

French, W. L., & Bell, C. H. (1984). *Organization development* (4th ed.). Englewood Cliffs, NJ: Prentice-Hall.

French, W. L., & Bell, C. H. (1995). *Organization development* (5th ed.). Englewood Cliffs, NJ: Prentice-Hall.

French, J.R.P., Jr., & Raven, B. H. (1959). The bases of social power. In D. Cartwright (Ed.), *Studies in social power.* Ann Arbor, MI: Institute for Social Research.

Garvin, D. A. (1993, July–August). Building a learning organization. *Harvard Business Review,* pp. 78–91.

Gellermann, W., Frankel, M. S., & Ladenson, R. F. (1990). *Values and ethics in organizational and human systems development: Responding to dilemmas in professional life.* San Francisco: Jossey-Bass.

Gersick, C.J.G. (1991). Revolutionary change theories: A multilevel exploration of the punctuated equilibrium paradigm. *Academy of Management Review, 16*(1), 10–36.

Gilchrist, A. (2000). The well-connected community: Networking to the edge of chaos. *Community Development Journal, 3*(3), 264–275.

Gold, M. (1992). Metatheory and field theory in social psychology: Relevance or elegance? *Journal of Social Issues, 48*(2), 67–78.

Gould, S. J. (1989). Punctuated equilibrium in fact and theory. *Journal of Social Biological Structure, 12,* 117–136.

Greenwald, J. (1996, December 23). Reinventing Sears. *Time,* pp. 53–55.

Handy, C. (1994). *The empty raincoat.* London: Hutchinson.

Hannagan, T. (2002). *Management: Concepts and practices* (3rd ed.). London: FT/Pearson.

Hannan, M. T., & Freeman, J. (1988). *Organizational ecology.* Cambridge, MA: Harvard University Press.

Harris, P. R. (1985). *Management in transition.* San Francisco: Jossey-Bass.

Hatch, M. J. (1997). *Organization theory: Modern, symbolic and postmodern perspectives.* Oxford: Oxford University Press.

Hedberg, B., Nystrom, P., & Starbuck, W. (1976). Camping on seesaws: Prescriptions for a self-designing organization. *Administrative Science Quarterly, 17,* 371–381.

Hendry, C. (1996). Understanding and creating whole organizational change through learning theory. *Human Relations, 48*(5), 621–641.

Hirschhorn, L. (1988). *The workplace within.* Cambridge, MA: MIT Press.

House, J. S. (1993). John R. French, Jr.: A Lewinian's Lewinian. *Journal of Social Issues, 49*(4), 221–226.

Huczynski, A., & Buchanan, D. (2001). *Organizational behaviour* (4th ed.). London: FT/Prentice-Hall.

Jaques, E. (1998). On leaving the Tavistock Institute. *Human Relations, 51*(3), 251–257.

Kanter, R. M. (1983). *The change masters.* New York: Simon & Schuster.

Kanter, R. M. (1989). *When giants learn to dance: Mastering the challenges of strategy, management, and careers in the 1990s.* London: Unwin.

Kanter, R. M., Stein, B. A., & Jick, T. D. (1992). *The challenge of organizational change.* New York: Free Press.

Kearney, A. T. (1989). *Computer integrated manufacturing: Competitive advantage or technological dead end?* London: Kearney.

Kimberley, J., & Miles, R. (Eds.). (1980). *The organizational life cycle.* San Francisco: Jossey-Bass.

Kippenberger, T. (1998a). Planned change: Kurt Lewin's legacy. *The Antidote, 14,* 10–12.

Kippenberger, T. (1998b). Managed learning: Elaborating on Lewin's model. *The Antidote, 14,* 13.

Kotter, J. P. (1996). *Leading change.* Boston: Harvard Business School Press.

Lewin, G. W. (Ed.). (1948a). *Resolving social conflict.* London: Harper & Row.

Lewin, G. W. (1948b). Preface. In G. W. Lewin (Ed.), *Resolving social conflict.* London: Harper & Row.

Lewin, K. (1939). When facing danger. In G. W. Lewin (Ed.), *Resolving social conflict.* London: Harper & Row.

Lewin, K. (1943a). Psychological ecology. In D. Cartwright (Ed.), *Field theory in social science.* London: Social Science Paperbacks.

Lewin, K. (1943b). The special case of Germany. In G. W. Lewin (Ed.), *Resolving social conflict.* London: Harper & Row.

Lewin, K. (1943–1944). Problems of research in social psychology. In D. Cartwright (Ed.), *Field theory in social science.* London: Social Science Paperbacks.

Lewin, K. (1946). Action research and minority problems. In G. W. Lewin (Ed.), *Resolving social conflict.* London: Harper & Row.

Lewin, K. (1947a). Frontiers in group dynamics. In D. Cartwright (Ed.), *Field theory in social science.* London: Social Science Paperbacks.

Lewin, K. (1947b). Group decisions and social change. In T. M. Newcomb & E. L. Hartley (Eds.), *Readings in social psychology.* New York: Henry Holt.

Lewin, M. (1992). The impact of Kurt Lewin's life on the place of social issues in his work. *Journal of Social Issues, 48*(2), 15–29.

Lewis, R. (1994). From chaos to complexity: Implications for organizations. *Executive Development, 7*(4), 16–17.

Lindblom, C. E. (1959, Spring). The science of muddling through. *Public Administration Review, 19,* 79–88.

Lorenz, E. (1993). *The essence of chaos.* London: UCL Press.

Macbeth, D. K. (2002). Emergent strategy in managing cooperative supply chain change. *International Journal of Operations and Production Management, 22*(7), 728–740.

MacIntosh, R., & MacLean, D. (2001). Conditioned emergence: Researching change and changing research. *International Journal of Operations and Production Management, 21*(10), 1343–1357.

Marrow, A. J. (1957). *Making management human.* New York: McGraw-Hill.

Marrow, A. J. (1969). *The practical theorist: The life and work of Kurt Lewin.* New York: Teachers College Press.

Marshak, R. J. (1993). Lewin meets Confucius: A re-view of the OD model of change. *The Journal of Applied Behavioral Science, 29*(4), 393–415.

Matthews, R. (2002). Competition, archetypes and creative imagination. *Journal of Organizational Change Management, 15*(5), 461–476.

Miller, D., & Friesen, P. H. (1984). *Organizations: A quantum view.* Englewood Cliffs, NJ: Prentice-Hall.

Mintzberg, H., Ahlstrand, B., & Lampel, J. (1998). *Strategy safari.* London: Prentice-Hall.

Mullins, L. (2002). *Management and organisational behaviour* (6th ed.). London: FT/Pearson.

Nonaka, I. (1988, November–December). Creating organizational order out of chaos: Self-renewal in Japanese firms. *Harvard Business Review,* pp. 96–104.

Olsen, B. D. (2002). Applied social and community interventions for crisis in times of national and international conflict. *Analyses of Social Issues and Public Policy, 2*(1), 119–129.

Peters, T. (1992). *Liberation management.* New York: Knopf.

Peters, T., & Waterman, R. H. (1982). *In search of excellence: Lessons from America's best-run companies.* London: Harper & Row.

Pettigrew, A. M. (1973). *The politics of organisational decision making.* Tavistock: London.

Pettigrew, A. M. (1979). On studying organizational culture. *Administrative Science Quarterly, 24*(4), 570–581.

Pettigrew, A. M. (1980). The politics of organisational change. In N. Bjorn-Anderson (Ed.), *The human side of information processing.* New York: Elsevier.

Pettigrew, A. M. (1985). *The awakening giant: Continuity and change in ICI.* Oxford: Blackwell.

Pettigrew, A. M. (1987). Context and action in the transformation of the firm. *Journal of Management Sciences, 24*(6), 649–670.

Pettigrew, A. M. (1990a). Longitudinal field research on change: Theory and practice. *Organizational Science, 3*(1), 267–292.

Pettigrew, A. M. (1990b). Studying strategic choice and strategic change. *Organizational Studies, 11*(1), 6–11.

Pettigrew, A. M. (1997). What is a processual analysis? *Scandinavian Journal of Management, 13*(40), 337–348.

Pettigrew, A. M., Ferlie, E., & McKee, L. (1992). *Shaping strategic change.* London: Sage.

Pettigrew, A. M., Hendry, C. N., & Sparrow, P. (1989). *Training in Britain: Employers' perspectives on human resources.* London: HMSO.

Pettigrew, A. M., & Whipp, R. (1993). Understanding the environment. In C. Mabey & B. Mayon-White (Eds.), *Managing change* (2nd ed.). London: The Open University/Paul Chapman Publishing.

Pfeffer, J. (1981). *Power in organizations.* Cambridge, MA: Pitman.

Pfeffer, J. (1992). *Managing with power: Politics and influence in organizations.* Boston: Harvard Business School Press.

Prigogine, I., & Stengers, I. (1984). *Order out of chaos: Man's new dialogue with nature.* New York: Bantam Books.

Quinn, J. B. (1980). *Strategies for change: Logical incrementalism.* Homewood, IL: Irwin.

Quinn, J. B. (1982). Managing strategies incrementally. *Omega, 10*(6), 613–627.

Raven, B. H. (1965). Social influence and power. In I. D. Steiner & M. Fishbein (Eds.), *Current studies in social psychology.* New York: Holt, Rinehart, and Winston.

Raven, B. H. (1993). The bases of power—Origins and recent developments. *Journal of Social Issues, 49*(4), 227–251.

Raven, B. H. (1999). Kurt Lewin address: Influence, power, religion, and the mechanisms of social control. *Journal of Social Issues, 55*(1), 161–189.

Romanelli, E., & Tushman, M. L. (1994). Organizational transformation as punctuated equilibrium: An empirical test. *Academy of Management Journal, 37*(5), 1141–1166.

Schein, E. H. (1988). *Organizational psychology* (3rd ed.). London: Prentice-Hall.

Schein, E. H. (1996). Kurt Lewin's change theory in the field and in the classroom: Notes towards a model of management learning. *Systems Practice, 9*(1), 27–47.

Senge, P. M. (1990). *The fifth discipline: The art and practice of the learning organization.* London: Century Business.

Shelton, C. K., & Darling, J. R. (2001). The quantum skills model in management: A new paradigm to enhance effective leadership. *Leadership and Organization Development Journal, 22*(6), 264–273.

Smith, M. K. (2001). Kurt Lewin: Groups, experiential learning and action research. *The encyclopedia of informal education.* Available: http://www.infed.org/thinkers/et-lewin.htm, 1–15.

Stace, D., & Dunphy, D. (2001). *Beyond the boundaries: Leading and re-creating the successful enterprise* (2nd ed.). Sydney: McGraw-Hill.

Stacey, R. D. (1993). *Strategic Management and Organisational Dynamics.* London: Pitman.

Stacey, R. D., Griffin, D., & Shaw, P. (2002). *Complexity and management: Fad or radical challenge to systems thinking?* London: Routledge.

Stickland, F. (1998). *The dynamics of change: Insights into organisational transition from the natural world.* London: Routledge.

Tetenbaum, T. J. (1998). Shifting paradigms: From Newton to chaos. *Organizational Dynamics, 26*(4), 21–32.

Tobach, E. (1994). Personal is political is personal is political. *Journal of Social Issues, 50*(1), 221–244.

Tschacher, W., & Brunner, E. J. (1995). Empirical-studies of group-dynamics from the point-of view of self-organization theory. *Zeitschrift für Sozialpsychologie, 26*(2), 78–91.

Waclawski, J. (2002). Large-scale organizational change and performance: An empirical examination. *Human Resource Development Quarterly, 13*(3), 289–305.

Warwick, D. P., & Thompson, J. T. (1980). Still crazy after all these years. *Training and Development Journal, 34*(2), 16–22.

Wastell, D. G., White, P., & Kawalek, P. (1994). A methodology for business process redesign: Experience and issues. *Journal of Strategic Information Systems, 3*(1), 23–40.

Watcher, B. (1993). *The adoption of total quality management in Scotland.* Durham, NC: Durham University Business School.

Watson, T. J. (1997). *In search of management.* London: Thompson International.

Wheatley, M. J. (1992). *Leadership and the new science: Learning about organization from an orderly universe.* San Francisco: Berrett-Koehler.

Whyte, J., & Watcher, B. (1992). *The adoption of total quality management in northern England.* Durham, NC: Durham University Business School.

Wilson, D. C. (1992). *A strategy of change.* London: Routledge.

Wooten, K. C., & White, L. P. (1999). Linking OD's philosophy with justice theory: Postmodern implications. *Journal of Organizational Change Management, 12*(1), 7–20.

Zairi, M., Letza, S., & Oakland, J. (1994). Does TQM impact on bottom line results? *TQM Magazine, 6*(1), 38–43.

CHAPTER SIX

Argyris, C. (1965). *Organization and innovation.* Homewood, IL: Irwin, 1965.

Barker, R., Wright, B. A., & Gonick, M. R. (1946). *Adjustment to physical handicap and illness* (Bulletin 55). New York: Social Science Research Council.

Ezriel, H. (1952, May). Notes on psychoanalytic group therapy: II. Interpretation and research. *Psychiatry, 15,* 119–126.

Jones, H. E., & Gerard, H. B. (1967). *Foundation of social psychology.* New York: John Wiley.

Kelley, H. H. (1967). Attribution theory in social psychology. In D. Levine (Ed.), *Nebraska Symposium on Motivation* (Vol. 15, pp. 192–238). Lincoln: University of Nebraska Press.

Rosenberg, M. (1967). *Psychological selectivity in self-esteem formation* (mimeographed). Washington, DC: National Institute of Mental Health.

CHAPTER SEVEN

Aguinis, H. (1993). Action research and scientific method: Presumed discrepancies and actual similarities. *Journal of Applied Behavioral Science, 29*(4), 416–431.

Argyris, C., Putnam, R., & Smith, D. (1987). *Action science: Concepts, methods, and skills for research and intervention.* San Francisco: Jossey-Bass.

Argyris, C., & Schön, D. (1991). Participatory action research and action science compared. In W. F. Whyte (Ed.), *Participatory action research.* Newbury Park, CA: Sage.

Brooks, A., & Watkins, K. (Eds.). (1994). *The emerging power of action inquiry technologies.* New Directions in Adult and Continuing Education series, *63.* San Francisco: Jossey-Bass.

Brown, L., Henry, C., Henry, J., & McTaggart, R. (1982). Action research: Notes on the national seminar. *Classroom Action Research Network Bulletin, 5,* 1–16.

Carr, W., & Kemmis, S. (1986). *Becoming critical: Education, knowledge and action research.* London: Falmer Press.

Chein, I., Cook, S., & Harding, J. (1948). The field of action research, *American Psychologist, 3,* 43–50.

Clark, A. (Ed.). (1976). *Experimenting with organizational life: The action research approach.* New York: Plenum Press.

Cohen, L., & Manion, L. (1980). *Research methods in education* (2nd ed.). Dover, NH: Croom Helm.

Cunningham, J. B. (1993). *Action research and organizational development.* Westport, CT: Praeger.

Dickens, L. (1998). *A theory of action perspective of action research.* Unpublished doctoral dissertation. Austin: The University of Texas at Austin.

Elden, M., & Chisholm, R. (1993). Emerging varieties of action research: Introduction to the special issue. *Human Relations, 46*(2), 121–141.

Elden, M., & Levin, M. (1991). Co-generative learning: Bringing participation into action research. In W. F. Whyte (Ed.), *Participative action research.* Beverly Hills, CA: Sage.

Foster, M. (1972). An introduction to the theory and practice of action research in work organizations, *Human Relations, 25*(6), 529–556.

Greenwood, D., Whyte, W. F., & Harkavy, I. (1993). Participatory action research as a process and as a goal. *Human Relations, 46*(2), 175–191.

Heller, F. (1976). Group feedback analysis as a method of action research. In A. Clark (Ed.), *Experimenting with organizational life: The action research approach.* New York: Plenum Press.

Kemmis, S. (1988). *The action research reader.* Victoria, Australia: Deakin University.

Kemmis, S., & McTaggart, R. (1988). *The action research planner.* Victoria, Australia: Deakin University.

Lewin, K. (1946). Action research and minority problems. *Journal of Social Issues, 2*(4), 34–46.

Lippitt, R. (1979). *Kurt Lewin, action research, and planned change.* Paper provided by the author.

McTaggart, R. (1991). Principles for participatory action research. *Adult Education Quarterly, 41*(3), 168–187.

Merriam, S., & Simpson, E. (1984). *A guide to research for adult educators and trainers.* Malamar, FL: Krieger.

Oja, S. N., & Smulyan, L. (1989). *Collaborative action research: A developmental approach.* Philadelphia: Falmer Press.

Perry, C., & Zuber-Skerritt, O. (1994). Doctorates by action research for senior practicing managers. *Management Learning, 25*(2), 341–365.

Peters, M., & Robinson, V. (1984). The origins and status of action research. *Journal of Applied Behavioral Science, 20*(2), 113–124.

Reason, P., & Rowan, J. (Eds.). (1981). *Human inquiry.* New York: John Wiley and Sons.

Sanford, N. (1970). Whatever happened to action research? *Journal of Social Issues, 26,* 3–23.

Seashore, S. E., & Bowers, D. (1963). *Changing the structure and functioning of an organization,* Doc. 33. Ann Arbor: Survey Research Center, University of Michigan.

Smith, K., & Berg, D. (1988). *Paradoxes of group life.* San Francisco: Jossey-Bass.

Trist, E. (1976). Action research and adaptive planning. In A. Clark (Ed.), *Experimenting with organizational life: The action research approach.* New York: Plenum Press.

Watkins, K. (1991). *Validity in action research.* Paper presented at the Annual Meeting of the American Educational Research Association.

Whyte, W. F. (1991a). *Social theory for action: How individuals and organizations learn to change.* Newbury Park, CA: Sage.

Whyte, W. F. (Ed.). (1991b). *Participatory action research.* Newbury Park, CA: Sage.

CHAPTER NINE

Bennis, W. G. (1963). A new role for the behavioral sciences: Effecting organizational change. *Administrative Science Quarterly, 8*(2), 125–165.

Cameron, K. (2002, August). *Organizational virtues: Implications for performance.* Symposium presented at the Academy of Management, Denver.

Cavanagh, G. F., & Moberg, D. J. (1999). The virtue of courage within the organization. In M. L. Pava & P. P. Primeaux (Eds.), *Research in ethical issues in organizations* (Vol. 1, pp. 1–25). Stamford, CT: JAI Press.

Chin, R., & Benne, K. D. (2000). General strategies for affecting change in human systems. In W. L. French, C. H. Bell, Jr., & R. A. Zawacki (Eds.), *Organization development and transformation: Managing effective change* (5th ed., pp. 43–63). New York: Irwin McGraw-Hill.

Cooperrider, D. L. (1986). *Appreciative inquiry: Toward a methodology for understanding and enhancing organization innovation.* Unpublished Ph.D. dissertation. Case Western Reserve University, Cleveland.

Cooperrider, D. L. (1999). Positive image, positive action: The affirmative basis of organizing. In S. Srivastva & D. L. Cooperrider (Eds.), *Appreciative management and leadership: The power of positive thought and action in organization* (Rev. ed., pp. 91–125). Cleveland: Lakeshore Communications.

Cooperrider, D. L. (2000). The inter-religious friendship group: A visible force for peace. *Weatherhead:* The magazine for the Weatherhead School of Management. Cleveland: Case Western Reserve University.

Cooperrider, D. L. (2001). *AI: The beginnings (toward a methodology for understanding and enhancing organizational innovation).* Cleveland: Lakeshore Communications.

Cooperrider, D. L., & Whitney, D. (1999). A positive revolution in change: Appreciative inquiry. In D. L. Cooperrider, P. F. Sorensen, Jr., D. Whitney, & T. F. Yaeger (Eds.), *Appreciative inquiry: Rethinking human organization toward a positive theory of change* (p. 18). Champaign, IL: Stipes Publishing.

Cousins, N. (1998). Therapeutic value of laughter. *Integrative Psychiatry, 3*(2), 112.

Folkman, S., & Moskowitz, J. T. (2000). Positive affect and the other side of coping. *American Psychologist, 55,* 647–654.

Fredrickson, B. L. (1998). What good are positive emotions? *Review of General Psychology, 2*(3), 300–319.

Fredrickson, B. L. (2000). Cultivating positive emotions to optimize health and well-being. *Prevention and Treatment, 2.*

Fredrickson, B. L. (2001). The role of positive emotions in positive psychology: The broaden-and-build theory of positive emotions. *American Psychologist, 56*(3), 218–226.

Fredrickson, B. L., Mancuso, R. A., Branigan, C., & Tugade, M. M. (2000). *Motivation and Emotion, 24*(4), 237–258.

Fry, R., Barrett, F., Seiling, J., & Whitney, D. (2001). *Appreciative inquiry and organizational transformation: Reports from the field.* Westport, CT: Quorum Books.

Gergen, K. J. (1997). Social psychology as social construction: The emerging vision. In C. McGarty & S. A. Haslam (Eds.), *The message of social psychology: Perspectives on mind in society* (pp. 113–128). Malden, MA: Blackwell.

Grudin, R. (1990). *The grace of GREAT things: Creativity and innovation.* New York: Tricknor and Fields.

Haidt, J. (2000). The Positive emotion of elevation. *Prevention & Treatment, 3.*

Hatfield, E., Cacioppo, J. T., & Rapson, R. L. (1994). *Emotion contagion: Studies in emotion and social interaction.* New York: Cambridge University Press.

Hock, D. (1999). *Birth of the chaordic age.* San Francisco: Berrett-Koehler.

Hubbard, B. M. (1998). *Conscious evolution: Awakening the power of our social potential.* Novato, CA: New World Library.

Isen, A. M., Daubman, K. A., & Nowicki, G. P. (1987). Positive affect facilitates creative problem solving. *Journal of Personality and Social Psychology, 52,* 1122–1131.

Jackson, S. E., & Dutton, J. E. (1988). Discerning threats and opportunities. *Administrative Science Quarterly, 33,* 370–387.

Kast, V. (1994). *Joy, inspiration, and hope.* New York: Fromm International.

Khandwalla, P. N. (1998). Thorny glory: Toward organizational greatness. In S. Srivastva & D. L. Cooperrider (Eds.), *Organizational wisdom and executive courage* (pp. 157–204). San Francisco: The New Lexington Press.

Kotter, J. (1998). Leading organizational change: Why transformation efforts fail. *Harvard Business Review of Change,* pp. 1–20.

Kung, H. (1996). *Great Christian thinkers.* New York: Continuum. (Originally entitled *Grosse Christliche Denker*)

Ludema, J. D., Wilmot, T. B., & Srivastva, S. (1997). Organizational hope: Reaffirming the constructive task of social and organizational inquiry. *Human Relations, 50,* 1015–1052.

May, R. (1975). *The courage to create.* New York: Norton.

Quinn, R. E. (2000). *Change the world: How ordinary people can achieve extraordinary results.* San Francisco: Jossey-Bass.

Schneider, K. J., & May, R. (1995). *The psychology of existence: An integrative clinical perspective.* New York: McGraw-Hill.

Srivastva, S., & Cooperrider, D. L. (Eds.). (1998). *Organizational wisdom and executive courage.* San Francisco: The New Lexington Press.

Tugade, M. M., & Fredrickson, B. L. (2004). Positive emotions and health. In N. Anderson (Ed.), *Encyclopedia of health and behavior.* Thousand Oaks, CA: Sage.

Weick, K. E. (1984). Small wins: Redefining the scale of social problems. *American Psychology, 39*(1), 40–49.

Whitney, D., & Cooperrider, D. L. (2000). The appreciative inquiry summit: An emerging methodology for whole system positive change. *OD Practitioner: A Journal of the Organization Development Network, 32*(1), 13–26.

Wright, R. (2001). *Nonzero: The logic of human destiny.* New York: Vintage Books.

CHAPTER ELEVEN

Katz, D., & Kahn, R. (1966). *The social psychology of organizations.* New York: Wiley.

Lorsch, J. W., & Sheldon, S. (1972). The individual in the organization: A systems view. In J. W. Lorsch & P. R. Lawrence (Eds.), *Managing group and intergroup relations.* Homewood, IL: Business One Irwin.

Mintzberg, H. (1994). *The rise and fall of strategic planning.* New York: Free Press.

Seiler, J. A. (1967). *Systems analysis in organizational behavior.* Homewood, IL: Business One Irwin.

CHAPTER THIRTEEN

Harvey, J. (1974). The Abilene paradox: The management of agreement. *Organization Dynamics, 17,* 16–43.

Janis, I. (1982). *Group think* (2nd ed. rev.). Boston: Houghton-Mifflin.

Schein, E. H. (1992). *Organizational culture and leadership* (2nd ed.). San Francisco: Jossey-Bass.

Senge, P. (1990). *The fifth discipline.* New York: Doubleday Currency.

Senge, P., Roberts, C., Ross, R. B., Smith, B. J., & Kleiner, A. (1994). *The fifth discipline field book.* New York: Doubleday Currency.

CHAPTER FOURTEEN

Beckhard, R., & Harris, R. (1967). The confrontation meeting. *Harvard Business Review, 45*(2), 149–155.

Bion, W. R. (1961). *Experiences in groups.* New York: Basic Books.

Bohm, D. (1990). *On dialogue.* Ojai, CA: David Bohm Seminars.

Dannemiller, K., & Jacobs, R. W. (1992). Changing the way organizations change: A revolution in common sense. *Journal of Applied Behavioral Science, 28,* 480–498.

Deming, W. E. (1992). *Quality, productivity, and competitive position.* Cambridge, MA: MIT Center for Advanced Engineering.

Emery, F. E. (1995). Participative design: Effective, flexible and successful, now! *Journal for Quality and Participation, 18*(1), 6–9.

Glidewell, J. C. (1970). *Choice points.* Cambridge, MA: MIT Press.

Jayaram, G. K. (1977). Open systems planning. In T. Cummings & S. Srivastra (Eds.), *Management at work: A Socio-technical systems approach.* San Diego: Pfeiffer.

Katz, D. T., & Kahn, R. L. (1978). *The social psychology of organizations.* New York: Wiley.

Latane, B., & Darley, J. M. (1976). Helping in a crisis: Bystander response to an emergency. Morristown, NJ: General Learning Press.

Le Bon, G. (1896). *The crowd: A study of the popular mind.* London: T. Fisher Unwin.

Lewin, K. (1943). Forces behind food habits and methods of change. *Bulletin of the National Research Council, 108,* 35–65.

Lippitt, R. (1980). *Choosing the future you prefer.* Washington, DC: Development Publishers.

Lippitt, R. (1983). Future before you plan. In R. A. Ritvo & A. G. Sargent (Eds.), *The NTL managers' handbook.* Arlington, VA: NTL Institute.

Main, T. (1975). Some psychodynamics of large groups. In L. Kreeger (Ed.), *The large group: Dynamics and therapy.* London: Constable.

Marrow, A. J. (1969). *The practical theorist.* New York: Basic Books.

Menzies, I.E.P. (1960). The functioning of social systems as a defense against anxiety. *Human Relations, 13,* 95–121.

Miller, E. J., & Rice, A. K. (1967). Systems of organization: The control of task and sentient boundaries. London: Tavistock Institute.

Oshry, B. (1996). *Seeing systems.* San Francisco: Berrett-Koehler.

Owen, H. (1992). *Open Space Technology: A user's guide.* Potomac, MD: Abbott.

Schindler-Rainman, E., & Lippitt, R. (1980). *Building the collaborative community: Mobilizing citizens for action.* Riverside: University of California Extension.

Senge, P. M. (1990). *The fifth discipline: The art and practice of the learning organization.* New York: Doubleday.

Trist, E. L., & Emery, F. E. (1960). *Report on the Barford Course for Bristol/Siddeley, July 10–16, 1960* (Tavistock Document No. 598). London: Tavistock Institute.

Trist, E. L., Higgin, G. W., Murray, H., & Pollock, A. B. (1963). Organizational choice: Capabilities of groups at the coal face under changing technologies. London: Tavistock.

von Bertalanffy, L. (1950). *General systems theory.* New York: Braziller.

Weisbord, M. R. (1987). *Productive workplaces: Organizing and managing for dignity, meaning, and community.* San Francisco: Jossey-Bass.

Weisbord, M. R. (1992). *Discovering common ground.* San Francisco: Berrett-Koehler.

Zimbardo, P. G. (1970). The human choice: Individuation, reason, and order versus deindividuation, impulse, and chaos. In W. J. Arnold & D. Levine (Eds.), *Nebraska Symposium on Motivation.* Lincoln: University of Nebraska Press.

CHAPTER FIFTEEN

Argyris, C. (1985). *Strategy, change and defensive routines.* Boston: Pitman.

Argyris, C., & Schön, D. A. (1977). *Theory in practice: Increasing professional effectiveness.* San Francisco: Jossey-Bass.

Argyris, C., & Schön, D. A. (1978). *Organizational learning: A theory of action perspective.* Reading, MA: Addison-Wesley.

Argyris, C., & Schön, D. A. (1996). *Organizational learning II: Theory, method, and practice.* Reading, MA: Addison-Wesley.

Boeke, K. (1957). *Cosmic view: The universe in 40 jumps.* New York: John Day.

Conniff, R. (2005). *The ape in the corner office: Understanding the workplace beast in all of us.* New York: Crown Business.

Deal, T. E., & Kennedy, A. A. (1982). *Corporate cultures: The rites and rituals of corporate life.* Reading, MA: Addison-Wesley.

Drucker, P. F. (1967). *The effective executive.* New York: HarperCollins.

Emery, F., & Trist, E. (1965). The causal texture of organizational environments. *Human Relations, 18,* 21–32.

Epstein, N. (2004). *Who's in charge here? The tangled web of school governance and policy.* Washington, DC: Brookings Institute.

Executive stress: Stress is chief among executives' health concerns. (2004, April). *Mayo Clinic Checkup Newsletter.*

Feagin, J. R. (2001). *White racism.* New York: Routledge.

Foray, D. (2004, September). *Economics of knowledge.* Cambridge, MA: MIT Press.

Gallos, J. V. (2002, December). The dean's squeeze: Myths and realities of academic leadership in the middle. *Academy of Management Learning and Education, 1:2,* 174–184.

Kaplan, A. (1964). *The conduct of inquiry: Methodology for behavioral science.* San Francisco: Chandler.

Kelleher, M. D. (1997). *Profiling the lethal employee: Case studies of workplace violence.* Westport: Praeger.

Lipnack, J., & Stamps, J. (1997). *Virtual teams: Reaching across space, time, and organizations with technology.* Hoboken, NJ: Wiley.

McGonagill, G. (2004, October). *The amygdala hijack.* Presentation to the Organization Workshop Trainers Meeting, Boston.

Natta, D. V., Jr., Liptak, A., & Levy, C. J. (2005, October 16). The Miller case: A notebook, a cause, a jail cell and a deal. *New York Times,* p. A1.

Oshry, B. (1992). *Space work: A systemic analysis of the causes of partnership breakdown.* Boston: Power + Systems, Inc.

Oshry, B. (1993). *The terrible dance of power.* Boston: Power + Systems, Inc.

Oshry, B. (1996). *Seeing systems: Unlocking the mysteries of organizational life.* San Francisco: Berrett-Koehler.

Oshry, B. (1999). *Leading systems: Lessons from the power lab.* San Francisco: Berrett-Koehler.

Oshry, B. (2000). *The Organization Workshop trainer's manual.* Boston: Power + Systems, Inc.

Oshry, B. (2003). *The Merging Cultures Workshop trainer's manual.* Boston: Power + Systems, Inc.

Rosenbaum, D. E. (2005, October 16). Study ranks Homeland Retrieved April 6, 2005, from http://www.nytimes.com/2005/10/16/politics/16homeland.html?ex=1287115200&en=cc23d476e5e70370&ei=5088&partner=rssnyt&emc=rss.

Sciolino, E. (2005, November 10). Chirac, lover of spotlight, avoids glare of France's fires. *New York Times,* p. A12.

Shorris, E. (1981). *The oppressed middle: Scenes from corporate life.* Garden City, NJ: Anchor Books.

Tannenbaum, A. S. (1974). *Hierarchy in organizations.* San Francisco: Jossey-Bass.

Wolfe, T. (1980). *The right stuff.* New York: Bantam.

CHAPTER SIXTEEN

Argyris, C. (1962). *Interpersonal competence and organizational effectiveness.* Homewood, IL: Irwin.

Beckhard, R. (1969). *Organization development: Strategies and models.* Reading, MA: Addison-Wesley.

Bolman, L., & Deal, T. (2003). *Reframing organizations: Artistry, choice, and leadership* (3rd ed.). San Francisco: Jossey-Bass.

Bradford, D., & Burke, W. (2005). The future of OD? In D. L. Bradford & W. W. Burke (Eds.), *Reinventing organization development: New approaches to change in organizations.* San Francisco: Pfeiffer.

Burke, W. (1997, Summer). The new agenda for organization development. *Organizational Dynamics, 26*(1), 7–20.

Burke, W., & Bradford, D. (2005). The Crisis of OD. In D. L. Bradford and W. W. Burke (Eds.), *Reinventing organization development: New approaches to change in organizations.* San Francisco: Pfeiffer.

Cohen, M., & March, J. (1974). *Leadership and ambiguity.* New York: McGraw-Hill.

Cummings, T., & Worley, C. (2005). *Organization development and change* (6th ed.). Cincinnati: South Western.

Cyert, R., & March, J. (1963). *A behavioral theory of the firm.* Upper Saddle River, NJ: Prentice Hall.

Deal, T., & Kennedy, A. (2000). *Corporate cultures: The rites and rituals of corporate life* (2nd ed.). Cambridge, MA: Perseus.

Fletcher, J., & Olwyler, K. (1997). *Paradoxical thinking: How to profit from your contradictions.* San Francisco: Berrett-Koehler.

Galbraith, J. (2001). *Designing organizations: An executive briefing on strategy, structure, and process* (2nd ed.). San Francisco: Jossey-Bass.

Gallos, J. V. (1989, November). Developmental diversity and the OB classroom: Implications for teaching and learning. *Organizational Behavior Teaching Review, 13*(40), 33–47.

Gallos, J. V. (2005, Spring). Career counseling revisited: A developmental perspective. *Career Planning and Adult Development, 21*(1), 9–23.

Greiner, L., & Cummings, T. (2004, December). "Wanted: OD more alive than dead!" *Journal of Applied Behavioral Science, 40,* 374–391.

Hammer, M., & Champy, J. (1993). *Reengineering the corporation.* New York: HarperCollins.

Harvey, J. (2005). The future of OD, or why don't they take the tubes out of grandma? In D. L. Bradford & W. W. Burke (Eds.), *Reinventing organization development: New approaches to change in organizations.* San Francisco: Pfeiffer.

Kuhn, T. (1996). *The structure of scientific revolutions* (3rd ed.). Chicago: University Of Chicago Press.

Lawrence, P., & Lorsch, J. (1986). *Organization and environment: Managing differentiation and integration* (Rev. ed.). Boston: Harvard Business School Press.

Maslow, A. (1954). *Motivation and personality.* New York: HarperCollins.

McGregor, D. (1960). *The human side of enterprise.* New York: McGraw-Hill.

Meyer, J., & Rowan, B. (1983). Institutionalized organizations: Formal structure as myth and ceremony. In J. Meyer & W. Scott (Eds.), *Organizational environments: Ritual and rationality.* Thousand Oaks, CA: Sage.

Mirvis, P. (1988). Organization development: Part 1. An evolutionary perspective. In R. W. Woodman & W. A. Pasmore (Eds.), *Research in organizational change and development* (Vol. 2, pp. 1 –57). Greenwich, CT: JAI Press.

Mirvis, P. (1990). Organization development: Part 2. A revolutionary perspective. In R. W. Woodman & W. A. Pasmore (Eds.), *Research in organizational change and development* (Vol. 4, pp. 1–66). Greenwich, CT: JAI Press.

Perrow, C. (1986). *Complex organizations* (3rd ed.). New York: McGraw-Hill.

Pfeffer, J. (1994). *Managing with power: Politics and influence in organizations.* Boston: Harvard Business School Press.

Schein, E. (2004). *Organizational culture and leadership* (3rd ed.). San Francisco: Jossey-Bass.

Schön, D., & Rein, M. (1994). *Frame reflection: Toward the resolution of intractable policy controversies.* New York: Basic Books.

Smith, H. (1988). *The power game.* New York: Random House.

Weick, K. E. (1979). *The social psychology of organizing.* New York: McGraw-Hill.

Weick, K. E. (1995). *Sensemaking in organizations.* Thousand Oaks, CA: Sage.

Wheatley, M., Griffin, P., Quade, K., & the National OD Network. (2003). *Organization development at work: Conversations on the values, applications, and future of OD.* San Francisco: Pfeiffer.

CHAPTER TWENTY

Argyris, C. (1970). *Intervention theory and method: A behavioral science view.* Reading, MA: Addison-Wesley.

Argyris, C. (1982). *Reasoning, learning, and action.* San Francisco: Jossey-Bass.

Argyris, C. (1985). *Strategy, change, and defensive routines.* Boston: Pitman.

Argyris, C. (1987). Reasoning, action strategies, and defensive routines: The case of OD practitioners. In R. W. Woodman & W. A. Pasmore (Eds.), *Research in organizational change and development* (Vol. 1). Greenwich, CT: JAI Press.

Argyris, C. (1990). *Overcoming organizational defensives: Facilitating orga-nizational learning.* Needham Heights, MA: Allyn & Bacon.

Argyris, C., Putnam, R., & Smith, D. M. (1985). *Action science: Concepts, methods, and skills for research and intervention.* San Francisco: Jossey-Bass.

Argyris, C., & Schön, D. A. (1974). *Theory in practice: Increasing professional effectiveness.* San Francisco: Jossey-Bass.

Bush, R.A.B., & Folger, J. P. (1994). *The promise of mediation: Responding to conflict through empowerment and recognition.* San Francisco: Jossey-Bass.

Moore, C. W. (1996). *The mediation process: Practical strategies for resolving conflict* (2nd ed.). San Francisco: Jossey-Bass.

CHAPTER TWENTY-TWO

Deal, T. E., & Nutt, S. C. (1980). *Promoting, guiding, & surviving change in school districts.* Cambridge, MA: Abt Associates.

Firestone, W. A. (1977). Butte-Angels camp: Conflict and transformation. In R. Herriot & N. Gross (Eds.), *The dynamics of planned educational change.* Berkeley, CA: McCutchan.

Frangos, S. (1996). *Team zebra.* New York: Wiley.

Kotter, J. P., & Cohen, D. S. (2002). *The heart of change: Real life stories of how people change their organizations.* Boston: Harvard Business School Press.

Machiavelli, N. (1961). *The prince.* New York: Penguin Books. (Originally published 1514)

McLennan, R. (1989). *Managing organizational change.* Upper Saddle River, NJ: Prentice-Hall.

Mitroff, I. I. (1983). *Stakeholders of the organizational mind: Toward a new view of organizational policy making.* San Francisco: Jossey-Bass.

Morganthau, T. (1985, June 23). Saying 'no' to new Coke. *Newsweek,* pp. 32–33.

Oliver, T. (1986). *The real Coke, the real story.* New York: Random House.

Owen, H. (1987). *Spirit: Transformation and development in organizations.* Potomac, MD: Abbott.

CHAPTER TWENTY-FOUR

Halberstam, D. (1986). *The reckoning.* New York: Morrow.

CHAPTER TWENTY-FIVE

Drucker, P. (1967). *The effective executive.* New York: Harper & Row.

Gabarro, J. J. (1979, Winter). Socialization at the top: How CEOs and their subordinates develop interpersonal contracts. *Organizational Dynamics, 7*(3), 2–23.

Gabarro, J. J., & Norman, N. J. (1975, August 4). Frank Mason. *Harvard Business School Case Services,* #6–476–019.

Gerttula, G. (1993, November 8). Tom Levick. *Harvard Business School Case Services,* #9–480–049.

Kotter, J. P. (1979). *Power in management.* New York: AMACOM.

Kotter, J. P., Schlesinger, L. A., & Sathe, V. (1986). *Organization: Text, cases, and readings on the management of organization design and change* (2nd ed.). Homewood, IL: Richard D. Irwin.

CHAPTER TWENTY-SIX

Bass, B. M. (1985). *Leadership and performance beyond expectations.* New York: Free Press.

Berlew, D. (1974). Leadership and organizational excitement. *California Management Review, 17*(2), 21–30.

Burns, J. M. (1978). *Leadership.* New York: HarperCollins.

Caggiano, C. (1992, November). What do workers want? *Inc.,* pp. 101–102.

Caudron, S. (1993, November 15). Motivation? *Industry Week,* p. 33.

Conger, J. (1998). *Winning 'em over: A new model for management in the age of persuasion.* New York: Simon & Schuster.

Decker, B. (1993). *You've got to be believed to be heard.* New York: St. Martin's Press.

Deering, A. Dilts, R., & Russell, J. (2002). *Alpha leadership: Tools for business leaders who want more from life.* London: Wiley.

Friedman, H. S., Prince, L. M., Riggio, R. E., & DiMatteo, M. R. (1980). Understanding and assessing nonverbal expressiveness: The affective communication test. *Journal of Personality and Social Psychology, 39*(2), 333–351.

Galinsky, E., Bond, J. T., & Friedman, D. E. (1993). *The national study of the changing workforce.* New York: Families and Work Institute.

Garvin, D. A. (1991, November–December). How the Baldrige Award really works. *Harvard Business Review,* pp. 80–93.

Goleman, D., Boyatzis, R., & McKee, A. (2002). *Primal leadership: Realizing the power of emotional intelligence.* Boston: Harvard Business School Press.

Hamel, G. (2000). *Leading the revolution.* Boston: Harvard Business School Press.

Handy, C. (1999). *The hungry spirit: Beyond capitalism.* New York: Broadway Books.

Hickson, B., Clayton, E. W., Entman, S. S., Miller, C. S., Githens, P. B., Whetten-Goldstein, K., & Sloan, F. A. (1994). Obstetricians' prior malpractice experience and patients' satisfaction with care. *Journal of the American Medical Association, 272,* 1583–1587.

Kaye, B. L., & Jordon-Evans, S. (1999). *Love 'em and lose 'em.* San Francisco: Berrett-Koehler.

King, M. L., Jr. (1983). I Have a Dream. In C. S. King (Ed.), *The words of Martin Luther King, Jr.* (pp. 95–98). New York: Newmarket Press. Reprinted by permission of Joan Daves, copyright © 1963 by Martin Luther King Jr.

Leider, R. J., & Shapiro, D. A. (2001). *Whistle while you work: Heeding your life's calling.* San Francisco: Berrett-Koehler.

Mintzberg, H. (1994, January-February). The rise and fall of strategic planning. *Harvard Business Review,* p. 109.

Mintzberg, H., & Norman, R. A. (2001). *Reframing business: When the map changes the landscape.* New York: Wiley.

Novak, M. (1996). *Business as a calling: Work and the examined life.* New York: Free Press.

Olofson, C. (1998, September). The Ritz puts on stand-up meetings. *Fast Company,* p. 62.

Palmer, P. J. (2000). *Let your life speak.* San Francisco: Jossey-Bass.

Pines, M. (1984). Children's winning ways. *Psychology Today, 18*(12), 58–65.

CHAPTER TWENTY-SEVEN

Collins, J. C., & Porras, J. I. (1994). *Built to last.* New York: HarperCollins.

Hamel, G., & Prahalad, C. K. (1989). Strategic intent. *Harvard Business Review, 67*(3), 63–76.

Hamel, G., & Prahalad, C. K. (1994). *Competing for the future.* Boston: Harvard Business School Press.

Lawler, E. E., & Galbraith, J. R. (1994). Avoiding the corporate dinosaur syndrome. *Organizational Dynamics, 23*(2), 5–17.

Ledford, G. E., Wendenhof, J., & Strahley, J. (1995). Realizing a corporate philosophy. *Organizational Dynamics, 23*(3), 5–19.

Locke, E., & Latham, G. (1990). *A theory of goal setting and task performance.* Englewood Cliffs, NJ: Prentice-Hall.

Mintzberg, H. (1994). *The rise and fall of strategic planning.* New York: Free Press.

O'Toole, J. (1993). *The executive's compass.* New York: Oxford University Press.

Prahalad, C. K., & Hamel, G. (1990). The core competence of the corporation. *Harvard Business Review, 68*(3), 79–91.

Selznick, P. (1957). *Leadership in administration.* New York: HarperCollins.

Weisbord, M. (1992). *Discovering common ground.* San Francisco: Berrett-Koehler.

CHAPTER TWENTY-EIGHT

Lawler, E. E. (1996). *From the ground up.* San Francisco: Jossey-Bass.

CHAPTER TWENTY-NINE

Block, P. (2004). *The empowered manager: Positive political skills at work* (2nd ed.) San Francisco: Jossey-Bass.

Davis, L. E., & Sullivan, C. S. (1980). A labor-management contract and the quality of working life. *Journal of Occupational Behavior, 1,* 29–41.

Elden, M. (1978). *Three generations of work democracy experiments in Norway: Beyond classical socio-technical analysis.* Institute for Industrial Social Research, Technical University of Trondheim, Norway.

Emery, F. E. (1980). Designing socio-technical systems for 'greenfield' sites. *Journal of Occupational Behavior, 1,* 19–27.

Emery, M. (1982). *Searching: For new directions, in new ways for new times.* Canberra: Centre for Continuing Education, Australian National University.

Garson, B. (1989). *The electronic sweatshop: How computers are transforming the office of the future into the factory of the past.* New York: Penguin.

Herbst, P. G. (1974). *Socio-technical design.* London: Tavistock.

Hickey, J. W. (1986, April). Productivity gain seen in labor-management reversal. *World of Work Report, 11*(4), 3–4.

Hirschhorn, L. (1984). *Beyond mechanization: Work and technology in a postindustrial age.* Cambridge, MA: MIT Press.

Lytle, W. O. (1997). *Starting an organization design effort: A planning and preparation guide* (Rev. ed.). Englishtown, NJ: BPW Publishing.

Lytle, W. O. (1998). *Designing a high-performance organization: A guide to the whole-systems approach.* Englishtown, NJ: BPW Publishing.

Lytle, W. O. (2002, Winter). Accelerating the organization design process, reflections. *The SoL Journal.* Cambridge, MA: MIT Press.

McFletcher Associates. (1983). *The work-style preference inventory.* Scottsdale, AZ.

Mohrman, S. A., Cohen, S. G., & Mohrman, A., Jr. (1995). *Designing team-based organizations.* San Francisco: Jossey-Bass.

Pasmore, W., Francis, C., Haldeman, J., & Shani, A. (1982). Sociotechnical systems: A North American reflection on empirical studies of the seventies. *Human Relations, 35*(12), 1179–1204.

Pava, C.H.P. (1983). *Managing new age technology: An organizational strategy.* New York: Free Press.

Trist, E. L., & Dwyer, C. (1982). The limits of laissez-faire as a sociotechnical strategy. In R. Zager & M. F. Rosow (Eds.), *The innovative organization.* New York: Pergamon Press.

Walton, R. E. (1982). The Topeka work system: Optimistic vision, pessimistic hypotheses, and reality. In R. Zager & M. P. Rosow (Eds.), *The innovative organization.* New York: Pergamon Press.

Weisbord, M. R., & Maselko, J. C. (1981, May). Learning how to influence others. *Supervisory Management, 26*(5), 2–10.

Zager, R., & Rosow, M. P. (1982). *The innovative organization: Productivity programs in action.* New York: Pergamon Press.

CHAPTER THIRTY-ONE

Cameron, K. S., & Quinn, R. E. (1999). *Diagnosing and changing organizational culture.* Reading, MA: Addison-Wesley.

Goffee, R., & Jones, G. (1998). *The character of a corporation.* New York: HarperCollins.

Hofstede, G. (1980). *Culture's consequences.* Thousand Oaks, Ca: Sage.

Hofstede, G. (1991). *Cultures and organizations.* London: McGraw-Hill.

Schein, E. H. (1987). *Process consultation: Lessons for managers and consultants.* Reading, MA: Addison-Wesley.

Schein, E. H. (1999). *Process consultation revisited.* Reading, MA: Addison-Wesley.

Van Maanen, J., & Barley, S. R. (1984). Occupational communities: Culture and control in organizations. In B. M. Staw & L. L. Cummings (Eds.), *Research in organizational behavior* (Vol. 6). Greenwich, CT: JAI Press.

CHAPTER THIRTY-TWO

Cascio, W. F. (2000). *Costing human resources: The financial impact of behavior in organizations* (4th ed.). Cincinnati: South-Western.

Feingold, D., Mohrman, S. A., & Spreitzer, G. M. (2002). Age effects on the predictors of technical workers' commitment and willingness to turnover. *Journal of Occupational Behavior, 23,* 1–20.

Lawler, E. E., III. (1973). *Motivation in work organizations.* Pacific Grove, CA: Brooks/Cole.

Locke, E. A., & Latham, P. G. (1990). *A theory of goal setting and task performance.* Upper Saddle River, NJ: Prentice-Hall.

Maslow, A. H. (1954). *Motivation and personality.* New York: Harper.

Maslow, A. H. (1968). Toward a psychology of being. New York: Wiley.

McCall, M. M., Jr., Lombardo, M. M., & Morrison, A. M. (1988). *The lessons of experience: How successful executives develop on the job.* San Francisco: The New Lexington Press.

Nelson, B. (1994). *1001 ways to reward employees.* New York: Workman.

CHAPTER THIRTY-THREE

Harrison, R. (1971). Role negotiation. In W. Burke & H. Hornstein (Eds.), *The social technology of organization development.* Washington, DC: NTL Learning Resources.

Hastings, C., Bixby, P., & Chaudhry-Lawton, R. (1987). *The superteam solution.* San Diego: University Associates.

Peters, T. (1987). *Thriving on chaos.* New York: Knopf.

CHAPTER THIRTY-FOUR

Army Leadership. (1997, April). *FM 22–100 initial draft,* p. iii.

Baldwin, T. T., & Ford, J. K. (1988). Transfer of training: A review and directions for future research. *Personnel Psychology, 41,* 63–101.

Bass, B. M. (1985). *Leadership and performance beyond expectations.* New York: Free Press.

Bennis, W. G., & Nanus, B. (1985). *Leaders: The strategies for taking charge.* New York: HarperCollins.

Boehm, V. R. (1985). Using assessment centers for management development—five applications. *Journal of Management Development, 4*(4), 40–51.

Briggs, G. E., & Naylor, J. C. (1962). The relative efficiency of several training methods as a function of transfer task complexity. *Journal of Experimental Psychology, 64,* 505–512.

Brown, J. S., & Duguid, P. (1991). Organizational learning and communities-of-practice: Toward a unified view of working, learning, and innovation. *Organizational Science, 2*(1), 40–57.

Conger, J. A. (1989). *The charismatic leader.* San Francisco: Jossey-Bass.

Conger, J. A. (1992). *Learning to lead.* San Francisco: Jossey-Bass.

Dalton, M. A., & Hollenbeck, G. P. (1996). *How to design an effective system for developing managers and executives.* Greensboro, NC: Center for Creative Leadership.

Edelstein, B. C., & Armstrong, D. J. (1993). A model for executive development. *Human Resource Planning, 16*(4), 51–64.

Ericsson, K. A., & Charness, N. (1994). Expert performance. *American Psychologist, 49*(8), 725–747.

Ericsson, K. A., Krampe, R. T., & Tesch-Romer, C. (1993). The role of deliberate practices in the acquisition of expert performance. *Psychological Review, 100*(3), 363–406.

Ericsson, K. A., & Smith, J. (1991). *Towards a general theory of expertise.* Cambridge, MA: Cambridge University Press.

Facteau, J. D., Dobbins, G. H., Russell, J.E.A., Ladd, R. T., Kudisch, J. D. (1995). The influence of general perceptions of the training environment on pretraining motivation and perceived training transfer. *Journal of Management, 21*(1), 1–25.

Hall, D. T., & Otazo, K. L. (1995). *Executive coaching study: A progress report.* Boston: Human Resource Policy Institute, Boston University School of Management.

Hollenbeck, G. P., & McCall, M. W. (1999). Leadership development: Contemporary practice. In A. I. Kraut & A. K. Korman (Eds.), *Evolving practices for human resources management: Responses to a changing world of work.* San Francisco: Jossey-Bass.

Huczynski, A. A., & Lewis, J. W. (1980). An empirical study into the learning transfer process in management training. *Journal of Management Studies,* pp. 227–240.

Kaye, B., & Jacobson, B. (1996, August). Reframing mentoring. *Training & Development,* pp. 44–47.

Kilburg, R. R. (1996). Toward a conceptual understanding and definition of executive coaching. *Consulting Psychology Journal, 48*(2), 134–144.

Kotter, J. P. (1990). *A force for change.* New York: Free Press.

Kouzes, J. M., & Posner, B. Z. (1987). *The leadership challenge.* San Francisco: Jossey-Bass.

McCall, M., Jr. (1998). *High flyers.* Boston: Harvard Business Press.

McCall, M., Jr., Lombardo, M., & Morrison, A. (1988). *The lessons of experience: How successful executives develop on the job.* Lexington, MA: Lexington Books.

McCauley, C. D. (1986). *Developmental experiences in managerial work: A literature review.* Technical Report no. 26. Greensboro, NC: Center for Creative Leadership.

McCauley, C. D., Moxley, R. S., & Van Velsor, E. (1998). *Handbook of leadership development.* San Francisco: Jossey-Bass.

Mohr, D. C. (1995). Negative outcome in psychotherapy: A critical review. *Clinical Psychology: Science and Practice, 2*(1), 1–27.

Naylor, J. C., & Briggs, G. E. (1963). The effect of task complexity and task organization on the relative efficiency of part and whole training methods. *Journal of Experimental Psychology, 65,* 217–224.

Noe, R. A. (1986). Trainees' attributes and attitudes: Neglected influences on training effectiveness. *Academy of Management Review, 11*(4), 736–749.

Schaffer, G. (1994, November). *Competency-based managerial and leadership development.* Boston: Proceedings of the National Conference on Using Competency Tools & Applications to Drive Organizational Performance.

Schmitt, N., Ford, J. K., & Stults, D. M. (1986). Changes in self-perceived ability as a function of performance in an assessment center. *Journal of Occupational Psychology, 59,* 327–335.

Sims, H. P., & Manz, C. C. (1982, January). Modeling influences on employee behavior. *Personnel Journal,* pp. 45–51.

Tichy, N. M., & Devanna, M. A. (1986). *The transformational leader.* New York: Wiley.

Waldman, D. A., Atwater, L. E., & Antonioni, D. (1998). Has 360 degree feedback gone amok? *Academy of Management Executive, 12*(2), 86–94.

Westley, F. (1992). Vision worlds: Strategic visions as social interaction. *Advances in Strategic Management, 8,* 271–305.

Wexley, K. N., & Thornton, C. L. (1972). Effect of verbal feedback of test results upon learning. *Journal of Educational Research, 66,* 119–121.

Woodruffe, C. (1993). What is meant by a competency? *Leadership & Organizational Development Journal, 14*(1), 29–36.

Young, D., & Dixon, N. (1996). *Helping leaders take effective action: a program evaluation.* Greensboro, NC: Center for Creative Leadership.

Yukl, G. (1994). *Leadership in organizations* (3rd ed.). Englewood Cliffs, NJ: Prentice-Hall.

CHAPTER THIRTY-SIX

Argyris, C. (1957). *Personality and organization: The conflict between system and the individual.* New York: HarperCollins.

Brown, J. S. (1989, Fall). High performance work systems for the 1990s. *Benchmark,* pp. 8–11.

Cherns, A. B. (1976). The principles of socio-technical design. *Human Relations, 29,* 783–792.

Hackman, J. R., & Oldham, G. R. (1980). *Work redesign.* Reading, MA: Addison-Wesley.

Hanna, D. P. (1988). *Designing organizations for high performance.* Reading, MA: Addison-Wesley.

Lawler, E. E. (1978). The new plant revolution. *Organizational Dynamics, 6*(3), 2–12.

Lawler, E. E. (1986). *High-involvement management: Participative strategies for improving organizational performance.* San Francisco: Jossey-Bass.

Lawrence, P. R., & Lorsch, J. W. (1967). *Organization and environment: Managing differentiation and integration.* Homewood, IL: Business One Irwin.

Likert, R. (1961). *New patterns of management.* New York: McGraw-Hill.

Nadler, D. A. (1981). Managing organizational change: An integrative approach. *Journal of Applied Behavioral Science, 17,* 191–211.

Nadler, D. A. (1989, Fall). Organizational architectures for the corporation of the future. *Benchmark,* pp. 12–13.

Nadler, D. A., & Tushman, M. L. (1988). *Strategic organization design.* Glenview, IL: Scott, Foresman.

Rice, A. K. (1958). *Productivity and social organization: The Ahmedabad experiment.* London: Tavistock.

Roethlisberger, F. J., & Dickson, W. J. (1939). *Management and the worker.* Cambridge, MA: Harvard University Press.

Sherwood, J. J. (1988). Creating work cultures with competitive advantage. *Organizational Dynamics,* 5–27.

Taylor, F. W. (1911). *The principles of scientific management.* New York: HarperCollins.

Trist, E. L., & Bamforth, R. (1951). Some social and psychological consequences of the long wall method of coal-getting. *Human Relations, 4,* 3–38.

Tushman, M. L., & Nadler, D. A. (1978). Information processing as an integrative concept in organization design. *Academy of Management Review, 3*(3), 613–624.

Walton, R. E. (1977). The diffusion of new work structures: Explaining why success didn't take. In P. H. Mirvis & D. N. Berg (Eds.), *Failures in organizational development and change: Cases and essays for learning.* New York: Wiley.

Weber, M. (1947). *The theory of social and economic organization.* New York: Free Press.

CHAPTER THIRTY-EIGHT

Argyris, C. (1985). *Strategy, change, and defensive routines.* Boston: Pitman.

Argyris, C. (1990). *Overcoming organizational defenses.* Englewood Cliffs, NJ: Prentice Hall.

Argyris, C., Putnam, R., & Smith, D. (1985). *Action science.* San Francisco: Jossey-Bass.

Argyris, C., & Schön, D. (1978). *Organizational learning: A theory-in-action perspective.* Reading, MA: Addison-Wesley.

Bennis, W., & Nanus, B. (1985). *Leaders.* New York: Harper & Row.

de Geus, A. P. (1988, March–April). Planning as learning. *Harvard Business Review,* pp. 70–74.

de Pree, M. (1989). *Leadership is an art.* New York: Doubleday.

Dumaine, B. (1989, July 3). What the leaders of tomorrow see. *Fortune,* pp. 48–62.

Forrester, J. W. (1965, Fall). A new corporate design. *Sloan Management Review* (formerly *Industrial Management Review*), pp. 5–17.

Fritz, R. (1989). *The path of least resistance.* New York: Ballantine.

Fritz, R. (1990). *Creating.* New York: Ballantine.

Greenleaf, R. K. (1977). *Servant leadership: A journey into the nature of legitimate power and greatness.* New York: Paulist Press.

Hampden-Turner, C. (1990). *Charting the corporate mind.* New York: The Free Press.

Hardin, G. (1968, December 13). The tragedy of the commons. *Science, 162,* 1243–1248.

Kim, D. H. (1989, June). *Toward learning organizations: Integrating total quality control and systems thinking.* Working Paper No. 3037-9-BPS. Cambridge, MA: MIT Sloan School of Management.

King, M. L., Jr. (1986, January–February). Letter from Birmingham jail. *American Visions,* pp. 52–59.

Kouzes, J. M., & Posner, B. Z. (1987). *The leadership challenge.* San Francisco: Jossey-Bass.

Mason, R., & Mitroff, I. (1981). *Challenging strategic planning assumptions.* New York: John Wiley & Sons.

Miller, L. (1984). *American spirit: Visions of a new corporate culture.* New York: William Morrow.

Mintzberg, H. (1987, July–August). Crafting Strategy. *Harvard Business Review,* pp. 66–75.

Mitroff, I. (1988). *Break-away thinking.* New York: John Wiley & Sons.

Peters, T., & Austin, N. (1985). *A passion for excellence* New York: Random House.

Sashkin, M., & Burke, W. W. (1990a). An end-of-the-eighties retrospective. In R. Masarik, (Ed.), *Advances in organization development* (pp. 347–349). Norwood, NJ: Ablex.

Sashkin, M., & Burke, W. W. (1990b). Organization development in the 1980s. *Journal of Management, 13*(2), 393–417.

Schein, E. (1985). *Organizational culture and leadership.* San Francisco: Jossey-Bass.

Selznick, P. (1957). *Leadership in administration.* New York: Harper & Row.

Senge, P. (1990). *The fifth discipline: The art and practice of the learning organization.* New York: Doubleday/Currency.

Stalk, G., Jr. (1988, July–August). Time: The next source of competitive advantage. *Harvard Business Review,* pp. 41–51.

Tichy, N. M., & Devanna, M. A. (1986). *The transformational leader.* New York: John Wiley & Sons.

Wack, P. (1985, September–October). Scenarios: Uncharted waters ahead. *Harvard Business Review,* pp. 73–89.

CHAPTER THIRTY-NINE

Batson, C. D. (1994). Why act for the public good? Four answers. *Personality & Social Psychology Bulletin: Special Issue: The Self and the Collective, 20,* 603–610.

Batson, C. D., & Oleson, K. A. (1991). Current status of the empathy-altruism hypothesis. In M. S. Clark (Ed.), *Prosocial behavior: Review of Personality and Social Psychology* (Vol. 12, pp. 62–85). Thousand Oaks, CA: Sage.

Blum, L. (1980). Compassion. In A. O. Rorty (Ed.), *Explaining emotions* (pp. 507–517). Berkeley: University of California Press.

Brody, H. (1992). *The healer's power.* New Haven, CT: Yale University Press.

Cameron, K. S. (1994). Strategies for successful organizational downsizing. *Human Resource Management, 33,* 189–212.

Cameron, K. S. (1998). Strategic organizational downsizing: An extreme case. *Research in Organizational Behavior, 20,* 185–229.

Cameron, K. S. (2003). Organizational virtuousness and performance. In K. S. Cameron, J. E. Dutton, & R. E. Quinn (Eds.), *Positive organizational scholarship.* San Francisco: Berrett-Koehler.

Cameron, K. S., Bright, D., & Caza, A. (2004). Exploring the relationships between organizational virtuousness and performance. *American Behavioral Scientist, 47,* 766–790.

Cameron, K. S., Dutton, J. E., & Quinn, R. E. (2003). An introduction to positive organizational scholarship. In K. S. Cameron, J. E. Dutton, & R. E. Quinn (Eds.), *Positive organizational scholarship.* San Francisco: Berrett-Koehler.

Cameron, K. S., Dutton, J. E., Quinn, R. E., & Wrzesniewski, A. (2003). Developing a discipline of positive organizational scholarship. In K. S. Cameron, J. E. Dutton, & R. E. Quinn (Eds.), *Positive organizational scholarship.* San Francisco: Berrett-Koehler.

Cameron, K. S., Freeman, S. J., & Mishra, A. K. (1993). Downsizing and redesigning organizations. In G. P. Huber & W. H. Glick (Eds.), *Organizational change and redesign.* New York: Oxford University Press.

Cassell, E. J. (2002). Compassion. In C. R. Snyder & S. J. Lopez (Eds.), *Handbook of positive psychology* (pp. 434–445). New York: Oxford University Press.

Clark, C. (1997). *Misery and company: Sympathy in everyday life.* Chicago: The University of Chicago Press.

Connelly, J. (1999). Being present in the moment: Developing the capacity for mindfulness in medicine. *Academic Medicine, 74,* 420–424.

Dalai Lama. (1995). *The power of compassion.* London: Thorsons.

Davis, M. H. (1983). The effects of dispositional empathy on emotional reactions and helping: A multidimensional approach. *Journal of Personality, 51,* 167–184.

Davis, M. H., & Kraus, L. A. (1997). Personality and empathic accuracy. In W. J. Ickes (Ed.), *Empathic accuracy* (pp. 144–168). New York: Guilford Press.

Dutton, J. E. (2003). Breathing life into organizational studies. *Journal of Management Inquiry, 12*(1), 5–19.

Dutton, J. E., Frost, P. J., Worline, M. C., Lilius, J. M., & Kanov, J. M. (2002, January). Leading in times of trauma. *Harvard Business Review, 80,* 54–62.

Dutton, J. E., Worline, M. C., Frost, P. J., & Lilius, J. M. (2003). *The organizing of compassion.* Unpublished manuscript. Ann Arbor: University of Michigan.

Ekman, P. (1973). Cross cultural studies of facial expression. In P. Ekman (Ed.), *Darwin and facial expression: A century of research in review* (pp. 169–222). New York: Academic Press.

Fineman, S. (Ed.). (2000). *Emotion in organizations.* Thousand Oaks, CA: Sage.

Follet, M. P. (1995). *Mary Parker Follet: Prophet of management* (P. Graham, Ed.). Boston: Harvard Business School Press.

Frank, A. W. (1992). The pedagogy of suffering. *Theory and Practice, 2,* 467–487.

Frost, P. J. (1999). Why compassion counts! *Journal of Management Inquiry, 8,* 127–133.

Frost, P. J. (2003). *Toxic emotions at work: How compassionate managers handle pain and conflict.* Boston: Harvard Business School Press.

Frost, P. J., Dutton, J. E., Worline, M. C., & Wilson, A. (2000). Narratives of compassion in organizations. In S. Fineman (Ed.), *Emotion in organizations* (pp. 25–45). Thousand Oaks, CA: Sage.

Frost, P. J., & Robinson, S. (1999, July-August). The toxic handler: Organizational hero—and casualty. *Harvard Business Review, 77,* 96–104.

Gittell, J. H., & Cameron, K. S. (2003). *Virtuous leadership, relationships and resilience: The role of relational and financial reserves in responding to crisis.* Unpublished manuscript, Brookline, MA: Brandeis University.

Hallowell, E. M. (1999, January-February). The human moment at work. *Harvard Business Review, 77,* 58–66.

Hatfield, E., Cacioppo, J. T., & Rapson, R. L. (1994). *Emotional contagion.* New York: Cambridge University Press.

Himmelfarb, G. (2001). The idea of compassion: The British vs. the French enlightenment. *Public Interest, 145,* 3–24.

Hochschild, A. R. (1983). *The managed heart: Commercialization of human feeling.* Berkeley: University of California Press.

Hutchins, E. (1990). The technology of team navigation. In J. Galegher, R. E. Kraut, & C. Egido (Eds.), *Intellectual teamwork* (pp. 191–220). Hillsdale, NJ: Lawrence Erlbaum.

Huy, Q. N. (1999). Emotional capability, emotional intelligence, and radical change. *Academy of Management Review, 24,* 325–345.

Huy, Q. N. (2002). Emotional balancing of organizational continuity and radical change: The contribution of middle managers. *Administrative Science Quarterly, 47*(1), 31–69.

Kahn, W. A. (1993). Caring for the caregivers: Patterns of organizational caregiving. *Administrative Science Quarterly, 38*(4), 539–563.

Kelly, J. R., & Barsade, S. G. (2001). Mood and emotions in small groups and work teams. *Organizational Behavior & Human Decision Processes, 86*(1), 99–130.

Kuhl, D. (2002). *What dying people want: Practical wisdom for the end of life.* Garden City, NY: Doubleday.

Lerner, M. J. (1980). *The belief in a just world: A fundamental delusion.* New York: Plenum.

Lilius, J. M., Worline, M. C., Dutton, J. E., Kanov, J. M., Frost, P. J., & Maitlis, S. (2003). *What good is compassion at work?* Unpublished manuscript. Ann Arbor: University of Michigan.

Mead, G. H. (1962). *Mind, self, and society from the standpoint of a social behaviorist.* Chicago: University of Chicago Press.

Meyerson, D. E. (1994). Interpretations of stress in institutions: The cultural production of ambiguity and burnout. *Administrative Science Quarterly, 39*(4), 628–653.

Meyerson, D. E. (2000). If emotions were honoured: A cultural analysis. In S. Fineman (Ed.), *Emotion in organizations* (pp. 167–183). Thousand Oaks, CA: Sage.

Moreland, R. L., & Myaskovsky, L. (2000). Exploring the performance benefits of group training: Transactive memory or improved communication? *Organizational Behavior & Human Decision Processes, 82*(1), 117–133.

Nussbaum, M. C. (1996). Compassion: The basic social emotion. *Social Philosophy and Policy, 13,* 27–58.

Nussbaum, M. C. (2001). *Upheavals of thought: The intelligence of emotions.* Cambridge, UK: Cambridge University Press.

Parkinson, B. (1996). Emotions are social. *British Journal of Psychology, 87*(4), 663–683.

Reich, W. T. (1989). Speaking of suffering: A moral account of compassion. *Soundings, 72,* 83–108.

Rinpoche, S. (1992). *The Tibetan book of living and dying.* London: Rider Books.

Rozin, P. (2001). Social psychology and science: Some lessons from Solomon Asch. *Personality & Social Psychology Review: Special Issue, 5,* 2–14.

Ryff, C., & Singer, B. (1998). The contours of positive human health. *Psychological Inquiry, 9,* 1–28.

Ryff, C., & Singer, B. (Eds.). (2001). *Emotion, social relationships, and health.* Oxford, UK: Oxford University Press.

Sandelands, L. E. (1998). *Feeling and form in social life.* Lanham, MD: Rowman & Littlefield.

Sandelands, L. E. (2003). *Thinking about social life.* Unpublished manuscript.

Sears, D. (1998). *Compassion for humanity in the Jewish tradition.* Northvale, NJ: Jason Aronson.

Shelp, E. E. (Ed.). (1985). *Theology and bioethics: Exploring the foundations and frontiers.* Hingham, MA: Kluwer Academic.

Shott, S. (1979). Emotion and social life: Symbolic interactionist analysis. *American Journal of Sociology, 84*(6), 1317–1334.

Solomon, R. C. (1998). The moral psychology of business: Care and compassion in the corporation. *Business Ethics Quarterly, 8,* 515–533.

Strack, F., Martin, L. L., & Stepper, S. (1988). Inhibiting and facilitating conditions of the human smile: A nonobtrusive test of the facial feedback hypothesis. *Journal of Personality and Social Psychology, 54*(5), 768–777.

Sutcliffe, K. M. (2000). Organizational environments and organizational information processing. In F. M. Jablin & L. L. Putnam (Eds.), *The new handbook or organizational communication: Advances in theory, research, and methods* (pp. 197–230). Thousand Oaks, CA: Sage.

Van Maanen, J., & Kunda, G. (1989). Real feelings: Emotional expression and organizational culture. In L. L. Cummings & B. M. Staw (Eds.), *Research in organizational behavior* (Vol. 11, pp. 43–103). Greenwich, CT: JAI Press.

von Dietze, E., & Orb, A. (2000). Compassionate care: A moral dimension of nursing. *Nursing Inquiry, 7,* 166–174.

Wanburg, C. R., Bunce, L. W., & Gavin, M. B. (1999). Perceived fairness of layoffs among individuals who have been laid off: A longitudinal study. *Personnel Psychology, 52,* 59–84.

Wegner, D. M. (1987). Transactive memory: A contemporary analysis of the group mind. In B. Mullen & G. R. Goethals (Eds.), *Theories of group behavior* (pp. 185–208). New York: Springer-Verlag.

Wegner, D. M. (1995). A computer network model of human transactive memory. *Social Cognition, 13*(3), 319–339.

Weick, K. E. (1999). That's moving: Theories that matter. *Journal of Management Inquiry, 8,* 134–142.

Weick, K. E., & Roberts, K. H. (1993). Collective mind in organizations: Heedful interrelating on flight decks. *Administrative Science Quarterly, 38*(3), 357–381.

Weick, K. E., Sutcliffe, K. M., & Obstfeld, D. (1999). Organizing for high reliability: Processes of collective mindfulness. *Research in Organizational Behavior, 21,* 81–123.

Worline, M. C., Dutton, J. E., Frost, P. J., Kanov, J. M., Lilius, J. M., & Maitlis, S. (2003). *Creating fertile soil: The organizing dynamics of resilience.* Unpublished manuscript. Ann Arbor: University of Michigan.

Wuthnow, R. (1991). *Acts of compassion: Caring for others and helping our-selves.* Princeton, NJ: Princeton University Press.

Zaslow, J. (2002, November 20). New index aims to calculate the annual cost of despair. *Wall Street Journal,* pp. D1, D12.

CHAPTER FORTY

Argyris, C. (1957). *Personality and organization.* New York: HarperCollins.

Argyris, C. (1962). *Interpersonal competence and organizational effectiveness.* Homewood, IL: Dorsey.

Argyris, C. (1965). *Organizations and innovation.* Homewood, IL: Irwin.

Argyris, C. (1970). *Intervention theory and method.* Reading, MA: Addison-Wesley.

Argyris, C. (1980). *Inner contradictions of rigorous research.* New York: Academic Press.

Argyris, C. (1981). *Reasoning, learning, and action.* San Francisco: Jossey-Bass.

Argyris, C. (1994). *Knowledge for action.* San Francisco: Jossey-Bass.

Argyris, C., Putnam, R., & Smith, D. (1985). *Action science: Concepts, meth-ods, and skills for research and intervention.* San Francisco: Jossey-Bass.

Argyris, C., & Schön, D. (1974). *Theory in practice: Increasing professional effectiveness.* San Francisco: Jossey-Bass.

Bushe, G., & Gibbs, B. (1990). Predicting organization development consulting competence from the Myers-Briggs Indicator and stage of ego development. *Journal of Applied Behavioral Science, 26,* 337–357.

Chandler, D., & Torbert, W. (2003). Transforming inquiry and action by interweaving 28 flavors of action research. *Action Research, 1,* 133–152.

Cohen, J. (1983). *Applied multiple regression/correlation analysis for the behavioral sciences.* Hillsdale, NJ: Erlbaum.

Cook-Greuter, S. (1999). *Postautonomous ego development: A study of its nature and measurement.* Doctoral dissertation. Cambridge, MA: Harvard Graduate School of Education.

Fisher, D., & Torbert, W. (1991). Transforming managerial practice: Beyond the achiever stage. In R. Woodman & W. Pasmore (Eds.), *Research in organizational change and development* (Vol. 5). Greenwich, CT: JAI Press.

Foster, P., & Torbert, W. (2005). Leading through positive deviance: A developmental action learning perspective on institutional change. In R. Giacalone, C. Jurkiewicz, & C. Dunn (Eds.), *Positive psychology in business ethics and corporate responsibility.* Greenwich, CT: Information Age.

Greiner, L. (1972). Evolution and revolution as organizations grow. *Harvard Business Review, 50*(4), 37–46.

Kegan, R. (1982). *The evolving self.* Cambridge, MA: Harvard University Press.

Kegan, R. (1994). *In over our heads: The demands of modern life.* Cambridge, MA: Harvard University Press.

Kohlberg, L. (1984). *Essays on moral development: Vol. 2. The psychology of moral development.* San Francisco: HarperCollins.

Leigh, J. (2002). *Developing corporate citizens: Linking organizational developmental theory and corporate responsibility.* Paper presented at Denver Academy of Management Symposium on New Roles for Organizational Citizenship.

Lippitt, G., & Schmidt, W. (1967). Non-financial crises in organizational development. *Harvard Business Review, 47*(6), 102–112.

Loevinger, J. (1982). *Ego development.* San Francisco: Jossey-Bass.

Manners, J., Durkin, K., & Nesdale, A. (2004). Promoting advanced ego development among adults. *Journal of Adult Development, 11*(1), 19–27.

Merron, K., Fisher, D., & Torbert, W. (1987). Meaning making and management action. *Group and Organizational Studies, 12,* 274–286.

Reason, P., & Bradbury, H. (Eds.) (2001). *Handbook of action research.* London: Sage.

Reason, P., & Torbert, W. (2001). The action turn: Toward a transformational social science: A further look at the scientific merits of action research. *Concepts and Transformation, 6*(1), 1–37.

Rooke, D., & Torbert, W. (1998). Organizational transformation as a function of CEOs' developmental stage. *Organization Development, 16*(1), 11–28.

Rooke, D., & Torbert, W. (2005, April). Seven transformations of leadership. *Harvard Business Review,* pp. 66–77.

Rudolph, J., Taylor, S., & Foldy, E. (2001). Collaborative off-line reflection: A way to develop skill in action science and action inquiry. In P. Reason & H. Bradbury (Eds.), *Handbook of action research.* London: Sage.

Sherman, F., & Torbert, W. (2000). *Transforming social inquiry, transforming social action.* Boston: Kluwer.

Torbert, W. (1976). *Creating a community of inquiry.* London: Wiley.

Torbert, W. (1987). *Managing the corporate dream: Restructuring for long-term success.* Homewood, IL: Dow Jones-Irwin.

Torbert, W. (1989). Leading organizational transformation. In R. Woodman & W. Pasmore (Eds.), *Research in organizational change and developments* (Vol. 3). Greenwich, CT: JAI Press.

Torbert, W. (1991). *The power of balance: Transforming self, society, and scientific inquiry.* Thousand Oaks, CA: Sage.

Torbert, W. (1994). Cultivating post-formal adult development: Higher stages and contrasting interventions. In M. Miller & S. Cook-Greuter (Eds.), *Transcendence and mature thought in adulthood: The further reaches of adult development* (pp. 181–203). Lanham, MD: Rowman & Littlefield.

Torbert, W. (1996). The "chaotic" action awareness of transformational leaders. *International Journal of Public Administration, 19,* 911–939.

Torbert, W. (1998). Developing wisdom and courage in organizing and sciencing. In S. Srivastva & D. Cooperrider (Eds.), *Organizational wisdom and executive courage.* San Francisco: New Lexington Press.

Torbert, W. (2000). A developmental approach to social science: Integrating first-, second-, and third-person research/practice through single-, double-, and triple-loop feedback. *Journal of Adult Development, 7,* 255–268.

Torbert, W., & Fisher, D. (1992). Autobiography as a catalyst for managerial and organizational development. *Management Education and Development, 23,* 184–198.

Torbert, W., & Associates. (2004). *Action inquiry: The secret of timely and transforming leadership.* San Francisco: Berrett-Koehler.

Wilber, K. (1999). *One taste: The journals of Ken Wilber.* Boston: Shambhala.

Zaslow, J. (2002, November 20). New index aims to calculate the annual cost of despair. *Wall Street Journal,* pp. D1, D12.

PART EIGHT

Stravinsky, I. (1970). *Poetics of music in the form of six lessons.* Cambridge, MA: Harvard University Press.

CHAPTER FORTY-ONE

Ackerman-Anderson, L., & Anderson, D. (2001). Awake at the wheel: Moving beyond change management to conscious change leadership. *OD Practitioner, 33*(3), 4–10.

Anderson, D., & Ackerman-Anderson, L. (2001). *Beyond change management: Advanced strategies for today's transformational leaders.* San Francisco: Jossey-Bass/Pfeiffer.

Argyris, C. (1973). *Intervention theory and method: A behavioral science view.* Reading, MA: Addison-Wesley.

Beck, D. E., & Cowan, C. C. (1996). *Spiral dynamics: Mastering values, leadership and change.* Cambridge, MA: Blackwell.

Berger, P., & Luckmann, T. L. (1966). *The social construction of reality.* London: Penguin.

Bergquist, W. (1993). *The postmodern organization: Mastering the art of irreversible change.* San Francisco: Jossey-Bass.

Blake, R. R., & Mouton, J. S. (1976). *Consultation.* Reading, MA: Addison-Wesley.

Bradford, D. L., & Burke, W. W. (2004). Introduction: Is OD in crisis? *Journal of Applied Behavioral Science, 40,* 369–373.

Bradford, D. L., & Burke, W. W. (Eds.). (2005). *Reinventing OD.* San Francisco: Jossey-Bass.

Bunker, B. B., & Alban, B. T. (Eds.). (2005). [Special issue on large group interventions]. *Journal of Applied Behavioral Science, 41*(1).

Chin, R., & Benne, K. D. (1976). General strategies for effecting change in human systems. In W. G. Bennis, K. D. Benne, R. Chin, & K. E. Corey (Eds.), *The planning of change* (3rd ed., pp. 22–45). Austin, TX: Holt, Rinehart and Winston.

Clarke, N. (2005). Transorganizational development for network building. *Journal of Applied Behavioral Science, 41*(1), 30–46.

Gellermann, W., Frankel, M. S., & Ladenson, R. F. (Eds.). (1990). *Values and ethics in organization and human systems development.* San Francisco: Jossey-Bass.

Lent, R. M., McCormick, M. T., & Pearce, D. S. (2005). Combining future search and open space to address special situations. *Journal of Applied Behavioral Science, 41*(1), 61–69.

Marshak, R. J. (1992). Politics, public organizations, and OD. *OD Practitioner, 24*(4), 5–8.

Marshak, R. J. (1993). Lewin meets Confucius: A re-view of the OD model of change. *Journal of Applied Behavioral Science, 29,* 393–415.

Marshak, R. J. (2001). Claiming your power and leadership as an OD practitioner. *OD Practitioner, 33*(4), 17–22.

Marshak, R. J. (2004). Morphing: The leading edge of organizational change in the twenty-first century. *Organization Development Journal, 22*(3), 8–21.

Marshak, R. J. (2005). Is there a new OD? *Seasonings: A Journal by Senior OD Practitioners, 1*(1). Available: www.odnetwork.org/publications/seasonings/article_marshak.html

Miller, F. A., & Katz, J. H. (2002). *The inclusion breakthrough: Unleashing the real power of diversity.* San Francisco: Berrett-Koehler.

Olson, E. E., & Eoyang, G. H. (2001). *Facilitating organizational change: Lessons from complexity science.* San Francisco: Jossey-Bass.

Searle, J. R. (1995). *The construction of social reality.* London: Allen-Lane.

Tenkasi, R. V., & Chesmore, M. C. (2003). Social networks and planned organizational change: The impact of strong ties on effective change implementation and use. *Journal of Applied Behavioral Science, 39,* 281–300.

Watkins, J. M., & Mohr, B. J. (2001). *Appreciative inquiry: Change at the speed of imagination.* San Francisco: Jossey-Bass.

Weick, K. E., & Quinn, R. E. (1999). Organizational change and development. In J. T. Spence, J. M. Darley, & D. J. Foss (Eds.), *Annual Review of Psychology, 50,* 361–386. Palo Alto, CA: Annual Reviews.

Wheatley, M. J. (1992). *Leadership and the new science.* San Francisco: Berrett-Koehler.

Worley, C. G., & Feyerherm, A. E. (2003). Reflections on the future of organization development. *Journal of Applied Behavioral Science, 39*(1), 97–115.

CHAPTER FORTY-TWO

Beckhard, R. (1969). *Organization development: Strategies and models.* Reading, MA: Addison-Wesley.

Beer, M., & Nohria, N. (2000). Cracking the code of change. *Harvard Business Review, 78*(3), 133–141.

Burke, W. W. (2002). *Organization change: Theory and practice.* Thousand Oaks, CA: Sage.

Burke, W. W. (2004a). Internal organization development practitioners: Where do they belong? *Journal of Applied Behavioral Science, 40*(4), 423–431.

Burke, W. W. (2004b). Organization development: What we know and what we need to know going forward. *OD Practitioner, 36*(3), 4–8.

Schein, E. H. (1988). *Process consultation. Its role in organization development* (Vol. 1, 2nd ed.). Reading, MA: Addison-Wesley.

Tichy, N. M., & DeRose, C. (2003). The death and rebirth of organizational development. In S. Chowdhury (Ed.), *Organization 21c: Someday all organizations will lead this way.* Upper Saddle River, NJ: Financial Times Prentice-Hall.

Wheatley, M., Tannenbaum, R., Griffin, P. Y., Quade, K., & Organization Development Network. (2003). *Organization development at work.* San Francisco: Pfeiffer.

Wirtenberg, J., Abrams, L., & Ott, C. (2004). Assessing the field of organization development. *Journal of Applied Behavioral Science, 40*(1), 465–479.

CHAPTER FORTY-THREE

Gittell, J. H. (2000). *Programmed and interactive coordination mechanisms: Toward a theory of complementarity.* Working paper. Boston: Harvard Business School.

Handy, C. (1992, November-December). Balancing corporate power: A new federalist paper. *Harvard Business Review, 70*(6), 59–73.

Kanter, R. M. (1989). *When giants learn to dance: Mastering the challenges of strategy, management, and careers in the 1990s.* New York: Simon and Schuster.

Kanter, R. M., Stein, B. A., & Jick, T. D. (Eds.). (1992). *The challenge of organizational change.* New York: Free Press.

CHAPTER FORTY-FOUR

de Vries, M.F.R. (1994, October). Making a giant dance. *Across the Board,* pp. 27–32.

The discreet charm of the multicultual multinational. (1994, July 30). *Economist,* pp. 57–58.

Donkin, R. (1994, September 30). Cultural restraints on missionary zeal. *Financial Times,* p. 12.

Evans, P. (1992). Management development as glue technology. *Human Resource Planning, 15*(1), 85–105.

Gee, F., Jick, T., & Paine, S. (1993). *Clifford Chance: The merger (A)* and *Clifford Chance: International expansion (B).* Case study, Fontainebleau, France: INCITE.

Main, J. (1990, December 17). Making global alliances work. *Fortune,* pp. 121–126.

Savona, D. (1992, November). When companies divorce. *International Business,* p. 6.

Zweig, P. L. (1993, November 8). Sachs' spectacular road trip. *Business Week,* pp. 56B–56E.

CHAPTER FORTY-SIX

Rigoglioso, M. (1996, April). Stewards of the seventh generation. *Harvard Business School Bulletin,* p. 55.

—⁓— Name Index

⟶ Subject Index